lonely planet

USA

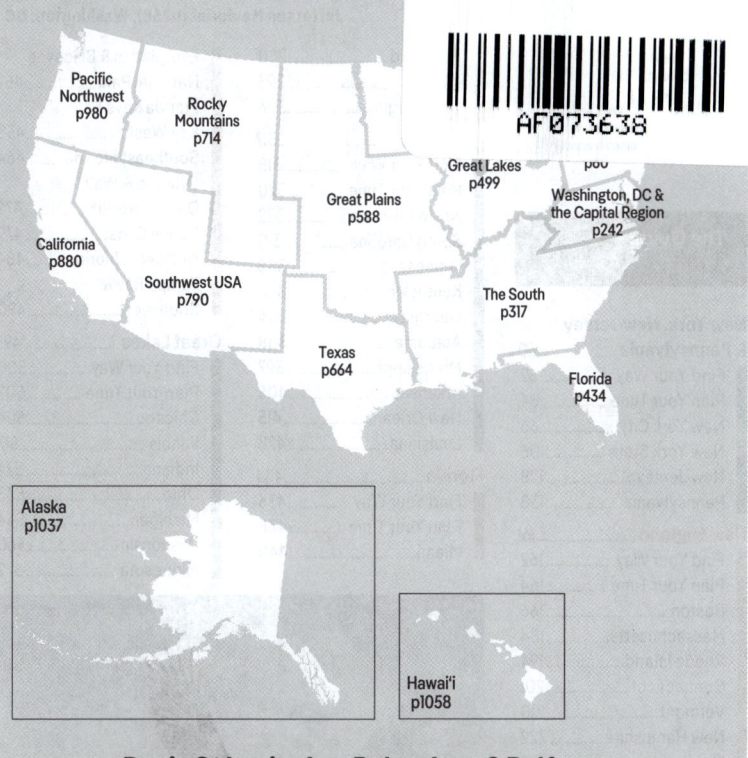

**Regis St Louis, Ann Babe, Amy C Balfour,
Sarah Etinas, Amelia Mularz, John Garry, Kevin Raub,
Jesse Scott, Helena Smith, Karla Zimmerman,
Mary Fitzpatrick, Anthony Ham, Lauren Keith**

CONTENTS

Plan Your Trip

The Journey Begins Here 6
USA Map 12
Our Picks 14
Regions & Cities 28
Itineraries 32
When to Go 42
Get Prepared 44
Trip Planner
National Parks 46
The Food Scene 50
The Outdoors 54

The Guide

**New York, New Jersey
& Pennsylvania** 60
  Find Your Way 62
  Plan Your Time 64
  New York City 66
  New York State 106
  New Jersey 128
  Pennsylvania 138

New England 161
  Find Your Way 162
  Plan Your Time 164
  Boston 166
  Massachusetts 184
  Rhode Island 194
  Connecticut 201
  Vermont 210
  New Hampshire 222
  Maine 229

**Washington, DC
& the Capital Region** 242
  Find Your Way 244
  Plan Your Time 246
  Washington, DC 248
  Delaware 271

Jefferson Memorial (p258), Washington, DC

  Maryland 280
  Virginia 293
  West Virginia 306

The South 317
  Find Your Way 318
  Plan Your Time 320
  North Carolina 322
  South Carolina 341
  Tennessee 353
  Kentucky 366
  Georgia 374
  Alabama 388
  Mississippi 397
  Arkansas 405
  New Orleans 415
  Louisiana 428

Florida 434
  Find Your Way 436
  Plan Your Time 438
  Miami 440

  Everglades & Biscayne
  National Park 452
  Florida Keys &
  Key West 458
  Southeast Florida 464
  Orlando & Walt
  Disney World® 472
  Space Coast 479
  Northeast Florida 484
  Tampa Bay &
  Southwest 490

Great Lakes 499
  Find Your Way 500
  Plan Your Time 502
  Chicago 504
  Illinois 517
  Indiana 524
  Ohio 533
  Michigan 544
  Wisconsin 560
  Minnesota 572

Bald eagle, Kenai Peninsula (p1052), Alaska

CLOCKWISE FROM TOP LEFT: KOSOFF/SHUTTERSTOCK, ROBERT HARDING VIDEO/SHUTTERSTOCK, FLORIDASTOCK/SHUTTERSTOCK

San Francisco (p886)

The Great Plains	588
Find Your Way	590
Plan Your Time	592
Missouri	594
Kansas	607
Oklahoma	614
Nebraska	624
Iowa	634
North Dakota	645
South Dakota	649

Texas	664
Find Your Way	666
Plan Your Time	668
Austin	670
San Antonio & the Hill Country	680
Dallas & Fort Worth	690
Houston & the Gulf Coast	697
West Texas & Big Bend National Park	706

Rocky Mountains	714
Find Your Way	716
Plan Your Time	718
Colorado	720
Wyoming	749
Montana	763
Idaho	777

Southwest USA	790
Find Your Way	792
Plan Your Time	794
Las Vegas	796
Nevada	802
Phoenix	808

Chicago (p504)

Grand Canyon National Park	813
Northern Arizona	821
Southern Arizona	835
Utah	843
New Mexico	863

California 880
Find Your Way	882
Plan Your Time	884
San Francisco & the Bay Area	886
Northern California: Redwoods & Wine Country	911
Yosemite, Lake Tahoe & Gold Country	925
Central California: The Coast & Sacramento	937
Los Angeles & the Deserts	949
Southern California: Disneyland to San Diego	967

Pacific Northwest 980
Find Your Way	982
Plan Your Time	984
Seattle	986
Washington	996
Portland	1011
Oregon	1021

Alaska 1037
Find Your Way	1038
Plan Your Time	1039
Juneau & the Alexander Archipelago	1040
Anchorage	1046

Hawai'i 1058
Find Your Way	1060
Plan Your Time	1062
O'ahu	1064
The Big Island of Hawai'i	1070
Maui	1075
Kaua'i	1079

FROM TOP RIGHT: GARRETT BROWN/SHUTTERSTOCK, ELENA VESELOVA/SHUTTERSTOCK

St Petersburg (p490), Florida

Toolkit
Arriving	1086
Getting Around	1087
Money	1088
Accommodations	1089
Family Travel	1090
Health & Safe Travel	1091
Food, Drink & Nightlife	1092
Responsible Travel	1094
LGBTQ+ Travelers	1096
Accessible Travel	1097
Nuts & Bolts	1099

Storybook
A History of The USA in 15 Places	1102
Meet the Americans	1106
The Birth of America's Vacation	1108
Riding the Rails Through the USA	1110
The Games That Bind Us	1112
Index	1114

Lobster roll (p50)

Lake Martin, Alabama (p388)

USA
THE JOURNEY BEGINS HERE

Some of my earliest travel memories revolve around America's national parks: marveling at Mesa Verde's ancient cliff dwellings, crawling through Mammoth Cave's chilly passageways and watching the fireflies dance around the family tent in the Great Smoky Mountains. Although I've traveled the globe since then, I'm convinced that the world's greatest treasures are right in my own backyard. More recently, I've been drawn to less tangible aspects of the US experience, perhaps owing to my move to New Orleans a decade ago. While there are some striking landscapes in the region (particularly the wetlands in Cajun Country), southern Louisiana is best known for its love of food and music, which come together in celebrations like Mardi Gras and Jazz Fest. More than anything, it's the strong sense of community that defines so much of the South. People you meet in passing take the time to chat, and all are welcomed in, no matter how short their stay.

Regis St Louis
@regisstlouis

The son of two Coloradans, Regis has spent half a lifetime exploring the world's wild places. He is the author of more than 100 Lonely Planet guides.

My favorite experience is boating across the mirror-like waters of Alabama's (p388) **Lake Martin**, an aquatic wonderland of towering bald cypress trees, ostentatious lotus flowers and great blue herons silently stalking the shoreline.

WHO GOES WHERE

Our writers and experts choose the places which, for them, define the USA.

Call me biased – I grew up in Wisconsin so I totally am – but **Lake Superior** (p557) just might be the most beautiful lake on the planet. At over 31,000 sq miles, it's so vast it could be mistaken for an ocean, and its rocky, rugged shoreline is a watercolor dream. I love it.

Ann Babe
annbabe.com

Ann writes about travel, culture and belonging.

Driving the **Peter Norbeck Scenic Byway** (p658) in the Black Hills of South Dakota is a blast. The Iron Mountain Rd section loops through the pines while the 14-mile Needles Hwy leg passes otherworldly granite spires. And oooh, those sketchy one-way tunnels.

Amy C Balfour
@AmyCBalfour

Amy writes about travel, food and adventure.

The **Ballard Locks** (p994) – officially known as the Hiram M Chittenden Locks – is one of my favorite places in Seattle. It doesn't look like much, but there's so much to see – feats of engineering, seasonal jumping salmon, blooming blossoms, and even the occasional harbor seal.

Sarah Etinas
sarahetinas.com

Sarah is a travel writer and editor.

A road trip once took me across Texas, the Southwest and California (pictured: Bixby Bridge, p944). I'll never forget seeing the ocean after having traversed so many dramatically different landscapes. Eye candy is selling it short. It was an eye feast.

Amelia Mularz
@ameliamularz

Amelia is a Midwest-born, LA-based writer who loves to tell stories about travel and design.

My favorite experience is climbing **Mt Beacon** (p115). On clear days, views stretch along the mountain-flanked Hudson to NYC's skyline, flickering 60 miles downriver – a grand diorama of America's diverse landscapes.

John Garry
@garryjohnfrancis

John is a writer, teacher, urban wanderer, mountain hiker and museum lover who eats out too much in Brooklyn, where he lives.

I've always been intrigued by off-the-grid places; what you find there is usually a version of something at its most raw. **Cordova** (p1052) is raw Alaska, where a sea-hardened population (just 2300 or so) self-sustains on moose, deer and salmon against an isolated backdrop of the Copper River Delta (pictured) and the Chugach Mountains.

Kevin Raub
@RaubontheRoad

Kevin is a Bologna-based travel journalist and the co-author of more than 125 Lonely Planet guidebooks.

My home base of **Fort Lauderdale** (p464), Florida, truly lives up to its 'Venice of America' nickname. Within a five-minute coast along its Las Olas Boulevard artery, you can be gawking at superyachts, strolling past designer boutiques and dipping your toes in the Atlantic. Beyond its white-sand-heaven reputation, I love how its artistic edge is becoming more visible.

Jesse Scott
@jesserobertscott

A Fort Lauderdale resident, Jesse has been writing about food and travel for 20-plus years.

Entering **Sacramento** (p937), I always have the paradoxical feeling that I'm entering a city and a forest at the same time. This California city has more than a million trees, cooling walkers on summer days, meeting in grand arches and framing the 1920s Craftsman homes and midtown Victorians. There are even city-center redwoods.

Helena Smith
@helenasmithpix

Helena loves to write about eco travel, community and the outdoors.

Chicago (p504) is my favorite place. That's why I've lived here for 35 years! Every time I take the L downtown, it's like the buildings pop up storybook-style. I love blue-green Lake Michigan spilling over the horizon, and old-school baseball at Wrigley Field. Then there are the beer gardens, free outdoor concerts at Millennium Park and water-squirting public art.

Karla Zimmerman
@karlazimmerman

Karla writes about travel and oddball sights.

Maryland (p280) is lovely around its edges, with the Eastern Shore a highlight. Secluded coves shelter picturesque waterside towns, quiet marshlands echo with the calls of ospreys, sunsets paint the skies and traditions endure. When you cross the Bay Bridge (pictured), you'll almost immediately feel slower-paced rhythms taking over, a oneness with the tides and the seasons, and a sense of tranquility and muted beauty.

Mary Fitzpatrick

Mary is an Africa-based writer with roots along the East Coast, where she returns frequently for visits.

I'm not sure what I expected as I headed to **Craters of the Moon National Monument** (p786) in Idaho. But standing in the middle of a blackened lava field, small volcanoes dotting the horizon, I felt like I was on the Big Island of Hawai'i. Until it started to snow. It was surreal, this volcanic landscape dusted in white, a reminder of just how diverse the Rocky Mountains region is.

Liza Prado

@liza.prado

Liza is a corporate lawyer turned travel writer and the author of over 60 books.

Hiking the Rim Trail in Utah's **Bryce Canyon National Park** (p858), I had one of those moments that only seem to happen in this remarkable state. All of a sudden, the Earth fell silent, there was no-one else around, and it felt like the landscape was holding its breath. And then, somewhere high on the rock walls, a single chickadee started to sing.

Anthony Ham

@AnthonyHamWrite

Anthony Ham writes about the wild places of our planet, from the deserts of Africa and the Arctic to the Amazon.

Nothing feels more like coming home than setting foot in the **Tallgrass Prairie National Preserve** (p610) in Kansas. When I was a kid, we took a road trip around Kansas, and this landscape has stuck with me ever since. When I listen to the wind, the meadowlarks and the snorting bison, it roots me right back here, no matter how long I've been away.

Lauren Keith

@noplacelike_it

Lauren is a guidebook author who grew up in Kansas. She's often found somewhere between the Midwest and the Middle East.

New York City (p66)

CONTRIBUTING WRITERS

Brett Atkinson
Alexis Averbuck
Ray Bartlett
Alison Bing
Dale Blasingame
Celeste Brash
Jade Bremner
Esther Carlstone
Rachel Chang
Gregor Clark
Julekha Dash
Suzie Dundas
Caroline Eubanks
Brandon Fralic

David Gibb
Michael Grosberg
Nicole Hagg
Ashley Harrell
Brian Healy
Carolyn Heller
Anita Isalska
Robert Isenberg
Sarah Kezele
Dylan Lalanne-Perkins
Alex Leviton
Stephen Lioy
Emily Matchar
Becky Ohlsen

Marisa Paska
Christopher Pitts
Britany Robinson
Jason Ruffin
Margot Seeto
Maya Stanton
Meena Thiruvengadam
Caroline Trefler
Julie Tremaine
Ryan Ver Berkmoes
Mara Vorhees
Terry Ward
Wendy Yanagihara

PLAN YOUR TRIP

Hawai'i

Kaua'i, Ni'ihau, Kapa'a, O'ahu, Wahiawa, Kailua, Moloka'i, Honolulu, Kahului, Lāna'i, Maui, Mauna Kea, Waimea (Kamuela), Kailua-Kona, Hilo, Hawai'i (Big Island)

Pacific Ocean

0 — 200 km
0 — 100 miles

Chicago
Bite into deep-dish pizza (p504)

New York City
Walk the Brooklyn Bridge at sunrise (p66)

Boston
Trace America's revolutionary past (p166)

Washington, DC
Explore the fabled Smithsonian collections (p242)

Great Smoky Mountains
Gaze across misty, blue-tinged peaks (p337)

Montgomery
Walk in the steps of Civil Rights icons (p393)

New Orleans
Join the party at Mardi Gras (p415)

Nashville
Dance with country fans at a honky-tonk (p359)

Miami
See cutting-edge street art (p440)

MN Duluth, Minneapolis, St Paul, Sioux Falls, Sioux City, Omaha, Lincoln, Topeka, Kansas City, Wichita, Tulsa, Little Rock, Dallas, Waco, Shreveport, Houston, Corpus Christi, Galveston, Baton Rouge, New Orleans, Jackson, Mobile, Pensacola, Tallahassee, Jacksonville, Daytona Beach, Orlando, Tampa, Fort Myers, Fort Lauderdale, Miami, Key West

Lake Superior, Sault Ste Marie, Green Bay, WI, Madison, Milwaukee, Lake Michigan, MI, Lansing, Detroit, Lake Huron, Lake Ontario, Buffalo, Rochester, Albany, Montpelier, VT, NH, Concord, ME, Augusta, Portland, MA, Boston, CT, RI, New York City, NJ, Philadelphia, Harrisburg, Baltimore, DE, MD, WASHINGTON, DC, Pittsburgh, Cleveland, Erie, PA, Toledo, Columbus, OH, Indianapolis, IN, Cincinnati, WV, Charleston, Richmond, VA, Norfolk, Raleigh, Charlotte, NC, Columbia, SC, Augusta, Charleston, Savannah, Atlantic Ocean, BAHAMAS, CUBA

Dubuque, Cedar Rapids, Des Moines, IA, Springfield, IL, St Louis, Louisville, Frankfort, KY, Jefferson City, MO, Springfield, Nashville, Knoxville, Memphis, Huntsville, Birmingham, Atlanta, GA, Columbus, Montgomery, AL, MS, LA, TN, AR, OK

Gulf of Mexico

0 — 1,000 km
0 — 500 miles

13

CAPTIVATING CITIES

The USA is home to mighty metropolises brimming with culture, cuisine and entertainment. You can admire the storied view over concrete canyons from skyscraper observatories or catch the latest avant-garde productions at small rep theaters. There are grand museums with art treasures from across the globe and thoughtfully designed parks where you can watch the world stroll past. Wherever you go, start local: pick a neighborhood to explore and dive in.

Bike-Friendly USA

Two-wheeled travel is increasingly popular in US cities, where you'll find many miles of dedicated bike lanes and easy-to-use bike-share programs.

Contactless Tickets

In many American cities, 'tap, ride and go' payment allows you to pay for a bus, tram or subway ride with the tap of a credit card.

Urban Forests

You're never far from nature even in dense city centers. Some parks, like Central Park in NYC, are even great places for seeing migrating birds.

San Francisco (p886)

BEST URBAN EXPERIENCES

Explore the many layers of **❶ San Francisco**, from its hidden mural-lined alleys to hilltop parks with magnificent panoramas. (p886)

Stroll the catwalk across the **❷ Brooklyn Bridge** for dazzling views of Manhattan and Brooklyn – and of the iconic bridge itself. (p67)

Spend the afternoon browsing record shops, booksellers and indie boutiques in the **❸ Wicker Park** neighborhood of Chicago. (p514)

Photograph the brilliantly colored street art of the **❹ Wynwood Walls**, an ever-evolving neighborhood installation in Miami. (p445)

Make a night of it in Las Vegas, where you can enjoy world-class shows on **❺ the Strip** even if you don't win big at roulette. (p801)

South Kaibab Trail (p817), Grand Canyon

NATIONAL PARKS

Often called 'America's best idea,' national parks protect both wilderness landscapes, unique geology and important historic sites, scattered amid the country's wide-ranging terrain. Whether watching bison on the move or strolling a virgin seashore, it's hard to think of a better way to spend your time in America than getting to know these remarkable places.

Learn Before You Go

The website *nps.gov* is the gateway to every national park in the country, with detailed info on attractions, history and planning tips.

Starring the American Wilderness

Get inspired by watching Ken Burns' excellent six-part documentary *The National Parks* (2009), which delves into the extraordinary story of America's park system.

BEST NATIONAL PARK EXPERIENCES

Admire the view of the Grand Canyon from aptly named Ooh Aah Point, reached by hiking the ❶ **South Kaibab Trail**. (p817)

Stroll a boardwalk path around thundering geysers, bubbling mud pools and hissing steam vents in ❷ **Yellowstone**. (p1090)

Hike amid verdant forests and shimmering waterfalls in the wilderness of ❸ **Great Smoky Mountains National Park**. (p337)

Gaze up at the massive sequoias in Yosemite's ❹ **Mariposa Grove**, with trees older than the Ancient Roman Empire. (p928)

Look for gators and great blue herons amid the mirror-like waters of the Florida ❺ **Everglades**. (p452)

SMALL TOWNS

Small towns have long occupied a large place in the national imagination – symbols of simplicity, nostalgia and neighborly pride. Across the US, these appealing settlements prove cities aren't the only havens of culture. Tight-knit art communities, mom-and-pop restaurants and streets leading to mountain trailheads and pristine lakes: these quiet corners serve charm in bite-size portions.

Tiny Town

America's smallest town is jh. It has just one resident: Elsie Eiler, who serves as the remote town's mayor, librarian, bartender, treasurer and sheriff.

What's in a Town?

What qualifies as a small town is fairly subjective, though the US Census Bureau generally considers any place with a population of 5000 or more a city.

Escaping the Crowds

Jarbidge, Nevada, is one of the nation's most remote small towns outside Alaska. It's over 100 miles to the nearest city.

BEST SMALL TOWN EXPERIENCES

Follow the Hudson River from ❶ **Beacon** to Hudson, two art-packed upstate New York towns surrounded by mountain trails. (p112)

Chase over 250 cascades in ❷ **Brevard**, North Carolina, known as the 'Land of Waterfalls,' then relax at a local brewery. (p334)

Inspect the paintings at ❸ **Grand Marais Art Colony** to see how the Minnesota hamlet's Lake Superior setting inspired creativity. (p583)

Stroll along the winding, hilly streets of ❹ **Eureka Springs**, an art-loving town of Victorian houses in the Ozarks of Arkansas. (p412)

Explore the shops and nearby creek trail in ❺ **Boerne**, one of many photogenic small towns in Texas' Hill Country. (p687)

BEHIND THE WHEEL

The open road awaits. As you hop into the driver's seat and hit the highway, you can chart a course through some of North America's most striking landscapes. Red-rock deserts of the West, the sultry swamplands of the South and the cliff-hugging Pacific Coast Hwy in California are a few fine starting points for the great American road trip. Be sure to veer off the interstate often to discover the bucolic 'blue highways' of lore.

Fill up the Tank

Keep the fuel tank topped up when you head onto the backroads – especially in remote parts of the West where gas stations can be few and far between.

Wildlife Safety

Be mindful of driving around dawn or dusk when wildlife is most active, and deer and other animals can wander onto the road.

Automobile Organizations

Join an automobile organization, like AAA, which will provide 24-hour roadside assistance and score you 10% savings at some motels and attractions.

Hwy 1 and Big Sur (p944), California

BEST ROAD TRIP EXPERIENCES

Admire the views over sea cliffs, misty forests and wave-battered beaches along a spectacular stretch of California's ❶ **Hwy 1**. (p944)

Pass through sun-bleached towns and desert wilderness en route to the stunning canyons in the ❷ **High Plains** of Texas. (p710)

Drive a stretch of historic ❸ **Route 66** in Oklahoma, home to more miles of the original road than any other state. (p614)

Stop for snacks at village general stores while rolling through the bucolic scenery of Vermont's ❹ **VT 100**. (p214)

Breathe in the clean mountain air while passing high-elevation forests and sparkling lakes on the ❺ **Cascade Lakes Scenic Byway**. (p1030)

Frenchmen Street (p423), New Orleans

THE AMERICAN SOUNDTRACK

From the soulful blues born in the Mississippi Delta to the bluegrass of Appalachia and Detroit's Motown sound – plus jazz, funk, hip-hop, country and rock 'n' roll – America has invented sounds integral to modern music. Walk in the footsteps of musical legends and hear tomorrow's stars in concert halls, honky-tonks and music clubs across the country.

Heart of Rock 'n' Roll

Rock 'n' roll has roots: Memphis is its birthplace, while Cleveland holds the hall of fame. Bethel, NY, hosted legendary rock concert Woodstock.

American Routes

For a deep dive into American music in all its beguiling forms, tune into American Routes, a weekly two-hour radio show (also a podcast) from New Orleans.

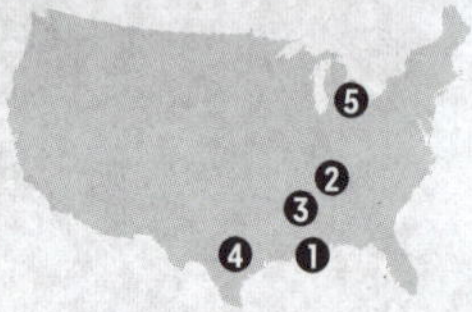

BEST LIVE MUSIC EXPERIENCES

Walk the club-lined strip of New Orleans' ❶ **Frenchmen Street**, ducking into music-filled bars. (p423)

Join country lovers for a night of dancing in a Nashville honky-tonk – like ❷ **Tootsie's Orchid Lounge**. (p361)

Listen to the soulful rhythms of up-and-coming blues stars at ❸ **Ground Zero** in the Mississippi Delta town of Clarksdale. (p400)

Take in the legendary music scene of Austin, Texas, starting with a show at the long-running ❹ **Continental Club** (p668).

Discover the latest talent in Motown (aka Detroit) on a visit to the indie-rock hub ❺ **Magic Stick**. (p547)

FABLED FESTIVALS

From small-town parades to big-city blowouts, festivals showcase creativity, community and culture. These aren't just parties – they're bucket list experiences worth planning a trip around – and although summer rules, you'll find major gatherings all year long. Whether honoring identity, celebrating history or joining a vast outdoor dance party, each event provides a glimpse of the loud, proud American spirit.

BEST FESTIVAL EXPERIENCES

Dance through the streets of New Orleans as carnival season crescendos into its bedazzling finale: ❶ **Mardi Gras**. (p415)

Admire prize-winning rabbits and sheep, eat your fill of corn dogs and catch the evening fireworks at ❷ **Iowa State Fair**. (p640)

Clink beer steins at ❸ **Oktoberfest Zinzinnati**, the nation's largest, honoring Ohio's German heritage with plenty of oompah. (p538)

See a showcase of Native American dance, art and crafts at the ❹ **Red Earth Festival**, which brings tribes to Oklahoma City. (p619)

Groove to the rhythms of Milwaukee's ❺ **Summerfest**, dubbed 'The World's Largest Music Festival' and going strong since 1968. (p563)

Independence Day

July 4 commemorates the Declaration of Independence with barbecues, parades and fireworks – particularly splendid in Washington, DC (p242), where marching bands parade down Constitution Ave.

Pride Month

Cities and small towns fly rainbow flags at parties and parades throughout June. The biggest celebration is in NYC, birthplace of the modern LGBTQ rights movement.

Federal Holidays

Check the calendar before making plans. On federal holidays, including US-specific holidays like Thanksgiving and Memorial Day, many businesses shut down, particularly in rural regions.

FROM LEFT: CAVAN-IMAGES/SHUTTERSTOCK, WIRESTOCK CREATORS/SHUTTERSTOCK

COASTAL TREASURES

Amid thousands of miles of shoreline, you'll find islands, seaside towns and some of America's loveliest beaches. There are plenty of surprises en route, from herds of wild horses descended from shipwreck survivors to remote national parks reached only by boat. Wherever you roam, it's hard not to feel like you've left the modern world behind as you head out to a place where nature rules supreme in a salt-tinged realm of sea, sand and sky.

Coastal Queen

Florida has more coastline than any other state in the contiguous US, including 825 miles of sugar-sand beaches and 350 miles of coral reefs.

Shark Tales

Over 50 shark species call the Atlantic's East Coast home, but encounters are extremely rare – despite horrors evoked by *Jaws*, filmed on Martha's Vineyard.

Dynamic Dunes

The Great Lakes have the world's largest collection of freshwater sand dunes, most prominent around Lake Michigan (home to a 400ft peak at Sleeping Bear).

Hanauma Bay, O'ahu (p1064), Hawai'i

BEST COASTAL EXPERIENCES

Swim, snorkel, paddle or dive around Florida Keys reefs at ❶ **John Pennekamp**, the nation's first underwater park. (p458)

Spot herds of wild horses trotting between dunes that dot ❷ **Assateague Island National Seashore** in Maryland. (p286)

Jump into Lake Michigan from ❸ **Door County, Wisconsin** – a remote 80-mile peninsula where wild waves crash along limestone cliffs. (p568)

Enjoy some Southern Cal beach time followed by arcade action and other vintage amusements at the ❹ **Santa Monica Pier**. (p958)

Immerse yourself in the paradise-like beauty of Hawai'i's ❺ **O'ahu**, from surfing off Waikīkī to snorkeling at Hanauma Bay. (p1066)

A MOVEABLE FEAST

Whatever your reasons for visiting, food is likely to play a starring role during your travels. This is the land of Maine lobster shacks, bagels and lox in Manhattan delis, tender brisket in Texas smokehouses and decadent Creole cooking in New Orleans. You also won't go thirsty in a region of abundant vineyards, craft breweries and home-grown bourbon (among many other spirits), not to mention Southern-style sweet tea and much-loved local coffee roasters all across the US.

Farmers Markets

Across the USA, farmers markets celebrate local veg, seafood, foraged mushrooms, inventive baked goods and more. Saturday morning is typically the big day.

Culinary Gifts

Edible souvenirs abound, including maple syrup from Vermont, smoked salmon in the Pacific Northwest and jams and honeys wherever you go.

Closing Time

Some small-town restaurants have limited opening hours, even in communities that are tourism-reliant. Always check timings in advance.

Wine-tasting room, Walla Walla (p1008), Washington

BEST FOOD EXPERIENCES

Indulge in a meal of African-influenced Low Country cuisine at ❶ **Hannibal's Kitchen** in Charleston, South Carolina. (p344)

Get your fill of the world's tastiest crustaceans at the five-day ❷ **Maine Lobster Festival** in Rockland. (p233)

Sip your way through Washington state's wine country on a visit to the tasting rooms of ❸ **Walla Walla**. (p1008)

Learn the art of preparing mouthwatering New Mexican dishes at the ❹ **Santa Fe School of Cooking**. (p868)

Bite into a heavenly slice of deep-dish pizza at ❺ **Giordano's**, which has been wowing Chicago diners since the 1970s. (p504)

Mission San José (p685), San Antonio, Texas

REMEMBERING THE PAST

Ancient peoples, revolutionaries and visionaries in the fight for civil rights have all played pivotal roles in shaping the American psyche. Today, hundreds of sites (many managed by the National Park Service) preserve the memory of watershed places and events in the nation's history, including 1000-year-old mound settlements, Spanish Missions and Civil War battlefields.

BEST HISTORY EXPERIENCES

Follow the nation's founding footsteps along Boston's ❶ **Freedom Trail**, exploring the city's role in the American Revolution. (p172)

Get a crash course in US history at the free-to-visit Smithsonian museums in ❷ **Washington, DC**. (p242)

Unearth the nation's dark history of slavery in ❸ **Montgomery**, Alabama, through memorials that inspire reflection. (p393)

Learn about the blending of cultures while exploring the Spanish Missions in ❹ **San Antonio**, Texas. (p680)

Wander through the oldest continuously inhabited settlement in the US at ❺ **Taos Pueblo** in New Mexico. (p870)

Talking History

American History Tellers is an excellent, highly engaging podcast with episodes that explore everything from the Salem witch trials to the hidden history of the White House.

Original Residents

People have occupied the North American continent for 12,000 years, possibly longer. Remnants of ancient civilizations like Georgia's Ocmulgee Mounds tell tales of complex Indigenous societies.

OFFBEAT AMERICANA

Leave the well-worn path behind to uncover the weirdest and wildest corners of these 50 states. Under-the-radar destinations may take extra effort to reach, but even a tiny detour sometimes reaps big rewards: outdoor art installations, roadside folk monuments, oddball museums and surreal landscapes – some of which are as memorable as the nation's more popular attractions.

BEST OFFBEAT AMERICANA EXPERIENCES

See evocative creations made by outsider artists at the ❶ **American Visionary Art Museum** in Baltimore. (p289)

Drive through Minnesota to find some of the nation's quirkiest stop-and-gawk sights, including the pork-praising ❷ **Spam Museum**. (p580)

Explore the kitschy wonders in ❸ **Amarillo**, Texas, including the Big Texan and the Cadillac Ranch. (p710)

Arrive during the rise of full moon at Kentucky's ❹ **Cumberland Falls** for the chance to see a moonbow – a rare after-dark rainbow. (p373)

Dig deep and dream big at ❺ **Crater of Diamonds** in Arkansas, where lucky visitors can keep whatever sparkling gems they find. (p410)

Roadside America

You'll find plenty of ideas for an excursion to see quirky monuments and attractions on the Roadside America app. There's also ample (free) content on the website.

National vs State Parks

Federally recognized national parks get all the glory, attracting swarms of visitors, but lesser-known state parks can rival their beauty. Give these underdog destinations a try.

Magnificent Springs

It's fitting that Ponce de León (allegedly) sought the fountain of youth in Florida. In fact, the state has over 1000 springs – among the densest concentrations on Earth!

REGIONS & CITIES

Find the places that tick all your boxes.

Great Lakes

OVERLOOKED BEAUTY IN THE USA'S HEARTLAND

Chicago, aka the Windy City, reigns over this region with its glittering skyline, electric arts scene and deep-dish Midwestern pride. Five mighty lakes link everything else – their coasts covered in gold dunes, moose-tracked forests, and cities like Milwaukee and Detroit, in mid-revival. Everything from quirky roadside attractions to pristine canoe paths through the wilderness awaits. **p499**

Great Plains

SURPRISING CITIES AMID PRISTINE PRAIRIE

Despite its lack of name recognition, the oft-overlooked Great Plains has wide-ranging appeal. You'll find a mix of vibrant cities and charming small towns, memorable settings for road trips (Route 66, the Great River Road), rich Native American heritage, and the otherworldly landscapes of the Badlands and the Black Hills. **p588**

Texas

BIG SKIES AND OPEN ROADS

The larger-than-life state makes a cinematic setting for road trips and big-city rambles. In the east, Austin, Dallas and Houston pack a lifetime's worth of exploring when it comes to art, culture and cuisine. Seaside adventures await on the long Gulf Coast, while further west lies a dramatic wilderness of deserts, mountains and canyons. **p664**

New York, New Jersey & Pennsylvania

SPRAWLING CITIES, HISTORIC HAMLETS AND NATURAL WONDERS

New York is packed with superlatives, ruled by cultural capital NYC – the nation's most populous city – and home to America's largest mountain-studded state park and the continent's most powerful waterfall. The rest of the region swings between seaside boardwalks, serene river towns, bucolic farms and Rust Belt cities on the rise. **p60**

New England

QUAINT VILLAGES, COLONIAL HISTORY AND ATLANTIC SHORELINE

Maine's rugged coast, Cape Cod's dune-framed peninsula and Rhode Island's white-sand beaches: New England's lobster-loving seaside is a summer oasis. Inland, mountains are dotted with farms supporting a locavore food scene that's vibrant in Vermont, epicenter of autumn leaf-peeping. It's all anchored by scholarly, sports-crazed Boston, built by America's revolutionaries. **p161**

Washington, DC & the Capital Region

US CAPITAL, MUSEUMS, BEACHES AND MOUNTAINS

'DC' is America's political powerhouse, adorned with monuments, parks and museums. Maryland and Delaware sit north, where salty shores connect to wooded mountains and diversity makes life blue-crab-meat sweet. To the south, Virginia is home of presidents, Civil War battlefields and the mountain-climbing Blue Ridge Pkwy. West Virginia spreads across Appalachia's wild wonderland. **p242**

The South

BIRTHPLACE OF AMERICAN MUSIC AND CIVIL RIGHTS

The South's syncopated rhythm echoes from Atlantic sandbars to colonial coastal cities, up Appalachian mountain trails and along Gulf Coast bayous. It rings out in New Orleans jazz clubs and Nashville honky-tonks; in crackling Memphis barbecues and bars pouring Kentucky bourbon. It's steeped in legend, both glorious and grim, central to America's soul. **p317**

Florida

BEACHES, CULTURE AND SUN-SOAKED TROPICS

This is America's sun-soaked playground, where art deco Miami hums with Latin flavor, the Everglades pulse with prehistoric life and the Keys stretch into a coral-dotted turquoise sea. Imaginations run wild in theme-park-happy Orlando, rockets launch along the Space Coast and tales of Spanish colonists linger in towns lined with moss-laden live oaks. **p434**

REGIONS & CITIES

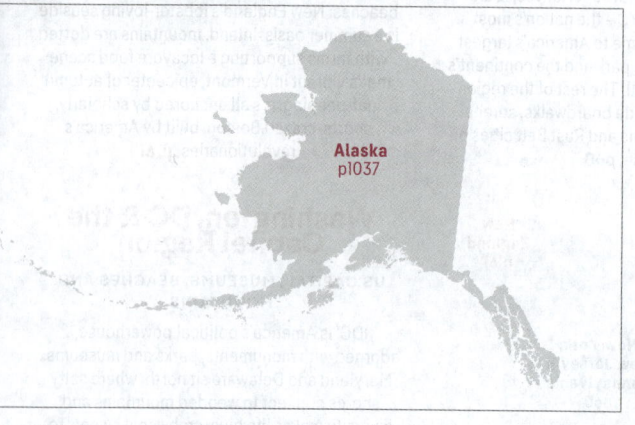

Hawai'i

ISLANDS OF ALOHA

Some 2500 miles west of California, the Hawaiian Islands loom large in the imagination with a mix of glorious beaches, verdant rainforests and sun-kissed mountaintops. There's much to discover beyond the landscapes, from shopping for artwork and accessories in Honolulu's Chinatown to touring a Kona coffee farm on the Big Island. **p1058**

California

THE LEISURELY LEFT COAST

The Golden State is like a nation unto its own with alluring oceanfront cities and countless famous icons – Hollywood, Napa Valley, Disneyland. You could spend many weeks exploring California's diverse wonders, from driving a seaside stretch of Hwy 1 to immersing yourself in nature amid the granite summits of Yosemite. **p880**

Alaska

NATURE, WILDLIFE AND MONUMENTAL ADVENTURES

Amid rugged wilderness, you can pack your days visiting glaciers, hiking mountain trails, going on wildlife-watching tours and kayaking across iceberg-dotted bays. There's lots to do in and around Anchorage, though you can also focus on the islands of the Southeast, with tiny towns backed by lush, forested slopes. **p1037**

Pacific Northwest

AN UNBEATABLE NATURE ESCAPE

The food- and arts-loving cities of Seattle and Portland make prime gateways to this wildly varied region of virgin beaches, temperate rainforests and snow-covered mountains (including active volcanoes). Rugged trails and scenic waterways provide numerous ways to get active, though vineyards and burgeoning cultural attractions are also major highlights. **p980**

Rocky Mountains p714

Rocky Mountains

EPIC BEAUTY MEETS OUTDOOR ADVENTURE

Towering peaks, alpine meadows and rushing rivers form the backdrop to big adventures in the Rockies. This is the place for legendary hiking, mountain biking, rafting and skiing, and its famous national parks offer outstanding wildlife-watching (bears, moose, elk and more). Mountain towns offer their own rewards, like galleries, indie shops and craft breweries. **p714**

Southwest USA p790

Southwest USA

ONE OF AMERICA'S GRAND EPICS

The sun-baked region of high deserts, chiseled peaks and age-old human settlements has rich Native American heritage and myriad natural wonders, including some 15 national parks. The towns and villages here are no less captivating, from timeless Santa Fe to serene Sedona, not to mention the one-of-a-kind desert metropolis of Las Vegas. **p790**

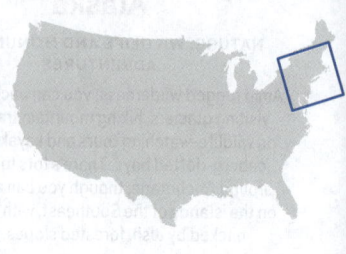

New York City (p66)

ITINERARIES

The Northeast by Rail

Allow: 8 days   **Distance:** 670 miles

You can forget about the hassle of driving on this scenic journey, traveling by Amtrak (and ferry) to some of the most dynamic cities and beguiling seaside towns in the Northeast. Along the way, you'll walk in the steps of American revolutionaries, see world-renowned art collections and explore cutting-edge cuisine.

❶ WASHINGTON, DC ⏱ 1 DAY

Start off in the capital (pictured, p242) with sunrise views from the steps of the Lincoln Memorial. Later, take in the famed planes in the National Air and Space Museum, followed by Native American lore at the National Museum of the American Indian – also the Mall's best place for lunch. Finish at the striking National Museum of African American History and Culture, with its century-spanning displays.

❷ PHILADELPHIA ⏱ 1 DAY

In Philly (pictured, p138), dash up the steps, Rocky Balboa–style, of the Philadelphia Museum of Art for a look at 20 centuries of treasures. Lunch at the Reading Terminal Market, with scores of food vendors. Spend the afternoon visiting Independence National Historical Park. Have dinner and drinks at Dandelion, an atmospheric spot near Rittenhouse Sq.

❸ NEW YORK CITY ⏱ 2 DAYS

Rise early for a morning walk over the Brooklyn Bridge, a cinematic spot to catch the NYC (pictured, p66) sunrise. Later, head to the Tenement Museum to learn about New York life of the past, then munch your way around the globe in the East Village. Catch a show that evening at the Public. Spend day two exploring leafy Central Park and the glorious Metropolitan Museum of Art.

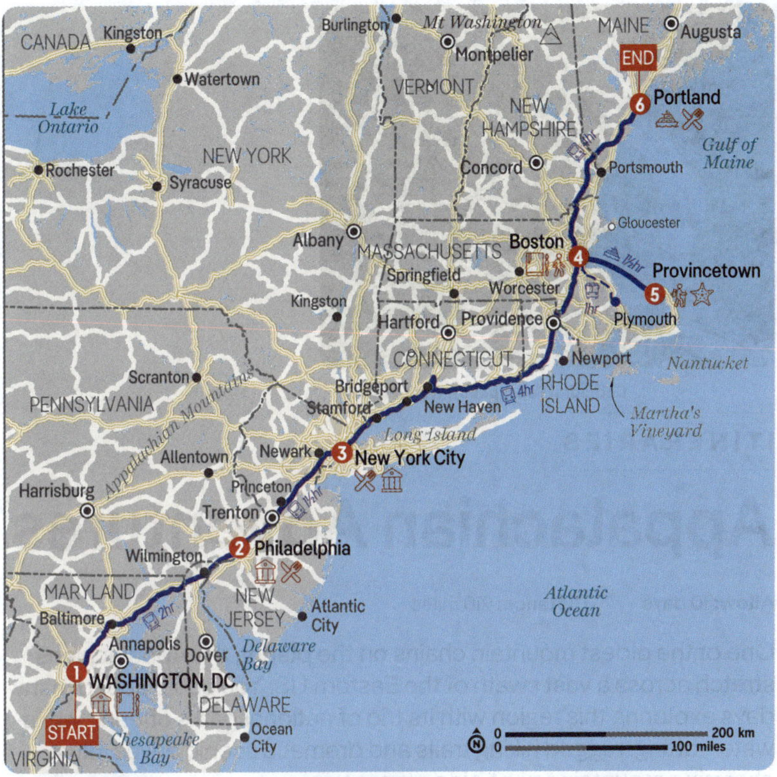

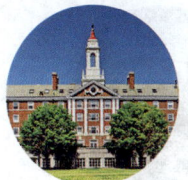

4

BOSTON 1 DAY

Learn about Boston's (pictured, p166) revolutionary past by walking the Freedom Trail, a 2.5-mile route that passes historic meeting halls and monuments. Feel the pulse of student life over at Harvard, then take a stroll along the Charles River Esplanade.

***Detour:** Step into the 17th century at the **Plimoth Patuxet Museums** (p183), where you can learn about the Pilgrims and the Wampanoag. ½ day*

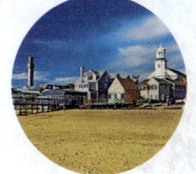

5

PROVINCETOWN 1 DAY

The boat ride from Boston provides a suitable introduction to the seaside town (pictured, p187) anchoring the north end of Cape Cod. Stretch your legs on a walk amid dunes, forest and marsh on the Province Lands Trail – also a good place to look for whales. Later, learn about island history at the Provincetown Museum, then have a waterfront meal at Fanizzi's by the Sea.

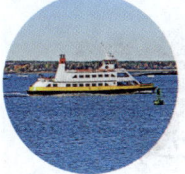

6

PORTLAND 2 DAYS

Breathe in the sea air in Portland (pictured, p231) on a stroll through the brick streets of the Old Port, then explore Maine history at the Wadsworth-Longfellow House. Have dinner at elegant Scales. On day two, get a taste of lobstering life with Lucky Catch Cruises or hop a ferry out to Peaks Island, and then indulge in freshly shucked perfection at Eventide Oyster Co.

FROM LEFT: JORGE SALCEDO/SHUTTERSTOCK, HAVESEEN/SHUTTERSTOCK, E.J.JOHNSON PHOTOGRAPHY/SHUTTERSTOCK

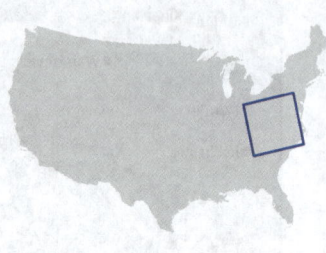

Cathedral Falls (p308), West Virginia

ITINERARIES

Appalachian Adventures

Allow: 10 days   **Distance:** 910 miles

One of the oldest mountain chains on the planet, the Appalachians stretch across a vast swath of the Eastern US. You could spend many days exploring this region with its trio of national parks offering white-water rafting, rugged hiking trails and dramatic scenic drives, plus charming mountain towns along the way.

1 HARPERS FERRY ⏱1 DAY

Just two hours' drive from Washington, DC, the little town of Harpers Ferry (p312) is a scenic gateway into Appalachia. Take in the lay of the land on a morning hike up the Maryland Heights Trail for sweeping views over three states. In the afternoon, delve into America's tumultuous history preceding the Civil War at free sites around town, including John Brown's Fort.

2 SHENANDOAH NATIONAL PARK ⏱1 DAY

Near the Virginia town of Front Royal, you'll reach the start of the Skyline Drive that takes you into the heart of Shenandoah National Park (p300). You'll pass lookouts and turnoffs to historic buildings. Alternatively, skip the scenic drive and focus on one of the park's most rewarding (and challenging) hikes: the climb to the top of Old Rag Mountain.

3 NEW RIVER GORGE ⏱2 DAYS

Spend a day getting to know one of America's newest national parks (p308). Immerse yourself in the region's natural beauty with a walk along the panoramic Endless Wall Trail. Or, brave the Bridge Walk for heart-pounding views over the rushing river. Later, take in the thundering Cathedral Falls. On your second day, go white-water rafting with Adventures on the Gorge.

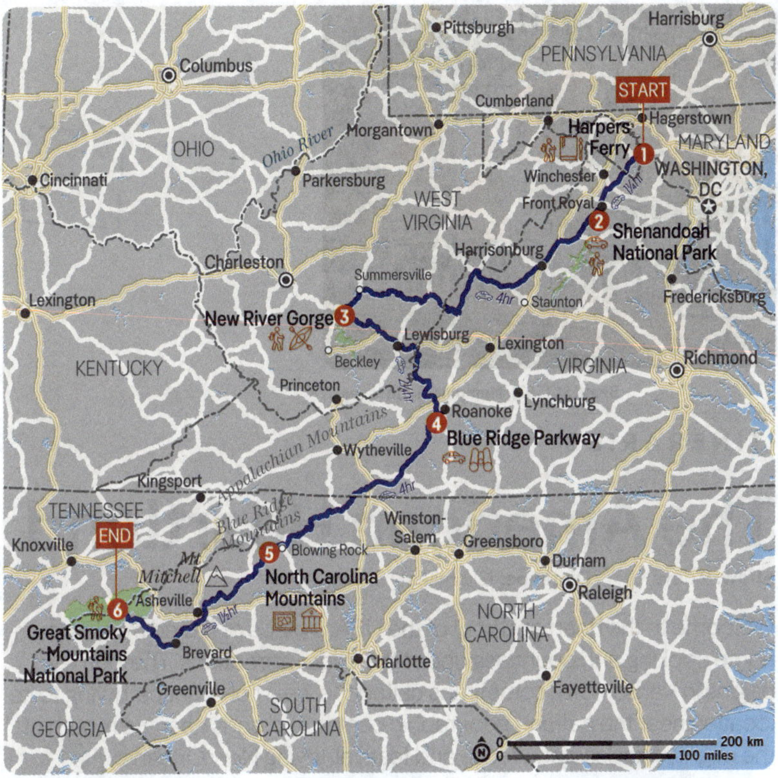

④
BLUE RIDGE PARKWAY
⏱ 1 DAY

Head to Roanoke, a lively mountain town and handy access point for the Blue Ridge Parkway (p300). Before hopping on the road, head up to the Mill Mountain Star, a city icon that affords far-off views of rolling mountain peaks. Next, hop on this road – among the most scenic in the Appalachians – and enjoy the views as you roll toward North Carolina.

⑤
NORTH CAROLINA MOUNTAINS ⏱ 3 DAYS

Start off the North Carolina Mountains (p333) adventure in Blowing Rock, a town of galleries and woodland walks from downtown. Continue to Asheville to explore the city's arts scene, with stops at the River Arts District and Noir Collective. On day two, visit the Biltmore, America's grandest private estate, then continue to Brevard for more craft and nature adventures.

⑥
GREAT SMOKY MOUNTAINS NATIONAL PARK ⏱ 2 DAYS

Greet the day atop the observation deck on Kuwohi, the highest point in the Smokies (p337), then hit the Alum Cave Trail for a rewarding hike amid lush forests and silvery streams. End the day with a drive along the pretty Roaring Fork Motor Nature Trail. On your second day, visit the old farmsteads and pioneer churches in Cades Cove.

FROM LEFT: BILANOL/SHUTTERSTOCK, CHANSAK JOE/SHUTTERSTOCK, TEAHLINT/SHUTTERSTOCK

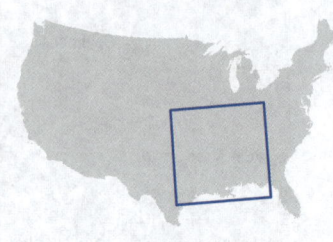

Beale St (357), Memphis, Tennessee

ITINERARIES

The American Heartland

Allow: 9 days   **Distance:** 1210 miles

Welcome to the heart and soul of the USA: a place of fabled music, down-home cooking and countless under-the-radar attractions. The journey begins in Kansas City, sometimes called the 'heart of America' owing to its location near the nation's geographic center, and ends near the mouth of the mighty Mississippi in food- and festival-loving New Orleans.

❶ KANSAS CITY ⏱ 1 DAY

Get the lay of the land in Kansas City (p601) from atop the lofty Liberty Memorial, followed by a journey through the excellent National WWI Museum below. Afterwards, feast on some of the country's best barbecue at Slap's BBQ. That evening, catch live jazz in the vibrant, historically Black neighborhood of 18th and Vine. Cap the night with bespoke cocktails at speakeasy-style Swordfish Tom's.

❷ ST LOUIS ⏱ 1 DAY

Explore St Louis' (p594) most imaginative side in the playfully art-centric City Museum. Next, see the Clydesdales at the Anheuser-Busch Brewery, learn about the past at the Old Courthouse and ride the tram to the top of the Arch for a fabulous view over the Mississippi.

Detour: Head across the Mississippi to explore the ancient mound-building civilization of **Cahokia** (p523). ½ day 🚗

❸ NASHVILLE ⏱ 2 DAYS

Wander through history at the interactive (and free) Tennessee State Museum, then delve into Nashville's (p259) musical heritage at the Country Music Hall of Fame & Museum. In the evening, follow the sound of twanging guitars to Tootsie's Orchid Lounge. On day two, head to East Nashville for forest strolls in Shelby Bottoms and shopping in the Fatherland District.

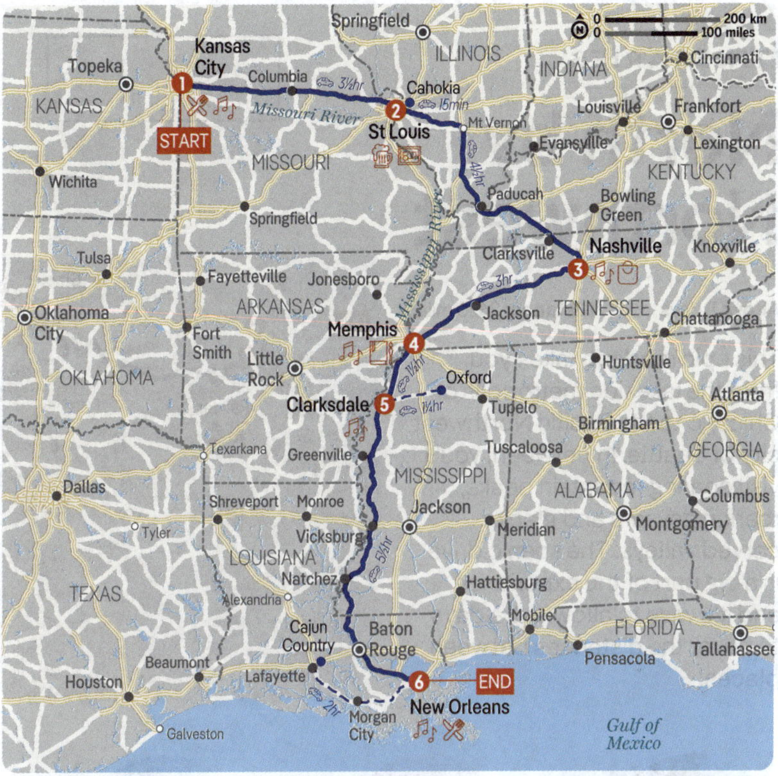

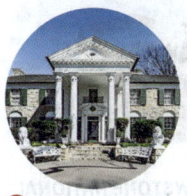

4

MEMPHIS 2 DAYS

Dive into the city's (p355) legendary music sites, including Sun Studio and Memphis Rock 'n' Soul Museum. That night, catch live music at BB King's on Beale St. On your second day, join Elvis fans at Graceland, then immerse yourself in the past at the National Civil Rights Museum. Later, take in the shops, cafes and bars of the creative Cooper-Young district.

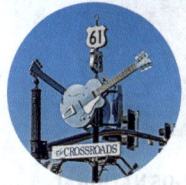

5

CLARKSDALE 1 DAY

After crossing into Mississippi, learn about the famous innovators who changed musical history at Clarksdale's (p399) Delta Blues Museum. Browse records and folk art at Cat Head, then spend the night listening to live blues at clubs like Red's and Ground Zero.

***Detour:** Drive east to **Oxford** (p285) to visit author William Faulkner's home and the leafy campus of Ole Miss.*

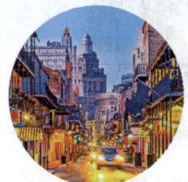

6

NEW ORLEANS 2 DAYS

Spend day one in New Orleans (p415) exploring the sights and sounds of the French Quarter. In the evening, catch live jazz on Frenchmen St. The next day, hop on the St Charles Avenue Streetcar for a ride out to Audubon Park. End the day over food and drinks in the backyard revelry of Bacchanal.

***Detour:** Visit **Cajun Country** (p431) for a Saturday morning dance, followed by a swamp tour. ½ day*

FROM LEFT: ROLF_52/SHUTTERSTOCK, HEIDI BESEN/SHUTTERSTOCK, F11PHOTO/SHUTTERSTOCK

ITINERARIES

North by Northwest

Allow: 11 days **Distance:** 2620 miles

This epic road trip takes you from the lakeside metropolis of Chicago to the Pacific Northwest city of Seattle. In between, you'll visit soaring mountain peaks, roaring geysers and glacier-carved valleys. The scenic drive is a big part of the experience, and it's wise to allow extra days to cover the distances between places.

① CHICAGO ⏱ 2 DAYS

Start the day in **Chicago** (p504) amid paintings and sculptures at the fabulous Art Institute, then go for a wander in the green oasis of Millennium Park. Catch live blues at the famed Buddy Guy's Legends. On day two, take a scenic boat tour aboard Chicago Architecture Center's *First Lady*, admire the views from the Willis Tower and enjoy some improv at Second City.

② BADLANDS NATIONAL PARK ⏱ 2 DAYS

Take your time exploring the extraordinary beauty of South Dakota's Badlands (p650). Get a feel for the setting on a scenic drive along Badlands Loop Rd, then take a closer look on a hike along the Notch Trail.

🚗 *Detour:* Drive west to the rock-carved faces of four American presidents at **Mt Rushmore** (p593) – also featured in a certain Alfred Hitchcock film. 1 day 🚗

③ YELLOWSTONE NATIONAL PARK ⏱ 2 DAYS

Pack your days with wonders on a journey through America's oldest national park (p758). Watch Old Faithful erupt, take a hike amid the otherworldly landscapes, spot bison and other wildlife and feel the mists of the thundering Upper Falls above the Yellowstone River.

🚗 *Detour:* Spend a day (or more!) taking in the spectacular beauty of **Grand Teton National Park** (p719), an easy drive south of Yellowstone. 1 day 🚗

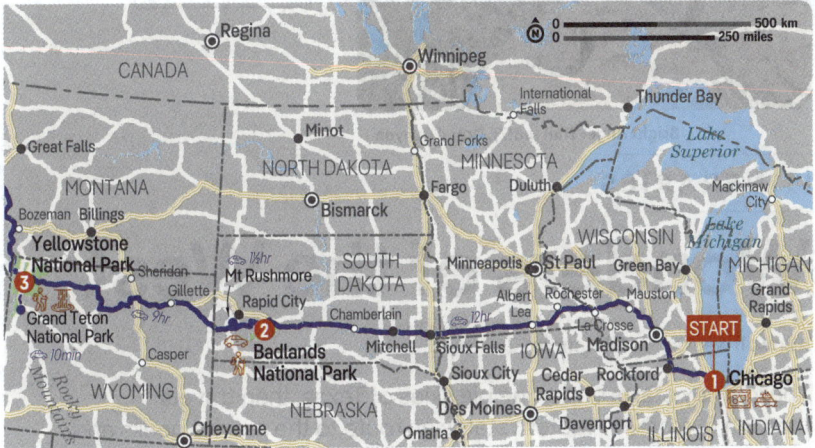

4 GLACIER NATIONAL PARK ⏱ 2 DAYS

Spend two action-filled days taking in some of the most dramatic scenery in the country. Prioritize a trip along the Going-to-the-Sun Rd, with its historic landmarks, overlooks and mountain passes – get an early start for the best chance to see wildlife. On your second day, tackle one of Glacier's (p772) memorable hikes. Alternatively, enjoy a view from the water on a kayak trip or boat cruise.

5 MT RAINIER ⏱ 1 DAY

Greet the dawn at Mt Rainier (p998) with an early-morning visit to Sunrise Point Lookout with its mesmerizing views of glaciers and the chiseled peaks of the Cascades. Stretch your legs on the scenic Sunrise Nature Trail, then make the drive to Paradise for views of wildflower-filled meadows. Continue to nearby Longmire, a former homestead with historic buildings that provide a window into the past.

6 SEATTLE ⏱ 2 DAYS

Experience Seattle's (p986) Asian heritage on a walk through the International District, then grab a bite at Pike Place Market and take in the views from atop the Space Needle. On day two, go whale-watching in Puget Sound or get an alternative view of Seattle on Bill Speidel's Underground Tour. Have dinner in Capitol Hill at Taylor Shellfish Oyster Bar, then catch live music at Chop Suey.

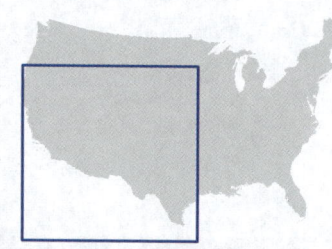

Bright Angel Trail (p817), Grand Canyon

ITINERARIES

Wonders of the West

Allow: 11 weeks   **Distance:** 2260 miles

The journey starts under the big skies of Texas, then travels through five other Western states en route to the granite peaks and ancient sequoias of Yosemite. You'll also see high deserts, red-rock mountains and one very famous canyon, along with two of the Southwest's most captivating cities.

❶ SAN ANTONIO ⏲ 2 DAYS

Spend the first day exploring San Antonio's (p680) blockbuster historic sites, including the Alamo and the Mission Trail, a collection of 18th-century churches south of town. On day two, check out the Mexican crafts (and snacks) at Historic Market Square, then take a stroll up the scenic River Walk, stopping to visit the San Antonio Museum of Art, followed by dining and shopping at the Pearl.

❷ BIG BEND NATIONAL PARK ⏲ 2 DAYS

Take a memorable hike in Big Bend (p708), a remote national park set amid mountains, desert and riverside. On day two, head off on a rafting or canoeing adventure along the Rio Grande, then rest your weary bones in Boquillas Hot Springs.

🚗 *Detour:* Make the drive northwest to **Marfa** (p708) for a dose of avant-garde art amid the cowboy country of West Texas.

❸ SANTA FE ⏲ 1 DAY

Fuel up for the day in Santa Fe (p867) with a breakfast burrito from Tia Sophia's. Next, hit the venerable sights of this fascinating high-desert town. Get an eyeful of history in St Francis Cathedral, tour the 17th-century San Miguel Mission and admire the seemingly miraculous staircase in the Loretto Chapel.

🚗 *Detour:* It's a breathtaking drive to **Taos Pueblo** (p870), where you can learn about Pueblo culture. ½ day

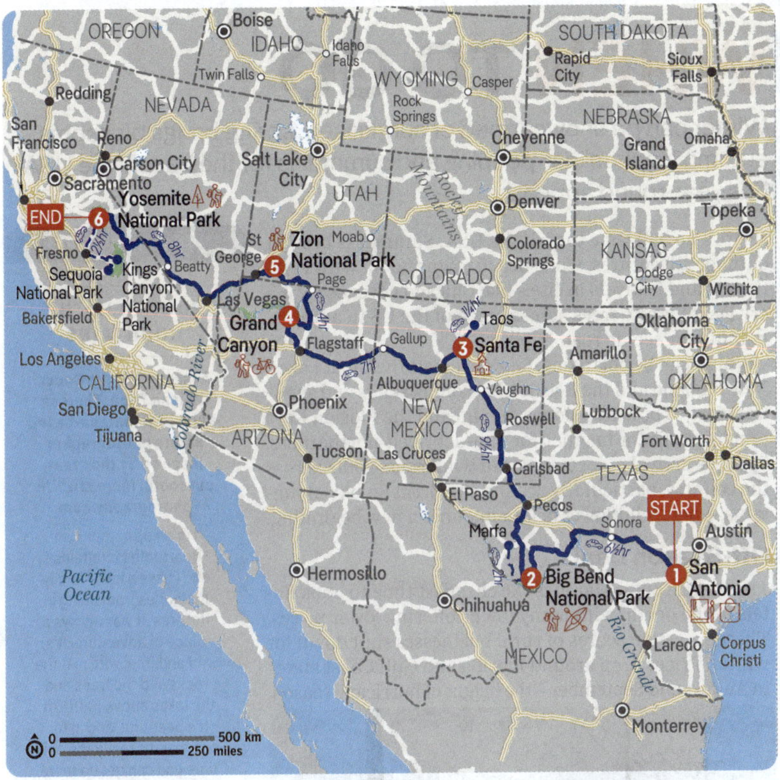

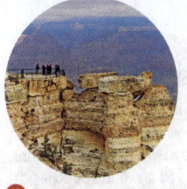

4

GRAND CANYON ⏱ 2 DAYS

Learn about the billion-year-old back story of the fabled mile-deep chasm at the Grand Canyon Visitor Center (p816). Admire the views from the many overlooks and hike a bit of the dramatic Bright Angel Trail. On day two, rent a bike for the ride to Hermits Rest. Alternatively, head up to Horseshoe Bend for a kayaking trip or a slot canyon tour.

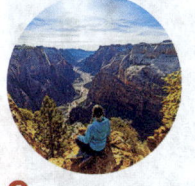

5

ZION NATIONAL PARK ⏱ 2 DAYS

Beat the crowds at Zion (p860) with a morning hike to Observation Point for canyon views. Later, walk to the Emerald Pools, a realm of photogenic grottos. The next day, take a scenic but easygoing stroll along the Riverside Walk. Or, you coulddress in proper attire, grab your walking stick and enter the river on a one-of-a-kind adventure through the Narrows.

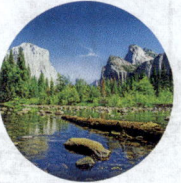

6

YOSEMITE NATIONAL PARK ⏱ 2 DAYS

Admire the beauty of Yosemite's (p928) granite monoliths like El Capitan, then head to the Mariposa Grove to marvel at the staggering 3000-year-old giant sequoias. On day two, tackle the challenging climb up Half Dome.

***Detour:** See more ancient trees on a day of hiking adventures at side-by-side **Sequoia & Kings Canyon National Parks** (p930). 1 day*

FROM LEFT: TFOXFOTO/SHUTTERSTOCK, JAKUB MACULEWICZ/SHUTTERSTOCK, NYOKKI/SHUTTERSTOCK

WHEN TO GO

Winter can be snowcapped or sun-kissed, spring brings blossoms, autumn inspires leaf-peeping and summer is for the beach: the USA has year-round appeal.

There's no bad time to visit the USA. Summer is best for outdoor adventures, when beach towns boom with vacationers and festivals in cities like Chicago never cease. Fiery leaves ignite trees across much of the US in autumn, making for scenic road trips.

Winter can be polarizing. Snow blankets the Great Lakes, New England and the Rockies, beckoning skiers and snowboarders to powdery slopes. Miami and the Florida Keys remain warm, a magnet for sun-deprived northerners. Spring's arrival is spectacular in wilderness spots across the country, particularly around the Great Smoky Mountains, where wildflower fields announce a new beginning.

Off-Season Deals

January through March is the cheapest time to book hotels in the north, with many towns offering lower prices. There's a catch: scores of rural businesses shut down for winter. Prices drop around Florida and Gulf Coast states in August and September – the height of hurricane season.

⊕ I LIVE HERE

SUMMER IN THE MOUNTAINS

A member of the Coeur d'Alene Tribe, Theresa White is a Montana-based nature photographer inspired by the great outdoors. *theresawhitephotography.com*

I grew up camping in Beartooth Mountains, and I have a lot of family memories from being in the area. It was always a place of adventure. It's wild and free, with just the rocks and the trees and the lakes above 10,000ft. It's beautiful, and in the summer it's really the only time you can get up there.

A hurricane makes land in Texas (p664)

HURRICANES

Powerful storms that form over warm ocean waters strike the US shoreline every year. Hurricanes are classified on wind speed (and lethality), from Category 1 (74mph) to Category 5 (157mph and up). Residents near the Atlantic and Gulf Coasts stay vigilant during hurricane season (June to November).

Weather Through the Year

JANUARY	FEBRUARY	MARCH	APRIL	MAY	JUNE
Average daytime max: **39.5°F (4.1°C)**	Average daytime max: **42.2°F (5.6°C)**	Average daytime max: **49.9°F (9.9°C)**	Average daytime max: **61.8°F (16.5°C)**	Average daytime max: **71.4°F (21.8°C)**	Average daytime max: **79.7°F (26.5°C)**
Days of rainfall: 3.64	Days of rainfall: 3.19	Days of rainfall: 4.29	Days of rainfall: 4.09	Days of rainfall: 3.96	Days of rainfall: 4.54

THROES OF WINTER

Owing to heavy snowfall in the Rockies, some mountain passes close from November to May. To reopen them, crews spend weeks clearing the roads, which requires bulldozers, graders with wedges and other heavy equipment to break up the dense snowpack.

Blockbuster Celebrations

Mardi Gras (p415) The mother of all street parties features one wild weekend of parades, costumes and merriment, plus other big celebrations during the weeks leading up to Shrove Tuesday. **February**

St Patrick's Day (p502) A local plumbers union dyes the Chicago River shamrock green – using a non-toxic, plant-based powder – just in time for a parade celebrating all things Irish in the Windy City. **March**

National Cherry Blossom Festival (p257) The star of DC's annual calendar celebrates spring's arrival with music, art, fireworks, cultural fairs, kite flying and a parade. The four-week event also commemorates Japan's gift of 3000 cherry trees in 1912. **March/April**

Summerfest (p563) Nine days of concerts (over three weekends) bring music lovers to Milwaukee's riverfront, with 12 different stages hosting a wide array of homegrown and global talent. **June/July**

Wacky & Wild Gatherings

Mermaid Parade (p64) Amid bedazzled floats, dancing groups and marching bands, artfully attired merfolk meander down Coney Island's Surf Ave during a party that celebrates summer's solstice. **June**

Chincoteague Pony Swim (p247) 'Saltwater Cowboys' herd semi-feral swimming ponies into Virginia's Assateague Channel, then auction the foals on Chincoteague Island. Onlookers coo over the cloppers' manes, bobbing above the water. **July**

Water Wars (p609) The best way to beat the heat in Kansas? Head to Humboldt for family-friendly water-fight parades and splash parks, where no one goes home dry. **August**

Half Moon Bay Art & Pumpkin Festival (p909) Join the fun in a California seaside town over pie-eating contests, outdoor concerts, a parade, fun run and photos beside prize-winning one-ton pumpkins. **October**

I LIVE HERE

THE MAGIC OF AUTUMN

Lonely Planet writer Gregor Clark has spent the past 25 years living in Middlebury and Brattleboro. @thewideopenroad

Vermont is gorgeous year-round, but nothing compares to a fall day when it approaches peak color. In the valleys, cornstalks glow gold amid green fields, while the mountainsides are a blaze of maples and white birches. This is my favorite time to climb Mt Mansfield, or to wander the beautiful trails at Shelburne Farms.

Miami Beach (p440)

SUNSHINE STATE

Don't tell anyone, but Florida barely scrapes into the 'top 10' list of America's sunniest states (Arizona ranks first). Nevertheless, the Sunshine State averages over 230 days of clear skies each year. Fort Myers tops the charts with around 270 days of annual sunshine.

JULY	AUGUST	SEPTEMBER	OCTOBER	NOVEMBER	DECEMBER
Average daytime max: **84.9°F (29.3°C)**	Average daytime max: **83.3°F (28.5°C)**	Average daytime max: **76.2°F (24.5°C)**	Average daytime max: **64.5°F (18.0°C)**	Average daytime max: **54.0°F (12.2°C)**	Average daytime max: **44.3°F (6.8°C)**
Days of rainfall: 4.60	Days of rainfall: 4.56	Days of rainfall: 4.31	Days of rainfall: 4.38	Days of rainfall: 3.58	Days of rainfall: 4.38

Glacier National Park (p772), Montana

GET PREPARED FOR THE USA

Useful things to load in your bag, your ears and your brain.

Clothes

Attire Outside the city, shorts and T-shirts are fine for casual restaurants, cafes and bars. Dress up a bit in the city and at more formal restaurants and nightspots.
Footwear Sandals or flip-flops are great for the beach. Bring versatile walking shoes for urban wanders, and decent hiking footwear if you're tackling tougher trails.
Rain Precipitation is a year-round possibility in most parts – pack a lightweight rain jacket or an umbrella.
Cold weather In the north, October through April can bring freezing temperatures, so carry a warm jacket, a hat, scarf and gloves if visiting then.

Manners

Northerners are known for being reserved and don't typically greet people they pass on the street.

In the south, people tend to smile at strangers and are much more likely to make time for a chat.

Sensitive topics like politics and religion are best avoided. You'll find more common ground talking about food and sports.

Swimwear Pack swimming gear and a quick-drying towel even if you're not beach-bound. Across the US are lakes, mountain rivers and freshwater springs.

📖 READ

The Rediscovery of America (Ned Blackhawk; 2023) Fascinating insight into centuries of history from a Native American perspective.

Demon Copperhead (Barbara Kingsolver; 2022) Brilliant retelling of Dickens' *David Copperfield*, set in present-day Appalachia.

The 1619 Project (edited by Nikole Hannah-Jones; 2021) Essayists and poets create a powerful portrait of the Black experience in America.

Olive Kitteridge (Elizabeth Stout; 2008) Pulitzer Prize–winning stories of richly drawn characters in a coastal Maine community.

Words

Ain't my first rodeo Not the first time someone has been in a particular situation (used in Texas and the West).
Angeleno Resident of Los Angeles.
Barking squirrel Another way to describe a 'prairie dog' in Wyoming.
Flatlander Term used by mountain dwellers to refer to residents of lower elevations.
Hooch Another word for moonshine, which is un-aged corn whiskey.
L (the 'el') Short for the elevated trains that make up Chicago's transit network.
Leaf-peeping Making a trip into a forested area known for its dramatic colors thanks to the changing leaves in autumn (usually October).
Legit Real, authentic (admirable).
Mealtime In some parts of the South and Midwest, the noon meal is called 'dinner' and the evening meal is called 'supper.'
Mid Something mediocre in nature.
Nor'easter Powerful coastal storm named after the winds that typically blow from the northeast; used in New England.
Santa Anas Strong, dry winds that blow from the desert across Southern California, which can cause wildfires to rage.
Snowbird A person who comes to live in Florida part-time during the winter months in order to escape the cold weather up north.
Y'all In the South, this conjunction of 'you' and 'all' is used to address more than one person.

📺 WATCH

Sinners (Ryan Coogler; 2025) Genre-bending film of blues, historical drama and vampires set in 1930s Mississippi.

Moonlight (Barry Jenkins; 2016) Oscar-winning coming-of-age tale set in a housing project in Miami.

12 Years a Slave (pictured; Steve McQueen; 2013) Accurate cinematic portrayal of slavery.

The National Parks: America's Best Idea (Ken Burns; 2009) The challenges and triumphs in creating the national parks.

Cold Mountain (Anthony Minghella; 2003) Civil War–era love story set in the North Carolina mountains.

🎧 LISTEN

This American Life (thisamericanlife.org) Weekly radio show (and podcast) with stories ranging from the humorous to the thought-provoking.

Cowboy Carter (Beyoncé; 2024) Pioneering album of country music and Americana that celebrates lesser-known Black artists of the past.

We Are (Jon Batiste; 2021) Grammy-winning album that channels feel-good vibes through soul, funk, gospel and brass.

Pet Sounds (The Beach Boys; 1966) Hailed as one of the greatest albums of all time, with lush harmonies and intricate instrumentation.

Yosemite National park (p928), California

TRIP PLANNER

NATIONAL PARKS

The US is home to over 60 national parks, plus 370-odd sites that are part of the national park system. No cross-country road trip would be complete without a visit to at least one of these remarkable natural treasures, rich in unspoiled wilderness, rare wildlife and history. Given the parks' enormous popularity, it's essential to plan ahead.

Admission Fees & Passes

Most national parks charge around $35 per vehicle to enter (some parks, like Hot Springs, are free). Given the cost, if you're headed to at least three national parks, buy an **America the Beautiful Pass** *(store .usgs.gov/pass; $80)*. It's valid for a year and gives you access to all national parks across the country, as well as national monuments and other federal recreation sites. Seniors, travelers with disabilities and members of the US military get discounted or free passes with the same benefits. Park visitors who are 62 and older can pay just $20 for the Senior Pass (or $80 for a lifetime pass). Kids in fourth grade in the US can also get a pass (providing free admission for the whole family).

Timed-Entry Tickets

Visitor numbers to the national parks have skyrocketed, and a growing number of parks have implemented mandatory timed-entry systems during peak periods. That means you won't be able to drive into the park if you don't have a reservation. Check individual parks for details about when reservations open; timed-entry tickets are released anywhere from 60 days to six months ahead of a visit. Some parks also release a limited number of tickets at 7pm for next-day visits. Arrange your ticket online *(recreation.gov)*, and note that the cost of an entry permit (typically $2 reservation fee) is in addition to park admission fees. Currently, the following parks have timed entry if visiting on these dates/hours:

WHEN TO GO

Seasonality is key if visiting mountain parks, where access is limited outside summer. Elsewhere, you'll have more flexibility with your travel itinerary.

Summer
From mid-June to mid-September, it's high season in most of America's national parks. These are the months when the roads through the Rockies, Sierras and Cascades are guaranteed to be open. It's also when the parks reach full capacity, so you'll need to plan well ahead.

Acadia Cadillac Summit Rd: May 21 to October 26
Arches 7am to 4pm April 1 to April 26, 7am to 4pm August 28 to October 31
Glacier Going-to-the-Sun Rd and North Fork: 7am to 3pm June 13 to September 28
Haleakalā Summit Rd to see the sunrise: 3am to 7am all year
Mt Rainier Sunrise Corridor: 7am to 5pm daily July to August, 7am to 5pm Saturday and Sunday September to mid-October
Rocky Mountain Most of the park: 9am to 5pm mid-May to mid-October; Bear Lake Rd: 5am to 6pm mid-May to mid-October
Shenandoah Old Rag Mountain Hike: March to November
Yosemite 6am to 2pm Memorial Day weekend, Labor Day weekend and mid-June to mid-August

If you can't secure a reservation, your best bet is to enter the park outside the ticket-limited hours (preferably early in the morning). Many parks (including those listed here) open 24 hours a day, seven days a week.

Spring & Autumn
If you don't have your sights set on summiting mountain slopes, spring and autumn can be lovely times to roam, with wildflowers in April and May, and blazing fall colors in late September and October.

ESSENTIAL PARK INFO

Permits
Permits are required for some activities, including canyoneering, overnight backpacking trips, rock climbing and rafting trips. Generally, you don't need a permit for day hikes in a national park. Some exceptions are the popular day hikes to Angels Landing (Zion), Half Dome (Yosemite) and Old Rag Mountain (Shenandoah). Apply well in advance for permits, which are sometimes based on a lottery system. Find more information on individual park websites. Most permitting is done online through *recreation.gov*.

Maps & Apps
National Park Service Excellent free app covering over 420 parks, with interactive maps, self-guided tours (including audio tours) and helpful planning tools.
AllTrails Lists of trails, reviews and current conditions. Free, but it's worth paying for AllTrails+ to download maps offline and get wrong-turn alerts.
Recreation.gov Indispensable app: reserve permits, campgrounds and passes for parks and other federal areas.
Merlin The free app will help you identify birds through photos you take or through sound alone – the press of a button will record birdsong near you and help identify the creatures in question.
what3words This company has given every 3 sq meters of the world a unique three-word address. Emergency services are increasingly using what3words to know exactly where to send help.
Paper maps It's always wise to travel with a paper map. National park visitor centers give out free reference maps, but for more detailed coverage, buy one of National Geographic's Topographic maps.

Shenandoah National Park (p300), Virginia

Ranger Programs

Many national parks offer free activities led by park rangers. This might entail anything from stargazing off a sandy beach in Acadia to a slough slog (walking through a swamp) in the Everglades. There are often talks about history, wildlife and archaeology, with daily offerings during the summer. Check out what's on offer before you head to a park (look up 'Things to Do' under the 'Plan Your Visit' tab on each park's website).

Lodging in the Parks

Some national parks have historic lodges, often built in the early 20th century in a style called National Park Service Rustic or 'Parkitecture.' Located in unbeatable spots mere steps from iconic landscapes and major trailheads, the lodges are unsurprisingly in high demand. Some offer both cabins and motel-style rooms – if you have a choice and the budget, opt for the pricier cabins, which have more personality. Rates are steep, and rooms are booked out far in advance. Check for cancellations to snag something at the last minute.

Camping

The national parks are dream destinations for campers. Reserve months ahead of your trip, particularly for sites in the national parks themselves. Use *recreation.gov* for federal lands and *reserveamerica.com* for state parks. Show up early in the day at campgrounds that are first-come, first-served. Free dispersed camping is allowed in some areas managed by the US Forest Service (USFS) and the Bureau of Land Management (BLM).

Camping in Joshua Tree National Park (p963), California

Best of the Rest

CLIMBING
Catch your breath after the ascent up **Longs Peak** (p731), a 14,259ft summit that towers above the surrounding mountains in the Rockies.

CAVING
See cathedral-sized chambers and cascade-like formations that glitter under lamplight on a tour through **Mammoth Cave** (p371).

RAINFOREST
Step into a forest of verdant splendor with moss, ferns and towering Sitka spruce in **Olympic National Park** (p999).

Gateway Towns

You'll find a mix of hotels and motels in towns just outside park entrances. Rooms fill up in the summer, but travelers without an itinerary can find rooms in towns a little further from the entrance gates.

How to Beat the Crowds

With over 330 million visitors each year, the national parks can sometimes seem unlikely places to enjoy a quiet connection with nature.

You can escape the biggest crowds if you avoid the peak season (mid-June to late August). Early spring (April) and autumn (October) can be great times to visit depending on the park, and you can even experience a rare side of some parks if you travel in winter.

Though most roads in Yellowstone are closed during the winter, some in-park lodges open from mid-December to mid-March, with snowcoaches (oversized, winterized buses) providing transportation into the park and tours to park highlights. Grand Teton allows more DIY adventures for cross-country skiers and snowshoers, with certain roads open all year.

EXPLORING STATE PARKS

If traveling during high season, consider visiting state parks rather than national parks. There are many spectacular spots for hiking and wildlife-watching that don't have the name recognition (or huge crowds) of national parks. This includes places like Baxter State Park in Maine, Palo Duro Canyon in Texas, Custer State Park in South Dakota, and hundreds of other places.

TRAIL SAFETY

Don't Go Alone
It's wise not to walk alone. Be sure to let someone know your plans: leave details of your intended route, the number of people in your group and the expected return time with someone responsible before you set off; later, announce your return.

Weather
Always check the weather forecast for the area for the next 24 hours. If bad weather is on the way, reschedule your outing.

Timing & Route Planning
Allow plenty of time to accomplish a walk before dark, particularly in spring and fall when daylight hours are shorter. Study the route carefully before setting out, noting possible alternate routes and the point of no return (where it's quicker to continue than to turn back).

Packing Essentials
Bring a relevant map, compass and whistle. Carry more than enough water for your journey. If traveling in grizzly-bear country, pack bear spray, know how to use it and make sure it's within easy reach (a hip holster is best).

DESERT	CANYONS	RAFTING	KAYAKING
Hike amid the mazelike rock formations, palm-filled oases and namesake desert plants of **Joshua Tree** (p963).	Peer back into prehistoric times at the wind-sculpted hoodoos, craters and mesas of little-visited **Canyonlands** (p795).	Hold on tight while splashing along the white water rushing through the **New River Gorge National Park & Preserve** (p308).	Glide beneath towering old-growth tupelos while paddling the inky black waters of **Congaree National Park** (p352).

Gumbo (p427), New Orleans

THE FOOD SCENE

Stellar ingredients, culinary creativity and global flavors: wherever you roam, you're never far from a memorable meal in the USA.

As a country of 340 million residents, with immigrants hailing from every corner of the globe, the US offers incredible diversity when it comes to cooking. Big cities are no longer the sole providers of great international cooking – you can find thoughtfully prepared Mexican, Thai and Indian dishes, among other fare, at small towns all across the US.

The American continent is also a land of plenty with richly productive farmland, vineyards in nearly every state, and three coastlines. Even if there was nothing else to see, it would still be worth your while traveling across this country simply because of the food.

Every region offers unique cuisine, and its locals will proudly tell you the best places to go to find those unmatched specialties. While there are plenty of award-winning dining rooms, the US also has humbler but no less memorable spots where recipes have been passed down through the generations to sublime effect in traditional dishes featuring locally sourced ingredients.

NYC & the Mid-Atlantic Feast

Owing to its huge immigrant population and voracious appetite for all things new and exciting, New York captures the title of America's greatest restaurant city. Its diverse neighborhoods serve up authentic Italian food and thin-crust pizza, all manner of Asian food, French haute cuisine and classic Jewish deli fare.

More uncommon cuisines are found here as well, from Ethiopian to Tibetan.

Best US Dishes

Lobster roll Lobster meat with mayo, typically served cold on a split bun. (New England)

Bagel with schmear and lox Bagel with cream cheese topped with smoked salmon. (NYC)

Shrimp and grits Locally caught shrimp mixed with hot, creamy stoneground grits. (the South)

Gumbo Stew of chicken and shellfish, or sausage and often okra. (New Orleans)

From New York down through Maryland and Virginia, the Mid-Atlantic states share a long coastline and a cornucopia of apple, pear and berry farms. New Jersey and New York's Long Island are famous for their potatoes. Chesapeake Bay's blue crabs are the finest anywhere, and Virginia salt-cured 'country-style' hams are served with biscuits (a buttery, scone-like baked good). In Philadelphia, you can gorge on 'Philly' cheesesteaks made with thin, sautéed beef and onions and melted cheese on a bun. And in Pennsylvania Dutch Country, stop by a farm restaurant for chicken pot pie, noodles and meatloaf-like scrapple.

New England Traditions

Seafood is king in New England: the North Atlantic offers up clams, mussels, oysters and huge lobsters, along with shad, bluefish and cod. New Englanders love a good chowder (seafood stew) and a nice old-fashioned clambake, an almost ritual meal where the shellfish are buried in a pit fire with corn, chicken, potatoes and sausages. Fried clam fritters and lobster rolls (lobster meat with mayonnaise served in a bread bun) are served throughout the region. There are excellent cheeses made in Vermont, cranberries (a Thanksgiving staple) harvested in Massachusetts and maple syrup tapped from New England's forests. Maine's coast is lined with lobster shacks; baked beans and brown bread are Boston specialties; and Rhode Islanders embrace traditional cornmeal johnnycakes.

FOOD & DRINK FESTIVALS

Maine Lobster Festival (pictured; p233; mainelobsterfestival.com; late July–early August) Feast on Maine's best-loved crustacean in the seaside town of Rockland during five days of food, music and crafts.

Kelseyville Pear Festival (p919; pearfestival.com; September) The small town in northern California throws a pear-centric party in September with pie-eating contests, live music and craft and food vendors.

National Cherry Festival (p554; cherryfestival.org; June/July) Traverse City, Michigan, spreads a feast of tart fruit, alongside an airshow, parade and a cherry pit-spitting contest.

Penn Cove Musselfest (p1001; penncovemusselfest.com; March) See chef demos, take a boat tour and tuck into some of the world's tastiest bivalves.

Original Gullah Festival (p350; originalgullahfestival.org; May) Learn about traditional Gullah culture, while indulging in hearty Lowcountry cooking.

New York pizza slices

Brisket	Enchiladas	Grilled Chinook salmon	California roll
Beef cut seasoned and cooked for eight hours or more. (Texas)	Corn tortillas layered with cheese and topped with green or red chile. (New Mexico)	Quite simply the richest, tastiest salmon on Earth. (Pacific Northwest and Alaska)	Sushi roll invented in 1960s LA using crab, avocado and cucumber. (California)

Southern Cooking

No region is prouder of its food culture than the South, which has a long history of mingling Anglo, French, African, Spanish and Native American foods in dishes such as slow-cooked barbecue, which has as many meaty and saucy variations as there are towns in the South. Southern fried chicken is crisp outside and moist inside. In Florida, dishes made with fish, shrimp and conch incorporate hot chili peppers and tropical spices.

Across the South, breakfasts are big, and treasured dessert recipes tend to produce big layer cakes or pies made with pecans, bananas and citrus. Light, fluffy hot biscuits are served well buttered, and grits (ground corn cooked to a porridge-like consistency) are a passion.

Louisiana's legendary cuisine is influenced by French and Spanish cultures, Afro-Caribbean cooking and Choctaw traditions. Bayou-born Cajun food marries native spices such as sassafras and chili peppers with provincial French cooking.

Southwestern Temptations

While Californians may disagree, many people feel that Texas and other parts of the Southwest have the best Mexican food in the USA. Regardless, it's no surprise that the culinary influence is widespread throughout Texas, New Mexico and Arizona. You'll find outstanding Mexican dishes from the traditional to Tex-Mex, in tacos, enchiladas, burritos, chimichangas and other dishes made of corn, or flour pancakes filled with all manner of grilled meats, beats and *nopal* (cactus).

West Coast Cuisine

Owing to its vastness and variety of microclimates, California is truly America's cornucopia for fruits and vegetables. The state's natural resources are overwhelming, with wild salmon, Dungeness crab and oysters from the ocean; robust produce year-round; and artisanal products such as cheese, bread, olive oil, wine and chocolate. Starting in the 1970s and '80s, star chefs such as Alice Waters and Wolfgang Puck pioneered 'California cuisine' by incorporating the best local ingredients into simple, yet delectable, preparations.

Further north, Pacific Northwestern cuisine references local Native American traditions, with a focus on seafood – especially salmon – and foraged mushrooms, fruits and berries. Seattle spawned the modern international coffeehouse craze with Starbucks – though these days Portland gets more attention for its excellent coffee scene, with some of the country's top roasters.

Tex Mex tacos

Specialties

Seafood

Oysters There are dozens of varieties from different regions. A few favorites include Wellfleet (Massachusetts), Pemaquid (Maine) and Hog Island (California).

Crab Seek out sweet-tasting Dungeness crab, found in abundance all along the Northwestern coast. Out east, smaller but delicious blue crabs are popular, especially from the Chesapeake Bay. Massive Alaskan king crab is pricey but worth a splurge.

Salmon The Pacific Northwest is salmon country, with five species found in the region's waters. The Chinook salmon is Oregon's state fish.

Grouper The mild, slightly sweet flavor of this fish makes for delicious blackened grouper sandwiches in Florida.

Barbecue Styles

Texas Beef, especially brisket, slow-cooked over oak (and sometimes mesquite for added flavor).

Memphis Known for its dry-rubs, though sauces are also used.

Oysters

Carolina The love for pork shows no bounds; vinegar-based sauces are common.

Kansas City Uses a variety of meats, with tomato-based sauces adding sweetness.

Sweet Treats

Pecan pie Buttery nuts layered atop a caramel-like custard filling.

Peach cobbler A deep-dish dessert with a thick crust and peach filling; best served warm with a scoop of vanilla ice cream.

Key lime pie Has a creamy, tangy filling made with key lime juice; best topped with a big meringue.

MEALS OF A LIFETIME

American Flatbread (p216) Amid gardens and an old barn, feast on wood-fired pizzas and craft brew at Vermont's Lareau Farm.

Grey (p384) An award-winning chef elevates family recipes in a former Greyhound bus station in Savannah.

Chez Panisse (p907) Where it all started – worship at the temple of Alice Waters in Berkeley.

Owamni (p574) Experience true North American Indigenous food made with Native American ingredients in Minneapolis.

Franklin Barbecue (p678) Bite into some of the world's best brisket at this legendary Austin spot.

Paradise Grille (p495) Dig your heels in the sand while munching a grouper sandwich and watching a Florida sunset.

THE YEAR IN FOOD

SPRING

Foragers head into the woods in search of tender fiddleheads and ramps (a kind of wild leek). In many places, the first local farmers markets begin (in warmer parts there are year-round markets).

SUMMER

Farmers markets fill with a bounty of fresh fruits and vegetables, and this is the prime season for food festivals. It's a popular time for heading to the coast for feasting on lobsters, clams and other delectable seafood.

AUTUMN

September and October are months of abundant autumn harvests (apples, squash, pumpkins, sweet potatoes) – a fine prelude to the biggest feast of the year during Thanksgiving (turkeys, cranberries, pumpkin pie).

WINTER

The northern winters don't bring an end to culinary riches since innovative farming techniques allow winter growing (cold-hardy greens). Make the most of long nights with feasts of crab, oysters and (on the Gulf) crawfish.

North Cascades National Park (p1000), Washington

THE OUTDOORS

Towering sequoias, red-rock canyons, snow-covered peaks and dramatic coastlines of unrivaled beauty: the USA has no shortage of spectacular settings for a bit of adventure.

No matter your weakness – hiking, rafting, mountain biking and more – you'll find world-class places to commune with the great outdoors. In some places, you can hit the trails or the waterways right from downtown, making for easy exploration. In other places, the wilderness is within just an hour's drive. National parks are great places to start, though you'll find state parks and countless other protected reserves in every pocket of the US, meaning you're never far from nature no matter where you roam.

Walking & Hiking

Outdoors-loving Americans take great pride in their formidable network of trails – over 190,000 miles at last count – and there's no better way to experience the countryside up close and at your own pace. A focal point in the east is the Appalachian Mountains. Numerous state parks and forests protect this ancient wilderness, and you'll find plenty of variety in trails across 14 states. On the legendary Appalachian Trail you can hike anything from a short section to the whole of its 2200 miles. In the west, the Rocky Mountains, passing through eight states, is another big draw. California offers a lifetime of hiking adventures – you can summit 14,000ft peaks, walk under the world's tallest trees and admire the glorious views from the Pacific Crest Trail, which runs for 2650 miles.

Alternative Activities

HORSEBACK RIDING
Don your cowboy hat and mount your steed for a memorable ride through Arizona's **Saguaro National Park** (p840).

TUBING
Watch the pretty riverside slip past on an easygoing float down the **Deschutes River** (p1028) in Bend, Oregon.

BIRDING
Aim binoculars skyward above **Cape May** (p130) as 400 avian species flap along the Atlantic Flyway during migration season.

FAMILY ADVENTURES

Count rainbows while sailing aboard the *Maid of the Mist*, a sopping-wet thrill ride at New York's **Niagara Falls State Park** (p126).

Watch the kids enjoy free-spirited play amid Tulsa's **Gathering Place** (p618), with its sprawling playgrounds, splash pads, beach and boathouse.

Go for a spin on the **C&O Canal** (p292), a smooth cycling trail that runs past leafy forests and scenic overlooks.

Don your headlamps before exploring Iowa's subterranean passageways in **Maquoketa Caves State Park** (p623).

Look for alligators and turtles on a guided boat ride through **Okefenokee Swamp** (p374), Georgia.

Crane your eyes skyward for a look at the world's tallest trees, while walking the forested paths of CA's **Redwood National Park** (p921).

Cycling & Mountain Biking

Cycling's popularity increases by the day, with numerous cities (including New York) adding cycle lanes each year and becoming more bike-friendly, while a growing number of greenways dot the countryside.

Mountain-biking enthusiasts will find trail nirvana in Crested Butte and Salida, Colorado; Moab, Utah; Bend, Oregon; Ketchum, Idaho; Helena and Big Sky Resort, Montana; and Marin, California, the last being where Gary Fisher bunny-hopped the sport forward by careening down the flanks of Mt Tamalpais on a home-rigged bike. Montana alone has thousands of miles of mountain-biking trails. There's some fine mountain biking in the east as well, especially in the Bentonville area of Arkansas.

On the Water

East of the Mississippi, West Virginia has an arsenal of white water. First, there's the New River Gorge National Park & Preserve, where you paddle through a deep gorge that's sometimes dubbed 'the Grand Canyon of the East.' There's also the Gauley, which is revered for its ultra-steep and turbulent chutes. Six more rivers, all in the same neighborhood, offer training grounds for less experienced river rats. North Carolina has two choice places for paddlers: the US National Whitewater Center outside Charlotte, and the Nantahala Outdoor Center near the Smokies.

Out west, there's no shortage of spectacular rafting, from Utah's Cataract Canyon, and a romp through the red rocks of Canyonlands National Park, to the Rio Grande in Texas, a lazy run through limestone canyons. For more serene adventures, hop in a canoe for outdoor pastimes in Minnesota's Boundary Waters. The Everglades is another prime paddling spot. The Northwest is ideal for sea kayaking, particularly around the San Juan Islands.

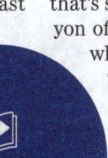

ACTION AREAS
See p56

Mountain Biking, Salida (p736), Colorado

SANDBOARDING
Rent a sandboard for a fun adventure sliding the slopes in Colorado's **Great Sand Dunes National Park** (p748).

HOUSEBOATING
Rent an easy-to-operate houseboat and head off for an adventure amid the islands of Minnesota's **Voyageurs National Park** (p584).

STARGAZING
Peer deep into outer space at the **McDonald Observatory** (p707) in Texas, home to some of America's clearest night skies.

SKIING
Hit the slopes of **Steamboat Springs** (p732), one of the best Colorado resorts for skiers of all levels.

ACTION AREAS

Where to find USA's best outdoor activities.

Cycling
1. Kingdom Trails (p220)
2. C&O Canal Towpath (p292)
3. DuPont State Forest (p335)
4. Bentonville (p409)
5. Moab (p848)
6. Tahoe Rim Trail (p934)
7. Phil's Trail (p1028)

National Parks
1. Acadia National Park (p236)
2. Grand Canyon National Park (p817)
3. Great Smoky Mountains National Park (p337)
4. Rocky Mountain National Park (p730)
5. Yellowstone National Park (p758)
6. Yosemite National Park (p928)
7. Zion National Park (p860)

THE USA
THE GUIDE

Pacific Northwest p980
Rocky Mountains p714
Great Lakes p499
New England p161
New York, New Jersey & Pennsylvania p60
Washington, DC & the Capital Region p242
California p880
Great Plains p588
Southwest USA p790
The South p317
Texas p664
Florida p434
Alaska p1037
Hawai'i p1058

Chapters in this section are organised by hubs and their surrounding areas. We see the hub as your base in the destination, where you'll find unique experiences, local insights, insider tips and expert recommendations. It's also your gateway to the surrounding area, where you'll see what and how much you can do from there.

Matanuska Glacier (p1049), Alaska
CHANSAK JOE/SHUTTERSTOCK

Researched and curated by by John Garry

New York, New Jersey & Pennsylvania

CITIES, HISTORIC HAMLETS & NATURAL WONDERS

These three neighboring states mix big-city riches with small-town simplicity. They're like an everything bagel – that iconic NYC treat – sprinkled with something for all tastes.

New York City – America's cultural capital – is the East Coast's focal point, with an origin story that echoes across state lines. Initially the Indigenous Lenape's stomping ground, the island they called 'Manahatta' saw its first shady real-estate transaction when the Dutch purchased the area in 1626, dubbing it New Amsterdam. The British barged in next, renamed it New York and vacated after losing the Revolutionary War. There was good reason to fight for the land. With its superior port and eventual waterway link to the Great Lakes, New York became the United States' financial and industrial powerhouse. Immigrants followed, lured by promises of prosperity, and the population boomed. It's no wonder NYC is called 'the city that never sleeps': density transformed it into a creative pressure cooker. There's something new to do on every corner.

Things might be sleepier outside NYC, but they're no less exciting. In New York State, mountains and rivers provide the backdrop for creative towns where a locavore food scene flourishes. In Pennsylvania, wild woodlands link Pittsburgh, the former 'Steel City' experiencing a rebirth, to Philadelphia, the heartbeat of colonial American history. New Jersey's farmsteads run from Pennsylvania's border to the Atlantic Ocean – a summertime fun zone lined with beaches and boardwalks.

The possibilities here are as diverse as the seasons: ever-changing and always ready with a colorful palette of adventures.

THE MAIN AREAS

NEW YORK CITY	**NEW YORK STATE**	**NEW JERSEY**	**PENNSYLVANIA**
The USA's electric cultural empire.	Rivers and mountains link artsy enclaves.	Atlantic coastline and Ivy League pedigree.	Forests connect cities amid a renaissance.
p66	**p106**	**p128**	**p138**

For places to stay in New York, New Jersey & Pennsylvania, see p158

THE GUIDE

NEW YORK, NEW JERSEY & PENNSYLVANIA

Left: Clayton House (p156) Pittsburgh; Above: the High Line (p85), New York City

Find Your Way

NYC and Philadelphia, linked together by trains, are best explored by foot and public transport. Nearly everywhere else requires a car. There's no better way to reach the region's serene mountain towns, state parks and sandy beaches.

CAR
Watch out for tiny-town speed traps and wild animals along country roads, particularly in upstate New York and the Pennsylvania Wilds. Expect wintry conditions between December and March. Phone service gets sketchy in rural towns; bring a map for GPS back-up.

TRAIN
All tracks lead to NYC. The high-speed Amtrak Acela links to Philly in an hour; more services reach Pittsburgh and Buffalo. NJ Transit rides to the Jersey Shore and Princeton. MetroNorth runs through the Hudson Valley. The Long Island Railroad zips to Montauk.

PLANE
Small airports make it possible to fly to destinations far from NYC, including Pittsburgh, Buffalo and NY state capital Albany near the Adirondacks. Flying cuts down dramatically on driving time, especially on trips to Buffalo and Pittsburgh, over six hours away.

Pennsylvania, p138
Forested parks fill gaps between edgy Philadelphia's historic sites, revitalized Pittsburgh's big-time museums, bucolic Lancaster's Amish country and the untamed Pocono Mountains.

Plan Your Time

The region's size can overwhelm. Each state is a mini universe; every city is a distinct planet. Stick to a geographic region based on your interests or explore it all on a whirlwind road trip.

Ellis Island (p72)

A Long NYC Weekend

● Spend your first day exploring Lower Manhattan. Follow immigrant footsteps on **Ellis Island** (p72), order global cuisine around **Chinatown** (p71), shop through the **SoHo** (p75), then dine and drink around the Lower East Side's **cocktail bars** (p80).

● Go uptown on day two. Start with a history crash course at the **Museum of the City of New York** (p95), skip through the **Met** (p96) to admire world-class art, then ramble across **Central Park** (p100) for pizza from **Mama's TOO!** (p98). Once satiated, hop on a **Citi Bike** (p71), roll down the Hudson River to Midtown and end the night with innovative theater at **Playwrights Horizons** (p90).

● Travel to Brooklyn for day three. Ogle NYC's skyline from **Brooklyn Bridge Park** (p99), then hop around **Williamsburg breweries** (p103) and dance 'til dawn at **Elsewhere** (p103).

Seasonal Highlights

Summer is action packed and autumn makes for fantastic road trips. Many rural regions and coastal treasures hibernate throughout winter, aside from upstate New York's ski-happy mountain towns. NYC perpetually buzzes.

JANUARY
Skiers hit slopes around Lake Placid and Hunter Mountain, while chilly weather in cities like NYC and Philly inspires indoor trips to museums. Budget travelers can find hotel deals throughout winter.

JUNE
Rainbow-splashed **Pride marches** in Philly and NYC bookend this festival-packed month. Nautical costumes flood Coney Island for the **Mermaid Parade** and Livingston Manor gets fishy mid-month for the **Trout Parade**.

JULY
Crowds bombard Jersey Shore boardwalks in Asbury Park and Wildwood. Surfers catch waves around Montauk. Hikers trace the gorge trails around Ithaca, jumping into cascade-splashed swimming holes as a post-trek reward.

Five Days from Philly to the Coast

● Choose from colonial history and contemporary culture during a short Philadelphia stint. Walk the halls of **Independence National Historical Park** (p142), peer at the **Barnes Foundation's** (p146) impressionist paintings and applaud the Gayborhood's **drag performers** (p140). With more time, eat around **Reading Terminal Market** (p144) and admire the mosaics at **Philadelphia's Magic Gardens** (p147).

● Drive to sister towns **New Hope** (p149) and **Lambertville** (p137) for a quiet afternoon of antiquing along the Delaware River.

● The Jersey Shore comes next. Explore Asbury Park first: traipse down the mile-long **boardwalk** (p132), dip your toes in the Atlantic and hear rock bands jam at the **Stone Pony** (p133).

● Finish at Cape May: tour **Victorian architecture** (p130) and peep at **birds along the beachscape** (p130).

A Week Driving Around New York State

● Zip north of NYC for outdoor adventures between spring and autumn. Hike around **Storm King's** outdoor sculptures (p112) and stroll Beacon's quaint **Main Street** (p113). Reserve a day for nearby Hudson: shop along **Warren Street** (p113), stop by art-packed **Olana** (p115) then see **Kaaterskill Falls** (p116), New York's tallest two-tiered cascade.

● The Adirondacks beckon next, with high-octane trekking to the peak of **Buck Mountain** (p119), a historic steamboat cruise along **Lake George** (p119) and Olympics history around **Lake Placid** (p120).

● Zoom to the Finger Lakes for a day or two, best spent **wine tasting** (p122) and at watering holes around the region's **gorges** (p122).

● Detour to the wondrous waterfalls of **Letchworth State Park** (p123) en route to **Niagara Falls** (p126) – the exclamation point on a week packed with captivating cascades.

THE GUIDE

NEW YORK, NEW JERSEY & PENNSYLVANIA

AUGUST
Summer's dog days invite vacationers around the Poconos and Catskills to hop in tubes and float down the Delaware River. Swimmers, kayakers and cruisers all bob around Lake George.

SEPTEMBER
Harvest season unfolds with foodie festivals throughout the region, including weekend markets at Bethel Woods. Twitchers flock to Cape May as migratory birds soar above its beaches. Sunflowers color Kane's fields gold.

OCTOBER
Leaf-peepers fawn over fiery forests in the Catskills and Adirondacks – but nothing burns brighter than the **Great Jack O'Lantern Blaze** in Hudson Valley spooktown Sleepy Hollow. Thousands gather in NYC for the **Village Halloween Parade**.

DECEMBER
NYC gets into the holiday spirit with Christmas markets, outdoor skating rinks and twinkling decorations. The jolly jamboree culminates in **Times Square's ball drop**, ringing in the new year.

65

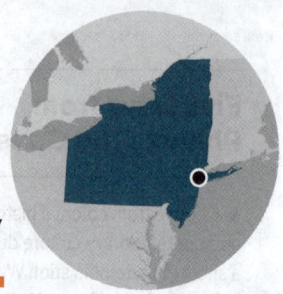

New York City

ARTISTIC EXCELLENCE | ENDLESS ENERGY | MELTING-POT MAGIC

GETTING AROUND

NYC is a pedestrian town, and strolling is a fantastic way to see the sites – as long as you follow the unspoken sidewalk rules: keep right, walk no more than two people across, and if you need to pause, step aside. Prefer speed? Cycle the city's 1500 miles of interconnected bike lanes using Citi Bike, NYC's bikeshare program. For longer distances, hop on the subway (run by the MTA; *mta.info*), zipping 1.4 million passengers daily between 462 stations spread across 665 miles of track. It's cheap, efficient and operates 24/7. Tap a smartphone or contactless bank card to go. Buses, also run by the MTA, are best for people with limited mobility.

Skyscraper canyons. Honking cabs. Rattling trains. Massive museums. Michelin-starred restaurants. The bright lights of Broadway. The list doesn't stop; New York doesn't either. It's the most populous metropolis in the United States, with 8.4 million residents. You'll find more subway stations here than in any other city worldwide, and you might hear 800 languages: NYC is the most linguistically diverse destination on Earth. This modern-day Babel boasts biblically tall towers, including One World Trade Center, the Western Hemisphere's highest building. There are 170-plus museums, 2300 green spaces and more than 20,000 restaurants spread across five boroughs. Many visitors start by exploring Manhattan, where the city's most captivating histories reveal themselves. From Indigenous Lenape land to Dutch settlement to global melting pot, NYC has remained resilient through wars, epidemics, economic crises and riots. Take a bite of the Big Apple and you'll barely scratch the surface. Spend a lifetime here and you'll still find yourself surprised.

Sail Away to Governors Island
Escape lower Manhattan's incessant buzz

Car-free, glamp-ready and laced with paths for strolling and cycling, **Governors Island** (*govisland.com*) might be a five-minute ferry ride from Manhattan's southern tip, but it's energetically worlds away. Choose your own adventure on this 172-acre pleasure pad, shaped like an ice-cream cone and sprinkled with activities for all palates.

To see the sites quickly, cycle the island's 7 miles of trails for panoramas of Lower Manhattan's skyline. Rent wheels from **Blazing Saddles** (*blazingsaddles.com/new-york; from $21*), or use one of three Citi Bike stations around the island.

Art enthusiasts can spend an afternoon admiring mammoth outdoor sculptures, such as the indigenous fruit trees populating the living *Open Orchard* earthwork. Kids can get

Brooklyn Bridge

a thrill zooming down the city's longest slide, a 57ft screamer on aptly named **Slide Hill**. When hunger calls, head to **Liggett Tce's food trucks** or a waterfront restaurant with New York Harbor views. To decompress, book a session at a Roman-style spa at **QC NY** *(qcny.com; from $98)*, where guests unwind in saunas and steam rooms, and soak up city views from a heated outdoor infinity pool.

Governors Island has seen tremendous transformations since Indigenous tribes fished here in the 1500s. It's now 100 acres larger, having been bulked up in 1912 with debris from the Lexington Ave subway excavation, and decorated with architectural remnants from two centuries as a military stronghold. **Fort Jay** and **Castle Williams**, completed in the early 19th century, are the most impressive – both served as prisons for Confederate soldiers during the Civil War.

Ferries depart from Lower Manhattan's **Battery Maritime Building** daily. Adult tickets cost $5; on weekends, all passengers ride free until 11am.

Stroll the Brooklyn Bridge

MAP P68

Architectural icon with breeze-buffeted views

When this marvel of modern engineering opened in 1883, it was the world's first steel suspension **bridge** *(nyc.gov)* and the first land link between Manhattan and Brooklyn, spanning 1596ft across the East River.

Longer NYC bridges have since snatched the spotlight, but this 1-mile-plus journey still inspires awe. Its elevated pedestrian path is like an open-air cathedral, with granite stones forming neo-Gothic arches that point toward the heavens, while at sunset, the latticework of steel-wire cables seems like stained glass. Reach the bridge's apex for picture-perfect frames of Manhattan's skyscrapers and Brooklyn's waterfront.

☑ TOP TIP

Improvising last-minute plans is possible – but it will limit your options. Book tickets to Broadway shows weeks or months in advance; reserve tables at trendy or high-end restaurants several weeks prior; schedule timed tickets to museums a week or so before arrival.

VIEWS FROM NEW YORK HARBOR

Captain Jonathan Boulware, president and CEO of South Street Seaport Museum. @seaportmuseum

New York is a maritime town. It was a port before it was a city, and its identity as a global destination is rooted in its port-ness. Until the middle of the 20th century, the first sight of New York that greeted new arrivals was from the harbor, looking at the lower end of Manhattan. It's possible to see that historic vista from two **South Street Seaport Museum** vessels: the 1885 *Pioneer* schooner, and the last surviving New York–built wooden tugboat, *WO Decker*. Trips last a couple of hours, starting at Pier 16 *($10-50)*.

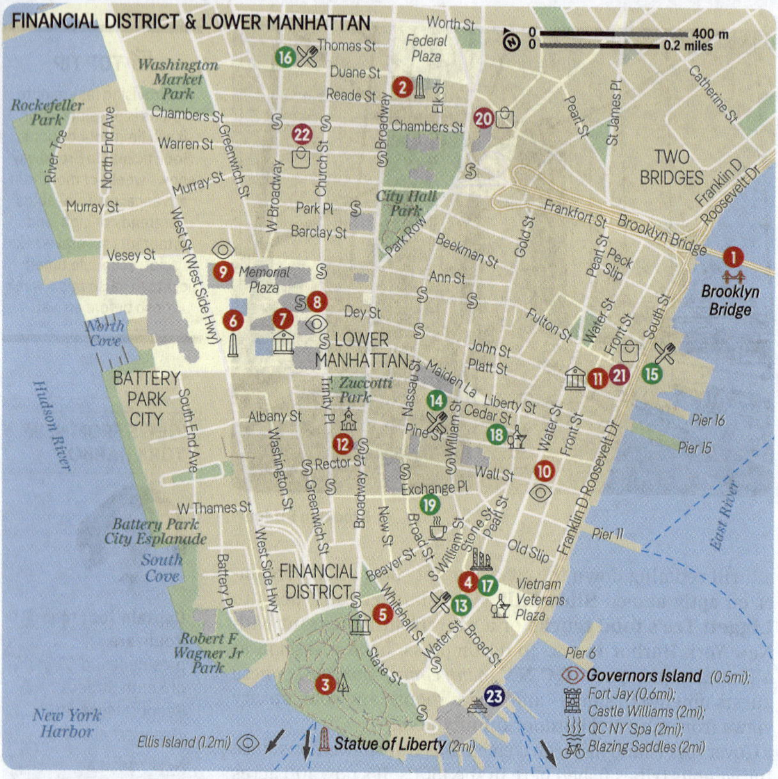

FINANCIAL DISTRICT & LOWER MANHATTAN

- **HIGHLIGHTS**
  1. Brooklyn Bridge
- **SIGHTS**
  2. African Burial Ground National Monument
  3. Battery
  4. Lovelace Tavern foundation
  5. National Museum of the American Indian
  6. National September 11 Memorial
  7. National September 11 Memorial Museum
  8. Oculus Center
  9. One World Trade Center
  10. Slave Market Historical Marker
  11. South Street Seaport Museum
  12. Trinity Church
- **EATING**
  13. Fraunces Tavern
  14. Manhatta
  15. Tin Building
  16. Tiny's & the Bar Upstairs
- **DRINKING & NIGHTLIFE**
  17. Dead Rabbit
  18. Overstory
  19. Split Eights
- **SHOPPING**
  20. CityStore
  21. McNally Jackson
  22. Philip Williams Posters
- **TRANSPORT**
  23. Battery Maritime Building

For a soul-stirring jaunt to Brooklyn, start at the bridge entrance at Manhattan's City Hall Park. The Brooklyn side has two exits: the first leads to Dumbo, with easy access to Brooklyn Bridge Park (p99); the second ends where leafy Brooklyn Heights meets Downtown Brooklyn. Expect large crowds from late morning to early evening, particularly in good weather.

Constructing the Brooklyn Bridge was no walk in the park. An estimated 27 people died during the 14-year process, including designer John Roebling, who contracted tetanus after his foot was crushed at Fulton Landing in the early stages of work. His son, Washington Roebling, took the baton, only to become bedridden with the bends (decompression sickness) after toiling away in underwater caissons used to excavate the riverbed for the bridge's towers. His wife, Emily, supervised most of the construction and became the first person to cross the bridge in a carriage, holding a rooster as a sign of victory.

See NYC from One World Observatory MAP P68
Soar to great downtown heights

The World Trade Center site's 16-acre campus is a symbol of NYC's resilience. There's the **National September 11 Memorial** and a connected **museum** (*911memorial.org; adult/youth $24/36*), a somber tribute honoring victims of the deadliest terror attack on US soil, alongside amazing modern architecture, including Santiago Calatrava's gleaming cream **Oculus**. The greatest testament to the city's recovery from 9/11 is **One World Trade Center** (aka Freedom Tower), which soars 1776ft above the plaza like a phoenix, claiming the title of tallest building in the Western Hemisphere.

The shimmering 104-floor spectacle is impressive from below, but wait until you reach the observation decks (*oneworldobservatory.com/tickets; from $54*) on levels 100 to 102. Floor-to-ceiling windows showcase a 360-degree panorama of all five boroughs and three adjoining states. If you need help identifying landmarks, interactive mobile tablets programmed in multiple languages are available, included in a combo ticket for a well-spent extra $10.

Purchase tickets online to avoid long queues and consider arriving early to beat the crowds (sunsets on clear days are particularly busy). The experience is more 'theme-park glam' than 'NYC grit,' but if you can stomach snaking security lines and wide-eyed visitors, it's worth the trip.

See SoHo's Artsy Side MAP P74
Free galleries and sidewalk surprises

Today's fashionistas lust over flagship stores around SoHo (South of Houston, pronounced 'How-stown'), but in the 1960s, many New Yorkers considered the area a wasteland – unless they were among the artists living and working in its industrial loft spaces. By the 1980s, these creative crowds turned the neighborhood into NYC's arty epicenter. Look beyond the storefronts for a couple of hours to spot SoHo's stylish origins.

UNIQUE NEW YORK SOUVENIRS

Fishs Eddy: Come to this Union Sq store for bold NYC-themed kitchenware, be it a 'Don't touch my nuts' squirrel dish or Lady Liberty mug. (*fishseddy.com*)

Only NY: This LES fashion shop's line of city-themed merch drips with local swagger. (*onlyny.com*)

CityStore: Find authentic-looking taxi medallions and FDNY tees inside the Manhattan Municipal Building. (*nyc.gov/site/dcas/about/citystore*)

Philip Williams Posters: Time flies while scanning museum-worthy stacks piled with 100,000 printed pieces in Tribeca, including vintage New Yorker covers. (*postermuseum.com*)

Quimby's Bookstore: In Williamsburg, leaf through boxes stuffed with locally made zines covering everything from Barbie's queer subtext to Aleister Crowley's unforgettable quotes. (*quimbys.com*)

 EATNG IN LOWER MANHATTAN: BEST MEALS MAPS P66, P72

Tin Building: Celebrated restaurateur Jean-Georges Vongerichten attracts crowds to this marketplace with 53,000 sq ft of food counters. *8am-10pm* $$

Manhatta: Splurge on the tasting menu or sip a cocktail bar-side – what's most important are the 60th-floor views. *hours vary* $$$

Frenchette: This contemporary French bistro is more Left Bank Paris than West Side Manhattan. *noon-10pm Mon-Fri, from 11am Sat, 11am-9:30pm Sun* $$$

Tiny's & the Bar Upstairs: American classics get doused with modern pizzazz at this pretty-in-pink 1810 townhouse. *hours vary* $$$

UNCOVER LOWER MANHATTAN'S COLONIAL PAST

In a city known for its relentless drive to be 'New,' a trove of old-world history hides in plain sight.

START	END	LENGTH
Battery	African Burial Ground National Monument	2 miles; 3 hours

Start at the ❶ **Battery's** waterfront, facing Lady Liberty, to consider how her lofty ideals compare with the city's complicated origins. Stop by the ❷ **National Museum of the American Indian** *(free)* on the park's eastern side to learn about 'Turtle Island' land before European takeover. Trace the park to ❸ **Pearl St**, the city's original shoreline before landfill expanded it outward, and jog east to ❹ **Fraunces Tavern** *(museum adult/child $10/5)*, where George Washington famously threw back a few pints. Across the street, look for the bones of ❺ **Lovelace Tavern's foundation**, buried beneath the sidewalk. Next stop is ❻ **Stone St**, which became the city's first cobblestone-paved passage in the 17th century. Three blocks northeast is a plaque marking the site of New York's ❼ **slave market**, opened in 1711. Slavery was introduced to the city in 1626; by 1730, 42% of the free population owned enslaved people. Walk west on ❽ **Wall St** (an actual defence wall in the 17th century) toward ❾ **Trinity Church** (resting place of Alexander Hamilton) and north along ❿ **Broadway** (built on an old Lenape route). End at the ⓫ **African Burial Ground National Monument** *(free)*, a memorial and museum honoring the estimated 15,000 African souls interred on-site. The mass grave is a reminder of the backs on which New York was built.

The African burial ground was unearthed in 1991 during construction of an office building.

Before Henry Hudson arrived in 1609, the Lenape paddled here in wood-carved canoes.

Built in 1670 and burned down in 1706, Lovelace Tavern wasn't rediscovered until 1979.

Begin at the **Leslie-Lohman Museum of Art** *(leslielohman.org; free)*, the world's first museum dedicated to LGBTQ+ themes. Charles Leslie and the late Fritz Lohman started showcasing their gay-centric art collection from a SoHo loft in 1969 – an assemblage that rapidly expanded as they rescued works by dying artists during the 1980s AIDS pandemic. Nearby, you'll find the **Drawing Center** *(drawingcenter.org; free)*, a nonprofit institute focused solely on drawings. Founded in 1977 as SoHo's art scene took shape, the free-to-visit museum is now a neighborhood fixture that's featured everyone from Michelangelo to Richard Serra.

Continue to the 2nd floor of 141 Wooster St to see the work of artist Walter de Maria – a room filled with 280,000lb of dirt. This is the **New York Earth Room** *(diaart.org; free; open noon-3pm & 3:30pm-6pm Wed to Sun)*, on view since 1980. It's a heady experience,. Finally, watch where you step while walking over the northwest corner of Prince St and Broadway (outside Prada) and you'll spot the work of sculptor Ken Hiratsuka, who carved roughly 40 sidewalks after moving to NYC in 1982. This design took about five hours of actual work, though its completion took two years (1983–84), as police patrols often disrupted Hirasuka's illegal chiseling.

Eat Everything in Chinatown   MAP P74
Dumplings, rolls, buns and bao

The most rewarding way to visit Chinatown is through your taste buds. Follow this 1-mile food tour past dangling duck roasts, paper lanterns and simple storefronts where food is the main attraction. Begin inside the East Broadway Mall, a largely abandoned shopping center beneath the Manhattan Bridge. Look past the grungy vestibules and let your nose lead you downstairs to **Fu Zhou Wei Zhong Wei Jia Xiang Feng Wei**, which roughly translates to 'The tastiest Fuzhou hometown-flavor restaurant.' Order the dumplings and decide if the food lives up to the name. Next stop is **Mei Lai Wah** *(@meilaiwahcoffeeshop)*, famous for pineapple buns with roast pork. There's often a line snaking outside this tiny shop. Once it's your turn, place an order at the digital kiosk inside and watch the kitchen staff prep to-go bags for ravenous hordes. Give your belly a break from the food frenzy in **Columbus Park**, once a part of Five Points – NYC's first tenement slums. Today, entering the leafy oasis is like a trip to Shanghai: spy spirited mah-jongg meisters, slow-motion tai-chi practitioners *(continues on p75)*

CYCLE THE CITY

Citi Bike *(citibikenyc.com)*, NYC's ubiquitous bikeshare program, offers single passes ($4.99 for 30 minutes) and day passes ($25 for unlimited 30-minute rides), allowing users to unlock bikes at one station and drop them off at any other station around the city. You can purchase day passes at station kiosks, but download the Citi Bike app for a better user experience. If you're new to urban biking, get your bearings along the Hudson River Greenway – a north–south bike path that rolls along Manhattan's west side. There are around 20 Citi Bike kiosks surrounding the laneway, so you can dock and explore the borough's pretty riverside parks. New Yorkers use this path for commuting. Act accordingly: obey traffic lights; slower traffic sticks to the right.

DRINKING IN LOWER MANHATTAN: BEST COCKTAILS   MAPS P66, P74

Overstory: This lofty lounge on the 64th floor is best for marveling at the city's sparkling lights. Reserve an outdoor table ($75 minimum spend). 5:45pm-midnight

Dead Rabbit: It's tough beating this three-floor bar named after a 19th-century Irish American gang – the Irish coffee is a knockout. 11am-2am, Sun-Thu to 3am Fri & Sat

Split Eights: Let the bartender decide what you should imbibe at this moody bi-level hang out where buttoned-up crowds let loose. 4:30pm-2am

Smith & Mills: Former carriage house turned cocktail bar and restaurant. Don't leave without seeing the loo, inside a 1902 cage elevator. 4-11pm Sun & Mon, to 1am Tue-Sat

Liberty Island's museum

TOP EXPERIENCE

Statue of Liberty & Ellis Island

'Lady Liberty' is New York's most enduring icon, her torch shining high above the harbor since 1886. A one-woman welcoming committee for millions of immigrants, 'Liberty Enlightening the World' (her official name) is an international symbol of freedom, justice and opportunity. Nearby is Ellis Island, America's immigration epicenter from 1892 to 1924, from where 40% of the US population can trace their ancestry.

DID YOU KNOW?

Lady Liberty was intended as an icon of emancipation, celebrating the end of slavery in the US, not immigration. Ellis Island didn't open its 'golden door' until six years after the statue was unveiled. The original idea was replaced by the sentiment of Emma Lazarus' 1883 poem 'The New Colossus,' on the pedestal, which welcomes 'huddled masses yearning to breathe free.'

Ride the Ferry

Start your journey along the water-splashed Battery, where crowds congregate for the 15-minute ferry ride to Liberty Island. Expect airport-style security screenings at the boarding station, with 30- to 90-minute waits during summer's high season. Once on board, grab a seat by the lower-level windows or on the upper-level railings for views of Governors Island (p66), the Verrazzano-Narrows Bridge and Manhattan's jagged skyline.

PRACTICALITIES
- cityexperiences.com/new-york/city-cruises/statue
- adult/child $25.50/16.50
- 1st ferry departs the Battery 9am
- last ferry departs Ellis Island 5:15pm

Visit the Museum

Step into Liberty Island's free museum – a 26,000-sq-ft complex completed in 2019 – for a riveting introduction. The statue's original torch, removed in 1984, is the visual pièce de résistance, while the most engaging exhibit digs into the statue's hypocrisy. In 1886, 'universal liberty' was a dream deferred for many Americans – women didn't have the right to vote and African Americans suffered through racist government policies during post–Civil War reconstruction. Even today, America maintains a complicated relationship with Lady Liberty's ideals.

Gaze at the Goddess

While staring at Lady Liberty's sea-green copper sheen, consider the fantastic feats it took to bring her to America. Designer Frédéric-Auguste Bartholdi's 450,000lb giantess was constructed in Paris between 1881 and 1884, with help from French engineer Alexandre Gustave Eiffel (of the eponymous tower), using 300 copper sheets, each about 7.8ft wide. She was transported to New York across the treacherous Atlantic in 214 crates, reassembled from 350 pieces over four months, then placed on a granite pedestal designed by architect Richard Morris Hunt, bringing her total height to 305ft.

Sail to Ellis Island

Traveling to Ellis Island begins as it did for roughly 12 million immigrants – on the water. The 27.5-acre plot of land is only accessible by ferry, which leaves from Liberty Island, sailing for 15 minutes to the National Immigration Museum. Get your camera ready: the trip from Liberty Island is particularly scenic.

Understand the United States

Immerse yourself in the complex tapestry of US immigration prior to Ellis Island's debut around the Main Building's 1st-floor museum. *Journeys: The Peopling of America, 1550–1890* traces the movement of people to and through the US as they built the blocks of the nation's foundation. Stories of displaced Native Americans, enslaved Africans and optimistic immigrants illuminate America's ongoing struggles with identity.

See an Immigrant's Point of View

On the Main Building's 2nd floor, you can visit *Through America's Gate*, an exhibition chronicling the step-by-step process for newly arrived immigrants on Ellis Island. Begin in the 338ft-long Registry Room, where thousands of hopefuls once gathered daily to wade through the tape of American bureaucracy. From here, wander through halls to learn about medical and legal inspections necessary to gain admittance to the US, including the 29 questions that would determine a person's future. While 98% of immigrants eventually made it into the country, 2% of people faced the personal and financial pain of rejection – which could account for more than 1000 people per month. Take a moment to examine pieces of salvaged walls, scrawled on by immigrants desperate to make their mark on America.

OYSTERS TO ELLIS

Native Americans called Ellis Island 'Kioshk' (Gull Island). The Dutch called it Oyster Island for its mass of mollusks. It was then dubbed Gibbet Island when criminals were hanged here in the 1760s. Today's name comes from Samuel Ellis, a merchant who took ownership in the 1770s. He unsuccessfully tried to rid himself of the property while alive. The upside? Now his name is famous.

TOP TIPS

● Statue Cruises is the only company that sells tickets to Liberty and Ellis islands; the box office operates inside the Battery's Castle Clinton and New Jersey's Liberty State Park. Book online to avoid queues.

● If you want to see the Statue of Liberty and Ellis Island in one day, hop on a ferry before 2pm.

● Liberty Island's food is expensive and mediocre. Pack lunch or snacks to enjoy on-site instead.

● Head to Ellis Island's lobby to check the schedule for free tours, to watch screenings of the 35-minute film *Island of Hope, Island of Tears*, and to pick up a free audio guide.

NEW YORK CITY NEW YORK, NEW JERSEY & PENNSYLVANIA

SOHO, CHINATOWN, NOLITA & LITTLE ITALY

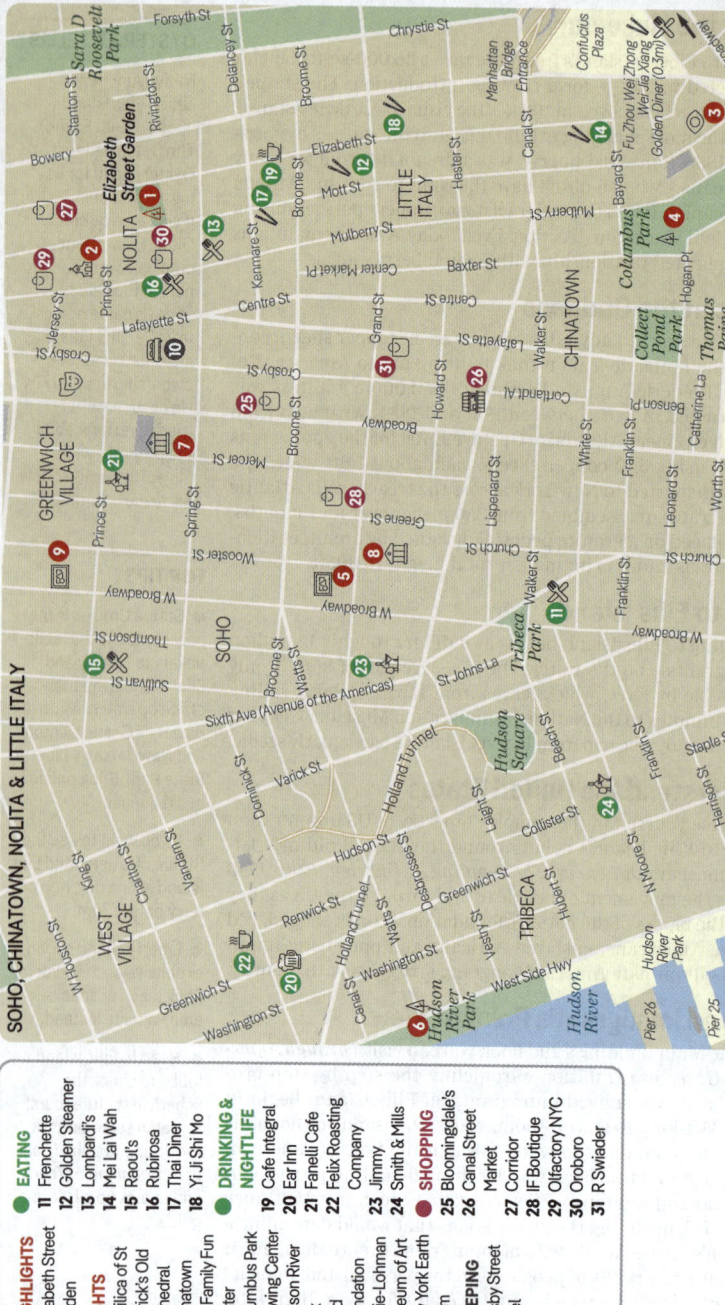

- ★ **HIGHLIGHTS**
  1. Elizabeth Street Garden

- ● **SIGHTS**
  2. Basilica of St Patrick's Old Cathedral
  3. Chinatown
  4. Columbus Park
  5. Drawing Center
  6. Hudson River Park
  7. Judd Foundation
  8. Leslie-Lohman Museum of Art
  9. New York Earth Room

- ● **SLEEPING**
  10. Crosby Street Hotel

- ● **EATING**
  11. Frenchette
  12. Golden Steamer
  13. Lombardi's
  14. Mei Lai Wah
  15. Raoul's
  16. Rubirosa
  17. Thai Diner
  18. Yi Ji Shi Mo

- ● **DRINKING & NIGHTLIFE**
  19. Cafe Integral
  20. Ear Inn
  21. Fanelli Cafe
  22. Felix Roasting Company
  23. Jimmy
  24. Smith & Mills

- ● **SHOPPING**
  25. Bloomingdale's
  26. Canal Street Market
  27. Corridor
  28. IF Boutique
  29. Olfactory NYC
  30. Oroboro
  31. R Swiader

(continued from p71)
and aunties gossiping over homemade dumplings. Continue to Elizabeth St's **Yi Ji Shi Mo**, a tiny counter famous for rice rolls. End your food tour with Chinatown's tastiest *bao* (steamed buns) at **Golden Steamer** on Grand St. Order the pumpkin – if they haven't already run out.

Expect Great Performances at the Public Theater
MAP P82

Downtown theater and cabaret
Broadway isn't the only place to see great theater. See what's playing at the **Public** *(publictheater.org)*, a legendary Off-Broadway house founded in 1954 that launched some of New York's biggest hits, including *Hamilton* in 2015. Today, you'll find a lineup of new works and reimagined classics, with Shakespeare on heavy rotation. Speaking of the bard, the Public also stages star-studded Shakespeare in the Park performances during the summer – free, if you can get tickets (try the TodayTix lottery: *todaytix.com*), and located in Central Park.

Next door is **Joe's Pub**, named for Public Theater founder Joseph Papp. Part bar, part cabaret venue, the intimate space serves up top-shelf entertainers, ranging from downtown icon Joey Arias to Broadway's biggest divas and heavy hitters (Adele even sang here). Take a chance on lesser-known names. Who knows? They might be New York's next big thing.

Shop 'til You Drop
MAP P74

Pop into SoHo's boutiques
Soho and its surrounds burst at the seams with sartorial splendor. Spend an afternoon following NYC's style fiends to the neighborhood's trendiest shops. Start by strutting down Broadway for global chains from Adidas to Zara and everything in between – including **Bloomingdale's** *(bloomingdales.com)*, a department store beloved by big spenders. Zigzag west toward West Broadway to try on designer labels at spots like **IF Boutique** *(ifsohonewyork.com)*, a SoHo fashion stalwart since 1978.

In Nolita (North of Little Italy), jewel-box boutiques sell unique threads, kicks and fragrances. Don't miss **Oroboro** (upscale-casual womenswear; *oroborostore.com*), **R Swiader** (gender-optional clothes plus a salon; *rswiader.com*) and **Corridor** (thick-knit plaids for gents; *corridornyc.com*).

HALF-SHELL HISTORY

Long before pizza became the cheap-eat treat for famished New Yorkers, a salty sea candy reigned supreme on the streets: oysters. Their thick beds lined the city's estuaries, plucked by the Indigenous Lenape then pillaged by European colonizers. NYC earned a reputation as the world's oyster capital, and some biologists estimate that New York Harbor contained half the world's supply. But by 1927, pollution and overharvesting killed the masses of meaty mollusks. Today, Hudson River Park is dedicated to repopulating their defunct reefs. In 2021, 11.2 million larval oysters were added to the Hudson River Park's Estuarine Sanctuary, and the Billion Oyster Project plans to restore one billion oysters back to New York Harbor by 2035.

 EATING IN SOHO & CHINATOWN: BEST MEALS — MAP P68

Thai Diner: Classic NY-diner style (chrome stools, spacious booths), retooled with Southeast Asian flavors. *11am-10:30pm Mon-Wed, to 11:30pm Thu-Sat, from 10am Sat & Sun* $$

Raoul's: Cool kids started lining up for Raoul's French-bistro classics in 1975. Order the peppercorn-crusted burger – if it's available. *5-11pm Mon-Fri, 11am-2:30pm Sat & Sun* $$$

Lombardi's: Opened in 1905 when Little Italy dominated the area, this Neapolitan-style parlor claims to be America's first pizzeria. *noon-10pm Sun-Thu, to midnight Fri & Sat* $$

Golden Diner: Trek to this Manhattan Bridge haunt for surprising takes on greasy-spoon grub, including Asian influences. *10am-10pm Tue-Sun* $$

SNAKE DOWN DOYERS ST

In a city dominated by an orderly grid, Doyers St – a curved block in Chinatown – refuses to conform. Named after Hendrick Doyer, an 18th-century Dutch immigrant who owned a distillery here, Doyers became the epicenter of Chinatown as it took shape in the late 1800s. By the end of the century, the street earned new monikers, including the 'Bloody Angle' – a reference to criminal activity. Throughout the early 20th century, warring tongs (Chinese gangs) attacked rivals by hiding behind the street's sharp bend – a cause for concern among anyone visiting nearby tenement buildings packed with gambling parlors and opium dens. Today, it's a peaceful pedestrian promenade; a colorful mural decorates the formerly blood-splattered street.

HERE NOW/SHUTTERSTOCK

For fantastic street vendors, skip to the stands on Prince St (between Mulberry and Mott) to see handmade jewelry and art. Searching for scents? Stop by **Olfactory NYC** (olfactorynyc.com).

You don't need to be a fashionista to enjoy the consumer circus. Bookstores such as **McNally Jackson** (mcnallyjackson.com) cater to literati, and you can choose between shopping and eating thanks to local vendors at **Canal Street Market** (canalstreet.market).

Find Solitude in a Secret Garden   MAP P74
Nolita's hidden public park

Cement-smacked SoHo and Nolita are largely devoid of green space, save for **Elizabeth Street Garden** (elizabethstreetgarden.com; 11am-6pm), a hidden oasis between Prince and Spring Sts. It started in 1991, when an antiques dealer leased the abandoned lot from the city, added landscaping and sprinkled its acre with outdoor sculptures. This whimsical spot is now a serene refuge for shop-weary New Yorkers. Grab a coffee from nearby **Cafe Integral** (cafeintegral.com) to sip in the shade of garden trees.

DRINKING IN SOHO: BEST BARS & CAFES   MAP P74

Ear Inn: See how SoHo looked before fashionistas took over at this 18th-century house-turned-drinking-den built for James Brown, George Washington's African aide. 11:30am-4am

Jimmy: Tipsy patrons spill onto the open deck at this sky-high hangout atop ModernHaus SoHo. 5-11pm Sun & Mon, to 1am Tue & Wed, to 2am Thu-Sat

Fanelli Cafe: A saloon from 1847, Fanelli bridges SoHo's past and present. The corner table looking down Prince and Mercer Sts is the envy of TikTok. 11am-late

Felix Roasting Company: Contemporary cafe culture meets Gilded Age at the Greenwich St branch of this java chain fit for an Astor. 7am-10pm

Elizabeth Street Garden

Explore the Tenement Life of Immigrants
MAP P78

Big stories in tiny apartments

Stand in one of the tenement apartments alongside eight or 10 fellow visitors on the popular tours at the **Tenement Museum** *(tenement.org; $30),* and you'll get an idea of what it was like living in these cramped quarters. Depending on which tour you choose, a docent will lead you through various rooms of the historically restored buildings and tell you the stories of people who lived there in the 19th and 20th centuries. The 'Tenement Women: 1902' tour, for instance, will take you into the small three-room apartment of the Levine family – where Jewish immigrant Jennie Levine managed the household while her husband ran a garment factory in the front room. Other tours explore the stories of immigrants from Germany, Puerto Rico, Italy and China, among other places, who lived here at various points. Tours are the only way to experience the museum, and they sell out daily, so book tickets in advance.

Taste NYC's Beloved Pastrami
MAP P78

Sandwiches at Katz's Delicatessen

Eating a pastrami sandwich on rye bread is one of those quintessential NYC experiences, and **Katz's** (established 1888; *katzsdelicatessen.com*) is the number-one place to do it. This kosher-style deli has all the trappings – neon signs, table seating, gruff but kind-hearted staff and usually a line out the door. (Movie buffs: this is where Meg Ryan faked her famous orgasm in the 1989 film *When Harry Met Sally.*) Get a ticket when you walk in and proceed to the various counters to order your meal. Keep that ticket to pay after you eat. You might be surprised by the prices *(around $28),* but the sandwiches are huge and best shared.

WHEN LITTLE ITALY WAS BIG

Mulberry St, named after the mulberry trees that once lined its sidewalks, became synonymous with Italy in the late 19th and early 20th centuries as millions of Italian immigrants funneled into the country. By 1910, roughly 10,000 Italian Americans crammed themselves into a two-mile radius of tenement buildings that Jacob Riis called the 'foul core of New York's slums.' After WWII, the community began a mass exodus and, as Chinatown expanded, Little Italy went from a brash boot to a slim sandal. But wiping out the Italian heritage is impossible: restaurants such as **Rubirosa** (*rubirosanyc.com*) ensure Mulberry St remains soaked in red sauce, and September's 11-day festival for the **Feast of San Gennaro** (*sangennaronyc.org*) revives its red, white and green glory.

EAST VILLAGE & THE LOWER EAST SIDE

⭐ **HIGHLIGHTS**	9 Russian & Turkish Baths
1 Tenement Museum	● **SLEEPING**
● **SIGHTS**	10 Public Hotel
2 Bowery Ballroom	● **EATING**
3 Hole	11 Abraço
4 International Center of Photography	12 Apollo Bagels
5 Merchant's House Museum	13 B&H Dairy
6 Museum at Eldridge Street	14 Cafe Mogador
7 New Museum	15 Dimes
8 Yiddish Walk of Fame	16 Essex Market
	17 Hanoi House
	18 Katz's Delicatessen
	19 Little Myanmar

20 Nowon
21 Punjabi Grocery & Deli
22 Rosella
23 Russ & Daughters
24 Scarr's Pizza
25 Smør
26 Soothr
27 Superiority Burger
28 Supermoon Bakehouse
29 Takahachi
30 Veselka
31 Yellow Rose
32 Yonah Schimmel's Knish Bakery

● **DRINKING & NIGHTLIFE**
33 Accidental Bar
34 Amor y Amargo
35 Attaboy
36 Lobby Lounge
37 Ruffian

● **ENTERTAINMENT**
38 Metrograph
39 Slipper Room

● **SHOPPING**
40 Only NY
41 Orchard Corset

Kvell over Jewish History

MAP P78

From knishes to temples

In the 19th and 20th centuries, about two million Jews left Europe for the US in response to anti-Jewish sentiment – and about 75% of them ended up in NYC. Most settled around the Lower East Side's tenements, which became the capital of Jewish life in America. Their descendants might've moved elsewhere, but their cultural impact remains. Spend a couple hours following their footsteps.

Start by looking for faded stars in the pavement on the **Yiddish Walk of Fame's** southeast corner (E 10th St and Second Ave) to spot names of Jewish thespians who thrived here pre-WWII. Back then, Second Ave was known as 'Yiddish Broadway.' Clock the Chase Bank that takes up the corner – it was once a Jewish deli.

Next, slip inside **B&H Dairy** *(bandhdairykosher.com)*, a slender greasy spoon open since the late 1930s, for a taste of a time when Second Ave was the land of milk and honey. Polish Catholic Ola Abdelwahed now runs the Jewish Kosher luncheonette with her Muslim Egyptian husband Fawzy, churning out Yiddish comfort classics (blintzes, matzo ball soup), arguably better than a *bubbe*.

Save some appetite for **Yonah Schimmel's Knish Bakery** *(knishery.com)*, which started selling its namesake Jewish dough pockets from a Coney Island pushcart in the 1890s. By 1910, the store opened on the LES, where it continues selling knishes stuffed with potatoes, cabbage, blueberry cheese and more.

Walk off your meal en route to the **Museum at Eldridge Street** *(eldridgestreet.org; adult/child $15/8)*, a landmark synagogue built in 1887 and the center of Jewish life for decades. The high-ceilinged sanctuary must have felt like a reprieve for the tenement-dwelling neighborhood residents of yore. Join a docent-led tour to appreciate the stunning stained glass (added in 2010) or explore on your own.

Pop into Orchard Street Storefronts

MAP P78

Shopping and strolling through the LES

In the early 1700s, there was actually an orchard on **Orchard St**, but in the late 1800s this became the Lower East Side's main shopping strip, with garment workers packed into tenement buildings and storefronts selling textiles. Nowadays, Orchard St is the hippest part of the neighborhood,

UNDERSTAND THE EAST VILLAGE & LOWER EAST SIDE

The East Village and Lower East Side (LES) are integral to NYC's multicultural melting pot, home to successive waves of immigrant communities, remnants of which linger around every corner. This is also where all the cool stuff happened – where the Beat Generation gravitated in the 1950s, the hippies came in the '60s, and where CBGB kick-started careers of punk and new-wave musicians including the Ramones. Things got sketchy in the '70s, coming to a head in the late 1980s with riots in Tompkins Square Park. The neighborhoods continue changing, but they remain Manhattan's most eclectic, creative places to be. New restaurants, cocktail bars and fashion boutiques now vie for attention amid the old-school delis and dives.

EATING IN EAST VILLAGE: BEST RESTAURANTS

MAP P78

Superiority Burger: The best veggie burger in town, plus mouthwatering pies and flavor-packed sides. *hours vary* $$

Veselka: This vestige of the area's Ukrainian past has been serving handmade *varenyky* (pierogis), borscht and goulash since 1954. *8am-midnight Mon-Sat, to 11pm Sun* $$

Rosella: Sustainably minded sushi earns this Japanese restaurant an A+. The menu features locally caught fish, all approved by Seafood Watch or NOAA. *5-10pm Wed-Sun* $$$

Yellow Rose: Flour tortillas give Tex-Mex taquerias their north-of-the-border flair at this outpost, far north of Texas. *noon-10pm Tue-Fri, 10am-4pm & 5-10pm Sat & Sun* $$

Essex Market

TOP SPOTS FOR DOWNTOWN NOSTALGIA

Merchant's House Museum: Tour this red-brick mansion from 1832 for an authentic look at 19th-century life.

Judd Foundation: Admire minimalist artist Donald Judd's five-story, cast-iron home, purchased in 1968 for a now-unthinkable $68,000.

Basilica of St Patrick's Old Cathedral: Descend into the catacombs on a guided tour of the Gothic Revival basilica, a 19th-century Irish Catholic stronghold.

Chinatown Fair Family Fun Center: This Mott St arcade has been going strong since 1940, delivering childhood sentimentality with Ms Pac-Man and more.

Metrograph: Serious cinephiles catch oldies and rare archival films at this LES throwback movie theater with an on-site restaurant and bar.

especially the stretch between Houston and Canal Sts, which is lined with indie boutiques, happening restaurants such as **Scarr's Pizza** *(scarrspizza.com)* and upstart art galleries. Wander this seven-block strip and you'll still find some yesteryear holdouts, including **Orchard Corset**, which opened in 1968 and caters to everyone from Orthodox Jews to trans women – all with the aspirations of Victorian silhouettes.

Sweat It out at the Russian & Turkish Baths

MAP P78

Spa day in a townhouse basement

Locals have been schvitzing at this slightly cramped downtown **spa** *(russianturkishbaths.com; $60)* since 1892. These days, it draws an eclectic mix of actors, students, couples, singles, Russian regulars and old-school locals. Everyone strips down to their skivvies or bathing suits (towels, cotton shorts and sandals are provided) and moves between steam rooms, saunas, an ice-cold plunge pool, the sun deck and the restaurant. Most hours are coed (clothing required), but there are blocks of men- and women-only hours (clothing optional). Massages, scrubs and Russian oak-leaf treatments are available, too. The cafe serves specials such as Polish sausage and blinis.

 DRINKING IN THE VILLAGE & LOWER EAST SIDE: OUR PICKS ─── MAP P78

Attaboy: Speakeasy vibes and bespoke cocktails – tell the barkeep what you like and they'll whip up the concoction of your dreams. Expect to wait. *5pm-3am*

Amor y Amargo: 'Love and Bitters' is a cocktail chemistry lab showcasing its namesake amaro selection. Bartenders offer advice on flavors. *3pm-midnight*

Accidental Bar: The sake sommeliers behind this Japanese juice joint with a hilariously descriptive menu to inspire indulgence. *5-11pm Sun, Tue & Wed, to midnight Thu-Sat*

Ruffian: If you're into funky orange wines, grab a stool at this intimate vino joint to taste Eastern European grapes and mostly vegetarian fare. *5pm-midnight Mon-Sat, 3-11pm Sun*

Grab a Snack at Essex Market
MAP P78

An LES food market

Street vendors have come together at what's known as the **Essex Market** *(essexmarket.nyc)* since 1818, though its newest location only opened in 2019. The most recent Grand St incarnation is a wide-ranging representation of the neighborhood with stalls selling everything from cheese, groceries, spices and Dominican food to ceviche, rice balls and more. Legendary lunch counter **Shopsin's** serves its wide-ranging menu of inventive diner fare in a tiny sit-down space. Downstairs, the **Market Line** food court has outposts of local institutions like Veselka (p79), as well as pizza, ramen, pho and sushi. If you're ordering counter food, head upstairs to dine in sunny, open-atrium seating. This makes a sensible pit stop while walking down Orchard St (p79), located two blocks west.

Sample NYC's Melting Pot
MAP P78

Gorge on global cuisine in the East Village

The diversity of worldwide cuisines in the East Village is jaw-dropping. Find what tickles your taste buds, then tour the world through food. **Nowon** *(nowonusa.com)* is a favorite for American Korean 'drinking food,' and some people say the northern-style pho at **Hanoi House** *(hanoihousenyc.com)* is better than anything in Vietnam. Nibble Nordic delicacies at **Smør** *(smornyc.com)* and its adjoining bakery, which serves freshly baked cardamom buns and egg sandwiches on fluffy brioche. Try Burmese specialties at **Little Myanmar** *(littlemyanmar.nyc)*, and if you like spicy Thai food, go to **Soothr** (pronounced 'sood'; *soothrnyc.com*). Meanwhile, **Cafe Mogador** *(cafemogador.com)* has been turning out Moroccan favorites since 1983 and **Takahachi** *(takahachi.net)* has been a stalwart for sushi and Japanese noodles since 1991. For quick, cheap eats, follow the cab drivers to **Punjabi Grocery & Deli** *(@punjabidelinyc)* for delectable vegetarian fare.

Admire the Whitney Museum's Permanent Collection
MAP P82

America's modern art masters

The **Whitney Museum of American Art** *(whitney.org; adult/25 & under $30/free)* opened as a showcase for homegrown artists in a W 8th St townhouse in 1930. After successive

(continues on p84)

EDGY ART, MUSIC & CINEMA

New Museum: Work by emerging and established contemporary artists inside a futuristic fortress that looks like a giant's Tetris game.

Hole: Art openings attract rowdy crowds at this bi-coastal gallery known for performances and special events.

Bowery Ballroom: Audiences adore this concert venue's intimate feel and great sound system. Head downstairs for drinks and mingling.

International Center of Photography: Rotating exhibits celebrate the humanitarian and political documentary work of world-class photographers.

Slipper Room: Squeeze in tight for hit-or-miss shows featuring comics, magicians, burlesque dancers and circus performers, often worth the gamble.

 EATING IN THE VILLAGE & LOWER EAST SIDE: BREAKFAST & COFFEE MAP P78

Abraço: Sip espresso while inhaling the dangerously addictive olive-oil cake inside this ground-level cafe. *8am-6pm Tue-Thu & Sun, to 9pm Fri & Sat* $

Supermoon Bakehouse: Lines of laminated pastries, including cruffins, look like designer jewelry at this shop where flavors change weekly. *10am-6pm Thu-Mon* $

Russ & Daughters: Feast on bagels and the city's best smoked salmon at this diner extension of a long-running Jewish delicatessen. *8:30am-2:30pm Mon-Thu, to 3:30pm Fri-Sun* $$

Apollo Bagels: Classic NY bagel texture (crispy exterior, chewy interior) with a twist: these are made with slightly tangy sourdough. *7am-5pm* $

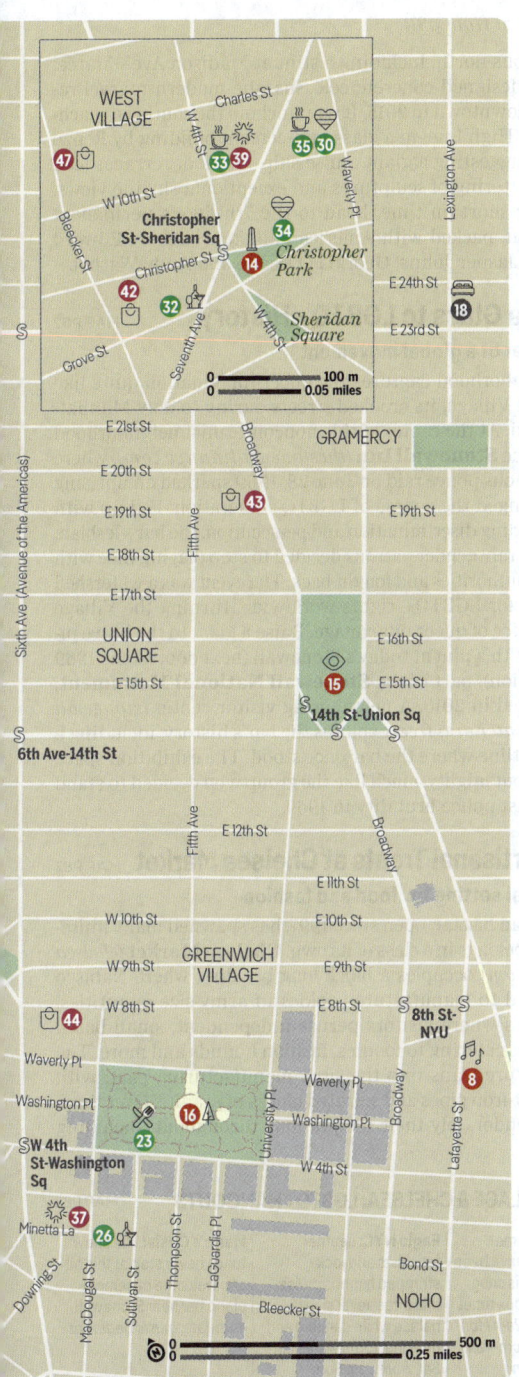

⭐ HIGHLIGHTS
1. High Line
2. Whitney Museum of American Art

● SIGHTS
3. 520 W 28th Street
4. Dia Chelsea
5. Gagosian
6. Gansevoort Peninsula
7. High Line Nine
8. Joe's Pub
9. Little Island
10. Pace Gallery
11. Paula Cooper Gallery
12. Pier 45
13. Pier 57
14. Stonewall National Monument
15. Union Square
16. Washington Square Park

● ACTIVITIES
17. Chelsea Piers Complex

● SLEEPING
18. Freehand
19. Hotel Chelsea
20. Jane Hotel

● EATING
21. Anixi
22. L'Industrie
23. NY Dosas
24. Semma
25. Shukette

● DRINKING & NIGHTLIFE
26. 124 Old Rabbit Club
27. Cubbyhole
28. Eagle NYC
29. Employees Only
30. Julius'
31. Le Bain
32. Marie's Crisis
33. St Jardim
34. Stonewall Inn
35. Té Company

● ENTERTAINMENT
36. Atlantic Theater Company
37. Comedy Cellar
38. Lucille Lortel Theatre
see 8 Public Theater
39. Smalls
40. Village Vanguard

● SHOPPING
41. Chelsea Market
42. Cueva
43. Fishs Eddy
44. Goods for the Study
45. Printed Matter, Inc
46. Screaming Mimis
47. Zuri

83

NYC'S HIPPEST MICRO-HOOD?

Is Dimes Sq the hippest new micro-hood in NYC? Does it even exist? Media coverage has debated whether this small Lower East Side corner around Division and Canal Sts is a publicity joke or a real thing, and talking about it has brought it into being. What we know for sure: **Dimes** *(dimesnyc.com)* was an immediate restaurant hot spot for cool downtown kids when it opened in 2013. We're still happy to hang out there if we can get a table. Dine elsewhere with the in-crowd at one of the area's fashionable bars and restaurants, including the chic **Lobby Lounge** inside **Nine Orchard Hotel** *(nineorchard. com)*. It might be a media-made gimmick, but it's cool – like the rest of the Lower East Side.

(continued from p81)

expansions north, including a stint at Madison Ave's Marcel Breuer–designed concrete colossus, the modern marvel returned downtown in 2015. It now anchors the southern reaches of the High Line in a glass-and-cement building by Renzo Piano, suggesting a giant cruise ship. Outdoor terraces lead to a smattering of sculptures and exceptional skyline views. If you're short on time, head to the 7th floor's permanent collection, packed with American all-stars such as Edward Hopper, Jasper Johns, Georgia O'Keeffe and Andy Warhol.

Raise a Glass to LGBTQ+ History   MAP P82
Epicenter of a global movement

No neighborhood captures the queer imagination quite like the West Village, its crooked streets daring to defy Manhattan's grid. At the center of this nonconformist neighborhood stands the **Stonewall Inn** *(thestonewallinnnyc.com)*, where an infamous police raid on June 28, 1969 sparked an uprising that changed the course of LGBTQ+ liberation. Fed up with never-ending discrimination and persecution, the bar's lesbian, gay and transgender patrons decided to stop playing nice with bigoted authorities and fought back. The event was a watershed moment for LGBTQ+ rights worldwide, turning the Village into a place of queer pilgrimage. Raise a glass to the brave pioneers with a pint at today's Stonewall (next door to the 1969 incarnation), part of the **Stonewall National Monument**, designated in 2016. A neighboring visitor center *(stonewallvisitorcenter.org; free)* explores the bar's history, including a silver outline where the bar once stood. The exhibition space is small but mighty, much like the group who decided to stand up against police brutality in 1969.

Find Artisanal Treats at Chelsea Market   MAP P82
Industrial setting for food and fashion

This urban bazaar, open since 1997, has spawned many imitators but belongs in a class of its own. **Chelsea Market** *(chelseamarket.com)* occupies a block-long building where Nabisco once used to manufacture cookies in army-size quantities. Today, it's where visitors peruse independent, small-batch delicacies catering to foodies, fashion hounds and more. The architecture leans into the site's manufacturing past, with huge cast-iron pipes and serrated blocks of granite. Over three dozen vendors ply their temptations throughout, including

DRINKING IN THE WEST VILLAGE & CHELSEA: LGBTQ+ HANGOUTS — MAP P82

Julius': One of NYC's longest-running gay joints, this cozy dive, famous for a 1966 civil rights 'Sip In,' is refreshingly unpretentious. *hours vary*

Cubbyhole: Femme-forward crowds have been cramming into this snug spot to play jukebox tunes since 1994. *4pm-2am Mon-Thu, to 4am Fri, 2pm-4am Sat, 2pm-2am Sun*

Eagle NYC: Leather fetishists and jock-strapped himbos cruise this three-level sleaze palace while dancing and drinking. *10pm-4am Mon-Sat, from 5pm Sun*

Marie's Crisis: The show tunes never stop at this all-are-welcome basement piano bar near Stonewall. *4pm-late, music begins at 5:30pm*

Lobster Place

Miznon (Israeli street food), the Lobster Place (good luck resisting its rolls), Fat Witch Bakery (brownies and other decadent hits) and Los Tacos No 1 (authentic Mexican tacos). Head to the covered sidewalk tables for outdoor seating. Once you've had your fill, check out Artists & Fleas, a small market where local artists sell their wares. It makes a great pit stop while wandering the High Line.

Skip down the High Line

MAP P82

Chelsea's elevated train-track park

Snaking between the Meatpacking District to Hudson Yards, 30ft above street level, the **High Line** *(thehighline.org)* is a fabulous example of industrial reuse. Once a 20th-century freight line linking slaughterhouses along the Hudson River, it's now an art-strewn pedestrian ribbon running between galleries, modern high-rises and swanky shopping centers.

The High Line's story began in the early 20th century, when the west side's booming industrial enterprises were served by perilous street-level tracks, earning Tenth Ave the nickname 'Death Avenue.' A two-story-high railway became the expensive solution, and the 'West Side Elevated Line' ran its first train in 1933. It wasn't long before the train line became a money pit and fell into disuse; in the 1990s, demolition was mooted. Enter

A VILLAGE THEORY

The Village's compact streets are chockablock with charm. To find out why this neighborhood beguiles, read *The Death and Life of Great American Cities*, a 1961 tome by urban-planning guru Jane Jacobs. Inspired by Greenwich Village, Jacobs was the first to expound ideas that are now commonplace: density spurs commerce and community, and city life takes place outdoors in a 'sidewalk ballet.' Her greatest adversary? Urban planner Robert Moses, a political Goliath who fought to build a highway through Jacobs' beloved neighborhood. While Moses transformed much of NYC's landscape, you can see who won this particular battle: the late Jacobs is immortalized with a plaque at 555 Hudson St ('Jane Jacobs Way').

DRINKING IN THE VILLAGE: BEST BARS & CAFES

MAP P82

Employees Only: This divine speakeasy-style bar ushered in a new era of haute mixology when it served its first egg-white cocktail in 2004. *6pm-4am*

St Jardim: Perched on a lively Village side street, this all-day cafe and natural wine bar is perfect for people-watching. *hours vary*

124 Old Rabbit Club: The reward for finding this craft-beer haunt (look for the word 'Rabbit') is rare brews and local ales. *6pm-2am Mon-Sat, 4pm-midnight Sun*

Té Company: Loose-leaf teas from Taiwanese farmers served alongside sweets so pretty they belong in a Wes Anderson film. *noon-6pm Tue-Fri, from 11am Sat & Sun*

Jersey City skyline from Little Island

FASHION, JOURNALS & ZINES IN THE VILLAGE & CHELSEA

Screaming Mimis: This funtastic shop carries an excellent selection of vintage, designer and flamboyant costume threads.

Cueva: Eclectic designs rotate inside this seasonally curated international menswear collection.

Zuri: Colorful racks of one-style-fits-all dresses made from ethically sourced fabrics from Kenya.

Goods for the Study: Hardcore journalers and sketch-pad savants go ga-ga for this assortment of paper and writing utensils.

Printed Matter, Inc: Trim shelves hide thousands of ideas packed into strange zines and artist monographs.

the Friends of the High Line, with a vision of an elegant park. Years of activism resulted in the jewel we enjoy today: a pedestrian catwalk, planted with 500-plus native species, wending its way above former factories and plenty of top-dollar real estate.

Begin your one- or two-hour journey near **Hudson Yards** (enter at 30th or 34th Sts), with super-tall skyscrapers shining eastward. Plant-packed railroad tracks evoke the industrial wilderness that preceded the park's creation. As the path narrows, you'll see tons of contemporary constructions, including starchitect Zaha Hadid's futuristic glass-and-metal apartment complex at **520 W 28th Street**.

For a bird's-eye view of Tenth Ave, sit on the amphitheater-style seats at 17th or 26th Sts and watch as cabs whiz by. If you prefer serene scenery, snag a train-wheel-tracked chaise longue on the Diller-von Furstenberg Sundeck – named after fashion queen Diane von Furstenberg and her billionaire husband Barry Diller, the pockets behind this entire project.

The High Line ends at the foot of the Whitney Museum (p81) and near a few other noteworthy areas, including Hudson River Park and the West Village's winding streets.

MEET THOSE DANCIN' FEET
Consider yourself a theater buff? Grab drinks alongside chorus kids at some of their favorite Midtown haunts and don't miss the **Museum of Broadway** (p90), a love letter to NYC show business.

Head up Hudson River Park MAPS P74, P82
The west side's green ribbon

Hudson River Park is the 550-acre shining star of Manhattan's modern green spaces, and its most popular sections hug the Village and Chelsea. Spend a sunny afternoon roaming around the waterfront.

Start at **Pier 45** (also called Christopher St Pier and beloved by queer crowds), where Speedo-clad gaggles gather to worship the sun – and each other. Walking north, there's **Gansevoort Peninsula**, completed in 2023 and billed as Manhattan's first public beach. Lounge in Adirondack chairs and admire David Hammons' ghostly *Day's End*, a skeletal art installation evoking the docks that once populated the riverfront.

Up next is **Little Island** *(littleisland.org)*, which appeared like a surrealist dream in 2021: 132 concrete pods shoot from the water like tulips, crowned by undulating green hills. Stroll the 2.4-acre folly's footpaths to enjoy gentle breezes and expansive views, or check the seasonal event schedule for live performances.

Pier 57 rounds out the park with its range of offerings, including City Winery's live music and Market 57's food vendors curated by the James Beard Foundation. (This is a great spot to try dim sum from Nom Wah Tea Parlor, a popular Chinatown restaurant.) Don't miss the rooftop – perfect for picnics and panoramas, including the best view you'll get of Little Island, backed by One World Trade Center.

Meet the Locals in Washington Square Park

MAP P82

A slice of Village life

Grab a seat in Greenwich Village's unofficial **town square** *(nycgovparks.com)* and you'll see it all: NYU students scurrying between classes, street vendors selling handmade clothes, fearless squirrels, socializing canines, speed-chess pros, brassy buskers, barefoot children splashing around the fountain – and possibly ghosts.

Centuries ago, this site was a marshy area crossed by Minetta Creek. Dutch colonists granted land rights (for a price) to settlers of African descent, who created a community known as Little Africa. Later, the plot became a public cemetery for the unidentified deceased. When the burial grounds turned into a space for military parades in the 1830s, real-estate developers followed and some of the city's toniest homes sprouted on the park's north border. Today, the park is dominated by the Stanford White–designed Washington Square Arch – 73ft of gleaming white Tuckahoe marble. Originally made of wood to celebrate the centennial of George Washington's inauguration in 1889, it proved so popular that it was replaced with stone six years later.

Head to the park's northwest corner to see an English elm considered one of Manhattan's oldest trees. Known as Hangman's Elm, its branches were used (according to legend) to hang traitors during the American Revolution.

QUEER PIER PAST

Ken Lustbader, co-founder and co-director of the NYC LGBT Historic Sites Project, explores the Greenwich Village waterfront's 20th-century history. *@nyclgbtsites*

This was one of the country's busiest ports, comprised of piers and beaux-arts-style shipping terminals. Eventually, those piers were abandoned and became urban ruins, which were appropriated by men who had sex with men, as well as gay artists who used the decrepit, deteriorating pier structures for public artwork and open-air sexual experimentation. Artist David Wojnarowicz was at the piers regularly, taking photographs, and even said, 'This is the real MoMA.' If you go there now, it's a sanitized version of a waterfront, without any of this history discernible in the current landscape.

EATING IN THE VILLAGE: RESERVATIONS RECOMMENDED

MAP P82

Semma: Experience summer in South India with the spicy chutneys and sauces on Michelin-starred Semma's menu (if you can snag a reservation). *5-10pm Mon-Sat* **$$$**

Shukette: The fluffy pita is an enticing teaser for what's to come: bites of delicious, shareable Middle Eastern delicacies. *5-11pm Mon-Sat, 4-10pm Sun* **$$**

Anixi: This faux-meat fortress is dressed to impress, with velvet curtains and crystal chandeliers as fancy as its Mediterranean-inspired menu. *hours vary* **$$**

L'Industrie: Wait in line for a pizza slice smothered in burrata and a cream-filled maritozzo, then bring it next door to Talea and pair it with a beer flight. *noon-10pm* **$**

APPLAUD PERFORMING ARTS

Village Vanguard: Turn a quiet Monday night into a big-band jamboree by seeing the Vanguard Jazz Orchestra at this prestigious jazz club.

Comedy Cellar: Talented regulars, including up-and-coming TV writers and personalities, have tested new material inside this chuckle den since the 1980s.

Atlantic Theater Company: This Off-Broadway house knows how to pick 'em: numerous shows here went on to win Best Musical Tony Awards.

Lucille Lortel Theatre: Clock the sidewalk stars in front of this Off-Broadway playhouse, including theater wordsmiths such as Neil LaBute and Charles Busch.

Smalls: Intimate basement jazz den that winks at Prohibition-era speakeasies.

If hunger calls, grab food from **NY Dosas** (*@nydosas; 11am–3pm Mon-Sat*), Sri Lanka–born Thiru Kumar's South Indian pushcart near the dog run. Chow down while taking it all in.

Ogle Art at Chelsea's Galleries   MAP P82
DIY contemporary-art crawl

Zigzagging through far-west Chelsea is like visiting a free contemporary-art museum. The area is home to NYC's densest concentration of galleries; most open to the public from 10am to 6pm Tuesday to Saturday. Spend a couple of hours seeing what's on view. A perfect starting point is **High Line Nine** (*highlinenine.org*). This thin strip mall linking 27th and 28th Sts is a gallery space where collectors spot up-and-coming artists. The eight floors of the **Pace Gallery** (*pacegallery.org*) showcase work by leading contemporary artists. Don't miss its smaller 4000-sq-ft space at 510 W 25th St – inside one of the many auto garages that once populated the area. Seeing exhibits at global chain **Gagosian** (*gagosian.com*) is akin to spinning around the Guggenheim – except everything is for sale. Check the website to see what's showing – perhaps Jeff Koons or Nam June Paik. The massive pieces inside the 20,000-sq-ft **Dia Chelsea** (*diaart.org*) would dwarf most jewel-box Manhattan galleries. Marvel at their size before perusing the picture-perfect art bookshop. End at **Paula Cooper Gallery** (*paulacoopergallery.com*), the eponymous founder of which started SoHo's gallery explosion in 1968, then moved to Chelsea in the 1990s before it became cool.

Climb Higher than King Kong   MAP P89
Tour Midtown's Empire State Building

There's a reason King Kong chose this tower above the rest. One World Trade Center might be taller. The Chrysler Building might be prettier. But when it comes to skyline landmarks, the **Empire State Building** (*esbnyc.com; adult/child from $44/38*) is NYC's queen. Built in a frenzied 410 days, this steel-framed, limestone-and-granite-clad art-deco emblem opened in 1931 as the world's tallest building – a title it held until 1970, when the Twin Towers eclipsed its height. Take the vertiginous elevator ride to spectacular city views.

The main observation deck on the 86th floor is outdoors. There's also a tiny room with floor-to-ceiling windows on the 102nd floor ($35 extra). While on the 86th floor, train binoculars on the nearby Chrysler Building to admire its deco details.

EATING IN MIDTOWN: BEST RESTAURANTS   MAP P93

Le Bernardin: French-born chef Eric Ripert has spent decades steering this restaurant to deceptively simple seafood heaven. Michelin agrees. Book ahead. *hours vary* $$$

Barbetta: Linger at this gorgeous Restaurant Row time warp for Piedmontese specialties such as gnocchi and risotto. *4:30–11pm Tue-Sat, plus noon-2pm Wed & Sat* $$$

Mercado Little Spain: Celebrity chef José Andrés brings the Iberian peninsula to the Hudson Yards mall, where kiosks and sit-downs serve Spanish cuisine. *11am–9pm* $$

Ace's Pizza: When hunger strikes around Rockefeller Center, head here for rectangular Detroit-style pizza slices. *11:30am-7pm Mon-Fri, to 6pm Sat & Sun* $

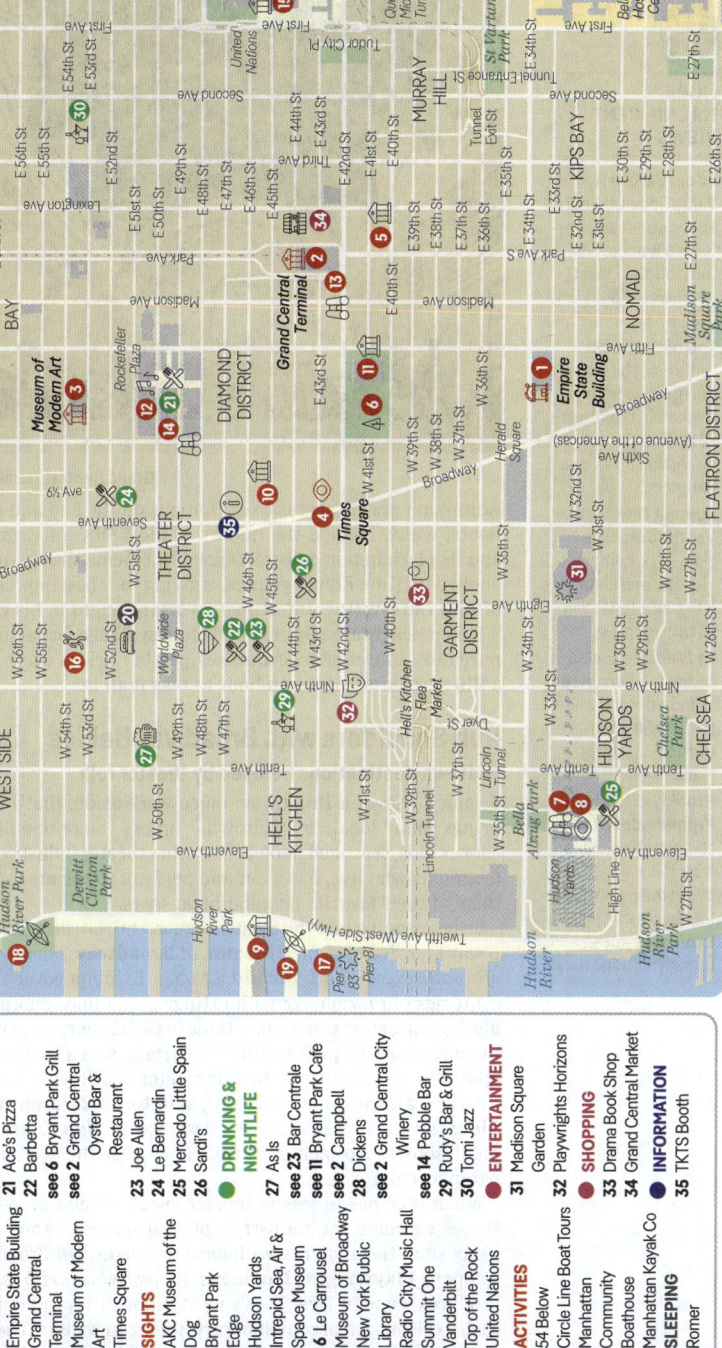

MORE MAGNIFICENT VIEWS

Edge: Gaze at Hudson Yards from 100 floors above street level, or test your nerves on the world's highest open-air building ascent.

Top of the Rock: Get a blockbuster perspective from Rockefeller Center's 70th floor, 850ft in the air with a 360-degree panorama.

Summit One Vanderbilt: Ride a glass-bottomed elevator and step into a city-reflecting infinity room.

Le Bain: Sip cocktails on the top floor of the Standard Hotel while partying in a club overlooking lower Manhattan.

Brooklyn Heights Promenade: Wow at Manhattan's skyline from this eight-block pedestrian strip atop the Brooklyn–Queens Expressway near Brooklyn Bridge Park.

Grand Central Terminal

Admission grants access to exhibitions on the 2nd and 80th floors, which include the history of the ESB's construction and its place in pop culture. If you like cinema shtick, snag a photo with King Kong's giant paw, giving your best impression of Ann Darrow (the unfortunate woman caught in his grip).

Timed tickets are required and often available for same-day purchase. Sunset offers exquisite light, but tickets come with a $10 surcharge. Allow an hour to take it all in.

Rub Shoulders with Broadway Babies MAP P89
Midtown destinations beloved by theater folk

Seeing a show on Broadway: office work aside, that's what brings many locals to Midtown – unless you're one of the chorus kids, seasoned hoofers and other theater industry professionals who live, hang out and perform in the area. Meet them at their favorite neighborhood spots.

Before running into the theater cognoscenti, brush up on your B'way knowledge at the **Museum of Broadway** (*themuseumofbroadway.com; adult/child $43/35*). Exhibits cover three centuries of razzmatazz with artifacts, costumes and props highlighting everything from *Annie* to *Oklahoma* and beyond. Visitors also get a peek behind the curtain with a 1st-floor exhibit showcasing the soup-to-nuts making of a Broadway show.

After learning your Do-Re-Mi, skip to the **Drama Book Shop** (*dramabookshop.com*) – designed by *Hamilton's* scenic designer – to pick up scripts and other theater-related paraphernalia.

When it comes to seeing theater, plenty of non-Broadway stages welcome the industry's biggest names – and you'll likely sit in the audience with local thespians. Off-Broadway company **Playwrights Horizons** (*playwrightshorizons.org*) produces some of New York's most innovative productions, each a celebration of contemporary American writers. Theater fans should also consider a cabaret and dinner at **54 Below** *(54below.org)*, where everyone from Tony Award winners to New York's up-and-coming stars belt the night away.

For a taste of old-school insider Broadway, stop by **Sardi's** *(sardis.com)* – a restaurant with walls covered in caricatures of famous patrons. After curtain call, you might spot actors clinking glasses at **Bar Centrale** *(barcentrale.com)* or **Joe Allen** *(joeallenrestaurant.com)*.

Time Travel at the Museum of Modern Art MAP P89
Admire art-world stars in Midtown

Name a notable artist from the 19th century onward – Van Gogh, Matisse, Picasso, Kahlo, Rothko, Warhol, Bourgeois – and **MoMA** *(moma.org; adult/child $30/free)* probably shows some of their best work among its 200,000-piece collection. For aesthetes, it's an encounter with the sublime; for the uninitiated, a cultural crash course. Attempting to see everything in MoMA's 630,000-sq-ft space could take half a day or more – a surefire way to experience museum fatigue. Instead, go through the collection chronologically, ensuring a glimpse of the big names on display. Pieces rotate through the galleries at least once a year, which means first-timers might miss some famous works, but repeat visitors will get a fresh experience.

Work your way down: floor 5 covers the 1880s–1940s. Count on seeing Van Gogh's swirling *Starry Night*, Monet's Impressionist water lilies and, if you're lucky, Frida Kahlo's gender-bending *Self Portrait with Cropped Hair*. Floor 4 tackles the 1940s–70s, with Jackson Pollock and Andy Warhol leading the charge. Don't miss Faith Ringgold's 1967 response to Picasso's *Guernica* in the shocking *American People Series #20: Die*. On floor 2 (1970s–present), there's Richard Serra's *Equal*, composed of 80-ton steel stacks, and works by NYC painter Jean-Michel Basquiat.

Timed tickets are required to guarantee museum entry; book online in advance.

Slow down at Grand Central Terminal MAP P89
Relive the railroad's golden age

Don't rush through this 1913 beaux-arts station hall like Metro-North's commuters. **Grand Central Terminal** *(grandcentralterminal.com)* evokes the romance of rail travel and it's worth

THEATER TICKET DISCOUNTS

Broadway tickets often have three-digit prices, but there are ways to score fabulous seats at a fraction of the cost. For the most options, visit the Theatre Development Fund's **TKTS Booth** under the red steps in Times Square's Father Duffy Sq, offering up to 50% off same-day shows and next-day matinees (lines can be long). Most shows hold lotteries, allowing select winners to purchase choice seats at bargain prices. Many productions also have rush tickets, slashing seat prices on a first-come, first-served basis – visit *playbill.com* for a show-by-show guide. The TodayTix app *(todaytix.com)* offers discounted pricing in all forms, including digital lotteries – the most convenient way to grab tickets before arriving in NYC. Want to avoid online fees? Purchase tickets directly from the box office.

DRINKING IN MIDTOWN: BEST BARS — MAP P89

Pebble Bar: This townhouse bar has done the unthinkable: create a cool cocktail scene in kitschy Rockefeller Center. *4pm-midnight Sun-Wed, to 2am Thu-Sat*

Tomi Jazz: Stumble into this Japanese jazz den after 6pm, when whiskey flows as freely as an improvised sax solo. *5pm-1am Sun-Thu, to 3am Fri & Sat*

As Is: Hell's Kitchen's beer heads agree – this hops den is tops, with 20 beers on tap. *3pm-late Mon-Fri, from noon Sat & Sun*

Dickens: Dine and drink inside this posh four-floor LGBTQ+ palace, an elevated answer to Hell's Kitchen cramped gay dens. *hours vary*

MIDTOWN TOURS & QUIRKY MUSEUMS

New York Public Library: Visit the magnificent Rose Reading Room to see its celestially painted coffered ceiling on a 15-minute tour.

Radio City Music Hall: Join the 60-minute Stage Door Tour for the inside scoop on the famous performance complex.

Madison Square Garden: Can't make it to a Knicks NBA or Rangers NHL game? Tour the complex instead.

AKC Museum of the Dog: The airy 1st-floor galleries contain paintings of dogs, and an upstairs library carries books on every breed.

United Nations: Go international on a tour through Le Corbusier and Oscar Niemeyer's mid-century masterpiece.

spending at least an hour falling in love with its treasures. Start by strolling across the marble-trimmed concourse to gaze at the vaulted aquamarine ceiling depicting the night sky's constellations. The starry wonder isn't original – it's a 1944 copy covering water damage in the first fresco designed by French painter Paul Cesar Helleu. A 1990s renovation added twinkling lights (part of Helleu's plan) and cleaned the ceiling. Follow Cancer's claws to the northwest corner to a tiny black rectangle: an original patch of soot, approximately 9 by 5 inches, caused by decades of air pollutants. While admiring the work, examine the layout. The zodiac is actually backwards. After its unveiling, railroad officials swatted away critics, saying it was painted from the perspective of God. For more hidden wonders, head to the Whispering Gallery (p255) between the Main Concourse and Vanderbilt Hall, where an acoustic quirk allows people to stand on opposite gallery corners and carry a conversation sotto voce. There's plenty to eat and drink, too – try **Grand Central Market** (fast casual), **Grand Central Oyster Bar & Restaurant** (fine dining), **Grand Central City Winery** and the **Campbell**, which features live jazz on weekend evenings.

Light up at Midnight
MAP P89
Times Square's nightly art show

There isn't a dimmer switch – **Times Square** (*timessquarenyc.org*) perpetually shines. It's a splash of Vegas, a soupçon of Disney and a digital deluge of American commercialism. Love it or loathe it, it's hard not to be mesmerized by the lights – particularly around midnight, when crowds thin out and the blinking billboards momentarily transform from ads into an immersive art experience.

Midnight Moment, the world's largest digital public art program, synchronizes 92 digital displays between 41st and 49th St for a three-minute, immersive contemporary art spectacle starting at 11:57pm. Works change monthly, featuring well-known names like Andy Warhol and contemporary boundary-breakers in the digital-art ecosystem. For the most mesmerizing view, climb the 27 red steps above the TKTS Booth at 47th St and watch art appear all around.

End the light show with a nightcap – perhaps a $4 draught from **Rudy's Bar & Grill** (*rudysbarnyc.com*) or a fancy cocktail from Pebble Bar (p91), both within walking distance.

Take a Break in Bryant Park
MAP P89
Eat, shop, skate and stroll

European coffee kiosks, alfresco chess games and outdoor events for the whole family make leafy, Parisian-style **Bryant Park** (*bryantpark.org*) a whimsical break from Midtown's mayhem. Office workers stream in at lunchtime, competing for tables with skyscraper views. There's also **Bryant Park Grill**, with a patio ideal for twilight cocktails, and neighboring **Bryant Park Cafe**, an alfresco hangout from mid-April

UPPER WEST SIDE & UPPER EAST SIDE

★ HIGHLIGHTS
1. American Museum of Natural History
2. Central Park
3. Metropolitan Museum of Art

● SIGHTS
4. American Folk Art Museum
5. Asia Society & Museum
6. Bethesda Fountain
7. Central Park Zoo
8. Cooper-Hewitt Smithsonian Design Museum
9. Dakota Building
10. Frick Collection
11. Jacqueline Kennedy Onassis Reservoir
12. Jewish Museum
13. Lincoln Center
14. Museum of the City of New York
15. Neue Galerie
16. New-York Historical Society
17. Nicholas Roerich Museum
18. North Woods
19. Park Avenue Armory
20. Ramble
21. Solomon R Guggenheim Museum
22. Strawberry Fields

● ACTIVITIES
23. Sheep Meadow
24. Wollman Skating Rink

● EATING
25. Cafe Luxembourg
see 15 Café Sabarsky
26. JG Melon
27. Le Pain Quotidien
28. Levain
29. Lexington Candy Shop
30. Mama's TOO!
31. Tatiana

● DRINKING & NIGHTLIFE
32. 2nd Floor Bar & Essen
33. Bemelmans Bar

● SHOPPING
34. Zabar's

● TRANSPORT
35. Central Park Bike Tours

THE EVOLUTION OF TIMES SQUARE

Long mythologized as the 'Crossroads of the World,' Times Square is what non–New Yorkers often picture as its emblem: commerce, crowds, digital billboards and around-the-clock entertainment. But being seen in this neighborhood wasn't always admirable. Starting in the 1960s, Times Square became a pit for peep shows, porn theaters and three-card-monte scammers. In 1981, *Rolling Stone* dubbed 42nd St the 'sleaziest block in America.' All that changed in the mid-1990s when city mandates downgraded the area's X-rating to a G. Now, roughly 360,000 people pass through Times Square daily – but don't confuse this strip for wholesome Main Street America. It's colorful, sure, but equally chaotic. Think Main Street on steroids. Locals avoid it at all costs.

Bryant Park (p92)

to November. Ping-pong, played on the northern side, can be intensely competitive. Kids whirl around on Le Carrousel's *($4)* 14 painted ponies. The scene is particularly popular in summer, when you can watch cinema by starlight at one of Bryant Park's free movie nights (bring a blanket and a picnic for thorough enjoyment). The park is great in cold weather, too: find unique gifts at the holiday market, open between Thanksgiving and Christmas, or ice skate all winter long on the city's largest free-admission rink. It's hard to believe this was a crime-ridden hellscape in the 1970s. Check the park website for detailed info on events.

Set Sail on the Hudson

MAP P89

Boating around Midtown and Chelsea

Midtown's most notable coastal assets are almost entirely on the west side. The **Intrepid Sea, Air & Space Museum** *(intrepidmuseum.org; adult/child $38/28)*, a hulking aircraft carrier that survived both a WWII bomb and kamikaze attacks, houses an impressive interactive military museum with videos, historical artifacts and frozen-in-time living quarters. The flight deck features fighter planes and military helicopters, which might inspire you to try the museum's high-tech flight simulators. On a pier just to the Intrepid's south, board a Circle Line tour for a floating perspective of the city's profile. The 90-minute Landmarks cruise *(circleline.com; from $43)* is essential for New Yorkers eager to see the skyline from afar. Next door to Circle Line, on Pier 94 (at 44th St), **Manhattan Kayak Co** *(manhattankayak.com; rentals $12)* offers a variety of kayaking and stand-up paddleboarding classes and tours. To try out kayaking on the Hudson for free, in a more limited area, head north to Pier 96 (at 55th St) and the **Manhattan Community Boathouse** *(hudsonriverpark.org)*.

There's also an exceptional architecture tour run by Classic Harbor Line, which teams up with the American Institute of Architects for a fun, informative, three-hour cruise aboard a 1920s-style commuter yacht that circumnavigates Manhattan (*sail-nyc.com; adult/student $112/88*). Expert guides narrate tales about riverfront towers while motoring underneath bridges and circling the Statue of Liberty. Tickets include a complimentary drink. Boats depart from **Chelsea Piers**.

Visit Austria at the Neue Galerie   MAP P93
Art and food with Viennese flair

Austrian and German art from 1890–1940 take center stage inside this Upper East Side **mansion** (*neuegalerie.org; adult/student $28/15*) from 1914 designed by Carrère and Hastings (the architects behind the New York Public Library and the Frick). The museum's most prized collection is a series of sketches and paintings by Gustav Klimt, including his gold-flecked 1907 *Portrait of Adele Bloch-Bauer 1,* acquired for a cool $135 million by cosmetics magnate and museum founder Ronald Lauder. (The 2015 film *Woman in Gold* recounts the painting's fascinating history, which includes looting Nazis, a feisty Bloch-Bauer heir and the obstinate Austrian government.) A connected bookstore is a museum unto itself, decorated with artist monographs and coffee-table books.

For an immersive Austrian experience, reserve a table at Vienna-style **Café Sabarsky**. With dishes such as goulash soup, roasted bratwurst and *topfentorte* (quark cheesecake), you might mistake the Upper East Side for Europe's Eastern Alps.

Cover Centuries of NYC History   MAP P93
Museum dedicated to local stories

The **Museum of the City of New York** (*mcny.org; adult/child $23/free*), housed in a Georgian Colonial Revival–style building near the top of Central Park, artfully illustrates the past, present and future of this ever-evolving city. At a minimum, spare 28 minutes to watch *Timescapes,* a multiscreen documentary that chronicles NYC's past 400 years from tiny Dutch trading center to international powerhouse. Other permanent exhibits explore centuries of social activism and feature notable New Yorkers such as poet Walt Whitman and urbanist Jane Jacobs.

MORE MAGNIFICENT UES MUSEUMS

Solomon R Guggenheim Museum: Architect Frank Lloyd Wright's iconic inverted ziggurat spirals up from Fifth Ave.

Cooper-Hewitt Smithsonian Design Museum: Andrew Carnegie's 64-room Georgian mansion devotes itself to historical and contemporary interior design.

Jewish Museum: Housed in a 1908 French Gothic chateau, this 30,000-piece collection spans 4000 years of Jewish culture.

Park Avenue Armory: This Gothic Revival behemoth features a 55,000-sq-ft performance space, plus designs by the likes of Stanford White.

Asia Society & Museum: One of America's preeminent institutions for pan-Asian art: Chola-period Indian bronzes, modern Japanese paintings etc.

 EATING & DRINKING ON THE UES: OUR PICKS   MAP P93

| JG Melon: No-frills, cash-only pub serving one of NYC's best burgers since 1972. Wash it down with a beefy Bloody Mary. *11:30am-3am* $ | Lexington Candy Shop: Order an egg cream at New York's oldest family-run luncheonette, serving diner delights since 1925. *7am-6pm Mon-Fri, 8am-6pm Sat, to 4pm Sun* $ | Bemelmans Bar: Sip Manhattans and admire murals by *Madeleine* illustrator Ludwig Bemelmans as pianists tinkle the ivories. *hours vary* | 2nd Floor Bar & Essen: Down creative drinks and shtetl-style bar bites in this speakeasy-esque hangout above a kosher deli. *5pm-midnight Tue-Thu, to 2am Fri & Sat* |

TOP EXPERIENCE

Metropolitan Museum of Art

This stately, two-million-sq-ft museum, founded in 1870, is an encyclopedic bastion of world-class art, celebrating 5000 years of human creativity. The Met's one-million-plus objects cover all corners of the globe with artifacts, paintings, sculptures, textiles and even an Egyptian tomb guarded by a moat. It's the Western Hemisphere's largest museum, overflowing with must-see treasures. Dive in.

DON'T MISS

- Temple of Dendur
- Leon Levy and Shelby White Roman Sculpture Court
- Van Gogh's *White Field with Cypresses*
- Damascus Room
- Leutze's *Washington Crossing the Delaware*
- Charles Engelhard Court
- Benton's *America Today*
- Cantor Rooftop Garden Bar

Egyptian Art

Time-travel through Egypt's history in 39 galleries covering the Paleolithic to Roman eras (c 300,000 BCE to 400 CE). Start at the **Tomb of Perneb**, a limestone burial chamber with intricately painted reliefs (Gallery 100). Next, after walking past pyramid pieces and funerary statues, pause at Gallery 136's mysterious *Fragment of a Queen's Face* (c 1390–1336 BCE) to appreciate the sculptor's laser-like precision. If you only see one thing, make it the **Temple of Dendur** (Gallery 131). This is the Western Hemisphere's only complete Egyptian temple, built over 2000 years ago on the banks of the Nile.

PRACTICALITIES

- metmuseum.org
- adult/student $30/17
- 10am–5pm Sun-Tue & Thu, to 9pm Fri & Sat

Greek & Roman Art

With more than 30,000 individual pieces, this is North America's most comprehensive assemblage of toga-wearing trophies. Start south of the **Great Hall** to gape at chiseled gods preening under a vaulted beaux-arts ceiling. All this eye candy might inspire staying put, but even greater treasures await in the sunlit **Leon Levy and Shelby White Roman Sculpture Court** (Gallery 162). Bonus points for spotting the headless **Three Graces** of Greek mythology – Beauty, Mirth and Abundance.

European Paintings

From Giotto to Gauguin, the Met has it all: religious iconography from the 13th century, every Dutch master you can name and a sweeping selection of 19th-century French Impressionists. Unlike *Starry Night* at MoMA (p91), you won't contend with crowds to see Vincent van Gogh's paintings here. Stand before his *White Field with Cypresses* (Gallery 822) to imagine a blustery day in Saint-Rémy-de-Provence. Don't leave without viewing self-taught artist Henri Rousseau's *The Repast of the Lion* (Gallery 825).

Islamic Art

Objects sacred and secular fill these 15 galleries dedicated to the Arabian Peninsula, Turkey, and Central and South Asia. The glazed-tile **mihrab** (prayer niche; Gallery 455) is a vision in blue, framed by the five pillars of Islam, written in Kufic. If you're a fan of interiors, stop by Gallery 461 to wow over gold-leaf embellishments in the 18th-century **Damascus Room**.

American Wing

This two-floor collection in the museum's northwest corner covers everything from colonial times to the early 20th century, including Emanuel Luetze's iconic *Washington Crossing the Delaware*, which looms large over Gallery 760. If you need a pick-me-up, stop by the American Wing Cafe in the **Charles Engelhard Court** – a glass garden filled with American-made sculptures and framed by a marble facade that once graced Wall St. Visit on Friday or Saturday for Date Night (5pm to 9pm), when live music sets a romantic scene.

Modern & Contemporary Art

Georgia O'Keeffe, Edward Hopper, Pollock, Dalí – the museum's southwestern corner is a who's who of art-world titans from the late 19th century onward. Particularly impressive is Thomas Hart Benton's *America Today* (Gallery 909), a room-sized mural depicting the US at the Great Depression's onset.

Special Events at the Met

Visit on Friday or Saturday evening, when the museum stays open until 9pm and live music drifts through the halls. Enjoy the aural art with drinks at the American Wing Cafe or Petrie Court Cafe. If you're here in summer, see the Costume Institute's spring fashion exhibit, following the annual celebrity-studded Met Gala – always a hit.

AN ANCIENT EMBLEM

Stop by Gallery 136 to meet William, a blue faience hippopotamus with an essential museum job: mascot. Discovered in an Egyptian tomb in 1910 and acquired by the Met in 1917, the hippo quickly became the museum's quirky frontman, earning his name from a British humor magazine. Ancient Egyptians feared the aggressive hippo, but here, little Billy is cute as a button.

TOP TIPS

● Beat the Great Hall's snaking ticket line by entering at 81st St.

● Don't try to see everything in one visit. Pick a few galleries or a handful of pieces and immerse yourself.

● Upon entering, join the virtual queue via QR code for temporary exhibits. These artist retrospectives and cultural deep-dives are often some of the city's most fantastic museum shows.

● Stream the Met's free audio guide, which includes a Highlights Tour – an exceptional resource available on your smartphone. Visit *metmuseum.org/audio-guide*.

● Docents offer free guided tours of specific galleries. Check the website or at the information desk for details.

GET CULTURED ON THE UPPER WEST SIDE

Lincoln Center: This travertine complex is home to renowned performance venues such as the Metropolitan Opera and New York City Ballet.

Nicholas Roerich Museum: A townhouse turned art temple featuring rich Tibetan landscape paintings by Russian-born Roerich (1874–1947).

Zabar's: Cheese, meats and freshly baked knishes: a bastion of gourmet kosher foodie-ism since 1934.

New-York Historical Society: NYC's oldest museum (1804) showcases 60,000-plus quirky and fascinating objects.

American Folk Art Museum: Kaleidoscopic quilts, hand-carved decoy ducks and other art celebrates homegrown, self-taught makers.

Step Inside a Gilded Age Jewel Box MAP P93
Fantastic art at the Frick

When industrialist Henry Clay Frick made plans to build an Indiana limestone mansion along Fifth Ave in the early 20th century, he intended to turn it into a museum after his death. You'll be glad he made good on his promise. Walk through the **Frick Collection's** palatial rooms *(frick.org; $30, no under 10s)*, fresh off a $220-million makeover completed in 2025, to find gilt-framed masterpieces by Western European artists like Bellini, Goya, Rembrandt, Turner and Vermeer. Unlike the Met's massive collection, this is the kind of place you can zoom around in an hour, before Gilded Age envy sets in.

Geek out over Bones & Bugs MAP P93
American Museum of Natural History

You could spend a lifetime (or at least a couple of hours) exploring this **cutting-edge science center** *(amnh.org; adult/child $25/14)* and can't-miss hit for kids. From the main entrance on Central Park West, enter the soaring Theodore Roosevelt Rotunda to spot skeletons of a barosaurus and allosaurus frozen in combat. The astounding Milstein Family Hall of Ocean Life contains interactive lessons about marine food chains – all under a suspended, 94ft-long replica of a blue whale. Budding entomologists should make a beeline for the David Family Butterfly Vivarium in the new Gilder Center, where fluttering specimens land on outstretched arms. Armchair astronauts will appreciate the Rose Center for Earth & Space, its spherical theater transporting visitors to faraway galaxies. And don't forget the hundreds of dinosaur fossils – they're on the top floor.

Feel the Pulse of Harlem's Soul MAP P93
Highlights of the Harlem Renaissance and beyond

Ever since the Harlem Renaissance jazzed up New York in the early 20th century, Harlem has been a cradle of Black culture, birthing talents and trends with global appeal. This is where Billie Holiday crooned, where Romare Bearden pieced together collages and where Langston Hughes penned his explosive poetry. Walk these streets and hear them sing.

In the 1920s, the rhythmic baton of Duke Ellington led Harlem's Jazz Age jamboree. Pay your respects to the big-band maestro at the tiny **National Jazz Museum** *(jmih.org; free)*

EATING ON THE UWS: OUR PICKS MAP P85

Levain: The original location of this cookie chain remains its most charming. Each dough ball is a 6oz lesson in decadence. Get the chocolate-chip walnut. *8am-8pm* $

Mama's TOO!: You'll understand why people crowd outside this bite-sized pizza shop after tearing into the Angry Nonna (a square slab of hot honey-drizzled pepperoni). *noon-11pm* $

Tatiana: Good luck getting a table at this Afro-Caribbean-inspired restaurant in David Geffen Hall, featured on nearly every NYC 'best' list. *5-10pm Mon-Sat* $$$

Cafe Luxembourg: Upper-crust locals have been knocking back cocktails and nibbling steak tartare at this French bistro since the 1980s. *hours vary* $$$

American Museum of Natural History

– a one-room, Smithsonian-affiliated love letter to improvisational tunes. Ellington's cream-white baby grand piano sits up front.

Harlem's heart beats loudest on 125th St, home to the **Apollo Theater**, where Ella Fitzgerald got her start. Skip the live performances – you're here instead for the **Studio Museum in Harlem** (*studiomuseum.org; free*). This incubator for promising artists of African descent is set to unveil a new five-story building in late 2025. Come here to spot the art world's next big thing.

End your Harlem tour by trawling **Malcolm Shabazz Harlem Market** on 116th St for its colorful African goods. Textiles, jewelry and musical instruments represent countries like Nigeria, Kenya and Ghana. The canopied bazaar is the heart of Little (or 'Le Petit') Senegal – home to scores of francophone immigrants who began building a community here around the 1980s.

Spend an Afternoon on Brooklyn's Waterfront

MAP P102

See NYC from Brooklyn Bridge Park

Jaw-dropping views and recreational activities, plus restaurants, stores and performance spaces: **Brooklyn Bridge Park** (*brooklynbridgepark.org*) is a one-stop shop for urban leisure. Devote a few hours to this 85-acre green space hugging the East River.

For a breezy introduction to Brooklyn's historic waterfront, hop on a Manhattan ferry (*ferry.nyc; $4.50*) at Midtown's 34th St or Fidi's Pier 11, sailing across the river like writer Walt Whitman in the 19th century. You'll land at **Fulton Ferry Landing**, where lines from his 1856 poem 'Crossing the Brooklyn Ferry' are engraved on the guard rails.

(continues on p103)

NEIGHBORHOOD BODEGAS

Some call them delis. Others call them convenience stores. If you're a New Yorker, the proper term is 'bodega' – an embodiment of the 'city never sleeps,' often open 24/7. A bodega is technically a store with no more than two cash registers that sells milk and mostly food – and isn't a specialty store, like a butcher. At their core, these corner shops are more like neighborhood lifelines for groceries, beer, cleaning supplies, lottery tickets, ATMs and the beloved BEC (bacon, egg and cheese). Bodegas first appeared in the early 20th century, opened by Puerto Rican and Cuban immigrants to serve their communities. Now, there are roughly 13,000 around town, mainly run by Dominican, Mexican, Yemeni and East Asian immigrants – and occasionally guarded by a resident 'bodega cat.'

Bethesda Fountain

TOP EXPERIENCE

Central Park

With 843 acres of meadows, ponds and woodlands, Central Park seems like Manhattan in its raw state. But every inch was built by human hands. And thank goodness it was: the majestic merger of nature and art provides a welcome respite from urban jungle living. Spend half a day getting lost on its curving pathways – deliberately designed as a break from Manhattan's grid.

DON'T MISS

- Central Park Zoo
- Sheep Meadow
- Strawberry Fields
- Bethesda Fountain
- Ramble
- Jacqueline Kennedy Onassis Reservoir
- North Woods
- Central Park Conservancy's guided tours

A Grand Project

In the early 1850s, this area of Manhattan was occupied by pig farms, a garbage dump, a bone-boiling operation and Seneca Village, the largest community of African American property owners in pre–Civil War New York. All that changed in 1858, when plans created by landscape designer Frederick Law Olmstead and architect Calvert Vaux began taking shape. Today, this people's park has over 18,000 trees, 136 acres of woodland, 21 playgrounds, seven bodies of water and more than 40 million visitors a year.

PRACTICALITIES

- centralparknyc.org
- free
- 6am–1am

Tour the South End

Most visitors enter Central Park from its southern edge at W 59th St. Walk along the **pond** at the southeast corner to spot ducks and geese flapping in the blue. In winter, crowds ice skate at **Wollman Skating Rink**, where Midtown's soaring skyscrapers provide a dramatic backdrop.

Continue northeast to the small but mighty **Central Park Zoo** *(adult/child $22.95/16.95)*, near E 64th St, the pavilions of which house penguins, grizzly bears, tropical birds and even a snow leopard. Kids (and most adults) will love petting goats in the children's area and watching sea lions sing for their supper.

Perhaps most popular in this part of the park is **Sheep Meadow** (near W 67th St), a 15-acre lawn where thousands picnic, toss Frisbees and bare their skin in summer. Spending a few hours people-watching here is a quintessential city experience.

A skip north is **Strawberry Fields** (near W 72nd St), a tear-shaped garden and moving memorial for John Lennon, assassinated in front of his home at the **Dakota** in 1980. It contains a grove of stately elms and a tiled mosaic that says simply, 'Imagine.'

Amble around Mid Park

Work your way east to **Bethesda Fountain**, then cross picture-perfect **Bow Bridge** to enter one of the park's most transporting sections. The **Ramble**, a 36-acre forest, features waterfalls, rocky outcroppings and unpaved paths through thickets of trees. Don't be surprised to see people pointing binoculars at nearby branches: this is a beloved birding destination. Central Park, located along the Atlantic Flyway (an important route for migrating birds), acts as a resting pad for weary winged travelers. Twitchers can spot more than 200 avian species resting among the leaves in spring and autumn.

Continue north and you'll arrive at the **Jacqueline Kennedy Onassis Reservoir**, stretching between 86th and 96th Sts. The 6.1-mile gravel path along its perimeter is the domain of runners, who navigate the loop in a strictly clockwise direction. Exercise deference if you walk the loop to snap a pic of skyscrapers reflected on the water's glassy surface.

Wind through the North End

Crowds thin out as you head uptown, making a wander through the **North Woods** particularly magical. This 40-acre arcadia on the upper reaches of Central Park feels more like the Adirondacks than the heart of Manhattan. Amble along the waterfall-linked **loch**, a gentle tree-hugged stream (accessible via the Glen Span Arch near W 103rd St), to spot scampering chipmunks and the occasional raccoon. If you wander deep enough, skyscrapers disappear and traffic becomes but a murmur.

EXPERT GUIDES

If navigating the park alone seems Sisyphean, join a tour led by the **Central Park Conservancy** *(centralparknyc.org; adult/child $33/free)*. Guided walks cover everything from woodland ecology to little-known park histories and iconic landmarks. Most tours (aside from low-cost, family-geared offerings) start around 10am and last roughly 1½ hours. Check the website for schedules; advanced booking is required.

TOP TIPS

● Speed through the park by cycling its 6.1-mile loop. For rentals, try **Central Park Bike Tours** *(centralparkbiketours.com; from $17)*. There's also **Citi Bike**, though the docking system makes it difficult to park and explore.

● If you didn't pack a picnic, dine alfresco near Sheep Meadow at casual **Le Pain Quotidien** *(lepainquotidien.com)*, or stop by a food cart for snacks and drinks (be prepared with cash).

● Turned around? Check the numbers at the base of park lamp posts. The first two digits indicate nearby cross streets; the second two note if you're east or west (even numbers mean you're on the park's east side).

NEW YORK CITY NEW YORK, NEW JERSEY & PENNSYLVANIA

BROOKLYN

★ HIGHLIGHTS
1. Brooklyn Bridge Park
2. Coney Island

● SIGHTS
3. Avant Gardner
4. Brooklyn Heights Promenade
5. City Reliquary
6. Deno's Wonder Wheel Park
7. Elsewhere
8. Empire Stores
9. Jane's Carousel

● SLEEPING
10. Pod Brooklyn
11. Wythe Hotel

● EATING
12. Bonnie's
13. Fornino at Pier 6
14. Laser Wolf
15. Lilia
16. Nathan's Famous
17. Smorgasburg

● DRINKING & NIGHTLIFE
18. 18th Ward Brewing
19. 3 Dollar Bill
20. Brooklyn Brewery
21. Grimm Artisanal Ales
22. House of Yes
23. Long Island Bar
24. Maison Premiere
25. Mood Ring
26. Pilot
27. SEY Coffee
28. Talea

● ENTERTAINMENT
29. Luna Park
30. Mermaid Parade

● SHOPPING
31. Quimby's Bookstore NYC

● TRANSPORT
32. Fulton Ferry Landing

(continued from p99)

Like so much of NYC, this landscape differs greatly from the time when Whitman wrote '...Brooklyn of ample hills was mine.' In the following decades, the Brooklyn and Manhattan Bridges became Big Apple landmarks. Red-brick buildings shot up along the waterfront, home to companies that manufactured goods such as cardboard boxes and Brillo pads. Commercial production didn't last long: by the 1970s, businesses left and the waterfront became a wasteland. Industrial facades, cobblestone streets and antique railroad tracks remain today, but the waterfront is otherwise transformed in a triumph of urban renewal.

Venture north of Fulton Ferry to soak in an East River panorama. For 360-degree views, spin around **Jane's Carousel** *(janescarousel.com; $3)*, a vintage 1922 treasure housed in a Pritzker Prize–winning acrylic box. Behind the carousel is **Empire Stores**, which houses the **Time Out Market** *(time out.com)*, a collection of bustling food stalls and bars, plus a selection of retail chains.

Crowds thin out south of Fulton Ferry. If you're willing to hoof it, stop by Pier 6 for alfresco eating options, including **Fornino** (unfussy wood-fired pizza; *fornino.com*) and **Pilot** (oysters and cocktails on a wooden schooner; *crew.fun/pilot; May-Oct*).

Feast Your Eyes on Quirky Relics   MAP P102
Williamsburg's kooky mini-museum

Walk through an antique subway turnstile into **City Reliquary** *(cityreliquary.org; adult/child $10/free)*, a tiny museum dedicated to Big Apple ephemera. The three-room collection contains an oddball mix of memorabilia: Lady Liberty figurines, Second Ave Deli signage and a shrine honoring Brooklyn Dodgers star Jackie Robinson. Seeing the jam-packed space takes 20 to 30 minutes tops – a bit steep at the ticket price, but worth it if you like marching to the offbeat. Check its online events calendar to catch occasional readings, burlesque shows and junk craft classes in the art-filled backyard.

Sip Craft Beer at Brooklyn Breweries   MAP P102
Williamsburg tap tour

When it comes to craft chemistry, Brooklyn is NYC's go-to scientist. Over a dozen breweries cater to all tastes, whether you prefer floral IPAs or tart goses. Spend a night hopping between Williamsburg and Bushwick to see which hops you like best.

THE BEST NIGHTLIFE VENUES IN BROOKLYN & QUEENS

Elsewhere: Rap, rock and rave music are just a few styles you'll hear inside this furniture factory turned concert venue in East Williamsburg.

Avant Gardner: Dust off your dance shoes before seeing a show at East Williamsburg's 80,000-sq-ft EDM palace.

3 Dollar Bill: Brooklyn's biggest queer bar packs its 10,000-sq-ft space with fantastic performances and a colorful crowd.

Nowadays: Transcendental tunes fly through the air during Mister Sunday, a May-to-October alfresco dance party beloved by techno heads.

House of Yes: Burlesque performers, drag artists and circus acts set the stage at this all-inclusive warehouse club.

DRINKING IN BROOKLYN: BEST BARS & CAFES   MAP P102

Maison Premiere: Visiting the green fairy at this absinthe-forward oyster-and-cocktail bar is like traveling to 19th-century New Orleans. *2pm-1am Mon-Fri, from noon Sat & Sun*

Mood Ring: Tattooed 20-somethings with a zeal for the zodiac get sweaty at this ultra-inclusive astrology-themed club. *6pm-2am Sun-Wed, to 3am Thu, to 4am Fri & Sat*

Long Island Bar: This retro 1951 juice joint is always abuzz with cool-cat clientele, sipping cocktails crafted by Cosmo inventor Toby Cecchini. *5pm-midnight Tue-Fri, from 2pm Sat & Sun*

SEY Coffee: A mad-scientist attention to detail ensures this Nordic-style coffee roaster produces impeccable brews. *7am-5pm Mon-Fri, from 8am Sat & Sun*

BROOKLYN'S HEADY HISTORY

Brooklyn is no stranger to beer. As German immigrants flooded New York in the 19th century, breweries sprang up around the borough, turning Kings County into Lager Elysium. By the turn of the 20th century, Brooklyn was home to nearly 50 breweries, and a 12-block stretch linking Williamsburg and Bushhwick earned the nickname 'Brewer's Row' thanks to its near-dozen suds-focused establishments. But as the decades marched on, business dried up. By 1976, all of Brooklyn's beer makers were gone. It took more than a decade to turn the tap back on and now Brooklyn is once again the leader of NYC's pint-sized revolution. In addition to Williamsburg, the Gowanus neighborhood is known for producing exceptional brews inside industrial spaces. Sop up the scene at **Threes Brewing** (threesbrewing.com).

Begin at **Brooklyn Brewery** (brooklynbrewery.com) – the granddad of Brooklyn's contemporary beer boom, open since 1996. Soak up suds in the taproom or book a guided tasting ($32.66) – reserve your spot online. Next up is **Talea** (talea beer.com) – New York's first women-owned brewery. Head to the original Williamsburg location to try fruit-forward beers in the pastel-tiled interior. **18th Ward Brewing** (18thward brewing.com) gets pretty packed whenever there's a concert at nearby Brooklyn Steel, but it's worth wading through the crowds to sample easy-drinking ales. End with bold flavors from **Grimm Artisanal Ales** (grimmales.com). It's nearly impossible to decide between the experimental IPAs, barrel-aged sours and chocolatey lagers. Order a flight to sample them all, best enjoyed on the rooftop terrace.

Get Topsy Turvy at Coney Island

MAP P102

Amusement rides on Brooklyn's 'riviera'

Tattooed mermaids, vintage roller coasters and greasy-food stands await at this gritty-glamorous escape along the Brooklyn waterfront. A one-hour trip from Midtown, **Coney Island** became a democratized day-tripper destination in turn-of-the-20th-century New York, promising sugar-sand beaches and cotton-candy clouds. Spend half a day admiring its charms.

The official season for this summer escape is Memorial Day to Labor Day, when you can expect big weekend crowds. Start by skipping down **Riegelmann Boardwalk**, a 2.5-mile waterfront promenade from 1923, to pass a sea of colorful characters, along with whirling carnival rides.

Riegelmann Boardwalk

Fancy getting flung into the air at 90mph? The Sling Shot awaits at **Luna Park** *(lunaparknyc.com; day pass from $48.60 or pay per ride $10)*. Perhaps the 56mph race around the 2233ft-long Thunderbolt is more your speed. Or you can go old-school – New Yorkers started shrieking down the wooden Cyclone's 85ft plunge in 1927, and the drop still thrills riders.

At **Deno's Wonder Wheel Park** *(denoswonderwheel.com; pay per ride)*, you can hop on the Wonder Wheel ($10). Around since 1920, Coney Island's oldest ride is also its most romantic: sweeping views from 150ft above ground are bound to make your heart pitter-pat.

If your stomach survives the thrills and spills, get a taste of tradition by biting into one of **Nathan's Famous** hotdogs at the flagship location on Surf and Stillwell *(nathansfamous. com)*. The beefy frank, snuggled in a toasted bun, has been a Coney classic since 1916.

WACKY & WONDERFUL FESTIVALS & EVENTS

Mermaid Parade: Artsy, eclectic crowds don nautical costumes to flip their fins down Surf Ave on Coney Island for June's summer solstice.

NYC Pride March: All of June is a rainbow-splashed extravaganza, culminating in one of the world's largest LGBTQ+ celebrations.

Village Halloween Parade: Thousands of outlandishly costumed ghouls stalk Sixth Ave during this spooky street fest on October 31.

Macy's Thanksgiving Day Parade: Massive helium-filled balloons float above high-kicking Rockettes and adoring throngs in November.

New Year's Eve: An army of merrymakers descend on Times Square to ring in the new year and see the iconic ball drop.

EATING IN WILLIAMSBURG: OUR PICKS

MAP P102

Lilia: This pasta restaurant in a former auto shop cranks out some of the best noodles in town. Getting reservations is notoriously tough. *4-10pm* $$$

Laser Wolf: Everything here is a feast: mezze appetizers, Israeli-style skewers and views of Manhattan from the Hoxton Hotel's terrace. *5-11pm Sun-Wed, to 1am Thu-Sat* $$$

Bonnie's: A Cantonese-American marriage of flavors, plus a rowdy wedding-party-style scene, especially if you're drinking the Long Island iced tea pot with eight servings. *5-10pm* $$

Smorgasburg: Every Saturday from April to October, foodies file into Marsha P Johnson State Park to sample hand-held treats at this open-air culinary bazaar. *11am-6pm* $$

New York State

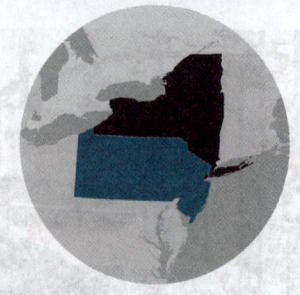

CULTURED ENCLAVES | FARMSTEADS | FORESTS

Places
Long Island p106
Hudson Valley p112
The Catskills p116
The Adirondacks p117
Finger Lakes p121
Letchworth State Park p123
Buffalo p124
Niagara Falls p126

GETTING AROUND

New York spans 54,554 sq miles. While buses and trains travel across large swaths of the state, covering a land mass this size requires a car. Renting wheels is cheaper outside NYC; take a train elsewhere to pick up a vehicle.

New York is more than its eponymous metropole. NYC accounts for 40% of the state's population, but it covers less than 1% of its area. Over half the state is blanketed in forests – a leafy universe lit by constellations of tiny towns, midsize cities and 180 state parks.

NYC residents consider anything north of NYC 'upstate' – a distinction hotly contested by everyone else. Follow the Hudson River north for the Hudson Valley, a network of arty towns and rural farmland. The Catskill Mountains rise west, with eccentric communities of outdoor enthusiasts. Jet northeast to the Hudson's source to reach the Adirondacks, home of the largest publicly protected park in the contiguous United States. Central New York sparkles with the Finger Lakes. Western New York draws crowds thanks to Niagara Falls, next to Buffalo, undergoing a Rust Belt revival. Downstate and east of NYC is Long Island, where suburban sprawl gives way to ritzy summer escapes lapped by the Atlantic.

Long Island
MAP P110

Views from Montauk Point Lighthouse

New York's **first lighthouse** *(montaukhistoricalsociety.org; adult/child $15/5)* is the exclamation point on Long's Island's eastern edge, standing 110ft above the sea-battered coast since 1796. Originally commissioned by President George Washington to warn sailors of the rocks below, it's now the photogenic heart of **Montauk Point State Park** *(parks.ny.gov; summer car fee $8)*, an 862-acre expanse of wooded trails and bluff-backed beaches. A small museum, located in the keepers' house from 1860, provides historical insight, and climbing the tower's 137 iron steps leads to 360-degree views. Stop by around sunrise or sunset (outside of museum hours) when the candy-colored tower gets painted burnt sienna by the light. For exquisite views from afar, head to **Camp Hero State Park** *(parks.ny.gov; summer car fee $8)* and hike east

Montauk Point Lighthouse

DIVE INTO MONTAUK

Montauk sizzles like a summer romance, burning hot from Memorial Day to Labor Day, then cooling off as winter's population shrinks from 40,000 to 4000. Falling in love with this Long Island escape is easy: the peninsula is kissed by beaches and wrapped with six state parks. It's New York's easternmost point – nicknamed 'The End' – and the state's last stop before jumping into the Atlantic, far from NYC's towers. The hamlet has seen its share of suitors: the Indigenous Montaukett, followed by English colonizers, fisherfolk and eventually Carl G Fisher, who tried turning Montauk into the 'Miami Beach of the North' in the 1920s. Although his plan failed, future generations succeeded, opening swanky restaurants serving summer's moneyed masses.

along the seaside bluffs – the lighthouse shines as a distant maritime beacon.

Surf with Montauk's pros

Montauk is the holy land of East Coast surfing, and catching waves at **Ditch Plains Beach** is akin to attending church. Unlike typical Atlantic Ocean waves that break quickly over sandy shores, Ditch Plains waves cascade over cobblestones, offering surfers minute-long rides to fine-tune their surfing skills. Seasonal variations add to the allure: summer brings gentle waves, while fall and winter unveil majestic swells fit for serious board disciples. There's a blend of clean and consistent surf, making it paradise for both beginners and experts. As a result, Montauk teems with seasoned surfers – and knowledgeable teachers – who genuflect before their boards year-round.

If you're eager to join this spiritual communion, **Sunset Surf Shack** (sunsetsurfshack.com; from $100) offers hour-long lessons complete with wetsuit, surfboard and instructor. Bring a towel, some water and a can-do attitude: hanging ten can be tough, but the promise of a wave-riding revelation can't be beaten.

 EATING & DRINKING IN MONTAUK: OUR PICKS

Bird on the Roof: Aussie-inspired brunch transitions to American-style dinner with pastas, curries, fish and inventive cocktails. *8am-2pm Sat & Sun, 5-11pm Thu-Sat* $$

Duryea's: Seasonal spot to catch the sunset while slurping oysters and sipping rosé. Connected to a market and boutique. *hours vary May-Sep* $$$

Montauket: Ideal location for soaking up sunsets with seafaring locals. Come early for window-facing seats. Seafood served in summer. *2pm-late, from noon Sat & Sun*

Montauk Brewing Company: Red-barn bastion for beer, founded by three local buds. Chill vibes. *2-6pm Mon, Thu & Fri, from noon Sat & Sun*

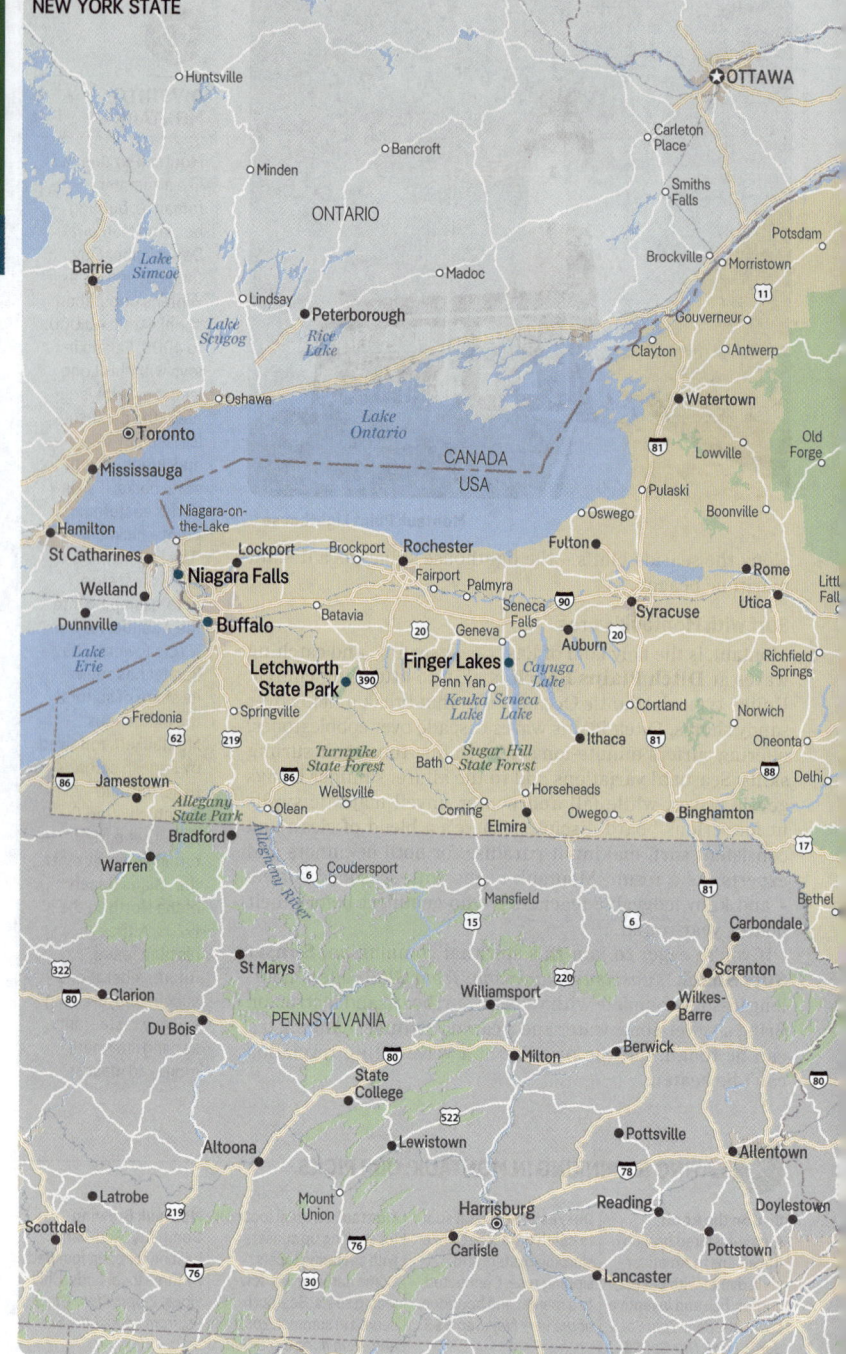

☑ TOP TIP

If NYC is your base and you're traveling sans car, visiting Beacon, Hudson and Montauk is possible via Metro-North and Long Island Rail Road *(mta.info)*. Metro-North trips along the Hudson River are splendid in fall, chugging past crayon-colored woodlands. **Amtrak** *(amtrak.com)* serves Buffalo; rideshares are easy to find upon arrival.

NEW YORK STATE NEW YORK, NEW JERSEY & PENNSYLVANIA

THE GUIDE

HIGHLIGHTS
1 Cherry Grove
2 Ditch Plains Beach
3 Montauk Point Lighthouse

SIGHTS
4 Amsterdam Beach Trailhead
5 Big Duck
6 Camp Hero State Park
7 Channing Daughters
see 1 Cherry Grove Community House and Theater
8 Dia Bridgehampton
9 Hither Hills State Park
10 Kirk Park Beach
11 LongHouse Reserve
12 Montauk Point State Park
13 Pollock-Krasner House
14 Sag Harbor Village Marina
see 14 Sag Harbor Whaling & Historical Museum
15 Shadmoor State Park
16 South Edison Beach
17 Sunken Forest

ACTIVITIES
18 Fire Island Pines
see 16 Sunset Surf Shack

SLEEPING
19 Breakers
see 16 Daunt's Albatross Motel

EATING
20 Almond
see 16 Amber Waves Farm
21 Doubles
22 Duryea's
see 14 Sag Pizza

DRINKING & NIGHTLIFE
see 18 Blue Whale
see 1 Ice Palace
23 Montauk Brewing Company

ENTERTAINMENT
see 22 Montauk
see 18 Sip-n-Twirl
see 14 Sag Harbor Cinema

SHOPPING
see 14 Sag Harbor Books

TRANSPORT
24 Sayville Ferry Service

Sag Harbor's whaling past and wealthy present

The 'un-Hampton': until a decade ago, that's how locals fancied Sag Harbor. While well-heeled Manhattanites reshaped towns such as East Hampton with status-symbol shops (Gucci, Rolex etc), Sag Harbor maintained its charm with locally owned boutiques and a dedication to historic preservation. Although some of the magic is waning (everything here is expensive), stroll down Main St to see why Sag Harbor remains a South Fork standout. Start at the **Sag Harbor Whaling & Historical Museum** *(sagharborwhalingmuseum.org; adult/child $8/3)*, erected in 1845 for a whaling tycoon. Whale blubber, used to make oil, earned locals big bucks throughout the 1830s and '40s, but the rush was brief. By the 1850s, overfishing sank the whale-oil market just as kerosene and petroleum gained popularity. Continue north to Main St's three-block shopping center and you'll see that money found its way back to town. Stop for slices at **Sag Pizza** *(sagpizza.com)*, snap a picture of art-deco **Sag Harbor Cinema** *(sagharborcinema.org)* and pop into **Sag Harbor Books** *(southamptonsagharborbooks.com)* to leaf through *Moby Dick* (author Herman Melville gives the village a shout-out). Sag Harbor's **marina** punctuates Main St's history. In summer, mansion-sized yachts line the docks – a nod to Sag's seafaring origins and recent wealthy upswing.

Find freedom on Fire Island

Muscular architecture, maritime forests and sweeping dunes lapped by the Atlantic: between May and September, there are myriad reasons to board the **Sayville Ferry** for a day trip to Fire Island, a slender sandbar off Long Island's coast. But the main draw? LGBTQ+ crowds.

Cherry Grove became 'America's first gay and lesbian town' around the 1930s and 1940s. Pay your respects at the **Cherry Grove Community House and Theater** *(artsprojectcg.org)*, where openly LGBTQ+ residents played important roles in civic life decades before the US elected queer politicians to office. Summer evenings center around the **Ice Palace** *(icepalace.club)*, a club and performance space graced by the likes of Liza Minelli, Patti LuPone and scantily clad men who come for Friday night's Underwear Party. If you prefer low-key to late night, take a detour to the **Sunken Forest** *(nps.gov)*. A 1.5-mile boardwalk loops through its 300-year-old collection of American holly trees, sassafras and juneberry, 'sunken' beneath protective dunes.

While Cherry Grove welcomes mixed LGBTQ+ crowds, including a strong sapphic contingency, neighboring **Fire Island Pines** is predominantly gay. Join the boys strutting its boardwalks to ogle eye-candy architecture. Many of the modernist homes were designed by architect Horace Gifford in the 1960s and '70s, using cedar and glass to complement the natural surroundings. The facade of **252 Bay Walk** looks like a proscenium arch for a seductive stage play; **482 Tarpon** boasts a deck that hovers above its neighbors – a voyeur's delight.

MONTAUK BEACH ACCESS

The secret is out – Montauk is spoiled with spectacular beaches, and though they're all open to the public, parking is usually restricted to permits issued by the Town of East Hampton. This includes beloved Ditch Plains. Permits for non-residents cost $500 – a steep price for a weekend getaway – though some beaches have reasonable day passes, such as **Kirk Park Beach** *($35)* and **Hither Hills State Park** *($10)*. Don't defy local laws – cops sniff out illegally parked cars like sharks smelling blood. Prefer free parking? Consider booking a hotel near popular **South Edison Beach** so you can walk to the seashore (try **Daunt's Albatross Motel**; p158), or hike the easy 1.5-mile trail to **Amsterdam Beach**.

MORE LGBTQ+ BEACH HAVENS

Fire Island is one of many communities that historically cater to queer summer crowds. There's also Ogunquit, Maine (p229), Provincetown on Cape Cod (p187), Asbury Park along the Jersey Shore (p128) and Rehoboth Beach, Delaware (p276).

All boardwalks here eventually lead to the **Blue Whale** (*pinesfi.com*), where gaggles gather around 5pm to babble over cocktails at 'Low Tea.' At 8pm, crowds flow to the adjacent pool deck for 'High Tea.' The final stop is **Sip-n-Twirl**, where music pulses until dawn.

Hudson Valley

Lose yourself in Beacon's steel canyons

Manhattan day-trippers arrive via Metro-North to drool over NYC's most sought-after commodity: space, superabundant at contemporary-art institution **Dia Beacon**. Roughly 300,000 sq ft of this former Nabisco box-printing factory devotes itself to minimalist paintings and mammoth sculptures that wouldn't fit through an NYC doorway. The most transportive works feel less 'contemporary art museum' and more 'aesthete's playground.' Winding through Richard Serra's rust-red *Torqued Ellipses* feels like hiking Arizona's Antelope Canyon, the sweet scent of Meg Webster's 8ft-tall *Wall of Beeswax* recalls a buzzy honey farm, and barbed-wire walls by Melvin Edwards add a tinge of danger while walking about. Free guided tours take place on Saturday and Sunday at noon and 1:30pm, though it's best to experience the museum at your own pace. Gliding through the galleries, lit by 34,000 sq ft of skylights, is a meditative experience. An on-site cafe serves treats; the gift shop is stacked with interesting art tomes.

Cornwall's outdoor sculpture park

Storm King Art Center (*welcome.stormking.org; adult/youth $25/15; open Apr-Nov*) marries what the Hudson Valley does best – nature and art. Hike around this pastoral park's 500 acres and you might wonder where one ends and the other begins. Colossal pieces sprout from manicured lawns and pop among the woodlands. Site-specific works also mimic the landscape, such as Maya Lin's *Storm King Wavefield,* an 11-acre earthwork undulating like a miniature Hudson Highlands.

Budget a few hours to adequately explore. Start by trekking around the North Woods, then walk counterclockwise, stopping by Menashe Kadishman's gravity-defying *Suspended* on your way to the top of Museum Hill, the park's highest point. Here you'll find the museum's shop and gallery space, housed in a Normandy-style château. Finish by meandering among native grasslands, creeks and allées, where you might spot white-tailed deer, box turtles and cottontail rabbits crawling

---

SPECTACULAR SIGHTS IN THE HAMPTONS

Shadmoor State Park: Montauk trails thick with black cherry trees lead to WWII bunkers and oceanside bluffs.

Pollock-Krasner House: Explore the paint-splattered studio and home of husband-and-wife abstract expressionists Jackson Pollock and Lee Krasner. Open May–October; reservations required.

Dia Bridgehampton: This shingle-style 1908 house has served as fire station, Baptist church and, now, exhibition space for minimalist Dan Flavin's fluorescent artwork.

Big Duck: Quirky detour where the North and South Forks split. Step inside the 20ft-tall Pekin duck from 1931.

LongHouse Reserve: More than 60 sculptures, including works by Yoko Ono and Willem de Kooning, sprout from this 16-acre garden.

EATING & DRINKING IN THE HAMPTONS: OUR PICKS

Amber Waves Farm: Charming roadside cafe and market on a working farm in Amagansett. Peep the goats, pick produce, sit swing-side. Great for kids. *8am-2pm* $$

Almond: Bridgehampton's boisterous French-style bistro, where white-collar crowds dine on roast chicken and raw bar delicacies. *from 5pm Tue-Sat, closing hours vary* $$$

Doubles: Amagansett's outpost for Caribbean-influenced food, including doubles (fried dough topped with a curried chickpea concoction). *11:30am-8pm* $$

Channing Daughters: The South Fork's most inventive boutique winery serves flights patio-side, overlooking 33 acres of vine-wrapped trellises. *11am-5pm*

Shadmoor State Park

ALL ABOUT BEACON

Bohemian Beacon's unofficial nickname is 'Brooklyn North' – a nod to the influx of people from NYC who've spent two decades transforming it into King's County's upstate cousin. Walk down Main St and all the Brooklyn-as-brand signifiers are present: artisanal boutiques, small-batch breweries, avant-garde art galleries and farm-to-table restaurants. But Beacon is more than NYC's facsimile. Sandwiched between the Hudson River and Hudson Highlands, it's a jump-off point for outdoor adventures, including a collection of heart-pumping mountain hikes. This small town is a perfect NYC getaway: take the 1½-hour train ride from Grand Central via Metro-North, then hoof it to Main St or hop on the Beacon Free Loop bus rolling through town.

around works by Roy Lichtenstein, Alexander Calder and Mark di Suvero.

If you want to zip through the park quickly, rent a bicycle ($20 to $30) or hop on the wheelchair-accessible tram loop. Getting here is easiest by car (25 minutes from Beacon), though it's possible to take a free museum shuttle from Beacon's train station (summer only) or catch a Coach bus (*coachusa.com*) from Manhattan. Plan a trip around leaf-peeping season (mid-September to early November), when trees put on an arboreal art show rivaling the sculptures.

Hudson's trendy heart

Uber-hip Hudson is beloved by NYC weekenders, who travel by car or train to cruise Warren St's antique stores, boutiques, galleries and restaurants. Join the crowds for a 1-mile stroll.

Start by snacking on a sourdough croissant from **Mel the Bakery** (*melthebakery.com*), or rev up your engine with java from **MOTO Coffee Machine** (*motocoffeemachine.com*), a coffee-and-motorcycle shop. You'll spot more than 10 art galleries along Warren St, including **Carrie Haddad's** (*carriehaddadgallery.com*) collection of notable locals. Peep the hidden upstairs hallway dedicated to Mark Beard's athletic nudes. There's an eclectic collection of upcycled decor at **LikeMindedObjects** (*likemindedobjects.com*), vintage home

EATING & DRINKING IN BEACON: OUR PICKS

Roundhouse: Standard seasonal fare served inside this hat factory–turned-hotel is just an appetizer for the views of a gushing Fishkill Creek waterfall. *hours vary* $$$

Noble Pies: The Hudson Valley apple pie is a salute to Americana, served with other sweet and savory selections at this regional chain. *9am-8pm Sun-Thu, to 9pm Fri & Sat* $

Hudson Valley Brewery: Lavender, dandelions and sour candy are a few flavors found in these funky ales – arguably Beacon's best. *noon-8pm Sun & Mon, to 10pm Thu-Sat*

Big Mouth Coffee Roasters: First-rate third-wave coffee, with art-adorned walls (for sale), ample seating and on-site bean roasting. *7am-6pm Mon-Fri, 8am-7pm Sat, to 5pm Sun*

GREAT HUDSON VALLEY MUSEUMS & GALLERIES

Boscobel House & Gardens: This 19th-century Federalist home showcases how the fledgling US remained tethered to British influence.

Art Omi: Wander 120 acres of outdoor sculptures among fields and forests in Ghent.

Magazzino Italian Art: Bold postwar Italian art fills this beautiful brutalist space. Wave to the museum's 14 Sardinian donkeys.

KuBe Art Center: Edgy 'Kunsthalle Beacon' transforms a former high school into an art gallery with cheeky rotating exhibits.

Kykuit: Four generations of oil-rich Rockefellers inhabited this Gilded Age mansion atop historic Sleepy Hollow.

furnishings at well-curated **FINCH Hudson** *(finchhudson.com)* and high fashion with an outdoorsy edge at **Meridian** *(meridian.vision)*. The antiques game is strong here, too. Pop into **Red Chair on Warren** *(redchair-antiques.com)* for Swiss, Belgian and French finds from the 17th, 18th and 19th centuries. At **Spotty Dog Books & Ale** *(thespottydog.com)*, you can thumb through novels while sipping beer. Throughout the journey, admire Hudson's beautiful bones. Warren St is chockablock with 19th-century architecture, including Federal, Queen Anne and Victorian homes.

America's first major art movement

Rapid industrialization and westward expansion captured the imaginations of most 19th-century Americans. But painter Thomas Cole (1801–48), an émigré from soot-smothered England, saw power in preservation. His prescient viewpoint became the canvas for America's first significant artistic fraternity – the Hudson River School, coined in the 1870s to classify a group of landscape artists who depicted the country's wild frontier as sublime. The Hudson Valley and Catskills served as Cole's local muses, and paintings of places such as Kaaterskill Falls (p1116) became his artistic form of proto-environmentalism. Visit his art-filled property in Catskill – the **Thomas Cole National Historic Site** *(thomascole.org)*,

EATING & DRINKING IN HUDSON: OUR PICKS

Lil' Deb's Oasis: Home to Hudson's avant garde, who gobble trendy takes on Mexican food while sipping from goblets of wine. *5-10pm Thu-Sun* $$

BackBar: Pack into a picnic table at this relaxed indoor-outdoor hangout for Southeast Asian plates and cocktails. *5-10pm Thu, noon-10pm Fri & Sat, noon-8pm Sun* $$

Quinnie's: Equal parts coffee shop, bakery, specialty market, sandwich shop and cocktail bar inside a lovingly renovated 1700s farmhouse on six grassy acres. *9am-4pm Fri-Tue* $

Half Moon: One-stop shop for last call (local beer), late-night munchies (pizza) and the occasional concert. *4pm-midnight Mon-Thu, to 1am Fri & Sat* $

Olana mansion

TOP HUDSON VALLEY HIKES

Download the AllTrails app *(alltrails.com)* for detailed info on each route.

Mt Beacon: Scale Mt Beacon's 1600-ft summit on a 4-mile return journey to breathtaking views of the Hudson Highlands.

Bull Hill: Trek past scenic overlooks and mysterious ruins on this 5.4-mile loop trail near Beacon.

Breakneck Ridge: Brace yourself for rocky scrambles and steep ascents on this 3.2-mile hike, accessible on summer weekends via Metro-North. Closed for maintenance until 2027.

Storm King Mountain: Circle the crown of this 1300ft peak on a 2.4-mile trail, different from the same-named art park.

Walkway over the Hudson: Stroll or roll across the world's longest elevated pedestrian bridge, a 1.3-mile link between Poughkeepsie and Highland.

a 10-minute drive from Hudson. The three-building compound showcases Cole's work inside his Federal-style home, framing distant mountains. Strolling the grounds is free; guided tours cost $20.

After seeing Cole's work, drive across the Rip Van Winkle Bridge to **Olana** *(olana.org),* a Gothic-Moorish mansion owned by Cole's protégé, Frederic Edwin Church (1826–1900). Church studied with Cole from 1844–1846 before making a name for himself with romantic landscapes of the Andes Mountains, icebergs and more distant landscapes most New Yorkers would never see in real life. Paintings aside, Church's standout work is this fairy-tale castle (completed in 1872), which he designed in collaboration with Central Park architect Calvert Vaux. Wandering the 250-acre estate, free and open to the public daily from 8am to sunset, is like stepping into one of his oil paintings. More than 5 miles of carriage roads roll from meadows to an artificial lake and on to expansive views of the Hudson River and Catskill Mountains. The home is even more impressive, with exterior brickwork and ceramic tiles nodding to the international curios displayed inside. Tours of the landscape *($12)*, house interior *($20)*, or a combo of the two *($40)* enhance the experience. Book tickets in advance.

EATING & DRINKING AROUND WOODSTOCK: OUR PICKS

Phoenicia Diner: Greasy-spoon aesthetics (chrome, terrazzo) and creative Catskills takes on classics, like po'boys with cornmeal-crusted trout. *8am-6pm Thu-Tue* $$

Silvia: An unpretentious take on farm-to-fine dining. Start with the horseradish-spiced mushroom lentil pâté; finish with a wood-smoked pork chop. *hours vary* $$$

Good Night: Slide into a plush velvet banquette for upscale Southeast Asian-inspired plates with plenty of crunch, spice and tang. *hours vary* $$$

West Kill Brewing: Sip beer made with locally grown and foraged ingredients on a historic 127-acre farm. Cinematic scenery. *noon-7pm Fri & Sat, to 6pm Sun*

COME TO THE CATSKILLS

The Catskill Mountains are a vast collection of rolling plateaus, including 600,000-acre Catskill Park, sculpted by streams, lakes and forests. The Hudson and Delaware Rivers frame the landscape, speckled with sleepy main streets where a cultural renaissance is underway, steadily moving westward across the region with rustic-chic resorts and a formidable art scene. If you're staying in the region, base yourself in or around the eastern Catskills town of Woodstock – not to be confused with the concert that rocked America's psyche in 1969, which took place in Bethel, 60 miles west. Woodstock blossomed from an art colony formed in 1902 and retains its creative edge. Wander along Tinker St for a taste – galleries, tchotchke shops and inventive restaurants.

Kaaterskill Falls

The Catskills

Stand in awe at Kaaterskill Falls

New York's **tallest cascade** (*catskillsvisitorcenter.org; free*) – a two-tiered stunner 90ft higher than Niagara Falls (p126) – has inspired artists for centuries. Washington Irving described its 'feathery foam' in *Rip Van Winkle*, and poet William Cullen Bryant evoked its 'palace of ice' in wintertime. Today, 100,000-plus annual visitors attempt to capture the 260ft local icon on camera. Follow their lead: if you only take one hike in the Catskills, this should be it.

Start at the Laurel House Rd parking lot and choose from routes catering to novice and experienced hikers alike. Take the easy 1000yd round-trip trail to the **Falls Viewing Platform** to see the glorious gusher from above. The 1.4-mile round-trip jaunt to the lower falls will get your blood pumping with its steep staircase (unsuitable in icy conditions). Tack on an extra mile by following the Kaatskills Creek downstream to **Bastion Falls**, or head to the Escarpment Trail for a 4.8-mile loop leading to **Inspiration Point**, where you can see Kaaterskill Clove, a slender cleft in the Catskills sculpted by glaciation and the persistence of Kaaterskill Creek.

 EATING & DRINKING IN THE WESTERN CATSKILLS: OUR PICKS

Heron: Nearby farms provide most ingredients at this Narrowsburg spot for southern-inspired American fare. Sublime outdoor-terrace views. *hours vary* $$

Cochecton Fire Station: Former pyro police pad turned contemporary cocktail joint with wood-fired pub grub. *3-8pm Mon & Tue, to 9pm Fri, noon-9pm Sat, noon-8pm Sun*

Katskeller: Sit at outdoor picnic tables to savor Neapolitan pizza and sides in Livingston Manor. Try the brook trout rillettes, a local creek delicacy. *hours vary* $$

Catskill Brewery: This Livingston Manor beer hang is famous for the bitter pinewood finish of its Devil's Path IPA. *hours vary*

America's modern Stonehenge

Quarrying bluestone was a profitable enterprise in the 19th-century Catskills. Cities from Albany to NYC used the durable, slate-blue sandstone for sidewalks until the 20th century, when cement took over. Many quarrying companies folded as a result, leaving square-cut scars across the landscape. Self-taught sculptor Harvey Fite turned some of those scars into the Catskills' most captivating artwork. After purchasing property surrounded by abandoned quarries, Fite started a 37-year project: **Opus 40** (1939–76), a whimsical 6.5-acre handcrafted earthwork, visible on his property-turned-sculpture-park from late March through late December *(opus40.org; adult/child $16/5, guided tours $31)*. Fite adapted Mayan stone-working techniques to create his serpentine structure – an open-air monument to Indigenous design and the majestic Catskill Mountains.

Feel Woodstock's beat in Bethel

In the summer of 1969, America was at war. Nixon commanded the Oval Office, LGBTQ+ patrons revolted against police brutality at Stonewall and soldiers lost their lives in Vietnam. But on Max Yasgur's dairy farm, nearly half a million people found peace – unless they tripped on the bad acid supposedly going around. This was the Woodstock Music and Art Fair, a three-day hippie happening that took the sleepy town of Bethel by surprise. Rock legends including Janis Joplin, the Grateful Dead and Santana electrified crowds. Jimi Hendrix riled audiences with a rousing rendition of 'The Star Spangled Banner,' turning the national anthem into a guitar hero's protest.

Though the crowds have long gone – save a few white-haired hippies who never left – the spirit lingers. Yasgur's farm is now **Bethel Woods Center for the Arts** *(bethelwoodscenter.org)*, where you can revive Woodstock's memory at outdoor summer concerts. There's also the seasonal **Museum at Bethel Woods** *(adult/child $22.69/5, cheaper if booked in advance; Apr-Dec)* bursting with music and images from Woodstock. For the full summer of '69 experience, consider booking a campsite during one of the shows. (Unlike Woodstock, where visitors camped for free on mud-slick farmland, this sanitized and markedly grassier version starts at $82 per night.) There's are also a weekend harvest festival throughout September and October, with plenty of artisans, food trucks and live music on display.

If you can't attend a summer concert, drive by to pay your respects. While lingering before the coffin-shaped monument near the field where history sang, commiserate with Joni Mitchell by listening to her wail 'Woodstock.' She missed the cultural capstone, too.

The Adirondacks

Climb every Adirondack mountain

Over 2000 miles of hiking trails weave their way through the Adirondacks, with options for all levels of outdoor enthusiasm.

MORE OUTDOOR ADVENTURES IN THE CATSKILLS

Overlook Mountain: Pass the charred remains of a 19th-century hotel on this 4.6-mile hike to views above Woodstock.

Delaware River: Tube, raft or kayak down gentle rapids with **Lander's River Trips**.

Sam's Point Area: Climb the Shawangunk Ridge on this 7-mile trek to panoramic overlooks, ice caves and 187ft-high Verkeerderkill Falls.

Peekamoose Blue Hole: Cool off during summer's dog days by braving Roundout Creek's icy, Caribbean-blue water.

Hunter Mountain: Shred slopes from late November to early April on 67 trails spread across 320 acres.

MORE WONDERFUL WATERFALLS

If you love chasing waterfalls, head to Ithaca, a Finger Lakes city graced with more than 100 gushing cataracts, including the East Coast's tallest single-drop waterfall, Taughannock Falls (p121).

TOUR THE WESTERN CATSKILLS' CUTEST TOWNS

The Catskills' revival as 'hickster' haven is most apparent while driving between tiny Delaware River towns where forests give way to walkable main streets.

START	END	LENGTH
Narrowsburg	Upward Brewing Company	22 miles; 3-4 hours

Begin on Main St in ❶ **Narrowsburg**, perched on a bluff above the Delaware. Breakfast sandwiches from Tusten Cup fuel some light shopping. Stop in River Gallery (landscape paintings), Narrowsburg Proper (market snacks) and One Grand Books (lit hand-picked by famous creatives). In summer, swimmers jump into the river from rocks below the sea-green Narrowsburg–Darbytown Bridge.

Drive along a portion of the Upper Delaware Scenic Byway (Rte 97) as it snakes along Pennsylvania's border toward ❷ **Callicoon**. The town's name, derived from the Dutch 'Kollikoonkill,' meaning 'Wild Turkey Creek,' is still fitting for a place resembling the set for a cowboy flick. Sample whiskey at distiller Catskill Provisions and peek inside Farmhouse Project, an elegant artisan shop and cocktail parlor. The town seems to quadruple in population for Sunday's farmers' market *(11am to 2pm)*, where local vendors hock honey, jam, baked goods, pottery and piles of organic fruit.

❸ **Livingston Manor**, unfurling along Willowemoc Creek, is the liveliest town of the bunch. Walk Main St to peruse shops and grab food: eye Homestedt's cabin-core collection; gobble biscuits from the Walk In, then drive to ❹ **Upward Brewing Company** to sip craft beer on its 120 acres, complete with ski-mountain-inspired chalet.

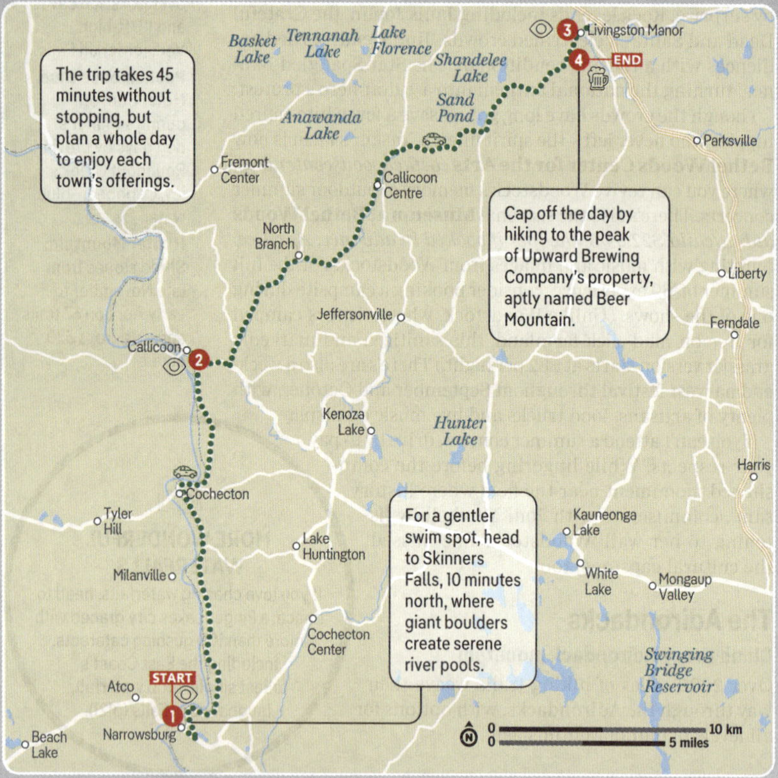

> The trip takes 45 minutes without stopping, but plan a whole day to enjoy each town's offerings.

> Cap off the day by hiking to the peak of Upward Brewing Company's property, aptly named Beer Mountain.

> For a gentler swim spot, head to Skinners Falls, 10 minutes north, where giant boulders create serene river pools.

Experienced hikers in the Lake George area will appreciate the 6.5-mile return route to **Buck Mountain**, which shoots 2000ft above Lake George's eastern banks. Crawl across granite slopes knotted with tree roots, littered with boulders and cut by gentle creeks to a spectacular view of the island-dotted lake below. Bonus points if you can spot the Sagamore Resort, a historic horseshoe-shaped hotel on the edge of Green Island. Use AllTrails for more info.

If you'd rather roll to picture-perfect panoramas, put the pedal to the metal on **Prospect Mountain** *(dec.ny.gov)*. Between late May and early November, drivers pay $10 to reach the summit, where views extend 100 miles on clear days. Hikers who tackle the arduous 3.2-mile woodland trail (steep and rocky with scrambles) reach the summit for free. Park along Smith St to access the trailhead.

Superlative paths near Lake Placid offer similar levels of accessibility. The 10-plus-mile trail to **Indian Head** leads to a low summit with a photogenic long shot of the Ausable River. From May to October, it's necessary to make parking reservations with **Adirondack Mountain Reserve** *(hikeamr. org; free)*. For views from the comfort of your car, drive up Whiteface Mountain, New York's fifth-highest peak (4867ft), on the **Whiteface Veterans' Memorial Highway** *(whiteface.com; $10)*, open from late spring to fall.

Be prepared to contend with ice and snow while hiking outside of summer. Most trails require crampons or snowshoes in winter.

Swim, kayak and cruise on Lake George

While touring the Adirondacks in 1791, Thomas Jefferson wrote, 'Lake George is without comparison, the most beautiful water I ever saw.' Spend a few hours floating around the lake and it's hard to disagree. In summer, join families on the 51-acre **Million Dollar Beach** *(dec.ny.gov; parking $10)* and wade into crystal-clear waters under the protective eye of a lifeguard. Water tends to reach 70°F to 75°F, with peak temperatures around late July and August.

If you'd rather explore the lake's wild shores without crowds, rent a kayak, canoe or stand-up paddleboard from **Lake George Kayak Co** *(lakegeorgekayak.com; per hour/half-day $35/75)*. There are tons of boat-rental companies around the lake, too, though not all are reputable and costs can be prohibitive. At **FR Smith & Sons** *(frsmithandsonsmarina.com)*

AMERICAN MYTHOLOGY

If you know the stories 'Rip Van Winkle' (the Catskills man who hit a 20-year snooze button) or 'The Legend of Sleepy Hollow' (Ichabod Crane's ill-fated meet-up with the Headless Horseman), you know Washington Irving, America's first celebrated wordsmith. Both tales, published in 1819, feature one of his favorite locations – the Hudson Valley – where he transformed a stone Dutch house with eclectic architectural styles. The property, **Sunnyside** *(hudsonvalley.org; adult/child $18/13)* is tour-worthy, as is the nearby town of Sleepy Hollow, renamed in 1996 to capitalize on his ghoulish account, sewn into American mythology. Visit around Halloween to see Van Cortlandt Manor's **Great Jack O'Lantern Blaze** *(pumpkinblaze.org; $20)*, when thousands of pumpkins light up the night.

 EATING & DRINKING AROUND THE ADIRONDACKS: OUR PICKS

Hitching Post & Tavern: It's all about cheese at this restaurant and market run by Nettle Meadow Farms, a purveyor of fantastic goat *fromage. hours vary* $$	**Deer's Head Inn:** The Adirondacks' oldest tavern (1808) serves American classics utilizing local ingredients, modernized with international zest. *5-9pm Wed-Sun* $$$	**Capisce Coffee & Espresso Bar:** Strong java, sandwiches and a small selection of local art and vintage clothes. *6am-4pm Mon, Tue & Thu-Sat, to noon Wed & Sun* $	**Paradox Brewery:** Sample craft beer made with pristine water from Adirondack Park's granite bedrock. *noon-8pm Wed & Thu, to 9pm Fri & Sat, to 6pm Sun*

JACK AIELLO/SHUTTERSTOCK

TROUT TOWN, USA

When spring blossoms erupt around the Catskills, fly fishers pull out their poles to catch trout. Fly fishing is a local tradition dating back to the 1890s, thanks to Theodore Gordon – 'Father of American Dry Fly Fishing' – who revolutionized the sport with new techniques (dubbed 'Catskill style') in rivers and creeks around Roscoe and Livingston Manor. Today, both towns wear their fishy history with pride. Roscoe calls itself 'Trout Town, USA' (find tackle shops along Old Rte 17), and Livingston Manor celebrates local legends at the **Catskill Fly Fishing Center & Museum** *(cffcm.com; $12)*. In June, Livingston Manor dons its best river drag for the wacky and wonderful **Trout Parade** *(livingston manorny.com)*, led by marching bands and giant trout puppets.

in Bolton Landing, a full-day affair on a four-person boat costs $522 – a price worth the pleasure of speeding off to a private cove. For a uniquely Lake George experience, see the sights from one of **Lake George Steamboat Company's** *(lakegeorgesteamboat.com)* historic cruise vessels, docked along the lake's south side. The most adorable of the bunch is ***Minnie-Ha-Ha*** *(adult/child $24.50/$12.50; May-Oct)*, one of America's last steam paddle-wheel ships, which toot-toots along the lake during an informative, family-friendly, one-hour tour. A calliope – the boat's 32-whistle steam organ – belts classic tunes between journeys from the top deck.

Go for gold in Lake Placid

Lake Placid, two-time host of the Winter Olympics, doesn't need snow to celebrate seasonal sports – the alpine village wears its athletic heritage like a badge of honor year-round. Spend a day following in the ski tracks of global champions at sites in and around town. Start at the **Lake Placid Olympic Museum** *(lakeplacidolympicmuseum.org; adult/youth $15/12)*, a small but mighty look at the 1932 and 1980 Games. The museum holds a little something for everyone: plenty of history, graphic and fashion designs from Olympics past, and a riveting video chronicling one of the most legendary Olympic upsets – the underdog US ice-hockey team's 1980 victory over the Soviet Union. There's also an interactive section where visitors can hop into a bobsled for a virtual thrill ride. Adrenaline junkies who prefer a real-life rush should soar to the **Olympic Jumping Complex** *(olympicjumpingcomplex. com)*, where ski jumpers zoom down steep ramps before taking flight. Take a similar (and safer) journey on the high-speed **Sky Flyer Zipline** *($45)*. Your final stop is **Whiteface Mountain** *(whiteface.com)*, where Olympic slalom stars raced for

Taughannock Falls

gold in 1980. Between the end of November and mid-April, visitors can purchase a day pass *($129)* and rent equipment *($71)* to test their skills on the East Coast's biggest vertical drop (3430ft). In summer, take the 15-minute **Cloudsplitter Gondola** *(adult/youth $30/25)* ride to the top of Little White Face, gliding above grassy slopes to a majestic view of Lake Placid and nearby Lake Champlain.

Finger Lakes
Trails to powerful plunges near Ithaca
More than 150 waterfalls grace gorges in a 10-mile radius around Ithaca, beating heart of the Finger Lakes region, with more gushers dazzling further afield. The most wow-worthy of the bunch is **Taughannock Falls** *(parks.ny.gov; per car $9)*, the East Coast's tallest single-drop waterfall, shooting 215ft into a canyon of gun-metal-gray shale. Follow the well-groomed and largely flat 1.8-mile out-and-back Gorge Trail to feel its power from below, then drive to the Taughannock Park Rd viewing platform to appreciate the landscape from above.

LAKE GEORGE: GATEWAY TO THE ADIRONDACKS

Lake George, the 'Queen of American Lakes,' is royal indeed. Crowned by pine-packed peaks and bejeweled with over 170 islands, humans have spent centuries admiring the 32-mile-long, spring-fed stunner. The Indigenous Haudenosaunee (or Iroquois Confederacy) and Mohicans came first and called it 'Andia-ta-roc-te' (lake that shuts itself in), followed by the French, then pushed out by the British, who renamed it after King George II in 1755. Gilded Age travelers built grand cabins here throughout the 19th century, and these days, summertime tourists descend upon the lake between Memorial and Labor Days. Along the queen's southern shores sits the village of Lake George, gateway to Adirondack Park – a 6-million-acre preserve with 46 mountains over 4000ft high.

 EATING AROUND ITHACA: OUR PICKS

Moosewood: America's longest-running vegetarian restaurant planted seeds for a farm-to-table revolution in 1973 and remains top tier. *11:30am-9pm Wed-Mon* **$$**

Hazelnut Kitchen: Regional ingredients get dressed to impress, but this dining room in Trumansburg remains casual and quaint. *5-8:30pm Thu-Sat* **$$$**

Creekside Cafe: Snug, low-key operation for breakfast sandwiches and sweets, located at the heart of Trumansburg's Main St. *9am-2pm Fri & Sat, to 1pm Sun* **$**

Cayuga Lake Creamery: Divert from vineyards for experimental homemade ice-cream flavors such as jalapeño popper, apple-cider sorbet and maple bacon. *hours vary* **$**

FUN IN THE FINGER LAKES

Look at a map of Central New York and you'll see 11 spindly bodies of water splayed out like a giant's hands. These are the glacier-gouged Finger Lakes, adorned with farmsteads and tiny towns. At the bottom of 39-mile-long Cayuga Lake, the hand's longest appendage, sits hippie-dippie Ithaca, bookended by Cornell University and Ithaca College. The city's academic underpinnings make it a magnet for free-spirit thinkers who dine and drink around the Commons, Ithaca's pedestrian strip below Cornell's campus. The city's tourism slogan since the 1970s, 'Ithaca is Gorges,' plays on the region's abundance of geological showstoppers: narrow canyons carved by creeks and lashed by some of the East Coast's most magnificent waterfalls.

For spectacular gorge trails, **Watkins Glen State Park** sets the gold standard. This 3-mile out-and-back trail climbs 832 stone steps to 19 cascades that appear plucked from the pages of a Tolkien tale. Closer to Ithaca, there's **Robert H Treman State Park**, which has a dozen cascades on its 4.5-mile Gorge and Rim Trail loop. **Buttermilk Falls State Park** packs 10 waterfalls into a similar 1.6-mile loop. Both showcase natural swimming holes at the base of frothy cataracts – perfect for a refreshing post-hike dip in summer. All state parks cost $10 per car.

In downtown Ithaca, you can drive by **Ithaca Falls**, a 150ft-tall, 175ft-wide powerhouse visible from Lake St, or hike through **Cascadilla Gorge** (cornellbotanicgardens.org; free), passing six feathery falls on a 1.2-mile round-trip path linked to Cornell.

To hike all the gorge trails, visit between late May and October. Taughannock Falls remains open year-round, but many paths close between winter and spring.

Unwind at verdant vineyards

Drive the pastoral perimeter of Cayuga and Seneca Lakes, decorated with neat rows of grape vines. Nearly 150 winemakers call the Finger Lakes home – a tradition that flowered in the 1960s when Ukrainian refugee Dr Konstantin Frank successfully planted vinifera grapes near Keuka Lake. While the region is best known for German-style rieslings, plucky vintners have recently shown potential for cultivating reds such as cabernet franc and pinot noir. Quality here varies drastically, so instead of hopping on one of the area's touted wine trails for an improvised tour, choose your stops judiciously. **Six Eighty Cellars** (sixeightycellars.com) is Cayuga Lake's west-coast-cool kid, with knowledgeable staff espousing the virtues of bubbly pét-nats and smoky chardonnays. Tastings come with a charcuterie board, which you can enjoy in the whitewashed tasting room or in an outdoor Adirondack chair overlooking Cayuga Lake. At **Forge Cellars** (forgecellars.com), located on a steep hill with heavenly Seneca Lake views, it's all about the local terroir. Sample rieslings that differ in only one way – the site upon which the grapes were grown. A map of local growing sites accompanies flights. **Lakewood Vineyards** (lakewoodvineyards.com) is best for budgets, with $5 flights – choose between samples of sweet or dry wines. Don't sleep on **Heart & Hands Wine Co's** (heartandhandswine.com) pinot noir, either. Need a chauffeur to usher you

DRINKING IN ITHACA: BEER, COCKTAILS & COFFEE

Personal Best Brewing: Come to this industrial, yeast-scented brewhouse for hop-forward suds; stay for the full-sized shuffleboard courts and board games. *hours vary*

Ithaca Beer Co: Flower Power IPAs grace taps in 15 states, but you'll only find kegs of its experimental ales here. *4-9pm Wed & Thu, from noon Fri-Sun*

Bar Argos: While Cornell's party crowds down shots around the Commons, sophisticated sippers head to Argos Inn's Victorian-style lobby for quiet cocktail contemplation. *4-10pm*

Press Cafe: Ithaca's coffee-fueled undergraduate digerati clack away on keyboards inside this bright, bohemian two-room cafe showcasing local art. *8am-6pm*

Lakewood Vineyards

between vineyards? Hire a ride through **Main St Drivers** *(mainstreetdrivers.com; from $48 per hour, 4hr minimum).*

Letchworth State Park
Gaze into the Grand Canyon of the East

The Genesee River has spent thousands of years carving Letchworth Gorge – the shale-and-sandstone centerpiece of 17-mile-long **Letchworth State Park** *(parks.ny.gov; per car $10)*, dubbed the 'Grand Canyon of the East,' one hour east of Buffalo by car. While the comparison to Arizona's stony celebrity is flattering, it belies the singular beauty on view here: 600ft-high cliffs topped by woodlands thick with hemlock, oak and sugar maple trees – a spectacular sight in fall. There are also three major cascades – the Upper, Middle (most magnificent) and Lower Falls. Though they are not as powerful as Niagara Falls, the park is less crowded and more wild, making it a worthwhile detour between Buffalo and Ithaca.

To experience the park on foot, follow the 14-mile out-and-back **Gorge Trail**. Don't be alarmed by the mileage – this is more of a steady stroll than a heart-pounding hike, following the gorge's scenic western rim.

The park also prioritizes accessibility. Parking lots and pullouts for cars are near all the top sights, and the **Autism Nature Trail** *(autismnaturetrail.com)*, a 1-mile route with eight sensory-friendly stations, provides autistic individuals a safe space to experience the great outdoors.

BEST OF THE REST AROUND THE FINGER LAKES

Corning Museum of Glass: Ancient Egyptian glassmaking, Dale Chihuly creations and glass-blowing demonstrations.

Town of Aurora: Century-old mansions line this manicured 2-mile strip along Cayuga Lake. Grab a walking tour brochure from **Inns of Aurora** (p158).

Women's Rights National Historical Park: Honor the First Women's Rights Convention in 1848, birthing a gender-equality movement.

Sunset View Creamery: 'Cow cuddling' with three to four gentle calves inside a hay-covered pen.

Finger Lakes Cider House: Swill ciders on a hillside farm or take a tour *($24)* to learn about bud-to-bottle production.

PIERRE WILLIOT/SHUTTERSTOCK

BUFFALO'S BACKSTORY

Its winters may be harsh, but Buffalo is a city in spring. After economic turmoil in the late 20th century, artists, preservationists and a squad of local cheerleaders are planting the seeds for Western New York's Rust Belt revitalization. Incorporated in 1832, Buffalo owes its origins to the Erie Canal, linking to NYC. When the artificial waterway opened in 1825, the city overflowed with riches and became an industrial boomtown. By 1901, it boasted more millionaires per capita than any American metropole. But after WWII, industries vanished, leaving behind their brick-and-cement skeletons. These bones are now the bedrock of Buffalo's rebirth, with visionaries turning abandoned buildings into breweries, museums, restaurants and parks.

Buffalo

Tour Buffalo's historic architecture

Buffalo's architectural landscape glimmers with riches from its industrial past. From the 19th century, there's **Delaware Park** *(bfloparks.org)*, designed by Frederick Law Olmsted (of Central Park and Niagara Falls fame), and the neighboring **Richardson Olmsted Campus** *(richardson-olmsted.com; guided tours from $20)*, featuring the Romanesque Revival Buffalo State Asylum for the Insane, now a boutique hotel. There's also downtown's **Buffalo City Hall** *(buffalony.gov; free)* from 1931: after enjoying its art-deco details from Niagara Sq, take an elevator to the 25th floor and walk up three flights for panoramic city views.

Thanks to local preservationists, Buffalo is also the greatest sanctuary, outside of Chicago, for Frank Lloyd Wright's organic architecture. The 1906, Prairie-style **Martin House** *(martinhouse.org; 75min tour of main structures $25, full 2hr tour $45)*, commissioned by self-made millionaire Darwin Martin, is most magnificent – even Wright called it 'a well-nigh perfect composition.' Book a guided tour to see interiors on the 30,000-sq-ft grounds. Exploring the building's Roman brick exterior and gardens is free, though a $15 audio tour enhances the experience. The interwar **Graycliff Estate** *(experiencegraycliff.org; adult/child $38/23)*, constructed as a Lake Erie summer home for the Martin family, awaits 30 minutes' drive south in Derby, NY. Standard 90-minute tours examine the property.

MORE RESPLENDENT WRIGHTS

Fans of Frank Lloyd Wright will fawn over **Fallingwater** (p156), his masterful creation outside Pittsburgh, Pennsylvania. For more Wright in NY, head to NYC's **Guggenheim** (p95), a circular departure from the city's blocky buildings.

Richardson Olmsted Campus

Wander Buffalo's waterfront

Efforts to rinse off Buffalo's Rust Belt image are most apparent throughout Canalside, a district transformed from bustling Erie Canal terminus to late-20th-century wasteland and now a recreation-packed park. Spend an hour exploring the area, or plan an adventure that lasts half a day.

Roaming around is half the fun: historical placards provide Erie Canal insight and *Shark Girl*, the 'fish out of water' statue by Casey Riordan, begs passersby to snap a selfie. Throughout summer, visitors can paddle around Elevator Alley (a stretch of river flanked by towering grain elevators) with rentals from **BFLO Harbor Kayak** *(bfloharborkayak.com; per hour $25)* or hop on the **Queen City Bike Ferry** *(queencityferry.com; $1)* for access to Lake Erie's serene Outer Harbor. Ride the **Buffalo Heritage Carousel** from 1924 *(buffaloheritagecarousel.org; $3)*, skate around New York's largest outdoor winter rink, **Ice at Canalside** *(buffalowaterfront.com; adult/child $8/5, skate rental $5)*, or cruise Lake Erie on a two-hour **Spirit of Buffalo** schooner tour *(buffaloboattours.com; adult/child $39/19)*. From this point of view, Buffalo's renaissance has arrived.

MORE BUFFALO MUSEUMS & TOURS

Buffalo AKG Art Museum: Modern and contemporary art inside a 1905 neoclassical temple, 1962 modernist addition and 2023 glass-walled wing.

Burchfield Penney Art Center: Admire dreamy landscapes by local watercolorist Charles Ephraim Burchfield.

Buffalo History Museum: Covers 12,000 years of local history.

Silo City Ground and Vertical Tours: Explore Buffalo leads seasonal 1½-hour explorations of abandoned and repurposed grain silos.

Buffalo Transportation Pierce-Arrow Museum: Revs up motorheads with its collection of vintage vehicles and local history.

 EATING & DRINKING IN BUFFALO: OUR PICKS

West Side Bazaar: Immigrant and refugee chefs show off their skills at this food hall featuring Congolese, Jamaican, Korean and more international eats. 11am-8pm Tue-Sat $

Dapper Goose: The goose is debonair indeed, with smart takes on shareable American plates and meaty mains served under pressed-tin ceilings. 5-9pm Tue-Sun $$$

Gabriel's Gate: The city's spicy, deep-fried Buffalo wings were invented at Anchor Bar (1964) but perfected here. 11:30am-midnight Mon-Fri, to 1am Sat & Sun $$

duende: Ghostly grain silos and gardens surround this industrial indoor-outdoor bar pouring drinks inside a 1940s American Malting Company office building. *hours vary*

Prospect Point Observation Tower

TOP EXPERIENCE
Niagara Falls

Prepare to be mystified: North America's most powerful falls dump roughly 700,000 gallons of water over three distinct cascades every second, plunging into the Niagara Gorge at 25mph. Their immensity is hypnotic, attracting conservationists, industrialists and thrill-seekers to the boundary between the US and Canada for centuries. Join thousands of onlookers, electrified by nature's spectacle each day.

DON'T MISS

Maid of the Mist

Prospect Point Observation Tower

Luna Island

Three Sisters Islands

Goat Island

Cave of the Winds

Niagara Falls Underground Railroad Heritage Center

Celebrate Niagara's Sculptors

Begin your journey at **Prospect Point**, overlooking the crest of the American Falls. More than 12,000 years in the making, Niagara's story begins with receding glaciers from the last ice age, which carved the Great Lakes, unleashed a deluge of melting ice and formed the Niagara River linking Lake Erie and Lake Ontario.

The verdant crown atop the park owes its existence to the Free Niagara movement, a cadre of 19th-century environmentalists appalled by industrial abuse of the natural wonder. Their fiery advocacy culminated in the establishment of Niagara

PRACTICALITIES
- niagarafallsstatepark.com
- 24hr
- prices and hours vary by activity

Falls as the nation's first state park in 1885. Follow the park's sinuous pathways, designed by Calvert Vaux and Frederick Law Olmsted, to experience the falls for free.

Feel the Powerful Falls

Though walking above the falls is pretty, sailing into the thundering cascades is the best way to appreciate their force. On the **Maid of the Mist** *(maidofthemist.com; adult/child $30.25/19.75; enter at Prospect Point)* boat tour, operating since 1846, visitors brave the water's icy embrace on a half-hour ride. Despite the experience's theme-park trappings (long entrance lines; exit through a gift shop), the ride provides heart-pumping, must-see perspectives. Be sure to don the blue ponchos provided and store your phone somewhere safe – floating near Horseshoe Falls, the largest waterfall, can be like cruising into a tempest. Tickets include access to the **Prospect Point Observation Tower** ($1.25 when sold separately, but a sensible post-ride pitstop), which extends over the gorge for panoramic views.

Find Your Favorite Viewpoint

From Prospect Point, follow Goat Island Rd to an archipelago above the gorge. On tiny **Luna Island**, peer over railings to gasp at the brink of Bridal Veil Falls. **Three Sisters Islands** offers a glimpse of the park's untamed origins, spread across rocky tufts lapped by whitecaps. **Goat Island** is the largest of the collection, featuring **Cave of the Winds** *(adult/child $21/17)*, a hurricane-worthy waterfall encounter 175ft down into the gorge. Instead of a cave (it collapsed in the 1950s), visitors walk along a series of wooden boardwalks built 20ft from Bridal Veil Falls' nonstop torrents. The entire boardwalk is only installed during summer, though thousands of nesting seagulls make it a worthwhile sight out of season

You can partially admire Horseshoe Falls from Goat Island's **Terrapin Point**, but for unobstructed views, consider traversing the **Rainbow Bridge** *(ezbordercrossing.com; cars $6, pedestrians $1)* to Canada (passports required). While parts of Canada's Niagara suffer from over-commercialization, the scenery from **Queen Victoria Park** *(niagaraparks.com)* is tops.

Dive into Local History

Niagara Falls' proximity to Canada, which abolished slavery three decades before the US, made it a haven for freedom-seeking enslaved African Americans in the 19th century. Crossing the Niagara Gorge became a promising path to liberty, turning Niagara Falls into a crucial stop along the Underground Railroad. To learn more about the town's abolitionist past, head to the **Niagara Falls Underground Railroad Heritage Center** *(niagarafallsundergroundrailroad.org; adult/child $15/10)*, five minutes north by car, which centers stories of self-emancipating freedom seekers in its immersive exhibit *One More River to Cross*.

DAREDEVIL DAMSEL

Annie Edson Taylor celebrated her 63rd birthday in 1901 by climbing into a barrel and plunging over Niagara Falls. She became the first person to survive the death-wish journey, escaping with but a cut on her head. The stunt, she hoped, would solve her financial woes. It didn't, and her fame lasted as long as the ride – just over 15 minutes.

TOP TIPS

● Arrive early to park near Prospect Point ($10 Monday to Thursday, $15 Friday to Sunday) or on Goat Island.

● If walking isn't your speed, hop on the Niagara Scenic Trolley – a vintage hop-on, hop-off bus that cruises around the park April to December *(adult/child $5/3)*.

● Cycle around Niagara Falls using the bikeshare Reddy program or **Sight See Rentals** *(sightseerentals.com; per day $25)*.

● Food sold around the park is mediocre and overpriced. Bring snacks or hold out for a meal at **Savor** *(sunyniagara.edu/nfci/savor)*, prepared by Niagara Falls Culinary Institute students.

● Purchase timed-entry tickets for Cave of the Winds in advance.

● Wear shoes you can get wet – waterproof is best.

New Jersey

BEACHFRONT ESCAPES | SUMMERTIME BOARDWALKS | HISTORIC TOWNS

Places
- Cape May p130
- Wildwood p131
- Asbury Park p132
- Long Beach Island p132
- Sandy Hook p133
- Princeton p134
- Lambertville p137

☑ TOP TIP
Weekend traffic along the Jersey Shore can be heinous. Get an early start to avoid highway pile-ups. If you're spending most of your time along the coast, know that many communities charge a beach-access fee. You'll have to pay between Long Beach Island north to Sandy Hook. Atlantic City and Wildwood are free.

Don't be fooled by everything you've seen on TV. Sure, some things from *The Real Housewives of New Jersey* and *The Sopranos* ring true – namely the thick Jersey accents (lose the 'New' to sound local). But it's not all McMansions and mobsters. Look beyond northern Jersey's labyrinthine highways and you'll see why it's called the Garden State. Farmland and green parks bloom between two important waterways: the Delaware River to the west and the Atlantic Ocean to the east, lapping 127 miles of coastline.

The state's hurricane of history goes from Indigenous Lenape territory to British colony to important battleground during the American Revolutionary War. After WWII, it became a destination for African Americans moving north, and industrial cities bolstered the country's economy. Most people come here to visit the Jersey Shore – running from super-sized boardwalks to tranquil summer towns – though inland hamlets steeped in history are equally worth exploring.

GETTING AROUND

The most common way to navigate Jersey is with a car. Don't get caught off guard at the gas station: this is the only US state where you can't pump fuel – an attendant will do it for you. Trains connect much of the state to NYC via **NJ Transit** *(njtransit.com)*. The North Jersey Coast Line stops at seaside towns including Asbury Park, while the Northeast Corridor Line runs through Princeton and links to Philadelphia. Ferries are also an option: ride the pedestrian-only **Seastreak** *(seastreak.com)* from NYC to Sandy Hook, or the **Cape May–Lewes ferry** *(capemaylewesferry.com)* to Lewes, near Rehoboth Beach, Delaware.

Cape May

See Victorians by the shore

Cape May, located on New Jersey's southern tip, is the only place in the state where the sun rises and sets over the water. It's idyllic. It should be no surprise, then, that it became one of the nation's first seaside resorts in the mid-18th century. Climb the 199 steps to the lookout at **Cape May Lighthouse** (capemaymac.org; adult/child $12/8) to understand what those early vacationers were after: sweeping gold beaches tumbling into the blue Atlantic.

Much of the lavish architecture built to house those trend-setting beach bums burned down in an 1878 fire, sweeping through 35 acres across town. When Cape May rebuilt, it was the height of the Victorian era – a style that characterizes today's landscape.

Take a **Cape May MAC trolley tour** (capemaymac.org; adult/child $20/15) for an overview of Cape May's architectural legacy. The guide points out Italianate and Queen Anne towers, shingled mansard roofs and distinctive Victorian colors, with asides about the town's history. The pastel-painted gingerbread homes, with wraparound porches and filigree trim, are outliers along the Shore – otherwise known for generic, contemporary condos.

If you're raring to see a historic home's interior, head to the whimsically designed **Emlen Physick Estate** from 1879 (capemaymac.org; adult/child $20/15), where 45-minute guided tours by volunteers provide details about how Cape May's upper class once lived.

Look to the sea and sky

Philadelphians and Jerseyites aren't the only ones who flock 'down the shore' (local lingo for heading to Jersey's coastline). Birds, butterflies and bottlenose dolphins also bum-rush Cape May throughout the year.

The town's peninsula is an important migratory crossroads – best appreciated in spring and autumn, when birds on the Atlantic Flyway pass through. If you're new to birding, get your bearings at the **Cape May Bird Observatory** (njaudubon.org/centers/cape-may-bird-observatory). Pick up binoculars and field guides in the bookstore, then hop on the observatory's mile-long loop trail in search of winged wonders.

If you're already a big-time bird-watcher, consider visiting in September and October, when Cape May's skies are ruled by peregrine falcons – predatory birds known for being some of the

JERSEY VINO

New Jersey's wine industry, youthful and growing, can trace its origins to Cape May's farmlands, blessed as they are with a long, frost-free growing season. But it was the 1981 New Jersey Wine Act, which stamped out restrictive Prohibition-era rules about winemaking, that allowed the industry to grow. The **New Jersey Wine Grower's Association** (newjerseywines.com) provides a wine 'passport' you can get stamped at some three dozen stops.

One of the seven wineries in Cape May County worth visiting is brother-run **Hawk Haven** (hawkhavenvineyard.com). They began growing grapes on their grandparents' farmland where lima beans once sprouted, experimenting and figuring out what the grapes naturally wanted to do. There's a food truck out back and live music on Friday nights in summer.

EATING IN CAPE MAY: OUR PICKS

Uncle Bill's Pancake House: Drawing crowds hungry for butter-drenched flapjacks since the 1960s. *8am-1pm* $

Taco Caballito: This open-air beachfront tequileria and taco joint has especially good service. Try the short-rib banh mi. *noon-10pm, to 11pm Fri & Sat* $

Mad Batter: Eat fluffy oat pancakes or rich clam chowder in this white Victorian B&B beloved for brunch. Live music nightly. *8am-9pm* $$

Lobster House: A classic waterfront seafood experience. Order from the raw bar or takeout window, or grab a wharfside table for a full-blown lobster. *11:30am-3pm & 4:30-10pm* $$$

Cape May Lighthouse

world's fastest animals. Head to **Cape May Point State Park** *(nj.gov/dep/parksandforests)* to watch them swoop through the air.

Autumn is also a fantastic time to spot monarch butterflies, which undertake the longest migration of any North American butterfly species, flitting from Canada to Mexico in six to eight months. Their arrival in Cape May can turn the landscape into a fluttering orange kaleidoscope.

In spring and summer, you might spot New Jersey's most iconic endangered bird – the piping plover. This migratory shorebird requires sandy beaches with few disturbances. Some areas have symbolic fencing with informational signs, marking nesting sites and reminding people to keep their distance. Be quiet and listen attentively – you might hear one peep (or 'pipe') before you see it.

As for marine life, bottlenose dolphins and migrating whales arrive around spring. Several companies run cruises out of the marina to spot them flipping their fins. Set sail with **Cape May Whale Watch & Research Center** *(capemaywhalewatch.com; 2hr Dolphin & Bird Watch tour from $40)*.

Wildwood

The Big Daddy of boardwalks

Wildwood's boardwalk is summer on steroids. **Morey's Piers** *(moreyspiers.com; packages from $45)*, probably the best and biggest of all the Jersey Shore's parks, takes up vast chunks of boardwalk real estate, with three amusement piers and two water parks. Locals debate whose is the better slice of pizza on the beach: **Sam's** *(samswildwood.com)* thin crust or **Mack's** doughy? **Wildwood's Honky Tonk** *(honkytonkww.com)*, a huge country bar with live music, is housed in a former boardwalk arcade. And since 1949, a miniature rubber-tired **tram** *(wildwood.com; $5)* runs the boardwalk's length, chirping 'Watch the tram car, please.' Cycling can also be fun – a

CINEMATIC JERSEY MOBSTERS

New Jersey's glittering shoreline has attracted centuries of beach bums – along with crime bosses, particularly in the 1920s, when rum runners used its coastal inlets, rivers and bays to offload illegal liquor during Prohibition, a phenomenon explored in the TV series *Boardwalk Empire* (2010–14). The show was inspired by real-life Atlantic City–based gangster Enoch 'Nucky' Johnson, who controlled and influenced politicians, businessmen and the heads of organized-crime families. He even helped host the Atlantic City Conference – the first-ever national meeting of the American mob. The end of Prohibition marked the end of Atlantic City's allure as a 'den of iniquity' – though it remains a gambler's Gomorrah.

BOAT RIDES ALONG THE SHORE

Tiki Bar Boat: Book a 1½-hour trip on the dry-grass-covered pontoon in Beach Haven. BYOB.

Miss Beach Haven: Join a three-hour fluke fishing tour several miles from Beach Haven.

Black Pearl Pirate Tours: Kids can go full Jack Sparrow, shooting water cannons at an accompanying boat.

Atlantic City Cruises: Dolphin-watching tours with a money-back guarantee of success; the captain provides background on wildlife.

Seastreak: Tours are run on four winter Saturdays; a wildlife expert educates passengers on a variety of birds and seals.

Convention Hall

12-mile bike path runs along the oceanfront. Pick up wheels from **Crest Bike Rental** (crestbikerental.com; adult single-speeds from $15).

For those interested in solitude, head to the beach access point at Rambler Rd, south of the boardwalk. There's free street parking nearby, plus clean bathrooms. For even more tranquility, visit **Hereford Lighthouse** (pronounced *heh*-ford; herefordinletlighthouse.com; free) from 1874, situated at the northern end of North Wildwood with a pretty garden.

Visit on Friday evenings to end your Wildwood day with a bang: fireworks light up the night sky.

Asbury Park

Relive the Jersey Shore's Jazz Age

Artsy and edgy Asbury Park is the Jersey Shore's jewel of renewal – a once-derelict haunt that's undergone a bohemian rebirth over the past decade, attracting a diverse crowd of artsy couples, young families and LGBTQ+ folks who arrive via New Jersey Transit from NYC. Mosey along the historic seaside boardwalk at the center of the renaissance.

Kicks things off by admiring the architecture. Enter the boardwalk near Fifth Ave to see **Convention Hall**, built between 1928 and 1930 by the same designers behind Manhattan's Grand Central Terminal. Continue south past sizzling food stands to see the gutted beaux-arts casino and carousel – ghostly reminders of the town's Jazz Age heyday.

Along your stroll, join retired pinball wizards rediscovering their youth at **Silverball Retro Arcade** (silverballmuseum.com/asbury-park; 1/6hr $17.50/20). There are over 160 restored arcade games – including a 'rotary merchandiser' from the 1930s. Placards above machines offer historical context.

If you want to join the beach brigade, you'll need to book a beach pass (apbeachpasses.com; weekdays $7, weekends & holidays $10) from Memorial Day to Labor Day.

Rock out in Asbury Park

Bruce Springsteen put this beach town on the map with his 1973 debut album *Greetings from Asbury Park* – and 50 years later, the locals still love grooving to 'The Boss.' Follow Springsteen's path to fame by heading to the **Stone Pony** *(stonepony online.com; tickets from $35)*, a boardwalk-adjacent rock club where he honed his sound in the '70s. Check the venue's Summer Stage schedule to see big-name acts perform under the stars from May through September. If you don't like the line-up, see who's playing at **Wonder Bar** *(wonderbarasbury park.com; tickets from $28)*, where up-and-coming acts rip through sets of rock, pop and punk.

Long Beach Island
Try Jersey's 'Chowda'

One of the best off-season times to visit Beach Haven is in early October for the **Chowda Cookoff** *(bhchowdercookoff. com)*, formerly known as the Chowda Fest. During this event, local restaurants go head to head, competing to have the best red or white chowder on Long Beach Island (or the best 'Jersey chowder,' a combo of red and white). There's usually a 'most unique chowder' category; one past noteworthy winner was clam-chowder ice cream – a fishy yet refreshing take on the summer dessert. The opening and closing ceremonies attract large crowds – it's often the last weekend when summer-home owners head 'down the shore.'

Sandy Hook
The Jersey Shore's northern tip

It's hard to believe Sandy Hook is only a 40-minute **ferry ride** *(seastreakferry.com; adult/child $49/22)* from NYC's Financial District. This stretch of the Jersey Shore's northern peninsula is a far cry from city life: from here, NYC's skyscrapers appear toy-sized.

Cyclists cruise along the peninsula's 7-mile multi-use path, while history buffs tour **Fort Hancock** *(nps.gov; day pass $20)* – an old army base, home to America's oldest operating **lighthouse**, built in 1764 (park rangers provide tours from 1pm to 4:30pm April to October). The most popular reason to venture here is for pristine beaches. For family-friendly fun, stick to Beaches B, C, D and E. North Beach tends toward the quiet side.

JOYOUS JERSEY FESTIVALS

Red, White & Blueberry Festival: Hammonton, the birthplace of the American blueberry, kicks off this June celebration with a massive pancake breakfast.

Atlantic City Air Show: Half a million people fly to AC in mid-August; come on warm-up day before to avoid the throngs.

Mutzfest: Fill up on mozzarella at Hoboken's most famous April festival. Have more room? Go pastry crazy.

Barefoot Country Music Festival: Wildwood books A-listers for beachfront performances on the third weekend in June.

Shadfest: Lambertville's April shindig honors fishing for shad (the largest in the herring family) with music, food and fun.

EATING AROUND ASBURY PARK: OUR PICKS

Ada's Gojjo: A curious combination of Dominican and Ethiopian in Asbury Park, with dishes from both cultures on the same menu. *noon-8pm Sun & Tue-Thu, to 9pm Fri & Sat* $

Starving Artist: Casual Ocean Grove spot with a large outdoor patio for breakfast, grilled fare and fried seafood; ice cream is available at the adjacent shop. *8am-2pm Thu-Tue* $

Heirloom at the St Laurent: One-of-a-kind mouthwatering dishes innovatively combining flavors and ingredients. *11am-2pm & 5-10pm Wed-Mon* $$$

Moonstruck: Has views of Wesley Lake, dividing Asbury and Ocean Grove, and an extensive, Italian-leaning menu. It's romantically lit up at night. *4-9pm Wed-Sun* $$$

SURFING THE JERSEY SHORE

Chris Sciarra, co-owner of Kona Surf Company in Wildwood. @konasurfcompany

We have beginner-friendly waves that can get really good, even 10ft to 15ft during hurricane season. The lowest swell is during the summer season. Generally, the further north, the better and bigger the waves are, around Belmar and spots in Monmouth County. The area's best breaks are Cape May's Cove and Poverty beaches; in Wildwood, at 10th and 2nd Sts in North Wildwood and at Diamond Beach south of Wildwood Crest.

Beginners: check out Jason Reagan's Cape May surf school *(jasonreagansurfschool.com)*, Randazzo surf school and camps *(randazzosurf.com)* in Margate and North Wildwood, and Tim Kaye's Surftopia *(thesurftopia.com)* in Wildwood for rentals and lessons.

If you want to throw caution (and your swimsuit) to the wind, head to **Gunnison Beach** – a naturist oasis on Sandy Hook's curved shaft. Locals say it's been a skinny-dipping sensation since Fort Hancock's army troop days, and now, on top of being a time-honored tradition, it's New Jersey's only legal clothing-optional shore. LGBTQ+ travelers take note – the beach's south side is a favorite among gay men, who bring elaborate beach set-ups for day-long fiestas. As for the rules, there are two to hold dear: this isn't a peep show, so don't stare, and if you don't want to get naked, get lost. As for packing – a towel, sunblock, water and snacks are musts. Bring an umbrella – shade is a hot commodity.

Princeton

Half a day with the Ivy League

Perfectly coiffed Princeton is packed with elegant architecture and anchored by its top-tier Ivy League university. The university's Nassau Hall, built in the mid-1700s, became one of the largest stone structures in the American colonies and briefly served as the nation's capital when the Continental Congress arrived in 1783. Like most seats of learning, Princeton is flush with brewpubs and chic boutiques – though it skews more 'bougie upper-crust' than 'penny-pinching collegiate.' Spend half a day studying its streets.

Start by following the footsteps of Princeton's smart set around the Collegiate Gothic **campus** on a self-guided tour. Head to *visitour.io/princeton-university* and choose the free standard Orange Key guide – a one-hour trip to 11 destinations around the campus's immaculate landscaping.

It's also worth peeking inside the **Princeton University Art Museum** *(artmuseum.princeton.edu; free)*, slated to re-open in a new, modern complex in fall 2025. The collection is like a mini version of NYC's Metropolitan Museum of Art, with 117,000 artworks spanning over 5000 years of global creativity. Budget an hour.

Once you're ready to graduate from college life, head to nearby Palmer Sq, edged with preppie stores, and stroll the surrounding streets for light shopping. Vinyl and CD lovers may lose track of time flipping through **Princeton Record Exchange's** *(prex.com)* 100,000 non-digitized musical selections. Bibliophiles and casual readers can make like a Princeton English major and wander the two floors of **Labyrinth Books** *(labyrinthbooks.com)*.

 EATING IN PRINCETON: OUR PICKS — MAP P135

Chuck's Spring Street Cafe: Wings are the thing at Chuck's: you can order up to 100 of these twice-cooked tangy buffalo-style ones at a time. *11am-9pm Tue-Sun* $

Little Chef Pastry Shop: The Haitian-born pastry chef here has been spinning out decadent croissants, napoleons and eclairs since 2003. *9:30am-3:30pm* $

Winberie's Restaurant & Bar: Aka 'the Princeton Pub'; has the town's best fried chicken, as well as other upscale comfort food. *11:30am-11pm* $

Mistral: Serves three- to four-course brunches and dinners, with flavors ranging from the Caribbean to Scandinavia. *5-9pm Mon-Fri, 11:30am-2pm & 4-10pm Sat & Sun* $$$

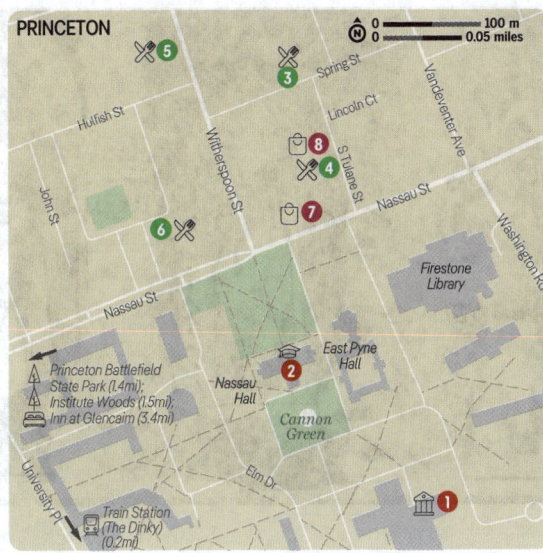

PRINCETON

SIGHTS
1. Princeton University Art Museum
2. Princeton University

EATING
3. Chuck's Spring Street Cafe
4. Little Chef Pastry Shop
5. Mistral
6. Winberie's Restaurant & Bar

SHOPPING
7. Labyrinth Books
8. Princeton Record Exchange

Walk through Revolutionary woods

Princeton Battlefield State Park *(nj.gov/dep/parksandforests; free)* is mostly a grassy field with some plaques and a historic house – but use your imagination, and a bloody scene unfolds. On January 3, 1777, General George Washington and his ill-equipped troops won a decisive battle here against British forces, the world's most powerful army at the time. Hundreds of men lost their lives. It's widely regarded as a turning point in the fight for American independence.

Sharing the same parking lot is **Institute Woods** *(ias.edu/about/campus-and-lands)* – a 600-acre slice of forested countryside. Washington and his troops marched through these woods before the Battle of Princeton. Later, Robert Oppenheimer, Albert Einstein and John Nash (to name a few intellectual luminaries) found the forest a beneficial refuge for contemplation. These days, the pathways are beloved for strolling and birding – it's an important stop for warblers during spring migration, when the number of avian species jumps from 42 to 200.

MORE AMERICAN REVOLUTION HISTORY

Follow George Washington's path to victory outside **Lambertville** (p137), where he crossed the Delaware River before coming to Princeton, and see the spot where he trained soldiers at Pennsylvania's **Valley Forge** (p148).

 EATING IN DINERS BEYOND PRINCETON: OUR PICKS

White Mana Diner: For Jersey kids, sitting at the circular linoleum counter is still a rite of passage at this pioneer of the fast-food hamburger. *8am-11pm* $

Tick Tock Diner: Aka 'The Tick,' this legendary diner in Clifton serves classics like disco fries covered in mozzarella and brown gravy. *7am-10pm* $

Shut up and Eat!: This Tom's River spot adds a dose of Jersey attitude with pajama-clad waitresses, snappy repartee and a cornucopia of kitsch. *6:30am-3:30pm* $

Summit Diner: Grab a swivel stool to chow down on traditional diner breakfasts and sandwiches at this railroad-car-designed greasy spoon. *5:30am-4pm* $

ANN KAPUSTINA/SHUTTERSTOCK

DINER DEMOCRACY

The diner is a chrome-covered bastion of Americana – an affordable, egalitarian 'greasy spoon' serving all-day breakfast alongside sandwiches, pies, wings and sides. Menus are novels. Coffees are bottomless. They're immortalized in Edward Hopper's *Nighthawks* painting and Suzanne Vega's song 'Tom's Diner.' Roughly 450 of these swivel-stool sanctuaries call New Jersey home – more than any other US state, making it the world's diner capital. In the past decade, however, many nostalgia-stuffed restaurants shuttered – victims of rising expenses and changing tastes. But the diner isn't done – it's adapting to the times. New additions to the scene incorporate international flavors, like **Golden Diner** (p75) in NYC; others celebrate locavore movements, like **Phoenicia Diner** (p115) in the Catskills.

America's magnificent Hindu temple

The 200ft spires of the **BAPS Swaminarayan Akshardham** *(usa.akshardham.org; free; timed reservations required for weekends and holidays)*, one hour south of Princeton, rise from green fields like limestone mountains – a modern echo of ancient Angkor Wat. Completed in 2023, this is the largest Hindu temple complex outside of India, with roughly 1.9 million cu ft of interlocking granite, marble and more decorative stones sourced worldwide. Its multiple buildings sprawl over nearly 180 acres and showcase some 10,000 statues – including the 49ft gold deity Nilkanth Varni, the child-yogi form of Bhagwan Swaminarayan, balanced on one leg. (According to followers, he held this yogic position for 2½ months in a Himalayan winter.)

New Jersey has one of the nation's largest Hindu populations, and the temple serves as an important place of pilgrimage. Within the Akshardham – which means 'divine abode' – you'll find intricate carvings depicting moments from Swaminarayan's life. Other Hindu deities have separate altars, and according to the scriptures and principles, they're fed, clothed and 'put to rest' several times daily.

There's also a secular edge to the site, with quotes from Martin Luther King Jr and Albert Einstein. In fact, it's a visitor-friendly experience, welcoming plenty of tourists more interested in architecture than spiritual experiences. Guided tours provide context, offered hourly on Monday, Wednesday, Thursday and Friday between 10am and 5pm; advanced booking recommended. Wearing shorts or sleeveless tops isn't permitted (sarongs are provided if needed). For food, drop into **Shayona Café** *(11am-8pm),* serving excellent vegetarian Indian fare.

Though the site is awe-inspiring, its construction was clouded in controversy. In 2021, the organization was accused of using forced labor to complete the complex – which required

BAPS Swaminarayan Akshardham

an estimated 4.7 million hours of work across 15 years. The plaintiffs withdrew their lawsuit in 2023, but not before the allegations attracted widespread news coverage.

Lambertville

Antique treasures on the Delaware

Lambertville, perched on the eastern banks of the Delaware River, is an antiques oasis, with half a dozen top-quality shops in town, along with art galleries and home-furnishing stores with mid-century-modern flair. You'll find most of the action around North Union St – though the area's biggest and oldest operation is 2 miles south on Rte 29 – the **Golden Nugget Antique Flea Market** *(gnflea.com)*, open since 1967. The outdoor tables and 20-plus specialist indoor stores are a haphazard cornucopia of potential *Antiques Roadshow* treasures. Haggle to your heart's content with vendors hawking furniture, books and a thousand other collectibles.

People often pair a trip to Lambertville with neighboring New Hope, PA (p157) – its sister town on the Delaware's western side.

Cycle through history

The 70-mile **D & R Canal trail** *(dandrcanal.org)* traces the 19th-century Delaware and Raritan Canal, built as an industrial shipping route. Now a linear parkway through Central New Jersey, it's a sensational spot for cycling. Rent bikes from **Pure Energy Cycling & Java House** in Lambertville *(pureenergycycling.com; per hour from $18)* then pedal 7 miles south to tour **Washington Crossing State Park** *(nj.gov; free)*, commemorating the site where George Washington and his men snuck across the Delaware in 1776. Wander the grounds to soak up the history, then head further south or loop back to Lambertville for a hearty meal.

BEST STATE FORESTS & PARKS

Visit *nj.gov/dep/parksandforests* for more park info.

High Point State Park: The state's highest point (1803ft), with views of the Delaware River and surroundings; great for camping and hiking.

Norvin Green State Forest: Awesomely isolated 5000-acre forest near the New York border; trails from moderate to difficult, with spectacular views.

Cheesequake State Park: A blend of pine barrens, salt- and freshwater swamps and forest. Choose between four easy to moderate trails, swimming and kayaking.

Kittatinny Valley State Park: Home to lakes with campsites, hiking and cycling paths. Part of the Appalachian Trail runs along the ridge.

Wharton State Forest: New Jersey's largest single tract of parkland forest in the Pine Barrens.

Pennsylvania

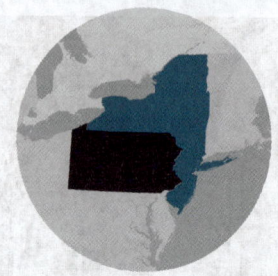

REVOLUTIONARY HISTORY | ARTS & CULTURE | RIVER TOWNS

Places
Philadelphia p138
Brandywine Valley p147
Valley Forge p148
Doylestown p148
New Hope p149
The Poconos p150
Lancaster p151
Gettysburg p152
Pennsylvania Wilds p152
Pittsburgh p154
Laurel Highlands p156

Sprawling Pennsylvania (PA) sits at an American crossroads, linking the East Coast's end to the Midwest's beginning. The Mason–Dixon line runs along its southern border – a symbolic divide between northern and southern sensibilities. In Philadelphia, colonial architecture from the American Revolution shares the skyline with contemporary skyscrapers. In Lancaster, sports cars whizz by horse-drawn buggies guided by Amish farmers. The Civil War's deadliest battle once raged in Gettysburg, now a peaceful park. Steel factories that fueled Pittsburgh's industrial days stand dormant as the Rust Belt city rises from the ashes. Between it all, patchworks of forests and rushing rivers link mountains and rural hamlets, where elk herds and eagles sometimes outnumber people. On top of covering some 46,000 sq miles, PA captures a diverse spectrum of American culture. It's got world-class art and outdoor adventures, queer communities and conservative towns. Equal parts Philly cheesesteak and Pennsylvania Dutch scrapple, the Keystone State defies tidy labels.

GETTING AROUND

Philadelphia is accessible from NYC and DC via Amtrak train and easy to navigate sans car. The rest of the state is sprawling: you need a set of wheels to see it all. GPS service can be sketchy away from major towns; a hardcopy map is a good backup. Gas station chains (Sheetz, Wawa, Rutter's) might be your best bet for food in remote regions.

Philadelphia
MAP P141

Discover world-changing documents

In the shadow of Independence Hall, the **National Constitution Center** (*constitutioncenter.org; adult/youth $19/15*) stands as a pilgrimage site for those seeking to understand democracy's roots and the challenges it faces.

The museum does a fantastic job dramatizing the US Constitution – an otherwise dry, dense document outlining the government's structure and the rights of citizens. Visits start with a theater-in-the-round presentation by a single actor explaining the evolution of the political experiment. 'The Story of We the People' exhibit narrates a captivating journey through the US Constitution. Interactive displays and multimedia presentations dive into detail about the founding

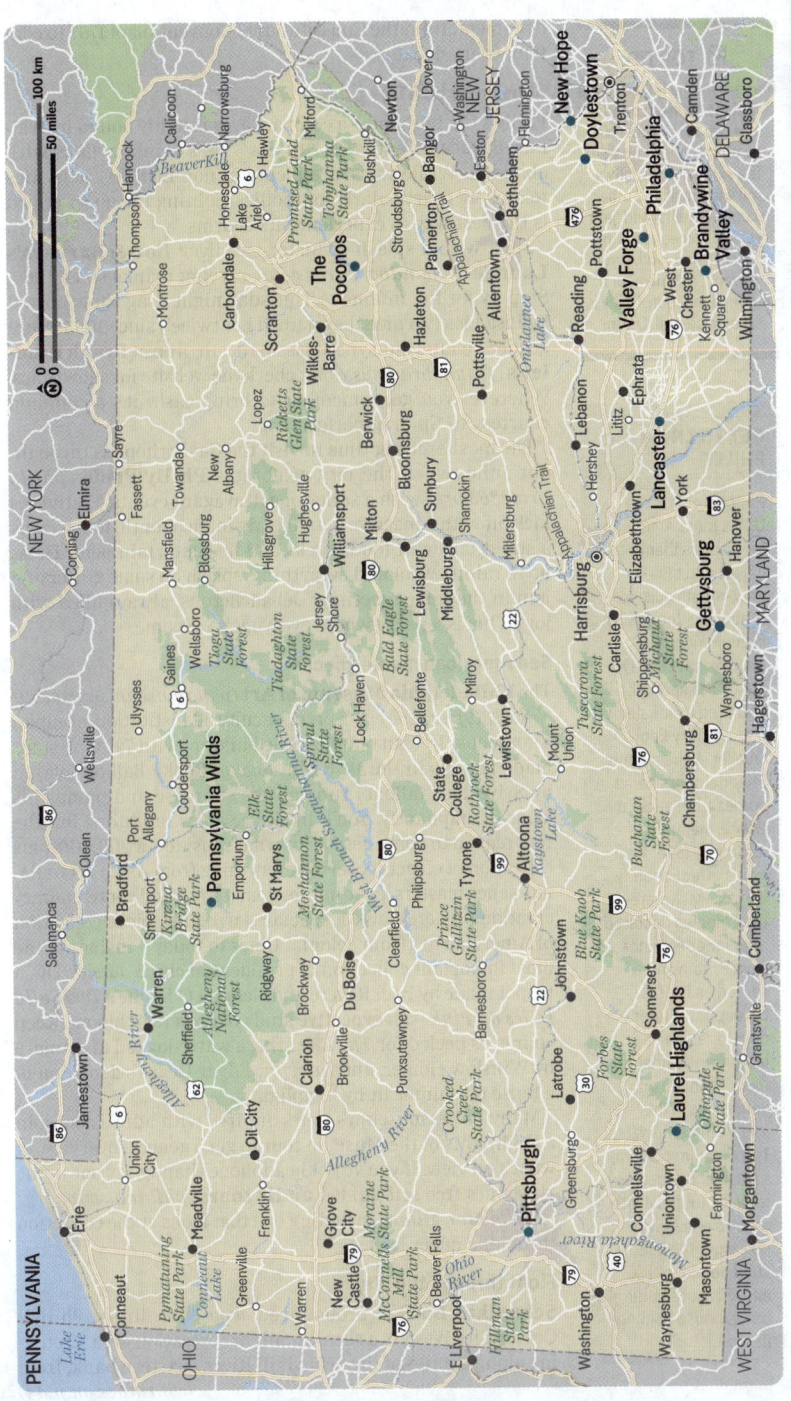

> ☑ **TOP TIP**
>
> Prepare for the Philadelphia dialect. 'Water' sounds like 'wooder,' 'youse' is the plural 'you,' a 'hoagie' is a sandwich (usually a roll with meat and other accoutrements) and 'jeet yet?' is someone asking if you've had food. If you haven't, ask them for a recommendation: Philly is foodie central. Dig in.

> **GET TO KNOW PHILLY**
>
> Philadelphia is the USA's most American metropolis thanks to it's art and melt-in-your-mouth cuisine, though it's the city's prominence in US history that usually steals the spotlight. Founded by idealistic 17th-century English Quaker William Penn, Philadelphia's name comes from ancient Greek, meaning 'brotherly love.' Philly, as it's affectionately known, was where the colonies declared their independence from Britain and served as the first US capital. It later developed into a leading industrial town, then fell on hard times in the mid-20th century. The economic boom, bust and 21st-century rebirth molded it into a scrappy survivor – no longer the middle child between NYC and DC, but a cultural powerhouse holding its own.

document, from the Constitutional Convention of 1787 to contemporary debates.

Show your LGBTQ+ pride

Philly's Gayborhood – a compact area roughly bound by Walnut, Spruce, Broad and 11th Sts – flies rainbow flags with abandon. While there are plenty of non-LGBTQ+ activities to do here (particularly for foodies), joining the queer crowd is the best way to experience its charms.

Start with a splash of history at divey **Bob & Barbara's Lounge** (bobandbarbaras.com), serving drinks since 1969. Stop by for the infamous Thursday night drag show hosted by Lisa Lisa ('so nice they named her twice') since 1995. More gender-bending lip-sync assassins death drop at **Frank Bradley's** (frankybradleys.com); check the website for showtimes. Wherever you go, remember to bring cash: it's a common courtesy to tip drag performers.

The most exciting time to visit the Gayborhood is throughout June, when the city celebrates **Philly Pride** (phillypride365.org) with a series of extravagant events. Festivities kick off with a massive march early in the month, followed by a street fair with food trucks and live entertainment. Dress up in rainbow-colored everything, splash on some glitter and join in the fun (sometimes debaucherous, always filled with joy). This is a party where everyone's welcome.

See American masterpieces

The **Philadelphia Museum of Art** (philamuseum.org; adult/child $30/free), the city's premier cultural institution, occupies a gorgeous Grecian temple–style building with 72 stone steps made famous in the 1976 film *Rocky*: Rocky Balboa (played by Sylvester Stallone) runs up the staircase and pumps his arms triumphantly. You'll likely see a few imitators. But the real reason to come here is for what's inside – a 200,000-plus collection of objects covering everything from Asian art to Renaissance masters, post-impressionist work and contemporary creations. There's also a spectacular 12,000-piece collection of American art from colonial times to today – including the most important collection of presidential china outside DC, a teapot made by Paul Revere and Georgia O'Keeffe's *Two Calla Lilies on Pink* – an evocative study of flowers in bloom. Keep your eyes peeled for *The Life Line*, a water-logged nightmare by Winslow Homer, and *Interior*, Edgar Degas's depiction of a tense encounter lit by lamplight.

Many of the museum's tours are free with admission; join a Highlights of the Museum tour to get a general overview of what's on view. If you've got headphones handy, try one of the museum's free self-guided **audio tours** (philamuseum.org/visit/visitor-guide), including one that looks at the collection through a queer lens.

Float through the city

Schuylkill Banks (pronounced *skool*-kill), lining Philly's Center City West, is a scenic outdoor recreation area stretching along 8 miles of the Schuylkill River's eastern bank, from

(continues on p144)

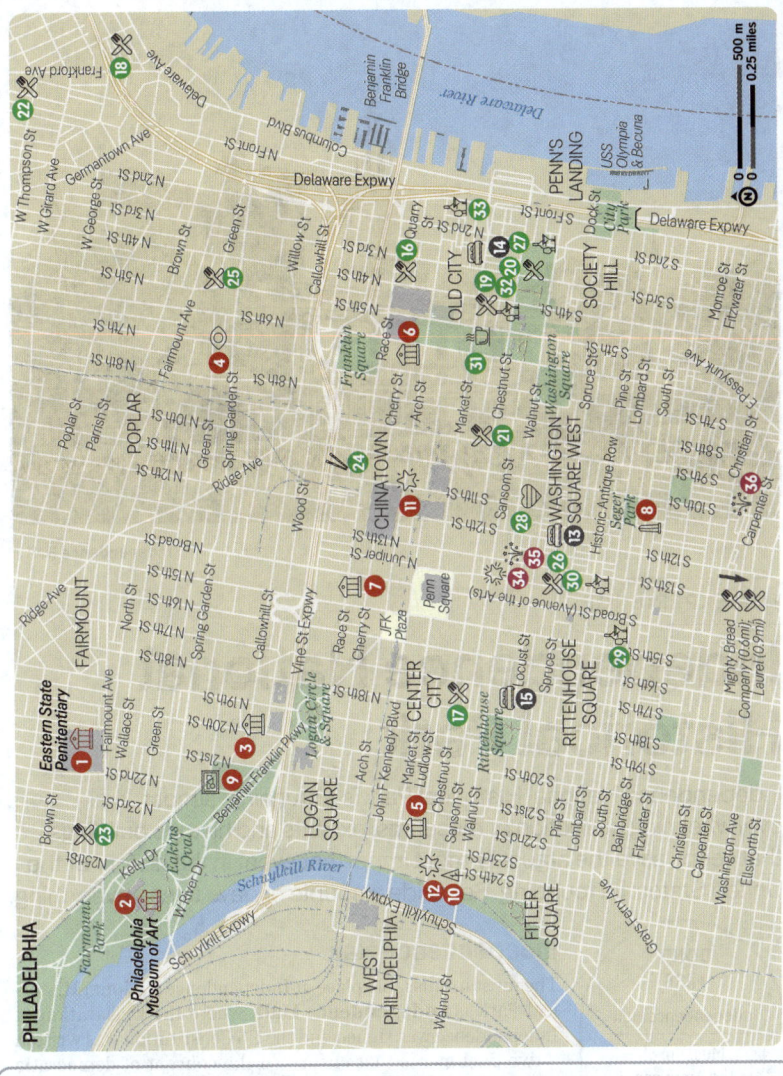

Independence Hall

TOP EXPERIENCE

Independence National Historical Park

Independence National Historical Park is a stunning, almost overwhelming collection of museums, exhibits and historic buildings that keeps alive the arguably most important event in the history of the United States: its founding. Set aside a couple of days to see everything.

DON'T MISS

Independence Hall

Museum of the American Revolution

Liberty Bell Center

Congress Hall

Benjamin Franklin Museum

Franklin Court

President's House Site

Independence Hall

The most unmissable place at Independence National Historical Park is **Independence Hall**, where the Declaration of Independence was signed and the US Constitution was written – two documents that enshrined the concept of democratic rule. Entry to this World Heritage site, a Georgian building that also served as the Pennsylvania State House, is by tour only. Inside, you'll visit the **Supreme Court Chamber**, which has been restored to look much as it did in those hallowed days of the country's founding.

PRACTICALITIES
- nps.gov/inde/index.htm
- hours vary by building; check the website
- free
- timed tickets required for tours; book ahead at nps.gov/inde/planyourvisit/fees.htm

Across the hall is the **Assembly Room**, with its photogenic green felt tabletops and hardwood chairs, where most of the building's notable events took place. The Declaration of Independence was approved here on July 4, 1776. George Washington sat in the chair at the center; Abraham Lincoln's body lay here in state for two days following his assassination in 1865.

Museum of the American Revolution

Enter this impressive, multimedia-rich **museum** *(amrevmuseum.org)* and virtually 'participate' in the American Revolution through interactive dioramas and 3D experiences, taking visitors from contentment with British rule to the eventual rejection of it. Learn about the events, people, cultures and religions that participated in one of the world's most important events. Lots of hands-on displays and video stories mean kids will have as much fun as adults. All entry tickets are timed; reserve them early online. A prime attraction is George Washington's battle tent, dramatically revealed after an engrossing presentation about it. Actors dramatize period scenes as well, though schedules vary. Check the website for details.

Liberty Bell Center

Originally called the State House Bell, the Liberty Bell was made in 1751 to commemorate the 50th anniversary of Pennsylvania's constitution. Mounted in Independence Hall, it tolled on the first public reading of the Declaration of Independence. The crack developed in the 19th century. The bell was retired in 1846 and now sits as the star attraction of the **Liberty Bell Center**.

Congress Hall

Near Independence Hall, **Congress Hall** served as the seat of the United States Congress from 1790 to 1800. It's where George Washington was inaugurated for his second term as president and John Adams took the oath of office as the nation's second president.

Franklin Court

The peaceful **Franklin Court**, accessible from Market and Chestnut Sts, is where Benjamin Franklin's home once stood. The house was demolished in 1812, but you can still get a good impression of its dimensions from the tubular steel 3D outline of the building designed by the architectural firm Venturi, Rauch and Scott Brown in 1976.

Benjamin Franklin Museum

The **Benjamin Franklin Museum** features a diverse collection of exhibits and artifacts related to his life and achievements. Explore interactive displays showcasing Franklin's inventions, scientific experiments and writings, including his famous Poor Richard's Almanack and contributions to the field of electricity. The exhibition, divided into five areas that focus on one of Franklin's traits, is cleverly laid out with interactive elements and plenty of famous quotations. In the courtyard, park rangers demonstrate the printing process Franklin would have used.

PRESIDENT'S HOUSE SITE

Across from the Liberty Bell Center, the **President's House Site** shows where the first two US presidents, George Washington and John Adams, had their presidential offices. Partially built redbrick walls mark the outlines of where the building once stood and frame a series of exhibits and archaeological remains that offer a window into the lives of the enslaved people who lived and worked here.

TOP TIPS

- Time your visit carefully to avoid crowds; weekday mornings are best.

- Consider bringing games for kids as lines can be long, including those for bathrooms.

- Bring snacks and plenty of water.

- You will be walking a lot, both inside the buildings and from spot to spot.

- Some exhibits (such as George Washington's tent) are only viewable as part of hourly timed viewings (every hour on the hour), but general admission includes this opportunity.

- The National Park Service can provide wheelchairs for loan.

- Check *nps.gov/inde* for any alerts and information.

GETTING AROUND PHILLY

Ditch the car: traffic and limited parking can make navigating the city nightmarish. The Old City's colonial-era streets are a pedestrian paradise. Take note: numbered streets generally run north–south; streets with tree names ('Walnut' etc) generally run east–west. For far distances, ride **SEPTA** (septa.org) – the city's bus, subway and trolley network. Purchase a day pass or SEPTA Key (a reusable, contactless card) to access the transport system. If you pay in cash, bring exact change. Philly also has a bikeshare program, **Indego** (rideindego.com; unlocking fee $4.50, plus 30¢ per ride, 24hr pass $15, plus 20¢ per ride), with options for single rides. Download the app to purchase passes, then cruise through town on over 200 miles of cycling lanes.

(continued from p140)

below the Fairmount Dam through a surprising location for a park: Philadelphia's tower-studded center.

One of the best ways to explore this urban oasis is on a guided kayak tour. Paddle with **Hidden River Outfitters** *(hiddenriveroutfitters.com; from $40)* to learn about the river's history and ecology from a seasoned guide. Prefer to float without effort? Riverboat tours are also available – check **Schuylkill Banks** *(schuylkillbanks.org/events/riverboat-tours; adult/child $25/12)* for dates.

Taste Philly's flavors

Reading Terminal Market *(readingterminalmarket.org)* isn't just a fancy grocer – it's a city institution dating back to 1893. The stalls attract everyone from blue-collar workers to billionaires, lured in by Philly's cultural melting pot of flavors. There are nearly 100 stalls – which may be overwhelming. Start with some favorites, then explore with your taste buds.

Dutch Eating Place sells Amish baked goods. **Hershel's East Side Deli** hocks juicy corned-beef sandwiches. **Pearl's Oyster Bar** serves freshly shucked oysters and snapping turtle soup. **Miller's Twist** is known for buttery pretzels. **Bassetts** is the country's oldest ice-cream company, established in 1861. If you wind up at **Sweet Nina's**, order the banana pudding. Note that Amish and Mennonite stalls are closed on Sundays.

EATING & DRINKING IN THE OLD CITY: BREAKFAST & LUNCH — MAP P141

Cafe Ole: The sunshine-yellow decor makes the great muffins, pastries and sandwiches taste even better. Great coffees, lattes and teas as well. *8am-6pm* **$$**

High Street Philadelphia: Fancy mushroom bowls, non-grain pasta and other delicious fare. *8am-5pm Mon, to 9pm Tue-Thu, to 9:30pm Fri & Sat, 10am-3pm Sun* **$$**

Fork: Seasonal, locally sourced ingredients are crafted into innovative dishes, and paired with a sophisticated atmosphere and excellent service. *11am-3:30pm & 5-9pm Tue-Sun* **$$$**

Forsythia: A French-inspired spot with plating as stunning to behold as it is to eat. Weekend brunch is sublime. *10:30am-2:30pm Sat & Sun, 5-10pm Mon-Sat, to 9pm Sun* **$$$**

Reading Terminal Market

A TASTE OF READING TERMINAL HISTORY

Philadelphia has always been a market city – but they weren't always indoors. So many outdoor markets once sprouted here that by the mid-1800s, residents complained about noise and unsanitary conditions. As a result, markets either closed or moved inside. The current Reading Terminal Market is the combined descendant of two markets once located on Market St's 1100 block. When the block was purchased by the Reading Railway, merchants refused to leave. After heated meetings between railway brass and merchant spokespeople, both sides reached a compromise: the vendors could stay. The market served Philadelphians for a century, until a decline in the 1970s forced closure. A newfound interest in farmer-grown fare rejuvenated the market to its current glory.

You could also snack while listening to Philly food lore on a 45-minute visit with **City Food Tours** (*phillysfoodtour.com; $25*). Tours begin at 10:30am and 2pm, starting with a snack and ending with an additional something to savor. During the tour, guests learn about the market's history as a guide spins colorful food-related yarns.

Eat tantalizing Italian in South Philly

In the late 19th century, Italian immigrants began settling in Philadelphia, mostly on 9th between Wharton and Fitzwater Sts. They brought with them culinary traditions, including a love for fresh produce, meats and cheeses.

As the Italian community grew, so did this **South 9th Street Italian Market** (*italianmarketphilly.org*), which became a hub for locals to purchase authentic Italian ingredients and goods. The market's fame expanded in the 1970s when it gained national attention through movies like *Rocky* and *Philadelphia*. It's also expanded beyond Italian goods and now includes shops from around the world. It even has a section known as Little Vietnam.

Today, visitors to the South 9th Street Italian Market can explore streets lined with vendors selling produce, seafood, meats, cheeses and pastries. Visit in mid-May for the annual **South 9th Street Italian Market Festival**. Highlights include the Procession of Saints and team attempts

DRINKING IN THE OLD CITY: BEST COCKTAILS, WINE & COFFEE — MAP P141

48 Record Bar: More casual than some of the Old City standbys, with a music-first vibe, friendly bartenders and creative cocktails. *5pm-2am, Tues-Sun*

National Mechanics: In the former Mechanics National Bank, now plying liquid gold – cocktails. *noon-10pm Mon & Tue, to midnight Wed, to 2am Thu & Fri, 10am-2am Sat, 10am-10pm Sun*

Panorama: Wine-focused restaurant with an extensive list of Italian wines, craft cocktails, classic Italian dishes and gorgeous city views. *5-9pm Tue-Thu, to 10pm Fri, 3-10pm Sat, to 9pm Sun*

La Colombe: A Philly chain gone big, La Colombe offers great specialty coffees, a signature 'draft latte' and excellent indie vibes. *7am-6pm*

PENNSYLVANIA, NEW YORK, NEW JERSEY & PENNSYLVANIA — THE GUIDE

FANTASTIC PHILLY MUSEUMS

Barnes Foundation: A reproduction of art collector Albert C Barnes' mansion holds a trove of work by Cézanne, Van Gogh and other European stars.

Rodin Museum: The only institution outside Paris devoted to French sculptor Auguste Rodin showcases 140 career-spanning pieces.

Mütter Museum: Dedicated to odd and disturbing medical conditions, this museum is not for the squeamish.

Pennsylvania Academy of the Fine Arts: Victorian Gothic architecture nearly overshadows what's inside: works by Winslow Homer, Andy Warhol, Mary Cassatt and more.

Edgar Allan Poe National Historic Site: Descend to the cellar of this small museum, which inspired Poe to write *The Black Cat* while living here.

Al Capone's cell, Eastern State Penitentiary

at climbing a 30ft pole greased with lard, with treats and money at the top.

Get spooked in a former prison

Eastern State Penitentiary (*easternstate.org; adult/child $21/17, cheaper if booked in advance*) is eerie year-round, but especially during Halloween, when the former prison transforms into a haunted attraction. It's worth a trip no matter the season. Beyond the spine-chilling setting, exhibits tackle issues like racial prejudice and overcrowding in the US, problems the nation continues to confront.

When it opened in 1829, the penitentiary was seen as a paragon of modern incarceration – praised by politicians, police officers and prison reformers alike. It offered something no other prison did at the time: solitary confinement, then seen as a miraculous solution to the unsafe practice of housing prisoners in dorms. But it was as costly as it was impressive, and as views on solitary confinement shifted, so did the prison's fortunes.

Though it housed infamous inmates like Al Capone and other high-profile criminals, Eastern State Penitentiary fell out of favor and began closing in 1960; it finally shuttered in 1971. Today, the empty cells, peeling paint and rusted bars

---

 EATING IN CHINATOWN & THE GAYBORHOOD: OUR PICKS — MAP P141

Nan Zhou Hand Drawn Noodle House: At this popular noodle shop, everything is good, but the bowls of cut noodles in savory broth are best. *11am-10pm* $

Vetri Cucina: One of Philly's priciest meals, this spectacular spot has a gourmet prix fixe that's divine. The wine pairings are highly recommended. *5-9pm* $$$

Dirty Franks: Friendly neighborhood bar with cheap drinks, dartboards and even reverse BYOB – bring your own food to eat with a beer from the bar. *1pm-2am Wed-Sun, from 4pm Mon & Tue*

Bike Stop: At this leather-and-chains gay biker bar, a Philly icon, it's not uncommon to see dudes walking around in a harness and little else. *4pm-2am Mon-Sat, from 2pm Sun*

are hauntingly photogenic – the kind of place that can pull you in for hours.

Marvel at mosaics

Philadelphia's Magic Gardens *(phillymagicgardens.org; adult/child $15/8)* is a South Philly folk-art wonderland that will mystify, mesmerize and perhaps even baffle. It's the ongoing life's work of mosaic mural artist Isaiah Zagar, who started beautifying the South St area with public installations in the 1960s. He started work on the Magic Gardens in 1994; the riot of artsy flotsam now covers half a block.

Zagar's psychedelic mirror murals, bottle walls and sculptures can be seen around the city; visiting the Magic Gardens helps you know what style to look for elsewhere. This spot also puts on small exhibitions of other artists' work, with a focus on mosaic and folk art by self-taught creatives. Guided tours *($25)* offer deeper insight into the museum itself, murals on surrounding blocks, or Zagar's 10,000-sq-ft Magic Gardens Studio – a mosaic-mired masterpiece about 25 minutes away on foot.

Brandywine Valley

Flowers and fountains in Kennett Square

The choreographed water-fountain shows at **Longwood Gardens** *(longwoodgardens.org; adult/youth $32/17, reservations required),* one of North America's largest and most spectacular petal palaces, blows even the Bellagio in Las Vegas away. Longwood occupies 1100 acres (400 open to the public) just outside the town of Kennett Square, an hour drive west of Philadelphia. Its superlatives include having the largest tulip collection outside the Netherlands, but no need to wait for spring blossoms. With one of the world's largest greenhouses and 11,000 kinds of plants, something is always in bloom.

Pierre du Pont, the great-grandson of the DuPont chemical-company founder, began designing this property in 1906 with the grand gardens of Europe in mind, especially those in France and Italy. In 2024, Longwood pumped $250 million into a new 17-acre makeover project, including the Mediterranean-inspired 'crystal palace,' designed to look like it's floating on water. The estate now has around 5 acres of glass-protected gardens, perfect for year-round exploration.

Horticulture heads will need a minimum of two hours to take it all in. Tickets don't allow you to leave and re-enter, so grab snacks and drinks at one of Longwood's eateries.

SEGREGATED CITY

Philadelphia is one of the most diverse cities in the US. It's also one of the most segregated. Among the nation's 30 biggest cities, Philly is second to Chicago in its level of residential segregation between Black and white residents, according to data collected by Brown University in 2021. In 2020, the Black Lives Matter movement brought renewed attention to these divisions. One of its targets was the statue of controversial former mayor and police commissioner Frank Rizzo, whose tough stance on crime led to deep rifts along racial lines. Activist Asa Khalif voiced the feelings of the wider Black community when he said the statue represented decades of oppression and violence. In 2020, the statue was removed from its prominent location facing City Hall.

EATING IN PHILLY: BRUNCH & LUNCH

MAP P141

Cleavers: Devour tasty cheesesteaks and a lot more at this popular sandwich spot using artisanal ingredients. *11am-9pm Sun-Wed, to 10pm Thu-Sat* **$$**

Little Pete's: Come to this spot near the Museum of Art for some of the finest Philly cheesesteaks in town, sold at reasonable prices. *7am-9pm* **$**

Silk City: A Spring Garden St fixture since the 1950s outfitted with classic diner booths and chrome. *4-10pm Mon-Wed, to 11pm Thu, to 2am Fri, 11am-2am Sat, to 10pm Sun* **$$**

Mighty Bread Company: Order to go and eat in nearby Columbus Square Park. The orange ricotta teacake is spectacular. *8am-6pm Mon, Thu & Fri, from 9am Sat & Sun* **$**

'SHROOM TOWN

That putrefying organic matter you smell around the Kennett Square area? It's the scent of money to mushroom farmers. Essentially a liquified manure and compost mix, it's the fertilizer that makes this area the 'mushroom capital of the world.' Legend says mushroom farming started here around 1880s, when two Quaker flower growers brought back some spores from Europe. These days, the region produces 60% to 64% of the country's mushrooms. Locals say they get used to the smell, but, periodically, their complaints lead to campaigns that pressure the industry to make changes. Mushrooms are fungi, so they're not grown outside like plants, but instead cultivated year-round inside 'mushroom houses.' **The Mushroom Cap** (themushroomcap.com) in Kennett Square sells locally produced mushrooms and mushroom-themed gifts.

Valley Forge
Washington's war refuge

Valley Forge National Historic Park *(nps.gov; free)* commemorates the 'birthplace of the Continental Army.' This is where, after the British occupation of Philadelphia, George Washington trained a rag-tag, short-term militia of nearly 12,000 into a cohesive force. It's also where 2000 continental soldiers died of disease and exposure during the famously devastating winter of 1777–78. That winter, Washington and the Continental Congress changed their recruitment strategy: they offered land and more money for those who'd commit to fight to the end.

Today, paths for cyclists and walkers border the park's 5.5 sq miles of rural beauty. Before taking to the trails or doing the self-guided audio tour, stop by the visitor center for some historical context. The scene is incongruously only minutes from the massive King of Prussia mall, which is about 45 minutes northwest of Philly. A 30-mile cycling path along the Schuylkill River connects Valley Forge to Philadelphia.

Doylestown
Museums dedicated to Henry Mercer

Henry Mercer was an archaeologist, ceramicist, amateur historian, inveterate traveler and polymath. He was also heir to his wealthy aunt's fortune, allowing him to indulge his passions and leave a lasting, eccentric and utterly fascinating legacy in Doylestown, an hour's drive north of Philly. His idiosyncratic architectural vision led to the construction of the 19,000-sq-ft, 44-room Gothic-Romanesque-Byzantine **Fonthill Castle** *(mercermuseum.org; adult/youth $20/10)*, where Mercer lived as a bachelor for 18 years until his death in 1930. The hour-long guided house tours reveal how every feature reflects Mercer's obsessive scholarly mind – like the 'main study,' with four working desks positioned for various periods of the day.

Next door, at the **Moravian Tile Factory** *(thetileworks.org; 30min tours from $15)*, is where Mercer established himself as 'America's foremost arts and crafts tile maker,' after fearing that pottery skills (and most others) were disappearing. The Spanish mission-style building houses a workshop with apprenticeships and residencies. It's also open to the public for enthusiastic tours, perfect for kids interested in playing with and molding clay *($75)*.

EATING IN PHILLY: UPSCALE DINNERS — MAPS P141

Dandelion: Great cocktails, a homey bar and excellent food like Welsh rarebit salutes the Union Jack. *11:30am-11pm Mon-Thu, to midnight Fri, 10am-midnight Sat, to 10pm Sun* $$

Laser Wolf: One of the neighborhood's top dining experiences in hip-and-happening Fishtown, with bold flavors and expertly crafted Middle Eastern dishes. *5-10pm* $$$

Laurel: Fancy French doesn't get much better, with menu options like black onion poached cod and duck with knotweed. Desserts look as spiffy as they taste. *5-10pm Tue-Sat* $$$

Elwood: Unique farm-to-table Pennsylvania Dutch dishes, like shad roe served on fine porcelain. Join weekends-only high tea. *5-9:30pm Thu & Fri, 11am-2pm & 5-9:30pm Sat & Sun* $$$

Valley Forge National Historic Park

But it's the one-of-a-kind **Mercer Museum** (mercermuseum.org; adult/youth $20/10), only a short drive away, that encapsulates Mercer's primary concern: postindustrial Americans were losing the knowledge and skills in how things were made. Look up upon entering the main building's six-story light-filled central hall. It's like a vision out of a Dr Seuss story, with every manner of object hanging from the walls and ceiling. Throughout, niches dedicated to every imaginable craft, from candlemaking to gunsmithing to beekeeping, are filled with tools and explanatory text on the crafts' history and evolution.

New Hope

Old charms in New Hope

Like its sister town Lambertville (p137), located across the Delaware River, New Hope is a quaint town that's overrun with visitors gorging at its cafes, ice-cream shops and restaurants between May and September. It all started as an artists' colony; Broadway playwright Moss Hart and lyricist Oscar Hammerstein both spent time here. Their influence lives on at the **Bucks County Playhouse** (bcptheater.org), a jewel-box theater presenting main-stage musicals and smaller cabarets

BEST WINERIES AROUND PHILLY

Penns Woods Winery: A family-run place with European-style blends and tastings paired with artisanal cheeses and meats.

Chaddsford Winery: Housed in a 17th-century dairy barn with a festive outdoor scene on weekends. Check out Brandywine River Museum nearby.

Va La Vineyards: A highly regarded and small-batch artisanal producer with more than two dozen varietals – mostly Italian, some fairly unique.

Wycombe Vineyards: A family-owned farm since the 1920s, it's relatively new to winemaking and offers friendly, personable attention during tastings.

Bishop Estate Vineyard & Winery: A charming farm-and-vineyard, with over two dozen varieties offered at tastings. Stay for the fire pits and live music.

 DRINKING IN PHILLY: MORE BARS

Ranstead Room: Look for the red lantern above a doorway, place your name on the reservations list, then wait to be escorted inside. *7pm–midnight Mon-Wed, to 2am Thu-Sat*

Harp & Crown: Upstairs has a long horseshoe bar; downstairs is a two-lane bowling alley and cozy gentleman's club–like space with leather armchairs. *4pm-midnight*

Monk's Cafe: Hops fans crowd this mellow wood-paneled place for Belgian and American craft beer – one of the best selections in the city. *11:30am-11:45pm Tue-Sun*

Philadelphia Distilling: Imbibe while learning how to craft great cocktails at this distillery and teaching lab. *4-10pm Thu, to 11pm Fri, 1-11pm Sat, to 9pm Sun*

WHERE TO SHOP IN NEW HOPE

Peddler's Village: Walk the lovely grounds of this outdoor 'mall,' lined with 60 boutiques and shops, many locally owned.

George Nakashima Woodworkers Studio: There are guided tours and floor pieces for sale at this internationally renowned furniture designer/craftsman's workshop.

Rice's Market: Flea market with indoor and outdoor spaces selling nearly everything, including antiques, clothing and fresh food.

Love Saves the Day: This smorgasbord of secondhand clothing, one-of-a-kind objects and other ephemera was formerly an East Village, NYC, mainstay.

Avigail Adam: This magical wonderland of a shop sells hand-crafted, ornately designed whimsical 'goddess' jewelry.

Central Market, Lancaster

throughout the year. Located between NYC and Philly, New Hope's abundance of sophisticated B&Bs makes it a favorite weekend getaway and a low-key alternative for LGBTQ+ travelers who aren't into party-hard Fire Island (p111). It's also ideal for a day trip: wander Main St to take it all in.

The Poconos
River tubing and waterfalls

The Pocono Mountains were once associated with cheesy TV ads featuring resorts with heart-shaped hot tubs for honeymooners. No longer. Today, charming towns like Milford, Hawley and Honesdale draw tourists from NYC and Philly, who flock to its idyllic forest trails and waterways. In summer, one of the best things to do here is tube down the Delaware River, rushing between NY's Catskills and PA's Poconos.

Tubing outfits like **Adventure Sports** (*adventuresport.com; from $53*) and **Kittatinny Canoes** (*kittatinny.com; from $40*) can drive you to a river-access point, rent you a tube, then pick you up further downstream. The current can be slow, which means you'll have to contend with some paddling. Expect to share the river with the occasional group of beer-chugging weekenders. Start early, set aside half a day and apply more sunblock than you think you should.

 EATING IN KENNETT SQUARE: OUR PICKS

La Michoacana: This place has been doling out homemade Mexican ice cream and popsicles for several decades. *noon-8pm* $

Market at Liberty Place: An excellent food court with Korean, Mediterranean, fried chicken and vegan offerings. *7am-10pm Sun-Thu, to 11pm Fri & Sat* $

Trattoria La Tavola: Exceptional Italian pastas, pizza, fish and meaty mains, along with tasty mushroom soup and fantastic service. *11:45am-9pm Sun-Thu, to 10pm Fri & Sat* $$

Talula's Table: This gourmet takeout cafe serves a highly sought-after eight-course tasting menu at dinnertime (booked out many months in advance). *7am-6pm* $$$

For dry land fun, it's easy to access several impressive waterfalls on PA's side of the Delaware. Most impressive is **Dingmans Falls**, the second tallest PA waterfall. The 130ft gusher comes into focus towards the end of a woodland walk along Dingmans Creek Trail, a 0.8-mile out-and-back boardwalk route.

Eat Scranton pizza

Often trotted out as shorthand for former President Joe Biden's working-class PA roots, Scranton – the largest city in the Poconos – is also known as the 'pizza capital of the world.' (Think twice before mentioning this to residents of NYC or New Haven, CT.) Some of the best spots are in Old Forge, just outside Scranton. Sample **Revello's** *(revellos.com)*, **Salerno's** *(salernoscafe.com)* or **Arcaro & Genell** *(arcaroandgenell.com)*, with its double-crusted white pizza that's a grilled cheese–pizza hybrid. In Exeter, a 20-minute drive from Scranton, taste test two very different styles: **Pizza L'Oven** *(pizzalovenexeter.com)* serves cheesy pan-fried Sicilian squares; **Sabatini's** *(sabatinis.com)* is more traditional, with a slightly sweet sauce.

In Scranton proper, try **Maroni's Pizza** *(maronispizza.com)* – a family-run favorite since 1982. For fans of *The Office* (set in Scranton), stop by **Alfredo's Cafe** *(alfredoscafe.com)* – it's referenced as the 'good pizza place' on the TV show.

Lancaster

Fun on the farm

The Amish are farmers, so it's no wonder the best things to do around lovely Lancaster relate to eating and enjoying the bucolic landscape's bounty. Spend a day getting your fill. For food, stop by Lancaster's **Central Market** *(centralmarketlancaster.com)* – the nation's oldest continually run farmers market, open since 1730. While not all vendors are Amish, nearly everyone has an interesting story to tell. Groff's Vegetables has been around for over seven decades. Kauffman Orchards is run by the family's fourth generation. Long's Horseradish has used the same grinder since 1889. S Clyde Weaver won awards for the best cheddar at the 2023 World Cheese Championship in Norway.

Learn more about the Pennsylvania Dutch simple life at **Amish Experience** *(amishexperience.com; adult/child from $26.95/19.95)* – a big operation along Old Philadelphia Pike. Choose your adventure: perhaps the informative guided

THE US NATIONAL BIRD

Look up while cruising the Delaware River and you might spot a bald eagle gliding above the treetops. With its white-feathered head, bright yellow beak and a wingspan sometimes reaching over 7ft, the bald eagle has symbolized American independence and strength since landing on the Great Seal in 1782. But by the mid-20th century, habitat loss and pesticide use brought the species to the brink of extinction. Thankfully, after decades of intensive restoration efforts, their numbers are once again soaring. Around 150 to 200 eagles winter in the Upper Delaware region, and every year, more stick around to rear their young throughout summer. They're not the only raptors enamored with the waterway: hawks, ospreys, kestrels and vultures all migrate through the area in spring and autumn.

 EATING IN DOYLESTOWN & NEW HOPE: OUR PICKS

Sprig & Vine: New Hope's all-vegan cafe serves innovative dishes like an oyster mushroom po'boy wrap and jerk-grilled tofu. *4-8:30pm Wed-Sat, 10am-2:30pm Sun* $$

Hattery Stove & Grill: Doylestown Inn's restaurant offers tacos, burgers, rack of lamb and a delicious pistachio-crusted salmon. *hours vary* $$

Terrain Cafe: Part of a Doylestown high-end garden center; offers a great daily 'brunch' and dinner complemented by an extensive wine selection. *11am-9pm Mon-Thu, 9am-10pm Fri-Sun* $$

Bowman's Tavern: This New Hope place has burgers and other elevated pub grub, along with live music nightly. *11:30am-9pm Tue-Sun* $$

BEST ARTISANAL SHOPS AROUND LANCASTER

Pennsylvania Guild of Craftsmen: Real-deal, well-curated Pennsylvania Dutch artisanal goods in Lancaster, with furniture, home decor, fabrics and kitchen goods.

Dutchland Galleries: High-quality original paintings by local artists, plus prints by well-known names, in Intercourse's Kitchen Kettle Village.

Mount Hope Wine Gallery: Join a tasting to sample its products, including Rumspringa craft beer and hard ciders.

Stoltzfus Meats: Specialty smoked meats, sausages and homemade bakery items.

Old Country Store: Locally handmade crafts (pillows, art, embroidery, quilts) and edibles like jam and canned goods.

minibus tour along backcountry roads or, our favorite, a visit to a working farmstead and home where you can chat and ask questions.

At **Old Windmill Farm** (oldwindmillfarm.com; from $22), 20 minutes from Lancaster, you can pet animals, milk a cow, go on a hayride and jump around a ball-pit-style barn filled with corn.

Gettysburg
The Civil War's bloodstained battlefield

This tranquil town, surrounded by rolling hills 55 miles west of Lancaster, is synonymous with one of the bloodiest conflicts in American history: the Civil War's 1863 Battle of Gettysburg. Over 50,000 people lost their lives, and the southern state–led Confederacy never recovered. Historians consider it the war's turning point. Later that year, President Abraham Lincoln delivered one of his most eloquent and powerful speeches – the 'Gettysburg Address' ('Four score and seven years ago...') – reinforcing the Union's mission of equality.

Tours of the **Gettysburg National Military Park** (gettysburgmuseum.com; tours up to 6 people from $82) last two to three hours, best done privately in your car with a licensed guide. The expert drives and talks, telling a detailed account of the fighting. Other options are downloadable audio tours and bus tours with guides.

The **museum** (adult/child $18/9) at the visitor center is a must-see, chronicling the war from its onset to Lincoln's assassination. Set aside a couple hours. Rangers also lead several free tours daily, including a 'history hike' and a cemetery visit. Check the visitor center's digital board for details.

Pennsylvania Wilds
Wow over Pennsylvania's Grand Canyon

The PA Wilds is a collection of deep forests, winding rivers and ancient mountains stretching over 3100 sq miles across the state's northern boundary. It's sparsely dotted with tiny, self-sufficient towns and the occasional lodge for hunting and fishing. It's worth passing through between spring and autumn to see Pine Creek Gorge – a 45-mile-long chasm plunging to depths of 1500 ft – dubbed the 'Grand Canyon of Pennsylvania.'

Views from behind the gorge's western side, near the visitor center at **Leonard Harrison State Park** (pa.gov), are more

EATING IN HONESDALE & HAWLEY: OUR PICKS

Be Kind Bakehouse: Casey Zier, Honesdale's best baker, makes inventive sweets from scratch, like pine needle cookies and blueberry-lavender cream pies. *9am-4pm Wed-Sat* $

Scarfalloto's Town House Diner: A popular Honesdale place with classic diner menu, portions and decor, with a toy train running throughout near the ceiling. *6am-8pm Wed-Mon* $

Dyberry Forks: This chef-run bistro in Honesdale has a wide-ranging menu, from chicken parma and burgers to sushi and ramen. *5-9pm Wed-Sun* $$

Glass: Eat out on the deck for stunning waterfall views in Hawley while enjoying anything from a porterhouse to a variety of small dishes. *5-9pm* $$$

Leonard Harrison State Park

panoramic than what you'll see on the east. To admire the gorge, hike the short-but-challenging Turkey Trail, a 2-mile out-and-back trek starting to the right of Leonard Harrison's visitor center. It descends to the valley floor, passing several waterfalls. At the bottom of the gorge is the **Pine Creek Rail Trail**, a mostly flat 62-mile former railroad bed that's good for cycling, hiking and even a kid-friendly **Ole Covered Wagon ride** (olecoveredwagon.com; adult/child $40/20). Stop by **Pine Creek Outfitters** (pinecrk.com) on Rte 6 near the park's visitor center: it's a one-stop-shop for all outdoor needs, including bike, kayak and canoe rentals.

See what's blooming in Kane

The quaint town of Kane, two hours between Pine Creek Gorge and Pittsburgh by car, is all mom-and-pop shops hidden in the Allegheny National Forest. Civil War General Thomas Kane founded the town in 1863 and built the Georgian Revival–style **Kane Manor Inn** (kanemanorinn.com) – an 18,000-sq-ft mansion from 1896, now a gorgeous B&B and the best place to stay in town.

These days, **Wilds Sonshine Factory** is putting Kane on the map as one of the world's few producers of sunflower spirits (wildssonshinefactory.org) – an earthy, honey-hinted liquor.

GETTYSBURG'S GREATEST FESTIVALS

Gettysburg Festival of Races: An April weekend of long-distance running through the battlefield's roads and fields.

Gettysburg Bluegrass Festival: Mid-May and mid-August weekends of top-flight contemporary and traditional bluegrass, in a farmland location.

Battle of Gettysburg Anniversary: The first week of July sees book signings, talks and other events.

National Apple Harvest Festival: Held on the first two weekends in October in Biglerville; celebrates apples with great food and live music.

Remembrance Day & Dedication Day: There's a history reenactors parade, talks and more on November 11 and 19 (the latter being the anniversary of Lincoln's cemetery address).

 EATING AROUND GETTYSBURG: OUR PICKS

Hollabaugh Bros: Stop by this lovely farmers market in Biglerville for sandwiches, pastries and fresh produce. *9am-5pm Mon-Sat, from noon Sun* $

Blessing: Slip into a comfy booth for a variety of Mexican dishes. The juicy birria tacos are a must. *10:30am-8:30pm Wed-Mon* $

Dobbin House: Gettysburg's oldest building houses this atmospheric restaurant, offering hefty portions of crab cakes and strip steaks. *11:30am-9pm* $$$

Hickory Bridge Farm Restaurant: Reserve a table for family-size portions of country-style fare at this B&B restaurant outside Gettysburg. *4pm-8pm Fri & Sat, 11:30am-3pm Sun* $$$

THAT'S SO PITTSBURGH

From slang like 'jag-off' (idiot) and 'yinz' (you all) to its singular food culture, Pittsburgh is proudly and defiantly distinct. One of its most iconic food offerings is the Primanti sandwich: two pieces of Mancini Italian bread stuffed with pastrami or roast beef, french fries and coleslaw. Its origins are labor related – it was basically a way for truck and train drivers to grab a full meal on the go without stopping work, as it could be held and eaten with one hand. Then there's the pickle-making Heinz legacy, which lives on in **Picklesburgh** (picklesburgh.com). This downtown July festival is dedicated to all things pickled: pickle pizza, pickle beer and even pickle doughnuts. Plastic vomit bags are kept on standby during the pickle-juice drinking contest. You've been warned.

A visitor center describes how sustainability and natural-resource conservation guided the project.

Stop by at night or weekends for a specialty cocktail at the bar and tasting room. The bar boasts the world's longest table made from a single piece of wood, carved from Pennsylvania's state tree, the Eastern hemlock. Ask to check out the nearby fields between mid-August and September, when sunflowers typically bloom.

Pittsburgh

MAP P155

Meet the Yinzers

Get to know Yinzers (a nickname for Pittsburghers) at this Smithsonian-affiliated **Heinz History Center** (heinzhistorycenter.org; adult/youth $20/11) with galleries spread across a six-story former ice warehouse. Interactive exhibits explore the classic PBS children's show *Mister Rogers*, filmed in town, and Heinz, the home-grown company behind the iconic ketchup. History buffs will appreciate galleries tracing the French and Indian War, which raged here in the 1700s, and a ground-floor exhibit honoring prominent local women. Sports fans: head straight to the floor with memorabilia celebrating Pittsburgh's beloved Steelers, Penguins and Pirates.

Feast on the Strip

Eating around Pittsburgh's Strip is a must-taste experience. This half-square-mile district north of downtown is peppered with dining institutions, offering an edible history of Pittsburgh's working-class comfort food. Visit on weekends, when it's the liveliest place in town.

One of the strip's anchor restaurants is **Primanti Bros** (primantibros.com), a Great Depression–era stalwart famous for adding fries to sandwiches. It's nearly impossible to grab a table when one of the city's sports teams is playing. **Jimmy & Nino Sunseri Co** (sunserisinthestrip.com), open since 1985, boasts the best pepperoni roll in the city. The spot gets so crowded in summer that the rolls are sold on the street; ask for the pepper-stuffed 'atomic roll.' Bubblegum-pink **Pamela's Diner** (pamelasdiner.com) is a favorite of former President Obama, known for its fruit-flavored pancakes.

The specialty markets and food halls are also worth sampling: there's **Novo Asian Food Hall** (novoasianfoodhall.com) for Japanese, Korean and more and **Wholey Fish Market**

EATING IN KANE: OUR PICKS

Texas Hot Lunch: A family-run place since 1914, with classic diner fare and Greek dishes like souvlaki and pita sandwiches. *7am-9pm* $

Bell's Meat & Poultry: Cobble together a lunch from this market's variety of cheeses and sausages, or Swedish specialities like pickled herring and crispbreads. *9am-5pm* $

Table 105: A casual, upscale eatery with artisanal pizza, juicy steaks and creatively conceived fish dishes. Sushi on Wednesday nights. *11am-9pm* $$

Flickerwood Wine Cellars: Thursday is pasta night; otherwise it's appetizers, charcuterie and subs served with the made-in-house wine. *noon-5pm Mon-Thu, 11am-9pm Fri & Sat, noon-6pm Sun* $$

PITTSBURGH

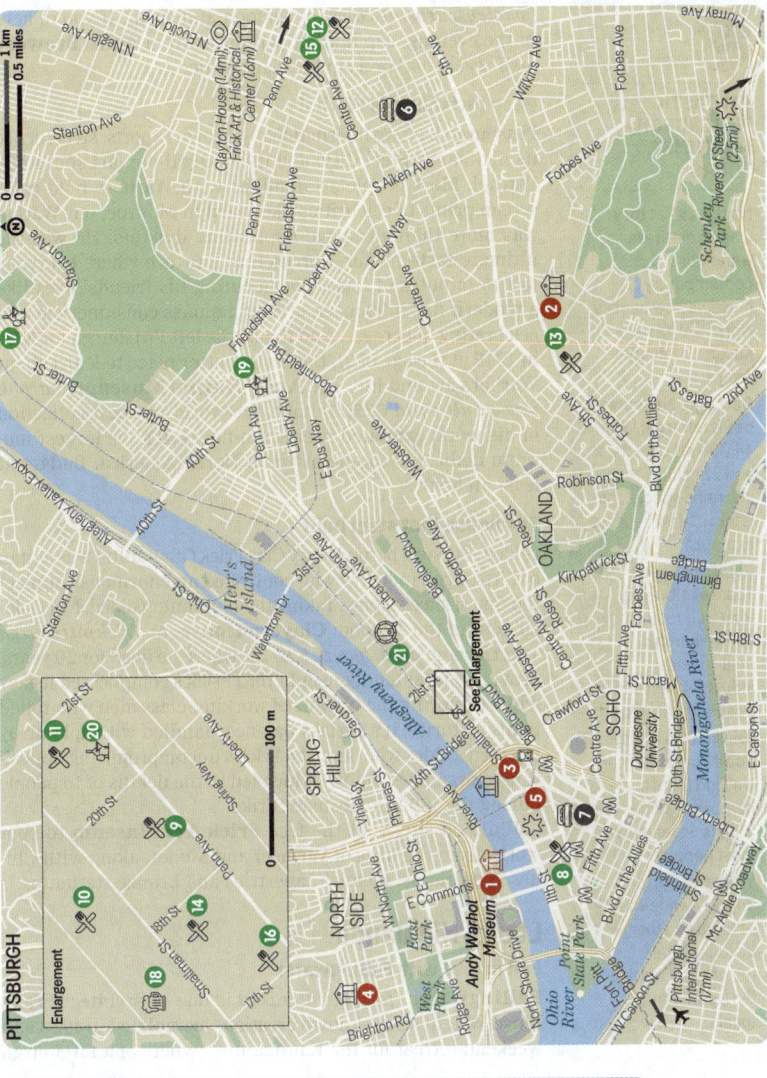

★	**HIGHLIGHTS**
1	Andy Warhol Museum
	SIGHTS
2	Carnegie Museums
3	Heinz History Center
4	Mattress Factory
	ACTIVITIES
5	Walk the Burgh Tours
	SLEEPING
6	Inn on Negley
7	Monaco
	EATING
8	Con Alma
9	Jimmy & Nino Sunseri Co
10	Novo Asian Food Hall
11	Pamela's Diner
12	Paris 66
13	Porch at Schenley
14	Primanti Bros
15	Square Café
16	Wholey Fish Market
	DRINKING & NIGHTLIFE
17	Allegheny Wine Mixer
18	Aslin Brewery
19	Brillobox
20	Lefty's
21	Wigle Whiskey Distillery

155

NEW YORK, NEW JERSEY & PENNSYLVANIA PENNSYLVANIA

THE GUIDE

FANTASTIC PITTSBURGH MUSEUMS & TOURS

Mattress Factory: Once a mattress warehouse, this contemporary art museum now houses works like Yayoi Kusama's infinity rooms.

Carnegie Museums of Pittsburgh: With 44,000 art objects and 22 million scientific specimens, it takes a few hours to explore.

Rivers of Steel: Tours explore the Rust Belt remnants of Pittsburgh's coal-fueled industrial past and postindustrial rebirth.

'Burgh Bits & Bites Food Tours: Culinary walking tours of a number of 'hoods; the Strip is deservedly most popular.

Walk the Burgh Tours: A wide variety of tours and themes, including films, history and whiskey, led by longtime locals.

(wholeyscurbside.com) for seafood and sushi. If you're here in the evening, cap it all off with beer from **Aslin Brewery** *(aslinbeer.com)* or a sip the 'daddy juice'.

Peep Pittsburgh's Warhols

Pittsburgh has two internationally known exports: steel (hence its nickname, Steel City) and its prodigal pop-art son, Andy Warhol. Most people are familiar with Warhol's bold-color screen prints of celebrities like Marilyn Monroe, but Warhol was more than an image-duplicating dynamo. He was the ultimate taste maker – predicting a future where everyone has 15 minutes of fame, documenting his friends' lives like a modern-day influencer, critiquing mass consumerism and celebrating queerness. And though he left Pittsburgh for NYC in 1949 at the age of 21, there's no better place to learn about Warhol's art and life. The **Andy Warhol Museum** *(warhol.org; adult/child $25/13)* holds the world's largest collection of his work, exhibited over seven floors. It's the largest museum dedicated to one artist in North America. Budget at least an hour.

The house that steel built

Gilded Age steel baron Henry Clay Frick (1849–1919) was a titan of Pittsburgh industry who controlled an enormous chunk of the American economy. Taking the 75-minute 'Gilded, Not Golden' tour of the 22-room **Clayton House** *(thefrickpittsburgh.org/clayton; adult/youth $22/12)*, where he lived for 20 years, provides enlightening insight into Frick's complicated legacy while exploring the travails of working-class men who toiled in his factories. It's a tricky balance, handled with aplomb by talented guides who describe Frick's uncompromising opposition to organized labor – which led to the deaths of 16 people during the 1892 Homestead Strike.

While on site, visit the free **Frick Art Museum** to spot works from the likes of Vermeer and Monet, along with Chinese porcelains, Flemish tapestries and bronze statuettes.

Laurel Highlands

Fall in love with Fallingwater

Fallingwater *(fallingwater.org)* is one of architect Frank Lloyd Wright's best-known creations, completed in 1938 as a weekend retreat for the Kaufmanns, owners of a Pittsburgh

---

 EATING IN PITTSBURGH: OUR PICKS — MAP P155

Square Café: Sunny East Liberty cafe with elevated diner food like brussels sprouts hash, banana foster waffles and strawberry Nutella crepes. *7am-3pm Wed-Mon* **$**

Con Alma: Equally notable for its Latin-inspired menu and its top-flight jazz musicians. Sip excellent cocktails while savoring it all. *5-10pm Mon-Sat, 4-9pm Sun* **$$**

Porch at Schenley: Ingredients from local gardens get served with flair in a casual-chic setting with a weekday happy hour. *7am-10pm Mon-Fri, from 10am Sat & Sun* **$$**

Paris 66: Order top-end French fare like *coq au vin* and steak frites while sitting in this cozy bistro. *3-9pm Wed-Fri, from noon Sat, 10am-2pm Sun* **$$$**

Andy Warhol Museum

department store. Tucked between two ridges of the Allegheny Mountains, 90 minutes south of Pittsburgh near Ohiopyle State Park, Wright wanted the home to look like it sprouted from the surrounding forest. Concrete cantilevers appear as continuations of rocky outcroppings over a waterfall, audible in every room. An ice-cold plunge pool, steps down from the living room, sits in a pristine trout stream. It's the epitome of Wright's organic architecture, blending human life with the natural world. Standard guided tours last an hour; reservations should be made far in advance. Tours of the grounds cost $18; the must-do architecture tour is $39. The house is closed in January, February and the beginning of March. An on-site cafe serves drinks and snacks.

Kentuck Knob (kentuckknob.com; adult/student $30/18), another Wright house, is also worth a visit, located 7 miles southwest of Fallingwater. Designed in 1953 and built into the side of a rolling hill, it's notable for its hexagonal design and honeycomb skylights. After a guided house tour, check out the panoramic views of the Youghiogheny River gorge and take the woodland trail passing around 30 sculptural works.

BEST HIKES IN OHIOPYLE STATE PARK

Visit *pa.gov* for more park info.

Ferncliff Trail: A short loop trail that's just over the bridge from Ohiopyle village, on the peninsula's and river's edge, with views of falls.

Great Gorge Trail: A popular 1.8-mile loop easily accessible from Ohiopyle, partly along old train tracks, with river views and spring wildflowers.

Baughman & Sugarloaf Trail Loop: Combining two routes into a 5.3-mile adrenaline pumper with a relatively steep ascent and descent. Do it for views from the overlook.

Old Mitchell Loop: A peaceful, meandering 2.2 miles through forests, past waterfalls and along meadows good for birding.

Laurel Highlands Hiking Trail: Overnight at shelters every 10 miles while hiking 70 miles along the Youghiogheny River from Ohiopyle to the Conemaugh Gorge.

 DRINKING IN PITTSBURGH: OUR PICKS

Lefty's: The city's dingiest dive bar has cup holders nailed to the wall. Crowds spill out onto the street in warm weather. *12:30pm-midnight*

Allegheny Wine Mixer: This high-end Lawrenceville wine bar has an extensive menu, smart staff and tasty nibbles. *5pm-midnight Tue-Thu & Sun, to 1am Fri & Sat*

Wigle Whiskey Distillery: Come to this North Side whiskey maker to sample the honey-colored liquor. *11am-7pm Mon & Tue, to 9pm Wed & Thu, to 10pm Fri & Sat, to 4pm Sun*

Brillobox: A busy Lawrenceville spot with live music, open-mic events and DJs, plus vegetarian-friendly food and a decent beer selection. *5pm-2am Tue-Sat*

Places We Love to Stay

$ Budget $$ Midrange $$$ Top End

New York City
MAPS P74, P78, P82, P89, P93, P102

Jane Hotel (West Village) $ Ship-cabin-sized rooms were initially constructed for sailors in 1908; *Titanic* survivors stayed here in 1912. Now it's a haunt for out-of-town hipsters.

Freehand (Midtown) $ Arty, affordable and located between Union Square and Midtown. Save bucks by bunking four to a room, or spread out with a king.

Harlem Flophouse (Harlem) $ Old-school style works its charm inside this Victorian brownstone, 15 minutes' walk north of Central Park. Most rooms share a bathroom, complete with antique claw-foot tubs.

Pod Brooklyn (Williamsburg) $ The perfect crash pad after a Brooklyn all-nighter.

Romer (Midtown) $$ It's a skip to Broadway, Central Park and Ninth Ave's glut of international restaurants. The best part: sage-green rooms provide a tranquil escape from Midtown mayhem.

Public Hotel (Lower East Side) $$ Studio 54's disco days are over, but you can still stay up all night in the neon glow of club co-founder Ian Schrager's slick, minimalist digs.

Hotel Chelsea (Chelsea) $$$ This iconic bohemian hang for big-name artists (Hendrix, Mapplethorpe, Madonna) got a plush 2022 revamp. Raise a glass to their ghosts in the Lobby Bar.

Crosby Street Hotel (SoHo) $$$ Vibrant patterns and colorful splashes adorn every room, making this serene hotel seem like it was plucked from a glossy fashion magazine.

Wythe Hotel (Williamsburg) $$$ With fab on-site French brasserie Le Crocodile, this factory-turned-upscale-hotel brings Parisian elegance to an industrial space.

New York State
MAP P110

Nest Hudson (Hudson) $ Rooms inside this 1920s arts-and-crafts-style building are tiny, but you'll likely spend your time strolling around Hudson's main drag, two blocks away.

Urban Cowboy Lodge (Central Catskills) $$ Step inside a Pendleton ad at this creekside lodge with a hearty on-site restaurant, forest footpath, wood sauna and antlers galore.

Herwood Inn (Woodstock) $$ All four rooms in this cheery lodge pay tribute to iconic female musicians (Joni Mitchell, Stevie Nicks etc); a 15-minute stroll from Woodstock's epicenter.

Daunt's Albatross Motel (Montauk) $$ Spartan but stylish: slate-gray floors, sea-green tiles and blonde wood like fine sand, designed to match Montauk's South Edison Beach two blocks away. Fantastic value.

Breakers (Montauk) $$ Whitewashed walls seem sun-bleached, just like the surrounding landscape as it spills into the ocean. Private cottages give 'summer camp' vibes. Walkable to Montauk restaurants.

Lodge at Schroon Lake (The Adirondacks) $$ Hotel rooms, private chalets and glamp sites nod to the region's 19th-century Great Camps above this lesser known, but no less stunning, Adirondacks lake.

Firelight Camps (Finger Lakes) $$ Glamp on the edge of Buttermilk Falls State Park in safari-style tents with plush bedding, balconies and electric heaters for cool nights.

Richardson Hotel (Buffalo) $$ Don't worry about ghosts inside this Gothic fortress, originally built as a 19th-century insane asylum – contemporary comforts ensure everyone sleeps soundly.

DeBruce (Western Catskills) $$$ It's hard to choose between Foster Supply Hospitality's five idyllic retreats, each catering to various budgets. Plus points here: exceptional food and Livingston Manor proximity.

Roundhouse (Beacon) $$$ With minimalist rooms overlooking Fishkill Creek and Main St, it's hard to believe this serene space once whirred with 19th-century manufacturing equipment.

Sagamore Resort (The Adirondacks) $$$ An icon of Lake George luxury since 1883, comprising a Colonial Revival mansion and multi-unit lodges perched on Green Island.

Inns of Aurora (Finger Lakes) $$$ This campus of historic homes revamped as cozy, museum-worthy accommodations is the pearl of Cayuga Lake; serene spa and top-tier restaurants included.

New Jersey

Hugh Inn (Cape May) $$ The eight individually designed rooms here have a mix of Victorian original detail and contemporary glam with bold colors. A sophisticated French bistro is attached.

Pan American Hotel (Wildwood) $$ Every room in this stylish retro air-travel-themed hotel has a balcony and sea views. There's a new restaurant, heated outdoor pool and fire pit.

St Laurent Social Club (Asbury Park) $$ The stylish rooms here feature fold-down beds and designer surfboards. There's a pool and bar, and the restaurant is one of the best around.

Inn at Glencairn (Princeton) $$ Five serene rooms in a renovated Georgian manor with old-world style and modern amenities.

Lambertville House (Lambertville) $$ The rooms here creak with age, but the four-poster beds, immaculate wooden furniture and lobby bar make up for it. Located in the heart of town.

Pennsylvania MAPS P141, P155

Apple Hostels (Philadelphia) $ The apple-green color scheme fits the name, but this Hosteling International–affiliated place is also strong on details such as kitchens, lounges and power outlets in lockers.

Alexander Inn (Philadelphia) $ Impeccably kept rooms have a subdued, slightly vintage style; some have old-fashioned half-size tubs. Original architectural details, including stained-glass windows, oak moldings and marble-tiled floors, add to the atmosphere.

Monaco (Pittsburgh) $$ This good downtown choice has exceptionally stylish room decor and a recommended basement restaurant.

Inn on Negley (Pittsburgh) $$ A Shadyside place with all the amenities and first-name-basis friendliness of a quiet B&B.

Porches on the Towpath (New Hope) $$ This cozy Victorian is relatively secluded, with porches, canal views and uniquely designed main-house rooms and others in an atmospheric 19th-century carriage house.

Darby (Poconos) $$ This stylish boutique lodging is located just over a bridge and the Delaware River from Narrowsburg, NY.

Rough Cut Lodge (PA Wilds) $$ Conveniently close to the PA 'Grand Canyon,' this place has homey room suites on one side of the road and more lodge-style riverside options on the other.

Red Caboose Motel (PA Dutch Country) $$ A fun novelty hotel between Lancaster and Philly, these motel rooms are wedged into a colorful collection of caboose cars.

Gettysburg Battlefield B&B (Gettysburg) $$ This atmospheric Civil War–era farmhouse has a wide variety of room configurations, morning 'history talks' and evening 'ghost talks.'

Franklin on Rittenhouse (Philadelphia) $$$ This 1911 mansion is a fine choice for small and local luxury. The place mixes old-world sophistication with contemporary touches, and its location can't be beat.

Wythe Hotel (p102), Williamsburg

For places to stay in New England, see p240

Above: Plimoth Patuxet Museum (p183); Right: Freedom Trail (p172)

THE MAIN AREAS

BOSTON
Revolutionary history and innovative artistry.
p166

MASSACHUSETTS
Dune-backed beaches, whale-watching and the Berkshire Mountains.
p184

RHODE ISLAND
Where land and sea are intertwined.
p194

Researched and curated by
Mary Fitzpatrick

New England

QUAINT VILLAGES, COLONIAL HISTORY AND ATLANTIC SHORELINE

Whether hiking amid spectacular fall foliage, spotting whales along the coast, exploring cosmopolitan Boston or immersing yourself in the region's past, New England never fails to captivate.

In the beginning were the Wampanoag, Abenaki and other First American peoples. Then came the Pilgrims at Plymouth Rock, the Revolutionary War's minutemen, abolitionist heroes, enslaved people seeking sanctuary along the Underground Railroad, and free-spirited thinkers and immigrants from almost every corner of the globe. Today, all these and more make up New England's rich cultural and historical mosaic. The region's history is the USA's history, and its images – of single-spired churches on manicured town greens, wave-battered lighthouses, cobbled streets and lobster pots stacked on wooden piers – have become iconic images of the country.

The musings of New England's poets and philosophers and its unparalleled collection of universities underpin a long tradition of progressive thinking and independent minds. Its museums and urban architecture showcase a dynamic artistic and cultural diversity. And then there is the scenery, which alone would be worth a visit. On the coast are small harbors, sandy coves, graceful windjammers, rugged islands and myriad kayaking spots. Inland are lively towns, rolling hills dotted with a patchwork of farms and orchards, winding lanes with old covered bridges and the Adirondack Mountains, beckoning outdoor adventure with their jagged peaks, blazing foliage and wealth of hiking paths and ski trails. Picturesque inns and B&Bs, and a thriving farm-to-table dining culture featuring abundant produce, locally made cheese and fresh seafood, make overnighting and eating a delight too.

WILLIAN SILVER/SHUTTERSTOCK

CONNECTICUT
Charming shoreline, river valleys and vibrant cities.
p201

VERMONT
Four-season celebration of nature.
p210

NEW HAMPSHIRE
Mountains, lakes and historic town centers.
p222

MAINE
North America's dramatic coastline.
p229

THE GUIDE

Find Your Way

New England packs so much into a relatively compact area. Pick a base or two and explore from there. Trains, buses and even ferries reach some major highlights, but you'll need a car to discover the region in-depth.

Maine, p229
Much more than a land of lobsters and lighthouses, Maine has enchanting seaside towns, remote island getaways and plentiful adventures on land and sea.

New Hampshire, p222
It's easy to fall for the Granite State, a gem of small, vibrant towns; expansive state parks and New England's highest mountains.

Vermont, p210
Lake Champlain and the Green Mountains provide a splendid backdrop for Vermont's historic villages, small farms and year-round opportunities for outdoor recreation.

TRAIN

You'll find trains along the coastal corridor and a few scenic routes in rural areas. **Amtrak's** (amtrak.com) **Downeaster** runs from Boston's North Station to Brunswick (Maine) via Exeter (New Hampshire) and Portland (Maine); its **Lake Shore Limited** and **Vermonter** trains serve destinations in Massachusetts, Rhode Island, Connecticut and Vermont.

BUSES, TAXIS & RIDESHARES

The T is Boston's subway/underground system. City buses also provide transportation – within Boston and in other big cities. Some areas have regional bus lines. Taxis and Uber are common in the largest cities, but you'll probably have to phone a cab in smaller towns.

BUS

Greyhound (greyhound.com) and regional carrier **Peter Pan** (peterpanbus.com) provide services within New England. Other bus companies plying routes within the region include **Concord Coach Lines** (concordcoachlines.com), with services from Boston to destinations in New Hampshire and Maine.

Boston, p166

With its rich history, grand architecture and world-renowned academic and cultural institutions, Boston makes a big splash for a mid-sized city.

Rhode Island, p194

The country's smallest state inspires big passion for local seafood, history and innovation, and 400 miles of coastal adventures.

Connecticut, p201

Follow meandering rock walls – first laid in the late 18th century to clear farmland – to historic cities, quaint coastal towns and industrial hubs.

Massachusetts, p184

Visit Cape Cod, New England's premier seaside destination, and explore central and western Massachusetts' artful mix of cultural, cosmopolitan, rural and rustic.

THE GUIDE

NEW ENGLAND

Plan Your Time

Summer is wonderful, but visiting in spring or late fall helps to avoid congested coastal roads and crowds. Away from the ski resorts, note that many places close in the winter off-season.

Cadillac Mountain (p236)

Pressed for Time

With less than a week in New England, split your time between Boston and Cape Cod. In **Boston** (p166), begin with a dip into the region's past by walking along the **Freedom Trail** (p172) and discovering the **Black Heritage Trail** (p175) before visiting the **Museum of Fine Arts** (p177) and the **Boston Athenaeum** (p175); the city has plenty more great museums to sample. Afterwards, find more Revolutionary history around **Concord and Lexington** or visit storied **Plymouth** (p182), where the **Plimoth Patuxet Museum** (p183) takes you back to the US's early days. Then take the **ferry** (p184) to Cape Cod's Provincetown for views from the **Pilgrim Monument** (p187), some **whale-watching** (p188) and your fill of salty sea air.

Seasonal Highlights

Summertime brings the crowds but also ample outdoor adventures and generally fine weather. Fall's fiery landscapes are a highlight, while winter offers skiing and snowboarding; spring brings buds and flowers.

JANUARY
Temperatures are chilly but New England's crisp, snowy panoramas are a highlight. Away from the busy ski resorts in the mountains, some hotels close, while others slash their prices in the off-season.

APRIL
Spring in New England can take a long time to arrive, but when it does come, it's lovely. Travel in this season can be ideal, with greening-up landscapes and fewer people.

MAY
May is a perfect travel month. Sights and hikes throughout the region remain less crowded, it's generally drier than in April, and whale-watching season begins along the coast.

More Than One Week

More than a week lets you take in three of New England's best mountain hikes. Start in Vermont's **Stowe** (p214) to get your bearings before heading off for a walk on **Mt Mansfield** (p216), the state's highest peak. From here, make your way into New Hampshire's White Mountains, basing yourself in **North Conway** and getting an early start for the ascent up **Mt Washington** (p226), New England's highest summit. If hiking up it doesn't appeal, you can drive up or take a cog train. No matter what you choose, the views are stunning. Finish with some time in Maine's **Acadia National Park** (p236), where you can hike (or drive) up the 1530ft **Cadillac Mountain** (p236).

A New England Road Trip

With several weeks, do a south-to-north road trip, spending a few days in **Connecticut** (p201) and **Rhode Island** (p194) before carrying on to Massachusetts. **Boston** (p166) will take as much reward as you can give it, but also visit other parts of **Massachusetts** (p184), including Cape Cod and the Berkshires. **Vermont** (p210) is a highlight, where driving the **Scenic Route 100** (p218) makes for a good introduction and puts you within range of **Smugglers Notch** (p215). In **New Hampshire** (p222), take in the White Mountains' scenery along the **Kancamagus Highway** (p228) before finishing in **Maine** (p229), perhaps taking a **windjammer cruise** (p233), driving the **Blue Hill Peninsula** (p234) and hiking **Mt Katahdin** (p238).

JULY
July – especially the weekend of July 4 – marks the start of the main tourist season, with summer festivals, beach weather, ice cream, barbecues and busy coastal roads.

SEPTEMBER
From mid-September into October, New England's famous, blazing fall foliage is at its prime. Check **Yankee Magazine** *(newengland.com)* for leaf-peeping maps, although it's guaranteed beautiful almost everywhere.

OCTOBER
October is full of traditional regional scenes. Farmers markets are laden with fresh fruits and other produce from New England's bountiful harvest, and farm-to-table dining is at its best.

DECEMBER
Cozy lodges, quiet landscapes and snowy ski trails make it easy to forget the cold. Many hotels have peak-season pricing from late December into early January, but watch for discounts in early December.

Boston

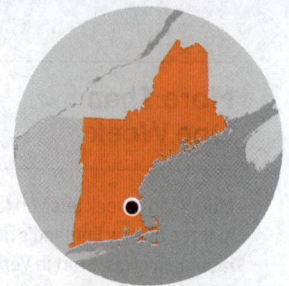

REVOLUTIONARY HISTORY | INNOVATIVE ARTISTRY | CHARLES RIVER

GETTING AROUND

From any airport terminal, take the silver-line bus to the Seaport District or **South Station** to connect with red-line subway trains, or take the free shuttle bus to the blue-line Airport Station, from where you can ride the subway into central Boston. Downtown is compact and walkable, with T stations everywhere. To reach **Faneuil Hall** (p173), take any line (except red) to Haymarket, State or Government Center. The blue-line Aquarium stop offers the easiest waterfront access. **Blue Bikes** (bluebikes.com) is Boston's bikeshare program, with hundreds of stations and bikes around the city and surrounding towns. Pay per half-hour or get an all-day pass.

It was the Puritans who set out in search of religious freedom and founded Boston as their 'shining city on a hill.' In the following century, the Sons of Liberty were born in Boston, where they caroused and rabble-roused until the colonies found themselves in the midst of the War of Independence. A hundred years later, it was Boston's writers and philosophers who were leading a cultural revolution, pushing progressive causes such as abolitionism and transcendentalism.

Today, innovation and higher education shape the city, with it's universities attracting scholars, scientists, philosophers and writers who feed off and contribute to the evolving culture and economy.

Besides being young, the residents of Boston are also diverse, with non-Hispanic whites making up almost half the population. The result is a rich cultural landscape, with music, food and festivals representing every corner of the world.

Boston packs a lot in. Plan your days, but leave time for detours (literally and figuratively).

Flowers, Fountains & Food Trucks   MAP P168
Find your way along the Greenway

A multilane elevated highway once separated downtown Boston from its scenic waterfront. Fortunately, it was relocated underground and replaced with the **Rose Kennedy Greenway** (rosekennedygreenway.org). This 1.5-mile linear park weaves a green, garden-filled path from the North End to Chinatown. Stroll along the Greenway to explore pollinator gardens, observe beehives (cautiously), patronize food trucks and admire an evolving array of public art.

At the northern end, residents and workers picnic on the lawn, while kiddos cool off in the Canal Fountains. For a more meditative experience, walk the **Labyrinth** in the Armenian Heritage Park further south. Nearby, young visitors make a beeline for the hand-carved sea turtles, peregrine falcons and other creatures on the whimsical **Greenway Carousel**. For

Chinatown Gate

lunch, food trucks often park at nearby **Dewey Sq Parks**, while **Trillium Garden** serves cold local drafts. Check the Greenway website for events throughout the year, such as the annual Boston Local Food Festival or the Winter Sauna Village.

Ocean Adventures
MAP P168
See the creatures of the sea

The **New England Aquarium** (neaq.org; adult/child $39/30) highlights marine life from around the region and across the globe. The centerpiece is the four-story Giant Ocean Tank, a Caribbean coral reef environment teeming with vibrant tropical fish. Additionally, there are penguins, sea lions, a giant octopus and more. Look also for exhibits about conservation efforts and sustainable seafood.

Of course, the best place to see the creatures of the sea (and all creatures, really) is in the wild. Whale-watching tours set off from Long Wharf to journey out to Stellwagen Bank, a breeding ground for whales, dolphins and marine birds. Whale sightings are practically guaranteed.

Art & Culture in Chinatown
MAP P168
More than delicious dining

Flanked by two marble lions, the **Chinatown Gate** marks the entrance to Boston's historically Chinese district, a neighborhood that still retains much of its cultural identity.

Chinese immigrants began arriving in Boston in the 1870s. Some of these early migrants pitched their tents in Ping On Alley, a narrow lane off Essex St; and as recently as the 1950s, this alley held a communal roasting oven that all the local residents and restaurants used.

While the original immigrants came from southern China, today the neighborhood is home to people with roots from all

(continues on p170)

☑ TOP TIP

Boston is a compact city that's wonderful for walking or cycling, with its main sights and activities contained within an area that's only about 3 sq miles. Otherwise, most of the main attractions are accessible by subway. Driving is not usually recommended due to bad traffic, tricky navigation and ornery Boston drivers.

BOSTON NEW ENGLAND

CENTRAL BOSTON

★ HIGHLIGHTS
1. Boston Common
2. Freedom Trail Foundation
3. Museum of African American History
4. Rose Kennedy Greenway

● SIGHTS
5. Boston Children's Museum
6. Boston Fire Museum
7. Boston Tea Party Ships & Museum
8. Brewer Fountain
9. Bunker Hill Monument
10. Castle Island & Fort Independence
11. Charlestown Navy Yard
12. Chinatown Gate
13. Copp's Hill Burying Ground
14. Dewey Sq Parks
15. Faneuil Hall
16. Granary Burying Ground
17. Greenway Carousel
18. Institute of Contemporary Art
19. King's Chapel & Burying Ground
20. Labyrinth
21. Make Way for Ducklings Statue
22. Massachusetts State House
23. Nichols House Museum
24. Old Corner Bookstore
25. Old North Church
26. Old South Meeting House
27. Old State House
28. Pao Arts Center
29. Park Street Church
30. Paul Revere House
31. Paul Revere Mall
32. Public Garden
33. Robert Gould Shaw Memorial

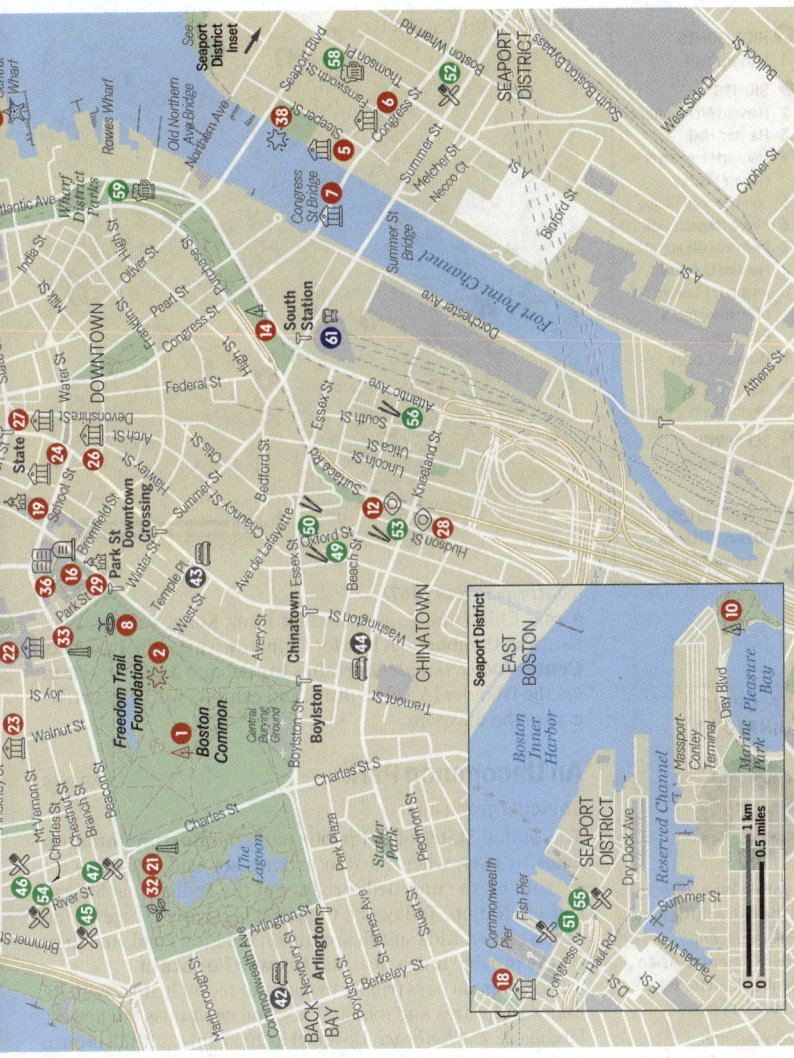

THE GUIDE
NEW ENGLAND BOSTON

34 USS Constitution
35 USS Constitution Museum

ACTIVITIES & TOURS
see 33 Black Heritage Trail
36 Boston Athenaeum
37 Community Boating
38 Martin's Park
39 New England Aquarium
40 Urban AdvenTours

SLEEPING
41 CitizenM North Station
42 College Club
43 Godfrey Hotel
44 HI Boston Hostel

EATING
45 75 Chestnut
46 Beacon Hill Books & Cafe
47 Cobblestones
48 Dovetail
49 Dumpling King
50 Hei La Moon
51 Legal Seafoods - Harborside
52 Row 34
53 Somenya
54 Tatte
55 Yankee Lobster Co
56 Zhi Wei Cafe

DRINKING & NIGHTLIFE
57 The Anchor
58 Trillium Brewing
59 Trillium Garden
60 Warren Tavern

TRANSPORT
61 South Station Bus Terminal

169

- **HIGHLIGHTS**
  1 Harvard Yard
- **SIGHTS**
  2 Harvard Art Museums
  3 Harvard Hall
  4 Harvard Museum of Natural History
  5 John Harvard Statue
  6 Massachusetts Hall
  7 Memorial Church at Harvard University
  8 Peabody Museum of Archaeology & Ethnology
  9 Widener Library
- **ACTIVITIES**
  10 Smith Campus Center
- **SLEEPING**
  11 Irving House at Harvard
- **INFORMATION**
  see 10 Harvard University Information Center

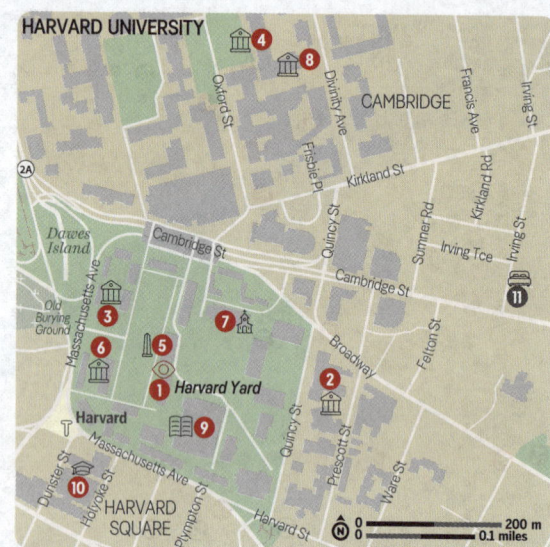

EXPLORING CHINATOWN

Cynthia Woo, Director of the Pao Arts Center (@paoartscenter), says 'There's more to Asian identity than traditional lion dances.'

Every autumn, Experience Chinatown organizes a mural festival, as well as other musical performances, gallery shows and arts events year-round.

Check out neighborhood murals, such as *Where We Belong*, painted by artist Ponnapa Prakkamaku near 79 Essex St.

(continued from p167)

across China and Asia, including Hong Kong, Taiwan, Vietnam and Cambodia. A hub for Chinatown arts, the **Pao Arts Center** *(paoartscenter.org)* aims to celebrate Asian American Pacific Islander (AAPI) culture and exhibits works by artists across the diaspora.

An Uncommon Park

MAP P168

Boston's green heart

The United States oldest public park, the **Boston Common** dates to 1634, when Puritan arrivals set aside pastures for grazing on the unceded territory of the Indigenous Massachusett Nation. Today, the Common is a leafy refuge in the urban center. Kids splash around on the Frog Pond, and food trucks provide lunch near the **Brewer Fountain**.

The Common pays tribute to past and recent history with its many sculptures and monuments. You can't miss the newest landmark, *The Embrace*. Unveiled in 2023, this 20ft-tall bronze sculpture of intertwining arms celebrates Martin Luther King Jr and his wife Coretta Scott King, who met as students at Boston University in the 1950s.

Blooms & Boats

MAP P168

The Public Garden's peaceful appeal

West of the Boston Common, the more formal and manicured **Public Garden** *(friendsofthepublicgarden.org; free)* opened in 1837 as the country's first public botanical garden. In 1877, entrepreneur Robert Paget started offering boat rides on the lagoon, on a boat driven by pedals and decorated with a swan.

(continues on p174)

TOP EXPERIENCE

Harvard University

Founded in 1636 to educate men for the ministry, Harvard is the country's oldest university, and remains one of its most prestigious. Alumni of the original Ivy League school include eight US presidents and dozens of Nobel laureates and Pulitzer Prize winners. For visitors, the campus contains some historic buildings clustered around Harvard Yard, as well as impressive architecture and excellent museums.

Johnston Gate

Touring the Grounds

While Harvard now occupies vast areas in Cambridge and Allston, its geographic and historic heart remains **Harvard Yard**. Flanking the main entrance at **Johnston Gate** are the two oldest buildings on campus. South of the gate, **Massachusetts Hall** (1720) houses the offices of the President of the University. North is **Harvard Hall** (1766). The focal point of the yard is the **John Harvard Statue**, where every Harvard hopeful has a photo taken (and touches the statue's shiny shoe for good luck).

The most imposing building in the Yard is **Widener Library** (closed to the public), which contains more than 5 miles of books. The **Memorial Church** was built in 1932 to honor the students and alums who died in World War I. Museums on the university's grounds include the **Harvard Art Museums** *(harvardartmuseums.org; free)*, the **Peabody Museum of Archaeology & Ethnology** *(peabody.harvard.edu; adult/child $15/10)* and the **Harvard Museum of Natural History** *(hmnh.harvard.edu; adult/child $15/10)*, which is famed for its botanical galleries, featuring some 3000 pieces of hand-blown, intricately crafted glass flowers and plants.

TOP TIPS

● Stop by the **Smith Campus Center**, where the lobby is lush with thousands of plants growing on the living walls.

● Free campus tours depart from the **Information Center** inside the Smith Campus Center.

● Get a self-guided tour booklet or download the mobile app from the website.

PRACTICALITIES
Scan this QR code for prices and opening hours

Old South Meeting House

TOP EXPERIENCE

Freedom Trail

Summon your inner Paul Revere and follow the redbrick road of the Freedom Trail, from the Boston Common to the Bunker Hill Monument. This 2.5-mile walking route is the best introduction to revolutionary Boston, tracing the locations of the events that earned the town its status as the 'Birthplace of the Revolution.'

DON'T MISS

Boston Massacre Monument

Granary Burying Ground

Faneuil Hall

Old North Church

Copp's Hill Burying Ground

Bunker Hill Monument

Walking the Trail

The Freedom Trail kicks off at the **Boston Common** (p170), the USA's oldest public park. Don't miss the memorial to Union officer **Robert Gould Shaw** and the all-Black 54th Regiment, who fought for the Union in the Civil War. Overlooking the Common is the **Massachusetts State House**, on land that was previously part of John Hancock's cow pasture. Go inside for a free tour.

PRACTICALITIES

Scan this QR code for an audio tour of the Freedom Trail, plus links to written information about each stop.

Next is **Park Street Church**, whose soaring spire has been a landmark since 1809. The church earned the moniker 'Brimstone Corner,' both for its usage as a gunpowder storage spot during the War of 1812 and for its fiery preaching. Next door, a pair of Egyptian Revival gates open to the **Granary Burying Ground**, the final resting place for revolutionary hero Paul Revere and many other Sons of Liberty, as well as the victims of the Boston Massacre.

At the corner of School St, the Georgian **King's Chapel** overlooks its adjacent burying ground – the oldest in the city. Check out its large bell, crafted by Paul Revere, and the governor's pew, once occupied by George Washington. On School St, a plaque commemorates the site of the country's first public school (1635). Note the statue of Benjamin Franklin, the school's most famous dropout. On the corner is the **Old Corner Bookstore**, the mid-19th century home of Ticknor & Fields, an influential publishing house that helped shape US literature. Just south is the **Old South Meeting House**, which saw the beginnings of the Boston Tea Party, one of the Revolution's most vociferous protests.

Turning north, walk to the **Old State House**, a striking redbrick edifice. Outside, gaze up at the balcony where the Declaration of Independence was first read to Bostonians in 1776; the cobblestone circle marks the site of the 1770 **Boston Massacre**, the Revolution's first violent conflict. Inside, peruse historic artifacts and listen to firsthand accounts of revolutionary events.

Just beyond is historic **Faneuil Hall** (1770), Boston's original market and public meeting place. Don't miss the insightful Boston Slavery Exhibit.

Now make your way across the Rose Kennedy Greenway and into North End to reach charming North Sq, home to Paul Revere. Tours of the **clapboard house** shed light on Revere's work and family life. North on Hanover St, **Paul Revere Mall** has a statue of the patriot and views of your next destination, the **Old North Church**. Boston's oldest house of worship, the 1723 church played a crucial role in revolutionary events. About 500ft further on, **Copp's Hill Burying Ground** is home to some of the city's oldest gravestones and is the resting place of Daniel Malcom, one of the Sons of Liberty – British soldiers used his headstone for target practice.

Now cross the Charlestown Bridge to the **Charlestown Navy Yard** (p181), home to the world's oldest commissioned warship, the **USS Constitution** (p181). Board for a tour of the upper decks.

Finish the Freedom Trail by climbing the 294 steps to the top of the **Bunker Hill Monument** – a 220ft granite obelisk – for views of the city, the harbor and beyond.

BEST GUIDED TOURS

Freedom Trail Foundation (thefreedomtrail.org) Guides in period costume cover the main Freedom Trail sites (not including Charlestown).

Boston by Foot (bostonbyfoot.org) 'Boston by Little Feet' is a truncated Freedom Trail tour designed for kids.

Ye Olde Tavern Tours (yeoldetaverntours.com) Combines education and libation at Boston's historic sites and pubs.

Photo Walks (photowalks.com) Covers the first 11 Freedom Trail sites, with plenty of time for pictures. Also offers custom-designed scavenger hunts for interactive explorations.

TOP TIPS

● The self-guided tour is excellent; scan the QR code on the previous page to access it.

● Pick up information and maps from the Boston Common information kiosk or the visitor center in Faneuil Hall.

● Many of the sites are free of charge; you can visit the Old State House and the Old South Meeting House with one ticket.

● The Freedom Trail Foundation offers seasonal tours, such as spooky lantern-lit tours in October and festive holiday tours in December.

DUCKS ON PARADE

In addition to the Swan Boats, the Public Garden has another waterbird landmark: sculptor Nancy Schön's **Make Way for Ducklings** statue, a whimsical parade of eight bronze ducklings following their mother, Mrs Mallard. Installed in 1987, the artwork pays tribute to Robert McCloskey's classic children's book of the same title – first published in 1941 – which tells the story of a duck family who came to live in the Public Garden.

See if you can quickly say the ducklings' names three times: Jack, Kack, Lack, Mack, Nack, Ouack, Pack and Quack.

The ducklings often get dressed up for special occasions, such as public holidays and Red Sox victories.

(continued from p170)

The design for the Swan Boats was inspired by the Wagner opera *Lohengrin* (1848), in which a heroic knight crosses a river in a boat pulled by a swan. Paget's descendants continue to operate this beloved Boston seasonal attraction, and the Swan Boats are still pedal-powered. In summer, the Friends of the Public Garden lead free one-hour tours of the blooms and artwork.

Genteel Beacon Hill

MAP P168

Local life in days gone by

Boston's Beacon Hill neighborhod, in the shadow of the golden dome of Massachusetts State House, is known for its celebrated history of Black activism and literary achievement, its political vibes and its narrow cobblestone streets lined with brick townhouses and gas lanterns. Take a tour here of the **Nichols House Museum** (*nicholshousemuseum.org; adults/students/children $16/8/free*) to admire the elegant interior of the 1804 townhouse and learn about the Nichols family who lived here. The star of the tour is former resident Rose Standish Nichols, who was a landscape designer, suffragette and all-round crafty woman. Her work is on display around the house.

EATING IN CHINATOWN: OUR PICKS

MAP P168

Hei La Moon: A top choice for dim sum, featuring everything from shrimp hargow to baked pork buns to custardy egg tarts. *11am-8pm Mon-Fri, from 10am Sat & Sun* $

Dumpling King: This takeout stall in the minuscule Avana Mall serves one thing – dumplings – and they're delicious. *10am-6pm* $

Zhi Wei Cafe: Lanzhou-style beef noodle soup is the specialty of this modern Leather District Chinese eatery. *11am-9pm Mon-Thu, to 10pm Fri & Sat, noon-9pm Sun* $$

Somenya: With or without soup, housemade soba and udon are highlights at this serene Japanese noodle shop. *noon-10pm Sun-Thu, to 10:30pm Fri & Sat* $$

Public Garden (p170)

Established in 1807, the **Boston Athenaeum** *(boston athenaeum.org; day pass $40)* is one of the oldest libraries in the country, with extensive collections of rare books and artworks. Reserve a spot on the one-hour guided Art & Architecture Tour to learn more about the building's cultural heritage, or purchase a day pass to commune with the spirits of Louisa May Alcott, Nathaniel Hawthorne and other literary forebears.

Beacon Hill's Black History

MAP P168

Black community in Boston

In the 18th and 19th centuries, a vibrant, free Black community lived on the north slope of Beacon Hill. The neighborhood's Abiel Smith School, dating to 1835, was the first public school for Black students in the United States. The building, now the **Museum of African American History** *(maah.org; adult/child $15/8)*, houses changing exhibits about Boston's Black heritage, with many items drawn from the museum's collection of over 3000 artifacts.

Next door, the African Meeting House (also part of the museum) is the oldest Black church in the US. Many anti-slavery activists spoke here, including newspaper publisher and

BLACK HERITAGE TRAIL

Delve deeper into the history of Beacon Hill on the **Black Heritage Trail** *(nps.gov/boaf)*, a route that connects sites related to the abolitionist movement, the Underground Railroad and other landmarks from the Black community who resided here in the 18th and 19th centuries.

Download the National Park Service (NPS) app *(nps.gov/subjects/digital/nps-apps.htm)* for an audio tour of the 1.6-mile route around Beacon Hill. Or take a free guided tour led by NPS park rangers. The trail begins at the bronze memorial opposite the Massachusetts State House (p172). The Robert Gould Shaw and Massachusetts 54th Regiment Memorial, sculpted by Augustus Saint-Gaudens and located opposite the State House, honors one of the first units of Black soldiers to serve in the US Civil War.

 EATING IN BEACON HILL: OUR PICKS — MAP P168

Cobblestones: Stop into this Charles St storefront for breakfast, sandwiches and several varieties of soups. *8am-6pm* **$**

Tatte: Take a break for coffee and pastries at this local bakeshop's Charles St branch. *7am-8pm Mon-Sat, to 7pm Sun* **$**

Beacon Hill Books & Cafe: Tiny bookshop cafe offering a small but creative breakfast and lunch menu, plus prix-fixe suppers ($$$). *9am-9pm Tue-Sat, 11am-5pm Sun* **$$**

75 Chestnut: Longstanding neighborhood eatery known for its seafood and steaks. *5-11pm Mon-Fri, from 10:30am Sat & Sun* **$$**

CHARLES RIVER BIKE PATH

The Charles River Esplanade is part of a longer cycling circuit that runs along both sides of the Charles River, between the Charles River Dam (at the Museum of Science) and the Mt Auburn St bridge at Watertown Sq, 5 miles west of Cambridge. The paved, off-road route provides a wonderful overview of Boston, offering glimpses of working waterfronts, spectacular cityscapes, inviting parklands and historic college campuses. The round trip is 17 miles, but 10 bridges in between offer ample opportunities to shorten the excursion.

Get a bicycle from Boston's bikeshare program, **Blue Bikes** (*bluebikes.com*), or rent from **Urban AdvenTours** (*urbanadventours.com*). If you're nervous about navigating on two wheels, the latter also offers guided bike rides along the route.

---

abolitionist William Lloyd Garrison, abolitionist leader Frederick Douglass and women's rights and anti-slavery advocate Maria W Stewart. Guided tours walk visitors through the history of Boston's Black community and its fight for rights and justice.

The Museum of African American History is the final stop on the Black Heritage Trail (p175).

Life on the Charles

MAP P178

Experience Boston's other waterfront

In the late 1880s, landscape architect Frederick Law Olmsted designed 'Charlesbank,' a riverside promenade featuring the region's first free outdoor gym. But it wasn't until Boston's river was dammed in 1910 that the parkland was transformed to a scenic recreation area. In the 1930s, Olmsted disciple Arthur Shurcliff expanded it, creating the foundation for the park now known as the **Charles River Esplanade** (*esplanade.org*).

With riverfront walking and cycling paths, the Esplanade extends from the Charles River dam to the Boston University Bridge and makes for a leafy location to walk, run or cycle, with river and city views.

Community Boating (*community-boating.org*) offers various ways to explore the river; they rent sailboats, kayaks and stand-up paddleboards to visitors between April and October, and it's a wonderful way to escape the crowds and see Boston from a different perspective. The dockmaster will briefly interview sailors to ensure they have prior experience before going out on the water.

Jazzy Beats & Good Eats

MAP P178

Black History in the South End

There was a time when the intersection of Mass Ave and Columbus Ave had a music club on every corner. This was the heyday of jazz – in the 1940s and 1950s – when a quarter of Boston's Black population lived in the South End. The only club remaining from this era is **Wally's Cafe**, which has been holding its own since 1947. Wally's was the first nightclub in Boston with an African American owner – one Joseph Walcott. Nowadays, Walcott's great-grandchildren run the place. Nothing fancy going on here, just pure live music – blues, jazz and funk – every night of the week.

The peak of jazz's popularity was also the era of segregated restaurants and hotels. History has it that visiting jazz musicians knew they could get a good meal up the street at **Charlie's Sandwich Shoppe**. This old-school diner has changed owners but still retains its welcoming atmosphere and retro decor. Photos and memorabilia record the many famous visitors over the years. It's only open for breakfast and lunch.

Museum of Fine Arts

Art on the Avenue

MAP P178

Admire art through the ages

Boston's premier art venue, the **Museum of Fine Arts** *(MFA; mfa.org; adult/child from $27/10)* occupies a handsome neoclassical building overlooking the Fens (aka the Back Bay Fens, a picturesque parkland). The museum's holdings encompass all periods, making it truly encyclopedic in scope (though there are a few genres where the museum excels). There's too much to see in one visit, so choose a wing or two to explore and enjoy at your leisure.

Art of the Americas: The pride of the museum is the four-story Americas wing, which includes 53 galleries with art from the pre-Columbian era (lower level) up through the 20th century (top level). On the first level, you'll find some treasures from colonial-era Boston, as well as an incomparable collection of paintings by John Singleton Copley. On the second level, a highlight is the gallery dedicated to John Singer Sargent.

European Art: The collection of European art in the museum's northern wing also covers all periods, with highlights from the Italian Renaissance. You'll find an impressive display of impressionists and postimpressionists, including one of the largest collections of Monet paintings this side of Paris.

GETTING AROUND FENWAY-KENMORE

Using public transportation, it can be quite tricky to get around the Fenway-Kenmore area to the west and southwest of central Boston, as the green line of the T forks into four branches. To stay on the right route, pay attention not only to the color of your subway train, but also its letter (B, C, D or E). To reach either Kenmore Sq or Fenway Park, take any of the green-line subway trains – except the E branch – to the Kenmore T station. Sights along Huntington Ave in Fenway are accessible from the E-branch (the Museum of Fine Arts stop) or from the orange line (Ruggles Station). The Massachusetts Bay Transportation Authority (MBTA) website *(mbta.com)* has a helpful trip planner.

 EATING & DRINKING NEAR THE WATER: OUR PICKS ——— MAP P168

The Anchor: Pleasant waterfront beer garden in Charlestown, with occasional live music and events. Open weekends only in winter (with igloos to keep you warm). *4-9pm Mon-Fri, to 9pm Sat-Sun*

Warren Tavern: A historic tavern on Charlestown's Main St that dates to 1780 and is named for revolutionary war hero Joseph Warren. Local beers and modern pub grub. *11am-1am* **$**

Dovetail: Hidden among the Navy Yard's granite warehouses, this is a delightful stop for lunch or dinner, featuring seafood and pasta. *hours vary* **$$**

Trillium Brewing: Sample brews in the tap room, eat in the dining room or chill on the rooftop at Trillium Brewing's Fort Point location. *noon-11pm Mon-Sat, to 10pm Sun* **$$**

BOSTON NEW ENGLAND

FENWAY-KENMORE

SIGHTS
1. Berklee Performance Center
2. Boston Symphony Orchestra
3. Charles River Esplanade
4. David Ortiz Drive
5. Fenway Park
6. House of Blues
7. Museum of Fine Arts
8. New England Conservatory
9. Red Room at Cafe 939

SLEEPING
10. Charlesmark Hotel
11. Copley Square Hotel
12. Oasis Guest House

EATING
13. Audubon
14. Charlie's Sandwich Shoppe
15. Kenmore
16. Phinista
17. Saltie Girl
18. Time Out Market

DRINKING & NIGHTLIFE
19. Bleacher Bar

ENTERTAINMENT
20. Wally's Cafe

The MFA has recently opened a new center of Netherlandish art, along with seven galleries showcasing Dutch and Flemish fabulousness. Feast your eyes on some 100 paintings by Golden Age masters, including five by Rembrandt.

Asia and the Ancient World: In the southwestern wing, the collection of Asian art includes exhibits in the serene Buddhist Temple room. In the southeastern wing, wide-ranging displays of ancient art include two rooms of mummies in the Egyptian galleries.

Contemporary Art: The Linde Wing for Contemporary Art is full of surprises. The pieces change regularly, with plenty of room given over to video, multimedia and other experiments. Look out for the remarkable *Black River*, a huge tapestry of discarded bottle caps by the Ghanaian artist El Anatsui.

Fenway Park, Inside & Out

MAP P178

America's oldest baseball park

Home of the Boston Red Sox since 1912, **Fenway Park** *(red sox.com)* is the oldest operating ballpark in the country and an obligatory pilgrimage site for baseball fans. The best way to experience it is to watch the Olde Towne Team do their stuff, from April through October. You can also learn about Fenway's history by taking a tour (year-round), where you visit the press box, the visiting team's locker room and the Green Monster seats.

Alternatively (or additionally), take a walk around the outside of Fenway Park to pick up some fun facts and local lore. Start at Gate A, the main entrance on Lansdowne St. The street is lined with bars, but the coolest place to pre-game is the **Bleacher Bar**. You enter from the street, but the bar is tucked beneath the bleachers, with a big window looking out onto center field.

Around the corner, outside of Gate B, is a series of statues of Red Sox legends. The touching sculpture *Teammates* depicts Ted Williams, Johnny Pesky, Bobby Doerr and Dom DiMaggio – four Hall-of-Famers who were teammates for seven years and friends for life.

West of the ballpark is **David Ortiz Drive**, named for the beloved Red Sox slugger in 2017. His big, red number 34 is also here, along with the retired numbers of other Red Sox greats.

BOSTON'S BEST MUSIC VENUES

Boston Symphony Orchestra: The queen of Boston cultural institutions successfully entertains listeners at the spectacular Symphony Hall.

New England Conservatory: The country's oldest music school and primary feeder to the Boston Symphony Orchestra. Students and faculty perform at Jordan Hall.

Berklee Performance Center: The main venue at the Berklee College of Music, where programs focus on contemporary music, especially jazz and modern American music.

Red Room at Cafe 939: This all-ages club is a more intimate Berklee venue.

House of Blues: The bigger, glossier successor to the very first House of Blues that Dan Aykroyd opened in Cambridge in 1992.

 EATING IN FENWAY-KENMORE: NEIGHBORHOOD FAVORITES ⎯ MAP P178

Phinista: A delightful French-Vietnamese cafe serving sweet crepes and savory *banh mi* (sandwiches). *8am-5pm, to 9pm Wed-Sun* **$**

Kenmore: The rare kitchen that is open late night (until at least 11:30pm). Best burgers in the 'hood. *10am-1am Sun, 11am-1am Mon-Wed, to 2am Thu-Sat* **$**

Time Out Market: The Landmark Center houses this excellent food hall with 15 eateries and two bars from local chefs and restaurateurs. *8.30am-10pm Mon-Thu, till 11pm Fri, 9am-10pm Sat & Sun* **$$**

Audubon: A sophisticated take on a 'local,' with great food and class but casual ambiance. *11:30am-1am Mon-Wed, to 2am Thu-Sat, to midnight Sun* **$$**

SEAPORT DISTRICT FOR KIDS

Boston Children's Museum: A multistory multimedia museum on the waterfront. Whether it's experimenting with bubbles, ball launchers or turtles, kids have plenty to challenge their minds and bodies. *(bostonchildrensmuseum.org; $24)*

Boston Fire Museum: Exhibits document firefighting through the centuries. There are antique firetrucks (great photo ops), firefighting equipment and displays of devastating blazes. *(bostonsparks.com/boston-fire-museum; free)*

Martin's Park: A shady oasis along the harbor walk with a replica wooden ship, timber maze and climbing sphere. The park honors Martin Richard, the youngest victim of the 2013 Boston Marathon bombings. *(martinsparkboston.org; free)*

Castle Island: Neither an island nor a castle, this historic site is actually a cape jutting out into Pleasure Bay with walking trails, fishing piers, family-friendly beaches, sea breezes and wonderful views. *(nps.gov/places/castle-island.htm; free)*

USS Constitution

Join the Revolution
Welcome to the tea party

MAP P168

On December 16, 1773, a gang of colonists snuck onto three ships moored at Griffin's Wharf and threw their precious cargo of tea into the Boston Harbor. This act of rebellion – to protest unfair taxes – became known as the Boston Tea Party, a key event that led to the Revolutionary War.

Full-scale replicas of two of these ships now comprise the **Boston Tea Party Ships & Museum** *(bostonteapartyship.com; adult/child from $36/26)*. After learning about the political climate at the time, visitors can board the vessels and throw crates of tea into the harbor in solidarity with their ancestors. The story continues inside the museum, with talking portraits and other presentations.

Art with a View
A dramatic setting for distinctive pieces

MAP P168

The **Institute of Contemporary Art** *(ICA; icaboston.org; adult/child $20/15)* is as notable for its waterfront architecture as for its collections. Designed by Diller Scofidio + Renfro, the building is cantilevered over the water, and its translucent spaces glow. Outside, sit on the wooden steps with views out to sea; inside, the glass-enclosed Founders Gallery offers even more expansive vistas.

Look for specially curated digital exhibits in the Mediathèque. This unusual gallery is suspended below the cantilever at a seemingly precarious angle. The result is a view of the water and nothing else – no land, no horizon, no context. It's at once mesmerizing and disorienting.

The ICA's permanent collection includes many 20th- and 21st-century art innovators, including photographer Robert Mapplethorpe, pop artist Yayoi Kusama and multimedia artist Paul Chan.

Sailing Vessels & Battleships
MAP P168

Discover the Charlestown Navy Yard

For nearly two centuries, the **Charlestown Navy Yard** *(nps.gov/bost/learn/historyculture/cny.htm; free)* was a hub of industry and innovation in the realm of shipbuilding and seafaring. Nowadays, this busy spot is a sort of living museum: the National Park Service (NPS) visitor center is a good place to start your explorations.

The main attraction is the 1797 **USS Constitution** *(nps.gov/bost/learn/historyculture/ussconst.htm; free)*, the country's oldest Navy ship. US Navy crew members give free tours of the historic ship (fondly termed 'Old Ironsides'), telling of its greatest feats and direst tragedies. Photo ID is required for security purposes.

Learn more about Old Ironsides at the **USS Constitution Museum** *(ussconstitutionmuseum.org; suggested donation from $10)*. Exhibits explore the birth of the US Navy during the Barbary Wars and the War of 1812, and a unique exhibit gives kids (or anyone) a chance to experience a sailor's life by scrubbing the boatdeck and furling a sail. The museum is also the headquarters of the USS Constitution Model Shipwright Guild.

The USS *Cassin Young* is a Fletcher-class WWII destroyer that was built right here in Charlestown. It participated in the 1944 Battle of Leyte Gulf, as well as the 1945 invasion of Okinawa. In season, guided tours explore the ins and outs of the battleship, or you can wander around the main deck independently.

Although most of the shipyard buildings are not open to the public, many of the old granite structures are still standing. The oldest building in the yard is the imposing Federal-style Commandant's House, dating to 1805.

Revolutionary Beginnings

The American Revolution's first battles

Students of history and lovers of liberty can trace the events of the fateful day – April 19, 1775 – that started a revolution. Follow the footsteps of the British troops and colonial minutemen who tromped out to Lexington to face off at sunrise on the village green, now known as **Battle Green**. The *Lexington Minuteman* statue stands guard at the southeastern end of Battle Green, honoring the bravery of the 77 minutemen who met the British here in 1775, and the eight who died.

SEAFARING IN MINIATURE

Paul Schmitt, Admiral of the USS Constitution Model Shipwright Guild *(usscmsg.org)*, talks about a unique museum experience.

The USS Constitution Museum is home to one of the largest ship-modeling clubs in the world, the USS Constitution Model Shipwright Guild. Members share a passion for maritime history and building fine scale models of all types.

On the museum's 1st floor, the club maintains a working model shop in which volunteer members demonstrate ship modeling to visitors, and in which we keep our extensive library of modeling books and plans. The museum and guild co-sponsor an annual ship model exhibit and competition, timed to coincide with the local winter school vacation.

EATING IN AND AROUND THE SEAPORT DISTRICT: SEAFOOD
MAP P168

Yankee Lobster Co: A seafood shack that has been specializing in the eponymous crustaceans since the 1950s. *11am-8pm Tue-Thu, to 8:30pm Fri & Sat, to 7pm Sun* **$$**

Row 34: A bustling seafood hall in a former warehouse. Snack on oyster sliders, smoked seafood spreads and (pricey) lobster rolls. *11:30am-10pm Mon-Sat, to 9pm Sun* **$$$**

Legal Seafoods - Harborside: Two words: roof deck. Come for the clam chowder, grilled fish, steamed lobster and sea views. *11am-10pm Sun-Thu, to 11pm Fri & Sat* **$$$**

Saltie Girl: Serves up seafood towers, lobster rolls and other specialties of the sea. *11am-10pm Mon-Wed, till 11pm Thu-Sat, till 9pm Sun* **$$$**

A REVOLUTIONARY RIDE

Starting near Alewife Station in Cambridge, the **Minuteman Bikeway** *(minutemanbikeway.org)* rail trail runs 6.5 miles from Cambridge to historic Lexington, skirting the shady woodlands and flat marshlands of Great Meadows. The route then traverses an additional 3.5 miles of idyllic scenery, terminating in the rural suburb of Bedford. At the end of the trail is Depot Park, which contains a vintage diesel car and an information center in the old freight house.

The unpaved Reformatory Branch extends the trail by an additional 4 miles, from Bedford to the Old North Bridge in Concord. Ride back along Battle Rd or take the commuter rail back to Cambridge or Boston.

Rent your bicycle from **Urban Adventours** (p176) or **Blue Bikes** *(bluebikes.com)*.

Overlooking the green, **Buckman Tavern** *(lexingtonhistory.org; adult/child $14/8)* was the minutemen's headquarters.

From here, the regulars marched west toward Concord. This whole area has been preserved as the **Minute Man National Historical Park** *(nps.gov/mima; free)*. The visitor center at the eastern end of the park shows an informative multimedia presentation depicting Paul Revere's ride from Boston to warn his compatriots about the British advance, as well as the ensuing battles. Within the park, Battle Road is a 5-mile wooded trail that connects the historic sites related to the battles, including Paul Revere's capture site and Hartwell Tavern.

Further west, the **Old North Bridge** *(nps.gov/mima; free)* is the site of the 'shot heard around the world' (as Ralph Waldo Emerson wrote in his poem, 'Concord Hymn'). This is where enraged minutemen fired on British troops and forced them to retreat to Boston. Daniel Chester French's first statue, *Minute Man*, presides over the park. Stop into the visitor center to see a video about the battle and admire the Hancock, the Revolutionary War brass cannon.

Lexington is about 12 miles west of downtown Boston, and Concord center is another 6 miles west. The Massachusetts Bay Transportation Authority (MBTA) operates buses 62 and 76 run from Alewife Station in Cambridge to Lexington; the MBTA commuter rail runs from North Station in Boston to Concord. There's no public transportation between the two towns.

Time Travel in Plymouth

Visit a 17th-century colonial village

During the winter of 1620–21, after arriving on the shores of Massachusetts, half of the Plymouth colonists died of disease,

Old North Bridge

privation and exposure to the elements. But new arrivals joined the survivors the following year, and by 1627 – just before an additional influx of settlers founded the colony of Massachusetts Bay – Plymouth Colony was on the road to prosperity.

The **Plimoth Patuxet Museum** *(plimoth.org; adult/child from $35/20)* have recreated the English Village with exacting authenticity. Everything here – costumes, implements, vocabulary, artistry, recipes and crops – has been painstakingly researched and remade. Historic interpreters, in costume and in character, explain the details of daily life and answer your questions as they work and play. And yes, you will be invited to participate. A highlight is the Craft Center, where you can help artisans as they weave baskets, throw pottery and build furniture using the techniques and tools of the early 17th century.

At the nearby **Historic Patuxet Homesite**, Indigenous people demonstrate the lifestyle of the Wampanoag Native Americans during the 17th century. You can go inside a *wetu* (traditional dome-shaped hut covered in bark), check out the furs (many) and furnishings (limited), observe cooking and growing techniques, and see the construction of a *mishoon* (dugout canoe). Unlike the actors at the English Village, these individuals are not acting as historic characters: they are Indigenous people speaking from a modern perspective. The large, open-air complex is open from late March through Thanksgiving Day.

Plymouth & Brockton *(p-b.com)* buses depart every hour from South Station (p169) for the one-hour trip to Plymouth. The bus stop in Plymouth is at the Park & Ride lot at Exit 13. From here, it's 15 minutes on the GATRA Mayflower Link to either Plymouth Center or the Plimoth Patuxet Museum. Allow at least half a day, if not a full day, to explore these sites.

MORE PLIMOTH PATUXET MUSEUMS

There are two additional living-history sites in Plymouth that are part of Plimoth Patuxet Museum.

The **Mayflower II** *(plimoth.org; adult/child $19/13)* is a replica of the small ship in which the Pilgrims made their fateful voyage from England to the New World, where 102 people lived together for 66 days as the ship sailed the stormy North Atlantic. Actors in period costume are on board, recounting harrowing tales from the journey. The ship is docked at State Pier.

A half-mile south on Town Brook, the **Plimoth Grist Mill** *(plimoth.org; adult/child $11/8)* is a working duplicate of an actual gristmill that was constructed in 1636. See how the water wheel powers the mill to grind corn, and take home a bag of freshly ground cornmeal to sample.

Massachusetts

DUNE-BACKED BEACHES | WHALE-SPOTTING | BERKSHIRE MOUNTAINS

Places
Falmouth p186
Sandwich p186
Provincetown p187
Nantucket Island p189
Sturbridge p189
Springfield & Around p190
The Berkshires p192

TOP TIP
If your time in Massachusetts is limited, get the essence of Olde Cape Cod by driving east along the historic **6A** (p191), known as the Old King's Highway, while beelining toward **Provincetown** (p187). To the west, a weekend in the **Berkshires** (p192) is a highlight.

Massachusetts – New England's most populous state – packs a lot into a small area. To the east are Cape Cod's lighthouses, dune-backed beaches, tranquil marshes and salty air – all far removed in feel from Boston's fast pace. Home to the USA's oldest continuous art colony and longest-running professional summer theater, the Cape continues to attract talented artisans of all types. Hikers and cyclists are drawn to the miles of pristine trails, while boaters, fishers, nature lovers and whale- and seal-watchers converge along the shore.

Turning westwards, the mighty Connecticut River cuts through central Massachusetts for more than 60 miles, connecting a series of appealing college towns. Further west, the Berkshire Mountains line up along the New York border, offering stunning panoramas and outdoor adventure. Eating and drinking is also a highlight in these parts, thanks to the area's delicious farm-to-table dining scene, supplied by bountiful farms and complemented by world-class summer festivals.

GETTING AROUND

A car is hands down the best way to get around. Budget, Avis and Enterprise all have local outlets. The **Cape Cod Regional Transit Authority** *(CCRTA; capecodrta.org)* operates buses throughout all 15 Cape municipalities, in addition to their **Dial-A-Ride Transportation** (DART), a door-to-door shared-ride service (Monday to Saturday). Check online for maps and schedules.

The **Steamship Authority** *(steamshipauthority.com)* runs several car and passenger ferries, and the **Bay State Cruise Company** *(baystatecruisecompany.com)* has a daily Boston-Provincetown ferry (May to October). The **Berkshire Transit Authority** *(BRTA; berkshirerta.com)* runs buses between Lenox and the other Berkshire towns.

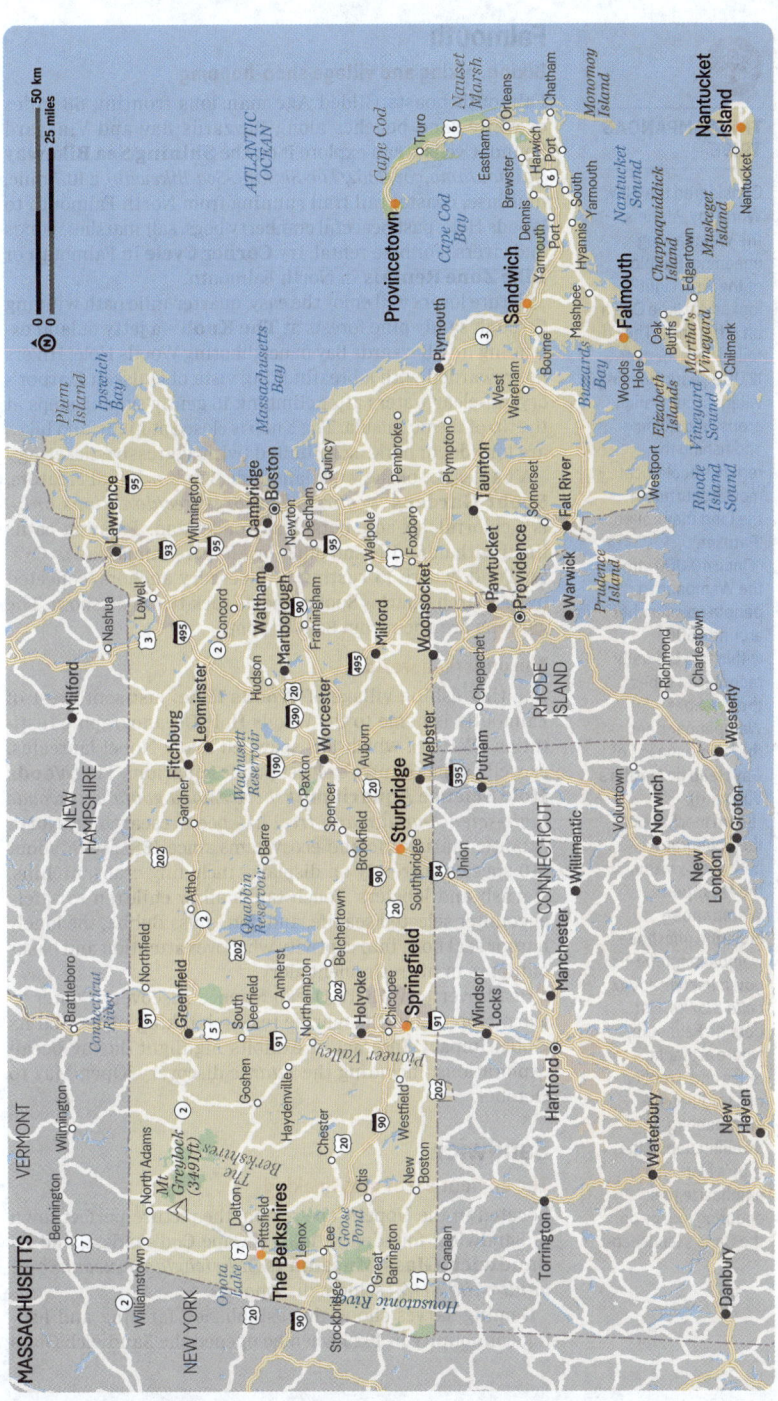

Falmouth

Biking, hiking and village shop-hopping

Falmouth boasts Gilded Age mansions fronting 68 miles of white-sand beaches along Buzzards Bay and Vineyard Sound. Cyclists can explore it on the **Shining Sea Bikeway** (*falmouthma.gov/1362/The-Shining-Sea-Bikeway*), a 10.7-mile, multiuse, coastal rail trail running from North Falmouth to Woods Hole, past peaceful cranberry bogs, salt marshes, ponds and rivers. For bike rental, try **Corner Cycle** in Falmouth or **Bike Zone Rentals** in North Falmouth.

Nature lovers will enjoy the easy, quarter-mile path winding through sandy pine forests at **The Knob** – a jetty of land extending into Buzzards Bay in neighboring Woods Hole. Hikers are rewarded with a breathtaking vista of Quissett Harbor's crystal-clear waters after climbing 16 gently sloping steps at the tip of the peninsula. The Knob is closed at night, and bikes are forbidden; parking is limited (with aggressive ticketing).

A namesake of the woodland hideaway's original creators, **Spohr Gardens** (*spohrgardens.org; free/donations only*) is a colorful, six-acre botanical wonderland. Twisting paths lined with daffodils and other bright perennials lead to Oyster Pond, where 13 rusting 18th-century anchors, collected by patriarch Charles Spohr, line its rock-trimmed shore. The gardens are open from 8am to 8pm.

The undersea world

The tiny fishing village of **Woods Hole**, just southwest of Falmouth, is home to the Woods Hole Oceanographic Institution (WHOI), which has spawned many Nobel laureates, as well as the country's oldest public aquarium. The **Woods Hole Science Aquarium** (*fisheries.noaa.gov/about/woods-hole-science-aquarium; free*) has been researching North Atlantic marine life and ecosystems since 1885, with about 140 species currently on display – including crabs, urchins, starfish and lobsters. Touch tanks allow children to safely encounter selected sea life, and don't miss Bubba, the lonely harbor seal born into captivity who loves attention and basks outdoors in his retirement glory.

Head over to WHOI's Ocean Science Discovery Center to learn more about the marine research taking place, and its global impact. Interactive exhibits highlight daring ocean explorations, including the *Titanic* discovery. Open May to October.

Sandwich

The ancient art of glassmaking

Located in the Upper Cape region, the picture-perfect town of Sandwich, founded in 1637, is Cape Cod's oldest, and its **Sandwich Glass Museum** (*sandwichglassmuseum.org; adult/child $14/3*) seldom disappoints.

Deming Jarves shook this established farming and fishing community in 1825 when he opened the Sandwich Glass

---

THE WAMPANOAG TRIBE

Considered the 'New World' by Pilgrims, the Wampanoag (meaning 'People of the First Light') looked at Cape Cod a bit differently. They'd toiled here for over 12,000 years, building villages, cultivating crops, and hunting and fishing the region's ecological mosaic, nurturing the land they called 'Patuxet.'

Once 40,000 strong, the Wampanoag people now number around 4500, within two federally recognized tribes: the Mashpee Wampanoags and the Wampanoags of Gay Head (in Martha's Vineyard).

Learn more about their cultural heritage by visiting the **Mashpee Wampanoag Museum** (*mashpeewampanoagtribe-nsn.gov/museum; adult/child $15/10*), just outside Falmouth, where artifacts, relics and a replica of a traditional Wampanoag dwelling depict the tribe's history and emphasize their enduring legacy on the Cape's landscape.

Provincetown

Manufactory. Employing 500 workers, it quickly became one of the US' largest glass factories. Today, the packed gallery showcases over 10,000 pieces sculpted by factory artisans, including exquisite beehive designs and decorated glassware rarely seen in today's conveyor-belt production lines.

Watch a brief documentary on the history of glassmaking, then witness a live glass-blowing demonstration as a sculptor creates a tabletop masterpiece in front of you. The museum is closed January.

Provincetown

Towering vistas and compelling history

Muster your energy and climb 116 steps and 60 ramps to the top of Provincetown's 252ft **Pilgrim Monument** *(pilgrimmonument.org; adult/child including Provincetown Museum $21/12)* for panoramic views of the picturesque town below, and the beaches and ocean waters stretching to the horizon. Built in 1910 to commemorate the first landing of the Mayflower Pilgrims in 1620 (and subsequent signing of the Mayflower Compact, a predecessor to the Constitution), it's the tallest all-granite tower in the country. The plaque in **Pilgrims' First Landing Park**, at the western terminus of

---

 EATING AROUND FALMOUTH: BEST FEASTS & TREATS

Betsy's Diner: Step back into simpler times with throwback pricing at this '50s-themed 1957 Mountain View diner. Great breakfasts and gluten-free options, too. *7am-2pm* $

Epic Oyster: Lip-smacking local oysters and fresh-from-the-waves seafood in a 1922 Tierney dining car: a fave Bob Dylan chill spot. *5-9pm Tue-Fri, from noon Sat* $$

Polar Cave Ice Cream Parlour: Embrace your inner child at this ice-cream parlor straight from a fairy tale. Dare to try the 'Death By Chocolate.' *hours vary* $

Ben & Bill's Chocolate Emporium: Decadent chocolates and ice cream, with gluten and lactose-free options. Try their summertime lobster-flavored cone. *hours vary* $$

TRAVELING ON A BUDGET

Pinching pennies? Vacationing in Cape Cod isn't cheap, but deals and discounts can still be scored. Try these tips.

Pitch a tent, rent a yurt or choose homestays with kitchens to prepare meals yourself. Eating out gets expensive, fast. Shop for groceries at Market Basket and buy booze from Trader Joe's to save on cash.

Prioritize free, outdoor activities: bring/rent bikes and hit beautiful trails and gardens, or beachcomb for treasures (but avoid parking at the beach).

Take advantage of highly discounted off-season rates, when lodging costs drop big-time. Check *capecoddailydeal.com* for special discounts and promotions.

Whale-watching

Commercial St, marks the historic spot where the Pilgrims first stepped aground.

At the base of the tower, the ADA-compliant **Provincetown Museum** highlights the chronology of the town's evolution. From its First Nations, the Wampanoags, and their encounters with the Pilgrims, to its development as a predominantly Portuguese fishing port and eventual emergence as a free-spirited arts, theater and LGBTIQ- embracing tourist hub, its story is celebrated with pride and reverence. The museum is open April to November (closed Mondays and Tuesdays), and there's plenty of parking.

On the **Town Green**, near the inclined elevator (an accessible uphill conveyance to the monument), the **Bas Relief** – an impressive 16ft-by-9ft bronze plaque erected in 1920 – marks the 300th anniversary of the Pilgrims signing the Mayflower Compact.

Whale-watching around Provincetown

The Cape's best whale-watching expeditions launch from **MacMillan Pier**, steps from Commercial St, with **Dolphin Fleet Whale Watch** *(whalewatch.com; adult/child/aged 4 and under $75/50/free)* a leading favorite. Each 3-4-hour excursion, running up to 10 times daily during peak season, is narrated and supervised by an experienced naturalist – who's

 EATING IN PROVINCETOWN: OUR PICKS

Tin Pan Alley: Our runaway favorite. Outstanding service, mouthwatering comfort foods and rockin' themed specials. A neighborhood eatery where you're part of their community. *11:30am-12:30am* $$

The Canteen: Cozy place with tasty comfort food. Don't miss the garlic-marinated pickles. *11am-4pm Sun-Thu, to 8pm Fri & Sat* $$

Relish: Great breakfast and lunch sandwiches, plus a bakery and salad bar. Best chicken salad sandwich, ever. *hours vary* $$

Fanizzi's: Wide views overlooking the bay. Don't miss their all-you-can-eat Sunday brunch smorgasbord. *11:30am-3:30pm & 4:15-9:30pm* $$

busy collecting and sharing data from each trip with scientific and educational institutions that support whale conservation efforts. You'll head 6 miles off coast to the **Stellwagen Bank National Marine Sanctuary** – a protected marine habitat home to whales, dolphins, seals and sharks – where you're virtually guaranteed to see acrobatic humpbacks breaching the waters next to your boat. Bring binoculars and sunblock – and be ready to get wet. The tours run April to October, and reservations are recommended. Breakfast, lunch and cocktails are available.

Explore beaches, forests and bogs

Bike, hike or skate the paved, 5.45-mile **Province Lands Trail** *(nps.gov/caco)* through pine forests, sandy dunes and marshy bogs for stunning views of Cape Cod Bay and the Atlantic Ocean. It's an intermediate-level challenge.

Start at the **Province Lands Visitor Center** (open May to October), where there's ample parking and ocean views from the observatory deck (open year-round) – watch for spouting and breaching whales in the distance. Begin the trail loop to the left, leading past **Provincetown Municipal Airport** toward **Race Point Beach** and then on toward **Herring Cove Beach**, where you can try to spot right whales during their spring and summer migration. Complete your loop to finish back at the visitor center.

Nantucket Island

Harpoons, whale tales and commanding views

About 30 miles south of Cape Cod is Nantucket Island, where the highlight is the **Whaling Museum** *(nha.org; adult/child $20/5)*. Covering the island's storied and proud heritage as whaling capital of the world, the museum is housed in a circa-1846 whale-oil candle factory, where exhibits depict life during the late-1700s peak of the once cutting-edge, financially lucrative whaling industry. Banned since 1986, commercial whalers previously supplied a much-coveted product used in lamp oil, candles, paint, soap, textiles, toys and rope. Nowadays, efforts continue across Cape Cod to protect whale species, promoting the resurgence of local populations. Don't miss the awesome views from the rooftop deck. The museum is open Monday to Saturday (and Sundays in summer), mid-February to December.

Sturbridge

Step back into 19th-century New England

Once you've explored the coast, turn your sights inland, where **Old Sturbridge Village** *(osv.org; adult/child $27/12, discounts available)* – about a 30-minute drive from Worcester in central Massachusetts – takes you back into a rural New England hamlet from the 1830s, complete with houses, shops, churches, schools and mills, all of which were transported from around the region. The museum covers some 240 acres, with houses and shops surrounding a green in the center, and

---

LONG POINT DREAMING

Ed Macri, co-owner of the exquisite Land's End Inn *(landsendinn.com)* B&B, shares a favorite activity.

One of Provincetown's most magical excursions is to **Long Point Beach**, a strip of sand ending the spiral of Cape Cod. There, you might share the beach with only seals, stand just yards from passing boats and enjoy breathtaking views of town. The easiest way to get there is via the Flyer's Shuttle at MacMillan Pier. Or trek across the breakwater, a short walk from our inn in the West End. After the 40-minute journey across, turn right and follow the beach until you reach Wood End Lighthouse. Just be sure to pack plenty of water and check the tides – the breakwater becomes impassable at high tide.

BEST CENTRAL MASSACHUSETTS HIKES

Scenic mountain ranges rise steeply on either side of the Connecticut River, offering moderate hikes with great panoramic rewards.

The **Mt Tom State Reservation** protects the Mt Tom Range on the west side of the river. Start near the visitor center for the challenging 4-mile hike up Mt Tom (990ft), or the easier 1.7-mile hike up to **Goat Peak**, which is topped with a lookout tower.

You can drive to the top of Mt Holyoke (942ft), in **Skinner State Park**, from May to September. Thankfully the 1.5-mile hike is not too strenuous, providing summiteers with expansive vistas over the Connecticut River Valley.

working farms and water-powered mills in the surrounding countryside.

Visitors are invited to wander and explore independently. Along the way, you'll meet 'interpreters' – historians dressed in period garb – who are hard at work tending their homes, farms and shops. The interpreters stay in character as they explain their tasks and tools. Check the schedule of daily events for possible cooking demonstrations, school lessons, house tours and more. Incredible handiwork is on display here, as the craftspeople demonstrate cabinetry, pottery, basket-weaving, blacksmithing and more. It's also interesting to see the farm animals – all 'heritage' breeds that are similar to the historical breeds from the 19th century.

Old Sturbridge Village is open year-round, Wednesday through Sunday, plus holiday Mondays. In December, it's open on select evenings only (for a Christmas by Candlelight program) but closed during its regular operating hours. It's best to avoid the village on weekdays from the end of April until mid-June, as this is a popular time for school field-trips.

Springfield & Around

An immersion in children's literature

If you're travelling with Dr Seuss fans, consider making a detour to visit the **Amazing World of Dr Seuss** (*seussinspringfield.org; adult/child $25/13*) in Springfield. The museum celebrates the life and work of Theodor Seuss Geisel (aka Dr Seuss), who was born and raised here. It offers hands-on kid's activities, original artwork displays and a moving collection of letters. Outside, the Dr Seuss Memorial Sculpture Garden includes bronze depictions of his most beloved characters.

Just 25 miles north on I-91, in Amherst, is the **Eric Carle Museum of Picture Book Art** (*carlemuseum.org; adult/child $15/8*), co-founded by Eric Carle, the author and illustrator of *The Very Hungry Caterpillar* (and about 70 other books). This superb spot displays book illustrations from around the world and the permanent collection of Carle's own vibrant work. Read-aloud story times and hands-on art projects engage visitors of all ages.

Both museums have excellent bookstores, but if you don't find what you're looking for, head 9 miles west to **High Five Books** (*highfivebooks.org*) in Florence (a village of Northampton).

DRINKING AROUND STURBRIDGE & WORCESTER: BEST BREWERIES

Rapscallion Pub: Beers from the brewery in Spencer are served in this cozy Sturbridge pub along with snacky food and live music. *4-10pm Mon-Thu, from noon Fri & Sat, to 8pm Sun*

Tree House Brewing Company: Highly touted New England IPAs and other beers are brewed and sold only on-site, 5 miles east of Sturbridge. *11am-8pm Mon-Thu, to 9pm Fri & Sat, noon-8pm Sun*

Wachusett Brewing Co: This Westminster outfit makes and serves ales and lagers in a brewhouse in the shadow of its namesake mountain. *noon-9pm Mon-Thu, to 10pm Sat, to 7pm Sun*

Jack's Abby: Winning awards for craft lagers since 2011, sample beers and wood-fired pizzas at this Framingham brewery, between Boston and Worcester. *noon-9pm Sun & Tue-Thu, to 11pm Fri & Sat*

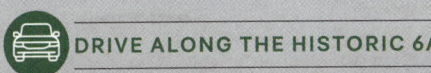

DRIVE ALONG THE HISTORIC 6A

Known as the Old King's Highway, this scenic road dissects villages that evoke the spirit of Olde Cape Cod, with galleries, antique shops, museums and charming historical properties.

START	END	LENGTH
Sturgis Library	Brewster Store	15 miles; 2 hours

Begin your journey at ❶ **Sturgis Library** in Barnstable. Dating to c 1644, it's the USA's oldest building housing a library – and holds a first-edition *Moby Dick*. Head east to ❷ **Old Jail**, a wooden prison that's held infamous pirates and is believed to be haunted. Admire historic captains' homes while driving east toward ❸ **Edward Gorey House**, a museum in Yarmouth Port once home to the delightfully twisted author, who was also an illustrator for Lewis Carroll and HG Wells. A bit further on, hang a left onto Center St for ❹ **Gray's Beach** in Dennis. Back on the Old King's Highway, continue east, turn right onto Scargo Hill Rd and follow signs to ❺ **Scargo Tower**. Climb atop this century-old, 30ft cobblestone tower for commanding views. Drive a mile back to 6A and park at ❻ **Cape Cinema**, an operating vintage theater and site of the 1939 world premiere of *The Wizard of Oz* thanks to Margaret Hamilton (the Wicked Witch), who'd played summer theater in the same arts complex at ❼ **Cape Playhouse**. This 540-seat, velvet-draped venue has been hosting Broadway-quality performances since 1927. Next door, ❽ **Cape Cod Museum of Art** presents established and up-and-coming Cape artists in a variety of media. Push on 5 miles east along 6A. ❾ **Cape Cod Museum of Natural History** in Brewster features compelling presentations on the region's geographic transformation, showcasing much of its colorful fauna. End your trip at ❿ **Brewster Store**, an 1866 general store that time has forgotten.

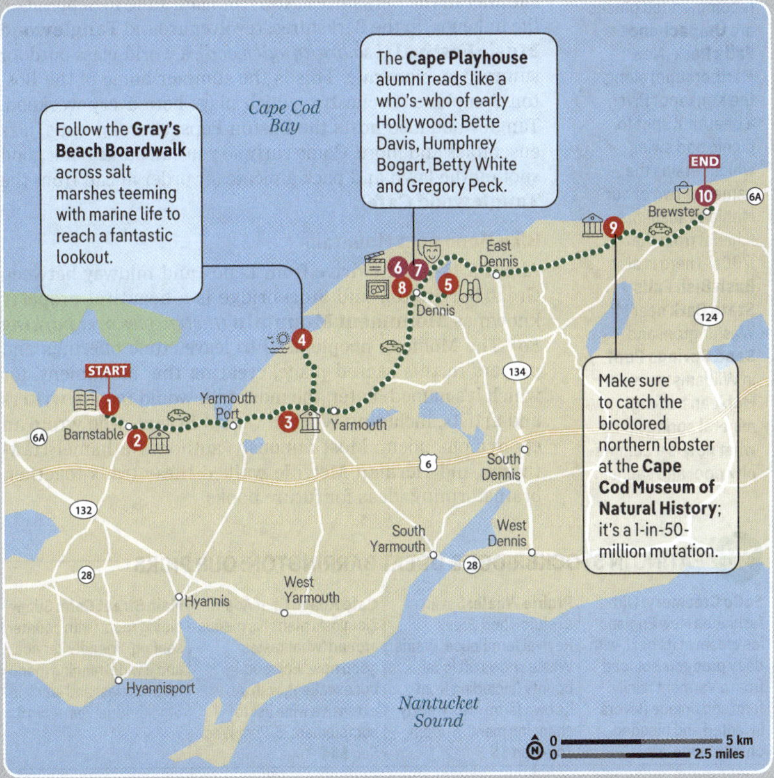

Follow the **Gray's Beach Boardwalk** across salt marshes teeming with marine life to reach a fantastic lookout.

The **Cape Playhouse** alumni reads like a who's-who of early Hollywood: Bette Davis, Humphrey Bogart, Betty White and Gregory Peck.

Make sure to catch the bicolored northern lobster at the **Cape Cod Museum of Natural History**; it's a 1-in-50-million mutation.

NATIVE AMERICAN HERITAGE

Bonney Hartley is the Historic Preservation Manager of the Stockbridge-Munsee Tribe *(mohican.com)*.

Mohican people are 'people of the waters that are never still,' and our Berkshire homelands reflect this quality of our heritage. The landscape is abundant with rivers, waterfalls and natural springs that our ancestors knew and loved. Some recommended places are **Umpachenee Falls Park** (New Marlborough) along the Konkapot River, a beautiful spot to picnic and swim, which retains the names of two of our Mohican *sachems* (chiefs) from the 1700s. There is also **Bash Bish Falls State Park** near Mt Washington, and **Sand Springs Pool** in Williamstown – a Mohican healing mineral spring filling what now is a community pool and sauna.

The Berkshires

Music under the stars

An evening of alfresco entertainment is one of the delights of summer in the Berkshires. And from late June to September, life in Lenox, in the Berkshires, revolves around **Tanglewood Music Festival** *(bso.org/tanglewood)*, a world-class outdoor summer music venue. This is the summer home of the Boston Symphony Orchestra, which plays here every weekend. Tanglewood also hosts the Boston Pops, choral groups, jazz ensembles and more. Come early so you can stake out a good spot on the lawn and pack a picnic (or order ahead from the **Tanglewood Cafe**).

Hike Monument Mountain

About a 15-minute drive from Lenox and midway between Great Barrington and Stockbridge is a beautiful property known as **Monument Mountain** *(thetrustees.org; parking $6)*. The Mohican people used to leave stone offerings and prayers in this sacred place, creating the 'monument' for which it's named. Later, the mountain would inspire writers and artists, including William Cullen Bryant, who wrote an eponymous poem. Most famously, authors Nathaniel Hawthorne and Herman Melville walked these trails together, brainstorming ideas for future books.

 EATING IN STOCKBRIDGE & GREAT BARRINGTON: OUR PICKS

SoCo Creamery: Old-fashioned New England ice cream at its best, with dairy products sourced from a Vermont family farm and unique flavors invented and blended on-site. *noon-10pm* $

Prairie Whale: Set in a refurbished Greek Revival farmhouse, Prairie Whale shows off local bounty (including from its own farm) in its weekly changing menu. *5-10pm Thu-Mon* $$

Cafe Adam: Chef Adam Zieminski plans his menus around 'what tastes good now.' Eclectic but excellent, with an extensive wine list to complement. *5-9pm Wed-Sun* $$$

Main Street Cafe: Sunny dining room (with counter seating), friendly service and a wide-ranging menu for breakfast and lunch in Stockbridge. *7am-4pm* $

Mt Greylock

You, too, might find inspiration at Monument Mountain, with its 3-mile hiking route to/from the summit at Squaw Peak (1642ft) via the Hickey Trail and a lookout at Devil's Pulpit. On a clear day, you'll see all the way to **Mt Greylock** (Massachusetts' highest peak) in the northwest and the Catskills in the east.

Visit a living museum

The Shakers were an 18th-century religious sect that practiced communal living, gender and racial equality, pacifism and celibacy (the latter explaining why they have all but disappeared). Their worship often included ecstatic trembling, which inspired their moniker, and they were also renowned for their work ethic and artistry.

In the late 18th century, Shaker communities sprouted up throughout the northeast, including the **Hancock Shaker Village** (hancockshakervillage.org; adult/child $20/8) in Pittsfield, which today remains as a living museum with original buildings, Shaker furniture and exhibits about community life (though no Shakers live here anymore). It's open daily from mid-April through October.

FARMS FOR EVERY SEASON

Berkshire Grown (berkshiregrown.org) is a guide to locally grown food, including pick-your-own, farmers markets, events and farm-to-table restaurants. Some of our favorites:

Windy Hill Farm: Come for blueberries in summer and apples in fall.

Lakeview Orchard: Pick your own sweet and tart cherries, raspberries, plums, redcurrants, blueberries and 15 varieties of apples.

High Lawn Farm: A dairy farm where you can purchase fresh-from-the-cow milk and cream, farmstead cheese, slow-churned butter and - yes! - dense ice-cream.

Hilltop Orchards: A traditional apple orchard, with pick-your-own apples and fresh cider. The Furnace Brook Winery is on-site.

 EATING IN LENOX: OUR PICKS

Chocolate Springs Cafe: This cozy cafe is filled with chocolate treats, from 'serious' hot chocolate to gelato, truffles and more. Also, see the chocolatiers at work. *9am-7pm* **$**

Haven Cafe & Bakery: With ingredients sourced from local farms, Haven offers a refined menu of fancy egg dishes for breakfast and sophisticated sandwiches for lunch. *8am-2pm Thu-Mon* **$$**

Bistro Zinc: A slick, modern setting (with a zinc bar) for decadent French classics, from *moules frites* to beef bourguignon. *11:30am-3pm & 5-9pm* **$$$**

Alta: Head to this classy eatery for decadent delights such as seared duck in salty caramel sauce or chipotle-braised pork cheeks. *5-9pm Sun, Mon, Wed & Thu, to 10pm Fri & Sat* **$$$**

Rhode Island

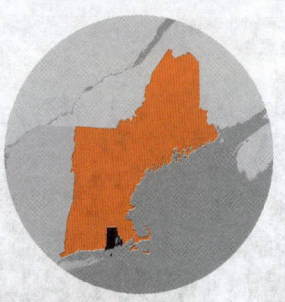

WATERSIDE WALKS | MUSEUMS | STATELY HOMES

Places
Providence p196
Newport p198

☑ TOP TIPS
You can drive almost anywhere in Rhode Island in under an hour. But give yourself time – those 1034 sq miles are dense with things to see and do. Also factor in extra time for navigating around inlets and across Narragansett Bay.

Puritan minister and theologian Roger Williams landed in what would become Rhode Island after he was banished from Massachusetts for his belief in the separation of church and state – opinions that officials deemed 'new and dangerous.' Williams and his wife fled to the tip of Narragansett Bay, where they befriended Native Americans and purchased a portion of their land, which they declared a place of religious freedom. Relationships with area tribes became more complicated as colonists continued arriving with big plans and an individualistic outlook. While conflict between neighboring colonies and tribes sowed chaos across Rhode Island for much of the 17th century, the colony's commitment to religious freedom opened up the waterways to a steady flow of both newcomers and commerce.

Today, the state holds on to that underdog energy. Between its shiny resort exteriors and a proud, ocean-worn heart is a willingness to try new things, innovate and welcome new ideas.

GETTING AROUND

It's helpful to have four wheels in Rhode Island, where major highways connect most destinations. Check out at least one of the state's nine designated scenic roadways. Parking is plentiful in Providence, but can be crowded in Newport. Both cities are enjoyably walkable and in Newport, popular attractions can be reached by the city's trolley, which offers a free hop-on-hop-off service from May through October, departing from the Newport Transportation Center.

From June to October, you can board the **Seastreak Ferry** *(seastreak.com)* to travel between Providence, Bristol and Newport. It's a slow but fun way to see three significant destinations.

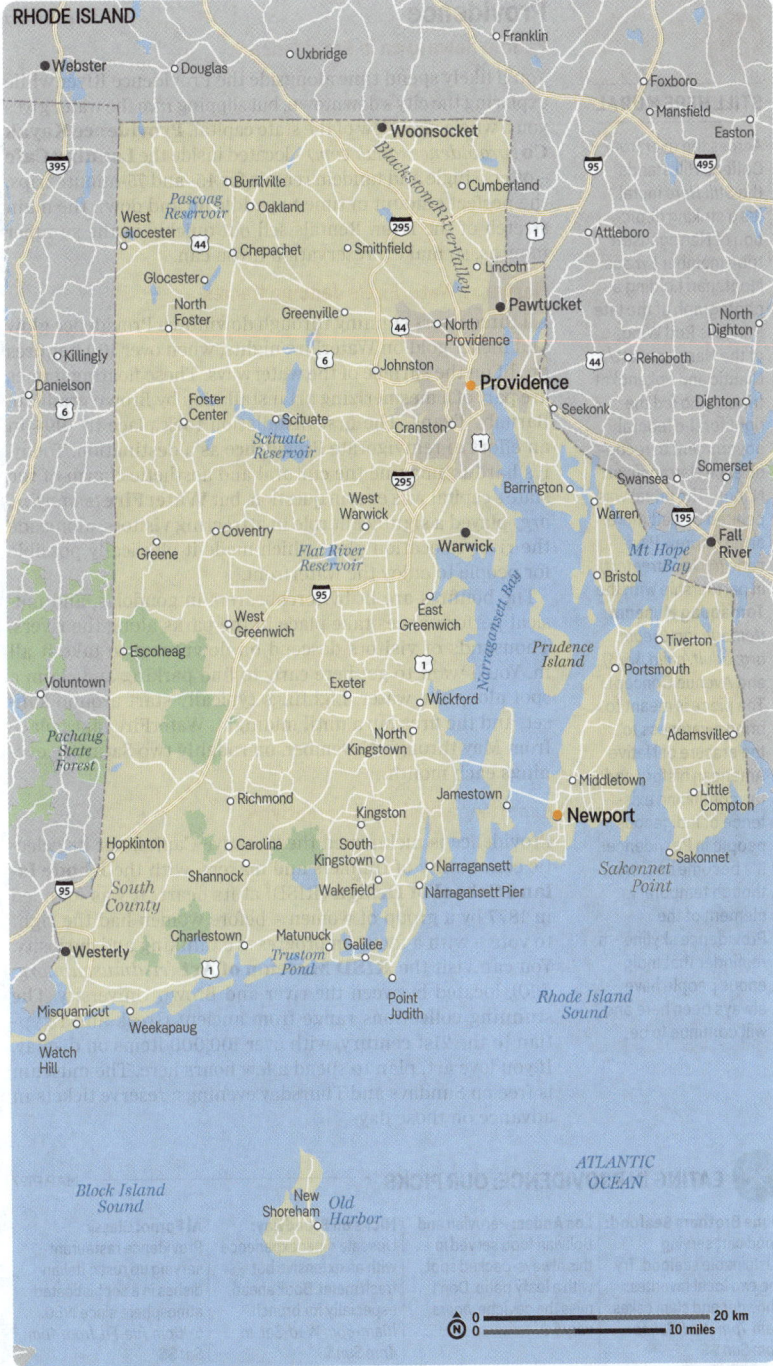

Providence

MAP P197

Paddle downtown in Providence

You'll likely spend time alongside the Providence River while exploring the city's downtown, but slipping *into* the water gives you a whole new view of the state capital. **Providence Kayak Co** *(providencekayak.com)* – located inside the **Landing Cafe** – offers single and tandem rentals for 45- and 75-minute trips, the perfect amount of time to paddle up and down the main stretch of the river. Rentals sell out quickly in the summer months, so make a reservation if you can.

Marvel at WaterFire's dancing flames

All three rivers running through downtown Providence glow and flicker gold on WaterFire nights, when over 100 bonfires are lit on the surface of the waterways. These floating flames are part of a mesmerizing art installation by Brown graduate Barnaby Evans. The first installation took place in 1994 in an effort to reinvigorate Providence as a destination. Today, it's hard to imagine the cultural and aesthetic charm of the state's capital was ever in question, but **WaterFire** *(waterfire.org)* played a significant role in attracting visitors, alongside the river relocation plan, which made it physically possible for people to enjoy the waterfront.

The bonfires are lit by torchbearers in gondolas, and musical performances take place in the parks along the rivers. Thousands of visitors descend on downtown to take it all in. You'll want to get here early to find parking and claim a spot along the water. Lightings typically start around sunset, and the fires burn until midnight. WaterFire takes place from May through November, on roughly two Saturday evenings each month.

Experience design and creativity

Providence is nicknamed the 'Creative Capital' for its eclectic community of thinkers and makers, with the **Rhode Island School of Design** (RISD) at its heart. It was founded in 1877 by a group of women – before women had the right to vote – with a focus on progressive thinking and curiosity. You can visit the **RISD Museum of Art** *(risdmuseum.org; $20)*, located between the river and Brown University. The stunning collections range from ancient Greek and Egyptian to the 21st century, with over 100,000 items on display. If you love art, plan to spend a few hours here. The museum is free on Sundays and Thursday evenings; reserve tickets in advance on those days.

STILL HERE MURAL

Across the river from College Hill stands the *Still Here* mural. It's a striking depiction of Narragansett tribe member Lynsea Montanari holding a photograph of the late Princess Red Wing, of the Narragansett/Niantic and Pokanoket tribes, who led the fight for the federal government to recognize the Narragansett Nation. The mural was painted by Baltimore artist Andrew Pisacane *(@Gaiastreetart)* in partnership with the **Tomaquag Museum** *(tomaquagmuseum.org; adult/child $6/3)* and Avenue Concept. The piece is meant to bring awareness to the erasure of Native American history and the continuing existence of Indigenous people in Providence. It's become an iconic, though temporary, element of the Providence skyline – a reminder that Indigenous people have always been here and will continue to be.

EATING IN PROVIDENCE: OUR PICKS

MAP P197

Dune Brothers Seafood: Food cart serving sustainable seafood. Try the two local favorites: chowder and clam cakes. *11am-7pm Wed-Sat, to 5pm Sun* $$

Los Andes: Peruvian and Bolivian food served in this always-packed spot with a leafy patio. Don't miss the ceviche. *hours vary* $$

Nicks on Broadway: Upscale diner experience with an extensive but fresh menu. Book ahead, especially for brunch. *10am-8pm Wed-Sat, to 4pm Sun* $

Al Forno: Classic Providence restaurant serving up rustic Italian dishes in a sophisticated atmosphere since 1980. *5-10pm Tue-Fri, from 4pm Sat* $$

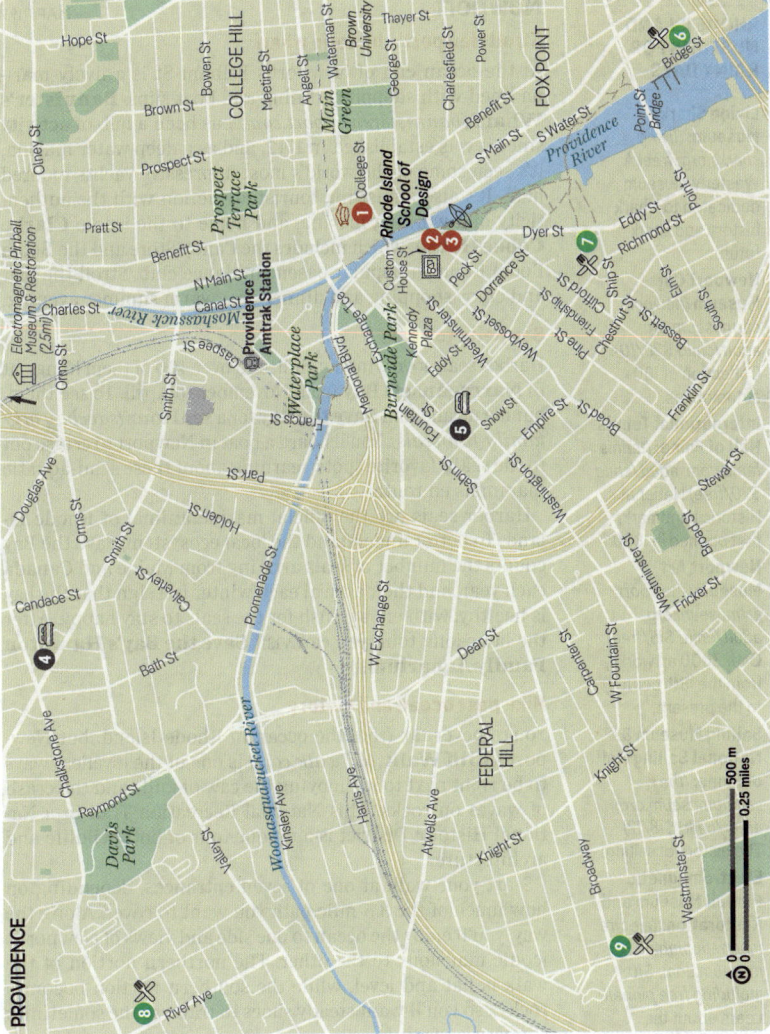

PROVIDENCE

★ HIGHLIGHTS
1 Rhode Island School of Design

● SIGHTS
see 1 RISD Museum of Art
2 Still Here mural

● ACTIVITIES
3 Providence Kayak Co.

● SLEEPING
4 Esperanto
5 Dean Hotel

● EATING
6 Al Forno
7 Dune Brothers Seafood
8 Los Andes
9 Nicks on Broadway

● DRINKING & NIGHTLIFE
see 3 Landing Cafe

Newport

MAP P199

RHODE ISLAND MUSEUMS FOR RAINY DAYS

Living Sharks Museum: *(livingsharks.org; free)* A Westerly museum dedicated to 'shark history and shark future.'

Newport Car Museum *(newportcarmuseum.org; adult/child $20/10)*: Collection of 100+ automobiles.

International Tennis Hall of Fame: *(tennisfame.com; adult/child $20/free)* National Historic Landmark, first opened in 1880.

Newport Art Museum: *(newportartmuseum.org; adult/child $15/free)* Over 3000 artworks, from the 18th century to the present.

Sailing Museum & National Sailing Hall of Fame: *(thesailingmuseum.org; adult/child $18/12)* The history of sailing.

Electromagnetic Pinball Museum and Restoration: *(electromagneticpinballmuseum.com; $10 including free pinball)* Learn about the craft behind pinball machines.

Stroll Newport's historic wharf

At the ocean end of Newport's Pelham St is a lively marina lined with shopping, dining and boat slips. **Bannister's Wharf** *(bannistersnewport.com)* has been a hub of activity since it was established in 1742, and as a deep water marina, it's seen some of the world's most impressive yachts moored here. It's also a bustling tourist attraction with the authenticity of a working marina, and home to the iconic **Clarke Cooke House**, which includes the Candy Store and the Boom Boom Room, a popular basement dance club. Stroll the pier and enjoy shopping and dinner on a warm summer evening.

Say hello to seals

Harbor seals love winter's chill, and over 400 of them hang out in **Narragansett Bay** from November to April. To see them, bundle up and join **Save the Bay** for a **seal tour** *(savebay.org/family-fun/seals)*. You'll board a boat in Newport to cruise out to the seals' favorite spots, learning about these semi-aquatic mammals en route.

Harbor seals are the official marine animal of Rhode Island. To better understand the local ecosystem, Save the Bay counts the number of seals arriving from Maine and Canada each year, and their arrival each winter is a sign that the bay is healthy, with enough fish for the seals to stay happy. After the hour-long tour, you can visit **Save the Bay's Hamilton Family Aquarium**.

Hike past ocean and history

You're never far from the ocean in Rhode Island, but Newport's **Cliff Walk** *(cliffwalk.com)* is one of the loveliest ways to be right next to it, enjoying the caw of gulls and the crash of waves on rocks. This National Recreation Trail in a National Historic District is a unique tour of both wildlife and architecture.

Start your walk at one of seven entrances, depending on how much of the 3.5-mile path you want to cover. Along the way, you'll enjoy the ocean to one side and views of Newport's iconic mansions to the other. The northern portion of the walk is flat and level, while the southern portion becomes rocky, so you'll want steady shoes to traverse the sometimes slippery surfaces.

EATING IN NEWPORT: SCRUMPTIOUS BREAKFASTS

MAP P199

Corner Cafe: A cozy spot for all-day breakfast. House specials like the Jimmy Pesto Especial are worth the wait. *hours vary* $$

Cru Cafe: The locally sourced menu rotates seasonally at this trendy cafe. Breakfast served all day. Bonus: BYOB. *8am-3pm* $$

Annie's: The best breakfast deal is right on Bellevue Ave. The classic diner menu includes budget basics and decadent options such as crab-cake Benedict. *7am-3pm* $

Coffee Grinder: For a light breakfast, enjoy an authentic Italian espresso coffee and a pastry with views of Newport Harbor. *7am-6pm Sun-Thu, to 7pm Fri & Sat* $

NEWPORT

HIGHLIGHTS
1. Bannister's Wharf
2. Cliff Walk
3. The Breakers

SIGHTS
4. International Tennis Hall of Fame
5. Marble House
6. Newport Art Museum
7. Rosecliff
8. The Elms
9. Sailing Museum & National Sailing Hall of Fame

ACTIVITIES
10. Save the Bay's Hamilton Family Aquarium

SLEEPING
11. Mill Street Inn

EATING
12. Annie's
13. Clarke Cooke House
14. Corner Cafe
15. Cru Cafe
16. Scales & Shells
17. The Red Parrot

DRINKING & NIGHTLIFE
18. Coffee Grinder

ENTERTAINMENT
19. Bowen's Wharf Seafood Festival

NEWPORT'S BELOVED FESTIVALS

Newport Folk Festival: Started in 1959, the summer event takes place on a peninsula in Fort Adams State Park.

Newport Jazz Festival: A multiday music fest that includes jazz and genre-defying artists, both well-known and up-and-coming; also in Fort Adams State Park.

Newport Oyster Festival: For one weekend in May, oyster growers and vendors gather at Bowen's Wharf for visitors to sample the local variety.

Bowen's Wharf Seafood Festival: In October, historic Bowen's Wharf hosts a cornucopi of local seafood along with live music.

Newport Pride: The annual June Pride march includes a bike parade, live performances and an inclusive, loving atmosphere.

Newport Folk Festival

Discover gilded-age extravagance

In the late 19th century, when robber barons were rolling in untaxed wealth, Newport became the most stylish summer destination. The wealthiest of New York and Philadelphia spent millions building extravagant mansions on rolling estates with views of the Atlantic Ocean. Today you can tour a handful of these opulent homes for a look inside the Gilded Age. Highlights include the **Breakers** – a Vanderbilt family property built in the Italian Renaissance style; **Rosecliff**, featuring a heart-shaped staircase and Newport's largest ballroom; **Marble House**; and **The Elms**. Regular house tours are self-guided, and you can download the Newport Mansions app *(newportmansions.org)* for an audio tour of each. If you're interested in going deeper, book a guided tour, like 'Beneath the Breakers', where you'll explore the subterranean levels of the house, or the 'Servant Life Tour' to see how 'the help' kept things running.

EATING IN NEWPORT: SEAFOOD FAVORITES

MAP P199

Flo's Clam Shack: Established in 1936, this casual spot serves scrumptious fried seafood from two locations: Middletown and Portsmouth. *11am-9pm* $

Scales & Shells: Exclusively serving seafood, this popular eatery sources locally. Snag a seat on the balcony for views of Thames St. *hours vary* $$

Clarke Cooke House (p198)**:** Refined dishes served with classic maritime elegance, on Bannister's Wharf with harbor views. *1:30pm-midnight Mon-Sat, from 11am Sun* $$$

Red Parrot: Lobster is the star of the Red Parrot's extensive menu, served on three levels with festive, family-friendly vibes. *11:30am-9:30pm Sun-Thu, to 10:30pm Fri & Sat* $$

Connecticut

CHARMING SHORELINE | RIVER VALLEYS | VIBRANT CITIES

Connecticut, perhaps more than any other New England state, is cloaked in clichés as a moneyed place where New Yorkers come to play tennis and ride horses. But people who know the state know of its grit, history and charm, from the dense woods where gnarled trees grow through 19th-century farm equipment to industry towns that have risen, fallen and risen again with the evolution of goods and technology.

Prior to the arrival of Dutch fur traders and English Puritan settlers, the Pequots, Mohegans, Paugussets and Schaghticokes called this land home. Despite a devastating genocide known as the Pequot War, surviving Pequots have maintained their culture and now own the famous Foxwoods Casino and other major businesses. While colonial history dominates, there are many opportunities to learn about the people who have been here for thousands of years while exploring a state dotted with picturesque coastal towns, rolling hills, covered bridges and medium-sized cities full of nightlife and culture.

Places

New Haven p203
Guilford & Madison p205
Essex p205
Mystic p206
Hartford p207
Northeastern Connecticut p209

☑ TOP TIP

New Haven was the United States' first city designed on a grid. While this layout should make it easy to navigate, one-way streets can make driving a frustrating endeavor. Take the train or ditch the car ASAP and explore on foot. Elsewhere, most towns have a walkable green or central district, but you'll want to drive to reach other areas of interest.

GETTING AROUND

Driving makes it easier to get to the central and northern parts of the state. I-95 will bring you up and down the coast, while I-91 is the main thoroughfare north. Take the scenic routes if you have time.

The **Metro-North Railroad** *(mta.info)* services the shoreline, from New York's Grand Central Terminal to New Haven. From there, you can continue along the coast via Shoreline East all the way to New London. The **Hartford Line** *(hartfordline.com)* connects central Connecticut to the coast.

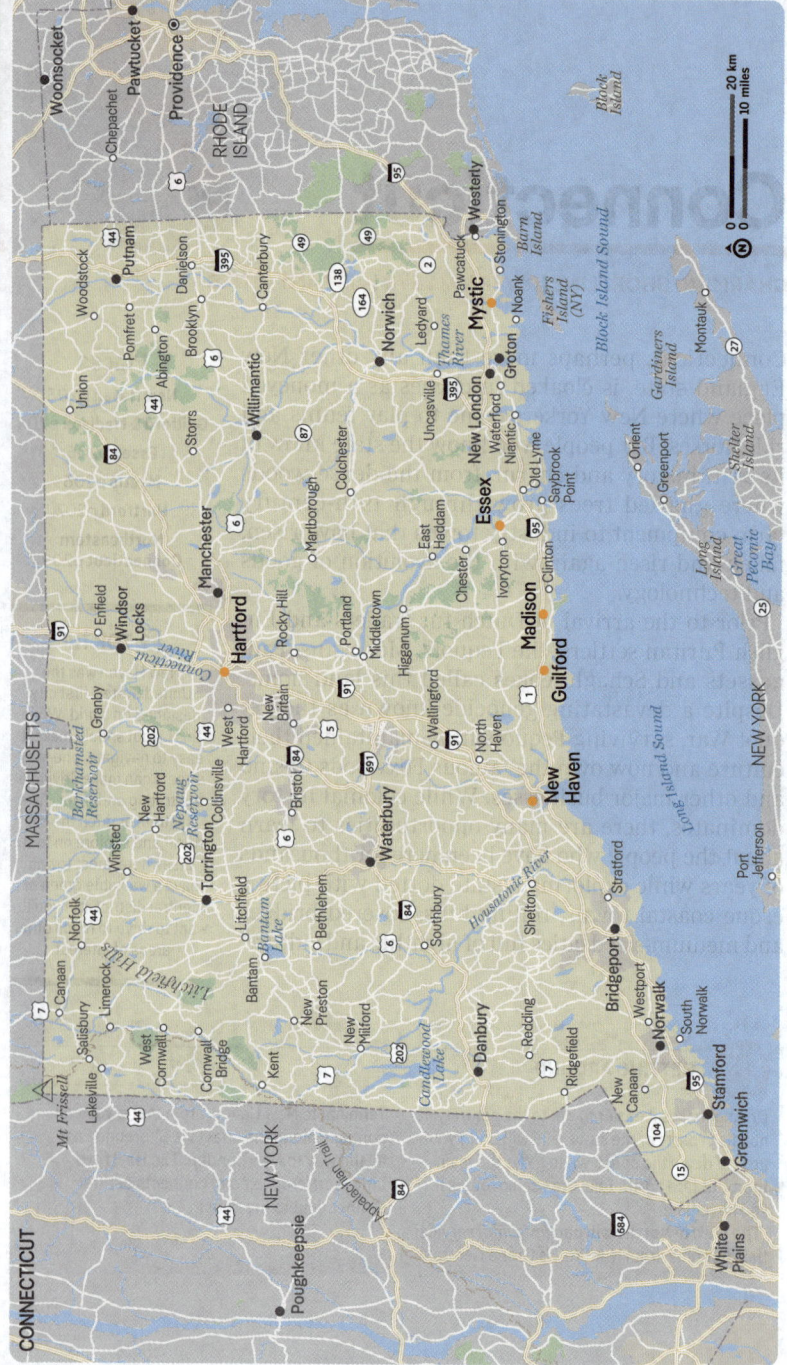

New Haven

MAP P204

Line up for pizza

New Haven pizza is a family affair. **Frank Pepe** opened his pizzeria *(pepespizzeria.com)* on Wooster Street in 1925. His nephew opened Pepe's long-standing rival, **Sally's Apizza** *(sallys apizza.com)*, on the same street in 1938. **Modern Apizza** *(modernapizza.com)* was already on the scene in 1934, and the three cemented the city's status as a pizza destination with a uniquely New Haven style: Neapolitan with an extra thin crust that's fired to a crispy, black char (don't call it burnt).

A visit to Pepe's or Sally's means lining up, even before they open, and then declaring yourself committed to one or the other. Don't expect an expansive menu of sides and drinks. All three serve the white clam pie pizza, invented by Pepe's and embraced by all.

The 'newest' pizza spot is **BAR** *(barnightclub.com)*, a restaurant-club-pub which opened in 1996 to serve a younger, hipper crowd; it's famous for the mashed potato pie.

All four are within a mile or two of each other, and walking between them is a great way to see the Wooster and East Rock neighborhoods.

Climb above the city

If you're looking for a bird's eye view of New Haven and some green reprieve from the city streets, **East Rock Park** is your spot. The summit, standing 350ft above Mill River, was formed 200 million years ago when molten rock erupted between stress cracks in the region's sandstone bedrock, then cooled and hardened into dolomite. The surrounding sandstone was softer, and erosion carved it down through the centuries, eventually making East Rock a distinguished rock face.

Climb the **Giant Steps Trail** to the summit, where you'll find the *Soldiers and Sailors* monument, commemorating New Haven residents who died in various wars. Enjoy the views over New Haven as it stretches to the Long Island Sound.

Go back in time at the Peabody

The dinosaur skeletons got a bit older during the four years that New Haven's **Yale Peabody Museum** *(peabody.yale.edu; free)* was closed for major renovations and expansion – but in that time, they found lots of new friends. The renowned natural history museum reopened in March 2024 with new

NEW HAVEN TRAIN STATIONS

New Haven has two train stations: **Union Station** and **State Street Station**.

Union Station is the larger of the two, with Amtrak, Metro-North and CTrail services, along with many bus and shuttle lines. The station itself is a bustling, beautiful hub of transportation, with classic wooden benches and a high ornamental ceiling. The ride from Union Station to Grand Central in New York City is just under two hours and runs regularly. Expect crowded trains at rush hour and around the holidays.

State Street is a smaller, newer station with only local service.

If you're heading to a train station in New Haven, make sure you know which one!

 EATING IN NEW HAVEN: BEYOND PIZZA MAP P204

Meat & Co.: Grab a thick, decadent sandwich at Meat & Co. and bring it next door for beer at East Rock Brewery. *11:30am-8:30pm Sun-Thu, to 9:30pm Fri & Sat* **$**

Camacho Garage: Housed in an old Shell gas station, this Westville favorite serves contemporary Mexican street food. *hours vary* **$$**

Heirloom: Located in The Study at Yale, the menu at this place is an exciting exploration of local seafood and farm-fresh produce. *7am to 9pm* **$$**

Junzi Kitchen: Healthy, filling meals prepared to order with authentic Chinese flavors – and made extra tasty with their signature chili oil. *11am-9pm* **$**

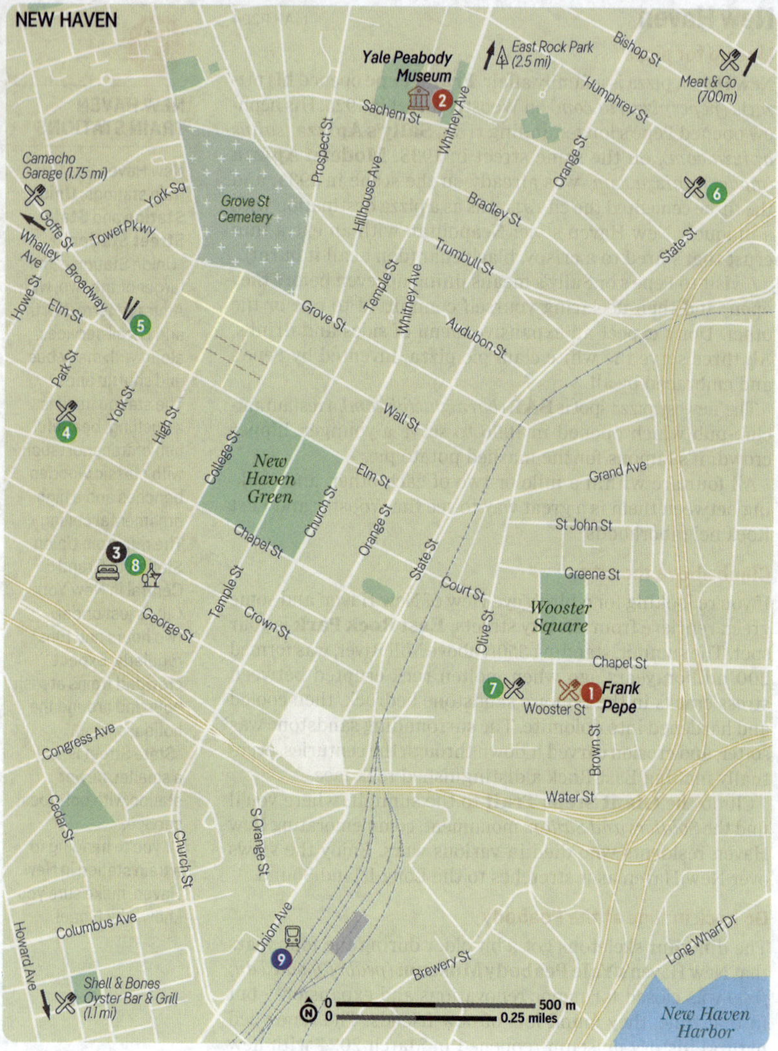

NEW HAVEN

⭐ HIGHLIGHTS
1. Frank Pepe
2. Yale Peabody Museum

⚫ SLEEPING
3. Blake Hotel

🟢 EATING
4. Heirloom
5. Junzi Kitchen
6. Modern Apizza
7. Sally's Apizza

🟢 DRINKING & NIGHTLIFE
8. BAR

🔵 TRANSPORT
9. Union Station

spaces, exhibits and an increased focus on accessibility. The cathedral-like building's two-story great hall was built to house the giant skeletons of extinct reptiles, including a beloved brontosaurus, and they continue to be a major draw. Today, the new and improved Peabody includes 14 million specimens and objects that map the history of life on Earth.

Guilford & Madison

A Connecticut shoreline sampler

Dive into a books and beaches theme when exploring Guilford and Madison, adjacent shoreline towns where you'll find thoughtfully curated independent bookstores and peaceful coastal spots to read. In Guilford, **Breakwater Books** *(breakwaterbooks.net)* sits on a vibrant town green with a row of boutiques, restaurants, a coffee shop and a chocolatier. Once you've picked your read, enjoy it on nearby **Jacobs Beach**.

From Guilford, take Rte 1 to the main strip of downtown Madison and **RJ Julia Booksellers** *(rjjulia.com)*. This cozy shop is packed with just about any genre you can imagine, and there's a cafe. If the sun is out, bring your book to nearby **Hammonasset Beach State Park**, with a 2-mile stretch of sand and water access.

You might also venture down one of the nature trails through the park's tidal marsh habitat. The National Audubon Society named Hammonasset a Globally Significant Bird Area for its high concentration of rare and endangered birds.

Essex

A turning point in travel

About a 40-minute drive from New Haven is Essex, where you can experience a slice of travel history by riding a **steam train** *(essexsteamtrain.com)* and riverboat for a tour of the Connecticut River Valley. Board a vintage coach pulled by a steam locomotive at Essex Station for the narrated 90-minute trip, during which you'll chug through thick forest and small towns, with a beautiful landscape gliding by your window.

At Deep River Landing, leave the train to board the *Becky Thatcher* riverboat to cruise along the Connecticut River. There are multiple open-air decks from which can view the riparian habitat of blue herons, egrets, cormorants and red-winged blackbirds. From February to March, you're likely to spot bald eagles as they migrate to the region from Canada.

THE OLD STONE HOUSE

About halfway between the Guilford Town Green and the marina sits the oldest house in Connecticut, set back from the road on a gently rolling lawn, and easy to miss as you drive by. Now officially called the **Henry Whitfield State Museum** (and also known as the Stone House), it was built in 1639 by Reverend Henry Whitfield, who lived there with his wife and children. The land was taken over by the Whitfields as part of an agreement with the Menunkatuck band of the Quinnipiac tribe; the settlers also used it as a defensive building, and it marked the start of tensions and the eventual displacement of the native people of coastal Connecticut.

 EATING ON THE CONNECTICUT SHORELINE: SEAFOOD

Lenny & Joe's Fish Tale: Lenny and Joe's is a festive summer favorite, thanks to the big patio with a merry-go-round and ice-cream shack. *11:30am-8:30pm Sun-Thu, to 9pm Fri & Sat* $$

Shell & Bones Oyster Bar & Grill: Decadent small plates and dinners are served on a beautiful waterfront patio in New Haven. *noon-10pm Mon-Thu, 11am-11pm Fri-Sun* $$$

Bill's Seafood: The perfect place to celebrate summer, with seafood and live music. Their Rhode Island and New England clam chowders are both delicious. *11am-9pm* $

Dog Watch Cafe: Sit on a dock in Stonington or play yard games in Mystic. Both locations have distinct vibes and scrumptious seafood. *11:30am-9pm* $$

PROTECTIVE SALT MARSHES

Salt marshes cover about 15,000 acres along Connecticut's shoreline, marking the transition from ocean to land. But the salt marshes have shrunk significantly in the past century. To ensure the state maintains this vital foraging habitat for birds, breeding habitat for saltwater fish and flood protection for coastal communities, **Audubon Connecticut** *(audubon.org)* is working on salt-marsh restoration up and down the Connecticut coast. Efforts include removing invasive plants and using dredged soil to rebuild target elevations that have suffered from erosion. You can enjoy the lively beauty of salt marshes from the Guilford Salt Meadows Audubon Sanctuary, Hammonasse Beach State Park, and the Stewart B. McKinney National Wildlife Refuge.

Choose between coach, 1st class or the caboose for the train. First-class passengers are able to purchase alcohol and non-alcoholic beverages. The boat is open seating/standing.

Mystic

Climb aboard wooden ships

About an hour's drive from New Haven is the **Mystic Seaport Museum** *(mysticseaport.org; adult/child $32/22)* – a hands-on exploration of Connecticut's maritime history, focused on the 1800s, when Mystic's whaling industry was thriving. But you won't just look at pictures and read placards about rigging wooden ships and forging iron harpoons; you'll watch people actually *do* these things. Come prepared for an indoor/outdoor experience: start with the indoor museum, which includes an art gallery and rotating exhibits on maritime history. Then wander the replica seaport village and the shipyard, where you can visit their historic ships.

The *Charles W Morgan* is the museum's most famous vessel. Built in 1841, this whaling ship once traversed much of the globe, breaking through sea ice in the Arctic circle and rounding Cape Horn to bring back the whale oil that fueled lamps and greased countless innovations of the Industrial Revolution. Today it's the only remaining wooden whaling ship in the world, and it sits out of the water at Mystic Seaport, meaning visitors can clamber aboard and glimpse what it would have been like to live onboard for months at a time.

It's easy to spend several hours at the museum. To make a full day of it, opt for the Mystic Seapass, which includes

Mystic Seaport Museum

entrance to both the Mystic Seaport Museum and the **Mystic Aquarium** *(mysticaquarium.org; adult child from $34/26)* just down the street.

Hartford

Tour Mark Twain's family home

Mark Twain was a man of big dreams and strong opinions, and visitors to the **Mark Twain House & Museum** *(mark twainhouse.org; adult/child $28/15)* in Hartford get a feel for that. All of the words he wrote and thought about travel, politics, racism, imperialism, public schools and more bounce timelessly between these walls that preserve his legacy.

The home was built in 1873, and Sam Clemens (Mark Twain was his pen name) moved in with his wife Olivia in 1874. It was their dream home, and the author later called the years they spent there with their daughters the family's happiest. He wrote some of his most popular books in the Hartford house, including *The Adventures of Tom Sawyer* (1876), *Adventures of Huckleberry Finn* (1884) and *A Connecticut Yankee in King Arthur's Court* (1889).

 EATING IN HARTFORD: OUR PICKS

Max's Trumbull Kitchen: A global menu paired with a long list of seasonal cocktails offers endless possibilities at this downtown location. *hours vary* **$$**

Black-Eyed Sally's Southern Kitchen & Bar: Award-winning Southern staples are served in a lively atmosphere with live music. *noon-8pm, bar open late* **$$**

Rockin Chicken: Succulent chicken is cooked in a charcoal rotisserie oven from Peru and served alongside other authentic Peruvian favorites. *11am-8pm* **$$**

Max Downtown: Upscale steakhouse classics. There's a dress code for the main dining area. *11:30am-9pm Mon-Thu, to 10pm Fri, from 5pm Sat* **$$$**

THE OLDEST NEWSPAPER

The *Hartford Courant* was first published in 1764, before the founding of the US. When the second owner died of smallpox, his widow, Hannah Bunce Watson, took over, becoming the country's first female publisher. For many years, the paper ran ads to aid in the capture of fugitive enslaved people. The northern state's early pro-slavery sentiments reflects a dark and often-overlooked aspect of Connecticut's history.

The ads ended in 1848 when the state officially outlawed slavery, but the paper remained a significant political voice. Around 1870, Samuel Clemens (Mark Twain) sought (unsuccessfully) to become a shareholder. Today, the *Hartford Courant* is the oldest continuously running newspaper in the country and it prints daily. The online version *(courant.com)* is a great resource for news and events.

He and his family loved Hartford, too. It was a city of intellectuals, with Harriet Beecher Stowe, author of *Uncle Tom's Cabin* (1852), their neighbor. 'All I should get for it would be the pleasure of living in Hartford among a most delightful society, and one in which [Livy] and I both would be supremely satisfied,' he once said, according to the Mark Twain House and Museum.

The only way to visit the house is on a tour, which is well worth it. They're offered seven days a week and sell out several days ahead of time, so book yours early.

Traverse art history

Any visit to downtown Hartford should include at least a couple hours at the **Wadsworth Atheneum** *(thewadsworth.org; adult/child $20/free)*, an art museum that's sprawling in both space and coverage. A cultural hub since the 19th century, the collection includes 50,000 pieces spanning 5000 years. While the original proposal was for an art 'gallery,' founder and Hartford native Daniel Wadsworth decided to make it an 'atheneum' instead – a cultural center dedicated not just to the preservation of fine art but also to history and education. Don't miss the Morgan Great Hall, where powerful American and European paintings from the 16th to 19th centuries climb deep blue walls to reach an arched white ceiling with dazzling skylights.

Roseland Park, Woodstock, in the Last Green Valley

Northeastern Connecticut
Enjoy fall foliage with Walktober

Connecticut's northeastern 'Quiet Corner' is also known as the **Last Green Valley** *(thelastgreenvalley.org)*. This region is a National Heritage Corridor, a wilderness more than 10 times bigger than Acadia National Park. In October, the area comes to life with fall colors and activities, including **Walktober**, a local event that's been taking place for over 34 years. Throughout the month, you can join dozens of guided walking tours in many of the Last Green Valley's 35 Connecticut towns. Tours range from historical walking tours and ghost tours to farm visits and river paddles.

FEAST ON FARM PRODUCE

Litchfield County, in the Berkshire foothills, is home to over 85,205 acres of farmland that produces fresh fruit and vegetables, as well as eggs, meat and dairy. For the freshest food, go straight to the farms or farmers markets in the area, where you can meet the growers and enjoy unique agricultural experiences. On Saturdays, the **Litchfield Hills Farm Fresh Market** *(litchfieldfarmersmarket.org)* is open indoors at the Litchfield Community Center from October through May. In July, pick your own berries at **Evergreen Berry Farm** *(evergreenberryfarm.com)* in Watertown. At **Lindell Flower Farm** *(lindellflowerfarm.com)*, admire rows of color and bring home your own bouquet; the farm store is open daily from 10am to 6pm.

EATING IN LITCHFIELD COUNTY: ALFRESCO DINING

Down the Hatch: Vacation vibes are strong at the only restaurant on Candlewood Lake. Enjoy fresh seafood and cocktails. *11:30am-midnight, Tue-Sun* $$

White Horse: British-inspired pub food next to the East Aspetuc River. Savor award-winning cooking on one of the four patios. *11:30am-9pm Mon-Thu, to 10pm Fri & Sat, 11am-8:30pm Sun* $$

West Shore Seafood: *The* place in Litchfield County for fried fish, shrimp baskets and lobster rolls. Pick up food at the window and enjoy in their all-weather tent or on the lawn. *hours vary* $

Hopkins Inn: Austrian fine dining, sitting above the shore of Lake Waramaug. Try the traditional Wiener schnitzel. *hours vary* $$$

Vermont

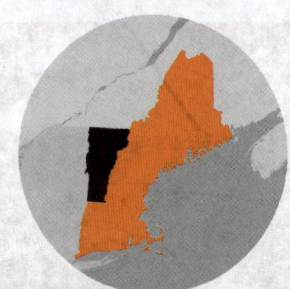

LAKE CHAMPLAIN | GREEN MOUNTAINS | HISTORIC VILLAGES

Places

Burlington p212
Middlebury & Around p213
Stowe & Around p214
Montpelier p217
East Burke p220
Peacham p221
Bennington p221

☑ TOP TIP

Travel in Vermont is slower than you'd expect from the state's diminutive size, which maxes out at 150 miles north to south, and 90 miles east to west. Allow extra time to navigate the mountainous terrain and rural roads.

With its blend of bucolic farmland, serene mountains and picturesque villages, Vermont is one of the country's most uniquely appealing destinations. Here in the nation's second-least-populous state, where the capital city (Montpelier) only has 8000 residents, and the largest (Burlington) tallies just shy of 45,000, nature always feels close at hand. Hikers, bikers, skiers and boaters flock year-round to Vermont's Green Mountain slopes, the expansive waters of Lake Champlain and the impressive network of parks and recreation trails.

Travelers invariably notice something different when they cross the state line. For starters, there's Vermont's total lack of billboards; you'll also see more mom-and-pop businesses, fewer big box stores and considerably less urban sprawl than in other parts of the country.

In a world where breakneck growth often prevails, Vermont takes a certain pride in its nonconformist approach and remains a haven for quirky creativity and community-mindedness. It's a bastion of the 'small is beautiful' aesthetic.

🧭 GETTING AROUND

Two superhighways serve Vermont. I-91 traces the state's eastern edge from Massachusetts to Canada, while I-89 cuts a diagonal swath northwest from New Hampshire to Lake Champlain and the Québec border. Western Vermont's main thoroughfare is US Hwy 7. Elsewhere, two-lane state highways and remote backroads prevail.

Amtrak (amtrak.com) operates two Vermont-bound trains: the **Ethan Allen Express**, running from New York City through the Hudson Valley to Rutland, Middlebury and Burlington; and the **Vermonter**, connecting Philadelphia, New York City, Connecticut, Massachusetts and Washington, DC, with nine Vermont stations between Brattleboro and St Albans.

Vermont Translines (vttranslines.com) and **Greyhound** (greyhound.com) offer long-distance bus services from Albany and Montréal, while **Dartmouth Coach** (dartmouthcoach.com) runs from Boston and New York City to neighboring New Hampshire. Within the state's borders, various regional operators provide shorter distance connections around places such as Burlington, Montpelier and Brattleboro.

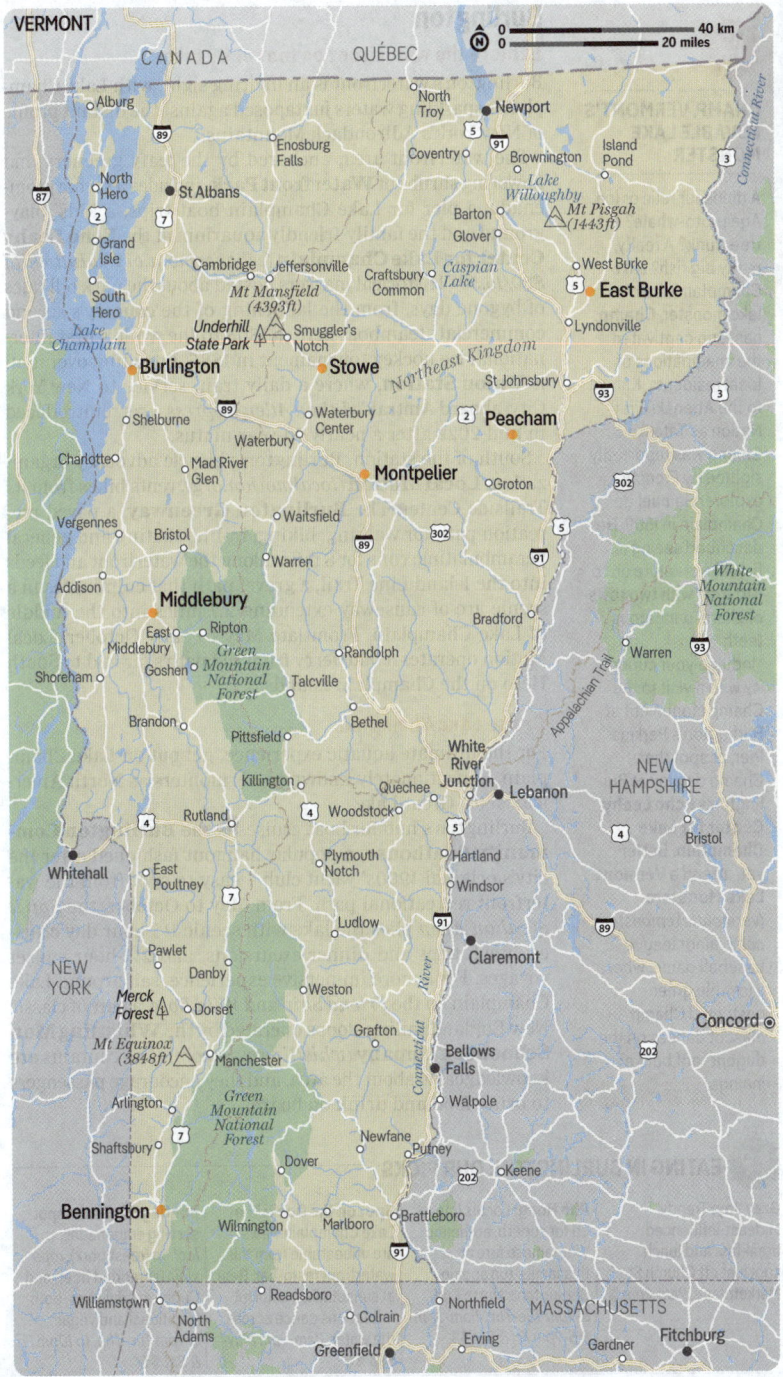

Burlington

Explore the waterfront on foot or by bike

Burlington's waterfront is an inviting sight, with Lake Champlain's sparkling waters juxtaposed against the distant profile of New York's Adirondack Mountains.

The waterfront area, anchored by the leafy greenery and flowering shrubs of **Waterfront Park**, includes a scenic promenade, a pier for Lake Champlain boat trips, a kids' playground and the family-friendly aquarium at the **Echo Leahy Center for Lake Champlain** (echovermont.org; adult/child $20/16.50). Historical markers posted about the park tell tales of bygone days, from the launching of the country's second commercial steamboat here in 1808 to the world's first international ice hockey tournament in 1886. Presiding over it all is **Union Station**, where a daily train service to New York City, aboard Amtrak's *Ethan Allen Express*, was reintroduced in mid-2022 after a nearly 70-year hiatus.

South of the station, Burlington's bicycle advocacy organization, **Local Motion** (localmotion.org), rents bikes from its Trailside Center. The **Burlington Greenway**, a paved recreation path for walking, biking, in-line skating and general perambulating, runs for 8 miles along the waterfront and feeds into the Island Line Trail, a gravel path that culminates in a scenic arc of causeway extending 2.7 miles into the middle of Lake Champlain. From late May to early October, Local Motion operates a bike ferry from the path's far end to South Hero on the Champlain Islands.

Cruise Lake Champlain

For the ultimate aquatic experience, get out on Lake Champlain – affectionately known to Vermonters as North America's sixth Great Lake.

Burlington's hub for boat cruises is the **Burlington Community Boathouse**, a popular hangout fashioned after the city's original 1900s' yacht club – easy to spot from the waterfront recreational path. From May to October, the *Spirit of Ethan Allen* plies the lake with scenic 1½-hour cruises, lunch trips and dinner excursions, and 2½-hour sunset voyages. For a more immersive experience, sail around Lake Champlain on the *Friend Ship* and *Wild Rose*, a pair of classic New England sailing sloops operated by the **Whistling Man Schooner Company** (whistlingman.com). The captains are knowledgeable about the area, and they encourage passengers to bring food and drink on board.

CHAMP, VERMONT'S LOVABLE LAKE MONSTER

A dinosaur relic or Ice Age proto-whale? A tree trunk? A really, really big fish? Lake Champlain's beloved lake monster, **Champ**, has long captivated the imaginations of local residents. Known to the Abenaki First Nation as Tatoskok, Champ was reportedly sighted by French explorer Samuel de Champlain in 1609. He described seeing a fish-like creature up to 10ft long with two rows of sharp, dangerous teeth.

Indulge your curiosity with a visit to the Champ Monument at Burlington's Perkins Pier, or spot the Champ display at Burlington's **Echo Leahy Center for Lake Champlain**. Better yet, attend a **Vermont Lake Monsters** (vermontlakemonsters.com) minor league baseball game, where a lovable green-costumed Champ mascot dances on the dugout roof between innings.

 EATING IN BURLINGTON: OUR PICKS

Grey Jay: Trendy Mideast-influenced breakfast and lunch spot just off Church St Marketplace. *9am-2pm* $

Pho Hong: Locals line up for superb, authentic Vietnamese fare at this family-run spot in Burlington's North End. *3-9pm Tue-Thu, 11am-3pm & 5-9pm Fri & Sat* $$

Spot on the Dock: The Lake Champlain views are unbeatable from this waterfront resto-bar. Best at sunset when colorful reflections dance across the water. *11am-9pm May-Sep* $$

Santiago's: Cuban spot serving empanadas, *lechón* (roast pork), *ropa vieja* (shredded beef) and Cuban sandwiches, both traditional and vegan. *5-9pm Tue-Thu, to 10pm Fri & Sat* $$

Lake Champlain

Burlington's **Community Sailing Center** *(communitysailingcenter.org)* rents out kayaks, canoes and paddleboards by the hour.

Serious paddlers with their own boats can explore dozens of miles of shoreline north and south of the city on the **Lake Champlain Paddlers' Trail**. There's no finer way to enjoy the water than on a multiday excursion, overnighting at one or more of the 600-plus camping spots around the lake.

Middlebury & Around

Walk the Robert Frost Trail

For nearly four decades, Robert Frost (1874–1963), the Poet Laureate of Vermont, spent the summer and fall near Middlebury (about an hour's drive from Burlington), growing apple trees, teaching and writing much of his poetry in a log cabin in **Ripton**, a beautiful hamlet set in the Green Mountains. For a taste of the landscape he loved and the poetry it inspired, take a walk on the **Robert Frost Interpretive Trail** *(fs.usda.gov)*, 10 miles southeast of Middlebury on VT 125. The roughly 0.75-mile loop traverses a wetland on boardwalks, then crosses the Middlebury River and loops through forests and meadows. Along the way, plaques display half a dozen of Frost's poems.

VERMONT'S BEST FARMSTANDS

Cedar Circle Farm: Shop this East Thetford farmstand for fruit and veggies, or pick your own in expansive fields stretching down to the Connecticut River.

Champlain Orchards: Renowned apple-cider producer southwest of Middlebury hosting pick-your-own-fruit-and-berries sessions, plus seasonal events.

Brattleboro Farmers Market: Folks gather here weekly to buy direct from farmers and enjoy live music beside the tree-shaded Whetstone Brook.

Jubilee Farmstand: This gargantuan barn in Huntington with a Camel's Hump mountain backdrop epitomizes Vermont's time-honored self-serve system (choose your produce, leave money in the cashbox).

Pete's Greens: Four-season organic farm selling direct to customers daily (May to October) in charming Craftsbury village.

 EATING BEYOND BURLINGTON: OUR PICKS

Middlebury Bagel & Deli: Family-run Middlebury institution specializing in homemade donuts, bagel sandwiches and made-to-order breakfasts. *6am-1pm, closed Thu & Sun* **$**

Rustic Roots: Delightful breakfast and lunch spot in an old gray farmhouse near the center of Shelburne village. *9am-2pm Wed-Sun* **$$**

Shelburne Farms Inn: Pioneering farm-to-table eatery serving breakfast and dinner in a lakeside mansion on a gorgeous historic estate. *8-11am & 5-8:30pm* **$$$**

Blue Paddle Bistro: Popular dinner spot on the Champlain Islands offering everything from burgers to lobster, plus a great Sunday brunch. *5-8pm Thu-Sat, 9:30am-1pm Sun* **$$$**

BEST FALL FOLIAGE SPOTS

Mt Mansfield: Head to Stowe, Jeffersonville, Cambridge, Smugglers Notch or Underhill State Park for panoramic views of the fiery foliage and (sometimes) snow-dusted summit of Vermont's highest peak.

Lake Willoughby: Enjoy the technicolor majesty of changing maples on the precipitous slopes of this fjord-like lake.

Mad River Valley: Gawk at gorgeous colors from VT 100, the backroads on the opposite side of the valley, or Mad River Glen's iconic single chairlift.

Merck Forest: Take in breathtaking Taconic Mountain vistas from Merck's barn meadow.

Grafton: Grafton's white clapboard houses are especially photogenic when contrasted against blazing maples and a brilliant blue October sky.

Trapp Family Lodge

A quarter mile further east, National Forest Rd 396 leads from the Robert Frost Wayside picnic area up to Frost's former cabin; today it's viewable from the outside only, but the lovely mountain views from here are well worth the detour. Continue east up VT 125 to find the distinctive yellow-frame buildings of the **Bread Loaf School of English** (*middlebury.edu/blse*), which Frost helped found while teaching at Middlebury College. In winter, Bread Loaf transforms itself into the **Rikert Outdoor Center** (*rikertoutdoor.com*), whose Frost Fields loop trail allows skiers to experience the poet's cabin in all its wintry glory.

Stowe & Around

Ski the USA's oldest Nordic trails

Among Vermont's 30 Nordic skiing venues, nothing compares to a day at **Trapp Family Lodge** (*vontrappresort.com*), 4 miles west of Stowe. Founded by the Von Trapp family of *The Sound of Music* fame, America's oldest cross-country center features 40 miles of groomed trails for every skill level; the Austrian-inspired eating and drinking options make for a dreamy all-day skiing experience.

For a delightful loop, start with an easy glide through snow-covered forest on Sugar Rd, then huff and puff your way

EATING IN STOWE: OUR PICKS

Piecasso: Stowe's go-to choice for pizza, après-ski or following a summer outing on the adjacent Stowe Recreation Path. *11am-10pm Fri & Sat, to 9pm Sun-Thu* $$

Bistro at Ten Acres: On a hillside west of town, this cozy spot serves soups, salads and mains, from veggie curry to meat and fish specials. *5-10pm Fri-Tue* $$$

Harrison's: Steaks, grilled pork chops, roast lamb, venison and seafood rule the menu at this traditional favorite in the heart of Stowe village. *4:30-8:30pm Wed-Sat* $$$

Michael's on the Hill: Gourmet choice in a sweet 19th-century hilltop farmhouse 6 miles south of Stowe. *5-9pm Wed-Mon* $$$

up the Parizo Trail to a junction with the Cabin Trail. From here, a more gentle climb leads to **Slayton Pasture Cabin**, where you can warm yourself by the fire with hot chocolate, homemade soup or chili.

Now comes the fun part! At the far end of Slayton Pasture, begin the ridiculously long and gradual descent down Haul Rd. At the bottom, you can pick up the Luce Trail to loop back to the lodge – but for a longer, even more blissful day out, cross Trapp Hill Rd and continue descending through open pastures to Lager Lane, home to the **Von Trapp Bierhall**. Here you can feast on bratwurst, schnitzel, sauerkraut mashed potatoes and roasted veggies, all accompanied by the Von Trapp's European-styled homebrews and finished off with Austrian desserts like Sachertorte.

Afterwards, Sleigh Rd is your gateway to several scenic (albeit uphill) loops back to the lodge.

Explore Vermont's most captivating mountain pass

Just 10 miles northwest of Stowe via VT 108, **Smugglers Notch** (2170ft) is one of Vermont's most scenic mountain passes. Named for the smugglers who used this route to transport goods between Vermont and British Canada prior to the War of 1812, it's the jumping-off point for numerous hiking trails, including the **Long Trail**, which runs for 272 miles between the Massachusetts and Québec borders.

The road up is an adventure in itself. Near the summit, cliffs and boulders encroach on the roadway from both sides, narrowing the state highway to a strip of asphalt barely wide enough for two vehicles. An obligatory stop en route is the **Barnes Camp Visitors Center**, where the recently constructed Smugglers Notch Boardwalk allows visitors in wheelchairs or with strollers to follow a short section of the Long Trail through a montane wetland to a viewpoint with lovely perspectives on the notch. Plaques along the way offer insights about the ecology and natural history. Hiking destinations from the notch include Sterling Pond and Elephant's Head to the northeast, and Mt Mansfield (p216) to the southwest.

Enjoy legendary ice-cream

In 1978, Ben Cohen and Jerry Greenfield took over an abandoned gas station in Burlington and, with a modicum of training, launched the outlandish flavors that forever changed America's ice-cream culture. Nearly half a century later, a tour of **Ben & Jerry's Ice Cream Factory** *(benjerry.com/about-us/factory-tours; adult/child $6/1)* – 1 mile north of

ROADS LESS TRAVELED

For a scenic adventure, try these less-traveled, unpaved Green Mountain crossings.

Hazens Notch Rd: This Revolutionary War-era route crosses a glacier-scoured notch, passing pretty wetlands and beautiful views of Jay Peak.

Lincoln Gap Rd: The 16-mile road from Bristol to Warren climbs ridiculously steeply through Lincoln Gap (2428ft). When closed in winter, it's popular with daredevil sledders.

Mt Tabor Rd: Surrounded by Green Mountain National Forest, the 15-mile journey from Danby to Landgrove grants access to the Appalachian Trail and White Rocks National Recreation Area.

Kelley Stand Rd: Stretching from East Arlington to Stratton, this 14-mile road climbs steeply up the Battenkill River's Roaring Branch before leveling into a landscape of high altitude ponds.

DRINKING IN STOWE: OUR PICKS

Alchemist Beer Cafe: Enjoy a draft Heady Topper with Jamaican fare at Vermont's renowned Alchemist Brewery. *11am-6pm*

Von Trapp Bierhall: Authentic Alpine food and German-style lagers are served under the soaring ceiling at this ski-in trailside beerhall. *11:30am-9pm*

Stowe Cider: Sample crisp, hard ciders in the tasting room, or pair them with a meal at the adjacent Shakedown Street BBQ. *4-9pm Wed & Thu, noon-9pm Fri & Sat, to 8pm Sun*

WhistlePig Pavilion: Sip Vermont's finest rye whiskey and cocktails après-ski or during the summer concert series at Stowe's Spruce Peak. *noon-7pm Sun-Thu, to 9pm Fri & Sat*

VERMONT'S LONG-DISTANCE HIKING & SKIING TRAILS

Long Trail: The USA's first long-distance hiking trail was built between 1912 and 1930. It traces the Green Mountains' ridgeline for 272 miles from Massachusetts to Canada. The **Green Mountain Club** (GMC; greenmountainclub.org) maintains more than 60 rustic lodges and lean-tos en route; for more info, visit GMC's headquarters south of Stowe. The Long Trail served as inspiration for the Appalachian Trail, and these two venerable routes coincide for nearly 100 miles in southern Vermont.

Catamount Trail: Running the length of Vermont from Readsboro to North Troy, the 300-mile Catamount Trail is the country's longest cross-country ski route. Its magnificent meander through the Green Mountains encompasses 11 ski touring centers, including some that offer lodging.

Waterbury off I-89 and about a 15-minute drive from Stowe – remains an obligatory stop. Half-hour tours start with a campy video that follows the company's long, strange trip to corporate gianthood; next, you'll head to a special glassed-in room to glimpse the production line in action. After chowing (very teeny) free scoops, linger a while to admire the informational displays about Ben & Jerry's efforts to change the world through community building and environmental leadership, one scoop at a time. In summer, cows roam among the solar panels and pastures outside.

Before you leave, make sure to climb the grassy knoll above the upper parking lot to see Ben & Jerry's Flavor Graveyard. Ringed by a neat white picket fence and framed by a grand purple archway, this tongue-in-cheek tribute to four-dozen ice-cream flavors that flopped features neat rows of headstones that honor forgotten concoctions like Dastardly Mash, Divinity Bovinity and Vermonty Python. Each memorial is lovingly inscribed with the flavor's brief lifespan on the grocery shelves of this Earth and a poem in tribute.

Admire 360-degree views of Vermont

Vermont's tallest mountain may look small by world standards, but a climb to the summit here is an unforgettable experience. **Mt Mansfield** (4393ft) encompasses a larger swath of above-the-treeline terrain than any place in Vermont, yielding spectacular views west to Lake Champlain and the Adirondacks, south along the Green Mountains' rugged spine, east to the White Mountains and north into Québec on a clear day. The peak's profile resembles a human face, as reflected in the anthropomorphic names (Adam's Apple, Chin, Nose, Forehead) shown on local trail maps. Mansfield is also home to 200 acres of fragile alpine tundra, the largest such expanse in Vermont. Stowe makes a fine base for Mt Mansfield.

Two classic approaches to the mountain are via the **Long Trail South** from Barnes Camp (p213) or the **Hell Brook Trail** from Smugglers Notch (p213; look for both trailheads west of Stowe on VT 108); however, the steep ascents here (2700ft over roughly 2 miles) are not for the faint of heart.

For a more moderate climb (2600ft over 3.3 miles) with awesome nonstop views, head for **Underhill State Park** (vtstateparks.com/underhill.html) on Mt Mansfield's western flank. Start with a gentle 1-mile climb on the CCC Rd, then bear left into the forest, cross several bridges and begin climbing in earnest on the **Sunset Ridge Trail**. Partway up the mountain, a worthwhile detour leads to Cantilever Rock,

EATING BEYOND STOWE: OUR PICKS

Red Hen Bakery: Roadside pit stop between Waterbury and Montpelier that's beloved for its delectable pastries, sandwiches and hearty organic bread. 7am-3pm $

Warren Store: Enjoy breakfast and lunchtime goodies on the deck or the steps overlooking the sculpted rocks and swimming hole below. 7:30am-5pm Fri & Sat, 8am-3pm Sun-Thu, closed Tue $

American Flatbread: Wood-fired pizzas and locally sourced salads served beside a roaring fire in winter or at picnic tables with mountain views in summer. 4-9pm Thu-Sun $$

Hen of the Wood: Waterbury's iconic gourmet eatery, featuring farm-to-table and wild-sourced ingredients. 5-10pm Wed-Mon $$$

Vermont State House

where you can pause for a snack on massive stone slabs. Back on the main trail, you'll soon emerge above the treeline. The summit looks deceptively close, but you've still got a solid hour of steady climbing; no worries – the jaw-dropping vistas offer ample compensation. You'll know you're getting close when you reach junctions with the Laura Cowles and Long Trail and begin crossing boardwalks through the tundra. From here, it's a short scramble to reach the 360-degree panoramas up top. Allow five to six hours for the round trip.

Montpelier

Visit the country's smallest capital city

With only 8000 inhabitants, Montpelier is the country's smallest capital city, and the only one without a McDonald's. Towering above town, the golden dome of the **Vermont State House** (statehouse.vermont.gov; free) is Montpelier's unmissable landmark. On weekdays, visitors can take a tour (docent- or self-guided, depending on whether the legislature is in session). In the lobby, look for the fossils of ancient sea creatures embedded in the 'black marble' (actually limestone) floor, quarried from an ancient reef on Isle La Motte in the Champlain Islands.

(continues on p220)

GETTING AROUND IN NORTH-CENTRAL VERMONT

Exploring north-central Vermont is easier with your own vehicle, as public transit is limited, with Burlington the most economical place to arrange rentals. If you don't have your own car, **Amtrak**'s once-daily *Vermonter* train to/from Washington, DC and New York City has stops in Montpelier and Waterbury. The **RCT** *(Rural Community Transportation; riderct.org)* bus 100 runs from Waterbury to Stowe. The **GMT** *(Green Mountain Transit; ridegmt.com)* bus 83 – the Waterbury Commuter – connects Waterbury with Montpelier (20 to 30 minutes), and bus 86 (the Montpelier Link Express) offers service from Montpelier and Waterbury to Burlington. From late December through March, GMT also runs a seasonal ski shuttle from Waitsfield to Mt Snow's Lincoln Peak.

DRINKING BEYOND STOWE: OUR PICKS

Lawson's Finest Liquids: Iconic Vermont brewery serving pints and pub grub around outdoor firepits and under the high ceilings of its Waitsfield brewpub. *noon-7pm Sun-Thu, 11am-8pm Fri & Sat*

Prohibition Pig: Waterbury microbrewery with an on-site restaurant specializing in scrumptious barbecue and Southern fare. *4-9pm Mon-Fri, from noon Sat & Sun*

Three Penny Taproom: Excellent cocktails and an ever-evolving assortment of top-notch beers on tap in downtown Montpelier. *11am-9pm Mon-Thu, to 10pm Fri & Sat*

Capitol Grounds: Montpelier's go-to spot for an early-morning java jolt; near the Vermont State House. *6:15am-2pm Mon-Fri, from 7am Sat & Sun*

DRIVING TOUR

Drive Vermont's Scenic Route 100

Weaving along the base of the Green Mountains through the rural heart of Vermont, VT 100 is one of New England's quintessential road trips. The route rambles past cow-speckled pastures, tiny villages with country stores and white-steepled churches, and verdant mountainsides crisscrossed with hiking trails and ski slopes. Even if your time is limited, don't miss the scenic 45-mile stretch between Stockbridge and Waterbury, an easy detour off I-89.

1 Wilmington
Nestled in the upper Deerfield Valley, historic Wilmington was chartered by New Hampshire governor Benning Wentworth in 1751. These days, it's best known as the access point for **Mt Snow** *(mountsnow.com)*, one of southern Vermont's best ski resorts and a summertime mountain-biking and golfing destination.

The Drive Head 44 miles north on VT 100, passing through the pretty villages of Jamaica and Londonderry.

2 Weston
The picture-postcard village of Weston (population 566) is renowned for its **Vermont Country Store**, run by five generations of the Orton family. This browsers' paradise is packed with vintage games, flannel nighties, Vermont-made cheeses, maple products, penny candies and more. Across the town green, catch a show at **Weston Theater Company** *(westontheater.org)*, Vermont's oldest professional theater.

The Drive A quick 10-mile hop up VT 100 brings you to Ludlow.

3 Ludlow
On the Green Mountains' eastern slopes, low-key Ludlow is home to family-friendly **Okemo Mountain Resort** *(okemo.com)*. With 100-plus trails, the east's longest superpipe, excellent snowmaking and

Plymouth Cheese Corporation

high-speed lifts, Okemo appeals to skiers and snowboarders of all levels.

The Drive VT 100 snakes north past a series of lakes to Plymouth Notch, where a one-mile detour on VT 100A leads to the **President Calvin Coolidge State Historic Site**.

4 Plymouth

President Calvin Coolidge's boyhood home of Plymouth is a Vermont village frozen in time, with its one-room schoolhouse, general store and barns gracefully arrayed among old maples on a bucolic hillside. Sample the venerable Vermont cheddar produced on-site at **Plymouth Cheese Corporation** (plymouthcheese.com).

The Drive VT 100 doglegs west past Killington ski area, then resumes a northward course through the wide-open White River Valley.

5 Rochester

Cradled between two Green Mountain ridges, Rochester is another classic Vermont village with a tidy town green. Settle in for home-baked snacks and browse the shelves at **Sugar Mama's** and **The Bookery**, a cozy spot spread across two historic farmhouses.

The Drive Continue 19 miles on VT 100, passing pretty **Moss Glen Falls** and watching for moose in Granville Gulf, the gateway to the Mad River Valley.

6 Warren

Warren's blink-and-you'll-miss-it village center revolves around the **Warren Store** (p216), a creaky-floored edifice boasting two levels of shopping bliss. Head upstairs for clothing, Vermont crafts and kids' games, or grab snacks and drinks from the downstairs deli's vintage ice chest, best enjoyed on the sunny deck overlooking the sculpted rocks along Freeman Brook; the mini-gorge here is perfect for a summertime dip. North of town, giant barns, covered bridges and old farmhouses dot the landscape on your 29-mile journey up the Mad River Valley to **Stowe** (p214).

WHY I LOVE MERCK FOREST

Gregor Clark, Lonely Planet writer

Merck Forest is that rarest of jewels – a 2700-acre tract of idyllic high pastures and mountains that has escaped the relentless march of development, thanks to the foresight of the folks that preserved it as an environmental education center in the 1950s. Traveling to Merck is a trip back in time; no motorized vehicles are allowed, and traditional, sustainable land stewardship practices are observed. Visitors can mingle with farm animals and admire sweeping Taconic Mountain vistas just 10 minutes from the parking lot, or travel deep into the forest on Merck's extensive trail network for overnights at rustic backcountry cabins. As a 16-year-old, I volunteered here with the Student Conservation Association, and totally fell in love – 20 years later, Merck inspired my move to Vermont.

Mountain biking, Kingdom Trails

(continued from p217)

Just down the street, the **Vermont Historical Society Museum**'s award-winning 'Freedom & Unity' exhibit walks visitors through 400 years of history. Here you can learn about Vermont's first people, the Abenaki, or discover the story of the region's 14-year stint as an independent republic (1777–91). The rest of downtown Montpelier is eminently walkable, with State and Main Sts hosting the lion's share of shops and restaurants.

East Burke

Mountain bike the Kingdom Trails

Passing through century-old farms and forest floors dusted with pine needles, the award-winning **Kingdom Trails** *(kingdomtrails.com)* network offers one of New England's best mountain-biking experiences. In winter, its dozens of miles of singletrack, doubletrack and dirt roads are also a magnet for cross-country skiing, snowshoeing and fat biking. Trail passes are available online; a day pass costs US$20/15 per adult/child.

One of the network's most striking sections any time of year is the high ridgeline along Darling Hill Rd, where miles of trail command far-reaching views over the Northeast Kingdom's mountains and meadows. From May to October, buy trail passes at the **Kingdom Trails Welcome Center** in **East Burke**. From December to March, head uphill to the **Nordic Adventure Center**. Trails are typically closed in April and November.

Peacham

Historic village and autumn foliage

One great joy of traveling in Vermont is the serene beauty of its historic villages. One such place is Peacham, founded in the late 1700s along the then-bustling Bayley-Hazen Military Rd. These days, the town's privileged hilltop setting and the pastoral beauty of its surrounding farmland remain largely untouched by modern development, making this a wonderful spot for aimless wandering – especially in early October, when blazing maples contrast with the lush, rolling fields. From Peacham's town center, scenic dirt roads fan out in all directions. Pull out your Vermont road atlas and build a loop of any length; pretty options include Academy Hill Rd, Green Bay Loop, County Rd, Town Rd South and Old Cemetery Rd.

Bennington

Get folksy with Grandma Moses

Bennington's standout **museum** *(benningtonmuseum.org; adult/child $16/free)* houses the world's largest public collection of works by Anna Mary Robertson Moses, aka 'Grandma' Moses, who spent most of her life on a farm just across the state line in Eagle Bridge, NY, and attained international fame as a folk artist in her later years, from ages 70 to 101. The Grandma Moses gallery – recently renovated, expanded and reopened to the public – displays the artist's trademark paintings of rural life, alongside textiles and furniture. The remainder of the museum showcases three centuries worth of Vermont paintings, decorative arts and folk art. Don't miss the extensive collection of local pottery, and the vintage Martin Wasp, a showstopper of a 1925 luxury car manufactured right here in Bennington.

VERMONT'S BEST COVERED BRIDGES

Vermont has more covered bridges per square mile than any other state. Here's a pontist's guide to our favorites:

Montgomery: The seven covered bridges in Montgomery village represent the densest concentration anywhere in Vermont.

Three-in-a-Row Bridges, Northfield: On Cox Brook Rd off VT 12, cross the Station, Lower and Upper Bridges within just 0.3 miles.

Cornish-Windsor Bridge: This 449ft span from Windsor, VT, to Cornish, NH, is the country's longest covered bridge.

Fisher Railroad Bridge, Wolcott: Off VT 15 is a bridge replete with a cupola, designed to disperse smoke from the steam engines that once rumbled through.

Bartonsville: This bridge has been resurrected by the community after floodwaters swept away its 19th-century predecessor in 2011.

EATING IN & BEYOND BENNINGTON: OUR PICKS

Blue Benn Diner: A Bennington classic since 1948, this iconic diner boasts individual jukeboxes in every booth. *6am-3pm Tue, Wed, Sat & Sun, to 8pm Thu & Fri* $

Pangaea: Cozy North Bennington resto-bar with half-formal, half-casual seating and a beautiful patio overlooking the river out back. *5-9pm Tue-Sat* $$

Phelps Barn Pub: Enjoy paella, duck breast or classic pub fare by the fireside in this comfy eatery. *5-8pm Tue-Sat* $$

TJ Buckley's: Brattleboro's intimate eight-table bistro, in a converted railway dining car, is famed for its gourmet, seasonal, farm-to-table cuisine. *6-9pm Thu-Sun* $$$

New Hampshire

MOUNTAINS | LAKES | HISTORIC TOWN CENTERS

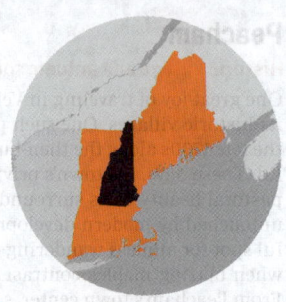

Places
Portsmouth p224
Mt Washington p226
White Mountains p228
Franconia p228

Jagged mountains, serene valleys and island-dotted lakes lurk in every corner of New Hampshire. The whole state begs for exploration, whether looking for loons near Winnipesaukee or trekking the upper peaks surrounding Mt Washington. Each season yields a bounty of adrenaline and activity: skiing and snowshoeing in winter (many slopes are open into spring), magnificent walks and drives through fall's fiery colors, and swimming in crisp mountain streams in summer.

Jewel-box historical settlements such as Portsmouth set a sophisticated tone, while small-town culture lives on in pristine villages like Peterborough and Littleton. There's even a bit of beach action, with the state making the most of its 18-mile shoreline.

Named in 1629 after the eponymous English county New Hampshire was one of the first American colonies to declare its independence from Britain in 1776. These days, it's known for its libertarian tendencies and one of the country's best-known mottos: 'Live Free or Die.'

☑ TOP TIPS

If your time in New Hampshire is limited, check out Portsmouth and the beaches, then head north to **Mt Washington** (p226) for year-round adventures (hiking, train rides, scenic drives and skiing).

GETTING AROUND

Historic town centers like Portsmouth are quite walkable, but to get between destinations, a car is very handy in this part of New England. You can often get the best rental rates in Manchester.

Concord Coach Lines *(concordcoachlines.com)* provide service between Boston (South Station and the airport) and various key towns in New Hampshire, including Concord and North Conway. There's also **Dartmouth Coach** *(dartmouthcoach.com)*, with quick service between Boston and Hanover.

For the White Mountains, Concord Coach Lines travel daily from Boston's South Station to North Conway (about 3¾ hours). US302 and NH16 run through the valley, joining in North Conway (where there's free parking) as the White Mountain Hwy.

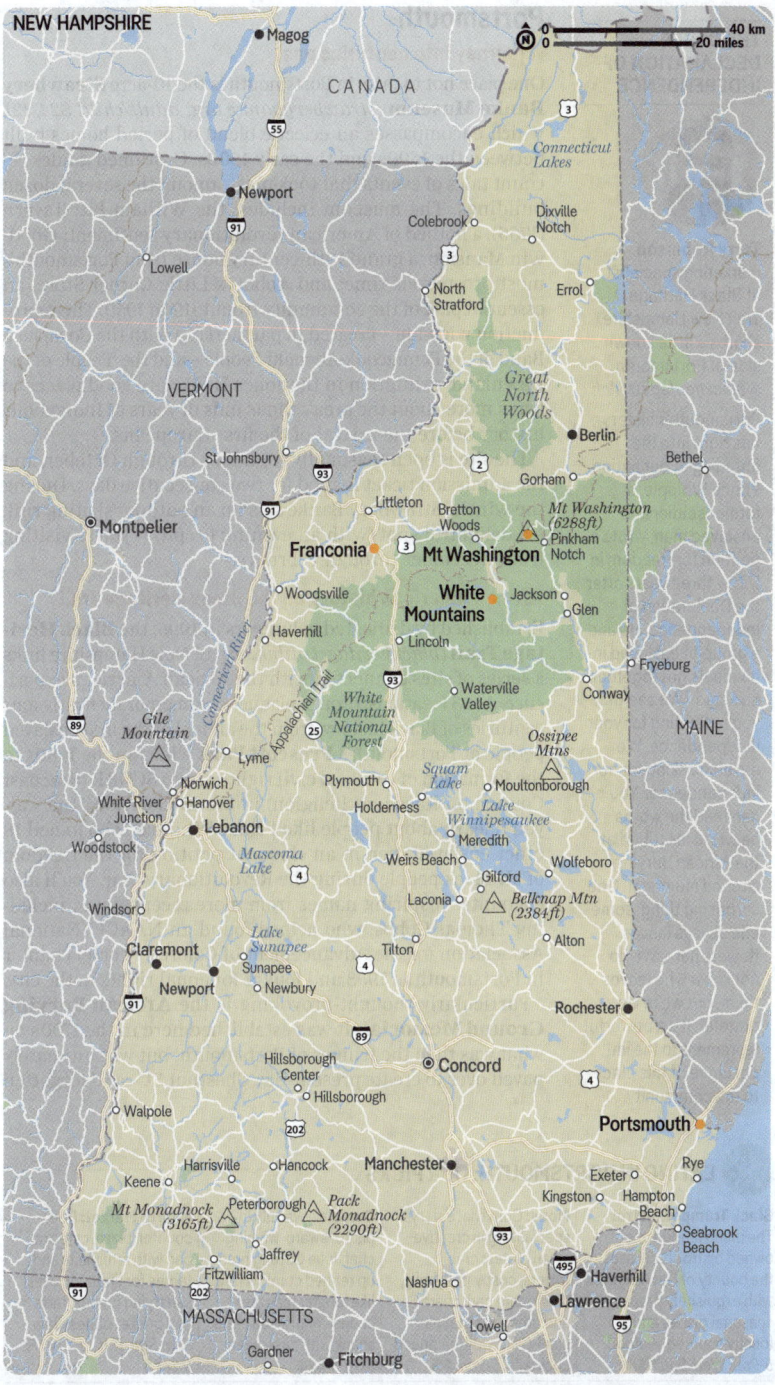

THE OTHER DECLARATION OF INDEPENDENCE

Terry Robinson, marketing specialist at Black Heritage Trail New Hampshire, shares a little known side of Portsmouth. @blackheritagetrailnh

Portsmouth's history ties right into the founding of our nation. Prince Whipple, a former soldier and enslaved man, wrote a petition for freedom in 1779 – three years after the Declaration of Independence. He and a group of enslaved individuals got together and said, 'We see that you're fighting for your independence. We are also asking for our independence.' You can read the words he wrote inscribed at the African Burying Ground Memorial. One surprising thing: someone always leaves flowers here. We do not know who leaves them, but we're very grateful. It's a powerful testament to the importance of this place to the community.

Portsmouth

A journey into centuries past

One place not to miss in Portsmouth is the 10-acre **Strawbery Banke Museum** *(strawberybanke.org; adult/child $24/12)*, which encompasses an eclectic blend of period homes built between the 1690s and the early 1800s. Costumed guides recount tales of events that took place among the several dozen buildings. The museum includes: the William Pitt Tavern (1766), a hotbed of American revolutionary sentiment; Goodwin Mansion, a grand 19th-century house from Portsmouth's most prosperous time; and Abbott's Little Corner Store, an essential part of the community from 1919 to 1950. The reproduction wigwam – created in partnership with the Cowasuck Band of the Pennacook-Abenaki People – and the 'People of the Dawnland' exhibition in the Jones House are good places to learn more about the area's thousands of years of Indigenous history before the arrival of the first Europeans.

The site is open seasonally from May through October, and the admission ticket is good for two consecutive days. During the winter, Strawbery Banke sets up an outdoor skating rink – a delightful spot (with an evening firepit) if you're visiting from December through February.

African American history on the Black Heritage Trail

Established by dedicated volunteers in 1995, the **Black Heritage Trail** *(blackheritagetrailnh.org)* of New Hampshire links a series of sites connected with the African American experience. At 23 locations, bronze plaques commemorate nearly four centuries of Black history, from the arrival of the first enslaved people at Portsmouth's **Prescott Park** wharf in the 1680s to the formation of the local civil rights group SCORR (Seacoast Council on Race and Religion) in the 1960s. Along the way, you'll learn about people like Prince Whipple, who joined 18 other enslaved men in an eloquent petition for the freedom of all Black people during the Revolutionary War. You'll also encounter inspiring names from more recent times, including Thomas Cobbs, who helped found an NAACP (National Association for the Advancement of Colored People) chapter in Portsmouth in 1958 and fought for equal rights in the city.

Particularly thought-provoking is the **African Burying Ground Memorial**. It was established here in the 1700s on what was then the fringes of Portsmouth, but was ultimately paved over to create present-day Chestnut St – and forgotten

---

 EATING IN PORTSMOUTH: OUR PICKS

Black Trumpet Bistro: The much lauded chef-owned bistro showcases the bounty of New England with exquisitely prepared seasonal dishes and locally sourced seafood. *5-9pm Wed-Sun* **$$$**

Moxy: Convivial eatery specializing in creative small plates: crab fritters, crispy pork belly, mushroom carbonara and other hits that pair nicely with well-balanced cocktails. *5-9pm* **$$**

Cure: In a warmly lit bistro, award-winning chef Julie Cutting fires up refined comfort fare like lobster mac and cheese or braised lamb shank with cassoulet. *5-9pm* **$$$**

Hearth Market: Deli counter, pizza, cafe and bar, with armchairs and tables for lingering over satisfying crepes, tarts and brisket plates. *8am-8pm Sun-Thu, to 10pm Fri & Sat* **$**

HISTORIC PORTSMOUTH ON FOOT

Peel back the centuries while taking the pulse of present-day Portsmouth on a walk amid the town's old lanes.

START	END	LENGTH
Market Square	Pier	1.5 miles; 30 min

Start in picturesque ❶ **Market Square**, Portsmouth's hub since the mid-1700s. The white spire of the ❷ **North Church** soars above the square's southeast side. It was built in 1854 to replace a meeting house built in 1713.

A few blocks southwest of there, the ❸ **African Burying Ground Memorial** is an impressive work that pays homage to the town's African and African American community, with many members laid to rest here between 1705 and 1803.

Wind your way past the ❹ **South Meetinghouse**, a fine Italianate design from the 19th century. Stop to admire the fresh catch of the day at ❺ **Sanders Fish Market**. Loop back along the ❻ **waterside lane** (Mechanic St), taking in the tranquil views to nearby Peirce Island. At the ❼ **Point of Graves Burial Ground**, peruse finely carved gravestones from the early 1800s.

Cross ❽ **Trial Gardens** and walk out onto the ❾ **pier**, where you can see a constant flurry of activity at the Portsmouth Naval Shipyard, going strong since 1800. From here, look for boats sailing under the movable Memorial Bridge, completed in 2013. The ribbon-cutting ceremony was led by Eileen Foley. At 95, the beloved former mayor reprised her role from 1923, when she cut the silk ribbon for the opening of the first Memorial Bridge as a five-year-old.

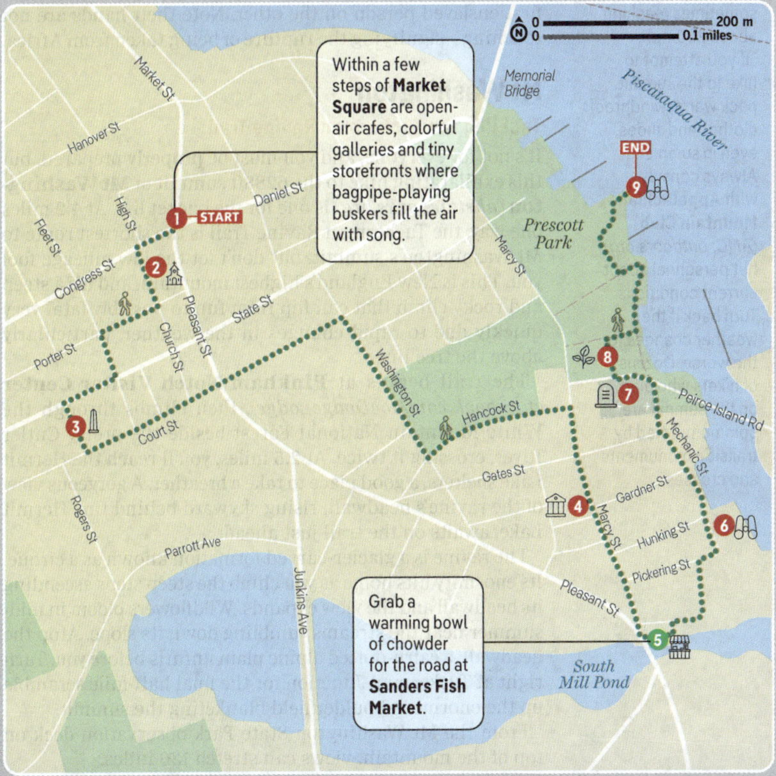

Within a few steps of **Market Square** are open-air cafes, colorful galleries and tiny storefronts where bagpipe-playing buskers fill the air with song.

Grab a warming bowl of chowder for the road at **Sanders Fish Market**.

NEW ENGLAND NEW HAMPSHIRE

MT WASHINGTON: KNOW BEFORE YOU GO

The mountain is renowned for frighteningly bad weather – the average temperature on the summit is 26.5°F (-3°C), while the mercury has fallen as low as -47°F (-43°C), but only risen as high as 72°F (22°C). Over 21ft of snow falls each year, and the climate can mimic Antarctica's. Hurricane-force winds blow every three days or so on average, sometimes reaching above 200mph.

If you attempt to hike to the summit, pack warm, windproof clothes and shoes, even in summer. Always consult with **Appalachian Mountain Club** (AMC; outdoors.org) hut personnel about current conditions. Turn back if the weather changes for the worse. Dozens of hikers who died on the summit are commemorated by trailside monuments and crosses.

as the city grew. The powerful statue anchoring the north end of the memorial represents Mother Africa on one side and the first enslaved person on the other. Note their hands are not touching – signifying the rupture of being taken from Africa.

Mt Washington

Tackling the Tuckerman Ravine Trail

It's not for everyone, and you must be properly prepared, but this exhilarating hike to the 6288ft summit of **Mt Washington** (nhstateparks.org) is one for the bucket list. At 4.2 miles one way, the Tuckerman Ravine Trail is the shortest route to Mt Washington's summit, but don't let the low mileage fool you. This is New England's highest mountain, and it's a steep and rocky climb that can flip from fun to possibly fatal very quickly due to rapid changes in the weather, particularly above the tree line.

The trail begins at **Pinkham Notch Visitor Center** (facebook.com/JoeDodgeLodge), then climbs through the White Mountain National Forest beside the pretty Cutler River, crossing it twice. At 2.5 miles, you'll reach the Hermit Lake shelters, a good place to take a breather. A gorgeous view of the ravine's headwall, rising skyward behind tiny Hermit Lake, awaits on the trail just ahead.

The ravine is a glacier-carved formation known as a cirque. Its enormity hits home as you climb the steep steps ascending its headwall and the view expands. Wildflowers bloom in midsummer near the streams tumbling down its slope. Atop the headwall, a cairn-dotted alpine plain unfurls before you. Turn right at Tuckerman Junction for the final half-mile scramble up the enormous boulder field blanketing the summit.

From the Mt Washington State Park observation deck on top of the mountain, views can stretch 130 miles.

Mt Washington Cog Railway

Train to the summit

Purists walk and the lazy drive, but the quaintest way to reach Mt Washington's summit is via the **Mt Washington Cog Railway** (thecog.com; adult/child from $84/61). From 1869 until 2008, coal-fired, steam-powered locomotives traveled the scenic 3-mile track up the mountainside. In more recent times, the coal-burning engines have been largely replaced by cleaner biodiesel locomotives, though the railway still operates two vintage steam engines in the warmer months.

Train lovers will undoubtedly enjoy the unique ride (and views), with an average grade of 25%, reaching 38% just below the tree line on the world's second steepest railroad trestle (the steepest is at Mt Pilatus, Switzerland). The round trip takes roughly three hours, with about one hour spent at the summit.

The train operates year-round but only goes as high as Waumbek Station (elevation 4000ft) from late fall through early spring.

Driving a legendary road

One of New England's top adventures, the serpentine drive up the 7.6-mile **Mt Washington Auto Road** (mt-washington.com/drive-yourself; adult/child $36/15) is not for the faint of heart. This private, narrow, alpine toll road gains more than 4000ft in elevation as it travels from the Pinkham Notch area to the parking lot just below the 6288ft summit. There are pull-offs along the way to admire the view (and cool your brakes on the descent). The price includes entry to the weather-focused Extreme Mount Washington Museum. 'This car climbed Mt Washington' bumper stickers are sold in the summit gift shop. For a guided audio tour, download the free Mt Washington Auto Road app before you arrive.

TOP OUTDOOR ADVENTURES

Rock Climbing: Go rock- or ice-climbing in White Mountain National Forest with **Eastern Mountain Sports Climbing School** (@easternmntnsports).

River Trips: Conway-based **Saco Bound** (sacobound.com) offer tubing and canoeing, from easygoing one-hour paddles to multi-day camping trips.

Skiing & Snowboarding: Appealing winter resorts include **Cranmore** (cranmore.com), with 56 trails and seven lifts; a mile east of North Conway.

Cross-country Skiing & Snowshoeing: Jackson XC (jacksonxc.org) is legendary: 60 miles of Nordic ski trails and 40 miles of snowshoeing.

Aerial Adventures: In addition to skiing, **Wildcat Mountain** (skiwildcat.com) rusn a summertime Ziprider – a chair suspended high above the ground, where you'll glide 45mph.

KANCAMAGUS PRACTICALITIES

The **Saco Ranger District Office** (Conway), the **White Mountains Visitor Center** (Woodstock) and the smaller **Lincoln Woods Visitor Center** are all good places to get maps and up-to-date info on trail conditions. Serious hikers will want to purchase a detailed map, such as the excellent, locally produced *Exploring NH's White Mountains* waterproof top map.

A day-use pass (*$5*) is required any time you leave your car. Passes are sold at visitor centers and at self-pay kiosks. US National Parks passes (and other federal passes) are also accepted. Place your pass on your dashboard.

Camping is first-come, first-served at five of six campgrounds along the Kancamagus Highway; reserve ahead at **Covered Bridge Campground**. Backcountry camping is free, but restrictions apply.

If you'd rather not drive, you can take a two-hour guided van tour, which allows a full hour on the summit. In summer, one-way shuttles for hikers are available on a first-come, first-served basis – but don't assume you'll nab a spot. The road may be closed in severe weather (even in summer).

White Mountains

Driving the Kancamagus Highway

One of New Hampshire's prettiest driving routes, the **Kancamagus Highway** immerses you in the forested beauty of the **White Mountains**. Winding for 35 miles between Lincoln and Conway, and paved only in 1964, the 'Kanc' is still unspoiled by commercial development. It offers easy access to US Forest Service (USFS) campgrounds, hiking trails and fantastic scenery.

Among the most popular spots to tramp through the forest is the **Lincoln Woods Trail**. Here you can head off on short hikes or multi-day treks into 'the Pemi' (the Pemigewasset Wilderness).

Wherever you're heading, the journey begins by crossing a suspension bridge. The Lincoln Trail then continues another 1.4 miles along an abandoned railway that parallels a mountain stream. Make it even more rewarding by going all the way to Franconia Falls (around 6.8 miles round trip). There are plenty of other options if you want to keep going. You'll find the trailhead about 5 miles east of Lincoln.

A 0.3-mile one-way stroll on the popular **Sabbaday Brook Trail** ends at **Sabbaday Falls**, a gorge waterfall that zigzags through narrow granite walls into lovely pools. Steps lead to overlooks with mesmerizing views of the flume. The trailhead is about 16 miles west of the Saco Ranger District Office in Conway, and the trail is accessible for people with disabilities.

Franconia

Visiting Robert Frost's farmhouse

In the mid-20th century, Robert Frost (1874–1963) was the USA's most renowned and best-loved poet. For several years he lived with his family on a farm near Franconia (about an hour's drive from North Conway), now known as the **Frost Place** (*frostplace.org; adult/child $7/free*). The years spent here were some of the most productive and inspired of his life.

The farmhouse has been kept as faithful to the period as possible, with numerous exhibits of memorabilia. In the forest behind the house is a 0.5-mile nature trail, with some of Frost's poems displayed along the way.

Maine

ACADIA NATIONAL PARK | SEASIDE TOWNS | ADVENTURES

New England's largest state boasts hundreds of miles of coastline encompassing sea cliffs, sandy beaches and craggy, wave-kissed shores. Offshore, there are countless islands for exploring, with scenic walks amid empty coves and misty, forested shorelines, while villages nearby boast year-round populations that fail to reach the triple digits. Inland, Maine has vast tracts of wilderness, with thick forests, mirror-like lakes and treeless, boulder-strewn peaks. Such a magnificent landscape offers near-countless adventures, and you can spend the day cycling along winding shore roads, kayaking beside curious harbor seals or hiking up above falcon nests to lofty mountaintop overlooks.

Given all that wilderness, it's not surprising that Maine residents are known for being independent and hardy. The state's history reaches back to the earliest Paleo-Indians, who hunted and fished here for thousands of years. The rugged, glacier-carved landscape was a serious challenge for early European colonists, and the region has remained sparsely populated up to the present.

Places

Portland p231
Boothbay Harbor p233
Rockland p233
Bar Harbor & Acadia National Park p236
Quoddy Head State Park p238
Baxter State Park p238

☑ TOP TIP

Take in the beaches of southern Maine, then work your way up the coast, stopping in harbor towns and the famous **Acadia National Park** (p236). With extra time, detour to the mountainous wilderness of **Baxter State Park** (p239).

GETTING AROUND

The **Downeaster**, operated by **Amtrak** *(amtrak.com)*, runs five times daily between Boston and Portland, a journey of about 2½ hours. The train also stops in Wells on the coast, a 15-minute drive to Ogunquit and a 20-minute drive to York.

Having your own wheels is essential if you want to explore beyond Portland (where several rental agencies, including Enterprise and Budget, have bases). **Concord Coach Lines** *(concordcoachlines.com)* has several stops in Maine on its routes between New York, Boston and Portland. The US 1 hwy parallels the coastline and offers scenic travel but can be quite slow (and gridlocked in the summer).

Portland

Adventures on Casco Bay

Gulls shriek overhead as the scent of the sea drifts through the streets like the fog off Casco Bay, and everywhere the salt-laced wind licks your skin. Portland – Maine's largest city – has capitalized on the gifts of its port history to become one of New England's most vibrant small cities. Its famous ferry service, **Casco Bay Lines** *(cascobaylines.com)*, heads out to six different islands year-round, delivering mail, freight and visitors. It's a picturesque journey no matter where you go. **Peaks Island**, just 17 minutes from Portland, is a popular day-trip destination for walking and cycling. A five-minute stroll from the dock, **Brad's Bike Rental** hires out two-wheelers and tandems for scenic spins around the island. There's a selection of scenic cruises, too – the three-hour mailboat run is a great way to see the bay's sights.

The trail of Henry Wadsworth Longfellow

The revered American poet Henry Wadsworth Longfellow (1807–82) grew up in Portland in a Federal-style house, built in 1785 by his Revolutionary War-hero grandfather. Open only during the summer (Tuesday to Saturday, June though October), the **Wadsworth-Longfellow House** *(mainehistory.org; adult/child $18/12)* has been impeccably restored to look as it did in the 1800s, complete with original furniture, artifacts and a lovely garden.

One part of the complex features the galleries of the **Maine Historical Society** *(mainehistory.org)*, included with admission to the Wadsworth-Longfellow house. Here you'll find some of Portland's best exhibits looking at life in the state. Recent topics focused on photojournalism and the 1936 flood, the early roots of Maine music and the building of the International Appalachian Trail. The galleries are open Tuesday to Saturday, February through December.

Epicenter of fine art

Founded in 1882, the **Portland Museum of Art** *(PMA; portlandmuseum.org; adult/child $20/free)* houses an outstanding collection of American works. Maine artists, including Winslow Homer, Edward Hopper, Louise Nevelson and Andrew Wyeth, are particularly well-represented. You'll also find a few works by European masters, including Monet, Degas, Picasso and Renoir. The temporary exhibitions are among the best in the state and often blaze new trails, such as the 2024 show *Jeremy Frey: Woven*, which was the first-ever major retrospective

PORTLAND'S BEST TOURS

Lucky Catch Cruises: *(luckycatch.com)* Live the life of a lobsterman or lobsterwoman – if only for 90 minutes – as a passenger aboard a commercial lobster boat.

Maine Island Kayak Co: *(maineislandkayak.com)* From its base on Peaks Island, this well-run outfitter offers fun half-day, full-day and sunset paddling trips.

Portland Schooner Company: *(portlandschooner.com)* Take a two-hour tour on an elegant early-20th-century schooner.

Summer Feet Cycling: *(summerfeet.net)* Combine cycling with sightseeing and local history on various tours (with lobster-roll stops thrown in for good measure).

Maine Day Ventures: *(mainedayventures.com)* Delve deeper on a guided walking tour: there are foodie excursions, history outings and working waterfront walks.

EATING IN PORTLAND: OUR PICKS

Scales: Cavernous dockside warehouse serving some of Portland's best seafood. Feast on Bangs Island mussels, seared scallops and pan-roasted halibut. *4:30-9:30pm* **$$$**

Central Provisions: Choose from masterfully prepared small plates that range from sea urchin to bone marrow toast. *11am-2pm & 5-9:30pm* **$$**

Green Elephant: Even carnivores shouldn't miss the vegetarian fare at this Zen-chic, Asian-inspired bistro with hits like king oyster mushroom tempura. *11:30am-2:30pm & 5-9:30pm* **$$**

Eventide Oyster Co: Portland's most celebrated raw bar has scrumptious Maine oysters and shellfish, shucked to order, plus an enticing menu of creative small plates. *11am-11pm* **$$$**

WALK THE OLD PORT

Stroll Portland's Old Port district and take in the history, cuisine, ambiance and views.

START	END	LENGTH
Bread & Friends	Portland Observatory	1.5 miles; 30 min

Fuel up for a day's walk in vibrant Portland with a stop at the charming neighborhood cafe and bakery ❶ **Bread & Friends**. Nearby, take a look at the bronze ❷ **statue** dedicated to local-boy-turned-movie-director John Ford. Find your way to ❸ **Wharf Street**, whose brick buildings and cobblestone paving embodies the historic yet unpolished allure of the Old Port District – there's even a brewpub here called ❹ **Gritty's**.

Near the corner of Fore and Moulton is the three-story building known as ❺ **Mariners' Church**, which dates back to 1829; it held a 3rd-floor chapel that catered to waterfront workers. In the basement, Daniel Colesworthy ran a bookshop and printer.

You'll soon spot the seagulls as you walk down to ❻ **Long Wharf**, which is dotted with bobbing vessels and a few curiosities on dry land. These include a giant slab of the ❼ **Berlin Wall**, complete with a Soviet hammer and sickle on one section. Two piers over, you can take in the bounty of the sea at the iconic ❽ **Harbor Fish Market**. Next door, head into the very first ❾ **Sea Bags** store, which takes old sail cloth and upcycles it into bags and totes. If you're not ready to call it a day, head up to the quiet East End and climb up the ❿ **Portland Observatory**. The seven-story brick tower, built in 1807, offers views over Casco Bay.

John Ford's Irish immigrant father once owned a grocery store across the street.

Robert Benjamin Lewis' groundbreaking *Light and Truth* (1836), which looked at history from an Afro-centric standpoint, was published in the **Mariners' Church** basement.

The **Harbor Fish Market** has live lobster tanks, 17 types of oysters and countless varieties of fish.

of a Wabanaki artist in a fine art museum in the US. The collections are spread across three separate buildings, with the majority of works in the postmodern Charles Shipman Payson building, designed by the firm of famed architect IM Pei. Check online for events throughout the year, including curator talks and family days with hands-on art activities. Admission is free Friday evenings (from 4pm to 8pm).

Boothbay Harbor

Paddling Boothbay's waterways

Once a beautiful little seafarers' village on a wide blue bay, Boothbay Harbor is now an extremely popular tourist resort in the summer, when its narrow and winding streets are packed with visitors. Still, there's good reason to join the holiday masses in this picturesque place. Overlooking a pretty waterfront, the large, well-kept Victorian houses crown the town's many knolls, and a wooden **footbridge** ambles across the harbor.

Maine Kayak rent out single and tandem kayaks for taking out on the water. The coast and secluded islands nearby make fine settings for spotting ospreys, harbor seals, bald eagles and plenty of other wildlife. A good destination is **Burnt Island**, about a 2-mile paddle south of Boothbay and set with rocky shores, maritime forest and an 1821 lighthouse. Pack a picnic and enjoy some downtime.

Rockland

Rock a bib at the Maine Lobster Festival

Boasting a large fishing fleet and a proud year-round population, the former shipbuilding center of Rockland has a vibrancy lacking in some of Maine's other mid-coast towns. Lobster fanatics won't want to miss the five-day **Maine Lobster Festival** *(mainelobsterfestival.com)*, held here in late July or early August. It's not just a homage to the crusty crustacean, however. There's also plenty of live music, parades, an art show and a fun run. Accommodations get booked up for many miles surrounding Rockland, so reserve well ahead.

Sail the High Seas

Although traveling by schooner largely went out of style at the dawn of the 20th century, adventurers can still explore the untamed Maine coast the old-fashioned way – aboard fast sailing ships, or windjammers. Nine of these multi-masted vessels anchor at **Rockland** and **Camden** and offer outings ranging from an overnight to nine days around Penobscot Bay and beyond. Travelers explore towns and islands along the way, stopping for hiking, sightseeing and shopping. They also take their meals on the boat (expect sunset dinners and plenty of lobster; the food is generally excellent). Four- to six-day cruises are the most common. For details of schooners, schedules and prices, visit the **Maine Windjammer Association** *(mainewindjammerfleet.com)*.

TOP FOUR BOOTHBAY HARBOR TOURS

Cap'n Fish's Cruises: *(boothbayboattrips. com)* Offers a big menu of boat trips, from whale-watching to scenic excursions to Eastern Egg Rock in search of puffins.

Balmy Days Cruises: *(balmydayscruises. com)* Balmy Days run sunrise trips, sailing adventures and mackerel fishing.

Maine Kayak: *(mainekayak.com)* Based in New Harbor, this outfit provides two-hour jaunts along the coast, as well as up Johns River to an oyster farm.

Boothbay Sailing: *(boothbaysailing. com)* Boothbay run two-hour sailing trips (including a sunset voyage) aboard one of two impressive schooners.

DRIVING TOUR

Drive the Blue Hill Peninsula

If you're looking for the soul of coastal Maine, head to the Blue Hill Peninsula. You'll find charming seaside villages, pretty walks through forest and along shoreline, and a vibrant artisan food scene. South of the peninsula lies Deer Isle, actually a collection of islands joined by causeways and linked to the mainland by a pretty suspension bridge. Old lobster towns, island walks and idyllic countryside views are all part of the allure.

1 Blue Hill

Start off in Blue Hill, a petite coastal town that's home to a number of artists and writers. Pick up an espresso from **Bucklyn Coffee**, check out artwork and Maine titles (or play chess or board games) at the **Blue Hill Public Library** *(bhpl.net; free)*. Head just north of town to reach Blue Hill's eponymous **mountain** *(bluehillheritagetrust.org)*, which, at 934ft, offers a fine vantage point over the peninsula. Several well-marked trails lead up to the summit, including the **Osgood Trail** (0.9 miles).

The Drive It's a 20-minute journey along forest-lined roads to Brooklin, with occasional glimpses of the Mt Desert Narrows off to the left.

2 Brooklin

The sleepy settlement of Brooklin in the southeastern corner of the Blue Hill Peninsula has some surprising finds. Don't miss the **Brooklin Candy Company**, a whimsical store with sweet treats from around the globe. Try heavenly Swedish elderflower candy, Australian Tim Tams or chocolate bars made with real crickets. Just up the

Stonington

road, you'll find more goodies (snacks, coffee, ceramics) at the **Brooklin General Store**. Next door, **Leaf & Anna** has loads of Maine-centric gift ideas, including stationery, market bags and bath products.

The Drive The 45-minute journey winds to Castine through forest and past white-washed churches, then skirts the Bagaduce River, with occasional glimpses of the wide waterway.

3 Castine

One of Maine's prettiest villages, Castine has a handsome town common ringed with historic buildings and a pleasant waterfront overlooking Penobscot Bay. Get a dose of local history at the **Castine Historical Society** (castinehistoricalsociety.org), visit the small anthropological collection at the **Wilson Museum** (wilson museum.org; free) and take a stroll in **Witherle Woods** (mcht.org). Pick up a snack and some new literature from the much-loved **Compass Rose Books**.

The Drive It's a little under an hour to Deer Isle, and you'll have some fine views of Penobscot Bay along the way, particularly from Deer Isle Bridge.

4 Nervous Nellie's Jams & Jellies

Famous for its jams made from Maine's berries, **Nervous Nellie's** is a shop but also a sprawling fantasyland. Wander the vivid installations of the *Wild West*, *Camelot* and the *Deep South*, the imaginative creations of artist Peter Beerits.

The Drive The 15-minute trip to Stonington follows the eastern shore, passing pockets of greenery and remote homesteads before reaching the southern edge of the island.

5 Stonington

Deer Isle's main town, Stonington, is a quaint settlement where lobster fisherfolk and artists live side by side. Wander the tiny Main St overlooking the water, and peek in shops and galleries, like the family-owned **Dry Dock**, with its pottery, artwork and clothing.

ACADIA NATIONAL PARK ESSENTIALS

Layout: Mt Desert Island covers the bulk of the national park. Other parts of the park are on the Schoodic Peninsula and Isle au Haut.

Entry Fee: A one-week vehicle pass costs $35.

Visitor Centers: Three miles northwest of Bar Harbor, Acadia's main gateway is **Hulls Cove Visitor Center**, which has maps, info and park passes. When Hulls Cove is closed (November to mid-April), head to the **Bar Harbor Chamber of Commerce**.

Navigating the Park: The 27-mile-long **Park Loop Rd** circumnavigates the eastern section of Mt Desert Island, passing many trailheads and points of interest. It's one-way in places.

Opening Days: The park is open year-round, although many roads (including the Park Loop Rd) close from around late November to mid-April.

Acadia National Park

Bar Harbor & Acadia National Park

Learn about the Wabanaki

In the waterfront town of Bar Harbor, the **Abbe Museum** *(abbemuseum.org; adult/child $18/10)* contains a fascinating collection of cultural artifacts related to Maine's Native American heritage – particularly the Wabanaki people, who inhabited Mt Desert Island for thousands of years before the Europeans arrived. You can see pottery, tools, combs and fishing implements spanning the last 2000 years. Contemporary pieces include finely wrought wood carvings, birch-bark containers and baskets.

Grand views over Acadia

The only national park in all of New England, **Acadia National Park** *(nps.gov/acad; one-week entry per person/vehicle $20/35)* offers unrivaled coastal beauty and numerous activities, from hiking and cycling woodland trails to rock climbing and kayaking. The gateway to the park is Bar Harbor, where you'll find elegant B&Bs, along with inviting restaurants, taverns and boutiques – particularly along Main St and Cottage St. Adventure outfitters here offer a wide range of gear and tours that allow visitors to make the most of the scenic spendor.

Don't leave the park without driving – or hiking – to the 1530ft summit of **Cadillac Mountain**. For panoramic views of Frenchman Bay, walk the paved 0.5-mile summit loop of the mountain. It's a popular place in the early morning, as it's touted as the first spot in the US to see the sunrise.

There are numerous paths to the top, leading from north, south, east and west. The easiest to access is the **Cadillac North Ridge Trailhead**, located about 3 miles southwest of central Bar Harbor (and about 3.5 miles south of **Hulls Cove Visitor Center**). From the trailhead, it's a moderate 2.2-mile (one-way) climb to the summit, with fine views of Eagle Lake to the west on the way up.

To avoid the hassle of driving, use Bar Harbor's free shuttle system, the **Island Explorer** *(exploreacadia.com)*; it runs from late June to mid-October.

Acadia's prettiest pond

On clear days, the glassy waters of the 176-acre **Jordan Pond** reflect the image of Penobscot Mountain like a mirror. A stroll around the pond and its surrounding forests and flower meadows is one of Acadia National Park's most popular and family-friendly activities. (Sorry, no swimming allowed.) Follow the 3-mile self-guided nature trail around the pond before stopping for refreshments at the **Jordan Pond House**.

There are numerous trails leading off from the lake, some easy, others strenuous. For a short but challenging climb up to a viewpoint overlooking the water, take the trail up to **South Bubble**, located in the northeast corner of the pond. It's steep, but it's only about 0.4 miles to **Bubble Rock**, a massive boulder that seems quite precariously perched over the mountain's ledge.

Hiking the wave-battered coast

Jutting out to sea on the eastern side of Acadia's **Sand Beach** is the forested headland known as **Great Head**. A 1-mile trail loops around the headland, providing spectacular views of the craggy coastline and the pounding surf hitting against the rocks below. It's a fairly easy hike through forest, then out along the exposed rock face.

Wild Gardens' flower power

Wander a serene trail and breathe in the heady aroma of the pine-scented air while exploring the national park's acre-sized **Wild Gardens of Acadia** *(nps.gov/places/wild-gardens-of-acadia.htm)*. Despite the small size, the gardens boast 13 of Acadia's biospheres in miniature, from bog and coniferous woods to meadow and heath. In all, over 400 plant species are present.

Hiking on the Schoodic Peninsula

About 45 minutes by boat from Bar Harbor across Frenchman Bay is the **Schoodic Peninsula**, which contains a quieter, less visited portion of Acadia National Park. From here, you can hike various trails (ranging from half a mile to 3 miles one-way) and enjoy great views of Cadillac Mountain and other high points of Mt Desert Island. There are also some 8 miles of packed gravel paths ideal for cycling. Although you can drive here in an hour, it's more enjoyable (and faster) to take the ferry operated by **Downeast Windjammer** *(downeastwindjammer.com)*, who have five departures daily (late May

TOP LOCAL TOURS

Acadia Mountain Guides Climbing School: *(acadiamountainguides.com)* The highly regarded outfitter and climbing school leads half- and full-day rock-climbing adventures in Acadia.

Acadian Boat Tours: *(acadianboattours.com)* Look for whales, porpoises, bald eagles, seals and more on a narrated two-hour nature cruise.

Maine State Sea Kayak: *(mainestatekayak.com)* Runs highly regarded half-day tours down the quieter west side of the island, with scenic paddling and downtime on a beach.

Lulu Lobster Boat: *(lululobsterboat.com)* Brush up on your lobster knowledge aboard a lobster boat while combining sightseeing and seal-watching.

Diver Ed's Dive-In Theater: *(diveintheater.com)* A family favorite, this adventure provides a boat trip with live viewing of undersea life, followed by hands-on interactions with small sea creatures.

EATING & DRINKING IN BAR HARBOR: OUR PICKS

Blaze: Warm, welcoming Blaze has wood-fired pizzas and high-end pub fare, plus outstanding jerk pork chops (the chef is Jamaican). *11:30am-8:30pm* $$

Thirsty Whale: A wood-lined tavern that draws locals and out-of-towners, who come for satisfying seafood, including delicious fried haddock sandwiches. *11am-midnight* $$

Barnacle: Much-loved local haunt with numerous Maine craft brews on tap, plus creative cocktails (try the spicy ghost pepper margarita) and oysters. *4pm-1am Wed-Sun* $$

Brasserie Le Brun: Dress up for this elegant bistro. Think French classics made with Maine ingredients: lobster bouillabaisse, duck breast cassoulet and roasted cauliflower. *4-10pm* $$$

OTHER ACADIA GATEWAYS

Apart from Bar Harbor, there are several other settlements on and near Mt Desert Island that make quieter bases for exploring the park. On the east side of Somes Sound, **Northeast Harbor** overlooks a waterfront sprinkled with yachts, and its tiny Main St is dotted with galleries and cafes, while the hillsides are lined with Gilded Age mansions and fantastical gardens.

Across the Sound, **Southwest Harbor** is a less upscale community that's home to a commercial fishing harbor. The heart of town is the intersection of Main St and Clark Point Rd, with its shops and restaurants.

About 10 miles north of Mt Desert Island, the bigger town of **Ellsworth** is further from the action, but has ample lodging and dining options.

to mid-October) between Bar Harbor and Winter Harbor. At the latter, the Island Explorer (p237) provides a free shuttle service looping around the southern end of the peninsula. You can take bikes aboard the ferry.

Quoddy Head State Park

Dramatic coastal trails

Anchoring the easternmost point in Maine (and thus the contiguous US), **Quoddy Head State Park** *(maine.gov/quoddyhead; day pass adult/child $4/1)* is best known for its jagged sea cliffs that offer unique views along the coast – at least when the weather is cooperating. Fog often blankets this lush peninsula, making for some cinematic shots of the historic, red-and-white striped **West Quoddy Head Lighthouse** *(westquoddy.com)*. There are various trails in the 541-acre park, most of which are fairly level but require constant vigilance while negotiating the uneven, sometimes slippery terrain. Follow the rocky shoreline along the **Coastal Trail**, then loop back through conifer woods, lichens and mosses along the **Thompson Trail**. It's worth making a short detour to the **Bog Trail**, a boardwalk that passes unusual flora, including carnivorous pitcher plants.

Baxter State Park

Views from the Mt Katahdin summit

Reaching the summit of Baxter Peak, better known as **Mt Katahdin** *(baxterstatepark.org; park entry per person $20)*, is on the bucket list of many New England hikers – and for good reason. Ascending Maine's highest peak – at an elevation of 5267ft – is one of the most challenging and rewarding day hikes in the state, particularly if you get here via the harrowing **Knife Edge Trail**.

Don't underestimate this hike, as there have been fatal accidents over the years (most from falls or lightning strikes), so make sure you're in good shape and adequately prepared. On the morning of the ascent, check the weather report at the ranger station; if rain or high winds are forecast, don't go. Start out early, as you'll need eight to 12 hours to complete the hike.

There are several ways to the top; all are rated by the park as 'very strenuous' and require scrambling over boulders above the tree line.

The most popular route is the **Hunt Trail** (also the final section of the Appalachian Trail), which leads up from Katahdin

EATING NEAR ACADIA: DESTINATION DINING

Thurston's Lobster Pound: Super fresh lobster and crab are the headliners at this waterfront lobster pound. Tie on a bib and dive in. *noon-8pm, late May-mid-Oct* $$

Aragosta at Goose Cove: Delicious, painstakingly prepared dishes sourced locally from farm and sea. The waterfront setting (with patio) is magical. Reservations essential. *hours vary* $$$

Islesford Dock Restaurant: Book ahead for this beautifully sited spot on Little Cranberry Island that serves lobster, mussels, oysters, veggie dishes and more. *hours vary* $$$

Tinder Hearth: Munch phenomenal pizzas in a weathered barn or out on the garden-fringed lawn. There are also morning croissants. Reserve ahead. *hours vary* $$

Penobscot River

Stream. This 5.2-mile (one way) hike past the scenic Katahdin Stream Falls involves a 4188ft elevation gain.

The hardest way to the top means taking the 3.2-mile **Helon Taylor Trail** (starting at Roaring Brook) up to Pamola Peak and continuing via the Knife Edge for the final 1.1 miles. This last bit lives up to its name, as you'll be walking along a narrow rocky traverse (4ft wide in parts), with steep drop-offs on both sides. It's more of a technical hike, and you'll need focus and agility. Those afraid of heights should steer clear.

Be sure to register at the gatehouse before setting out on the hike, and after you've returned safely. Also note that if you plan to hike from any of the Katahdin trailheads, be sure to make a day-use parking reservation (DUPR) online (baxterstatepark.org; $5) up to two weeks before your visit.

Canoeing on serene ponds

Most people come to Baxter to hike, but it's also a great place for idyllic paddling. You can spend the morning on mirror-like waters against the backdrop of mountain peaks, with the chance to spy beavers, moose and bald eagles. The park rents out canoes for a mere $1 per hour (or $8 per day). These are available at over two-dozen locations, including **Daicey Pond**. Check with park rangers (some canoes require a key) for availability when you arrive.

World-class rafting on the Penobscot

The white water draws adventure-seekers to the **Penobscot River**, which churns through Baxter State Park, within view of soaring Mt Katahdin. You can join an epic rafting trip with **North County Rivers** (northcountryrivers.com), spending six hours on the Penobscot and traveling 12 miles as you navigate class IV rapids and a few stretches of class V. The season runs from mid-May through mid-September. Trips meet at the **Big Moose Inn**, roughly halfway between the town of Millinocket and the entrance to Baxter State Park.

BAXTER STATE PARK ESSENTIALS

Gateways: The town of Millinocket is a handy base for exploring Baxter if you're staying in the park. It has a handful of simple hotels, cafes and restaurants, as well as places selling hiking gear.

Visitor Centers: In Millinocket, the **Baxter State Park Authority Headquarters** doles out information and has essential hiking maps for sale.

Entry Fee: One-day entry costs $20, a season pass costs $50.

Overnighting in the Park: There are 11 campgrounds, plus bunkhouses and basic cabins, and numerous backcountry sites. Make reservations up to four months in advance.

Lodges: There are also various private campgrounds and lodges, ranging from rustic to high-end.

TRAVELLING TO BAXTER

If you're traveling without a car, you can take an evening bus from Bangor to Medway (70 minutes), operated by **Cyr Bus Line** (johntcyrandsons.com). From there, the **Appalachian Trail Hostel** (p241) runs a shuttle to their location in Millinocket, located 30 minutes' drive outside Baxter State Park.

Places We Love to Stay

$ Budget $$ Midrange $$$ Top End

Boston MAPS P168, P170, P178

HI Boston Hostel $ The private rooms with en suite baths, the enormous guest kitchen and the ample hanging-out space highlight this modern 430-bed urban hostel near Chinatown.

CitizenM North Station $ You'd have to sleep on the hockey rink to be closer to TD Garden events; this cheeky, high-tech hotel is in the North Station complex.

Charlesmark Hotel $ The pocket-sized rooms in this narrow six-story hotel don't have much light, but they're smartly designed, and the Copley Square location couldn't be more central.

College Club $ Part private club and part B&B (open to all), this traditional 1864 townhouse has six cozy singles sharing hall baths, plus six spacious en suite doubles.

Irving House at Harvard $ Right behind Harvard Yard, this warm and welcoming inn offers smart rooms. Top marks for the excellent breakfast. Inquire about shared bathrooms to save money.

Godfrey Hotel $$ Only a block from the Boston Common, this 242-room downtown hotel has a bike share program, a George Howell coffee shop and service-centered staff.

Copley Square Hotel $$ In Boston's second oldest continuously operating hotel, the traditional guest rooms have been smartly updated. Guests can help themselves to coffee in the communal kitchen.

Oasis Guest House $$ This Euro-style guesthouse occupies four bow-front townhouses on a tree-lined lane in Back Bay. Rooms are modest but comfortable, including cheapies with shared bathrooms.

Longfellow's Wayside Inn $$ Operating since 1716, this wonderfully old-fashioned inn was the setting for Longfellow's collection of poems, *Tales of a Wayside Inn*. Located west of Concord in Sudbury.

3 Waves $$ Promises a relaxing stay, with six lovely rooms, incredible service and some unique wellness amenities, plus easy access to the beach; in Plymouth.

Massachusetts

Cornell Inn (Lenox) $ Unbeatable value for designer rooms, impeccable service and a prime location overlooking a picturesque pond; a few blocks from the town center.

AutoCamp Cape Cod (Cape Cod) $ Boutique camping. Fully equipped Airstream trailers and accessible cabins, near Cape Cod's Shining Sea Bikeway. Clubhouse has an indoor fire pit, tuck shop and restaurant.

Dunes' Edge Campground (Provincetown) $ Family-friendly RV/tent sites and rustic bungalows on 17 acres of pines and dunes near Provincetown. Close to National Seashore. Busy, so book early. Mid-May to September.

Masthead Resort (Provincetown) $$ Historic inn with rustic cottages and renovated suites. Lounge on Adirondack chairs overlooking the bay. Year-round value.

Woods Hole Inn (Woods Hole) $$ Nineteenth-century beauty, with downhome charm and comfort, complemented by upscale decor, offering 14 bright rooms. Mornings start with scrumptious home-cooked breakfasts, served with a smile.

Rhode Island MAPS P197, P199

Dean Hotel (Providence) $ A design-focused boutique hotel, the Dean features a beer hall, karaoke bar and cocktail den.

Esperanto (Providence) $ A backpackers' hostel with private rooms and shared dorms with up to five beds. The staff are friendly and helpful.

Mill Street Inn (Newport) $ Exposed brick and high ceilings harken back to its former mill days. Studio and one-bedroom suites are great value.

Atlantic Beach Hotel Newport (Newport) $$ Clean, modern rooms sitting right on Easton's Beach. The rooftop sundeck is a nice place to lounge.

Connecticut MAP P204

Quiet Corner Inn (Brooklyn) $ Budget accommodation in northeast Connecticut that doesn't cut corners. The rooms are simple, clean and comfortable.

Inn at Mystic (Mystic) $ Overlooking Mystic Harbor, this quaint inn includes some little luxuries, such as rooms with ocean views and fireplaces.

Simsbury 1820 House (Hartford) $$ A historic country inn with modern amenities. Hotel bikes are available for riding the Rail Trail.

Blake Hotel (New Haven) $$ This boutique hotel offers downtown luxury in apartment-style rooms with kitchens.

Vermont

Inn at Long Trail (Killington) $ Rustic hikers' lodge smack in the middle of Vermont's illustrious Long Trail, and convenient if you're driving the scenic Route 100.

Hostel Tevere (Stowe) $ Charming four-room hostel in an old farmhouse a stone's throw from the Mad River Valley ski slopes.

Burton Island State Park (St Albans City) $ Book early for the simple lean-tos and cabins lining the lakeshore at this family-friendly state park on an island in the middle of Lake Champlain.

Stowe Motel & Snowdrift (Stowe) $ Halfway between Stowe village and the slopes, this well-priced motel on the Stowe Recreation Path has swimming, lawn games and free bikes and snowshoes for guests.

Green Mountain Inn (Stowe) $$ Relax in a front porch rocker and watch the world go by from this historic inn in the heart of Stowe village.

Lang House (Burlington) $$ Long-established B&B in a Victorian home perched on the hillside between downtown Burlington and the University of Vermont.

Trapp Family Lodge (p214) (Stowe) $$$ High on a hillside above Stowe, this Austrian-inspired lodge lures guests with beautiful mountain views and a world-class Nordic ski center.

New Hampshire

Colonial Motel (North Conway) $ Budget-friendly family-run motel offers good value for its simple but well-maintained rooms, less than a mile south of North Conway's center.

Sailmaker's House (Portsmouth) $$ Breezy blue accents, crisp white linens and hardwood floors set a maritime vibe at this 10-room boutique inn near Strawbery Banke in Portsmouth.

Hotel Portsmouth (Portsmouth) $$ A short walk from the town center, the 32-room Queen Anne-style inn dates from 1881 and has beautiful rooms and common areas.

Cranmore Inn (North Conway) $$ Decor is classic but feels modern at this central three-story North Conway option; the seasonal pool is the perfect antidote to a day of hiking.

Spruce Moose Lodge (North Conway) $$ A short walk from town, Spruce Moose has charming rooms set inside a spruce-green 1850s home, plus fabulous home-cooked breakfasts.

Kearsarge Inn (North Conway) $$ Just off Main St, this lovely choice evokes a bygone era, with rooms kitted out with antique-style furnishings and gas fireplaces.

Maine

Appalachian Trail Hostel (Baxter State Park) $ A favorite of thru-hikers, this welcoming spot in Baxter State Park has a mix of shared and private accommodations, plus a room in a converted school bus.

Seawall Campground (Mt Desert Island) $ Our pick of Acadia's three campgrounds, Seawall is on the quieter side of Mt Desert Island and has 200 shaded sites, including a handful of walk-ins.

Black Elephant Hostel (Portland) $ Portland's first (and currently only) hostel has vibrantly colorful interiors and a friendly social vibe that's ideal for meeting other travelers.

Inn at St John (Portland) $$ Portland's oldest continuously operating inn (opened 1897) has a European vibe, with attractive accommodations, including budget-friendly vintage rooms with shared bathrooms.

Tugboat Inn (Boothbay) $$ You can't get much closer to the water without sleeping with the fishes at this pleasant motel-style inn in the heart of Boothbay.

LimeRock Inn (Rockland) $$ This eight-bedroom mansion in Rockland, built in 1890, has been lovingly furnished with a tasteful mix of antique and modern furniture.

Little Fig Hotel (Bar Harbor) $$$ Friendly Bar Harbor inn with spacious rooms in a contemporary style and grab-and-go tea, coffee and snacks available around the clock.

Copley Square Hotel (p178), Boston

Researched and curated by
Mary Fitzpatrick

Washington, DC & the Capital Region

US CAPITAL, MUSEUMS, BEACHES AND MOUNTAINS

From cosmopolitan Washington, DC to West Virginia's remote mountain towns, DC and the Capital Region pack incredible diversity into a relatively small and easily explored area.

There are few places in the US where the juxtaposition of bustling urban centers and quiet rural byways is as stark as in Washington, DC and the Capital Region. Within a few hours' drive of the nation's capital, with its world-class museums, African American history, monuments, theaters, markets and restaurants, you'll find winding backroads, expansive estates and rolling wine country. Throughout, the attractions are almost limitless. Wander the cobbled streets of Annapolis. Move on to the Eastern Shore, where watermen make a living from the bounty of the Chesapeake Bay. Carry on further to walk for hours on long Delaware beaches around Rehoboth, before turning inland to follow in the footsteps of Harriet Tubman and the underground railroad, or to learn about Native American history. To the west, visit Civil War battlefields, and to the south, step back into the colonial era at Virginia's Mount Vernon and Colonial Williamsburg. Visit Revolutionary-era mansions in Fredericksburg and chateau-like estates in Delaware's Brandywine Valley, and then follow those twisting, turning West Virginia mountain roads past forested slopes and fast-flowing rivers, taking in the views and seeing why the state is 'almost heaven.' All the while, you'll experience the Capital Region's unique mix of gracious southern hospitality and bustling northern practicality while gathering enough road-trip memories to last a lifetime.

KYLE J LITTLE/SHUTTERSTOCK

THE MAIN AREAS

WASHINGTON, DC
Capital of the USA.
p248

DELAWARE
Beaches, art and history.
p271

MARYLAND
Eastern Shore waterways and colonial history.
p280

VIRGINIA
Beach walks and mountain drives.
p293

WEST VIRGINIA
Heart of Appalachia.
p306

For places to stay in Washington, DC & the Capital Region, see p314

THE GUIDE

WASHINGTON, DC & THE CAPITAL REGION

Left: Virginia Beach (p301); Above: US Capitol Building (p254)

Find Your Way

The Capital Region, sandwiched between Atlantic beaches, Chesapeake Bay coves and Appalachian mountain valleys, packs so much into every corner. Start in one of its hubs and revel in exploring.

West Virginia, p306

Raft wild rivers, hike shady trails and lose yourself in the forests and small towns of this resilient state.

CAR

Driving is often the only way to reach out-of-the-way destinations and to enjoy the region's many scenic roads. Within urban areas, heavy traffic and parking challenges make walking, bikeshares, local bus and taxi or rideshare services better options.

TRAIN

Many of the region's major cities have frequent rail connections, making train a useful way to arrive. Amtrak services Washington, DC, Baltimore, Wilmington, Harpers Ferry and Richmond, and local commuter rail provides additional routes.

TAXIS & RIDESHARES

Taxis are easy to find in major cities. Rideshare apps Uber and Lyft are also available, though away from city centers, it can be hard to find drivers. Only use licensed cabs and certified rideshares.

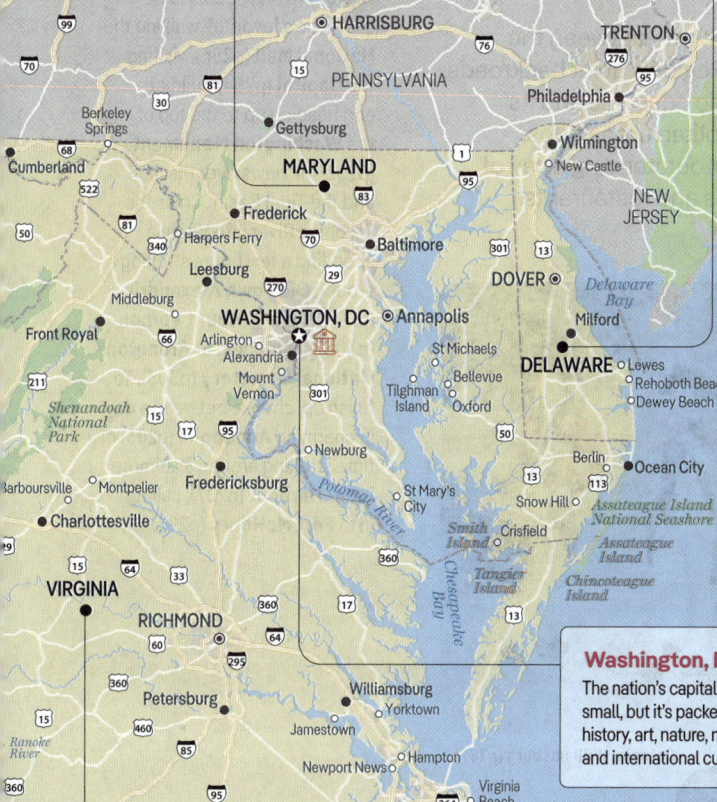

Maryland, p280
Explore Maryland's colonial- and Civil War–era history and discover its urban hubs against a backdrop of tidal marshes and quiet coves.

Delaware, p271
Get acquainted with the nation's second-smallest state, filled with surf and sand, blooming gardens and centuries-old buildings.

Washington, DC, p248
The nation's capital is relatively small, but it's packed with history, art, nature, museums and international culture.

Virginia, p293
Storied pasts come alive and mountain, ocean and historic city landscapes intertwine, with fall mountain foliage a highlight.

THE GUIDE

WASHINGTON, DC & THE CAPITAL REGION

Plan Your Time

Split your time between the Capital Region's quiet backroads, its Atlantic coastline and its cosmopolitan urban hubs, with their outstanding array of museums and restaurants.

Colonial Williamsburg (p289)

Pressed for Time

Focus on the Capital area, taking in at least some of the museums (the **National Museum of Natural History** (p249) seems to be everyone's favorite), walking the **National Mall** (p256), visiting the **Capitol** (p254) building and heading up to the top of the **Washington Monument** (p252) for views over the mall and the Tidal Basin. Cross the Potomac River into Virginia, spending a few hours strolling around **Old Town Alexandria** (p304), visiting **Mount Vernon** (p305) or stopping at **Arlington National Cemetery** (p303). To finish up, choose between a day in charming **Annapolis** (p283) or time strolling around Baltimore's **Inner Harbour** (p287), calling in at **Fort McHenry** (p290).

Seasonal Highlights

DC and the Capital Region has year-round appeal, with springtime cherry blossoms, summer beach days, brilliant fall foliage, snow-dusted winter forests, and festivals and concerts throughout.

JANUARY
January can be chilly and damp, but it's also an ideal time to visit DC's **Smithsonian museums** crowd-free.

APRIL
Try to catch DC's cherry blossoms in bloom, or drive the greening slopes of the Blue Ridge Parkway (p300).

JUNE
Watch for arts festivals in Delaware and elsewhere in the region, and enjoy the beaches ahead of July's crowds.

One Week to Travel

Spend a week sampling the region's beaches and eastern reaches. Start at tiny **Lewes** (p278), taking in its charms, before continuing south along Rte 1 to **Rehoboth** (p276) and other Delaware beaches. Continue on to Maryland's **Ocean City** (p286), allowing at least a day to detour to **Assateague** (p280) and perhaps also **Chincoteague National Wildlife Refuge** (p247). If you're travelling in the summer, there will be plenty of traffic, but you can try to catch the pony swim at Chincoteague. Finish with a few days exploring Maryland's **Eastern Shore** (p285), spending your final evening in **Annapolis** (p283).

Take a Road Trip

After several days in **Washington, DC** (p248) getting your fill of capital vibes, head northwest towards **Antietam National battlefield** (p290), **Harpers Ferry** (p312) and **Cumberland** (p291), with perhaps some cycling along the **C&O Canal** (p292) or from **Morgantown** (p311) to **Charleston** (p342). It's then just a short hop to the **New River Gorge** (p308) and some rafting. Carry on, then on to **Charlottesville** (p298) and **Virginia wine country** (p298). Continue on to **Colonial Williamsburg** (p298) before finishing up with time at **Virginia Beach** (p301).

JULY
July 4 fireworks blend into summer beach days, heaping plates of Maryland blue crabs and the Chincoteague pony swim.

SEPTEMBER
Check out crab festivals along Maryland's Eastern Shore and the Mothman festival in West Virginia.

OCTOBER
Drive through Virginia and West Virginia to surround yourself with the best of the region's fall foliage.

DECEMBER
Catch the tree-lighting ceremony in DC and hit the slopes at West Virginia's ski resorts.

Washington, DC

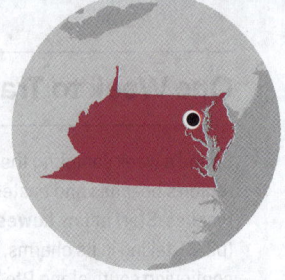

NATION'S CAPITAL | CHERRY BLOSSOMS | MUSEUMS

GETTING AROUND

DC is a walkable city with great public transportation and an expansive **bikeshare program** *(capitalbikeshare. com)*. The best way to explore is to lace up your favorite sneakers and hit the pavement. For longer stretches, the District's famous Metro system is really as good as it sounds, allowing you to get cheaply and easily to nearly anywhere in the city, including both airports, on comfortable, fully ADA-compliant trains.

☑ **TOP TIP**

Keep an eye on DC's social calendars (such as *The Washington Post*'s Weekend section) to make the most out of some of the famous sites, such as the White House and the Kennedy Center.

Washington, DC is a diverse urban center that's easy to navigate, friendly and safe, and has so much to do. It's the United States' capital, and was purpose-built to be so more than 230 years ago on the banks of the Potomac and Anacostia rivers, with Maryland and Virginia donating land to the cause.

The city grew over time, becoming a hub for freed slaves in the mid-1800s and eventually, thanks to immigration and international workers, the culturally diverse and forward-thinking place that it is today.

It's easy to fill your days here with all kinds of activities. You could visit DC just for the museums – the Smithsonian Institution alone has 17 free museums – or simply to explore the history of the nation, its government and its majestic monuments. Then there are all the gorgeous parks, too-cool live-music joints, incredible theater productions and amazing art.

Performing Arts

MAP P249

Discover the Kennedy Center

The **John F Kennedy Center for the Performing Arts** *(kennedy-center.org)*, aka the Kennedy Center, is one of the United States' premier cultural institutions and is home to the National Symphony Orchestra, the National Opera and the National Ballet. The Kennedy Center also hosts symphonies, operas, ballets, theater and live-music shows by national and international artists. There are free daily performances on the smaller Millennium Stage. Don't miss the Reach, a 2019 addition to the center with rehearsal and performance spaces, directly accessible from the Rock Creek Park trail by a stylish pedestrian bridge.

American Craft

MAP P249

Decorative arts at the Renwick Gallery

The **Renwick Gallery** *(americanart.si.edu/visit/renwick; free)*, located near the White House, is a museum dedicated

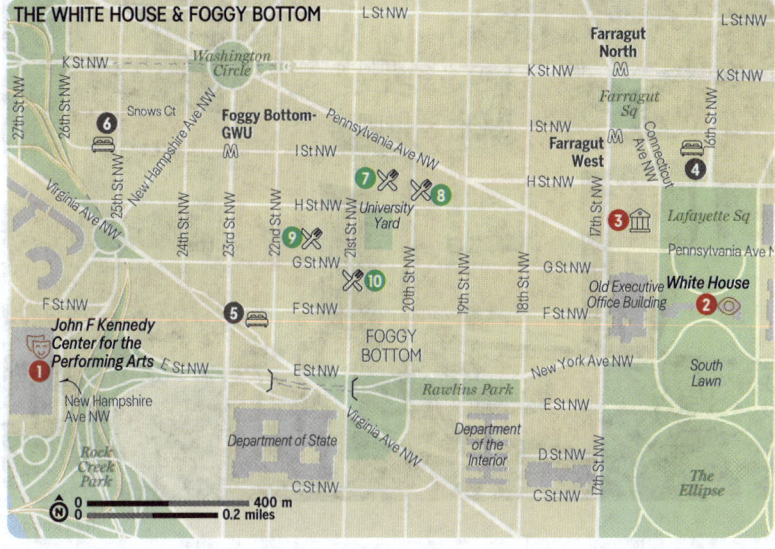

to American crafts and decorative arts from the 19th century to the present. The museum, which is a branch of the Smithsonian American Art Museum, is generally devoted to exhibiting American craft art, though it tends to extend the definitions of craftsmanship and artistic expression, promoting innovative contemporary works that range from the 'Art of Burning Man' to 'Wonder,' a large-scale sculptural exhibit designed to provoke exactly that.

Say Hi to Henry

MAP P252

And the butterflies, too

The free **National Museum of Natural History** (*naturalhistory.si.edu; free*) is one of the most lauded museums in the world and, with so much on offer, it's no wonder. Besides Henry, the giant African elephant greeting you in the Rotunda, museum highlights include the Hope Diamond, the Hall of Fossils (think dinosaurs), the butterfly pavilion filled with living butterflies, and Egyptian mummies – and that's not even a quarter of it all.

From Africa to the World

MAP P252

African American history and culture

Opened in 2016, the **National Museum of African American History and Culture** (*nmaahc.si.edu; free*), often called the Blacksonian, is one of the country's foremost museums dedicated to African American culture and history. Designed by Ghanaian-British architect David Adjaye, it includes exhibits on slavery and freedom, African American impact on sports, music and film, and the 'Power of Place,' a powerful exhibition about belonging.

★ HIGHLIGHTS
1 John F Kennedy Center for the Performing Arts
2 White House

● SIGHTS
3 Renwick Gallery

● SLEEPING
4 Hay-Adams Hotel
5 Hotel Hive
6 River Inn

● EATING
7 Captain Cookie & the Milk Man
8 Founding Farmers
9 GW Delicatessen
10 Tonic at Quigley's

Red Room

TOP EXPERIENCE
The White House

A central piece of American identity, 1600 Pennsylvania Avenue NW is both the workplace and residence of the President of the United States of America. You can visit, though due to strict national-security measures, you'll need to do a lot of planning. Getting to walk around this bucket-list site, however, is worth the effort.

DON'T MISS

- Blue Room
- China Room
- Rose Garden
- President's Park
- National Christmas Tree Lighting Ceremony
- White House Garden

The White House Complex

The **White House** was designed by Irish-born architect James Hoban. Its construction took more than eight years, though President John Adams and his wife Abigail moved in in 1801, before it was complete. The North and South Porticoes were added in the 19th century, followed by the 2nd story and the West Wing in the early 1900s. In the 1950s, the entire 55,000-sq-ft building was remodeled to avert structural problems.

PRACTICALITIES

Scan this QR code to learn more about how to arrange a visit.

The White House complex of today is owned by the National Park Service, and includes a six-story Executive Residence, the West Wing (which holds the president's offices), the Eisenhower Executive Office Building (site of the staff offices) and the Blair House guest residence.

House Tours

White House tours take you through all the public rooms in the East Wing, including the Blue Room, Red Room, Green Room, State Dining Room and China Room, and also give you a view of the Rose Garden. While there are no official tour guides, there are Secret Service members posted in every room who can help to answer questions about the house's architecture and history.

To book a tour, US residents must submit a request through their Congress member between 21 and 90 days in advance – tours are subject to availability and security clearance. Foreign visitors should contact their country's embassy in DC. If your tour is confirmed, you'll get a scheduled time between 9:30am and 12:30pm, Tuesday to Saturday. The self-guided tours are free and last about 45 minutes. You'll need an ID card to enter (only valid US-issued ID cards or passports are accepted) and note that there are no restrooms available during the tour, so plan accordingly (especially if you're with kids).

There is a (very long) list of banned items, which can be found online. These include detachable-lens cameras, video cameras and tobacco products. There's no on-site storage, so your best bet is to leave your bag in your hotel before heading out.

Garden Tours & President's Park

Touring the White House Garden is another spectacular, albeit rarer, option. Garden tours only take place twice a year, in October and April, are announced only a week or two in advance and last for just two consecutive days. Free tickets for the timed tours are distributed outside of the White House Visitor Center on the day, starting at 8:30am.

If you don't manage to secure a garden tour, take a walk around the President's Park instead. This is an 18-acre natural setting surrounding the White House that's full of statues, memorials and other important structures. President's Park is open to the public for free.

Holiday Events

The White House hosts two truly special holidays events that are amazing to experience. The first is the Easter Egg Roll, which has been a tradition since 1878 (although it now takes place on the Monday after Easter). The second is the National Christmas Tree Lighting Ceremony, held in December since 1923. Tickets to both events are free, but available by lottery only. Check *recreation.gov* for more info.

BLACK LIVES MATTER PLAZA

In June 2020, during the George Floyd protests, the MuralsDC program painted 16 bright-yellow letters on 16th St NW, just in front of the White House. The 35ft-tall letters spelled out 'Black Lives Matter' and, at the work's unveiling, Mayor Muriel Bowser declared the street would be renamed Black Lives Matter Plaza. In 2025, the letters were painted over due to pressure from the Trump administration.

FUN FACTS

- It takes 570 gallons of white paint to cover the outside surface of the White House.

- The White House became wheelchair accessible in the 1930s, during Franklin D Roosevelt's presidency. There is a movie theater, bowling alley, flower shop and dentist office on the grounds.

- According to lore, Presidents Herbert Hoover and John Quincy Adams both kept pet alligators in the White House.

- The White House Briefing Room used to be a swimming pool.

- Franklin D Roosevelt hosted a toga party at the White House (photos exist).

- The White House has 412 doors, 147 windows, 28 fireplaces, seven staircases and three elevators.

HIGHLIGHTS
1. Lincoln Memorial
2. National Air and Space Museum
3. National Museum of African American History and Culture
4. National Museum of Natural History
5. Vietnam Veterans Memorial

SIGHTS
6. Artechouse
7. Hirshhorn Museum
8. International Spy Museum
9. Jefferson Memorial
10. Korean War Veterans Memorial
11. Martin Luther King Jr Memorial
12. National Gallery of Art
13. National Museum of African Art
14. National Museum of Asian Art
15. National Museum of the American Indian
16. National WWII Memorial
17. Washington Monument

EATING
see 4 Atrium Cafe
18. Camp Wharf at the Firepit
19. Eat at America's Table
see 15 Mitsitam Native Foods Cafe
20. Officina
see 3 Sweet Home Café

Get a Bird's-eye View
MAP P252

Ride 50 stories to the top

One of DC's most iconic structures is a 555ft-tall, Egyptian-style obelisk built to honor the first President of the United States. The **Washington Monument** *(nps.gov/wamo)* is the world's tallest freestanding stone structure and offers amazing views of the National Mall, Capitol building and Lincoln Memorial. Reserve tickets in advance *($1)* or get free same-day tickets

(continues on p256)

EATING ON THE NATIONAL MALL: MUSEUM CAFES
MAP P252

Sweet Home Café: At the Blacksonian, this acclaimed eatery serves soul and Southern food, grilled favorites and on-the-go sandwiches. *11am-3pm Tue-Sun, from noon Mon* $$

Mitsitam Native Foods Cafe: In the National Museum of the American Indian, serving dishes inspired by Western Hemisphere Indigenous groups. *11am-4pm* $$

Eat at America's Table: Traditional American eatery in the National Museum of American History, serving burgers, hot dogs, barbecue favorites, Tex-Mex and classic salads. *11am-4pm* $$

Atrium Cafe: The Natural History Museum's ground-floor cafe is a large, family-friendly affair with craft burgers and seasonal market specials. *11am-3pm* $$

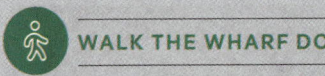

WALK THE WHARF DC

Completed in 2022, the Wharf DC has quickly become the district's waterfront hot spot, where dining, shopping, leisure and live music come together.

START	END	LENGTH
Recreation Pier	High Water Mark	0.5 miles; 1 hour

Start your tour at ① **Recreation Pier**, where you can rent a kayak or stand-up paddleboard, then head over to ② **Pearl Street Warehouse**, a live-music haven with a name that is a nod to the largest-known attempted escape from enslavement in America – it took place in 1848 aboard a 65ft schooner called *The Pearl*. (The incident didn't end well for the 77 enslaved people, though it did inspire both Harriet Beecher Stowe and Abraham Lincoln to work towards ending slavery.)

Walk over to ③ **Transit Pier**, a floating dock outside the Anthem theater that's host to outdoor events, shows, markets, the summer Sunset Cinema and the district's only over-water ice-skating rink in winter. Stop by the ④ **Market Docks**, where you can explore DC by water on a City Cruise lunch boat or monument tour, or on a beautifully restored 1950s runabout (retro-fitted with an electric motor) from Retro Boat Rentals DC. Afterwards, refuel with delicious cooked crabs or fresh clam chowder from the ⑤ **Municipal Fish Market**, the country's oldest continuously running open-air fish market. It's been in operation, without fail, since 1805. While here, take a gander at the ⑥ **High Water Mark**, a public art installation that takes an honest look at the damage presented by climate change. Colorful buoys are suspended in the air, marking historic and possible future flood levels within DC's floodplain, as predicted by 2020 climate-change models. It's an important reminder of the impact humans are having on the natural world.

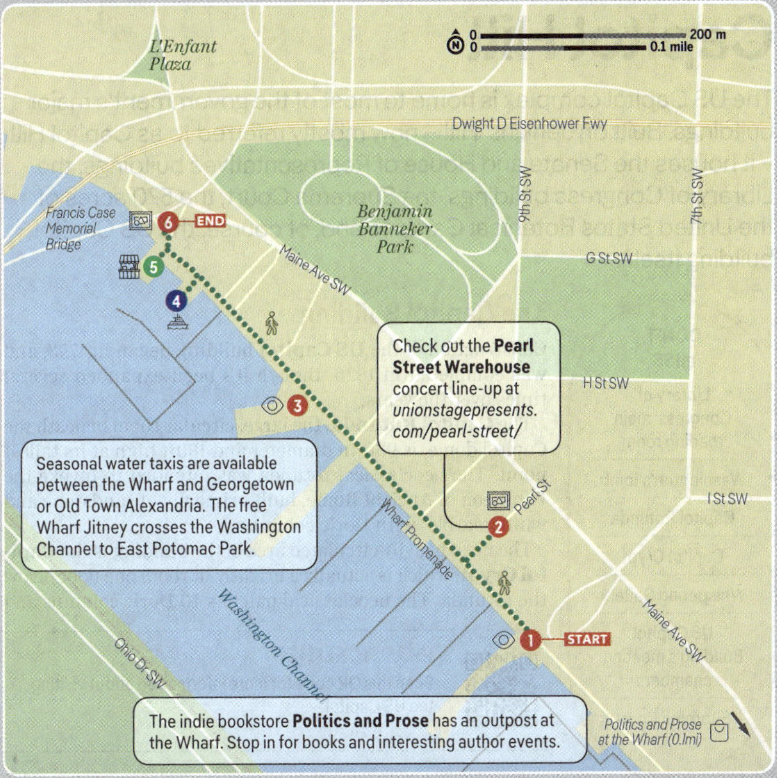

Check out the **Pearl Street Warehouse** concert line-up at *unionstagepresents.com/pearl-street/*

Seasonal water taxis are available between the Wharf and Georgetown or Old Town Alexandria. The free Wharf Jitney crosses the Washington Channel to East Potomac Park.

The indie bookstore **Politics and Prose** has an outpost at the Wharf. Stop in for books and interesting author events.

Politics and Prose at the Wharf (0.1mi)

Library of Congress

TOP EXPERIENCE

Capitol Hill

The US Capitol complex is home to most of the government's major buildings. Built on Jenkins' Hill – now mostly referred to as Capitol Hill – it houses the Senate and House of Representatives buildings, the Library of Congress buildings, the Supreme Court, the 570 acres of the United States Botanical Gardens and, of course, the US Capitol building itself.

DON'T MISS

Library of Congress' main reading room

Washington's tomb

Capitol Rotunda

Capitol Crypt

Whispering Gallery

US Capitol Building's meeting chambers

Supreme Court

The Capitol Building

Construction of the **US Capitol** building began in 1793, and was completed in 1826, though it's been expanded several times over the years.

The **Capitol Rotunda**, the large, circular room beneath the Capitol dome, is 96ft in diameter and 180ft high at its tallest point. The neoclassical rotunda was intended to invoke the Pantheon of Ancient Rome, built primarily of sandstone and white marble, with Doric columns.

The most heavily circulated area of the building is the **Capitol Crypt**, which is actually a brightly lit room one floor below the rotunda. The neoclassical hall has 40 Doric columns and

PRACTICALITIES

Scan this QR code for more information about visiting the US Capitol.

sandstone floors, and is centered on the exact spot where the city's (original) four quadrants meet.

The **National Statuary Hall's** half-dome shape has some unique acoustics that have earned it the name 'Whispering Gallery.' There are some spots in which a person on the other side of the room can be heard more clearly than one next to you, meaning a whispered secret might be unintentionally heard across the room. In the same hall you'll find a collection of 100 statues of renowned citizens from across history – two from each US state (though only 12 are of women). The largest is a 15,000lb statue of Hawaiian King Kamehameha I, standing at 9ft, 10in tall, donated by his island state.

Every visitor to the Capitol building will inevitably pass through **Washington's tomb** – or rather, the tomb that wasn't. The area beneath the crypt was originally reserved for George Washington's remains, though his final wish was to be buried at his home in **Mount Vernon** (p305), so the tomb remains empty.

You can also watch the government in session in the **meeting chambers** from the galleries with a pass procured from your senator or representative or, for noncitizens, from the appointment desks on the upper level. Tours of the Capitol building can also be organized through your congressperson (ideally) or through the **US Capitol Visitor Center** (*visitthecapitol.gov*). There are often walk-up tours available, though reservations are strongly recommended.

The Library of Congress

The **Library of Congress** (*loc.gov*) is said to be the world's largest library, with approximately 173 million books, maps, photographs, films, recordings and manuscripts on file in more than 470 languages. Established in 1800, the library, which is housed in three separate buildings, functions primarily to research questions presented by Congress members through the Congressional Research Service.

In the Thomas Jefferson Building, you'll find the **main reading room**, a grand research center that's the library's main attraction. See it from above on a self-guided tour (by appointment) or visit the main floor, which is open twice a day (Tuesday to Friday). Credentialed researchers can freely use the space and its resources.

Every Friday in July and August, movies from the National Film Registry are shown on the southeast lawn during the annual **Summer Movies on the Lawn** event.

Supreme Court

The **Supreme Court** (*supremecourt.gov*) building is home to the US's judicial branch of government and is the site where monumental, country-changing decisions are handed down. Download a PDF from the website and take a self-guided tour through the majestic Great Hall, past the ground floor's two self-supporting gold and marble spiral staircases, and into the courtroom, where you can sit in on a case or listen to opinions being handed down (seating is first come, first served).

FROM JUNGLE TO DESERT

In the middle of humid, steamy (or cold, wet) Washington is the **United States Botanic Garden** (*usbg.gov*), one of the oldest botanical gardens in North America. Although unassuming from the outside, its glass-encased conservatory contains rare and endangered plants from around the world on display in a profusion of greenery and color. Exhibits are thoughtfully divided by species or biome, meaning that in just a few steps you can explore plants from tropical rainforests and then surround yourself with the succulents of the US's arid Southwest, immerse yourself in medicinal plants or take a tour through the orchid collection, where all the orchids are watered by hand.

TOP TIP

● Many of the buildings on Capitol Hill are connected by underground passageways, some of which are open to visitors. Walk through the tunnel that connects the library's Thomas Jefferson Building to the Capitol Hill Visitor Center. There is an underground subway system for Congress members, built in 1909. Some Capitol Hill tours will take you on it, so ask your congressperson if that's possible.

THE NATIONAL MALL

Also known as 'America's Front Yard,' the National Mall has more than 1000 acres of green space running from the Lincoln Memorial in the west to the US Capitol building in the east. The sprawling park is lined by some of the Smithsonian Institution's most popular museums, along with memorials to war veterans and past American leaders. The National Mall is also a hot spot for activist rallies, a space for festivals and events and a place to celebrate some of the nation's biggest holidays, such as July 4. There are few restaurants on the strip, so if the weather is sunny, pack a picnic to enjoy while museum-hopping.

National Air and Space Museum

(continued from p252)

for the minute-long elevator ride up – expect lines in summer. There's a small museum at the top and, on the two-minute ride down, look for the memorial stones gifted from different states on the monument's inner walls.

Eclectic Art Galleries

MAP P252

From Asia to Africa

For a global art immersion, start at the Smithsonian's **National Museum of Asian Art** *(asia.si.edu; free)*, which is split between two galleries – the Freer Gallery of Art and the Arthur M. Sackler Gallery – situated in two separate but contiguous buildings. This century-old institution was the Smithsonian's first art museum and includes works from China, Korea, Japan, Southeast Asia, South Asia and the Middle East from as far back as the Neolithic period. Head also to the **National Museum of African Art** *(africa.si.edu; free)*, which was originally located in Frederick Douglass' former townhouse before it was acquired by the Smithsonian and moved to a purpose-built building. The collection expanded beyond traditional sub-Saharan art to include modern works, becoming the first museum in the US with a sustained focus on contemporary African art.

Indigenous Stylings

MAP P252

From Indigenous communities to the world

The curvilinear, limestone building of the **National Museum of the American Indian** *(americanindian.si.edu; free)* was designed entirely by Native American architects. It's one of DC's most visually striking structures, and is home to one-third of one of the world's largest collections of objects, archives and photographs of Indigenous populations from the

American continents. The Smithsonian museum covers Indigenous populations across North and South America, and all of its exhibitions, landscaping and structures are designed in collaboration with Indigenous communities.

Let Your Mind Soar
MAP P252

Fly high at the Air and Space Museum

It isn't just one of the most popular museums in the city – year after year, the Smithsonian's **National Air and Space Museum** *(airandspace.si.edu; free)* is one of the most visited museums in the world. Exploring the planet's largest collection of aviation and space artifacts is true immersion into all things airborne. See the Wright Flyer that took the world's first successful flight in 1903, as well as the Spirit of St Louis, the first airplane to fly nonstop from New York to Paris. There are several Mars Rovers on display, and even one of George Lucas' original X-wing fighters (a highlight for *Star Wars* fans).

The Man Who Had a Dream
MAP P252

Monument to MLK

Along the Tidal Basin, at 1964 Independence Ave SW (an address honoring the Civil Rights Act of 1964), is the fourth DC monument built in honor of a non-president, and the first for a person of color. The centerpiece of the **Martin Luther King Jr Memorial** *(nps.gov/mlkm; free)* is a 30ft-high statue of Dr King, carved from the 'Stone of Hope,' which is emerging from two large boulders called the 'Mountain of Despair' – references from King's 'I Have a Dream' speech: 'Out of the mountain of despair, a stone of hope.' There is also a 450ft-long Inscription Wall with quotes from King's speeches and sermons.

See the Cherry Blossoms in Bloom

Favorite spring festival

Visit DC around March or April and you're likely to experience one of the city's star attractions: cherry blossoms. Walk around the Tidal Basin and delight in the light-pink blooms, then check out the events of the **National Cherry Blossom Festival** *(nationalcherryblossomfestival.org)*, such as live-music performances, outdoor markets and a parade. According to the festival's organizers, 'forecasting peak bloom

AN ART GALLERY TOUR

The National Mall's federally owned **National Gallery of Art** *(nga.gov; free)* is home to a classical art collection featuring works by Miró, Mondrian, da Vinci, Monet, Kandinsky and more. The museum and its delightful sculpture garden are free and often host events, such as an outdoor ice-skating rink in winter, or Jazz in the Garden on Friday evenings in summer. Also stop by the Smithsonian's **Hirshhorn Museum** *(hirshhorn.si.edu; free)* inside a 'brutalist donut' (as it's often lovingly called) – a 1960s construction by architect Gordon Bunshaf that's endowed with the contemporary and modern-art collection of Joseph H Hirshhorn, featuring works by Picasso, Matisse, Cassatt, Pollock and Rothko, among other artists.

EATING IN FOGGY BOTTOM: OUR PICKS
MAP P249

Founding Farmers: Farm-to-table eatery cooperatively owned by growers. One of the city's best brunch spots. *7am-10pm Mon-Thu, to 11pm Fri, 8:30am-11pm Sat, to 10pm Sun* $$

Tonic at Quigley's: Once a local drugstore and soda fountain, now a favorite for classic American cuisine. *11:30am-10pm Mon-Wed, from 11am Thu-Sun* $

GW Delicatessen: Of all GWU's sandwich spots, only this one serves an absurd amount of bacon in your BLT. *6:30am-5pm Mon-Fri, 8am-4pm Sat & Sun* $

Captain Cookie & the Milk Man: Former food truck serving the best ice cream, cookies and milkshakes around. *9am-midnight Mon-Thu, to 1am Fri, 11am-1am Sat, to midnight Sun* $

THOMAS JEFFERSON

Thomas Jefferson wore many hats. He wrote the Declaration of Independence's first draft and was the US's secretary of state and third president, along with being a scientist, linguist, diplomat, scholar and a farmer. His **memorial** *(nps.gov/thje; free)*, designed by John Russell Pope and constructed between 1939 and 1943, is meant to recall the Pantheon of Rome and has a 19ft-high bronze statue of Jefferson inside (which was installed four years after the monument's inauguration).

The location of Jefferson's Memorial by the Tidal Basin was a controversial move, as it meant removing some cherry trees, which sparked a protest by 50 local women that came to be known as the Cherry Tree Rebellion.

is almost impossible more than 10 days in advance,' and once the buds open, they only last about two weeks. While seeing them is never guaranteed, it's a wonderful surprise when it does happen.

President Lincoln's Memorial   MAP P252

Shrine to America's 16th president

You've seen it on the back of a penny or a $5 bill, but the **Lincoln Memorial** *(nps.gov/linc; free)* is something altogether different when seen in person. The neoclassical, Parthenon-like structure was idealized by architect Henry Bacon, while the 19ft-tall white-marble statue inside was designed by Daniel Chester French and carved by New York's Piccirilli brothers. The memorial is full of symbolism. For example, the 36 supporting columns represent the US states existing when Lincoln died. Inside, you'll find some of Lincoln's words, including the entire 1863 Gettysburg Address, etched into the walls.

Arrive from the east – entering across the Reflecting Pool best illuminates the scene – and, after you've taken it all in, head around back to watch one of the city's best sunsets over the Potomac.

Across the 38th Parallel & Beyond   MAP P252

Remembering America's overseas wars

The **Korean War Veterans Memorial** *(nps.gov/kwvm; free)*, built in 1995, has two long walls that come together like the point of a triangle over the Reflecting Pool of Remembrance. In the middle, you'll find 19 stainless-steel statues from all branches of the armed forces. When they reflect against the shining granite walls, an optical illusion doubles them into 38 statues, the same number as the parallel that divides North and South Korea.

Dedicated in 2004, the **National WWII Memorial** *(nps.gov/wwii; free)* is a circular, open-air construction with a central fountain surrounded by 56 columns (representing each of the states, territories and the District) and two 43ft-tall arches along the perimeter – one for the Atlantic, the other for the Pacific. There are also two hidden 'Kilroy was here' inscriptions, a cartoon-like graffiti used by American troops during WWII to indicate that friendlies were in the area. Try finding them.

EATING IN PENN QUARTER & CHINATOWN: OUR PICKS   MAP P259

Zaytinya: Greek-Turkish joint by renowned chef José Andrés with floor-to-ceiling windows. *11:30am-10pm Mon, to 11pm Tue-Thu, to midnight Fri, 11am-midnight Sat, to 10pm Sun* $$$

Immigrant Food: Adorable cafe below Planet Word, serving global dishes and creative cocktails. *11am-9pm Tue-Thu, to 10pm Fri, 11:30am-10pm Sat, to 3pm Sun* $$

China Boy: No-frills, cash-only Chinese takeout that has never disappointed anyone, ever. *9:30am-5pm* $

Cuba Libre: Cuban cuisine and a rum bar in a Havana-style dining room; salsa nights are the true draw. *4-9pm Mon, Tue & Thu, to 3am Fri, noon-3am Sat, to 9pm Sun* $$

PENN QUARTER & CHINATOWN

HIGHLIGHTS
1. National Archives

SIGHTS
2. American Art Museum
3. Capital One Arena
4. Museum of Illusions
5. National Building Museum
6. National Children's Museum
7. National Museum of Women in the Arts
8. Planet Word

SLEEPING
9. Motto by Hilton

EATING
10. Busboys & Poets
11. China Boy
12. Cuba Libre
see 8 Immigrant Food
13. Zaytinya

ENTERTAINMENT
14. National Theatre
15. Shakespeare Theatre Company
16. Warner Theatre
17. Woolly Mammoth Theatre Company

The 2-acre **Vietnam Veterans Memorial** (*nps.gov/vive; free*) was less well received in its early days, due to American architect Maya Lin's somber design. The two black granite walls engraved with names of the fallen were called a 'nihilistic slab of stone,' yet, after some adaptations, the design was built and inaugurated in 1982.

Charters of Freedom

MAP P259

We hold these truths

The **National Archives** (*visit.archives.gov; free*) is home to the country's most significant documents – notably the

> **SMITHSONIAN FOLKLIFE FESTIVAL**
>
> The Smithsonian Folklife Festival in July brings together artists, musicians, storytellers and chefs from around the world for a gathering and celebration on the National Mall.

 EATING AROUND DC: DISTINCTIVE BITES — MAPP252, P26

Tsehay: This crowd-pleaser is an homage to owner Selam Gossa's late mother's Addis Ababa cafe, with authentic ingredients and hand-ground spices. *4-10pm Mon-Wed, noon-10pm Thu-Sun* $$

Camp Wharf at the Firepit: Adorable Airstream trailer serving make-your-own s'mores kits by a wood-burning firepit. *6-10pm Thu, to 11pm Fri, 5-11pm Sat, to 10pm Sun* $

All-Purpose Riverfront: Italian-American artisanal pizzas; popular for its egg-topped breakfast pizzas on weekends. *5-9pm Tue-Thu, to 10pm Fri, 11am-10pm Sat, to 9pm Sun* $

Officina: Three-story Italian nirvana: cafe, bar, Italian market, 2nd-floor trattoria and rooftop terrace. *11am-9pm Sun & Tue-Thu, to 10pm Fri & Sat* $$

THEATERS & VENUES

Warner Theatre: Has been hosting everything from concerts and comedy shows to Broadway favorites since 1924; the theater itself is a work of art. *warnertheatredc.com*

National Theatre: One of America's oldest continually operating theaters (since 1835), and the oldest one still presenting Broadway productions. *the nationaldc.org*

Shakespeare Theatre Company: Has two locations in Penn Quarter – both offer classic and contemporary takes on Will's writings. *shake speretheatre.org*

Capital One Arena: Hosts everything from high-profile sporting events to headlining concerts, Cirque du Soleil shows, monster-truck rallies and NBA playoff games. *capital onearena.com*

Woolly Mammoth Theatre Company: Known for its original, thought-provoking productions. *woolly mammoth.net*

Declaration of Independence, the Constitution and the Bill of Rights. Explore permanent and rotating exhibits and the public vaults – just don't forget a sweater, as temperatures are kept cool to preserve the parchment. In summer, reserve timed-entry tickets online.

Art Abounds

MAP P259

American artistic heritage

Start your day at the **American Art Museum** (*si.edu/ museums/american-art-museum; free*), which celebrates the US's rich artistic heritage from colonial times to now, featuring iconic American artists such as Louise Nevelson and Winslow Homer. In the same building is the **National Portrait Gallery**, with a permanent collection of American portraits that offer a unique look at national identity (Oprah, Michelle Obama and Beyonce are all in there).

Several blocks north is the **National Museum of Women in the Arts** (*nmwa.org; adult/child $21/free*), focusing on the contributions of female artists and featuring pioneering works that challenge traditional narratives.

Child's Play

MAP P259

Museums for kids and families

In DC's Penn Quarter, north of Pennsylvania Ave, are some fun museums for kids. **Planet Word** (*planetwordmuseum. org; by donation*) is an interactive language arts museum that compares languages and dialects from around the world, posing interesting questions about why we say things the way we do. The **National Children's Museum** (*national childrensmuseum.org; $19*) is an interactive play space that's intellectually stimulating and great for burning off excess energy. The **National Building Museum** (*nbm.org; adult/child $10/7*) is an underrated gem, with exhibits that range from understandable architecture to LEGO structures. Finally, hit up the **Museum of Illusions** (*moiwashington.com; adult/ child $24/19*), a weird and wild no-holds-barred favorite for kids from three to 73.

Contemporary Culture

MAP P261

Art spaces sprout in SW

Contemporary art has found a home in Southwest DC, thanks to spots such as the **Rubell Museum** (*rubellmuseum.org/dc; adult/child $15/10*), displaying pieces from one of the world's largest private collections of contemporary art (Keith Haring and Yayoi Kusama are on the list). Entrance is free for DC residents or members; Wednesday to Friday is pay what you wish. The **Culture House DC** (*culturehousedc.org; free, donations appreciated*) is an uber-colorful church turned cultural center, run on the principle that 'art is a catalyst for change.' Stop also at **Artechouse** (*artechouse.com; adult/child $22/16*), where digital art and technology come together to create truly immersive experiences – think colorful interactive projections,

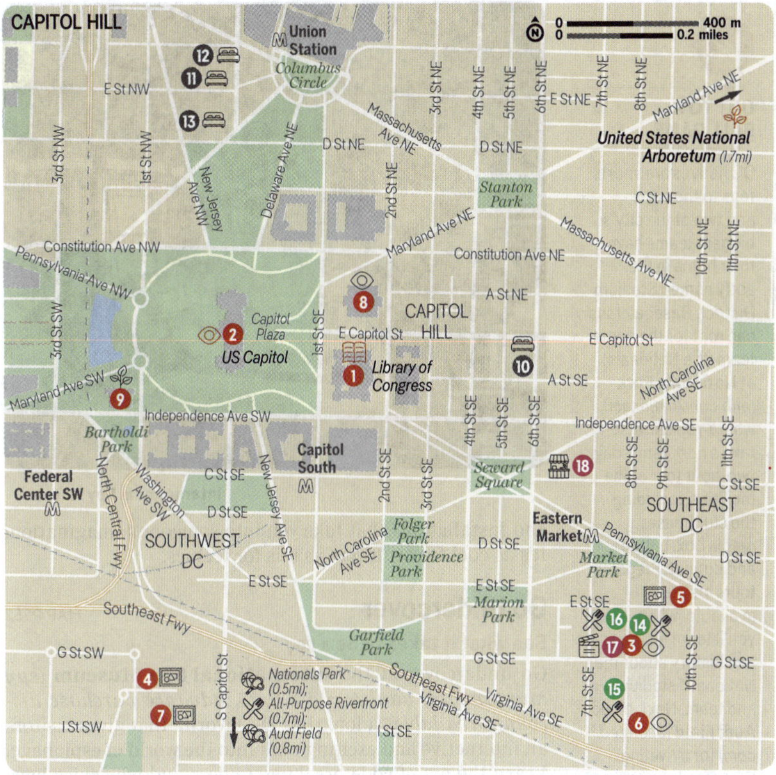

CAPITOL HILL

- ⭐ **HIGHLIGHTS**
  1. Library of Congress
  2. US Capitol
- 🔴 **SIGHTS**
  3. Barracks Row
  4. Culture House DC
  5. Hill Center
  6. Marine Barracks
  7. Rubell Museum
  8. Supreme Court
  9. United States Botanic Garden
- ⚫ **SLEEPING**
  10. Friends Place on Capitol Hill
  11. Kimpton George Hotel
  12. Phoenix Park Hotel
  13. YOTEL Washington DC
- 🟢 **EATING**
  see 13 Art and Soul
  14. Belga Cafe
  15. Pineapple & Pearls
  16. Ted's Bulletin
- 🔴 **ENTERTAINMENT**
  17. Miracle Theatre
- 🔴 **SHOPPING**
  18. Eastern Market

🍴 EATING ON CAPITOL HILL: OUR PICKS

MAP P261

Art and Soul: Seasonal, locally sourced Southern comfort food with a view of the Capitol dome. *7:30am-3pm Mon, to 9pm Tue-Fri, 9am-9pm Sat, to 8pm Sun* $$

Pineapple & Pearls: Fine dining with two Michelin stars, four courses, a disco-chic dress code and no disappointments. *6-9pm Wed & Thu, 5-10pm Fri & Sat* $$$

Belga Cafe: Belgian-French brasserie serving savory waffles and stuffed truffle brie. *5-9:30pm Mon, from noon Tue-Thu, noon-10pm Fri, 9:30am-10pm Sat, to 3:30pm Sun* $$

Ted's Bulletin: American eats done right, with homemade pop tarts and boozy milkshakes. *7am-10pm* $

OUT TO A BALL GAME

DC natives are sports fans to the core, and two of the city's biggest teams have their home in the aptly named Stadium District. Baseball fans can root for the home team (the Nationals) at **Nationals Park** *(mlb.com/nationals)*, where you can also take a non-game-day, two-hour tour of the facilities, including the clubhouses, media box, bullpen and dugout. Pregame tours are also available, where you'll learn fun facts and history about the Nationals' stadium and team. Next, hit up **Audi Field** *(dcunited.com)* for a riveting DC United soccer match, or cheer on the women of the Washington Spirit. Audi Field is also home stadium for the DC Defenders UFL team.

International Spy Museum

and installations that take you into someone's imagination. It's as cool for art lovers as it is for techies.

Go Undercover

MAP P252

See what it takes to be a spy

Go undercover at the **International Spy Museum** *(spymuseum.org; adult/child $37/23, advance purchase discounts available)*, a longtime DC favorite that gives visitors an interactive and exciting peek into the world of espionage. Learn the art of code breaking, understand why spies have to dress the part, and find out why we have spies in the first place. The museum even confronts controversial topics such as counterfeiting, torture and secret surveillance in a multi-perspective manner that sparks instant debate. Check out an immense collection of the coolest spy gadgets, or head to the 5th floor, where you'll find fascinating stories of the world's most famous spies.

Historic & Culinary Hot Spots

MAP P261

Visit Eastern Market and Barracks Row

Eastern Market is as much a historic stop as it is a culinary one. Stop by the 19th-century brick building for all your meat, poultry, seafood, baked-good, flower and deli needs, or visit one of the short-order spots for a meal (don't miss the Market Lunch's wildly popular crab cakes). Head also to **Barracks Row**, an olde-times main street full of shops, restaurants and cool sites. Stop by the birthplace of American composer John Philip Sousa, catch a flick at the **Miracle Theatre** and check out the artwork at the **Hill Center**, an art gallery in a renovated Civil War–era hospital before catching the evening parade at the **Marine Barracks** *(barracks.marines.mil)* every Friday from May through August.

Festival Day
Celebrate Adams Morgan Day

DC's longest-running neighborhood festival is a vibrant celebration of community and culture. Adams Morgan Day has been held on 18th St on the second Sunday in September for the past 45 years, showcasing the area's food, music, art and music. You'll find local artists and international cuisine lining the street, and for entertainment, expect everything from drag-queen story time, reggae bands and gospel miming to go-go fitness, flag football clinics and dance collectives. There's also live music, DJ performances and a dedicated kids zone with activities for the little ones.

The festival, organized entirely by volunteers, welcomes residents and visitors alike to meet the neighborhood's businesses and enjoy the local offerings – but mostly to celebrate living in one of DC's most diverse neighborhoods.

Furry Friends   MAP P264
A menagerie at the National Zoo

Established in 1889, the 163-acre **Smithsonian's National Zoo** *(nationalzoo.si.edu; free)*, just north of Adams Morgan in Rock Creek Park, is home to more than 2100 animals from nearly 400 different species – elephants and sea lions to sloths, bison and orangutans.

The lovely meandering pathways take you through regional exhibits, such as the American Trail, where California sea lions, North American beavers and red wolves live; the Great Ape House, where you'll find gorillas and orangutans (a high-wire trail allows them to travel over the heads of visitors to their second home at the 'Think Tank'); and the Africa Trail, where you can spot cheetahs, zebras, warthogs, gazelles, lesser kudu and ostriches.

Tree Spotting   MAP P261
Azaleas, bonsai and Corinthian columns

Established in 1927, the 450-acre **United States National Arboretum** *(usna.usda.gov; free)* is a perfect DC escape into nature. Wander along the 9 miles of parkland roads, stopping to visit attractions such as the National Bonsai and Penjing

(continues on p267)

STUDIO THEATRE

Studio Theatre *(studiotheatre.org)* is a nonprofit theater company whose 1978 creation was a catalyst for the Logan Circle neighborhood's revitalization. The company, which began in a former warehouse, now has a multimillion-dollar building (renovated in 2021–22) spanning half a city block. Its thought-provoking, contemporary shows feature national and international players, and the troupe also offers apprenticeships, in-house residencies, student-priced matinees and myriad community-engagement programs. It also has some of the most accessible offerings of any DC theater, with wheelchair-accessible areas in all its theaters, as well as free assistive-listening devices and regularly scheduled sign-language-interpreted and audio-described performances.

 EATING IN ADAMS MORGAN & THE U STREET CORRIDOR: OUR PICKS   MAP P266

Rita Loco: Counter-service burritos, tacos and cocktails, with a popular upstairs patio. *5pm-midnight Tue-Thu, to 1:30am Fri, noon-1:30am Sat, to 6pm Sun* $

Busboys & Poets: Bookshop, coffee shop and world-food cafe, serving as a neighborhood cultural hub. *8am-10pm Mon-Thu, to 11pm Fri, 9am-11pm Sat, to 10pm Sun* $

Compass Rose: Eclectic international restaurant in a brick townhouse with a cool bar. *5pm-midnight Mon-Thu, to 1am Fri & Sat, 11am-10pm Sun* $$

Chercher: In a townhouse just outside of DC's 'Little Ethiopia,' with a mouthwatering menu plus flavorful off-the-menu stews and other dishes. *4-10pm Tue-Thu, from noon Fri-Sat* $$

Howard University

TOP EXPERIENCE

Black Broadway

Until NYC's Harlem took over in 1920, DC was the cultural and social capital of Black America, boasting the largest urban Black population in the country. A strong society of Black-owned and -run businesses, newspapers, civic groups and churches sprouted along the U Street Corridor, along with the country's first Black University, transforming DC into a Black cultural and intellectual epicenter.

DON'T MISS

- Howard University
- Howard Theatre
- Lincoln Theatre
- Dunbar High School
- Duke Ellington's Statue
- Ben's Chili Bowl
- Meridian Hill Park

Howard University

The country's first African American research **university** *(howard.edu)* opened in 1867, quickly becoming a magnet for Black intellectuals from around the country. Howard University was an anchor for the community that would become the largest and most prosperous Black middle class of its time.

Howard Theatre

When the **Howard Theatre** *(thehowardtheatre.com)* opened in 1910, it was dubbed the largest colored theater in the world and received all the greats of the era – Louis Armstrong, Billie

PRACTICALITIES

For an in-depth history of Black Broadway, scan this QR code.

Holliday, Ella Fitzgerald, Duke Ellington and Nat King Cole all graced the stage. The theater remained a hot spot for Black American culture until the 1980s, when it was neglected and shuttered, before being reborn in 2012 as the cultural powerhouse it remains today.

Lincoln Theatre

Shortly after it opened more than 100 years ago, the **Lincoln Theatre** *(thelincolndc.com)* became the epicenter of Black Broadway. The theater had a 1600-seat auditorium and movie theater backed by the Lincoln Colonnade, a big-band dance hall that became the place to meet on U St.

Dunbar High School

The first high school for African Americans in the nation, **Dunbar High School**, opened in 1870, and had such an incredible reputation that families from all over the country shipped their children to DC to study. Teachers often had doctorate degrees and were some of the highest-paid African Americans in the country, as the federal government paid Black and white teachers in the District the same wages. High percentages of the student graduates went onto college, an extreme rarity at the time.

Duke Ellington's Statue

Before becoming famous in Harlem, the king of jazz, Edward Kennedy 'Duke' Ellington, was born and raised in Washington, DC, where he quickly became a well-known musician. A statue, entitled *Encore*, sits outside the Howard Theatre in honor of the hometown hero.

Langston Hughes Residence

From 1924 to 1926, poet Langston Hughes lived in a small house on S St while working odd jobs to help support his family. His first book of poems was published after his time at the DC residence (now a private home) and the rest, as they say, is history.

Thurgood Marshall Center

The 12th St YMCA was the first YMCA established in the nation for 'colored men and boys.' The original 1853 structure was designed by William Sidney Pittman, one of the nation's earliest Black architects, and Langston Hughes once had a room here. The building was fully restored and renamed the **Thurgood Marshall Center** *(tmcsh.org)*, a community center with some historical displays inside.

Old Whitelaw Hotel

The **Old Whitelaw Hotel** was a community masterpiece. Funded by Black investors and built by Black entrepreneurs and craftsmen, the gray-brick hotel was named for its builder, John Whitelaw Lewis (and not for the 'white laws' that segregated the city). In its heyday, the Whitelaw attracted Washington's Black elite, though it deteriorated into a drug den in the 1960s and '70s, before being fully restored into apartment buildings in the early '90s, as it remains today.

A BOWL OF CHILI

A late addition to the scene is the area's most important culinary landmark: **Ben's Chili Bowl**. Opened in 1958 by wife-and-husband team Virginia and Ben Ali, Ben's quickly became a watering hole for Washington's Black community and, with the Lincoln Theatre next door, for entertainers as well.

TOP TIPS

● When you're ready for a rest, stop at the corner of 10th and U Sts and contemplate the **African American Civil War Memorial**, a striking monument designed by sculptor Ed Hamilton. Its centerpiece depicts a sailor and a soldier going off to war while loved ones wave them away.

● Read through the Wall of Honor, where you'll find the names of the 209,145 Black men who served in the Civil War.

● Head to **Meridian Hill Park** (aka Malcom X Park), a 12-acre park with cascading waterfalls and a sculpture garden. The park was ground zero during segregation – white DC lay to the west, while Black DC was to the east.

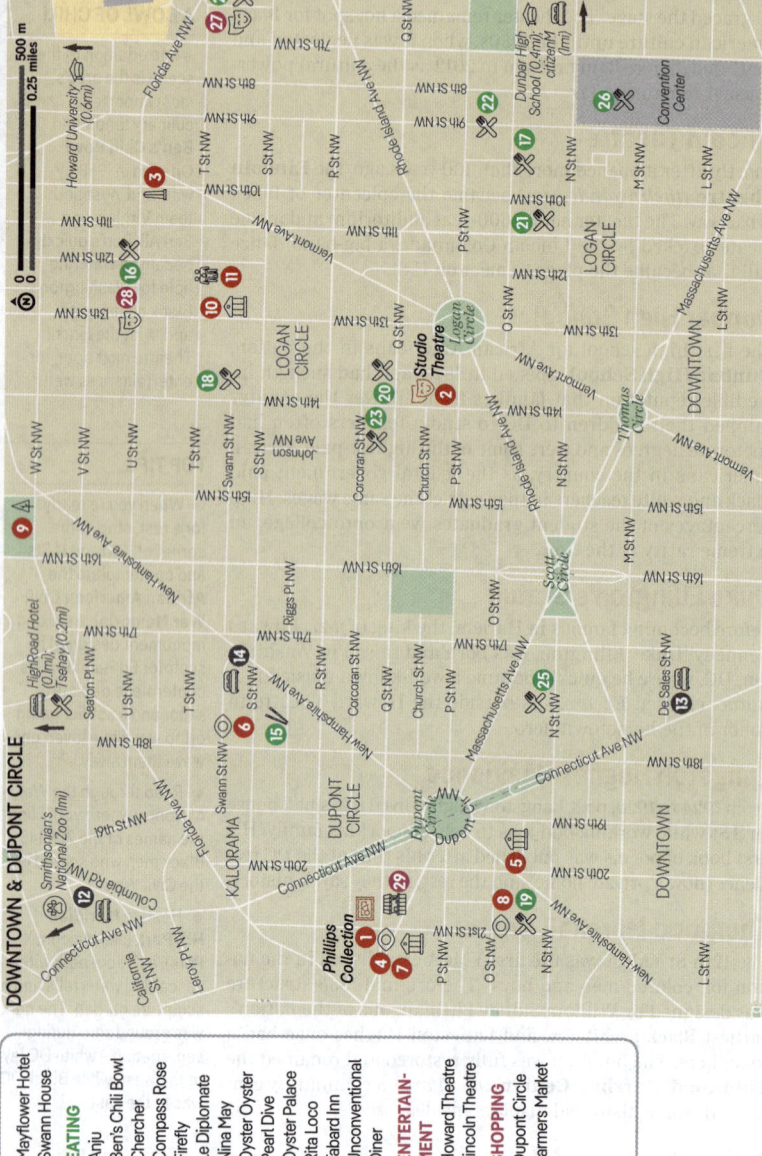

(continued from p263)
Museum (a collection of the legendary minute Japanese and Chinese trees), the National Herb Garden, the Gotelli Conifer Collection, the azalea collection and the Flowering Tree Walk.

Then there are the columns – 22 huge Corinthian sandstone columns that somewhat awkwardly supported the US Capitol's frieze from 1828 until 1958, when the building was renovated and the columns were replaced. In the 1980s, the ousted columns were cleverly reassembled in the Ellipse Meadow of the National Arboretum, where they became a favorite (and very Instagram-worthy) tourist attraction.

Modern Art, Storied History MAP P266

America's first modern-art museum

Founded in 1921 by Duncan Phillips, the **Phillips Collection** *(phillipscollection.org; adult/child $20/free)* is considered to be America's first modern-art museum. It was founded on the pioneering idea of (in Phillips' words) 'a museum where one could encounter the art of the past and the present on equal terms' and features works by artists such as O'Keeffe, Van Gogh and Renoir, in a space where visitors can connect deeply with each piece of art on display. Reserving tickets in advance is encouraged, although walk-ins are welcome.

Market Mornings MAP P266

Farm-fresh produce with community vibes

Every Sunday from 8:30am to 1:30pm, Dupont Circle transforms into the lively outdoor **Dupont Circle Farmers Market** *(freshfarm.org),* where colorful stalls offer a diverse selection of farm-fresh produce, locally sourced meats and cheeses, fresh-baked goods and artisanal products. In peak season, more than 50 vendors make up what the *Financial Times* called 'one of the top farmers markets in the country.'

This beloved community gathering began in 1997 and has become a weekend staple for locals and visitors alike, who come not just to shop but also for the community atmosphere. Arrive early to get the best produce, but stay later to try goods such as artisanal bourbon or to get a fresh-made meal on-site.

COOLEST HISTORIC BUILDINGS

Mayflower Hotel: The 1925 'Hotel of Presidents' has been host to countless prominent people and events throughout the last century.

Heurich House: This Gilded Age mansion turned museum was built for German immigrant Christian Heurich, whose brewery was once DC's second-largest employer.

Mansion on O Street: Actually four historic row houses stuck together, the 'mansion' is a black hole of oddities, memorabilia, hidden doorways and funky stuff.

Larz Anderson House: This 1905 beaux-arts Gilded Age mansion, now a museum, takes opulence to a new level.

Embassy Row: Many of Massachusetts Ave NW's chic residences – once known as Millionaires Row – were converted into embassies and social clubs after the Great Depression, giving birth to Embassy Row.

EATING IN DOWNTOWN & DUPONT CIRCLE: BEST RESTAURANTS — MAP P266

Tabard Inn: DC's oldest restaurant, with a Michelin Star–studded chef in a Civil War–era-style dining room. *8am-3pm, plus 5-9pm Sun-Wed, 5-10pm Thu-Sat* $$$

Oyster Oyster: Chic, carefully sourced, plant-based cuisine with a sustainability ethos. *5:30-8:30pm Tue-Sat* $$$

Le Diplomate: Old-style French cafe with Hemingway-in-Paris vibes and an excellent brunch. *11:30am-3pm & 5-11pm Mon-Thu, to midnight Fri, 9:30am-midnight Sat, to 11pm Sun* $$$

Anju: Homey Korean joint with comfy seating and comfort food to match. *5-9pm Mon-Thu, to 10pm Fri, 11am-1:30pm & 5-10pm Sat, to 9pm Sun* $$

Spend a Day in Georgetown's Book Hill

MAP P269

Hilltop stop for intellectuals and artists

Start your day at Book Hill's namesake attraction, perusing the shelves of independent booksellers such as **Bridge Street Books** (bridgestreetbooks.com), or the used and rare-edition treasure trove that is the **Lantern Bookshop** (lanternbookshop.org). Next, wander in and out of some of the numerous art galleries lining Wisconsin Ave, such as the **Washington Printmakers Gallery** (washingtonprintmakers.com), **Addison/Ripley Fine Art** (addisonripleyfineart.com) and **Gallery Article 15** (article15gallery.com) for vibrant Congolese art.

After browsing the shops, it's time to refuel. Grab some noodles at the colorful and quirky **Oki Shoten**, followed by a creamy cone from old-school ice-cream shop **Thomas Sweet**, a mouthwatering pastry from **Boulangerie Christophe**, or a cookie from Oprah's favorite French bakery, **Maman**.

Still feeling stressed? Locals rave about the affordable acupressure and massages at **Meridian Health and Relaxation**, located at the top of Book Hill – think 30-minute massages for less than $30.

Scientific Discovery

MAP P269

Historic laboratory

Nestled among Georgetown's quiet streets is an important scientific site: the **Volta Laboratory and Bureau** (nps.gov/places/volta-bureau.htm), which was Alexander Graham Bell's research center. Built in 1893, after Bell won 50,000 francs from the French government for his invention of the telephone, the Volta Bureau was dedicated to the 'increase and diffusion of knowledge relating to the deaf,' a cause Bell took on for his mother, who was nearly deaf, and his wife, Mabel Gardiner Hubbard, who was deaf. The building is currently closed to the public.

May the Force Be with You

MAP P269

Gargoyle hunting at the National Cathedral

Officially named the Cathedral Church of St Peter and St Paul, the neo-Gothic **Washington National Cathedral** (cathedral.org) is just north of Georgetown. From the day the cornerstone was laid in 1907, the cathedral took 83 years to complete, and is the sixth-largest cathedral in the world. It has 215 stained-glass windows – standouts include the Space Window, which

---

NIGHTLIFE IN GEORGETOWN

Blues Alley: This landmark jazz supper club has hosted all the greats, from Ella Fitzgerald and Count Basie to Dizzy Gillespie and Tony Bennett. *bluesalley.com*

Sovereign: This Belgian resto-bar has more than 50 beers on tap, with 300 bottles and rare brews to boot. *thesovereigndc.com*

El Centro D.F.: Authentic Mexican fare and mezcal served in a two-story space with a happening back patio. *eatelcentro.com*

Mr. Smith's: Georgetown's favorite karaoke piano bar since 1965, with American-style fare and classic decor. *mrsmiths.com*

Clydes: This well-loved saloon still serves cold beers in the location in where it opened in 1963. *clydes.com*

 EATING BRUNCH: OUR PICKS

MAP P266

Nina May: Hyper-local farm-to-table American cuisine with outdoor seating and weekend brunch. 5-9:30pm Tue-Thu, to 10:30pm Fri, 10am-10:30pm Sat, to 9:30pm Sun $$

Firefly: American comfort food served around a large indoor tree, boasting one of the area's best brunches. 7-11am & 4-10pm Mon-Fri, 9am-3pm & 5:30-10pm Sat, 9am-3pm Sun $$

Unconventional Diner: Contemporary-chic New American diner with a nod from Michelin, serving brunch until late afternoon. 9am-10pm $$

Pearl Dive Oyster Palace: Southern-inspired oyster house serving lip-licking seafood. 4-10pm Mon, Wed & Thu, 11am-11pm Fri & Sat, to 10pm Sun $$

- **SIGHTS**
  1. Volta Laboratory & Bureau
- **ACTIVITIES**
  2. Key Bridge Boathouse
  3. Meridian Health & Relaxation
  4. Thompson Boat Center
- **SLEEPING**
  5. Graham Georgetown
- **EATING**
  6. Bluefin Sushi
  7. Boulangerie Christophe
  8. Chaia
  9. Good Stuff Eatery
  10. Il Canale
  11. Maman
  12. Oki Shoten
  13. Thomas Sweet
- **DRINKING & NIGHTLIFE**
  14. Clydes
  15. El Centro D.F.
  16. Mr. Smith's
  17. Sovereign
- **ENTERTAINMENT**
  18. Blues Alley
- **SHOPPING**
  19. Addison/Ripley Fine Art
  20. Bridge Street Books
  21. Gallery Article 15
  22. Lantern Bookshop
  - see 3 Washington Printmakers Gallery

Washington National Cathedral (p268)

PAINTING STORIES

In 2007, DC's Department of Public Works started a Murals Program, aimed to beautify walls in every part of the city. The initiative has resulted in 141 murals across the district, each depicting or supporting important themes from the area, including a handful of murals that memorialize DC's Black history and immigrant stories around DC's U St area. Some favorites include *The Wailin' Mailman: A Portrait of Buck Hill* by Joe Pagac (a masterpiece more than 70ft high) and *The Torch*, in which Aniekan Udofia tells the story of 'the torchbearers who illuminate the way,' including Harriet Tubman, Muhammed Ali and the Obamas (it's located on the alley wall of Ben's Chili Bowl (p265)).

contains a rock from the moon, and the Rose Window, made of more than 10,500 pieces of glass. The grounds are home to one of the city's few remaining old-growth forests, but the most fun activity at the cathedral is gargoyle spotting. Among the 112 gargoyles on its exterior are an alligator, an American rattlesnake, a raccoon and Darth Vader.

Paddle the Potomac

MAP P269

A wetter way to explore DC

The Potomac River is a renowned rowing and kayaking spot, and if you're keen to join in, the **Thompson Boat Center** *(boatingindc.com)* and the **Key Bridge Boathouse** *(boatingindc.com)* are the two main spots to rent watercraft. Whether you're a master kayaker or looking simply to cruise, either boating center will help you find the best way to get on the water. Both locations provide paddling and safety instructions and gear, and offer introductory classes for those who've never paddled. At Thompson, you can even learn to row a scull, or rent one if you're already a rower.

EATING IN GEORGETOWN: OUR PICKS

MAP P269

Il Canale: Thin-crust, wood-fired pizza done to perfection from a place named one of the US's top 100 pizza spots. *11am-10:30pm Mon-Thu, to 11pm Fri & Sat, to 10pm Sun* $$

Bluefin Sushi: Serving high-grade sushi and sashimi in a tiny canal-front dining room for nearly 30 years. *4-9pm Tue, noon-9:30pm Wed-Sat, 1-9pm Sun* $$

Good Stuff Eatery: Nothing but burgers, fries and shakes served just right by Spike Mendelsohn of *Top Chef* fame. *11:30am-10pm Mon-Sat, 11am-9pm Sun* $

Chaia: The chic vegan and vegetarian tacos of farmers-market fame have found an adorable red-brick-and-mortar location. *11am-9pm* $

Delaware

BEACHES | HISTORY | NATURE

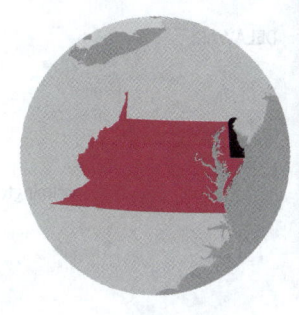

In just two hours you can drive from Delaware's southern beaches to its countryside estates in the Brandywine Valley bordering Pennsylvania, passing historic towns and nature reserves en route. Its diminutive size has earned it a few nicknames, including 'small wonder' and the Diamond State. Delaware's precious rivers, bays and ocean attracted European colonists and it played an integral role in shaping US history. It was the first state to ratify the US Constitution in 1787, which had a domino effect on the other 12 states.

Delaware's commitment to preserving its history is evident throughout the state, with numerous museums and walking tours featuring costumed re-enactors. Historical attractions also recount the arduous struggle for African American residents. Delaware was an essential conduit for the Underground Railroad, with Harriet Tubman and other abolitionists relying on its safe houses and forests to secure freedom as they escaped north.

Places
Wilmington p273
Dover p276
Milford p276
Rehoboth Beach p276
Sussex County p277

☑ TOP TIPS
Beach lovers should head straight to Delaware's southern end to soak up the joy of being surrounded by surf, sand and saltwater taffy.

GETTING AROUND

Driving is the most efficient way to travel around Delaware, allowing you to explore off-the-beaten-path towns, parks and attractions. **DART** *(dartfirststate.com)*, Delaware's transit system, operates more than 60 bus routes in the state's three counties: New Castle in the north, Kent in the middle (encompassing Dover and Milford) and Sussex in the south, including Rehoboth and Lewes. DART has seasonal routes connecting Dover and Wilmington with the beach and also runs seasonal buses from park-and-ride stops on Coastal Hwy (SR1) to Rehoboth Beach. Wilmington is well connected to other east-coast hubs by Amtrak.

Wilmington

MAP P274

Explore Wilmington's riverfront

Once the site of thriving shipbuilding businesses, Wilmington's Christina River continues to benefit the city today as a prime recreation spot. The **Riverfront Wilmington** *(riverfrontwilm.com)* features an accessible boardwalk with restaurants, museums and parks. You'll find joggers, rowers and cyclists, as well as folks enjoying more leisurely activities such as playing cornhole at the seasonal beer garden or just enjoying the water views.

At the north end, the 1.3-mile stretch begins at the **Du Pont Environmental Education Center**, the elevation of which provides a bird's-eye view of the 212-acre tidal marsh and wildlife refuge below. Abundant trees and cooling breezes make it a good place for respite on warmer days.

Walk south on the riverfront path for an impressive view of the city skyline, passing Minor League Baseball venue **Frawley Stadium**, the **Delaware Children's Museum** *(delawarechildrensmuseum.org; $12)*, and food stalls in a restored warehouse at **Riverfront Market**. Just across Market St lies **Tubman Garrett Riverfront Park**, a popular spot for city festivals, anchored by a moving statue depicting abolitionists Thomas Garrett and Harriet Tubman guiding the enslaved people through the Underground Railroad.

Tour a Swedish ship and church

A mile north of Tubman Garrett Riverfront Park, the **Kalmar Nyckel Shipyard** features a replica of a Dutch tall ship that brought Swedish and Finnish settlers to Wilmington in 1638 and laid the foundation for the city's robust shipbuilding business. The site's **Copeland Maritime Center** *(kalmarnyckel.org; adult/child $10/5)* highlights the area's first European settlement and the city's maritime history with educational videos, artifacts, model ships and a log-cabin replica. Check the schedule for free deck tours and ticketed sailings in Wilmington or New Castle, and step out on the museum balcony for a prime view of the river and boat when it's docked.

Scandinavians buried their dead and worshipped at the church and cemetery at **Old Swedes Historic Site** *(oldswedes.org; free)* down the street. Enter through Hendrickson House, a 1722 stone home owned by a Swedish American family that was moved from its original location in Pennsylvania. Old Swedes is one of the oldest Protestant churches in North America; its sparkle comes from crushed oyster shells

MUSIC CITY

Eunice LaFate, local artist and owner of LaFate Gallery. *@lafategallery*

Bob Marley's family is establishing a museum in Wilmington to honor him, his Jamaican heritage and reggae music. He lived here in the 1960s and early '70s. He and I are from the same place in Jamaica – St Ann Parish. There is a park in Wilmington called One Love Park (named after the Marley song) at W 24th and N Tatnall Sts. I have a permanent wall in my gallery for Marley. The annual People's Festival Tribute to Bob Marley features music, storytelling and food. Music fans should also visit during the annual Clifford Brown Jazz Festival in June. Thousands of people come from all over. It's big.

 EATING IN WILMINGTON: OUR PICKS — MAP P274

Bardea Food & Drink: Italian James Beard–nominated eatery serving pizza, pasta and seafood, with an adjoining seasonal garden and steakhouse. *5-9pm Mon-Thu, to 11pm Fri & Sat* **$$**

DECO Wilmington: Food hall with vegan comfort food, pizza, chicken and waffles, livened up with art markets, karaoke and trivia. *hours vary by vendor* **$**

Oath 84: Black-owned New American restaurant carrying creative meat and seafood small plates. *4-10pm Tue-Fri* **$$**

Jessop's Tavern: Colonial-era decor, pub fare and Belgian beer in a 350-year-old building in historic New Castle. *11:30am-9pm Mon-Thu, to 10pm Fri & Sat, to 8pm Sun* **$$**

WILMINGTON

● SIGHTS
1 Copeland Maritime Center
2 Delaware Children's Museum
3 Delaware History Museum
4 Old Swedes Historic Site
5 Tubman Garrett Riverfront Park

● SLEEPING
6 Hotel du Pont

● EATING
7 Bardea Food & Drink
8 DECO Wilmington
9 Oath 84
10 Riverfront Market

from the Christina River that builders added to the mortar. Inside, white pews contrast with colorful stained-glass windows. Visitors get to try their hand at pulling the heavy church bell during tours.

A window to the past

The **Delaware History Museum** *(dehistory.org; adult/child $10/5)* and **Mitchell Center for African American Heritage** chronicle the state's journey over hundreds of years, starting with its earliest residents, the Lenni Lenape Native American tribe, and continuing with the fight for freedom faced by African Americans. Permanent exhibits reside in an art-deco former-Woolworth building connected to the brick-covered Old Town Hall, Delaware's first government building, completed in 1799.

Delaware held enslaved people during the Civil War and was among the last of the states to ratify the 13th Amendment abolishing slavery, so the road to freedom and equality here was an arduous one for African Americans. That struggle is chronicled, from the Underground Railroad's route through the state, to the end of segregation in public schools, to the role of churches.

TOUR THE BRANDYWINE VALLEY'S ESTATES

The French-style sprawling estates in the Brandywine Valley – known as château country – are a testament to the outsized legacy of the industrialists and philanthropists of Delaware's Du Pont family.

START	END	LENGTH
Nemours Estate	Winterthur	13 miles; 1-2 hours

Start at ❶ **Nemours Estate**, a 15-minute drive north of Wilmington, flanked by towering black-and-gold iron gates, one hailing from Wimbledon Manor and the other with the initials of Catherine the Great. Helpful staff guide visitors through the bedrooms and elaborate reception hall outfitted with 18th- and 19th-century paintings, wall tapestries and du Pont family portraits. There are 25-minute tours of the 200-acre garden filled with statues, a pool and a maze of evergreen trees.

It's a 10-minute drive to the indoor-outdoor ❷ **Hagley Museum & Library**, which features dozens of stone structures, waterwheels and a coal-fired steam engine that whisks you back to the 19th-century gunpowder factory founded by El du Pont. One highlight is a booming black powder–explosion demonstration.

Drive slowly along narrow winding roads to the ❸ **Mt Cuba Center**. This botanical garden blooms with various native plants and habitats along newly ADA-accessible, fragrant garden paths. Set out on one of the trails or take a horticultural class.

After this, it's five minutes' drive to ❹ **Winterthur Museum, Garden & Library**, where tens of thousands of furniture items, porcelain and other decorative objects are spread throughout rooms in the former home of Henry Francis du Pont. One of the two buildings resembles the original mansion and the other is a conventional museum. Signs show what's in bloom each month in the garden, which can be viewed from a tram.

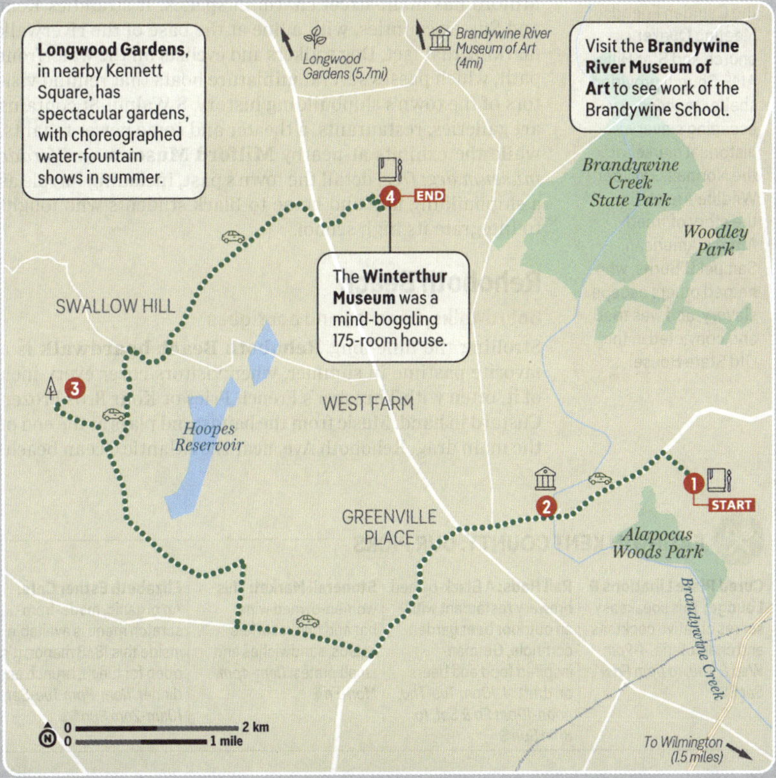

Longwood Gardens, in nearby Kennett Square, has spectacular gardens, with choreographed water-fountain shows in summer.

Visit the **Brandywine River Museum of Art** to see work of the Brandywine School.

The **Winterthur Museum** was a mind-boggling 175-room house.

Dover

Relive history in the downtown

Downtown Dover's half-acre, tree-filled lawn surrounded by historic buildings, known as the **Dover Green**, holds most of the town's treasures. It's where suffragettes demanded the right to vote and legislators voted to ratify the US Constitution. **First State Heritage Park** *(destateparks.com)* storytellers dressed in 18th-century garb recount these pivotal moments during walking tours held Wednesday through Saturday.

Visitors can also tour the former and current homes of the **Delaware General Assembly**. Built in 1791, the Georgian-style Old State House features an exhibit on free Black man Samuel D Burris, who was tried and convicted for helping enslaved people escape. Members of the State House and Senate met in the two chambers upstairs until 1933, when the new Legislative Hall was built. Murals depicting scenes from Delaware history, painted by artist John Lewis, were added to the chambers of the **Delaware Legislative Hall** in 1987 to memorialize the 200th anniversary of Delaware signing the US Constitution.

Milford

A charming main street

With several attractive buildings and a scenic riverwalk, Milford has main-street charm in spades. It straddles Kent and Sussex counties, with a line at the base of the riverwalk marking that fact. Dog walkers and cyclists fill the waterfront path, which passes several miniature boats that remind visitors of the town's shipbuilding history. S Walnut St contains art galleries, restaurants, a theater and some newer tenants, while the exhibits at nearby **Milford Museum** *(milforddemuseum.org; free)* detail the town's past, including its role as a shipbuilding hub and home to Black students who fought to integrate its high school.

Rehoboth Beach

Boardwalks, beaches and boutiques

Strolling the mile-long **Rehoboth Beach boardwalk** is a favorite pastime in summer, when visitors cover every inch of it, often with Thrasher's French Fries or Kohr Bros Frozen Custard in hand. Music from the bandstand plays at the end of the main drag, Rehoboth Ave, near the Atlantic Ocean beach.

HARRIET TUBMAN'S LEGACY

Kent County is home to six sites associated with abolitionist Harriet Tubman, whose journeys rescued 70 enslaved individuals. Tubman relied on a network of safe houses, trails and waterways (the Underground Railroad) in Maryland and Delaware to reach the free state of Pennsylvania. The 6000-acre Blackbird State Forest is said to be one of her landmarks during her passages, while the Camden Friends Meeting Quaker church and Star Hill AME Church provided shelter to those escaping slavery. A historical marker at the Norman G Wilder Wildlife Area tells the story of freed African American Samuel D Burris, who helped others escape slavery, and was tried and convicted in the Old State House.

EATING IN KENT COUNTY: OUR PICKS

Cured Plate Libations & Lounge: This speakeasy serves creative cocktails and charcuterie. *4-9pm Wed & Thu, to 11pm Fri & Sat* $$

Rail Haus: A Black-owned brewery restaurant with an outdoor beer garden, cornhole, German-inspired food and beers on draft. *4-10pm Tue-Thu, noon-10pm Fri & Sat, to 8pm Sun* $

Stonerail Market: This women-owned wine bar and market offers salads, sandwiches and small plates. *11am-4pm Mon-Fri* $

Elizabeth Esther Cafe: An organic, made-from-scratch menu is available inside this 1868 manor; it's open for lunch, brunch and dinner. *11am-8pm Tue-Sat, 10am-2pm Sun* $$

Delaware Legislative Hall

Arrive early to grab a parking spot and plop your umbrella on the beach before sunbathers and swimmers swallow every available space. It's worth venturing past the souvenir shops near the beach to peruse the assortment of independent stores. The long-standing **Browseabout Books** features author signings, while **Buddhas & Beads** sells crystals, jewelry and antiques. Venture down the storybook-like **Penny Lane Mall** to grab a sweet crepe or savory croissant from **Cafe Papillon**.

Sussex County

Explore the Delaware beach towns

While Rehoboth commands the most name recognition, Sussex County contains a cluster of waterside hamlets stretching 24 miles along the Coastal Hwy from Lewes to Fenwick Island, passing through Dewey Beach and Bethany Beach. Explore each for a few hours or days.

Filled with remarkably well-preserved historic homes and blooming gardens, Lewes (p278) looks like it's been plucked from the English countryside. After driving past Rehoboth, the road turns narrow, with the rushing Atlantic Ocean waves on one side and serene bay waters on the other. Party hot spots and live-music venues such as the Starboard, Bottle &

BEST FOR ART & FILM LOVERS

Cinema Art Theater: The Rehoboth Beach Film Society operates this two-screen movie hall showcasing foreign and independent movies from emerging filmmakers.

Rehoboth Art League: With exhibits, lectures and festivals, this nonprofit continuously hosts events for art lovers.

Clear Space Theatre Company: Featuring plays and Broadway musicals, this regional theater company also holds acting classes for all ages.

Milton Theatre: Live bands, musical theater and a Pride festival are just some of the events held at this two-story building, constructed in 1910.

Clayton Theatre: Classic and first-run movies are shown at this single-screen movie theater, with its retro marquee lit at night.

EATING IN SUSSEX COUNTY: UPMARKET MEALS

Henlopen City Oyster House: Arrive early to grab a seat at this popular no-reservations eatery offering a wide fish selection and a raw bar. *noon-9pm Mon-Sat* **$$$**

Cafe Azafran: Garlic shrimp, ratatouille and other Mediterranean dishes are on offer here, with a sister cafe in Lewes. Check for weekly specials. *5-8:30pm Mon-Sat* **$$$**

One Coastal: A James Beard–nominated chef sources ingredients from local farms and waters to deliver standout meat and seafood dishes. *5-9pm Tue-Sun* **$$$**

Blue Hen: A hotel restaurant with a daily-changing menu, weekly specials and good happy-hour specials. *4-8:30pm Mon-Thu, to 9pm Fri & Sat* **$$$**

NATURE SPOTS BEYOND THE BEACH

Lavender Fields at Warrington Manor: The lavender fields are the main attraction, but don't skip the native-plant gardens and the shop selling lavender products.

Delaware Seashore State Park: With 6 miles of oceanfront and 20 miles of bay shoreline, this is a prime spot for all water activities.

Georgetown–Lewes Trail: This bicycle and pedestrian trail will add its final leg in fall 2025, making it 17 miles to connect the towns of Lewes and Georgetown.

Gordons Pond Trail: The loop traverses its namesake saltwater lagoon and Cape Henlopen State Park, where you'll see sand dunes and remnants of the former WWII military base.

Prime Hook National Wildlife Refuge: At this migratory bird sanctuary you might spot bald eagles, ospreys or waterfowl.

DAVID KAY/SHUTTERSTOCK

Cork and Rusty Rudder overflow with singles in the summer. The 15-minute drive to **Bethany Beach** takes you across the Charles W Cullen Bridge, the slanted pylons of which resemble a ship's sails and are lit up an ocean-blue. Stop in Delaware Seashore State Park, or at the Big Chill Beach Club restaurant, for a prime bridge view.

Collectively called 'the quiet resorts,' Bethany Beach and **Fenwick Island** have a tranquil atmosphere that draws families. The half-mile boardwalk in Bethany contains a couple of arcades, souvenir shops and restaurants with beach views, while mini golf and a water park are the highlights of Fenwick's small boardwalk. The gentle waters of **Assawoman Bay** make an excellent spot for beginners to rent kayaks, paddleboards and sailboats from Coastal Kayak.

Walk through historic Lewes

The picturesque town of **Lewes** packs five centuries of architecture into its historic district, which contains a mishmash of styles from colonial to Federal and Victorian. The Dutch settled here in 1631, earning Lewes the 'first town in the first state' moniker. Its Dutch history is on display at the free **Zwaanendael Museum** *(history.delaware.gov/museums;*

EATING IN SUSSEX COUNTY: OUR PICKS

Fish On: One of a dozen restaurants under local SoDel Concepts' domain, with a happy hour and seafood specials daily. *5-9pm* $$

Confucius Chinese Cuisine: Long-standing Chinese spot with shareable Hunan dishes, including salt-and-pepper shrimp and roasted Peking duck. *5-9pm Thu-Mon* $$

Raas: Indian cuisine in a 125-year-old Victorian home with traditional and unique fare, including chili olive naan and a dedicated street-fare menu. *noon-9pm Tue-Sun* $$

Off the Hook: Standout farm-to-table small plates and seafood dishes with a daily happy hour and weekday specials. *11:30am-9pm* $$$

Bethany Beach

free), where the striking red-and-white shutters take after a town hall in the Netherlands.

Park your car or bicycle and explore the town on a **walking tour** *(historiclewes.org)* with Lewes Historical Society. Engaging storytellers in period costumes take you past landmarks such as the **Ryves Holt House** *(historiclewes.org/locations/ryves-holt-house-museum; free)*, Delaware's oldest building. You can also pop into the 18th- and 19th-century buildings at the organization's main Shipcarpenter St campus, including a former school, doctor's office and a tavern that sells cocktails made from colonial-era recipes on the first Friday of each month.

Lewes' main thoroughfare, 2nd St, houses an eclectic assortment of independent stores selling antiques, vintage jewelry and art, women's clothes and books. A leisurely walk toward the water leads to the picturesque **Lewes Canalfront Park** *(lewescanalfrontpark.org)*, where you can tour the last lighthouse boat made for the US Lighthouse Service, the **Lightship Overfalls** *(overfalls.org; adult/child $5/free)*.

En route to or from Lewes, it's worth making the 23-mile detour to the **Delaware Botanic Gardens** *(delawaregardens.org; adult/child $15/free)* at Pepper Creek, where the central 2-acre meadow is filled with native plants that change throughout the year.

WHY I LOVE LEWES

Julekha Dash, Lonely Planet writer

After my husband and I moved from Lewes, I still visit at least every other month. While the highway traffic and businesses have quadrupled in the last 20 years, the heart of Lewes remains unchanged. The calm waters of Savannah Beach appeal to a nervous ocean swimmer like me, and even during high season you can find a stretch of sand to call your own. I've spent many afternoons at Cape Henlopen State Park walking the 3-mile loop past sand dunes, wetlands and the lookout point where the Delaware Bay meets the Atlantic Ocean. I love taking visitors on boat tours from the Lewes Canal to the Delaware Bay to spot dolphins, waterfowl and lighthouses, or on the Cape May–Lewes Ferry.

Maryland

CHESAPEAKE BAY | WILD HORSES | HISTORY

Places
Annapolis p282
St Mary's City p282
Cambridge p284
Ocean City p286
Assateague Island p286
Baltimore p287
Antietam National Battlefield p291
Cumberland p291

☑ TOP TIP

Annapolis and the Eastern Shore make an ideal focus if you only have a day or two in the state. With more time, linger along the coast, discover Baltimore or head west towards Antietam and Cumberland.

Straddling the historical divide between north and south, Maryland mixes southern charm with northern savvy, its attractions rimmed by a long eastern shoreline and rolling western highlands. Wild horses wander the dunes and coastal grasses of Assateague Island. Spring redbuds and fall foliage brighten the slopes of the Allegheny Mountains around Cumberland. Watermen ply their trade amid the coves and waterways of Chesapeake Bay, and 19th-century drum rolls seem to echo across the now-peaceful expanses of Antietam's Civil War battlefields. In Baltimore, the state's commercial hub, creative chefs dish up some of the Mid-Atlantic's most exciting cuisine, while in Annapolis, Maryland's picturesque waterside capital, a fine collection of 18th-century buildings set the backdrop for museums, eateries and international-class boat shows. Wherever you go, you'll find something for every taste and budget, wrapped up in a small enough package that you can sample it all with ease.

 GETTING AROUND

Check *visitmaryland.org* for scenic byway routes. Bay Runner Shuttle links Baltimore and BWI Airport with Ocean City, Cambridge and Cumberland. Flixbus connects Washington, DC and Annapolis. **MUST Bus** *(mustbus.org)* has a handful of eastern routes, and Shore Transit links Salisbury (which is served by Greyhound and the Bay Runner Shuttle) with Crisfield, Berlin and Ocean City, but you'll need a car to really explore the Eastern Shore. **Maryland Transit Administration** *(mta.maryland.gov)* has commuter bus info for Baltimore. MARC commuter trains also link Washington, DC with Baltimore, and Amtrak's Capitol Limited runs between Washington, DC and Cumberland. Downtown Annapolis is eminently walkable. In Baltimore, the **Water Taxi** *(baltimorewatertaxi.com)* has free connector service around the Inner Harbor in good weather and a paid route to Fort McHenry. There's also the free Charm City Circulator bus serving downtown neighborhoods.

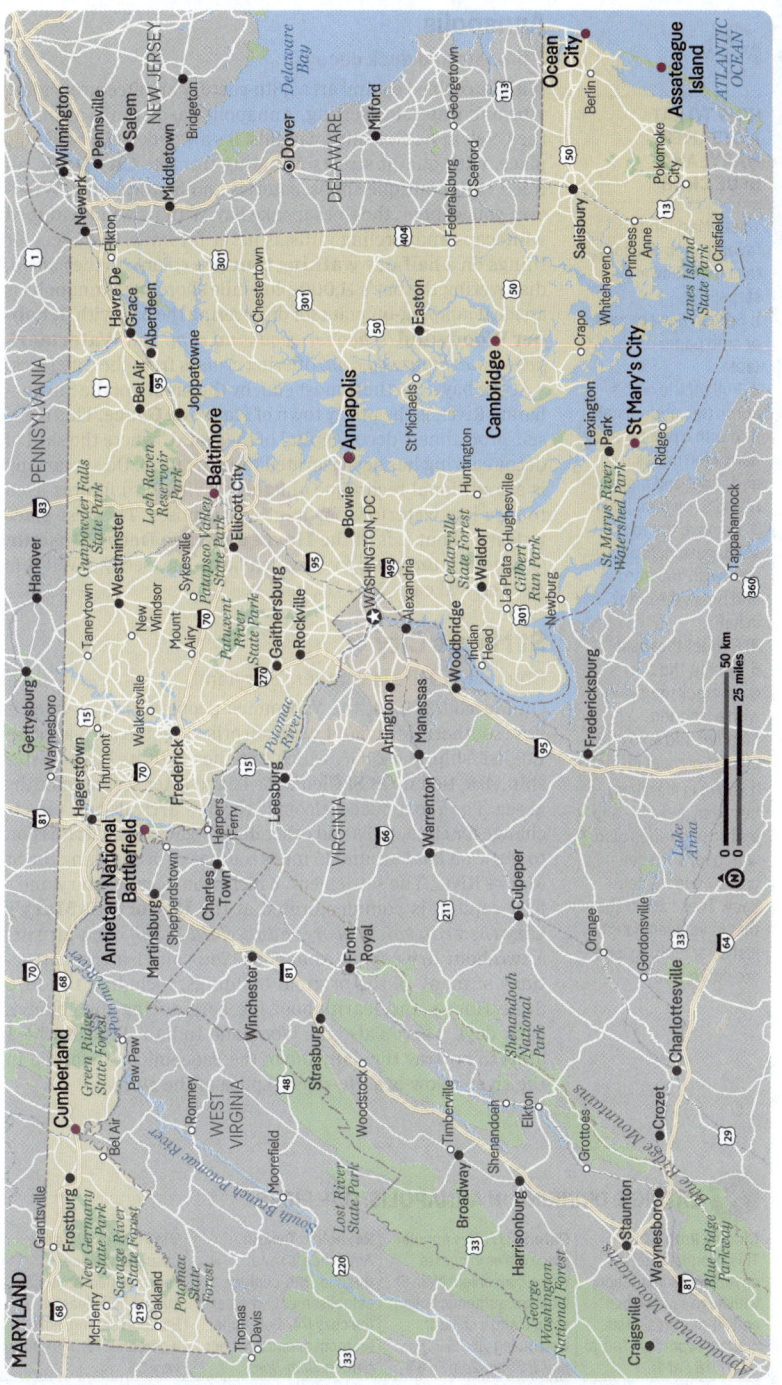

Annapolis

Sailboats and duck decoys

With its cobbled central area, 18th-century architecture, sailing vibe and waterside setting, Annapolis easily ranks as one of the USA's most charming capitals. It's a wonderfully walkable place, with quaint streets radiating from its **City Dock**, all lined with boutique shops, eateries and historic inns. Wherever you wander, the Chesapeake Bay, with its wind-whipped whitecaps and circling gulls, is never far away. Get a feel for things on a half-day **walking tour** or explore further afield, discovering the bay's 11,000-plus-mile shoreline. Annapolis is an ideal jumping-off point for discovering the bay, with **Schooner Woodwind** *(schoonerwoodwind.com)* and **Watermark** *(watermarkjourney.com)* offering cruises from the City Dock.

At the bay's northernmost end, by the mouth of the Susquehanna River, is the pretty town of **Havre de Grace**. This is the self-proclaimed 'decoy capital of the world,' where the skill of decoy carving has been elevated to an art form. Decoy carving is a traditional technique of hand-carving bird figures used to lure live waterfowl for hunting purposes. The best place to learn about it is at the **Havre de Grace Decoy Museum** *(decoymuseum.com; free),* which hosts the Decoy & Wildlife Art Festival each May.

St Mary's City

Colonial-era life in southern Maryland

On March 23, 1634, the Yaocomico people living in what is now southern Maryland were surprised by the arrival of an English ship, the *Dove*, which together with its larger sister ship, *Ark*, tied up at St Clement's Island after several months at sea. The Yaocomico welcomed the new arrivals and – in exchange for cloth, tools and other items – gave them permission to settle on land around 15 miles southeast, overlooking the St Mary's River. The settlement, which soon became Maryland's first capital, is commemorated at the **Historic St Mary's City** *(hsmcdigshistory.org; adult/child $10/6)* open-air site, a two-hour drive from Annapolis. You can visit reconstructions of many of the original buildings, including the 1676 State House, and learn about life here during the colony's early days. There's also the Woodland Indian Hamlet, which aims to portray the daily life of the Yaocomico. Anchored in the river below is a life-sized replica of the *Dove*.

HOW TO EAT A STEAMED MARYLAND BLUE CRAB

To eat Maryland's favorite crab delicacy, take the following steps:
1. Spread newspapers or crab paper on the table.
2. Pull off the crab's apron (the abdominal flap with a point that's narrow on males, and wider and more rounded on females).
3. Remove the top shell, guts, gills and yellowish 'mustard' and break the crab in half.
4. Extract the meat.
5. Finally, the best part: crack the claws with a wooden hammer and enjoy the chunks of meat inside.

If you're in Maryland between mid-May and early September, also watch for softshell crabs – a local delicacy. These are crabs that have just been caught just after molting, and are eaten whole.

 EATING & DRINKING IN ANNAPOLIS: OUR PICKS

Chick & Ruth's Delly: This informal eatery is an Annapolis institution, with huge sandwiches and all-day breakfasts. *6:30am-10pm Sun-Thu, to 11pm Fri & Sat* $

Osteria 177: This popular place draws in guests with a convenient Main St location, authentic Italian cuisine and a chilled, welcoming vibe. *5-10pm, plus 11:30am-2pm Fri* $$

Reynold's Tavern: Ambience is key at this mid-18th-century establishment, whether in the cozy 1747 Pub, upper tearoom or outdoor beer garden. *11am-11pm*

Vin 909: An intimate, casual ambience, seasonal neo-American cuisine and pleasant Eastport setting make this a perennial favorite. *hours vary* $$

ANNAPOLIS ON FOOT

The best way to explore Annapolis' cobbled streets and dock area is on foot. You may need a car for attractions away from the centre.

START	END	LENGTH
State House	WWII and Gold Star Families Memorial	6 miles; 3-4 hours

Maryland's late-18th century ❶ **State House** (open daily for self-guided tours with photo ID) is the oldest state capitol in continuous legislative use. Atop its dome, an upside-down acorn symbolizes wisdom. Nearby is Church Circle, with ❷ **St Anne's Episcopal church** (1692). From here, follow Franklin St to the ❸ **Banneker-Douglass-Tubman Museum**, highlighting the achievements of Marylanders of African American ancestry. It's named after orator and abolitionist Frederick Douglass, Harriet Tubman (p284) and Benjamin Banneker, an astronomer and mathematician. Return past Church Circle before turning southeast on ❹ **Main St**. At its eastern end is ❺ **City Dock** and the ❻ **Kunta Kinte–Alex Haley Memorial**, commemorating Kunta Kinte's 1767 arrival at this spot. The surrounding Story Wall has quotes on reconciliation and healing. Just beyond is the boat-turnaround channel known as ❼ **Ego Alley**. Bordering this is Compromise St, leading over Spa Creek to Eastport and the ❽ **Annapolis Maritime Museum**. Back at City Dock, pass ❾ **Market Sq** en route to the ❿ **US Naval Academy**, where you can walk or arrange driving tours in one of the academy's electric vehicles. Diagonally opposite is ⓫ **St John's College**, one of the US's oldest post-secondary institutions. From here, it's about 2 miles (but worth it) across the Severn River bridge to the ⓬ **WWII and Gold Star Families Memorial**, overlooking the Severn River, with the names of 6000-plus Marylanders who lost their lives during the war.

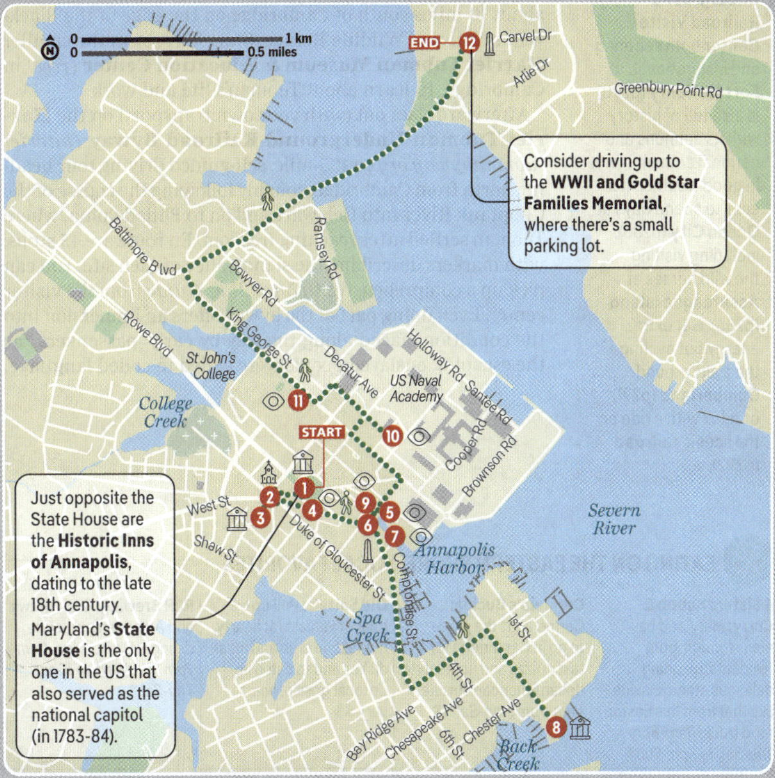

Consider driving up to the **WWII and Gold Star Families Memorial**, where there's a small parking lot.

Just opposite the State House are the **Historic Inns of Annapolis**, dating to the late 18th century.

Maryland's **State House** is the only one in the US that also served as the national capitol (in 1783-84).

About 10 miles south of St Mary's City, where the Potomac River flows into Chesapeake Bay, is **Point Lookout State Park** *(dnr.maryland.gov/publiclands; $7)*, the site of a medical center for wounded Union soldiers during the Civil War and now a quiet area of pines and marshes. Its camping area is currently closed for renovations, but the setting is peaceful and, in season, there's a half-day ferry excursion to and from Smith Island, which lies about two hours southeast of Point Lookout in the bay.

Cambridge
The underground railroad

The underground railroad was a secret network of people and safe houses that offered support and assistance to enslaved people trying to escape bondage by fleeing north or into Canada. During the early to mid-19th century, hundreds of mostly unsung heroes, Black and white, helped what is estimated to be thousands of enslaved people to reach freedom. One of the most famous 'conductors' of the underground railroad was Harriet Tubman (1822–1913), who was born near Cambridge. After managing to escape, she repeatedly travelled back to the Eastern Shore to help family and friends to safety. Her story is movingly portrayed in the excellent **Harriet Tubman Underground Railroad Visitor Center** *(nps.gov/hatu; free)*, about 10 miles south of Cambridge on the edge of the Blackwater National Wildlife Refuge. Start here, or in the smaller **Harriet Tubman Museum & Education Center** *(free)* in Cambridge, to learn about Tubman's life and work.

Afterwards, set out (with your own transport) on the **Harriet Tubman Underground Railroad Byway** *(harriettubmanbyway.org)*, a 125-mile, self-guided driving tour heading north from Cambridge, roughly following the course of the Choptank River into Delaware and on to Philadelphia, where Tubman settled after reaching freedom. En route are 45 stops, with markers describing the significance of each site. You can pick up a comprehensive *Driving Tour Guide* from the visitor center. Even doing part of the byway offers an immersion into the conditions faced along the way by early 'passengers,' as the escaping enslaved people were called in coded language.

MARYLAND FOR KIDS

Maryland offers so much for kids of all ages. Get to know its waterways on a sightseeing **cruise** *(watermarkjourney.com)* in Annapolis or Baltimore, or watch a boat being constructed at the Chesapeake Bay Maritime Museum in St Michaels. The **Maryland Science Center** (p288) has displays for all ages. History-loving teens will likely find the **Harriet Tubman Underground Railroad Visitor Center** both sobering and inspirational. **Fort McHenry** (p290) is also full of history with its cannons and national anthem story. In good weather, it's easy to spend days at **Ocean City** (p286), including visiting the wild horses at **Assateague Island** (p286). Get extra energy out cycling the trails around **Cumberland** (p291) or relax with a ride on the scenic **railroad** (p292).

 EATING ON THE EASTERN SHORE: LOCAL FAVORITES

4 Sisters Kabob & Curry: Maryland has many foreign-born residents, meaning delicious ethnic cuisine like that from this Easton food truck. *11am-8pm Tue-Sat, to 6pm Sun* **$**

Carmela's Cucina: Carmela's is the place to go in Cambridge for tasty pizza and homestyle ItalianAmerican cuisine. *11am-9pm Mon-Sat* **$$**

Old Salty's: Pull up by boat or vehicle for hearty, homestyle crab and meat dishes and to catch up on local gossip. *hours vary* **$$**

RaR Brewing: Craft brews and American pub-style dining in Cambridge. *11am-9pm Sun-Wed, to 10pm Thu-Sat* **$$**

EASTERN SHORE MEANDERINGS

The pace slows down as soon as you get over the Bay Bridge. Maryland's Eastern Shore is worth as much time as you can give it.

START	END	LENGTH
Annapolis	Assateague Island	187 miles; 2-3 days

From Annapolis, follow Rte 50 to ❶ **Easton** and then Rte 33 to ❷ **St Michaels**, with its shop- and eatery-lined main street and the Chesapeake Bay Maritime Museum. Continue towards tiny ❸ **Bellevue**, catching the seasonal vehicle ferry (dating to 1683) across the Tred Avon River to ❹ **Oxford**, also dating to 1683 and one of Maryland's oldest towns. Continue southeast towards ❺ **Cambridge**, where the historic center has plenty to offer, including the Choptank River lighthouse (a replica of the original 1870s structure). Continue along Rtes 16 and 335 to ❻ **Blackwater National Wildlife Refuge**, which offers a haven for birds migrating along the Atlantic Flyway – one of the USA's four major migratory bird flyways. Neighboring Blackwater is the moving ❼ **Harriet Tubman Underground Railroad Visitor Center**. Rejoin Rte 50 near Vienna, following it to Salisbury and then exiting towards ❽ **Crisfield**, a working watermen's town known for its September crab festivals – the Hard Crab Derby and the Tawes Crab and Clam Bake. Crisfield is the departure point for boats to ❾ **Smith Island**, 7 miles offshore. The ferry can be booked at Captain Tyler Motel near the dock. Smith Island is known for its distinctive old English accent and its traditional way of life. Back on the mainland, finish with time at ❿ **Ocean City** and ⓫ **Assateague Island**, where you can arrange kayaking with Assateague Outfitters (*assateagueoutfitters.com*).

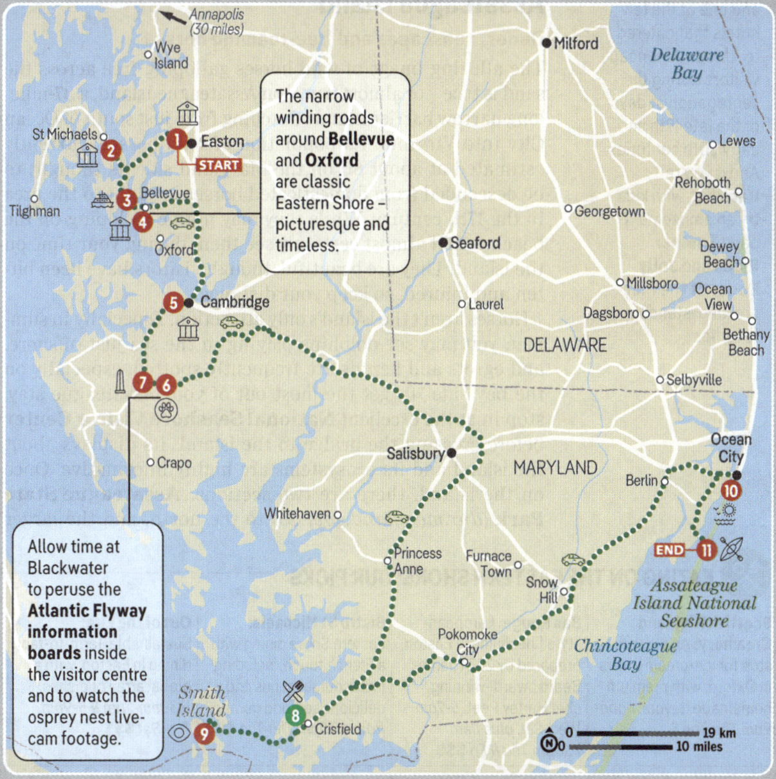

> The narrow winding roads around **Bellevue** and **Oxford** are classic Eastern Shore – picturesque and timeless.

> Allow time at Blackwater to peruse the **Atlantic Flyway information boards** inside the visitor centre and to watch the osprey nest live-cam footage.

Ocean City

Beach and boardwalk fun

Especially in August, it can seem as if the entire population of the Washington, DC metropolitan area has descended on Ocean City for a holiday, but don't let that dissuade you from a visit. In the low season, you'll have the long, wide beach almost to yourself, and even in season, the sea air, surf and cooler temperatures are a balm. If you're a fan of boardwalks, Ocean City's 2-mile-plus **boardwalk** is one of the region's best, with a smooth, wooden, wheelchair-friendly surface (beach wheelchair rentals are also available), the Giant (Ferris) Wheel, arcades, rides, waterslides and amusements. If this doesn't appeal, the surrounding area offers quieter pursuits. Tiny **Berlin**, about 9 miles inland from Ocean City, has a walkable historic town center with narrow streets lined with boutiques and shops.

Ocean City has ridesharing services (Uber and Lyft) and the Ocean City Beach Bus runs along the Coastal Hwy to 144th St (no winter service), making it easy to get around. In summer season, there's also the Boardwalk Tram and a Park & Ride lot in West Ocean City, with free shuttle service to/from South Division St at the boardwalk's southern end.

Assateague Island

Dunes, seascapes and free-roaming horses

The alluring image of wild horses galloping free across the sand is true – or almost true – on Assateague Island, a 37-mile-long narrow barrier island stretching from just south of Ocean City into Virginia. Its population of wild horses, currently estimated at about 80 on the Maryland side, is thought to be descended from domesticated horses brought to the area in the 17th century. While they may not be galloping on the beach, you'll almost certainly see them during your time on the island. They are beautiful, though visitors have been bitten and injured, so keep your distance.

Horses aren't the island's only attraction. Especially in summer, you may see dolphins playing in the sea just offshore, and egrets and herons are frequently spotted, especially on the bay side. To get the most out of your Assateague stay, stop in at the excellent **National Seashore Visitor Center** before crossing the bridge to the island. Its displays about the island and its ecosystems are highly informative. Once on the island, there are two sections: **Assateague State Park** *(dnr.maryland.gov; $5)* to the north, and the larger

---

OCEAN CITY ATTRACTIONS

Apart from walking for miles along the beach, there's plenty more to do in Ocean City. Visit the small **Life-Saving Station Museum** for a historical overview and stroll the boardwalk, grabbing an ice cream along the way. Wander past the historic **Henry Hotel** (currently closed, but slated for renovation). Dating to the late 19th century, it's one of Ocean City's oldest buildings and one of the few hotels that catered to African American visitors during the segregationist days of the late 19th and early 20th centuries. And if you're travelling with kids, try an amusement park: **Trimper Rides** and **Jolly Roger at the Pier** are long-standing favorites.

 EATING ON THE EASTERN SHORE: OUR PICKS

Scottish Highland Creamery: An essential stop for ice-cream lovers in Oxford, with premium homemade flavors. *noon-9pm Thu-Tue* $

Bas Rouge: European-style fine dining in Easton, prepared by 2024 James Beard award–winning chef Harley Peet. *5-9pm Wed-Sat, plus 11am-1:30pm Thu & Fri* $$$

Bistro St Michaels: Eastern Shore dining with a French touch, including multicourse menus and a delicious seafood gumbo. *from 4:30pm Thu-Tue* $$$

Out of the Fire: Sustainable, farm-to-table dining in Easton, with a global array of dishes. *11:30am-2pm & 5-9pm Tue-Sat* $$$

Baltimore's Inner Harbor

Assateague Island National Seashore (nps.gov/asis; per week per person/vehicle free/$25) to the south. During the warmer months, you can rent bicycles and kayaks in the park from **Assateague Outfitters** (assateagueoutfitters.com), and hiking is possible year-round. There are campsites on both the bay and ocean sides, including rustic walk-in (or kayak-in) sites. Make bookings up to six months in advance as spots fill quickly, and bring mosquito repellent. Note that backcountry (walk-in) campsites can't be reserved. While winter visits are for the hardy, the island's magic and serenity are easier to feel with fewer visitors around. Summer brings warmth and crowds, while spring and fall are both lovely, with fewer visitors and insects.

Baltimore

MAPS P288, P290

A day around the Inner Harbour

Baltimore's **Inner Harbor** is a destination in itself and a convenient jumping-off point for exploring the city. If it's a clear day, start with a bird's-eye view of the city from the **Top of the World** (viewbaltimore.org; adult/child $8/5) observation deck at the Baltimore World Trade Center before choosing between the nearby **National Aquarium** (aqua.org; adult/child $50/40) – one of the USA's best – and visits to the Inner Harbor's historic ships. In addition to the *USS Constellation*,

BEST MARYLAND FESTIVALS

Maryland Renaissance Festival: Held near Annapolis on weekends from late August through October. *rennfest.com*

Kunta Kinte Heritage Festival: In Annapolis; commemorates Maryland's African and African American heritage (September). *kuntakinte.org*

Baltimore Pride: Takes place over a week in June. *baltimorepride.org*

Annapolis Boat Show: There are now several, but the October sailboat show remains one of the best. *annapolisboatshows.com*

Deal Island Skipjack Race: Skipjack races, seafood and a parade (September).

Watermen Appreciation Day: At Chesapeake Bay Maritime Museum (August).

Maryland Crab Cake Festival: Sample Maryland's best crab cakes at Carroll County Farm Museum (October).

 EATING IN & AROUND OCEAN CITY: OUR PICKS

Berlin Farmers Market: The emphasis is on fresh, homemade and artisanal. *9am-1pm Sun May-Sep* $

Island Creamery: Try flavors such as java jolt and key lime pie, all homemade at the Chincoteague (Virginia) main shop. *11am-9pm Sun-Thu, to 10pm Fri & Sat* $$

Blacksmith Restaurant & Bar: A Berlin favorite, with craft beer, well-prepared farm-to-table dishes and a laid-back vibe. *11:30am-9pm Mon-Sat* $$

Ripieno's Italian Bistro: Probably Ocean City's best (and biggest) pizzas. Also has sandwiches, subs and platters. *10am-9pm Mon-Thu, to 10pm Fri & Sat* $$

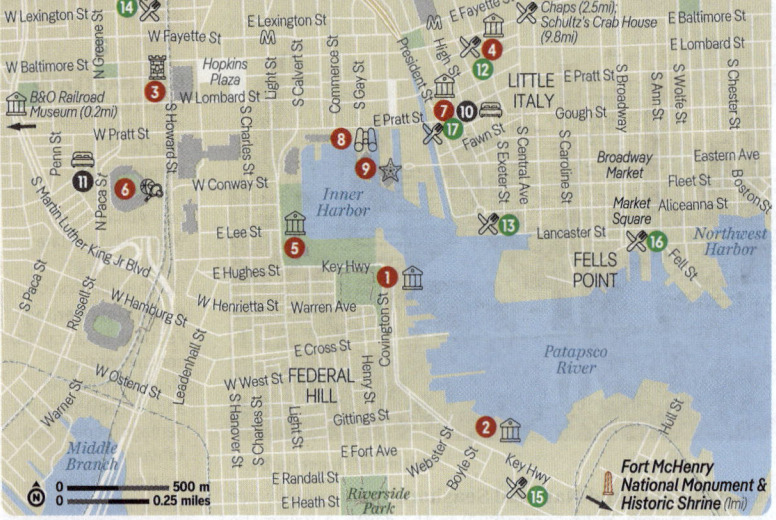

BALTIMORE

SIGHTS
1 American Visionary Art Museum
2 Baltimore Museum of Industry
3 Bromo Seltzer Tower
4 Jewish Museum of Maryland
5 Maryland Science Center
6 Oriole Park at Camden Yards
7 Reginald F Lewis Museum
see 7 Star-Spangled Banner Flag House
8 Top of the World Observation Deck

ACTIVITIES
9 National Aquarium

SLEEPING
10 BlancNoir
11 Rachael's Dowry B&B

EATING
12 Attman's Deli
13 Charleston
14 Faidley Seafood
see 14 Lexington Market
15 Locust Point Steamers
16 Thames Street Oyster House
17 Vaccaro's Italian Pastry

FREDERICK DOUGLASS

Frederick Douglass, the famed abolitionist, writer, orator and civil-rights activist, was born around 40 miles east of Annapolis on the Eastern Shore, near Tuckahoe Creek, but came to Baltimore for five years as a child to work in the shipyards at Fells Point, and again when he was 18. It was from Baltimore that he escaped by train to Pennsylvania and freedom.

the US Navy's last sail-only warship (notable also for its role in working to halt the foreign slave trade), these include the *USS Torsk* submarine, the lightship *Chesapeake* and US Coast Guard Cutter 37, all of which you can board and tour.

Continuing around the west side of the Inner Harbor, you'll reach the **Maryland Science Center** (mdsci.org; adult/child $30/22) and Davis Planetarium, which are particularly good stops if you're traveling with kids. There's also an adventure playground next door. Just beyond is Baltimore's Federal Hill

EATING & DRINKING IN BALTIMORE: A CITY SAMPLER — MAPS P288, P290

La Cuchara: Well-prepared Basque cuisine in an atmospheric setting. *5-9pm Sun-Thu, to 10pm Fri & Sat* $$

Thames Street Oyster House: Get your fill of oysters and other seafood at this iconic Fells Point eatery. *hours vary* $$

WC Harlan: Vintage, speakeasy-style cocktail bar in Remington neighborhood. *5pm-midnight Mon-Wed, to 1am Thu-Sat*

Charleston: Take advantage of the small-plate approach to maximize your culinary experience. *5:30-9pm Mon-Thu, 5-9:30pm Fri & Sat, to 8:30pm Sun* $$$

neighborhood and the community-oriented **American Visionary Art Museum** *(avam.org; adult/child $16/10)*. Featuring the work of self-taught artists, including homemade robots and matchstick models, this place will challenge your ideas of both museums and art. Nearby is the **Baltimore Museum of Industry** *(thebmi.org; adult/child $15/8)*, a fascinating place focused on the city's entrepreneurs and inventors, with live demos and hands-on activities. Once finished, head around to the harbor's east side, past cruise operators and paddle boats, to Fells Point, a former shipbuilding hub known for its multicultural neighborhoods, cobbled streets, restaurants and pubs. In the evenings, Fells Point is as good as it gets around the Inner Harbor. Another option is to catch an Orioles game at nearby **Oriole Park at Camden Yards** *(orioles.com)* stadium.

Museum round-up

Baltimore has enough museums to keep you busy for months. The city's art museums are a highlight, starting with the **Baltimore Museum of Art** *(artbma.org; free)*, known for its collections of Matisse and African art. About 3 miles south of here, in the Mount Vernon neighborhood, is the equally wonderful **Walters Art Museum** *(thewalters.org; free)*, with permanent collections that span continents and millennia, from ancient Egypt to Renaissance Europe, with illustrated Islamic manuscripts and an impressive collection of medieval arms and armor. From here, it's about 1.5 miles southeast to the edge of the Little Italy neighborhood – well worth a stroll, if only to sample a pastry at **Vaccaro's Italian Pastry** – and the **Reginald F Lewis Museum** *(lewismuseum.org; adult/child $12/9)* of African American history and culture. For more on African American history, check out the simple but thought-provoking **National Great Blacks in Wax Museum** *(greatblacksinwax.org; adult/child $18/15)*, spotlighting famous people such as Jackie Robinson as well as lesser-known figures such as Maryland-born explorer Matthew Henson. For more niche interests, try the **B&O Railroad Museum** *(borail.org; adult/child $20/12)* with its old locomotives and roundhouse, or the **Evergreen Museum** *(museums.jhu.edu; adult/child $12/10)*, offering glimpses into upper-class Baltimore life during the 1800s. Surrounding it are expansive, landscaped grounds and the campuses of several universities. The **Jewish Museum of Maryland** *(jewishmuseummd.org; adult/student/child $10/6/4)*, just reopened after extensive renovations, offers tours of two well-preserved synagogues that open doors into the history of Jewish Baltimore.

BALTIMORE INSIDER TIPS

Jon Patrick Leary, a lifelong Baltimorean, recommends the following places for visitors. *facebook.com/jon.p.leary*

Attman's Deli: It's 100-plus years of age and like NYC.

Club Charles: Come for cocktails. Blondie, Johnny Depp, John Waters and Ric Ocasek have been here – you never know who you'll meet.

Bromo Seltzer Tower: Climb behind the big clock face – really neat.

Lexington Market: One of the country's oldest markets.

Schultz's Crab House: An old-school rarity, about 10 miles from Baltimore in Essex.

Koco's Pub: The best crab cakes around.

Baltimore Museum of Industry: A tourist destination, but still well worth a visit.

 EATING IN BALTIMORE: BEST FOR LOCAL FLAVOR — MAPS P288, P290

Faidley Seafood: This long-standing place at Lexington Market is famous for its crab cakes and other seafood. *10am-5pm Mon-Thu, to 5:30pm Fri & Sat* **$$**

R House: This sleek food hall in Remington offers an array of cuisines, including Egyptian, Korean and Italian. *8am-10pm Sun-Thu, to 11pm Fri & Sat* **$**

Chaps: The go-to stop for pit beef (grilled, sliced top-round on a kaiser roll with 'tiger sauce' and onion slice). *10:30am-9pm Sun-Thu, to 10pm Fri & Sat* **$**

Locust Point Steamers: A classic Baltimore crab house, with a hometown vibe and tasty seafood. *11am-9pm Sun-Thu, to 9:30pm Fri & Sat* **$$**

CHARLES ST

If you could pick one Baltimore street that encapsulates all the city has to offer, it would likely be Charles St, which runs north from the Inner Harbor for about 5 miles. En route, it takes you through the Bromo and Station North arts districts, historic Mount Vernon with its 178ft Washington Monument (climb to the top for views), several historic churches, including the neoclassical Basilica of the Assumption, the Walters Art Museum and the Baltimore Museum of Art before coming to the Johns Hopkins University campus. Just west of campus is Hampden, known for its hipster-creative working-class vibe and the vintage shops and eateries lining 'The Avenue' (W 36th St).

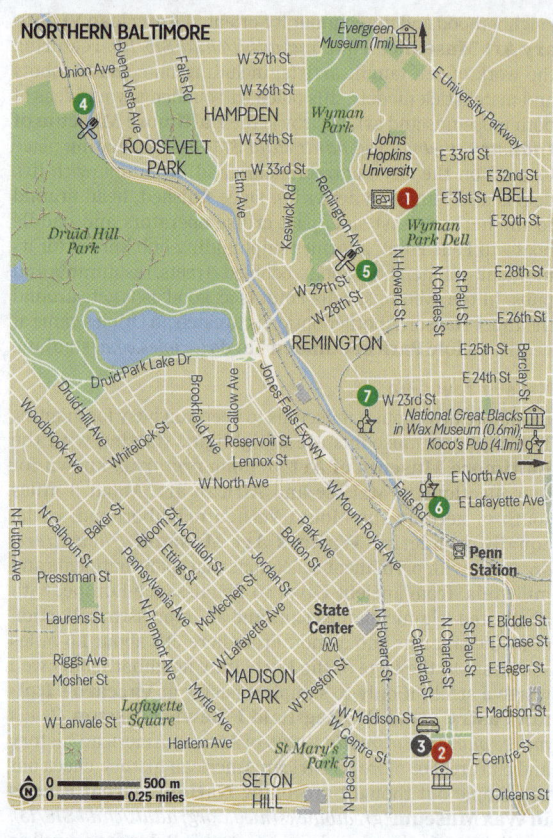

SIGHTS	SLEEPING	DRINKING & NIGHTLIFE
1 Baltimore Museum of Art	3 Hotel Revival	6 Club Charles
2 Walters Art Museum	**EATING**	7 WC Harlan
	4 La Cuchara	
	5 R House	

O say can you see...

On a dark, rainy night in September 1814, American lawyer Francis Scott Key found himself stuck on a ship in the Patapsco River, watching as the British attacked Fort McHenry as part of their efforts to seize control of Baltimore. When dawn finally came, Key's incredulity, pride and gratitude at seeing the giant (30ft by 42ft) American flag still waving over the fort, despite the heavy shelling, prompted him to pen the stanzas of a poem, which he called 'The Defense of Fort M'Henry.' The poem's title was later changed to 'The Star-Spangled Banner' and, in 1931, its words became the US national anthem. The whole series of events is commemorated at the **Fort McHenry National Monument and Historic Shrine** (nps.gov/fomc; adult/child $15/free), starting with a short but moving film that concludes with a stirring rendition of the anthem, followed by time to wander the grounds and take in the views over the harbor. In town, at the **Star-Spangled Banner Flag House** *(flaghouse.org; adult/child $8/6)*, you can visit the place where seamstress Mary Pickersgill made the original Fort McHenry flag, which is now on display in the Smithsonian's National Museum of American History in Washington, DC.

Antietam National Battlefield

Hear the echoes of the Civil War

In the open, rolling farm country on the edge of Sharpsburg, about 25 miles northwest of Frederick, is **Antietam National Battlefield** *(nps.gov/anti; per person/vehicle $10/$20)*, where, in 1862, an estimated 23,000 people were killed or injured in what is considered the bloodiest single-day conflict in US history. The battle marked the end of the southern attack aimed at Maryland and Washington, DC. It was also a significant turning point in the Civil War, and served as a springboard for Abraham Lincoln's Emancipation Proclamation. Today, surrounded by the battlefield's bucolic expanses, it's difficult to imagine the battle's carnage and suffering. To relive some of the history and learn more about Antietam, start at the visitor center, where there is an informative welcome film. It's then easy to explore the battlefield on a self-guided driving tour, taking advantage of informative plaques at each of the designated stops. Alternatively, you can arrange in advance to take a guided tour. However you visit, don't miss the Dunker Church, Burnside Bridge and the Observation Tower, with wide views over the surrounding area. If you want to immerse yourself even more in Civil War history, the smaller **Monocacy National Battlefield** *(nps.gov/mono; free)*, site of a decisive battle for the national capital, is about 25 miles southeast of Antietam on Frederick's southeastern outskirts, and also well worth a stop. It has short walking trails and a similar self-guided-drive setup.

Cumberland

Crossroads of America

Tiny Cumberland's historical designation as 'Crossroads of America' might seem an exaggeration, but the more you delve into the area's rich history, the more apt the name becomes. Start at the **Allegany Museum** *(alleganymuseummd.org;*

GLEN ECHO CAROUSEL

If you're departing Washington, DC and heading northwest towards Frederick or Antietam, take time for a detour to Maryland's **Glen Echo Park** *(glenechopark. org; free)*. Its historic (and still operational) carousel – at its best on the park's annual Carousel Day in late April – became a focal point for the Civil Rights movement in 1960, when Black and white protesters joined forces and picketed for several months against Glen Echo's segregationist policies, until the park's owners finally announced that the park would open to all visitors. The 2024 documentary film *Ain't No Back to a Merry-Go-Round* tells the story in detail.

EATING & DRINKING IN FREDERICK: CREATIVE CUISINE & CRAFT BEER

Carroll Creek Breweries: Get introduced to Frederick's craft-beer culture at this cluster of breweries around Carroll Creek's eastern side. *hours vary*

Ordinary Hen: Enjoy cornbread, squash-and-dumplings and other Appalachian-inspired cuisine, plus live music Fridays at the outdoor Shed. *11am-3pm & 5-9pm Thu-Sat, 4-8pm Sun* **$$**

Wine Kitchen: Local beef cuts of distinction, plus seafood and vegetarian options and curated wine pairings. *noon-9pm Tue-Thu & Sun, to 10pm Fri & Sat* **$$**

Bentztown: Southern cuisine goes upmarket at this place, where music is as much a draw as the menu. *11am-10pm Mon, Wed, Thu & Sun, to 1am Fri & Sat* **$$**

CYCLING THE C&O CANAL

One of the Mid-Atlantic's great cycling trails runs between Washington, DC and Pittsburgh, first following the C&O Canal (184 miles) and then the Great Allegheny Passage (GAP; 149 miles). Cumberland's Canal Pl is the meeting point of the two. The three-season ride can be done in either direction, is mostly flat (with some gradual ascents/descents around Cumberland) and is a great mix of nature and scenery. En route, there's rustic but free trail camping and a mix of public and private campgrounds. Alternatively, you can detour into nearby towns to stay at a hotel. Many cyclists do the trail independently, but if you want to arrange a tour, **Wheelz Up Adventures** in Cumberland can help with bike rentals and tours.

Curtis' Coney Island Famous Weiners

free) where the Crossroads of America exhibit covers everything from Cumberland's earliest inhabitants to its pivotal transportation position during the French and Indian War to the development of the C&O Canal and the B&O Railroad. From here, make your way over to the **Crossroads of America mural**, which stretches for 200ft along the wall in front of the train station. The plaza just beyond the mural marks the starting point for cycling both the C&O Canal towpath to Washington, DC and the Great Allegheny Passage trail to Pittsburgh, Pennsylvania. Back at the train station, check out the **Cumberland Visitor Center and Museum** before taking the **Western Maryland Scenic Railroad** *(wmsr.com)* – these days, a historic diesel train – to Frostburg (4½ hours return, including about 1½ hours in Frostburg). Finish up back in Cumberland with a walk around the historic central pedestrian area focused around Baltimore and Center Sts. It's lined with late-19th-century buildings and, especially in the summer, serves as Cumberland's town hub, with a farmers market and frequent sidewalk festivities.

EATING IN CUMBERLAND: LOCAL FAVORITES

Caporale's Bakery: Don't miss the pepperoni rolls, ramp rolls and other delicacies at this old-style Cumberland institution. *10am-5pm Mon & Wed-Fri, 9am-3pm Sun* $

Curtis' Coney Island Famous Weiners: Serving hot dogs, burgers and its signature Coney Island sauce to a loyal clientele for over a century. *9am-8pm Mon-Sat* $

Crabby Pig: Crab cakes, cream of crab soup, pulled pork sandwiches and other seafood and meat dishes. *11am-9pm Tue-Sat, to 8pm Sun* $

Ristorante Ottaviani: Enjoy wine tastings and well-prepared Italian-American cuisine in downtown Cumberland. *5-9pm Tue-Thu, to 10pm Fri & Sat, 4-8pm Sun* $$

Virginia

BEACHES | HISTORY | SHENANDOAH MOUNTAINS

In a famous line from the musical *Hamilton*, Thomas Jefferson celebrates returning home from France in the late 1700s by proclaiming his love for his sweet home, Virginia. Anyone who spends any time exploring Virginia and engaging with Southern-charm-filled locals will surely fall in love with the state, too.

From the misty peaks of the Blue Ridge Mountains to the serene ripples of Chesapeake Bay, the state offers an array of natural beauty. Virginia's past is as varied as its geography: it's where the first English settlement of Jamestown was established, and the site of crucial Civil War battles. Bustling urban epicenters, from the capital of Richmond to the DC-adjacent Arlington, brim with architectural landmarks, while Virginia's coastal towns exude a nautical heritage that's a mix of quaint and captivating.

Whether you're tracing the founding fathers' footsteps, exploring wine country or hiking Appalachian trails, Virginia will enchant with its stories and scenery.

Places

Richmond p295
Williamsburg p297
Charlottesville p298
Blue Ridge Parkway p300
Shenandoah National Park p300
Virginia Beach p301
Norfolk p302
Chincoteague National Wildlife Refuge p302
Arlington p303
Fredericksburg p304
Alexandria p304
Mount Vernon p305

☑ TOP TIP

Plan a few days in each region – the coastal plains and Virginia Beach, the central Piedmont region and Richmond, the Blue Ridge Mountains and points west – to experience Virginia's unique zing.

GETTING AROUND

Renting a car is the easiest way to navigate the state's entirety. Take note, particularly in Northern Virginia and along major highways, of HOV lanes (often requiring two or more passengers per vehicle) and snag an E-Z Pass toll pass to navigate rush-hour traffic. Amtrak connects the entire state, from Roanoke and Danville in the southwest to Norfolk in the southeast and Alexandria in the north. The trains connect with other major Virginia systems, including Virginia Railway Express and Metro.

Richmond and Charlottesville have bikeshare programs and the Greater Richmond Transit Company (GRTC) has free Pulse buses serving most tourist routes.

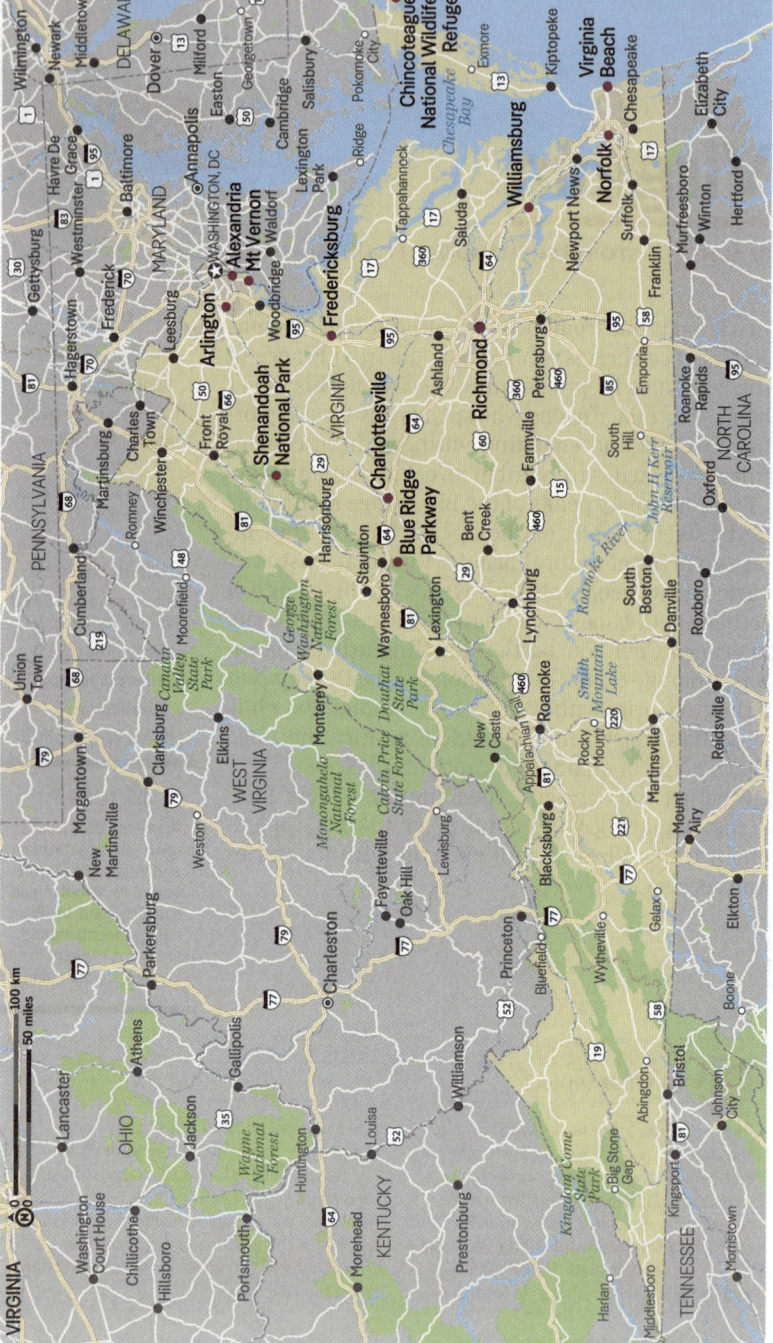

Richmond

Museum hop in the downtown

Begin at the **Virginia Museum of Fine Arts** *(vmfa.museum; free)*, where a highlight is the permanent 'Fabergé and Russian Decorative Arts' exhibit, with nearly 300 gold and precious-metal-draped objects. Hit also the free Institute for Contemporary Art (ICA) at Virginia Commonwealth University, with its modern sculpture garden.

The **Branch Museum of Architecture and Design** *(branchmuseum.org; suggested $5)*, housed in a stately brick castle of sorts on Monument Ave, has rotating exhibits focusing on a range of topics, including the origins of Richmond's cityscapes and international women's-rights posters. The hands-on **Science Museum of Virginia** *(smv.org; adult/child $18/15)* captivates curious minds of all ages. You can generate tornadoes, or test your reflexes against the speed of light in interactive labs. The **American Civil War Museum** *(acwm.org; adult/child $18/9)* includes personal artifacts and narratives conveying various wartime characters, with its exhibits often focusing on one of three perspectives – the north, the south or African American. The museum is housed in the former Tredegar Iron Works building; cannons made on its grounds fired the first shots at Fort Sumter in South Carolina to kick off the Civil War.

Stroll the cobblestoned Shockoe Bottom

From your first step on Shockoe Bottom's cobblestones, you know the streets have been a setting for the extraordinary through the centuries. This is where George Washington mapped out a national system of transportation canals, laying the groundwork for America's infrastructure. It's where Thomas Jefferson signed the Virginia Statute for Religious Freedom, a cornerstone of American civil liberties. And it's where Abraham Lincoln famously arrived by canoe to witness the historic fall of the Confederacy. Knowing Shockoe Bottom's lore makes it a magical stop.

The neighborhood's hub is **17th Street Market**, which regularly hosts art shows as well as a bimonthly farmers market. A communal favorite is the Richmond Night Market (second Saturday of every month), with an artisan village, live art activations and jam sessions from local bands. The **Tobacco Company** *(www.thetobaccocompany.com)* is a three-level, charm-filled restaurant that was once a – you guessed it

LIVE-MUSIC VENUES IN RICHMOND

The National: Has large capacity, an intimate feel, stunning architecture and a state-of-the-art sound system.

The Camel: Catch up-and-coming local talent in a cozy setting, with yummy smashburgers, too.

Canal Club: Industrial chic, adjacent to Canal Walk, with indoor and outdoor performance spaces.

Richmond Music Hall at Capital Ale House: Mid-size venue with a big sound that's attached to a craft-beer haven.

Altria Theater: Historic space with opulent features and arguably the best sight lines and acoustics in town.

EATING IN RICHMOND: OUR PICKS

Stella's: Intimate Greek eatery with authentic flavors evoking a homemade charm in every bite. Reservations recommended. *11:30am-3pm Mon-Fri, plus 4-10pm Mon-Sat* $$$

Lunch.SUPPER!: Southern fare featuring locally sourced ingredients. You can't miss the deer-antler chandelier and ornate decorations. *11am-9pm Mon-Fri, from 10am Sat & Sun* $$

Pho Tay Do: Vietnamese cuisine in a quirky house setting, with authentic pho and other dishes. Cash only. *10am-6pm Mon, Tue & Thu-Sat, to 5pm Sun* $$

Hot for Pizza: A divey den, boasting drink deals and a lineup of pies with ingredients like fennel sausage and oyster mushrooms. *11am-2am Mon-Sat, from noon Sun* $$

VIRGINIA WASHINGTON, DC & THE CAPITAL REGION

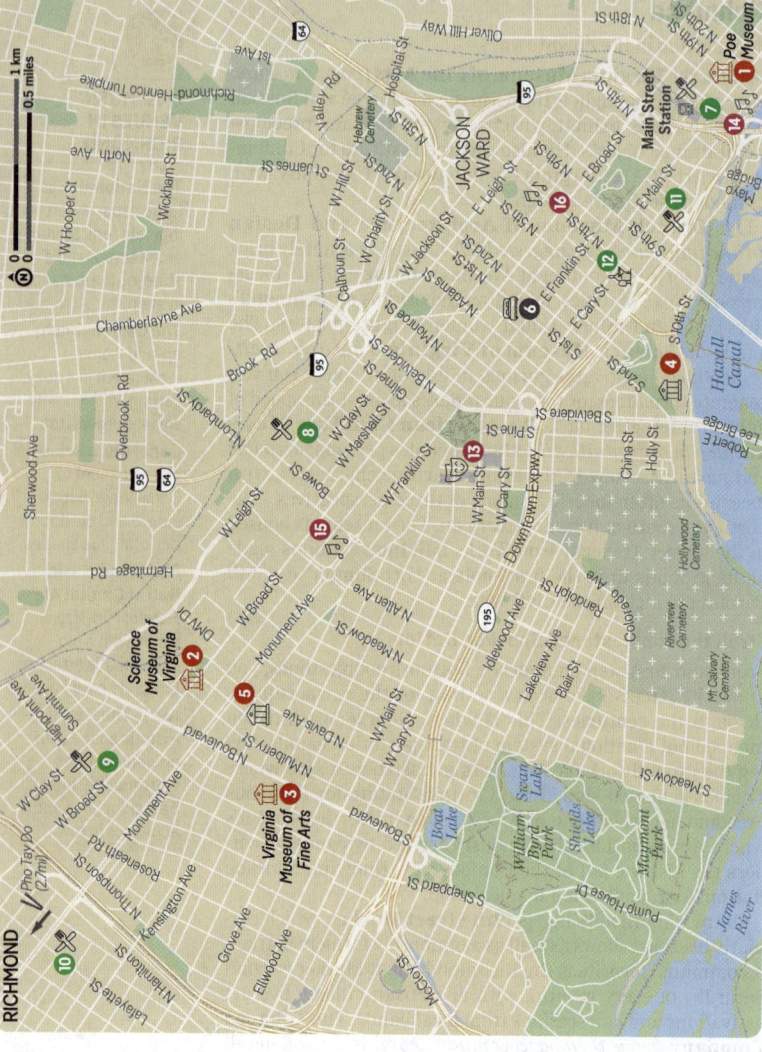

★ HIGHLIGHTS
1. Poe Museum
2. Science Museum of Virginia
3. Virginia Museum of Fine Arts

● SIGHTS
4. American Civil War Museum
5. Branch Museum of Architecture and Design

● SLEEPING
6. Linden Row Inn

● EATING
7. 17th Street Market
8. Hot for Pizza
9. Lunch.SUPPER!
10. Stella's
11. Tobacco Company

● DRINKING & NIGHTLIFE
12. Capital Ale House

● ENTERTAINMENT
13. Altria Theater
14. Canal Club
15. The Camel
16. The National

– tobacco warehouse. The pecan-crusted lollipop lamb chops, brass elevator and central walnut staircase dazzle 'round the clock. The **Poe Museum** *(poemuseum.org; adult/child $10/free)* is a living homage to famed Richmond resident, Edgar Allan Poe, offering insights into his enigmatic life and the theories surrounding his demise. The courtyard space – dubbed the Enchanted Garden, which was inspired by Poe's 'To One in Paradise' poem – is a quiet oasis and regularly hosts 'UnHappy Hours' sponsored by local breweries.

Williamsburg

Hitch a wagon ride in Colonial Williamsburg

Williamsburg was Virginia's capital during the American Revolution and today's **Colonial Williamsburg** *(colonialwilliamsburg.org; adult/child $32/9)* is a living time capsule that transports locals and visitors alike to the 1700s. Throughout the 300-plus-acre area, historical reenactors with powdered wigs and tricorn hats wander about as horse-drawn carriages roll by. For a carriage ride *(from $10)*, head to the Colonial Williamsburg Visitor Center.

By wagon or foot, prioritize a stop at the Governor's Palace. Amid its three-story brick grandeur, note all the pineapple accents – an emblem of hospitality and wealth in the mansion's 1700s heyday and beyond. From the palace, head just west to the Capitol building – this is where the House of Burgesses initially proposed US independence from the British in 1776. A final stop is the Public Gaol, where you can learn about colonial-era crime and punishments. Take note of the historic pillory, a wooden structure with slots for criminals' heads and hands. It was common for passersby to hurl tomatoes and other objects at criminals, so come to this photo op – and the other pillories scattered about Colonial Williamsburg – creatively.

Unexpected historical pizzazz

Don't let Williamsburg's generally refined vibe fool you – there's some quirkiness to explore here. Hit the **Virginia Musical Museum** *(virginiamusicalmuseum.com; free)*, which celebrates the state's musical heritage through a collection of rare musical instruments and memorabilia celebrating Virginia-bred icons. Learn all about the likes of country-pop legend Patsy Cline and the 'Queen of Jazz,' Ella Fitzgerald. Among the more unique items is the country's first talking doll and a 1790 Joshua Shudi harpsichord – one of two in existence today. The **College of William & Mary** is the US's second-oldest institution of higher education (Harvard is the oldest). Stop at the Crim Dell Bridge – local lore promises eternal love to those who kiss atop its burgundy-and-gold-railed steps and, if you cross the bridge alone, well, you're doomed to solitude. While at William & Mary, check out the Wren Building, which has survived three major fires since its 1700 inception and is the oldest college building still in use in the country.

When hunger inevitably beckons, **Charly's Airport Restaurant** is a quirky and unexpected find. Situated at Williamsburg Jamestown Airport, it allows you to watch smaller and

WILLIAMSBURG WALKING TOURS

Ultimate Pirate Tour: All-ages tour that delves into the history of pirates and their impact on early colonies.

Murder Tour and Pub Crawl: Learn about the town's seedy, murderous history while sipping on a libation at each pub.

Haunted Williamsburg: Candlelight tour in which you get to enter historic buildings in Colonial Williamsburg.

We Shall Overcome: Hear inspiring stories of African Americans while visiting the Williamsburg landmarks connected to their stories.

Taste of Williamsburg: Williamsburg's best bites and craft drinks are the focus of this tasty tour.

TIPS FOR NAVIGATING WILLIAMSBURG

At approximately 9 sq miles, Williamsburg is compact and largely walkable. Colonial Williamsburg is particularly easy to stroll, with wide, pedestrian-friendly expanses.

Beyond its colonial core, the Williamsburg Area Transit Authority (WATA) serves key tourist attractions such as Jamestown, Busch Gardens and the College of William & Mary. WATA has an all-day pass for $3 and is particularly handy for venturing beyond Colonial Williamsburg. Pay cash for the all-day pass on the bus (credit cards are not accepted).

There's a fee to enter buildings and experience educational programming in Colonial Williamsburg. Odds are that you may want to pair your visit with a Yorktown trek, a Busch Gardens trip or more, and a variety of discounted packages are available at *colonialwilliamsburg.org*.

sometimes vintage aircraft depart and land as you nosh on homestyle plates. Round out a day of the extraordinary at the **Archaearium** (*historicjamestowne.org*; adult/child $15/5), an archaeology museum dedicated to America's first English colony, Jamestown. The museum has more than 2000 artifacts, including Native American arrowheads and tobacco pipes bearing the names of prominent settlers.

Charlottesville

Exploring past and present

In the foothills of the Blue Ridge Mountains, Charlottesville is as ahhhh-worthy visually as it is historically. It is home to the **University of Virginia**, which was founded by Thomas Jefferson in 1819 and remains a centerpiece of the city's architectural and cultural story. The university's Rotunda and vast lawn are quintessential landmarks, embodying Jefferson's vision of an 'academical village.' President James Monroe's home, **Highland** (*highland.org*; adult/child $18/13), is notably in Charlottesville as well. Just outside of town is **Monticello** (*monticello.org*; adult/child from US$22/8), Jefferson's historic home with graceful grounds that you can stroll on your own, capped by the main house, for which you'll need to take a guided tour. Afterwards, spend time exploring Charlottesville's pedestrian-friendly **Downtown Mall**. It's a brick- and column-draped experience with pops of energy coming in the form of buzzing breweries, the facade of the ever-glowing **Paramount Theater** (*theparamount.net*) and more. The mall is a seven-block stretch, with the Ting Pavilion and Omni Charlottesville Hotel as its east and west anchors. Between them, hit **Lone Light Coffee** for a coffee concoction or sweet treats such as bourbon vanilla-infused ice cream.

Uncork Virginia's wine wonderland

Charlottesville wasn't named *Wine Enthusiast*'s Wine Region of the Year in recent times for no reason. The city and surrounding Albemarle County are home to more than 40 wineries, producing everything from the heartiest of merlots to light hybrids. Companies such as **Central Virginia Wine Tours** (*centralvirginiawinetours.com*) offer transportation and winery hops. If you're plotting your own wine adventure, start at **Blenheim Vineyards** (*blenheimvineyards.com*). The property dates to 1730 and was started as a sustainable winery by world-renowned musician

EATING IN WILLIAMSBURG: HISTORIC TAVERNS

King's Arms Tavern: Authentic colonial dining, blending 18th-century recipes with modern flavors. *11am-2pm daily, plus 4:30-8pm Thu-Mon* $$$

Christiana Campbell's Tavern: George Washington's favorite local seafood spot. Come for the crab cakes, stay for the balladeers. *4-8pm Tue-Sat* $$$

Chowning's Garden Bar: Relaxed open-air dining with a colonial twist, offering classics such as burgers and hot dogs. *11am-5pm Thu-Sat* $$

Raleigh Tavern Bakery: Fresh ginger cake, sandwiches and baked treats from this bakery with wood-fired ovens. *9am-5pm* $

DRIVE THROUGH WARTIME & COLONIAL HISTORY

This tour takes you through some of Virginia's most historic sites against a scenic tidewater backdrop.

START	END	LENGTH
Yorktown Battlefield	Historic Jamestowne Island Loop	30 miles; 4-5 hours

Begin at ❶ **Yorktown Battlefield** to soak in Revolutionary War history seeped into the ground. This 1781 battle was a turning point in the war, leading to its end and the USA's independence from Great Britain. Make your way towards ❷ **Nelson House**, one-time residence of Thomas Nelson Jr, a signatory of the Declaration of Independence. Most features in the Georgian home are original. If you visit when enough staff are present, a tour of the interior is possible. Wind your way through the streets of ❸ **Yorktown's historic waterfront**, where restored 18th-century homes line the streets. Water St leads to the ❹ **French Memorial**, a tribute to the French soldiers who lost their lives in battles in and around Yorktown. Hop on the ❺ **Colonial Parkway** from here. This 23-mile scenic drive weaves its way through pine and hardwood forests, tidal estuaries along the James and York rivers and through Williamsburg on its way to Jamestown. Overlooks dot the parkway. Head to Jamestown Island where you'll find the ❻ **Jamestown Settlement**. Exhibits and outdoor re-creations tell the story of America's beginnings, including its Indigenous people and the arrival of English colonists in 1607. Around the corner from the settlement, you'll find ❼ **Jamestown Glasshouse**, where modern glassblowers hold demonstrations while utilizing tools and techniques similar to those used in the 17th century. Just a bit further and you can cruise the ❽ **Historic Jamestowne Island Loop**, discovering the beauty of the island's marshy landscape.

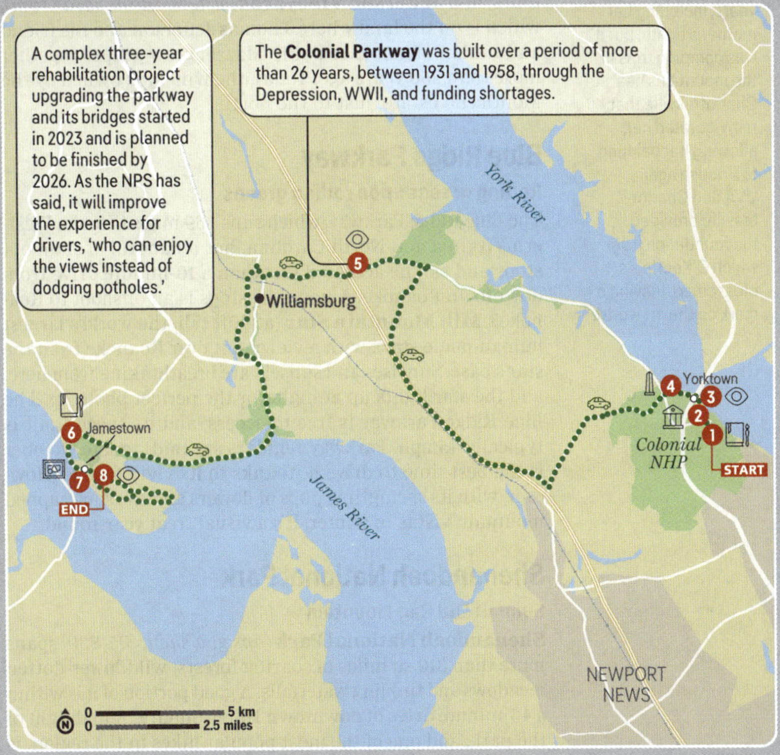

A complex three-year rehabilitation project upgrading the parkway and its bridges started in 2023 and is planned to be finished by 2026. As the NPS has said, it will improve the experience for drivers, 'who can enjoy the views instead of dodging potholes.'

The **Colonial Parkway** was built over a period of more than 26 years, between 1931 and 1958, through the Depression, WWII, and funding shortages.

PROFESSOR O'KEEFFE

We can thank the hallowed halls of the University of Virginia for inspiring Georgia O'Keeffe to be the artist we recognize today. O'Keeffe spent summers at UVA studying art, eventually teaching some courses herself. It was under her teachers' mentorship that she began exploring the abstract, drawing inspiration from the Blue Ridge Mountains and campus life. O'Keeffe endured many trials over those years, including her mother's death, but it was camping trips in the mountains near Charlottesville that reinvigorated her, allowing her painting to flourish again. UVA and Charlottesville provided the foundation from which O'Keeffe's art blossomed, leaving a mark on the art world.

and local icon Dave Matthews. Others to take in include **King Family Vineyards**, situated on a former thoroughbred horse farm; **Pippin Hill** (*pippinhillfarm.com*), which is a rolling-hills staple with farm-to-table dinners and estate tours; and **Jefferson Vineyards** (*jeffersonvineyards.com*), which is on the land where Thomas Jefferson and his friend and Italian winemaker Philip Mazzei grew grapes together more than 250 years ago. Today, the winery is owned by the Monticello estate, just to the north.

Blue Ridge Parkway

Rolling greens upon rolling greens

The Blue Ridge Parkway, which runs 469 miles through Western Virginia and North Carolina, has a handful of standout stops and can be accessed less than a 10-minute drive from downtown Roanoke. Among the stops is an offshoot to Roanoke's **Mill Mountain Star** (at 90ft tall, the world's largest human-made star), with a viewpoint over Roanoke from the star's base. Sunrises and sunsets are breathtaking from here, and the star lights up at night for the perfect photo op. The Blue Ridge Parkway is free to access, and its speed limit is typically 45mph. Parkway regulars say mid- to late October is the best time to drive it, thanks to its vivid foliage. However, with its springtime pops of flowers and the snowcapped mountain vistas in winter, it's a visual treat year-round.

Shenandoah National Park

Summit Old Rag Mountain

Shenandoah National Park (*nps.gov/shen, $15-$30*) spans more than 310 sq miles of soaring forests, wildflower-dotted meadows and tinkling waterfalls. A good portion of it is within a 45-minute drive of downtown Harrisonburg. A highlight of the park, and one of the most popular hikes in the region, is

Old Rag Mountain

Old Rag Mountain. You'll need to snag a day-use ticket in advance during peak season (March 1 through November 30). Allow seven hours for the hike – there are two different routes you can take, amassing approximately 2500ft in elevation. Along the way, count on some rock scrambles and boulder hiking. On completion, you'll be rewarded with 360-degree views of the valley, which glows yellow and orange during the fall foliage season.

Appreciate views on Skyline Dr

With 105 miles of mountain bliss, this public road through Shenandoah National Park provides awe-inspiring views from the crest of the Blue Ridge Mountains. There is no shortage of opportunities for snapping photos, with 75 overlooks along the way.

Virginia Beach

A non-bored walk

This much is certain: you might be on vacation, but you'll still want to wake early, plop it on the **Virginia Beach Boardwalk** adjacent to white sands and take in a sunrise. Beyond that, there is so much to explore along the boardwalk. Starting in the south at 2nd St and running north to 40th St, it

THE JM IN JMU

James Madison, born in Virginia in 1751 and nicknamed 'Father of the Constitution,' helped write the US Constitution and the Bill of Rights. Madison also cowrote the Federalist Papers, pushing for the Constitution's approval. As the fourth president, he led the nation during the War of 1812 and helped negotiate the Treaty of Ghent. Back home in Virginia, he was involved in founding the University of Virginia and served in the state's House of Delegates and the US House of Representatives. His legacy is closely tied to Virginia's history and politics. Today, Harrisonburg's own James Madison University bears his name as tribute.

 EATING IN HARRISONBURG: FARM-TO-TABLE RESTAURANTS

| **Rocktown Kitchen:** Locally sourced, seasonal American cuisine in an elevated yet casual dining venue. *11am-2:30pm & 5-9pm Tue-Sat* $$$ | **Local Chop & Grill House:** Organic ingredients from neighborhood farms in the historic City Produce Exchange building; extensive whiskey selection. *4-11pm Mon-Sat* $$$ | **Magpie Diner:** A 1950s service station turned modern diner, with locally roasted coffee and craft cocktails alongside seasonally inspired classic dishes. *8am-2pm Tue-Fri, from 9am Sat & Sun* $$ | **Little Grill:** Cozy spot offering a menu for vegetarians and those seeking locally sourced organic-meat options. *hours vary* $ |

spans 3 miles and is nearly 30ft wide in most spots. Among its quirkier highlights: just north of 30th St is Neptune's Park, where you'll find a large statue of the Roman god. At 38th St is the Navy Seal Monument, a life-size statue of a serviceman donning a swimsuit, flippers and weapon. At 25th St is the *Norwegian Lady* statue, commemorating a nearby shipwreck from the 19th century. For bird enthusiasts, the Atlantic Wildfowl Heritage Museum is housed in a small cottage near 12th St and is loaded with waterbird art, relics and exhibits, leaving you to surely say, 'What the...duck!' by the end.

Climb Cape Henry Lighthouse

There are many firsts pertaining to the 90ft-tall, red- and tan-bricked **Cape Henry Lighthouse**. Beyond being near the first landing site of English settlers in the US, the lighthouse also marks the first public-works project of the US government, overseen by Alexander Hamilton. The lighthouse is on the Fort Story military base, so you'll need to provide ID at the base's gate and then shuttles (which run every 15 minutes) take non-military civilians directly to the lighthouse. On arrival, there are 191 steps to climb to enjoy 360-degree coastal views from the cozy lantern room.

Norfolk

Explore naval history

It's only appropriate that Norfolk, about a 20-minute drive from Virginia Beach, has a naval museum on a ship. Part of the **Nauticus** maritime discovery center, the Battleship *Wisconsin* includes interactive spaces that you can stroll through, including an on-ship hospital with a surgery center, barber shop and even a brig where misbehaving sailors were temporarily jailed. There's also a sailing center on-site where you can take a craft for a guided spin on the water, with a unique perspective on downtown Norfolk's skyline. For a more relaxed time on the water, Half Moone Cruise and Victory Rover Naval Base Cruises are next door and offer narrated cruises of the city's coastline.

Chincoteague National Wildlife Refuge

Horsing around on the Eastern Shore

It's an otherworldly scene here, with wild horses roaming, chomping on marsh grasses and slurping up water from ponds, and **Chincoteague National Wildlife Refuge** *(fws.gov; pedestrian & cyclist/vehicle per day free/$10)* is the epicenter

---

SURF'S UP, DUDE

Virginia Beach is home to the world's oldest continuously run surfing competition, the Coastal Edge East Coast Surfing Championship, locally known simply as ECSC. For more than 60 years, competitive surfers have flocked to the area to claim their place on the podium, creating an event that has morphed into so much more. The weeklong festival, typically held in August, delights with showcases in longboard, shortboard and stand-up paddleboarding. Through the years, other beach-favorite activities such as volleyball and street skating, live music, arts-and-crafts vendors and more have been added to the festival lineup, making ECSC an event for more than just wave riders.

DRINKING IN VIRGINIA BEACH: ORANGE CRUSHES

Waterman's Surfside Grille: The OG – Waterman's vodka, fresh OJ, a splash of Sprite, enjoyed at the beach. *hours vary*

Shack on 8th: Crush on Classic Orange to Honey Habanero among patio vibes with fire pits and yard games. *4pm-late Thu & Fri, from noon Sat & Sun*

Back Deck: Indulge in refreshing crush variations at this laid-back bayside waterfront venue. *11am-10pm*

Chix on the Beach: Beachfront crushes with the personal touch of lime and cranberry. *11am-10pm Sun-Thu, to 2am Fri & Sat*

Arlington National Cemetery

of the action. In the refuge, which is located mostly on the Virginia side of Assateague Island (p286), about a two-hour drive from Virginia Beach, nearly 300 ponies wander through the forests and prairies and it's not uncommon to see colorful shorebirds and bald eagles soaring in the sky. **Assateague Explorer** *(assateagueexplorer.com)* has a Pony Express Nature Cruise, which lasts about two hours and coasts safely up to the horses. Perhaps the most unique pony spectacle in the region, held on the last consecutive Wednesday and Thursday in July, is the annual Pony Penning, where the area's ponies are guided to swim across the Assateague Channel to Chincoteague Island, where select foals are auctioned off. This sale helps to humanely control the pony population and proceeds benefit veterinary care for the herd.

Arlington

In solemn tribute

Arlington National Cemetery *(arlingtoncemetery.mil; free)* is a 693-acre military cemetery where over 400,000 people, including more than 300,000 veterans, lie at rest. The country's most famous cemetery isn't just a place to reflect or grieve – it's also a solemn but scenic walk through the nation's military history. Main sites include Arlington House, the former residence of Robert E Lee, and the gravesite of President

NAVIGATING IN & AROUND VIRGINIA BEACH

If you're sticking to the beach, strolls and a periodic rideshare (Uber or Lyft) will do the trick. Hampton Roads Transit operates an Atlantic Ave trolley that runs parallel to the boardwalk. There are plenty of touristy bike shops along the boardwalk area with hourly rentals as well as day packages in the $40 range.

For ventures beyond Virginia Beach, you'll need a car. Norfolk is an east–west straight shot along Interstate 264. The drive to Virginia's Eastern Shore has at its core a 17-plus-mile journey across the Chesapeake Bay Bridge-Tunnel. Within the over-under-water stretch, there are two 1-mile sections of tunnel. There's a $22 fee (round trip) on the Bridge-Tunnel, which is best navigated with an E-Z Pass.

EATING IN CAPE CHARLES: OYSTERS

Oyster Farm Seafood Eatery: Raw and steamed offerings, with a deck overlooking Chesapeake Bay. *4-8pm Wed & Thu, 11:30am-8pm Fri & Sat, to 3pm Sun* **$$$**

The Shanty: Cottage vibe with local oyster selections, rice bowls and orange miso-glazed calamari. *11:30am-9pm* **$$**

Hook @ Harvey: Open for dinner, with a bistro setting, rotating fare and ever-fresh seafood catches. *5-9pm Tue-Sat* **$$$**

Coach House Tavern: Tucked into a golf community, this neighborhood restaurant has fresh oysters served on the half shell. *hours vary* **$$**

> **WHY I LOVE FREDERICKSBURG**
>
>
>
> **Jesse Scott**, Lonely Planet writer
>
> Consider me one of those dudes that's ultra-proud to be where he's from. Hint: it's Fredericksburg. In my 37 years, I've seen this town blossom from a sleepy Civil War town to one with a rockin' culinary scene, a broadminded and artsy vibe and rad public spaces. Rte 3 is now nuts with shopping and there's even a baseball team. Who woulda thought? Hurkamp Park has the giant word LOVE to take photos with – it's painted a different vibe each season. This town is full of love – people say hi to you on the streets, and generations want to tell you how proud they are to be from 'the 'Burg.' I don't blame them.

John F Kennedy, with its eternal flame. The most notable site, however, is the Tomb of the Unknown Soldier, a tribute to the unknown fallen soldiers of the US's major wars. The neoclassical white-marble sarcophagus is guarded 24 hours a day.

To find a specific grave or memorial, download the ANC Explorer app, which has maps and photos down to individual tombstones.

Fredericksburg

Historic-house hopping between revolutionary residences

The 'midpoint between Washington, DC and Richmond' and George Washington's boyhood home, beautifully preserved, heritage-filled Fredericksburg is home to numerous historic homes, some of which are open to the public and host regular tours.

Chatham Manor *(nps.gov)* looms over the Rappahannock River and dates back to 1771. During the Civil War, it was a hospital and Union headquarters, with famous visitors such as Abraham Lincoln and Walt Whitman. There are free walking tours of the grounds, including a stop with views of Fredericksburg's steeple-filled skyline. **Mary Washington House** *(washingtonheritagemuseums.org)* is a larger, white-paneled downtown home where George Washington's mother lived toward the end of her life (from 1772–1789). Beyond rooms set up to replicate Mary's lifestyle, the lush-yet-quaint gardens offer a lovely and colorful stroll, particularly in springtime.

Kenmore *(kenmore.org)* is another standout residence, constructed in 1775 by Fielding Lewis and his wife, Betty, who was George Washington's sister. At the time of its construction, it was an architectural marvel for its ornate plasterwork and ceilings, which have been tastefully restored through the years. If you plan to visit both Kenmore and Mary Washington House, buy a combo ticket at Kenmore for discounted entry.

Alexandria

A walk fit for a king

Old Town Alexandria is a nationally designated historic district and its core, King St, puts much of its zest on display, particularly between the King St Metro station and the Potomac River waterfront. Among the highlights is **Torpedo Factory Art Center**, a former munitions plant and now an art gallery. Inside, you can weave through the galleries of 70-plus local artists. For Alexandria-themed tchotchkes, the **Old Town Shop** has Americana-inspired ornaments, puzzles and charms. The **Alexandria Visitor Center** has some fun keepsakes, too, including an ever-evolving collection of history-themed candles. Eastward, King St culminates at a waterfront park with views of DC's skyline.

Mount Vernon

Mount Vernon
Walk in Washington's footsteps

Mount Vernon (*mountvernon.org; adult/child $28/15*) was George Washington's most famous home, built by his dad in 1734. George and his wife, Martha, lived here for 40-plus years, with George dying here in 1799. To enter the grounds, you'll need to purchase a pass, with an additional fee to access the main mansion. There are a number of add-ons available from there – the best are a 45-minute boat excursion on the Potomac River and, for *Hamilton* lovers, a look at how Washington's life correlated with the famed Broadway show's songs.

Highlights in the mansion include Washington's private study and the majestic New Room. You'll also want to check out the farm space, with costumed interpreters depicting how Mount Vernon's workers sheared sheep, harvested crops and more. Mount Vernon was also once home to hundreds of enslaved people and among the more moving moments at the mansion is a small, replica slaves' cabin.

COBBLE, COBBLE

Embracing the historical whimsy of Old Town's cobblestone streets is no challenge. It's like stepping back in time. This style of paving wasn't chosen for its charm – during construction, cobblestones were affordable and readily available as merchant ships used river-rounded rocks as ballast in Alexandria. However, their durability posed challenges. Alignment issues and erosion meant ongoing maintenance, which eventually became unsustainable. Cobblestones eventually became a thing of the past in Alexandria as brick and other sturdier materials became more common. Ongoing preservation efforts, including the repaving of some cobblestones in 1979, have contributed to local conservation.

EATING IN ALEXANDRIA: BEST RIVER VIEWS

Vola's Dockside: Premier riverfront dining, with seafood, tacos, American classics and a mid-century-modern throwback in the Hi-Tide Lounge. *hours vary* **$$$**

Ada's on the River: Seafood and steaks surrounding a custom wood-burning oven with views of the Potomac. *hours vary* **$$$**

BARCA: Mediterranean fare, tapas and a wine bar situated on a pier. *hours vary* **$$**

Jula's on the Potomac: American classics on the 4th floor, with a terrace overlooking the river. *hours vary* **$$$**

West Virginia

WHITE-WATER | APPALACHIA | FORESTED SLOPES

Places
Charleston p307
New River Gorge p308
Hatfield-McCoy Trails p309
Point Pleasant p309
Sutton p310
Morgantown p311
Harpers Ferry p312
Berkeley Springs p313

'The sun doesn't always shine in West Virginia,' President John F Kennedy once said, 'but the people do.'

Kennedy wasn't alone in his affection for the Mountain State. 'Take Me Home, Country Road' is one of John Denver's most enduring ballads, and countless writers have waxed poetic on this wild and wonderful land. Yes, West Virginia has seen plenty of drama over the years, from the Hatfield-and-McCoy blood feud to the complicated legacy of coal mining, but open-minded visitors will find the best of Appalachia in these textured highlands. Nearly 80% of West Virginia is blanketed in forest, and its six national parks are a paradise for temperate wildlife – as well as birders, hikers and anglers. West Virginia's reputation for hospitality is also well earned, and locals tend to wear their hearts on their sleeves. As you fall into its down-home rhythms, you'll likely find yourself shining, too.

GETTING AROUND

With its odd shape and rolling topography, West Virginia is best explored 1 mile at a time. Drives can be long and service stations scattered, so keep an eye on the fuel gauge. While Greyhoud connects most major towns, tickets aren't cheap and the winding routes burn time: Morgantown to Charleston takes almost 10 hours. A car makes things easier and is necessary to really explore southern West Virginia. The tougher your vehicle, the better – while highways are well maintained, secondary roads have their share of potholes, and you don't have to stray too far to hit gravel and severe inclines. Central Charleston and Morgantown are walkable, and there are local buses.

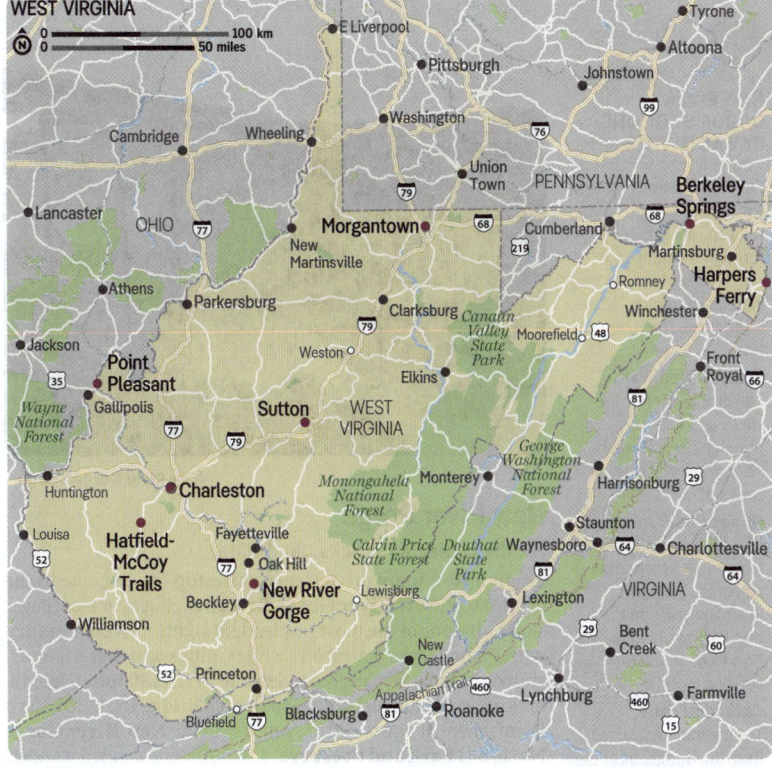

Charleston

A dusty district turned hip

Charleston, West Virginia's low-key capital, stands at the confluence of the Elk and Kanawha rivers and is hours from any major city, yet it packs a lot into its walkable central area. **Capitol St** is a tree-lined commercial strip with vintage storefronts, brick-paved sidewalks, brewpubs and restaurants. You can amble across downtown Charleston in no time, but the neighborhood is rich in historic architecture and commemorative plaques. The most recent addition is **Slack Plaza**, a beautiful pedestrian concourse, playground and splash pad. Two whimsical sculptures of fiddling musicians welcome you to the plaza, and real-life instrumentalists play here in the warmer months. Downtown Charleston is best enjoyed in the summer, when the streets are busy and food trucks are out, but Slack Plaza also has a skating rink in the winter. Just a few blocks away is the **Clay Center for the Arts and Sciences** (theclaycenter.org; free), where you'll find a theater, art museum and planetarium in one facility – perfect for families and kids.

☑ TOP TIP

Driving from Virginia, you can explore West Virginia's history in roughly chronological order – from the colonial getaway of Berkeley Springs (p313), head to Harpers Ferry (p312) for a lesson in abolitionism or Morgantown (p311) for a course on the Industrial Revolution. Then hike in the footsteps of Hatfield and McCoy (p309) before finishing at Charleston.

NEW RIVER GORGE'S TOP ONE-DAY ACTIVITIES

Fayette Station Rd: This one-way road spirals 8 miles through the gorge. The 40-minute drive includes a trestle bridge over the New River.

Endless Wall Trail: The hiking is tame; the views are epic. This popular 2.4-mile walk skirts a spectacular series of cliffs.

Bridge Walk: Join this tour *(bridgewalk.com)* to conquer acrophobia and cross the New River Gorge Bridge on a narrow catwalk. Don't worry; you're safely clipped in.

Cathedral Falls: Twenty minutes' drive from the bridge, this waterfall makes for a spectacular selfie. Park in the lot and you're steps away.

Bridge Day: Mark your calendars: the bridge is closed to motor traffic on the third Saturday of October. Pedestrians, vendors and BASE jumpers rejoice.

New River Gorge Bridge

New River Gorge

Hit the trails...and rocks...and water

About a 70-minute drive from Charleston, you'll come to the iconic steel **New River Gorge Bridge** arcing over New River Gorge. It's one of the most resplendent sights in West Virginia, with its image recreated on T-shirts, mugs and more. The architectural masterpiece, completed in 1977, is 3030ft in length, making it the longest single-span arch bridge in the Western Hemisphere. It's also a fitting gateway to the **New River Gorge National Park and Preserve**, a 70,000-acre wooded wonderland. The park is a magnet for hikers, campers, rock climbers and mountain bikers, especially in summer. Motor activities are also common here, with routes for 4WDs and snowmobiles and, after a good winter storm, snowshoers and cross-country skiers take over the trails. But even in the busiest months, you can find peace and solitude among the corrugated hills. The New River itself extends 53 miles through the protected landscape, with waters that range from calm and glassy to frothing class III rapids. The waterway's length attracts kayakers and white-water rafters from around the world, and the varying conditions appeal to both newbies and veterans. Many tour operators are based in Fayette County, but the largest and most dynamic is **Adventures on the Gorge**

EATING & DRINKING IN CHARLESTON: OUR PICKS

Adelphia Sports Bar: Bustling bar and dining room with a diverse pub menu and lots of TVs. *11am-11pm Mon-Wed, to midnight Thu-Sat, 1-10pm Sun* $$

Black Sheep Burrito & Brews: Upmarket Mexican fusion restaurant with reasonable prices, plus cocktails. *11am-9pm Mon-Thu, to 10pm Fri & Sat, 11am-3pm Sun* $$

Hale House: Refined bistro with a brick dining room and menu of 240 varieties of bourbon. Head downstairs to the Volstead speakeasy. *4-10pm Mon-Sat* $$

Fife Street Brewing: Lively taproom with high ceilings and big windows, on a lively pedestrian walkway. *11am-10pm* *(adventuresonthegorge.com)*, based in Lansing. This outfit can arrange class-V rafting trips, family ziplining and accommodations in its luxury cabins.

Fayetteville, a tiny historic town on the western side of New River Gorge, is just a mile from the bridge and makes a good base. Its Court St is lined with bistros, outfitters and antebellum houses, and visitors typically stop here to grab lunch and get their bearings. The town is ringed with hotels, lodges and campgrounds, and plenty of visitors bed down in Fayetteville while spending daylight hours in the park.

Hatfield-McCoy Trails
Hike through history

It's strange to think that these peaceful paths were once the backdrop for a bitter blood feud, with members of the Hatfield and McCoy clans spending 28 years treading these very routes in their quest for shotgun justice. What started as an argument over land rights in the 1860s ballooned into an interfamilial conflict, and at least 20 lives were lost in West Virginia's woodlands before its ceasefire in 1891. Founded in 2000, the **Hatfield-McCoy Trails** *(trailsheaven.com; permit $50)* extend more than 1000 miles through the southwestern quarter of the state, spanning nine counties.

Such a vast network has plenty of segments and trailheads, but the closest to Charleston is the **Ivy Branch trail system**. An entry point in the town of **Julian** stands about a half-hour drive from the capital, and you'll find a sizable parking lot and welcome center. From here, you can access 60 miles of rugged, wending paths.

Point Pleasant
A living folk hero?

West Virginia has many folk heroes, but none of them excites the imagination like the Mothman. This insect-human hybrid made its debut in *The Mothman Prophecies,* a 1975 memoir by John A Keel, which takes place in the small riverside town of Point Pleasant, about an hour's drive northwest of Charleston. The Mothman has gone on to win worldwide attention among cryptozoologists, and many a local has claimed to spot this winged, 10ft-tall critter in the wild. The legend inspired a 2002 feature film, *The Mothman Prophecies*, starring Richard Gere. A year later, a Mothman statue was unveiled in the middle of Point Pleasant. The statue stands directly in front of

OUTDOOR EXCURSIONS IN NEW RIVER GORGE

Bill Chouinard, pilot, vacation-rental operator and owner of Wild Blue Adventure Co *wildblueadventurecompany.com*

Fayette County is the epicenter of multisport days in the US. I moved here nearly 30 years ago, dropping out of college with $300 and a one-way ticket to the world-class climbing at New River Gorge.

I've spent almost three decades climbing, kayaking, mountain biking, running, paragliding, BASE jumping and now flying here. This place is more than just our home. It's fuel for daily inspiration, exploration and adventure. The thing that really makes this place stand out is the people – an incredible mix of locals and transplants drawn here by a common interest in the outdoors and everything it offers.

EATING IN FAYETTEVILLE: BEST GRUB

The Stache: Come for the toys and knickknacks; stay for the eclectic ice cream and candy. *11:30am-6pm* $

Wanderlust Creativefoods: Elegant and sophisticated plates in a cozy setting, with decor highlighted with attractive woodwork. *4-9pm Thu-Sun* $$

Southside Junction Tap House: LGBTQ+-friendly corner bar in an old brick building. Craft beers, burgers and live music. *3-11pm Mon, Tue, Thu & Fri, 2-11pm Sat, to 9pm Sun* $$

Pies & Pints: Funky pizzas and a dizzying range of beers on tap in a polished modernist venue. *11am-9pm Sun-Thu, to 10pm Fri & Sat* $$

YARNS SPUN ABOUT THE HATFIELD-MCCOY FEUD

Blood Feud: The Hatfields & McCoys Novelist Lisa Alther presents an authoritative nonfiction biography of the Hatfields and McCoys and their multigenerational feud.

The Feud: The Hatfields & McCoys Dean King describes the peaceful coexistence between the two families before the Civil War wrenched them apart.

The McCoys Before the Feud: A Western Novel This fictional account by author Thomas A McCoy imagines his ancestors' less-known exploits in the American West.

The Coffin Quilt Ann Rinaldi's young-adult novel illustrates life in 1870s Appalachia through the eyes of young Fanny McCoy.

Hatfields & McCoys Kevin Costner and Bill Paxton star as rival patriarchs in this action-packed History Channel miniseries.

the **World's Only Mothman Museum** *(mothmanmuseum.com; adult/child $5/2)*, a small storefront that houses newspaper clippings, artwork and other ephemera. In the third week of September, the whole thing is commemorated with the annual Mothman Festival.

Sutton

Supernatural sightings and Bigfoot

About an hour's drive northeast of Charleston, in Sutton, is some more food for the imagination. The **Flatwoods Monster Museum** *(braxtonwv.org/the-flatwoods-monster; free)*, a former soda fountain, features the Flatwoods Monster, a 10ft-tall extraterrestrial with a red face and flowing gown that locals claimed to have spotted in 1952. The town embraces this strange episode with a sign that reads 'Home of the Green Monster,' a reference to the creature's green outfit. Just a block away is the **West Virginia Bigfoot Museum** *(wvbigfootmuseum.org; free)*, a roomy exhibition space dedicated to all things Sasquatch. This newest addition opened in 2021 and displays art, artifacts and testimonials from Bigfoot lore.

 DRINKING IN CHARLESTON: LOCAL HAUNTS

Red Carpet Lounge: Local favorite, with a sizable patio out back and bargain prices. *11am-midnight Mon-Wed, to 1am Thu, to 2am Fri, noon-2am Sat, 1pm-midnight Sun*

Bar 101: Busy bar with craft beer, pub menu, regular DJs and throbbing dance floor. *11:30am-12:30am Mon-Thu, to 2am Fri, 1pm-2am Sat, to midnight Sun*

ROQ: Atmospheric lounge specializing in cocktails, live music and salsa dancing. Thoughtful menu, including flatbreads. *4pm-late Tue-Fri, from 5pm Sat*

Vino's Bar & Grill: Upstairs is a West Virginia lounge with a Manhattan streak; downstairs is a casual hangout. DJs, pool and pinball. *4pm-2am Tue-Fri, from 8am Sat*

Morgantown Rail Trail, Mon River Trail (p304)

Morgantown
Stroll High St

Most of the culture and nightlife in Morgantown, former coal capital and home of West Virginia University (WVU), is squeezed into High St, a long commercial corridor just east of the Monongahela River. On the north end, WVU campus crowns a hilltop with stately brick buildings, and students trickle down steep walkways to the restaurants, bars and galleries below. Weekends can get rowdy, as WVU has a long-standing party-school rep. One exception is First Friday, a family-friendly showcase of local artists and gourmands. The lynchpin of First Friday is the **Monongalia Arts Center** *(MAC; monartscenter.com),* an historic gallery and performance venue.

The **Metropolitan Theatre** *(morgantownmet.com)* is an active show space for concerts, plays and comedians. Each year, some 35,000 theatergoers travel from across the tristate area, most to catch touring musicians. The auditorium dates back to 1924, when it served as a vaudeville stage. Nearby stands a statue of TV star Don Knotts, a beloved native son.

THE ORIGINAL MORGAN

Morgantown is named after its tough-as-nails founder, Colonel Zackquill Morgan, who was born in Wales and fought in both the French and Indian War and the American Revolution. Morgan and his wife, Catherine Garretson, weren't just early settlers in the region; they were the first known colonists to build a home on the land that would become West Virginia. In his postwar life, Morgan commissioned a courthouse and public square, and he personally opened the town's first tavern. In 2016, some 221 years after his death, a statue of Morgan was unveiled on Spruce St. It was sculpted by artist Jamie Lester, who also created the Don Knotts monument around the block.

 DRINKING IN MORGANTOWN: BEST BARS

Gibbie's Pub & Eatery: Deep hangout with multiple bars, an impressive local beer selection and generous patio. Lots of local regulars. *11am-2:30am*

Apothecary Ale House & Cafe: Hip pub with vintage interior and wide selection of brews on tap. *11am-midnight Mon-Thu, to 1am Fri & Sat, noon-8pm Sun*

Metropolitan Billiard Parlor: Basement pool hall with a small bar and lots of vintage decorations. A local institution since Prohibition. *5-11pm Sun-Wed, to midnight Thu-Sat*

Sports Page: Immensely popular sports bar with TVs, wings baskets and a locally famous iced tea. *7pm-3am Thu, from 5pm Fri, 11am-3am Sat, noon-3am Sun*

The river itself – the 'Mon' – has always been the lifeblood of Morgantown, first for industry and now for recreation. Cycle or jog along the **Mon River Trail**, which snakes along the river for 19.5 miles, ending in the town of Reedsville, or rent a kayak or stand-up paddleboard from **Morgantown Adventure Outfitters** (*adventurewv.wvu.edu*) between April to October.

Harpers Ferry
Explore a Blue Ridge paradise

To call Harpers Ferry, about a three-hour drive from Morgantown, a special place is a serious understatement. Here, the beloved Shenandoah River merges with the Potomac on its journey to Chesapeake Bay. Three states – Maryland, Virginia and West Virginia – huddle together, and you can hopscotch across multiple borders without breaking a sweat. This valley has received more than its share of natural and structural beauty, thanks to rolling hills, soaring cliffs and two railroad bridges that span the wide waters. Even its architecture excels: the Historic District's stone houses, federalist brick facades and cobbled streets look virtually unchanged since hoop skirts were in fashion.

Harpers Ferry was also the backdrop for John Brown's final standoff. In 1859, the radical abolitionist attempted to attack the town, raid its armory and free enslaved people across the region. Instead, Brown's men embedded themselves in a local engine house and clashed with the US Army. Brown was tried and executed, but he became a hero of the anti-slavery movement.

You can see this story in three dimensions at the **John Brown Wax Museum** (*johnbrownwaxmuseum.com*), which vividly brings this final struggle to life. Check before visiting, as the museum's fate was uncertain at the time of research. The center of the action was **John Brown's Fort** (*nps.gov; free*), the name given to the little brick firehouse he used as a stronghold. The 'fort' has been moved slightly from its original location, but visitors can still tour the structure, and Harpers Ferry is packed with other monuments from the era. The town was literally designed for walking, but note that some streets are steep and not ideal for wheelchairs.

OUTDOOR ACTIVITIES AROUND HARPERS FERRY

Maryland Heights Trail: This 6.5-mile trail has some tough climbs, but hikers are rewarded with unparalleled views of the town and valley.

River tubing: The lazy currents are ideal for floating downriver in an inflatable tube. Come summer, make arrangements with **River Riders** (*riverriders.com*).

Ziplining: Fly along seven ziplines through the canopy, or walk an elevated skybridge, at **Harpers Ferry Adventure Center** (*harpersferryadventurecenter.com*).

C&O Canal towpath: This segment of rail trail is part of a 333-mile bike route between Pittsburgh and Washington, DC.

Bolivar Heights Battlefield: These peaceful meadows and forest were hotly contested during the Civil War. See the cannons, fences and still-visible trenches.

EATING IN HARPERS FERRY: UNIQUE VENUES

Rabbit Hole Gastropub: Craft cocktails and gourmet dining in a discerning country-charm setting. Beautiful porch and stone walls. *noon-8pm Mon-Thu, 11am-9pm Fri-Sun* **$$**

Kelley Farm Kitchen: West Virginia's first plant-based restaurant, set in a farmhouse. Riffs on traditional entrees and great ramen. *4-8pm Wed, from 11am Thu-Sat, noon-4pm Sun* **$$$**

Barn of Harpers Ferry: Converted barn with regular live concerts and creative libations. Food served Fridays and Saturdays. *4-11pm Wed-Sun* **$$**

Yatai Hibachi Food Trailer: Pan-Asian food truck. Claim a picnic table and watch chef Made Sudira work the hibachi. *11am-8pm Wed-Sat, noon-7pm Sun* **$$**

Harpers Ferry

Berkeley Springs
Soak in waters fit for a president

Not only did George Washington sleep here, he also bathed in Berkeley Springs – indeed, he was such a fan of the area, he bought up much of its real estate. Travelers have flocked to the town's 74°F thermal pools since colonial times, and Indigenous people likely enjoyed the mineral-rich waters long before that. Berkeley Springs is a two-hour drive from Morgantown and an hour's drive northwest of Harpers Ferry, but the mineral baths and quaint downtown are well worth the trip.

The town has two full-service retreats: **Atasia Spa** *(atasiaspa.com)* and Renaissance Spa at the **Country Inn** *(thecountryinnwv.com)*. You can also find warm waters in **Berkeley Springs State Park** *(berkeleyspringssp.com)*, home to the Old Roman Bath House. This historic brick structure contains a 750-gallon private mineral bath, where four adults can soak for up to an hour. All facilities offer a complete menu of facials, massages and other wellness services.

The town's main drag is, naturally, named Washington St, and its handful of shops and restaurants should occupy most visitors for an afternoon or two.

TOP SKI RESORTS OF WEST VIRGINIA

Canaan Valley: This state park has a sizable lodge, cabins and tent sites. There are 47 ski trails in the winter, plus an 18-hole golf course in summer. *canaanresort.com*

Snowshoe Mountain Resort: A beloved resort modeled on Alpine villages, boasting 14 lifts and 60 ski trails. Fire-tower visits and mountain biking are popular in summer. *snowshoemtn.com*

Winterplace Ski Resort: An intimate four-season resort in southern West Virginia, with 28 trails, nine lifts and 16 lanes of snow tubing. *winterplace.com*

Timberline Mountain: A great place for beginners and crowd-shy skiers. Timberline has 37 easygoing trails and a 20-room boutique hotel. *timberlinemountain.com*

 EATING AROUND BERKELEY SPRINGS: BEST BITES

Naked Olive Lounge: This Berkeley Springs olive-oil tasting room triples as a gourmet food market and LGBTQ+-friendly cocktail lounge. *11am-11pm Fri & Sat, noon-6pm Sun* **$$**

Cacapon Mountain Brewing: Follow your spa session with a craft beer in an upbeat Berkeley Springs taproom. Kitchen window available for bites. *4-8pm Thu, noon-8pm Fri & Sat, to 6pm Sun* **$$**

Lot 12 Public House: Savor chef Damien Heath's masterful dishes and thoughtful wine pairings in a converted, century-old Berkeley Springs house. *5-9:30pm Fri & Sat, to 9pm Sun* **$$$**

Prima Marina: Riverside restaurant in Moundsville serves up hoagies, freshwater-fish platters and beautiful Ohio River sunsets. *11am-8pm Tue-Sat, to 3pm Sun* **$$**

# Places We Love to Stay

$ Budget $$ Midrange $$$ Top End

Washington, DC
MAPS P249, P259, P261, P266, P269

Friends Place on Capitol Hill $ This Quaker guesthouse is possibly the friendliest and most affordable hostel in the city.

HighRoad Hotel $ One of the city's better budget options, with clean rooms, dorms and stylish decor in the heart of Adams Morgan.

Hotel Hive $$ Affordable, friendly and convenient (albeit with small rooms), with a bar and rooftop.

River Inn $$ Although not on the river, this quiet hotel near the Kennedy Center offers well-appointed suites and kitchenettes.

Motto by Hilton $$ The Motto offers 245 small, clean rooms in a great location with a rooftop bar.

Phoenix Park Hotel $$ Clean rooms, respectable amenities and solid service close to Union Station and Capitol Hill.

YOTEL Washington DC $$ Four-star contemporary business hotel with a rooftop pool and cool outdoor terrace, steps from Capitol Hill.

citizenM $$ Small but super-high-tech rooms and thoughtfully decorated common areas – perfect for single travelers.

American Guest House $$ Twelve-bedroom B&B in a home-style environment with comfortable rooms, friendly staff and great breakfast.

Swann House $$ Historic B&B with spacious rooms, aesthetically pleasing minimalist decor, impeccable service and a seasonally open outdoor swimming pool.

Mayflower Hotel $$$ Nicknamed the Hotel of Presidents for good reason – expect service worthy of a head of state.

Hay-Adams Hotel $$$ Expect old-school elegance at this luxurious heritage hotel with White House views.

Kimpton George Hotel $$$ Creamy-white rooms adorned with presidential pop art near Union Station. Kid- and pet-friendly.

Graham Georgetown $$$ Modernist boutique hotel in the middle of Georgetown with contemporary decor and rooftop lounge that's perfect for sundowners.

Delaware
MAP P274

Home2 Suites by Hilton (Dover) $$ A suite hotel within walking distance of downtown Dover attractions, with free breakfasts and an indoor pool.

Hilton Garden Inn Dover (Dover) $$ Close to Dover's casino, with an indoor pool and rooms with microwaves and mini fridges.

Causey Mansion Bed & Breakfast (Milford) $$ This landmark 18th-century building, set on a 3-acre property in Milford, is sprinkled with art, fountains and antique period details.

Hotel Rodney $$ (Lewes) In downtown Lewes, this historic hotel has fun furnishings and a British-style gastropub.

Hotel du Pont $$$ (Wilmington) Luxury Wilmington property with a spa, opulent lobby and food court in an Italian Renaissance building that debuted in 1913.

Avenue Inn & Spa $$$ (Rehoboth) One block from the beach in Rehoboth, with a spa and James Beard semi-finalist restaurant, the Blue Hen (p275).

Maryland
MAPS P288, P290

Assateague Island Campground (Assateaugue Island) $ Basic facilities and sometimes-crowded camping, but you'll wake to unobstructed views of the sea or bay.

Days Inn Ocean City Oceanfront (Ocean City) $ A good beachfront location at the northern end of the boardwalk, with helpful staff. The beach-facing rooms are worth the extra money.

King Charles Hotel (Ocean City) $ This aging but functional hotel is near the boardwalk.

Inn on Main (Annapolis) $$ In a central Main St location above Chick & Ruth's Delly (p282), with small, homey rooms. Breakfast included.

Historic Inns of Annapolis (Annapolis) $$ Enjoy Annapolis' 18th-century architectural heritage at three historic inns: Maryland Inn, Governor Calvert House and Robert Johnson House.

Whitehaven Hotel (Whitehaven) $$ This early 19th-century house overlooks the Wicomico River near Blackwater National Wildlife Refuge.

Rachael's Dowry B&B (Baltimore) $$ Spacious rooms in a restored historic house near Camden Yards.

Hay-Adams Hotel (p249), Washington, DC

BlancNoir (Baltimore) $$ In Little Italy, easy walking distance from the Inner Harbor, with spotless, comfortable rooms.

Hotel Revival (Baltimore) $$ Well located in the heart of the trendy Mount Vernon neighborhood, and billing itself as the city's only boutique art hotel.

Inn on Decatur (Cumberland) $$ This biker-friendly B&B is near the trails in Cumberland. Management also runs the nearby budget- and cyclist-friendly 9 Decatur Guest House.

Virginia
MAP P296

Linden Row Inn (Richmond) $$ Victorian-style inn with modern comforts. Enjoy the terrace and garden before making your way on foot to bustling Broad St.

Cedars of Williamsburg (Williamsburg) $$ Georgian architecture, cozy rooms, friendly service and walkable to downtown.

Liberty Trust (Roanoke) $$ Restored downtown bank incorporating original features such as a tasting room in the original vault.

Hotel Madison (Harrisonburg) $$ Comfortable accommodations with refined touches close to downtown. Catch views of the city or the mountains and nods to James Madison.

Ironclad Inn (Fredericksburg) $$ Historic residence turned inn walkable to downtown, with an Ironclad Distillery bourbon tasting room.

Boar's Head Resort (Charlottesville) $$$ Modern amenities and outdoor activities with a classic appeal, surrounded by the rolling foothills of the Blue Ridge Mountains.

Hilton Virginia Beach Oceanfront (Virginia Beach) $$$ Private balconies, panoramic ocean views, prime boardwalk location and a rooftop pool and bar.

West Virginia

Outpost (Fayetteville) $ Cabins, tent platforms and RV hookups – this Outpost is ready for almost any kind of outdoors enthusiast. Regular fireside jams for music fans.

Brass Pineapple Inn (Charleston) $$ This century-old inn was formerly a private home, and rooms retain an Edwardian homeyness. Some have claw-foot tubs. Room service on silver trays.

Glen Ferris Inn (Glen Ferris) $$ A lovely way station for travelers for nearly two centuries, just a stone's throw from photogenic Kanawha Falls. Home-style restaurant.

Country Inn (p313; Berkeley Springs) $$ Built in 1933, this Greek Revival–style estate is Berkeley Springs' keystone. Two restaurants, live music and a firepit.

Hotel Morgan (Morgantown) $$$ Distinguished flagship hotel in the middle of Morgantown, fully renovated in 2020. Anvil + Ax is a gorgeous cocktail lounge on the 1st floor.

1799 Inn (Harpers Ferry) $$$ When the Harpers Ferry armory was being built in 1799, workers stayed in this very house. The beautiful rooms thoughtfully blend old and new.

THE GUIDE

THE SOUTH

For places to stay in the South, see p432

Above: Vicksburg National Military Park (p403); Right: Sun Studio (p355)

THE MAIN AREAS

NORTH CAROLINA
Enchanting cities, mountains and islands.
p322

SOUTH CAROLINA
Coastal allure and charming Charleston.
p341

TENNESSEE
The epicenter of country and blues.
p353

KENTUCKY
Bourbon distilleries, racehorses, wilderness.
p366

GEORGIA
Urban attractions and seaside beauty.
p374

Researched and curated by
Regis St Louis

The South

BIRTHPLACE OF AMERICAN MUSIC AND CIVIL RIGHTS

Explore the nation's most misunderstood region, a dynamo of music, culture and history, set against a backdrop of vibrant towns and cinematic natural beauty.

The South is a land of ancient mountain peaks, alluvial plains and remote islands where wild horses still roam. It was one of the first regions of the US to be considered its own distinct place, not merely for its geography, but its literature, cuisine, lilting accents and above all its history – one that is long and beautiful in places, cruel and harrowing in others.

Jazz, blues, country and even rock and roll were born in the South. Music pilgrims come to visit famous sites like Graceland and Sun Studio to connect with the people and events that shaped history. Meanwhile fans of those distinct American sounds fill the clubs of Clarksdale, Memphis, Atlanta, Nashville and New Orleans to hear the great performers of today.

The human presence in the South dates back thousands of years, evident in the ruins left behind by the ancient mound builders. Native American tribes still retain strong ties to the land (visible in towns like Cherokee), while national park sites preserve the battlefields of the Civil War, as well as pivotal places in the fight for Civil Rights.

Despite all its heartache, the South has always been a hotbed of creativity, which you can explore in rural settlements and urban neighborhoods alike.

It's also a place of unbridled outdoor adventure, whether biking the Ozarks, rafting Appalachian mountain rivers or hiking wilderness trails all across the region.

ALABAMA	**MISSISSIPPI**	**ARKANSAS**	**NEW ORLEANS**	**LOUISIANA**
The heart of the Civil Rights movement.	Historic sites and the Delta blues.	Mountain biking, hiking and kayaking.	Food-loving city of jazz and joie de vivre.	Cajun music amid lush wetlands.
p388	**p397**	**p405**	**p415**	**p428**

Find Your Way

The South encompasses plains, forests, mountains and coastline, plus small towns and big cities found across the landscape. If time is limited, focus on a state or two rather than trying to see it all.

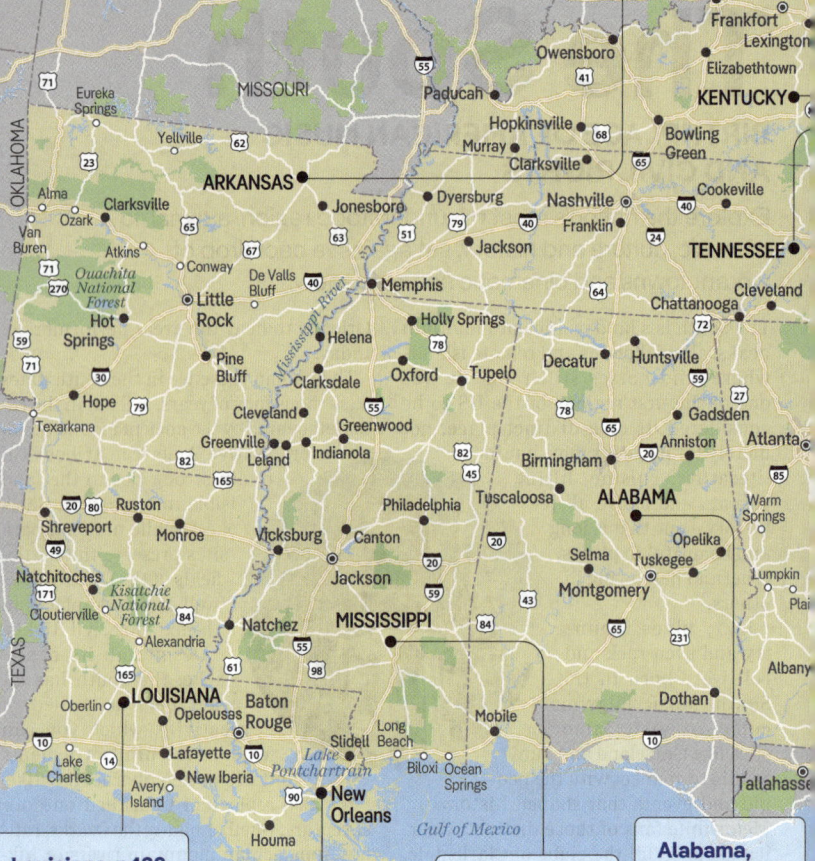

Arkansas, p405
Visit the Natural State for incredible mountain biking, hiking and canoeing, plus grand art museums, arts-minded communities and progressive college towns.

Louisiana, p428
Walk where ancient mound-builders dwelled, work the floorboards at a Cajun dancehall, and spy alligators and ibises on a wildlife-filled swamp tour.

New Orleans, p415
Home to French and Spanish colonial architecture and fiery jazz clubs, NOLA captivates with its decadent cuisine, buzzing nightlife and music-fueled festivals.

Mississippi, p397
The birthplace of the blues has juke joints and heritage museums, Civil War sites and serene towns perched alongside the USA's mightiest waterway.

Alabama, p388
Journey into the past at Civil Rights sites in Birmingham and Montgomery, then launch into the future in Huntsville (aka Rocket City).

Kentucky, p366

See the Derby in Churchill Downs, sip fine bourbons at famed distilleries, and trek the forests and falls of the Red River Gorge.

Tennessee, p353

Nashville's legendary music scene hogs the limelight, though there's also blues in Memphis, hiking in Chattanooga and mountain adventures in the Smokies.

North Carolina, p322

Go island-hopping in the Outer Banks, get active in the Appalachian mountains, and explore the arts in Asheville, Charlotte and Durham.

South Carolina, p341

Wonderful beaches are a big draw, as is charming Charleston. There are also islands, Gullah culture and paddling adventures in Congaree National Park.

Georgia, p374

Explore lively neighborhoods in Atlanta, see the Ocmulgee Mounds, get a taste of Savannah and unwind on picturesque islands like Jekyll and Cumberland.

CAR
Getting behind the wheel gives you the freedom to explore beyond city centers. The South is a fine place for a road trip, whether tracing the Mississippi on the Blues Highway or discovering mountain towns across Appalachia.

BUS
Without a car, your best bet for navigating this vast region is Greyhound (greyhound.com), which links major towns across the South. Megabus (us.megabus.com) also operates a few routes, mostly in Arkansas, Georgia and the Carolinas.

TRAIN
Various long-haul routes operated by Amtrak pass through the South. While not all that practicable, these train journeys offer outstanding scenery. One route links New Orleans with Memphis, while another connects numerous cities between New Orleans and NYC including Birmingham, Atlanta and Charlotte.

Plan Your Time

Don't try to cram in too much, though with a week or more to spare, you can see a few different regions of the South, including coastline, mountains and music-filled city neighborhoods.

Fort Sumter (p339)

24 Hours in the Big Easy

Head straight for **New Orleans** (p415), one of the most fascinating cities in the country. Start with a morning stroll in the **French Quarter** (p418). Get a dose of history at the **Historic New Orleans Collection** (p417) and learn about primitive medical practices at the **New Orleans Pharmacy Museum** (p417). Have lunch at the legendary Creole spot of **Dooky Chase** (p422), then board a vintage streetcar along Canal St to **City Park** (p427). Have beignets and chicory coffee at **Cafe Du Monde** (p427), stroll the Spanish moss-draped live oaks lining the bayou and visit the sculpture garden. In the evening, treat yourself to a meal in the delightful hideaway of **N7** (p423). Later, join the jazz-loving crowds on **Frenchmen Street** (p423).

Seasonal Highlights

The South is a year-round destination, with hiking, biking and aquatic adventures in the warmer months, abundant cultural offerings in the winter, and big celebrations and music fests throughout the year.

FEBRUARY

Head to the South to escape the winter chill. It's the most festive time of the year in New Orleans, which hosts several weeks of revelry (parades, costuming, music, merriment) leading up to **Mardi Gras** (p415).

APRIL

Clarksdale, Mississippi, draws blues fans from far and wide to its fabulous **Juke Joint Festival** (p400). You can catch outdoor concerts at stages around town and keep the party going at old-school music venues by night.

MAY

With spring in full bloom, pull out the pastel hues and head-turning hats for a trip to the Kentucky Derby. The exciting race is preceded by two weeks of celebration during the **Kentucky Derby Festival** (p368).

Seven Days in Georgia & the Carolinas

Start off in photogenic Savannah with a stroll through the **Historic District** (p384) and a tour of the **Owens-Thomas House & Slave Quarters** (p385). Crossing into South Carolina, visit **St Helena Island** (p348) to learn about Gullah culture, then enjoy some beach time at **Hunting Island State Park** (p349). Continue to **Charleston** (p342), one of the South's most beguiling cities. Take a deep dive into the past at the **International African American Museum** (p344) and the **Aiken-Rhett House** (p344), then see where war erupted at **Fort Sumter** (p347). Next up is **Wilmington** (p324), North Carolina, with its vibrant **river district**. Drive to Cedar Island and take the ferry to **Ocracoke** (p327), gateway to beaches and island lore on the Outer Banks.

10-day Road Trip from Appalachia to Mississippi

Begin in **Asheville** (p333), a bohemian town of crafts and breweries in the North Carolina Mountains. Enjoy outdoor adventures near **Brevard** (p335), then learn about the **Cherokee** in the town named for them (p336). It's a short drive into **Great Smoky Mountains National Park** (p337) for hikes amid forests, streams and waterfalls. Dust off your cowboy boots (or buy a pair) in **Nashville** (p359), country music capital, then continue west to **Memphis** (p355) for blues and barbecue. The theme continues south in **Clarksdale** (p399), where you can enjoy a night of Delta blues in juke joints like **Red's** and **Ground Zero** (p400). Head east into Alabama to visit the country's most powerful Civil Rights memorials, including the **Birmingham Civil Rights Institute** (p392) and Montgomery's **Legacy Sites** (p394).

JUNE
Summer days offer unrivaled adventures, especially in the mountains of North Carolina and Tennessee, where there's great mountain biking and hiking, as well as white-water adventures down the **Nantahala** (p336).

SEPTEMBER
With the summer crowds subsiding, it's a good time to head to the coast (but be mindful of hurricanes). You'll still find warm, pleasant temperatures along **Cape Lookout National Seashore** (p325) in North Carolina's Outer Banks.

OCTOBER
The forests in the upper South blaze with red, yellow and orange during the height of autumn. A prime place to experience the beauty is on the trails in the **Great Smoky Mountains National Park** (p337).

NOVEMBER
In the South, college football is practically a religion. Seeing a home game at any Southeastern Conference stadium is not something you'll forget, especially if you watch the Alabama Crimson Tide take the field in **Tuscaloosa** (p393).

North Carolina

WILD COASTLINE | APPALACHIAN PEAKS | ARTS & CRAFTS

Places
- Wilmington p324
- Beaufort p324
- Cape Lookout National Seashore p325
- Outer Banks p326
- Charlotte p329
- Winston-Salem p331
- Greensboro p331
- Durham p331
- Chapel Hill p331
- Carrboro p333
- Saxapahaw p333
- Asheville p333
- Blowing Rock p335
- Brevard p335
- Cherokee p336
- Bryson City p336
- Great Smoky Mountains National Park p337

☑ TOP TIPS
On the Outer Banks, many restaurants have limited hours or close from November to March; call ahead to ensure your destination is open.

Blessed with islands and mountains, dynamic cities and arts-loving small towns, North Carolina seems to have it all. The state of 11 million residents also boasts astonishing diversity and a road trip here can take in everything from famous Civil Rights sites (Greensboro) to communities with deep-rooted Native American heritage (Cherokee).

The coast is synonymous with the Outer Banks – affectionately dubbed OBX – the chain of barrier islands that remain largely underdeveloped despite their popularity with summer vacationers. This is the region for visiting landmark lighthouses, seeing herds of wild horses and exploring hundreds of miles of windswept beaches.

Central North Carolina, also known as the Piedmont, is home to buzzing cities and appealing college towns (like Durham and Chapel Hill). West of there, the Appalachian Mountains hold some of the tallest peaks east of the Mississippi, and make a memorable setting for hiking, mountain biking, wildlife watching, rafting and numerous other outdoor adventures.

 GETTING AROUND

Charlotte and the Triangle cities (Raleigh, Durham, and Chapel Hill) all have public bus systems, though using them takes some planning as they may be infrequent or limited. There are also intercity buses operated by Greyhound. Amtrak has several rail lines through North Carolina, connecting Raleigh, Durham, Greensboro and Charlotte by train. The North Carolina Ferry System *(ferry.ncdot. gov)* runs the state's ferry routes, including three to Ocracoke Island. Island Express Ferry Service *(islandexpressferryservices.com)* provides additional boats to the islands of the Cape Lookout National Seashore. Once on the islands, getting around by bicycle is an excellent option (especially in summer, when vehicular traffic can be a nightmare).

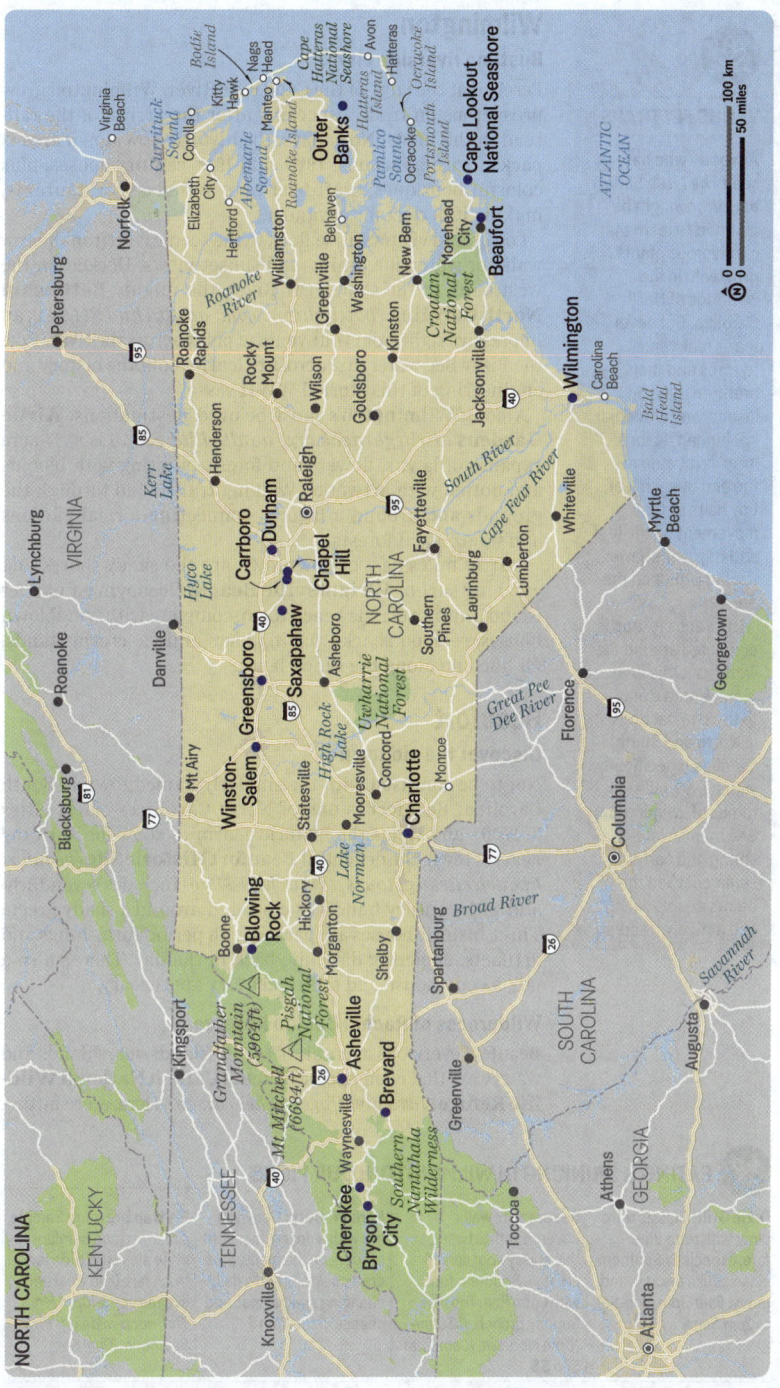

Wilmington
Bustling riverside city

Perched at the edge of the Cape Fear River, Wilmington grew prosperous on trade, especially after the arrival of the railroad in the 1840s. Nowadays, the historic downtown area is packed with handsome 18th- and 19th-century houses, plus colorful boutiques, craft-beer bars and classy restaurants, making it perfect for a wander.

Locals and visitors alike flock to the scenic riverfront boardwalk for waterside dining and sunset views. Docked on the west bank of the Cape Fear River, the mighty **Battleship North Carolina** (battleshipnc.com; adult/child $14/6) is an impressive sight from your vantage point across the river. Take the Bizzy Bee water taxi across to learn about the history and engineering of this storied WWII vessel.

Among Wilmington's most beloved destinations, **Airlie Gardens** (airliegardens.org; adult/child $10/3) is a 67-acre expanse of lawns, flowers and forest, bursting with blooms and dotted with artworks. Walking trails wind through the grounds and around a lagoon, connecting formal gardens and ungroomed forests.

Just 10 miles east of downtown are the sandy shores and crashing surf of **Wrightsville Beach**. Occupying a barrier island, this is a classic beach town, complete with windblown houses, seafood shacks, fishing piers and ice-cream stands, all lined up along the sandy lanes.

Beaufort
Discover the old town

Not to be confused with the similarly named town in South Carolina, Beaufort is one of North Carolina's oldest cities (c 1709), and it has the historic charm to show for it. In the heart of town, the delightful **Beaufort Historic Site** (beaufort historicsite.org; tours adult/child $15/6) includes seven 18th- and 19th-century buildings clustered around a shady green. Three historic houses are packed with period furnishings and artifacts, depicting daily life back in the day. There's also a jail, a courthouse and a 19th-century apothecary.

Wilderness of Rachel Carson Reserve

Beaufort overlooks a mosaic of scenic islands, marshlands and waterways that comprise the **Rachel Carson National Wildlife Refuge** (fws.gov/refuge/rachel-carson). Here, ever-shifting

---

VENUS FLYTRAPS

Anybody who has seen *The Little Shop of Horrors* might be alarmed to learn that carnivorous plants grow wild in the wetlands of North Carolina. But never fear – real Venus flytraps and their brethren feast on insects and arachnids, not human flesh. A 'trap' is located at the end of each leaf; tiny hairs detect movement on the leaf and trigger its 'jaws' to clamp shut on the prey.

The Venus flytrap is cultivated around the world, but this unique plant is native only to the coastal bogs in North and South Carolina (specifically, within a 60-mile radius of Wilmington). See them in late spring and early summer, when the plants are blooming and actively trapping.

EATING & DRINKING IN WILMINGTON: OUR PICKS

Dixie Grill: Classic retro diner with retro diner fare, especially Southern classics like biscuits and gravy. *8am-3pm Mon-Sat, to 2pm Sun* $

Savorez: Its walls covered with artwork, this classy spot serves creative Southern food with Latin flair. Tops for Sunday brunch. *11:30am-10pm Mon-Sat, 10am-2pm Sun* $$

Fork 'N' Cork: Convivial bar with a dozen decadent burgers on the menu, plus craft cocktails and a daily-changing special mac and cheese. *11am-11pm* $

Flytrap Brewing: Sample American and Belgian-style ales alongside food-truck fare (and weekend live music). *3-10pm Mon-Thu, noon-midnight Fri & Sat, noon-10pm Sun*

Battleship North Carolina

islets and shoals provide refuge for wild horses, river otters and water birds. The best way to experience this blissful place is to rent a kayak or take a tour with **Beaufort Paddle** *(beaufort paddle.com; half-day rental single/double $60/75, tour adult/ child $65/45)*. Pull your kayak up onto the sandy beach at the western end of Town Marsh to explore several different habitats on two 1-mile loop trails. Be sure to bring water, as there are no facilities and little shade in the reserve.

You can also visit the Rachel Carson Reserve in the comfort of a covered boat with **Water Bug Tours** *(waterbugtours. com; adult/child $20/10)*. No paddling required!

Cape Lookout National Seashore

Explore the rugged coastal beauty

The most rewarding day trip from Beaufort, **Cape Lookout National Seashore** *(nps.gov/calo)* is a 56-mile stretch of windswept, wave-beaten barrier islands. The jumping-off point is Harkers Island, which is 17 miles east of Beaufort. There's a visitor center with a few exhibits, but most folks just hop on the Island Express Ferry Service *(islandexpressferry services.com; adult/child $30/20)* and head out to the islands.

Your first stop is **Shackleford Banks**, a starkly beautiful place strewn with wildflowers and home to wild 'Banker'

BLACKBEARD THE PIRATE

Fierce and fearsome, Blackbeard terrorized ships up and down the East Coast in the early 18th century. In 1718 his fleet blockaded the port of Charleston, SC, demanding food and supplies and holding the city hostage for several weeks. Shortly thereafter, Blackbeard surrendered to the North Carolina governor, promising to change his ways. The reformed pirate settled down with his new wife in Bath.

This period of respite did not last long, however. Blackbeard soon returned to piracy, with the Royal Navy in hot pursuit. On November 22, 1718, Lieutenant Robert Maynard ambushed the pirate at Ocracoke Inlet, arresting or executing his crew. Blackbeard's head was cut off and hung from the bow of Maynard's ship, an ignominious end for a notorious swashbuckler.

 EATING & DRINKING IN BEAUFORT: OUR PICKS

Turner Street Market: A quick, central place for fresh sandwiches, salads or hot breakfast. *7am-2pm* $

Black Sheep: A lovely waterfront setting to nosh on crusty pizzas with tasty toppings. Extensive drink menu too. *11am-9pm Wed-Sun* $$

Beaufort Grocery: Cozy, convivial bistro serving homemade soups and sandwiches by day, fancy dinners by night. *11:30am-9:30pm Thu-Sat & Mon, 10am-2pm Sun* $$$

Backstreet Pub: Cool cubbyhole with a breezy courtyard. Weekend live music, midweek 'Hoot Nite' jam sessions. *noon-close Mon-Sat, from 5pm Sun*

Ocracoke Lighthouse

BEST ART GALLERIES IN OCRACOKE

Village Craftsmen: Run by the 10th generation of Howards on Ocracoke, this gallery features local arts and crafts and plenty of history.

Down Creek Gallery: This place overlooking Silver Lake offers fine art by Ocracoke and Hatteras artists, including paintings, pottery, glasswork and more.

Bella Fiore: Creative gifts and accessories, including scarves, bags, hats and exquisite handcrafted jewelry.

Over the Moon: Packed with quirky and clever gifts, art from recycled materials and funky arts and crafts.

Art Ocracoke: Island-inspired pieces, especially paintings of lighthouses, beaches and resident creatures.

ponies. Trails crisscross the island, but they can be marshy depending on the tide. Pack a picnic and spend a few hours birding, pony-spotting and snapping pics of the supremely picturesque landscape.

From here it's a short ride to **Cape Lookout** with its distinctive diamond-patterned lighthouse. Wide and wild, the beach here is prime for swimming and beachcombing. 'Beach shuttles' take passengers around the abandoned buildings of Cape Lookout Village and down to the Point, the southernmost tip of the cape.

Outer Banks

Shipwrecks and wild beaches

Hatteras and neighboring Ocracoke Islands make up the **Cape Hatteras National Seashore**, a preserve of sand dunes and salt marshes, including 70 miles of glorious, undeveloped beaches. At the southern end of Hatteras, a few laidback beach towns cater to families, fisherfolk and surfers, but it's pretty quiet outside of the summer months.

The seafloor here is strewn with thousands of shipwrecks, earning it the nickname 'Graveyard of the Atlantic.' Every wreck has a story, and many are told at the **Graveyard of the Atlantic Museum** (graveyardoftheatlantic.com; free)

 EATING ON HATTERAS ISLAND: OUR PICKS

Buxton Munch: Cheerful longtime favorite serving up nosh-worthy fish tacos, avocado wraps and crabby patties. *11am-3pm Tue-Sat* $

Orange Blossom Bakery: Filling breakfast sandwiches and irresistible pastries. A Buxton institution and worth the wait. *6:30-11am* $

Tavern on 12: Wildly popular local spot for elevated pub fare, including crab cakes, po' boys and Hatteras-style clam chowder. *11am-8pm Tue-Sun* $$

Oceanas Bistro: Islanders congregate at this Avon haunt for delectable 'grillers' (open-faced quesadillas), many featuring local seafood. *8am-10pm* $$

in Hatteras. Artifacts, photographs and video footage bring the history to life – not just the disasters but also the heroic lifesaving efforts of local villagers.

The **Hatteras Island Ocean Center** *(hioceancenter.org; free)*, is an indoor-outdoor nature center that's all about life in the marsh. See it up close as you walk along the scenic boardwalk and trail that wind through the salt marsh and maritime forest. Look for birds including herons, egrets, kingfishers, ibises and ospreys, as well as turtles, snakes and skinks. It's particularly lovely in the early morning and late afternoon.

Go carefree (and car-free) on Ocracoke

Take the ferry to Ocracoke Island to frolic on untamed beaches, explore the historic village and immerse yourself in local lore. The island's unofficial historian, Philip Howard, is a descendent of William Howard, the first European owner and settler of Ocracoke. Howard narrates two entertaining walking tours that are available for download at Ocracoke Navigator *(ocracokenavigator.com)*. Follow the tour 'Around Creek' to see the historically important sites northeast of Rte 12, such as the **British Cemetery** and the **Ocracoke Preservation Museum** *(ocracokepreservation.org; free)*. Southwest of Rte 12, the tour 'Down Point' includes the **Ocracoke Lighthouse** and grand **Berkley Manor**, built by inventor, industrialist and local icon Sam Jones. Packed with anecdotes and quirky characters, the tours offer fascinating insights into Ocracoke history, culture and island life. Both tours start at the Village Craftsmen *(villagecraftsmen.com)*.

A well-groomed (but poorly marked) half-mile trail traverses **Springer's Point Preserve** *(coastallandtrust.org)*, a lush and scenic area of maritime forest, salt marsh and sandy beach. Look for the side-by-side graves of the former property owner, the aforementioned Sam Jones, and his beloved horse Ikey D. The route ends at the waterfront, where herons, egrets and ibises nest nearby.

Searching for the Lost Colony

In the 1580s – more than two decades before Jamestown – English settlers came to Roanoke Island to establish the first British colony in the Americas. The first English-American baby, Virginia Dare, was born in 1587. The site of this settlement is part of the **Fort Raleigh National Historic Site** *(nps.gov/fora)*. Unfortunately, the colony struggled from the get-go, and the governor had to return to England for supplies. By the time he made it back, his 116 compatriots had disappeared, almost without a trace. The fate of the 'Lost Colony' remains one of the United State's greatest mysteries.

Exhibits at the visitor center delve into the settlement's backstory and the theories behind its disappearance. Nearby are the remains of the earthen fort that was constructed by colonists in 1585. The next stop in your 'Lost Colony' experience is **Roanoke Island Festival Park** *(roanokeisland.com; adult/child $11/8)*, an indoor-outdoor living history museum on the Manteo waterfront. Back at Fort Raleigh,

FREEDMEN'S COLONY

Mike Anderson is an interpretive park ranger at Fort Raleigh National Historic Site *@fortraleighnps*

While Fort Raleigh National Historic Site is best known for the 16th-century Lost Colony, my favorite piece of the park's history is the 19th-century Freedmen's Colony, which was a safe haven for thousands of freedom-seekers during the Civil War. The goal of the Freedmen's Colony was to help formerly enslaved people claim their rights, by reuniting families, providing education, creating jobs and giving opportunities for property ownership. This story sheds light on the role of Roanoke Island in the struggle for freedom from slavery. Visitors can learn more by participating in a ranger program, exploring the exhibits at the visitor center or walking the Freedom Trail.

BEST HIKES IN THE OUTER BANKS

Nags Head Woods Preserve: Eight trails cross the maritime forest, thick with ancient oaks, hickories and birch.

Kitty Hawk Woods: Nearly 2000 acres of maritime forest, swamp and freshwater wetlands, rich with bird and animal life.

Dogwood Trail: A 5-mile paved path loops around Duck Woods Country Club, alongside a picturesque creek in Southern Shores.

Currituck Banks Maritime Forest Trail: A 1-mile trail snakes through salt marsh and maritime forest, ending at Currituck Sound. Lovely for sunsets.

Freedom Trail: This 1.3-mile route connects Fort Raleigh to Croatan Sound, with signposts detailing the history of the Freedmen's Colony.

the highlight of Manteo's historical experiences is surely the Tony-winning play the **Lost Colony** (thelostcolony.org; adult/child from $25/12; late May-Aug), performed at the outdoor theater. This extravagant musical dramatization features Native American dance, Elizabethan costumes and epic battle scenes.

Flounder and dunes on Nags Head

Many a fisher has been known to while away a summer day (or a summer) waiting for a bite at **Jenette's Pier** (jennettespier. net; adult/child fishing $14/7, walk-on $2/1, rod rental $12). Anglers of all ages and backgrounds line the rails, nurse cold drinks, cast their lines and share stories about big catches and near misses. It's fun to watch and even more fun to join in. All-inclusive 'family fishing' lessons (adult/child $20/10) are available for first-timers.

Five miles north of the pier, **Jockey's Ridge State Park** (ncparks.gov/jockeys-ridge-state-park) is a vast, desert-like landscape comprising the tallest dune system on the East Coast. Miles of sandy hills roll all the way to Roanoke Sound. Tracks in the Sand is an out-and-back, 1.2-mile trail that traverses the dunes. For a bit more adventure, rent a sandboard from **Kitty Hawk Kites** (kittyhawk.com; $25) and sled down. The steeper the hill, the faster you go. Prepare to get sandy.

Powerful winds mean that kite-flying at Jockey's Ridge is a popular pastime. The summit is also a premier spot to watch the sunset over the sound.

Historic flight from Kitty Hawk

On December 17, 1903, Wilbur and Orville Wright launched the world's first successful airplane flight at Kitty Hawk (now Kill Devil Hills). The 12-second flight is memorialized at the impressive **Wright Brothers National Memorial** (nps.gov/wrbr; adult/child $10/free). The First Flight Boulder marks the takeoff point, with additional markers showing the distances of their four increasingly successful flights that day. The on-site visitor center has a full-size reproduction of the 1903 flyer, as well as excellent exhibits about Wright family life, the brothers' scientific process and their competitors in the race to fly.

Village and equine life in Corolla

The centerpiece of this little village is **Historic Corolla Park** (visitcurrituck.com), a pleasant manicured space dotted with museums and historic buildings, including a

EATING & DRINKING IN THE OUTER BANKS: OUR PICKS

Art's Place: Fab local spot in Kitty Hawk for beers and burgers, plus live music on the outdoor stage. 7am-9pm $$

Kill Devil Grill: In a historic diner car, this casual place serves sophisticated Southern-influenced fare. 11:30am-9pm Tue-Sat $$

Corolla Beer Garden: Tiny wooden shack with a big shady garden and 14 beers on tap, plus occasional live music. 2pm-sunset Apr-Oct

Blue Moon Beach Grill: Not on the beach but still a fabulous stop in Nags Head for seafood and sandwiches. 11:30am-9pm Wed-Mon $$

Whalehead Club

fabulous art-nouveau 'cottage,' dubbed the **Whalehead Club** *(adult/child $7/5)*. A 45-minute audiotour of the house gives insights about the history of the property and shows off its art-nouveau ornamentation. Nearby, the red-brick **Currituck Beach Lighthouse** *(obcinc.org; adult/child $13/free)* still shines its beacon to warn ships away from the barrier islands. You can climb the 220 steps to the top, which offers 360-degree views of sea and sound.

Wild mustangs roam freely on the beaches and dunes north of Corolla. If you don't have a 4WD, **Corolla Outback Adventures** *(corollaoutback.com; $68)* and **Wild Horse Adventure Tours** *(wildhorsetour.com; $65)* offer excursions that bounce you down the beach and over the dunes in the back of an open-air truck in search of the feral creatures.

Charlotte
Museums and galleries galore

North Carolina's largest city, Charlotte has an increasingly big and boisterous arts scene, with once-empty industrial zones now teeming with record stores, galleries, vintage boutiques and concert venues. A single block holds three of the best art spaces, all under the umbrella of the Levine Center for the Arts. The impressive **Mint Museum Uptown** *(mintmuseum.org;*

WILD-HORSE HISTORY

Nobody knows exactly how the wild Spanish mustangs ended up in the Outer Banks, but historians believe they arrived with the first Spanish explorers, as early as 1526. Others theorize that some horses swam ashore from shipwrecks – or were deliberately offloaded as extra weight when ships ran aground on the sandbars. In any case, the so-called Banker horses have flourished on the Outer Banks for hundreds of years, with a peak population of 5000 animals in the early 20th century.

Nowadays, the **Corolla Wild Horse Fund** *(corollawildhorses.com)* manages and protects the herd of about 100 members in Corolla. Visitors can learn more (and meet rescued and rehabilitating horses) at its Betsy Dowdy Equine Center *(10am-2pm Wed Jun-Sep)* in Grandy.

EATING IN CHARLOTTE: OUR PICKS

Mert's Heart & Soul: Homey soul food and Lowcountry cuisine diner. Don't miss the salmon cakes or the shrimp and grits. *11am-8pm* $$

Optimist Hall: Buzzy food hall with global offerings; crispy okra fries at Botiwalla and buns at Bao & Broth are highlights. *7am-9pm* $

Alexander Michael's: In an old blue house, this beloved Uptown tavern has welcoming vibes and comfort food with a twist. *11am-10pm Tue-Sat* $$

Supperland: In a former church, 'Supperland' describes itself as 'Southern steakhouse meets church potluck.' *5-10pm Mon-Thu, to 11pm Fri & Sat, brunch 10:30am-1:30pm Sat & Sun.* $$$

THE GREENSBORO SIT-INS

On February 1, 1960, four Black college students sat down at a whites-only lunch counter at Greensboro's Woolworth's department store. When asked to leave, they refused; they sat until the store closed that night. The next day, more students joined. Soon, hundreds of Black students were participating in what became known as the Greensboro Sit-Ins. These sit-ins quickly spread to other cities in the South, where segregation persisted in stores, restaurants, buses and schools. Sit-ins became boycotts of stores with segregated lunch counters, and owners began losing revenue. By July the Greensboro Woolworth's had taken a major financial hit and agreed to desegregate. Sit-ins as a form of nonviolent protest would continue throughout the Civil Rights movement.

Duke University

adult/child $15/free) has galleries surrounding a four-story atrium. Just across the way is the **Bechtler Museum of Modern Art** *(bechtler.org; adult/child $10/5)*, with a small-but-mighty collection of work by mid-20th-century modernists like Giacometti, Miró and Picasso. A block away is the ochre modernist building of the **Harvey B Gantt Center** *(ganttcenter.org; adult/child $9/7)*, with a small permanent collection and rotating exhibitions of contemporary Black works.

Raft the urban environment

Northwest of Charlotte, on the banks of the Catawba River, the **US National Whitewater Center** *(whitewater.org)* is all about outdoor adventure – especially the kind that gets you extremely wet. The main attraction is the artificial river, where visitors run rapids in kayaks or guided rafts *($59)*. But an all-access day pass *(adult/child $79/69)* will also get you climbing, ziplining, stand-up paddleboarding, doing yoga and more. Reserve your rafting time when you buy tickets, ideally for the first trip of the day – these can fill up.

 EATING IN DURHAM: OUR PICKS

Guglhupf: Crowds pack the patio of this German-style bakery-cafe for schnitzel and *schnecken* (sweet rolls), washed down with pilsner. *8am-8pm Tue-Sat, to 3pm Sun* **$$**

Little Bull: Creative Mexican-American comfort food like *birria* (stewed meat) dumplings and steak with peanut salsa draw raves. *5-10pm Wed-Sun, plus 11am-2:30pm Sun* **$$$**

King's Sandwich Shop: Order at the window and take your chili dog and milkshake to a picnic table at this 82-year-old institution. *11am-4pm Mon-Sat* **$**

Zweli's: Bright cafe in a renovated tobacco warehouse serving Zimbabwean classics like piri piri chicken and greens in peanut-butter sauce. *5-9pm Tue-Thu, 11am-8pm Sun* **$$**

Winston-Salem

Peer back to the 18th century

Members of a German-speaking Protestant sect called the Moravians settled in what's now Winston-Salem in the late 1700s. Today, **Old Salem** *(oldsalem.org; adult/child $30/16)* is a living history museum extending across several blocks south of downtown. It's free to admire the architecture, shop for crafts or buy cookies at the wonderful, wood-fired Winkler Bakery. But you'll have a much richer experience if you pay for access to the on-site museums, houses and workshops, where costumed guides demonstrate Moravian traditions such as gardening, doctoring and gunsmithing.

Greensboro

Pioneers of the Civil Rights

In the Woolworth's building that was the site of the original Greensboro Sit-Ins, the powerful **International Civil Rights Center & Museum** *(sitinmovement.org; self-guided tour $15)* is dedicated to the history and legacy of the USA's Civil Rights movement. You can take a self-guided tour of the permanent exhibit, with pictures, videos and artifacts including the original Woolworth's lunch counter, but spending the extra $5 for the guided tour is well worth it.

Durham

A Day at Duke

In the town of Durham, **Duke University** is one of the country's most prestigious institutions of higher learning, with a splendiferous Gothic-style campus to match. The main attraction for visitors is **Sarah P Duke Gardens** *(gardens.duke.edu; free)*, an expansive 55 acres of koi ponds, terraced flower gardens and magnolia groves. Descend the original terrace where seasonal flowers are planted in luscious tapestries, wander the graceful bridges and stone paths of the Asiatic Garden, and picnic on the wide lawns.

Durham's coolest attraction has to be the **Duke Lemur Center** *(lemur.duke.edu; adult/child $17/12)*, a research and conservation institute that's home to the largest collection of lemurs outside their native Madagascar. Visits are by guided tour only, and must be reserved weeks if not months in advance.

Chapel Hill

College days

Strolling along a brick path through a shady quad surrounded by antebellum buildings: this is the **University of North Carolina** *(unc.edu)*, the US's oldest public university. You can easily spend half a day walking the historic campus, visiting photo hot spots like the Old Well (drinking from it is said to bring straight As), the flower-filled Coker Arboretum, and the Davie Poplar, which was already a century old when UNC was founded in 1793.

THE TRIANGLE

Raleigh, Durham, Chapel Hill: three points on the isosceles triangle that give the region its name. The three cities are deeply interconnected but also have their own identities. **Raleigh** has all the things you'd expect of a state capital: government workers bustling around downtown on their lunch hour, big museums full of kids on field trips, steak houses serving rib eyes to movers and shakers. **Durham** is diverse and progressive, with a downtown of old brick tobacco warehouses now full of restaurants, bars, bookshops and tech-company offices. College town **Chapel Hill** has long been nicknamed 'The Southern Part of Heaven,' and in the spring when the dogwoods and cherry trees bloom on campus and the sky is Carolina blue, it's easy to see why.

DOWNTOWN DURHAM ON FOOT

Wander among the stylishly renovated warehouses of this tobacco town turned arty hot spot.

START	END	LENGTH
Brightleaf Sq	Durham Bulls Athletic Park	1.2 miles; 2 hours

Begin at ❶ **Brightleaf Square**, where two historic brick tobacco warehouses are home to restaurants, boutiques and a charming antiquarian bookstore.

Walk southeast down Main St, noting the massive 1948 ❷ **Chesterfield Building**, one of the last cigarette factories to be built in Durham.

After 0.5 miles you'll come to ❸ **Five Points**, where Main St meets Chapel Hill St. Continue past the pretty brick and stone storefronts and restaurants on Main until you reach Corcoran St. Here you'll find the ❹ **21c Hotel**, with edgy public art in an old bank tower designed by the architects of the Empire State Building.

Go north on Corcoran to CCB Plaza, where the iconic bronze ❺ **bull statue** (its official name is *Major*) is the subject of thousands of Instagram posts.

Half a block east on Chapel Hill St is the ❻ **Durham Hotel**, in a mid-century modern bank building.

Turn right on charmingly cobblestoned ❼ **Orange St**, then again on ❽ **Parrish St**, once known as 'Black Wall St' for its many Black-owned banks and businesses in the late 1800s and early 1900s.

Two blocks south, at 201 Pettigrew St, is the splendid Italianate ❾ **Old Bull Building**. Finished in 1874, it's downtown's oldest edifice. Continue south to the restaurant- and shop-filled ❿ **American Tobacco Campus**, across from the beloved ⓫ **Durham Bulls Athletic Park**.

> The *Life is So Beautiful. Life is So Hard* mural in the Brightleaf Sq parking lot is a quote from author and Duke professor Kate Bowler.

> The Five Points area has some of Durham's best restaurants, from Italian to tapas to fried chicken and waffles.

> On the American Tobacco Campus, the iconic Lucky Strike water tower has presided over downtown since the 1930s.

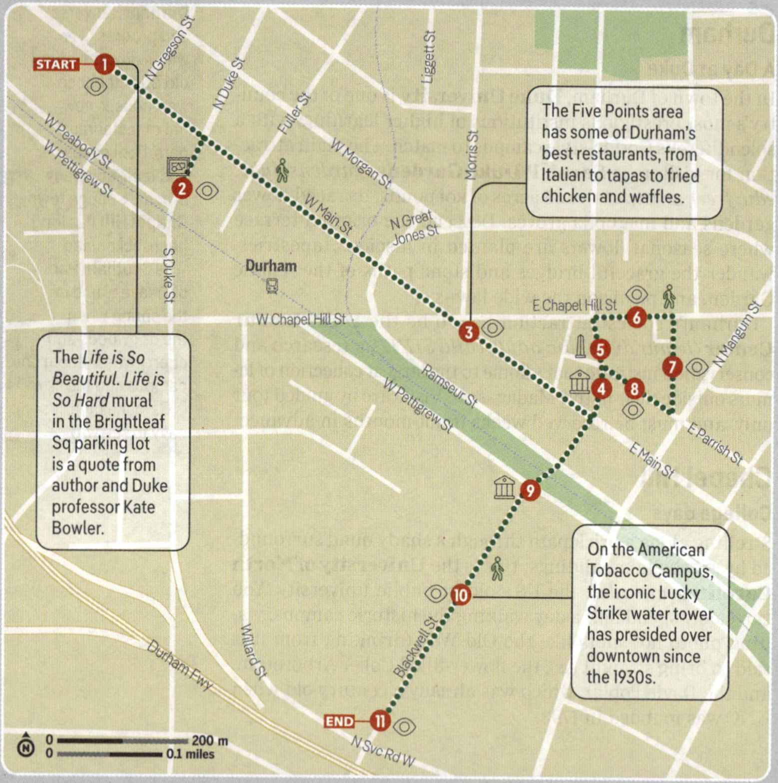

Carrboro
NC's most charming small town

Chapel Hill's little sister, Carrboro, is a former mill town turned progressive paradise. It's adjacent to Chapel Hill – get there by walking west on Franklin St. Once called West End, it was long the working-class neighbor to the wealthier college town next door. But things have changed. Today the old mill is Carr Mill Mall, whose co-op grocery, the **Weaver Street Market**, is the spiritual center of town, with locals eating and dancing on the lawn all day. Other major attractions of Carrboro include the **farmers market**, which draws crowds on Saturday mornings and Wednesday afternoons, the many coffee shops and bars, and the two-day Carrboro Music Festival, with some 100 bands playing at venues around town in early fall.

Saxapahaw
Explore a mill village

On the Haw River west of Chapel Hill, the village of Saxapahaw was a cotton mill town until the 1990s, when it was largely abandoned. It's been redeveloped now, and is a popular weekend destination for lunch and river activities like stand-up paddleboarding. Draws include the **Haw River Ballroom**, a music venue with a riverside deck in the mill's old dye room; the biscuits at **Saxapahaw General Store**, a laid-back gourmet cafe in an old gas station; and the trails and whale-shaped slide at **Saxapahaw Island Park**.

Asheville
Artists and artisans

The North Carolina Mountains have deep craft-making traditions. See the imagination on full display by heading to the galleries and collectives of Asheville. Occupying a prime position on Pack Sq and Biltmore Ave, the **Asheville Art Museum** *(ashevilleart.org; adult/child $20/10)* has a stellar collection of 20th- and 21st-century American art, with a focus on the Southeast.

Nearby, the **Noir Collective** *(noircollectiveavl.com)* is a pillar of the historic Black business district, and a great place to discover emerging and established artists, artisans and designers from Asheville's Black community. You'll find paintings, graphic T-shirts, jewelry and incense, as well as books.

BEST LIVE MUSIC SPOTS IN ASHEVILLE

Orange Peel: A showcase for big-name indie bands since 2002. Seats a thousand-strong crowd.

Asheville Music Hall: Upstairs is AMH; One Stop is downstairs. Diverse sounds from funk, reggae and jazz to rock tribute bands.

Grey Eagle: All-ages club that's a great place to catch rising and established stars playing bluegrass, rockabilly, folk and blues.

Jack of the Wood Pub: Welcoming tavern with a small stage where you can catch Irish folk and Appalachian music jams.

Highland Brewing Co: A 10-minute drive from downtown, Asheville's largest independent brewery hosts mountain music and other sounds.

 EATING & DRINKING IN ASHEVILLE: OUR PICKS

| **Huli Sue's:** Perfect barbecue stars in smokehouse salads and pulled-pork sandwiches. Also blackened-fish tacos, poke bowls and tropical cocktails. hours vary *hours vary* **$$** | **Chai Pani:** Like a colorful Bollywood film, with small plates perfect for sharing; try the okra fries or kale *pakoras* (fritters). *11am-3pm & 5-9pm* **$$** | **Cúrate:** Convivial hangout celebrating the elegant simplicity of Spanish tapas, with an occasional Southern twist. *4-10:30pm Tue-Thu, from 11am Fri-Sun* **$$$** | **Battery Park Book Exchange & Champagne Bar:** Raise a glass in Asheville's most atmospheric drinking den. *hours vary* |

> ### BLACK CULTURE IN ASHEVILLE
>
>
>
> **Alexandria Ravenel**, co-founder of Noir Collective (p333), shares insight on the heritage of Black Asheville *@noir collectiveavl*
>
> The YMI Cultural Center has been here for over 130 years, and it sits central to what is now called the historic Black business district. Before my time there were a lot of Black-owned businesses on South Market St and Eagle St. YMI was at the heart of all that activity, and it still plays a vital role in what's sometimes called 'the Block.' It offers extensive programming on workforce development and housing opportunities, with space for youth projects. With a beautiful gallery space and a state-of-the-art ballroom, YMI also does a great job in keeping the culture going strong in Black Asheville, with lecture series, town halls and jazz nights.

Some of the old buildings of downtown now hold galleries. At the **Woolworth Walk**, you can browse works by dozens of creators in a 1938 Woolworth store.

Badly affected by flooding from Hurricane Helene in 2024, the **River Arts District** *(RAD; riverartsdistrict.com)* nevertheless continues to play a vital role in the city's creative community. Start the journey through RAD at the **Odyssey Gallery of Ceramic Arts** *(odysseygalleryofceramicarts.com)*, which features the wide-ranging work of nearly two dozen artists.

Beer City USA

A walk through the South Slope Brewing District is an easy introduction to 'Beer City USA' – an apt nickname for a metropolitan area with more than 50 breweries and cideries catering to a population of just 95,000. The massive **Wicked Weed** *(wickedweedbrewing.com)* mothership, with over two dozen taps, is a stalwart of Biltmore Ave. Never mind the menacing logo at **Burial** *(burialbeer.com)*: this friendly joint whips up some of Asheville's finest and most experimental Belgian-leaning styles. Step inside the multistory **Green Man** *(greenman brewery.com)* for English-style ales. Its original Dirty Jack's taproom has a scruffy, everybody's-welcome appeal; it's also a favorite of soccer fans.

Beyond the city limits you'll find some appealing options. Some 18 miles south of Asheville, **Sierra Nevada** *(sierranevada.com/visit/mills-river)* is a massive brewery from the California-based icon with great food, 23 taps, daily tours, a patio and live music on weekend afternoons from 2pm to 5pm.

America's grandest mansion

The largest privately owned home in the US, Biltmore House was completed in 1895 for shipping and railroad heir George Washington Vanderbilt II, and modeled after a French Renaissance–style chateau. **Biltmore** *(biltmore.com; adult/child from $85/50)* is extraordinarily expensive to visit, but you could spend the better part of a day exploring this 8000-acre estate with its dazzling art-filled house (which you'll see on a self-guided tour), gardens and satellite areas including the farmyard and winery, plus 22 miles of hiking trails. Buy your tickets in advance, and arrive right at opening time to make the most of the experience. You can also eat at the Biltmore: there are numerous options around the estate, from casual cafes and bustling taverns to decadent, multicourse meals at the Dining Room.

 EATING & DRINKING IN BREVARD: OUR PICKS

Square Root: Award winner with a creative menu including local mountain trout, cedar plank salmon and wok-fried brussels sprouts. *11am-9pm Tue-Sat* **$$$**

Oskar Blues: Wide variety of brews (and food-truck burgers) on a spacious covered patio, plus live music weekends. *noon-8pm Sun-Thu, to 9pm Fri & Sat* **$**

185 King Street: Proudly calls itself 'Brevard's Backyard,' with outdoor seating, craft beers and live music. *4-9pm Tue-Fri, noon-9pm Sat & Sun* **$**

Wood & Vine: Atmospheric spot for innovative wines, plus oysters, wood-fired pizzas and truffle ravioli. *4:30-8pm Tue-Sat* **$$**

Biltmore

Blowing Rock
Forested beauty

The stately and idyllic mountain village of Blowing Rock makes a scenic base for exploring North Carolina's forests and mountains – among the tallest in the Eastern USA. Just a few minutes' walk from Main St, the **Glen Burney Falls Trail** takes you past a series of waterfalls, where you can admire the silvery streams pouring over slick smooth boulders amid birdsong and rhododendron.

The highest of the Blue Ridge Mountains, **Grandfather Mountain** *(grandfather.com; adult/child from $25/10)* is famous for the Mile High Swinging Bridge (though a mile above sea level, the bridge stretches just 80ft above a chasm). There's also a nature center with rescued wildlife, and plenty of walks. The challenging Grandfather Trail to Calloway Peak (2.4 miles one way) takes you scrambling up ladders and holding on to cables as you ascend steep slopes.

If you're just here to hike, you can head instead to **Grandfather Mountain State Park** *(ncparks.gov; free)*. Access its 13 miles of wilderness trails at Mile 300 on the Blue Ridge Pkwy.

READING THE NORTH CAROLINA MOUNTAINS

Cold Mountain: (Charles Frazier; 1997) Adventure, savagery and heartache as a soldier journeys home during the Civil War.

The Caretaker: (Ron Rash; 2023) Friendship, love, betrayal and the legacy of war in 1950s Blowing Rock.

Even As We Breathe: (Annette Saunooke Clapsaddle; 2020) Set in the 1940s and focused on a young Cherokee man on a journey of discovery.

When These Mountains Burn: (David Joy; 2020) Masterfully told tale of addiction and redemption against the devastating fires of 2016.

Big Lies in a Small Town: (Diane Chamberlain; 2020) Mystery and murder in a small NC town; narrated by two women born in different times.

Brevard
Hiking, biking and gallery-hopping

It's easy to fall for Brevard, a charming little mountain town with a downtown full of indie shops, craft breweries, cafes and wine bars. Take in the art scene at the **Lucy Clark Gallery** *(lucyclarkgallery.com)*, with works in fabric, metal, textiles and ceramics by 45 artists.

Serious mountain bikers give high marks to the 86 miles of trails in **DuPont State Forest**, a 10,000-acre reserve located about 11 miles southeast

DRIVING THE BLUE RIDGE

The scenic **Blue Ridge Parkway** (p300) winds its way past overlooks and hiking trails for 469 miles in North Carolina and Virginia. Sections of the NC side were badly damaged by Hurricane Helene in 2024. Check road closures on nps.gov/blri.

SEQUOYAH'S SYLLABARY

Although he could neither read nor speak English, Sequoyah (1770–1843) became obsessed with the 'talking leaves' (words on paper) and felt they were somehow key to white settlers' power. After working assiduously for nearly a decade, he invented a writing system for the Cherokee language, which he unveiled in 1821. Consisting of 86 characters, the Cherokee Syllabary became widely adopted by the tribe within a decade. Literacy spread quickly, and five years after the appearance of the syllabary, thousands of Cherokee could read and write – far surpassing the literacy rates of the white settlers around them. Sequoyah became something of a folk hero for the Cherokee, and his achievement is astonishing: it's the only recorded instance of one person singlehandedly creating a system of writing.

---

of Brevard. Rent bikes and enjoy a post-ride craft brew at the **Hub** *(thehubpisgah.com)*.

For more great outdoor experiences, head to **Pisgah National Forest**. Pick up maps at the Pisgah Visitor Center, a 10-minute drive from Brevard, then take a hike. Among many options, the trail to **Looking Glass Rock** is a strenuous, mostly uphill journey (around 6 miles round trip) to a sweeping panorama over the Blue Ridge Mountains. Afterwards, cool off by zipping down **Sliding Rock** *($5)*, a natural 60ft slide of smooth, gently sloping granite into an 8ft deep pool at the bottom.

Cherokee
Vibrant native community

North Carolina's westernmost tip is blanketed in parkland, sprinkled with tiny mountain towns and rich in Native American history. At the **Museum of the Cherokee People** *(motcp.org; adult/child $15/8)*, you can learn about Cherokee history and see works by living Cherokee artists and craft makers. Across the street, **Qualla Arts & Crafts** *(quallaartsandcrafts.org)* sells high-quality baskets, beadwork, wooden carvings, copper jewelry, pottery, finger weavings and paintings. There's also a small gallery displaying the work of legendary makers of the past.

Run by the nonprofit Cherokee Historical Association, the **Oconaluftee Indian Village** *(cherokeehistorical.org/oconaluftee-indian-village; adult/child $25/15)* transports visitors back to the 1700s in a recreated settlement. Cherokee guides will take you through the open-air space, stopping at various stations where you can learn about tribal craft traditions, hunting and weapon-making.

Bryson City
Taking a scenic train ride

The **Great Smoky Mountains Railroad** *(gsmr.com)* chugs from Bryson City out into the wilderness on one of two memorable train trips *(from $65)*, each lasting around four hours. Special seasonal excursions are offered throughout the year, including a holiday-themed Polar Express from early November through December.

Rafting and other adventures

A true crossroads for adventure, the **Nantahala Outdoor Center** *(noc.com)* specializes in wet and wild rafting trips down the Nantahala River. The center's 500-acre main campus also offers ziplining and mountain biking, and it has its own lodging and dining options. The standard, three-hour guided trip **($70)** sweeps eight-person groups on yellow rafts through the dramatic Nantahala Gorge. The scenery is superb, with dense forest lining both banks of the broad, ever-frothing river.

Mountain Farm Museum

TOP EXPERIENCE

Great Smoky Mountains National Park

The Smokies are a magical place to reconnect with nature. Days here are spent hiking past shimmering waterfalls and picnicking beside boulder-filled mountain streams, followed by evenings watching fireflies on the move. Lofty summits offer mesmerizing viewpoints over the rolling mountains, while the dense forests and open valleys create memorable opportunities for spotting elk, black bears and numerous bird species.

DON'T MISS
Oconaluftee Visitor Center
Mountain Farm Museum
Charlies Bunion
Alum Cave Trail
Kuwohi
Roaring Fork Motor Nature Trail
Rainbow Falls
Cades Cove Loop

Gateway to the Southern Smokies

Just 2 miles north of Cherokee, NC, the inviting, modern **Oconaluftee Visitor Center** straddles a vast open meadow by the Oconaluftee River. Inside, interpretive displays inform visitors about the area's attractions, and volunteer staff give suggestions about hikes and present talks on wildlife.

Out back, the open-air **Mountain Farm Museum** (*free*) is a recreation of a Great Smokies farmstead, providing a glimpse into the everyday lives of hardworking mountain people in the 19th and early 20th centuries. The field beyond the fence is a prime grazing spot for elk – come early or late in the day to spot them.

PRACTICALITIES
- nps.gov/grsm
- admission (parking pass) $5/15 per day/week
- 24hr

OVERNIGHT HIKES

There are scores of options for overnight hikes in the Smokies, including the granddaddy of backpacking trips, the Appalachian Trail. There are few dedicated loop routes in the Smoky Mountains, though the many intersecting trails allow you to plan a loop without having to end far from your starting point. A backcountry permit and campsite reservation are required for all backcountry stays in the park *(nps.gov/grsm/planyourvisit/backcountry-camping.htm)*.

RETURN OF THE ELK

Before European settlement, an estimated 10 million elk ranged across the future United State, including southern Appalachia. By the mid-1800s the region's elk were wiped out by habitat loss and overhunting. In 2001 after years of study and planning, the park reintroduced a small herd of elk to the Smokies. Today the population numbers around 300, and they range throughout the park; look for them in the Oconaluftee Valley.

Alum Cave Trail

Horseback Rides & Wagon Trips

Smokemont Riding Stables *(smokemontridingstable.com)* offers two different rides. On the one-hour River Crossing Trail *($50)*, you will indeed get to splash through the water during a scenic 3-mile loop. The 2½-hour Waterfall and Riverside Trail *($125)* visits Chasteen Creek Cascade. Smokemont also offers a 40-minute wagon ride *($30)*. Reserve ahead.

Hiking to Charlies Bunion

For a taste of the US' oldest long-distance trail, make the journey to **Charlies Bunion**, which offers a stunning panorama over a vast swath of the Smokies. From **Newfound Gap**, this 8-mile out-and-back jaunt follows the Appalachian Trail along the North Carolina–Tennessee border before reaching an outcropping with an awe-inspiring overlook.

Ascent to Alum Cave

The 4.6-mile (out-and-back) **Alum Cave Trail** is one of the Smokies' most popular, thanks to its scenic beauty and variety. A few steps off the busy main road you'll find yourself in a gorgeous green forest where canopies of rhododendrons overhang the rushing waters of Walker Camp Prong. The path's wide and flat first mile offers a delightful stroll with minimal exertion. At 1.4 miles the route crosses a log bridge and spirals up through Arch Rock, a photogenic cleft navigated by graceful stone steps. From here a more pronounced climb, punctuated by breathtaking views of the valley below, leads to Alum Cave (2.3 miles), a dramatic overhang of sandy-hued stone that contrasts fetchingly with the surrounding forest and serves as a convenient umbrella during rainstorms. Most people retrace their steps from here, but you can continue

2.7 miles further on the steep trail toward the summit. The views just keep getting better, while strategically placed cables serve as handholds for navigating slippery stretches of rock underfoot. At trail's end (5 miles), turn right on the Rainbow Falls Trail to reach LeConte Lodge, Mt LeConte's summit and a pair of classic viewpoints: Cliff Tops and Myrtle Point.

Overnighting on the Mountain

Spending the night in the **LeConte Lodge** is a bucket-list goal for many in-the-know Smokies visitors. The rustic cabins clustered at 6400ft above sea level offer the national park's only indoor accommodation. While amenities are generally simple – bunk beds, kerosene lamps, front-porch rockers, a washbasin and a shared outhouse – the effort of getting here makes it all the sweeter. The only way in is on foot, tackling one of several steep trails – none less than 5 miles – to reach your accommodation.

Reservations are awarded by lottery. In September the lodge accepts reservation requests (via *lecontelodge.com/reservations*) for the following season (March through November), with winners notified on October 1. Lodging and meals per person costs $190 ($104 for children).

Greet the Dawn at Kuwohi

At 6643ft, **Kuwohi** (formerly known as Clingmans Dome) is the highest point in Great Smoky Mountains National Park. In 1959 the National Park Service added a space-age viewing platform near the summit, which affords 360-degree views of the Smokies' grandeur. A magical time to visit is in the early morning on a clear day, when the sun crests the mountains' eastern slopes and mists hang in the valleys below. You'll also enjoy the experience without the sizable crowds that come

GHOST TOWN IN THE FOREST

From 1910 until the creation of the park in 1934, Elkmont saw the rise of small vacation homes, complete with large porches, bold colors and plenty of natural wood details. Today you can experience a remnant of the whimsical world created a century ago with a visit to **Daisy Town** (aka Elkmont Historic District), a painstakingly restored cluster of structures near the Elkmont Campground. Afterwards, continue uphill and onto the **Jakes Creek Trail** to see more ghostly ruins, including solitary chimneys, moss-covered steps and low stone walls, as well as one restored two-story house you can enter.

Kuwohi

TOP TIPS

- Gatlinburg (Tennessee) and Cherokee (North Carolina) are the closest towns to the park, and good places to arrange last-minute lodging.

- There are no restaurants in the park so be sure to pack a picnic.

- Arrive early in the morning at popular trailheads (like Alum Cave). Parking lots can fill up by 8am, leaving you out of luck. Alternatively, book a ride on a shuttle with **A Walk in the Woods** *(awalkinthewoods.com)* from Gatlinburg.

- The best way to travel the 11-mile Cades Cove loop is by bicycle on vehicle-free Wednesdays (mid-June to September). You can rent bikes on site.

later in the day. Kuwohi is reached from Newfound Gap via a 7-mile spur road. From the parking lot it's a taxing half-mile climb (up a paved trail) to the viewing platform, with an elevation gain of 300ft.

The Climb to Ramsey Cascades

For those with the stamina to tackle it, the beautiful climb to **Ramsey Cascades**, the park's highest waterfall, is one of the Smokies' most rewarding hikes. Ascending 2280ft over 4 miles, the Ramsey Cascades Trail starts in the remote Greenbrier section of the park, 11 miles east of Gatlinburg via the mostly unpaved Greenbrier and Ramsey Prong Rds. Along the way, you'll pass through old-growth forest with some massive tulip trees.

Driving the Roaring Fork Motor Nature Trail

The Roaring Fork area is named for one of the park's biggest and most powerful mountain streams and is well loved for its waterfalls, glimpses of old-growth forest and excellent selection of preserved cabins, gristmills and other historic structures. The one-way 5.5-mile **Roaring Fork Motor Nature Trail** begins and ends a short distance from downtown Gatlinburg.

A worthwhile add-on is the hike to **Rainbow Falls**, one of the park's most dramatic – and one sure to give you a good workout. From the trailhead, it's a 2.8-mile uphill trek with 1600ft of elevation gain. Your reward is one of the Smokies' highest waterfalls, cascading 90ft down a cliff immersed in forest. The fine stone-slab bridge over LeConte Creek makes for a delightful place to soak up the view.

Other fine routes here include the walk to **Grotto Falls**, most easily accessed via a 1.4-mile section of the **Trillium Gap Trail**. Beyond the beauty of the falls themselves, this outing offers two unique features: the chance to walk behind the 25ft cascades (a classic Smokies photo op) and the rare opportunity to cross paths with llamas carrying supplies to and from LeConte Lodge. Llamas travel the Trillium Gap Trail on Monday, Wednesday and Friday.

Time Travel on Cades Cove Loop

Thanks to its history, wildlife and pastoral scenery, the 11-mile **Cades Cove Loop** has become one of the Smokies' most sought-after tourist destinations. Alas, its popularity all too often translates into traffic congestion. To fully appreciate Cades Cove's majesty without the crowds, set off at dawn or in the late afternoon.

The one-way road encircles land used as a hunting ground by the Cherokee before English, Scots-Irish and German settlers arrived in the 1820s. These determined newcomers built cabins and churches while clearing the valley's trees for farmland. Mills, forges and blacksmith shops soon followed, creating a thriving community. Today the creaky cabins, mossy spring houses, weathered barns and tidy cemeteries whisper the stories of the families who made this place their home.

South Carolina

CULTURE & HISTORY | GOLDEN BEACHES | SOUTHERN CHARM

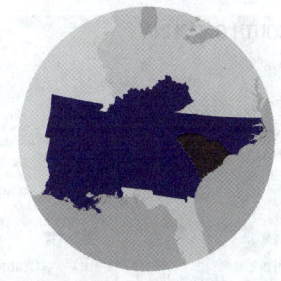

There's a reason South Carolina ranks among the country's fastest-growing states. Yes, affordable housing and the low cost of living are factors, but the state's natural beauty and welcoming vibes surely play a part too. Most travelers begin along the Lowcountry coast, home to splendid historic cities such as Beaufort and Charleston as well as wide sandy beaches studded with dunes and palms. Along the barrier islands you can immerse yourself in Gullah culture, its language and stories created by the formerly enslaved, who held onto West African traditions through centuries of hardship.

Innovative cities including Greenville and Columbia are hubs of culinary and cultural expression in the state's interior. Museums, plantations and galleries in these destinations and along the coast are re-examining the state's past and sharing more comprehensive accounts. There's also plentiful scope for outdoor adventure amid landscapes ranging from rugged state parks in the mountains to spooky blackwater swamps to sun-kissed salt marshes.

Places

Charleston p342
Beaufort p348
St Helena & Hunting Islands p348
Myrtle Beach p349
Columbia p350
Greenville p350
Congaree National Park p352

☑ TOP TIP

Dress up like greenskeeper Carl Spackler and jump into the ocean on January 1 during the Bill Murray Look-a-Like Polar Plunge on Folly Beach. This subzero swim pays homage to Charleston's most distinguished resident, Bill Murray, with participants attempting to resemble him in various roles.

 GETTING AROUND

Driving your own vehicle is the best way to explore the state, though if you're just stopping through Charleston, you can explore its compact and pedestrian-friendly downtown on foot.

Amtrak (amtrak.com) runs through South Carolina on four routes. The *Silver Meteor* links NYC and Miami, with stops in Florence, Charleston and Savannah, GA. The *Palmetto* connects Charleston with New York City and Savannah. The *Silver Star* stops in Columbia, while the *Crescent* links Greenville and Clemson.

Greyhound (greyhound.com) has stations in Charleston, Columbia, Florence, Georgetown, Greenville and Myrtle Beach. Megabus (us. megabus.com) stops in Florence and Columbia.

Charleston

MAP P343

Step back in time

Cobblestone streets, hidden alleyways and photogenic homes straight from the 1800s set the stage for rewarding exploring in Charleston, one of the South's most fascinating cities.

The **Charleston Museum** (*charlestonmuseum.org; adult/teen/child $15/12/6*) may be the oldest museum in the country – it opened in 1773 – but it certainly isn't stuffy. Exhibits spotlight various periods of the city's long and storied past. Artifacts include a whale skeleton, tags worn by the enslaved and the 'secession table' used for the signing of the state's secession documents before the Civil War.

EATING IN CHARLESTON: SOUTHERN FARE

MAP P343

Marina Variety Store: A long-standing, down-home kinda place, with harbor views and Southern hospitality as warm as the buttermilk biscuits. *7am-9pm Wed-Sat, to 2pm Sun* $

Poogan's Porch: The homemade buttermilk biscuits are out of control and the chicken and waffles are second to none. Boozy brunchers have plenty of options. *9am-3pm & 4:30-9:30pm* $$

Slightly North of Broad: Lowcountry comfort dishes reinvented with flair. Try the peach salad with prosciutto, goat cheese and pecans. *11am-2:30pm & 5-10pm* $$$

FIG: Foodie favorite known for welcoming staff, efficient but unrushed service and sustainably sourced nouvelle Southern fare. *5-10:30pm Tue-Sat* $$$

Charleston

- **HIGHLIGHTS**
  1. Old Slave Mart Museum
- **SIGHTS**
  2. Aiken-Rhett House
  3. Charleston Museum
  4. International African American Museum
  5. Marion Square
- **ACTIVITIES**
  6. Gateway Walk
- **SLEEPING**
  7. Andrew Pinkney Inn
- **EATING**
  8. Chez Nous
  9. FIG
  10. Marina Variety Store
  11. Poogan's Porch
  12. Slightly North of Broad
  13. Ordinary
- **DRINKING & NIGHTLIFE**
  14. Bin 152
  15. Blind Tiger
  16. Citrus Club
  17. Fiat Lux
  18. Henry's on the Market
  19. Palmetto Lobby Bar
  20. Pavilion Bar
  21. Prohibition
  22. Rooftop at the Vendue
- **SHOPPING**
  23. Charleston City Market
- **INFORMATION**
  24. Fort Sumter Visitor Education Center at Liberty Square

With its grand homes and manicured gardens, Charleston is awash in aesthetic charms. But the city owes much of its beauty and success to an economy that was once driven by enslaved labor. On the grounds of an open-air market that auctioned men, women and children, the simple but powerful **Old Slave Mart Museum** (oldslavemart.org; $7) spotlights the day-to-day realities and horrors of the slave trade in the years leading up to the Civil War. It was the largest of 40 or so similar auction houses in the city.

More than 250,000 enslaved Africans entered the United States in Charleston, and many disembarked at Gadsden's

Wharf beside the Cooper River. The wharf is now home to the striking **International African American Museum** (*iaamuseum.org; adult/child $22/10*), which shares the stories of the African American diaspora through interactive exhibits, firsthand recollections, eye-catching artifacts and compelling art. Gullah-Geechee culture is also featured – be sure to step into the recreated Praise House and watch the short film about the uplifting Moving Hall Star Singers, a multigenerational gospel group from Johns Island.

The only surviving urban townhouse complex in the city, the 1820 **Aiken-Rhett House** (*historiccharleston.org; adult/child $15/7*) gives a fascinating glimpse of antebellum life on a 45-minute self-guided audiotour. The Historic Charleston Foundation has conserved but not restored the home, so when you step through the ornate doors of this tangerine-colored mansion, once home to South Carolina governor William Aiken, it feels like time-traveling to 1858. The collection of books, furnishings, art and architectural details, though worn, is largely intact.

Be sure to also take a peek in the **Charleston City Market** (*thecharlestoncitymarket.com*), which stretches four blocks along Meeting St in the French Quarter. It's one of the nation's oldest markets, getting its start in 1804.

Ghosts in the graveyard

If you're a fan of spooky Southern Gothic fiction, welcome to your unhappy place. The **Gateway Walk** is a loose, natural-feeling corridor that ribbons through downtown's hustle and bustle, but the weathered headstones, walled pathways and live oaks are an instant portal to another, quieter time. The silence is occasionally broken by church bells ringing in the distance. Defying the melancholy? Wildflowers deliver bursts of color in spring.

The western entry is on Archdale St at St John's Lutheran Church. If the gate is closed, begin next door at the Unitarian Church. A memorial to the enslaved workers who built the church rises near the entrance. The path winds through the graveyard and its intentionally overgrown foliage and concludes at St Philips Episcopal.

Afterwards, take a breather from the Gothic intensity by heading south to the Battery. A promenade follows along the harbor and offers views of Fort Sumter, while live oaks provide shade for cannons and statues of military heroes in the adjacent garden. Flanked by historic homes and the harbor, the area is a pretty spot to relax.

AFRICAN AMERICAN HERITAGE IN CHARLESTON

For a list of Black-owned restaurants and businesses, pick up the free Explore Black History booklets found around town or visit *exploreblackcharleston.com*. The website has an interactive map, and it shares itineraries that spotlight destinations with connections to Black history. Located 1 mile north of the International African American Museum, **Hannibal's Kitchen** (*hannibalkitchen.com; 11am-8pm Mon-Sat*) serves soul food, including Gullah-Geechee standards such as shrimp-and-crab rice (its signature dish) and collard greens. Opened by family patriarch Robert 'Hannibal' Huger in 1985, the restaurant is now managed by his granddaughters.

EATING IN CHARLESTON: OUR PICKS

MAPS P343 & P346

Edmund's Oast: Charleston's highest-brow brewpub serves Southern faves and a long list of cocktails and draft beers. *11am-10pm $$*

Leon's Oyster Shop: In a converted old body shop reimagined as an industrial-chic eatery, Leon's is a local favorite for oysters, fried chicken and scalloped potatoes. *11am-10pm $$*

Ordinary: Inside a cavernous 1927 bank building, this buzzy seafood hall and oyster bar feels like the best party in town. *5-10:30pm Wed-Mon $$*

Chez Nous: A diminutive restaurant with a short menu of dishes and wines from southern France, northern Italy and northern Spain. *11:30am-3pm & 5-10pm $$*

STROLLING HISTORIC CHARLESTON

Three centuries of history jostles for attention between Broad St and the Battery, which means wandering off course is entirely expected.

START	END	LENGTH
Old Exchange & Provost Dungeon	Four Corners of Law/ St Michael's Church	1.5 miles; 1 hour

Begin at the ❶ **Old Exchange & Provost Dungeon**, where costumed guides lead tours of the dungeon where Stede Bonnet, the Gentleman Pirate, and Revolutionary War prisoners were once held.

Walk south to the pastel beauty of ❷ **Rainbow Row**, a block of redone 1730s merchant stores that inspired the birth of the Preservation Society of Charleston in the 1920s.

Follow Tradd St to Church St and turn right. The ❸ **Heyward-Washington House**, where the first president slumbered in 1791, is on your left.

Head south to East Battery and the ❹ **Edmondston-Alston House**, where tours pass intricate woodwork and family artifacts.

Continue south to approach the ❺ **Battery & White Point Garden**, named for the fortifications that lined the seafront and for the mounds of oyster shells once piled over the point.

Cut through the park and walk north along Meeting St to the ❻ **Williams Mansion**, formerly known as the Calhoun Mansion. Famed for its opulent decor, this Gilded Age manor is Charleston's largest single-family residence.

Continuing north, the ❼ **Nathaniel Russell House** appears on the left. You can see its free-flying spiral staircase on a tour.

At the ❽ **Four Corners of Law**, notice St Michael's Church, representing God's law, on the southeastern corner.

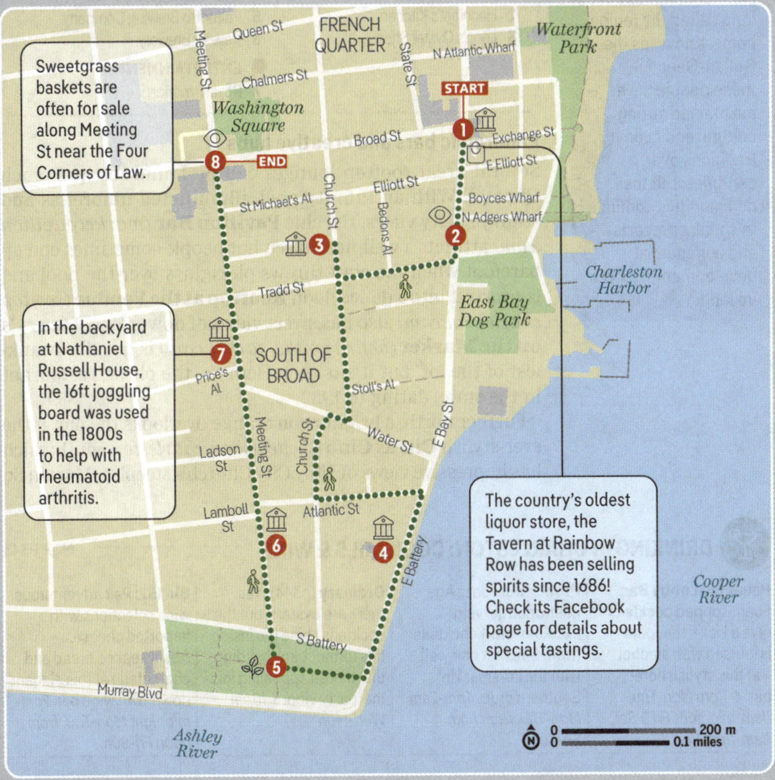

Sweetgrass baskets are often for sale along Meeting St near the Four Corners of Law.

In the backyard at Nathaniel Russell House, the 16ft joggling board was used in the 1800s to help with rheumatoid arthritis.

The country's oldest liquor store, the Tavern at Rainbow Row has been selling spirits since 1686! Check its Facebook page for details about special tastings.

345

DEFINING THE LOWCOUNTRY

Much of South Carolina's southeastern coastline, dubbed the Lowcountry, is a patchwork of barrier islands marked by small inlets and salt marshes as well as stretches of shimmery, oyster-gray sand and wild, moss-shrouded maritime forests. Bridges link to some of these islands, but many can be reached only by boat or ferry. Descendants of West African enslaved have long called the region home. Known as the Gullah-Geechee, these people have maintained strong cultural and culinary traditions over centuries, but their communities continue to shrink as resorts and commercial developments gobble up land.

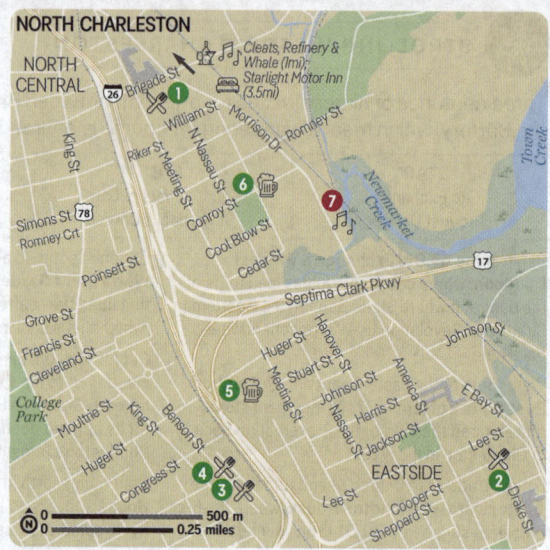

- **EATING**
  1. Edmund's Oast
  2. Hannibal's Kitchen
  3. Leon's Oyster Shop

- **DRINKING & NIGHTLIFE**
  4. Little Jack's Tavern
  5. Palmetto Brewing Company
  6. Revelry Brewery

- **ENTERTAINMENT**
  7. Royal American

Panoramic bars and creative hubs

Several great rooftop lounges can be found in the French Quarter. With an infinity pool, illuminated umbrellas and stunning city views, the chic **Pavilion Bar** (marketpavilion.com) attracts a well-heeled set, but people sometimes end up barefoot when the staff throws plexiglass over the pool and converts it into a dance floor. **Rooftop at the Vendue** (rooftopcharleston.com) also has sweet views of downtown. **Henry's on the Market** (henrysonthemarket.com) is not the swankiest of the lot, but it sits atop Henry's, the oldest restaurant in the state, dating to 1932.

Further north, a bright neon orange overlooks the bar at the ever-stylish **Citrus Club** (thedewberrycharleston.com), which has impressive views of Holy City Church's steeples, Marion Sq

DRINKING IN CHARLESTON: COCKTAILS & WINE — MAP P343

Palmetto Lobby Bar: Foam-topped cocktails give a kick – the foam is infused with alcohol – at this stylish hotel bar. *4-11pm Mon-Thu, 11am-midnight Fri & Sat, 11am-11pm Sun*

Prohibition: Jazz Age gastropub serving excellent craft cocktails (from $16) that pair well with the lip-smackin' Southern grub. *4pm-2am Mon-Thu, from 11am Fri-Sun*

Ordinary (p344): Yes, there are oysters, but the cocktails shine too inside this former bank building that has an appealing join-the-party vibe. *5-10pm Wed-Mon*

Bin 152: Pair adventurous wine selections with imported cheese, freshly baked bread and charcuterie at this elegant downtown wine bar. *2pm-midnight Mon-Thu, from noon Fri-Sun*

and the Ravenel Bridge from its perch atop the Dewberry. Around the corner, admire the artwork in the Hotel Bennett's lobby before gliding up to **Fiat Lux** *(hotelbennett.com),* where you'll enjoy views of **Marion Square** with your cocktails.

A few miles further north, the **Refinery** *(therefinerychs.com)* is a special place to watch live music. Check for upcoming shows at this 2000-person outdoor venue beside the railroad tracks in North Charleston. Other tenants in this creativity hub include the **Whale**, a bar with a lengthy craft-beer list, and the sports bar **Cleats**.

An infamous fort

Grab a seat on the upper deck for the boat ride across Charleston Harbor to **Fort Sumter** *(nps.gov/fosu; free),* where the first shots of the Civil War were fired. Upon arrival you'll disembark the ferry and walk to the fort. Travelers on the first ferry of the day may be asked to help raise the US flag, while those on the last may be asked to lower it. National park rangers and docents are available to answer questions and share information about the history of the site and its role in the Civil War. Buy tickets *(fortsumtertours.com; adult/child $40/26)* ahead of your visit to avoid missing out. Expect to spend about 2¼ hours total on your trip, including the ferry rides. Boats depart from both Liberty Square (in downtown Charleston) and Patriots Point.

Before hopping on the ferry, stop by the **Fort Sumter Visitor Education Center at Liberty Square** *(free)* to see exhibits about the roots of the conflict that led to South Carolina's secession, the Civil War and the war's aftermath.

Reachable by car, **Fort Moultrie** *(nps.gov/fosu; adult/child $10/free)* offers a deeper dive into the region's coastal defense systems, as its exhibits and structures span nearly 200 years. Across the street from the fort, the visitor center has an information desk staffed by park rangers, along with a theater, a museum and a bookstore.

Kayaking the coast

Numerous companies lead tours and boat trips through the marshes and along the coasts of Charleston County's sea islands. **Adventure Harbor Tours** *(adventureharbourtours.com)* runs harbor cruises, sunset excursions and fun trips to uninhabited Morris Island – great for shelling. Trips leave from the marina at Ashley Point in Charleston. Well-established **Coastal Expeditions** *(coastalexpeditions.com; kayak tour*

CHARLESTON'S LIVE-MUSIC VENUES

Liv Brownstein, Charleston musician and College of Charleston student, shares her favorite music venues.

At Folly Beach, **Chico Feo** is a relaxed kind of place. The tacos are really good. On Monday it has an open-mic night where lots of bands or solo people go and play all original music. It's super cute, outdoors and right off the beach.

Every single night there's something happening at **Pour House**. The farmers market on Sunday has live music.

On the way to North Charleston at the top of the peninsula, **Royal American** is an indoor-outdoor venue. It has food and a sit-down area. Lots of different kinds of bands come here and there's a lot of rock music.

🍸 DRINKING IN CHARLESTON: BREWERIES & PUBS

MAPS P343 & P346

Palmetto Brewing Company: The city's first microbrewery (since Prohibition, anyway) produces an amber ale, a pilsner and a couple of IPAs. 4-10pm Mon-Thu, noon-10pm Sat, noon-7pm Sun

Revelry Brewery: Knock back artfully crafted cold ones on the fairy-lit and fire-pit-heated rooftop with Ravenel Bridge views. noon-10pm Mon-Thu, to 11pm Fri & Sat, to 8pm Sun

Blind Tiger: This atmospheric bar seduces with stamped-tin ceilings and good pub grub. Enjoy your cocktail in the expansive courtyard. 4-11pm Mon-Thu, 11am-midnight Fri & Sat, 11am-11pm Sun

Little Jack's Tavern: A classy neighborhood cocktail bar and restaurant, with one helluva hamburger. noon-10pm

BEST SEA ISLANDS NEAR CHARLESTON

Isle of Palms: The 7-mile stretch at Isle of Palms is well suited to families, and there's a playground steps from the beach.

Sullivan's Island: A broad commercial-free swath of sand south of Mount Pleasant. Come here to decompress and avoid the crowds.

Folly Beach: A favorite of locals, this festive spot with good surfing feels most like a beach town (particularly around Center St).

Kiawah: A mostly private island, but visitors can enjoy a family-friendly beach day at **Kiawah Beachwater Park**.

Edisto Beach State Park: A gorgeous, uncrowded beach with oak-shaded hiking trails. Stop for gossip and fried seafood baskets at Whaley's Store

adult/child from $48/38) leads kayak tours through the salt marshes at Shem Creek and along the Kiawah River, where full-moon trips are on the schedule. They also rent kayaks.

Sunsets and nature walks in Mount Pleasant

Mount Pleasant, originally a summer retreat for Charlestonians, sits just north of the Cooper River from Charleston. It has a historic downtown, and some great spots for catching the sunset, including along Shem Creek, where folks drink beer on restaurant patios and soak up views of the creek and Charleston Harbor. You can also stretch your legs and scan for dolphins along the dock-lined **Shem Creek Boardwalk**, which overlooks the marsh. For an easygoing vibe after your walk, settle in with a beer on the deck at **Red's Ice House** *(redsicehouse.com)*.

Beaufort

Learn Reconstruction Era history

The southern half of the South Carolina coast is a tangle of islands cut off from the mainland by inlets and tidal marshes. From 1861 to 1900, Beaufort and the surrounding sea islands became a hub for organization, education and self-determination for the formerly enslaved, who comprised 80% of the local population. Established by Congress in 2019, the **Reconstruction Era National Historical Park** *(nps.gov/reer)* covers the history of this era at three separate sites – all free – near Beaufort. Start at the **Old Beaufort Firehouse Visitor Center** downtown where you'll find a few exhibits as well as details about the other locations and scheduled park programs.

The best way to experience this evolving park is by listening to the stories and history shared by rangers. Check the online calendar for program times.

St Helena & Hunting Islands

Gullah culture and history

St Helena Island, east of Beaufort, has the highest concentration of Gullah people in the state and is the best place to learn about their culture. The **Penn Center** *(penncenter.com; tours $15-20)* has a museum that's a great starting point. Exhibits cover Gullah culture and trace the history of the center.

South Carolina's best seaside state park

The lush and inviting **Hunting Island State Park** *(southcarolinaparks.com/hunting-island; adult/child $8/4)* impresses

EATING IN BEAUFORT: OUR PICKS

Lowcountry Produce: A fantastic market for picnic supplies with an equally appealing cafe. Try an Oooey Gooey, a grilled pimento-cheese sandwich with bacon and garlic-pepper jelly. *11am-2:30pm* $

Blacksheep x Sabbatical: This small wine shop and restaurant serves an eclectic selection of toasts, sips and sandwiches downtown. *11am-6pm Tue-Sat* $

Old Bull Tavern: Delicious food and cocktails amid a low-lit, worldly aesthetic. Menu changes daily but always features playful American and European comfort dishes. *5-9pm Tue-Sat* $$

Ribaut Social Club: Celebrate a special occasion inside a refurbished mansion a short walk from downtown. Seafood dishes shine. *5-7:45pm Tue-Sat* $$$

SkyWheel, Myrtle Beach

with its acres of spooky maritime forest and tidal lagoons. The bone-white beach is littered with seashells and the occasional shark tooth. The Vietnam War scenes from *Forrest Gump* were filmed in the marsh, a nature-lover's dream. Climb the lighthouse *($2)* for coastal views.

Myrtle Beach

Sand and boardwalk fun

Stretching for 60 miles along South Carolina's north coast, Myrtle Beach is famously overdeveloped, but there's plenty of fun to be had if you're willing to embrace the kitsch. Get the lay of the land by taking a spin on the **SkyWheel** *(skywheelmb. com; adult/child $20/16)*, which overlooks the 1.2-mile coastal boardwalk. Get your fill of mini-golf, T-shirt shops and arcade games along the **boardwalk**. When you need a break, enjoy a nature fix at **Myrtle Beach State Park** *(southcarolina parks/myrtle-beach.com; adult/child $8/4)*. Unfurling along an undeveloped mile of coastline 3 miles south of central Myrtle Beach, this park is a pretty destination for walking the two short (half-mile) nature trails through maritime forest. There's also a long pier that's ideal for fishing *(fishing pass for adults/children $8/3)* and rods are available for rental *($25 for the day)*.

A day at Brookgreen Gardens

A true storybook setting, **Brookgreen Gardens** *(brookgreen. org; adult/child $22/12)* in Pawleys Island has the largest collection of American figurative statuary in the United States. Botanical gardens, art galleries, Gullah-Geechee sites and a Lowcountry Zoo are also highlights on the 9100-acre property, founded by Archer and Anna Hyatt Huntington in 1931. Lowcountry classics, including salt marshes, live oaks and longleaf pines, provide the outer-garden backdrop.

FAMILY FUN IN MYRTLE BEACH

Family Kingdom: Old-fashioned amusement-and-water-park combo overlooking the ocean.

Market Common: Vast retail and entertainment hub with disc golf and the wonderful, all-abilities Savannah's Playground for the toddler set.

Broadway at the Beach: Outdoor mall with shops, restaurants, rides, a Ripley's aquarium, a Wonderworks funhouse and a movie theater.

Myrtle Beach Boardwalk & Promenade: Go old school: walk the piers, play arcade games, ride the SkyWheel and eat some ice cream on the 1.2-mile promenade.

Topgolf: Yep, it's a national chain, but this multilevel golf-game outpost offers bays that are cooled or heated year-round.

GULLAH CULTURE

Starting in the 16th century, African people were transported from the so-called Rice Coast (Sierra Leone, Senegal, Gambia and Angola) to a remarkably similar landscape of swampy coastlines and tropical vegetation. These new African Americans were able to retain many of their homeland traditions after the fall of slavery and well into the 20th century. The resulting culture of Gullah (also known as Geechee in Georgia) has its own language, an English-based Creole with many African words and sentence structures, and traditions including storytelling, art, music and crafts. Gullah culture is celebrated during the Original Gullah Festival in Beaufort, while **Gullah-N-Geechie Mahn Tours** (*gullahngeechietours. com*) stop at sites on St Helena Island.

Columbia
River adventures

The Saluda and Broad Rivers merge just northwest of state capital Columbia, joining forces to create the Congaree River. June through August you can inner tube down the Lower Saluda to the Congaree, floating past Riverbanks Zoo. **Palmetto Outdoor** (*palmettooutdoor.com; tube & shuttle $20*) will rent you a tube and shuttle you upriver from the West Columbia Riverwalk & Amphitheater beside the Gervais Bridge. After your float, which runs about three hours, walk to **Savage Craft Ale Works** for a pint and river views from its rooftop.

Greenville
South Carolina's prettiest town center

In photogenic Greenville, the Reedy River twists through the city center, and its dramatic falls tumble beneath the sleek Liberty Bridge at Falls Park. Downtown Main St rolls past a lively array of indie shops, great restaurants and craft-beer pubs. Public art on Main honors town founders and features a whimsical collection of objects, from suitcases to mice. Good bets for shopping are **Mast General Store** (*mastgeneral store.com*), a regional outdoor shop and old-fashioned candy

EATING & DRINKING IN MYRTLE BEACH: OUR PICKS

Earth Cafe: Tuck into the salads, wraps and smoothies at this hip and healthy place. *8:30am-4pm Mon & Tue, to 10pm Wed-Sun $$*

Hook & Barrel: Join the fun at this natty central bar where seafood is the showstopper. *4-9pm Mon-Thu, to 9:30pm Fri & Sat $$$*

New South Brewing: Try the bestselling Dirty Myrtle DIPA at this hyperlocal craft brewery – at it since 1998. *4:30-7pm Mon-Fri, 1-5pm Sat & Sun*

Atlas Tap House: Scruffy but friendly, with numerous craft beers on tap, near the boardwalk. Top-notch happy-hour tacos (from $1). *4pm-2am*

Greenville

emporium, and nearby **Poppington's** *(poppingtons.com)*, known for its imaginatively flavored gourmet popcorn. **M Judson Booksellers** *(mjudsonbooks.com)* is a sunny woman-owned bookshop (with cafe) in the old courthouse, while the patio at **Soby's** *(sobys.com)* is the place to see, be seen and savor Southern favorites like shrimp and grits. The chocolate-chunk cookies are a delicious complement to your latte at **Coffee Underground** *(coffeeunderground.info)*. Main St downtown closes to cars every Saturday morning May through October for the **Saturday Market** *(saturdaymarketlive.com)*.

Cycle the Swamp Rabbit Trail

You can walk it, jog it or skate it, but the most popular way to experience the fabulous **Swamp Rabbit Trail** – a former railway corridor – is on two wheels. The best section of the paved, tree-shaded greenway stretches 22 miles along the Reedy River, linking downtown Greenville with Furman University and the town of Travelers Rest. Pretty bridges, cafes and breweries dot the path. Expect the round-trip ride to take half a day. You can rent bikes in downtown Greenville from **Reedy Rides** *(reedyrides.com)* or a city bikeshare with **Greenville B Cycle** *(greenville.bcycle.com)*.

SWEETGRASS BASKETS

Sweetgrass baskets are for sale across the Lowcountry. These eye-catching coiled baskets have been made by hand by the Gullah-Geechee since the 18th century, when they were used by the enslaved on the region's rice plantations, and the craft of sweetgrass weaving was passed down through the generations. Today the baskets are often intricately patterned and are considered pieces of decorative art. Designs may vary by family. Learn more about the history behind sweetgrass baskets at the Sweetgrass Basket Pavilion – where they are also for sale – beside the Mount Pleasant Visitor Center and Memorial Waterfront Park. The park also hosts the annual Sweetgrass Festival in late July.

 EATING IN GREENVILLE: OUR PICKS

Soby's: Book yourself one of the intimate brick-walled banquettes at this bastion of New Southern cuisine. *5-9pm, plus weekend brunch* **$$**

Trappe Door: Descend beneath E Washington St for rib-sticking Belgian food and an extensive beer list. *5-10pm Sun-Thu, to 11pm Fri & Sat* **$$**

Jianna: Savor rustic Italian cuisine and oysters galore in this cheerful 2nd-floor restaurant near Falls Park. *5-9pm Tue-Fri, from 11am Sat & Sun* **$$**

Anchorage: Local food and booze reign supreme in West Greenville – particularly true at the Anchorage. Look for its bright, enormous mural depicting produce. *5-9:30pm* **$$**

TOP EXPERIENCE

Congaree National Park

Thick with knobby bald cypress trees, moss-covered tupelos and tangled Spanish moss, the swampy interior of Congaree National Park is a Southern Gothic setting at its most elemental. Home to the largest old-growth forest in the Southeastern USA, the park is on a plain fed by the floodwaters of the Congaree and Wateree Rivers. This eerie wonderland is 20 miles southeast of Columbia.

Boardwalk Trail

TOP TIPS

- Pack a picnic or snacks for your visit. There are no restaurants in the park and few options nearby.

- Some ranger-led tours require a reservation and have limited availability. Check the park website to see what's on.

- Don't forget the bug spray.

PRACTICALITIES
- nps.gov/cong
- park 24hr; visitor center 9am-5pm
- admission free

Boardwalk Trail

The most efficient way to explore the floodplain here is to walk the 2.6-mile **Boardwalk trail**, an elevated walkway that loops through the park's old-growth bottomland forest. This easy route passes beneath loblolly pines, water tupelos and bald cypresses, and it provides up-close views of the dark Dorovan muck, an 8ft-deep mix of clay and dead leaves. The trail also swings past boggy Weston Lake.

Paddling Through a Primeval Landscape

For an even more interactive experience, join a half-day guided paddling trip on the Cedar Creek Canoe Trail. This 15-mile water trail meanders through the park's old-growth forest, which provides thick shade. Look for otters, deer, snakes and even alligators while kayaking or canoeing along the marked path. The soundtrack may be the ratatatat of pileated woodpeckers doing their thing and the spooky calls of barred owls. Guided trips take about three hours and cost around $100 per person. Palmetto Outdoor (p350) among other approved outfitters lead trips. It's a relatively easy excursion, but some paddling experience is helpful and will keep you from holding up the group. Outings depart from the South Cedar Creek Canoe Landing, which is a seven-minute drive from the park visitor center.

Tennessee

BLUES & COUNTRY | FORESTED PEAKS | CAPTIVATING CITIES

Most states have one official state song. Tennessee has 11 – and for good reason: this place has music deep within its soul. Here, you can find the mountain twang of folk music in Appalachia, bluesy rhythms of African American communities in the western Delta, and those polished country chords for which Nashville is famed.

The state's three geographic regions are represented by the three stars on the Tennessee flag. Each has its own unique beauty: the heather-colored peaks of the Great Smoky Mountains; the lush green valleys of the central plateau around Nashville; and the sultry lowlands near Memphis.

Apart from visiting fabled recording studios and hallowed Graceland, the Volunteer State is the place for art and culture, dining and nightlife, from Memphis to Chattanooga. Follow this with some nature time amid forested trails, shimmering waterfalls and rocky overlooks – the perfect complement to big-city rambles.

Places
Memphis p355
Nashville p359
Chattanooga p362
Rainbow Lake Wilderness Area p364
Knoxville p365

☑ TOP TIPS

While traveling through Tennessee, be sure to tune in to its excellent radio stations. The nonprofit, community-run WYXR (91.7 FM) in Memphis plays blues, hip-hop, jazz and indie rock. In Nashville, WNXP (91.1 FM) plays wide-ranging grooves with a focus on Music City's local talent. In Chattanooga check out WUTC (88.1 FM) for live local music.

GETTING AROUND

In Memphis, MATA *(matatransit.com)* operates buses as well as a vintage trolley line that runs up Main St (passing Beale St along the way). In Nashville, WeGo Public Transit *(wegotransit.com)* has decent service for getting around town (Rte 4 is useful for getting from downtown to East Nashville). You can also get around town on Nashville's good bikesharing network *(nashville.bcycle.com)*. Memphis and Nashville both have Uber and Lyft. For city-to-city transport, Greyhound is about your only option, though you can take the scenic train to New Orleans if you're heading south from Memphis.

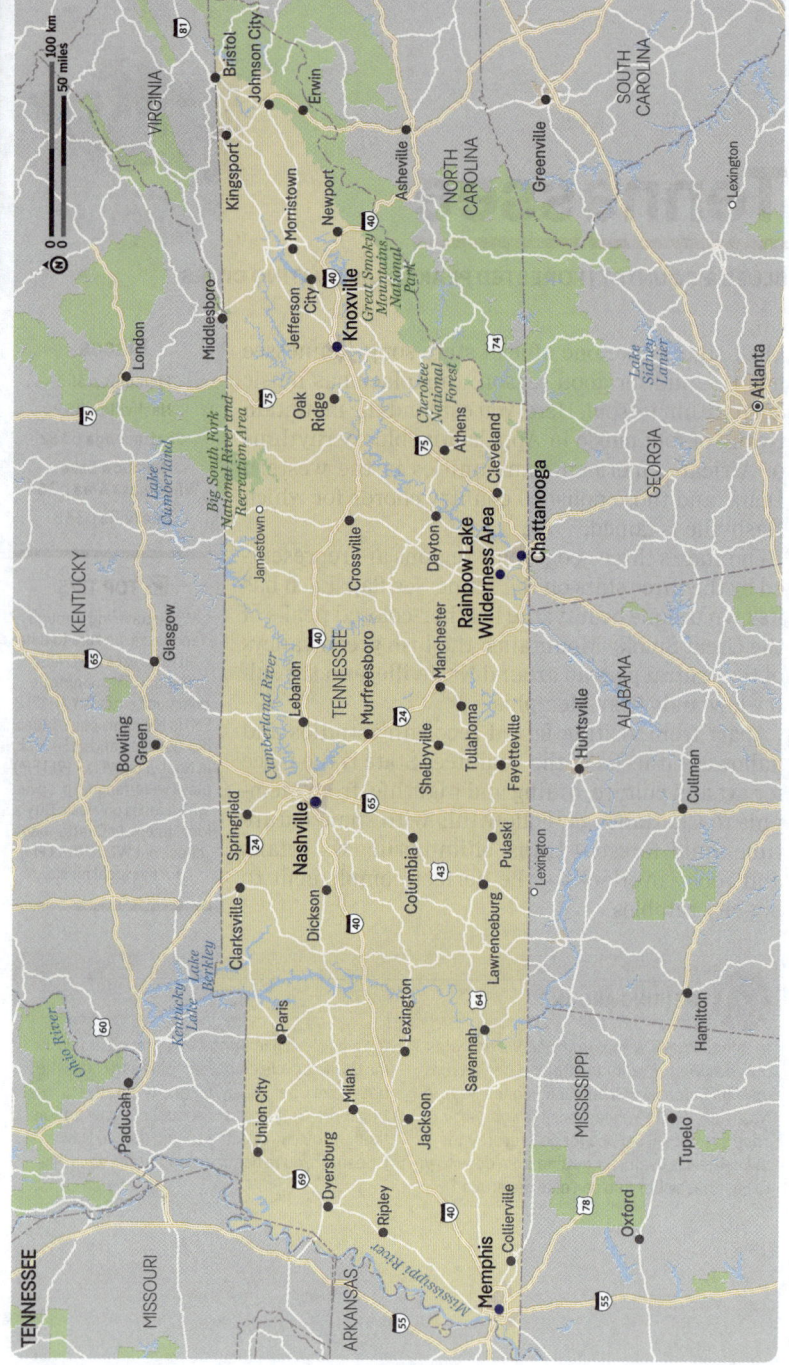

Memphis

MAP P356

The fight for Civil Rights

Housed partly inside the Lorraine Motel, where Martin Luther King Jr was fatally shot on April 4, 1968, is the gut-wrenching **National Civil Rights Museum** (*civilrightsmuseum.org; adult/child $20/17*). Its engaging and compelling exhibits chronicle the struggle for African American freedom and equality from the earliest days of slavery in the United States. Both Dr King's cultural contribution and his assassination serve as prisms for looking at the Civil Rights movement, its precursors and its continuing impact on American life. The turquoise exterior of the 1950s motel and two preserved interior rooms, which are on view, remain much as they were at the time of King's death.

Musical pioneers who changed history

Memphis draws music-loving pilgrims who come to pay their respects in a city famed for its connection to rock and roll. A good place to start is the **Memphis Rock 'n' Soul Museum** (*memphisrocknsoul.org; adult/child $14/11*) which takes you through the evolution of the genre, from the rural music of Black Americans singing gospel, field hollers and work songs, through the early days of blues recordings and into the emergence of rock and roll itself. Exhibitions and objects (a sharecropper's wagon piled high; an early vinyl-playing juke box; dazzling costumes worn by performers) bring the past to life, and there are lots of listening stations along the way where you can hear songs by innovators like BB King, the Staple Singers and Carl Perkins.

At **Sun Studio** (*sunstudio.com; adult/child $20/15*), you can see (and hear) where the magic happened. Starting in the early 1950s, Sun's Sam Phillips recorded blues artists such as Howlin' Wolf, BB King and Ike Turner, followed by the rockabilly dynasty of Jerry Lee Lewis, Johnny Cash and, of course, the King himself (who started here in 1953). Packed 45-minute tours (hourly from 10:30am to 4:30pm) take you into the tiny studio, where you'll hear original tapes of historic recording sessions. Guides are full of great stories, and you can pose for photos on the 'X' where Elvis once stood and touch the microphone used by so many legends. Go early; tours sell out.

Wanna feel the funk? Head to the **Stax Museum of American Soul Music** (*staxmuseum.com; adult/child $20/16*), aka Soulsville USA, a museum on the site of the old Stax recording

BACKSTAGE PASS

If you want to visit all of Memphis' major music sites, be sure to buy the **Backstage Pass** (*$108*), which is sold at **Rock 'n' Soul** and **Stax**. It gives admission to Graceland, Stax, Sun Studio and the Memphis Rock 'n' Soul Museum (saving you 20% vs buying tickets individually), and you can use it over multiple days. Elvis fans have plenty of other options, including VIP tours with a private guide and access to special collections (*$145 to $250*). You can further the experience by staying at the **Guest House at Graceland**, a 450-room resort featuring lots of Elvis touches (Priscilla Presley had a big hand in the design).

EATING IN MEMPHIS: OUR PICKS

MAP P356

Charlie Vergos' Rendezvous: Tucked along a downtown alley, this place has been serving its famous dry-rub ribs since 1948. *11am-9pm Tue-Sat* **$$**

Blues City Cafe: Buzzing spot on Beale St with a big menu, including turnip greens, skillet shrimp and juicy ribs, plus live music nightly. *11am-1am* **$$**

The Four Way: A 1940s landmark serving the best soul food in Memphis, from fried green tomatoes to catfish filets with yams, greens and cornbread. *11am-5pm Wed-Sun* **$**

Majestic Grille: This classy former 1913 movie palace has a broad menu of flatbreads, steaks and seared tuna, as well as weekend brunch. *11am-9pm* **$$**

MEMPHIS

★ HIGHLIGHTS
1. Graceland
2. National Civil Rights Museum
3. Stax Museum of American Soul Music
4. Sun Studio

◉ SIGHTS
5. Cooper-Young
6. Crosstown Concourse
7. Formal Gardens
see 5 Jay Etkin Gallery
8. Memphis Brooks Museum of Art
9. Memphis Rock 'n' Soul Museum
10. Memphis Zoo
11. Old Forest State Natural Area
12. Overton Park
13. Overton Park Shell
14. Overton Square

● SLEEPING
15. Arrive
16. Guest House at Graceland
17. Peabody

● EATING
18. Blues City Cafe
19. Charlie Vergos' Rendezvous
20. Four Way
see 5 Imagine Vegan Cafe
21. Majestic Grille

● DRINKING & NIGHTLIFE
see 5 Bar DKDC
see 5 Celtic Crossing
22. Earnestine & Hazel's
23. Eight & Sand
see 5 Java Cabana
24. Loflin Yard
25. Memphis Chess Club
26. Silky O'Sullivan's
see 5 Young Avenue Deli

● ENTERTAINMENT
27. BB King's
28. Blues Hall
see 14 Lafayette's Music Room
see 28 Rum Boogie
29. Wild Bill's

● SHOPPING
see 5 901 Comics
see 5 Burke's Book Store
see 5 Goner Records

studio. Dive into soul-music history with photos, displays of '60s and '70s stage clothing, a Soul Train dance floor complete with musical accompaniment and video, and Isaac Hayes' 1972 Superfly Cadillac, outfitted with shag-fur carpeting and 24-karat-gold exterior trim.

The world of Elvis Presley

Some 8 miles south of downtown, **Graceland** *(graceland. com; adult/child $84/48, parking $10)* is hallowed ground for Elvis lovers, who come to visit the King's former home and the sprawling museum complex adjoining it. Though born in Mississippi, Elvis Presley was a true son of Memphis, raised in the Lauderdale Courts public-housing projects, inspired by blues clubs on Beale St, and discovered at Sun Studio. In the spring of 1957, the already-famous 22-year-old spent $100,000 on a colonial-style mansion, named Graceland by its previous owners. A visit here starts with a short film, after which you'll receive a video tablet and headphones, then hop on a shuttle and head to the mansion. The tablet gives audio commentary (by John Stamos) as you make your way through the ostentatiously decorated home, complete with a 15ft couch, numerous TVs and some wildly imagined rooms (like the Jungle Room, which has shag carpet on floor and ceiling alike and a once-functioning artificial waterfall). The self-guided house tour ends near his grave. Next, you'll head to the entertainment complex, which houses Elvis' car museum, an exhibit on his time in the army, and a near-exhaustive lineup of memorabilia – including a beautifully displayed collection of his jumpsuits, in all their bedazzled glory. Don't miss Elvis' planes parked nearby.

Exploring Cooper-Young & Overton

Some 5 miles southeast of downtown, **Cooper-Young** *(cooperyoung.com)* is a vibrant district sprinkled with restaurants, shops and drinking spots. Everything is within a few blocks of the intersection of Cooper and Young Sts. You can browse for new and used vinyl at **Goner Records** *(goner-records.com)*, find some fresh or vintage comics and/or action figures at **901 Comics** *(facebook.com/901comics)* and discover new authors around the corner at the famed **Burke's Book Store** *(burkesbooks.com)*, which opened back in 1875. It has a special section on Memphis authors and local history, with used and new titles. You'll find works from artists with a Memphis connection as well as African carvings at **Jay Etkin Gallery** *(jayetkingallery.com)*.

LIVE MUSIC SPOTS

Beale St's music clubs draw mostly tourists, but this is the place for classic blues. Check the Memphis Flyer *(memphisflyer.com)* for shows elsewhere.

BB King's: The original Beale St nightclub from the blues legend brings a fine lineup of talented performers.

Rum Boogie and Blues Hall: Two adjoining spots on Beale St host popular blues nights; one cover *($5)* gets you into both.

Silky O'Sullivan's: Dueling pianos (and requests) make for a kitschy fun time on Beale St.

Lafayette's Music Room: Famous venue for quality performances (and good Southern fare) in an intimate setting near Overton Sq.

Wild Bill's: A gritty hole-in-the-wall juke joint with utterly authentic original blues. It's 4 miles northeast of downtown.

 DRINKING IN MEMPHIS: OUR PICKS — MAP P356

Memphis Chess Club: Inviting rainy-day escape with good coffees, snacks and craft beer, plus board games including, of course, chess. *7am-8:30pm Mon-Sat, from 8am Sun*

Earnestine & Hazel's: This brothel turned dive bar has a 2nd floor of claw-foot tubs and tattered furniture. The Soul Burger is legendary. *5pm-late Wed-Sun*

Eight & Sand: DJs spin vinyl beneath a soaring record wall in this lounge-bar in the Central Station Hotel. *4-11pm Sun-Thu, to 1am Fri & Sat*

Loflin Yard: A massive junkyard-aesthetic beer garden with local beers on draft, barrel-aged cocktails, smoked brisket and other temptations. *4-10pm Wed & Thu, 11am-1am Fri & Sat, 11am-10pm Sun*

BEST ATTRACTIONS IN OVERTON PARK

Old Forest State Natural Area: Get a taste of the wilderness on the paved (1.4 mile) and unpaved (4 miles) trails lacing through this verdant old-growth forest.

Overton Park Shell: Spread a picnic blanket on the grass and enjoy free concerts from May through October, with food and drink for sale.

Formal Gardens: See what's in bloom or join a free yoga or tai chi class.

Memphis Brooks Museum of Art: Tennessee's oldest museum has excellent temporary exhibitions, plus live music, film screenings and art workshops (nude drawings, watercolors, printmaking).

Memphis Zoo: Earns high marks for its well-organized layout, fair prices and chance to feed giraffes.

Bicentennial Capitol Mall State Park

Stop for coffee at **Java Cabana**, a welcoming gathering place day and night (especially Thursdays at open mic from 7pm to 10pm). Grab a bite in the neighborhood. **Imagine Vegan Cafe** (*imaginevegancafe.com*) serves meat-free versions of Memphis classics, including a decadent barbecue sandwich. There's live music and good pub fare at spots like **Young Avenue Deli** (*youngavenuedeli.com*), and cocktails and live bands (especially soul) at **Bar DKDC** (*bardkdc.com*), plus some fine bars with terraces – like **Celtic Crossing** (*celticcrossingirishpub.com*) for nursing cold drinks amid a laid-back crowd.

About a mile north of Cooper-Young, Overton is another restaurant- and bar-filled district, with a dozen spots – many with patios. The epicenter is **Overton Square** (*overtonsquare.com*), where you can catch free film screenings, food festivals and other periodic events.

Seven blocks north of the neighborhood is **Overton Park** (*overtonpark.org*), a beloved green space that draws a wide cross section of Memphis to walking trails, sports fields, outdoor concerts, a zoo and more.

Wander a vertical village

One of Memphis' best-loved recent developments, the **Crosstown Concourse** (*crosstownconcourse.com*) transformed a massive (and long abandoned) Sears distribution center (built

EATING IN NASHVILLE: OUR PICKS — MAP P360

Acme Feed & Seed: A multilevel original on Broadway with Southern cooking, live music and rooftop parties (plus Sunday yoga). *4:30-11pm Mon-Thu, 11am-2am Fri-Sun* $$

Puckett's Restaurant: The Nashville original of this small chain boasts a barn-like decor, huge menu (breakfasts, Southern, sandwiches, barbecue) and nightly concerts. *7am-10pm* $$

Peg Leg Porker: Fall-off-the-bone ribs and tender pulled pork at this barbecue icon in the popular Gulch neighborhood. *11am-9pm Mon & Tue, to 10pm Wed-Sat* $

Black Rabbit: Beautifully prepared local rainbow trout, bone-in pork chop, creative cocktails and happy hour specials. Reserve ahead. *4-11pm Mon-Fri, 10am-midnight Sat* $$$

in 1927) into a live-work-entertainment complex with indie restaurants, shops and community organizations. Stop in the Memphis Listening Lab *(memphislisteninglab.org; free)* to hear rare grooves on vinyl; it also hosts music-related listening sessions, artist talks and book signings. On the same level (2nd floor), you can peek in a few galleries, or catch a periodic concert at the intimate Green Room *(crosstownarts.org/music/green-room)*. Next door, you can order cocktails from the small stylish drinking den, the Art Bar *(5pm to midnight)*. Restaurants and snack spots are sprinkled along the 1st floor. Top choices include the beautifully designed Bao Toan *(baotoanmemphis.com)* for elevated Vietnamese fare and creative cocktails, and Global Cafe *(globalcafememphis.com)* with cuisine from far-flung regions of the world. At Crosstown Brewing *(crosstownbeer.com)*, you can linger over microbrews (including their excellent IPA Traffic), munch on pizza and burgers, and catch trivia nights, live music and adult spelling bees.

Nashville

MAP P360

Discovering downtown Nashville

Tennessee's biggest city and capital is packed with intriguing attractions – not all of which revolve around Nashville's dynamic music scene. Before hitting the country-music bars, start your explorations at the **Tennessee State Museum** *(tnmuseum.org; free)*, where you'll find free parking and excellent multimedia exhibits spanning the ages (including well-done short films introducing different periods). You could spend several hours time-traveling through displays on natural history, First Peoples, the Civil War, World Wars and the battle for Civil Rights.

Next door is the **Nashville Farmers Market** *(nashvillefarmersmarket.org)*, where a large food hall has wood-fired pizza, Korean bowls, crepes, hot chicken, vegan tacos and more. Across the street, you can stroll through **Bicentennial Capitol Mall State Park** with its history-laden plaques and fountains, and make your way (up a steep hill) to the **Tennessee State Capitol** *(capitol.tn.gov; free)*. There you can wander through the lavishly decorated rooms or take a guided tour *(free, departing on the hour)* for more insight into Tennessee history and governance.

A few blocks south of the capitol, head inside the grand **Nashville Public Library** on Church Street *(library.nashville.org;*

TOP MUSIC SITES IN NASHVILLE

Country Music Hall of Fame & Museum: At the great cathedral of country music, you can gaze at Carl Perkins' blue suede shoes, Elvis's gold Cadillac and Taylor Swift's tiered gown from the Eras Tour.

Grand Ole Opry: Hosts the *Grand Ole Opry*, a lavish tribute to classic Nashville country music, every Tuesday, Friday and Saturday night from February through October.

Ryman Auditorium: See a show in the fabled venue where countless legends have performed.

Station Inn: Catch live bluegrass nightly at this long-running venue.

Johnny Cash Museum: Small but comprehensive collection of Johnny Cash artifacts and memorabilia.

Bluebird Cafe: Never mind the strip mall location, some of the best up-and-coming singer-songwriters in country music play here. Reserve ahead.

 DRINKING IN NASHVILLE: OUR PICKS

MAP P360

6th & Peabody: Always a lively time at this sprawling indoor-outdoor space with a moonshine distillery, microbrewery and taco shop. *11am-10pm Mon-Wed, to 11pm Thu-Sun*

Close Company: In a redesigned candlelit warehouse in hip Germantown, you can sip inventive elixirs and munch on pastry pockets. *4pm-midnight*

Monday Night Brewing: Another favorite in Germantown, with an industrial-chic interior, huge patio and delicious house-made brews. *noon-10pm Mon-Sat, noon-8pm Sun*

Patterson House: Go early to score a spot at this intimate lounge with a Gatsby-esque vibe serving Nashville's best cocktails. *4pm-2am*

DOWNTOWN NASHVILLE

★ HIGHLIGHTS
1. Country Music Hall of Fame & Museum

● SIGHTS
2. Bicentennial Capitol Mall State Parkl
3. Johnny Cash Museum
4. Riverfront Park
5. Tennessee State Capitol
6. Tennessee State Museum

● ACTIVITIES
7. Nashville Public Library

● SLEEPING
8. Union Station Hotel

● EATING
9. Acme Feed & Seed
10. Assembly Food Hall
11. Black Rabbit
12. Peg Leg Porker
13. Puckett's Restaurant

● DRINKING & NIGHTLIFE
14. 6th & Peabody
15. Patterson House

● ENTERTAINMENT
16. Robert's Western World
17. Ryman Auditorium
see 16 Stage on Broadway
18. Station Inn
19. Tootsie's Orchid Lounge

● SHOPPING
20. Boot Country
21. Nashville Farmers Market

free). Head up to the 2nd floor to check out the Civil Rights Collection, a permanent exhibit with a symbolic lunch counter and various on-demand videos you can watch that spotlight different aspects of the movement.

From there it's an easy walk to Lower Broadway, which is thumping with shops, restaurants and honky-tonks. If you're in the market for Nashville's quintessential footwear, visit **Boot Country** *(twofreeboots.com)*, where it's 'buy one pair, get two pair free.' There are loads of dining options nearby, but for the indecisive, head to **Assembly Food Hall** *(assembly foodhall.com)* with dozens of vendors (and several bars) firing up a wide array of high-quality delicacies.

Hit the honky-tonks

The heart of Nashville's live music scene is Lower Broadway, a four-block stretch of downtown lined with music-filled bars, their bold neon signs lighting the way. The most venerated of the honky-tonks, **Tootsie's Orchid Lounge** *(tootsies.net)*, is a blessed dive oozing boot-stomping, hillbilly, beer-soaked grace with stages on each of its three floors. Nearby, **Robert's Western World** *(robertswesternworld.com)* is a cut above other joints, and a must for folks making a country

- **SLEEPING**
  1 Waymore's
- **EATING**
  2 Bad Idea
- **DRINKING & NIGHTLIFE**
  3 Bongo East
  4 Red Door Saloon East
  5 Urban Cowboy Public House
- **SHOPPING**
  6 Abode Mercantile
  7 Daydream Records
  8 Defunct Books
  see 7 Ellie Monster
  9 Fanny's House of Music
  10 Goodbuy Girls
  see 10 Three Wolves Trading Post

  EATING & DRINKING IN EAST NASHVILLE: OUR PICKS — MAP P360

Urban Cowboy Public House: Stylish lounge and inviting patio make a memorable setting for inventive cocktails and wood-fired pizzas. *4-11pm* $$

Redheaded Stranger: Nashville's finest tacos, topped with ingredients like brisket, red hatch chilies and poblano peppers. Best enjoyed on the front terrace. *10am-10pm* $

Red Door Saloon East: Classic dive in bar-dotted Five Points with indoor and outdoor seating and plenty of love for the (Chicago) Bears. *11am-3am*

Bad Idea: Strange and wonderful mashup of Lao cuisine meets wine bar, set (naturally) in a converted church sanctuary. *5pm-midnight* $$$

BEST NASHVILLE NATURE ESCAPES

Centennial Park: Just west of downtown, with a full-size replica of the Parthenon and an easy trail around a lake.

Riverfront Park: Steps from downtown, you can go for a stroll or a run along the Cumberland River.

Cheekwood: The numerous gardens combine themes (Japanese, water, wildflower) with art, and surround a straight-out-of-a-Jane-Austen-novel house, where exhibitions are held regularly.

Shelby Bottoms: Boasts over 10 miles of multi-use trails including a paved trail that winds alongside the scenic Cumberland River.

Warner Parks: Picturesque overlooks, 200-year-old stone walls, old-growth forest and over 60 miles of trails, plus a nature center, play areas for kids, and regular events.

music pilgrimage. Performances start at opening and goes all night. At the **Stage on Broadway** *(thestageonbroadway.com)*, you can join the rockin' and rowdy crowd who come for three levels of dance floors. A huge wall mural depicting some of country's legends fills one side of the honky-tonk, and above the door you can see a painting of the Highwaymen that once belonged to Waylon Jennings. All are welcome by day; it's age 21 and up after 6pm.

Urban exploring in East Nashville

For inspiration, join the creative kids across the Cumberland River in East Nashville, a district known for its unique vintage shops, record stores and creative gift boutiques. At the Five Points Alley, you can browse for used titles at **Defunct Books** *(defunctbooks.com)*, try on vintage cowgirl boots and other Western essentials at **Goodbuy Girls** *(goodbuygirls nashville.com)* and discover unusual Native American jewelry at **Three Wolves Trading Post** *(@threewolvestrading)*. Refuel at nearby **Bongo East** *(bongojava.com)* – it's also a great rainy-day spot with loads of board games on hand. Nearby, **Fanny's House of Music** *(fannyshouseofmusic.com)* is a welcoming bungalow of music where down-to-earth staff can you help you find your next new or vintage guitar, banjo or ukulele. There's also a small collection of vintage clothing and accessories.

Several blocks south of there the Fatherland District *(fatherlanddistrict.com)* is another indie shopping spot. Pick up western and retro-styled clothing at **Ellie Monster** *(elliemonster.com)*, hunt for old vinyl at **Daydream Records** *(@daydreamrecordshop)* and pick up assorted gifts (fragrances, jewelry, whimsical socks) at **Abode Mercantile** *(abodemercantile.com)*.

Chattanooga

Art and river life in downtown Chattanooga

It's easy to fall for the charms of Chattanooga, a Tennessee River town with a dynamic arts scene and a great love of the outdoors. At the **Bluff View Art District** *(bluffviewartdistrictchattanooga.com)*, you can wander through a sculpture garden overlooking the river. Amid the greenery are over a dozen works, including pieces by Richard Serra and Leonard Baskin. Nearby, the **River Gallery** *(river-gallery.com)* showcases paintings, ceramics, glasswork and jewelry by numerous artists, many with local

EATING & DRINKING IN CHATTANOOGA: OUR PICKS

Niedlov's Cafe & Bakery: Heavenly pastries, outstanding coffees and flavor-rich sandwiches on perfectly baked breads. *7am-6pm Mon-Fri, to 4pm Sat* **$**

STIR: Artfully designed space in the historic Chattanooga Choo Choo complex, serving oysters, fish tacos, veggie bowls and steak frites. *11am-midnight Mon-Fri, from 10am Sat & Sun* **$$**

Hi-Fi Clyde's: Play ping pong, catch live music on weekend nights or linger over smoked wings and brisket nachos at this friendly corner bar. *11am-midnight Sun-Thu, to 2am Fri & Sat* **$**

1885 Grill: Tuck in to shrimp and grits, rainbow trout or fried chicken while relaxing on the tree-shaded patio opposite the Incline Railway station. *11am-9pm* **$$**

View from Lookout Mountain

ties to Chattanooga. Take a break at various restaurants in the area, including **Rembrandt's Coffee House** *(@rembrandtscoffeehouse)*, with its shaded courtyard.

Anchoring the district is the **Hunter Museum of American Art** *(huntermuseum.org; adult/child $20/free)*, set in a striking building of elegant curving steel (like a mini Bilbao Guggenheim) adjoining an early-20th-century mansion. There's a fine permanent collection of 19th- and 20th-century works, along with Chattanooga's best temporary exhibitions.

It's a short stroll from here, via a pedestrian bridge over the Parkway, to the **Tennessee Aquarium** *(tnaqua.org; adult/child $40/30)*. This impressive destination spotlights the inhabitants and ecology of the Tennessee River as it flows from the Appalachian Mountains to the Mississippi Delta. Exhibits in the Ocean Journey building display saltwater marine life. Crowd-pleasers include river otters, penguins and leaping lemurs.

Next to the aquarium, take the Passage, a lane that leads down to the river. Here, water cascades down the steps and into a small wading pool. It's a great spot for kids to cool off. Just below is **Ross's Landing** *(nps.gov/places/ross-s-landing.htm)*, a stretch of greenery that was the starting point of the Trail of Tears. Artwork memorializes the forced removal of the Cherokee in 1838.

For hands-on adventures in downtown, head to the nearby **High Point Climbing** *(highpointclimbing.com; adult/child $31/29)*, a requisite stop for rock climbers. The large center has bouldering walls and dozens of routes for top-rope climbing as well as auto-belay climbs covering a wide range of levels.

Trails and rails on Lookout Mountain

Some of Chattanooga's oldest and best-loved attractions are 6 miles southwest of downtown at Lookout Mountain, near the Georgia state line. Visitors come to ride the **Incline Railway**

GATEWAYS TO THE SMOKIES

Eastern Tennessee is a popular base for visiting Great Smoky Mountains National Park (p337).

Gatlinburg: At the entrance to the national park. Lures visitors with pancake breakfasts, moonshine distilleries and various odd museums and campy attractions, plus the mountaintop adventure park of Anakeesta.

Pigeon Forge: Some 10 miles north of the park entrance, the buzzing, often congested town of Pigeon Forge is another handy base, with myriad amusements, including the Dolly Parton theme park of Dollywood.

Townsend: A smaller settlement to the park's west; handy for reaching the Cades Cove section, some 16 miles away.

You can also access the park via the scenic North Carolina town of Cherokee (p336).

BEST ADVENTURES IN CHEROKEE NATIONAL FOREST

The 660,000-acre **Cherokee National Forest** in Tennessee's east offers unrivaled adventures.

Cherokee Rafting: Splash through family-friendly rapids on the Ocoee River or go epic on class III and IV rapids of the Olympic section.

Cherohala Skyway: See spectacular mountain scenery on the 43-mile drive from Tellico Plains (TN) to Robbinsville (NC).

Conasauga River Blue Hole: Snorkel the clear waters of the Conasauga River, home to over 39 different fish species.

Raft One: A one-stop shop for rafting trips, ziplines, horseback riding and mountain bikes for hire.

Benton Falls Trail: One of countless hikes in the Cherokee, this 3-mile out-and-back route takes in Appalachian forests and a 65ft waterfall.

Rock City trail

(ridetheincline.com; adult/child $22/10), which chugs up a steep slope to a lofty neighborhood. From the top, you can stroll (head right 0.3 miles) to **Point Park** *(adult/child $10/free)*, a 10-acre site full of monuments and fine views that played a pivotal role in a Civil War battle. It's part of the Chickamauga & Chattanooga National Military Park *(nps.gov/chch)* run by the National Park Service, and you can learn more about the battle at the free visitor center and museum facing the entrance to Point Park. There are also numerous scenic hikes in the area, including the 3-mile out-and-back journey along the Bluff Trail to Sunset Rock. Access the trailhead in Point Park or start at the base of the hill at Cravens House (free parking) – the oldest surviving structure on Lookout Mountain and a major focal point during the battle.

Other attractions on Lookout Mountain include stunning **Ruby Falls** *(rubyfalls.com; adult/child $29/19)*, the world's longest underground waterfall. Next to it is **High Point Zip Adventure** *(rubyfalls.com; $22)* with some 700ft of ziplines and a 40ft climbing tower. Four miles south of there (in Georgia) is **Rock City** *(seerockcity.com; adult/child $43/33)*, a garden marked by dramatic rock formations and a clifftop overlook.

Rainbow Lake Wilderness Area

Waterfalls and lookouts

Near the settlement of Signal Mountain, some 20 minutes' drive north of downtown Chattanooga, the **Rainbow Lake Wilderness Area** *(free)* is home to bouncy suspension bridges, waterfalls, scenic overlooks and many miles of trails lacing through the area. Those out for a short-ish, easy-going excursion to the reserve's highlight can start at the Ohio Ave trailhead and make the 1.5-mile (round-trip) hike to Rainbow Lake. After rains, the water cascades 20ft over the dam, creating a lovely waterfall, and you can swim in the pool below.

For a longer outing, instead of heading straight to the lake, take the Bee Branch Trail, which will take you over an Indiana Jones–style suspension bridge. Turn left right after crossing the bridge and follow it down to Rainbow Lake. Afterwards, continue along the Cumberland Trail. This will take you past the spur trail to Rainbow Falls. For adventurers only, this super steep descent (0.1 miles) along slippery terrain has ropes that you'll need to hold on to to make it safely down and back. The reward: one of the region's most beautiful waterfalls, an 80ft cascade into a shimmering pool that you may have entirely to yourself (don't forget swimwear). Continuing on the Cumberland Trail you'll pass the Julia Falls overlook with its jaw-dropping views over the Tennessee River as it winds past Raccoon Mountain. The trail ends near Signal Point (another parking area/trail access point), where you can complete the loop by walking 0.5 miles on the road (it's a pleasant, little trafficked neighborhood).

Knoxville

Delving into the past in a World's Fair city

Dubbed a 'scruffy little city' by the *Wall Street Journal* before the 1982 World's Fair, Knoxville is these days a polished destination when it comes to the arts and outdoor attractions. The visual centerpiece is the **Sunsphere** *(worldsfairpark.org/sunsphere; adult/child $10/5)*, a golden orb atop a tower built for the Fair. You can take the elevator to the 4th-floor observation deck to see the skyline. Nearby, you'll find green space, fountains and a waterway, along with the **Knoxville Museum of Art** *(knoxart.org; free)*, well worth visiting for its impressive collection of East Tennessee artists. Seek out the turbulent works by the Delaney brothers, as well as spiritually charged mixed-media pieces by Bessie Harvey and the miniaturized wonderland of the Thorne Rooms.

Next, stroll a few blocks east to the **Museum of East Tennessee History** *(easttnhistory.org; adult/child $10/free)*. Interactive displays cover the Civil War (when many in the region sided with the Union against the Confederacy), 'hillbilly' stereotypes and mountain music, and the little-known role East Tennessee played during WWII, when the 'secret city' of Oak Ridge was created to refine uranium for the atomic bomb.

Afterward, walk through the sculpture-filled Charles Krutch Park and up to **Market Square**, where you'll find an assortment of outdoor cafes, restaurants and bars with tables on the plaza.

About 1.5 miles east of Market Sq, the **Beck Cultural Exchange Center** *(beckcenter.net; free)* is a great place to learn about African American history in Knoxville. The converted mansion houses rooms full of historic photos and artifacts, and kindly staff will put on a documentary about the destruction of Black neighborhoods owing to urban renewal. Next door, a museum dedicated to the artist Beauford Delaney is in the works.

MOONSHINE

Eastern Tennessee has deep ties to moonshine – un-aged whiskey, often sourced from corn. Moonshine earned its modern reputation during Prohibition, when alcohol production and consumption was banned in 1920. Enforcement, however, was difficult, and making illegal spirits provided extra income for Appalachian home distillers. To hide the smoke from their stills, the distillers made their corn liquor at night, under the light of the moon, hence the name moonshine. Although Prohibition was repealed in 1933, moonshining was a good way for families to make extra cash during the Depression, which continued across the 1930s. NASCAR racing is a descendant of the wild automobile chases of the era, when federal agents chased the souped-up cars used by the bootleggers to deliver their product.

Kentucky

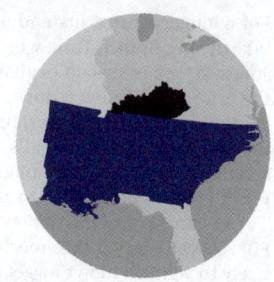

THOROUGHBREDS | BOURBON | RUGGED WILDERNESS

Places
Louisville p368
Bardstown p369
Lexington p369
Frankfort p370
Mammoth Cave National Park p371
Red River Gorge p372
Daniel Boone National Forest p373

☑ TOP TIPS

Kentucky's farmers markets offer great ways to experience the state's bounty. Louisville has two excellent ones: **Bardstown Road** *(bardstownroadfarmersmarket.com; Sat year-round)* and **Douglas Loop** *(douglassloopfarmersmarket.org; Sat Apr-Dec).* Lexington also has several farmers markets *(lexingtonfarmersmarket.com)* including a **downtown market** *(Sat year-round).*

Horses thunder around racetracks, bourbon pours from distilleries and banjos twang in Kentucky, a geographical and cultural crossroads that's part North, part South, part genteel and part country cousin. Every corner is easy on the eye, but there are few sights more beautiful than the rolling limestone hills around Lexington, where long-legged steeds nibble under poplar trees on multimillion-dollar farms. Bourbon distilleries also speckle the countryside, prime for scenic road tripping to swirl and sniff a dram at the source. It's like an offbeat version of California's Napa Valley, but with fewer crowds and headier alcohol. Outdoor adventures prevail in the state's unspoiled parks and forests, which offer some dazzling attractions – including the world's largest caverns and thundering waterfalls that glisten with moonbows at certain times of the month. And while big cities like Louisville have farm-to-table restaurants, cocktail bars and a vibrant music scene, most of Kentucky is made up of small towns, including its delightful state capital, Frankfort.

GETTING AROUND

Kentucky is generally a tough place to get around without a car. In Louisville **TARC** *(ridetarc.org)* runs a decent bus network that can get you around town (though not always all that quickly). Downtown is quite walkable, and route numbers 4, 6 and 29 run from there to Churchill Downs (with frequent service during the Kentucky Derby). In Lexington, there's a smaller bus network run by Lextran *(lextran.com).* During racing season in April, buses connect Lexington's transit center (Vine St) with Keeneland. You'll find decent rideshare service from both Uber and Lyft in Louisville and Lexington.

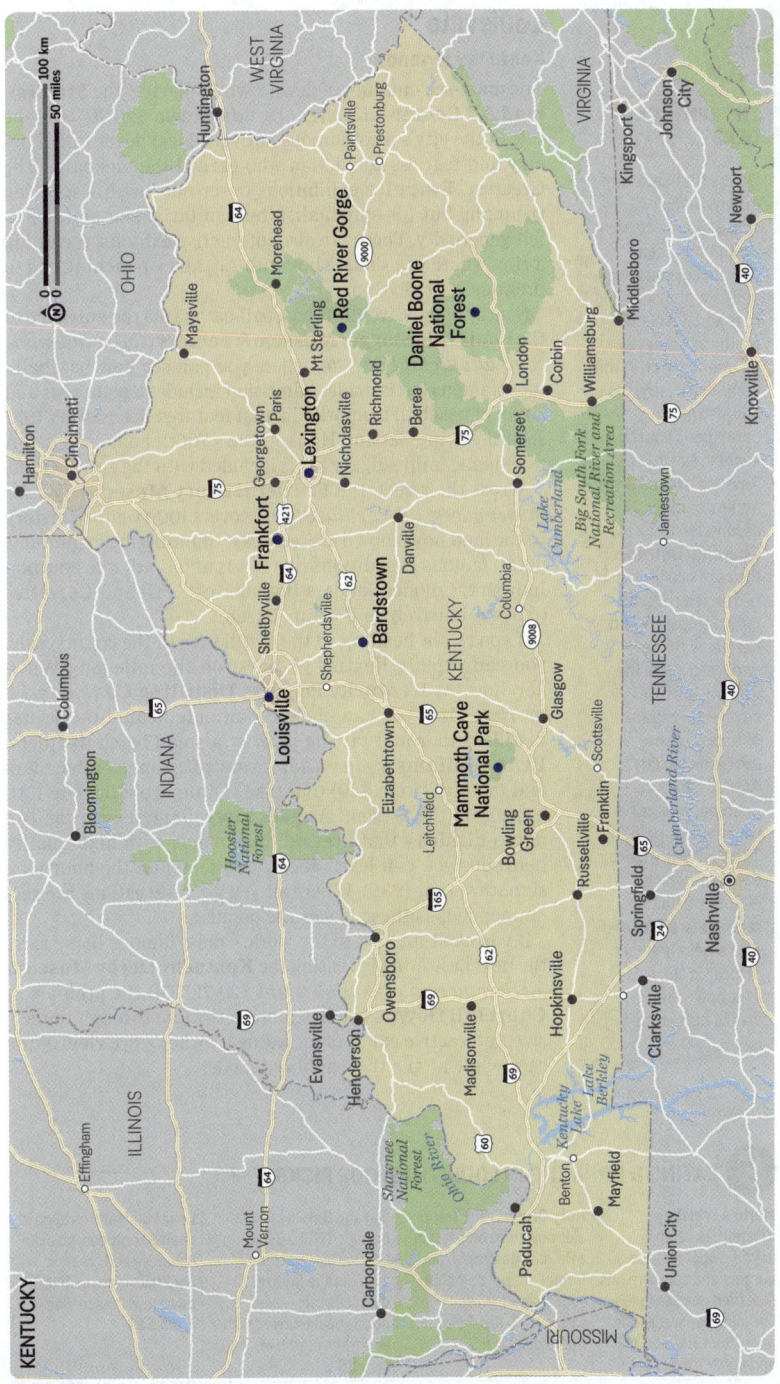

Louisville
Kentucky legends

The must-see museum of downtown Louisville, the **Muhammad Ali Center** *(alicenter.org; adult/child $20/10)* tells the tale of the city's most famous native: a local boxer full of poetry and fearless conviction who earned the nickname The Greatest. Evocative exhibitions cover not just his sporting triumphs but his spirituality, humanitarianism and heartfelt generosity. There are also interactive exhibits, including a ring where you shadowbox with Ali, and a punching bag to practice your rhythm.

Nearby, a massive 120ft baseball bat marks the entrance to the **Louisville Slugger Museum & Factory** *(sluggermuseum.com; adult/child $24/16)*, where you can see how baseball's most famous bat is made. Admission includes a plant tour and a hall of baseball memorabilia that features Babe Ruth's 1927 record-setting bat and Hank Aaron's 700th home run bat. A take-home mini-slugger bat is included with the entrance fee.

Across the street, the **Frazier History Museum** *(fraziermuseum.org; adult/child $16/10)* covers 1000 years of history in the land now known as Kentucky. Illuminating exhibitions detail famous expeditions like Lewis and Clark, the bourbon industry, Colonel Sanders (founder of KFC) and Corvettes (made exclusively in Bowling Green).

If you're not heading to the distilleries in the countryside, you can explore Kentucky's finest on the mile-long Whiskey Row. At **Kentucky Peerless Distilling Co** *(kentuckypeerless.com)*, you can book a 75-minute behind-the-scenes distillery tour and tasting *($32)* at a small-batch distillery. **Evan Williams** *(evanwilliams.com)* offers memorable tours and tastings (from $20) that take visitors from the late 18th century to the present. **Angel's Envy** *(angelsenvy.com)* is a micro-distillery that lives up to its name, with high-quality bourbons you can learn about (and taste) on the hour-long signature tour ($30). Wherever you go, reservations are recommended, as these places are popular.

If you can't make it to the world's most famous horse race, the next best thing is visiting the **Kentucky Derby Museum** *(derbymuseum.org; adult/child $20/12)*. On the grounds of **Churchill Downs** you'll explore derby lore through immersive, interactive exhibits including a jockey's-eye view of the race while atop a thoroughbred model.

THE KENTUCKY DERBY

On the first Saturday in May, a who's who of upper-crust USA put on their seersucker suits and most flamboyant hats and descends for the 'greatest two minutes in sports': the Kentucky Derby, the longest-running continuous sporting event in North America, when 20 horses thunder around the track at **Churchill Downs** for the race of a lifetime.

After the race, the crowd sings 'My Old Kentucky Home' and watches as the winning horse is covered in a blanket of roses. Then everyone parties. Actually, they've been partying for a while by this point. The **Kentucky Derby Festival**, which includes a balloon race, a marathon and the largest fireworks display in North America, starts two weeks before the big event.

EATING & DRINKING IN LOUISVILLE: OUR PICKS

Merle's Whiskey Kitchen: Buzzing, anytime spot for tacos, burgers and southern hits (like fried chicken), plus live music on weekends. *11am-10pm Tue-Thu, to midnight Fri & Sat* **$**

Holy Grale: Drink Trappist ales and slurp mussels in a Belgian gastropub and former chapel complete with stained-glass windows. *5-10pm Mon-Fri, from 2pm Sat & Sun*

Garage Bar: In buzzing bar-lined NuLu (New Louisville), this former auto garage fires up delicious brick-oven pizzas best enjoyed with an Atrium craft beer. *hours vary* **$$**

Proof on Main: Indulge in charred octopus, chicken Milanese and creative cocktails in an art-filled downtown space. *8am-10pm* **$$$**

Muhammad Ali Center

Bardstown

On the bourbon trail

The elegant streets of Bardstown in Central Kentucky make an excellent base for exploring the nearby bourbon distilleries. Learn about the spirit's history from pre-colonial days through Prohibition and up to today at the **Oscar Getz Museum of Bourbon History** *(facebook.com/whiskeymuseum; free)*, then head to top-notch distilleries in the area like **Willett** *(kentuckybourbonwhiskey.com)*, where you can learn about production methods and family history on a 75-minute tour *($27)*, with samples throughout the experience. On a former tobacco farm, **Preservation Distillery** *(preservationdistillery.com)* offers intimate tours *($24)* of its small-batch operations. Plan your visit around the **Kentucky Bourbon Festival** *(kybourbonfestival.com)*, featuring three days of tastings, panel discussions and workshops in early September. If you don't have a designated driver, consider booking a tour with **Mint Julep Experiences** *(mintjuleptours.com; from $200)*, which includes three distillery tours and tastings, lunch and transportation.

Lexington

Horsing around

Kentucky's second largest city is often dubbed the horse capital of the world, owing to the staggering number of thoroughbred farms in the area. Some 10 miles north of downtown Lexington, you can get a deeper understanding of equine culture at the **Kentucky Horse Park** *(kyhorsepark.com; adult/child $28/14)*. Apart from the excellent museum documenting horses and their deep impact on human history (warfare, colonization, farming, transportation), the sprawling complex has shows and activities throughout the day – from horse-drawn trolley rides to draft horse and champion presentations, where you

THE LAND OF BOURBON

Silky, caramel-colored bourbon whiskey was likely first distilled in Bourbon County, north of Lexington, around 1789. Today 95% of the world's bourbon is made in Kentucky, thanks to the state's pure, limestone-filtered water, which contains a high proportion of minerals (like calcium and magnesium) that are optimal for distilling. Bourbon must contain at least 51% corn, and be stored in charred oak barrels for a minimum of two years. The char is essential for imparting those notes of vanilla, caramel and toffee, not to mention the smokiness. While connoisseurs drink it straight or with water, you must try a mint julep, the archetypal Southern drink made with bourbon, simple syrup and crushed mint.

A LEGENDARY FRONTIERSMAN

Lee Muncy, historical interpreter and member of the Sons of the American Revolution @sar.org

Before the Revolution, Daniel Boone was an employee of the British-run Transylvania Company, and he helped cut out a trail through the Cumberland Gap of the Appalachian Mountains down in Virginia. He ultimately founded Boonesborough, one of the first settlements in Kentucky. After the Revolutionary War, Boone moved to Missouri, which is where he was living when Lewis and Clark came to see him before their great expedition in 1802. They told him they were going in search of the Pacific Ocean. Boone said he'd already been there. Sure enough, when Lewis and Clark met various Indian tribes, a lot of them talked about that guy from Kentucky.

Mammoth Cave National Park

can meet the four-legged stars of the park. Check the schedule before heading here to avoid missing out.

Lexington is also home to **Keeneland** *(keeneland.com)*, with exciting thoroughbred races run in April and October, and opportunities to watch morning training sessions *($22)* or take a behind-the-scenes tour *($50)*.

Frankfort

Small-town charm

One of the south's most appealing little towns, Frankfort lies along the banks of the idyllic Kentucky River and its brick streets are dotted with indie shops, cafes and local restaurants. The diminutive capital of Kentucky also has a handful of museums where you can explore the past. Start off at the **Kentucky Historical Society** *(history.ky.gov; adult/child $8/6)*, where you can spend an hour or more learning about the lives of its former inhabitants, including Native Americans, pioneers, enslaved people, Civil War soldiers and moonshiners. There are lots of curious items here, like the pocket watch President Abraham Lincoln carried in 1860. Your admission ticket gives you access to two other nearby sites: the **Old State Capitol**, which was the seat of power from 1830 to 1910, and the **Kentucky Military History Museum** – the best place to find out about the state's involvement in wars dating back to the 1800s.

It's also worth visiting the **Capital City Museum** *(capitalcitymuseum.org; free)* for its displays on surprising events, like the assassination of Senator William Goebel, with accurately detailed mannequins gathered around the supine figure, who died in this building back in 1900.

When you need a break, take a stroll along West Broadway and intersecting St Clair Street. You can browse for regionally made crafts and artwork at **Completely Kentucky** *(completelykentucky.com)*, pick up new (and secondhand) reading material at **Poor Richard's Books** *(poorrichards booksky.indielite.org)* and purchase new and used records – as well as guitars – at **Musket's Music Station** *(muskets musicstation.com)*. Enjoy coffee, snacks and yet more books at the **Kentucky Coffeetree Cafe** *(kentuckycoffeetree.com)* or head 1½ blocks southwest of there to **Engine House** *(enginehouse1868.com)*, a former fire station that today serves Frankfort's best lattes and cold brews.

Frankfort also has some distilleries near town. The legendary **Buffalo Trace** *(buffalotracedistillery.com)*, the nation's oldest distillery, has lovely grounds you can wander, in addition to free tastings. **Castle & Key** *(castleandkey.com; tour $30)* is among the most photogenic distilleries with its medieval-looking buildings.

Mammoth Cave National Park
Caving, hiking, horseback riding and canoeing

Home to the longest cave system on earth, **Mammoth Cave National Park** *(nps.gov/maca)* has more than 400 miles of surveyed passageways. It's at least three times longer than any other known cave, with vast interior cathedrals, bottomless pits and strange, undulating rock formations.

Excellent ranger-guided tours *(adult/child from $23/19)* explore the subterranean expanse. Book ahead if possible *(at recreation.gov)* as they do sell out, especially in summer and on weekends, and some tours are offered only at specific times on certain days of the week.

Jaunts range from hour-long strolls to strenuous, day-long spelunking adventures *(adults only)*. The **Frozen Niagara Tour** is the easiest of the bunch. There are several options that take place by lantern light, including **Star Chamber**, **Great Onyx** and **Violet City** – a nostalgic way of experiencing these caverns.

If you're short on time, opt for the self-guided **Discovery Tour** *(adult/child $12/9)*, where you can explore at your own pace through large open passageways dotted with artifacts from the cave's early days. There's also one accessible tour, where you can visit (via elevator) several impressive formation-filled rooms with no stairs involved.

In addition to the caves, the park contains 85 miles of trails. You can head off on memorable hikes, like the moderate 2.5-mile loop along the **Green River Bluffs** and **Heritage Loop** trails, where you'll enjoy some wonderful views over the dense forests. You can also experience the woodlands by horseback: family-owned **Double J Stables** *(doublejstables.com; rides $40-75)* offers scenic one- and two-hour trail rides.

Some 30 miles of the Green and Noilin Rivers wind through the national park. Several outfitters rent out kayaks and canoes, including **Adventures of Mammoth Cave** *(adventures ofmammothcave.com; canoe or kayak $65)*. They'll provide shuttle transport to the launch, where you can leisurely paddle your way along a 7.5-mile stretch of forest-lined riverside. Allow three to four hours to complete the journey.

RED RIVER GORGE ESSENTIALS

Info & Dining: Tiny Slade has a handy visitor center *(gopoco. org/visitor-center)* with maps and trail recommendations. Fill up at **Miguel's** *(7am-9:45pm)* on breakfasts, pizza and sandwiches, or cabin-like **Sky Bridge Station** *(noon-9pm Mon-Sat, to 6pm Sun)* for burgers and craft beer.

Roads: Many trailheads are reached off Hwy 77 and Hwy 715, which form a 33-mile loop near Slade.

Trails:

Rock Bridge Arch A 1.5-mile loop passing a small waterfall and shallow pool, where kids (and dogs) love to splash about.

Chimney Top This easy 0.7-mile trail is a scenic outing for all levels, as is the neighboring Princess Arch Trail.

Auxier Ridge A 4.5-mile out-and-back hike with great views. Many nearby trails too. Access it via Tunnel Ridge Rd.

THE MOONBOW

Cumberland Falls is one of the few places in the world to see a moonbow. Also called a lunar rainbow, this brilliant display forms in the water's mist when conditions are right. It can only happen during a full moon and on the two days before and after the full moon. There must also be clear skies and abundant mist (with decent wind). None of this would be possible without the atypical location of the falls – they face north with water cascading in a northward direction. Plan your visit sometime between dusk and midnight when the moon hangs low in the sky. The park website has dates for when the phenomenon occurs each month and it can happen throughout the year.

Red River Gorge

Hikes and cave paddles

A vast tract of cliffs, trickling streams and natural arches set amid dense forests, the **Red River Gorge** *(redrivergorge.com)* is Kentucky's top spot for outdoor activities. Hikers will find numerous trails traversing the forest of hemlock and white pine, past wild rock formations and thickets of rhododendron. Bordering the gorge area is the **Natural Bridge State Resort Park** *(naturalbridgestatepark.com; free)*, where you can hike a 1-mile trail up to the 65ft high, 78ft wide sandstone bridge. Take the narrow stairs up to the top and keep going (along the Laurel Ridge Trail) to reach a sweeping overlook across the forested landscape. From here, you can complete the loop via the Battleship Rock Trail, which will take you past high cliffs and fern-covered rock shelters. Alternatively, you can ride the **Sky Lift** *(naturalbridgeskyliftandgiftshop.com; adult/child $17/14)* up to a viewpoint near the natural bridge.

For a different perspective on this unusual geological region, book an excursion with **Gorge Underground** *(gorgeunderground.com; tour $55)*. You'll take a one-hour guided kayaking visit through a century-old, now-flooded limestone mine where you might see bats winging past and massive trout swimming below. Helmet and headlamp included, but dress warmly (thick socks) for the chilly subterranean temperatures.

Cumberland Falls

Daniel Boone National Forest
Natural wonders in Cumberland Falls

Part of the vast Daniel Boone National Forest in eastern Kentucky, **Cumberland Falls State Resort Park** *(cumberland fallsstatepark.com; free)* is a verdant expanse of densely forested ridges on either side of the meandering Cumberland River. The star of the show is the thundering **Cumberland Falls**, a 69ft tall, 125ft wide cascade that's sometimes dubbed 'the Niagara of the South.' Viewing platforms run along the east side of the falls, and some 17 miles of trails wind through the pristine forests surrounding them. One of the best short hikes is the 1.5-mile (round trip) out-and-back hike to **Eagles Falls**, a hidden cascade on the west side of the river. You can also tack on another half mile by following signs for the loop trail. A short drive (or walk) from the falls (and also part of Cumberland Falls State Resort Park), you'll find camping, cabins and lodge rooms as well as a simple old-fashioned restaurant. Just up the road, **Sheltowee Trace Adventure Resort** *(ky-rafting.com)* offers many activities: rafting, kayaking and ziplines. Also in the area, **Cumberland Falls Horse Stables** lead 45-minute rides *($25 per person)* through the forests. These depart hourly from 10am to 6pm.

Georgia

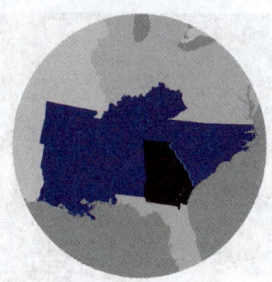

ARTS & CULTURE | CAPTIVATING NEIGHBORHOODS | ISLAND ESCAPES

Places
Atlanta p375
Athens p382
Macon p382
Okefenokee National Wildlife Refuge p383
Savannah p384
Georgian Coast p384

☑ TOP TIP

A good Southern meal needs to be washed down with iced tea, and the default here is always sweet (ask for unsweetened if you have a lower sugar tolerance). Most soul food spots will likely send you home with another one to go.

When it comes to the Peach State, Atlanta hogs headlines (a film industry upstart, Fortune 500 epicenter and sporting powerhouse) while everything else seems to fly bewilderingly under the radar (Georgia has beaches?). That's just fine by natives, who'd love nothing more than to keep Georgia's other gems, including the northern mountains – and their surrounding foothills and upcountry – to themselves. Other lesser-known attractions pockmark the hinterlands, including the wildlife-rich landscape of the Okefenokee Swamp and the astonishing Native American legacy of Ocmulgeee Mounds.

Along the coast, Savannah has long captivated out-of-towners with its mix of history, creativity and culinary prowess, not to mention a heavy dollop of Southern charm. Nightlife thrives year-round and there are bustling watering holes aplenty. Savannah is also the gateway to picturesque sea islands lapped by salt tides and peppered with marshes, estuaries and beaches. These islands have a lost-in-time, almost Gothic, beauty; every corner seems to drip with sweat and Spanish moss.

 GETTING AROUND

In Atlanta the four-line **MARTA** train system is generally a plus-sign shape, with two north–south lines (red and gold) and two east–west ones (blue and green). The Atlanta Streetcar line circles between Centennial Olympic Park and King Historic District, and there's an extensive bus system. You can explore Savannah's historic core by foot or the free DOT shuttle. A car is also your best bet for getting around coastline. Bus service is fairly limited though Greyhound and Megabus connect Atlanta to both Athens and Savannah, among other places.

Atlanta

MAPS P376, P378, P379

Exploring downtown

Some of Atlanta's biggest attractions all fall within a peach's throw of each other in the downtown area.

The city was a key focal point during th Civil Rights movement, and the **National Center for Civil & Human Rights** *(civilandhumanrights.org; adult/child $20/16)* shines a light on the past. One of the most powerful (and popular) installations is the interactive Lunch Counter Sit-In Simulation, inviting visitors to sit and gain an idea of the patience necessary to be part of nonviolent protests.

EATING IN DOWNTOWN ATLANTA: OUR PICKS

MAP P376

Food Shoppe: Creole specialties like shrimp and grits in easy-to-transport Walk & Eat bowls. Try Angie's bread pudding. *8:30am-8pm* **$**

Aviva by Kameel Downtown: Organic Mediterranean dishes in a corner of the Hub at Peachtree Center. *11am-3pm Mon-Fri* **$$**

Alma Cocina: Modern Mexican cuisine; guacamole and salsa samplers, and street tacos including chicken tinga. *11:30am-3pm & 5-10pm Mon-Fri, 5-10pm Sat, to 9pm Sun* **$$$**

Kwan's Deli & Korean Kitchen: Bustling deli with everything from bibimbap and katsu to Italian sandwiches and chicken wings. *10:30am-3pm Mon-Thu, to 8pm Fri & Sat* **$**

ATLANTA'S FOOD TRUCKS

Chase Davis, an Atlanta chef who launched King Kabob in 2015, shares his insight on the city's food trucks @thekingkabob

The Atlanta food-truck scene is special for its rich diversity, offering cuisines from around the world, often fused with Southern flavors reflecting the city's cultural melting pot. It thrives in vibrant, community-centered spaces like food-truck parks and festivals, creating a lively social atmosphere. Apart from **King Kabob**, one must-visit food truck is the **Kitchen**, which serves Asian-soul fusion delights such as Korean barbecue tacos. For dessert, don't miss the **Experience**, offering decadent Southern-style sweets including peach-cobbler milkshakes.

DOWNTOWN ATLANTA

⭐ HIGHLIGHTS
1 National Center for Civil & Human Rights

🔴 SIGHTS
2 Centennial Olympic Park
3 Georgia Aquarium
4 SkyView
5 World of Coca-Cola

⚫ SLEEPING
6 Glenn Hotel

🟢 EATING
7 Alma Cocina
8 Aviva by Kameel Downtown
9 Food Shoppe
10 Kwan's Deli & Korean Kitchen
11 Sun Dial Restaurant & View

🟢 DRINKING & NIGHTLIFE
12 Atlantucky Brewing
13 Der Biergarten
14 RT60
see 6 SkyLounge

Next door, the **World of Coca-Cola** *(worldofcoca-cola.com; adult/child from $23/19)* is an ode to the beloved beverage – some 1.9 billion servings are enjoyed across 200-plus nations daily. Start by entering The Loft, packed with more than 200 relics of the brand's history, before watching a six-minute film about its global impact, and then entering the museum for exhibits on its formula, history and pop culture impact.

Nearby, the **Georgia Aquarium** *(georgiaaquarium.org; from $43)* is packed with wonders from the sea, including one of the world's largest single aquatic exhibits (a tank holding

DRINKING IN DOWNTOWN ATLANTA: OUR PICKS

MAP P376

Atlantucky Brewing: Craft-brew bar in Castleberry Hill opened by rapper Nappy Roots; affordable beers on tap in a beer hall–like space. *3-10pm Wed-Sun*

SkyLounge: Covered rooftop in the Glenn Hotel; cocktails on weeknights and small plates on weekends. *4-9pm Mon-Thu, 6pm-midnight Fri & Sat*

RT60: Hard Rock Hotel's 34th-floor bar rocks, well, hard. DJs and drinks including a mini martini flight and sangria tower. *4pm-midnight Mon-Wed, to 2am Thu-Sat, to 11pm Sun*

Der Biergarten: Ascending the staircase feels like walking into Germany: lagers, wine and cocktails alongside Wiener schnitzel and wurst. *4-9pm Wed-Fri, from noon Sat & Sun*

TOP EXPERIENCE

Martin Luther King Jr National Historical Park

America's Civil Rights movement was powered by the fearless leadership of Martin Luther King Jr, who believed in peaceful protest as a means to action. Long before he gave his most famous 'I Have a Dream' speech in Washington, DC, he was a boy spending his formative years in the neighborhood along Atlanta's Auburn Ave that is now the Martin Luther King Jr National Historical Park preserved as a time capsule to his legacy.

Ebenezer Baptist Church

Understand the Context of King's Life

Since the park site is spread out over a few blocks, make the **visitor center** your starting point to get oriented. The information desk will also provide the times for that day's programs, including must-hear talks inside the Ebenezer Baptist Church. The main exhibit, 'Courage to Lead,' outlines King's life and the growth of the Civil Rights movement, culminating in a life-size rendition of the Freedom Road walkway with marchers of every age.

Walk in King's Footsteps

On the next block, at 501 Auburn Ave, is a brown-and-beige **Queen Anne Victorian house** built in 1895. This is where King's mother grew up and where King himself was born. Birth Home tours are available on a first-come, first-served basis on the day of the tour. On the corner, peek in at Fire Station No 6, which served the segregated neighborhood.

One of the most moving experiences at the historical park is sitting in the pews of the **Ebenezer Baptist Church**, where King was baptized and also where he was ordained as a minister when he was 19, eventually becoming co-pastor with his father.

TOP TIPS

● On the way to the visitor center, stop and smell the roses. They're one of five major World Peace Rose Gardens in the world.

● Find the side-by-side tombs of Dr and Mrs King amid the fountains at the King Center for Nonviolent Social Change.

PRACTICALITIES

● nps.gov/malu
● 9am-5pm
● free

TINY DOORS ATL

Atlanta has its own brand of geocaching in the form of **Tiny Doors ATL** (tinydoorsatl.com). Launched by artist Karen Singer in 2014, the project consists of more than 30 colorful little art pieces in the shape of doors hidden throughout the city. Her three main criteria are to make them all accessible, public and free. For instance, a trio of doors is hidden in one art piece in Centennial Olympic Park. (Hint: search for colorful scenery and don't forget to look up.) Also keep your eyes open at the Krog Street Tunnel, the Trap Music Museum and State Farm Arena.

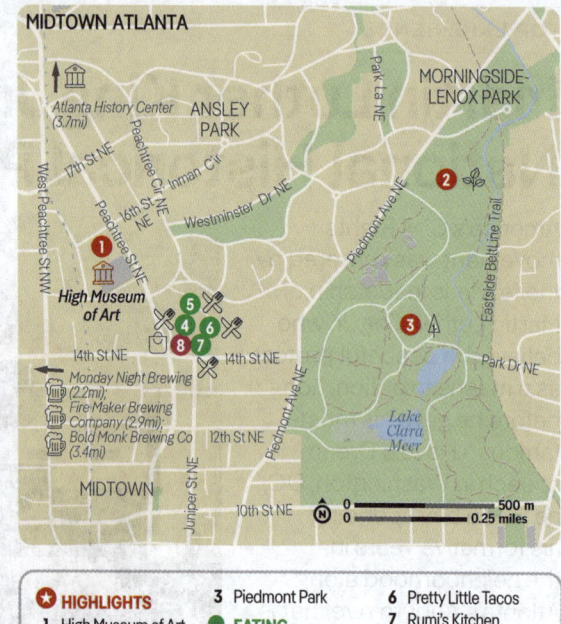

MIDTOWN ATLANTA

- ★ **HIGHLIGHTS**
  1. High Museum of Art
- ● **SIGHTS**
  2. Atlanta Botanical Garden
  3. Piedmont Park
- ● **EATING**
  4. Delilah's Everyday Soul
  5. Holeman & Finch
  6. Pretty Little Tacos
  7. Rumi's Kitchen
- ● **SHOPPING**
  8. Colony Square

6.3 million gallons of water). Highlights include standing in the shadows of the beluga whales in Cold Water Quest, eyeballing great hammerhead sharks in Sharks! Predators of the Deep and climbing through a tunnel to come face-to-face with African penguins.

Anchoring these attractions is 22-acre **Centennial Olympic Park** (gwcca.org/centennial-olympic-park), which commemorates the 1996 Games and serves as the city's central plaza.

On the southeast corner of the park, you can enjoy dazzling views over the city by taking a spin on the **SkyView Ferris wheel** (skyviewatlanta.com; adult/child $19.50/14.45). It rises 20 stories high in 42 sealed, climate-controlled gondolas with floor-to-ceiling windows.

For dining (or not) with a view, there's the Westin Peachtree Plaza, home to the upscale **Sun Dial Restaurant & View**

 EATING IN MIDTOWN ATLANTA: BEST COLONY SQUARE EATS — MAP P378

Pretty Little Tacos: Started as a food truck and quickly known for juicy birria tacos. *11am-9:30pm Mon-Thu, to 10:30pm Fri & Sat, to 8:30pm Sun* **$**

Delilah's Everyday Soul: Oprah Winfrey called the mac 'n' cheese here the best in the country. *11am-10pm Mon-Thu, to 11pm Fri & Sat, to 9pm Sun* **$$**

Rumi's Kitchen: Bustling Persian favorite; kebabs and labne are among popular picks. *11:30am-10pm Mon-Thu, to 11pm Fri, 11am-11pm Sat, to 10pm Sun* **$$$**

Holeman & Finch: Cozy lounge with elevated pub food, in chic digs with a dress code. *11am-10pm Sun-Wed, to midnight Thu-Sat* **$$**

EASTSIDE ATLANTA

- **HIGHLIGHTS**
  1. Martin Luther King Jr National Historic Park
- **SIGHTS**
  2. Historic Fourth Ward Park
  3. Jimmy Carter Presidential Library & Museum
  4. Krog Street Tunnel
- **EATING**
  5. Krog Street Market
  6. Ponce City Market
  7. Vortex
- **DRINKING & NIGHTLIFE**
  8. Euclid Avenue Yacht Club
  9. Nine Mile Station
  10. Porter
  11. Star Community Bar
  12. Village Coffee House
- **ENTERTAINMENT**
  13. Skyline Park
- **SHOPPING**
  14. Little Five Points

(sundialrestaurant.com; adult/child $10/5), which rotates on the 72nd floor. Between 11am and 9pm daily, visitors can take in the panorama.

Art and greenery in Midtown

Hailed as the Southeast's most renowned art destination, the **High Museum of Art** *(high.org; $23.50)* boasts a vast collection ranging from classic European paintings to contemporary works, with an emphasis on artists of the South. Of particular note is the folk and self-taught gallery, as well as its many rotating exhibitions showcasing the work of Black artists. For a personalized (and fun) experience, the museum's site *heartmatch.org* lets you swipe on art you like (much like a dating site) and generates a custom map.

A short walk south of the museum, **Colony Square** *(colonysquare.com)* feels like Midtown's living room, with its beauty spas, yoga, Pilates and a robust calendar of events. Step into the buzzy 20,000-sq-ft Politan Row food hall, where each of the dozen or so options is chef-driven with a local twist. There are also lively sit-down restaurants and bars. Top off the day by catching a flick at IPIC Theaters, which serves food and cocktails at your seat.

HIPPIE HAVEN

Bart Pond is a musician and a Little Five Points resident since 2010.

Little Five is Haight-Ashbury with Southern charm and hospitality. The murals here are constantly changing. This isn't graffiti; it's art. You learn who the artists are through their tags – this one is the Junkyard Chef and this is Paul Athol. Even the sidewalks have them. I can't give away all my secrets, but they have messages and if you follow them they'll lead you to two secret venues. There's other kinds of art too, like this sticker on the back of the street sign. A guy just puts free stories up. This one starts, 'My child was possessed by a demon who injured him through his rotting baby teeth....'

A few blocks east of there, the nearly 200-acre **Piedmont Park** *(piedmontpark.org)* has woods, wetlands and walking paths, plus a race track and the 11.5-acre Lake Clara Meer. Along the park's northwestern side is the 30-acre **Atlanta Botanical Garden** *(atlantabg.org; adult/child $29/26)*. There, the Cascades Garden is anchored by a topiary goddess sculpture, while the Kendeda Canopy Walk allows visitors to walk 40ft up among the trees. Piedmont Park is a popular site for events such as the Atlanta Dogwood Festival *(dogwood.org)* in April.

Experience the cutting edge at Little Five Points

At **Little Five Points**, a skeleton head with psychedelic eyes welcomes customers into the **Vortex** *(thevortexatl.com)* bar and grill, while the **Village Coffee House** *(instagram.com/villagecoffeehouselittle5)* has a retro photo booth outside and a rack of vintage clothes for sale inside. Tattoo parlors and smoke shops are interspersed among a metaphysical crystal store and a record shop, while in between there are vintage boutiques for every kind of shopper, imaginative bars and some dazzling street art.

 DRINKING IN ATLANTA'S LITTLE FIVE POINTS: OUR PICKS — MAP P379

Euclid Avenue Yacht Club: Standard dive-bar fare in an eclectic environment. *noon-3am Mon-Sat, to midnight Sun*	**Star Community Bar:** All about its characters, with events from honky-tonk dance lessons to drag competitions. *5pm-2:30am Mon-Thu, 1pm-2:30am Fri & Sat, to midnight Sun*	**Vortex:** Entered through a skeleton's mouth, this bar delivers on memorable clientele. *11am-midnight Sun-Thu, to 2am Fri & Sat*	**Porter:** Relatively clean-cut Porter has 60 craft brews on draft and a massive beer cellar. *5pm-midnight Wed-Fri, from 11am Sat & Sun*

Skyline Park mini golf

Explore Atlanta BeltLine's Eastside Trail

Any time of day along the **Atlanta BeltLine's Eastside Trail** *(beltline.org)* there will be folks running, biking, walking their dogs and riding scooters. In essence, this 3-mile section of what will eventually be part of a 22-mile loop around the entire city is proof of what all of Atlanta could soon become. A colorful starting point is the mural-covered **Krog Street Tunnel** connecting Cabbagetown and Inman Park. Heading north, just to the left the paved trail soon comes into view. You'll walk past **Krog Street Market** *(thekrogdistrict.com)*, an enticing food hall in an 1889 building. Let your instincts guide you, whether it's stopping off at a brewery for a pint or taking a break to watch the daredevils in the skatepark. You'll soon arrive near **Historic Fourth Ward Park** *(h4wpc.org)* and the vast **Ponce City Market** *(poncecitymarket.com)*, one of the biggest and best food halls in the South. Don't miss the rooftop, where you'll find **Skyline Park** *(poncecityroof.com/skyline-park; from $7)*, with boardwalk games, mini golf, a three-story slide and Heege Tower for even higher views. Also up top is the **Nine Mile Station** *(9milestation.com)* beer garden, which has private igloos in the cooler months.

The city's past through living history

Set on 33 acres, the **Atlanta History Center** *(atlantahistorycenter.com; adult/child $27/15)* is unlike other city historical society museums. With a rare in-the-round painting, a mansion made famous by a movie franchise, blooming gardens, sunken woods, historic buildings and a farm – with sheep and goats. – this Buckhead neighborhood museum is creating its own history as much as it's preserving the city's. Follow the events that shaped Atlanta through exhibits on how railroads set the city's foundation (even climb aboard a restored Texas

THE BEER BUS

Hopping from brewery to brewery is a great way to get to know the city, with each brewery offering its own unique atmosphere. The Upper Westside has emerged as the newest favorite concentration for breweries in the city. A cluster of them have established an Ale Trail and offer rides on the **Atlanta Beer Bus** *(atlantabeerbus.com; free)*, which runs alternating routes on Sunday. From 1pm to 7pm riders can start from any one of the area breweries and pick up a passport and get a beer at each spot. The stops include **Fire Maker Brewing Company** *(firemakerbeer.com)*, **Bold Monk Brewing Co** *(boldmonkbrewingco.com)* and **Monday Night Brewing** *(mondaynightbrewing.com)*.

BEST OUTDOOR FUN IN NORTHERN GEORGIA

Tallulah Gorge State Park: Both easygoing and challenging hikes amid forests and waterfalls, plus a dramatic suspension bridge.

Unicoi State Park & Lodge: See sublime cascades, including Anna Ruby Falls in the Chattahoochee-Oconee National Forest.

Brasstown Bald: Ascend Georgia's highest point (elevation 4784ft); it's a paved, 0.6-mile hike uphill walk from the parking lot.

Blood Mountain: Get a taste of the Appalachian Trail on this iconic, moderately difficult 4.4-mile (round-trip) day hike from Neel Gap to the 4452ft mountaintop.

Vogel State Park: One of Georgia's oldest parks sits at the base of Blood Mountain and has many trails, including an easy 1-mile (round-trip) walk to Trahlyta Waterfall.

locomotive) and another on Atlanta 1996 (meet the fuzzy blue Olympic mascot, Izzy).

Explore the Jimmy Carter Presidential Library

Set in the midst of 30 acres of landscaped greenery between a pair of lakes, the **Jimmy Carter Presidential Library & Museum** *(jimmycarterlibrary.gov; adult/child $12/free)* feels like a peaceful sanctuary in the center of Atlanta. Inside, interactive exhibits trace Carter's path from his modest roots to the Oval Office, including a replica of the White House space as it was during his tenure. Also fascinating is the exhibit on the Camp David meetings: the secret negotiations between Israel and Egypt. Don't miss the chance to pose behind the presidential podium on the way out.

Athens

Visit Georgia's finest college town

One of the USA's quintessential college towns, beery, artsy and laid-back Athens is home to the **University of Georgia** and its fiercely followed football team. If you don't manage a ticket for a game at **Dooley Field at Sanford Stadium** (look on *seatgeek.com*), head downtown and pick a bar – they'll all be packed. You can freely wander the 760-acre campus. The **Athens Welcome Center** *(athenswelcomecenter.com)* produces a self-guided walking tour.

For a different take on the Athens' experience, head to the excellent **Georgia Museum of Art** *(georgiamuseum.org; free)*. Here you can gawk at modern sculpture in the courtyard garden as well as the tremendous collection from American realists of the 1930s.

At the 323-acre **State Botanical Garden of Georgia** *(botgarden.uga.edu; free)* at the University of Georgia, 3 miles south of town, gorgeous winding outdoor paths lead to an amazing collection of plants, including rare and threatened species, across eight specialty gardens. There are nearly 5 miles of top-notch woodland walking trails, too. If you're toting little ones, the interactive children's garden features a treehouse, a fossil wall, a granite map of Georgia and more.

Macon

Walking the Ocmulgee Mounds

Poised to become the country's newest national park, **Ocmulgee Mounds** *(nps.gov/ocmu; free)* has Indigenous ceremonial

EATING & DRINKING IN & AROUND ATHENS: OUR PICKS

| **Mama's Boy:** Fluffy, buttery biscuit sandwiches are the calling card of this detour-worthy Southern breakfast bastion off the North Oconee Greenway. *7am-2.30pm* $ | **Last Resort Grill:** Southwestern-inspired plates satiating Athens for 30 years. Fantastic patio. *hours vary* $$$ | **Hendershots:** Quintessential Athens coffeehouse; also a great bar and live-music venue. *hours vary* | **Creature Comforts Brewing Co:** In a former tire shop, the three-bar, 54-tap brewery is the epitome of everything great about Athens. *hours vary* |

Okefenokee National Wildlife Refuge

mounds dating back thousands of years with special ties to the Muscogee (Creek) people who lived here before their removal on the Trail of Tears. The park has a museum with artifacts recovered from a 1930s archaeological dig that was the largest in US history. You can also climb the stairs to the top of the Great Temple Mound Complex, which offers views of the Ocmulgee River and beyond. Try to time your visit to catch a ranger-led tour, held on alternating weekends throughout the year. Better yet, plan your trip around Ocmulgee's cornerstone annual events, such as the **Lantern Light tours** (March) and the **Ocmulgee Indigenous Celebration** (September).

Okefenokee National Wildlife Refuge
Primeval wetlands

The **Okefenokee National Wildlife Refuge** *(fws.gov/refuge/okefenokee; $5)* is the nation's largest blackwater swamp – 'blackwater' refers to the tea-like hue created by the ancient peat at the bottom. Spanning 354,000 acres of rivers, lakes and islands, the swamp's name comes from the Indigenous word for 'land of the trembling earth.' Several creatures call the area home, including thousands of alligators and more than 200 species of bird, plus endangered indigo snakes and wood storks. There are a few short trails here (all less than a mile), but the best way to experience this watery landscape is by boat. Guided 90-minute boat tours are operated by **Okefenokee Adventures** *(okeswamp.org; adult/child $35/30)* and you can also rent canoes *($50)* and kayaks *($30 to $50)*.

For a driving tour, pick up a brochure at the **Bolt Visitor Center** to make the scenic 7-mile Swamp Island Drive by car or bicycle. Along the way, signs indicate several trails including the 1.5-mile (round-trip) boardwalk to the old Chesser Island Homestead. There are also markers pointing out the habitats of alligators, black bears and woodpeckers.

MOTHER OF THE BLUES

If there's one artist to add to your Georgia soundtrack, it's **Gertrude 'Ma' Rainey**, who was born in Columbus in 1886. She started singing at a young age, following in the footsteps of her parents, performing at a talent show at the famed Springer Opera House at age 14. She joined the touring circuit, performing around the country in her unique style, a mix of jazz and blues with her signature raspy voice. Rainey returned to her hometown in 1933, where she retired and is now buried. Her former home still stands, and tours *(parks.columbusga.gov/parks/ma-rainey-home)* are offered on an appointment basis. Don't miss the award-winning 2020 film *Ma Rainey's Black Bottom*, set in 1920s Chicago.

Savannah

Step back in time in the Historic District

Savannah's Historic District is home to 18th- and 19th-century homes, fascinating museums and monuments, and world-class restaurants, all enveloped by a canopy of Spanish-moss-laden live oaks. After taking a stroll around the neighborhood, head to the **Telfair Academy** *(telfair.org; adult/child $30/10)*, considered Savannah's top art museum. Ensconced in the historic and captivating Telfair family mansion, the gallery is filled with 19th-century American works and a smattering of European pieces. Admission includes unlimited entries to the **Jepson Center** (which focuses on 20th- and 21st-century art) and the early-19th-century **Owens-Thomas House** for a week.

Visit the Plant Riverside District

Stepping into the generator hall at this former power station (now a JW Marriott hotel) in the **Plant Riverside District** *(plant riverside.com)* is a big 'Whoa!,' especially if you're walking in from the riverfront or the leafy Historic District. Throngs of people flow past as they explore the vast space, and there's an enormous chrome-dipped dinosaur hanging overhead. Glittering geodes and minerals beckon in every direction.

Galleries, boutiques and exuberant works of art fill the cavernous lobby, which exudes steampunk cool with its mix of modern amenities and original power-plant fixtures. After checking out whimsical creations at art-minded shops like **18Loves Art** *(18loves.com)*, head skyward to the **Myrtle & Rose Rooftop Bar** or the nearby **Electric Moon Skytop Lounge** for drinks overlooking the river. For something more structured, check out the indoor music venue here, **District Live**, which hosts touring acts with regional and national followings.

Georgian Coast

Beachcombing on Tybee Island

Savannah's favorite getaway is **Tybee Island**, with its eclectic art shops, laid-back cafes and pretty beaches. For sheer beauty, set your sights on **North Beach**, a beautiful swath of white sand. With fewer services and a vibe that feels more remote, this stretch of shoreline is a great place to relax – though you can also get active, climbing the 178-step staircase that corkscrews to the top of the **Tybee Island Light Station**

BEST HISTORIC HOUSE TOURS

Mercer-Williams House: Tour the 1st floor of Savannah's most notorious house.

Flannery O'Connor Childhood Home: This stone row house on Lafayette Sq is where the literary great was born in 1925 and lived until she was 13.

Juliette Gordon Low Birthplace Museum: Childhood home of the founder of the Girl Scouts of the USA, which runs the museum.

Sorrel Weed House: Fans of the paranormal can get their thrills at one of Savannah's spookiest mansions.

Owens-Thomas House & Slave Quarters: Completed in 1819 by British architect William Jay, this gorgeous villa exemplifies English Regency-style architecture, known for its symmetry.

EATING IN SAVANNAH: OUR PICKS

Treylor Park: Amid a retro-chic aesthetic, enjoy fried chicken on a biscuit paired with an excellent cocktail. *11am-1am Mon-Fri, from 10am Sat & Sun* **$**

Mrs Wilkes Dining Room: Once you're seated family-style, the kitchen unloads the likes of fried chicken, beef stew and black-eyed peas. *11am-2pm Mon-Fri* **$$**

Grey: A wonderfully retro makeover of a 1930s Greyhound bus terminal, serving up deliciously inventive 'Port City Southern' cuisine. *5-9pm Tue-Sun, also 11am-3pm Sun* **$$$**

Starland Yard: For alfresco dining and drinking, stop in this lively food-truck park, which offers plenty of variety, plus events (live music, line dancing). *5-10pm Mon-Wed, noon-9pm Thu-Sun* **$**

WALKING SAVANNAH'S SQUARES

One of the joys of visiting Savannah is walking around the Historic District amid some of the most beautiful residential architecture in the country.

START	END	LENGTH
Forsyth Park	Johnson Square	1¾ miles; 2 hours

Begin at the iconic fountain in ❶ **Forsyth Park**. Continue north on Bull St toward the intersection with Wayne St, where a statue of General Casimir Pulaski soars above ❷ **Monterey Square**. Walk north and turn right on cobblestoned Jones St, flanked by Greek Revival homes and live oaks. Turn left on Abercorn to see the spectacular ❸ **Cathedral Basilica of St John the Baptist**. Head north to Colonial Park Cemetery. Wander past Gothic tombs and monuments, then turn west on E Perry St. A bronze statue of Savannah founder James Oglethorpe oversees the action from ❹ **Chippewa Square**. The park-bench scenes in *Forrest Gump* (1994) were shot on the north side along Hull St (the actual bench was a prop). Keep truckin' north on Bull St to ❺ **Wright Square**, burial site of Tomochichi, the Yamacraw tribe leader who befriended Oglethorpe and helped him establish the colony. Head west to ❻ **Telfair Square**, where the Telfair Academy and the Jepson Center border Barnard St. Continue north, cross busy Broughton St and continue to ❼ **Ellis Square**, a hub of commerce from the 1730s through the 1950s. In the 1850s it housed a market for the sale of enslaved human beings. Head east down St Julian St toward Bull St and end at ❽ **Johnson Square**, Savannah's first and largest square.

Thanks to the work of the Colonial Dames of Georgia, a boulder made of granite from Stone Mountain honors Tomochichi in **Wright Square**.

Running east–west, **Jones Street** is famed for its cobblestones and high-stooped Greek Revival homes tucked under a canopy of live oaks.

The remains of Revolutionary War hero General Nathaniel Greene were exhumed in 1902 from **Colonial Park Cemetery** and reinterred in Johnson Square.

BEST ANNUAL EVENTS ON TYBEE ISLAND

SCAD Sand Arts Festival: Students from the Savannah College of Arts & Design create magical sand sculptures on South Beach in August.

Tybee Island Beach Bum Parade: Come prepared with a water gun – no one's safe at this giant traveling water fight – which is oh so welcome on hot days. Held mid-May.

Tybee Turtle Trot: Coinciding with sea-turtle nesting season in late April, this 5km beach run is a fundraiser for turtle-preservation efforts.

Fourth of July: Catch the spectacular fireworks show, with views anywhere along the eastern beaches.

Pirate Fest: Dress up like your favorite buccaneer and party like it's 1699 at this four-day fest in mid-October.

(tybeelighthouse.org; adult/child $12/10; closed Tue), where even more glorious views await. Tickets include admission to the adjacent lighthouse keeper's cottage and museum.

Exploring Wormsloe & Gullah-Geechee culture

Just south of Savannah, the **Wormsloe State Historic Site** (gastateparks.org/Wormsloe; adult/child $12/6) spotlights the state's earliest history. On a visit here, you can learn all about this colonial estate, founded in the 1730s. Stop by the visitor center to buy admission tickets and pick up a property map. You'll also board the tram that shuttles between the visitor center and the park museum via Live Oak Ave, which was originally flanked by more than 400 moss-draped oaks. Property highlights include the ruins of the original tabby house (tabby is a crude concrete composed of oyster shells and lime mortar), the Colonial Life Area, where interpreters in period costumes may be on hand to demonstrate Colonial-era crafting and tool work, and an observation deck overlooking a pretty stretch of marsh.

Nearby, the **Pin Point Heritage Museum** (chsgeorgia.org/pin-point-heritage-museum; adult/child $15/7) spotlights the culture of the Gullah-Geechee people in the secluded village of Pin Point. The community, which was established by first-generation formerly enslaved, thrived for nearly 100 years.

DRINKING IN SAVANNAH: OUR PICKS

Two Tides Brewing Co: A small quirky brewery and cafe with an adventurous beer list and good coffees, plus a cocktail bar downstairs. *7am-10pm Sun-Thu, to midnight Fri & Sat*

Savannah Smiles Dueling Pianos: It's a deliciously kitschy good time at this sing-along nightspot, where patrons decide what's played on stage. *7pm-2am Thu-Sat*

Artillery: Mixologists craft novel, quality cocktails in this opulent space where 19th-century eclecticism meets modern design. *4-11pm Mon-Thu, to midnight Fri & Sat*

El-Rocko Lounge: You'll feel the '70s-inspired swank but then realize that the vibe is absolutely chill. DJs keep the energy high. *5pm-midnight Mon-Wed, to 3am Thu-Sat*

Wormsloe State Historic Site

Vibrant arts-loving Brunswick

Some 80 miles south of Savannah, the town of Brunswick dates from 1771, and has a multicultural vibe with West Indian flavors and a rich local art scene. Check out the new restaurants, bars and tasting rooms that have opened on the main drag, Newcastle St, and if you're sticking around for the night, catch a performance at the **Historic Ritz Theatre** *(goldenislesarts.org)*, which hosts plays, concerts and films.

Captivating Jekyll Island

An easy 20-minute drive from Brunswick, Jekyll Island has miles of beaches, wilderness and historic buildings. Get the lay of the land at **Mosaic Jekyll Island Museum** *(jekyllisland.com; $10)*, which shares the history of the island across a half dozen or so historic time periods, with evocative exhibits – sweetgrass baskets, a miniature portrait and a Red Bug flyer – highlighting the varied stories. Trolley and historic tours *(from adult/child $20/15)* depart the museum throughout the day, including the new Millionaire Motorcar Tour *(up to four people $125)* in a 1930s Model T replica.

Beaches & wild horses of Cumberland Island

More remote, Cumberland Island is the southernmost barrier island in Georgia, and was once an exclusive playground for the elite. Visitors can access it via daily ferries *(cumberlandislandferry.com; adult/child round trip $40/30)* from tiny St Marys and explore the ancient 17-mile-long stretch of moss-covered oak forests, salt marshes and untouched beach. Wild horses roam, sea turtles hatch, and the ruins of a once-grand mansion still stand, begging to be discovered. Reserve well ahead for the ferry.

JEKYLL ISLAND: NEED TO KNOW

An exclusive refuge for millionaires in the late 19th and early 20th centuries, Jekyll Island is a 4000-year-old barrier island with 10 miles of beaches. These include photo darling Driftwood Beach, famed for its fallen skeleton trees. Today the island is an unusual clash of wilderness, preserved historic buildings, modern hotels and a massive campground. And, oddly, it's all part of **Jekyll Island State Park** *(jekyllisland.com)*, complete with a $10 per day parking fee payable upon entry. It's also an easily navigable place – you can get around by car, horse or bicycle.

Alabama

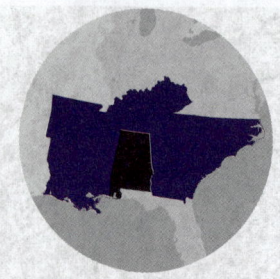

CIVIL RIGHTS | OUTER SPACE | OFFBEAT ADVENTURES

Places
Huntsville p388
The Shoals p390
Birmingham p392
Montgomery p393
Moundville Archaeological Park p395
Mobile p395
Fairhope p396

☑ TOP TIP

Several regions in Alabama (including Muscle Shoals, Huntsville, Montgomery and Birmingham) offer an All-in-One Ticket, allowing you to visit multiple attractions over a set time period at a substantial saving. Purchase it online *(alabama.travel/attraction-tickets)*.

The land of red soil and lilting accents, Alabama is a complicated and oft misunderstood place. Follow a meandering road trip across the state and you'll see cotton fields and vast forests, peaceful riverside towns and booming cities (Huntsville) fueled by burgeoning aerospace and tech industries. And Alabama's nature reserves encompass both sandy Gulf beaches and wooded canyons dotted with waterfalls.

As elsewhere in the South, locals' love for the state runs deep – and not just when it comes to college football. Alabamans take pride as being the birthplace of the Civil Rights movement, where pioneers like Martin Luther King, Rosa Parks and John Lewis inspired people around the globe to fight for a more just and inclusive society. The state is also home to an incredible musical heritage (visit Muscle Shoals for the inside scoop), and the oldest Mardi Gras celebrations in the country – with colorful parades rolling through the Franco-Caribbean streetscape of Mobile.

Huntsville

Culture and green spaces downtown

The birthplace of Huntsville was the gushing **Big Spring**, which produces some 7 million gallons of fresh water each day. A scenic **park** surrounds the meandering waterway, which also anchors downtown Huntsville. You can go for a pleasant stroll here, or feed the ducks, geese and koi fish (strategically placed dispensers dole out pellets for 25 cents).

 GETTING AROUND

Decent intercity transportation is lacking across Alabama, though it is possible to reach some urban areas (including Birmingham, Mobile and Montgomery) by slow Greyhound bus. You'll find walkable centers in some cities, though you'll need a car to reach many sites. Huntsville and Montgomery also have a bikeshare network, Blue Bikes (find details on *tandem-mobility.com*). In 2025, Amtrak re-established train service between Mobile and New Orleans, with two daily departures (morning and evening) in each direction.

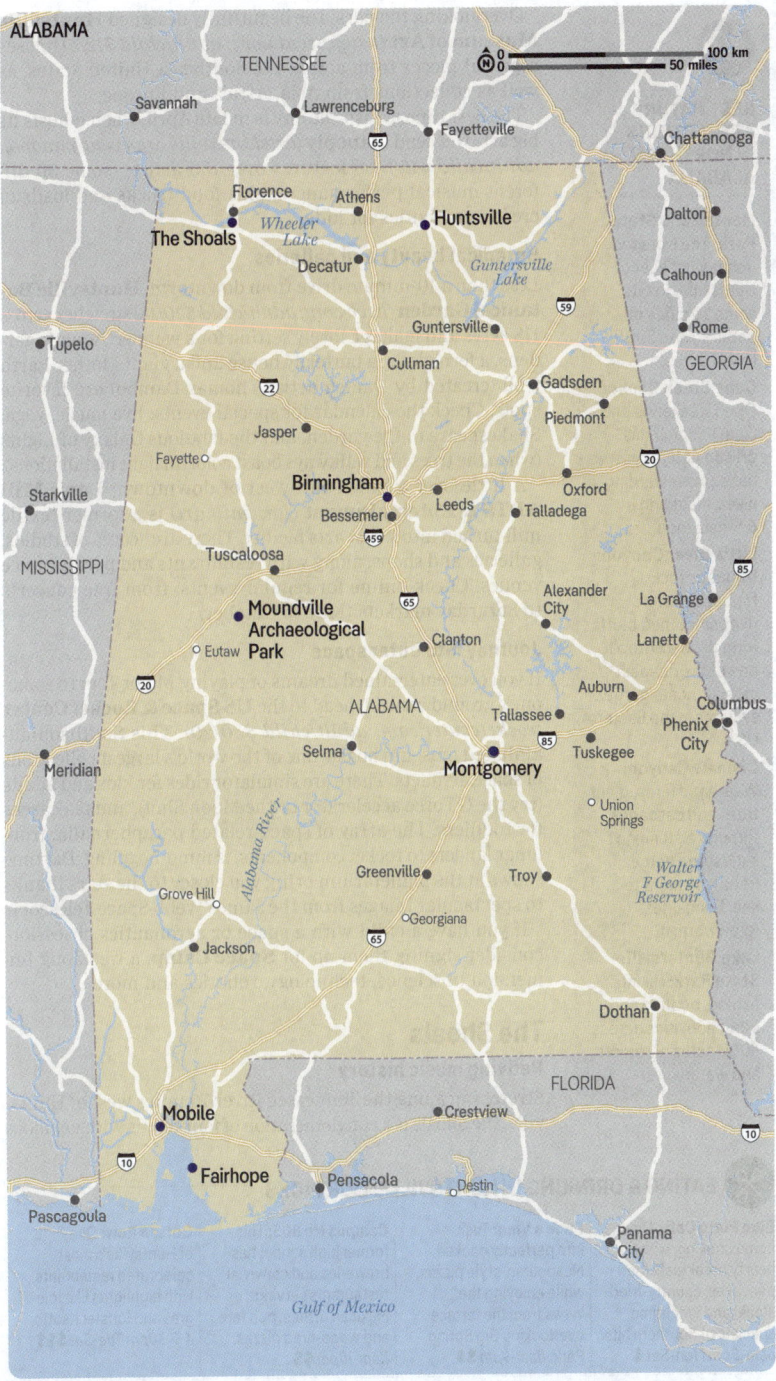

BEST NATURE ATTRACTIONS IN NORTHERN ALABAMA

Monte Sano State Park: The forested upland just east of Huntsville boasts some 20 miles of paths across 2000 lovely acres.

Cane Creek Canyon: Open weekends only (7am to 5pm), this private nature reserve has some rewarding hikes, including a 6.5-mile loop.

Little River Canyon: Dramatic rock formations and river-smoothed bluffs form the backdrop to one of the deepest, most intricate gorge systems in the Eastern USA.

Dismals Canyon: Walk amid ferns, giant trees and cascades through a stunning sandstone gorge. Return by night to see 'Dismalites' (glowworms).

Lake Guntersville State Park: Hiking, fishing, boating and other activities across 6000 acres of forests and waterways.

Overlooking the park, the beautifully designed **Huntsville Museum of Art** *(hsvmuseum.org; adult/child $12/5)* houses regional pieces from across the Southeast United States, as well as collections from Asia, Africa and Europe.

The best time to visit the city is in late April, when it hosts its big arts weekend. **Panoply** *(artshuntsville.org/event/panoply; adult/child $15/free)* features over 100 artists, some 30 different musical performances, plus food trucks and loads of creative activities for kids.

Botanical beauty and galleries

Less than a 10-minute drive from downtown, **Huntsville Botanical Garden** *(hsvbg.org; adult/child $20/13)* stretches across 118 acres and makes a lovely setting for a wander. Aquatic gardens, a fern glade, a butterfly house and a giant Mother Earth troll (created by Danish artist Thomas Dambo) are favorite spots. Check the calendar for special events: live music, yoga, Shakespeare in the garden, and the fabulous Galaxy of Lights (when the trees and walkways boast colorful light installations).

A little over a mile southwest of downtown, **Lowe Mill ARTS & Entertainment** *(lowemill.art)* is a former textile mill turned into a vast arts facility. There are scores of studios, galleries and shops, along with restaurants and performance venues. Check online for regular events, from free concerts to Saturday markets (May to October).

Journey into outer space

If you ever entertained dreams of playing Major Tom to someone's ground control, head to the **US Space & Rocket Center** *(rocketcenter.com; adult/child $30/20)*. This Smithsonian-affiliated museum boasts one of the world's largest collections of space artifacts. There are simulator rides for kids and adults (try the G Force accelerator or the Moon Shot), and play areas for toddlers. The array of space-related paraphernalia, from lunar landers to rocket components, is mind-boggling. Daytime shows at the planetarium bring you closer to the stars thanks to spectacular images from the James Webb Space Telescope.

If you have a child with a space or aeronautics obsession, consider signing them up for **Space Camp**, a weeklong immersion in science, technology, robotics and more.

The Shoals

Reliving music history

Stretching along the Tennessee River 70 miles west of Huntsville, the Shoals is a conglomeration of four towns with nebulous

EATING & DRINKING IN HUNTSVILLE: OUR PICKS

Blue Plate Cafe: Down-home cooking, with hearty breakfasts (berry pancakes, country-fried steak) and lunchtime specials of Southern hits. *6am-8pm Mon-Sat* **$**

Pane e Vino: Tuck into perfectly cooked Neapolitan-style pizzas, while enjoying the views from the terrace overlooking Big Spring Park. *11am-9pm* **$$**

Campus No 805: This former high school has breweries and convivial restaurants serving Mexican dishes, pub fare and wood-fired pizzas. *11am-10pm* **$$**

Cotton Row: One of Huntsville's most celebrated restaurants, with highlights like foie gras and lobster risotto. *4-9:30pm Tue-Sat* **$$$**

US Space & Rocket Center

boundaries and little-known but captivating attractions. Beginning in the 1960s, this lightly populated region became ground zero for some of the most important music production of an era. At **Muscle Shoals Sound Studios** (*muscleshoals soundstudio.org*), you can learn all about the legends that recorded here, including the Rolling Stones, Bobby Womack, Paul Simon and countless others. On a small, intimate guided tour *(adult/child $25/12)*, you'll hear some wild stories from the recording days and listen to iconic songs made right in the studio. Hour-long tours typically run throughout the day, Tuesday through Saturday.

A couple miles south, you can take a similar guided tour through **Fame Studios** (*famestudios.com; adult/child $20/15*), where Wilson Pickett recorded 'Mustang Sally' and Aretha Franklin cut 'Do Right Woman' – among many, many other tracks.

Complete the musical journey with a visit to the **Alabama Music Hall of Fame** (*alamhof.org; adult/child $15/8*), which has instruments, attire and even an over-the-top golden convertible belonging to some of the musical stars that emerged from the state.

Learn about a sightless pioneer

Helen Keller – to this day perhaps the most beloved native of Alabama – was blind and deaf from the age of 19 months. With the aid of companion Anne Sullivan, Keller would go on to attend Radcliffe College, earn a degree and become a noted writer, lecturer and activist for pacifist and socialist causes. The **Helen Keller Birthplace** (*helenkellerbirthplace.org; adult/child $10/5*), her childhood home, is maintained with personal mementos, and guides on hand are happy to share pivotal episodes from Helen's life. *The Miracle Worker*, a play based on Keller's autobiography, is performed here at select dates in June and July.

THE MUSCLE SHOALS SOUND

Chase Brandon, sound engineer at Muscle Shoals Sound Studio, describes the versatile musicians that everyone wanted to record with back in the '60s and '70s @*muscleshoals soundstudio*

The Swampers have been described as very soulful musicians. They confused a lot of people because they looked kind of nerdy. You might see them and think country music, but they were totally into soul and R&B. In the '60s they worked almost exclusively with Black artists doing R&B records: Aretha Franklin, Wilson Pickett, Percy Sledge, the Staple Singers. In the '70s, the Swampers evolved from this one-genre rhythm section, and they recorded with a huge variety of artists: Boz Scaggs, Lulu, Duane Allman, Bob Seger and Paul Simon among many others.

Birmingham

MAP P393

Civil Rights history

One sight not to miss in Alabama is the **Birmingham Civil Rights Institute** (bcri.org; adult/child $15/13), which takes you on a journey through one of the country's most tumultuous periods. A maze of moving audio, video and photography exhibits tells the story of racial segregation and the Civil Rights movement, with a focus on the activities in and around Birmingham.

Nearby, you can learn about the horrifying bombing of the **16th Street Baptist Church** (16thstreetbaptist.org; adult/child $10/5), when four Black children were killed in 1963. Visits are by hourly tour (10am to 3pm Tuesday to Saturday). Today the rebuilt church is a memorial and house of worship (services 11am Sunday).

Across the street, in **Kelly Ingram Park**, walk in the footsteps of those who risked it all to bring an end to segregation. Various sculptures and monuments depict a moment in the Civil Rights struggle. In one space, the path becomes a gauntlet of snarling police dogs, while further along, a water cannon is aimed at visitors.

Around the corner from the park, the **AG Gaston Motel** was where Civil Rights leaders, including Martin Luther King Jr, stayed while in town. It's now run by the National Park Service, with exhibits about the dynamic entrepreneur AG Gaston, a pillar of the Black community.

Showtime!

Going strong since 1927, the **Alabama Theatre** (alabamatheatre.com) is one of the anchors of cultural life in downtown Birmingham. Built as a 2000-seat movie palace, the architectural landmark hosts plays, concerts, big-name comedians and classic films – often followed by audience sing-alongs with the Mighty Wurlitzer (a red-and-gold pipe organ). Across the street, the **Lyric** (lyricbham.com) is a former vaudeville theater that offers a similar line-up of concerts, comedy and dance.

Up the road, the **Sidewalk Film Center** (sidewalkfest.com) is an artfully designed space set beneath the Pizitz Building. Its two theaters screen independent films, and you can while away the evening in the bar and comfy lounge areas before or after catching a film.

Two miles east of downtown, **Saturn** (saturnbirmingham.com) is a sleek live-music venue with a '70s-meets-outer-space aesthetic. There's a fine roster of talent featuring up-and-coming indie rock stars (shows are ages 18 and up). Music aside, there are pinball machines, video consoles and board

---

BIRMINGHAM'S BEST OUTDOOR ATTRACTIONS

Sloss: Wander past soaring, iron-producing blast furnaces that powered Birmingham's economy from 1882 to 1971.

Vulcan: On a hill above Birmingham, a cast-iron statue of the Roman god of metal-working celebrates the city's industrial past. Head up the observation tower for wide views.

Railroad Park: A much-loved downtown green space where all are welcome to regular events (zumba, yoga, line dancing, outdoor concerts).

Red Mountain Park: Some 16 miles of trails including overlooks along forested ridge lines, 8 miles southwest of downtown.

Oak Mountain State Park: Hiking and mountain-biking on over 100 miles of trails in Alabama's largest state park (adult/child $5/2). It's 18 miles south of downtown.

EATING & DRINKING IN BIRMINGHAM: OUR PICKS

MAP P393

Fish Market: Casual spot for fresh-off-the-boat seafood, including crab legs and red snapper. 11am-8:30pm Mon-Sat $$

Essential: Trendy spot with a creative menu and popular weekend brunches. 11am-9pm Mon-Fri, 9am-2pm & 5-9pm Sat & Sun $$

Collins Bar: A beautiful space for sipping handmade cocktails under a Birmingham-centric periodic table of the elements. 4pm-midnight Mon-Sat

House of Found Objects: Bubble machines, a video booth, costumes (ask about cookie monster) and a backroom, entered via a birth canal. 4pm-midnight Tue-Sat

- **HIGHLIGHTS**
  1. Birmingham Civil Rights Institute
  2. Sloss
- **SIGHTS**
  3. 16th Street Baptist Church
  4. AG Gaston Motel
  5. Kelly Ingram Park
  6. Railroad Park
- **SLEEPING**
  7. Elyton Hotel
- **EATING**
  8. Fish Market
  9. The Essential
- **DRINKING & NIGHTLIFE**
  10. Collins Bar
  11. House of Found Objects
- **ENTERTAINMENT**
  12. Alabama Theatre
  13. Lyric
  14. Sidewalk Film Center

games. You can even stop in early (from 8am) if you're after coffee and warm pastries.

Across the road from Saturn, **Avondale Brewing Company** (avondalebrewing.com) pours out the good times courtesy of hazy IPAs, farmhouse ales and easy-drinking lagers. It also has a large outdoor concert venue, where all ages can catch rock, indie and country bands.

Montgomery

In the footsteps of Martin Luther King and Rosa Parks

Martin Luther King Jr had other job offers, but he and his wife Coretta Scott were drawn to Montgomery, and he served as pastor to a dynamic church – with a long history of progressivism – from 1954 to 1960. Now known as the **Dexter Avenue King Memorial Church** (dexterkingmemorial.org), this beautifully designed house of worship draws visitors who want to feel close to an inspiring man – and a congregation – that changed history. Call ahead for a guided tour ($10), which touches on King's leadership during the Civil Rights movement. All are welcome at Sunday services, which begin at 10:30am.

ROLL TIDE!

In the fall, the battle cry of 'Roll Tide' is ubiquitous across Alabama. The 'Tide,' in this case, is the Alabama Crimson Tide, the name of the University of Alabama's football team in Tuscaloosa (an hour's drive from Birmingham), which supposedly derives from a celebrated game of yesteryear. During the 1907 Iron Bowl against Auburn University (still one of the most fiercely contested college-sports rivalries in the country), the Alabama players, dressed in white jerseys, held off their much-favored opponents to a tie while playing in a slurry of red mud.

Seeing Alabama take the field in 100,000-seat **Bryant-Denny Stadium** is a near spiritual experience for avid football fans. Games usually sell out, but you can find resale tickets on StubHub and other sites.

TOP EXPERIENCE

Legacy Sites of Montgomery

Three different sites in Montgomery explore one of the most important topics in US history: the legacy of slavery. Through powerful exhibitions, memorials and monuments, visitors come face to face with 400 years of racial injustice, extending from the first people kidnapped in Africa, through the Jim Crow laws of the post–Civil War era to the rise of mass incarceration today.

The Legacy Museum

TOP TIPS

● You needn't visit all three sites on one day. Your ticket grants admission on subsequent days.

● Free shuttles connect the three sites and the boat launch. A good plan is to park at the Legacy Museum and take the shuttle from there.

The Legacy Museum

Allow at least two hours to wander amid evocative **exhibitions** that bring the horrors of enslavement to life: a wall of waves crashing over the heads of the captured and drowned, jars containing dirt gathered at sites where innocents were lynched, and dramatizations of families being split apart. There are film clips, sound recordings, screenings in small theaters and lots of interactivity – including simulated one-on-one encounters with incarcerated people.

National Memorial for Peace & Justice

On a 6-acre site, a grassy courtyard frames 800 steel **monuments**, each suspended from a metal pole and bearing the names of lynching victims from a particular county. In all, these sculptures memorialize 4400 Black people violently killed across the south and beyond between 1877 and 1950.

Freedom Monument Sculpture Park

Though you can drive there, it's more memorable to take the boat ride (included with admission) to reach the **Freedom Monument Sculpture Park**. The journey alludes to the (involuntary) voyage taken by over 12 million enslaved Africans, nearly two million of whom would die along the way. Once at the park, a path winds past brilliantly conceived sculptures that touch on the traumas of everyday life for those without freedom.

PRACTICALITIES

● legacysites.eji.org
● $5
● 9am-6pm Wed-Sun

For deeper insight into Martin Luther King's life in Montgomery, visit the **Dexter Parsonage Museum** *($10)*, open Friday and Saturday from 10am to 4pm. You'll watch a short introductory film, then take a docent-led tour through the house where King and his family lived. There's an intimacy to the well-preserved 1950s-era spaces, and it's hard not to feel the great man's presence in rooms like his office, with some of his books on theology, philosophy and activism.

King would make history thanks in large part to Rosa Parks. In 1955, activist Parks refused to give up her seat in the whites-only section of a public bus. The **Rosa Parks Museum** *(facebook.com/TroyUniversityRosaParksMuseum; adult/child $7.50/5.50)*, set in front of the bus stop where Parks took her stand, delves into the story behind her courageous stand. Parks, along with Martin Luther King, helped launch the Montgomery bus boycott, which inspired countless communities across the South to stand up to injustice during the Civil Rights movement.

Moundville Archaeological Park
Traces of an ancient civilization

One of the largest and best-preserved sites of the pre-Columbian Mississippian civilization, the 326-acre **Moundville Archaeological Park** *(moundville.museums.ua.edu; adult/child $8/6)* preserves the grassy remains of a mound city. Within the complex you find 29 mounds of varying sizes, arranged in a manner that suggests a highly stratified social structure. The excellent on-site museum is filled with pre-Columbian art, including pottery and disks inscribed with underwater panthers, feathered serpents and skulls. The site is about an hour's drive southwest of Birmingham.

Mobile
Exploring downtown Mobile and the waterfront

The only sizable coastal city in Alabama, Mobile (moh-*beel*) was founded in 1702 – 16 years before New Orleans – and its walkable downtown is awash in history. Speaking of New Orleans, Mobile throws some impressive Mardi Gras parades itself, with bead-tossing, marching bands and abundant merrymaking over several weekends leading up to the big day in February (or early March).

Get your bearings by taking a stroll through the old streets. Conti and Dauphin are dotted with restaurants and pubs, with live music spilling out of doors come sundown. Along the way, stop in scenic green spaces like Bienville Sq and Cathedral Sq, and take in the grandeur of the

REMEMBERING MARTIN LUTHER KING

Nikki Tucker Davis, Deacon at Dexter Avenue King Memorial Baptist Church *dexterkingmemorial.org*

For our church in those days, Dr King was just our pastor. He was very approachable. The kids loved him, the members loved him. When he announced that he was resigning in order to go do more work, he was tearful and emotional, just as our membership was tearful and emotional. He was a funny, caring, charismatic man, who brought forth these big ideas. My uncle, who is 101 years old, was at that first meeting when Mrs Rosa Parks was arrested. He talked about how dynamic Dr King was when he spoke. He moved a whole community, and that spread. That inspiration went throughout this state, and then it spread throughout the world.

 EATING & DRINKING IN MONTGOMERY: OUR PICKS

Martin's Restaurant: Casual spot in a strip mall that's famed for its fried chicken. *11am-7pm Mon-Fri, 10:45am-2:30pm Sun* **$**

Central: Fine dining on wood-fired dishes with international accents, served in an atmospheric 19th-century setting. *5:30-9pm Tue-Sat* **$$$**

Red Bluff Bar: Family-friendly outdoor spot with pub fare, live music and sweeping river views. *4-10pm Tue-Fri, from 1pm Sat & Sun* **$**

Tower Taproom: Lively spot downtown with pour-your-own craft beers, juicy burgers, wings and salads. *11am-9pm Mon-Fri, 2-10pm Sat* **$**

BEST OUTDOOR SITES ON THE GULF COAST

Audubon Bird Sanctuary: On Dauphin Island, a 3-mile trail wends through maritime forest, sand dunes and wetlands – a prime bird habitat.

Gulf State Park: A lovely spot to enjoy the seaside, with beaches, a small nature center (open weekdays) and 28 miles of hiking and cycling trails.

Fort Morgan State Historic Site: Explore this fascinating relic from the past – built during the War of 1812 to protect against potential British invasion of Mobile Bay.

Bon Secour National Wildlife Refuge: Ospreys, alligators and sea turtles can all be found here, along with four trails and a lovely beachfront.

Graham Creek Nature Preserve: Some 10 miles of trails (including accessible boardwalks), plus kayaks for rent.

Cathedral Basilica of the Immaculate Conception *(mobile cathedral.org).*

A good place to learn about the city is the **History Museum of Mobile** *(historymuseumofmobile.com; adult/child $14/11),* with interactive exhibits covering Indigenous people, colonial times, slavery, Civil War days, shipbuilding during WWII and the Civil Rights era. Admission also gives you access to the nearby colonial **Fort Condé**, with both reconstructed and original rooms dating back to the early 18th century.

Nearby, the **National Maritime Museum of the Gulf** *(nmmog.org; adult/child $14/11)* has interactive exhibits on nautical topics like sailing, piloting big vessels, shipwreck exploration and navigation skills. It's a hit with kids.

Three miles east of downtown, the **USS Alabama** *(uss alabama.com; adult/child $18/6)* is a 690ft behemoth famous for escaping nine major WWII battles unscathed. It's worth taking the self-guided tour just to experience the awesome size and might of the 'Lucky A.'

Fairhope

Small-town charm

On the eastern shore of Mobile Bay, the small town of Fairhope has a quaint and pedestrian-friendly center where the order of the day is browsing independent shops, gallery-hopping and enjoying a fine array of food and drinks. You can park at the (free) lot on Oak Ave, then head into the **Eastern Shore Art Center** *(esartcenter.org; free)* for a look at painting, photography and sculpture by local and regional artists. From there, it's a five-minute walk south to the **Fairhope Museum of History** *(free),* where you can peer at a vintage 1935 fire engine, learn about the founders' utopian ideals and see photos of important figures from the Civil Rights era.

Half a block further along, you'll reach the heart of Fairhope (Section St and Fairhope Ave). There's prime shopping within one block in any direction. Staff at the beloved bookstore **Page & Palette** *(pageandpalette.com)* can help you find some new reading material, or head to the back for coffee, cocktails or (later in the day) live music. Music fans should stop in **Dr Music Records** *(drmusic123.com),* which is packed with new and used vinyl. If you have kids in mind, **Fantasy Island Toys** *(fantasyislandtoys.com)* stocks puzzles, board games, dolls and lots of other eye-catching items for children of all ages.

The big event of the month is the **First Friday Art Walk**, when you can catch art openings, live music and special store events (6pm to 8pm).

 EATING IN MOBILE & FAIRHOPE: OUR PICKS

Wintzell's: A Mobile classic since 1938, there's no better spot for fresh or grilled oysters and other Gulf seafood. *11am-9pm Tue-Sun $$*

Loda Bier Garten: Landmark on Mobile's lively Dauphin St, with comfort food, outdoor tables and over 100 draft beer choices. *11am-midnight $*

Panini Pete's: Follow the brick walkway under Fairhope's 'French Quarter' sign to this charming back courtyard, with fabulous beignets and panini. *8am-2:30pm $*

Tamara's: Fairhope's favorite restaurant boasts a wide-ranging menu for brunch, lunch and dinner, and unrivaled happy hour deals (3pm to 5:15pm). *10am-9pm Wed-Mon $$*

Mississippi

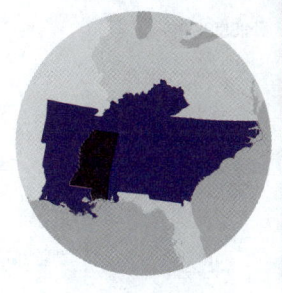

THE BLUES | SOUL FOOD | HISTORY

Flanked by the mighty Mississippi River along its entire western border, the Magnolia State encompasses many identities. You'll find palatial mansions and rural poverty; haunting cotton flats and verdant hill country; sandy beaches on the coast and serene farmland in the north. Often mythologized and misunderstood, this is the land with some of the rawest history in the country – evidenced in the powerful Civil Rights sites in Jackson.

Mississippi is also a place of exceptional artistry. You can see it for yourself in the one-room juke joints of the Delta (especially Clarksdale), where blues players sing heartfelt ballads of love and sorrow that echo the creative spirit that reaches back to the earliest forms of American music. There's folk art on display in shops and galleries across the state, and a rich literary heritage. Richard Wright, Tennessee Williams and Eudora Welty were all born in Mississippi, as was William Faulkner, whose grand house in Oxford draws literary pilgrims from across the globe.

Places
Mississippi Delta p399
Oxford p400
Jackson p401
Vicksburg p402
Natchez p403

☑ TOP TIP
Clarksdale is the big draw for live music, with lots happening on Friday and Saturday nights (it's quieter other days). Check the Cathead store's website *(cathead.biz/music-calendar)* for blues performances in Clarksdale. Find out what's happening elsewhere in Mississippi at *visitmississippi.org/events*.

 GETTING AROUND

Most visitors explore the state by car, but there is an Amtrak train (the *City of New Orleans* line) that passes through Mississippi on its run from the Big Easy to Memphis on to Chicago. The train stops in downtown Jackson, and as well as Marks, which is 18 miles east of Clarksdale – reach out to **CDRY Touring and Cab Services** *(facebook.com/cdrytouringandcabservice)* for a ride. Drivers who want to get off the beaten path can plan their route around scenic byways like Hwy 61 (aka the Blues Highway) or the Natchez Trace Pkwy.

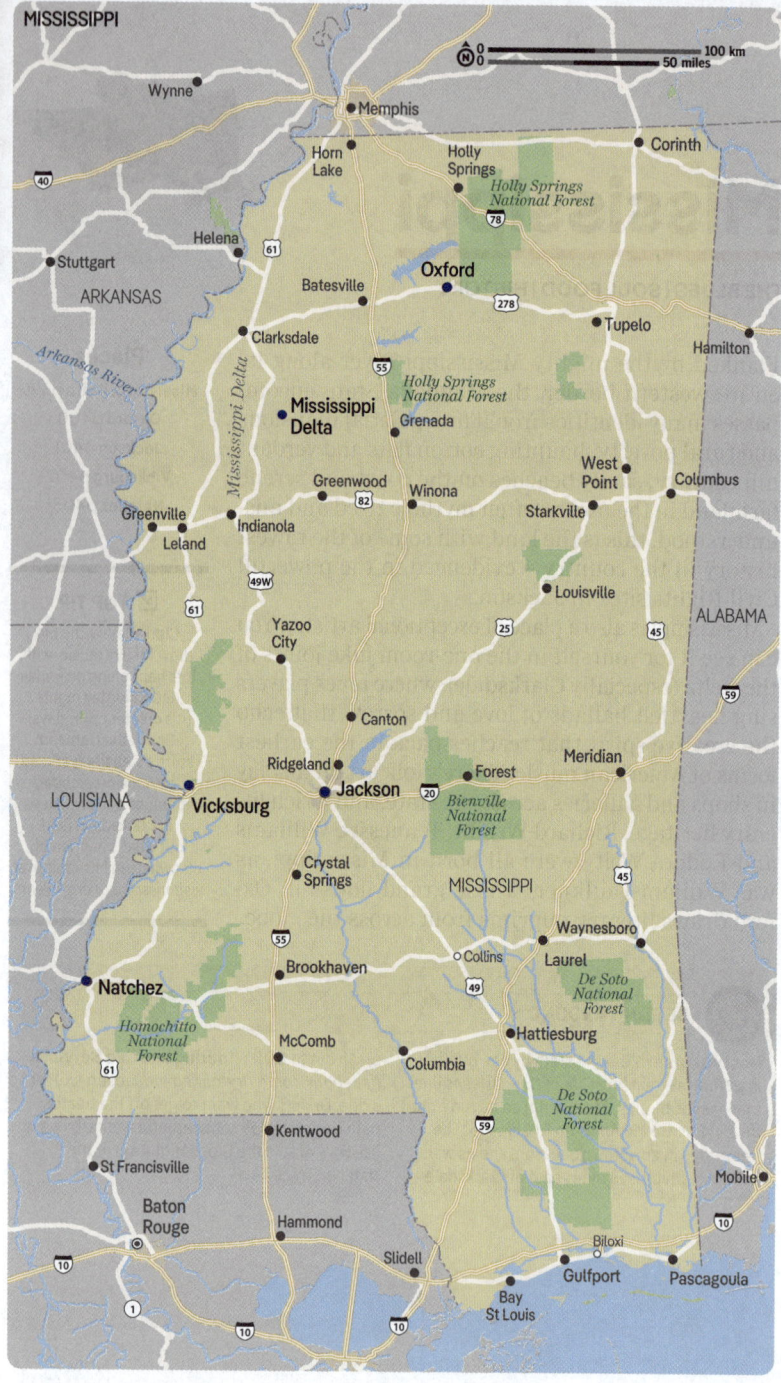

Mississippi Delta

Tracing the Blues Highway

Hwy 61, which follows along the course of the Mississippi River, is often called the Blues Highway for its connection to the USA's rich musical heritage. If you're driving down from Memphis, the **Gateway to the Blues Museum** *(tunicatravel.com; admission $10)* provides a fine introduction to the Delta. Stepping inside the weathered building (modeled after an old-fashioned juke joint), you'll find musical instruments and artwork that reference Muddy Waters, WC Handy and other blues greats. There's also a mini recording studio, where you can record your own song.

Leave ample time for Clarksdale, then continue the journey south to Leland. Take a stroll through the tiny downtown, checking out the various trail markers describing some of the talent (Johnny Winter, James 'Son' Thomas, Charley Booker) connected to the town. Afterwards, visit the **Highway 61 Blues Museum** *(adult/child $7/free),* which has a collection of photos, memorabilia and folk art affiliated with Delta blues singers. The folks who run the place are usually willing to regale you with local stories and blues lore.

Before leaving Leland, check out the **Birthplace of Kermit the Frog** *(free).* Local luminary Jim Henson, the creator of the Muppets, spent the first 12 years of his life in Leland, and his creative work is celebrated at this small exhibit on the bank of Deer Creek. Head onto the deck overlooking the slow waters and bottomland forest, and it's easy to imagine the inspiration for a certain green felt frog.

Take a 15-mile detour east off Hwy 61 to reach Indianola, another sleepy town with deep blues roots. Music fans come here to visit the **BB King Museum** *(bbkingmuseum.org; adult/child $15/10),* which charts the life of the pioneering musician through photographs, film footage, interviews and, of course, music. There are lots of guitars to gawk at (he even gave one to the pope) as well as vehicles (a Rolls Royce, El Camino, and his sleek touring bus). On the grounds attached to the museum, you can see King's final resting place, surrounded by the lyrics of his songs.

Catching live blues in Clarksdale

The scrappy epicenter of the Delta blues scene, Clarksdale is also the region's most useful base. You'll want to spend the night so you can hit the music scene (cover charges range from $10 to $20). Get an overview at the **Delta Blues Museum** *(deltabluesmuseum.org; adult/child $15/10),* which has a small but

SONGS OF THE DELTA

Wilsherie Hopson is a pianist, singer and author of *Recluse: Neglect, Survival, Recovery* @starjukezeta2k1112

Gospel and blues intertwine in Clarksdale. Most blues singers start off in the church. People begin at a young age – often in the choir. It's the foundation for the music scene in Clarksdale, which then becomes our own expression of life, celebration and heartache. The blues are a form of storytelling. There are a lot of great artists here – people like Edna Nicole. We call her 'the sweetheart of the Delta.' Her recent single 'Delta Dirt' basically describes the Delta in one song. You've got to listen to it.

EATING IN CLARKSDALE: OUR PICKS

Our Grandma's House of Pancakes: Start your day off with a hearty breakfast made with care at this old-fashioned charmer. *7am-1pm* $

Hooker Grocer & Eatery: Named after bluesman John Lee Hooker, this inviting place serves up brisket sliders, catfish platters and other comfort classics. *5-9pm Wed-Sun* $$

Abe's Bar-B-Q: Facing the crossroads, Abe's fires up Clarksdale's best pulled pork, plus nicely spiced tamales. *10am-8pm Mon-Sat, 11am-1:30pm Sun* $$

Meraki: The convivial community coffeehouse makes a fine place to recharge over cappuccinos, breakfast sandwiches and occasional live music. *7am-2pm Sun-Thu, to 8pm Fri & Sat* $

BIRTHPLACE OF THE BLUES

The alluvial plains that stretch across the low-lying stretch of Mississippi are a patchwork of cotton fields, lush bayous and lonely roads. American music took root in this place, evolving from the simple but soul-stirring songs developed by Black sharecroppers on cotton fields in the early 1900s. Musician and promoter WC Handy, dubbed the 'Father of the Blues,' helped popularize the 12-bar sound after hearing a sharecropper pluck his guitar with a knife and sing a repetitive tune while the two waited for a train in 1903. Across the Delta today, blues pilgrims can dig deep into the music's genesis and development. Historic interpretive markers pepper the region, noting key sites on the Mississippi Blues Trail *(msbluestrail.org)*.

Square Books

well-presented collection of memorabilia (including guitars from John Lee Hooker and BB King). The shrine to Delta legend Muddy Waters includes the actual cabin where he grew up.

Clarksdale is home to half a dozen atmospheric places to catch live blues. Co-owned by actor Morgan Freeman, **Ground Zero** *(groundzerobluesclub.com)* is a huge and friendly hall with a dance floor surrounded by tables. Bands take to the stage Wednesday to Saturday, and there's good food available. Going strong since the 1980s, the famous **Red's** *(facebook.com/RedsBluesLounge)* has neon-red lighting, which makes a moody backdrop for watching the blues players howl. Another battered juke joint not to miss is **Bad Apple Blues Club** *(facebook.com/badappleblluesclub)*, with memorable afternoon sessions (3pm to 6pm Wednesday to Saturday).

Another requisite stop in Clarksdale is **Cat Head** *(cathead.biz)*, a colorful, all-purpose, blues emporium. Shelves are jammed with books, face jugs, local folk art and blues records. Owner Roger Stolle seems to be connected to everyone in the Delta, and knows when and where the bands will play. Stop here for his weekly 'Sounds Around Town!' music calendar, also posted on the website.

In mid-April, the **Juke Joint Festival** *(jukejointfestival.com)* draws blues lovers to four days of live music from an array of talented musicians. Saturday is the big day, with some 17 outdoor stages scattered around an eight-block stretch of Clarksdale. Daytime events are free, but it's worth buying a wristband *($60)* to get access to nighttime performances at over two dozen venues.

Oxford

Faulkner and Ole Miss

Mississippi's most famous college town has a attractive town center, with restaurants, bars and shops encircling the main square (aka **Courthouse Square**). Start the day with a cafe latte among the collegiate at **Heartbreak Coffee Roasters** (two blocks north of the square), then pick up some new reading material at the excellent **Square Books** *(squarebooks.com)*, one of several booksellers facing the old courthouse.

From here, you can drive or stroll into the campus of the University of Mississippi, better known as Ole Miss. It's about a half mile from Courthouse Sq to the **University of Mississippi Museum** *(museum.olemiss.edu; free)*, where you'll find an intriguing collection of Southern folk art, American luminaries (like Georgia O'Keeffe) and some surprising ancient Greek and Roman works. It's another half mile from here to the Grove, the park-like epicenter of the pretty campus. Alternatively, the museum is also the starting point for a pretty 0.6-mile walk along the easy-going **Bailey Woods Trail**. The path ends at the edge of **Rowan Oak** *(rowanoak.com; adult/child $5/free)*, the grand manor home of William Faulkner, one of America's most lauded 20th-century writers. On a self-guided tour, you can peer in beautifully preserved rooms (some with original furnishings) and learn curious episodes from the author's life – like angrily writing drafts for *A Fable* on the walls of his office after the fan kept blowing his pages around.

Jackson

History and the fight for Civil Rights

You could easily spend half a day exploring the powerful **Mississippi Civil Rights Museum** *(mcrm.mdah.ms.gov; adult/child $15/8, Sun free)* located just a few blocks from the old domed capitol building. Whether it's a voice from overhead yelling at you to 'keep on moving,' graphic photos of lynchings hitting you with a gut punch, or the towering wall of mugshots of Freedom Riders stopping you in your tracks, the exhibits at this compelling museum keep you on high alert. The national Civil Rights movement is explored through the lens of the fight for racial equality in Mississippi, with eight exhibit halls tackling the key eras through photos, film footage, news clippings and interactive screens.

Your ticket also gives you admission to the adjoining **Museum of Mississippi History** *(mmh.mdah.ms.gov)*. For a broader context on the state's history, start here – watch the 10-minute film narrated by Mississippi's favorite native son Morgan Freeman, then wander through the thoughtfully presented galleries. Noteworthy displays, which are often supplemented by informative videos, cover prehistoric mound builders, the Chickasaw and Choctaw tribes and their legends,

BEST MISSISSIPPI MUSIC FESTS

Bentonia Blues Festival: Going strong for over 50 years, this admission-free fest draws blues fans to Bentonia (34 miles north of Jackson) over three days in late June.

Juke Joint Festival: Clarksdale's big mid-April gathering features dozens of bands playing at outdoor stages by day, and packing into the clubs by night.

King Biscuit Blues Festival: The huge October jam happens across the river in Helena, Arkansas, though everyone stays in nearby Clarksdale, and top blues performers play here afterwards.

Bright Lights: In September, several venues in Jackson's Belhaven district host this music and arts fest, featuring jazz, soul, indie-rock and blues.

Double Decker Arts Festival: Catch over a dozen bands playing over one fun weekend in Oxford in late April.

EATING & DRINKING IN JACKSON: OUR PICKS

Brent's Drugs: By day, enjoy burgers and milkshakes at a '50s-style diner. By night visit the hidden bar (Apothecary) for well-made cocktails. *hours vary* $

Elvie's: In a restaurant-packed corner of upscale Belhaven, this stylish gastropub showcases imaginative cooking from Gulf and pasture. *8am-2pm & 4:30-9pm Tue-Sat* $$$

Saltine: A spacious indoor-outdoor spot for seafood, especially oysters, which you can enjoy raw or wood-fired with creative toppings. *11am-10pm* $$

Bean: A delightful coffeeshop with breakfast bowls, avocado toast and sweet pastries, plus a bigger Saturday brunch menu. *7am-6pm* $

THE SIEGE OF VICKSBURG

In 1863 General Grant set his sights on Vicksburg, a city deemed vital to the Civil War's success. The challenge: Vicksburg sat high on bluffs over the Mississippi and was heavily fortified by the Confederates. After several unsuccessful attacks, the Union army laid siege, aiming to starve the city into submission. Under constant shelling, civilians dug shelters underground, making Vicksburg – as one resident described it, 'so honeycombed with caves that the streets look like avenues in a cemetery.' With provisions scarce, mules were eaten, dogs and cats went missing, and even rats were skinned and sold at the market. After 47 days, the Confederates surrendered, and the Union army took control of Vicksburg, which proved a turning point in the war.

the cotton industry, the barbaric practice of slavery, the Civil War and Mississippi's rich cultural heritage.

About a mile west of Mississippi Civil Rights Museum, the **Smith Robertson Museum** *(jacksonms.gov/smith-robertson-museum adult/child $7/4)* is housed in the state's first public school for African American children. The alma mater of the famed novelist Richard Wright, the former school offers insight and explanation into the pain and perseverance of the African American legacy in Mississippi.

Around 3½ miles northwest of there, the **Medgar and Myrlie Evers Home** *(nps.gov/memy; free)* is the ranch-style house where Civil Rights activist Medgar Evers lived with his young family from 1956 until 1963. You can freely wander through the home (don't forget to peek in the fridge), and learn about one of the rising stars in the fight for Civil Rights who was murdered here – shot in the back by a sniper while standing in the carport in 1963. It's run by the National Park Service, with tours hourly from 9am to 4pm (except noon).

Vicksburg

Strolling Mississippi's prettiest town center

Washington St (aka Hwy 61) between Clay and Main Sts is lined with historic buildings that today house galleries, cafes and tiny museums – the fine backdrop to a few hours of exploring. Parking is free on the street.

Get a dose of history at the **Vicksburg Civil War Museum** *(vicksburgcivilwarmuseum.org; adult/child $10/3.50)*. One of the region's only African American–owned Civil War museums gives insight into the conflict, with a special focus on Black soldiers, freedmen and abolitionists.

Just up on the right, **Lorelei Books** *(loreleibooks.com)* is an atmospheric little shop, where you can discover new titles – and there's a good selection from regional authors. Next door, **Highway 61 Coffeehouse** (open 7am to noon) is a cozy spot to curl up with your new book. Upstairs, you'll find one of the best folk art galleries in the state. The **Attic Gallery** *(atticgalleryvicksburg.com)* is packed from floor to ceiling with extraordinary works (paintings, sculptures, mixed media) created by self-taught artists.

One block up, the **Lower Mississippi River Museum** *(free)* explores the region's deep ties to the famous waterway, from the ancient peoples that hunted and fished here to the devastating floods of the 20th century. Head through the galleries to reach the MV *Mississippi IV*, a dry-docked research vessel that you can wander through (a favorite of young visitors).

EATING & DRINKING IN VICKSBURG: OUR PICKS

Walnut Hills: Savor rib-sticking, down-home Southern food, served family-style (solo diners enjoy the round table). *11am-9pm Mon & Wed-Sat, to 2pm Sun* $$

10 South: Take in the views while munching salads, shrimp and grits or hearty sandwiches from this rooftop spot. *5-9pm Tue-Sun, plus 11am-2pm Sat* $$

Key City Brewery: Satisfying house-brewed beers, plus creatively topped pizzas, swordfish and perfectly crispy fries. *4-10pm Mon-Thu, from 11am Fri-Sun* $$

Sun Izakaya: Buzzing new addition, with good sushi, soba and Japanese snacks like *takoyaki* (fried octopus balls). *11am-2:30pm & 4-9:30pm Mon-Sat* $$

USS Cairo Museum

Across the street, visit the small **Catfish Row Museum** *(catfishrowmuseum.org; free)*, which touches on Vicksburg history – including the fight for Civil Rights. Don't miss the drumset of the Red Tops, a group symbolizing the unifying force of the era. More recent is the evocative *Faces* mural painted by Vicksburg artist Kennith Humphrey.

Speaking of murals, it's well worth heading downhill to Levee St, for a look at the **Vicksburg Riverfront Murals** *(riverfront murals.com)*. Created to beautify the city's flood wall in the early 2000s, the 32 works spotlight key people and events in Vicksburg's past: Civil War, natural disasters (like the tornado of 1953) and cultural luminaries (famed Bluesman Willie Dixon).

Driving into the past

Vicksburg controlled access to the Mississippi River, and its seizure was one of the turning points of the Civil War. At the **Vicksburg National Military Park** *(nps.gov/vick; car $20)*, you can follow a 16-mile driving tour that passes artfully carved memorials and historic markers explaining battle scenarios and key events from the city's long siege. Get an overview at the visitor center, where you can watch a 20-minute film and peruse displays about the siege. Afterwards, follow the road to some 15 numbered stops. Don't miss the **USS Cairo Museum**, which covers the ironclad gunboats used by Union forces, including the salvaged USS *Cairo*. For audio commentary along the way, download the free NPS app and follow the Vicksburg self-guided park tour.

Natchez

Centuries of history in a riverside city

Sprawled across a bluff overlooking the Mississippi, the old city of Natchez (settled in 1716) is packed tight with historic buildings – some transformed into museums, restaurants and shops.

NATCHEZ' COMPLICATED PAST

Before the Civil War, the cotton plantations on the eastern banks of the Mississippi River produced the most millionaires in the US – all on the backs of enslaved Africans. In Natchez, plantation owners built over-the-top estates. By the time the Civil War came to Natchez, the town surrendered to Union forces without a fight (interestingly, locals voted against secession in 1861). Abolition stripped plantation owners of their income, but their estates remain frozen in time. Some plantations have been transformed into B&Bs, although it's far more enlightening to visit the federally managed sites (including Melrose) that are part of the Natchez National Historical Park *(nps.gov/natc)*.

THE NATCHEZ TRACE

If you're driving through Mississippi, it's worth planning at least part of your trip around one of the oldest roads in North America: the **Natchez Trace Parkway** (nps.gov/natr). This 444-mile road, today administered by the National Park Service, traces a route once used by Native American tribes and runs from the edge of Natchez, Mississippi, to just outside of Nashville, Tennessee. It's a lovely, scenic drive that traverses a wide array of Southern landscapes: thick forests, soggy wetlands, gentle hill country and long swaths of farmland. There are more than 50 access points to the parkway and a helpful visitor center outside Tupelo. There are no stoplights or stop signs to ruin your ride.

Swamp along the Natchez Trace Parkway

Before delving into the town center, stop at the **Grand Village of the Natchez Indians** (mdah.ms.gov; free). A visitor center displays pottery, tools and fragments of baskets while shedding light on the Mississippian people that lived here for over a thousand years (roughly CE 700 to 1730). Afterwards, take a stroll across the grassy expanse (once a plaza) to see the bare mounds that were previously topped with a temple and a chief's residence.

Fast forward through the years to the 19th century, with a visit to the **Melrose Estate** (nps.gov/places/melrose.htm; free), a sprawling Greek Revival mansion and former plantation. You can freely wander the grounds, but to see inside the house, you'll need to book a guided tour (recreation.gov; adult/child $11/1). Rangers do a decent job describing life for both the plantation-owning McCurran family as well as the enslaved.

Next head into central Natchez and continue your visit on foot. The **Natchez Museum of African American Culture and History** (visitnapac.net; free) highlights Black Mississippians who helped shape the state's history, including the writer Richard Wright and musician Clarence 'Bud' Scott. There are also exhibits on slavery, the cotton industry and Civil Rights.

A few blocks away, the displays inside the **William Johnson House** (free) show what life was like for free African Americans in the pre-Civil War South. When you need a break from the heavy weight of the past, head down to the river and admire the views along the half-mile **Natchez Bluff River Trail**.

EATING & DRINKING IN NATCHEZ: OUR PICKS

Camp Restaurant: Fun atmosphere, good pub grub (pork belly tacos, catfish) and craft beer on tap with Mississippi River views. *11am-8pm* $$

Frankie's on Main: Tuck in to high-end southern cooking inside a grand Greek Revival dining room (and former 1826 bank). *11am-10pm Tue-Sat* $$$

Pig Out Inn: Barbecue fans can't leave Natchez without trying smoky pork or brisket at this casual spot. *11am-9pm Mon-Sat, to 7pm Sun* $

Smoot's Grocery: Listen to blues while sipping tall bloody Marys at this river-facing bar. *6-10pm Thu & Fri, 1pm-late Sat, noon-6pm Sun*

Arkansas

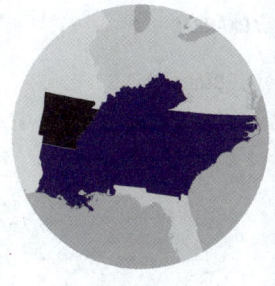

MOUNTAIN BIKING | HIKING | ARTS & CULTURE

Bridging the Midwest and the Deep South, 'the Natural State' exemplifies its nickname with swift-rushing rivers, dark leafy hollows and the crenelated granite outcrops of the age-old Ozark Mountains. The most impressive scenery lies in Arkansas' upper half, but the entire state is blessed with exceptionally well-presented (and generally admission free) state parks and tiny, empty roads crisscrossing dense woodlands and rolling farm fields.

Adventure comes in many forms, from paddling the Buffalo River on day-long or multiday excursions to mountain biking the rugged woodland trails in Bentonville. There are caves to explore and forested paths that lead to towering waterfalls and dramatic overlooks. You can even dig diamonds in one of the state parks – or take it easy with a bit of hydrotherapy in the rejuvenating waters of Hot Springs. Nature aside, Arkansas' towns and small cities are a delight to explore, especially Little Rock, Fayetteville, Bentonville and Eureka Springs.

Places

Little Rock p405
Hot Springs National Park p408
Tri-Peaks Region p409
Crater of Diamonds State Park p410
Fayetteville p410
Eureka Springs p412
Bentonville p413
Ozark Mountains p414

☑ TOP TIP

Be sure to visit at least one Arkansas state park (arkansasstateparks.com) while you're here. The state's 52 parks (most admission free) have an outstanding reputation, and many offer camping and good-value cabin accommodations. Some also have restaurants – like Petit Jean, with its fireplace and sweeping views.

Little Rock

MAP P407

See Clinton's legacy

Former President Bill Clinton served nearly 12 years as governor of Arkansas, so it's fitting that Little Rock houses the

---

 GETTING AROUND

Amtrak's *Texas Eagle* train, which runs from Chicago to Los Angeles, makes stops in Arkansas, including in Little Rock (the station is about 1.4 miles west of the River Market District). Greyhound buses also connect a few cities, but having a car is essential if you plan to explore beyond town centers. Arkansas' roads are generally in good shape, though take things slowly when traveling the narrow mountainous thoroughfares in the north of the state. Parking is free in most places, with the exception of downtown Little Rock and Fayetteville, as well as the streets near Hot Springs National Park.

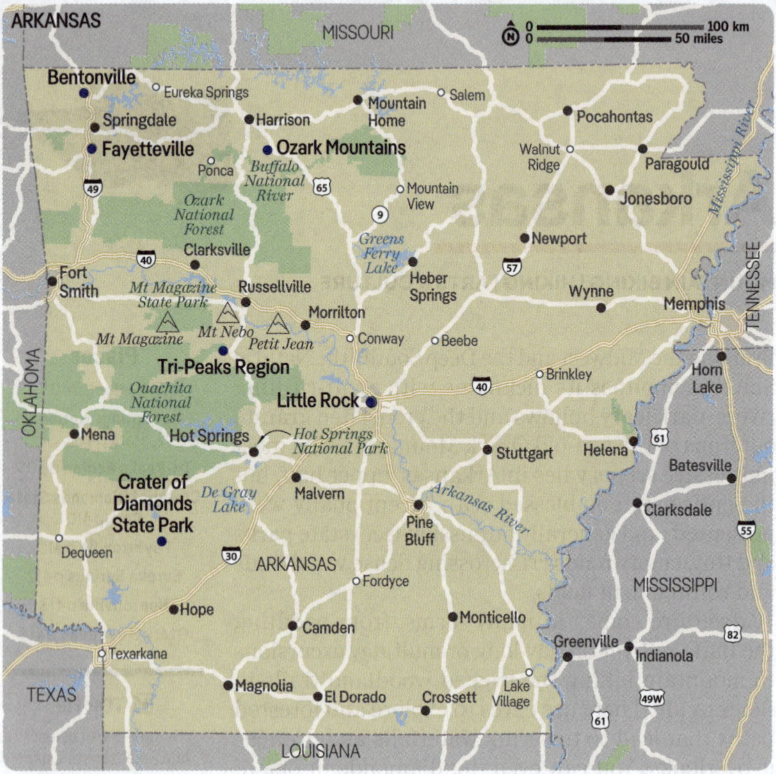

Clinton Presidential Center (*clintonlibrary.gov; adult/child $12/7*). The excellent museum serves as a time capsule of the 1990s when the boy from Hope (Arkansas) was in the White House. Start off with a video about Clinton (narrated by the man himself), then check out the displays of photos and videos highlighting different aspects of his presidency, from his successes bringing down the national debt to his relationships with world leaders (including Nelson Mandela). Speaking of relationships, there's scant attention paid to a certain affair with a White House intern, though his impeachment is mentioned in passing. You can also wander through full-scale replicas of the White House Cabinet Room and the Oval Office, and see gifts from visiting dignitaries

EATING & DRINKING IN LITTLE ROCK: OUR PICKS

MAP P407

Community Bakery: A well-loved gathering space for coffees, flaky bakery items and soups, sandwiches, quiches and daily specials. *7am-8pm* $

Flying Fish: Feast on catfish, barbecue shrimp and fried oyster po'boys at this Cajun-style seafood joint with a vintage diner interior. *11am-9pm* $$

Brood & Barley: Atmospheric gastropub in North Little Rock serving bistro fare (steamed mussels, sliders) along with creative cocktails. *11am-11pm Mon-Sat* $$

Lost Forty Brewing: Little Rock's top craft brewer has a rotating array of IPAs, seasonal brews and Belgian-style ales, plus good pub grub. *11am-9pm* $$

LITTLE ROCK

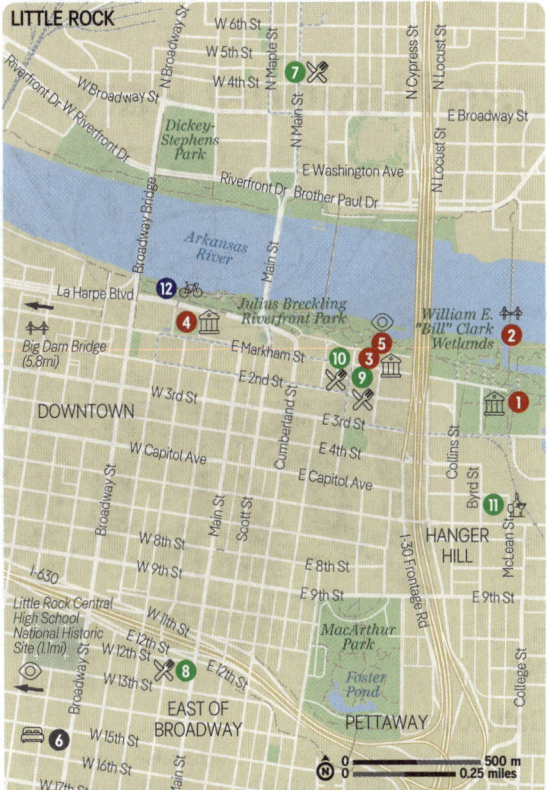

NEIGHBORHOODS OF LITTLE ROCK

River Market District: Waterfront trails, playgrounds and nearby attractions (a theater, restaurants, cafes) on President Clinton Av.

Main Street Corridor: Running south of the waterfront, this stretch of Main St has restaurants and a pocket park that hosts occasional events.

North Little Rock: Just across the Arkansas River from the Riverfront District. Stroll across the pedestrian-only Junction Bridge and head over to Main St, which is filled with shops and eateries (between West Broadway and East 6th Sts).

SoMa: Short for South Main, SoMa is a vibrant neighborhood of galleries, indie shops, restaurants and even a distillery; it's best between West 12th and West 16th Sts.

SIGHTS
1. Clinton Presidential Center
2. Clinton Presidential Park Bridge
3. Museum of Discovery
4. Old State House Museum
5. Witt Stephens Jr Nature Center

SLEEPING
6. Rosemont Cottages

EATING
7. Brood & Barley
8. Community Bakery
9. Flying Fish
10. Ottenheimer Market Hall

DRINKING & NIGHTLIFE
11. Lost Forty Brewing

TRANSPORT
12. Arkansas River Trail

(and also look at menus from state dinners). Don't miss those metal binders – you can peruse Clinton's schedule for every day he was in office.

Explore the riverfront

Stretching along the south bank of the Arkansas River, Little Rock's **River Market District** contains sculpture gardens, playgrounds and even a small wetlands sanctuary. Pedestrian paths wind along the riverfront, providing fine views for the strollers and cyclists passing through. Various bridges cross the river, including the **Clinton Presidential Park Bridge**, a scenic car-free path located near the Clinton Presidential Center.

TOP EXPERIENCE

Hot Springs National Park

Famed for its warm geothermal waters, Hot Springs is both a tiny national park and a charmingly low-key mountain town. Native Americans called this region the Valley of the Vapors, while Euro-American settlers were drawn to the springs' alleged healing powers. Today, restored bathhouses offer insight into the past (several offer old-school treatments), and trails lace through the surrounding woodlands.

Fordyce Bathhouse

TOP TIPS

● Free ranger-led tours from Fordyce Bathhouse happen Thursdays to Mondays (typically 10am and 2pm).

● Behind Bathhouse Row, the **Grand Promenade** passes flowing springs (and a hot-water fountain off Reserve St).

● Near Bathhouse Row, **Maxine's** *(maxineslive.com)* has deep dish pizzas, burlesque shows and live music.

PRACTICALITIES
● nps.gov/hosp
● Fordyce Bathhouse Visitor Center 9am-5pm Thu-Mon
● free

Bathhouse Row

The heart of the National Park is **Bathhouse Row**, a collection of architecturally striking buildings where the upper class once came for several weeks of treatments. Get the lowdown at the 1915 **Fordyce Bathhouse**, which serves as the NPS visitor center and a museum. The well-preserved building has stained-glass, Greek statues and a vintage gymnasium. To experience it for yourself, book an old-fashioned hydrotherapy treatment a few doors down at the **Buckstaff Bathhouse** *(buckstaffbaths.com; from $45)*; reserve well ahead.

Hiking Trails

The park has 26 miles of trails, many of them are short and scenic, and they link up to form a network across the town's mountains. For a pleasant outing, you can hike up from Bathhouse Row via the Peak Trail (0.6 miles) to **Hot Springs Mountain Tower** *(hotspringstower.com; adult/child $14/11)*; there an elevator goes up to a 216ft observation deck. Or skip the expense and continue along the Hot Springs Mountain Trail, the Gulpha Gorge Tail, the Goat Rock Trail and the Upper Dogwood Trail, before completing the loop on the Hot Springs Mountain Trail – all in, a 5-mile (2½-hour) loop.

Cyclists and runners can put in some mileage along the **Arkansas River Trail**, which hugs both sides of the river for 15.6 miles (the **Big Dam Bridge** to the west and the Clinton Presidential Park Bridge to the east are key anchors).

A prime spot for learning about Arkansas' natural world is the **Witt Stephens Jr Nature Center** *(agfc.com/things-to-do/nature-centers/little-rock; free)*. Exhibits explore all of the state's ecological zones, and include small aquariums with fish and even an alligator.

Young travelers will also enjoy the nearby **Museum of Discovery** *(museumofdiscovery.org; adult/child $14/12)*. The fun science-and-natural-history center is perfect for families. Inside hands-on galleries, you can lie on a bed of nails, meander through a kaleidoscope tunnel, climb amid netting and tunnels in a tower, and feel the rumble and roar of a tornado.

For a dose of Arkansas history, visit the **Old State House Museum** *(arkansasheritage.com/old-state-house-museum; free)*, which covers key events of the past since the 1830s. There's a special collection on dresses worn by first ladies, and several galleries devoted to Arkansas governors, including Sarah Huckabee Sanders, who spent time in the governor's mansion as both a teenager (as daughter of Governor Mike Huckabee) and in more recent years as the state's first female governor.

When hunger strikes, stop in the **Ottenheimer Market Hall** *(10am to 2pm Monday to Saturday)*. The spacious food hall has some tempting good-value lunch options, including sushi, Thai cuisine, Middle Eastern cooking, barbecue and fish and chips.

Tri-Peaks Region
Trails, waterfalls and scenic drives

Stretching between the Ouchita and Ozark mountain ranges in the verdant Arkansas River Valley, the Tri-Peaks region is home to three impressive mountains, each protected by its own state park – there's no admission fee at any of them, though you'll have to pay extra for camping or overnighting in a rustic cabin.

The easternmost is **Petit Jean**, which is Arkansas' oldest state park (founded 1923). This is a great place for a hike, followed by a meal with a panoramic view in the old lodge (you can also overnight in a cabin). Some 20 miles of trails wind through this 2658-acre park. The most famous is the moderately challenging Cedar Falls Trail, a 2-mile out-and-back excursion leading to an impressive 90ft waterfall. To see the falls from overhead, you can drive to the Cedar Falls Overlook. Speaking of drives, don't miss the short ride along Red Bluff Dr, which has several fine viewpoints including the Mary Ann Overlook offering glimpses of Mt Nebo and Mt Magazine.

A twisting 25 miles northwest of Petit Jean, **Mt Nebo** may lack vertical glory (topping out at 1350ft) but the valley views are still outstanding from this leafy state park. There are some 32 miles of hiking and biking routes here. On foot, the moderate Rim Trail (a 3.5-mile loop) offers grand views that stretch nearly 100 miles on clear days. The mountain biking is excellent (though you'll need to BYO bike since there's no rental nearby);

TOP FESTIVALS IN ARKANSAS

Ozark Folk Festival: Eureka Springs' big jam fest features flat-picking, mandolin playing and jig dancing over three days in early September.

Hot Springs Documentary Film Festival: Nine days of innovative films in October, plus discussions, parties and even wellness events like hiking and meditation.

Bentonville Bike Fest: Held in May, this major cycling event features competitions, skill workshops, demonstrations, kid activities and group rides.

Bentonville Film Festival: In June, this is a week-long showcase of underrepresented voices in cinema. Don't miss outdoor screenings at The Momentary.

Bean Fest & Championship Outhouse Races: Live music, bean feasting and people-powered potty races happen in Mountain View one weekend in October.

THE LITTLE ROCK NINE

In 1954, the US Supreme Court issued a landmark decision that outlawed segregation in public schools. Despite the ruling, many cities, including Little Rock, bucked the law and kept African Americans out of all-white schools. Change came when nine brave Black students – later known as the Little Rock Nine – enrolled at Central High School in 1957. The backlash was severe. Arkansas governor Orval Faubus sent the state's National Guard to block their entrance. They also faced an angry mob. President Dwight Eisenhower eventually got involved and sent the US Army to guard the students. Learn more about those tumultuous times by visiting the small **Little Rock Central High School National Historic Site** *(nps.gov/chsc; free)* near the still-functioning high school.

you'll find everything from the beginner friendly Miller's Goat Trail (5.3 miles) to the experts-only Lizard Tail (1.9 miles), not to mention the rewarding intermediate-level Chickalah Loop Trail (4.8 miles), among the best in the park.

Another 35 miles west of Mt Nebo, you'll reach **Mt Magazine**. Home to Arkansas' highest point (at 2753ft), this state park is a draw for hikers seeking bragging rights. The climb up Signal Hill takes you there, and it's a fairly easy 1.8-mile loop, with just over 250ft of elevation along the way. If you don't have time for a walk, the **Mt Magazine Scenic Byway** traverses the park and includes some memorable vistas of forests, lakes and valleys along the way as it connects Havana with Webb City along Hwy 309.

Crater of Diamonds State Park

Dig for diamonds

Some 60 miles southwest of Hot Springs, the **Crater of Diamonds State Park** *(adult/child $15/7)* is a one-of-a-kind place where you can dig through a 37-acre field (a former volcanic crater) in search of rocks, minerals and gemstones. Some 35,000 diamonds have been unearthed here, including an 8.5 karat one in 2015 worth a cool $1 million. On the downside, you'll be digging in the dirt on an exposed field in often scorching temperatures. You can bring your own gear, or rent tools from the park (shovel, box screen, bucket).

Fayetteville

Arts and culture

Nestled in the woodsy hills of the Ozarks, Fayetteville is the state's third largest town, fueled by the youthful energy of the **University of Arkansas**. On Fayetteville's west side, the leafy campus has wide-ranging cultural offerings, from classic and cutting-edge plays at the **University Theater**

Crater of Diamonds State Park

(theatre.uark.edu/productions) to concerts at the **Faulkner Performing Arts Center** (faulkner.uark.edu).

The town's love of the arts isn't limited to the university. In the center, the **Walton Arts Center** (waltonartscenter.org) stages Broadway musicals, comedy shows, rock concerts and even puppet theater. Nearby, **TheaterSquared** (theatre2.org) stages more avant-garde shows, with a packed calendar of more than 350 performances and events each year.

Walkng around downtown Fayetteville

Fayetteville's attractive downtown is has plenty of indie shops, restaurants and cafes. A good place to begin the exploration is at **Fayetteville Historic Square** – especially lively on Saturday mornings during the weekly **farmers market** (fayettevillefarmersmarket.org; 7am-2pm). Nearby, you can browse for quality home items, outdoor gear and gourmet provisions at **City Supply** (citysupplyfayetteville.com). You can also pick up some vinyl at **Block Street Records** (facebook.com/blockstreetrecords), and recharge over lattes and bakery items at **Little Bread Company** (littlebread.com).

Later in the day you can enter a hallowed electric realm at **Pinpoint** (pinpointfayetteville.com), a bar full of pinball machines, or drink quality bourbon cocktails at **Vault** (vault.bar; the mint juleps are ideal warm-weather refreshment).

PRIME MOUNTAIN BIKING SPOTS

Dave Neal, owner of Mojo Cycling, shares his favorite rides for first-time visitors to the Bentonville area @mojocycling.com

A good starting point is Bella Vista, just north of Bentonville. In the Back 40, there's a little entry park called Blowing Springs. It has numerous short trails that vary in technicality. There are beginner trails, where I taught my kids to ride, and more robust and tough trails too. There's also camping in the middle of it. So you can stay there and roll right out of your tent and on to a trail. Another great spot is called the Castle, found in Slaughter Pen. There are trails for all different levels here, and also a skills park where you can really progress as a rider.

 EATING & DRINKING IN FAYETTEVILLE: OUR PICKS

Hammontree's Grilled Cheese: Inviting spot for elevated comfort food: panko-fried artichoke hearts, French onion soup and decadent sandwiches. *11am-9:30pm Mon-Sat* $

Cheers at the OPO: Upscale Southern comfort fare (fried green tomatoes, wood-fired meats) inside a grand building that was a former post office. *11am-10pm Wed-Sun* $$

Farmer's Table: An old house turned restaurant with outstanding locally sourced dishes. Best choice for breakfast. *7am-3pm Tue-Sun, plus 5-9pm Fri & Sat* $$

Maxine's Tap Room: An atmospherically lit drinking den with well-crafted cocktails and regional microbrews. *4pm-2am Mon-Sat, from 6pm Sun*

STROLLING EUREKA SPRINGS

One of the Ozarks' most photogenic towns, Eureka Springs is a hilly enclave of winding streets, Victorian architecture and eye-catching shops.

START	END	LENGTH
Crescent Hotel	Eureka Springs Historical Museum	1 mile; 1½ hours

Park just above the town at the ❶ **Crescent Hotel**. Step inside this still-functioning 1886 grande dame, which is full of vintage character. Head to the top-floor Skybar for a bite or drinks on the terrace. Walk out the back through the hotel grounds and cross the street to ❷ **St Elizabeth**, a striking limestone church built in 1909. Turn left out of the church, and find the ❸ **Magnolia Path**. Descend through the trees and keep going downhill (at times on a wooden sidewalk). You'll eventually end up on Spring St, which takes you past vine-draped ❹ **Harding Spring**, one of many picturesque springs for which the town is famed. Further along, you can pick up handmade watercolors and other creative supplies at ❺ **Adventure Art**. Across the road, ❻ **MoJo's Records** stocks quality vinyl, and there's a cafe attached.

Keep following Spring St as it winds and curves down the hillside, and you'll soon be in the heart of town, with colorful shops and galleries, cafes and restaurants. Finish at the ❼ **Eureka Springs Historical Museum**, where you can learn about local history. If you don't want to walk back up the hill, hop on the trolley (red line; $4), which will take you back to your starting point.

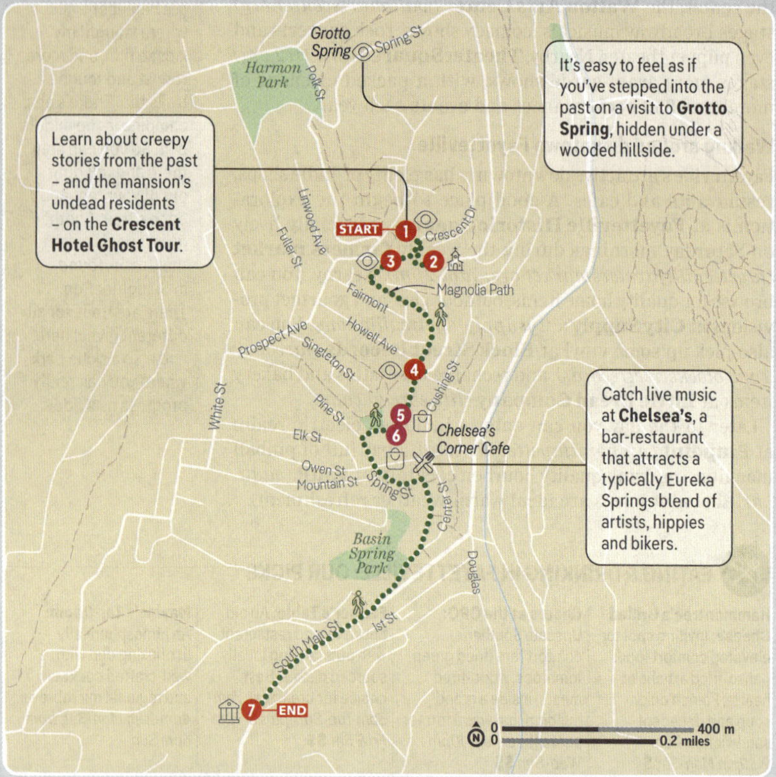

> Learn about creepy stories from the past – and the mansion's undead residents – on the **Crescent Hotel Ghost Tour**.

> It's easy to feel as if you've stepped into the past on a visit to **Grotto Spring**, hidden under a wooded hillside.

> Catch live music at **Chelsea's**, a bar-restaurant that attracts a typically Eureka Springs blend of artists, hippies and bikers.

For the unadulterated student-life experience, head a few blocks northwest to **Dickson Street**. Between University and Thompson Aves, you'll find live music spots (**George's Majestic Lounge**, the **Piano Bar**), buzzing little cafes and inviting stores – like the excellent **Dickson St Bookshop** (*dicksonstreetbooks.com*).

Bentonville

Ride the fabled trails

One of the best places for mountain biking in the US east of the Rockies, the Bentonville area has over 160 miles of pathways and bikeways, streetside bicycle paths and looped trails. You could spend many days happily exploring this system with its free well-marked trails, each rated beginner (green), intermediate (blue) or expert (black diamond).

With limited time focus your attention on **Slaughter Pen**, with its 40-plus miles of single track of all levels. Between berms, big rocks and forests, you'll get a great taste of local nature. You can access the Pen via the All American Trail, a mountain-biking route that connects to the Crystal Bridges Museum. Another highlight is **Coler Mountain**, with its 17 miles of varied trails (best accessed via NW 3rd St, about 1.8 miles west of Bentonville City Sq).

Pick up a free map of the entire network at the visitor center or at outfitters like **Mojo**, which rents high-quality mountain bikes (*mojocycling.com; 4hr rental $40-100*).

Be sure to also check out the **Ledger**, a rare bikeable building (follow the jewel-carrying insect mosaics up six stories of ramps). Stop for a pick-me-up on the ground floor at **Airship Coffee**.

See cutting-edge art in the Crystal Bridges Museum

Sprawling across a series of creek ponds fed by mountain streams, the enormous **Crystal Bridges Museum** (*crystalbridges.org; free; closed Tue*) is an unexpected find, to say the least. The curved pavilions, designed by acclaimed architect Mosh Safdie, house extensive collections that are connected by glass-encased tunnels, and the experience consistently filters sunlight through and across the grounds. The permanent collection focuses on artists active in the USA – everyone from Harlem Renaissance painter Jacob Lawrence to Osage photographer Ryan RedCorn. Special exhibitions (with admission prices) roam the globe, with recent retrospectives devoted to Yayoi Kusama, KAWS and Diego Rivera. Surrounding the museum, sculptures by renowned artists punctuate several leafy trails, including the **Art Trail**.

BENTONVILLE'S BEST ART & CULTURE EXPERIENCES

Skyspace: James Turrell's sky-centric circular chamber features a mesmerizing light installation beginning 45 minutes before sunrise and 10 minutes before sunset.

Bachman-Wilson House: Wander through this small, ingeniously designed home, dreamed up by the great Frank Lloyd Wright. Reserve a free ticket through *crystalbridges.org/calendar/frank-lloyd-wright-tours*.

Museum of Native American History: Impressive collection of artifacts made by cultures across the Americas.

Amazeum: A huge kids' museum with loads of fun, hands-on activities.

Walmart Museum: Learn the story behind Walmart.

Momentary: The factory-turned–creative hub has art exhibitions, live music and a top-floor cafe-bar.

 EATING & DRINKING IN BENTONVILLE: OUR PICKS

Meteor Cafe: Sunny, anytime spot with well-pulled espressos and tasty breakfast tacos, plus pizzas and margaritas later on. *7am-10pm* $

Wright's Barbecue: The famed destination for brisket, pulled pork, fall-off-the-bone ribs and other smoky decadence. *10:30am-8pm Tue-Sat* $$

Hub: A favorite post-ride gathering spot for Tex-Mex, craft beers and events (live music Fridays, trivia night Wednesdays). *11am-10pm Tue-Sun* $$

Table Mesa Bistro: One of many appealing spots overlooking Bentonville's photogenic main square, serving creative bowls, Mexican fare and burgers. *8am-9pm Mon-Sat, 9am-8pm Sun* $$

TOP HIKES IN THE OZARKS

Go after the rains to see waterfalls in all their flowing majesty.

Hemmed-in Hollow Falls: From the Compton Trailhead, make the 2.5-mile descent to this stunning 209ft waterfall. It's a challenging return (over 1300ft elevation gain).

Big Bluff & the Goat Trail: Start at the Centerpoint Trail to eventually reach (via exposed ledges in places) a fantastic view over the Buffalo River (6 miles return, with 1000ft elevation gain).

Hawksbill Crag: A moderate 2.7-mile out-and-back hike to cinematic Hawksbill Crag (aka Whitaker Point).

Glory Hole Falls: This moderate 2-mile return hike takes you to an unusual waterfall that pours through a hole in a rockface.

Alum Cove: Make the fairly easy 1.2-mile loop to see a natural rock bridge spanning over 130ft.

Buffalo National River

Ozark Mountains

On the trail in Devil's Den

Tucked in the lush Lee Creek Valley, some 25 miles south of Fayetteville, the **Devil's Den State Park** *(free)* is a favorite getaway for hiking, trail running, mountain biking and camping. The route not to miss is the relatively straightforward 1.5-mile Devil's Den Trail, which courses past waterfalls (flowing after the rains), dense greenery and the eerie rock formations that give the state park its name.

Paddle the Scenic Buffalo National River

Designated the nation's first national river, the **Buffalo** rolls west to east for 135 glorious miles through the heart of northern Arkansas. Along the way, the rushing waters pass by ochre cliffs and granite outcroppings, while lapping at small sandy beaches that fringe deep tracts of Ozark forest. For a memorable DIY adventure, rent a kayak or canoe for the day ($72 to $102) from **Buffalo Outdoor Center** *(buffaloriver.com)* in Ponca and make the 10-mile paddle to **Kyle's Landing**. They also offer shuttle service *(from $46),* which means they'll drive your car to your arrival point, so you can head off when you finish the day's paddle. This wild river is also a great spot for multiday trips, and you can camp at designated campsites along the way. Check the National Park site *(nps.gov/buff)* for more details.

Into the Underworld at Blanchard Springs Caverns

The spectacular **Blanchard Springs Caverns** *(blanchardsprings.org),* 15 miles northwest of Mountain View, were carved by an underground river. It's a little-known, mind-blowing spot in Arkansas. Guided tours *(adult/child $15/10)* like the accessible one-hour Dripstone Trail and the 1½-hour Discovery Trail (more challenging, with its 700 steps) are offered regularly. Reserve ahead through *recreation.gov.*

New Orleans

CREOLE COOKING | FIERY JAZZ | EUROPEAN ARCHITECTURE

No matter how many cities on this planet you visit, you'll never find one quite like New Orleans. When it comes to food, live music and celebration, New Orleanians have perfected the art of living large. Creole chefs have honed recipes for gumbo, jambalaya, char-grilled oysters, crawfish and decadent seafood combinations from the bountiful Gulf Coast. The city is famed for Mardi Gras and its weeks of parades, bands and costuming, but there's revelry throughout the year – from the myriad performances at Jazz Fest to the merriment of Halloween. The birthplace of jazz is also a great place to enjoy the vibrant, ever-evolving soundtrack that defines the Big Easy.

The starting point for the New Orleans experience is undoubtedly the French Quarter, with its centuries-old architecture, historic restaurants and cobblestone streets both elegant (Royal) and louche (Bourbon). Outside the Quarter, you'll find fascinating, largely local-centric neighborhoods, including the bohemian-loving Bywater, the grand Garden District and the Marigny – the epicenter of NOLA's live music scene.

Celebrating New Orleans' Style
Fun times during Mardi Gras and Jazz Fest

Mardi Gras *(mardigrasneworleans.com)* is about many things: massive floats rolling through packed streets, hilariously costumed krewes shimmying in unison to vintage disco and vast marching bands blasting out heart-pounding rhythms. There are also walking parades open to all (with a costume), and joining in is the best way to experience New Orleans' biggest celebration.

The parade season is a 12-day period beginning two Fridays before Fat Tuesday (in February). Early parades are charming, neighborly processions that whet your appetite for later events, which increase in size and grandeur until the spectacles of the

GETTING AROUND

New Orleans has a flat, fairly compact center. Streetcars, buses, bikeshares and rideshares connect different parts of the city. Within neighborhoods, walking is one of the best ways to get around. Riding one of New Orleans' historic streetcar lines is a must. The most scenic is the St Charles Ave line, which runs from the the edge of the French Quarter, passing through the Garden District, Uptown and lovely Audubon Park. Two slightly different lines follow Canal St to Mid-City, including the City Park line, which takes you to the entrance of New Orleans' biggest green space.

NEW ORLEANS THE SOUTH

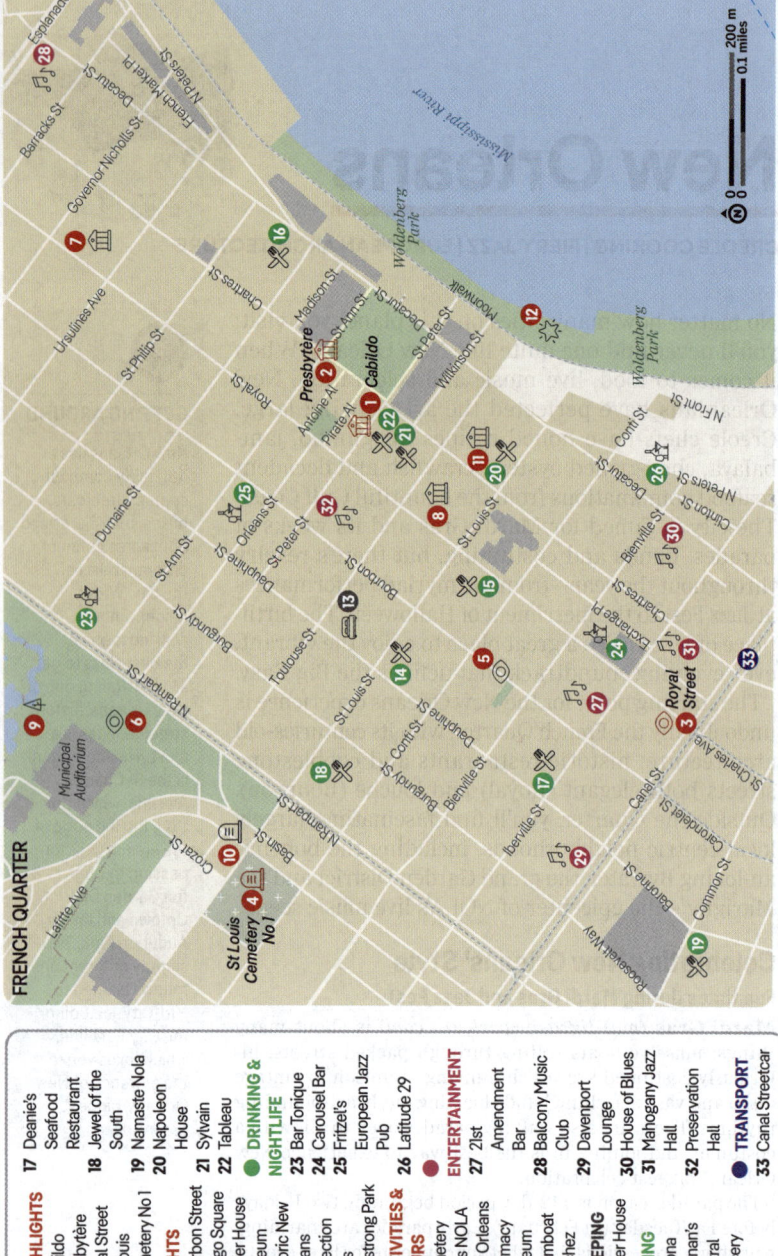

FRENCH QUARTER

★ HIGHLIGHTS
1. Cabildo
2. Presbytère
3. Royal Street
4. St Louis Cemetery No 1

SIGHTS
5. Bourbon Street
6. Congo Square
7. Gallier House
8. Historic New Orleans Collection
9. Louis Armstrong Park

ACTIVITIES & TOURS
10. Cemetery Tours NOLA
11. New Orleans Pharmacy Museum
12. Steamboat Natchez

SLEEPING
13. Olivier House

EATING
14. Bayona
15. Brennan's
16. Central Grocery
17. Deanie's Seafood Restaurant
18. Jewel of the South
19. Namaste Nola
20. Napoleon House
21. Sylvain
22. Tableau

DRINKING & NIGHTLIFE
23. Bar Tonique
24. Carousel Bar
25. Fritzel's European Jazz Pub
26. Latitude 29

ENTERTAINMENT
27. 21st Amendment Bar
28. Balcony Music Club
29. Davenport Lounge
30. House of Blues
31. Mahogany Jazz Hall
32. Preservation Hall

TRANSPORT
33. Canal Streetcar

superkrewes emerge during the final weekend. Download the WDSU Parade Tracker app to see what's on when.

Held in late April and early May, the New Orleans **Jazz & Heritage Festival** *(nojazzfest.com)* features a fabled lineup of bands and soloists from a wide range of genres. Local talent adds to the national and international superstars, and there's also outstanding food, a folklife village and kids' activities. In January, the musical acts are announced and tickets go on sale. Get info and buy tickets on the website. It all happens in Mid-City at the Fair Grounds Race Course.

Delve into New Orleans' History & Culture

MAP P416

A quartet of thought-provoking museums

A combination of preserved buildings, museums and research centers all rolled into one, the **Historic New Orleans Collection** *(hnoc.org; free)* presents a series of regularly rotating exhibits – among the most insightful in the city. Don't miss the French Quarter Galleries, with multimedia displays ranging from Native American settlement to 18th-century French colony to buzzing modern cultural hub.

The former seat of power in colonial Louisiana, the **Cabildo** *(louisianastatemuseum.org; adult/child $11/9)* gives a fine overview of the past with its collection that covers everything from Native American tools (1st floor) to 'Wanted' posters for escaped enslaved people (3rd floor).

Next door to the Cabildo, the 1791 **Presbytère** *(louisiana statemuseum.org; adult/child $11/9)* focuses on both the positive and negative aspects of life in New Orleans, namely Mardi Gras revelry and devastating hurricanes – in particular Hurricane Katrina.

Set in one of the country's oldest apothecaries, the **New Orleans Pharmacy Museum** *(pharmacymuseum.org; adult/child $10/7)* has cabinets full of assorted elixirs once thought to be therapeutic, along with frightening-looking hypodermic needles and bone saws. Book ahead for 45-minute guided tours *(adult/child $20/17)* that shed light on the epidemics, nefarious 'cure-alls' and primitive medical treatments (opium, leeches, mercury injections) of centuries past.

THE CARIBBEAN CONNECTION

Following a 1791 revolt led by enslaved people, thousands of slaveholders fled St Domingue (now Haiti) with their 'property' (enslaved human beings) to Louisiana, which bolstered French-speaking Creole traditions. At the same time, thousands of the formerly enslaved also relocated from St Domingue to New Orleans as free people of color. By 1810, some 10,000 of these islanders had come to the city, doubling the total population and tripling the population for the free people of color. This influx from St Domingue also injected an indelible trace of Caribbean culture that remains in evidence to this day. Their most obvious contribution was the practice of voodoo, which became popular in New Orleans during the 19th century.

EATING IN THE QUARTER: CASUAL DINING

MAP P416

Napoleon House: A 1797 building packed with history; its atmospheric courtyard is a magical spot for classic Creole cooking. *11am-10pm* **$$**

Sylvain: In a stylish carriage house, Sylvain is a convivial spot for well-executed comfort fare. *10:30am-3pm Fri-Sun, plus 4-11pm daily* **$$**

Central Grocery: Famed for its muffuletta, a massive sandwich stuffed with meat, cheese and olive salad. Get it to go and eat by the river. *9am-5pm* **$**

Deanie's Seafood Restaurant: Temptations run from BBQ shrimp to charbroiled oysters. *11am-9:30pm Thu-Mon, from 4pm Tue & Wed* **$$**

A PROMENADE IN THE FRENCH QUARTER

Explore the historic heart of New Orleans, taking in eclectic architecture, iconic monuments and a grand sweep of riverside.

START	END	LENGTH
Jackson Square	Riverfront	1 mile; 1½ hours

Start on Chartres St on the edge of 1 **Jackson Square**, which is quiet in the morning but later in the day bubbles with activity (buskers, tarot readers, tour groups). From here, you can take in some of the Quarter's grand architecture, including 2 **St Louis Cathedral**. Though the current building dates from the 1850s, previous iterations of the church date as far back as 1718.

At 3 **632 1/2 St Peter Street**, you can peer up at the 2nd-floor balcony of the house, where Tennessee Williams lived in 1946 and 1947. It was here that he wrote his famed *A Streetcar Named Desire*. Head around the corner and continue along elegant 4 **Royal St**, which has plenty of architectural eye candy, before making your way to the 5 **French Market**, which has numerous food and craft stalls. A trading post for centuries, the present 19th-century structure was designed by Joseph Abeilard, one of the USA's first African American architects.

New Orleanians have an abiding affection for Joan of Arc, manifest in the gilded 14ft, 2700-pound 6 **statue** that was gifted to the city by the people of France in 1964. Cross Decatur and head up to the 7 **riverfront**. From here you can amble along the muddy Mississippi enjoying fine views across the water.

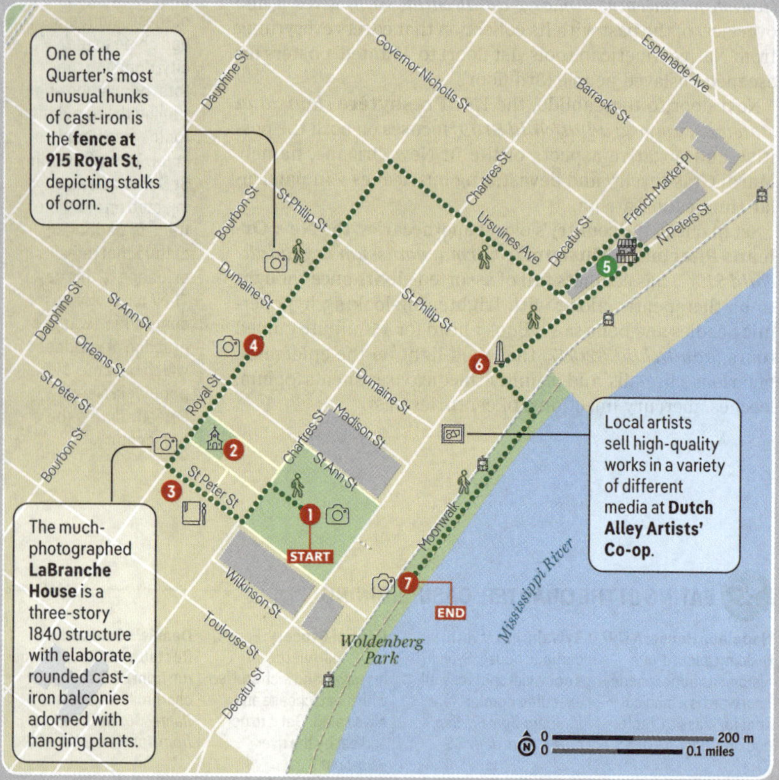
One of the Quarter's most unusual hunks of cast-iron is the **fence at 915 Royal St**, depicting stalks of corn.
The much-photographed **LaBranche House** is a three-story 1840 structure with elaborate, rounded cast-iron balconies adorned with hanging plants.
Local artists sell high-quality works in a variety of different media at **Dutch Alley Artists' Co-op**.
Governor Nicholls St
Esplanade Ave
Barracks St
Dauphine St
Chartres St
French Market Pl
N Peters St
Ursulines Ave
Decatur St
St Philip St
Bourbon St
Dumaine St
St Ann St
Orleans St
St Peter St
Royal St
Madison St
Moonwalk
Mississippi River
Wilkinson St
Toulouse St
Woldenberg Park
START
END
0
200 m
0.1 miles

Strolling Royal Street

MAP P416

Architecture and eye-catching shops

Royal Street, with its handsome storefronts stretching beneath cast-iron balconies, is one of the Quarter's prettiest thoroughfares. Several blocks of the strip are dedicated to antiques stores and art galleries, making Royal a sort of elegant 19th-century outdoor shopping arcade. The stretch between Bienville and Orleans closes to traffic between 11am and 4pm (until 7pm weekends), when musicians, performers and other buskers set up shop (don't forget to tip).

Cruising the Mississippi

MAP P416

Fun times on a paddlewheeler riverboat

For an old-fashioned dose of slow travel, book a trip along the Mississippi in an old paddle wheeler. Two main boat companies offer similarly themed cruises, including history-themed tours *(adult/child $42/17)*, jazz brunches *(adult/child $69/35)* and dinner excursions with live music (adult/child $95/40). The **Steamboat Natchez** *(steamboatnatchez.com)* departs from a pier near the base of Toulouse St, while the **Creole Queen** *(creolequeen.com)* sails from the river end of Poydras St, behind the Four Seasons Hotel.

Portal into the Past

MAP P416

Take a historic house tour

Get a deeper understanding of New Orleans by taking a guided tour through one of its house museums (reserve these ahead). The **Gallier House Museum** *(hgghh.org; adult/child $17/14)* exemplifies a style unique to the French Quarter thanks to the innovations of famed architect James Gallier Jr, who designed the house in 1860. Guides point out unique features like double skylights and indoor plumbing with hot and cold running water – cutting-edge technology at the time. You'll also learn about the residents, including the four enslaved people – Laurette, Rose, Julienne and Francois – who occupied the quarters out back.

The Legendary Jazz Spot

MAP P416

An evening at Preservation Hall

Housed in a former art gallery dating from 1803, **Preservation Hall** *(preservationhall.com; $25)* is one of New Orleans' most storied live-music venues, but it's unlike other places in town. You must purchase tickets online before coming, shows

TOP LIVE MUSIC SPOTS IN THE QUARTER

21st Amendment Bar: A great jazz bar that rarely has a cover charge (one drink minimum) on Iberville.

House of Blues: Home to several different live music venues, this national chain stages some excellent bands – not just blues.

Davenport Lounge: The Davenport is inside the Ritz Carlton and offers quality jazz to a well-dressed crowd.

Balcony Music Club: This buzzing spot on Decatur St has live music daily with a wide range of acts – jazz, blues, rock and funk.

Mahogany Jazz Hall: This somewhat newish space has vintage vibes and outstanding performances from the likes of trumpeter Leroy Jones.

 EATING IN THE QUARTER: FINE DINING

MAP P416

Jewel of the South: Tucked behind a cottage, the courtyard here is as enchanting as the cuisine. *5-11pm Wed-Mon, from 11:30am Fri & Sat* **$$$**

Bayona: A slow-food pioneer, Bayona is classy but unpretentious. *6-8:30pm Tue-Sat, plus 11:30am-1:30pm Thu-Sat* **$$$**

Brennan's: One of the grandes dames of Creole dining, Brennan's has famous dishes (Gulf fish amandine) and decadent breakfasts. *9am-9pm* **$$$**

Tableau: Book a table on the balcony for memorable views while indulging in haute-Creole cuisine and crème brûlée. *11am-9pm Wed-Sun* **$$$**

THE BOURBON-POWERED ECONOMY

Locals love to hate on **Bourbon St** – which can indeed be crass and malodorous – and yet it plays a vital role in the city's economy. Each year New Orleans welcomes over 18 million visitors, who spend some $9 billion during their stay. An estimated 80% of those visitors come to Bourbon St, pumping tens of millions of dollars into the local economy. It also supports over 7000 jobs compressed into 20 square blocks straddling both sides of the street – a job density that is nearly 100 times more productive than the rest of New Orleans. The real estate value of the street is also no small matter, with estimates hovering around $500 million.

run just 45 minutes and happen several times nightly, and all ages are welcome.

Behaving Badly on Bourbon Street
Neon-lit debauchery

Like Vegas and Cancún, the main stretch of **Bourbon Street** is where the great id of the repressed American psyche is let loose into a seething mass of karaoke, strip clubs and bachelorette parties. It's one of the tackiest experiences in the world, but there's never a dull moment here, and you can't come to New Orleans and not visit the place.

At St Philip St, Bourbon shifts from a Dante's Inferno–style circle of neon-lit hell into an altogether more agreeable stretch of historical houses, diners and bars, many of which cater to the LGBTQ+ community. Great spots here include Lafitte's, the oldest continuously operating gay bar in the country.

Tour St Louis Cemetery No 1
City of the dead

New Orleans is famed for large above-ground necropolises. The most impressive is **St Louis Cemetery No 1**, with its artfully designed tombs and burial sites of famed residents (like Voodoo practitioner Marie Laveau). Access is by guided tour only. Book with **Cemetery Tours NOLA** (*cemeterytourneworleans.com; adult/child $25/18*). The 45-minute tour departs from across the street at Basin St Station (*basinststation.com*), which also has exhibits on city history.

The Heart of the Backstreet
Explore the culture of the Tremé

The Tremé sits at the heart of New Orleans Black culture, and is a great place to learn about the city's deep-rooted traditions. Start your visit at the small **Backstreet Cultural Museum** (*backstreetmuseum.org; adult/child $25/10*) on St Philip St. Mardi Gras Indian suits grab the spotlight with dazzling flair – and finely crafted detail – in this informative space, which examines many of the distinctive elements of African American culture in New Orleans.

Everyone Is a Star
A DIY music experience

Created by a group of local artists and tinkerers, **Music Box Village** (*musicboxvillage.com, adult/child $15/7*) is not just

DRINKING IN THE QUARTER: OUR PICKS

Carousel Bar: Go early to snag a seat at the spinning carousel, a 1949 landmark inside the Hotel Monteleone. *11am-midnight*

Fritzel's European Jazz Pub: A Bourbon St original, this atmospheric spot often has live music. *4pm-midnight Mon, noon-2am Tue-Sun*

Bar Tonique: Walking a fine line between lounge and dive bar, this place shakes excellent cocktails in a low-lit setting. *noon-2am*

Latitude 29: Hallowed ground for Tiki lovers, Latitude 29 serves delicious rum cocktails. *3-9pm Sun-Thu, noon-11pm Fri & Sat*

THE MARIGNY, BYWATER & THE TREMÉ

THE GUIDE

THE SOUTH NEW ORLEANS

★ **HIGHLIGHTS**
1 Frenchmen Street

● **SIGHTS**
2 Backstreet Cultural Museum
3 Peter & Paul
4 Rathbone Mansions

● **SLEEPING**

● **EATING**
5 Bacchanal
6 Dooky Chase
7 Gabrielle
8 Lil' Dizzy's
9 N7
10 Satsuma
11 Sneaky Pickle
12 St Roch Market
13 Willie Mae's Scotch House

● **DRINKING & NIGHTLIFE**
14 Bar Redux
15 BJ's

● **ENTERTAINMENT**
16 Blue Nile
17 Cafe Negril
18 d.b.a.
19 Music Box Village
20 Snug Harbor
21 Spotted Cat
22 Vaughan's

● **SHOPPING**
23 Art Garden

☑ TOP TIPS

From March through early May, you can catch free concerts in Lafayette Sq in downtown. These happen Wednesdays from 5pm to 8pm (ylcwats.com). Bring an appetite – food vendors serve up all sorts of decadence.

421

BIRTHPLACE OF JAZZ

Bridging the French Quarter and Tremé, leafy **Louis Armstrong Park** hosts small festivals throughout the year. Near the south end of the park, a small inconspicuous plaza known as **Congo Square** played a vital role in the musical heritage of New Orleans – and the world beyond. During colonial days, enslaved people were permitted to gather here on Sundays, their only day of rest. Their gatherings were a celebration of West African rituals, and largely revolved around song and dance. Though the practice was shut down when US settlers took over the city, the memory remained, and by the late 19th century, brass bands were blending African rhythms with classical music. The innovative sounds eventually evolved into the well-known music of jazz.

a place to play music – the venue itself can be played. Made from recycled metal, pipes and wood, the village looks like something from a Mad Max film and everything makes noise. Come ding, dong, spin, whizz and slap the village to make your own music, or see a live performance where musicians collaborate to produce a truly unforgettable sonic experience.

The Beloved Bywater Bar Scene MAP P421

Bacchanal and the Barmuda Triangle

Quiet by day, the eastern edge of the Bywater wakes up at night with some of the city's best neighborhood watering holes. At **Bacchanal** (bacchanalwine.com), you walk into an unassuming entrance to discover a wine bar with fine cheeses. Grab what you like, then head to the backyard where a live jazz band is playing. There's also a cocktail bar upstairs.

Other beloved neighborhood dives are nearby. **Vaughan's** (@vaughansloungenola), has a fun vibe with Mardi Gras colors and Mexican *papeles picados* flags overhead. **BJ's** (@bjslounge) fashions itself as the neighborhood living room; it has a full calendar of live music. Enter below the neon 'Bar' sign to **Bar Redux** (@barreduxnola), another dive bar with performers in the garden along with finger-lickin-good Creole fried wings and gumbo.

 EATING IN TREMÉ: OUR PICKS ——————————— MAP P421

Gabrielle: This little cottage doles out rich Cajun plates of braised rabbit, slow-roasted duck and other favorites. *5-10pm Wed-Sat* $$$

Lil' Dizzy's: Join the crowds at this legendary lunchtime Creole buffet on the corner of Claiborne. *11am-3pm Mon-Sat* $

Willie Mae's Scotch House: Serves up signature fried chicken – among the world's best! *hours vary* $

Dooky Chase: New Orleans' most famous destination for Creole cooking has been dazzling diners (President Obama included) since 1941. *11am-3pm Tue-Fri, plus 5:30-9pm Fri & Sat* $$

Frenchmen Street

Go Bar-hopping on Frenchmen Street MAP P421
Join the jazz-fueled street party

Lined with music venues, street jazz and perhaps a piano on wheels, **Frenchmen Street** is a chaotic cacophony and loads of fun. A who's who of legendary jazz musicians frequently play here, including Kermit Ruffins and John Boutté. Top events are usually held at **Snug Harbor** (*snugjazz.com*), **d.b.a.** (*dbaneworleans.com*), the **Spotted Cat** (*spottedcatmusicclub.com*), **Blue Nile** (*bluenilelive.com*) and **Cafe Negril** (*cafenegrilnola.com*).

Take a break from the music to browse the arts and crafts for sale at the **Art Garden** night market (*artgardennola.com; 7pm-midnight Thu-Sun*).

Art Gazing Downtown MAP P424
A top museum and gallery district

The **Ogden Museum of Southern Art** (*ogdenmuseum.org; adult/child $11/6*) illuminates unique facets of the South in all its complexity. Rotating exhibitions showcase lots of intriguing subjects, from photography on the streets of New Orleans to the overlooked communities of Appalachia. The permanent collection (3rd floor) has 18th-century portraits

SECOND LINES!

Second Line refers to New Orleans' neighborhood parades, especially those put on by the city's African American Social Aid and Pleasure (S&P) clubs. The S&P members deck themselves out in flash suits, hats and shoes, and carry decorated umbrellas and fans. This snazzy crowd, accompanied by a hired band, dances through the city. This is the First Line. Marching behind it is the Second Line: the crowds that gather to celebrate the music. Hundreds, sometimes thousands, of people dance in the Second Line, stopping for drinks and food along the parade route. All are welcome to join. Second Lines occur every Sunday from September through May. To find the parade route, check out WWOZ's Takin' It to the Streets section (*wwoz.org*).

 EATING IN THE MARIGNY & BYWATER: OUR PICKS MAP P421

| **Sneaky Pickle:** Mostly vegan pub with excellent mac 'n' cheese, smoked tempeh Reubens and carrot juice Micheladas. *11am-9:30pm Wed-Mon* **$$** | **St Roch Market:** Food court in an 1875 market with cuisine from Cuba, Italy, Malaysia and elsewhere. *7am-9pm Sun-Thu, to 10pm Fri & Sat* **$$** | **Satsuma:** Bohemian, exposed-brick cafe with a shaded garden and sandwiches for breakfast and lunch. *8am-2pm* **$** | **N7:** Memorable French, Japanese and fish tapas served in a romantic, twinkly-lit garden. *5-9pm Mon-Thu, 11:30am-2:30pm & 5-10pm Fri-Sun* **$$$** |

GARDEN DISTRICT, LOWER GARDEN & CENTRAL CITY

Among the most photogenic corners of the city, the **Garden District** exudes Old Southern excess with its historic mansions, lush greenery, chichi bistros and upscale boutiques (namely along Magazine St). Between the Central Business District (CBD) and the Garden District, the **Lower Garden District** is somewhat like its upriver neighbor but not quite as posh. There's a slightly more bohemian vibe, and plenty of bars and restaurants. Up above St Charles Ave, **Central City** is very much in transition. While there are large stretches of urban blight, there is also a dynamic concentration of community activist organizations rebuilding what was once one of the city's most important African American neighborhoods (Oretha Castle Haley is the main thoroughfare).

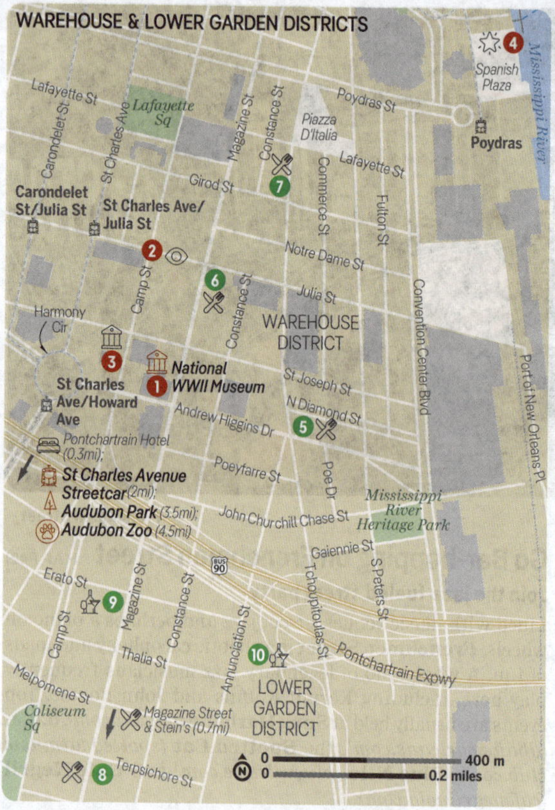

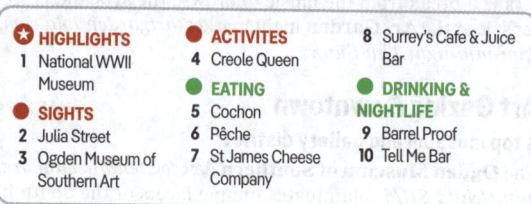

WAREHOUSE & LOWER GARDEN DISTRICTS

★ HIGHLIGHTS
1 National WWII Museum

● SIGHTS
2 Julia Street
3 Ogden Museum of Southern Art

● ACTIVITES
4 Creole Queen

● EATING
5 Cochon
6 Pêche
7 St James Cheese Company
8 Surrey's Cafe & Juice Bar

● DRINKING & NIGHTLIFE
9 Barrel Proof
10 Tell Me Bar

by French artists, lush Louisiana landscapes of the 1800s and socialist-realist artists of the 1930s.

Sometimes referred to as Gallery Row, **Julia Street** (between St Charles and Tchoupitoulas) is the heart of the Warehouse Arts District *(artsdistrictneworleans.com)*, with a smattering of galleries dotting the old buildings along this one-way thoroughfare. Things are liveliest on the first Saturday of the month *(6pm to 9pm)*, when there are special exhibitions and free wine.

See WWII in all its complexity

MAP P424

A sprawling, immersive museum

The **National WWII Museum** (*nationalww2museum.org; adult/child $36/26*) drops you straight into the action. Wall-sized photographs capture the confusion of D-Day. Riveting oral histories tell remarkable stories of survival. A walk through the snowy woods feels eerily cold. Exhibits like these make this grand facility engaging; artifacts, battles and war strategies are humanized through personal recollections and heat-of-the-moment displays. You could easily spend a full day (or more) here, so plan your visit carefully.

The must-see film of the museum is *Beyond All Boundaries*, which takes a 4D look at the USA's involvement in the war on a panoramic 120ft-wide screen. Get ready for rumbling seats and a dusting of snowflakes. Oscar-winning actor Tom Hanks narrates this evocative 48-minute experience, which runs on the hour from 10am to 4pm daily.

HIGHLIGHTS
1 City Park

SIGHTS
2 Botanical Gardens
3 New Orleans Museum of Art
4 Sydney & Walda Besthoff Sculpture Garden

ACTIVITIES
5 City Putt
6 Louisiana Children's Museum

DRINKING & NIGHTLIFE
7 Cafe du Monde

ENTERTAINMENT
8 Carousel Gardens
9 Jazz & Heritage Festival
10 Storyland

EATING IN THE CBD & WAREHOUSE DISTRICT: OUR PICKS
MAPS P416, P424

Namaste Nola: Despite the hotel setting, this place fires up beautiful Indian fare, including a rich paneer tikka masala. *11am-3pm & 5-10pm Thu-Tue* **$$**

Cochon: Donald Link pays homage to his Cajun culinary roots, serving meats smoked and wood-fired to perfection. *11am-10pm* **$$**

Pêche: One of New Orleans' best seafood restaurants lets the high-quality ingredients speak for themselves. *11am-10pm* **$$$**

St James Cheese Company: Heavenly cheesy sandwiches like Gruyère with caramelized onions. *11am-6pm Mon-Sat, to 4pm Sun* **$**

BEST KID-FRIENDLY SPOTS IN CITY PARK

Louisiana Children's Museum: Interactive exhibits, huge grounds and an enormous outdoor play area. Take your kids here on a hot day.

Storyland: Chase small children past life-size replicas of storybook characters at what might be the gentlest tourist attraction around.

City Putt: Home to two separate courses, this 36-hole putt-putt is the only minigolf attraction in the city.

Couturie Forest: A spaghetti tangle of pleasant trails wind past waterways and the 'highest point in New Orleans.'

Carousel Gardens: There are rides, a merry-go-round, a mini-roller coaster and plenty of fun to be had.

St Charles Avenue Streetcar

Strolling & Shopping on Magazine MAP P424
Indie boutiques, cafes and restaurants

Magazine Street is by far Orleans' best shopping strip. As a center for commercial activity it begins in the Lower Garden District, near the intersection with Felicity St. From here, you can follow Magazine west all the way to Audubon Park and shop or window browse in antiques stores and boutiques almost the entire way. The densest concentration of shops and restaurants lies around these intersections: Jackson, Washington, Louisiana and Napoleon.

Ride the St Charles Avenue Streetcar MAP P424
Vintage DIY adventure

Some of the grandest homes in the US line St Charles Ave, shaded by enormous oak trees. Clanging through this bucolic corridor comes the iconic **St Charles Avenue Streetcar**, running since 1835. It's a delightfully nostalgic way to get across town. Hop on at Canal – or anywhere along the line (there are stops every few blocks) and ride it to Audubon Park. Pay the $1.25 fare in cash ($3 for an all-day pass), or via the city's Le Pass app.

 EATING & DRINKING IN THE GARDEN DISTRICT: OUR PICKS — MAP P424

Surrey's Cafe & Juice Bar: Colorful neighborhood charmer offering outstanding breakfasts like shrimp and grits. *8am-3pm Thu-Mon* $

Stein's: The famed deli is an unrivaled spot for bacon, egg and cheese bagels and pastrami on rye. *8am-5pm Tue-Fri, from 9am Sat & Sun* $

Barrel Proof: A festive bourbon-centric option with corrugated iron walls, a long dark wood bar and fine cocktails with a creative edge. *4pm-1am*

Tell Me Bar: This well-hidden natural wine bar has a beautiful indoor and outdoor design and unusual wines from around the globe. *4-11pm*

Walk Amid Leafy Audubon Park

MAP P424

Verdant oasis and zoo

Audubon Park is a grand green space, run through with live oak trees, walking and cycling paths and a picturesque little lake, all framed by some lovely houses. Students lounge on the grass under Spanish moss while joggers lope by, dog owners play with their pets, golfers tee off and friends share an outdoor sundowner.

Appropriately enough, the **Audubon Zoo** (*audubonnature institute.org; adult/child $30/25*) is inside Audubon Park. It's a large place with sections including African, Asian and South American landscapes and fauna, and kids will find some of the world's most popular animals here, from elephants to giraffes. During the summer months, part of the zoo becomes a dedicated water park for youngsters. Don't miss the Louisiana Swamp section: a wet wonderland of bald cypresses and Spanish moss, carefully landscaped to reflect the natural wonders of southern Louisiana bayou country.

A Day at City Park

MAP P425

Art, sculpture and hands-on hijinks

City Park is so big that it includes two of the city's most wonderful museums, plus a sculpture garden, botanical garden and lots of walking paths. You can get there on the streetcar – take the **Canal Street line** (board the No 48 'City Park/Muse' route).

A good place to begin at **Cafe Du Monde** (*shop.cafe dumonde.com*). Order beignets and coffee with chicory, while listening to birdsong. Afterwards, take a stroll along the narrow bayou, which is lined with huge centuries-old live oak trees.

A short hop from there, the elegant **New Orleans Museum of Art** (*NOMA; noma.org; adult/child $20/free*) was opened in 1911 and is well worth a visit for its special exhibitions, gorgeous marble atrium and galleries of African, Asian, Flemish, Italian and American Southern art.

The **Sydney & Walda Besthoff Sculpture Garden** (*free*) is just outside NOMA, amid a wooded quilt of streams, pathways, lovers' benches and, of course, sculpture – mainly of the contemporary sort. For even more greenery – and countless flower species – head to the **Botanical Garden** (*adult/child $12/6*).

LEGENDARY GUMBO

Candi Vanardo, sous-chef at Deelightful Roux School of Cooking, gives insight into New Orleans' quintessential dish. *chefdeelavigne.com*

The secret to gumbo is your roux and filé. If there is no filé – ground sassafras leaves – then it is not gumbo. The filé gives it a certain taste, texture and color. They say gumbo should look like the Mississippi River, and filé has that ability that makes it kind of dredgy. What you put in it depends on where you grew up. People put different things in their gumbo. For me, there's going to be filé, seafood, smoked sausage, hot sausage – this is a 9th Ward gumbo we're talking about. For seafood, I use shrimp, blue crab or even snow crab.

Louisiana

BLACK HISTORY | CAJUN CULTURE | WETLANDS & WILDLIFE

Places
Plantation Country p429
Lafayette p430
Tabasco p431
Poverty Point p431

French and Spanish explorers alike were drawn to the magnificent Mississippi River, and both countries would lay claim to the region, which was ultimately named after French king Louis XIV in the 17th century. Even after Louisiana was purchased from France by the fledgling United States in 1803, it retained its francophone roots thanks to the generations of Europeans living here, along with the influx of French-speaking Acadians (later known as Cajuns) and Haitians in the years following the St Domingue Revolution.

Not surprisingly, Louisiana feels completely different from other parts of the country. Cajun and Creole music still spills out of dance halls along the bayou, and you may feel like you're entering another realm while boating through fertile wetlands of alligators, birdsong and soaring bald cypress trees. There are also ample opportunities to explore the past, whether visiting a Native American mound-building settlement (and present-day World Heritage Site) or learning about the enslaved people who helped build this nation.

☑ TOP TIP

The best time to visit Lafayette is during **Festival International de Louisiane** *(festivalinternational.org)*. Held on the last weekend in April, the free music event (simply called 'Festival' in these parts) brings incredible talent from far-flung corners of the world to the multiple stages set up around town.

 GETTING AROUND

Most travelers explore Louisiana by car as it's quite difficult to get around without your own wheels. If you're flying in, New Orleans is the best place to arrange affordable rentals. If you don't plan on doing much traveling within the state, rail fans can take one of three weekly departures aboard Amtrak's *Sunset Limited*, which connects New Orleans with Los Angeles. The train makes several stops in Louisiana, including in New Iberia and Lafayette, though once there you'll still need a vehicle to get around (Uber and Lyft both operate in Lafayette, however).

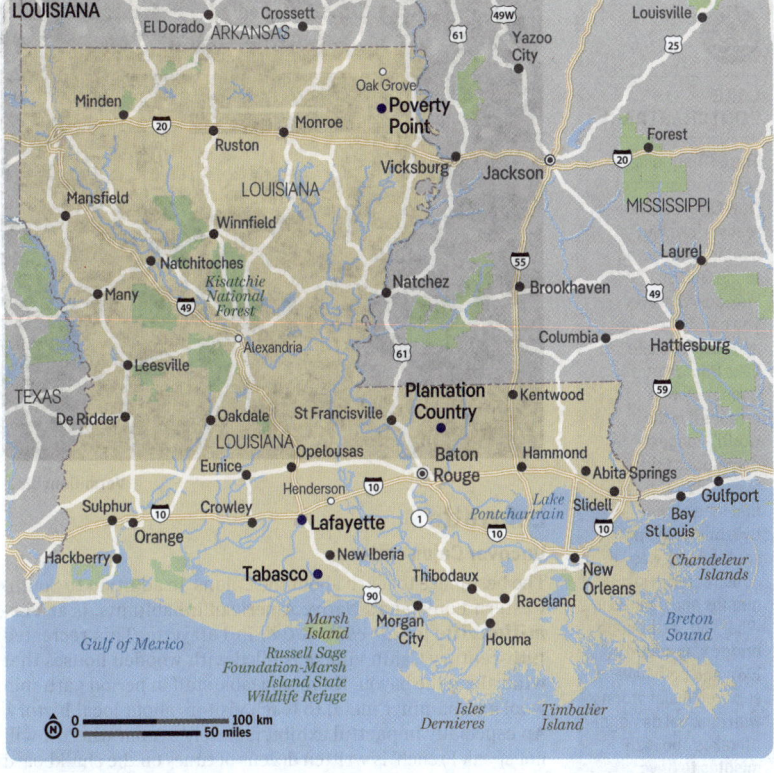

Plantation Country

See the other side of plantation life

The excellent **Whitney Plantation** *(whitneyplantation.org; adult/child guided tour $32/18, self-guided tour $25/11)* rewrites the script with 1½- to two-hour guided tours that focus on the lives of the enslaved. It isn't easy history to hear, but the guides do a wonderful job – many of them locals whose ancestors may have worked on the plantation. Guided tours are offered Wednesday to Monday at 10:45am, 12:45pm and 2:15pm. Self-guided tours with an audio device or app are available from 9:30am to 3pm.

Another 10-minutes' drive up the road, the **Laura Plantation** *(lauraplantation.com; adult/teen/child $28/20/15)* also does a remarkable job of contextualizing the life of both the free and enslaved on the Duparc Sugar Plantation. Guides rely on historical records and the first-hand accounts of Laura Locoul, a Creole woman who grew up here. Guided tours, available in English and French, last about 75 minutes and run every 20 to 40 minutes from 10am to 3:20pm.

LAKE PONTCHARTRAIN

The 630-sq-mile waterbody north of New Orleans is not really a lake, but an estuary connected to the Gulf of Mexico. Whatever you call it, it's huge, and the 23.8-mile Lake Pontchartrain Causeway that crosses it is the world's longest continuous bridge over water. The first lane of the twin bridge, going southbound, was constructed in just 14 months and opened in 1956. The northbound bridge was added in 1969, and both have survived major storms with minimal damage.

It takes about 25 minutes to drive across the bridge. Unsurprisingly, you won't see land for most of the journey. Driving northbound is free, but you'll have to pay a $6 toll on the drive back.

Vermilionville

Lafayette

Uncover Cajun culture

The best place to learn about the Cajuns, in addition to Southwestern Louisiana's Native American inhabitants, is at **Vermilionville** (adult/child $10/6) in Lafayette. This recreated 19th-century Cajun village is filled with wooden houses that wind along the bayou. Knowledgeable staff in period garb spin wool and hammer metal to teach visitors about local history. An especially impactful exhibit is the classroom where 'I will not speak French' is written dozens of times on the chalkboard – for decades, French was banned in public schools. There's plenty to read and an excellent restaurant if you're hungry. Check the calendar for live music on weekends.

Dance to Cajun & Creole rhythms

If you overnight in Lafayette, be sure to check out the town's renowned music scene. At the **Blue Moon Saloon** (bluemoonpresents.com), you can catch one of the best backyard jam sessions in town (it's also a guesthouse). For something a little different, head to **Pat's Fisherman's Wharf** (patsfishermanswharf.com) in Henderson (a 25-minute drive east of Lafayette), where Cajun bands draw dance-loving crowds on Saturdays (8:30pm) and Sundays (4:30pm) at the **Atchafalaya Club**.

Some 10 miles east of Lafayette, tiny Breaux Bridge is famous for its Saturday morning zydeco breakfasts at **Buck & Johnny's** (buckandjohnnys.com; $10). The Cajun-meets-Italian restaurant has a dining hall that vibrates with zippy zydeco (a genre that blends Creole, R&B and blues) from 8:30am to 11:30am. It's an uproarious time as young and old bob and spin on the dance floor – the $20 for bottomless mimosas certainly helps. If you can't make it on Saturday, Buck & Johnny's also has live music from around 6pm to 9pm on Thursdays, Fridays and Saturdays.

Go boating in the swamp

Touring the swamps and bayous ('streams' in the Choctaw language), on the lookout for alligators and bald eagles, is a bucket-list experience. Recommended outfitters such as **Cajun Country Swamp Tours** (*cajuncountryswamptours.com; $25*) will take you on a two-hour boat excursion to see alligators, yellow-crowned herons and other wetland wildlife on Lake Martin, some 15 miles east of Lafayette. If you prefer to get a bit of a workout while you sightsee, **Champagne's Swamp Tours** (*champagnesswamptours.com*) rents kayaks (*$20 per person per hour*). You can paddle your way across mirror-like waters and stop in secluded spots where you'll hear nothing but the sound of the birds.

Tabasco

Birds & Hot Sauce

Near the town of New Iberia, you can visit Avery Island, home to one of the country's most famous hot sauces, **Tabasco** (*tabasco.com; adult/child $16/13*). Avery is not really an island but rather a salt dome that extends 8 miles below the surface. The salt mined here goes into Tabasco sauce, as do locally grown peppers. You'll learn all this on a self-guided tour that takes you from seed to sauce, with tastings at the end. Afterwards, you can walk or drive through **Jungle Gardens** (included with Tabasco admission), with its 250 acres of moss-covered live oaks and subtropical jungle flora. There's an amazing array of waterbirds (especially snowy egrets, which nest here in astounding numbers) as well as turtles and alligators.

Poverty Point

Engineers of the ancient world

Louisiana has just one UNESCO World Heritage Site, and it remains little known, even to many state residents. Near the Mississippi border, some four hours north of New Orleans (and just an hour northwest of Vicksburg, p402), **Poverty Point** (*povertypoint.us; admission $4*) preserves the monumental earthworks built by a highly organized society some 3400 years ago. In the visitor center, you can browse exhibits and pick up a map for a self-guided tour of the site. A 2.6-mile walking trail takes you past 20 points of interest and through various landscapes (including a stretch of forest and a view over the Bayou Macon), and up a 72ft mound built by hand from some 15 million bushels of earth brought from elsewhere. If you're not up for the walk, you can instead do a more condensed 2-mile driving tour of the site passing 11 points of interest – ask rangers for this separate driving tour guide.

CAJUNS & CREOLES

You may be excused if you're confused by the terms Cajun and Creole – they are confusing indeed. The initial definition of a Creole was someone born in the European colonies who spoke a Romance language and practiced Catholicism, though it later became associated with people of mixed European, African and Native American ancestry. Cajun derives from Acadian, the French-speaking people who settled in Louisiana after the British exiled them from what's now eastern Canada in Le Grand Dérangement (The Great Displacement; 1755–64). In the present day, most people identifying as Cajuns are white, while Creoles are Black or of mixed race, though the two cultures have historical and genealogical connections that are often overlooked.

Places We Love to Stay

$ Budget $$ Midrange $$$ Top End

North Carolina

Crews Inn (Ocracoke) **$** An authentic old island home, with five lovely light-filled rooms named for its original inhabitants, plus the delightful innkeeper's cottage out back.

Dunhill Hotel (Charlotte) **$** Small, historic Uptown hotel with a quiet lobby and rooms that nod to the 1920s.

Arrive (Wilmington) **$$** This stylish boutique operation has modern, bright rooms, a creative restaurant and an inviting courtyard, complete with lawn games.

Atlantic Inn (Hatteras Island) **$$** A century-old property in Hatteras that's been revamped and reopened as a classy, comfortable lodging with a vintage vibe.

Princess Anne Boutique Hotel (Asheville) **$$** Offers handsomely furnished rooms and spacious suites in a quiet, leafy neighborhood.

South Carolina MAPS P343, P346

Starlight Motor Inn (Charleston) **$** Spare but snazzy, this revamped motor court in North Charleston has a pool and an on-site pub.

Andrew Pinkney Inn (Charleston) **$$** Two restored historic buildings hold bright, comfy rooms. Complimentary wine social and breakfast in upper-level atrium. Great value.

Old Village Post House (Mt Pleasant) **$$** This pale-yellow-and-blue clapboard house is a down-home, relaxing option tucked into a historic fishing community.

Swamp Rabbit Inn (Greenville) **$$** Fun six-room inn in a '50s-era former boarding house downtown. Feels like a hostel but features colorfully decked-out private rooms.

Tennessee MAPS P356, P360, P361

Crash Pad (Chattanooga) **$** Nicely run hostel with dorms and private rooms, guest kitchen-lounge and a courtyard in a great Southside location near restaurants and bars.

Arrive (Memphis) **$$** Beautiful redesign of an industrial building just steps from the train station. Great ground-floor cafe and bar.

Peabody (Memphis) **$$** A 464-room downtown property with classically furnished rooms and a lobby where ducks are marched in daily to swim about in the fountain.

Waymore's (Nashville) **$$** In uber-hip East Nashville, this 93-room hotel hits all the right notes, with artfully minimalist rooms and a rooftop bar with skyline views.

Hotel Chalet (Chattanooga) **$$** On the grounds of the historic train station, this revamped classic has stylish rooms set in Victorian railcars.

Union Station Hotel (Nashville) **$$$** This soaring Romanesque gray-stone castle (and former train station) boasts grand common areas and contemporary rooms with playful accents.

Kentucky

DuPont Lodge (Daniel Boone National Forest) **$** Near Cumberland Falls, this forest-fringed lodge has pleasant rooms, and you can also bunk in a rustic cottage with a fireplace.

Jailer's Inn (Bardstown) **$$** In a former jail from 1819, you'll find a B&B kitted out with wallpaper-covered rooms with antique furnishings. Good cooked breakfasts.

21c Museum Hotel (Louisville) **$$$** Art-focused option featuring edgy design details and changing exhibitions in common areas, plus inviting rooms with ample natural light.

Georgia MAP P376

Thunderbird Inn (Savannah) **$** A vintage-chic 1964 motel offering complimentary popcorn and frosted breakfast donuts in the lobby, and RC Colas and Moon Pies in every room.

Glenn Hotel (Atlanta) **$$** This 1920s neoclassical revival building boasts a cozy boutique feel and one of Downtown's best rooftop bars, SkyLounge.

River Street Inn (Savannah) **$$** Historical-chic rooms with hardwood floors and four-poster beds – the best ones have balconies. The building dates to 1817.

Rivet House (Athens) **$$$** In the repurposed Mill District, this 50-room newcomer turned a former denim factory into Athens' hippest hotel. Great Italian restaurant, cool bar, no breakfast.

Alabama MAP P393

106 Jefferson (Huntsville) **$$** Stylish, newish boutique hotel in a great downtown location, with mid-century modern-style rooms and a rooftop bar.

Elyton Hotel (Birmingham) **$$** In a grand 1909 building, this boutique beauty has crisp white rooms with pops of color and contemporary art. Great downtown location.

SpringHill Suites (Montgomery) **$$** Though part of the Marriott chain, this historic property is no cookie-cutter, with industrial chic style in a walkable downtown setting.

Malaga Inn (Mobile) **$$** Tastefully designed rooms with a Victorian-era vibe are set in two converted townhouses from the 1860s. Lovely courtyard and a central location.

Mississippi

Auberge Clarksdale Hostel (Clarksdale) **$** Perfect downtown setting and a convivial traveler vibe (the lounge has a turntable and guitars) with simple dorms and private rooms.

Shack Up Inn (Clarksdale) **$** Stay outside of town in refurbished sharecropper cabins or the creatively renovated cotton gin. There are loaner guitars and a barnlike bar.

Natchez Grand Hotel (Natchez) **$** Contemporary design with 119 rooms in a great central location. Book a room with views of the Mississippi River.

Corners Mansion Inn (Vicksburg) **$$** Delightful B&B with a welcoming host, atmospheric rooms, homemade breakfasts and river views from the front porch swing.

Arkansas   MAP P407

Gold-Inn (Hot Springs) **$** A delightfully renovated vintage hotel with colorful rooms and a swimming pool less than a mile from Bathhouse Row.

Bike Inn (Bentonville) **$** A welcoming base for mountain bikers, with suites and simple cabins with shared bathrooms, and there's a sauna and gear for hire.

Rosemont Cottages (Little Rock) **$$** In the vibrant Soma district, you can stay in attractive, uniquely designed cottages and suites that ooze southern charm.

Treehouse Cottages (Eureka Springs) **$$$** Amid pine forest, these delightful stilted wooden cottages make a charming hideaway. Some boast Jacuzzi tubs and wrap-around decks.

New Orleans   MAPS P416, P421, P424

Rathbone Mansions (Tremé) **$** These pre–Civil War mansions have hardwood floors, four-poster beds and an art-deco-meets-the-19th-century vibe at a very forgiving price point.

Olivier House (French Quarter) **$$** 1838 gem offering wide-ranging options, from the economical to the elaborate, with balconies, exposed brick and antique furnishings.

Peter & Paul (Marigny) **$$** Like a page from an architecture magazine, with 71 antique-filled rooms spread across several buildings: a 19th-century Catholic schoolhouse, rectory, convent and church.

Pontchartrain Hotel (Garden District) **$$** On St Charles, this grande dame has handsomely furnished rooms with old-fashioned charm. There's great dining, live music and a rooftop bar.

Louisiana

Blue Moon Saloon (p430) (Lafayette) **$** A draw for music lovers with fun (but loud) backyard jam sessions; boasts a friendly backpacker vibe, with dorms and private rooms.

Bayou Cabins (Breaux Bridge) **$** Quintessential Cajun spot on a bayou with 14 historic cabins boasting retro furnishings (ranging from 1949 wallpaper to century-old cypress flooring).

Maison Mouton (Lafayette) **$$** An oasis amid flower-filled gardens and live oaks with 12 rooms spread over historic cottages dating back to 1820.

Union Station Hotel, Nashville

Researched and curated by
Jesse Scott

Florida

BEACHES, CULTURE AND SUN-SOAKED TROPICS

Shoreline rhythms, lively cities and wild backwaters shape a state of contrasts – electric, eccentric and steeped in stories old and new.

Florida refuses to be just one thing. At first glance, it's all sunshine and shoreline – a long, lanky canvas brushed with pastel lifeguard towers, sea oats swaying in Atlantic winds, and sunsets that melt into the Gulf. But scratch below the sunburn and you'll find a land of contrasts: cosmopolitan and kitschy, wild and refined, proudly weird and endlessly welcoming.

Start in Miami, where art-deco façades glitter against Latin beats, Wynwood murals blaze bold, and Cuban cafes fuel locals and night owls alike. Glide south into the Everglades, where the modern world disappears in a sweep of sawgrass, cypress domes and prehistoric silence pierced by the bellow of a gator. Keep going and you hit the Keys – a coral-capped chain where time slows, the water glows and sundowners are a ritual.

In Southeast Florida, high-rises kiss the sea while retirees, creatives and snowbirds mingle in brunch lines. Central Florida is another universe altogether – especially in Orlando, where theme parks aren't just attractions, but their own gravity. Along the Space Coast, rockets streak skyward, reviving dreams of the cosmos. Tampa blends Gulf Coast breezes with cigar-rolling heritage, and in the northeast, moss-draped oaks line brick streets in cities like St Augustine and Jacksonville, where history lingers in the humid air. Florida dazzles, defies and demands a closer look.

THE MAIN AREAS

MIAMI
Swagger, style and cityscape sizzle.
p440

EVERGLADES & BISCAYNE NATIONAL PARK
Wild silence reigns in the grasslands.
p452

FLORIDA KEYS & KEY WEST
Island breezes, sunsets and conch-fried freedom.
p458

SOUTHEAST FLORIDA
Coastal luxury and ever-evolving charm.
p464

For places to stay in Florida, see p496

FOKKEBOK/GETTY IMAGES

THE GUIDE

FLORIDA

Left: Alligator in Everglades National Park (p452); Above: South Beach (p440), Miami

ORLANDO & WALT DISNEY WORLD®
Imagination, fantasy and thrills beyond rides.
p472

SPACE COAST
Launchpads, surf towns and stars align.
p479

NORTHEAST FLORIDA
Colonial echoes, oak canopies, golden shores.
p484

TAMPA BAY & SOUTHWEST
Sun-drenched cities, art and calm waters.
p490

Find Your Way

Stretching more than 500 miles from the Gulf Panhandle to the Keys, Florida fans out into beaches, swamps and cities – with distinct regions spanning coasts, wetlands, islands and inland theme-park country.

Orlando & Walt Disney World®, p472
Theme parks reign, but Orlando surprises with a vibrant LGBTQ+ scene, cultural events and international flair beyond the thrill rides.

Tampa Bay & Southwest, p490
Tampa buzzes with nightlife, while St. Pete shines with arts, beaches, and offshore islands for a laid-back Gulf escape.

Everglades & Biscayne National Park, p452
These wild wetlands teem with gators, birds and beauty. A rare pocket of primordial nature tucked between Florida's cities and suburbs.

BUSES

Although cars are recommended for getting around Florida, **Greyhound** (*greyhound.com*) runs intercity buses between 40 cities. They might move at the pace of a sea turtle, but they're more economical and eco-friendly. **Megabus** (*megabus.com*) also serves Miami, Orlando and Jacksonville.

TRAINS

Amtrak offers limited service within Florida, but other rail services pick up the slack. **Tri-Rail** (*tri-rail.com*) connects cities in the south, while **SunRail** (*sunrail.com*) serves 16 stops in Central Florida. **Brightline** (*gobrightline.com*) offers economical high-speed service connecting Miami and Orlando.

PLANES

Florida has many international and regional airports, so there's always a fast way to get around. **Southwest Airlines** (*southwest.com*) is a popular go-to for quick city hops. Otherwise, save the airport hassle and drive or use commuter rail services instead.

Plan Your Time

With everything from untamed wilderness to world-renowned theme parks, planning a Florida trip means first choosing your vibe – beachy, wild, cultural, whimsical or a little of it all – and letting the Sunshine State do the rest.

Iconic South Florida

Start in **Fort Lauderdale** (p464) and cruise its scenic waterways via water taxi, stopping at Bonnet House or the Riverwalk for breezy bites and people-watching. Next, dive into Miami's color-splashed culture: admire the murals of **Wynwood Walls** (p445), dig into Cuban flavors in **Little Havana** (p448), and dance the night away in **South Beach** (p440). Then head west for a day with the gators in **Everglades National Park** (p452) – get on the water in a canoe or kayak to view wildlife. Finally, cruise the Overseas Highway to the Florida Keys. Start in **Key Largo** (p458) for snorkeling or a slice of key lime pie, then roll south to **Islamorada** (p462) or funky **Key West** (p459), where sunsets, street performers and rum punches make for a perfect finale.

Christ of the Abyss (p460), John Pennekamp Coral Reef State Park

Seasonal Highlights

Florida's subtropical climate means year-round adventures – from turtle hatchings and rocket launches to food fests and art fairs.

JANUARY
Art Deco Weekend transforms Miami's Ocean Dr, manatees gather near Tampa, and dry weather is ideal for Everglades hikes and stone crab feasts.

FEBRUARY
Dry, crisp days for patio dining on Gulf oysters or spotting roseate spoonbills and nesting bald eagles in wetlands.

MARCH
Spring break fills beaches, citrus is at its peak – sip fresh OJ or try key lime pie.

Gulf Coast Swing

Start in **Tampa** (p492) with riverfront walks, Cuban sandwiches in **Ybor City** (p492) and a nightcap at a rooftop bar. Then hop to **St Petersburg** (p494) to admire Dalí's surreal genius, hunt murals downtown and sip small-batch beers at breweries aplenty. Afterward, it's off to the sands: unwind on the family-friendly beaches of **St Pete Beach** (p495). From here, you're at the epicenter of some of the Gulf's most prized beaches – head south to **Pass-a-Grille Beach** (p495) and take a ferry out to the unspoiled Shell Key. Make sure to spend an evening at nearby **Clearwater Beach** (p495), where its Pier 60 nightly sunset celebrations – with entertainers galore – rival those in Key West.

Theme Park Parade

Kick things off with two days at **Walt Disney World®** (p475), diving into the world's most beloved theme-park empire. Zoom through space, soar on banshees and sing along with animatronic dolls (you know the ones). Next, give the grown-ups their due: take in downtown Orlando's **Leu Gardens** (p476) or cool off at **Wekiwa Springs State Park** (p474). **Universal Orlando Resort** (p477) is next – where Diagon Alley, Marvel heroes and Jurassic coasters collide. Cap things off with a day at **SeaWorld Orlando** (p478) or **LEGOLAND Florida** (p476) in Winter Haven – ideal for kids and anyone still clinging to their inner child. End your trip with a breezy evening at **Disney Springs** (p475), where souvenirs and chef-driven fare await.

MAY
Sunrise beach walks are magical, mangoes ripen in South Florida and rising heat calls for mid day breaks indoors or by water.

JULY
Fireworks light up St Augustine's bayfront and Tampa's **Riverwalk**. Expect daily afternoon thunderstorms and steamy heat.

OCTOBER
Universal's haunted houses and costumed crowds fill Orlando for Halloween, while migrating butterflies flutter over wildflower patches and coastal dunes statewide.

DECEMBER
Boat parades in the Keys, Miami's **Art Basel** draws global crowds, and cool, dry weather is ideal for beach strolls and spiny lobster dinners.

Miami

FIRE, FLAIR, FLAVOR – MORE THAN BEACHES

GETTING AROUND

South Beach is best explored on foot – it's compact, vibrant and packed with visual treats. The free Miami Beach Trolley is a breezy option for hopping between SoBe, Mid-Beach and North Beach. To explore the broader city, rideshares, the Metrorail and the free Metromover in downtown Miami make it easy to zip between neighborhoods.

☑ TOP TIP

From college reunions and spring break to foodie, music and art festivals, Miami is ground zero for large-scale gatherings in every season. Check the calendar before you arrive – the vibe is often dictated by the theme of whatever event is on, and Miami tends to go all-in on whatever it's celebrating.

Miami is a city of many moods – a place where Caribbean heat, Latin flair and coastal cool collide. Yes, Miami Beach still shines with its signature art-deco glow, oceanfront energy and ever-buzzing nightlife. But cross the causeways and you'll find a wider city with just as much pulse. Wynwood's street art and indie galleries rival any major art capital, Little Havana hums with café cubano culture and domino games, and Coconut Grove offers breezy bayside calm beneath lush tropical canopies. Whether it's sunrise yoga in South Beach, a foodie crawl through Calle Ocho or sunset cocktails in Brickell's glassy high-rises, the typical Miami experience isn't one-size-fits-all. It really is a choose-your-own-adventure city, where beach mornings, museum afternoons and all-night dance floors coexist with jungle gardens, historic districts and family-run bakeries. Don't just stay put in Miami – explore. Miami rewards the curious with culture, rhythm and sunshine around every colorful corner.

Lay of the Sandy Land

MAP P441

Beaches beyond South Beach

When it comes to sun, sand and surf, Miami Beach covers all the bases – and with a different vibe to look forward to depending on the stretch where you choose to unfurl your beach towel.

South Beach is without a doubt the section of sand most people think of when they hear the words 'Miami Beach,' but there's far more coast to saunter along out here. Unless otherwise noted, the numbered streets here all extend off Collins Ave (A1A), which runs north and south parallel to the beach itself.

Mid-Beach spans the sands from 23rd to 63rd Sts. It's not like the crowds out here stop preening and showing off – this is still model/influencer territory – but many have shifted from posting TikToks of their nights at the club to boosting reels of their nights with their growing families. The Mid-Beach area is attached to

(continues on p443)

MIAMI BEACH

★ HIGHLIGHTS
1. Faena Hotel Miami Beach
2. Fontainebleau
3. Freehand Miami
4. Miami Beach Boardwalk
5. South Beach

● SIGHTS
6. Art Deco Museum and Welcome Center
7. Bass Museum
8. Jewish Museum of Florida-FIU
9. Mid-Beach
10. Romero Britto Fine Art Gallery
11. Wolfsonian-FIU

● SLEEPING
12. Kimpton Surfcomber

● EATING
13. Abbalé Telavivian Kitchen
14. Baires Grill
15. Forte dei Marmi
16. Lilikoi
17. Macchialina
18. MILA
19. RAO's
20. Stubborn Seed

ART-DECO AMBLE

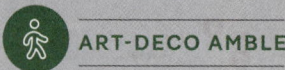

Spend a morning walking around South Beach to admire the world's largest collection of 1920s and 1930s art-deco buildings.

START	END	LENGTH
Art Deco Museum	Wolfsonian-FIU	1 mile; 1 hour

Some 800 art-deco buildings here are listed on the National Register of Historic Places, and you'll encounter many of them whether you set out on a purposeful stroll past bold facades and whimsical tropical motifs or not.

Start at the ❶ **Art Deco Museum** for background and exhibits on art-deco style. Stroll north along Ocean Dr between 12th and 14th Sts to spot some of the area's most famous art-deco hotels. ❷ **The Leslie** is known for its boxy shape and 'eyebrows' (cantilevered sunshades) that wrap around the building; ❸ **The Carlyle** has modernist styling; and the graceful ❹ **Cardozo South Beach**, built by Henry Hohauser and now owned by Gloria and Emilio Estefan, is recognized for its sleek, rounded edges.

When you arrive at 14th St, peek inside the ❺ **Winter Haven Hotel** to admire its fabulous terrazzo floors, made of stone chips set in mortar and polished to a shine. Then turn left down 14th St to Washington Ave and the ❻ **US Post Office**, located at 13th St, known for its curvy block of white art-deco and stripped classical style.

Finish your amble nearby at the ❼ **Wolfsonian-FIU**, an excellent design museum in the former Washington Storage Company, where wealthy snowbirds of the '30s stashed their pricey belongings before heading back north.

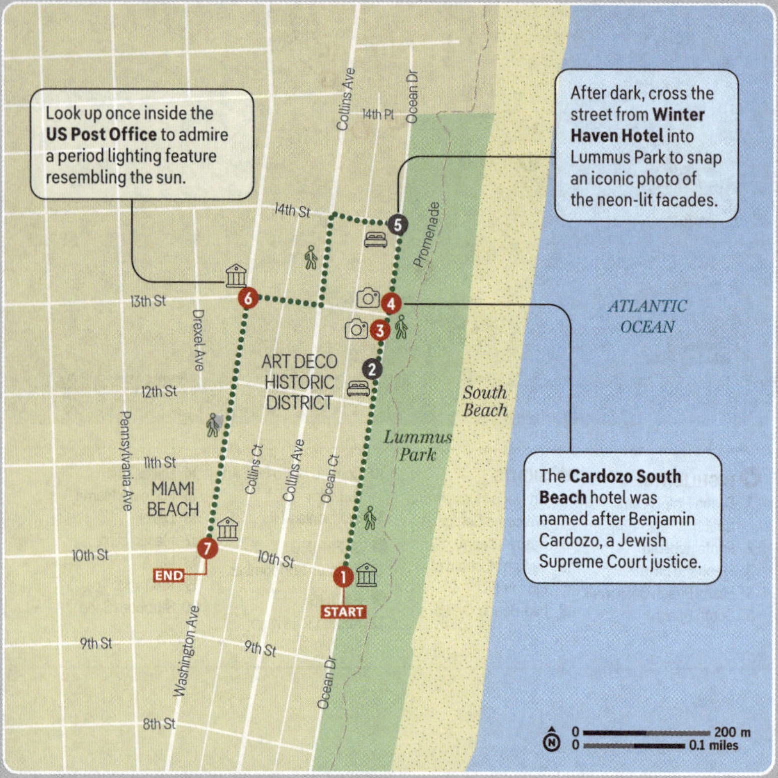

Look up once inside the **US Post Office** to admire a period lighting feature resembling the sun.

After dark, cross the street from **Winter Haven Hotel** into Lummus Park to snap an iconic photo of the neon-lit facades.

The **Cardozo South Beach** hotel was named after Benjamin Cardozo, a Jewish Supreme Court justice.

(continued from p440)
a lot of the area's big luxury hotels, such as the **Fontainebleau** and **Faena Hotel Miami Beach**. On the bay side of the beach is North Bay Rd, where you can see (well, glimpse over the walls) some of the area's largest mansions. This area includes the official **Miami Beach Boardwalk** *(miamibeachboardwalk.com; free)*. It runs between 21st and 46th Sts, where Orthodox Jews often mix with social media mavens.

North Beach extends from 63rd St to 87th Tce. The beaches here are smaller and more family-friendly, although this is also where you'll find **Haulover Beach** (4.5 miles north of 71st St); the northern section of this beach park is clothing-optional and has been popular with naturists since the 1990s.

Free Downtown Tour up High
Metromover groovin'

What's that train whirring overhead through some of Miami's densest real estate? The answer is the **Metromover** *(miamidade.gov/global/transportation/metromover.page; free)*, an elevated, electric monorail meant to alleviate the traffic woes of Downtown and Brickell. The Metromover did not succeed in doing this, as anyone who has driven in South Florida can attest. But it's a beloved, complete rail line that moves thousands of passengers each month – for free! It also happens to be a pretty cool way to see central Miami from above, which is a nice thing, given the city's 'skyscraper canyon' landscape.

The Metromover opened in 1986 and sports that distinctive, so-modern-it-looks-dated appearance of public works from that period. Its three lines – the Omni Loop, Inner Loop and Brickell Loop – span 4.4 miles and connect major Downtown spots like **Bayfront Park**, the **Kaseya Center** (where the Miami Heat play) and the **Adrienne Arsht Center for the Performing Arts**, among others. The mover is a particularly good way of seeing the full architectural span and beauty of the **Freedom Tower** (p446), modeled after the Giralda bell tower in Seville.

MIAMI BEACH'S BEST MUSEUMS & GALLERIES

The Bass: Founded in 1964, this contemporary art museum sits in a 1930s art-deco building *(thebass.org)*.

Jewish Museum of Florida-FIU: Florida Jewish history is celebrated within two art-deco buildings, one a former synagogue *(jmof.fiu.edu)*.

Wolfsonian-FIU: A museum, library and research center devoted to art and design *(wolfsonian.org)*.

Romero Britto Fine Art Gallery: This gallery of the eponymous visual artist from Brazil bursts with color, inside and out *(shopbritto.com)*.

Art Deco Museum: Dive into the major design styles that influenced Miami Beach: Mediterranean revival, art-deco and Miami Modern *(mdpl.org)*.

 EATING IN MIAMI: MIAMI BEACH

Lilikoi: Laid-back, indoor-outdoor spot for healthy, mostly organic, veg-friendly dishes. *8am-3pm* **$$**	**Macchialina:** Rustic-chic Italian trattoria with all the ingredients for a terrific night out. *6-11pm Mon-Thu, from 5pm Fri-Sun* **$$**	**Abbalé Telavivian Kitchen:** Mediterranean-inspired weekend brunch and shared mezze plates. *11am-10pm Mon-Thu, to 11pm Fri, 10am-11pm Sat, to 10pm Sun* **$$**	**Baires Grill:** Argentinean *parrillada* (barbecue) alongside *milanesas* just like in Buenos Aires. *noon-11pm Sun-Thu, to 11:30pm Fri & Sat* **$$**
MILA: Omakase-style rooftop bar, this swanky restaurant takes guests on a culinary odyssey. *hours vary* **$$$**	**Stubborn Seed:** Michelin starred and James Beard awarded for its adventurous haute-American cuisine. Reserve. *6-10pm Sun-Thu, to 11pm Fri & Sat* **$$$**	**RAO's:** Italian restaurant in Loews Miami Beach Hotel. Raw bar, antipasti and southern Neapolitan cuisine. *5:30-10pm Sun-Thu, to 11pm Fri & Sat* **$$$**	**Forte dei Marmi:** Led by a two-Michelin-starred chef, this coastal Italian spot evokes a Tuscan villa in a Mediterranean revival building. *hours vary* **$$$**

DOWNTOWN & BRICKELL

★ HIGHLIGHTS
1 Adrienne Arsht Center for the Performing Arts
2 Bayfront Park
3 Pérez Art Museum Miami

● SIGHTS
4 Brickell Key Park

5 Freedom Tower
6 Kaseya Center
7 Maurice A. Ferré Park
see 5 Museum of Art & Design
8 Watson Island Park

● SLEEPING
9 Dunns Josephine

● EATING
10 NIU Kitchen
11 Quinto
12 River Oyster Bar
see 3 Verde

● DRINKING & NIGHTLIFE
13 Blackbird Ordinary

14 Elleven Miami
15 Rosa Sky
see 11 Sugar

● SHOPPING
16 Bayside Marketplace

● TRANSPORT
17 Port of Miami

🍴 EATING IN MIAMI: DOWNTOWN — MAP P444

Quinto: Sexy rooftop in the EAST Miami hotel with tropical greenery, incredible cocktails and fusion fare. *hours vary* $$

Niu Kitchen: Stylish, living room–sized restaurant serving Catalan cuisine and a killer wine list. *6-10pm Tue-Thu & Sun, to 10:30pm Fri & Sat* $$

Verde: Inside the Pérez Art Museum Miami is a local favorite for tasty market-fresh dishes in an atmospheric setting. *11am-4pm Fri-Mon, to 8pm Thu* $$

River Oyster Bar: A few paces from the Miami River, this buzzing little spot whips up excellent plates of seafood. *noon-10:30pm* $$

The high-rises of Brickell make for a shiny sight from the Metromover, and the Omni Loop offers great views of Biscayne Bay, the Miami River and the **Pérez Art Museum Miami**. Trains run from 5am to midnight every day, arriving roughly every three minutes (more frequently during rush hour).

The Metromover isn't the only elevated rail line in town. Miami's **Metrorail** links Downtown with residential neighborhoods like Coral Gables and Coconut Grove. Beneath it runs the **Underline** – a planned $146 million, 10-mile-long linear park to be completed in 2026. The section from Brickell to Vizcaya Station was unveiled in 2024. You'll find weekly community yoga classes staged on the Underline, an outdoor gym, a meditation garden, and a walking and biking path to explore.

Get out on the Water

MAP P444

Cruise on Biscayne Bay

The Atlantic Ocean might be a causeway away from Downtown Miami, but you can still get out on the area's sparkling waterways from Downtown's shoreline when you head out on a boat tour with one of the companies operating from **Bayside Marketplace**.

For a serious rush, **Thriller Miami Speedboat Adventures** (*thrillermiami.com; $45*) offers 45-minute 'Miami Vice–style' tours (Don Johnson sightings not guaranteed) aboard its fleet of three catamarans that take you across Biscayne Bay and past the mansions of Fisher Island and Star Island.

Island Queen Cruises (*islandqueencruises.com; $35, child 4-12 $25, child under 4 $5*) offers a slower-paced, 90-minute sightseeing jaunt on a private ship with an open upper deck and air-conditioned salon during which you'll cruise pass sites like **Millionaire's Row**, Miami Beach and the **Port of Miami**.

On both tours, it's impressive to catch sight of Downtown Miami's shoreline and skyscrapers from the turquoise waters, showcasing just how truly tropical the city is.

Color Pop & Shop

MAP P446

Walk the Wynwood Walls

One of the most photographed locations in Miami (if social media hashtags are anything to go by), **Wynwood Walls** (*thewynwoodwalls.com; adult/child $12/5*) is a collection of murals and paintings laid out over an open courtyard that bowls people over with its exuberant colors and commanding

DOWNTOWN MIAMI'S BEST PARKS

Bayfront Park (p443): Downtown Miami's green heart spans 32 acres fronting Biscayne Bay. It has two performance venues, playgrounds and picnic areas.

Watson Island Park: Follow the MacArthur Causeway to this small park with grand views of Downtown Miami's spectacular skyline.

Brickell Key Park: Beautifully landscaped, waterfront park with picnic areas, palms and walking trails.

Maurice A Ferré Park: A 21-acre urban park featuring the longest waterfront bay walk in Miami, a jogging and strolling favorite.

Margaret Pace Park: Waterfront park on Biscayne Bay with basketball courts, picnic tables, outdoor gym equipment, playground and walking trails.

DRINKING IN MIAMI: PARTYING PICKS

MAP P444

Rosa Sky: Rooftop cocktail bar in Brickell with jaw-dropping views of the Downtown Miami skyline. *4:30pm-2am Tue-Sat, 2pm-1am Sun*

Blackbird Ordinary: Late-night drinking spot in Brickell with excellent cocktails that draw a neighborhood crowd. *3pm-5am*

Elleven: Multi-level club and social playground spread over 20,000 sq ft. Great cocktails and huge party vibes. *hours vary*

Sugar: Come for creative cocktails and Biscayne Bay views on the tropical rooftop deck of the EAST Miami hotel. *hours vary*

IMMIGRATION ICON AMID SKYSCRAPERS

Impossible to miss along Biscayne Blvd, the richly ornamented **Freedom Tower**, completed in 2025, is one of two surviving towers modeled after the Giralda bell tower in Spain's Cathedral of Seville. As the 'Ellis Island of the South,' it served as an immigration processing center for almost half a million Cuban refugees in the 1960s. Placed on the National Register of Historic Places in 1979, the tower houses the **Miami Museum of Art & Design** (MOAD; moadmdc.org), with exhibits ranging from contemporary sculpture to historical photography. The tower and MOAD are scheduled to reopen to the public in late 2025 with a re-imagined visitor experience celebrating the tower's 100th anniversary.

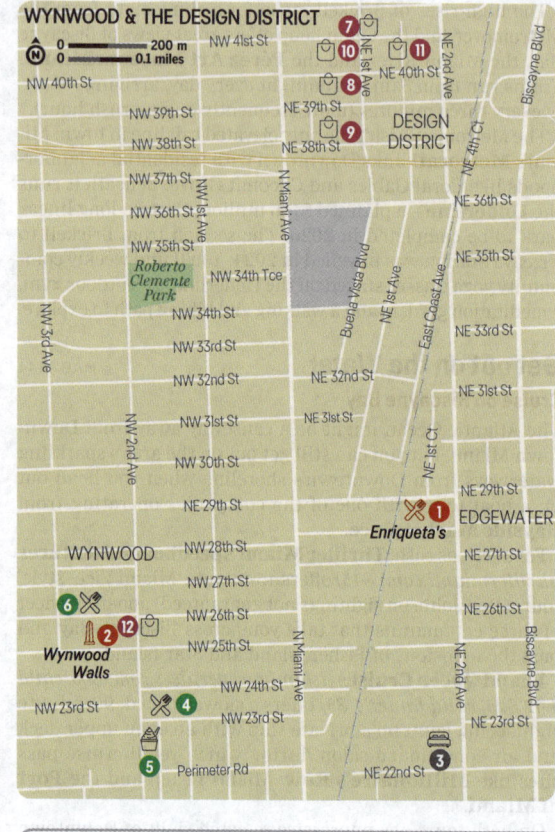

WYNWOOD & THE DESIGN DISTRICT

⭐ **HIGHLIGHTS**
1 Enriqueta's
2 Wynwood Walls

⚫ **SLEEPING**
3 Arlo

🟢 **EATING**
4 1-800-Lucky
5 Dasher & Crank
6 Zak the Baker

🔴 **SHOPPING**
7 Acne Studios
8 Alice + Olivia
9 GANNI
10 Golden Goose
11 Maison Francis Kurkdjian
12 Wynwood Walls Shop

 EATING IN MIAMI: WYNWOOD — MAP P.446

Enriqueta's: No-frills Cuban diner with daily specials, great Cuban sandwiches and coffee. *7am-3pm Mon-Fri, to 2pm Sat* $

1 800 Lucky: Miami's take on an Asian hawker market, with tons of street food and Wynwood neon to boot. *noon-1am Mon-Thu, to 3am Fri-Sun* $

Zak the Baker: Artisan and kosher bakery helmed by a Miami native, known for its pastries and BLTs on croissants. *7am-5pm Sun-Fri* $

Dasher & Crank: Quite literally churns out ice cream, ranging from passion fruit sorbet to (of course) mojito. *noon-11pm Mon-Thu, to midnight Fri-Sun* $

presence. What's on offer tends to change with the coming and going of major arts events, such as Art Basel, but it's always eye-catching, interesting stuff, and the energy that congregates around the Walls is buzzy and exciting. Depending on your worldview, the Walls are either a triumph of Wynwood's unwritten mission of bringing street-generated contemporary art to the masses…or a triumph of the commercial forces that have taken the creative energy of the street and repackaged it for conspicuous consumption. Are we thinking too hard about it? Maybe, but that's the point of art, right? In any case, if you want to take a little piece of the Walls home, pop into the on-site shop. You can also learn the spray paint basics and create your own piece of graffiti here with the **Wynwood Graffiti Experience** (*wynwoodartwalk.com; adult/child $42/34*).

The Soundtrack Goes Clickety-Clack MAP P448
Doing Domino Park

Perhaps Little Havana's most evocative reminder of street life from Cuba is **Máximo Gómez Park** (*miami.gov; free*). More commonly called Domino Park, it's a tree-shaded, gated oasis on Calle Ocho. The big iron gates are open between 9am and 6pm daily. Regulars file in from around the neighborhood and across Miami, and the competitive banter and strategizing get going as cups of Cuban coffee are sipped. The sound of seasoned players trash-talking over games of dominoes is harmonized with the quick clack-clack of slapping tiles – though photo-taking tourists do give an odd spin to the experience, not that the players pay them any heed. In fact, they don't seem to mind people watching them at all – if anything, they feed off the crowd's energy.

The heavy cigar smell and a sunrise-bright mural of the 1994 **Summit of the Americas** add to the atmosphere. You might spend a few minutes here passing through or get sucked into watching a game for longer. The walkways around the park are decorated with domino-inspired tiles and there are benches where you can sit for a spell to soak up the ambience of it all in the shade. The neighborhood's cult ice creamery, **Azucar** (*azucaricecream.com*), is right across the street if all the spectating makes you peckish.

THE DESIGN DISTRICT'S BEST SHOPS

Acne: Italian leather and Japanese denim are among the elite raw ingredients in this cult Swedish atelier's stable.

Alice+Olivia: Women's clothing boutique known for designer denim and beautiful print dresses.

Golden Goose: There are sneakers, and then there is this beloved high-fashion Italian brand known for its emblematic star.

Maison Francis Kurkdjian: Pop in for a signature scent from this luxury French perfumery. Candles and scented body lotions round out the offerings.

GANNI: If it's cool enough for Copenhagen's cool girls, you'll find the Scandinavian fashion favorite here.

EATING IN MIAMI: LITTLE HAVANA — MAP P448

Sanguich de Miami: Gourmet takes on Cuban sandwiches have 'em lining up at this cult neighborhood spot owned by first-gen Cuban Americans. *10am-6pm* $

Old's Havana Cuban Bar & Cocina: Snag a table in the tropical garden of this Calle Ocho *cocina* to feast on *picadillo*, *ropa vieja* and *vaca frita*. *11am-11pm Sun-Thu, to midnight Fri & Sat* $$

Sala'o Cuban Restaurant & Bar: With live music every night, this Calle Ocho eatery does specialties like *rabo encendido* (oxtail). *noon-midnight Sun-Wed, to 2am Thu, to 3am Fri & Sat* $$

Versailles: Miami's not-to-miss Cuban restaurant on Calle Ocho, famed for sit-down feasts and walk-up window *cafecitos*. *hours vary* $$

VIERNES CULTURALES

Every third Friday of the month, from noon until late, **Viernes Culturales** (Cultural Fridays) turns Little Havana into a street festival celebrating art, music and culture. Expect live music on stage, and galleries open until 11pm to celebrate the neighborhood's creativity and *joie de vivre*. The action plays out in the **Little Havana Historic District** along Calle Ocho, between SW 15th and 17th Aves, and features cigar rollers, local arts and crafts for sale, *mucho* music and dancing under the stars. The event draws thousands of revelers – come ready for a good time, and you'll fit right in the mix.

- 🟥 **HIGHLIGHTS**
  1. Máximo Gómez Park
- 🟢 **EATING**
  2. Azucar Ice Cream
  3. Old's Havana Cuban Bar & Cocina
  4. Sala'o Cuban Restaurant & Bar
  5. Sanguich de Miami
- 🟥 **ENTERTAINMENT**
  6. Viernes Culturales
- 🟥 **SHOPPING**
  7. Little Havana Visitors Center

Beauty at the Biltmore

MAP P449

Take a free tour of a grande dame

In the most opulent neighborhood of one of the showiest cities in the world, Coral Gables' **Biltmore Hotel** (biltmorehotel.com) has a classic beauty that seems impervious to the passage of time. Sure, you could book a room to fully bask in its beauty – or save some pennies and reserve a spot on one of the free tours of this National Landmark Hotel. Led by guides from the **Dade Heritage Trust** (dadeheritagetrust.org; free), tours take place every Sunday at 2pm.

This elaborate hotel spans 150 acres, encompassing tropical grounds, tennis courts, a massive swimming pool, and a restored 18-hole golf course. Inside, you could spend a few days occupied by the many activities on offer. One example:

 EATING IN MIAMI: CORAL GABLES & COCONUT GROVE — MAP P449

Coral Bagels: They are bagels, and they are cheap, and they are also very, very good at this family-owned shop. *7am-3pm* $

PLANTA Queen: This bright, beautiful queen is a vegan's dream, serving plant-based Asian-inspired fare. *hours vary* $$

Matsuri: Miami doesn't want for trendy sushi spots, but this strip-mall hideaway trades in the real deal. *hours vary* $$

Threefold Cafe: Cheerful cafe with Down Under vibes, espresso drinks, divine eggs Benedict and a memorable salmon salad. *7:30am-3pm Mon-Thu, to 4pm Fri-Sun* $$

CORAL GABLES & COCONUT GROVE

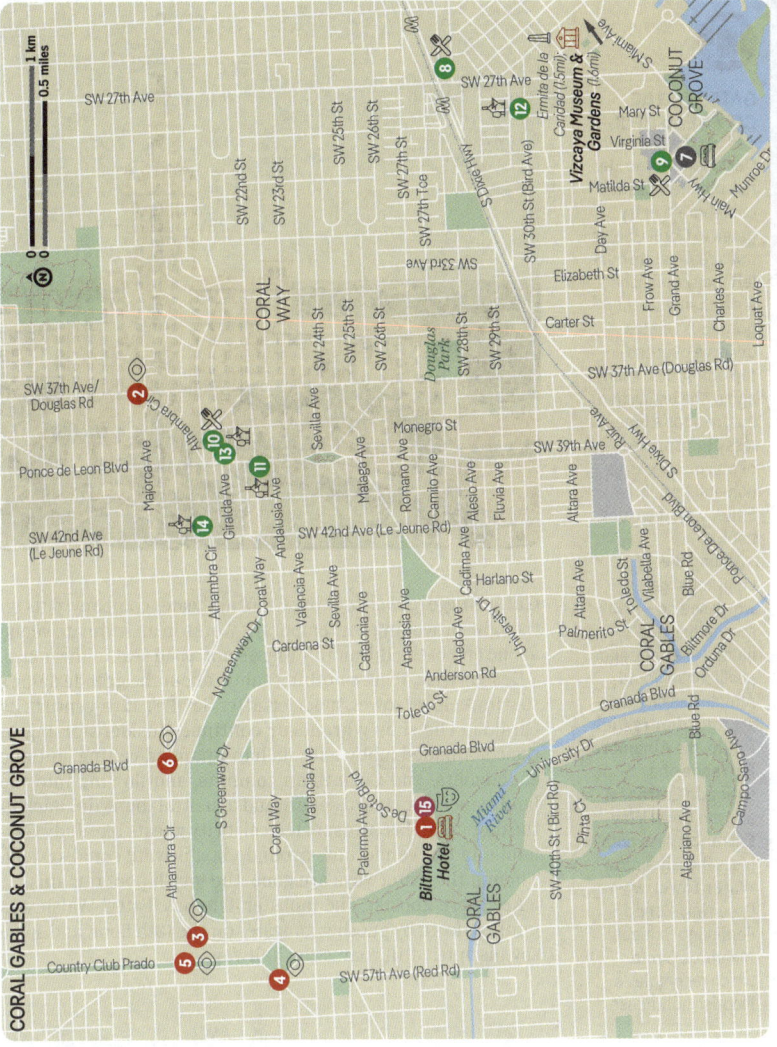

THE GUIDE

FLORIDA MIAMI

HIGHLIGHTS
1. Biltmore Hotel

SIGHTS
2. Alhambra Entrance
3. Alhambra Water Tower
4. Coral Way Entrance
5. Country Club Prado
6. Granada Entrance

SLEEPING
7. Mr C

EATING
8. Coral Bagels
9. PLANTA Queen
10. Threefold Cafe

DRINKING & NIGHTLIFE
11. Copper 29
12. Happy Wine in the Grove
13. The Bar
14. The Globe

ENTERTAINMENT
15. GableStage

449

GATES TO THE CITY BEAUTIFUL

Designer George Merrick planned a series of elaborate entry gates to Coral Gables, but a real-estate bust left many unfinished. It's a shame, as the gorgeous Gables deserve over-the-top entrances. Then again, the unfinished nature adds a timeless atmosphere... or maybe speaks to humanity's hubris? Either way, they look cool.

Among the completed gates worth seeing – many resembling and named after entrance pavilions to grand Andalusian estates – are the **Country Club Prado**, the **Alhambra Entrance**, the **Granada Entrance** and the **Coral Way Entrance**. Also notable is the **Alhambra Water Tower**, where Greenway Ct and Ferdinand St meet Alhambra Circle, which resembles a Moorish lighthouse.

FELIX MIZIOZNIKOV/SHUTTERSTOCK

GableStage (*gablestage.org*), a local theater company, puts on thought-provoking contemporary works in an intimate venue at one end of the Biltmore – there's not a bad seat in the house.

Design-wise, there's nothing subtle about the grande dame's soaring central tower, modeled after Seville's 12th-century La Giralda. The showy grandeur continues inside, starting in the colonnaded lobby with its hand-painted ceiling, antique chandeliers, and Corinthian columns, and flowing into the landscaped courtyard set around a central fountain. Back in the day, gondolas transported celebrity guests like Judy Garland and the Vanderbilts around via a private canal system. Though the waterways are gone, the lavish pool remains.

Are there ghosts? The mobster Thomas 'Fatty' Walsh was gunned down by another gangster on the 13th floor, and some say his spirit still roams the hallways.

 DRINKING IN MIAMI: CORAL GABLES & COCONUT GROVE ——— MAP P449

The Bar: Count on this spot to be divey, laid-back and big on cold brews and burgers. Very affordable, too. *3pm-3am*

Copper 29: Retro gastropub on the Miracle Mile with DJs, craft cocktails and bottle service for those who wouldn't have it any other way. *hours vary*

The Globe: A lively bar, Euro cafe undertones and Saturday-night live jazz make it a perennial pick. *hours vary*

Happy Wine in the Grove: Happy-hour tapas at this neighborhood spot go down even better when you have hundreds of wine labels on offer. *hours vary*

Biltmore Hotel (p449)

The Magic City's Magic Mansion   MAP P449
Go full golden age at Vizcaya

Back in 1916, industrialist James Deering started a Miami tradition of making a ton of money and building ridiculously grandiose digs. He employed 1000 people (then 10% of the local population) and stuffed his home with Renaissance furniture, tapestries, paintings and decorative arts.

You'll want a few hours to see all there is to see at **Vizcaya Museum & Gardens** (*vizcaya.org; adult/child $25/10*). The Coconut Grove mansion fronts Biscayne Bay and is a classic of Miami's Mediterranean-revival style. The largest room is the informal living room, sometimes dubbed 'Renaissance Hall' for its works dating from the 14th to 17th centuries. The music room is intriguing for its beautiful wall canvases from northern Italy, while the banquet hall's regal furnishings evoke the grandeur of European imperial dining rooms. On the south side of the house, a series of gardens, modeled after the formal Italian gardens of the 17th and 18th centuries, form a counterpoint to the wild mangroves beyond. Sculptures, fountains and vine-draped surfaces give an antiquarian look to the grounds, and an elevated **Garden Mound** terrace provides a fine vantage point over the greenery. You can access a free, informative audio tour by downloading the Vizcaya app.

A CHURCH WITH TIES TO THE ISLA

The Catholic diocese purchased some bayfront land from Deering's Villa Vizcaya estate and built a shrine here for its displaced Cuban parishioners. Built in 1967, **Ermita de la Caridad** is a beacon, facing the homeland, 290 miles due south, as well as a lighthouse for those Miamians who long for a land they may never have visited. This isn't the only way this church, Santuario Nacional de Nuestra Señora de la Caridad, engages with Cuba. A mural depicts the island's history, and a Spanish-language presence is the norm for the congregation. Outside the church is a grassy stretch of waterfront that makes a fine picnic spot.

Everglades & Biscayne National Park

WILD WETLANDS | GATORS GALORE | WATER ADVENTURES

GETTING AROUND

A car is essential for exploring Everglades National Park, with its far-flung entrances and sprawling terrain. From Shark Valley to Flamingo, most sites require driving, but once inside, you can explore by tram, bike, foot, canoe, or kayak – with rentals through park-approved vendors. Over at Biscayne National Park, it's all about the water – you'll need to book a guided boat tour to truly experience it. Most departures leave from the Dante Fascell Visitor Center, located near Homestead.

Stretching across South Florida, Everglades National Park is a vast, otherworldly wilderness of marshes, mangroves and slow-moving sawgrass sloughs. Whether by tram, bike, kayak or on foot, there's no wrong way to explore it. Shark Valley, about 40 miles west of Miami, offers a 15-mile paved loop perfect for tram rides, cycling and wildlife-watching. The Gulf Coast Visitor Center in Everglades City launches boat tours through the bird-rich Ten Thousand Islands. Near Homestead, Royal Palm provides easy-access trails and alligator sightings, while Flamingo, farther south, is a launchpad for paddling Florida Bay and camping under the stars. Just east of Homestead lies another natural marvel: Biscayne National Park. Though 95% underwater, it's a snorkeler and paddler's paradise, with coral reefs, shipwrecks and uninhabited keys offering a watery contrast to the Everglades' swampy sprawl. Together, these two parks show off South Florida's wild side – above the waterline and below.

Primordial Wilderness Vistas

Cycle or tram Shark Valley

A major destination for many visitors to the Everglades, **Shark Valley** *(nps.gov; pedestrian/motorcycle/car $20/30/35)* is named not for its marine life but rather its location at the headwaters of the little-known Shark River, which drains into the Gulf of Mexico. The big draw is the 15-mile paved loop trail that leads into Shark River Slough. You'll pass small creeks, tropical forest and 'borrow pits' (human-made holes now used as basking spots for gators, turtles and birdlife). Herons stalk prey along the water, and clouds shimmer like mirror images on the vast expanse of the River of Grass.

Closed to cars, the pancake-flat trail is perfect for bicycles. The halfway point is the spiraling 45-ft-high **Shark Valley Observation Tower**, a brutalist concrete structure with dramatic 360-degree views of the landscape. If you don't feel

EVERGLADES & BISCAYNE NATIONAL PARK

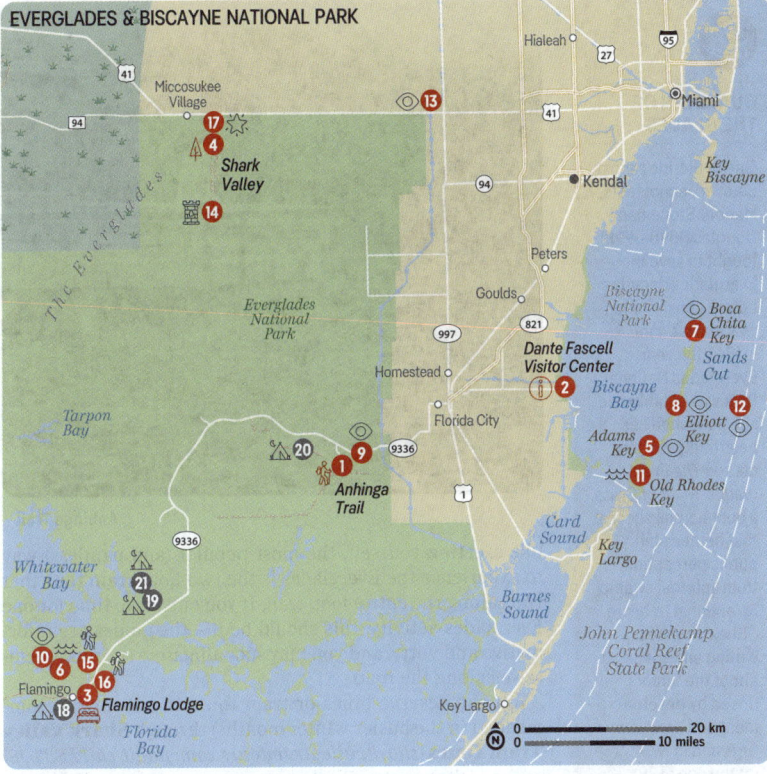

★ HIGHLIGHTS
1. Anhinga Trail
2. Dante Fascell Visitor Center
3. Flamingo Lodge
4. Shark Valley

● SIGHTS
5. Adams Key
6. Bear Lake
7. Boca Chita Key
8. Elliott Key
9. Ernest F Coe Visitor Center
10. Homestead Canal
11. Jones Lagoon
12. Mandalay Shipwreck
13. Miccosukee Casino & Resort
14. Shark Valley Observation Tower

● ACTIVITIES
15. Bear Lake Trail
16. Christian Point Trail
see 1 Gumbo Limbo Trail
17. Shark Valley Tram Tours

● SLEEPING
see 7 Boca Chita Key Campground
see 8 Elliott Key Campground
18. Flamingo Campground
19. Lard Can Campsite
20. Long Pine Key Campground
21. Pearl Bay Chickee

● INFORMATION
see 3 Flamingo Visitor Center
see 1 Royal Palm Visitor Center

☑ TOP TIP

The culinary landscape is sparse in Everglades National Park. Snacks and drinks are available at visitor centers, but the restaurant at the Flamingo Lodge (p496) is the sole sit-down option. Your best bet is to stock up and pack a cooler in nearby Homestead, Florida City, Miami or near the Miccosukee Casino & Resort.

Anhinga Trail

GUARDIAN OF THE GLADES

One of Florida's most beloved iconoclasts, Marjory Stoneman Douglas (1890–1998), fought to save the Everglades decades before conservation was mainstream. In 1947, the year Everglades National Park was established, she published her beautifully written classic *The Everglades: River of Grass*, a commercial success that helped shift public perception from 'infernal swamp' to 'national treasure.'

She continued writing and speaking about the threats posed by development and agriculture, and in 1969 (at the age of 79), founded Friends of the Everglades – a nonprofit that still plays a pivotal role in garnering political and financial support for restoration.

like exerting yourself, the most popular (and painless) way to experience the Everglades is the two-hour tram tour that runs along the entire loop trail. If you only have time for one Everglades activity, this should be it – the guides are informative and witty, and you may spot alligators sunning themselves along the road.

You can reserve bikes or tram tours in advance (recommended in the busier winter months) through **Shark Valley Tram Tours** *(sharkvalleytramtours.com; adult/child $33/18)* at the visitor center. Plan to go early in the day to beat both the heat and the crowds.

An Overnight Serenade

Camp on an above-water chickee

Everglades National Park has two drive-in campgrounds, accessible via the Homestead entrance: the 274-site **Flamingo Campground** *(flamingoeverglades.com/campgrounds; per night $33-60)* and the 108-site **Long Pine Key Campground** *(flamingoeverglades.com/campgrounds; per night $33-60)*.

And then there are chickees. What's a chickee, you ask? In Everglades-speak, it's a wooden platform built above the water where you can set up a tent. It's like having your own little island with seemingly endless horizon – sunrises and sunsets are unobstructed, and depending on the day, you may see gators coasting by, wading birds galore and frogs crooning you to sleep.

Most chickee sites are found near the **Flamingo Visitor Center** *(nps.gov/ever/planyourvisit/gbvc; per night $20-35)*. You'll need a few things in addition to your camping gear: a backcountry camping permit (available at any park visitor center), bug repellent for the inevitable mosquitoes, and a canoe, since the platforms are only reachable by water. Canoes and kayaks can be rented from several spots around the park. Off the Hell's Bay Trail, a handful of chickee sites sit within a 5-mile paddle, including **Lard Can** and **Pearl Bay Chickee** *(nps.gov; $21, plus per person per night $2)*.

Beaches, Boardwalks & Prairies
Check off quick hikes aplenty

You'll find fewer than three dozen trails in the entirety of Everglades National Park, many of which are short interpretive trails less than a mile long. Yet the trails you'll find are ones you won't soon forget. Regardless of where your Everglades hiking adventure takes you, you can be sure the route will be flat. Just make sure to pack sun-protective clothing, sunscreen and bug repellent for any Everglades hike to mitigate sun- or mosquito-related headaches.

For a moderate hike with a little history, **Bear Lake Trail**, located 2 miles north of the Flamingo Visitor Center in Homestead, is the top choice. Trickling alongside the trail, you'll see the **Homestead Canal**, which was constructed in 1922 to funnel freshwater from the marshland out to sea. The project's (dubious) goal? To create a drier piece of land for future development. The result? Just the opposite, as saltwater entered what had been a freshwater ecosystem, forever making a hybrid habitat in that portion of the park. The 3.3-mile trail features more than 50 different tree species, with hardwood hammocks towering above, culminating in a sweeping vista of **Bear Lake**, dotted with mangrove islands. Wear sturdy hiking shoes to navigate the thick grass patches and downed branches.

Christian Point Trail is for experienced hikers with its multifaceted terrain and takes upwards of three hours for the 3.2-mile experience. You'll find the trailhead 1 mile north of the Flamingo Visitor Center – and once you set out, you'll discover that the trail's difficulty stems from its jagged terrain, including thick mangrove patches and sporadic debris from hurricanes of yesteryear. A stretch of open prairie offers a welcome respite on dry days. If rain is in the forecast or the area has seen recent downpours, prepare for a muddy experience. Even the flattest prairies are a slushy mudfest, so bring the right pants and boots.

For families and a gentle saunter, the **Anhinga Trail** is 0.8 miles. This pristinely paved trail, with portions of well-kept and railed wooden boardwalks hovering over the marshland, is perhaps your easiest and best chance to see turtles and a hearty selection of the Everglades' bird species. To access the Anhinga Trail trailhead, venture to the **Ernest F Coe Visitor Center** *(nps.gov/ever/planyourvisit/coedirections)* in Homestead and head approximately 4 miles south to the **Royal Palm Visitor Center** *(nps.gov/ever/planyourvisit/royal-palm)*. The trailhead is about 50ft behind the building. If you're itching for a bonus hike, the 0.4-mile **Gumbo Limbo Trail**, draped in massive hammock trees, is a stone's throw from the visitor center.

ALLIGATORS & CROCS COEXISTING

While Florida and the Everglades receive a lot of hype around the number of American alligators lurking below the surface of freshwater ecosystems, it's not so well known that American crocodiles are also native to the Sunshine State. In fact, this is the only place in the world where alligators and crocodiles coexist. Though it's less common to spot a crocodile due to their lower population and elusive habits, the lucky few who do differentiate the two by their color and snout. Alligators tend to be darker with broad snouts and only live in freshwater, while crocodiles are lighter with narrow snouts and can thrive in both fresh and saltwater environments.

LORE AMID THE LUSHNESS

There's no shortage of lore surrounding Everglades National Park. Its history and remoteness are the perfect backdrop to stories of mystery and paranormal activity. Al Capone was rumored to have made moonshine in the desolate Lost City. Hauntings have been reported on aircraft built with scraps from the Eastern Airlines Flight 401 crash. Several murders were allegedly committed by Ed Watson, an Everglades farmer, and townsfolk took justice into their own hands and killed him – his farm is said to be haunted. Today, you can backcountry camp at Watson Place, view memorials for plane crashes, and visit the now-abandoned, hard-to-find Lost City.

FRANCISCO BLANCO/SHUTTERSTOCK

Gliding Above & Below the Surface
Boating, kayaking and making a splash

Most travelers come for a day's adventure in **Biscayne National Park**, which could entail kayaking, snorkeling or island exploring. The Biscayne National Park Institute, located at the **Dante Fascell Visitor Center** *(nps.gov/bisc)*, offers a variety of excursions, all of which are best reserved in advance. Wherever you go in Biscayne, you're likely to see plenty of seabirds, from cormorants perched on mooring posts and flocks of brown pelicans flying in formation to steely-eyed osprey gliding just above the water. Pods of bottlenose dolphins zip across the horizon, while crabs and lizards scuttle among the roots of red mangroves along the water's edge.

The **Heritage of Biscayne cruise** *(biscaynenationalpark institute.org; adult/child $83/49)* takes you across the bay and past **Adams**, **Elliott** and **Boca Chita Keys**. Aboard this half-day tour, guides bring the islands' past to life, sharing stories of some of the people who lived here over the years. There was Israel Jones, an African American man who settled on Porgy Key in the 1850s and transformed it into one of South Florida's most prosperous key-lime and pineapple farms. His descendants were instrumental in helping preserve the islands for future generations (instead of taking a hefty payout from developers).

Industrialist Mark Honeywell, on the other hand, left his mark on Boca Chita Key. After founding his eponymous

Kayaking through mangroves

thermostat and home-heating company, he purchased the key as a holiday retreat, constructing an ornamental lighthouse and a chapel, and polishing up old Spanish cannons that were fired to welcome guests to the lavish parties he loved to host. The cruise typically stops at Boca Chita, where you can admire the views from atop the lighthouse, walk a short nature trail amid the mangroves and relax on the island's tiny beach.

For a closer look at the park's natural beauty, you can sign up for one of several **paddling tours** *(1½hr $39)*. Hidden between Totten Key and Old Rhodes Key, **Jones Lagoon** has calm, clear waters fringed by mangroves. After a 30-minute motorboat ride from the mainland, you'll hop onto a stand-up paddleboard (which offers better visibility of marine life than a kayak) and look for great blue herons, great egrets and roseate spoonbills as you glide silently along. In the aquamarine waters below, you might spy sea turtles, baby sharks, rays, upside-down jellyfish or sea stars.

Snorkeling trips *(3½hr $115)* offer you immersion in Biscayne's most biologically diverse ecosystem. On a half-day trip, you'll visit two different sites, exploring coral reefs, a shipwreck or a bayside mangrove, where you can see soft coral and sea sponges. Scuba-certified divers can opt for a six-hour trip with two **dives** *($298)*. There's also the option to explore half a dozen sunken ships on the park's Maritime Heritage Trail. Three of the vessels are suited for scuba divers, while the others, especially the **Mandalay**, a two-masted schooner that sank in 1966, can be accessed by snorkelers.

A PARTY ON STILTS

Stiltsville's history is shrouded in mystery, but it was once a hot spot for parties and socializing. The collection of wooden shacks on stilts, only accessible by boat, hovers above the water of Biscayne Bay. Stiltsville began when its original core shack was built in the 1930s, and in its heyday, it was home to as many as 27 buildings. Some were social clubs or fisheries, others weekend getaways. Only a handful remain due to the exposed location and havoc-wreaking storms. In 1985, the area became a part of Biscayne National Park. Use of the houses is by permit only, but the structures are preserved to highlight the park's marine resources and remain a reminder of the area's history.

Florida Keys & Key West

ISLAND-HOPPING | SUNSET CELEBRATIONS | QUIRKY CHARM

GETTING AROUND

Getting around the Florida Keys is best done by car, especially if you're exploring the full stretch from Key Largo to Key West. From Miami, Miami-Dade Transit's bus 301 reaches Key Largo in about 90 minutes, but beyond that, public transport options thin out. Most towns are compact and walkable, but a car or bike is best for reaching beaches, state parks and waterfront eateries. Rideshare services like Uber and Lyft operate throughout the Keys, though availability can dip late at night or during low season. Boat rentals and charters are also widely available.

☑ TOP TIP

For a quieter sunset than Mallory Square, head to the pier at Fort Zachary Taylor Historic State Park. Bring a blanket and snacks to watch the sun dip into the Gulf with fewer crowds.

The Florida Keys stretch like a lazy smile across the southern tip of Florida, offering an island-hopping escape packed with natural wonders, fresh seafood and offbeat charm. While Key Largo greets you with mangroves and the coral treasures of John Pennekamp Coral Reef State Park, the journey only entices further as you follow the Overseas Highway south. Islamorada reels in anglers with world-class sportfishing and breezy waterfront bars, while Marathon has family-friendly beaches and dolphin encounters. Big Pine Key slows the pace with quiet nature trails and glimpses of the elusive Key deer. Then there's Key West – the irreverent, free-spirited finale where pastel streets, live music and historic homes channel tropical nostalgia and sunset celebration. Just 70 miles farther west, accessible only by boat or seaplane, lies Dry Tortugas National Park, home to 19th-century Fort Jefferson and pristine snorkeling waters. Together, the Keys deliver a sun-soaked, sea-sprayed adventure unlike anywhere else in the US.

Soaking up Scenery & Sun

Diving into the John Pennekamp Coral Reef State Park

John Pennekamp (*floridastateparks.org; vehicle $8, plus per person 50¢*) holds the distinction of being the USA's first underwater park. It includes 170 acres of dry parkland here and more than 48,000 acres (75 sq miles) of water – the vast majority of the protected area is ocean. Before heading out onto or into the water, be sure to enjoy the pleasant beaches and stroll the park's nature trails.

Three trails are short, flat and more educational than strenuous. The **Mangrove Trail** is a good boardwalk introduction to this ecologically awesome species (the trees, often submerged in water, breathe via long roots that act as snorkels). At a whopping 0.6 miles long, the **Grove Trail** is the longest and winds through tropical fruit groves that occasionally attract butterflies. If you're curious about the trees of the Keys, have

FLORIDA FLORIDA KEYS & KEY WEST

★ HIGHLIGHTS
1. Fort Zachary Taylor State Park
2. Islamorada Brewery & Distillery
3. John Pennekamp Coral Reef State Park

SIGHTS
4. Mallory Square
5. No Name Pub
6. Robbie's Marina
7. Sloppy Joe's Bar
8. Anne's Beach
9. Curry Hammock State Park
10. Duval Street
11. Higgs Beach
12. Indian Key Historic State Park
13. Lignumvitae Key Botanical State Park

see 13 Matheson House
14. Sombrero Beach

SLEEPING
15. Havana Cabana
16. Isla Bella
17. John Pennekamp Coral Reef State Park
18. NYAH Key West
19. Playa Largo Resort & Spa
20. Seashell Motel & Key West Hostel

EATING
21. Blue Heaven
22. Kermit's Key Lime Shoppe
23. Key Largo Conch House
24. Key West Original Conch Fritters
25. Lazy Days

see 2 Lorelei
see 19 Sol by the Sea
26. Sunset Pier

DRINKING & NIGHTLIFE
see 2 Florida Keys Brewing Company
27. Jimmy Johnson's Big Chill

CORAL BLEACHING

Coral reefs develop over thousands of years, with tiny reef-building coral polyps coming together and growing many layers of hard exoskeleton. Their color comes from the symbiotic relationship with zooxanthellae, a microscopic algae that live in coral tissue and produce food and oxygen for the coral. When water temperatures become too hot or coral gets stressed, it loses its zooxanthellae and appears white or bleached. If the coral goes too long without its main energy source, they can starve and die. Coral bleaching leads to larger issues, like loss of biodiversity and increased risks of coastal flooding. Widespread restoration efforts in the Keys continue to focus on preventing and repairing one of Florida's important natural resources.

a saunter around the **Wild Tamarind Trail,** where many of the hardwoods are labeled.

Stick around for nightly campfire programs. The **visitor center** is informative and well run, with a small saltwater aquarium and nature films providing a glimpse of what's below those waters. To really get beneath the surface, take a 2.5-hour, glass-bottom-boat tour aboard a catamaran to **Molasses Reef**, where you'll see filigreed flaps of soft coral, technicolor schools of fish, dangerous-looking barracuda and massive yet graceful sea turtles.

The park's most famous attraction is the **Christ of the Abyss**, a coral-fringed, 8.5ft, 4000-pound bronze sculpture of Jesus – a replica of one off Italy's Portofino Peninsula. On calm days, the park offers snorkeling trips to the statue, 6 miles offshore. You can also arrange diving excursions, which are obviously a big draw, or paddle through several miles of 'blue' trails among the mangroves.

Feed Very, Very Big Fish

Shopping at Robbie's and exploring beyond

Islamorada's scruffy jewel, **Robbie's Marina** *(robbies.com)*, covers all bases: it's a local flea market, tacky tourist shop, sea pen for tarpons (massive fish), waterfront restaurant and jumping-off point for fishing expeditions – all wrapped into one driftwood-laced compound. Boat rentals and tours are also available.

When you park, you'll first encounter the market section of Robbie's, showcasing crafts and art from around the islands. It's a good spot for picking up a unique piece of memorabilia. If folks aren't perusing paintings, they might be knocking back beers while enjoying the waterfront view. If it all feels like a bit of sensory overload, you can escape the bustle by renting a kayak *(kayakthefloridakeys.com; per day $50-60)* for a peaceful paddle through nearby mangroves, hammocks and lagoons. In fact, this is a major launch point for paddlers heading to Indian Key and Lignumvitae Key, two state parks accessible only by boat.

Now lonely and eerie, **Indian Key** was once a thriving town with a warehouse, docks, streets, a hotel and about 40 to 50 permanent residents. It was even the first seat of Dade County – now dominated by metro Miami, which is just a wee bit larger on the population scale. **Lignumvitae Key Botanical State Park** is a 280-acre island of virgin tropical forest ringed by alluring waters. The official attraction is the

EATING IN THE KEYS: OUR PICKS

Key Largo Conch House: Fresh seafood abounds at this waterfront restaurant. For an authentic Keys taste, start with conch fritters. *8am-9pm* $$$

Sol by the Sea: Opt for the 'water table' experience for sunset dining around a table in the water. *11am-10pm Mon-Fri, from 10am Sat & Sun* $$$

Lorelei: Relax and enjoy drinks, bites and live music on the Islamorada waterfront. Try the key lime peppercorn snapper. *7am-10pm* $$

Lazy Days: Take your pick of award-winning seafood and ocean-view dining: tables in the Islamorada sand, on the patio or indoors. *11am-10pm* $$$

HERITAGE TRAIL ROAD TRIP

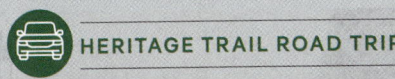

Cruise the Upper Keys on the Overseas Highway. Pull off the road for biker bars, seafood grills and blissful beaches along the way.

START	END	LENGTH
Dagny Johnson Key Largo Hammock Botanical State Park	Long Key State Park	45 miles; 8 hours

How many of the 84 protected species of plants and animals – including the elusive American crocodile – can you count at ❶ **Dagny Johnson Key Largo Hammock Botanical State Park**? Drive south next along the Overseas Highway to ❷ **John Pennekamp Coral Reef State Park**. Stroll along the Mangrove Trail, a short loop adjacent to the park's paddling trail. After, whet your whistle at the ❸ **Caribbean Club**, the oldest bar in the Upper Keys, just a six-minute drive from the state park.

As you make your way further south, satisfy your sweet tooth with a slice of authentic key lime pie at ❹ **Blond Giraffe Key Lime Pie Factory**.

Down the road in Islamorada, pause to snap a photo with the 30-ft-high sculpture of Betsy the Lobster at ❺ **Rain Barrell Village** and explore art by local artisans.

Following the highway further south brings you to the ❻ **History of Diving Museum** where you can nerd out on the history of underwater exploration. After working up an appetite learning about diving, fuel up with craft bites and brews at ❼ **Islamorada Brewery**. Keep it classic with a draft of the subtly citrus Sandbar Sunday or taste the Keys with the key lime and coconut-y No Wake Zone. Wrap up your road trip at ❽ **Long Key State Park** with a geocaching session.

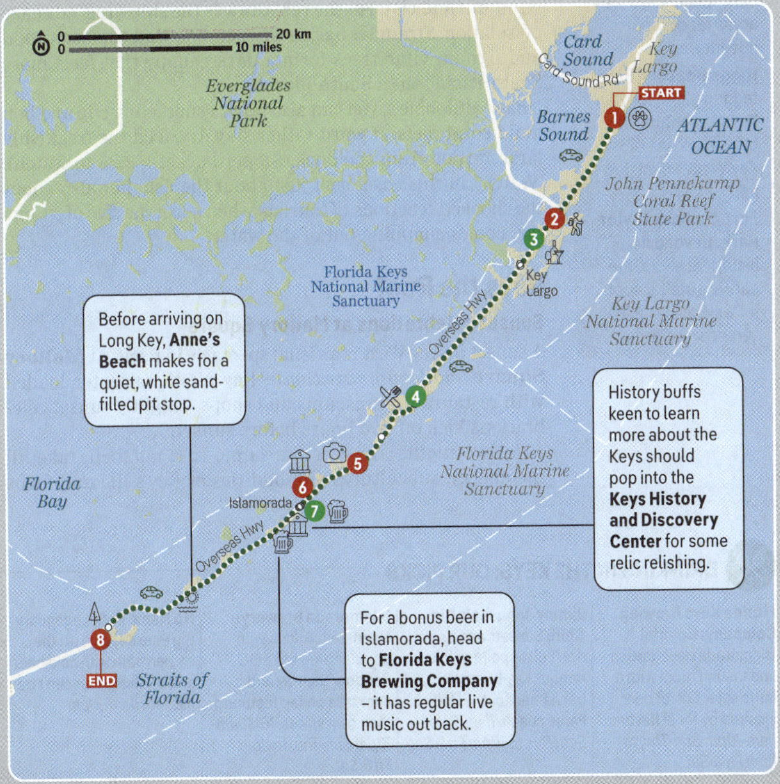

Before arriving on Long Key, **Anne's Beach** makes for a quiet, white sand-filled pit stop.

History buffs keen to learn more about the Keys should pop into the **Keys History and Discovery Center** for some relic relishing.

For a bonus beer in Islamorada, head to **Florida Keys Brewing Company** – it has regular live music out back.

BEST BEACHES IN THE KEYS

Anne's Beach: Family-friendly Islamorada beach with calm shallow waters, pavilions, a boardwalk and restrooms.

Sombrero Beach: This tranquil Marathon beach has shaded picnic spots, barbecue pits, a playground, volleyball courts and plenty of space to unwind.

Curry Hammock: Between Duck Key and Marathon, this park sports 1000 lush acres for outdoor adventures.

Higgs Beach: If Fido tagged along for your Keys adventure, this beach has one of Key West's best dog parks.

Fort Zachary Taylor Park: Beyond its historical allure, the park is a stellar spot for a swim in shallow, serene waters.

1919 **Matheson House** (*floridastateparks.org; $2.50),* with a windmill and cistern; the real draw is the shipwrecked sense of isolation. Strangler figs, mastic, gumbo-limbo, poisonwood and lignum vitae trees form a dark canopy that feels more South Pacific than South Florida.

Back at Robbie's, you can also book a snorkeling trip and bob amid coral reefs. If you'd rather stay dry, feed the freakishly large tarpon from the dock ($3 per bucket, $2.25 to watch). 'Watch,' in this case, isn't just about the fish, but also about the shocked reactions of tourists when a fish the size of a large dog comes snapping out of the water.

Rays the Roof

Sunset celebrations at Mallory Square

A sunset in Key West is a visual spectacle in itself. At **Mallory Square** *(mallorysquare.com)* – Key West's epicenter, loaded with restaurants, museums and shops – nightly sunset celebrations kick off two hours before sunset.

No two nights are ever the same. In a nutshell, take all the energy, subcultures and oddities of Key's life and focus

DRINKING IN THE KEYS: OUR PICKS

Florida Keys Brewing Company: Colorful Islamorada beer garden and tasting room with a large selection of beer inspired by local flavors. *11am-10pm Sun-Thu, to 11pm Fri & Sat*

Jimmy Johnson's Big Chill: Sunsets and drinks don't disappoint at this famous Key Largo tiki bar named for the Hall of Fame coach. *11am-9pm Sun-Thu, to 10pm Fri & Sat*

Islamorada Brewery: Neon-yellow icon with popular brews like OG Sandbar Sunday and cocktails on tap featuring their own spirits. *10:30am-10pm Sun-Thu, to 11pm Fri & Sat*

No Name Pub: Legendary Big Pine Key pub off the beaten path with cold beer and a fish dip that can't be missed. *11am-10pm*

Mallory Square

them into one torchlit, family-friendly (but playfully edgy), sunset-infused street party. The result of all these raucous forces is cinematic and a bit tourist-clogged. The waterfront setting is magnificent, and food vendors often gather here. Among the oft-kitschy activities, you can watch a dog walk a tightrope, a man swallow fire, and British acrobats tumble and sass each other. The showmanship and camaraderie of the performers are matched by the crowd's energy and the fading light of day.

Then – lucky you – you'll find yourself right at the top of **Duval Street**, ready for the **Duval Crawl**. Duval is Old Town Key West's main drag, a conglomeration of neon and historic buildings. Its upper reaches are packed with bars and restaurants, while the southern end has more galleries and gift shops – though it certainly doesn't lack for bars and restaurants either. From Mallory Square, you'll want to pace yourself as two of Duval's biggest dive bars, **Hog's Breath Saloon** (*hogsbreath.com*) and **Sloppy Joe's Bar** (*sloppyjoes.com*), are right there.

WHY I LOVE THE FLORIDA KEYS

Jesse Scott, Lonely Planet writer

I've called Fort Lauderdale home for nearly a decade. We have pristine beaches and stretches of world-class resorts. Honestly, a beach is the last place I want to vacation. But the Keys hit differently. Key West has a bohemian-historic vibe that is seldom found in South Florida and worth the jaunt. Talking to the story-filled locals fuels my soul. As do the ever-orange sunsets – a memorable one being a recent dinner with my wife at the Playa Largo resort. We sat at a 'water table' – literally a table anchored in shallow waters, noshing fresh ceviche and watching kids frolic on floating cabanas nearby. The Keys are a true escape, even if you're a local.

EATING IN KEY WEST: ICONIC SPOTS

Sunset Pier: The views from this spot, poised for best sunset dining, are undeniable. *11:30am-8:30pm $$$*

Key West Original Conch Fritters: Skip the sit-down meal and snag a classic Key West snack from this stand at the heart of Mallory Square. *10:30am-6pm $*

Kermit's Key Lime Shoppe: A popular place to relish all things key-lime flavored. The frozen, chocolate-dipped key-lime-pie bar is a hit. *10am-9:30pm $*

Blue Heaven: Customers (and free-ranging fowl) flock to dine on Caribbean fare in a ramshackle tropical garden. *8am-2:30pm & 5-10pm $$*

Southeast Florida

SUNNY BEACHES | LGBTQ+ HOT SPOTS | WATER EXCURSIONS

GETTING AROUND

Getting around Southeast Florida is easiest by car, but alternatives abound – especially in urban areas. In Fort Lauderdale, skip pricey parking and hop on LauderGO! shuttles or the free electric Micro Mover to reach spots like Las Olas, downtown and the beach. In West Palm Beach, the free downtown trolley connects the waterfront with key districts. Brightline, a sleek high-speed rail, links Fort Lauderdale, West Palm Beach and beyond, making coastal travel a breeze. In Vero Beach, consider biking waterfront trails or strolling its walkable downtown.

Southeast Florida, stretching from Vero Beach to Fort Lauderdale, blends laid-back beach towns, vibrant cultural hubs and sun-soaked luxury into a scenic coastal corridor like few others. Once known as the raucous spring-break capital, Fort Lauderdale has gracefully outgrown its party-hard past. Today, it's a polished, palm-fringed city of yachts, waterfront dining and stylish hotels lining the A1A and well inland. With 300 miles of inland waterways and more than 50,000 registered yachts, it's earned nicknames like the 'Yachting Capital of the World' and the 'Venice of America.' But Southeast Florida doesn't stop here. Head north and you'll find West Palm Beach, where historic charm meets a buzzing arts and dining scene, particularly along Clematis St and in the Warehouse District. Further up, Vero Beach offers a quieter coastal retreat with white-sand beaches, elegant resorts and a small-town vibe that's long attracted artists and snowbirds alike. From glossy marinas to turtle-tracked shores, Southeast Florida delivers sun, style and evolving appeal.

Catch Some Rays

MAP P465

Enjoy the largest beach in Lauderdale

Fort Lauderdale's sandy shoreline, stretching for miles along the Atlantic, is conveniently sectioned into smaller portions, each radiating its own unique personality and flavor. The largest and most popular of the bunch is **Fort Lauderdale Beach**. It's swank and chic, targeted by Instagrammers. At its heart is **Fort Lauderdale Beach Park**, sporting volleyball and basketball courts, a playground, restrooms and showers. The promenade's always hopping with rollerbladers and joggers, while yoga groups stretch on the beach. Luxury hotels, surf-inspired stores and oceanfront restaurants abound, with plenty of parking *($6/hr)* nearby.

FORT LAUDERDALE

🟠 **HIGHLIGHTS**	**SLEEPING**
1 Bonnet House	7 Conrad Fort Lauderdale Beach
🟠 **SIGHTS**	8 Snooze Hotel
2 Fort Lauderdale Beach & Promenade	9 The Grand Resort & Spa
3 Fort Lauderdale Beach Park	🟢 **EATING**
4 Hugh Taylor Birch State Park	10 Bohemian Latin Grill
5 Riverwalk	11 Café Seville
🟠 **ACTIVITIES**	see 8 Casablanca Cafe
6 Jungle Queen Riverboat	12 Coyo Taco
	13 Greek Islands Taverna
	14 Heritage

15 MAASS	21 Ramrod
16 Mykonos	see 16 Swizzle Rum Bar
17 Southport Raw Bar	22 The Manor
see 7 Takato	23 Wreck Bar
see 7 Vitolo	🟠 **SHOPPING**
🟢 **DRINKING & NIGHTLIFE**	24 Out of the Closet
see 10 4:30 Boardroom Bar	25 Pride Factory
18 Ann's Florist & Coffee Bar	🔵 **INFORMATION**
19 Elbo Room	26 Pride Center
20 Georgie's Alibi Monkey Bar	🔵 **TRANSPORT**
	27 LauderGO! Water Trolley

THE STINGING PORTUGUESE MAN O' WAR

Fort Lauderdale's beaches are generally considered safe, with lifeguards patrolling the most popular stretches. One thing to watch out for, though, is the Portuguese man o' war. This jellyfish-like creature is actually a species of siphonophore, and while usually not deadly, it delivers a painful sting. It resembles a small, blue-tinted plastic bag or balloon and can be found floating in the water or washed up on shore. If you see one, stay a few feet away: its long tentacles can still sting even after it's dead.

Bonnet House Museum & Gardens

Biking & Beaching

MAP P465

The hidden Hugh Taylor Birch State Park

One of the best-kept secrets in all of Southeast Florida, **Hugh Taylor Birch State Park** *(floridastateparks.org/hughtaylorbirch; vehicle $6)* is great for all things outdoors. Tucked between the ocean and intracoastal waters, it provides the best of both worlds. Bike the 2-mile Perimeter Trail, kayak through mangroves or sunbathe on hidden shorelines. The park is also accessible by the city's **Water Taxi** *(watertaxi.com; per day adult/child $38/18, after 5pm $25/18)*, departing from 11 stops in Fort Lauderdale and another 15 in nearby Pompano Beach and Hollywood Beach.

A Waterfront Stroll

Admire the Intracoastal Waterway

The Atlantic might steal most of the attention, but Fort Lauderdale is endowed with over 300 miles of inland waterways, too. Take in views of the New River with a stroll along the **Riverwalk** footpath, spotting historical homes, luxury condos and art sculptures en route. Allow a couple of hours to stroll the circular route or, if you succumb to the heat, hop aboard the free **LauderGO! Water Trolley**, which makes

 EATING IN SOUTHEAST FLORIDA: FORT LAUDERDALE BEACH — MAP P465

MAASS: Fort Lauderdale's first Michelin-starred restaurant wows with contemporary American fare. *5-10pm Mon-Thu, from 11:30am Fri-Sun* $$$

Takato: Ocean views and pan-Asian dishes at Conrad Fort Lauderdale Beach. Pair duck bao buns with a lychee martini. *8-10:30am & noon-10pm Sun-Thu, to 11pm Fri & Sat* $$$

Vitolo: This high-end Italian restaurant has all of the classics. Don't miss 4pm to 6pm happy hour. *noon-10pm Sun-Thu, to 11pm Fri & Sat* $$$

Casablanca Cafe: Perfect date-night spot where the architecture and ocean views are as charming as the Mediterranean food is delicious. *hours vary* $$$

eight stops. Bicycle and Segway rentals are also available, but narrow paths and sharp turns present a challenge when it's crowded.

Water Taxis to Luxury Boats
MAP P465
Cruise the waterfront

Swap your walk for a cruise along Fort Lauderdale's inland waterways. The **Jungle Queen Riverboat** *(junglequeen.com; adult/child $31.50/21, parking $13)* offers 90-minute, fully narrated cruises showcasing homes of the rich and famous – an area dubbed 'Millionaire's Row.' For something more intimate, the locally owned **Rent a Boat Fort Lauderdale** *(rentaboat fortlauderdale.com; 4hr for up to 10 people from $400)* offers private deck boat and pontoon rentals, with or without a captain. The most affordable option is the **Water Taxi** *(watertaxi.com; per day adult/child $38/18, after 5pm $25/18)*, which provides lighthearted, narrated cruises around town between 10am and 10pm. Hop on and off at 10 different stops.

History & Nature Unite
MAP P465
An orchid oasis at Bonnet House

Bonnet House Museum & Gardens *(bonnethouse.org; adult/child $25/8)* is a plantation-style, oceanfront homestead. Its 35 acres of subtropical gardens feature one of America's most esteemed orchid collections. The buildings were designed by professional artist and self-taught architect Frederic Bartlett in the early 1920s. Frederic's second wife, Evelyn, deeded the property to a historical trust before her death in 1997 to secure it against greedy developers. Thanks to her, you can enjoy nature trails winding through five distinct ecosystems on the area's last bastion of undeveloped shoreland. (Watch for spider monkeys in the treetop canopies.)

LGBTQ+ Hot Spot
MAP P465
Explore Wilton Drive

Wilton Drive (sometimes called 'The Drive') is abundant with queer-friendly restaurants, shops and watering holes. LGBTQ+ nightclub **Georgie's Alibi Monkey Bar** *(alibiwiltonmanors.com)* is perpetually packed, while **The Manor** *(themanorcomplex.com)* is a glamorous club featuring flashy chandeliers and more bars than you can shake a stick at. Younger crowds often spill onto its second level.

If leather's your thing, you'll enjoy the raunchy cowboy vibe at **Ramrod** *(ramrodbar.com)*, a popular hangout since 1994, where patrons rock to edgy tunes in a medieval dungeon-style setting.

Eager to shop? Neighborhood thrift shop **Out of the Closet** *(outofthecloset.org)* sells size 12 stilettos and offers free HIV testing while you browse. You'll also find quite a selection of gay clientele–geared clothing around the corner at **Pride Factory** *(pridefactory.com)*.

CELEBRATE FLORIDA'S LGBTQ+ CAPITAL

Despite the state government's push for anti-LGBTQ+ legislation in 2023 and 2024, Fort Lauderdale remains a thriving LGBTQ+ community and a popular queer holiday destination. LGBTQ+ retirees and remote workers flock to Wilton Manors and neighboring Victoria Park, cementing its status as the hub for LGBTQ+ nightclubs, bars, restaurants and social clubs. A rainbow-painted 'Love Wins' bridge welcomes visitors to Wilton Manors, where street lamps glow with artistic wire sculptures. The local **Pride Center** *(pridecenterflorida.org)* distributes information on area highlights.

But the LGBTQ+ pride really comes to life during the **Greater Florida Pride Parade and Festival** *(pridefortlauderdale.org)*, with floats, costumes and a celebration of diversity and love.

GREAT LOCAL HANGOUTS

Captain Danny Grant, owner of Floridian Coastal Charters *(floridiancoastal charters.com)*, shares his favorite spots to eat and drink.

4:30 Boardroom Bar: Awesome saloon in the north entertainment district with strong drinks and a surf-skate-hot-rod-inspired setting. Free vintage car show Saturdays.

Bohemian Latin Grill: A friendly couple serving up the tastiest Latin food in town. They'll even deliver to your bar stool next door at the Boardroom Bar.

Southport Raw Bar: Locals love grabbing fresh oysters and a pitcher at this casual waterfront restaurant with tasty seafood.

Café Seville: Every dish is a winner, with traditional Spanish cuisine and great wine. Start with *gambas as ajillo* (garlic seafood dish) and *ensalada maite* (palm hearts). Reserve.

A Fort Lauderdale Tradition MAP P465
Elbo Room

Hopping since 1938, this famed two-level beach bar is the ultimate throwback. Immortalized in the 1960 film *Where the Boys Are*, it became a magnet for spring breakers and a rite of passage for an entire generation of college students. Today, the legendary **Elbo Room** *(elboroom.com)* – often called the world's best beach bar – might feel lonely and forgotten by day, but by night, it morphs into a loud, brash party zone. The crowds pack so tightly it's nearly impossible to reach the bar (cash only). Elbo Room may be showing some wrinkles, but it's unlikely this old-school favorite will ride into the sunset anytime soon.

Brunch with Swimming Mermaids MAP P465
Showtime at the Wreck Bar

Frank Sinatra strutted the hallways at the historic **Wreck Bar** *(boceanresort.com/dining/the-wreck-bar)* when it opened in the 1950s at B Ocean Resort. The bar's nautical theme,

EATING & DRINKING: DOWNTOWN FORT LAUDERDALE MAP P465

Mykonos: A Greek island–inspired riverwalk spot serving seafood and small plates. *5-10pm Sun-Thu, to 11pm Sat & Sun* **$$$**

Coyo Taco: Enjoy 50% off select tacos on Taco Tuesdays! Don't miss the incredible smoky cauliflower tacos. *11am-9pm Sun-Thu, to 11pm Fri & Sat* **$**

Swizzle Rum Bar: Feel the speakeasy vibes when you cozy up in a booth with the best craft cocktails in town. *6pm-2am Mon-Thu, to 3am Sat & Sun*

Ann's Florist & Coffee Bar: Grab lunch and flowers, plus floral-inspired drinks and snacks from the back bar. *8am-11pm Mon-Sat, 9am-9pm Sun* **$$**

Clematis Street

with its chiseled wood bar and briny decor, suggests you're in a 1600s Spanish galleon. But it's the aquarium portholes behind the bar that reveal some extraordinary sights: on Saturday and Sunday mornings, mermaids and mermen put on a magical, family-friendly show ($15 excluding food and drinks). Enjoy standard American brunch fare as they swim past. The mermaids also make brief appearances during Thursday and Friday dinners. For an adults-only (ages 21+) mermaid show, reserve a Saturday dinner show ($40 excluding food and drinks).

The Heart of West Palm Beach

MAP P470

A night out on Clematis Street

Stroll over to **Clematis Street** *(clematisstreet.org),* a vibrant entertainment strip dripping in history. Henry Flagler, the founder of West Palm Beach, was florally obsessed, naming downtown streets after plants and flowers – in this case, a bright purple buttercup. During the day, the street isn't all that busy, with shops and midday restaurants being the primary draw. But when night falls, things turn up a notch.

☑ TOP TIP

Avoid extra driving and parking fees by selecting accommodations based on what matters most. For beach access, stay at a hotel along A1A. For restaurants, nightlife and shopping, opt for a place near main corridors like Las Olas Blvd in Fort Lauderdale.

 EATING IN SOUTHEAST FLORIDA: GREATER FORT LAUDERDALE — MAP P465

| **Heritage:** Innovative takes on Italian favorites: think sweet-and-sour calamari and short rib masala pizza. *11:30am-3pm & 5-11pm Wed-Sun* **$$** | **YOT Bar & Kitchen:** Watch yachts sail by as you enjoy cinnamon buns and lobster rolls at this riverfront brunch hot spot. *hours vary* **$$** | **Larb Thai-Isan:** This casual Thai restaurant between Fort Lauderdale and Pompano Beach is beloved by visitors and locals alike. *11:30am-10pm Wed-Mon* **$** | **Greek Islands Taverna:** You can't go wrong at this family-owned restaurant, which offers perhaps the best Greek food in town. *11am-10pm Mon-Sat, from noon Sun* **$$** |

MEET THE JAEGA PEOPLE

Prior to colonization, the Native American tribe known as the Jaega called West Palm Beach – and the rest of modern-day Palm Beach County – their home. They were hunter-gatherers who relied heavily on marine resources such as fish, shellfish and sea turtles, as well as skilled canoeists and traders.

Unfortunately, the Jaega people were decimated by European diseases and warfare in the 18th century, and there are no known descendants of the Jaega people today. However, their legacy lives on via the archaeological sites and artifacts found in Palm Beach County.

- ★ **HIGHLIGHTS**
  1. Blind Monk
- ● **SIGHTS**
  2. Centennial Square
  3. Clematis Street
- ● **SLEEPING**
  4. Hilton West Palm Beach
  5. The Ben
- ● **EATING**
  6. Galley
  7. Hullabaloo
  8. Kapow Noodle Bar
  9. Proper Grit
  10. Spruzzo
- ● **DRINKING & NIGHTLIFE**
  11. Clematis Social
  12. Juicy
  13. Spazio
- ● **ENTERTAINMENT**
  14. Respectable Street

Clematis' trendy dining and drinking options have exploded, stealing attention from their flashy nightclub neighbors. The manga-themed **Kapow Noodle Bar** (*kapownoodlebar.com*) pairs artfully crafted drinks with contemporary pan-Asian bites. Next door at **Hullabaloo** (*sub-culture.org/locations/hullabaloo*), musician-inspired cocktails are always a blast. Nearby, **Juicy** (*juicywpb.com*) is a popular spot known for using the highest-quality ingredients in its internationally inspired drinks, while rooftop bar **Spruzzo** (*spruzzowestpalm.com*) offers panoramic views to go with its top-notch drinks and Mediterranean plates.

 EATING IN SOUTHEAST FLORIDA: WEST PALM BEACH — MAP P470

Blind Monk: A classy, romantically lit tapas and wine bar. Pop in during happy hour for a chill and affordable night out. *5-10pm Mon-Sat* $$

Okeechobee Steakhouse: Florida's oldest steakhouse perfects Kansas City strip steak and key lime pie. *11:30am-10pm Mon-Fri, 4-10pm Sat, to 9pm Sun* $$$

Galley: Enjoy trendy bistro fare on an outdoor patio with an aromatic fire pit. Best smoky Old Fashioned cocktails around. *5-10pm* $$$

Proper Grit: Cozy and intimate. Try the hanging bacon and sticky citrus boar rib appetizers before your pick of flavor-bomb mains. *7am-10pm* $$$

Looking for live music? **Clematis Social** *(clematissocial wpb.com)* has long been the go-to spot, with its Billboard Hot 100 songs and large dance floor. Then, there's **Respectable Street** *(sub-culture.org/locations/respectable-street),* known for its punk rock vibes, and **Spazio** *(lynoras.com/spazio),* where EDM fans find their home. Last but not least, the free live-concert series **Clematis by Night** takes the stage at **Centennial Square** on Thursday evenings from 6pm to 9pm.

Spot Gentle Giants

MAP P470

Learn about magical manatees

After discovering that warm-water outflows from their Riviera Beach generating station attracted manatees in winter, Florida Power & Light opened an eco-discovery center to honor these gentle giants. **Manatee Lagoon** *(visitmanateelagoon.com; free)* provides educational exhibits and two levels of observation decks for visitors to view these docile sea cows – along with nurse sharks, sea turtles and other colorful marine life – as they swim freely through the Intracoastal Waterway. The best viewing is from November to March.

Stroll Through the First US National Wildlife Refuge

MAP P470

Explore the Pelican Island National Wildlife Refuge

Established in 1903 in Vero Beach to protect pelicans from feather hunters, **Pelican Island National Wildlife Refuge** *(fws.gov/refuge/pelican-island; free)* encompasses 5445 acres of protected water and land. With more than 218 species of birds, the area's a huge hit with bird-watchers. Almost 8 miles of nature trails lead walkers through multiple habitats packed with greenery and wildlife. Even better, the Centennial Trail is ADA-accessible, ending at an observation tower.

All of that said, bird-spotting can be difficult for newbie ornithologists, so consider a free guided tour. Taking place each Wednesday from January to April, these tram tours come with an expert local guide and a pair of binoculars. Call 772-581-5557 to reserve.

FLORIDA CITRUS PRODUCTION

It is widely believed that Spanish explorer Ponce de Léon introduced orange trees to Florida near St Augustine in the mid-16th century. It wasn't until 1763, however, that a man named Jesse Fish started the first commercial orange grove in the same area. For about 100 years, this grove – and many more – continued to thrive in the warm north Florida sun. But in the late 1800s, northern Florida was hit with devastating freezes, decimating most of the state's citrus crops. Some farmers left, while others migrated further south to the warm and soil-rich Indian River, where many of the world's best oranges are grown today.

 EATING IN SOUTHEAST FLORIDA: VERO BEACH

Tres Hermanos: Hole-in-the-wall eatery in the back of a Mexican grocery store with incredible, authentic tacos. *7am-7pm Mon-Sat* **$**

Citron Bistro: Innovative American fare with a breezy patio and can't-miss weekend brunch. *11am-3pm & 5-8pm Mon-Sat, from 9am Sun* **$$**

Mama Hue: Unassuming strip-mall spot serving pan-Asian food. Must-try pad thai and tapioca dumplings. *10am-8pm Mon-Wed & Fri, from noon Sat & Sun* **$$**

Pepper & Salt BBQ: Under-the-radar BBQ restaurant known for tender, flavorful brisket – with a side of creamy mac and cheese, of course. *10:30am-3pm Wed-Sat* **$$**

Orlando & Walt Disney World®

STUNNING GARDENS | IMMERSIVE MUSEUMS | THEME PARK UTOPIA

GETTING AROUND

For the most part, you'll need a car to get around Orlando. There are some exceptions to the rule, like the adorable I-Ride Trolley on International Dr and the LYMMO bus in downtown Orlando. Rideshares are widely available in Greater Orlando and can be more economical. For a more sustainable option, Orlando has electric bikes and scooters (from $1 per ride) through Lime, Bird and Veo.

☑ TOP TIP

Prepare for Orlando's heat, humidity and daily summer thunderstorms. Dress is typically casual in this Theme Park Capital of the World, so pack lightweight, breathable clothing, comfortable shoes, a rain poncho and a wide-brimmed hat to keep the sun off your face.

Most visitors to Orlando rarely venture beyond the fabricated worlds of Disney and Universal Orlando. Yet beyond the theme park thrills, the city of Orlando is home to several fantastic gardens and nature preserves, plus a delightfully slower pace.

Prior to 1965, when Walt Disney announced plans to build Walt Disney World®, Orlando had been a sleepy city. Its historic core, Old Orlando, is located along Church St between Orange and Garland Aves. Wetlands make up much of Greater Orlando, its landscape dotted with lakes, including the largest, Lake Apopka. The rainy season lasts from May to late October, and northern sunseekers flock during its delightful warm and dry season, from November through April. While the average visitor to Orlando spends their vacation indulging in theme-park food, locals know that just a few miles outside of these tourist attractions is a gateway to true Central Florida charm.

Black History & Culture

African American heritage at Wells'Built Museum

In the center of Orlando's historic Parramore district, the small **Wells'Built Museum** *(wellsbuilt.org; $5)* is dedicated to the city's African American history and culture. It's housed in the former Wells'Built Hotel, opened in 1926 by Dr William Monroe Wells to host African American performers forbidden from staying in the city's segregated accommodations. Count Basie, Cab Calloway, Billie Holliday, Ella Fitzgerald and Duke Ellington all spent a night under its roof. On the top floor, a hotel room remains frozen in time, complete with furniture and decor that would have greeted guests in the 1930s.

ORLANDO & WALT DISNEY WORLD®

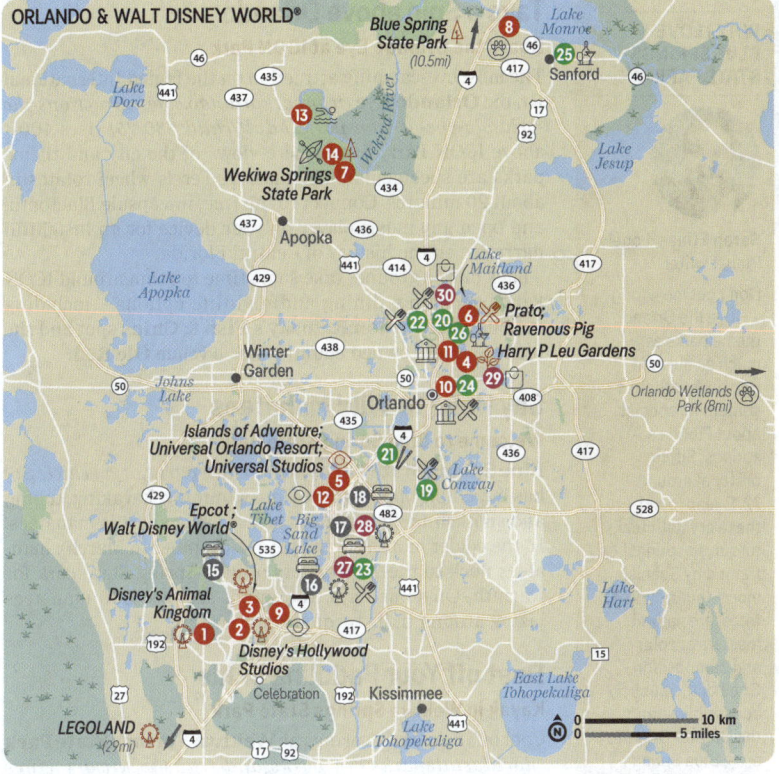

⭐ HIGHLIGHTS
1. Disney's Animal Kingdom
2. Disney's Hollywood Studios
3. Epcot
4. Harry P Leu Gardens
5. Islands of Adventure
6. Prato
- see 6 Ravenous Pig
- see 5 Universal Orlando Resort
- see 5 Universal Studios
- see 3 Walt Disney World®
7. Wekiwa Springs State Park

🔴 SIGHTS
8. Central Florida Zoo & Botanic Gardens
9. Disney Springs
10. Orange County Regional History Center
11. Orlando Science Center
- see 5 Universal CityWalk
12. Volcano Bay
- see 10 Wells' Built Museum

🔴 ACTIVITIES
13. Kelly Park
14. Nature Adventures

⚫ SLEEPING
- see 6 Alfond Inn
- see 12 Cabana Bay Beach Resort
15. Disney's Polynesian Village Resort
- see 10 Grand Bohemian Hotel
16. Hilton Garden Inn Lake Buena Vista
17. Rosen Inn at Pointe Orlando
18. Villatel Orlando Resort

🟢 EATING
19. Bombay Street Kitchen
- see 17 Gordon Ramsay Fish & Chips
20. Hunger Street Tacos
21. Isan Zaap
22. Mediterranean Deli
- see 17 Ole Red
23. Selam Ethiopian & Eritrean Cuisine
24. Swine & Sons

🟢 DRINKING & NIGHTLIFE
- see 17 Icebar
- see 24 Otto's High Dive
25. Suffering Bastard
26. The Courtesy

🔴 ENTERTAINMENT
- see 15 Magic Kingdom
27. SeaWorld
- see 17 Orlando Eye
28. Universal Epic Universe

🔴 SHOPPING
29. Atomic Horror
30. Bossa N' Roll Records
- see 6 Frank
- see 6 Gasp
- see 6 Winter Park Farmers' Market

WHY I LOVE BLUE SPRINGS STATE PARK

Sarah Etinas, Lonely Planet writer

Don't get me wrong – I love the Orlando theme parks as much as the next person, but there's something special about Florida's springs. Sitting pretty at around 72°F year-round, these crystal-clear, turquoise springs, framed by Spanish moss–laden cypress trees, are natural masters of color and composition. Of all of the publicly accessible springs in the Greater Orlando area, Blue Springs State Park is my personal favorite. Each winter, it's easy enough to check the park's Facebook page for an update on the daily manatee count – the number occasionally reaches 400 – and drive on over for an afternoon watching the manatees float on by.

Take a Spin above Orlando
Board the Orlando Eye at ICON Park

The most eye-catching attraction on the famed International Dr, the **Orlando Eye** *(iconparkorlando.com/attractions/the-orlando-eye-at-icon-park; adult/child $30/25)* rises 400ft above ICON Park, from where views of the city and theme parks are spectacular. The massive Ferris wheel rotates in about 20 minutes. Connect to the free, in-capsule Bluetooth, and open any music player on your device for an insightful narrative on the history of Central Florida.

Back on the ground, take some time to roam around ICON Park's shopping, dining and nightlife options – including famous chef **Gordon Ramsay's Fish & Chips** spot and the Blake Shelton–owned country-music venue **Ole Red**.

Say Hello to Wild Manatees
Welcome to Blue Spring State Park

Blue Spring State Park *(floridastateparks.org; vehicle $6)* has incredible opportunities for swimming, kayaking, tubing and snorkeling. But what sets this spring apart is manatees. In the colder months of the year (November to March), manatees flock to the 72°F waters of Blue Spring State Park for warmth. On some days, you might see over 500 manatees lazing around in its turquoise waters.

Dust off Your Paddling Skills
Kayak in Wekiwa Springs State Park

Cool off in emerald springs at **Wekiwa Springs State Park** *(floridastateparks.org/parks-and-trails/wekiwa-springs-state-park; vehicle $6)*, about 20 miles northwest of downtown Orlando in Apopka. Spot some of the 190 species of birds recorded here while hiking miles of trails meandering through woods, swamplands and along the banks of the Wekiva River.

You can rent a kayak or canoe from **Wekiwa Springs Adventures** *(wekiwaspringsadventures.com; 2hr from $40)* to paddle the scenic, still waters. It's actually possible to kayak 8.5 miles from the state park, through neighboring **Rock Springs Run State Reserve** *(floridastateparks.org; vehicle $3)*, into **Kelly Park** *(ocfl.net; vehicle $3)*. Along the way, enjoy the beauty of the turquoise waters and the fairytale-like, Spanish moss–laden trees, all while keeping an eye out for birds, fish, turtles, and the occasional alligator. Be sure to arrive early, as parking regularly reaches maximum capacity.

 EATING IN ORLANDO: CHEAP EATS

| **Bombay Street Kitchen:** Casual Indian spot known for great food and value. Don't miss the kale chaat and street special dosa. *11:30am-3pm & 5-10pm* $ | **Swine & Sons:** Fill up on Southern comfort classics like breakfast biscuits, fried pickles and spicy fried chicken sandwiches in Winter Park. *hours vary* $ | **Mediterranean Deli:** Greek sandwiches here are affordable and flavor-packed. *10:30am-5:30pm Mon-Sat* $ | **Isan Zaap:** Delicious northeastern Thai cuisine, with dishes like *som tum* (Thai papaya salad) and *laab* (minced pork). *11:30am-10pm* $$ |

TOP EXPERIENCE

Walt Disney World®

Where else can you dine in a castle, race through space and shake hands with a mouse in one day? Walt Disney World® is a storytelling spectacle with four theme parks, two water parks and a slew of hotels, restaurants and entertainment all working to make magic. From nostalgic rides to cutting-edge attractions, it's a choose-your-own-adventure playground for kids, grown-ups and superfans.

Fireworks at Disney's Magic Kingdom

Themed Lands, Legendary Rides

Start with Cinderella Castle at **Disney's Magic Kingdom®**, where fairy tales come to life and fireworks dazzle nightly. Over at **EPCOT®**, it's a race through the cosmos on *Guardians of the Galaxy: Cosmic Rewind* or a stroll through 11 countries in World Showcase. **Disney's Hollywood Studios®** delivers *Star Wars* drama and *Toy Story* whimsy, while **Disney's Animal Kingdom®** pairs thrills with wildlife encounters, from Everest coasters to jungle safaris.

Getting Around

Spanning 47 sq miles, Walt Disney World Resort is a city unto itself. Hop between parks by Monorail, Disney Skyliner, water taxi or bus. Rideshares and Minnie Vans offer extra convenience, but driving remains popular – just factor in time to transfer from parking areas to park gates.

Beyond the Parks

Shopping and dining districts like **Disney Springs®** tempt with Cirque du Soleil shows, chef-driven restaurants and one-of-a-kind shops. At resort hotels, you'll find everything from African savannas with roaming giraffes to poolside Polynesian luaus.

TOP TIPS

- Arrive early or stay late to enjoy cooler temps and lighter crowds.

- Lightning Lane passes save major time on high-demand rides.

- For the best castle fireworks view, claim a Main Street spot at least 30 minutes early.

PRACTICALITIES

- disneyworld.disney.go.com
- 9am-10pm
- prices vary

Stroll a Flora-Filled Oasis
Take in Harry P Leu Gardens

Stroll the 50-acre **Harry P Leu Gardens** *(leugardens.org; adult/child $15/10)*, an impressive botanical oasis just minutes from downtown Orlando. The plant collection includes primitive cycads, bright red hibiscus and almost 400 species of palm trees. The citrus grove's 50 different kinds of citrus trees highlight Florida's agricultural bounty, while a native wetland garden attracts wading birds and other wildlife. Tours of the 18th-century **Leu House** run every 30 minutes: former owner Mary Jane Leu loved roses, and her collection of old garden roses (those existing before 1867) forms the most extensive formal rose garden in Florida. Bring provisions for a lakeside picnic.

Say Hello to Wildlife in the Wild
Birding in the Orlando Wetlands

The artificial **Orlando Wetlands Park** in Christmas, about 30 miles east of downtown Orlando, was designed to provide advanced treatment for reclaimed water. An education center houses seasonal exhibits that include live animals and interactive displays. From the center, set off on the 2-mile **Birding Loop**, one of many trails that wind through the park. Not all trails are open to cyclists, but many are accessible for horseback riders. Be cautious of alligators on the trails – they're especially attracted to the sun-warmed, lime-rock surfaces that line many trails.

A Colorful World Built with Iconic Bricks
LEGO's relaxed theme-park experience

Manageable crowds and lines, interactive and educational exhibits, a fun, colorful backdrop and a water park make **LEGOLAND** *(legoland.com/florida; adult/child under 2 from $74/free)* a fantastic destination for families looking for a more stress-free vacation.

Located in Winter Haven, about 50 miles southwest of downtown Orlando, LEGOLAND has attractions geared toward children aged two to 12. At **Ford Driving School**, kids can drive cars through a pretend town, while **Miniland** is a grand LEGO-made model of iconic American landmarks and cities. Don't miss the **Imagination Zone**, an interactive learning

BEST BOUTIQUES & SHOPPING IN ORLANDO

Winter Park Farmers' Market: Shop for local goods like cheeses, flowers, baked goods and produce at this Saturday morning market.

Gasp: Winter Park boutique selling stationery, accessories and home decor from artists and creators. Girly-pop core at its finest.

Frank: Gift shop in Winter Park showcasing curated goods like precious-stone jewelry and coconut wax candles.

Bossa N' Roll Records: Leaning into old-school Orlando, this Maitland store boasts a well-curated vinyl selection.

Atomic Horror: A haven for horror enthusiasts in Baldwin Park with memorabilia and merch from horror film franchises.

 DRINKING IN ORLANDO: OUR PICKS

The Courtesy: Speakeasy vibes and crafted drinks at Greater Orlando's first cocktail bar. *4pm-midnight Tue-Thu, to 1am Fri & Sat, to 10pm Sun*

Suffering Bastard: Savor tropical cocktails at this tiki bar in the Sanford suburb. *5-10pm Wed, Thu & Sun, to midnight Fri & Sat*

Otto's High Dive: Known more for its rum than cuisine, the guava pastelito and coquito cocktails are incredible. *4pm-midnight Tue-Sat, 11am-10pm Sun*

Icebar: Sit on an ice-cold seat and sip icy drinks at this out-of-the-ordinary ice bar. *5pm-midnight Mon-Thu, to 2am Fri & Sat, to 1am Sun*

TOP EXPERIENCE

Universal Orlando Resort™

Welcome to the ultimate movie-lovers' playground, where rides, lands and shows bring blockbusters to life. Universal Orlando Resort features three epic theme parks – Universal Studios Florida™, Islands of Adventure™ and Epic Universe™ – plus splash-filled Volcano Bay™ and Universal CityWalk™. From dodging dinosaurs to casting spells or racing Mario, it's nonstop action and storytelling at every turn.

How to Train Your Dragon, Isle of Berk

Movie Magic in Every Direction

Universal Studios is where the silver screen springs to life. Race alongside Harry Potter through Gringotts, laugh with the Minions and blast aliens with Men in Black. Grab a Butterbeer in Diagon Alley or spot the fire-breathing dragon atop the wizarding bank. Over at Islands of Adventure, ride the Jurassic World VelociCoaster, soar with Spider-Man or brave Hagrid's Magical Creatures Motorbike Adventure. Don't skip E.T. Adventure – a charming classic still loved today.

Brand-New Worlds Await

The 2025 debut of Epic Universe introduced five new lands. Highlights include Super Nintendo World, complete with Mario Kart races, and Dark Universe, a moody realm of reimagined monsters. The Isle of Berk invites *How to Train Your Dragon* fans to soar through the sky, while the Wizarding World's Ministry of Magic blends 1920s Paris with wizard-filled London. Celestial Park, the park's radiant hub, offers intergalactic rides and a futuristic promenade.

Soak, Stroll & Snack

Cool down at Volcano Bay, a tropical water park with slides, splash pads and the Krakatau Aqua Coaster – all accessed with wristbands that hold your place in line. Come evening, unwind at CityWalk with mini golf, global eats, cocktails and entertainment. It's also the easiest way to walk between parks.

TOP TIPS

- Stay at a Universal Premier Hotel to receive complimentary Express Passes (a serious time-saver).

- Catch the Hogwarts Express between parks – it's different each way, and you'll need a park-to-park ticket.

- Arrive 30 minutes before park opening and head straight to Hagrid's or Mario Kart.

PRACTICALITIES

- universalorlando.com
- tickets from $119
- generally 9am–9pm

ORLANDO FAMILY ATTRACTIONS

Jeff Stanford, Orlando local and VP of Marketing at Orlando Science Center (osc.org), shares his favorite family attractions.

Orlando Science Center: There's something for kids of all ages...exhibits for infants and toddlers, dinosaurs and live animals for young kids, a Maker's Space and a giant-screen theater for teens.

Central Florida Zoo & Botanic Gardens: Besides animals, they've got a train, ziplines and merry-go-rounds. It's big enough to spend the day, but small enough to feel like an intimate experience.

Orange County Regional History Center: There's more to Orlando than theme parks. The OCRHC is a nice spot to learn about Orlando's history.

LEGOLAND (p476)

center where skilled LEGO builders are on hand to help children of all ages build their next block masterpiece.

An Emphasis on Conservation & Sustainability

Consider the new SeaWorld Orlando

SeaWorld (seaworld.com/orlando; adult/child under 2 from $143/free) is one of the largest theme-park franchises in Orlando. When the 2013 documentary *Blackfish* was released, alleging SeaWorld's mistreatment of its captive orcas, things took a turn, both in visitor numbers and in SeaWorld's practices. Today, SeaWorld Orlando works hard on education and conservation, rehabilitating hundreds of marine animals and implementing sustainable practices across its Orlando parks.

Oddly enough, SeaWorld Orlando is also making a name for itself in the thrill-ride world with ocean-themed roller coasters like Mako and Pipeline. SeaWorld Orlando's water park **Aquatica** (2-day combined ticket with SeaWorld adult/child under 2 $215/free) holds its own, too.

 EATING IN ORLANDO: OUR PICKS

Hunger Street Tacos: This spot is a contender for Greater Orlando's best tacos. The brisket or fried avocado tacos are top-notch. *11:30am-8pm Mon-Sat* $$

Selam Ethiopian & Eritrean Cuisine: From lentil samosa starters to the concluding coffee ceremony, Selam is a treat. *noon-9pm Mon, Wed & Thu, to 10pm Fri-Sun* $$

Ravenous Pig: Innovative takes on locally sourced American gastropub fare. The restaurant is a long-time local favorite. *hours vary* $$

Prato: Modern takes on Italian classics, celebrating local and sustainable ingredients. Don't miss the meatball appetizer. *hours vary* $$$

Space Coast

ASTRONAUTS | BEACHES | UNTAMED REFUGE

Florida's Space Coast is where cosmic dreams and coastal charm reign. Titusville and Kennedy Space Center form the epicenter of interstellar intrigue, a place where you don't just watch rockets launch, you feel them shake the earth. Since NASA planted its flag here in 1958, this stretch of Merritt Island has been launching missions, telescopes and imaginations skyward. But there's more to the region than space-age feats. Cape Canaveral is home to active launchpads, pristine beaches and the scenic Canaveral National Seashore. Just south, Cocoa Village adds a dose of vintage Florida with walkable streets, galleries, waterfront dining and a healthy dose of small-town soul. Nature and technology coexist here: one minute you're kayaking among manatees in the Indian River Lagoon, the next you're walking beneath a Saturn V rocket. Whether you're here for liftoffs, lattes or lagoons, the Space Coast delivers a down-to-earth adventure with out-of-this-world appeal (literally).

Secrets of Space Travel

Stratospheric fun at Kennedy Space Center

No visit to the Space Coast is complete without spending several hours – or a couple of days – at ground zero for America's space program, **Kennedy Space Center Visitor Complex** *(kennedyspacecenter.com; adult/child $75/65)*, where decades of interstellar history has been made. Part of a working launch facility, this popular attraction offers something for anyone who's ever stared at the sky and wondered.

Embark on the 90-minute bus tour (included with admission) for close-as-you-can-get views of launch facilities (unless you're an astronaut) and the massive Vehicle Assembly Building (the world's largest one-story building, its 465ft-high doors also the largest in the world). Tours stop at the Apollo/Saturn V Center, where you'll see the largest rocket ever flown (one of just three remaining), which transported astronauts to the moon, and many other Apollo mission artifacts.

GETTING AROUND

There's considerable distance between the space attractions and the surrounding wildlife refuge and national seashore, so you'll definitely want your own car to explore. If you're coming over from Orlando for the day, **Gray Line Orlando** *(graylineorlando. com)* offers round-trip sightseeing excursions from Disney, Kissimmee and Orlando to Kennedy Space Center Visitor Complex aboard comfortable buses.

☑ TOP TIP

Looking for an epic spot to watch space launches? Head to **Scobie Park** in Titusville, a postage-stamp-sized park across from NASA's launching pads. Two Hi-Spy viewing machines are at your disposal for even closer views – free of charge! Download the Next Spaceflight *(nextspaceflight.com)* app for up-to-date launch schedules.

SPACE COAST

HIGHLIGHTS
1. Crydermans Barbecue
2. Dixie Crossroads
3. Fat Snook
4. Kennedy Space Center
5. Merritt Island National Wildlife Refuge
6. Pompano Grill

SIGHTS
7. Cocoa Riverfront Park
8. Jetty Park
9. Scobie Park

ACTIVITIES
10. Island Watercraft Beach Rentals

SLEEPING
11. Beachside Hotel & Suites
12. Courtyard Titusville Kennedy Space Center
see 12 Hyatt Place Titusville/Kennedy Space Center
see 8 Jetty Park Campground

EATING
13. Café Margaux
14. Fishlips Waterfront Bar & Grill
15. Flavour Kitchen & Wine Bar
16. Milpa Tacos y Tortillas
17. Orleans Bistro & Bar
18. Pier 220 Seafood & Grill
see 9 Tree of Life Cuban Bakery

DRINKING & NIGHTLIFE
19. Coconuts on the Beach
20. Ellie Mae's Tiki Bar
21. Rikki Tiki Tavern
22. Village Bier Garten
23. Wine Lady

SHOPPING
24. Antilles Trading Company
25. Antiques & Collectibles Too
26. Carolyn Seiler Studios

TRANSPORT
27. Port Canaveral

Or perhaps taking in a movie at the IMAX Theater and catching some thrills aboard one of four immersive rides at Gateway: The Deep Space Launch Complex – starring the awesome Red Planet ride that takes you to Mars – is more your speed.

Immerse yourself in deeply cerebral experiences, from the US Astronaut Hall of Fame's films and multimedia exhibits to touring the actual Space Shuttle Atlantis that's on display. For goosebumps and an adrenaline rush, board the immersive Shuttle Launch Experience or Spaceport KSC flight simulators. Kids (ages two to 12) enjoy space-themed activities at Planet Play, while exhausted parents enjoy a drink at its bar lounge. You can even meet NASA astronauts, hearing all about their training and experiences during daily scheduled Astronaut Encounters – just be sure to check the center's event calendar in advance if you've got your heart set on meeting a certain someone. Pet kennels are available on-site (with proof of vaccinations).

A Perfect Beach Day
Great surf and pristine sands in Jetty Park

More than your average park, fabulous **Jetty Park** *(shop.port canaveral.com; day pass $15)* is a 35-acre oasis located on the water's edge right in **Port Canaveral**. While it's perfect for enjoying a beautiful day at the beach, watching cruise ships pass by, some extend their visit by camping in a tent or RV under star-filled skies at its excellent on-site campground.

Day passes must be bought online in advance, as no payment is accepted at the gate. Pets are only permitted with registered campers.

When there's a launch scheduled from Cape Canaveral – which happens regularly these days – views from the park's golden strip of beach and 1200ft-long fishing pier are as good as they get for watching rockets blast off over the Atlantic.

The sloping sandbar just offshore makes Jetty Park a popular surf break for consistent wave action, and you'll usually find a gaggle of surfers scanning the horizon, waiting for a behemoth to roll in. If you're tempted to paddle out, you can rent boards from **Island Watercraft Beach Rentals** *(island watercraftbeachrentals.com)*, which also offers umbrellas, chairs, kayaks and other beach-day essentials.

When the fishing pier isn't closed due to hurricane damage and refurbishments, you'll find throngs of anglers trying to hook red fish, jack, Spanish mackerel and more.

WHERE TO WATCH A LAUNCH

Chris Eckles, who works in the commercial space industry on Cape Canaveral, shares locations he loves for catching a launch.

Westgate Cocoa Beach Pier: It's hard to beat a perch over the ocean at the tiki bar at the end of the pier, something frosty in hand, while scoping the horizon.

Port St John Boat Ramp: Right on the Indian River in Port St John, the boat ramp at the end of Fay Blvd has great views across to the launch pads.

Harbor Heights Beach: Grab a spot on the sand at this Cape Canaveral beach or head out for a surf and look north to see the streak in the sky at launch time.

🍽 EATING IN THE SPACE COAST: TITUSVILLE

Dixie Crossroads: A local favorite for wild ocean-caught seafood and steaks. Don't miss their buttery, broiled rock shrimp. *11am-9pm* **$$**

Pier 220 Seafood & Grill: Historic spot on the Indian River Lagoon. Tasty grouper tacos and peel-and-eat shrimp. *10:30am-9pm Sun-Thu, to 10pm Fri & Sat* **$$**

Orleans Bistro & Bar: Shrimp and crawfish get the Cajun treatment at this fashionable New Orleans–style spot. Try the Nola Boil. *11am-midnight Sun-Thu, to 1am Fri & Sat* **$$**

Tree of Life Cuban Bakery: Enjoy authentic Cuban sandwiches, coffees and other treats in the spirit of Old Havana. *hours vary* **$$**

SPACE COAST STATE PARKS & REFUGES

Sebastian Inlet State Park: Pristine beaches, great waves, one of Florida's best fishing piers and a secluded snorkeling cove.

Archie Carr National Wildlife Refuge: Stretching more than 20 miles along the coast, an important habitat for nesting loggerhead sea turtles.

Merritt Island National Wildlife Refuge: Originally acquired for NASA's Space Program, 218 sq miles of hiking trails and a self-guided wildlife drive.

Indian River Lagoon State Park: Featuring lots of native plants, birds and sea life, it's popular with kayakers, boaters and water waders.

Something particularly fun to do here is bidding adieu to skyscraping cruise ships bound for the Bahamas and other ports of call as they pass along the shoreline on their way out of Canaveral Barge Canal into the wide-open Atlantic.

Antiquing & Cafe-Hopping

Explore historic Cocoa Village

Lest you think the Space Coast is all rockets, surfers and wildlife, you can also find one of Florida's most atmospheric downtowns for cafe-hopping, boutique shopping and antiquing here. Drive roughly 8 miles inland (west) from Cocoa Beach – crossing the sparkling waters of the Banana River and Indian River Lagoon – to reach Cocoa Village, a former riverfront trading post turned eclectic, artsy town.

A leafy urban oasis by the lagoon's edge, it's lined with historic buildings housing independent restaurants and cafes, wine bars and shops. Start your explorations at **Cocoa Riverfront Park**, where an amphitheater overlooking the Indian River often hosts concerts and festivals. The surrounding park affords a scenic view of the river and is a nice spot to sit for a spell atop benches painted with images of flamingoes and octopuses by local artists, watching boats sail by.

 DRINKING IN THE SPACE COAST: BEST TIKI BARS

Rikki Tiki Tavern: Cocktails in a colorful setting above rolling surf at the end of Westgate Cocoa Beach Pier. *11am-9pm Sun-Thu, to 10pm Fri & Sat*

Ellie Mae's Tiki Bar: Friendly neighborhood place in Cape Canaveral with tiki cocktail specials and smoked fish dip. *hours vary*

Coconuts on the Beach: Classic, lively oceanfront tiki bar, steps from the sand in Cocoa Beach. Killer piña coladas! *11am-10pm*

Fishlips Waterfront Bar & Grill: Watch passing cruise ships from this nautical rooftop tiki bar in Port Canaveral. Frosty drinks, pub grub. *hours vary*

Cocoa Riverfront Park

Then venture a few blocks inland to explore the village's cute shops and eateries.

Carolyn Seiler Studios (*carolynseiler.com*) is a wonderful artist co-op housed inside a colorful cottage where you can shop for things like glass jewelry, coasters, wind chimes and paintings created by more than 30 local artisans. **Antiques & Collectibles Too** (*facebook.com/actcocoavillage*) has a maze of rooms filled with things like estate jewelry, decades-old Disney snow globes, rare chess sets and vintage NASA mission patches. And don't miss **Antilles Trading Company** (*antillestradingcompany.com*), a pirate oddities store featuring an adjoining museum with timeless artifacts and pirate-related interactive exhibits.

Favorite spots for a drink or meal include German-themed **Village Bier Garten** (*villagebier.com*), **Milpa Tacos y Tortillas** (*milpataco.com*) for Oaxacan and Baja-style fare, and boutique wine store and tasting bar **Wine Lady** (*thewineladycocoa.com*). If you love barbecue, don't miss **Crydermans** (*crydermansbarbecue.com*) for succulent meat that pairs wonderfully with local craft beers and ciders. Just look for the gigantic cow mural – sporting sunglasses, of course.

HOMETOWN SURFING LEGEND

Look for a statue of the Space Coast's most famous surfer on the median strip approaching downtown Cocoa Beach on the A1A heading south. It pays homage to Kelly Slater, who was born in Cocoa Beach and surfed the area's beach breaks from the age of five. In fact, the area's consistently imperfect-shaped waves are often attributed with Slater's prowess – as they were more challenging beasts to master than perfect ones! A Cocoa Beach legend, this record-holding, 11-time World Surfing League champion still occasionally visits the Space Coast, so you never know when or where you might spot him along a casual paddle out (especially if surf's up at Sebastian Inlet).

EATING IN SPACE COAST: COCOA BEACH

Pompano Grill: A tiny, sweet hideaway for steak, seafood and crème brûlée. Family-run and welcoming. *5:30-8:30pm Tue-Thu, 5-9pm Fri & Sat* **$$**

Flavour Kitchen & Wine Bar: Exquisite dishes by affable Chef Jason. The seafood paella rocks, but so does everything else! *hours vary* **$$**

Fat Snook: Gourmet seafood restaurant in south Cocoa Beach, with a scratch kitchen and Caribbean-inspired dishes. *4-9pm Tue-Sun* **$$$**

Café Margaux: Casual elegance in Cocoa Village, serving French and European-inspired cuisine with fab wine pairings. *11:30am-9pm Mon-Sat* **$$$**

Northeast Florida

STORIED STREETS | BEACH BREAKS | RIVERFRONT BUZZ

GETTING AROUND

You'll need a car to visit many of Jacksonville's attractions and beaches – rent wheels or get a taxi, Uber or Lyft. Local buses *(jtafla.com)* are reliable, but don't cover all areas. There's a free elevated monorail downtown with a few stops, and the St Johns River Taxi takes you to some riverfront parks, docks, hotels and the TIAA Bank Field. Historic neighborhoods like Riverside, San Marco and Avondale are great places to wander on foot, as is the entirety of St Augustine.

Northeast Florida blends historic intrigue, beachside energy, and just the right dose of Southern hospitality. Jacksonville, the state's most populous city, sprawls with surprising ease – a mix of towering downtown, walkable historic districts and vast stretches of sand. Despite its size, Jax still feels like a tight-knit town, where tailgating is a ritual, fishing poles are standard gear and beach days come with live music and cold drinks. Just 40 miles south lies St Augustine, the oldest continuously occupied city in the US, where cobblestone streets, centuries-old forts and Spanish colonial architecture set a storybook scene. You can stroll the Castillo de San Marcos, sip from the legendary Fountain of Youth or simply wander among boutiques and wine bars. From Atlantic Beach's relaxed surf scene to St Augustine's old-world allure, Northeast Florida is a region where the past meets the present and every day ends with an ocean breeze.

Beach-hopping

MAP P485

Pick your Jacksonville beach experience

Jacksonville has lots of entertainment, dining and shopping opportunities, but when residents want to relax, they head to beaches 20 miles east. Smaller towns dot the white sandy shoreline, each offering different coastal vibes.

Jacksonville Beach is a popular weekend getaway for Jacksonvillians, with its wide range of indoor and outdoor activities. Kids love **Adventure Landing Jacksonville Beach** *(jacksonville-beach.adventurelanding.com)* with its Shipwreck Island Waterpark, go-karts, mini golf and arcade. Popular **South Beach Park** *(jacksonvillebeach.org)* boasts Sunshine Playground, a skate park, grills, volleyball courts, walking trails and a seasonal splash pad.

People in their 20s and 30s flock to Jacksonville Beach to dance, hit a bar or soak up live entertainment. All ages enjoy sunbathing, swimming and surfing. Colorful surfboards, boats and pelicans usually dot the Atlantic's blue-gray waves. Enjoy

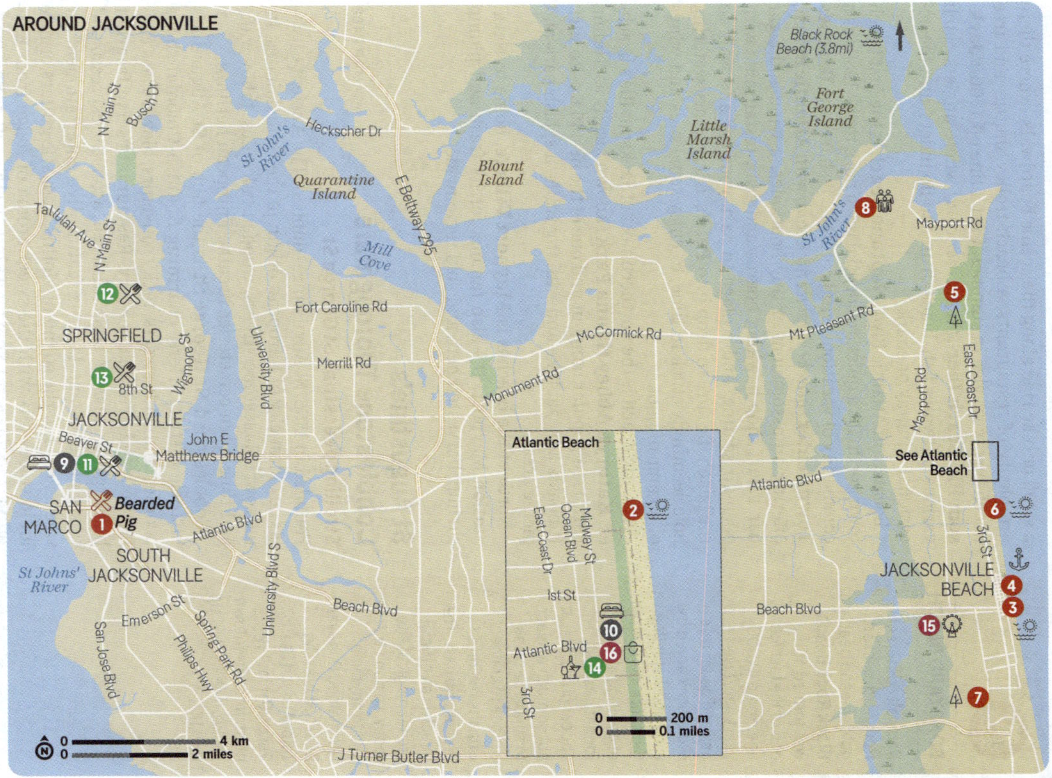

FLORIDA NORTHEAST FLORIDA

AROUND JACKSONVILLE

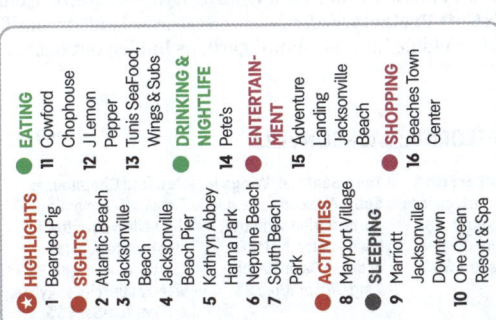

★ HIGHLIGHTS
1. Bearded Pig

● SIGHTS
2. Atlantic Beach
3. Jacksonville Beach
4. Jacksonville Beach Pier
5. Kathryn Abbey Hanna Park
6. Neptune Beach
7. South Beach Park

● ACTIVITIES
8. Mayport Village

● SLEEPING
9. Marriott Jacksonville Downtown
10. One Ocean Resort & Spa

● EATING
11. Cowford Chophouse
12. J Lemon Pepper
13. Tunis SeaFood, Wings & Subs

● DRINKING & NIGHTLIFE
14. Pete's

● ENTERTAINMENT
15. Adventure Landing Jacksonville Beach

● SHOPPING
16. Beaches Town Center

☑ TOP TIP

Avoid interstates and major roads during weekday rush hours (7am to 9am and 4pm to 6pm), when accidents happen and delays can triple travel times. Jacksonville trouble spots include I-95 downtown; east-west routes like Butler, Southside and Blanding Blvds; and the Main St, Buckman and Acosta bridges.

BONEYARD BEACH

Radically different from hard-packed, golden-sand beaches, **Black Rock Beach** was formed at the end of the last ice age, some 10,000 years ago. Live oak and cedar tree skeletons carved by wind and water line the shore, comprised of geological soil formations that appear primordial. It's not so much a beach to sunbathe on as a place to connect with the region's prehistoric past. The beach is an official archaeological site today, so don't try taking anything. Nicknamed Boneyard Beach, it is at Big Talbot Island State Park, 20 minutes north from downtown Jacksonville, off State Rd A1A.

a stroll or bike ride along the scenic boardwalk, where there are plenty of restaurants, a beach-trolley shuttle, and free beach-buggy service in summer. Cast a line off 1300ft **Jacksonville Beach Pier** *(thejaxpier.com)* where anglers catch various saltwater fish, black drums to flounders, and the occasional stingray or shark.

Located off Atlantic Blvd, **Neptune Beach** is the first beach town north. It's a quiet, residential town born in the 1930s as a community of vacation rental cottages. It shares the **Beaches Town Center** *(beachestowncenter.com)* with **Atlantic Beach**, offering an assortment of tiny boutiques, a wine and cigar bar, a surf shop hawking boards and gear, restaurants with open-air seating, and a place to park your car and walk to the beach. Be sure to drop into **Pete's**, a legendary watering hole seemingly stuck in time, to enjoy some suds and wings or a game of pool.

Atlantic Beach is the northernmost of Jacksonville's beaches. **Kathryn Abbey Hanna Park** (known locally as 'Hanna Park') is a popular hangout and one of the best places to surf. It boasts a plaza, bike and walking trails, a splash park and picnic areas.

North of the beaches is **Mayport Village**, home to Naval Station Mayport. It's also famous for its fresh and plump shrimp, harvested here and sold regionwide.

St Augustine's Cobblestone Thoroughfare

MAP P488

Strolling pedestrian St George St

Founded in 1565, St Augustine – dubbed 'The Ancient City' – is the oldest city of European origin in the United States. Its narrow, cobblestone streets, wooden balconies, tabby walls and time-worn cemeteries breathe European heritage.

Cobblestoned **St George St** is the hub of St Augustine's historic district. Here, charming Spanish-Colonial shops peddle handmade sweets, tacky souvenirs, blown-glass confections and artisanal jewelry. Restaurants serve fragrant baked goods, glasses of Spanish red, aromatic espresso and tapas plates. Some taverns feature live entertainment on weekends, and the sound of violins, acoustic guitars or melodic voices mix with the sweet aroma of fudge from **Kilwins** *(kilwins.com)*. Stop for a vintage-style soft pretzel from **Ben's Soft Pretzels** *(order.benspretzels.com)* and devour it at a bistro table in the tranquil gardens hidden out back. If

---

EATING IN NORTHEAST FLORIDA: JACKSONVILLE

MAP P485

Bearded Pig: Casual local spot after sports games, serving smoked ribs, wings, pulled pork and tasty sides. *11am-9pm Tue-Sun* **$$**

J Lemon Pepper Fish & Chicken: Three locations cooking up ginormous portions at good-value prices. *hours vary* **$$**

Tunis Seafood, Wings & Subs: A Jax fave, serving the best fried shrimp in town – or try the lamb gyro or delish Cajun Ranch wings. *10am-10pm* **$$**

Cowford Chophouse: Timelessly romantic, this stylish downtown steakhouse boasts a rooftop lounge with views of the city's skyline. *4-10pm Tue-Sat* **$$$**

St George St

you're ready to imbibe, tip one back at **Prohibition Kitchen** (pkstaug.com), a gastropub with rockin' live music and the longest bar in town.

Dating to the 1700s, you'll also find the **Oldest Wooden School House Museum & Gardens** (oldestwoodenschoolhouse.com; adult/child $8/7) here, steps from the **Colonial Quarter**. The street is only open to pedestrians. Cabs and trolleys stop at either end, bookended by city gates and the historic **Cathedral Basilica of St Augustine**. Built in 1797, the cathedral was remodelled under the guidance of renowned architect James Renwick Jr after a ravaging fire spared its coquina foundation in 1887.

A short walk from the southern end is **Plaza de la Constitución**, with giant oak-shaded eateries and galleries, and the small, open-air covered **Slave Market**, named for one of its unfortunate historical purposes. There's a ton of history here – each block packed with so many stories that it would take a weekend to stop and read all the memorial plaques.

Consider strolling across the majestic **Bridge of Lions**. Built in 1927 and restored in 2010, two marble lion statues still guard its crossing. The far side of the bridge affords a fantastic view of downtown, red Spanish tile roofs and quaint B&Bs lining the bayfront.

TROLLEY TOURS

Hands down, the easiest – and most fun – way to navigate the nation's oldest city, and score a lay of the land, is by old-fashioned trolley. Along the route, riders are regaled with interesting anecdotes and amusing tales about the businesses and historic sites they're passing.

The **Old Town Trolley** (trolleytours.com/st-augustine; adult/child $37/18) has 22 stops and offers 90-minute tours, as well as ghost tours. Tours include hop-on-and-off privileges, so passengers can stop to enjoy food and attractions along the way. **Ripley's Red Train Tours** (ripleys.com/attractions/ripleys-red-train-tours-st-augustine; adult/child $24/13) offers similar excursions, with 20 stops and an opportunity to visit Ripley's Believe-It-Or-Not Odditorium.

 EATING IN NORTHEAST FLORIDA: ST AUGUSTINE — MAP P488

Floridian: Old Florida hipster vibes with courtyard dining, a cozy bar and an eclectic menu with gluten-free and vegan/veg options. 11am-late Wed-Mon $$

St Augustine Fish Camp: Seafood so scrumptious there's usually a line, but it's worth the wait. Your taste buds will agree. hours vary $$

Lotus Noodle Bar: This Japanese-French styled hideaway is a foodie's paradise. Intimate dining. Reservations required. 5-9pm Tue-Thu, to 10pm Fri & Sat $$

Chez L'Amour: Dimly lit restaurant/bar with live jazz, speakeasy charm, mouthwatering tapas-style cuisine and delectable desserts. hours vary $$$

ST AUGUSTINE

⭐ HIGHLIGHTS
1. Castillo de San Marcos National Monument
2. St Augustine Eco Tours

● SIGHTS
3. Bridge of Lions
4. Cathedral Basilica of St Augustine
5. Colonial Quarter
6. Fountain of Youth
7. Mission Nombre de Dios
8. Oldest Wooden School House
9. Plaza de la Constitución
10. St George St

● ACTIVITIES
11. Old Town Trolley Tours
12. Red Train Tours
13. St Augustine Distillery

● SLEEPING
14. St George Inn
15. Villa 1565

● EATING
16. Ben's Soft Pretzels
17. Chez L'Amour
18. Floridian
19. Kilwins
20. Lotus Noodle Bar
21. St Augustine Fish Camp

● DRINKING & NIGHTLIFE
22. Auggie's Draft Room
23. Dog Rose Brewing
24. Prohibition Kitchen
25. Rendezvous

Old Fort, Older Mission: Fountain of Youth?

MAP P488

Exploring 'The Ancient City's' rich history

Meander sacred grounds at **Mission Nombre de Dios** *(mission andshrine.org; free)*, once thought to be the original landing site of Ponce de Léon, the Spanish explorer who discovered 'La Florida.' Although that's been rebuked, there's no disputing the site's historical significance: it was here that Pedro Menéndez de Avilés founded St Augustine in 1565, 55 years before the Pilgrims arrived. The first parish mass was held upon their arrival, with a thanksgiving dinner attended by Indigenous Timucuans.

Nowadays, a **Great Cross**, erected to commemorate the mission's 400th anniversary, towers 208ft above trails, foot bridges and saltwater marshes. Perfect for peaceful reflection, the serene **Memorial Pathway** passes archaeological excavations, a bell tower, crumbling tombstones, rustic buildings, statues and cascading fountains.

Nearby, the dog-friendly **Fountain of Youth Archaeological Park** *(fountainofyouthflorida.com; adult/child $23/10)* attracts visitors curious about its mythical springs. Sadly, it's all historical folklore, but indulge in a free cup o'youth nevertheless. Navigate your way through free-roaming peacocks, exploring a recreated Native Timucua village, and catching reenactors firing cannons and muskets.

Plagued by pirate attacks, military onslaughts, disease, pillaging, raiding and burning, St Augustine has flown five flags during its existence. One British invasion in 1702 saw every building torched to the ground except the formidable **Castillo de San Marcos** *(nps.gov/casa; adult/child $15/free)*, known locally as 'the fort,' which once contained defensive moats.

Built between 1672 and 1695, the imposing fort is the only extant 17th-century military construction in the country. It's also one of two fortresses in the world to be built in coquina, a locally quarried porous rock composed of tiny seashells compressed into limestone and capable of withstanding cannon fire (the other fortress is nearby **Fort Matanzas**). While the fort has changed hands a few times, it's never fallen, even while housing upwards of 1500 people during the English siege.

Allow at least two hours to visit the mostly accessible grounds on a self-guided tour. Parking costs $2.50 per hour.

BOTTLENOSE DOLPHINS

Spotted year-round, those fins slicing through the surface of the Matanzas River likely aren't sharks but, rather, common bottlenose dolphins – popular residents of St Augustine's inshore waters. Highly social, these intelligent, naturally acrobatic and playful sea creatures can live into their fifties, reach 6-12ft and weigh up to 400lb. Living in groups known as pods, they emit clicking noises to navigate, source food and avoid predators. To see and 'hear' these fascinating ocean-dwellers within their natural habitat, join marine naturalists at **St Augustine ECO Tours** *(staugustine ecotours.com; prices vary)* on a scenic tour aboard vessels equipped with underwater microphones.

 DRINKING IN NORTHEAST FLORIDA: ST AUGUSTINE TAPROOMS — MAP P488

Dog Rose Brewing Co: Fun gathering spot with a huge selection of handcrafted ales. Live music too. *noon-10pm Sun-Thu, to midnight Fri & Sat*

Rendezvous: Globetrot your way around 350 international beers at the city's 'original beer pub.' Family-friendly. *hours vary*

Auggie's Draft Room: Sample and sip at your own pace with 24 self-serve taps to choose from. *11am-8pm Sun-Thu, to 11pm Fri & Sat*

St Augustine Distillery: If you're a fan of premium bourbons, gins, vodkas and wines, you'll love this tour with generous samplings. *10am-6pm*

Tampa Bay & Southwest

WATERFRONT PATHWAYS | GULF HISTORY | GLOBAL MUSEUMS

GETTING AROUND

The TECO Streetcar has downtown routes, including to Ybor City, it's free and runs daily. Rent electric scooters or e-bikes through the Lime and Spin apps downtown. The Hillsborough Area Regional Transit Authority (HART) has bus routes throughout downtown and surrounds, including to Tampa International Airport. Downtown's Marion Transit Center is a hub for services to the zoo, Busch Gardens and the Henry B Plant Museum.

Few places in Florida fuse historic grit, artistic verve and breezy beach life quite like the Tampa Bay region. Tampa, with its brick-paved Ybor City and cigar-chomping past, pulses with a blend of Latin flavor and modern swagger. Its Riverwalk winds past concert halls, museums and sleek towers, while old neighborhoods like Seminole Heights trade in mid-century bungalows and craft beer. Across the bay, St Petersburg feels sun-splashed and soul-fed – a city where glass art, indie cafes and massive Salvador Dalí paintings live steps from marinas and banyan trees. Then there's St Pete Beach, a stretch of pure, powdery bliss where vintage motels and tiki bars keep things delightfully unpolished. This is where Florida loosens its collar a bit, ditches pretense and shows off its depth. It's a region shaped by salt air, immigrant legacies and rebellious creativity. It's where the Gulf isn't just scenery, it's a region's lifeblood.

River Views & Parks Aplenty
MAP P491

All along the Tampa Riverwalk

Stretching along the Hillsborough River, Tampa's best-loved green space takes you past palm-fringed parks and shimmering skyscrapers, always within view of the waterway where dolphins and manatees can be seen frolicking in the shadow of high-rises. For the full experience, you can join the runners, cyclists and skateboarders who traverse the full 2.5 miles, starting in either **Water Works Park** *(tampa.gov; free)* in

DRINKING IN TAMPA & SOUTHWEST: YBOR CITY
MAP P491

Gaspar's Grotto: Pirate-themed bar in the heart of the historic district with live entertainment and outdoor dining. *7am-2am Mon-Sat, from 11am Sun*

Ybor City Tap House: Live music and TVs tuned to whatever game is on draw sports fans, with 65 craft brews on tap. *hours vary*

Dirty Shame: Classic dive bar with darts, billiards and a loyal local crowd. A huge range of beers on tap, plus bottles and cans. *hours vary*

Castle: Ybor City's most famous nightclub has multiple floors and DJs, and crowds from goth to fetish and everything in between. *10:30pm-3am, Fri & Sat*

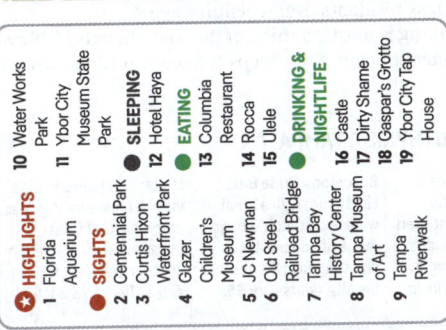

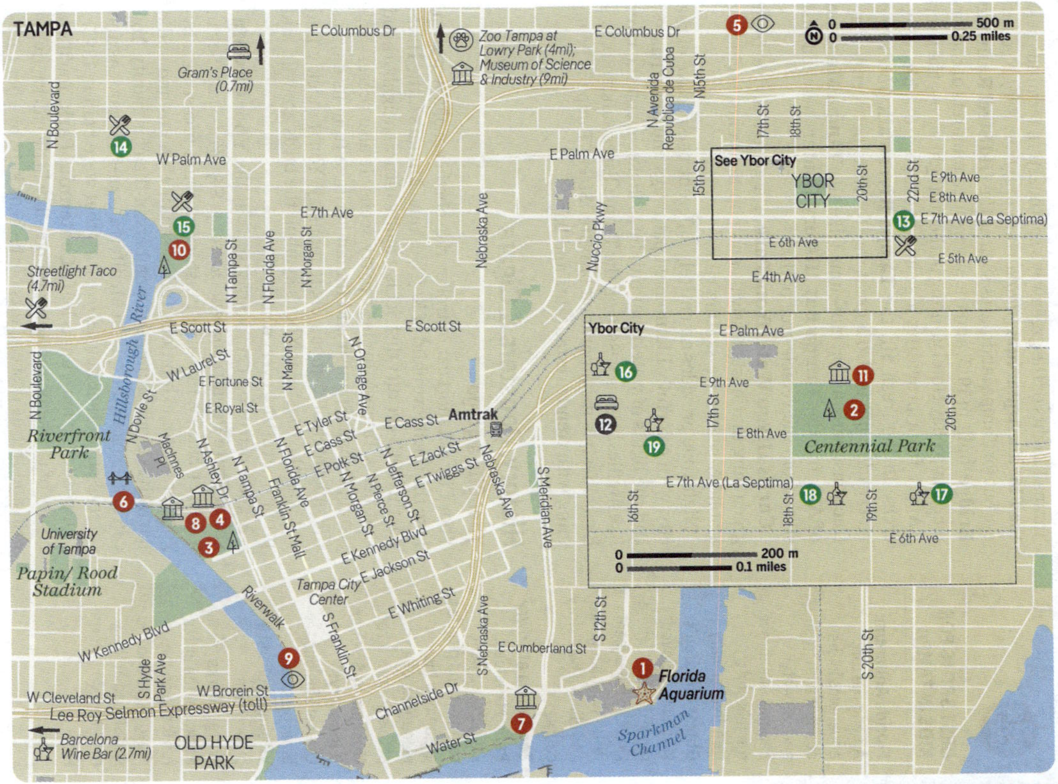

HIGHLIGHTS
1. Florida Aquarium

SIGHTS
2. Centennial Park
3. Curtis Hixon Waterfront Park
4. Glazer Children's Museum
5. JC Newman
6. Old Steel Railroad Bridge
7. Tampa Bay History Center
8. Tampa Museum of Art
9. Tampa Riverwalk
10. Water Works Park
11. Ybor City Museum State Park

SLEEPING
12. Hotel Haya

EATING
13. Columbia Restaurant
14. Rocca
15. Ulele

DRINKING & NIGHTLIFE
16. Castle
17. Dirty Shame
18. Gaspar's Grotto
19. Ybor City Tap House

Tampa Heights or the greenway's southeastern terminus near the **Florida Aquarium** (*flaquarium.org; from $30*). Keep an eye out for Tampa landmarks such as the **Old Steel Railroad Bridge**, built in 1915, and the silver-hued minarets of the former Tampa Bay Hotel glinting in the sunlight across the river.

Apart from providing a scenic backdrop to a bit of exercise in the fresh air, the **Tampa Riverwalk** (*thetamparriverwalk.com*) is also a great way to travel between key attractions, with major museums (like the **Tampa Museum of Art** and the **Tampa Bay History Center**) perched just steps from the vehicle-free path.

Curtis Hixon Waterfront Park is a gorgeous riverfront green lung that hosts festivals and pop-up events, including a holiday-season ice-skating rink.

Nighttime provides an entirely different perspective of the city, with colorfully illuminated pathways and underpasses, and the lights of waterfront buildings flickering on the river like fireflies. Also accessed off the Tampa Riverwalk, the city's lively lifestyle neighborhood of Water Street Tampa is brimming with trendy restaurants and bars.

History, Roosters & Cigars

MAP P491

Ybor City a go-go

Ybor City is a short car or trolley ride northeast of downtown. Like the illicit love child of Key West and Miami's Little Havana, this 19th-century district is a multicultural neighborhood that hosts Tampa's liveliest party scene. It also preserves a strong Cuban, Spanish and Italian heritage from its days as the epicenter of Tampa's cigar industry. You'll quickly find out why the rooster is Ybor's symbol: the birds are wild and proudly strutting everywhere.

A good place to begin your visit is at the **Ybor City Museum State Park** (*ybormuseum.org; $4; Wed-Sun*). Set in a former bakery, this small history museum preserves a bygone era, with exhibitions full of striking photos and audio narratives from prominent members of the community. You can also explore the quaint Mediterranean-style gardens and three cigar-worker houses (*casitas*) that were built in 1895.

Opposite the museum is leafy **Centennial Park**. You'll see plenty of chickens, roosters and possibly little chicks, living wild and free as descendants of the hens kept by Ybor City's working-class residents over a century ago.

Cigar making is mostly a thing of the past, though **JC Newman** (*jcnewman.com; free*) keeps the old traditions alive at

BEST SPOTS FOR KIDS IN TAMPA

Florida Aquarium: Among the top aquariums in the country, with fresh and saltwater habitats, mangrove tunnels and a free-flying aviary.

Glazer Children's Museum: Beloved rainy-day spot where kids can build giant forts, steer a tugboat and climb a two-story course.

Zoo Tampa at Lowry Park: Manatees, kangaroos, giant tortoises and giraffes are among the menagerie of animals at this nonprofit zoo.

Museum of Science & Industry: Optical illusions, brain puzzles, a VR simulator and a planetarium.

Water Works Park: Let the littles run loose on the playground and splash pad at this riverfront downtown park.

EATING IN TAMPA BAY & SOUTHWEST: TAMPA

MAP P491

Streetlight Taco: Passionfruit margaritas and fabulous carnitas and brisket tacos in South Tampa. *11:30am-9pm Sun-Thu, to 10pm Fri & Sat* **$**

Rocca: Known for its tableside mozzarella cart, this Michelin-starred Italian in Tampa Heights is perfect for date night. *5-9pm Tue-Thu & Sun, to 10pm Fri & Sat* **$$$**

Barcelona Wine Bar: Lively spot with a great weekend brunch, a huge range of Spanish tapas and sangria in the south of the city. *hours vary* **$$**

Ulele: This native Florida-inspired restaurant serves gator tail, Gulf Coast oysters and locally caught grouper. *11am-10pm Sun-Thu, to 11pm Fri & Sat* **$$**

St Pete Pier

TOP TIP

Visitors are often surprised to learn that Tampa itself is not on the beach. Clearwater Beach, one of the closest Gulf of Mexico beaches to Tampa, lies roughly 25 miles due west, with more options to the north and south.

SPARRING OVER A SANDWICH

Miami and Tampa both claim to have invented the American version of the Cuban sandwich – and the 'right' way to make the meaty wonder. If you've sunk your teeth into one in each city, you might have noticed the differences. Tampa lore credits the sandwich's origins to Ybor City, where it was made to feed Cuban cigar factory workers. And Tampa's version uses crispier bread on the outside while still fluffy inside and also adds Genoa salami to the usual mix of roasted pork, ham, Swiss cheese, dill pickles and mustard (the salami is said to be a nod to Ybor City's Italian immigrants).

its recently restored El Reloj building. You can peruse the museum or book a guided factory tour *(adult/child $15/12)* and see the art of hand-rolling cigars in action.

End your day with a meal at **Columbia Restaurant** *(columbiarestaurant.com)*, a striking Spanish-Cuban restaurant that's been going strong since 1905. The Cuban sandwich is legendary.

Stroll, Eat & Splash

MAP P494

Chill out on St Pete Pier

Before it reopened during the summer of 2020 after being completely renovated, the **St Pete Pier** *(stpetepier.org)* was a beloved but eyesore-inducing landmark on downtown's horizon. The new version of the pier, however, is nothing short of spectacular – all Scandinavian-inspired clean and contemporary lines interjected with beautiful public spaces that include a splash pad, marine-themed playground, **Tampa Bay Watch Discovery Center** *(tbwdiscoverycenter.org; adult/child $8/3)* with interactive conservation exhibits, and a sandy beach with plenty of spots for lounging on Tampa Bay.

You can easily while away a half-day or longer here, pausing for lunch or at least a tiki-themed cocktail with views of the city at **Pier Teaki** *(teakstpete.com/pier-teaki)* rooftop restaurant, or tossing out a fishing line from a dedicated platform on the pier. It's free to stroll the pier, which sprawls across a 26-acre district that hosts things like pop-up pickleball clinics and roller-skating rinks throughout the year.

 EATING IN SOUTHWEST: ST PETERSBURG ──── MAP P494

Hangar: Casual spot for burgers and wings with direct views over the bayfront runway of Albert Whitted Airport. *8am-9pm* $

Juno & the Peacock: Sceney corner spot near the Vinoy resort with an incredible raw bar and cocktails. *11am-10pm Mon-Fri, from 10am Sat & Sun* $$$

El Cap: St Pete's most iconic spot for a burger or hot dog has been grilling them up since 1964. *11am-9pm Sun-Thu, to 10pm Fri & Sat* $

Mullet's Fish Camp: Choose from 15 types of fish served with house-made sauces at this South St Pete go-to. *hours vary* $$

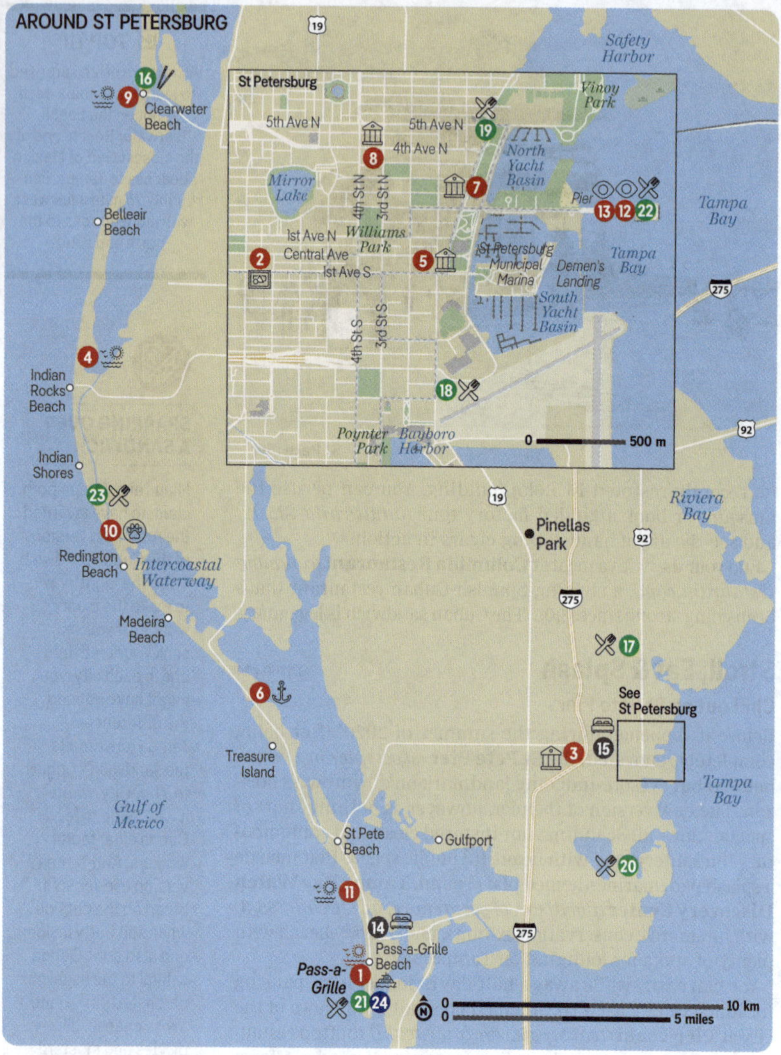

AROUND ST PETERSBURG

★ HIGHLIGHTS
1. Pass-a-Grille

● SIGHTS
2. Chihuly Collection
3. Imagine Museum
4. Indian Rocks Beach Nature Preserve
5. James Museum of Western & Wildlife Art
6. John's Pass Village
7. Museum of Fine Arts
8. Museum of the American Arts & Crafts Movement
9. Pier 60
10. Seaside Seabird Sanctuary
11. St Pete Beach
12. St Pete Pier
13. Tampa Bay Watch Discovery Center

● SLEEPING
14. Don CeSar
15. Moxy St Petersburg Downtown

● EATING
16. Carreta on the Gulf
17. El Cap
see 16 Frenchy's Original Cafe
18. Hangar
19. Juno & the Peacock
20. Mullet's Fish Camp
21. Paradise Grille
22. Pier Teaki
23. Salt Rock Grill

● TRANSPORT
24. Shell Key Shuttle

The Downtown Looper and Central Avenue Trolley make stops along the pier's length, in case you just want to view it as a drive-by.

White-Sand Beach Bliss

MAP P494

Clear waters and...Clearwater Beach, too

The closest Gulf of Mexico beachfront to the city is **St Pete Beach**, a mere 15-minute drive (on a good day) from bustling Central Ave in St Petersburg. The shoreline's key landmark is the towering Moorish Mediterranean **Don CeSar** hotel, a historic confection built in 1928 that's known to locals as the 'pink palace.'

The extra-wide beach itself ranks high for its natural beauty, and draws plenty of sunseekers who come for lounging by the waterside, long walks by the crashing waves and fiery sunsets. Proximity to the city has made this the most developed of the barrier-island beaches, with resorts, motels and restaurants just a few steps from the dune-backed sands.

Heading south from St Pete Beach, **Pass-a-Grille** anchors the southern end of Long Key. Here you'll find the most idyllic barrier-island beach, a narrow stretch of sand backed only by beach houses and metered public parking. You can watch boats coming through Pass-a-Grille Channel, hop aboard the **Shell Key Shuttle** *(shellkeyshuttle.com; round trip adult/child $30/15)*, which departs at 10am, noon and 2pm (2pm departure weekdays only) to unspoiled Shell Key, and retire for food and ice cream in the laid-back village center (essentially 8th Ave).

Slender barrier islands continue north of St Pete, harboring a handful of communities, from the tourist traps of **John's Pass Village** to the quieter, family-oriented Indian Rocks Beach. This is where you'll find the **Indian Rocks Beach Nature Preserve** *(indian-rocks-beach.com)*, which has a short boardwalk trail winding through mangroves out to a viewpoint of Boca Ciega Bay.

About a 15-minute drive north from there brings you to **Clearwater Beach**. It's hugely popular with tourists, particularly around **Pier 60** *(sunsetsatpier60.com)*, and hosts a nightly sunset celebration complete with buskers, and arts and crafts for sale.

Apart from beaches, the barrier-island chain is home to the largest wild-bird hospital in North America, the **Seaside Seabird Sanctuary** *(seasideseabirdsanctuary.org; free)*, which is home to over 100 sea and land birds for public viewing. You'll see a resident population of injured pelicans, owls, gulls, parrots and birds of prey, including a bald eagle. Several thousand birds are treated and released back to the wild annually. For a fine view over the beach, climb up the observation tower nestled in the back of the property.

BEST MUSEUMS & GALLERIES IN ST PETERSBURG

Museum of the American Arts & Crafts Movement: A local philanthropist founded the world's only museum that is dedicated to this historic movement.

James Museum of Western & Wildlife Art: Works by primarily living artists evoke the spirit of the West. The museum's façade is designed to resemble a sandstone mesa.

Museum of Fine Arts: Art representing ancient civilizations and modern masters makes up a world-class collection.

Chihuly Collection: Permanent collection of 18 installations by celebrated glass artist Dale Chihuly.

Imagine Museum: One-of-a-kind glass-art museum featuring works by American and international artists.

 EATING IN SOUTHWEST: ST PETE BEACH

MAP P494

Paradise Grille: Casual walk-up spot on Pass-a-Grille Beach with tasty seafood, cold drinks and picnic tables overlooking the sand. *7am-8:30pm* **$**

Salt Rock Grill: Classy Indian Shores dinnertime spot renowned for local seafood and steaks. *4-10pm Mon-Fri, from noon Sat & Sun* **$$$**

Frenchy's Original Cafe: Famous grouper-sandwich spot at Clearwater Beach and other locations. *11am-10pm* **$$**

Carreta on the Gulf: Sandpearl Resort's signature restaurant serves divine sushi and seafood. *7am-midnight Sun-Thu, to 1am Fri & Sat* **$$$**

Places We Love to Stay

$ Budget $$ Midrange $$$ Top End

Miami
MAPS P441, P444, P446, P449

Freehand Miami $ Dorms and private rooms, two craft cocktail bars and an outdoor pool, about a mile north of the South Beach nightlife.

Kimpton Surfcomber $$ With a recently renovated pool, happening beach bar and poolside cabanas in Miami Beach.

Dunns Josephine $$ In historic Overtown, themed rooms celebrate the lives of notable Black figures like Ella Fitzgerald and Langston Hughes.

Arlo $$ With gorgeous murals inside and out, this high-rise hotel in Wynwood has beautiful common spaces that draw the neighborhood in.

Faena Hotel Miami Beach (p435) **$$$** Scenic, super-luxurious beachfront and art-centric hotel with restaurants, nightlife and entertainment on-site.

Mr C $$$ Rooms with European glamour wow at this Coconut Grove property. Its rooftop pool gazes out on Biscayne Bay.

Everglades & Biscayne National Park
MAP P453

Flamingo Campground (p454) **$** Drive-in campground in Everglades National Park with heated showers, grills, and access to fishing and hiking.

Elliott Key Campground $ A hiking trail and fishing on the island in Biscayne National Park. Restrooms and cold showers available. Access by boat only.

Boca Chita Key Campground $ Waterfront views, picnic tables, grills and toilets on-site in Biscayne. Access by boat only.

Flamingo Lodge $$ Comfortable accommodations deep in the Everglades. Waterfront rooms, dining on-site, rentals, glamping tents, and tours available.

Florida Keys & Key West
MAP P459

John Pennekamp Coral Reef State Park $ The park has campsites that can accommodate both tents and RVs. Restrooms, hot showers and coin laundry on-site.

Seashell Motel & Key West Hostel $ Basic dorm-style housing conveniently located near Old Town Key West.

NYAH Key West $$ Adult-only, elevated, dorm-esque lodging, plus a continental breakfast. Private rooms available.

Playa Largo $$$ This Key Largo oceanfront resort is the classic combination of luxury and seclusion.

Isla Bella $$$ Comfortable oasis where every room overlooks the water in Marathon. Relax with waterfront amenities or dabble in water sports at the marina.

Havana Cabana $$$ Adults-only hotel with vibrant influences of the art and culture of Cuba, plus Key West's largest pool.

Southeast Florida
MAPS P465, P470

Snooze Hotel $ Fort Lauderdale beachfront accommodation complete with a rooftop deck and complimentary beach gear.

Grand Resort & Spa $$ An LGBTQ+-friendly resort, just steps from Fort Lauderdale Beach.

Historic Driftwood Resort $$ A fun, unique and nostalgic beachfront hotel in Vero, built in the 1920s using locally sourced driftwood.

Conrad Fort Lauderdale Beach $$$ Every room in this luxe, all-suite beachfront resort comes with an Italian marble bathroom, deep-soaking tub, and private balcony or terrace.

The Ben $$$ This luxury boutique hotel in West Palm Beach is part of the Marriott Autograph Collection. A block from Clematis St, many balconies overlook Palm Harbor Marina and the Intracoastal Waterway.

Hilton West Palm Beach $$$ This luxury property exudes style and grace: modern suites, resort-style pool, superb restaurants, full-service spa and complimentary valet parking.

Orlando & Walt Disney World®
MAP P473

Rosen Inn at Pointe Orlando $ A basic, affordable accommodation right in the middle of the action of I-Drive.

Hilton Garden Inn Lake Buena Vista $ An affordable resort, a 1-mile walk from Disney Springs® and the rest of the Walt Disney World® action.

Alfond Inn $$ Charming shops and restaurants

Faena Hotel Miami Beach (p443)

surround this artsy Winter Park boutique hotel.

Universal's Cabana Bay Beach Resort $$ An affordable Universal Orlando Resort hotel with retro-style single rooms and family suites.

Grand Bohemian Hotel $$$ In the heart of downtown Orlando, this AAA Four Diamond Resort combines luxury and a great location.

Disney's Polynesian Village Resort $$$ A volcano-inspired pool and lush grounds at this village resort transport guests to Fiji. Two monorail stops from the Magic Kingdom.

Villatel Orlando Resort $$$ Less hotel, more playful neighborhood, centrally located on I-Drive. Boredom never hits with amenities like water slides, pickleball courts, golf simulators and basketball.

Space Coast MAP P480

Jetty Park Campground $ Tent and full-service RV campsites at Port Canaveral with shuffleboard, playground and pier. Watch cruise ships passing by.

Hyatt Place Titusville/ Kennedy Space Center $$ Three-star hotel with a free daily breakfast buffet and outdoor pool.

Beachside Hotel & Suites $$ Retro surf vibes, balconies with ocean views in Cocoa Beach, and a water park with deck-side bar – oodles of family fun! On-site laundry; breakfast included.

Courtyard Titusville Kennedy Space Center $$$ Riverfront hotel with an outdoor pool and rooftop deck with launchpad views.

Northeast Florida MAPS P485, P488

Villa 1565 $ Classic Spanish architecture meets modern hospitality. Clean rooms surround a courtyard, home to a 650-year-old oak tree that pre-dates St Augustine.

Marriott Jacksonville Downtown $$ A four-star Water St hotel that's upscale and has a bar, bistro, pool and fitness area.

St George Inn $$ Centrally located, bodacious boutique inn offering apartment-style kitchenette suites with balconies overlooking St George St and the fort.

One Ocean Resort & Spa $$$ Atlantic Beach resort with oceanfront spa, swimming pool, pool bar and restaurant.

Tampa Bay & Southwest MAPS P491, P494

Gram's Place $ This small, welcoming hostel in Seminole Heights is for travelers who prefer personality over perfect linens.

Moxy St Petersburg Downtown $$ Right on Central Ave with a lively rooftop restaurant and bar, plus a podcast studio guests can use on the ground floor.

Hotel Haya $$$ Boutique hotel in Ybor City, offering art-filled rooms, a pool, and a great restaurant and cafe.

Don CeSar (p495) $$$ Iconic 'pink palace' resort on St Pete Beach with a Gulf-front pool and bar.

THE GUIDE

GREAT LAKES

For places to stay in Great Lakes, see p586

Above: Pictured Rocks National Lakeshore (p558); Right: Chicago (p504)

THE MAIN AREAS

CHICAGO
Art, architecture and chowhounds' playground.
p504

ILLINOIS
Land of Lincoln, Wright and Route 66.
p517

INDIANA
Race cars and towering sands.
p524

OHIO
From big cities to Amish villages.
p533

*Researched and curated by
Karla Zimmerman and Ann Babe*

Great Lakes

OVERLOOKED BEAUTY IN THE USA'S HEARTLAND

Unspoiled, uncrowded national parks mix it up with cool cultured cities and pie-baking small towns.

Here we are: the middle of the country. No mountains. No oceans. Flyover territory, right?

Don't be fooled by all the corn. Behind it lurks surfing beaches and Tibetan temples, car-free islands and the green-draped night lights of the aurora borealis. The Great Lakes takes its knocks for being middle-of-nowhere boring, so consider the moose-filled wilderness areas and Hemingway, Dylan and Vonnegut sites to be its little secret.

Roll call for the region's cities starts with Chicago, which unfurls what is arguably the country's mightiest skyline. Milwaukee keeps the beer-and-Harley flame burning, while Minneapolis shines a hip beacon out over the fields. And Detroit rocks, plain and simple.

The Great Lakes themselves are huge, like inland seas, with beaches, dunes, resort towns and lighthouse-dotted scenery. Dairy farms and fruit orchards blanket the region, meaning fresh pie and ice cream aplenty. And when the scenery does flatten out? There's always a goofball roadside attraction, such as the Spam Museum or the world's biggest ball of twine, to revive imaginations.

Most visitors come in summer when the weather is fine for hiking, biking, canoeing and kayaking in the local lakes and forests. Snowmobiling and cross-country skiing take over in the butt-freezing winter (as do eating and drinking in warm taverns). Whatever the season, a true slice of America awaits in the heartland.

MICHIGAN
Beaches, vineyards and forested islands.
p544

WISCONSIN
Pretty landscapes and lots of cheese.
p560

MINNESOTA
Lakes and wilderness aplenty.
p572

THE GUIDE

GREAT LAKES

Minnesota, p572
Hiking, paddling and other outdoor adventures abound, from the moose-teeming northern wilderness to urban areas like Minneapolis and Duluth.

Wisconsin, p560
Beyond the beery cities lies a vast expanse of shimmering islands, lakefront beaches, forested trails and good-time bashes to help celebrate it all.

Illinois, p517
An ancient city, moss-draped swamp and architecture hotbed emerge from the farmland, along with presidential sites and Route 66 corn dogs and kitsch.

CAR
You'll need your own wheels to travel with ease. There's no other way to get to smaller towns and far-flung parks. Even between major cities, trains and buses are scant. And within cities (except Chicago) public transportation is patchy.

TRAIN
Amtrak trains run in the region, but with fairly limited service. Chicago is the hub. Trains go to Milwaukee (seven daily), Minneapolis (two daily), Detroit (three daily), Cleveland (one daily) and Indianapolis (three per week).

FERRY
Two car ferries can save time when driving around Lake Michigan. The *Lake Express* goes between Milwaukee, WI, and Muskegon, MI, in 2½ hours. The SS *Badger* goes between Manitowoc, WI, and Ludington, MI, in four hours.

Find Your Way

The region is vast, around 1000 miles across from east to west. We've picked the places that capture the Great Lakes' down-to-earth culture and quietly sublime landscapes and presented them here state by state.

Michigan, p544

With four of the five Great Lakes kissing its shores, Michigan has beaches and sand dunes galore, plus the history-rich city of Detroit.

Chicago, p504

The heart of the Great Lakes beats in this cloud-scraping metropolis, a cultural stew of art, nightlife and star restaurants with laid-back style.

Ohio, p533

Vibrant cities mix it up with horse-and-buggy Amish communities, moonshine-making hill towns, party islands and a mist-threaded national park.

Indiana, p524

A trek over sand dunes and a hike through the 'Little Smoky Mountains' are among the unexpected pleasures in this state known for car culture.

Plan Your Time

Factor long distances into your planning. For instance, driving from Cleveland to Minneapolis (east to west across the region) is an 11-hour journey on the Interstate. Rural highways add even more to travel times.

Garden of the Gods (p515)

Great Lakes Weekend

You can swoop in for a few days and explore one of the cool Great Lakes cities. Chicago is the obvious choice to walk around (and ride the clackety L trains) and take in the **art** (p505), **architecture** (p507), **blues clubs** (p511) and very large **pizza** (p504). Tack on trips to **Wrigley Field** (p511) and an **improv comedy club** (p511), too. Detroit is another great candidate, where you can check out the **public art** (p545), art-deco **architecture** (p548), jazz and **Motown sounds** (p547) and **car-making history** (p549) with a foray to nearby Dearborn. Minneapolis also gives a solid feel for the region. Spend a couple of days enjoying its **rock clubs** (p577), **art museums** (p573) and **lake fun** (p577), along with jaunts to historic Twin City, **St Paul** (p578) and **Prince's pad** (p578) in the suburbs.

Seasonal Highlights

Whenever you visit, the Great Lakes region is having a party somewhere. Music festivals, food fairs, cultural bashes and snow carnivals fill the calendar.

JANUARY

It's cold and snowy, but that doesn't stop locals from donning parkas and heading out to snowmobile, cross-country ski, curl and party at outdoor events, such as the **St Paul Winter Carnival** (p577).

MARCH

St Patrick's Day celebrations make merry in Cleveland, Detroit, Milwaukee and especially Chicago (p504), which famously dyes its river green. Bundle up, because it's usually still cold outside for these shenanigans.

MAY

As the weather warms, wildflowers start to bloom. Indiana Dunes bursts with lupines, mayapples and many more, while Holland explodes in color at its **Tulip Time** (p554) festival.

Four Days to Travel Around

With four days, you can add some outdoor action. Chicago is close to beachy, bird-filled **Indiana Dunes National Park** (p529) and to the **Lake Michigan Shore Wine Trail** (p555) vineyards in southwestern Michigan. Detroit is within range of the soaring sands and blue waters at **Sleeping Bear Dunes National Lakeshore** (p553). Minneapolis is not too far from the wolf-howling wilderness of the **Boundary Waters** (p583) and to the waterfall-laden parks along **Hwy 61** (p581). Cleveland is a stone's throw from time-warped communities in Ohio's **Amish Country** (p541), where horse-drawn buggies rule the roads, and from the misty woods of **Cuyahoga Valley National Park** (p536).

A Weeklong Stay

A week lets you dig deeper into the area. You can combine a couple of cities and their surrounding sights, or strike out for further-flung regions. Michigan's Upper Peninsula takes you into the sparsely populated northern forest where mountain bikers hang out in **Marquette** (p559), and kayakers paddle at **Pictured Rocks National Lakeshore** (p558). A trip in the south along the Ohio River can include **Cincinnati's Brewing Heritage Trail** (p537), southern Indiana's caves and **scenic river towns** (p531) and southern Illinois' rugged **Shawnee Hills** (p523). To really get away from it all, remote **Voyageurs National Park** (p584) and **Isle Royale National Park** (p557) are among the least-visited wilderness areas in the country, where stars, moose, peace and quiet thrive.

JUNE
By mid-month the region is in full swing. It's finally warm, beer gardens hop, beaches splash, and parties such **Summerfest** (p563) rock most weekends.

JULY
The Great Lakes slowly get warm enough to swim in without teeth chattering. Blueberries and peaches are ready to pick, while the **National Cherry Festival** (p554) celebrates Michigan's favorite fruit.

SEPTEMBER
Peak season winds down in the region. But the coolness in the air also means Oktoberfest celebrations are on tap in cities like Columbus and Milwaukee. Cincinnati's **Oktoberfest** (p538) is the nation's biggest.

OCTOBER
Road trips to see fall colors are a big to-do. Hot spots include Door County, Hwy 61, Brown County and the Shawnee Hills. Bountiful harvests mean fresh apples, pumpkins and corn at markets.

Chicago

VISIONARY ARCHITECTURE | LAKEFRONT ALLURE | MUSIC SCENE

GETTING AROUND

The L (a system of elevated and subway trains) is the best way to travel around Chicago. Its eight color-coded lines are easy to use and get you to most sights and neighborhoods. An unlimited-ride day pass costs $5. Buy it at any L station or via the Ventra app *(ventrachicago.com)*, which also is useful for showing train times. Driving can be tough due to heavy traffic and scarce (and expensive) parking.

☑ TOP TIP

Advance bookings are wise, especially during weekends. Most restaurants take reservations via their websites using Tock, OpenTable or Resy. For museums, buying tickets online in advance can often provide cost savings over same-day purchases.

Chicago is the star of the Great Lakes, a big, teeming, tall-skyscraper buzz of energy. While it is the USA's third-largest city, home to 2.7 million people, its low-key cultured awesomeness tends to fly under the radar. It doesn't brag about its star art collections or reasonably priced food scene that rivals the coasts in Michelin stars. It doesn't gloat over its trendsetting architecture and blow-the-roof-off bands on stages nightly. Its sand-and-surf beaches pop up with typical Midwestern modesty. Which is why so many visitors find the city a surprise – an urbane, multicultural metropolis for all.

The top sights are downtown, around the area known as the Loop. But you'll want to head out into further-flung neighborhoods for the best eating and drinking. Great districts to scope include Wicker Park, Pilsen, Logan Square and Andersonville – all jam-packed with inventive storefront restaurants – and the West Loop, where the buzziest dining venues huddle.

Get a Hefty Slice

MAP P510

Try deep-dish pizza

Chicago's foremost food is deep-dish pizza, a hulking mass of crust that rises two inches above the plate and cradles a molten pile of toppings. Try it at **Lou Malnati's** *(loumalnatis. com)*, which lays claim to inventing the cheesy behemoth. **Giordano's** *(giordanos.com)* makes 'stuffed' pizza: a bigger, doughier version of deep dish. A third version is pan pizza, similar to deep dish, but the crust is baked differently and has a ring of crisp, caramelized cheese. **Pequod's Pizza** *(pequodspizza.com)* makes a mighty one.

One piece is practically a meal wherever you go. Expect to wait 40 minutes or so for the hefty pies to cook.

🟠 HIGHLIGHTS	7 Crown Fountain
1 Art Institute of Chicago	8 Grant Park
2 Millennium Park	9 Lurie Garden
🟠 SIGHTS	10 Maggie Daley Park
3 American Writers Museum	11 Museum of Contemporary Photography
4 Chicago Architecture Center	12 Museum of Illusions
5 Chicago Cultural Center	13 Nichols Bridgeway
6 Cloud Gate	14 Pritzker Pavilion
	15 Riverwalk
16 Rookery	21 HI-Chicago
17 St Regis Chicago	**🟢 EATING**
18 Willis Tower	22 Native Foods
🔴 ACTIVITIES	**🟢 DRINKING & NIGHTLIFE**
19 Chicago Architecture Center First Lady River Cruise	23 Cindy's
⚫ SLEEPING	**🔴 ENTERTAINMENT**
20 Hampton Inn Chicago Downtown/N Loop	24 Buddy Guy's Legends
	25 Chicago Theatre
	26 Goodman Theatre

Explore the Art Institute's Masterpieces MAP P505

Impressionist paintings star

Allocate at least a few hours to wander through the **Art Institute of Chicago** (artic.edu; adult/child $32/free), the USA's second-largest art museum. The main action happens on the 2nd floor. Stand in awe like Ferris Bueller in front of Georges Seurat's *A Sunday Afternoon on the Island of La Grande Jatte* (Gallery 240). In the adjoining rooms see color-swirled

BEST FAR-FLUNG & OVERLOOKED MUSEUMS

Griffin Museum of Science & Industry: Check out the submarine, coal mine and other mind-blowers at the Western Hemisphere's largest science museum.

Museum of Contemporary Art: The Art Institute's brash, rebellious challenger has a collection that always pushes boundaries.

Museum of Illusions: See your head on a platter and walk on walls at this kid-friendly, date-night favorite.

American Writers Museum: Bibliophiles will have a grand time at the word waterfall, typewriters, book lounge and other hands-on exhibits.

Insect Asylum: Wonderfully offbeat collection of vintage taxidermy and insect aquariums, plus yoga classes surrounded by snakes.

canvases by Monet, Renoir and Van Gogh. It takes a while to get through the impressionist and postimpressionist paintings – there are more here than anywhere outside of France. Nearby, Edward Hopper's lonely, neon-lit diner in *Nighthawks* (Gallery 262) and Grant Wood's stern-faced couple in *American Gothic* (Gallery 263) hang in side-by-side galleries.

To take a break from crowds, stroll downstairs to the Thorne Miniature Rooms (Lower Level, Gallery 11) to peer into 68 teeny-tiny, dollhouse-like interiors.

Then head to the light-drenched Modern Wing and up to the 3rd floor to gape at the blue, elongated figure of Pablo Picasso's *The Old Guitarist* (Gallery 391). From here the pedestrian-only **Nichols Bridgeway** arches over into Millennium Park, a fine add-on experience before or after your Art Institute jaunt.

Art by Day, Music by Night

MAP P505

Play in Millennium Park

Located downtown next to the Art Institute, **Millennium Park** *(millenniumpark.org; admission free)* has abundant free and arty sights. The mega draw is **Cloud Gate** – aka the Bean – Anish Kapoor's 110-ton, mirror-smooth sculpture. Go ahead: walk right up to it, feel it, ponder the skyline

EATING IN CHICAGO: LEGENDARY BITES

MAPS P508, P510

Mr Beef: No-frills spot that cooks the spicy, drippy Italian beef sandwich made famous in the TV show *The Bear*. *10am-4pm Mon-Sat* $

Al's #1 Italian Beef: Another longstanding Italian beef purveyor, where queues can be shorter than Mr Beef. *10:30am-midnight Mon-Sat, to 8pm Sun* $

Wieners Circle: Chicago-style hot dogs (with onions, tomatoes, pickle, relish) in a raucous late-night ambience. *11am-2am Sun-Thu, to 4am Fri & Sat* $

Billy Goat Tavern: Mythic subterranean joint for 'cheezborgers,' immortalized in a *Saturday Night Live* skit. *hours vary* $

Lurie Garden

MORE GREAT PARKS

Lincoln Park: Join locals on the running paths, athletic fields and beaches in Chicago's largest green space.

Grant Park: Grassy downtown sprawl dotted by spectacular Buckingham Fountain, which performs an hourly water show.

Northerly Island: Stroll or cycle around this prairie-like refuge, with great skyline views, floating alongside the Museum Campus.

Alfred Caldwell Lily Pool: Enchanting oasis of water lilies and dragonflies that feels like you've stumbled into Monet's Giverny garden.

Montrose Point Bird Sanctuary: Beachside woods known as the Magic Hedge for the 300 bird species that fly through here.

reflection and snap a picture. Then mosey onward to Jaume Plensa's **Crown Fountain**. Its two glass-block towers have video images of Chicagoans spouting water, gargoyle-style. On hot days, it's like a water park when everyone jumps in to cool down. Kids, especially, love it.

For a peaceful patch away from the crowd, seek out the **Lurie Garden**, abloom with prairie flowers. A little river runs through it, where folks kick off their shoes and dangle their feet.

Stay until evening and you might see a Nigerian juju band or a dream pop trio at **Pritzker Pavilion**, the swooping silver band shell designed by architect Frank Gehry. Free concerts take place most nights in summer. For all shows, but especially those by the Grant Park Orchestra, folks bring blankets, food, wine and beer. It's a summer ritual, as the sun dips, corks pop and gorgeous music fills the twilight air. Allow extra time to get in for evening events, as all visitors must go through a security/bag check.

Soak up Chicago's Architecture

MAP P505

Hop on a boat tour, then roam the Riverwalk

Follow the crowds to the docks beneath Michigan Ave, at the north end of the Loop, and climb aboard the **Chicago Architecture Center's First Lady** *(architecture.org; from $56)*. Yes, it's touristy, but it's also marvelous. Grab a seat on deck and look up as you glide under stunning skyscrapers. Docents' design lessons carry on the breeze, so you'll know your beaux arts from international style by journey's end. The boat cruises along the Chicago River for 90 minutes.

Afterward, building buffs can add to their knowledge by ascending to street level and browsing inside the **Chicago Architecture Center**, where

GET YOUR KICKS ON ROUTE 66

A sign across the street from the Art Institute announces the beginning of **Route 66** (p522), which makes a fun road trip through Illinois.

LINCOLN PARK & OLD TOWN

- **SIGHTS**
  1. Alfred Caldwell Lily Pool
  2. Lincoln Park
  3. Lincoln Park Zoo
  4. North Avenue Beach
  5. Peggy Notebaert Nature Museum

- **EATING**
  6. Galit
  7. Wieners Circle

- **DRINKING & NIGHTLIFE**
  8. Old Town Ale House

- **ENTERTAINMENT**
  9. iO Theater
  10. Kingston Mines
  11. Second City
  12. Steppenwolf Theatre

EATING IN CHICAGO: OUR PICKS

MAPS P505, P512, P515

mfk: Spanish dishes and sunny cocktails in a teeny, romantic space that feels like the seaside in Spain. *5-9:30pm Mon-Sat, 4-8:30pm Sun* $$$

Tortello: Bowls of supreme comfort at this cute storefront: fresh pasta made before your eyes. *4:30-9pm Mon, from 11:30am Tue-Thu, from 8am Fri-Sun* $$

Duck Duck Goat: Chinese-inspired dim sum, mains and cocktails from star chef Stephanie Izard. *4:30-10pm Mon-Thu, to 11pm Fri & Sat, 11am-3pm Sat & Sun* $$

Loaf Lounge: Small, sunny bakery-cafe where locals clamor for breakfast sandwiches and the choc cake made famous in *The Bear*. *8am-4pm Wed-Mon* $

exhibits provide a quick primer on local structures and visionaries. Excellent walking tours that explore by theme (art deco, women architects) also depart from here.

Or stay by the water and amble along the 1.25-mile long **Riverwalk** *(chicagoriverwalk.us)*, chock-full of alfresco bars and restaurants from which you can gaze out and admire Chicago's built environment.

Get High in the Sky

MAP P505

Views from the top observatories

For superlative-seekers, **Willis Tower** *(theskydeck.com; adult/child from $32/24)* is it: Chicago's tallest (and the USA's second-tallest) skyscraper, rising 1450ft into the heavens. On the 103rd-floor Skydeck, glass-floored ledges jut out in midair, giving a knee-buckling perspective straight down. Before ascending, you'll make your way through fun interactive exhibits about Chicago, so snap a photo with the giant deep-dish pizza and stand on the replica Second City stage. Timed tickets are available online.

You'll find **360 Chicago** *(360chicago.com; adult/child from $30/20)* on the 94th floor of 875 N Michigan Ave (formerly known as the John Hancock Center). Set next to Lake Michigan, it provides unfettered panoramic vistas. The hair-raiser here is TILT *($9)*, a set of floor-to-ceiling windows that you stand in as they move and tip out over the ground. Nighttime views are particularly impressive, especially during the fireworks shows at nearby Navy Pier.

Navy Pier's Crowd-Pleasers

MAP P510

Ferris wheel, fireworks and views

Amble out on half-mile-long **Navy Pier** *(navypier.org; free)* and a carnival's worth of amusements vie for your attention, from the cloud-brushing **Centennial Wheel** *(adult/child $20/18)* to the horse-bobbing carousel *($6)*, ice-cream shops and margarita-slinging beer gardens. Then again, you can always just promenade along the dock's perimeter and enjoy the cool breezes and stellar skyline views. Crowds amass in summer for the fireworks show on Wednesday and Saturday nights.

Polk Bros Park, by the pier's entrance, has performance lawns for free concerts and movies. Competing tour boats depart from the pier's southern side. Set sail on **Windy** *(lakeshoresail.com; adult/child $49/34)*, a tall-masted

BEST ARCHITECTURE ICONS

Marina City: The twin corncob towers were completed in 1968 and look like something from a space-age *Jetsons* cartoon.

Tribune Tower: The neo-Gothic cloud-poker is inlaid with stones from the Taj Mahal, Great Pyramid, Parthenon and more.

Wrigley Building: Its shimmering white terracotta, French Renaissance details and famous clockface are the stuff of postcards.

St Regis Chicago: Look up at the city's third-tallest tower to see the 'blow-through floor' that reduces sway in the blue-glass skyscraper.

Rookery: Looks hulking and fortresslike outside, but it's light and airy inside, thanks to Frank Lloyd Wright's atrium overhaul.

DRINKING IN CHICAGO: OUR PICKS

MAPS P505, P508, P515

Old Town Ale House: Unpretentious neighborhood favorite for jovial late nights near the Second City comedy club. *3pm-4am*

Cindy's: Best rooftop in town. Set on the 13th floor of the Chicago Athletic Association Hotel, it unfurls awesome park and lake vistas. *hours vary*

Goose Island Taproom: Chicago's first craft brewer (now Anheuser-Busch owned) retains its indie spirit here. *noon-8pm Wed, Thu & Sun, to 10pm Fri & Sat*

CH Distillery: Polished facility that makes vodka, aquavit, amaro and Malört (Chicago's local liquor that's famous for tasting awful). *hours vary*

NEAR NORTH & GOLD COAST

SIGHTS
1. 360 Chicago
2. Centennial Wheel
3. Chicago Children's Museum
4. Marina City
5. Museum of Contemporary Art
6. Navy Pier
7. Oak Street Beach
8. Polk Bros Park
9. theMart
10. Tribune Tower
11. Wrigley Building

ACTIVITIES
12. Windy

SLEEPING
13. Acme Hotel

EATING
14. Al's #1 Italian Beef
15. Billy Goat Tavern
16. Giordano's
17. Lou Malnati's
18. Mr Beef

DRINKING & NIGHTLIFE
19. Library at Gilt Bar
20. Three Dots & A Dash

SHOPPING
21. Harry Potter Shop

TRANSPORT
22. Shoreline Water Taxi to Museum Campus

schooner, or hop on the **Shoreline Water Taxi** (shoreline sightseeing.com; adult/child $16/10) to the Museum Campus.

Feel the Blues

MAPS P505, P508

Drop by an authentic club

The electric blues is Chicago's claim to music fame. When Muddy Waters and friends plugged their guitars into amplifiers here in the 1940s, sound reached new decibel levels. Chicago became the hub for the groundbreaking genre.

EATING IN CHICAGO: MICHELIN-STARRED

MAPS P505, P508, P515, P516

Smyth: Homey spot with three well-earned stars for creative, perfectly executed seafood, seasonal produce and sweets. 5-9pm Tue-Sat $$$

Galit: Lively Middle Eastern restaurant winning raves for its cocktails and tasting menu made for sharing. 5-9pm Tue-Thu, to 9:30pm Fri & Sat $$$

Moody Tongue: Brewery with beers such as Shaved Black Truffle Lager that pair perfectly with New American plates. 5-10pm Wed-Sat $$

Kasama: Walk-in Filipino bakery by day; 13-course, modern Filipino tasting menu by night. bakery 9am-3pm Wed-Sun, dinner Thu-Sun $$$

The nation's best players trade licks at **Buddy Guy's Legends** (*buddyguy.com; $15-25*), just south of downtown. The memorabilia-filled room is relatively small, putting you close to the string-benders on stage. Free, all-ages acoustic shows take place at dinner time.

In Lincoln Park, **Kingston Mines** (*kingstonmines.com*) is similarly priced and a bit larger, with two stages where blues bands wail into the wee hours. More crackling grooves fill the air at **Rosa's Lounge** (*rosaslounge.com*), a real-deal little club with top local players and serious fans who dance the night away. It's further flung in Logan Square.

Improv Night Out
Laugh-out-loud comedy

MAPS P508, P515

Improv comedy began in Chicago, and the city remains a hub for the genre. Seeing a show is raucous fun, as performers create sketches based on suggestions (often alcohol fueled) that the audience shouts out. Polished ensembles riff on politics and pop culture nightly at **Second City** (*secondcity.com; from $41*), the most famous venue. **iO Theater** (*ioimprov.com; from $30*) is another established spot, where the Improvised Shakespeare Company ad-libs wacky plays in Elizabethan verse. **Den Theatre** (*thedentheatre.com; tickets from $20*) is a relative newcomer, with fringy, offbeat shows. iO and Den typically have more availability. Book all tickets in advance.

Catch a Game at Wrigley Field
The Cubs' historic ballpark

MAP P512

About 5 miles north of downtown, **Wrigley Field** (*cubs.com; around $60*) pops up smack in the middle of a residential neighborhood – aka Wrigleyville – surrounded on all sides by houses, rollicking bars and even a fire station. The ballpark charms with its lived-in environs, as well as its 1914 old-school features, like the hand-turned scoreboard, ivy-covered outfield walls and distinctive neon entrance sign. Seeing a game here, amid diehard Cubs fans, is a blast.

Gates open 1½ hours before the game's start time. It's good to arrive an hour or so early to browse around inside. Check out the Walk of Fame behind the bleachers in right field to learn about Cubs greats through the ages. Watch players take batting practice. Grab a hot dog and Old Style beer: the quintessential Wrigley foods.

Outside, the grassy plaza just north of the main entrance is **Gallagher Way**. On nongame days it's open to the public

BEST EXPERIENCES FOR KIDS

Lincoln Park Zoo: Watch chimpanzees swing, lions roar and penguins waddle, then feed chickens at the on-site farm, all for free.

Peggy Notebaert Nature Museum: Underrated spot to immerse in gentle thrills, such as the butterfly haven, frog marsh and wilderness walk.

Harry Potter Shop: Buy a wand or belly up to the Butterbeer Bar in this theatrical store that steeps you in the wizard's world.

Chicago Children's Museum: Excavate dinosaur bones, climb a ropey schooner and make art, then enjoy the carnival rides on surrounding Navy Pier.

Maggie Daley Park: Take your pick among the free playgrounds, including an enchanted forest to wander through, and a ship to pretend-sail.

 DRINKING IN CHICAGO: BEST COCKTAILS

MAPS P510, P513

Three Dots & a Dash: Fun tiki bar with rum flights and its own speakeasy, the Bamboo Room. *4pm-midnight Sun-Wed, to 1am Thu & Fri, 2pm-1am Sat*

Matchbox: Teeny corner bar in West Town pouring martinis, gimlets, pisco sours and other classic drinks since 1945. *3pm-2am*

Library at Gilt Bar: World-class libations with velvet booths, vintage art and speakeasy vibes. *4-10:30pm Sun-Thu, to 11pm Fri & Sat*

Nobody's Darling: Inclusive, off-the-beaten-path bar stirring cocktails so delicious they were named Beard Award finalists. *hours vary*

BEST ROCK & JAZZ CLUBS

Green Mill: Timeless jazz institution with velvet-cushioned booths where gangster Al Capone used to hang out.

Metro: Chicago's premier loud-rock club and a tastemaker for more than 40 years. Bands on the way up thrash first.

Salt Shed: Cool indoor/outdoor venue carved from the old Morton Salt factory, where edgy, genre-spanning artists play.

Hideout: Feels like a retro basement, but with alt-country and indie-pop bands twanging on the small stage under twinkling lights.

Empty Bottle: Scruffy standby that reigns supreme for nightly shows, ranging from indie rock to punk to psych-pop. Cheap beer!

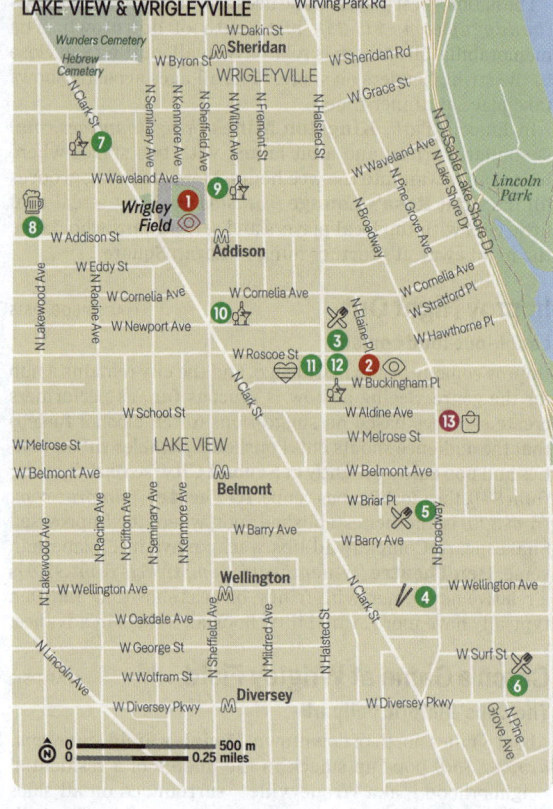

⭐ HIGHLIGHTS
1. Wrigley Field

🔴 SIGHTS
2. Northalsted

🟢 EATING
3. Chicago Diner
4. Crisp
5. Fancy Plants Cafe
6. mfk

🟢 DRINKING & NIGHTLIFE
7. GMan Tavern
8. Guthrie's Tavern
9. Murphy's Bleachers
10. Nisei Lounge
11. Roscoe's Tavern
12. Sidetrack

🔴 ENTERTAINMENT
see 7 Metro

🔴 SHOPPING
13. Unabridged Bookstore

 DRINKING IN CHICAGO: TOP WRIGLEYVILLE WATERING HOLES — MAP P512

Nisei Lounge: Festive dive bar to try the Chicago Handshake (an Old Style beer and shot of Malört). *5pm-1:30am Mon-Thu, from 11:30am Fri-Sun*

Guthrie's Tavern: Neighborhood hangout with a glassed-in back porch, patio chairs and board games. *3pm-2am Mon-Fri, from 11am Sat & Sun*

Murphy's Bleachers: Lively, classic saloon steps from the entrance to Wrigley Field's bleacher seats. *11am-2am Mon-Thu, from 9:30am Fri-Sun*

GMan Tavern: Features cool vinyl tunes, eclectic beer and live music beloved by the rock-and-roll crowd. *3pm-2am Mon-Fri, from noon Sat & Sun*

and hosts free movie nights and concerts. On game days it's a beer garden for ticket holders, and kids can run around or cool off in the splash pad.

Buy tickets at the Cubs' website or from online ticket broker StubHub (stubhub.com). Upper Reserved Infield seats are usually pretty cheap. The bleachers are fun. Ninety-minute stadium tours ($30) are also available most days in season.

Northalsted Pride

MAP P512

Hot spots in Chicago's LGBTQ+ hub

Northalsted – sometimes referred to as Boystown, its original name – lies along several blocks of N Halsted and Broadway streets, a short distance east of Wrigley Field. Rainbow crosswalks stripe the intersections, and rainbow pylons rise from the sidewalks. The pylons are part of the Legacy Walk, a mile-long outdoor museum that tells the stories of global LGBTQ+ icons.

Halsted St holds several thumping bars, as well as thrift and fetish shops to add sass to one's wardrobe. On Broadway, **Unabridged Bookstore** (unabridgedbookstore.com) is a community linchpin that stocks everything from gay parenting to queer spirituality titles.

● **SIGHTS**
1 Montrose Beach
2 Montrose Point Bird Sanctuary

● **EATING**
3 Hopleaf

● **DRINKING & NIGHTLIFE**
4 Big Chicks
5 Nobody's Darling
6 SoFo Tap

● **ENTERTAINMENT**
7 Green Mill
8 Neo-Futurist Theater

 DRINKING IN CHICAGO: BEST LGBTQ+ BARS MAPS P512, P513

Sidetrack: Community stalwart with thumping dance music for gay and straight crowds alike. *3pm-2am Mon-Fri, 1pm-3am Sat, noon-2am Sun*

Roscoe's Tavern: Casual bar in front, dance club in back and sun-splashed patio outdoors. *4pm-2am Sun-Thu, from noon Sat & Sun*

Big Chicks: Weekend DJs, a fun dance floor and art displays draw both men and women; cash only. *4pm-2am Mon-Fri, from 9am Sat & Sun*

SoFo Tap: Known for its dog-friendly patio, dartboards, karaoke and bear nights. *5pm-2am Mon-Thu, from 3pm Fri, from noon Sat & Sun*

BEST THEATERS

Check with Hot Tix *(hottix.org)* for discounted theater tickets to shows around the city.

Steppenwolf Theatre: Award-winning drama club of John Malkovich, Tracy Letts, Laurie Metcalf and other Hollywood stars.

Goodman Theatre: A crucible for new and classic dramas that often head to Broadway.

Chicago Theatre: Century-old stunner with an enormous glittering marquee that's an official city landmark and great for photos.

Chopin Theatre: This 1918 venue is full of vintage charm, hosting oddball, thought-provoking plays, concerts and literary events.

Neo-Futurist Theater: The hyper troupe makes a manic attempt to perform 30 original plays in 60 minutes.

To see the area at its peak, visit at night. The neighborhood mellows during the day when it's mostly about shopping (weekdays) and brunch (weekends).

Rock the Shops in Wicker Park

MAP P515

Stock up on stylish wares

A short distance northwest of downtown, the Wicker Park neighborhood brims with record shops, bookstores and vintage marts perfect for an afternoon trawl. Flick through bins of sad-core, post-rock and indie-tronica at **Reckless Records** *(reckless.com)*. Pick up a fringe jacket and Bionic Woman lunchbox at **Kokorokoko** *(kokorokokovintage.com)*. Browse the used tomes filling three floors at **Myopic Books** *(myopic bookstore.com)*. Loads of bars and dining venues pop up in between. Milwaukee Ave is the main vein, flanked by Blue Line L stations at Damen and Division. Wednesday through Saturday afternoon is the sweet spot when most shops are open.

Mosey Along the 606

MAP P515

Neighborhood trail above street level

The **606** *(the606.org)* is an urban-cool elevated path along a repurposed train track now dotted with trees, benches and artworks. Bike or stroll past factories, clattering L trains and locals' backyard affairs. It's great for a morning or afternoon escape.

The trail unfurls for 2.7 miles parallel to Bloomingdale Ave, with its eastern end on Ashland Ave (in Wicker Park), and its western end on Ridgeway Ave (in Humboldt Park). Access points pop up every quarter mile, so it's easy to get on or off the path. Bars and restaurants beckon at ground level.

Blue Line L stations at Western and Damen are within a quick walk. For those wanting to cycle, Divvy bikeshare stations are on Ashland Ave by the trail's eastern end and Milwaukee Ave near **Small Cheval** *(smallcheval.com)*, a festive little shack serving up burgers, fries, milkshakes and beers.

Museum Campus Marvels

MAP P516

Dinosaurs, sharks and asteroids await

Three top-draw museums line up in a row on a lakefront stretch just south of downtown. The mammoth **Field Museum** *(fieldmuseum.org; adult/child $30/23)* houses everything but the kitchen sink. The collection's rock star is Sue, the largest Tyrannosaurus rex yet discovered, who menaces

---

EATING IN CHICAGO: VEGETARIAN & VEGAN

MAPS P505, P512, P515

Native Foods: Cheery venue for vegan burgers, tacos, hot chicken and meatball sandwiches. *10:30am-8pm Mon-Sat, 11am-7pm Sun* $

Fancy Plants Cafe: Cute vegan spot for a carrot lox bagel, seitan sausage sandwich or smoked lentil lasagna. *8am-4pm* $

Handlebar: Bike-messenger hangout with veg and fish dishes, plus a great back patio for beers. *10am-midnight Mon-Fri, from 9am Sat & Sun* $$

Chicago Diner: Vegetarian comfort food stalwart with vintage red tables and booths. *11am-10pm Mon-Fri, from 10am Sat & Sun* $$

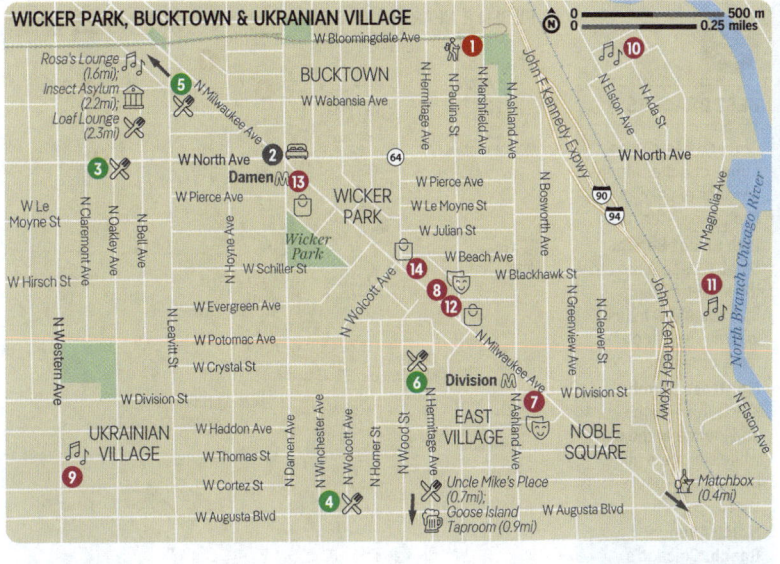

- **ACTIVITIES**
1 The 606
- **SLEEPING**
2 Robey
- **EATING**
3 Handlebar
4 Kasama
5 Small Cheval
6 Tortello
- **ENTERTAINMENT**
7 Chopin Theatre
8 Den Theatre
9 Empty Bottle
10 Hideout
11 Salt Shed
- **SHOPPING**
12 Kokorokoko
13 Myopic Books
14 Reckless Records

the 2nd floor with her toothy companions. Mummies, gemstones and taxidermy lions are also among the stash of 40 million artifacts.

Next door, the **Shedd Aquarium** (*sheddaquarium.org; adult/child from $39/29*) packs in families that come to gawp at the 32,000 aquatic creatures that live here, including sharks – separated from you by just 5in of Plexiglas – stingrays and rescued sea otters. Building renovations through to 2027 mean some galleries might be closed when you visit.

Space enthusiasts will get a big bang out of the **Adler Planetarium** (*adlerplanetarium.org; adult/child $25/13*) with its collection of sundials and the *Gemini 12* space capsule. To see all three museums in a day, start with Shedd, followed by Field and then Adler.

Cycle the Lakefront

Wind-in-your-hair ride

Lake Michigan edges the city from north to south. It's huge, a freshwater 'sea'; its frothy waves rippling over the horizon with no end in sight. The 18-mile Lakefront Trail is a beautiful route along the water, rolling by beaches, parks and harbors. It's split into separate lanes for walkers and cyclists. Pedaling the path is a blast, a great way to blend into the local scene.

BEST FREEBIES

Chicago Cultural Center: Pop in to see terrific art exhibitions, foreign films and the world's largest Tiffany glass dome.

Chicago Greeter: Have a local take you on a two- to four-hour walking tour; book at least two weeks in advance. *chicagogreeter.com*

Art on the Mart: An ever-changing light show projected on a huge building by the Riverwalk each night.

Museum of Contemporary Photography: Small but top-tier venue for works by Henri Cartier-Bresson, Sally Mann, Ai Weiwei and others.

National Museum of Mexican Art: Politically charged paintings and folk art in Pilsen.

BEST BEACHES

Chicago has 22 free public beaches along 26 miles of Lake Michigan waterfront.

12th Street Beach: Small crescent next to the Museum Campus that somehow hides in plain sight and remains serene.

Montrose Beach: Kayak, bird-watch and lounge at the bar while sailboats glide by the dune-backed shore.

North Avenue Beach: Chicago's favorite party beach, with a bar, cafe, volleyball courts, and bicycle and kayak rentals.

Oak Street Beach: Sandy beach downtown for swimming and sunbathing in the shadow of skyscrapers.

Margaret T Burroughs Beach: Play all day at this fab strand with a boat harbor, fishing dock and watercraft rentals.

PILSEN & NEAR SOUTH SIDE

- **SIGHTS**
  1. 12th Street Beach
  2. Adler Planetarium
  3. Field Museum
  4. Margaret T Burroughs Beach
  5. National Museum of Mexican Art
  6. Northerly Island

- **ACTIVITIES**
  7. Shedd Aquarium

- **EATING**
  8. 5 Rabanitos

- **DRINKING & NIGHTLIFE**
  9. Moody Tongue

Get a bike from Divvy (*divvybikes.com; day pass $18*). Be prepared for crowds on summer weekends, especially heading north, where there are more beaches.

EATING IN CHICAGO: AROUND THE WORLD

MAPS P512, P513, P515, P516

Crisp: Loud music, bright colors and picnic-style tables set the scene for Korean fried chicken and mixed vegetable bowls. *11:30am-9pm Tue-Sun* $

Uncle Mike's Place: Join construction workers, artsy youth and senior citizens chowing rice porridge and Spam at this fab Filipino breakfast diner. *6am-2pm* $$

5 Rabanitos: Unusual spice combinations and addictive salsa and mole make the dishes shine. *11am-9pm Mon-Fri, 9am-10pm Sat, 9am-9pm Sun* $$

Hopleaf: Cozy tavern for Belgian-style mussels, *frites* (fries) and beers from the 68 taps. *noon-11pm Sun-Thu, to midnight Fri & Sat* $$

Illinois

HISTORIC SITES | RURAL LANDSCAPES | WRIGHT DESIGNS

Outside of mighty Chicago, urbanity falls away fast and Illinois opens into a wide horizon of corn and soybean fields. Flat farmland covers three-quarters of the state, with the only real exception coming in the hilly northwest and knobby, bluff-strewn far south.

Road-tripping in Illinois turns up scattered shrines to local hero Abe Lincoln. Then there's Oak Park, the town with the most Frank Lloyd Wright–designed buildings of anywhere in the world. Historic Route 66 slices across the state, leaving a trail of corn dogs, pies and roadside oddities in its wake. Galena in the northwestern region delights with rolling hills and grazing horses near the Mississippi River (which forms most of Illinois' western boundary). Southern Illinois changes up the scene completely, with thick forests, wild rock formations and a cypress swamp for outdoor adventures.

Places

Oak Park p517
Springfield p519
Galena p521
Cahokia Mounds p523
Shawnee Hills p523

☑ TOP TIP

People tend to forget that Illinois is an agricultural powerhouse. Farm stands are common along the roads in rural areas. Keep an eye out for peaches and apples in southern Illinois, apples in western Illinois, and pumpkins and sweet corn in northern and central Illinois.

Oak Park

See Wright buildings galore

The western Chicago suburb of Oak Park is a repository of famed architect Frank Lloyd Wright's early solo work. Wright lived here for two decades, from 1889 to 1909, and was only 22 years old when he built his Oak Park home, the first house he ever designed. Soon he was drawing up plans for several neighbors. Twenty-five Wright-devised buildings

GETTING AROUND

The main Interstates are I-90 and I-94 that head north to Wisconsin (tolls), I-55 that links Chicago to St Louis following historic Route 66 (no tolls), I-80 that goes east–west passing Chicago to the south (some tolls), and I-57 that runs from Chicago to southern Illinois (no tolls). Amtrak runs a handy train between downtown Chicago and downtown Springfield five times a day. Those trains roll onward to St Louis.

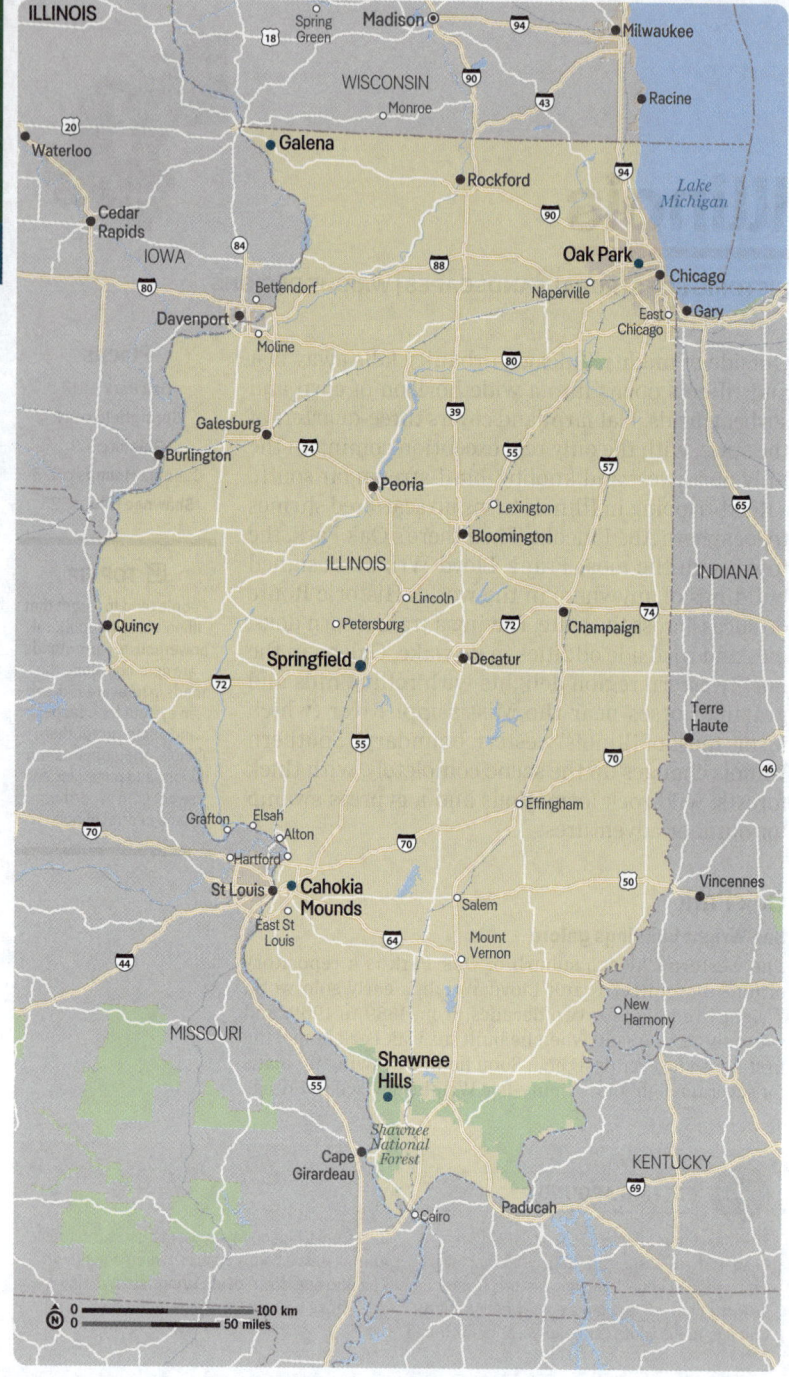

eventually popped up here, the largest concentration anywhere in the world.

The **Frank Lloyd Wright Home & Studio** (*flwright.org/tour/home-and-studio; tours $24*) is the main sight, accessible by guided tour only. It's best to book tickets online in advance. While walk-ups are welcome, slots tend to fill up. The hour-long walk-through reveals a fascinating place filled with original Wright-designed furniture and geometric details that made his Prairie-style architecture distinctive. Look for personal additions, such as the fireplace carved with his family motto: 'Truth is life.'

A half-mile away, Wright's 1908 **Unity Temple** (*flwright.org/explore/unity-temple; tours $18-20*) defies traditional ecclesiastical architecture. Like many of his buildings, the church's entrance is slightly hidden, leading visitors on what he called a 'path of discovery.' Inside, the sanctuary feels much warmer, splashed with sunshine-yellow walls and actual rays streaming in through the skylights.

Monday through Saturday mornings are the best time to visit and take in both sights. If driving, street parking is easy to find. Metra and L trains also have stations nearby.

Where Hemingway grew up

Frank Lloyd Wright wasn't the only influential artist in Oak Park at the turn of the century. Writer Ernest Hemingway grew up in the suburb. He was born in the 2nd-floor bedroom of a sprawling Queen Anne home on Oak Park Ave – a few blocks away from Wright's studio – in 1899. The house has been restored to look as it did then, with old family photos and frilly Victorian decor. Visits to the **Hemingway Birthplace** (*hemingwaybirthplace.com; adult/child $20/free*) are by hour-long guided tour only, offered Thursday through Saturday afternoons, as well as Saturday mornings.

In 1906, the family moved nearby to 600 N Kenilworth Ave. **Hemingway's Boyhood Home** is still a private residence, so you can't go inside, but a plaque marks the location.

Springfield

Follow in Abe Lincoln's footsteps

Illinois' small state capital has a serious obsession with Abraham Lincoln, who spent 24 years here as a young lawyer. A four-block neighborhood of old homes, gravel streets and wooden boardwalks near downtown has been preserved as the **Lincoln Home National Historic Site** (*nps.gov/liho;*

BEST ILLINOIS STATE PARKS

Starved Rock: Hike among 18 waterfall-filled canyons, each slicing through tree-covered, sandstone bluffs (north-central Illinois).

Mississippi Palisades: Hikers and rock-climbers love it, thanks to its Mississippi River-front real estate and dramatic limestone cliffs (northwest Illinois).

Matthiessen: Smaller and less crowded than nearby Starved Rock, but with similar scenery and sunflower fields (north-central Illinois).

White Pines Forest: Getaway to smell the pines, count the stars and stay in rustic log cabins (north-central Illinois).

Giant City: Popular for hiking and climbing amid the striking rock formations and towering trees (southern Illinois).

EATING & DRINKING IN OAK PARK: OUR PICKS

Spilt Milk: Excellent bakery for picking up a quiche, sandwich, scone or slice of creamy, flaky-crust pie. *8am-5pm Mon-Sat, to 2pm Sun* **$**

Hemmingway's Bistro: A few buildings south of Ernest's birthplace, this elegant spot serves French favorites. *11am-8:30pm* **$$$**

Citrine Cafe: Devour Mediterranean-influenced pastas, pizzas and seafood dishes, dreamed up by the Serbia-born owner. *hours vary* **$$$**

Kinslahger Brewing Company: Gorgeous taproom in a retro 1920s building where crisp lagers rule the taps. *4-10pm Wed-Fri, from 2pm Sat & Sun*

WRIGHT SIGHTS WALKABOUT

Gape at some of the 25 buildings Frank Lloyd Wright designed early in his career while living in Oak Park.

START	END	LENGTH
Frank Lloyd Wright Home & Studio	Unity Temple	0.75 miles; 45 minutes

Start at ❶ **Frank Lloyd Wright Home & Studio** (p511), the only house you can go inside. (The others are privately owned and not accessible.) Head south on Forest Ave, where Wright-designed residences line both sides of the street. One of the most unusual is ❷ **Nathan G Moore House** at 333 Forest Ave. In 1895, attorney Nathan Moore requested a home in Tudor Revival style, which Wright begrudgingly accepted as his first independent commission because he needed the money. Across the street at 318 Forest Ave, the 1902 ❸ **Arthur Heurtley House** looks much more classically Wright: a low roof, long horizontal lines and leaded glass windows.

Turn east on Elizabeth Ct to find ❹ **Laura Gale House** (6 Elizabeth Ct) tucked away among mature trees. It seems modest, but Wright said the residence's cantilevered balconies were the 'progenitor of Fallingwater' in Pennsylvania, perhaps his most famous construction.

Backtrack to Forest Ave. Wright considered ❺ **Frank W Thomas House** at 210 Forest Ave the first of his Prairie-style homes. Outside the gate of ❻ **Austin Gardens**, a bust of Wright is carved from a boulder.

Continue south on Forest Ave until the intersection with Lake St and turn east. At the corner of Lake and Kenilworth is the hulking concrete block of Wright's ❼ **Unity Temple** (p511).

After a fire in 1922, Wright completely redesigned the Moore House, but kept the English manor influence.

Wright designed his Home & Studio to fit around the ginkgo tree already growing in the east courtyard. It's still there.

Wright used concrete for Unity Temple to save money. Lightning struck the prior church, and funds to rebuild were limited.

free). Begin at the park visitor center to get a ticket to enter Lincoln's 12-room abode on a 30-minute ranger-led tour. The house is the only one Lincoln ever owned, and 80% is original, looking as it did when Abe and wife Mary lived here from 1844 until they moved to the White House in 1861.

The modern **Abraham Lincoln Presidential Library & Museum** *(presidentlincoln.illinois.gov; adult/child $15/6)* contains the most complete Lincoln collection in the world. Real-deal artifacts, such as Abe's shaving mirror and presidential seal join whizbang exhibits and Disneyesque holograms that keep the kids agog.

Lincoln's immortal line 'A house divided against itself cannot stand…' was delivered in the **Old State Capitol** *(dnrhistoric. illinois.gov; free)* in the days before the Civil War. Detailed tours outline his early political life, including the dramatic Lincoln–Douglas debates in 1858.

After his assassination, Lincoln's body was returned to Springfield, where it lies today. **Lincoln's Tomb** *(dnrhistoric. illinois.gov; free)* sits in Oak Ridge Cemetery, 2 miles north of downtown. Mary and three of their four sons are buried here, too.

The sites – except the tomb – are in Springfield's center, so park once and walk. All are open daily, except the old capitol (closed Sunday and Monday).

Galena

Evocative mid-1800s boomtown

Tucked in Illinois' northwest corner near the Mississippi River, tiny Galena spreads across wooded hillsides amid rolling, barn-dotted farmland. The town was named after the lead sulfide found here, and was the location of the first mineral rush in the US in the 1820s. At its peak, Galena was the lead-mining capital of the world and had nearly as many residents as Chicago. It was the wealthiest city in Illinois, still reflected in the redbrick mansions in Greek Revival, Gothic Revival and Queen Anne styles that line the streets.

Galena was also home for a short time to Ulysses S Grant, the 18th US president and commanding general of the Union Army during the Civil War. Grant moved to Galena in 1860 to work in his father's leather goods store. When he came back to town following the Civil War, Galena residents gifted him with a two-story brick Italianate-style **home** *(granthome. org; adult/child $5/3)*, fully furnished. However, he left for Washington, DC, shortly after and rarely returned. Today, the

WHAT IS A HORSESHOE SANDWICH?

It's on restaurant menus across Springfield but rarely seen anywhere else: the horseshoe sandwich. Loosen your belt before devouring this calorific concoction: an open-faced stack that consists of thickly sliced toasted bread topped with meat, French fries and a Welsh rarebit cheese sauce. It was first served at Springfield's Leland Hotel in 1928.

Hamburger is now the most common meat option for a horseshoe, but originally it was bone-in ham. Some places offer multiple meat options, including Angus beef, chicken breast, corned beef, buffalo chicken, ground lamb, pulled pork, brisket and even a veggie burger. Fortunately, many menus also offer it as a 'ponyshoe' (a smaller size).

EATING & DRINKING IN SPRINGFIELD: OUR PICKS

Luminary Kitchen & Provisions: Its weekly-changing, seasonal menus of New American plates are a treat. *4-9pm Wed-Sat, 10am-2pm Sun* **$$$**

D'Arcy's Pint: Many say this Irish pub makes the best horseshoe sandwich, along with burgers and shepherd's pie. *11am-9pm Tue-Sat* **$$**

Obed & Isaac's: Set in a 150-year-old mansion, this brewery offers sunny rooms for drinking and is also known for its horseshoes. *11am-10pm*

Wakery: Welcoming, artsy space that pours coffee by day and nonalcoholic cocktails, beers and wines by night. *7-11am & 4-10pm Mon-Fri*

ROUTE 66 RAMBLE

Take a drive into yesteryear on the Mother Road past neon-lit diners and oddball roadside attractions.

START	END	LENGTH
Begin Historic Route 66 sign (Chicago)	Cozy Dog Drive In (Springfield)	220 miles; 6 hours

The nostalgic highway rolls for 2400 miles from Chicago to Los Angeles. No time for it? Drive the section between Chicago and Springfield to sample it in a day.

Snap a photo with the ❶ **Begin Historic Route 66 Sign** at the northwestern corner of Adams St and Michigan Ave in downtown Chicago. Head a mile southwest and fuel up for the journey at ❷ **Lou Mitchell's**, a classic diner.

Motor west to Ogden Ave (aka Old Route 66) and onward through Chicago's western suburbs. Much of Route 66 has been superseded by I-55, so you'll get funneled onto the Interstate eventually. In Bolingbrook take Joilet Rd/IL-53, which parallels I-55. Now you're back on Old Route 66 to mosey into Wilmington to see the ❸ **Gemini Giant** – a 28ft fiberglass astronaut that stands guard along the road.

Continue to Pontiac to check out the free, tchotchke-filled museum at the ❹ **Route 66 Association of Illinois**. Proceed on the Interstate or Old Route 66 beside it until tiny Atlanta, where ❺ **Tall Paul** – a sky-high statue of lumberjack Paul Bunyan – clutches a hot dog. The town's ❻ **American Giants Museum** has even more hulking fiberglass creations. Stay the course to Springfield and finish at ❼ **Cozy Dog Drive In**, where the corn dog was born.

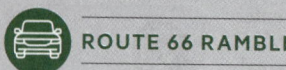

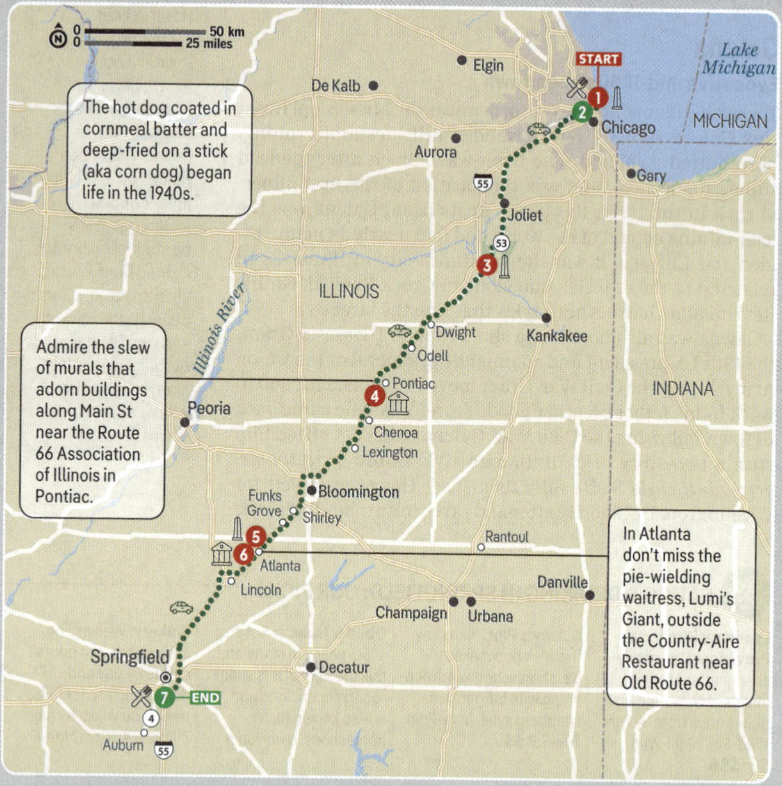

The hot dog coated in cornmeal batter and deep-fried on a stick (aka corn dog) began life in the 1940s.

Admire the slew of murals that adorn buildings along Main St near the Route 66 Association of Illinois in Pontiac.

In Atlanta don't miss the pie-wielding waitress, Lumi's Giant, outside the Country-Aire Restaurant near Old Route 66.

house retains about 90% of its original furnishings, including Grant's favorite green chair, which made it to the White House and back, and Julia Grant's 15lb Bible dating from 1865.

Cahokia Mounds

Ancient city near the Mississippi River

A stone's throw from St Louis, MO, **Cahokia Mounds State Historic Site** *(cahokiamounds.org; free)* is where the largest ancient city in North America once stood. At its peak, c 1100, some 20,000 people lived here – more than London during the same era. It's worth an hour or two of self-guided rambles around the lonely grounds.

About 70 earthen mounds survive, including the massive, 100ft-tall Monk's Mound, which you can climb and see the Gateway Arch and St Louis skyline on a clear day. 'Woodhenge,' a circle of poles used for highly accurate solar observations and date keeping, also impresses.

Shawnee Hills

Where eerie swamp meets vineyards

In the southern part of Illinois, near the border with Kentucky, the forested Shawnee Hills juts up, looking a lot like mini mountains. The rugged area makes for a great weekend break for nature lovers, especially in fall when the trees explode in color.

Start in **Shawnee National Forest** *(fs.usda.gov/shawnee; free)* and its dramatic sandstone rock formations known as **Garden of the Gods** for short trails to big views. About 65 miles southwest, the scenery shifts unexpectedly to Southern-style swampland, complete with moss-draped trees and croaking bullfrogs at **Cypress Creek National Wildlife Refuge** *(fws.gov/refuge/cypress-creek; free)*. **Cache Bayou Outfitters** *(cachebayououtfitters.com; tours adult/child $45/18)* takes you into it by canoe or kayak.

Another surprise in the area: multiple wineries. Sample the wares on the 40-mile **Shawnee Hills Wine Trail** *(shawneewinetrail.com)*. **Blue Sky Vineyard** *(blueskyvineyard.com)* is a sweet stop for a cabernet-style red while listening to live music on the patio.

Finally, if beer is your thing, **Scratch Brewing** *(scratchbeer.com)* hides amid horse-grazing pastures at Shawnee forest's western edge. Bark, berries and herbs foraged from the farm are thrown into the wild ales and sours. The bohemian microbrewery is open Friday through Sunday only.

STAGECOACH TRAIL

For a scenic detour, hop on the 26-mile Stagecoach Trail as an alternative to US 20 for the stretch of the route between Lena and Galena. The twisty road runs through the small communities of Nora, Warren, Apple River and Scales Mound, tempting a longer trip with vineyards and farm-fresh cheese along the way.

The Stagecoach Trail has been a road since the 1830s, and a stagecoach company once operated two daily services that carried passengers, post and parcels between Chicago and Galena. The railroads made the Stagecoach Trail obsolete within two decades. Cars later made the train line obsolete – passenger service ended in 1981. Today the former train station is the **Galena Country Visitor Center**, which has a free parking lot.

EATING & DRINKING IN GALENA: OUR PICKS

Fritz & Frites: This romantic little bistro serves a compact menu of German and French classics. *4-8pm Sun, Wed & Thu, to 9pm Fri & Sat* **$$**

Otto's Place: Breakfast classics and lunchtime sandwiches served in a historic building with pressed-tin ceilings. *8am-2pm Fri-Sun, to 1pm Mon & Thu* **$**

Fried Green Tomatoes: Try the lasagna or the espresso-encrusted steak in the building once owned by Grant's father. *hours vary* **$$$**

Galena Taphouse: Pours beers made within 200 miles of Galena and serves Asian-influenced dishes. *11:30am-10pm Sun-Thu, to midnight Fri & Sat*

Indiana

RACING SPECTACLE | RIVER RIDES | SOARING SANDS

Places
Indianapolis p526
Auburn p528
South Bend p528
Indiana Dunes National Park p529
Fairmount p530
Brown County p531
Ohio River Scenic Byway p531

 TOP TIP

Go stargazing at Kemil Park at the Indiana Dunes! It's the one part of the park that's open 24 hours, and it's designated an International Dark Sky Community and outfitted with telescopes.

The state revs up around the Indy 500 race, and cars are cherished in Auburn and South Bend. Otherwise, it's often about the slower-paced pleasures in corn-stubbled Indiana: cycling through its center, pie-eating in Amish Country, meditating in Bloomington's Tibetan temples and admiring big architecture in small Columbus. The northwest has moody sand dunes to climb, while the south has caves to explore and rivers to canoe. A quirky labyrinth, bluegrass music shrine and famed, lipstick-kissed gravestone also make appearances across the state.

For the record, folks have called Indianans 'Hoosiers' since the 1830s, but the word's origin is unknown. One theory is that early settlers knocking on a door were met with 'Who's here?' which soon became 'Hoosier.' It's certainly something to discuss with locals, perhaps at a local cafeteria.

Fun fact: Indiana is called 'the mother of vice presidents' for the six veeps it has spawned.

GETTING AROUND

Indianapolis International Airport is the state's largest airport by far, though, depending on where you're going, Louisville, KY, is also an option. There are a couple of smaller airports, including in South Bend. Amtrak stops in Indianapolis en route to Chicago and New York City. Going by Megabus or Greyhound is faster. Driving is fastest; Hwy 46 connects Bloomington, Nashville and Columbus. I-65 and I-69 are the main regional interstates. Within Indianapolis, **IndyGo** *(indygo.net)* runs the local buses – with two BRT lines so far: Red from Broad Ripple to University of Indianapolis, and Purple from downtown to Lawrence – and **Pacers Bikeshare** *(pacersbikeshare.org)* has bike stations along the Cultural Trail downtown.

INDIANA'S BEST FESTIVALS

Parke County Covered Bridge Festival: Known for its 31 covered bridges, which are celebrated for 10 days each year starting the second Friday of October.

Bill Monroe's Bluegrass Festival: In Morgantown, a bluegrass festival every June named after the finger-picking hero.

Abbey Road on the River: Over Memorial Day weekend at Jefferson's Big Four Pedestrian & Cycling Bridge, the world's largest Beatles and '60s music festival.

Little 500: Bloomington biking bonanza in April, where cyclists ride one-speeds for 200 laps around a quarter-mile track.

Johnny Appleseed Festival: In honor of the pioneering nurseryman, an apple-themed festival in September in Fort Wayne.

Indianapolis Motor Speedway Museum

Indianapolis

The greatest spectacle in racing

Indy's super-sight is the **Indianapolis Motor Speedway** *(indianapolismotorspeedway.com)*, about 6 miles northwest of downtown and home of the 'Greatest Spectacle in Racing,' the Indy 500. Stop in at the **Indianapolis Motor Speedway Museum** *(imsmuseum.org; adult/youth/child $25/18/free)*, which features some 75 racing cars (including former winners) and championship trophies. Limited availability golf-cart tours *(adult/youth $55/35)* of the grounds and track are available from April to October (OK, you're not exactly burning rubber in a golf cart, but it's still fun to pretend while you take a lap!). A short walk from the Speedway, the **Dallara Experience Hub** *(dallara experiencehub.com; $15-30)* is where you can peek at how the speedsters are made, and try a 10-minute driving simulator.

The big race itself is held on the Sunday of Memorial Day weekend and attended by 350,000 crazed fans. If you'll be in town, Grandstand tickets can be hard to come by, so plan ahead. Try general admission, or the prerace trials and practices, for easier access and cheaper prices.

The nation's premier kids' museum

If you're traveling with kiddos, the **Children's Museum of Indianapolis** *(childrensmuseum.org; adult/youth $32/27)* is

 EATING IN INDY: OUR PICKS

Milktooth: Breakfast lovers of the world unite for dishes like sweet sourdough waffles and savory Dutch baby pancakes. *10am-3pm Fri-Mon* **$$**

St Elmo's: Indy's oldest (1902), best steakhouse. Legendary shrimp cocktail, perfectly grilled beef. *4-10pm Mon-Thu, to 11pm Fri, 3-11pm Sat, 4-9pm Sun* **$$$**

Tinker Street: Fork into seasonal dishes at this New American favorite. Vegetarian and gluten-free options are plentiful. *5-9pm Mon-Thu, to 10pm Fri & Sat, to 8pm Sun* **$$$**

Bluebeard: Named after the Kurt Vonnegut book, James Beard-nominated fine-dining spot with daily changing menu. *11am-10pm Mon-Thu, to 11pm Fri & Sat, 5-10pm Sun* **$$$**

a must. It's the world's largest kids' museum, sprawled over five floors holding incredible exhibitions on dinosaurs, space stations and so much more. Indoors, it's centered around a stunning 43ft sculpture by Dale Chihuly that teaches tykes to blow glass (virtually!); and outdoors, the 7.5-acre Sports Legends Experience is the playground of your dreams.

An outing to Newfields

The 152-acre **Newfields** campus houses the **Indianapolis Museum of Art** (*discovernewfields.org; adult/youth/child $20/13/free*), home to a terrific collection of European art (especially Turner and postimpressionists), African tribal art, South Pacific art, Chinese works, Robert Indiana's original pop-art *Love* sculpture and the largest gallery dedicated to contemporary and modern design in the US.

The campus also includes the **Virginia B Fairbanks Art & Nature Park**, with striking modern sculptures set amid 100 acres of woodlands. The park has its own entrance and is free, and open daily from sunrise to sunset – perfect for an art fix without the admission price. Adjacent to the Madeline F Elder Greenhouse, a seasonal **beer garden** offers a rotating tap list, including an exclusively brewed saison from Sun King Brewery.

Cycle from the Monon Trail to the Indy Cultural Trail

A 26-mile former rail track turned walking and cycling path, the **Monon Trail** (*bikethemonon.com*) plies through some of Indianapolis' coolest districts, stretching from Sheridan in central Indiana, through the North Indy suburb of Carmel, to hip Broad Ripple and eventually to downtown. Rent a set of wheels (outfitters listed on the Monon Trail site), then head to an access point – major ones with parking, restrooms and other infrastructure are located at, among others, 75th St, 96th St and Carmel Central Park (11th St).

At 10th and Lewis Sts, link up with the **Cultural Trail**, an 8-mile urban bike trail that goes through six downtown cultural districts, including Mass Ave, Mile Square and several public art projects. Along the route, several museums are worth a stop. The **Indiana War Memorial** (*indianawarmemorials.org; free*) is a 210ft-tall mausoleum-evoking limestone tribute honoring Hoosier veterans of WWI, while the **Eiteljorg Museum** (*eiteljorg.org; adult/youth $20/12*) features Native American basketry, pots and masks, as well as a Western painting collection with works by Frederic Remington and Georgia O'Keeffe. Eiteljorg is located within the

INDIANA'S CAFETERIA SCENE

Cafeterias are an Indiana tradition, where diners grab a tray, slide it along a metal railing, and load it up with plates of hot and cold dishes. Fried chicken, meatloaf, mac 'n' cheese, freshly baked rolls and sugar cream pie are all beloved staples. One of Indiana's first cafeterias opened in 1900, with many more arriving on the scene in the decades that followed, like Gray Brothers Cafeteria in 1944 and MCL Cafeteria in 1950. Since then, many of Indiana's time-honored neighborhood cafeterias have disappeared – but Gray Brothers and MCL still remain.

DRINKING IN INDY: OUR PICKS

Sun King Brewery: Indy's young and hip swill pints, flights and growlers, and spill onto the patio in summer. 11am-9pm Mon & Tue, to 10pm Wed-Sat, to 8pm Sun

Slippery Noodle Inn: Indiana's oldest bar (1850), with stints as various venues; now a blues club. 11am-1am Mon-Fri, noon-2am Sat, 4pm-midnight Sun

Centerpoint Brewing Company: True-to-style beers in a former race-car-engine factory and mail-sorting facility. 3-9pm Mon-Wed, to 10pm Thu, noon-10pm Fri & Sat, noon-8pm Sun

Metazoa Brewing Co: Pet-friendliest brewery: on-site dog park, donates 5% of profits to animal/wildlife organizations. 1-10pm Mon-Wed, from 11am Thu-Sat, 11am-9pm Sun

MORE OF INDIANA'S TOP STATE PARKS & FORESTS

Falls of the Ohio State Park: This park has only rapids, no falls, but is of interest for its 390-million-year-old fossil beds.

Clifty Falls State Park: Large, wooded space in Madison with excellent hiking, waterfall views, creeks, canyons and campgrounds.

Turkey Run State Park: Known for its hiking, particularly the ladders of Trail 3, along with horseback riding, swimming and camping.

Mounds State Park: Featuring 10 prehistoric earthworks, largest is the Great Mound, built around 160 BCE by the Adena and Hopewell peoples.

Clark State Forest: Indiana's oldest state forest, which includes part of Indiana's longest hiking trail, the Knobstone Trail.

White River State Park *(whiteriverstatepark.org)*, the urban green space that encompasses seven city attractions, including the Indianapolis Zoo, Indiana State Museum and NCAA Hall of Champions.

Finally, the **Kurt Vonnegut Museum & Library** *(kurtvonnegutlibrary.org; $12/8)* pays homage to the famous author born and raised in Indy, who was an anti-censorship and peace activist. The museum, free the first Monday of the month, exhibits artifacts from his life.

Auburn

Check out classic cars

Classic-car connoisseurs should stop in Auburn, about 50 miles southeast of Amish Country, where the Cord Company produced the USA's favorite autos in the 1920s and '30s. Two remarkable car museums, the **Auburn Cord Duesenberg Automobile Museum** *(automobilemuseum.org; adult/student $15/10)* and the **National Auto & Truck Museum** *(natmus.org; adult/child $12/7)*, are conveniently lined up next door to one another for your car-viewing pleasure. The former has a 120-strong inventory of early roadsters – including Babe Ruth's Auburn 8-88 Roadster and Frank Lloyd Wright's orange Cord L-29 – in a beautiful art-deco setting that was once part of the original Auburn Automotive Company. The latter has a bit of everything, from toy cars to gas pumps to vintage rigs. You can also purchase a 'campus pass' for combined admission *($25/15)*.

South Bend

From horse-drawn carriages to motor vehicles

South Bend's automotive legacy stems from its homegrown carmaker Studebaker (later the Studebaker-Packard Corporation), which started off by manufacturing horse-drawn wagons and carriages in the 1850s, before transitioning to motor vehicles to put out its first electric car in 1902 and first gas-powered car in 1904. The **Studebaker National Museum** *(studebakermuseum.org; adult/student/child $11/7/free)* is where you can get a sense of the industry's evolution through the ages, as you meander through three floors of shiny vehicles that range from vintage carriages to a gorgeous 1956 Packard.

 EATING IN NORTHERN INDIANA: OUR PICKS

Rise'n Roll: Now a northern Indiana chain, it started here in Middlebury; all because of the sought-after cinnamon-caramel donuts. *7am-4pm Mon-Sat* $

Village Inn Restaurant: Sublime pies in Amish Country, baked in the wee hours of the morning. Burgers, meat loaf and other mains. *5am-8pm Mon-Fri, to 11am Sat* $

Octave Grill: In Chesterton, burgers made with grass-fed beef, paired with a wonderful selection of rotating craft beers. *3-9pm Mon & Thu-Sat. to 8pm Sun* $

Rocco's: A South Bend institution, ladling marinara sauce since 1951. After football games, lines of Notre Dame alums run out the door. *4:30-10:30pm Tue-Sat* $

TOP EXPERIENCE

Indiana Dunes National Park

In addition to being the state's most visited site, attracting 3.5 million visitors per year, sunny beaches, rustling grasses and woodsy campgrounds are the Indiana Dunes' claim to fame. The area is hugely popular on summer days with sunbathers from Chicago and towns throughout Northern Indiana. Beyond its beaches, the area is noted for sweet hiking trails that meander up the dunes and through the woodlands.

National Park Trails

The Dunes, which became the USA's 61st national park in 2019, stretch along 15 miles of Lake Michigan shoreline (swimming allowed). A short walk away from the beaches are several hiking paths; the best are the Bailly-Chellberg Trail (2.5 miles) that winds by a still-operating 1870s farm; and the Heron Rookery Trail (2 miles), where blue herons flock (though there's no actual rookery).

Plants & Wildlife

Oddly, all this natural bounty lies smack-dab next to smoke-belching factories, yet it still boasts remarkable features: it has 1100 native species of plants; dunes formed after melted glaciers, which top out at 192ft; and 370 species of birds. Birding and fishing are popular, as is beachcombing (beach glass collecting allowed, fossil and pebble collecting prohibited).

State Park & Three Dune Challenge

The **state park** is a 2100-acre, shoreside pocket within the national park; it's located at the end of Hwy 49, near Chesterton. Don't miss the **3 Dune Challenge**, a 1.5-mile, 552ft vertical climb to the park's three highest dunes: Mt Jackson (176ft), Mt Holden (184ft) and Mt Tom (192ft). It starts on Trail 8, by the **Indiana Dunes State Park Nature Center**.

TOP TIPS

- America the Beautiful Pass holders are covered to enter the national park area, but not the state park area, of the Indiana Dunes.

- For the state park, entrance is free on weekdays, November to mid-April.

- Kemil Beach is one section of the park that's open 24 hours, for stargazing.

PRACTICALITIES

- indianadunes.com
- national park 6am-11pm, state park 7am-11pm
- 7-day pass per car $12-25

Tour the University of Notre Dame

Founded in 1842, the **University of Notre Dame** (nd.edu) is often touted as one of the USA's prettiest higher education campuses. To get a good look at it, a free walking tour is recommended (it departs from the **Eck Visitors Center**; times vary and tours are limited to the first 25 people who sign up in person). But if you're short on time, at least pop into the stunning Basilica of the Sacred Heart (a neo-Gothic cathedral awash in stained-glass windows and murals painted by Vatican artist Luigi Gregori); the Golden Dome (the university's main admin building – often considered the nation's leading collegiate landmark – with a gorgeous rotunda topped with a 4400lb statue of Mary); and the Grotto of Our Lady of Lourdes (a recreation of the original in France). All three are next to each other on the north side of God Quad.

Fairmount
Hunt down James Dean's hometown

Pocket-sized Fairmount is but a few streets surrounded by farmland, but it's on the international map as the hometown of 1950s actor James Dean, one of the original icons of cool (he was born 10.5 miles north in Marion but raised by his relatives in Fairmount). Fans can follow Dean's footsteps, from birth to death.

Start at the **James Dean Museum** (thejamesdeanmuseum.com; adult/child $10/free), where you can see the world's largest collection of his personal belongings, ranging from his baby crib and high-school car, to his 1955 Triumph TR5 Trophy 500cc and 1947 Czech 125cc motorcycles, and more. (You'll also notice tributes to Garfield creator Jim Davis, Fairmount's other famous figure.) Other spots include the **James Dean Birth Site Memorial**, a 6ft-tall black granite monument erected in 2015 to honor the spot where the House of Seven Gables once stood; the farmhouse where Jimmy grew up; and his often lipstick-kissed **gravestone** in Park Cemetery. There's also a privately owned **James Dean Gallery** (jamesdeangallery.com; free) with several rooms of memorabilia in an old Victorian home downtown. Every September, Fairmount celebrates the **James Dean Festival** – thousands of fans pour in for three days of music, classic cars, a James Dean lookalike contest and other events honoring the Hollywood legend.

TIBETAN CULTURE IN BLOOMINGTON

The 14th Dalai Lama's brother Thubten Jigme Norbu came here from Eastern Tibet, teaching at Indiana University in the 1960s; Tibetan temples, monasteries and culture followed in his footsteps. In 1979, Thubten Jigme Norbu founded the colorful, prayer-flag-covered Tibetan Mongolian Buddhist Cultural Center to introduce the people of Indiana to Tibetan culture and to support Tibetan exile communities. The center, in southern Bloomington, is a draw for its traditional stupas, gift shop, open meditation sessions and various workshops and retreats. Across the city, in northern Bloomington, the Gaden Khachoe Shing Monastery is another place of peace. And downtown, Tibetan fare features at restaurants like Little Tibet.

DRINKING IN NORTHERN INDIANA: OUR PICKS

3 Floyds Brewing: In Munster, Zombie Dust, a flowery pale ale; and Dark Lord, a legendary Russian imperial stout, have a cult following. noon-7pm Tue-Sat

18th Street Brewery: Warehouse in Hammond for saisons, sours and IPAs. Also in Gary. noon-9pm Mon-Thu, 11am-10pm Fri & Sat, 11am-6pm Sun

Mad Anthony's Auburn Tap Room: Taproom in a historic downtown building with big windows and exposed-brick walls. 11am-10pm, to 11pm Fri & Sat

Crooked Ewe Brewery: Find a wealth of hops-heavy IPAs at this riverside brewpub in South Bend. Elevated bar fare, including vegan options. noon-9pm, to 10pm Fri & Sat

Brown County State Park

Brown County

Indiana's largest state park

A few miles southeast of Nashville, **Brown County State Park** *(browncountystatepark.net; $9/day)* is Indiana's largest state park, known as the Little Smoky Mountains for its steep wooded hills and fog-cloaked ravines. Trails stripe the 15,700-acre stand of oak, hickory and birch trees, and give hikers, mountain bikers and horseback riders access to the area's green hill country. The mile-long **Ogle Hollow Nature Preserve Trail** is a good place to see the rare yellowwood tree and its fragrant blossoms. And **Bean Blossom Overlook** is one of the best spots to take in the color-shifting treetops across Brown County.

Ohio River Scenic Byway

A river town, a cave and Lincoln's boyhood home

The Ohio River marks the state's southern border – and Ohio's and Indiana's, too – with the Ohio River Scenic Byway winding its way through nearly 1000 miles of lush and hilly landscape along the churning waterway. Indiana's 303-mile portion *(ohioriverbyway.com)* of the 943-mile route comprises Hwys 56,

ARCHITECTURAL HERITAGE IN COLUMBUS

When you think of the USA's great architectural cities – Chicago, New York, Washington, DC – Columbus, IN, doesn't quite leap to mind, but it's a remarkable gallery of design. Since the 1940s, Columbus and its leading corporation, Fortune 500 engineering company Cummins, have commissioned some of the world's best architects, including Eero Saarinen, Richard Meier and IM Pei, to create both public and private buildings. More than 70 notable structures and public art pieces span a wide area. Some of the most famous are **First Christian Church**, a brick-and-limestone Modernist masterpiece; and **Miller House & Garden**, the mid-century-modern residence of Cummins president J Irwin Miller – both designed by Saarinen.

EATING & DRINKING IN SOUTHERN INDIANA: OUR PICKS

Samira: Tasty Afghan food in downtown Bloomington: excellent kebabs, vegetarian dishes and lunch buffet. *5-9pm Mon-Sat, plus 11am-2pm Thu & Fri* $$

Henry Social Club: New American fine dining and the best bar in Columbus for a boutique cocktail, set in an open-concept kitchen. *5-9pm Tue-Sat* $$$

Exchange Pub + Kitchen: In New Albany, upmarket pub with an industrial-chic ambience. Burgers do not disappoint. *11am-10pm, to 11pm Fri & Sat, to 9pm Sun* $$$

Wood Shop: In Bloomington, this is the experimental sister site of more mainstream Upland Brewing Co next door – it's the all-sours brewery where funk flows. *5-9pm Fri & Sat*

INDIANA'S HARMONIST & UTOPIAN HISTORY

In southwest Indiana, the Wabash River forms the border with Illinois. Beside it, south of I-64, captivating New Harmony is the site of two early communal-living experiments. In the 1814, the Harmony Society, a German Christian sect led by George Rapp, developed a sophisticated, self-sufficient, model community here while awaiting the Second Coming. In 1825, the Welsh utopian Robert Owen acquired the town, renaming it New Harmony. By 1827, it had failed and dissolved. Today, New Harmony retains an air of contemplation, if not otherworldliness, which can be felt at the town's information center, the Atheneum; the Roofless Church; and the Labyrinth, a recreation of the Harmonists' original hedge-maze design.

Lincoln Boyhood National Memorial

156, 62 and 66, and makes for a scenic drive, with stops at a beautifully preserved mid-19th-century river town, a cave with astonishing underground formations and Abraham Lincoln's boyhood home.

Of all the charms along this stretch, few outdo the convivial and cozy vibe of small town **Madison** *(visitmadison.org)*. Home to the largest contiguous National Historic Landmark District in the US, Madison is a hub of Federal, Greek Revival and Italianate-style architecture along its postcard-perfect Main St. Grab a burger at **Hinkle's** *(hinkleburger.com)*, an old-school diner in action since 1933; and a beer at **Mad Paddle Brewstillery** *(madpaddle.com)*, a couple of blocks south.

Heading west, **Milltown** is where you can access the beautiful **Blue River**, a tributary of the Ohio River that's perfect for a paddle. **Cave Country Canoes** *(cavecountrycanoes.com)* puts on half-, full- or two-day trips (prices vary depending on the group size). About 4 miles west, a plunge into **Marengo Cave** *(marengocave.com; adult/child 40min tour $23/14, 60min tour $26/16, combination tour $32/2)* is highly recommended. The privately owned landmark offers tours walking past stalagmites and other ancient formations.

Then, off I-64 and 4 miles south of **Dale**, the **Lincoln Boyhood National Memorial** *(nps.gov/libo; free)* is where young Abe, who grew up to become the 16th US president, lived from age seven to 21. The memorial also includes admission to a working pioneer farm, open in the summer, that's modeled after the Lincoln farm but is not the original. A 1-mile trail loop from the memorial takes in the highlights.

Ohio

CITY CHARM | ERIE ISLANDS | AMISH COUNTRY

The nation's seventh most populous state has big cities Cleveland, Cincinnati and Columbus that lead its urban charge, rolling out a spread of kicky dining options, IPA-loving breweries and one-of-a-kind museums. Northern Cleveland exudes a feisty, rock-and-roll vibe, while southern Cincinnati feels more languorous and European. Columbus – the largest of the three, with a population of over 900,000 – is the polished tech and art hub that rises up in the middle, home to Ohio State University. Meanwhile, Ohio's rural side is way off the grid, from the horse-and-buggy-filled roads of its enormous Amish community to the moonshine makers in its southeastern hills. It makes for an intriguing mash-up, with just a short drive between wildly different lifestyles. In between, the roadways lead to the world's fastest roller coasters, rocking party islands, beatnik towns, pie shops and a mist-draped national park.

Places
Cleveland p534
Cuyahoga Valley National Park p536
Cincinnati p537
Columbus p538
Sandusky p539
Kelleys Island p540
Ohio Amish Country p541
Logan p542
Dayton p542

☑ TOP TIP

Camp overnight in Hocking Hills State Park! It's Ohio's favorite park for good reason, and there are abundant campsites available, with spectacular scenery all around.

GETTING AROUND

Cleveland Hopkins International Airport is Ohio's busiest airport – linked to downtown by the Red Line train – followed by Columbus, Cincinnati and Dayton. John Glenn Columbus International Airport is 10 miles east of downtown, while Cincinnati/Northern Kentucky International Airport is in Kentucky. Cleveland, Cincinnati and Sandusky are on Amtrak train routes; Columbus is not. Regardless, Megabus and Greyhound are cheaper and faster. Driving is best. For Cuyahoga Valley, the national park is just off I-77. Amish Country lies between Cleveland (80 miles north) and Columbus (100 miles southwest), with I-71 and I-77 flanking the area. US 33 leads to Logan, and US 23 to Chillicothe and the Hopewell mounds. Within Cleveland, the **RTA** (riderta.com) runs buses and trains. Within Cincinnati, there are **Metro** (go-metro.com) buses, a **streetcar** (cincinnatibellconnector.com) and **Red Bike** (cincyredbike.org) stations.

Cleveland

From the Beatles to the Rolling Stones

Cleveland's top attraction, the **Rock and Roll Hall of Fame & Museum** *(rockhall.com; adult/youth/child $39.50/29.50/free)*, is like an overstuffed attic bursting with groovy finds: Jimi Hendrix's Stratocaster, Prince's Cloud #2 Blue Angel Guitar, Keith Moon's platform shoes, John Lennon's Sgt Pepper suit and a 1966 piece of hate mail to the Rolling Stones from a cursive-writing Fijian. It's more than memorabilia, though. Multimedia exhibits trace the history and social context of rock music and the performers who created it.

EATING IN CLEVELAND: OUR PICKS

Citizen Pie: Wood-fired Neapolitan-style pizzas, with a mighty smoked pepperoni. Second location in Ohio City. *noon-9pm Tue-Sat, to 8pm Sun* $

Mitchell's Ice Cream: Mitchell's revamped an old movie theater. Watch through big glass windows as staff blend the rich flavors. One of 10 locales. *11am-10:30pm* $

Abundance Culinary: Four types of dumplings, along with rice, noodles and mains, plus Sichuan-inspired cocktails. *8am-10pm Tue-Thu, to 11pm Fri & Sat* $$

Zhug: Upmarket Mediterranean mezze (braised lamb, smoked calamari and roasted vegetables) in casual environs. *4-10pm Mon-Thu, to 11pm Fri & Sat* $$$

Why is the museum in Cleveland? Because this is the hometown of Alan Freed, the disc jockey who popularized the term 'rock and roll' in the early 1950s, and because the city lobbied hard and paid big. Be prepared for crowds.

Explore the arts and entertainment

Cleveland's fine and performing arts are sure to keep you entertained day and night. Begin at the **Cleveland Museum of Art** *(clevelandart.org; free; closed Mondays)*, a mammoth collection of European paintings; African, Asian and American art; and special paid exhibitions – all set around a dazzling, light-drenched atrium. Head to the 2nd floor for works from Impressionists, Picasso and surrealists. Interactive touchscreens are stationed throughout, providing fun ways to learn more; download the free ArtLens app for additional content. Free guided tours depart at 1pm and 1:30pm each day; they're limited to 15 participants, so advance tickets are recommended.

Nighttime is show time at the city's **Playhouse Square** *(playhousesquare.org)*, the nation's second-largest theater district. Several stages comprise the elegant performing arts center, which hosts theater, opera, ballet and beyond. Take note of the massive sparkler dangling above: that's North America's largest outdoor chandelier, 44ft tall and shining with 4200 faux crystals.

A walk on the West Side

The West Side is home to some of Cleveland's hippest neighborhoods. Start your day at the **West Side Market** *(westsidemarket.org)*, a European-style market overflowing with greengrocers and their produce, as well as purveyors of Hungarian sausage, Italian cannoli and Polish pierogi. The surrounding **Ohio City** is an ultra walkable little enclave known for its historic buildings, vibrant street art, cute boutique shops, delicious dining scene and several breweries, including the tried-and-true **Great Lakes Brewing Company** *(greatlakesbrewing.com)*, cozy **Bookhouse Brewing** *(bookhouse.beer)* and Eastern European newcomer **Hansa Brewery** *(hansabrewery.com)*. Also here, in a pocket called Hingetown, is **Transformer Station** *(clevelandart.org; free; open Thursday to Sunday)*, a Cleveland Museum of Art–affiliated gallery that showcases emerging artists, new media and live music at a repurposed industrial substation.

Nearby, the west bank of the Flats is home to the **Greater Cleveland Aquarium** *(greaterclevelandaquarium.com;*

LAY OF 'THE LAND'

Nicknamed 'The Land,' Cleveland is bisected by the Cuyahoga River, which divides the West and East sides. The city's center is at **Public Square**, with most major attractions downtown on the lakefront. Nearby, the Warehouse District and the Flats are abuzz with a youthful vibe. Eastward are Asiatown, University Circle, Little Italy, Coventry Village and Collinwood. Westward are hip Ohio City and Tremont, straddling I-90; the western bank of the Flats; and Gordon Square Arts District, a fun pocket along Detroit Ave between W 56th and W 69th Sts. Cleveland's public transit system, the RTA, is a handy network of buses, a three-line train service and a trolley that runs between Public Square and the Wolstein Center.

DRINKING IN CLEVELAND: OUR PICKS

Noble Beast Brewing Co: A homey place for German-style ales and pub fare. *11:30am-11pm Tue-Thu, to midnight Fri & Sat to 10pm Sun*

Millard Fillmore Presidential Library: Tell your pals you're going to a presidential library. It's actually a dive bar in Collinwood. *4pm-2:30am Mon-Fri, from noon Sat & Sun*

Jerman's Cafe: One of Cleveland's oldest bars, opened in 1908 by a Slovenian immigrant. Just a few beers on tap. *noon-1am Mon & Tue, to 2am Wed-Sat, 1pm-midnight Sun*

Great Lakes Brewing Company: Second-biggest craft-beer maker in the state wins prizes for its brewed suds. *11:30am-10pm Mon-Thu, to 11pm Fri & Sat, 11am-5pm Sun*

TOP EXPERIENCE

Cuyahoga Valley National Park

The Cuyahoga River worms over a forested valley, earning its Native American name of 'crooked river' (or possibly 'place of the jawbone'). Either name is evocative, and hints at the mystical beauty that Ohio's only national park engenders on a cool morning, when the mists thread the woods and all you hear is the honk of Canadian geese and the fwup-fwup-whoosh of a great blue heron flapping over its hunting grounds.

Brandywine Falls

TOP TIPS

● Parking lots at the Ledges and Brandywine Falls fill up quickly. Opt for mornings, evenings and weekdays.

● The Boston Mills Visitor Center is a good starting point.

● If you cycle, hike or run along the towpath trail in one direction, ride the train back for just $5.

The Ledges

This overlook is probably the most photographed place in the park, with an unobstructed vista looking west over the valley to eternity. There's a loop trail nearby, a little over 2 miles in length, that's a nice leg stretcher.

Brandywine Falls

Long considered one of the park's best attractions, this pretty spill of ice-cold water sits in a wooden idyll, and is accessed via a 1.5-mile round-trip hike that features some light elevation gain (160ft).

Ohio & Erie Canal Towpath Trail

The park's main trail follows the old Ohio & Erie Canal, which once served as one of the primary historical arteries into the American west. Boats pulled by mules ran adjacent to this path, now an ideal thoroughfare for hikers and cyclists, intersecting with many of the park's other trails.

Cuyahoga Valley Scenic Railroad

An old-school iron carriage (*cvsr.org; adult/child from $25/20*) chugs along a pleasant course from Akron to Independence, going through the heart of the park, with a depot midway at Peninsula. The most expensive seats have glass-topped domes, and special themed rides are offered, too. A full round trip takes around 3½ hours.

PRACTICALITIES

● nps.gov/cuva
● 24hr
● free

adult/child $20/14), a fun and interactive experience for the littles in tow, while **Tremont** and its bevy of trendy bars are a treat for the bigs. In summer, white-sand **Edgewater Park Beach** comes alive with sunbathers, swimmers and concession stands. Finish at nearby **Gordon Square Arts District** *(gordonsquare.org)* for dinner at **Blue Habanero** *(bluehabanerocleveland.com)*, a show at the **Cleveland Public Theatre** *(cptonline.org)* or live music (and a loaded hot dog!) at **Happy Dog** *(happydogcleveland.com)*.

Cincinnati

Get acquainted with Over-the-Rhine

At downtown's northern edge, the historic **Over-the-Rhine** (OTR) neighborhood is home to an impressive collection of 19th-century Italianate and Queen Anne buildings that have morphed into trendy dining venues, bars and shops. Begin at **Findlay Market** *(findlaymarket.org)*, the wrought-iron-framed structure in continuous operation since the 1850s; and mosey around the more than 50 stalls, where you can find meat, cheese, pastries, produce, flowers and more. For a truly local experience, cross the street to **Eckerlin Meats** *(eckerlinmeats.com)* and try some homemade *guetta*, a pan-fried patty made of ground meat and steel-cut oats, often served for breakfast in a sandwich or omelet. It's a unique food you won't find anywhere else besides Cincinnati and Northern Kentucky.

From there, it's on to **Cincinnati's Brewing Heritage Trail** *(brewingheritagetrail.org)*. Findlay marks one of two trailheads – the other being at Grant Park – for this fun three-quarter-mile route that takes you past classic brewhouses and historic saloons in the neighborhood. Markers along the way tell how Cincy was one of the nation's leading beer producers in the late 1800s. Download the free app for a self-guided tour or book a guided tour.

Go museum-hopping

Cincinnati has several museums of note close to downtown, not far from the riverfront, that make for a full day of history and arts. Starting in the West End, begin at the **Cincinnati Museum Center** *(cincymuseum.org; adult/child $19.50/12.50)*, a complex that includes the **Museum of Natural History & Science** (with a cave inside!), a children's museum and a history museum. The complex occupies the 1933 Union Terminal, an art-deco jewel still used by Amtrak; its interior features fantastic murals made of local Rookwood tiles.

OHIO'S QUIRKY SIGHTS

World's Largest Rubber Stamp (Cleveland): At Willard Park, Claes Oldenburg's 70,000lb 'Free' stamp sculpture is a photo-op favorite.

American Sign Museum (Cincinnati): An awesome cache of flashing, lightbulb-studded beacons in an old parachute factory.

World's Largest Cuckoo Clock (Sugarcreek): A 23ft-tall clock lets loose every half-hour, when a mechanical Bavarian couple dances a polka.

Christmas Story House (Cleveland): The original house of the 1983 film *A Christmas Story* sits in Tremont, complete with a leg lamp.

Paul A Johnson Pencil Sharpener Museum (Logan): One man's trove of 3400 pencil sharpeners, reportedly the USA's largest.

 EATING IN CINCINNATI: OUR PICKS

Eagle OTR: Serving modern soul food, including fried chicken with spicy honey, white cheddar grits and spoon bread. *11am-10pm Sun, to 11pm Mon-Thu, to midnight Fri & Sat* **$**

Bee's Barbecue OTR: Tasty brisket, ribs, pulled pork and other offerings in casual environs with welcoming staff. *11am-11pm Tue-Thu, to midnight Fri & Sat, to 9pm Sun* **$$**

Bridges: Build your own Nepali rice bowl with meat/vegan toppings at this homey spot in Northside. Other locations: downtown, Elmwood. *11am-9pm Mon-Thu, to 10pm Fri & Sat* **$$**

Sotto: Italian fine dining tucked in a downtown basement. Reservations are a must. *11am-2pm & 4-10pm Mon-Thu, to 11pm Fri, 4-11pm Sat, 4-9pm Sun* **$$$**

Over in downtown Cincy, the **National Underground Railroad Freedom Center** *(freedomcenter.org; $16.50/11.50)* details the city's history as a prominent stop on the Underground Railroad and a hub for abolitionist activities. The center displays artifacts along the historical road from slavery to freedom, and also covers modern struggles for civil rights. A few blocks north is the **Contemporary Arts Center** *(contemporaryartscenter.org; adult/child $12/free)*, displaying modern art in an avant-garde building designed by Zaha Hadid.

Eastward, round out the day at the **Cincinnati Art Museum** *(cincinnatiartmuseum.org; free)*, where its impressive collection spans 6000 years, with an emphasis on ancient Middle Eastern and European art.

Cross the Ohio River by foot

The mighty Ohio River is the border between Ohio and Kentucky, with a couple of notable bridges connecting Cincinnati to its southern neighbors. For those interested in a little jaunt into Kentucky, it's simple and straightforward to go via one bridge, then return via the other, while also enjoying the lovely green space that flanks the river on each side. Begin by walking around the well-tended **Smale Riverfront Park**, then take the **John A Roebling Suspension Bridge** *(roeblingbridge.org)* across to Covington, KY. A forerunner of John Roebling's famous Brooklyn Bridge in New York, the elegant 1867 spanner features Romanesque arches and draped cables that are highly photogenic. From Covington, it's an easy 30-minute walk through General James Taylor Park to Newport, where you can take the pedestrian-only **Purple People Bridge** *(purplepeoplebridge.com)* back to Cincy. You'll be deposited at **Sawyer Point**, a nifty park dotted by whimsical monuments and flying pigs.

Columbus

Stroll through a German village

Wandering through this remarkably large, restored all-brick **German Village** *(germanvillage.com)*, a half-mile south of downtown, feels like you've entered the 19th century. The historic village, first platted in 1814, is complete with cobbled streets, beer halls, cute boutique shops, arts-filled parks, and Italianate and Queen Anne architecture. The **German Village Society** has archives and maps.

Bibliophiles should stop in at the **Book Loft** *(bookloft.com)*, a sprawling bookshop occupying a block of pre–Civil War

OHIO'S BEST FESTIVALS

Cleveland Kurentovanje: The city's large Slovenian population gathers at this multiday spring festival, where a parade is led by Kurenti, the mythical monsters who chase away winter.

Bockfest Cincinnati: Each March, traditional Bock beers flow at venues across Over-the-Rhine.

Oktoberfest Zinzinnati: Beer, bratwursts and mania. It's the US' largest Oktoberfest celebration, with well over half a million revelers convening at Sawyer Point.

IngenuityFest: In Cleveland, a three-day fall festival full of art, technology and creative experiences.

Blink: Large-scale light projections and interactive art feature at this four-day event in Cincinnati in the fall.

DRINKING IN CINCINNATI: OUR PICKS

Uncle Leo's: Friendly bartenders will serve you a 'spaghett' – Miller High Life with, usually, Aperol. *4-11pm Mon-Wed, to 1am Thu, to 2am Fri, noon-2am Sat, noon-11pm Sun*

Rhinegeist Brewery: One of Ohio's biggest breweries. Try Truth IPA or 20 other brews on tap. Picnic tables and a rooftop. *3-10pm Mon-Thu, noon-1am Fri & Sat, noon-9pm Sun*

Longfellow: Cozy and candlelit cocktail bar in a vintage building with creaking hardwood floors and exposed brick walls. *4pm-2am Wed-Fri, from 2pm Sat & Sun*

Low Spark: Easygoing spot; cocktails served at a bar set around an illuminated fish tank. *4pm-midnight Mon-Wed, to 2:30am Thu & Fri, noon-2:30am Sat, noon-10pm Sun*

John A Roebling Suspension Bridge

buildings, where you're guaranteed to get lost in the labyrinth of 32 rooms stacked to the rafters with bestsellers, children's books, manga, memoirs and more. After, head over to **Schmidt's** *(schmidthaus.com)* to shovel in Old Country staples like sausage and schnitzel, but save room for the whopping half-pound cream puffs.

Peep at Ohio's biggest planetarium

COSI *(cosi.org, adult/child from $30/25)*, an acronym for the Center of Science and Industry, ranks high in the pantheon of children's museums around the country, with 300-plus hands-on exhibits that include a dinosaur gallery (with a mechanical T. rex), space gallery (with a replica space station to explore) and high-wire unicycle ride. Ohio's largest planetarium, a native prairie, live science shows and a 3D theater round out the whopping spread. Check the calendar for special events, too, like COSI Farm Days and COSI After Dark.

Sandusky

Get topsy turvy and go round and round

In summer the good-time resort region of Erie Lakeshore is one of the busiest places in Ohio. Boaters come to party, daredevils come to ride roller coasters, and outdoorsy types

TOP ART SPOTS IN COLUMBUS

Otherworld: Futuristic, fantastical art museum: 32,000 sq ft of immersive mixed-reality installations.

Short North Arts District: Hosts a gallery hop the first Saturday of each month, featuring exhibitions, live performances and vendors.

Columbus Museum of Art: Highlights include Edward Hopper's *Morning Sun* and several works by Henri Matisse and Pablo Picasso.

Franklinton Fridays: Area galleries, studios and bars put on an art crawl on the second Friday of each month, with food and entertainment.

Wexner Center for the Arts: Ohio State University's contemporary arts center has cutting-edge art exhibits, films and performances.

EATING & DRINKING IN COLUMBUS: OUR PICKS

DK Diner: Classic diner experience in Grandview: omelets, corned beef hash, and biscuits and gravy. *6am-3pm Mon & Tue, to 9pm Wed-Fri, 7am-9pm Sat, 7am-3pm Sun* $

Hoyo's Kitchen: *Hoyo* is 'mother' in Somali, and the siblings running this venue use Mom's recipes. It's in North Market Downtown. *11am-7pm Tue-Sat, to 5pm Sun* $$

Service Bar: It's in Middle West Spirits Distillery, so signature cocktails are made with bourbon fresh from the tanks. Also serves food. *5-10pm Wed & Thu, from 4pm Fri & Sat*

Land-Grant Brewing Co: Couple of dozen taps, and flights. Rotating food-truck line up. *3-10pm Mon-Wed, 11am-10pm Thu, 11am-midnight Fri & Sat, 11am-8pm Sun*

CANTON: BIRTHPLACE OF THE NFL

You may be wondering why the **Pro Football Hall of Fame** is located in Canton, Ohio. It's because Canton is where the American Professional Football Association, which later became the National Football League (NFL), was founded on September 17, 1920. Back then, Canton had its own team, the very successful Canton Bulldogs, who played in the Ohio League, winning titles in 1916, 1917 and 1919, before joining the national league and becoming a 1922 and 1923 champion there too – the NFL's first two-time champion. The Bulldogs' players included the legendary Jim Thorpe. All that and the people of Canton campaigned mightily for it.

Cedar Point

come to cycle and kayak. The season lasts from mid-May to mid-September – and then just about everything shuts down.

For kids (and adults) who love a thrill, a stop at **Cedar Point** *(cedarpoint.com; from $70)* is a must. As one of the world's top amusement parks, it's known for its 18 adrenaline-pumping roller coasters, with such stomach-droppers as Steel Vengeance, which provides 27 seconds of weightlessness, the most 'airtime' of any coaster on the planet.

Nearby, the whimsical **Merry-Go-Round Museum** *(merrygoroundmuseum.org; adult/youth/child $10/6/free)* features a fully refurbished, vintage Allan Herschell carousel headlined by lead horse, the c 1915 Stargazer. Children will delight in taking a spin atop antique ponies, or maybe a lion, an elephant, a pig or an ostrich – and even a less traditional sea monster. In addition to enjoying the museum's centerpiece, you can also go on a tour to learn about merry-go-round history and culture, and watch artisans at work as they restore period pieces.

Kelleys Island

Gargantuan glacial grooves

For a tamer experience, Kelleys Island offers pretty 19th-century buildings, pleasant beaches and scenic landscapes.

 EATING & DRINKING ON THE ERIE LAKESHORE: OUR PICKS

Topsy Turvey's Bar & Grill: Wharf-side venue with Lake Erie perch, homemade chili, and Cuban and other sandwiches. *11am-8pm Mon-Fri, from 9am Sat & Sun* **$$**

Village Pump: Old-school Kelleys Island tavern. Tuck into fried perch, walleye bites and lobster chowder. Brandy Alexander is the house cocktail. *11am-9pm* **$$**

Forge: In an old blacksmith shop in Put-In-Bay. Stoke your taste buds with crepes and more. *9am-10pm Mon, Thu & Fri, from 8am Sat & Sun, 5-10pm Wed* **$$**

Beer Barrel Saloon: A Put-In-Bay pub with plenty of space for imbibing – its bar is 406ft long, billed as the world's longest. *noon-11pm*

Get there by ferry *(kelleysislandferry.com; round-trip adult/ youth/child $24/16/free)*, which departs from Marblehead (about 30 minutes one way). Once deposited on the island's south shore, take a moment to appreciate the petroglyphs of **Inscription Rock**, not far from the ferry terminal. Native Americans who used the island as a hunting ground carved symbols into this boulder sometime between 1200 and 1600. It's not known exactly who made them, but historians believe they're the work of either the Late Prehistoric Period Sandusky culture, or the Erie, Cat, Neutral or other Indigenous peoples living in the region when Europeans arrived.

On the island's north shore, another wonder awaits: glacial grooves raked through the limestone. Created some 18,000 years ago, they're the largest and most easily accessible glacial grooves in the world, with gouges some 400ft long, 35ft wide and up to 10ft deep. If you're looking to camp overnight, **Kelleys Island State Park** features a popular ground with over 100 tent and RV sites, 6 miles of hiking trails with birds flitting by and a secluded, sandy beach.

Ohio Amish Country

Spend time in the USA's second-largest Amish community

A sojourn in the region provides pleasures of a slow kind. **Kidron**, on Rte 52, makes a good starting point, and if it's a Thursday, there's no better place than **Kidron Auction** *(kidronauction.com)*. Follow the buggy lineup down the road to the livestock barn. Hay and straw get auctioned at 10:15am, followed by cows at noon, pigs at 1pm, and sheep and goats after that. Next up is **Lehman's** *(lehmans.com)*, the Amish community's main purveyor of modern-looking products that use no electricity, housed in a 32,000-sq-ft barn.

About 25 minutes south, at **Yoder's Amish Home** *(yoders amishhome.com; adult/child $15/10)*, tour a local home, one-room schoolhouse and barn, before taking a buggy ride through a field. Over near Berlin, stop in at **Heini's Cheese Chalet** *(bunkerhillcheese.com)* to grab abundant samples of its 100% natural, unpasteurized cheeses, then stock up on all the Gouda, bleu, cheddar and other varieties you could want. Across the street, **Kauffman's Country Bakery** *(kauffmans countrybakery.com)* has the fresh bread to pair with it. Pick up a couple of loaves, and maybe a cinnamon pretzel doughnut or mint fudge brownie while you're at it.

Further southwest at **Hershberger's Farm & Bakery**, gorge on dozens of kinds of pie, homemade ice-cream cones and

MORE ABOUT THE AMISH

Rural Wayne and Holmes counties are home to the USA's second-largest Amish community. Visiting here is like entering a preindustrial time warp. Descendants of conservative Dutch-Swiss religious factions who migrated to the USA during the 18th century, the Amish continue to follow the Ordnung (way of life), in varying degrees. Many adhere to rules prohibiting the use of electricity, telephones and motorized vehicles. They wear traditional clothing, farm the land with plow and mule, and go to church in horse-drawn buggies. Others are not so strict. Keep in mind the Amish typically view photographs as taboo, so don't take photos of people without permission.

EATING & DRINKING IN AMISH COUNTRY: OUR PICKS

Mrs Yoder's Kitchen: In Mt Hope, enjoy homey Amish fare in simple environs. Order mains à la carte, or fill up a plate at the buffet. *11am-7pm Mon-Sat* $

Boyd & Wurthmann Restaurant: In Berlin, sample pancakes, pies and Amish specialties such as country-fried steak. Cash only. *5:30am-3:30pm Mon-Thu, to 7:30pm Fri & Sat* $

Park Street Pizza: It seems all of Sugarcreek is here at night. Wood-fired pies with farm-grown ingredients. *3-9pm Tue-Thu, from 11am Fri & Sat, 11am-8pm Sun* $

Wooly Pig Farm Brewery: Part of a 90-acre Fresno farm. Sit outside or in the tasting room for German-style beers. *1-9pm Wed & Thu, to 10pm Fri, noon-10pm Sat, noon-7pm Sun*

MORE OF OHIO'S TOP STATE PARKS & FORESTS

Malabar Farm State Park: This park in Lucas has a lot going on: hiking and horse trails, tractor-drawn farm tours and more.

John Bryan State Park: The highlight at this Yellow Springs park is Clifton Gorge, cut by the pretty Little Miami River.

Hueston Woods State Park: In College corner, golfing, horseback riding, fishing, camping, a nature center and a covered bridge.

Mohican-Memorial State Forest: Between Cleveland and Columbus, more than 4000 acres of forest with over 50 miles of hiking and cycling trails.

South Bass Island State Park: Set atop white cliffs on the island's southwest side, featuring a fishing pier, small rocky beach and watercraft rentals.

seasonal produce from the market inside. Pet the farmyard animals *($8)* and take pony rides *($5)* and draft horse rides *($6)* outside.

Logan
Ohio's most beloved park

Twelve miles southwest of Logan is Ohio's most popular park, **Hocking Hills** *(ohiodnr.gov; free)*. Splendid to explore in any season, it's especially lovely in autumn. Thirty miles of hiking trails meander through the forest past waterfalls and gorges. Two of the park's most famed spots are **Ash Cave** and **Old Man's Cave**, where several short paths (less than a half-mile) deliver scenic payoffs beset with cascades. Nearby **Cedar Falls** has a half-mile trail edged by steep rock walls that leads to a peaceful waterfall and pool. You can also rent a boat and paddle the Hocking River. The visitor center has maps and exhibits of the area's unique geology. There are also cabins and campsites for spending the night.

Also inside Hocking Hills is the **John Glenn Astronomy Park** *(jgap.info; free)*, where visitors have the awe-inspiring opportunity to gaze up at some of the country's darkest skies. The park features 12 telescopes – including one of Ohio's largest – that allow earthlings obsessed with the universe to peer at stars, planets, the moon, nebulae, galaxies and comets, with astronomers and other star experts nearby to interpret what you're seeing. Programs, which are free but should be reserved in advance, take place on Friday and Saturday nights, weather permitting, from March through November. Check the park's Facebook page for the most up-to-date information.

In addition to the small, retractable-roof observatory, there is the adjacent Solar Plaza that has been designed to capture the sun's rays during solstices and equinoxes – a tradition practiced at Stonehenge, England; Chaco Canyon, New Mexico; and elsewhere for centuries.

Dayton
On the aviation trail

Dayton leans hard on its 'Birthplace of Aviation' tagline, and the Wright sights definitely deliver. Begin your day of aircraft admiration on the West Side at the **Dayton Aviation Heritage National Historical Park** *(nps.gov/daav; free)*, where the visitor center, **Wright Cycle Company shop** and

---

EATING & DRINKING IN SOUTHEASTERN OHIO: OUR PICKS

Union Street Diner: Fueling Athenians for decades; everything from omelets and hash browns to chicken-fried steak, pies and milkshakes. *8am-2pm* $

Little Fish Brewing Co: Taproom and beer garden in Athens. Saisons and sours are the specialty. *noon-10pm Tue-Thu, to 11pm Fri, 11am-11pm Sat, 11am-10pm Mon*

Brewery 33: In Logan, sip craft beer, agave cocktails, cider or mead. Dogs bring their humans for the outdoor seating. *noon-9pm Mon-Thu, to 10pm Fri & Sat, to 8pm Sun*

Hocking Hills Moonshine: A stop at this Logan distillery won't disappoint. Friendly staff will give you a tour with very affordable samples, too. *11am-8pm Mon-Sat*

Ash Cave, Hocking Hills

original site of the Wright Brothers' home are all within a one-block radius, between W 3rd and 4th Sts, and S Williams and Shannon Sts. The visitor center screens a film about the Wright Brothers in the original location of their second print shop, while the cycle company presents exhibits in the original building of their fourth bike shop – yes, Orville and Wilbur were busy men.

A couple of miles south in **Carillon Historical Park**, the **Wright Brothers National Museum** is where you'll see the 1905 Wright Flyer III biplane and a replica of the Wright workshop. And about 10 miles northeast is the **Huffman Prairie Flying Field**, looking much as it did in 1904. Walk the 1-mile trail that loops around, pausing at the history-explaining placards. Indoors to out, it's a surprisingly moving experience to see the cluttered workshop where Orville and Wilbur conjured their ideas and the lonely field where they tested their plane.

Then there's the **National Museum of the US Air Force** *(nationalmuseum.af.mil; free)*, a mind-blowing expanse with miles of planes, rockets and more. Located at Wright-Patterson Air Force Base, the staggering complex of hangars holds just about every aircraft you can think of from through the ages – from a Wright Brothers 1909 Flyer to a Sopwith Camel (WWI biplane). Be sure to visit Building 4 for spacecraft and presidential planes (including the first Air Force One).

The aircraft-themed attractions don't stop there. Finish off your day with a cold one at **Warped Wing Brewing Company** *(warpedwing.com)*, which takes its name from the Wright brothers' breakthrough concept of wing-warping.

OHIO'S ADENA & HOPEWELL HERITAGE

Long before the Europeans came, the Ohio River Valley was the Native home in the Early and Middle Woodland periods (200 BCE to 500 CE) of the, respectively, Adena and Hopewell peoples, whose legacies can still be seen in the huge geometric earthworks and burial mounds they left behind. Of all the mounds that dot Southeastern Ohio, Serpent Mound in Peebles, 50 miles southwest of Chillicothe, is perhaps the most captivating. The giant, uncoiling snake stretches over a quarter of a mile and is the largest effigy mound in the world. South of Columbus, about 3 miles north of Chillicothe, variously shaped ceremonial mounds spread over 13-acre Mound City, a mysterious town of the dead. It's part of the **Hopewell Culture National Historical Park**.

Michigan

BEACH TOWNS | WINE COUNTRY | DYNAMIC DETROIT

Places
Detroit p545
Dearborn p549
Kalamazoo p550
Lansing p550
Ann Arbor p551
Grand Rapids p551
Charlevoix & Petoskey p552
Sleeping Bear Dunes National Lakeshore p553
Michigan's Wine Country p555
The M-22 p555
Mackinac Island p556
Isle Royale National Park p557
Pictured Rocks National Lakeshore p558
Marquette p559
Porcupine Mountains p559

More, more, more – Michigan is the Midwest state that cranks it up. It sports more beaches than the Atlantic seaboard. More than half the state is covered by forests. And more cherries and berries get shoveled into pies here than anywhere else in the USA. Plus Detroit is one of the Midwest's most exciting cities, reinventing itself daily with street art and fresh architecture.

Michigan occupies prime real estate, surrounded by four of the five Great Lakes – Superior, Michigan, Huron and Erie. Islands – Mackinac, Manitou and Isle Royale – freckle its coast and make top touring destinations. Surf beaches, colored sandstone cliffs and trekkable sand dunes also woo visitors.

The state consists of two parts split by water: the larger Lower Peninsula (LP), shaped like a mitten; and the smaller, lightly populated Upper Peninsula (UP), shaped like a slipper. They are linked by the gasp-worthy Mackinac Bridge, which spans the Straits of Mackinac.

 GETTING AROUND

Detroit has an enormously busy airport that serves as a Midwest hub. Within Detroit, the **QLine streetcar** *(qlinedetroit.com)* and the **People Mover** *(thepeoplemover.com)* provide some handy transport. Grand Rapids, Lansing and Traverse City have smaller air facilities. Amtrak stops throughout the Lower Peninsula's southern half, including in Detroit, Grand Rapids, Ann Arbor, New Buffalo and Holland. Megabus and Greyhound are faster and more widespread. Per usual, driving is fastest. I-75 is the only Interstate that enters the Upper Peninsula. Ferries to Isle Royale National Park sail from Houghton and Copper Harbor. On the west, the ferries that sail across Lake Michigan to/from Wisconsin dock in Muskegon and Ludington. On the region's eastern edge, Michigan has four border crossings to Canada, with the busiest at Detroit.

Detroit

MAP P546

Admire Rivera, Picasso and local artists

From fine art to street art, Detroit is a creative wonderland. First, **Detroit Institute of Arts** *(dia.org; adult/child $20/8)* holds one of the world's premier art collections, and its centerpiece is Diego Rivera's mural *Detroit Industry*, which fills an entire room and reflects the city's blue-collar labor history. Beyond it are Picassos, Caravaggios, suits of armor, modern African American paintings, puppets and troves more spread through 100-plus galleries. A 10-minute walk south, the **Museum of Contemporary Art Detroit** *(mocadetroit.org; adult/child $12/free)* is set in an abandoned, graffiti-slathered auto dealership. Heat lamps hang from the ceiling over peculiar exhibits that change every few months. Music and literary events take place regularly. The on-site cafe–cocktail bar is popular.

For street art, head to the **Lincoln Street Art Park**, an industrial site abutting a recycling facility where you'll see vivid graffiti, murals and sculptures made from found objects. It's a quintessential slice of urban-cool, DIY Detroit that's always changing, as local artists continue to add to it. DJ-fueled dance parties take place on occasion; keep an eye on its Facebook page.

☑ TOP TIP

Don't leave Michigan without trying a pasty! Driving around the Upper Peninsula, you'll see plenty of shops selling the local meat-and-vegetable pot pies brought over by Cornish miners 160 years ago.

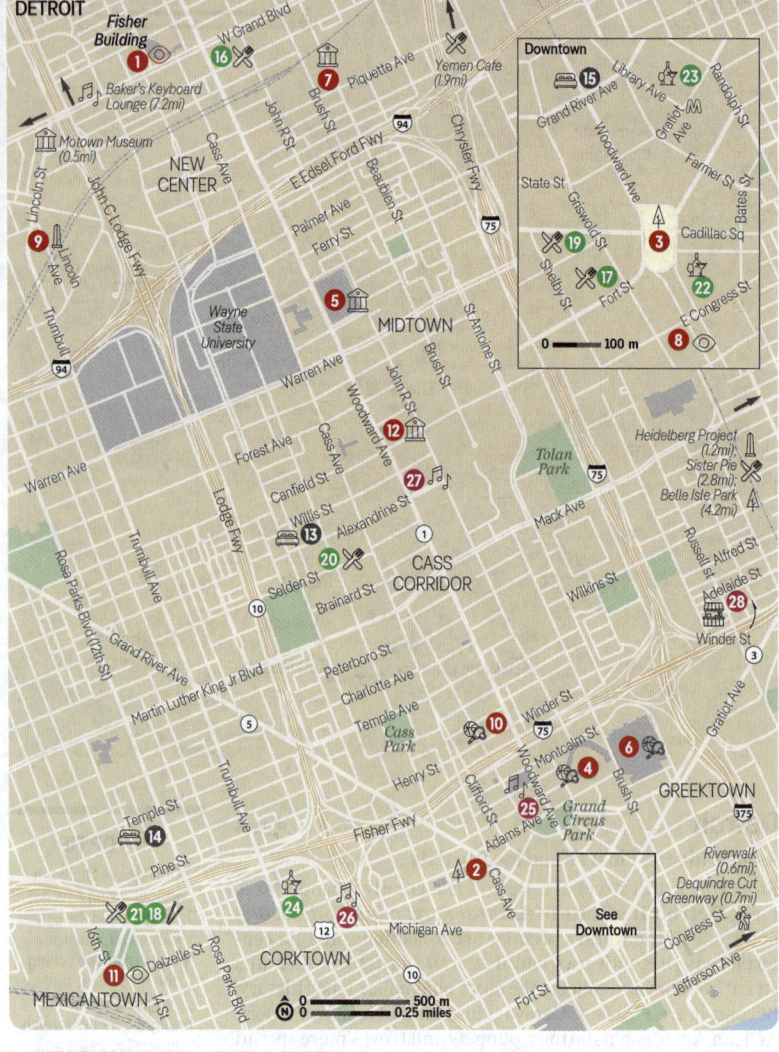

★ HIGHLIGHTS
1 Fisher Building

● SIGHTS
2 Beacon Park
3 Campus Martius Park
4 Comerica Park
5 Detroit Institute of Arts
6 Ford Field
7 Ford Piquette Avenue Plant
8 Guardian Building
9 Lincoln Street Art Park
10 Little Caesars Arena
11 Michigan Central Station
12 Museum of Contemporary Art Detroit

● SLEEPING
13 El Moore Lodge
14 Hostel Detroit
15 Shinola Hotel

● EATING
16 Baobab Fare
17 Dime Store
18 Ima
19 Lafayette Coney Island
20 Selden Standard
21 Slows Bar BQ

● DRINKING & NIGHTLIFE
22 Grand Trunk Pub
23 Standby
24 UFO Bar

● ENTERTAINMENT
25 Cliff Bell's
26 Lager House
27 Magic Stick

● SHOPPING
28 Eastern Market

And then there's the **Heidelberg Project**: polka-dotted streets, houses covered in Technicolor paint blobs, strange doll sculptures in yards – this is no acid trip, but rather a block-spanning art installation. It's the brainchild of artist Tyree Guyton, who wanted to beautify his rundown community and has been at it for nearly 40 years. It's an ever-evolving work in progress, and now it's undergoing a transformation from a founder-driven project to a community-focused one, celebrating emerging artists.

Eat your heart out at the Eastern Market

The sprawling, multi-shed **Eastern Market** (easternmarket.org) bills itself as the largest historic market district in the US, with more than 200 vendors. Whether it's produce, cheese, spices, flowers or beyond, you're sure to find nearly anything your heart desires. Saturday is the main market day, open 6am to 4pm year-round, but you can also turn up Monday through Friday to browse the specialty shops and cafes that flank the halls on Russell and Market Sts. In addition, from June through September, and in November and December, there are scaled-down markets on Tuesdays and craft markets on Sundays. Stop in at the Welcome Center for maps, directories, recipes and more information.

The sounds of jazz, Motown and beyond

Go on a musical tour of Detroit. By day, hit the **Motown Museum** (motownmuseum.org; adult/youth/child $20/17/free; closed Mon), where you can take a tour of the row of modest houses where Berry Gordy launched Motown Records – and the careers of Stevie Wonder, Diana Ross, Marvin Gaye and Michael Jackson – with an $800 loan in 1959. Gordy and Motown split for Los Angeles in 1972, but you can still step into humble Studio A and see where the famed names recorded their first hits. Then by night, bask in the smooth sounds of two of Detroit's most historic jazz clubs, the legendary **Baker's Keyboard Lounge** (bakerskeyboardloungedet.com) and **Cliff Bell's** (cliffbells.com). Continuously operating since 1934, Baker's is the world's oldest jazz club, a character-filled time capsule of a space with a small stage and curving art-deco bar, styled as piano keys. Cliff Bell's, meanwhile, is an elegant, candlelit space decked out in mahogany and brass, that started in 1935, before shuttering for a spell between 1985 and 2006. And if rap, rock and indie are more your jam, then **Magic Stick** (majesticdetroit.com) is the place for you.

MOTOR CAPITAL OF THE WORLD

French explorer Antoine de La Mothe Cadillac founded Detroit in 1701. Sweet fortune arrived in the 1920s, when Henry Ford began churning out cars. He didn't invent the automobile, as is sometimes mistakenly believed, but he did perfect assembly-line manufacturing and mass-production techniques. The result was the Model T, the first car the USA's middle class could afford to own. Detroit quickly became the motor capital of the world. General Motors (GM), Chrysler and Ford were all headquartered in or near Detroit (and still are). But Japanese competitors shook the industry in the 1970s. Detroit entered an era of deep decline, losing about two-thirds of its population.

EATING IN DETROIT: OUR PICKS

MAP P546

Sister Pie: Owner Lisa Ludwinski (a 2019 James Beard Award finalist) and her female bakers create amazing treats at this corner storefront. *10am-3pm Sat & Sun* $

Dime Store: A cozy, diner-esque venue with sandwiches, truffle mayo-dipped fries and eggy brunch dishes on the menu. *8am-3pm Mon-Tue & Thu-Sun* $

Slows Bar BQ: Southern-style barbecue in Corktown, with three-meat combo plates. Vegetarians have a couple of options, too. *11am-9pm, to 10pm Fri & Sat* $$

Selden Standard: Farm-to-table restaurant serving small plates, including fresh-caught fish, roasted vegetables and house-made bread and butter. *5-10pm* $$$

Support the home team

Detroit is the only US city to host all its major league men's sports teams in the heart of downtown. What's more, they're all in the same neighborhood. If you're in Detroit for a game, spectating can be an affordable and fun way to experience the local sports fandom. Head to **Ford Field** to cheer on Detroit's National Football League (NFL) team, the Lions; **Comerica Park** for its Major League Baseball (MLB) team, the Tigers; and **Little Caesars Arena**, which hosts both the Pistons (National Basketball Association; NBA) and Red Wings (National Hockey League; NHL).

Appreciate architectural grandeur

From Michigan Central Station (the beaux-arts rail terminal designed by the architect of New York's Grand Central) to art-deco beauties like the Fisher and Guardian buildings, Detroit is full of architectural grandeur that harken back to its heyday.

In Corktown, take in the transformation of **Michigan Central Station** *(michigancentral.com; free)*, which after closing in 1988, was left to fall into decline, becoming a symbol of the city's shattered economy. In 2018, Ford Motor Company bought it, and in 2024, it reopened as a new innovation campus. The Station is the focal point of the broader Michigan Central, a 30-acre tech and culture hub with workspace, commercial space, restaurants, parks and plazas. Visitors can book a 90-minute tour journeying through the Station's restoration.

Downtown, the **Guardian Building** *(guardianbuilding.com)* was originally commissioned as a 'cathedral of finance.' Indeed, this distinctive, 40-story, redbrick building with green and white accents was the world's tallest masonry structure when it opened in 1929. The interior is a colorful explosion of marble, mosaic and murals that draw from Aztec, art deco and local influences. For a behind-the-scenes peek of the building's history, arrange a tour through **City Tour Detroit** *(citytourdetroit.com; adult/child $12/6)*.

North, in New Center, the **Fisher Building** *(fisherbuilding.city)* is a 1928 masterpiece from the man who built Detroit, Albert Kahn. Its imposing art-deco exterior is made from Minnesota granite and Maryland marble, while its interior rivals any Italian cathedral – from the soaring vaulted ceilings, featuring an array of intricate, hand-painted patterns, to the sparkling mosaics by Hungarian artist Géza Maróti and gleaming marble on the walls. **Pure Detroit** runs tours *(puredetroit.com; $15)*.

FROM MOTOWN TO ROCK CITY

Motown Records and soul music put Detroit on the map in the 1960s, while the thrashing punk rock of the Stooges and MC5 was the 1970s' response to that smooth sound. By 1976, Detroit was dubbed 'Rock City' by a Kiss song. In the early 2000s hard-edged garage rock pushed the city to the music-scene forefront, thanks to homegrown stars such as the White Stripes, Von Bondies and Dirtbombs, while Eminem gave Detroit its rap bona fides. And then there's techno, the electronic dance music that DJs in the city created in the mid-1980s; heavy on synthesizer melodies and complex machine rhythms, it became a global sensation. One of the world's largest electronic music festivals still takes place in the city annually in honor of the style.

DRINKING IN DETROIT: OUR PICKS

MAP P546

Standby: Hiding in the Belt alleyway, an innovative resto–bar presenting creative cocktails. *5pm-1am Sun, Wed & Thu, to 2am Fri & Sat*

Lager House: Corktown staple: live music, extensive beer list, tasty New Orleans–style grub. *1pm-midnight Mon-Thu, to 2am Fri, 9am-2am Sat, 9am-midnight Sun*

Grand Trunk Pub: Once the Grand Trunk Railroad ticket hall. Vast food and drink menu. *11am-10pm Mon-Wed, to midnight Thu, to 1am Fri & Sat, 10am-10pm Sun*

UFO Bar: A hip hangout featuring cheap beer, grilled cheese sandwiches, indie music and retro vibes. *4pm-2am Tue-Sun*

Guardian Building

The first Ford Model T

More than sand dunes, beaches and Mackinac Island fudge, Michigan is synonymous with cars. To trace the state's automotive history, begin in Detroit with a look at the **Ford Piquette Avenue Plant** *(fordpiquetteplant.org; adult/youth/child $20/10/free)*, the landmark factory where Henry Ford cranked out the first Model T. Admission includes a detailed tour by enthusiastic docents, plus loads of shiny vehicles from 1904 onward.

You can see other iconic vehicles in Dearborn, Kalamazoo (p550) and Lansing (p550).

Dearborn

Historical tour of vintage cars

In Dearborn, the quintessential **Henry Ford Museum of American Innovation** *(thehenryford.org; adult/youth/child $38/28.50/free, parking extra, discounted for paying online)* is loaded with vintage cars, including the first one Ford ever built, the 1896 gas-powered Quadricycle. The museum also contains a fascinating wealth of American culture, such as the chair Lincoln was sitting in when he was assassinated, the presidential limo in which Kennedy was killed, the hot-dog-shaped Oscar Mayer Wienermobile and the bus on which Rosa

---

DETROIT'S BEST PARKS, PLAZAS & PEDESTRIAN WAYS

Belle Isle Park: Floating in the Detroit River, parkland with trails, kayaking, a glass-domed conservatory, beach, aquarium and maritime museum.

Riverwalk: From Hart Plaza to Mt Elliott St, this 3-mile riverfront path passes several parks and outdoor theaters.

Beacon Park: Gathering place featuring food trucks, local vendors, and free concerts and yoga.

Campus Martius Park: In the heart of downtown, a plaza with a fountain, stage, restaurant and bar, plus an ice rink in winter and sandy beach in summer.

Dequindre Cut Greenway: Halfway along the Riverwalk, near Orleans St, a 1.5-mile path juts north, offering a pleasant passageway to Eastern Market.

EATING IN DETROIT: OUR PICKS

Lafayette Coney Island: A 'coney' is a hot dog smothered with chili and onions. It's a Detroit specialty. *9am-midnight, to 2am Fri & Sat* $

Yemen Cafe: Hamtramck favorite serving amazing Arabic food like slow-cooked lamb *haneeth*, *fahsah* (stew) and hummus. *8am-1am* $$

Baobab Fare: Mouthwatering Burundian restaurant. Signature dish is *nyumbani*: a slow-simmered beef and tomato sauce. *11am-9pm Tue-Sun* $$

Ima: Modern *izakaya* experience: outstanding ramen, udon, gyoza, sushi and more. Sake and beer as well. *11am-10pm Mon-Thu, to 11pm Fri, from noon Sat & Sun* $$

DETROIT'S BLACK ROLLER-SKATING CULTURE

Roller-skating remains a beloved pastime in Detroit, and the Black skating community has long been at the center of the city's unique and innovative skating style. In a time when skating rinks barred/limited Black skaters, one family broke barriers when they opened the first Black-owned skating rink, RollerCade, in 1955. In the late 1950s through early 1970s, Black skating culture grew hand in hand with Motown; Detroit-style skating characterized by synchronized movements that follow the beat. RollerCade is still in operation, and many other roller rinks, communities and events have popped up on the scene, like Motown Roller Club and Soul Skate Detroit. The biannual festival draws the world's best skaters and is next slated for May 2026.

University of Michigan Union building

Parks refused to give up her seat. At the adjacent **Ford Rouge Factory Tour** *(adult/youth/child $26/19.50/free ; closed Sun)*, you can watch F-150 trucks roll off the assembly line; while in **Greenfield Village** *(adult/youth/child $41/30.75/free)*, you can ride in a Model T from 1923. Combination tickets are available. Across the parking lot, the separate interactive **Automotive Hall of Fame** *(automotivehalloffame.org; adult/youth/child $10/4/free; Thu-Sun)* focuses on the people behind notable cars, such as Mr Ferdinand Porsche and Mr Soichiro Honda.

Kalamazoo
Diner and drives

If you're on the car trail and you've got the time, head north of Kalamazoo along Hwy 43 to Hickory Corners and stop at the **Gilmore Car Museum** *(gilmorecarmuseum.org; adult/youth/child $20/12/free)*. Comprising some 20 buildings, this massive museum is filled with nearly 400 vintage autos, including 15 Rolls-Royces dating back to a 1910 Silver Ghost. Take a ride in a classic car, have a hot dog at the Blue Moon Diner and even stay overnight at a rented campsite. Check the calendar in advance, as there are lots of special car shows, seasonal festivals and live music events happening year-round.

Lansing
A riverside route through Michigan's capital

Tour Michigan's capital city by following the **Lansing River Trail** *(lansingrivertrail.org)*, a 16-mile route of paved paths and bridges that run alongside the Grand and Red Cedar rivers. Linking several parks, museums, a farmers market and a zoo, the trail system makes for a convenient way to explore some of the city's top attractions, either by bike or on foot.

Start at **Turner Dodge Park** and head south through **Old Town**, Lansing's arts and entertainment district, and stop at **Brenke Fish Ladder**, a peaceful sculpture-dotted park that's great for picnicking. Keep going and you'll reach the city's indoor farmers market, a science center and the **RE Olds Transportation Museum** *(reoldsmuseum.org; adult/ youth/child $10/7/free)*. Featuring a whopping garage full of shiny vintage cars that date back nearly 140 years, the museum, closed Mondays, leads guided 45-minute tours every Friday and Saturday at 1pm *(free with admission)* and hosts the Car Capital Auto Show each summer.

Further south, where the Grand and Red Cedar rivers converge, head east to **Potter Park Zoo**. From there, continue to follow the Red Cedar River eastward toward **Michigan State University**, or opt to veer south and link up with Sycamore Creek. This is the most naturally scenic part of the trail network, with acres of wetlands, wildflower-blanketed meadows and woodlands. (**Fenner Nature Center** makes for a good place to take it all in.) And for those who can't get enough of RE Olds, his tombstone is nearby too, tucked within **Mount Hope Cemetery**.

Ann Arbor
Michigan's most popular college town

Spend some time in the liberal and bookish little city that's home to the **University of Michigan**. Ann Arbor's walkable downtown is loaded with free-trade coffee shops, bookstores and brewpubs. If it's Saturday, peruse the **Farmers Market**: a bounty of goods from the surrounding farms and orchards, offering up everything from spicy pickles to cider to mushroom-growing kits. Make a stop at **Zingerman's Delicatessen** for one of the best Reuben sandwiches you'll ever have. From there, head south toward campus, where you can check out, all for free, the **University of Michigan Museum of Art** – there's a nice collection of Asian ceramics, Tiffany glass and modern abstract works – and the **University of Michigan Museum of Natural History**. Finish with a stroll through **Nichols Arboretum**, a 123-acre oasis of greenery that features a restored prairie landscape and North America's largest peony garden.

Grand Rapids
Tour one of the USA's best beer cities

Once voted the USA's best beer city, Grand Rapids now has 40 craft breweries in and within a half-hour drive of town.

MORE OF MICHIGAN'S BEST MUSEUMS

Great Lakes Shipwreck Museum: Displaying the vestiges of the vessels that have sunk on 'Shipwreck Coast,' the UP stretch from Munising to Whitefish Point.

Broad Art Museum: A parallelogram of stainless steel and glass, designed by Zaha Hadid in East Lansing.

Arab American National Museum: In Dearborn, home to one of the largest Arab American communities, showcasing the artifacts of well-known Arab Americans.

Grand Rapids African American Museum & Archives: Commemorating the contributions of local African Americans to history and culture.

Grand Rapids Public Museum: Established in 1854, Michigan's oldest museum features history, science and a 1928 carousel.

 EATING & DRINKING IN CENTRAL MICHIGAN: OUR PICKS

Downtown Market Grand Rapids: Stylish food hall. Standouts are Fish Lads and Love's Ice Cream. *11am-7pm Mon-Thu, to 8pm Fri, 10am-8pm Sat, 10am-7pm Sun* **$**

Chez Olga: A taste of the Caribbean in Grand Rapids; try curried goat, jerk chicken and creole tofu and more. Looks like a hobbit house! *5-9pm Mon, from 11am Tue-Sat* **$$**

Stella's Lounge: Grand Rapids restaurant. Award-winning stuffed burgers and other bar fare, including vegan options. *4pm-midnight Mon & Tue, from noon Wed-Sun, to 1am Fri & Sat* **$**

Naing Myanmar Family Restaurant: Lansing takeout spot. Traditional dishes from Burma, Malaysia and Thailand. Small grocery attached. *11am-8pm Tue-Sat* **$**

MORE DUNES IN MICHIGAN

They don't call Michigan's 300-mile western shoreline the Gold Coast for nothing.

Warren Dunes: Three miles of beachfront, with climbable dunes 260ft high.

Nordhouse Dunes: Within the Huron-Manistee National Forest, one of Lake Michigan's wildest stretches of shoreline.

Rosy Mound Natural Area: Boardwalk over wooded dunes to the lakeshore; interpretive signs along the way.

Silver Lake Dunes: Only dunes in Michigan where you're allowed to drive your own off-road vehicle.

Arcadia Dunes: Equipped with a universally accessible trail. The Baldy trailhead is here.

Saugatuck Dunes State Park: Dunes over 200ft tall, where visitors can book Saugatuck Dune Rides.

The **Beer City Brewsader app** *(experiencegr.com)* shows you where they are, and allows you to check in at each brewery you visit – when you reach eight, a free Brewsader T-shirt comes your way.

Top picks in Grand Rapids include **Vivant Brewery** for Belgian-style beers in an old chapel, the huge rock-and-roll-style **Founders Brewing Co**, **Mitten Brewing Company** and its wide-ranging brews in a cool old firehouse, and inventive neighborhood gem **Harmony Brewing Company**.

If you prefer a guided experience, book a tour through the popular **Grand Rapids Beer Tours** *(grbeertours.com; incl samples from $70)*. These van tours stop at three or four breweries, where a guide leads you through production facilities and tastings.

Charlevoix & Petoskey
Visit Hemingway's haunts

A number of writers have ties to northwest Michigan, but none are as famous as Ernest Hemingway, who spent the summers of his youth at his family's cottage on Walloon Lake. Go on a self-guided tour of the area to view the places that made their way into his writing. The **Michigan Hemingway Society** *(michiganhemingwaysociety.org)* has all the info you need. In Petoskey, stop at the **Little Traverse History Museum** *(petoskeymuseum.org; adult/child $5/free)* to see a collection that includes rare 1st-edition books the author autographed for a friend when he visited in 1947. Then head over to the nearby **City Park Grill** *(cityparkgrill.com)* to toss back a drink and enjoy some fresh-caught fish at the bar where Hemingway was reportedly a regular.

In Boyne City, there is the **Horton Bay General Store** *(hortonbaygeneralstore.com)*, which readers will recognize for its 'high false front' from Hemingway's short story *Up in Michigan*. The old-time shop now sells sandwiches, charcuterie, ice cream, spirits and wine on the 1st floor, and runs an inn on the 2nd floor. Next door, the **Red Fox Inn**, now listed on the National Register of Historic Places, is where Hemingway would stay with his fishing buddy Vollie Fox. It now operates a shop, with erratic hours, offering Hemingway books and memorabilia.

EATING ON THE GOLD COAST: OUR PICKS

Morning Star Café: Cooking up the best breakfast in Grand Haven. The Michigan blueberry pancakes are a winner. *6:30am-2:30pm* $

Spanglish: Mexican recipes made with Michigan ingredients in Traverse City, with lots of vegetarian and vegan options. *11am-6pm Tue-Sat* $

Paisley Grille: Fried chicken, burgers, fish and chips, and other fantastic gastropub fare at a Grand Haven favorite. *11am-9pm, to 10pm Fri & Sat* $$$

Chandler's: In Petoskey, upmarket fare – from sushi rolls to steak. Extensive wine list. Wine cellar seating available. *11am-9pm Mon-Thu, to 11pm Fri, 9am-9pm Sat & Sun* $$$

TOP EXPERIENCE

Sleeping Bear Dunes National Lakeshore

Extraordinary lake views from atop colossal sand dunes? Water blue enough to be in the Caribbean? Miles of unspoiled beaches? Secluded islands with mystical trees? All here at Sleeping Bear Dunes, along with lush forests, terrific day hikes and glass-clear waterways for paddling. The national park stretches from north of Frankfort to just before Leland, on the Leelanau Peninsula. Several cute towns fringe the area.

Empire Bluff Trail

Manitou Islands

The forest-cloaked **Manitou Islands** provide an off-the-beaten-path adventure. North Manitou is known for star-speckled backcountry camping, while South Manitou is terrific for wilderness-rich day trips. Kayaking and hiking are the big to-dos, especially the 7-mile trek to the Valley of the Giants, an otherworldly stand of cedar trees on South Manitou.

Dune Climb

The park's most popular attraction, this **climb** is up a 200ft-high dune to then run or roll down. Gluttons for punishment can keep slogging all the way to Lake Michigan, a strenuous 1½-hour trek one way.

Trails

The 22-mile paved **Sleeping Bear Heritage Trail** goes from Empire to Bohemian Rd (aka County Rd 669), and makes for a mostly gentle walk/bike ride – though there are some larger hills at the southern end. Trailheads with parking lots are located roughly every 3 miles; the one at Bar Lake Rd, near Empire, is a good place to embark.

The 1.5-mile round-trip **Empire Bluff Trail** rambles through peaceful beech-maple forest and eventually reaches a high bluff with grand views over Lake Michigan. Sunsets are awesome. It's moderately difficult, with a couple of sets of stairs to go up and down.

TOP TIPS

● If you're an America the Beautiful Pass holder, your entrance is already covered.

● This national lakeshore is cashless.

● Planning to camp in summer? Don't rely on first-come, first-served, as sites are likely to be sold out. Reserve online up to six months in advance.

PRACTICALITIES
● nps.gov/slbe
● 24hr
● 7-day pass per car $25

MICHIGAN'S BEST FESTIVALS

National Cherry Festival: A Traverse City tradition since 1931. Nearly 500,000 visitors watch parades, taste cherry pies and crown the National Cherry Queen each first week of July.

Movement: One of the world's largest electronic music festivals is held in Detroit over Memorial Day weekend.

Great Lakes Surf Festival: At Muskegon's Pere Marquette Beach in August, a day of surf lessons, yoga, art, music and more.

ArtPrize: Global artists display pieces throughout Grand Rapids over an annual 16-day period to win juried and popular-vote prizes.

Tulip Time: Holland blooms with millions of tulips – celebrated for nine days in early May, with Dutch food and cultural events at venues around town.

Holland

Tulips, windmills and more

You don't have to cross the ocean for tulips, windmills and clogs. Michigan's Holland has the whole kitschy package, plus a beautiful beach and a destination brewery. In early May, it's **Tulip Time** – the name of Holland's popular nine-day festival that takes over the town with parades, traditional clog dancing, a marketplace with Dutch foods and crafts, and other cultural events. If you haven't timed your trip with the festival, but the tulips are still in bloom, you can see them at **Veldheer Tulip Gardens** *(veldheer.com; adult/child $14/free)*. Outside of tulip season, it's free to check out the wooden-shoe factory, traditional blue-and-white pottery workshop and – somewhat oddly amid the Dutch items – a small buffalo herd.

From there, stop at **Windmill Island Garden** *(holland.org; adult/child $13/6)* to see an original working Dutch windmill, before enjoying lunch at the family-run **DeBoer's Bakkerij and Restaurant** *(deboerbakery.com)*, where the dishes are more Dutch-influenced than true Dutch, but nonetheless tasty. Klompen cakes (like pancakes with caramelized apple or other fruit added), eggs Benedict and croquettes star on the menu. It's touristy, but lots of locals eat here too. Finish with

DRINKING ON THE GOLD COAST: OUR PICKS

Pigeon Hill Brewing Company: In Muskegon, pale ales, IPAs and nitro stouts bubble from the taps. *11am-10pm Mon-Thu, to 11pm Fri & Sat, noon-9pm Sun*

Beards Brewery: A couple of home brewers opened Beards in Petoskey, and they know their stuff. Outside patio overlooking the bay. *11:30am-10pm Tue-Sun*

Odd Side Ales: Experimental suds in Grand Haven, like Tiramisu Bean Flicker and Imperial Mayan Mocha Stout. *11:30am-10pm Mon-Thu, to midnight Fri & Sat, to 9pm Sun*

Beer Church: In a former Methodist church in New Buffalo, signature brews include Pontius Pilate IPA and Crooked Cross cream ale. Wine and cocktails, too. *8am-midnight*

Holland tulip field

a pint at **New Holland Brewing Pub on 8th** *(newholland brew.com)*, known for its robust beers, such as Tangerine Space Machine and Dragon's Milk stout.

Michigan's Wine Country
Viticulture along the shore

Michigan has five main wine regions, aka American Viticulture Areas (AVAs) – Fennville, Lake Michigan Shore, Leelanau Peninsula, Old Mission Peninsula and Top of the Mitt – and four of them produce 95% of the state's wines. Those are Lake Michigan Shore, which actually encompasses Fennville; and Leelanau and the next door Old Mission peninsulas, near Traverse City. With so much great wine around, where to go? If you love a bold red, stick down south; if riesling is your thing, head up north; or, of course, there's nothing wrong with doing both.

Hop on the **Lake Michigan Shore Wine Trail** *(miwine trail.com)*, the stretch of I-94 and I-196 between New Buffalo and Saugatuck (and east to Kalamazoo) where about 15 member wineries are clustered.

Up in the Leelanau Peninsula AVA, there's the **Leelanau Peninsula Wine Trail** *(lpwines.com)* connecting 21 member wineries – go on a guided or self-guided bike tour with **Grand Traverse Bike Tours** *(grandtraversebiketours.com)*. Nearby, north of downtown Traverse City, the **Old Mission Peninsula Wine Trail** *(ompwinetrail.com)* links together 10 more. Tasting prices vary by winery, but range from $5 to $15 for four to six tastes.

The M-22
One of Michigan's most scenic drives

Take a ride along the M-22, arguably Michigan's most scenic drive, with dramatic vistas over Lake Michigan. The pretty

MICHIGAN'S TOP SPOTS FOR WINTER ACTIVITIES

Eben Ice Caves: Fantastical caves form when snow melts and freezes over a cliff's edge, glowing green-yellow from the tannins.

Muskegon Luge Adventure Sports Park: One of the nation's only public luge tracks, with cross-country ski and snowshoe trails, too. Clinics and rentals available.

Boyne Mountain Resort: More than 400 acres of skiing in Boyne Falls, including 63 downhill trails and 11 lifts.

Porkies Winter Sports Complex: Downhill skiing with a 787ft vertical drop, plus 26 miles of cross-country trails. Beginner-friendly.

Munising Snowmobile Trail System: Billed as the 'Snowmobile Capital of the Midwest,' this city has 10 trails that cover 300 miles.

NEED TO KNOW: THE UPPER PENINSULA

Residents of the UP, aka 'Yoopers,' consider themselves distinct from the rest of the state – they've even threatened to secede in the past. Rugged and isolated, with hardwood forests blanketing 90% of its land, the UP is edged by Lakes Huron, Michigan and Superior. Only 45 miles of Interstate highway slice through the trees, punctuated by a handful of cities, of which Marquette is the largest. The Keweenaw Peninsula is the UP's northernmost bit; its largest town Houghton is the jump-off to Isle Royale National Park, with ferries and seaplanes departing in summer. Further ahead on Hwy 26 is the turnoff for the Brockway Mountain Dr, which goes along the spine of the eponymous crag to reach the Copper Harbor, where another ferry sails for Isle Royale.

route goes from Manistee to Traverse City, hugging more than 100 miles of coastline, passing Sleeping Bear Dunes National Lakeshore (p553) and plenty of fun diversions along the way. Don't miss **Fishtown** *(lelandmi.org)*, a tiny commercial fishing village in **Leland** from the early 1900s and one of the few to be preserved on the Great Lakes shore. Wander among the shanties and see fish being cleaned and smoked, then pick up some to try at **Carlson's Fishery** *(carlsonsfishery.com)*.

Stop off for some grub in **Northport** – you can't go wrong at **Fischer's Happy Hour Tavern** *(fischershappyhour.com)*, a vintage tavern tucked in the woods, where the broasted (it combines broiling and roasting) chicken and fish are excellent – before stopping off for some suds in **Suttons Bay**. For beer, head to the outdoor beer garden at the **Hop Lot Brewing Company** *(hoplotbrewing.com)*; for cider, **Tandem Ciders** *(tandemciders.com)*.

At M-22's end in **Traverse City**, aka Michigan's 'cherry capital,' treat yourself to a slice of **Grand Traverse Pie Company's** top-selling cherry crumb pie (or one of its other seven or so pies with cherries). There are also guided kayak pub crawls via outfitters like **Paddle for Pints** *(paddleforpints.com; from $99)* or **Paddle TC** *(paddletc.com; from $69)*. Prices don't include the alcohol.

Mackinac Island

Ditch your car for two wheels

Mackinac's location in the straits between Lake Michigan and Lake Huron made this 3.8-sq-mile island a prized port in the North American fur trade, and a site the British and Americans battled over many times. To get here, catch the ferry from either Mackinaw City or St Ignace.

In 1898, cars were banned to encourage tourism, and 80% of the island is state parkland. Edging the island's shoreline is Hwy 185 (aka Lake Shore Rd), the only Michigan highway that doesn't permit cars. The best way to view the incredible scenery along this 8-mile road is by bicycle; bring your own or rent one at one of the many businesses. You can loop around the flat road in an hour. Along the way, you'll see the huge limestone **Arch Rock** *(mackinacparks.com)*, curving 150ft above Lake Huron and providing dramatic photo opportunities; and **Fort Mackinac** *(adult/child $17/10.25)*, built in 1780 by the British and one of the best preserved military forts in the country. Costumed interpreters, and cannon and rifle firings entertain the kids. Stop at the tearoom for a bite and

(continues on p559)

EATING IN THE UP: OUR PICKS

Syl's Cafe: In Ontonagon, breakfast is Syl's glory. Lunch and dinner don't disappoint either. The UP specialty (pasties) is available anytime. *7:30am-9pm* $

Falling Rock Cafe & Bookstore: New/used books, live music and wi-fi with your sandwich and coffee in downtown Munising. *8am-4pm, to 6pm Thu, to 8pm Fri & Sat* $

Jampot: In Eagle Harbor, bearded, black-robed monks from a nearby monastery sell homemade jams, coffee and pastries. *noon-4pm Tue-Thu, 10am-5pm Fri & Sat* $

Lake Superior Brewing Company: Whitefish and pizzas with house-made brews at this pub in Grand Marais. Also called the Dunes Saloon. *noon-midnight* $$

TOP EXPERIENCE

Isle Royale National Park

Totally free of vehicles and roads, Isle Royale National Park – a 210-sq-mile island in Lake Superior with 2000 moose roaming through the forest – is certainly the place to go for peace and quiet. It gets fewer visitors in a year than Yellowstone National Park gets in a day. The island is laced with 165 miles of hiking trails that connect dozens of campgrounds along Superior and inland lakes.

Greenstone Ridge Trail

At 42 miles, Greenstone Ridge Trail is the longest on Isle Royale, a grand backpacking adventure that spans the entire length of the island from Rock Harbor in the east to Windigo in the west. You can hike it in either direction, but most people start in Rock Harbor and take five to seven days to complete the epic wilderness trek.

The moderately difficult route pays off big time with forest solitude, fab lookouts over the wave-based coast and abundant moose and red fox sightings. The only accommodations along the way are basic campgrounds with pit toilets, so you have to carry all food and gear. Whether you finish in Windigo or Rock Harbor, it's easy to arrange boat transportation back to your starting point.

Stoll Trail

This easy 4.4-mile loop begins at Rock Harbor Lodge (p587) and meanders through old-growth forest and along shoreline bluffs to Scoville Point, an outcrop that unfurls dramatic views of Lake Superior and the craggy landscape. Keep an eye out for moose and osprey.

TOP TIPS

● It may be more cost efficient for groups to purchase a season pass *($60)*, which covers the pass holder, plus three more adults.

● If you're an America the Beautiful Pass holder, you're already covered to enter Isle Royale.

● Pay entrance fees online in advance; otherwise, it's credit card only on-site.

PRACTICALITIES
● nps.gov/isro
● 24hr mid-Apr to Oct
● daily adult/child $7/free

TOP EXPERIENCE

Pictured Rocks National Lakeshore

Stretching along Lake Superior, Pictured Rocks National Lakeshore is a series of wild cliffs and caves, where blue and green minerals have streaked the red and yellow sandstone into a kaleidoscope of color. In between Grand Marais in the east to Munising in the west, you'll find lakeside hikes, kayak trips and boat tours that feature brilliant ways to take in the area's shipwrecks, waterfalls and artist's-palette geology.

Au Sable Point Light Station

TOP TIPS

● If you are an America the Beautiful Pass holder, you're already covered to enter Pictured Rocks.

● This national lakeshore is cashless.

● Cell service is spotty here, so be sure to download maps ahead of time.

Sights

Top sights (from east to west) include the c 1874 **Au Sable Point Light Station** and its surrounding shipwrecks; agate-strewn **Twelvemile Beach**, accessed via the campground; hike-rich **Chapel Falls**, **Chapel Rock** and **Chapel Beach**; and view-worthy **Miners Castle**, one of the lakeshore's most distinctive rock formations.

Cruises

Boats with both deck and enclosed seating glide along the shore for 40 miles, passing many of Pictured Rocks' most popular sights. Rides last between two and three hours – the sunset option is particularly lovely – and depart from Munising's city dock. Book through **Pictured Rock Cruises** (*picturedrocks.com*); reserving ahead is wise.

Kayaking

Kayaking is popular in Pictured Rocks and no wonder, given that you paddle beneath sheer, color-stained bluffs with names like Lovers Leap, Flower Vase and Caves of the Bloody Chiefs. The duck's-eye view of the geologic features is awesome. Experienced paddlers can go it alone, but conditions are often wavy and windy. Newbies should go with a guide. Several operate out of Munising, with trips from just a few hours to all day. **Pictured Rocks Kayaking** (*picturedrockskayaking.com*) has good ones for beginners.

PRACTICALITIES
● nps.gov/piro
● 24hr
● 7-day pass per car $25

(continued from p556)

a million-dollar view of downtown and the Straits of Mackinac from the outdoor tables. The fort admission price also allows you entry to five other museums in town along Market St, including the **Mackinac Art Museum**, which houses Native American arts, historic maps and island photography.

Marquette

Outdoor adventures in nature's playground

The Upper Peninsula's largest (and snowiest) town, lakeside Marquette draws the outdoor enthusiasts. Forests, beaches and cliffs provide a playground spitting distance from downtown for skiing, hiking, biking, boating and beyond.

The easy **Sugarloaf Mountain Trail** and the harder, wilderness-like **Hogsback Mountain Trail** both have panoramic views, while the **Noquemanon Trail Network** *(noquetrails.org)* is highly recommended for mountain biking and cross-country skiing.

For water-sports enthusiasts, **Down Wind Sports** *(shop downwindsports.com)* rents all kinds of gear and has the lowdown on kayaking, fly-fishing, surfing, ice climbing and other adventures.

In the city, on a peninsula jutting out into Lake Superior, the high bluffs of **Presque Isle Park** make a great place to catch the sunset.

Porcupine Mountains

Roam Michigan's largest state park

Michigan's largest state park, **Porcupine Mountains** *(michigan dnr.com; per day $11)*, with 90 miles of trails, is a wilderness winner. 'The Porkies,' as they're called, are so rugged that loggers bypassed most of the range in the early 19th century, leaving the park with the largest tract of old-growth forest between the Rocky Mountains and Adirondacks. Along with 300-year-old hemlock trees, the Porkies are known for waterfalls, 20 miles of undeveloped Lake Superior shoreline, black bears lumbering about, and the view of the park's stunning Lake of the Clouds, the area's most photographed sight. After stopping at the **visitor center** to pay the park entrance fee, continue to the end of Hwy 107 and climb 300ft via a short path for the stunning view of the shimmering water. Lengthier trails depart from the parking lot.

MORE OF MICHIGAN'S TOP STATE PARKS

Tahquamenon Falls State Park: The Upper Falls' 50ft drop flows with hemlock-tinted waters, while the Lower Falls' series of small cascades swirl around an island.

Petoskey State Park: Beautiful beach featuring indigenous Petoskey stones (honeycomb-patterned fragments of ancient coral).

Grand Haven State Park: A 48-acre urban park that's all beach: popular in summer for swimming, a boardwalk and a tall red lighthouse.

Holland State Park: Has a Lake Michigan beach for sunset gaping, along with an inland Lake Macatawa beach where watercraft can be rented.

Ludington State Park: Once inside, simply pull over on the roadside and make a break for the beautiful beach. Trail system and lighthouse, too.

 DRINKING IN THE UP: OUR PICKS

Keweenaw Brewing Company: In Houghton, quality pints, including Widow Maker black ale and Pick Axe blonde ale. *3-10pm Mon-Wed, 11am-midnight Thu-Sat, noon-8pm Sun*

Blackrocks Brewery: Set in a cool refurbished house in Marquette, making deliciously hoppy beers, heavy on American IPAs. *4-11pm Mon, from noon Tue-Sun*

Ore Dock Brewing Co: Across from the docks in downtown Marquette, with laid-back bar, sidewalk seating, often food trucks out front. *noon-11pm, to midnight Fri & Sat*

Drifa Brewing Company: South of downtown Marquette, a dog-friendly brewery with tasty pours, ample outdoor seating area, and food truck. *noon-10pm, to 11pm Thu-Sat*

Wisconsin

FUN TRADITIONS | BEER BONANZA | WATER ADVENTURES

Places
Milwaukee p560
Racine p564
Madison p564
Wisconsin Dells p566
Spring Green p566
Door County p568
Green Bay p569
Apostle Islands p570

☑ TOP TIP

Buy a Wisconsin state park annual pass. It costs $38 per vehicle, whereas a day pass costs $16 per vehcle, so if you're visiting for more than two days it pays off quickly. Buy it online or at any of the parks.

Wisconsin is cheesy and proud of it. Its cow-speckled farmland pumps out more cheddar, Gouda and other pungent wedges than any other US state, and local license plates read 'America's Dairyland' with udder dignity.

So embrace the cheese thing, because there's a good chance you'll be here for a while. Wisconsin has a ton to offer: exploring the rocky coastline and lighthouses of Door County, kayaking through sea caves at Apostle Islands National Lakeshore, touring Green Bay's football shrine of Lambeau Field and driving along the bluff-framed Great River Rd. Families soak up the Wisconsin Dells' kitschy water parks, while architecture buffs marvel at Frank Lloyd Wright's forever home. The state's two largest cities, Milwaukee and Madison, welcome by offering bountiful beer, markets and locavore eats. At week's end, the whole state throws a party known as the Friday night fish fry, a quintessential Wisconsin experience.

Milwaukee

MAP P562

Brewery tours in Brew City

Milwaukee's enduring relationship with beer is no accident. The city was settled by Germans in the 1840s, and many started breweries. A few decades later, the introduction of bulk-brewing technology turned beer production into a major industry here, with Pabst, Schlitz, Blatz and Miller leading the way.

GETTING AROUND

The main Interstates are I-94 (runs east–west, connecting Milwaukee to Chicago and Minneapolis), I-90 (runs east–west near Madison) and I-43 (runs north–south, connecting Milwaukee to Green Bay). Wisconsin has no toll roads. Note that roads into Door County and the Wisconsin Dells often get jammed on summer weekends.

Amtrak runs a popular train between downtown Milwaukee and Chicago seven times per day; the trip takes 1½ hours and is often faster than driving.

Going on a brewery tour is a beloved Milwaukee activity, and visits typically include several samples. Make all bookings in advance.

Historic **Miller Brewing Company** (millerbrewerytour.com; tours $20) is the granddaddy of the scene. Though the mass-produced beer may not be your favorite, the factory impresses with its sheer scale: you'll visit the packaging plant where thousands of cans are filled each minute and the warehouse where half a million cases await shipment. It's closed Tuesday and Wednesday.

Much-loved **Lakefront Brewery** (lakefrontbrewery.com; tours $13-16) puts on 50-minute tours daily. Guides have a

EATING IN MILWAUKEE: OUR PICKS

Pitch's Lounge & Restaurant: Retro spot that's been family-run since 1942. Don't miss the baby back ribs. *5-9pm Wed, Thu & Sun, to 10pm Fri & Sat* **$$**

Uncle Wolfie's Breakfast Tavern: The brunch crowd lines up for biscuits and gravy, French toast and Bloody Marys. *8am-2pm Tue-Thu, to 3pm Fri-Mon* **$$**

Comet Cafe: Locals of all types pile in for meatloaf smothered in beer gravy and some of Milwaukee's best mac and cheese. *9am-9pm* **$$**

Odd Duck: Boisterous room for inventive, locally sourced small plates and cocktails; lots of vegetarian options. Reserve ahead. *3pm-midnight Tue-Sat* **$$$**

Milwaukee

HIGHLIGHTS
1 Milwaukee Art Museum

SIGHTS
2 America's Black Holocaust Museum
3 Bobblehead Hall of Fame and Museum
4 Bradford Beach
5 Bronze Fonz
6 Discovery World at Pier Wisconsin
7 Harley-Davidson Museum
8 Pabst Mansion

SLEEPING
9 Ambassador
10 Brewhouse Inn & Suites
11 County Clare Irish Inn

EATING
12 Comet Cafe
13 Milwaukee Public Market
14 Odd Duck
15 Pitch's Lounge & Restaurant
16 Swingin' Door Exchange
17 Uncle Wolfie's Breakfast Tavern

DRINKING & NIGHTLIFE
18 Best Place
19 Bryant's Cocktail Lounge
20 Central Standard Craft Distillery
21 Don's TV & Repair
22 Lakefront Brewery
23 Third Space Brewing

ENTERTAINMENT
24 German Fest
see 24 Irish Fest
see 24 Polish Fest
see 24 PrideFest
see 24 Summerfest

great sense of humor, and they take you right up to the bottling line. It's super-fun.

Pabst doesn't brew in Milwaukee anymore, but you can head to **Best Place** (bestplacemilwaukee.com; tours $14-25), a dark-wood tavern in the former brewery headquarters, to tour the company's historic premises.

Chow down at a fish fry

Friday is the hallowed day of the 'fish fry' all over Wisconsin. This communal meal of beer-battered cod, French fries and coleslaw came about years ago, providing locals with a cheap meal to socialize around and celebrate the end of the working week. Milwaukee is a terrific place to take part in the convention, as it's still going strong at many local bars and restaurants.

Lakefront Brewery (p561) hosts a popular fish fry in its beer hall that includes a polka band letting loose. **Swingin' Door Exchange** *(swingindoorexchange.com)* goes beyond the norm with its throwback, dark-wood ambience and elevated side dishes like spicy vermouth carrots. At **South Shore Terrace** *(southshoreterrace.com)*, you'll eat your fish in a sprawling lakefront beer garden.

Renegade bikes at the Harley Museum

Celebrate more than a century of motorcycles at the **Harley-Davidson Museum** *(harley-davidson.com/museum; adult/child $25/11)*. The company was founded in Milwaukee in 1903 when schoolmates William Harley and Arthur Davidson built and sold their first motorcycle. This museum has hundreds of motorcycles that show the styles through the decades, including the flashy rides of Elvis and Evel Knievel and 'Serial Number One,' the oldest known Harley in existence. Even nonbikers will enjoy the interactive exhibits and leather-clad crowds.

Art inside and out

On the shore of Lake Michigan, the **Milwaukee Art Museum** *(mam.org; adult/child $27/free)* showcases more than 32,000 works, including fabulous folk and outsider art and a sizeable collection of paintings by Wisconsin native Georgia O'Keeffe.

The museum building is a work of art itself and features a stunning winglike addition by Spanish architect Santiago Calatrava. Called the Burke Brise Soleil, the moveable shade is made of 72 steel fins spanning 217ft, slightly larger than a Boeing 747's wings. They spread wide with the museum opening at 10am, flap at noon and close at 5pm (8pm on Thursdays). Head to the suspension bridge outside for the best view of the action.

Sights along the RiverWalk

Edged by Lake Michigan and crisscrossed by three rivers, Milwaukee was made for waterfront wandering. The RiverWalk path cuts through downtown along both sides of the Milwaukee River. Don't miss the **Bronze Fonz** on the RiverWalk's east side, just south of Wells St. The Fonz, aka Arthur Fonzarelli, was a character from the 1970s TV show *Happy Days*, which was set in Milwaukee. It's a quintessential photo op.

MILWAUKEE'S BEST FESTS

Summerfest: The 'world's largest music festival' brings 600 rock, blues, country and alternative bands over nine days in June and July.

German Fest: Get ready for the dachshund derby, oompah bands, lots of beer drinking and shouts of 'Prost!' in late July.

Irish Fest: In mid-August, crowds amass for corned beef and cabbage, fiddle music, step dancing and beer guzzling.

Polish Fest: Get your fill of vodka tastings, polka dancing and cooking classes over three days in mid-June.

PrideFest: Beer drinking, live music, a dance pavilion and a family stage are all part of the June festivities.

DRINKING IN MILWAUKEE: OUR PICKS

MAP P562

Bryant's Cocktail Lounge: Opened in 1938, Milwaukee's oldest cocktail bar has no menu, just knowledgeable bar staff who mix up magic. *hours vary*

Don's TV & Repair: Swig boozy shakes named after old gaming consoles, mimosas served in a cute little bathtub and huge old fashioneds. *hours vary*

Central Standard Craft Distillery: Creates its own vodka, brandy, bourbon and whiskey, best enjoyed on the 5th-floor rooftop. *hours vary*

Third Space Brewing: The huge beer garden is an excellent choice for summertime sips, often accompanied by live music. *hours vary*

Onward as you head south is the **Milwaukee Public Market** (*milwaukeepublicmarket.org*), packed with local vendors selling cheese, sandwiches, beer and frozen custard each day.

Continue south along the path and you'll be in the heart of the **Third Ward**, an old warehouse district that's now a hub of galleries, boutiques and cool-cat dining venues powered by area farms, orchards and creameries. Pick a waterside bar or cafe to while away an afternoon or evening.

Racine

Unexpected architecture stop

By most accounts, the southeastern city of Racine is an unremarkable industrial town, but it has two key Frank Lloyd Wright sights. Start at the **SC Johnson Administration Building & Research Tower** (*reservations.scjohnson.com; tours free*), where Wright designed several striking buildings. Ninety-minute tours cover the 1939 Admin Building, with tall, flared columns in its vast Great Workroom and 43 miles of Pyrex glass-tube windows letting in soft, natural light. You'll also see the 1950 Research Tower – where Raid, Off and other famous products were developed – which features 15 floors of curved brick bands and more Pyrex windows.

About 5 miles north, **Wingspread** (*reservations.scjohnson.com; tours free*) is the house Wright designed for HF Johnson Jr, one of the company's leaders. It's the last and largest of Wright's Prairie-style abodes, completed in 1939, with 500 windows and a 30ft-high chimney. Tours for both sights run Wednesday through Sunday (reduced in winter) and must be booked in advance.

Racine makes a great stop between Milwaukee and Chicago.

Bite into a mega pastry

Racine is a prime place to sample the tire-sized state pastry known as the 'kringle.' The oval-shaped confection consists of 32 or more layers of flaky dough filled with fruits and nuts and baked until golden brown. Racine became a hub for the treat in the late 1800s, when the recipe came over with the many Danish immigrants who settled in the city. The kringles at family-owned **O&H Danish Bakery** (*ohdanishbakery.com*) are addictive wonders in flavors such as cranberry cream cheese, chocolate pecan and almond.

Madison

Wander the college district for art, beer and books

Madison is a pretty combination of small, grassy state capital and liberal, bookish college town. But it's that college – the University of Wisconsin and its 50,000 students – that dominates the scene and invites an afternoon hangout (which may well lead to an evening hangout).

The **Memorial Union** (*union.wisc.edu*) is the gathering spot. The sun-splashed terrace, set on Lake Mendota, could not be more perfect for a pitcher of beer and brat (local parlance for bratwurst). You can rent kayaks and paddleboards,

MORE MILWAUKEE TO-DO'S

America's Black Holocaust Museum: Founded by a lynching survivor, the museum presents a moving story of Black resilience despite centuries of oppression.

Bobblehead Hall of Fame and Museum: You know the bouncy-noggin dolls that look like celebrities? More than 10,000 of them bob here.

Pabst Mansion: Tour the Gilded Age grandiosity of beer baron Captain Frederick Pabst.

Discovery World at Pier Wisconsin: The lakefront science and technology museum features aquariums and a cool Les Paul electric guitar exhibit.

Bradford Beach: Legions of locals swim, play volleyball and lick frozen custard at this sandy strand a few miles north of downtown.

State Street, Madison

WISCONSIN'S BEST TRAILS

Ice Age Trail: Zigzags 1200 miles up and down the state, revealing icy springs, pine woods and bluff-top views. *iceagetrail.org*

400 State Trail: Gentle 22-mile cycling path between Elroy and Reedsburg that rolls through a farm-studded river valley.

Elroy-Sparta State Bike Trail: This 33-mile rail-trail meanders up hills, through old tunnels and alongside pastures; connects to the 400 State Trail.

Oak Leaf Trail: a 135-mile paved path that takes in parks, forests and lakefront vistas around Milwaukee.

CAMBA Trail System: The Chequamegon Area Mountain Bike Association has 250 miles of northern Wisconsin trails for beginners and experts.

or walk the trail around the lake. In winter the action moves indoors to the fireplace-warmed beer hall.

Nearby, the **Chazen Museum of Art** *(chazen.wisc.edu; free)* goes way beyond the norm for a university collection. The 3rd floor holds most of the genre-spanning trove: everything from the Old Dutch Masters to Picasso sculptures and Andy Warhol pop art.

State St links the campus to the Capitol. The mile-long, pedestrian-only road is lined with poets' cafes, parked bicycles and stores selling Free Tibet stickers through clouds of jasmine incense. Several locavore and international restaurants also fold in to the scene.

Graze through the Farmers Market

On Saturdays mornings from mid-April to early November, a food bazaar takes over Madison's Capitol Square. The **Dane County Farmers Market** *(dcfm.org; free)* is one of the nation's most expansive markets, famed for its artisan cheeses and breads. Keep your eyes peeled for Bleu Mont Dairy, which makes fantastic cheeses in a climate-controlled cave; and Stella's Bakery, which makes warm, pliable cheese bread. Street musicians and arts-and-crafts vendors add to the bohemian festival atmosphere. It gets crowded, but you can always find a tree-shaded grassy spot for respite.

 EATING IN MADISON: OUR PICKS

Mickie's Dairy Bar: Diner near campus that's been slinging breakfast for generations. Try the cinnamon roll French toast. *7am-2pm Wed-Sun* $

Tipsy Cow: Popular spot near Capitol Square for hobnobbing over burgers and beers from small-batch producers. *11am-10pm Mon-Sat* $

Lucille: Concocts inventive pizzas and cocktails across three stylish floors. *3-11pm Mon-Wed, 11am-11pm Thu & Sun, 11am-1am Fri & Sat* $$

Old Fashioned: Woodsy, retro spot for eating walleye, cheese soup and other Wisconsin specialties. *11am-9pm Mon-Thu, to 10pm Fri & Sat* $$

BEST WEIRD WISCONSIN SIGHTS

House on the Rock: Abode stuffed to mind-blowing proportions with wonderments, like whirring music machines, an enormous carousel and glass-walled 'infinity room.'

National Mustard Museum: Born of one man's ridiculously intense passion, it houses around 6000 mustards and kooky condiment memorabilia.

Dr Evermor's Sculpture Park: Found objects welded into a hallucinatory world of futuristic birds, dragons and other bizarre structures.

Cow Chip Throw: In September in Prairie du Sac, 800 competitors fling dried manure patties.

Concrete Park: A lumberjack's extraordinary folk art, featuring 200-plus whimsical, life-size sculptures.

If you're in town on a nonmarket day, get your fix at **Fromagination** *(fromagination.com)*, a shop that carries loads of hard-to-find local cheeses.

Wisconsin Dells

Water parks, both constructed and natural

About an hour's drive north of Madison, the **Wisconsin Dells** *(wisdells.com)* is an epicenter of kitschy diversions, including more than 20 water parks, water-skiing thrill shows, epic mini-golf courses and Ripley's Believe It or Not oddities. Practically every Midwestern family has splashed through a weekend here.

But beyond the carnival-like attractions, the Dells offers a nature fix amid limestone gorges and rushing rivers. **Dells Boat Tours** *(dellsboats.com; adult/child $40/20)* glide into the scenery; the Upper Dells trip is particularly lovely. Or head to nearby **Mirror Lake State Park** *(dnr.wisconsin.gov; vehicle day pass $16)* to hike amid sandstone bluffs that surround a glassy lake where you also can rent kayaks and pontoon boats. In winter, cross-country skiers glide over 18 miles of groomed trails, and ice fisherfolk set up on the lake. Even architecture buffs get a thrill here: Frank Lloyd Wright's Seth Peterson Cottage is tucked in the woods, and visitors can rent it if they get on the waiting list two years in advance.

Spring Green

Explore Frank Lloyd Wright's Taliesin

Renowned architect Frank Lloyd Wright chose the rolling green hills and valleys of southwestern Wisconsin for his dream home. He built **Taliesin** *(taliesinpreservation.org; tours from $35)* in 1911 in his signature Prairie style using low horizontal lines and local materials like limestone and river sand. Tours take you inside the house (actually the third Taliesin incarnation, after fires burned the first two), resplendent with warm, natural light and his clever custom-built decor. Longer jaunts go to other parts of the 800-acre estate, such as the Hillside Studio where he taught his apprentices. Wright lived at Taliesin on and off for almost 50 years.

Buy tickets in advance. Park at the visitor center. A shuttle bus takes you to the house. Even if you're not going on a tour, you can park and walk on the public trails that depart from the visitor center. Taliesin is an hour's drive east of Madison.

See a play in the woods

So you're in Spring Green to see Frank Lloyd Wright's mega sight. Why not stay into the evening for a magical show at **American Players Theatre** *(americanplayers.org; tickets from $66)*? The critically acclaimed troupe stages classical productions at an outdoor amphitheater in the woods. There's nothing like seeing *A Midsummer Night's Dream* under a silvery moon. Bring a picnic – it's tradition to hang out and nibble before the show. **Wander Provisions** *(wanderprovisions.com)* is a good place to stock up.

ROLLING ON THE GREAT RIVER ROAD

The Mississippi River forms Wisconsin's southwestern border, and alongside it runs the timeless, cheese-and-pie-laden Great River Rd.

START	END	LENGTH
Ellsworth Cooperative Creamery	La Crosse	105 miles; 5 hours

The Great River Rd follows Old Man River throughout its 2300-mile flow from Minnesota to Louisiana. Wisconsin's sections are among the prettiest. Start inland at 1 **Ellsworth Cooperative Creamery**, the state's largest cheese-curd producer. Bite a curd, and hear it squeak: a Wisconsin rite of passage.

Head south 15 miles to WI-35. Now you're on the River Rd, curving past bluffs until you reach 2 **Stockholm Pie & General Store**. Study the blackboard: double lemon, triple chocolate pecan, butterscotch cream? The slice will fuel you 6 miles to Pepin, where *Little House on the Prairie* fans can stop at the 3 **Laura Ingalls Wilder Museum**, and foodies at renowned, book-stuffed 4 **Harbor View Cafe**.

Stay on WI-35 a short distance to the 5 **Nelson Cheese Factory**. The shop carries a stash of Wisconsin cheese and rich ice cream. Take the bridge across the river to Wabasha, MN, where the 6 **National Eagle Center** gives the lowdown on the mighty birds, about 100 of which flock here each winter.

From Wabasha, stay on Hwy 61 on the Minnesota side for 60 miles, passing bucolic farms and green hills. Cross the bridge to La Crosse, WI. Get your camera ready for the 7 **World's Largest Six-Pack**, then explore the bars and shops of La Crosse's historic downtown.

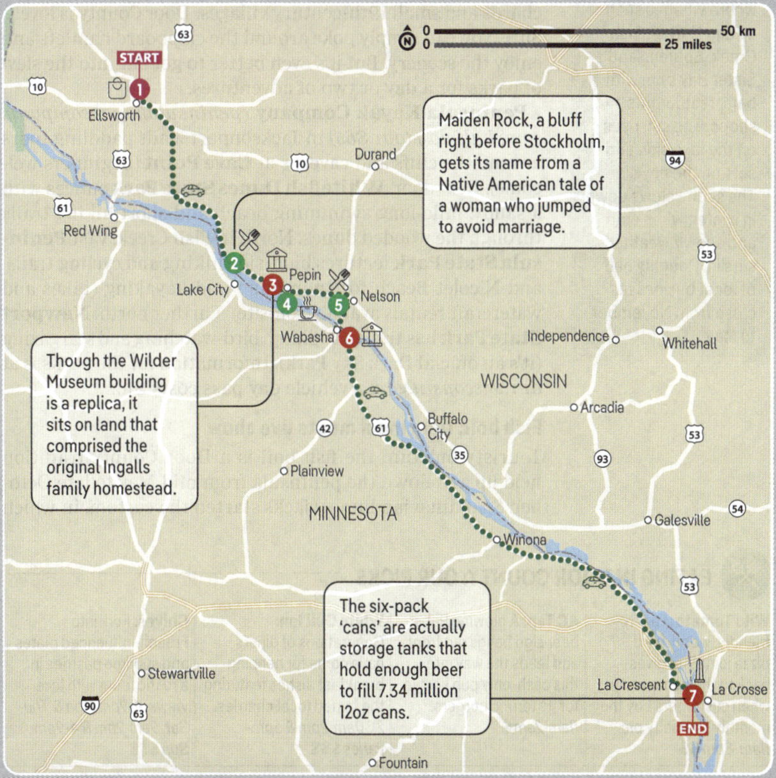
0 50 km
0 25 miles
START
Ellsworth
Durand
Red Wing
Lake City
Pepin
Nelson
Wabasha
Independence
Whitehall
WISCONSIN
Arcadia
Buffalo City
Plainview
MINNESOTA
Winona
Galesville
Stewartville
La Crescent
La Crosse
END
Fountain
Maiden Rock, a bluff right before Stockholm, gets its name from a Native American tale of a woman who jumped to avoid marriage.
Though the Wilder Museum building is a replica, it sits on land that comprised the original Ingalls family homestead.
The six-pack 'cans' are actually storage tanks that hold enough beer to fill 7.34 million 12oz cans.

DOOR COUNTY ORIENTATION

Door County spreads across a narrow peninsula jutting 75 miles into Lake Michigan. Sturgeon Bay, at the southern end, is the county seat and its only real city. Going north, the side of the peninsula that borders Lake Michigan is the more scenic 'quiet side,' and home to the communities of Jacksonport and Baileys Harbor. The side that borders Green Bay is busier, where villages such as Egg Harbor, Fish Creek, Ephraim and Sister Bay brim with bars, restaurants and shops. The sun rises on the lake side and sets on the bay side. The scene slows down in winter, when cold and snowy weather sets in. Roughly half of local businesses close from November to May.

Lambeau Field, Green Bay

Door County

Hike, bike and paddle the parks

With its rocky coastline, picturesque lighthouses, cherry orchards and small 19th-century villages, Door County is lovely. Sure, you can simply poke around the clapboard hamlets and enjoy the scenery. But it's even better to get out into the slew of parks for a day or two of adventures.

Peninsula Kayak Company (*peninsulakayakcompany.com; half-day tour $65*) in Jacksonport leads paddling tours around the cliffs and caverns at **Cave Point** (beginners welcome). Next door, **Whitefish Dunes State Park** entices with a sandy, mile-long swimming beach and short hiking trails through the wooded dunes. North in Fish Creek, vast **Peninsula State Park** features bluff-side hiking and cycling trails, and Nicolet Beach for swimming and kayaking (bikes and watercraft rentals available on-site). Further north, **Newport State Park** has tranquil hiking, bird-watching and stargazing (it's an official Dark Sky Park). Information for the parks is at *dnr.wisconsin.gov*; a vehicle day pass costs $16.

Fish boil: fiery meal meets live show

Touristy but fun, the fish boil is a Door County tradition held up and down the peninsula from mid May to late October. Scandinavian lumberjacks started the custom, in which

EATING IN DOOR COUNTY: OUR PICKS

Wild Tomato: Family-friendly, wood-fired pizza joint that gives back to the community when customers buy the monthly specialty pie. *11am-8pm* $$

AC Tap: A glowing Pabst beer sign hangs out front and leads the way into this cash-only pub known for its terrific burgers. *11am-2am* $

White Gull Inn: Generations of diners have come for heaping breakfast dishes featuring the famed local cherries. *7:30am-2pm & 5pm-varies* $$$

Chives: Fork into French-influenced plates and sublime pastries in a rustic room with lake views. *4-9pm Mon & Thu-Sat, 9am-2pm & 4-9pm Sun* $$$

whitefish, potatoes and onions are cooked in a cauldron over an open flame outdoors. Stand around the firepit while the 'boil master' prepares the ingredients and shares local lore. Then they douse the flames with kerosene, and whoosh! A fireball creates the requisite 'boil over' (which gets rid of the fish oil), signaling dinner is ready. Several restaurants host dinnertime fish boils. The **Old Post Office Restaurant** *(old postoffice-doorcounty.com; adult/child $28.50/18)* in Ephraim puts on a lively one, with a bonus of great sunset views.

Sail to Washington and Rock islands

If Door County starts to feel crowded, steer to its tip for your getaway. Hop aboard the **Washington Island Ferry** *(wisferry.com; adult/child/car $15/8/30)* at Northport Pier for the 30-minute crossing. The time-warped little isle, settled by Icelandic villagers in the 1800s, beckons with some 700 residents, lavender fields, rugged beaches and small resorts. You'll need a car (or bicycle) to get around. The ferry sails year-round. While the crossing is generally smooth, it does go through the strait known as 'Death's Door,' so named by Native Americans and early French explorers due to the treacherous currents that sank many a ship in past centuries. That's where Door County gets its moniker. Modern navigation aids have rendered the strait far less threatening today.

More remote is teeny Rock Island, which has no roads or facilities. It's a true escape for forest hiking and bird-watching. You also can explore the 1858 lighthouse, where volunteers offer free tours daily. The **Rock Island Ferry** *(wisferry.com; adult/child $15/6)* makes the trip from Washington Island's Jackson Harbor in 15 minutes, sailing from late May to mid-October. Leave your car in the parking lot by the dock. It's possible to visit both islands in one long day trip. Bring cash for small purchases like snacks or souvenirs.

Green Bay

Tour fabled Lambeau Field

The Green Bay Packers are legendary as the National Football League's smallest-market team but one of its most successful, winning 13 league championships and four Super Bowls (so far). The franchise is unique as the only community-owned nonprofit team in the NFL; perhaps pride in ownership is what makes the fans so die-hard.

The Packers' storied history makes a half-day visit to Lambeau Field worthwhile even if you aren't a hard-core supporter.

STELLAR SUNSETS

Betsy Riley, co-owner of Square Rigger Lodge (p587) in Jacksonport, shares top spots to see Door County's famous sunsets.

Stabbur Beer Garden at **Al Johnson's** Swedish restaurant is a fun place to watch the sky ignite. Or walk across the street to the waterfront park for a closer view. My grandparents would go there often in the evening. They'd plan their day around the sunset.

Shipwrecked Brew Pub has an outdoor patio and sits above the water, so you have a great lookout over Green Bay and boats in the marina.

Ellison Bluff County Park feels off the beaten path – there are never many people there – but it's near the highway. With no buildings around, it's a gorgeous wide-open place to see the sun drop.

 DRINKING IN DOOR COUNTY: OUR PICKS

Pearl Wine Cottage: Cute-as-a-button white bungalow serving European wines alongside cheeses and charcuterie. *4-9pm Thu-Sun mid-May-Oct*

Mink River Basin: Tucked-away bar that's been around for ages with fun games (Pac-Man!) and good beers, whiskies and food. *noon-2am*

Peach Barn Farmhouse & Brewery: Sprawling outdoor space to play lawn games and hear live music while sipping sours and lagers. *11am-8pm*

Bayside Tavern: Locals and visitors mix it up over burgers and beers in this festive, time-honored pub with a lively patio. *11am-2pm*

WHY SO CHEESY?

Wisconsin produces 3.5 billion pounds of cheese per year – a quarter of America's hunks. That's thanks to 5000 state dairy farms and their 1.3 million cows, according to the Department of Agriculture.

Most farming and cheesemaking happens in Wisconsin's hilly southwest. Here, in what's known as the Driftless Region, glaciers did not flatten the landscape as elsewhere in the state, but left hills, valleys and limestone-rich soil – poor for crop farming but perfect for roaming dairy herds that produce distinctive sweet milk.

Immigrants from Germany, Switzerland and Scandinavia who settled in Wisconsin in the 1800s put their old-country cheesemaking skills to work. The state has been America's Dairyland ever since.

The hour-long 'classic' **stadium tour** *(lambeaufield.com; adult/child $23/14)* takes in the luxury boxes and lets you walk through the tunnel out onto the field. Guides provide great stories of Packers lore. Tours happen daily year-round (except on game days). Afterward mosey around the Titletown district adjacent to Lambeau, which has live music, markets and other free events open to the public.

Apostle Islands

Kayaking and sea-cave adventures

Forested and windblown, trimmed with cliffs and caves, **Apostle Islands National Lakeshore** *(nps.gov/apis; free)* floats off Wisconsin's northern tip in Lake Superior. Kayaking around the 21-isle archipelago is very popular, paying off with stacks of red-rock arches and pillars rising from the water. Sea caves along the mainland near Meyers Beach and the craggy shores of Devils and Sand islands are the showstoppers. Conditions get rough and winds strong, so it's wise to go with a guide. Reputable companies offering half- and full-day outings include **Lost Creek Adventures** *(lostcreekadventures.org; tours from $80)* and **Trek & Trail** *(trek-trail.com; tours from $75)*.

The resort town of Bayfield has everything you need. The **National Lakeshore Visitors Center** *(nps.gov/apis)* downtown can help with camping permits. The islands themselves have no facilities. June through September is prime time to paddle.

Take a boat tour or hike

You don't have to be in a kayak to enjoy the Apostle Islands. Hop on a sightseeing boat with **Apostle Islands Cruises** *(apostleisland.com; tours adult/child $55/34)* instead. The

Devils Island, Apostle Islands National Lakeshore

three-hour 'grand tour' sails to sea caves and lighthouses, and you can bring your own wine and snacks on-board.

Or hike the first 2 miles of the Lakeshore Trail near **Meyers Beach**, which has terrific sea-cave views from land. Brave souls also can swim at Meyers Beach, but the water is breathtakingly cold. It's near Cornucopia, west of Bayfield, along Hwy 13.

Day trip to Madeline Island

The **Madeline Island Ferry** (madferry.com; return adult/child/car $21/10/38) makes the 25-minute trip multiple times per day from downtown Bayfield to bohemian **Madeline Island** and its walkable village of La Pointe. To go beyond, bring your car or rent a bicycle from **Motion to Go** (motion-to-go.com; per hr $12) by the dock. Pedaling around the island is pure joy.

Big Bay State Park (dnr.wisconsin.gov; vehicle day pass $16) beckons with a pretty beach, cliff-view hiking trails and stargazing. Or walk and forage for mushrooms in lovely **Madeline Island Wilderness Preserve** (miwp.org; free).

SUPPER CLUBS

Supper clubs are a type of time-warped restaurant, common in the upper Midwest. They took off in the 1930s, after Prohibition ended and people once again sought places to socialize over a drink. Most supper clubs today retain a retro vibe. Hallmarks include a woodsy location, mounted fish on the walls, a radish-and-carrot-laden relish tray on the table, a surf-and-turf menu and a mile-long, unironic cocktail list topped by the brandy old-fashioned (brandy, bitters, sugar, soda water, orange slice and cherry). Wisconsin has the most supper clubs by far, though Minnesota and Michigan also uphold the tradition. See wisconsinsupperclubs.com for locations around the state.

 EATING & DRINKING IN BAYFIELD: OUR PICKS

Hoop's Fish & Chips Dockside: Fresh fish, beer and wine served alfresco, plus live music on weekends. 11am-7pm Mon-Sat, to 6pm Sun $

Manypenny Bistro: Diner-esque venue for breakfast sandwiches, burgers, lake fish, wood-fired pizzas and Turkish kebabs. 7am-9pm $$

Fat Radish: Farm-to-table meat, fish and veg dishes in a log cabin in Washburn, just south of Bayfield. 11am-8pm Wed & Thu, to 9pm Fri & Sat $$$

Copper Crow Distillery: Tasting room on Native land for cocktails with house-made vodka and rum. 3-7pm Thu & Fri, 1-7pm Sat, noon-4pm Sun

Minnesota

WILDERNESS TRAILS | LAKES | ROCK STARS

Places
Minneapolis p572
Chanhassen p578
St Paul p578
Duluth p580
North Shore p581
Hibbing p583
Boundary Waters p583
Voyageurs National Park p584

☑ TOP TIP

The state is nicknamed 'Minnesnowta' for a reason. It's not uncommon for it to snow in late April or even early May. Then again, it can swing the other way and boil in summer. Moral of the story: bring layered clothing options.

Minnesota really is the land of 10,000 lakes (and then some). All that water is a boon for travelers. Adventurous types can wet their paddles in the Boundary Waters, where nighttime brings a blanket of stars and the lullaby of wolf howls. Voyageurs National Park unfurls another remote landscape, where roads vanish and the boreal backcountry is accessible only by boat. Hwy 61 slices into the cliffy, falls-filled North Shore. For a state with such vast tracts of unspoiled wilderness, Minnesota flies under the radar as an outdoor adventure hub. But that it is.

Urban explorers get the prize of Minneapolis, the biggest, coolest town on the prairie, with swanky art museums, rowdy rock clubs, progressive dining establishments and edgy theaters. It's always happenin,' even in winter. And for those looking for middle ground – a cross between the big city and big woods – the dramatic, ship-laden port of Duluth beckons.

Minneapolis
MAPS P574, P576

Follow Prince's purple path

Minneapolis' most famous former resident is the music star Prince. Even before his death in 2016, visitors flocked to town to follow his trail.

Hot spots include First Avenue (p577), the downtown music club that featured in the film *Purple Rain*. Nearby, a 100ft-tall

---

🧭 GETTING AROUND

The main Interstates are I-94 (runs east-west, connecting Minneapolis to Milwaukee and Chicago), I-90 (runs east-west through southern Minnesota) and I-35 (runs north-south, linking the Twin Cities and Duluth). Minnesota does not have toll roads, though express lanes on Twin Cities highways charge a fee for use. Hwy 61, the scenic road along Lake Superior north of Duluth, gets jammed on summer weekends. Amtrak trains go twice daily to Chicago and Milwaukee.

MINNESOTA

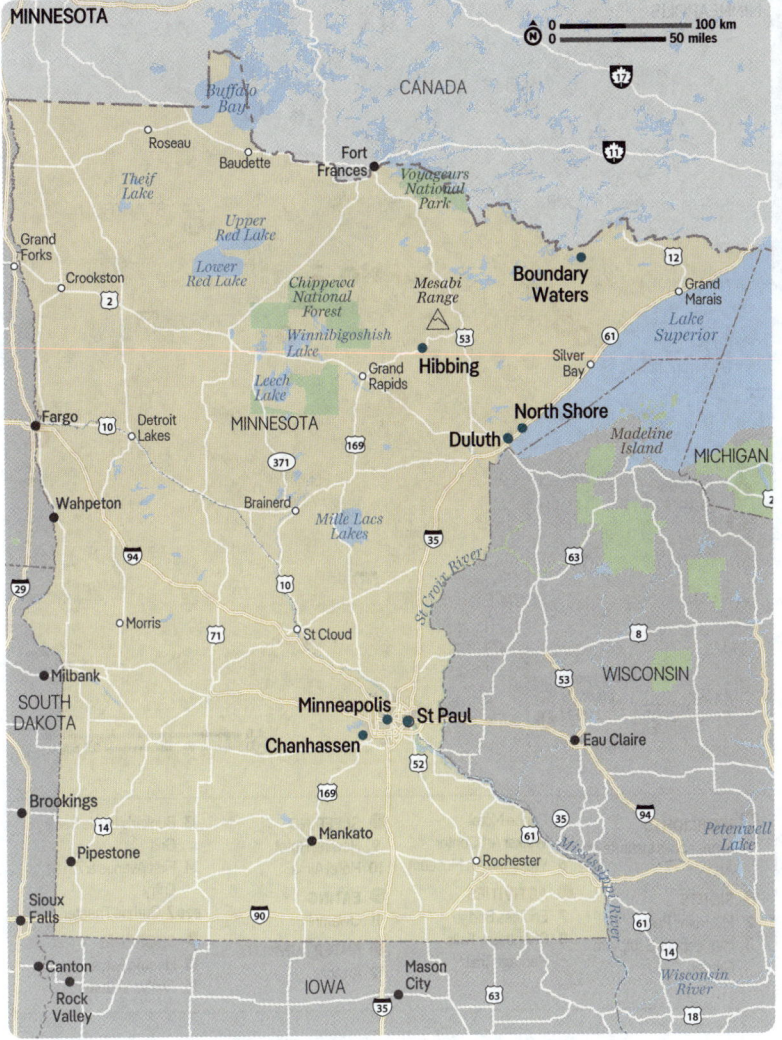

mural of Prince rises on the wall of a parking ramp. Hard-core fans can also seek out Prince's childhood home and more using the city's 'purple path' map *(minneapolis.org/princes-minneapolis)*.

The mega sight for fans is Paisley Park (p578), Prince's mansion in Chanhassen, 20 miles southwest of Minneapolis, complete with the Prince Tribute Tunnel.

Go on an art bender

Minneapolis takes its art seriously. Near downtown, the **Walker Art Center** *(walkerart.org; adult/child $18/free)* is one of

MINNEAPOLIS

HIGHLIGHTS
1. Minneapolis Institute of Art

SIGHTS
2. Mill Ruins Park
3. Minneapolis Sculpture Garden
4. Prince Mural
5. Walker Art Center
6. Weisman Art Museum

ACTIVITIES
7. Endless Bridge
8. St Anthony Falls Heritage Trail

SLEEPING
9. Hewing Hotel
10. Hotel Alma

EATING
11. Owamni

ENTERTAINMENT
12. Armory
13. Bunker's Music Bar & Grill
14. First Avenue & 7th St Entry
see 7 Guthrie Theater

SHOPPING
15. Electric Fetus
16. Twelve Vultures

EATING IN MINNEAPOLIS: CIVIC-MINDED RESTAURANTS — MAPS P574, P576

Owamni: Sun-splashed venue that only uses indigenous ingredients like corn, beans, wild game and native plants. *11am-9pm Tue-Fri, from 10am Sat & Sun* $$$

Mama Safia's Kitchen: Somali restaurant serving chicken, goat and spiced rice; it was rebuilt by the community after 2020's civil unrest. *7am-10pm* $$

Trio Plant-Based: Breezy vegan soul-food place decorated with photos of civil-rights heroes. *noon-6:45pm Tue-Thu, to 7:15pm Fri & Sat* $$

All Square: It's all about grilled cheese sandwiches at this little spot that helps recently incarcerated people get back on their feet. *11am-8pm Tue-Sat* $

the nation's top five for modern works. Most of the permanent collection is post-1960, heavy on Andy Warhol soup-can prints and Jasper Johns flag images. It's free on Thursday evenings. The **Minneapolis Sculpture Garden** *(walkerart.org; free)* sits next door, where Claes Oldenburg's beloved *Spoonbridge & Cherry* presides over the 11-acre grounds alongside a whimsical blue rooster and the Robert Indiana *Love* monument. It's delightful to meander.

South of downtown, the **Minneapolis Institute of Art** *(new.artsmia.org; free)* spans centuries and continents, with everything from Tibetan tangkas to Rembrandt paintings to 2000-year-old Mexican jade masks in its warren of galleries. You could spend the entire day here. The **Weisman Art Museum** *(wam.umn.edu; free)* on the University of Minnesota campus is smaller but equally impressive, thanks to its gleaming, Frank Gehry–designed building. It holds a quick-browse mash-up of ceramics, Korean furniture and 20th-century American art. Note: most museums are closed on Monday and Tuesday.

For the local art scene, check out the **Northeast Minneapolis Arts District** *(northeastminneapolisartsdistrict.org)*. Located north of downtown, the area teems with artist lofts and open-house events.

George Floyd Square: site of history and healing

George Floyd was killed by police in May 2020 outside a convenience store at the corner of E 38th and Chicago Aves in south Minneapolis. His death, which became a symbol for racial injustice and police brutality, sparked worldwide protests. Since then, the site – now known as **George Floyd Square** – has become a place to reflect and pay respects to Mr Floyd. People bring rocks, paintings, dolls, candles, beads, flowers and poems as offerings to the ever-changing memorial that has taken over the intersection. Murals, raised fist sculptures and raw art installations in locals' lawns extend for a block in each direction and add to the sobering feel. The square itself is a pedestrian-only zone.

Say Their Names Cemetery, another community-built memorial, lies a few blocks northwest, near where E 37th St and Columbus Ave meet. White cardboard headstones rise up in an empty lot and pay homage to everyone from Floyd to Emmett Till, Breonna Taylor and more than 100 other Black Americans killed by police.

Late morning or afternoon are good times to visit, though the sights are always open.

MINNEAPOLIS: GET YOUR BEARINGS

Minneapolis is relatively spread out. Neighborhoods include the North Loop (stylish warehouse district abutting downtown), Uptown (lively area south of downtown near Bde Maka Ska and other popular lakes), Northeast (art studios, breweries and dive bars northeast of downtown), East and West Banks (home to University of Minnesota's 50,000-plus students near downtown) and Powderhorn (where Floyd Square is in south Minneapolis). St Paul lies 10 miles east of Minneapolis, while the airport and Mall of America lie 10 miles south.

Handy Blue Line trains connect the mall, airport and downtown Minneapolis. Green Line trains connect Minneapolis to St Paul. A Metro Transit *(metrotransit.org)* day pass costs $4.

EATING IN MINNEAPOLIS: OUR PICKS
MAP P574, P576

Hola Arepa: Margaritas and Venezuelan-style arepas. Colorful, festive ambience. *4-10pm Tue-Thu, to 11pm Fri, 10am-11pm Sat, to 10pm Sun* **$$**

Heather's: Bright cafe whipping up from-scratch French toast, burgers, vegan tofu bowls and more. *9am-9pm Mon-Sat, to 8pm Sun* **$$**

Young Joni: Hip industrial space that fuses two seemingly unrelated types: pizza and Korean food. There's a hidden bar in back. *hours vary* **$$**

Creekside Supper Club: Retro knotty pine walls, vintage signs and classic fare like prime rib and martinis. *4-9pm Tue-Fri, 10am-2pm & 4-9pm Sat & Sun* **$$$**

MINNESOTA GREAT LAKES

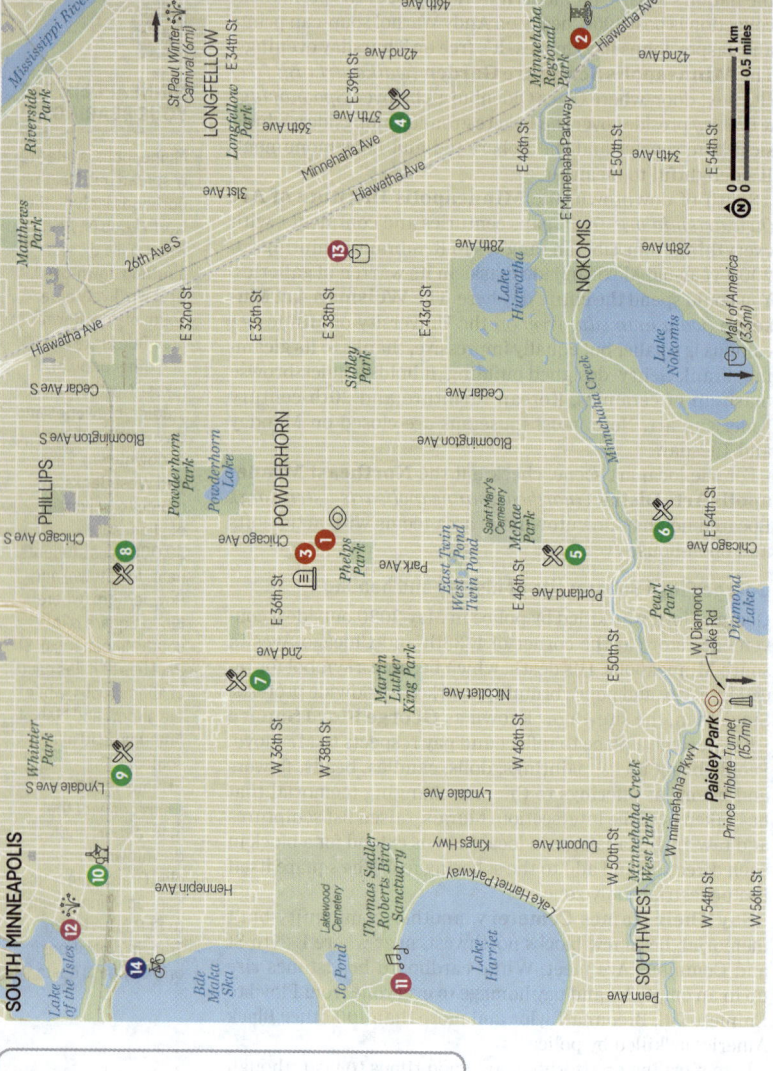

SIGHTS
1. George Floyd Square
2. Minnehaha Falls
3. Say Their Names Cemetery

EATING
4. All Square
5. Creekside Supper Club
6. Heather's
7. Hola Arepa
8. Mama Safia's Kitchen
    see 2 Sea Salt Eatery
9. Trio Plant-Based

DRINKING & NIGHTLIFE
   see 5 Sidecar at the Tap
10. Troubadour Wine Bar

ENTERTAINMENT
   see 9 Jungle Theater
11. Lake Harriet Band Shell
12. Luminary Loppet

SHOPPING
13. Tropes & Trifles

TRANSPORT
14. Wheel Fun Rentals

Riverfront views: mill ruins, a waterfall and more

The Mississippi River slices through downtown Minneapolis, flanked by parkland and a waterside trail. Join the many locals who are out for a stroll.

The cobalt-blue **Guthrie Theater** *(guthrietheater.org)* is a striking place to start. Check to see if the building is open (closed Mondays and most mornings) and then make your way up the escalator to the **Endless Bridge**. The cantilevered walkway juts out over the river and offers a knockout view. Onward along the water is brooding **Mill Ruins Park**, steeped in history from when Minneapolis led the world in flour milling. From here, pick up the **St Anthony Falls Heritage Trail**, a 1.8-mile path that crosses the car-free Stone Arch Bridge, providing a terrific view of cascading St Anthony Falls.

Jump in a lake

Minnesota is dubbed the land of 10,000 lakes, and Minneapolis claims over 22 of them. **Bde Maka Ska** (a Dakotan name) and **Lake Harriet** are among the most popular, where everyone flocks to revel in the summer sunshine. Both have beaches, cafes, walking and cycling paths, and kayaks and stand-up paddleboards from **Wheel Fun Rentals** *(wheelfunrentals.com; per hr $15-25)*. The castle-like **Lake Harriet Band Shell** is always abuzz with free concerts and films. Both lakes are conveniently located a short distance southwest of downtown.

Further north **Lake of the Isles** and **Cedar Lake** are two quieter neighborhood lakes, surrounded by grand historic homes that make for some astonishing scenery.

Summer is the busiest time, but locals are out in all seasons. Autumnal walks around the lakes are particularly marvelous.

Catch a show

The city buzzes with creative energy that spills over into an active nightlife. Downtown's **First Avenue & 7th St Entry** *(first-avenue.com)* – where native son Prince grooved in *Purple Rain* – is the epicenter of the music scene. It's two venues in one: First Avenue is the main room featuring national acts; smaller 7th St Entry is for up-and-comers who play a stage-dive away from the crowd. Stars painted on the building's exterior show the famed names who've rocked here over the years.

The historic **Armory** *(armorymn.com)* pops on the weekends with punk, metal and alt-rock bands downtown. Nearby in the North Loop, **Bunker's Music Bar & Grill** *(bunkersmusic.com)* is a scruffy winner that puts funk, blues or reggae bands on stage six nights a week (closed Mondays).

Theater buffs should see what's on at the **Guthrie Theater** *(guthrietheater.org)*, where Minneapolis' top-gun troupe mounts bold-themed classic and new works downtown. **Jungle Theater** *(jungletheater.org)* offers a more intimate experience, staging high-quality productions in Uptown.

Urban escape to Minnehaha Falls

It's hard to believe a 53ft-tall waterfall crashes down into a limestone gorge just 15 minutes from downtown Minneapolis. But **Minnehaha Falls** *(minneapolisparks.org; free)*

WINTER FESTS

Krista Westendorp, writer, outdoor enthusiast and 40-year Twin Cities resident, shares her favorite winter events.

St Paul Winter Carnival: Cold and snow don't stop locals from being outside. The St Paul carnival has been going for 140 years. It starts in late January, with ice-carving competitions, snow sculptures, parades, winter biking and more over 10 days. It's an annual highlight.

Luminary Loppet: This enchanted evening walk (held every February) goes around Lake of the Isles, lit by 1200 candle luminaries, past intricate ice sculptures. Hot cocoa and s'mores are served along the trail, and the walk ends at a party with food trucks, music and beer. Other parks also host candlelit trail events throughout winter with bonfires and refreshments.

BEST TWIN CITIES SHOPPING

Mall of America: The USA's largest shopping center goes beyond stores with a zipline, mini-golf course and amusement park inside.

Electric Fetus: Prince used to browse at this indie record store, with a great selection of local music and cool gifts.

Twelve Vultures: Theatrical curiosity shop where shelves hold taxidermy foxes, moose antlers, antique-framed insect specimens and more.

Birchbark Books: Native-owned indie bookstore that's a cozy community hub, with creaking wood floors and handwritten staff recommendations.

Tropes & Trifles: Dedicated to romance novels; lots of cheeky gifts supplement the spicy book selection.

does exactly that. Gawp over the ledge from the top or take the stairs down to the bottom and explore the cascade from a different angle. It's particularly stunning in winter when it freezes over and you can walk right around it.

The sublime waterfall sits in the middle of a park with 193 acres of woodlands, bluffs and riverside trails to roam around. Afterward, angle for a seat at **Sea Salt Eatery** (seasalt mpls.com), an open-air seafood spot right by the falls that's open daily April through October. Fish tacos, raw oysters, crab-cake sandwiches and pitchers of beer are available to help you replenish.

Chanhassen

Pay tribute to Prince at Paisley Park

Paisley Park (paisleypark.com; tours from $75), Prince's mansion in Chanhassen, is a stark white building at the highway's edge, and looks like an unsexy office building outside, but inside is a different story. Ninety-minute tours take in the recording studio, soundstage and music club where he hosted his famous late-night bashes.

Outside the building, the **Prince Tribute Tunnel** is an underpass beneath the highway that leads directly toward Paisley Park, which is behind a wire fence. Along the fence, fans have affixed purple love locks, purple guitars, purple flowers, poems and other offerings. The underpass itself is covered in purple drawings and graffiti. It's all quite moving. To reach the tunnel, it's easiest to park at Lake Ann Park and follow the pedestrian path under the road, which heads to Riley Creek Tunnel (its official name).

St Paul

F Scott Fitzgerald's early haunts

St Paul, Minnesota's capital city, is smaller and quieter than its twin to the west, Minneapolis. Strolling through its historic neighborhoods is a delightful way to spend a morning or afternoon.

St Paul's most celebrated literary son is *The Great Gatsby* author F Scott Fitzgerald (1896–1940). The genteel area around Cathedral Hill – named for the colossal church that marks the spot – is his old stomping ground. The **Fitzgerald birthplace**, a Pullman-style apartment, is on Laurel Ave. Nearby, the brownstone at **599 Summit Ave** is where he lived when he

DRINKING IN MINNEAPOLIS: OUR PICKS

MAP P574, P576

Surly Brewing: Family-friendly beer hall with outdoor, dog-friendly beer garden. *3-10pm Mon-Thu, to midnight Fri, 11am-midnight Sat, 11am-11pm Sun*

Troubadour Wine Bar: Low-lit charmer for globally sourced reds and whites amid soulful live music. *5-10pm Mon-Thu, to midnight Fri & Sat*

Dogwood Coffee: Neon-clad industrial space to fuel your day with an espresso and game of ping-pong. *7am-7pm Mon-Fri, 8am-6pm Sat & Sun*

Sidecar at the Tap: Casually chic room for cocktails made with attention to detail. *4-11pm Tue & Wed, to midnight Thu-Sat, to 10pm Sun*

Paisley Park

CULINARY SPECIALTIES

Hearty comfort foods hit the tables in Minnesota. Keep an eye on local menus for walleye, Minnesota's state fish, which offers a mild, white meat. Nutty-tasting, native wild rice often turns up in breads and soups. The Jucy Lucy appears in pubs around the Twin Cities. It's a burger stuffed with a molten core of American cheese, made by pinching two patties around the yellow slices and grilling to greasy perfection. A 'hot dish' (aka casserole) typically includes ground beef, potatoes or pasta, green beans or corn, and a canned cream soup. Tater tots commonly top it. Lutefisk, dried cod that's rehydrated with lye and then cooked, is popular during the winter holidays. The gelatinous dish is an acquired taste.

published *This Side of Paradise*. Both are private residences, so you can't go inside. Plaques mark the sites.

From here, continue along Summit Ave toward the cathedral to gape at the Victorian homes rising from the tree-lined street. Gilded Age vibes abound. Walk another half-mile or so toward the Mississippi River for more in the Irvine Park district, which is replete with fountains, gardens and turreted manors. It's next to W 7th St, an eating and drinking hub.

Learn to curl

For those uninitiated in northern ways, curling is a winter sport that involves sliding a 42lb granite stone (sort of like a jumbo hockey puck) down the ice toward a bull's-eye. It's popular in Minnesota, and there are rinks all over the state. The friendly folks at the **St Paul Curling Club** *(stpaulcurlingclub.org)* don't mind if you stop in to watch the action. Heck, they'll probably invite you to share a microbrew in the upstairs bar. It's the USA's largest club, and open daily in the evening from mid-October to late May.

EATING & DRINKING IN ST PAUL: OUR PICKS

Cecil's Deli: Kosher, family-run classic where locals devour huge sandwiches and matzoball soup at close-packed tables. *9am-8pm* **$$**

Hyacinth: Intimate, date-night restaurant serving modern takes on pasta, risotto and other buttery Italian dishes alongside cocktails. *5-9pm Tue-Sun* **$$$**

Nina's Coffee Cafe: In a rambling historic building full of nooks and crannies beloved by writers and cardamom-infused-latte fans. *6:30am-5pm*

Emerald Lounge: Sip creative cocktails (including alcohol-free ones) in plush seats amid vintage, green-toned decor. *4-10pm Tue-Thu, to 11pm Fri & Sat*

BEST QUIRKY MINNESOTA SIGHTS

Spam Museum: Learn all about the peculiar blue-tinned meat that has fed armies and inspired legions of haiku writers.

Darwin Twine Ball: The 'World's Largest Built by One Person': Francis A Johnson wrapped the 17,400lb whopper over 29 years.

Paul Bunyan Statue: The lofty lumberjack and his blue ox, Babe, tower over Bemidji's visitor center, which displays Paul's giant toothbrush inside.

Greyhound Bus Museum: See buses from yesteryear in an art deco–style terminal in Hibbing, where Greyhound Lines originated.

Mary Tyler Moore Statue: Photo op with the beloved 1970s TV character who put Minneapolis on the pop-culture map.

Duluth

Freighter-filled, eclectic port town

Duluth is a brawny shot-and-a-beer port town that immerses visitors in its storied history as a major shipping center. Start downtown at the **Aerial Lift Bridge**, Duluth's landmark that raises its mighty arm to let horn-bellowing freighters into the harbor. About 900 vessels per year glide through. Pop in to the **Maritime Visitor Center** (lsmma.com; free), next to the bridge, where computer screens tell what time the big ships come and go. Cool model boats and exhibits on Great Lakes shipwrecks also make it a top stop. From here you're a block from **Vikre Distillery** (vikredistillery.com), which makes gin with Northwoods-foraged botanicals. Free tours take place on Monday and Friday (reserve ahead), while the festive tasting room is open every afternoon. Or hop on the Lakewalk outside the maritime center and amble along the paved path that edges Lake Superior. It's part of the long-distance Superior Hiking Trail (p582).

For a hip scene of indie breweries, cider makers and restaurants, ramble through the Lincoln Park Craft District, west of downtown.

EATING & DRINKING IN DULUTH: OUR PICKS

OMC Smokehouse: Buzzing industrial space for revered, slow-cooked meats and local craft brews; try the pulled pork. 11am-9pm Sun-Thu, to 10pm Fri & Sat $$

New Scenic Cafe: Fork into refined meat and fish dishes in a cozy wood-paneled room with partial lake views. 11am-9pm Wed-Sun $$$

Ursa Minor Brewing: Lively indoor-outdoor taproom serving pilsners, hazy IPAs, fruited sour ales and pizzas. 11am-10pm Sun-Thu, to 11pm Fri & Sat

Duluth Cider: Choose among 14 hard ciders in this cool taproom carved from an old livery. noon-10pm Mon-Thu, to 11pm Fri & Sat, 11am-8pm Sun

Gooseberry Falls State Park

North Shore
Highway 61: nature at Lake Superior's rugged edge

Hwy 61 traces Lake Superior's shoreline, winding through red-tinged cliffs and towering firs from Duluth to Canada's edge. Several state parks dot the way, offering spectacular gorges, waterfalls and pine-scented hiking trails, much of it easily accessible from roadside parking lots. The route is 150 miles, drivable in three hours, but most folks make a weekend out of it, overnighting in little towns that speckle the landscape. Crowds amass on summer weekends.

After Duluth and Two Harbors, Hwy 61 ramps up its riches. First, there's pie at **Rustic Inn Cafe**, which wafts berry crumb, lemon meringue and a dozen other flaky-crust flavors from its log cabin at road's edge. **Gooseberry Falls State Park** appears a few miles onward. It's always busy, thanks to its five cascades, scenic gorge and easy trails, including the 2-mile Gooseberry River Loop. Another gorgeous landscape arrives 41 miles later at **Temperance River State Park**, where the waterway roars through a twisting gorge a short hike from the road.

Grand Marais (p582) has good eats, drinks and a lighthouse before hitting **Judge CR Magney State Park**. Here you can view Devil's Kettle, the famous falls where the Brule River splits around a huge rock. Half of the flow drops 50ft in a typically gorgeous North Shore gush, but the other half disappears down a hole and flows underground. Where it goes is a mystery – scientists have never been able to determine the water's outlet. It's a moderately breath-sapping 1.1-mile walk each way.

The road nears its end at **Grand Portage National Monument** (nps.gov/grpo; free), a reconstructed 1788 trading post

TALL TALES

While the legend of Paul Bunyan is heard throughout the northern USA, it's particularly prevalent in Minnesota. Stories of the giant lumberjack with superhuman strength were told in logging camps in the late 1800s and gained widespread popularity in the early 20th century when companies began using the character in ads. Famous feats by Paul and his trusty blue ox, Babe, are myriad. For instance, Paul scooped out the Great Lakes when Babe was thirsty and needed water. And Babe created the Mississippi River when his tank wagon leaked while paving icy logging roads, with the trickle forming the Mississippi. Minnesota leads the USA in Bunyan statues with 11, including the 2.5-ton colossus in Bemidji.

MINNESOTA'S UNOFFICIAL STATE BIRD

Look in any souvenir shop up north, and you'll see a postcard or T-shirt that says 'Minnesota State Bird' with an image of a big, nasty mosquito underneath. These bloodsuckers are relentless in summer. They're drawn to carbon dioxide and body heat, which is why they feast on hikers and paddlers. But mosquitos aren't the only biters in action: black flies sink their teeth into your skin with a sharp pinch. No amount of swatting keeps them away. They annoy mostly in May and June, a bit earlier in the season than mosquitos. Both pests buzz throughout Minnesota, but they're most brutal in the north, where forests and wetlands provide ideal breeding grounds. Use repellent and a net hat to deter them.

Grand Marais Lighthouse

and Ojibwe village. The site is impressively lonely and windblown, open in summer only. **Isle Royale Ferries** *(isleroyaleboats.com; adult/child $100.50/90.50)* also depart from Grand Portage for the 90-minute ride to Isle Royale National Park.

Information for the state parks is at *dnr.state.mn.us*. A vehicle day pass costs $7. An annual pass costs $35. Much of the hiking in the parks is along the Superior Hiking Trail.

Superior Hiking Trail adventure

The 300-mile **Superior Hiking Trail** *(shta.org)* follows the lake-hugging ridge line between Duluth and the Canadian border. Along the way it passes dramatic red-rock overlooks and the occasional moose and black bear. Trailheads with parking lots pop up every 5 to 10 miles, making it ideal for day hikes. The **Superior Shuttle** *(superiorhikingshuttle.com)* makes life even easier, picking up trekkers anywhere along the route as needed (reserve ahead). Overnight hikers will find 94 backcountry campsites and several lodges to cushion the body come nightfall; the trail website has details. The whole footpath is free, with no reservations or permits required. It's easiest to start in the south, where the terrain is more gentle. Thru-hikes take two to four weeks.

Artsy getaway to Grand Marais

Pretty little Grand Marais beckons toward the northern end of Hwy 61 (p581). It makes an excellent base for exploring the parks and trails along Lake Superior, as well as for venturing into the Boundary Waters. Several bars, restaurants, art galleries and antique shops in the tidy downtown give it a 'big city' feel.

GETTING TO ISLE ROYALE

While you can get to **Isle Royale National Park** (p557) from Minnesota, there is greater access from Michigan, which is the state that Isle Royale is officially part of.

Grand Marais' artistic pretensions are genuine. The **Grand Marais Art Colony** *(grandmaraisartcolony.org)* started in 1947 and exists to this day, luring painters, potters and print makers. Do-it-yourself enthusiasts can learn to build boats, sail a schooner and forage for mushrooms at the **North House Folk School** *(northhouse.org)*. If nothing else, make time for the 20-minute walk along the breakwater to **Grand Marais Lighthouse**. The path departs adjacent to **Artist's Point**, a dramatic-looking flat-rock area that is especially luminous as the sun sets.

Gunflint Trail scenic drive

The **Gunflint Trail** *(gunflinttrail.com)*, aka County Rd 12, slices inland through the pines from Grand Marais to Saganaga Lake. The paved, 57-mile-long byway dips into the Boundary Waters area and presents excellent hiking, picnicking and moose-viewing opportunities. It takes 1½ hours to drive one way, but you'll want longer to make stops at roadside pull-offs like the **Moose Viewing Trail**, a 0.3-mile walk to a lake where antlered pals sometimes gather. There aren't any towns along the route, but there are several lodges tucked in woods if you want to grab a meal or snack.

Hibbing

Explore the Iron Range

An area of red-tinged scrubby hills rather than mountains, the ore-rich Iron Range stretches across northeastern Minnesota. Hibbing is the largest town in the region with a couple of claims to fame. For one, Bob Dylan grew up here. See the papier-mâché Bob and small collection of memorabilia at the **Hibbing Public Library** *(hibbingmn.gov)*. It also provides a free walking tour map to find sites like his **Boyhood Home**, where he lived from 1948 to 1959, when he left for Minneapolis. It's privately owned, but good for a discreet photo.

The **Hull Rust Mine Viewpoint** *(hibbingmineview.org)* is the other must-see. Follow the signs that lead a few miles north of town, and behold the enormous, 3.5-mile-wide, open-pit mine spread below. The mind-blowingly huge display trucks give a sense of scale; go ahead and climb up. It's one of the largest iron-ore mines in the world.

Boundary Waters

Canoeing unspoiled wilderness to sleep under the stars

Legendarily remote and pristine, the Boundary Waters Canoe Area Wilderness is one of the world's premier paddling regions.

BOB DYLAN'S MINNESOTA ROOTS

Robert Zimmerman was born in Duluth in 1941. His family moved to Hibbing when he was still quite young. As a teenager he listened to radio stations from Chicago and Little Rock, which played the kind of music that few people in Hibbing knew. His first group, the Golden Chords, won a mere second prize at the local talent show. Bobby made frequent trips to big-city Minneapolis, where he hung around the university area, going to jazz joints and coffeehouses. He enrolled at the University of Minnesota for a year, but dropped out and headed to New York City's folk scene. By 1962 he had legally changed his name to Bob Dylan and never looked back.

 EATING & DRINKING IN GRAND MARAIS: OUR PICKS

Fisherman's Daughter at Dockside Fish Market: The morning boat's fresh haul is your fish and chips by lunchtime. *11am-8pm $$*

My Sister's Place: Tuck into sandwiches, burgers and fish dishes in this woodsy spot with an old-time saloon atmosphere. *11am-8pm $$*

World's Best Donuts: Staff nobly arrive at 3am to fry and glaze; join the queue for the chocolatey, cream-filled results. *7am-3pm Thu-Mon $*

Voyageur Brewing Co: Brewpub with a lake-view deck for knocking back sturdy stouts and ales. *11:30am-9pm Sun-Wed, to 10pm Thu-Sat*

TOP EXPERIENCE

Voyageurs National Park

Northern Voyageurs National Park, which marks the border between the USA and Canada, is a mosaic of land and water. Get ready for boating in summer, snowmobiling in winter and starry dark skies year-round. You'll have much of the landscape to yourself, as this is one of the USA's least-visited parks.

TOP TIPS

- Visit late July to mid-August for warmest lake temperatures and fewest biting insects.

- Boat tours operate mid-June to September; reserve at *recreation.gov*.

- Evening boat tours are often timed to coincide with stargazing tours; check *nps.gov/voya*.

PRACTICALITIES
- nps.gov/voya
- open year-round
- free

Summer Action

During the late May to September peak season, people come to Voyageurs to boat, fish, swim and spot wildlife. Moose, wolves and black bears prowl the forest. Visitor centers at Rainy Lake (open year-round), Kabetogama Lake, Crane Lake and Ash River (all open seasonally) have the lowdown on programs and boat tours. The 2½-hour **Rainy Lake Grand Tour** *(adult/child $50/25)* gives a feel for the scene, as does the **North Canoe Voyage** *(adult/child $15/7.50)* aboard a 26ft birchbark vessel like 17th-century fur traders (aka voyageurs) once paddled. For a true park experience, many visitors rent a houseboat from **Ebel's Voyageur Houseboats** *(ebels.com)* or **Voyagaire Houseboats** *(voyagaire.com)*.

Dark Skies & Winter Fun

Voyageurs is an International Dark Sky Park. The upper parking lot at **Rainy Lake Visitor Center** is an excellent place to stargaze. You might even glimpse the green-draped northern lights (more common in winter). Also prevalent in winter: snowmobiling. Voyageurs is a hot spot for the sport, with 110 miles of staked and groomed trails slicing through the pines. Snowshoeing and cross-country skiing on the trails also are popular.

More than 1000 lakes and streams speckle the piney, 1.1-million-acre expanse, rich in wildlife and sweeping solitude. If you're willing to dig in and canoe for a while, it'll just be you and the moose, bears, wolves and loons that roam the landscape.

The area draws hard-core outdoor adventurers, with most coming for at least four or five days to get away from it all. But it's possible to glide in for a day, too.

However long you plan to stay, know that this is real-deal backcountry and you need to be prepared. Outfitters can help. Ely (pronounced *ee*-lee), the main gateway into the Boundary Waters, has scores of them. The super-knowledgeable folks at **Piragis Northwoods Company** *(piragis.com)* have been around for decades and can set you up with canoes and gear for day trips, overnight stays, guided trips and more. **Ely Outfitting Company** *(elyoutfittingcompany.com)* is another good one.

Entry into the Boundary Waters requires a permit. Day-trip permits are free and can be obtained from the kiosk wherever you enter, no advance booking needed. Overnight permits *(recreation.gov; per trip adult/child $16/8, plus reservation fee $6)* are issued by the US Forest Service and best obtained in advance online. They're limited, and paddlers start snapping them up in January when they are released for the year. It gets a bit complex, as permits are for a specific entry location, of which there are many throughout the vast expanse, some of which require advanced paddling skills. Check *friends-bwca.org* for info. Outfitters are a good resource to help with this, too.

Late May through September is the paddling season, with July and August the peak times. Besides Ely, you can also access the Boundary Waters from Grand Marais by following the Gunflint Trail.

Meet a Boundary Waters rebel

Dorothy Molter lived for 56 years in a cabin in the Boundary Waters' midst, 18 miles from the nearest road. When the Forest Service tried to obtain her land, she refused to move, sparking a long legal battle. Dorothy won and remained in her cabin, paddling, hiking and fishing for whatever she needed. She became famous for providing medical assistance (she was trained as a nurse) and homemade root beer to anyone who dropped by. She died at age 79 (while hauling firewood!) and her friends brought her homestead by dogsled to Ely. It's now a root-beer-selling **museum** *(rootbeerlady.com; adult/child $7/4.50)* that lets you look around her badass abode.

WILDLIFE SPOTTING

Minnesota's northern region, including the Boundary Waters and Voyageurs National Park, holds the star wildlife. Between 13,000 and 18,000 black bears roam the local forests, according to the Department of Natural Resources (DNR). They're relatively common to spot, especially in the fall. Moose are more elusive. The DNR estimates around 4000 rustle through the north woods. Early morning or evening is the best time to see them. Minnesota has the largest population of wolves in the lower 48 states, with some 2900 prowling the area. They're rare to see, but you might hear their eerie howl at night. The loon, Minnesota's state bird, hangs out in the multitude of lakes in summer. Their haunting wail often is heard at night.

Places We Love to Stay

$ Budget $$ Midrange $$$ Top End

Chicago MAPS P505, P510, P515

HI-Chicago $ Chicago's most stalwart hostel is immaculate and adds a staffed information desk, lounge and stocked kitchen to the mix.

Hampton Inn Chicago Downtown/N Loop $$ Features the chain's much-loved amenities in retro environs.

Publishing House Bed & Breakfast $$ Vintage West Loop building with 11 mid-century modern rooms named after Chicago writers.

Robey $$ Sunny rooms stack a 12-story, art-deco tower in Wicker Park, complete with rooftop swimming pool.

Acme Hotel $$ Industrial-chic fills this energetic, 130-room Near North hotel.

Illinois

Inn at 835 (Springfield) $$ Rooms of the four-poster bed, claw-foot bathtub variety occupy a 1908 arts-and-crafts-style luxury apartment building.

Shawnee Forest Cabins (Herod) $$ Settle into a cozy log cottage, with hot tub and firepit, in the peaceful woods.

Indiana

Pepin Mansion (New Albany) $ Standing supremely along New Albany's historical Mansion Row, this 1851 Italianate abode features ornate hand-painted ceilings, original hardwood flooring and gas chandeliers.

Riverboat Inn & Suites (Madison) $ Parts of this historic inn on the river date back to 1929 (it was a former button factory). Riverfront patio bar and free breakfast.

Hotel Broad Ripple (Indianapolis) $$ This Scandinavian-accented boutique hotel is a cozy getaway in hip Broad Ripple, offering spacious rooms right along the Monon Trail.

Story Inn (Nashville) $$ This former general store dating to 1851 (tin roof and metal facade still intact!) drips with countrified rustic charm, offering rooms, cottages and a farm-to-table restaurant.

Riley's Railhouse (Chesterton) $$ Occupying a decommissioned 1914 freight station, this is a railway-themed boutique B&B with rooms inside a renovated depot and railcars. Train enthusiasts will love it – 86 pass per day!

Oliver Inn (South Bend) $$ Elegant nine-room B&B in a Queen Anne–style home dating to 1886. Corner turrets, curved-glass bay windows, claw-foot tubs, and spindles and balustrades abound.

Ironworks Hotel (Indianapolis) $$$ With design touches forged from industrial parts from an abandoned Wisconsin iron foundry, this hotel has several restaurants, a gym and 120 fantastic rooms.

Ohio

Symphony Hotel (Cincinnati) $ Nine rooms in a traditional Italianate building, each named after a classical composer, and each chock-full of period antique decor. Breakfast included.

Clifford House B&B (Cleveland) $$ If you don't like animals, this beautiful Ohio City B&B isn't for you. If you do, Henry the dog and Connie the cat are ready for you! Jim the human cooks up a scrumptious breakfast and is great fun to chat with. Free parking.

Inn at Brandywine Falls (Cuyahoga Valley) $$ An 1848 Greek Revival country home situated in a gentle sweep of pastoral prettiness. Six rooms, of which the Granary suite is particularly lovely. Breakfasts are delicious.

Inn at Honey Run (Millersburg) $$$ In Amish Country, 25 rooms occupy the lodge-like main building, while 12 'honeycomb' rooms are built right into the hillside Frank Lloyd Wright–style. Adults only.

Metropolitan at the 9 (Cleveland) $$$ Upscale Marriott-branded property with 156 good-sized rooms, a rooftop bar and a subterranean cocktail lounge set in the building's old bank vaults.

Hotel Kilbourne (Sandusky) $$$ Near the ferry dock, a boutique hotel complete with rooftop bar, a Mexican restaurant and a gift shop, all on-site.

Michigan MAP P546

Hostel Detroit (Detroit) $ An old building rehabbed using recycled materials and painted in vivid colors inside and out. Dormitories, private rooms and shared bathrooms and kitchens.

Landmark Inn (Marquette) $$ This elegant, six-story hotel fills a historic lakefront building and has a couple of resident ghosts.

El Moore Lodge (Detroit) $$ A unique option in Midtown with a friendly vibe, its 11 rooms occupy a turreted 1898 building that's been renovated;

reclaimed wood and tiles feature in the interior.

Shinola Hotel (Detroit) $$$ Detroit's homegrown brand known for luxury watches extends to this stylish hotel downtown. The 129 rooms have mid-century modern decor, big windows and Bluetooth speaker systems.

Perry Hotel (Petoskey) $$$ Grand historic place where Hemingway once stayed (in 1916 after a hiking trip in the region). Count on comfy beds, vintage furniture and a cozy on-site pub.

Grey Hare Inn (Traverse City) $$$ An intimate, three-room B&B on a working vineyard, with French-style decor and bay views. Free wine tastings.

Glen Arbor B&B (Sleeping Bear Dunes) $$$ The owners renovated this century-old farmhouse into a sunny, French country inn with eight themed rooms.

Burnt Toast Inn (Ann Arbor) $$$ Colorful house with a lovely garden, big porch and five rooms that mix sturdy antiques with edgy art. On a leafy street walkable to downtown. Free parking and breakfast.

Rock Harbor Lodge (Isle Royale) $$$ The island's sole lodge, offering 60 rooms with lake views in the main building, as well as 20 cabins with kitchenettes.

Wisconsin MAP P562

Julie's Park Cafe and Motel (Door County) $ Long-standing, crowd-pleasing budget option in Fish Creek right next door to Peninsula State Park.

Ambassador (Milwaukee) $$ Renovated art-deco gem near Marquette University, chock-full of polished marbled floors, bronze elevator doors and more period details.

County Clare Irish Inn (Milwaukee) $$ Rooms have a snug cottage feel, with four-poster beds, white wainscot walls and whirlpool baths; there's an on-site pub.

Hotel Ruby Marie (Madison) $$ A 19th-century railroad hotel retrofitted with modern conveniences while retaining vintage charm; free breakfast and happy-hour drinks.

Graduate Madison (Madison) $$ Near State St's action, this 72-room hotel wafts a hip academic vibe with its mod-meets-plaid decor and book-themed artwork.

Square Rigger Lodge (Door County) $$ Guests return year after year to this Jacksonport motel winner that features a private sand beach.

Beachfront Inn (Door County) $$ Cute Bailey's Harbor lakefront motel that earns extra points for its pool, nighttime beach bonfires and nearby pubs.

Charmant Hotel (La Crosse) $$ Sweet renovation of a 1898 candy factory into 67 rooms with exposed brick walls, wood floors and industrial-cool charm.

Brewhouse Inn & Suites (Milwaukee) $$$ A 90-room hotel set in the old Pabst Brewery complex. The large chambers have steampunk-type decor.

Old Rittenhouse Inn (Bayfield) $$$ Looking for lace, creaky floorboards and a romantic escape? This inn fills two Victorian homes atop a hill with lake views.

Minnesota MAP P574

Mountain Inn (Lutsen) $ Well-run motel with spacious rooms that are nothing fancy, but they're great value for the Lake Superior area.

Adventure Inn (Ely) $ A blue ribbon to the cute tidy motel rooms, which are walkable to eats and drinks in downtown Ely.

Canopy Mill District (Minneapolis) $$ Ornamental historic building downtown, where contemporary rooms have high, timbered ceilings and exposed brick.

Hewing Hotel (Minneapolis) $$ Rustic-vibe chambers feature wood-beam ceilings, deer-print wallpaper and plaid wool blankets; near downtown's action.

Celeste of St Paul (St Paul) $$ Located downtown, this lovingly restored former convent offers 72 smart, lofty rooms and a bouncy bar.

Hungry Hippie Farm & Hostel (Grand Marais) $$ Pretty farmhouse 8 miles east of Grand Marais, with six rustic-chic private rooms that share bathrooms.

Northern Rail Traincar Inn (Two Harbors) $$ It doesn't get much cooler than 14 rooms built into renovated train boxcars.

Ash Trail Lodge (Orr) $$ Family-owned business that offers little cabins and great home cooking right next to Voyageurs National Park.

Hotel Alma (Minneapolis) $$$ Seven light-wood, Nordic-style rooms set above Alma (the Beard Award–winning restaurant-cafe); delicious breakfast pastries provided.

Researched and curated by
Lauren Keith and Amy Balfour

The Great Plains

SURPRISING CITIES AMID PRISTINE PRAIRIE

The Great Plains are happy to transition you between east and west, but don't you dare dismiss this as flyover country.

If you slow down, the Heartland invites you in and shares some of the country's finest history, scenery and adventure. Each of its seven states has enough to stop you in your tracks; the only hard part is figuring out how to experience as much as possible in this vast region that makes up 15% of the country.

The USA's two longest rivers, the Missouri and the Mississippi, cut through the Plains, and many of the region's cities got their start along these mighty routes. Dams have tamed them since then, but wild – and federally protected, thanks to their outstanding scenery – waterways can still be found in Missouri's Ozarks and Nebraska's Niobrara Valley.

Other gripping landscapes include the dreamy colors of the badlands in the Dakotas and the bison-studded prairies also found there, as well as in Kansas and Oklahoma. Meanwhile, the Great Plains cities are quietly cool and self-confident – many have been undergoing a renaissance as they spruce up former warehouse districts and embark on new infrastructure projects that make it easier to travel here.

Does this region have the national parks of Utah, the coastline of California or the big cities of the East? No, but if you've come this far, you know that's not why you're here. Open your mind in these wide-open spaces, and you're bound to be captivated by what you discover.

RIVERNORTHPHOTOGRAPHY/GETTY IMAGES

THE MAIN AREAS

MISSOURI
The Show Me State has a ton to show off. **p594**

KANSAS
Wide open spaces and unexpected attractions. **p607**

OKLAHOMA
Deep Native history and cool Route 66 cities. **p614**

NEBRASKA
Still at the heart of travelers' trails. **p624**

For places to stay in the Great Plains, see p662

THE GUIDE

THE GREAT PLAINS

Bison, Custer State Park (p119)

IOWA
Heartland beauty and a cycling hot spot. **p634**

NORTH DAKOTA
Explore the grasslands that inspired Theodore Roosevelt.
p645

SOUTH DAKOTA
Mt Rushmore, bison and badlands. **p649**

THE GREAT PLAINS THE GUIDE

Find Your Way

Distances in the Great Plains are vast, and having your own wheels is the best way to rack up the miles. Interstates crisscross the region; the smaller state and federal highways are slower but more scenic.

TRAIN

Amtrak (*amtrak.com*) runs four long-distance routes across the Great Plains. Arriving by train (particularly from the hub city of Chicago) is an option, but getting around is not, with the exception of the *Missouri River Runner* between St Louis and Kansas City.

CAR

A car is essential for getting around the Great Plains, as well as within its cities, which lack comprehensive public transport networks. Car rental companies usually have locations in airports and downtown districts.

AIR

The major cities in each of the Great Plains states have airports, including **St Louis, Kansas City, Omaha, Oklahoma City** and **Des Moines.** However, they generally connect to larger hubs like Denver, Chicago and Dallas instead of one another.

North Dakota, p645
Find the celebrity woodchipper in Fargo, mingle with dinosaurs in Chamberlain, and hike the landscapes that Theodore Roosevelt called 'the romance of my life.'

Iowa, p634
Admire architectural treasures in Des Moines and Mason City, cycle statewide trails, follow Lewis and Clark, and soak up the bucolic scenery that inspired American Gothic.

South Dakota, p649
Squint at presidents at Mt Rushmore then drive past shaggy bison, granite spires and ponderosa pines in the Black Hills. National parks spotlight caves and badlands.

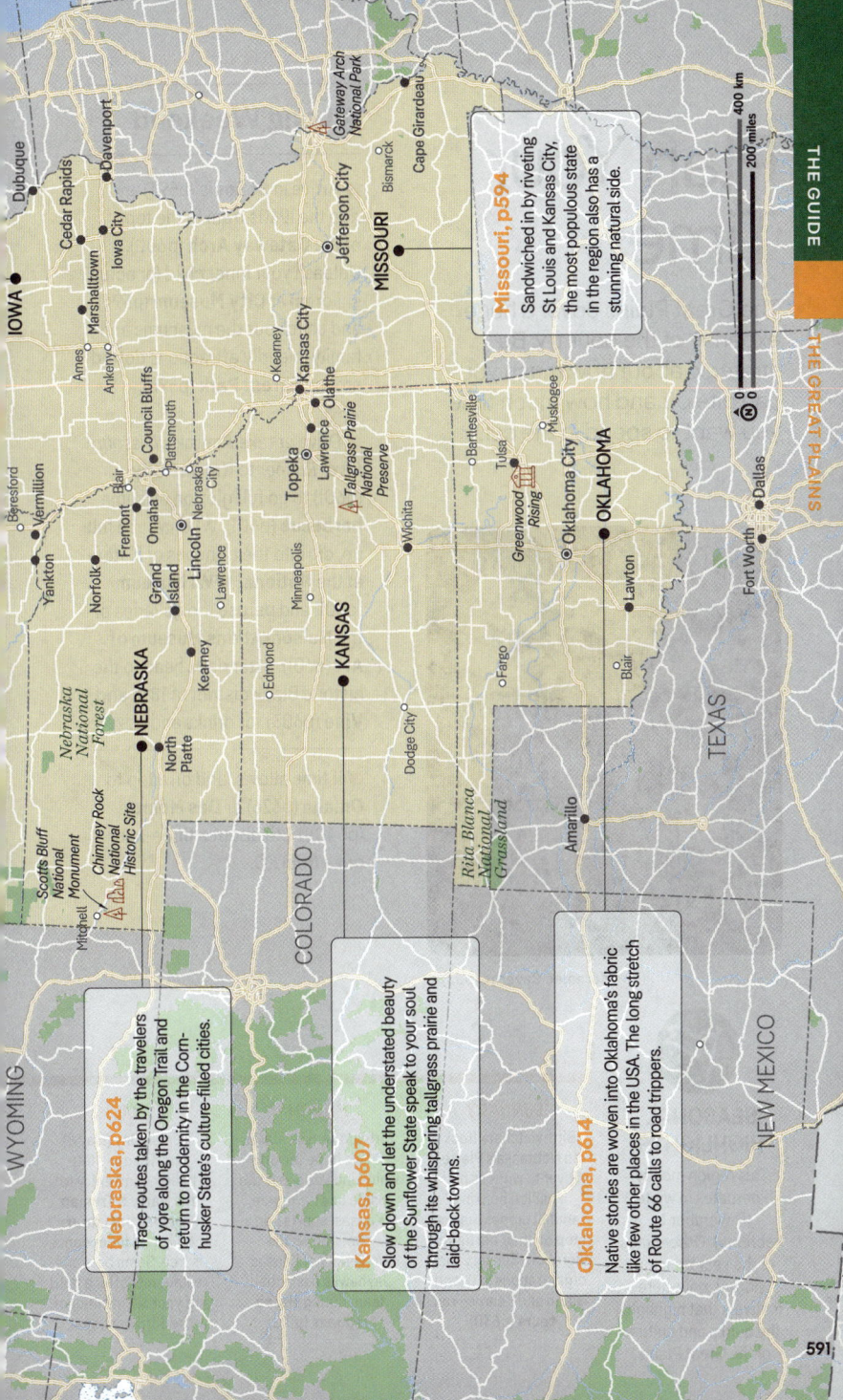

Plan Your Time

The Great Plains cover a huge expanse of the country. Be strategic about how much you can bite off and how much time you want to spend in the car.

Meramec Caverns (p57)

A Long Weekend

● Arrive in **St Louis** (p594) and ride the 1960s tram to the top of the **Gateway Arch** (p600). Unleash your inner child (or actual children) at **City Museum** (p594) and check out the museums and family-friendly attractions dotted around **Forest Park** (p598).

● Drive or take Amtrak's *Missouri River Runner* to **Kansas City** (p601) to go full glutton on some **barbecue** (p601). When you're full up, dig into the trenches of history at the **National WWI Museum** (p601) and peruse the galleries of the **Nelson-Atkins Museum of Art** (p601). After dark, head to the historic Black district of **18th and Vine** (p603) for drinks and jazz.

● If time allows, add on a trip to **Omaha** (p626) or **Des Moines** (p640), both about a three-hour drive from KC.

SEASONAL HIGHLIGHTS

This region mostly hibernates in winter (November to February). Other times of the year bring out vibrant, only-here festivals that highlight the quirks and culture of the Great Plains.

FEBRUARY
Bird-watchers flock to Nebraska's Platte River to witness half a million honking sandhill cranes make a stop on their northerly migration. Conservation organizations in Grand Island and Kearney run **tours** (p630).

MARCH
Tornado season starts, but we hope the only whirlwind you see is the inside of a Lawrence, Kansas, sports bar, cheering on the University of Kansas Jayhawks basketball team during **March Madness** (p1113).

MAY
Truman Day (May 8) is a Missouri state holiday, and entry to the **Harry S Truman Presidential Library** (p604) in Independence is free. Some bars and restaurants offer a third off your bill in honor of the 33rd president.

A Week in the Plains

● After a few days in **St Louis** (p594), snake up the Mississippi River to Iowa along the **Great River Road**, stopping in **Dubuque** and **Davenport** (p635). Pause in the folksy **Amana Colonies** (p638), established as 19th-century German religious communes, with a museum, shops and a boutique hotel.

● Take the back roads or hop on I-80 to **Des Moines** (p640) for art and architecture. Cross the state line to **Omaha** (p626) to explore shops, bars and restaurants in the **Old Market** (p626).

● Leave city life behind on your way to **Badlands National Park** and **Mt Rushmore** (p558) in South Dakota, stopping in Nebraska to float the Niobrara River near **Valentine** (p633) or just having lunch at **Monowi Tavern** (p633), run by the town's sole resident.

Route 66

● Marking its 100th anniversary in 2026, Route 66 is one of the USA's most iconic road trips. The Mother Road clocks up many miles through three Plains states. Spend a week or more checking out the cool cities and oddball small towns along the way.

● After seeing the sights of **St Louis** (p694), have a concrete at Ted Drewes (p697) and hit the road. **Meramec Caverns** (p697), the largest commercial cave in Missouri, is a classic stop.

● **Kansas** (p607) contains just 13 miles of the Mother Road but has diversions aplenty.

● Budget most of your time for Oklahoma. Stop at roadside attractions like the **Blue Whale** (p618) and get waylaid in **Tulsa** (p614), the 'capital of Route 66,' then carry on through **Oklahoma City** (p620) toward Texas.

THE GUIDE

THE GREAT PLAINS

JUNE
School's out, and summer fun is starting. Get weird on the water at Wichita's **Riverfest** (p609), celebrate **Pride** in cities across the region and mark **Juneteenth** on Tulsa's Black Wall Street (p614).

JULY
Road-tripping families scoot across Missouri, Kansas and Oklahoma along historic Route 66, while cyclists set off on **RAGBRAI** (p644), a weeklong noncompetitive 470-mile bike ride that traverses Iowa.

AUGUST
The **Iowa State Fair** (p640) in Des Moines is legendary, even inspiring a Broadway musical. More than a million visitors come to eat deep-fried Twinkies, coo over farm animals and check out the famous butter sculptures.

OCTOBER
Admire prismatic fall foliage along the **Great River Road** (p640), which traces the Mississippi River along Iowa's eastern edge through quaint waterfront towns. Peak leaf-peeping times are in mid- to late October.

Missouri

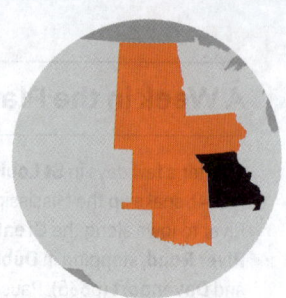

FINGER-LICKING BARBECUE | COOL MUSEUMS | WILD RIVERS

Places
St Louis p594
Kansas City p601
Independence p604
St Joseph p604
The Ozarks p605

☑ TOP TIP

Which state is Kansas City in? Well, both Kansas (KCK) and Missouri (KCMO). Don't get it wrong like many national politicians and musicians shouting it on stage. We include Kansas City in this book, but we've noted when places are on the Kansas side of the state line.

With more forest and fewer farm fields than neighboring states, Missouri might not seem like a natural fit in the Great Plains. Limestone canyons, more caves than anywhere else in the country and glacial-blue springs that feed undammed rivers aren't what many travelers expect, but the Show Me State deserves to brag about its outdoor attractions, as well as its cities.

The most populous Plains state likes to mix things up. St Louis (STL) and Kansas City (KC) are on opposite ends of the state, both with excellent museums, must-devour foods, and diversions for music fans and sports nuts. Expect to spend at least a few days soaking up the sights in each.

From St Louis, Route 66 cuts its way diagonally across the state, delivering hokey roadside detours. No matter where you go, you're sure to find an adventure worthy of Missouri native Mark Twain as you explore the state.

St Louis

Run wild at the City Museum

City Museum *(citymuseum.org; $20)*, perhaps St Louis' most boring-sounding attraction, is one of the coolest things to do in the entire region, so don't you dare let the dull name put you off. The Ferris wheel and school bus on the roof surely hint at the hilarity inside this museum gone maximalist.

 GETTING AROUND

International airports in Kansas City and St Louis bookend Missouri, making the state the easiest entry point by air into the Great Plains. You can travel between these two cities aboard Amtrak's *Missouri River Runner*, but if you're going further afield, you'll need a car.

Often congested, I-70 connects St Louis and Kansas City, while I-44 paved over much of Route 66 between St Louis and the Kansas–Oklahoma border. Roads in the Ozarks are often scenic, winding, two-lane roller coasters.

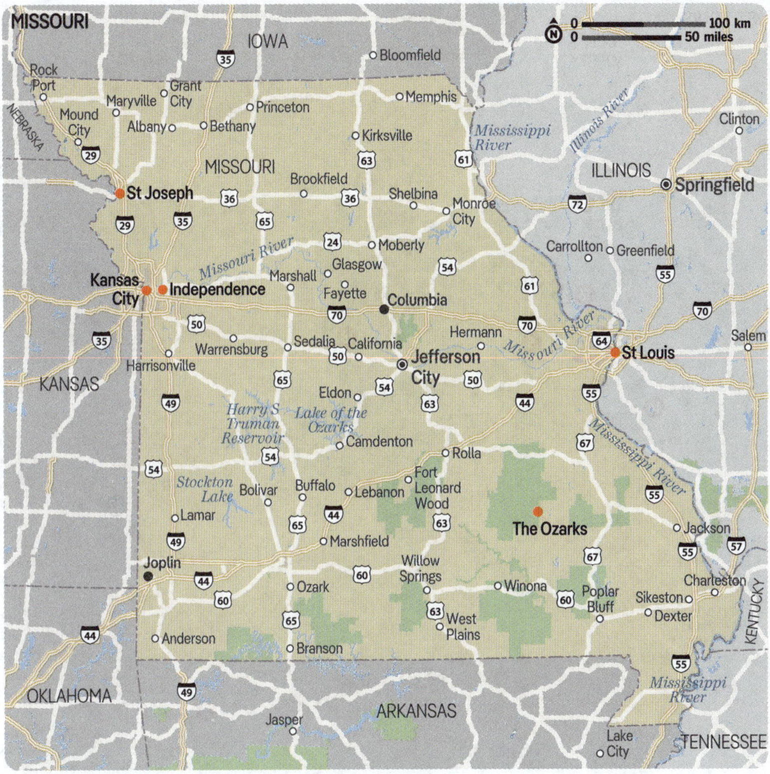

Part playground, part architectural salvage, part art installation, this fun house is a wild ride – literally. Seven- and 10-story slides cascade through the industrial building, a century-old former warehouse for the International Shoe Company. Relics from demolished buildings – many designed by architect Louis Sullivan, the 'father of skyscrapers' and mentor to Frank Lloyd Wright – are portals to other floors (and maybe even other worlds).

It costs $8 extra to visit the roof, but it's worth it. The modern art is sure to crack a smile, from a 'sausage man' made of bronze to *Bop Bear,* a punching bag resembling a bear-shaped honeypot that first debuted at Burning Man and is now a hit with kids.

 EATING IN ST LOUIS: OUR PICKS

City Foundry: Upscale food hall with 17 globetrotting stalls, plus shops, mini-golf and escape rooms, in an old motor factory. *10am-9pm* $$

Blood & Sand: This former members-only club has opened to us commoners with a signature tasting menu and killer cocktails. *5-11pm Mon-Sat* $$$

Broadway Oyster Bar: Suck down crawfish and other Cajun treats at this New Orleans–style joint that's part bar, part live-music venue, but all restaurant. *11am-10pm* $$

Katie's Pizza & Pasta: Phenomenal Italian food right outside Busch Stadium in Ballpark Village. *11am-10pm Mon-Thu, from 10am Sat & Sun* $$

ST LOUIS

★ HIGHLIGHTS
1 City Museum

● SIGHTS
2 Busch Stadium
3 Energizer Park
4 Enterprise Center
5 Forest Park
6 Gateway Arch National Park
7 Missouri Botanical Garden
8 Missouri History Museum
9 Museum at the Gateway Arch
10 National Blues Museum
11 Old Courthouse
12 St Louis Art Museum
13 St Louis Science Center
14 St Louis Zoo
15 Union Station

● ACTIVITIES
16 Big Muddy Adventures
17 Gateway Arch Riverboats
18 Steinberg Skating Rink

● SLEEPING
19 St Louis Union Station Hotel

● EATING
20 Blood & Sand
21 Boathouse at Forest Park
22 Broadway Oyster Bar
23 Charlie Gitto's
24 City Foundry
25 Imo's
26 Katie's Pizza & Pasta
27 Pappy's Smokehouse
28 Park Avenue Coffee

● DRINKING & NIGHTLIFE
29 4 Hands Brewing Co
30 Anheuser-Busch Brewery
31 Blueprint Coffee at High Low
32 Just John Club
33 None of the Above

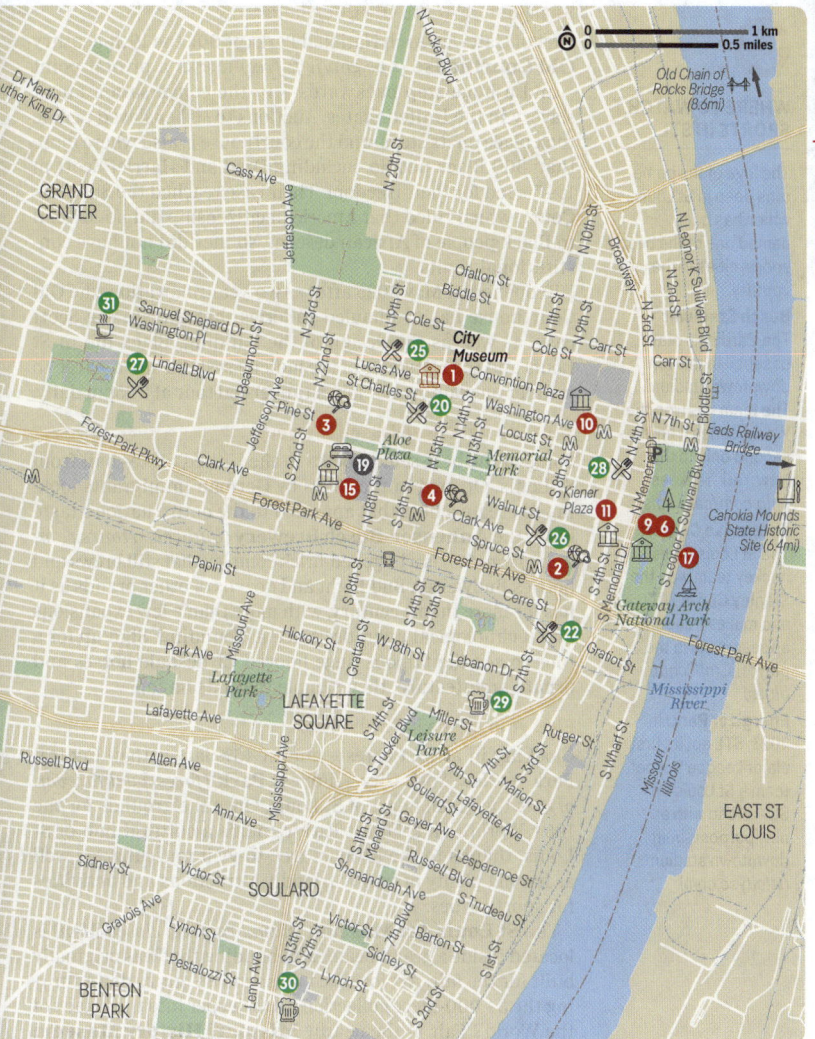

ROUTE 66 STOPS IN MISSOURI

Old Chain of Rocks Bridge: Now open only to pedestrians and cyclists, this mile-long span over the Mississippi River north of St Louis opened in 1929.

Ted Drewes: Save room for a concrete, a cup of thick frozen custard, invented at this St Louis institution in 1959. *(teddrewes.com)*

Meramec Caverns: Hugely popular and totally corny, these caves are filled with stalactites and Civil War history. *(americascave.com; adult/child $29.50/16)*

Uranus Fudge Factory: No pun is left unexcreted at this shameless roadside attraction. *(uranusgeneralstore.com)*

WHERE TO WATCH SPORTS IN STL

The love of the game runs deep in St Louis, which has been named one of the best sports cities in the country.

Busch Stadium: The Cardinals play baseball in this fun downtown stadium. The team has won the World Series 11 times, second only to the New York Yankees. *(mlb.com/cardinals)*

Enterprise Center: The St Louis Blues hockey team won the Stanley Cup in 2019 and makes frequent appearances in the playoffs. *(nhl.com/blues)*

Energizer Park: In 2023, STL got its first Major League Soccer team – St Louis City SC – along with a new purpose-built downtown stadium. *(stlcitysc.com)*

Seek justice at the Old Courthouse

Part of Gateway Arch National Park (p600), the 19th-century **Old Courthouse** *(nps.gov/jeff; free)* marks a pivotal point – and a huge step backwards – in the conversation about slavery in the United States. Auctions to sell enslaved people took place on its steps, and the courthouse is also where more than 300 Black people, including Dred and Harriet Scott in 1847, sued for their freedom. Their case reached the Supreme Court, which ruled that American citizenship did not extend to Black people of African descent, so they did not have constitutional rights.

Reopened in May 2025 after a two-year renovation, the Old Courthouse has overhauled galleries that explain the Scott case, as well as the design of the building, Black life in St Louis and the relevance of the judicial system. You are free to wander on your own or join a ranger-led tour at 2:15pm daily.

Tour the Anheuser-Busch Brewery

Some of the best-selling beers in the United States hail from St Louis. Opened in the 1850s by German immigrants looking to create a beer that appealed to the entire nation's taste buds, the **Anheuser-Busch Brewery** *(budweisertours.com; tours from $15)* is a huge red-brick complex that still brews and bottles Budweiser, Bud Light and dozens of other brands as it has for more than a century, with more than a few expansions and technological upgrades since its founding. Sign up for a tour to see the famous huge-hooved Clydesdale horses and ornate architecture, then sample the suds on tap.

Find your space in Forest Park

Clocking in at 1371 acres – almost 45% larger than Central Park in New York City – **Forest Park** *(forestparkforever.org)* is the green heart of St Louis. Once the grounds for the 1904 World's Fair, Forest Park remains a cultural hub of St Louis, thanks to the array of free-to-visit museums, as well as having plenty of family-friendly attractions and activities for sporty types.

The **St Louis Art Museum** *(slam.org; free; closed Mon)* is located inside a grand beaux-arts building that was originally built for the fair. Art lovers could spend an entire day admiring the 34,000-piece collection. Dive deeper into the legacy of the World's Fair at the nearby **Missouri History Museum** *(mohistory.org; free; closed Mon)*, whose showcase exhibit is

EATING IN ST LOUIS: ICONIC STL FOODS

Charlie Gitto's: Said to be the spot that invented toasted ravioli in 1947 when a chef dropped them in oil instead of water. *5-9pm Sun-Thu, to 10pm Fri & Sat* $$$

Imo's: This local chain is a prolific purveyor of St Louis–style pizza: cracker-thin, square-cut crust topped with Provel cheese. *10am-11pm or later* $

Park Avenue Coffee: Treat yourself to a slice of gooey butter cake. This cafe does them in several flavors, such as red velvet and pumpkin caramel. *7am-2pm Mon-Fri* $

Pappy's Smokehouse: Food Network called these the best BBQ ribs in the country, and our sticky fingers agree. *11am-4pm or later Wed-Mon* $

Forest Park

MORE STL SIGHTS

Missouri Botanical Garden: Walk around a 14-acre Japanese garden, a Victorian-style hedge maze and the geodesic Climatron. *(missouribotanicalgarden.org; adult/child $16/free)*

National Blues Museum: Explore the deep history of this influential music genre. *(nationalbluesmuseum.org; adult/child $15/10)*

National Museum of Transportation: Huge railroad locomotives, historic cars cooler than your rental and more that moves. *(tnmot.org; adult/child $16/8)*

Union Station: Family-friendly attractions in this former train station include a 200ft-tall Ferris wheel, a shark-filled aquarium and a ropes course. Adults can watch the light show in the Grand Hall, now a hotel bar (p642). *(stlouisunionstation.com)*

a scale model of the 1904 grounds. The museum's gift shop is one of the best places in town for STL souvenirs you never knew you needed, like a toasted ravioli fridge magnet.

Kids will be more drawn in by the critters at the **St Louis Zoo** *(stlzoo.org; free)* and the interactive displays and demonstrations at the **St Louis Science Center** *(slsc.org; free; closed Tue & Wed)*. From mid-November to early March, lace up your ice skates to glide on the **Steinberg Skating Rink** *(steinbergrink.com)*, the largest in the Midwest.

Fuel up for a big day out at the **Boathouse at Forest Park** *(boathousestl.com)*, the park's waterside cafe, where you can dine outdoors next to the ducks. Next door, rent paddle boats, canoes, kayaks, stand-up paddleboards – or bikes for landlubbers – from **Big Muddy Adventures** *(paddleforestpark.com)*.

DRINKING IN ST LOUIS: OUR PICKS

4 Hands Brewing Co: STL's largest craft brewery is down the road from big brother Bud, with a lively taproom. *11am-10pm or later Mon-Sat, to 8pm Sun*

Side Project: Hopheads must visit this suburban brewery that's been ranked as one of the best in the world multiple times. *4-8pm Mon, Wed & Thu, from 1pm Fri-Sun*

None of the Above: Sleek speakeasy below City Foundry (p595) started by a James Beard–winning chef. Look for the red light. *5pm-1am Wed-Mon*

Blueprint Coffee at High Low: This 'literary cafe' serves live music, art exhibitions and a creative atmosphere alongside coffee and pastries. *8am-4pm*

TOP EXPERIENCE

Gateway Arch National Park

The world's largest arch soars 630ft above the smallest national park in the United States. Set within a green space near the Mississippi River, long an unofficial divider between east and west, the Arch is a symbol of St Louis, promoting the city's historic role as the 'Gateway to the West.' The museum presents nuanced views on manifest destiny and white western migration.

TOP TIPS

● Save $3 on tram tickets with the **America the Beautiful** national park pass. Combo tickets for cruises also net small savings.

● Going through airport-style security is required to visit the museum and take the trams.

● Tram tickets often sell out; book online in advance.

PRACTICALITIES

● gatewayarch.com; nps.gov/jeff
● museum free; tram ride from $12
● museum and tram open 9am-6pm; grounds 5am-11pm

Museum at the Gateway Arch

The fascinating, free-to-visit **Museum at the Gateway Arch** will take up the majority of the time you spend at this national park. It's filled with interactive exhibits that detail the history of St Louis, provide updated perspectives on westward expansion, and dive into the architectural and engineering feats required for the arch's construction.

Tram to the Top

A visit to the Gateway Arch isn't complete without whizzing to the top in one of the small trams that feel like 1960s space capsules straight out of *The Jetsons*. They take four minutes to trundle to the top, releasing passengers into a narrow viewing area with windows that provide unbeatable views over the city.

Gateway Arch Riverboats

Churn up the 'Big Muddy' (the Mississippi River) on replica 19th-century steamboats on a narrated cruise with **Gateway Arch Riverboats**. Unfortunately, this stretch of river isn't particularly scenic, but it's still a fun way to see the city, and it's the only way to get on the fast-flowing water of the country's most fabled river.

Kansas City

Remembering the Great War

The United States' congressionally designated national museum of the Great War isn't in Washington, DC, but in the heart of the country in Kansas City. Enter the impressive, modern **National WWI Museum** *(theworldwar.org; adult/child $19.50/11.50; closed Mon Sep-May)* on a glass walkway over a field of red poppies, the symbol of remembrance of WWI. Through detailed and engaging displays, learn about a war that is almost forgotten by many Americans.

Outside, the **Liberty Memorial** towers nearly 270ft above the lawn, and you can ride an elevator to the top (for an extra $6) to see the city from on high. The view of Union Station (p599) from the top of Liberty Memorial and the courtyard below is the most photographed angle of Kansas City. The courtyard is free for all to access – you don't have to visit the museum.

Artsy outing at Nelson-Atkins

One of the top galleries in the region, the **Nelson-Atkins Museum of Art** *(nelson-atkins.org; free; closed Tue & Wed)* is a cherished city treasure and a must-visit for culture vultures. The globe-trotting collection spans continents, showing off ancient Egyptian coffins, Chinese bronzes and works by European masters (including pieces by Monet and Caravaggio).

But the most iconic pieces aren't in the museum at all – they are outside on the lawn. Four 18ft-tall badminton shuttlecocks playfully plunge into the grass on either side of the museum building, which represents the net, and they feature on countless KC souvenirs.

Nearby, the smaller **Kemper Museum of Contemporary Art** *(kemperart.org; free; closed Mon & Tue)* has edgy rotating exhibitions and an excellent cafe.

Track down KC's best barbecue

Kansas City was once home to some of the largest stockyards in the country, second only to Chicago, and smoked meat is still big business. KC's status as one of the best places in the USA to eat barbecue is thanks to Henry Perry, a Black pitmaster who opened a restaurant in the early 1900s. Although Perry's restaurant no longer exists, he trained apprentice pitmasters who carried on his craft at the thriving institutions of **Gates Bar-B-Q** *(gatesbbq.com)* and **Arthur Bryant's** *(arthurbryantsbbq.com)*.

WHERE TO WATCH SPORTS IN KC

Kansas City is the smallest city to host the 2026 World Cup games. To say that this place is sports mad is an understatement.

Arrowhead Stadium: Even before Taylor Swift, the Kansas City Chiefs were hitting the headlines, winning the Super Bowl three times between 2020 and 2024. *(chiefs.com)*

Kauffman Stadium: The Royals baseball team hits homers at The K. *(mlb.com/royals)*

CPKC Stadium: The first arena in the world purpose-built for a professional women's sports team opened for the KC Current's soccer stars in 2024. *(kansascitycurrent.com)*

Children's Mercy Park: Sporting KC, the men's soccer team, plays on the Kansas side. *(sportingkc.com)*

EATING IN KANSAS CITY: OUR PICKS

Antler Room: Local ingredients go global in seasonal small plates, which might include fresh pasta, potato gyoza or grilled octopus. *5–10pm Wed-Sun* **$$**

Baba's Pantry: Nowhere else in town does hummus, falafel and chicken shawarma as good as this Palestinian-American deli. *11am-7pm Mon-Sat* **$**

Green Dirt on Oak: The charcuterie boards are works of art and mostly sourced from its own farm in Weston, about 30 miles northwest. *10am-10pm Wed-Sun* **$$**

Corvino: Sit in the darkened dining room for a decadent New American dinner, starting with the signature seaweed doughnuts. *5–10pm Sun-Thu, to 11pm Fri & Sat* **$$$**

KANSAS CITY

● SIGHTS
1. American Jazz Museum
2. CPKC Stadium
3. Kemper Museum of Contemporary Art
4. Museum of BBQ
5. National WWI Museum
6. Negro Leagues Baseball Museum
7. Nelson-Atkins Museum of Art
8. Rock Island Bridge
9. Union Station

● EATING
10. Antler Room
11. Arthur Bryant's
12. Corvino
13. Gates Bar-B-Q
14. Green Dirt on Oak
15. Joe's Kansas City Bar-B-Que
16. Slap's BBQ

● DRINKING & NIGHTLIFE
17. Boulevard Brewery
18. Hamburger Mary's
19. J Rieger
20. Missie B's
21. Swordfish Tom's
22. Tom's Town
23. Vine Street Brewing Co

● ENTERTAINMENT
24. Mutual Musicians Foundation

Kansas City barbecue has deep roots but continues to evolve, with a new generation of pitmasters firing up the smokers for their own takes on tradition. The Z-Man sandwich (sliced brisket, smoked provolone cheese and onion rings on a Kaiser roll) from **Joe's Kansas City Bar-B-Que** *(joeskc.com)* holds legendary status, best devoured at its original location in a gas station on the Kansas side of the state line. Vegetarians should try the version with portobello mushroom. Elsewhere in KCK, **Slap's BBQ** *(slapsbbqkc.com)*, well, slaps. (Its name is actually an acronym that stands for 'Squeal Like a Pig.') Burnt ends – the fatty charred ends of brisket, like smoked beef crackling – are a Kansas City invention and a must-order here and at any spot worth its sauce.

Before you fill your stomach, feed your mind at the world's first **Museum of BBQ** *(museumofbbq.co; $12)*, opened in March 2025. It dissects the history of KC barbecue and other major regional styles. More importantly, it has a 'bean' ball pit.

Feel the soul of Black Kansas City

The historic Black district of **18th and Vine** was a cradle of jazz music and is still a focal point of Black culture in KC.

Learn about musicians – including Kansas City native Charlie 'Bird' Parker – instruments and styles at the **American Jazz Museum** *(americanjazzmuseum.org; adult/child $10/6)*, which also has an jazz club called the **Blue Room** for live performances throughout the week, some of which are free. Jazz-loving night owls should head to **Mutual Musicians Foundation** *(themutualmusiciansfoundation.com; midnight–5am Fri & Sat)*. When performers wrap up their evening shows elsewhere, they head to Mutual Musicians to jam. Sessions don't get going until midnight or later, and Mutual Musicians is the only place in the entire state that's allowed to sell alcohol all night, thanks to a special exemption from the Missouri legislature.

Next to the American Jazz Museum, the **Negro Leagues Baseball Museum** *(nlbm.com; adult/child $10/6; closed Mon)* covers the lesser-known history of Black teams, such as the KC Monarchs and New York Black Yankees, that flourished until baseball became fully integrated.

Vine Street Brewing Co *(vinestbrewing.com; closed Tue)*, Missouri's first Black-owned brewery, opened in 2023 and is already a neighborhood staple. Sip a pint of Jazzman, a black lager that's the brewery's signature pour, at its premises in a graffitied limestone former public-works building.

This district has been undergoing major and much-needed improvements, including a new pedestrian plaza for better

KC WITH KIDS

Rabbit hOle: Tumble into the magic of children's literature at this one-of-a-kind art-filled celebration of kids' books. *(rabbitholekc.org; $16)*

Union Station: It's still a working train station, but it also contains Science City, a planetarium and a five-story-tall movie screen. *(unionstation.org)*

Kansas City Zoo & Aquarium: Colorful fish, sharks and a giant Pacific octopus fill a 650,000-gallon aquarium opened in 2023. *(kansascityzoo.org; from $20)*

Wonderscope: Children's museum best suited for under-10s. *(wonderscope.org; $16)*

Deanna Rose Children's Farmstead: Pet farm animals and bottle-feed baby goats in the Kansas-side suburb of Overland Park. *($5)*

DRINKING IN KANSAS CITY: OUR PICKS

Swordfish Tom's: KC's best cocktail bar is hiding down an alleyway. Descend the stairs into a darkened basement boiler room. *4pm-1:30am Tue-Sat*

J Rieger: This historic distillery was closed during Prohibition but resurrected a century later by the founder's great-great-great-grandson. *3-10pm Wed-Sat*

Tom's Town: Distillery named for a 1930s political boss with an art deco–style bar and a weekend-only speakeasy. *4-10pm or later Mon-Fri, noon-midnight Sat*

Boulevard Brewery: A conglomerate now owns KC's original craft brewer, but locals still love sipping Boulevard Wheat. *noon-9pm Mon-Sat, 10am-6pm Sun*

INDEPENDENCE TO THE FRONTIER

Nicknamed the 'Queen City of the Trails,' Independence was a major launching point for the Santa Fe, California and Oregon Trails.

National Frontier Trails Museum: This free museum covers the history of the three main trails, as well as the Mormon Trail. Mormons still have a major presence in Independence, which church leader Joseph Smith declared as Zion. *(ci.independence.mo.us/nftm)*

SantaCaliGon Days: Named after the three trails, this late-summer fun fair brings amusement park rides and food vendors to Independence's historic square. *(santacaligon.com)*

Pioneer Trails Adventures: Tour the main sites of Independence in a covered wagon. *(pioneertrailsadventures.com)*

---

walkability, renovations of the century-old Boone Theater – set to become a Black Movie Hall of Fame – and a planned expansion of the Negro Leagues Baseball Museum to include more exhibit space, a seven-story hotel and rooftop bar.

Independence

Get to know the only president from Missouri

Harry Truman, the 33rd US president, grew up in **Independence**, a suburb east of Kansas City. Reopened in 2021 after a $29 million update, the **Harry S Truman Presidential Library and Museum** *(trumanlibrary.gov; adult/child $12/5; closed Sun)* is a behind-the-scenes look at his life, legacy and the world at large in the 1940s and '50s. Exhibits include somber artifacts, such as the safety plug from the atomic bomb dropped on Nagasaki, Japan, to more lighthearted items like the famous 'The Buck Stops Here!' sign.

Join a National Park Service ranger on a tour of the **Harry S Truman National Historic Site** *(nps.gov/hstr; free; 9am-4pm Wed-Sun)* to see the simple life Harry and his wife, Bess, lived in their basic but charming wood house. The former president lived here from 1919 to 1972, and it's furnished with their original belongings. Visits are by a 30-minute tour only, and you must pick up a first-come, first-served free ticket from the **Harry S Truman National Historic Site Visitor Center**, about half a mile away.

St Joseph

From the Pony Express to psychiatry

St Joseph (usually abbreviated to St Jo) was another major departure point for westward-bound 19th-century pioneers headed for the goldfields of California or the Oregon territory. No matter their origin or final destination, travelers converged in St Jo, once the westernmost American city accessible by rail and a river port for steamboats.

As the eastern terminus of the Pony Express, which first set off from here in April 1860, St Jo served as a lifeline that connected east and west. The **Pony Express National Museum** *(ponyexpress.org; adult/child $10/5)* is located in the stables from which the horse riders once departed. Time your visit for June for the annual **Re-Ride**, when riders gallop along the historic route and still carry letters in a leather mochila.

Nearby, the imposing 1858 **Patee House** *(ponyexpressjessejames.com; adult/child $8/5)* was a luxury hotel and the Pony

---

EATING & DRINKING IN INDEPENDENCE: OUR PICKS

Dixon's Famous Chili Parlor: Open since 1919, Dixon's is a diner that served Truman; wonder if he got the chili or all-you-can-eat tacos. *10am-9pm Mon-Sat* $

Clinton's Soda Fountain: Little has changed from when Truman got his first job. Come for ice cream and phosphate sodas. *11am-5pm Tue-Sat* $

3 Trails Brewing: This welcoming brewery is a hub for the community and hosts lots of events. *4-10:30pm Wed & Thu, to midnight Fri, noon-midnight Sat, to 7pm Sun*

Sentinel Room: Top-notch cocktail bar with a huge whiskey selection in a former newspaper office. *3-10pm Tue-Thu, to midnight Fri, noon-midnight Sat*

Ethnic Enrichment Festival

Express headquarters. It now showcases the city's rich story with exhibits full of historic memorabilia. Behind it is the modest house of notorious outlaw **Jesse James** *(extra $5/3)*. He was murdered here, and the bullet hole is still visible in the wall.

Continue the dark tourism trend at the **Glore Psychiatric Museum** *(stjosephmuseum.org; adult/child $12/8)*. Housed in the former State Lunatic Asylum No 2, this museum gives a frightening and fascinating look at lobotomies, the 'bath of surprise' and other discredited mental health treatments.

The Ozarks

Hike the hills and float in wild rivers

Ozark hill country spreads across southern Missouri and extends into northern Arkansas and eastern Oklahoma. Flashy Branson receives the lion's share of tourists, but the region's true charms lie not in town but further afield in the rolling hills and deep clefts where spring-fed rivers carry legions of happy campers floating downstream.

Two wild rivers, the Current and the Jacks Fork, wind through 80,000 acres of raw natural beauty in the **Ozark National Scenic Riverways** *(nps.gov/ozar; free)*, the first national park established to protect a waterway. Numerous natural springs feed the river; the most famous and accessible is **Big Spring**, which releases some 286 million gallons a day. **Blue Spring** is harder to get to but even more stunning, with surreal cerulean waters that almost look glacial. Swimming in the springs isn't allowed, but you can jump in the river nearby.

Another scenic swimming spot is **Johnson's Shut-Ins State Park** *(mostateparks.com; free)*, where the Black River swirls through canyon-like gorges (shut-ins). Find outfitters and rental services for river activities in the towns of **Van Buren** and **Eminence**. Summer weekends get busy and boisterous.

Hikers can tackle portions of the 430-mile **Ozark Trail** *(ozarktrail.com)*, parts of which follow the Current River. For a good half-day hike, head to **Taum Sauk Mountain State Park** *(mostateparks.com; free)*, where you can scale the state's

BEST MISSOURI FESTIVALS

National Tom Sawyer Days: Head to Hannibal, the childhood hometown of Mark Twain, to watch competitive fence painting and more in July. *(hannibaljaycees.org)*

Mardi Gras: The second-largest Mardi Gras celebrations in the country take place in the St Louis neighborhood of Soulard. *(stlmardigras.org)*

Ethnic Enrichment Festival: Diverse clubs in KC set up booths to share their food and culture in August. *(eeckc.org)*

Birthplace of Route 66 Festival: The nation's largest celebration of the Mother Road takes place every August in Springfield. *(route66festivalsgf.com)*

Maifest: Celebrate spring in the German-heritage town of Hermann in May. *(maifesthermann.org)*

Blue Spring (p605)

LGBTQ+ MISSOURI

In 2024, Missouri ranked last – along with 23 other states – in a Human Rights Campaign survey of LGBTQ+ equality, but that doesn't necessarily mean queer travelers should avoid the state.

St Louis and Kansas City have the most welcoming attitudes and dedicated gay bars. Try **Hamburger Mary's** (hamburgermarys.com) and **Missie B's** (missiebs.com) in KC, and **Just John Club** (justjohnnightclub.com) and other nearby LGBTQ+ bars in the Grove neighborhood of STL. The college town of Columbia, home to the University of Missouri, was the first Missouri city to ban conversion therapy for LGBTQ+ youth. These three cities, along with Springfield, have Pride festivities in June.

highest peak, 1772ft Taum Sauk Mountain (a flat walk from the already elevated parking lot) and see the state's tallest waterfall, 132ft Mina Sauk Falls.

See Branson's artificial and natural amusements

Hokey, family-friendly **Branson** is an unabashedly shameless tourist resort. The main attractions are **Silver Dollar City** (silverdollarcity.com; 1-day pass adult/child $92/82) – a huge Old West–themed amusement park – and the more than 45 theaters hosting country music, magic and comedy shows. **Branson's Famous Baldknobbers** (baldknobbers.com; adult/child from $46/23) is the musical comedy show that started it all in 1959. Three generations of the Mabe family – and a lot of 'friends' – cover country and gospel tunes, dance and offer up cornball comedy.

Drive just a few minutes out of town and you'll find yourself close to the Ozark wilderness again, though in a more manicured form. Man-made **Table Rock Lake** is a popular destination for boating and fishing, and you can rent motorboats and pontoons from multiple marinas. Much of the conserved land around Branson is thanks to Johnny Morris, the Missouri-born CEO of Bass Pro Shops. **Top of the Rock** (bigcedar.com/top-of-the-rock; adult/child from $45/20) lets you drive a golf cart along limestone cliffs and into a cave (which, of course, has a bar inside), while **Dogwood Canyon** (dogwoodcanyon.org; adult/child from $19/14) offers opportunities for hiking, cycling, horseback riding, fishing and hopping onto a trailer for nature tour.

 EATING IN BRANSON: OUR PICKS

Keeter Center: Staffed by students at the College of the Ozarks, this country-chic farm-to-table restaurant gets top marks. *10:30am-8pm Mon-Sat* $$

Gettin' Basted: Grilled by award-winning pitmasters, brisket, pulled pork and burnt ends are the stars at one of the best places to eat on Branson's '76 Strip.' *11am-9pm* $

Full Throttle Distillery: Devour barbecue and comfort food at this motorcycle-themed spot that makes its own moonshine. *7am-10pm or later* $$

Pie Safe: Kitschily charming Victorian-styled cafe serving miniature pies and other baked goods alongside flavored lattes. *10am-6pm Mon-Sat* $

Kansas

PRESERVED PRAIRIE | AVIATION HISTORY | OUTSIDER ART

Wicked witches, yellow-brick roads and tornadoes powerful enough to erase entire towns are popular images of Kansas, but visions of amber waves of grain spreading as far as the eye can see are closer to reality.

What Kansas might lack in mind-boggling scenery, it makes up for in quirky, soul-stirring stops. The rolling hills and limitless horizons have an evocative, understated beauty, particularly evident in places like the beguiling Tallgrass Prairie National Preserve. Gems abound, from the superb space museum in Hutchinson to the college-town cool of Lawrence.

The largest city in the state is Wichita, a 19th-century cow town that became the 'Air Capital of the World' as a major aircraft manufacturer. This transformation is emblematic of how the whole state continues to reinvent itself in weird and wonderful ways while still drawing on history and tradition – no matter where you go in Kansas, it's unlikely to be at all what you expected.

Places
Atchison p607
Lawrence p609
Topeka p609
Abilene p610
Flint Hills p610
Wichita p611
Hutchinson p612
Lucas p613
Dodge City p613

☑ TOP TIP

For discounts on tolls on the Turnpike, request a free K-TAG online *(ksturnpike.com)* before your trip, which will be mailed to you. Toll tags from some other states, such as Best Pass, Pikepass, EZ TAG and SunPass, can also be used here. Tolls cannot be paid with cash.

Atchison

Birthplace of America's finest female aviator

Famed flier Amelia Earhart broke many barriers and records. She was the first female pilot to fly solo nonstop across the Atlantic, and she disappeared in 1939 attempting to become the

GETTING AROUND

You need a car to get around Kansas. Two interstates cross the state in different directions, coming together near Kansas City: I-35, linking Wichita and Kansas City; and I-70, which shoots through Lawrence, Topeka and points west. Sections of both interstates are toll roads, called the Kansas Turnpike.

Wichita Dwight D Eisenhower National Airport is the busiest airport in Kansas (Kansas City's airport is in Missouri) and has services from regional hubs, such as Dallas, Denver and Chicago. Amtrak's *Southwest Chief,* which runs from Chicago to Los Angeles, stops in Lawrence, Topeka and Dodge City.

KANSAS THE GREAT PLAINS

THE GUIDE

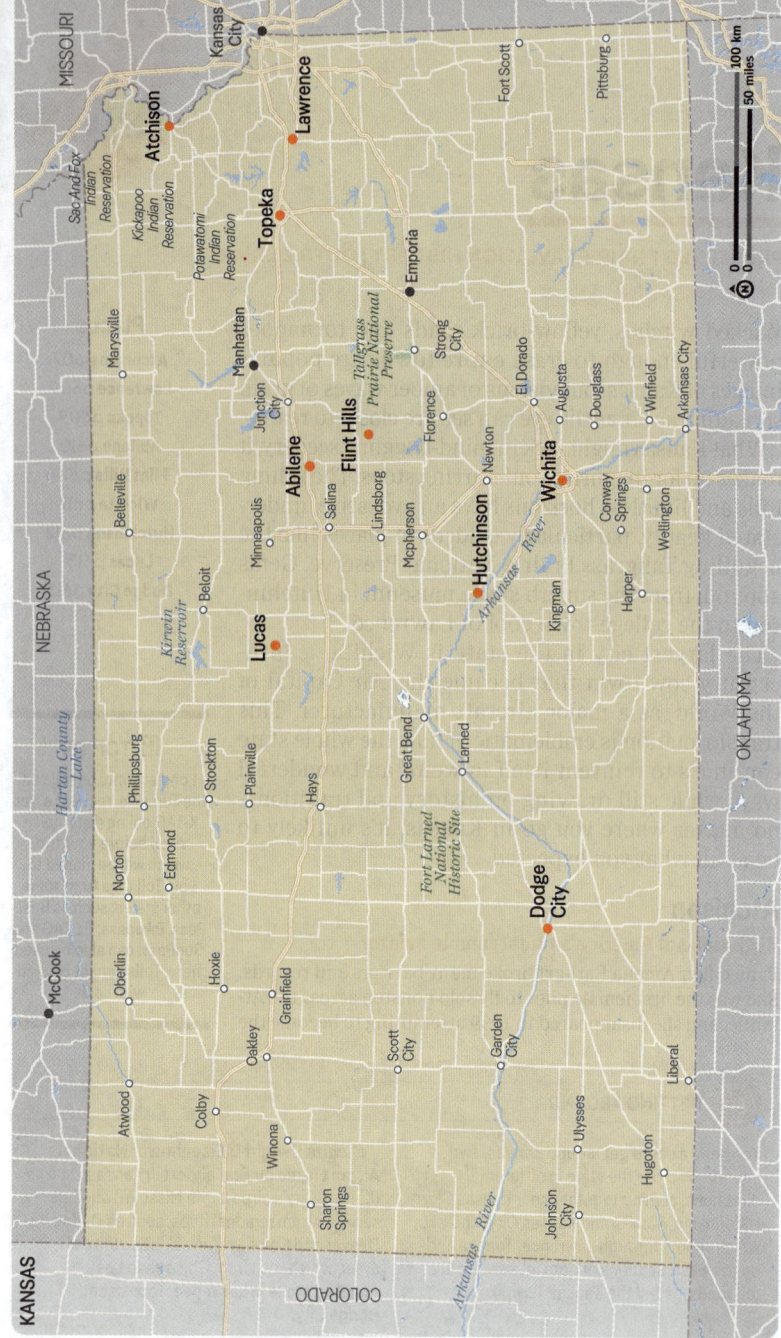

608

first woman aviator to circumnavigate the globe. She championed gender equality and women pursuing male-dominated careers in engineering and science. Her body and plane were never found, which fuels speculation to this day.

Aptly located at Atchison's tiny airport, the **Amelia Earhart Hangar Museum** *(ameliaearharthangarmuseum.org; adult/child $15/8; closed Mon & Tue)* opened in 2023 and shows off *Muriel,* the only surviving Lockheed Electra 10-E plane, exactly like the one Earhart flew on her final voyage.

You can also visit the **Amelia Earhart Birthplace Museum** *(ameliaearhartmuseum.org; guided/self-guided tour $15/12),* the 1861 Gothic Revival home where she grew up.

Lawrence
College-town vibes in Kansas' coolest city

Lawrence has been an island of progressive politics since its inception. Founded by East Coast abolitionists in 1854, it became a battlefield in the clash between pro- and antislavery factions. The city's free-thinking spirit continues, fueled in no small part by the huge student body at the University of Kansas (KU). It's one of the country's most vibrant college towns.

The appealing downtown centers on **Massachusetts St** (abbreviated to Mass), lined with historic buildings home to the city's best restaurants, coffee shops, bars and stores. It's an excellent place to spend an afternoon shopping and bar-hopping.

The KU campus is at the top of Mt Oread, aka 'the Hill,' and it's worth stopping by the **Spencer Museum of Art** *(spencerart.ku.edu; free; closed Sun & Mon)* to check out the exhibitions, and globe-trotting and century-spanning works.

Topeka
The push to desegregate public schools

Kansas' vital role in the country's race relations is documented in the otherwise humdrum state capital of Topeka. Set in the former Monroe Elementary School, one of Topeka's four segregated primary schools for Black students, **Brown v Board of Education National Historical Park** *(nps.gov/brvb; free; closed Sun & Mon)* tells the story of the famous 1954 Supreme Court case that threw out the 'separate but equal' doctrine, in the context of the wider Civil Rights movement.

BEST KANSAS FESTIVALS

Riverfest: Wichita's biggest festival includes a city-wide scavenger hunt, 'cowboy bathtub' races and a cardboard boat regatta in June. *(wichitariverfest.com)*

Walnut Valley Festival: This September bluegrass festival near Winfield draws more visitors than the town's population. *(wvfest.com)*

Water Wars: Everyone in Humboldt participates in a town-wide water fight in August. *(facebook.com/waterwars.humboldt)*

Lawrence Busker Festival: Fire breathers, dancers, magicians and other street performers take over downtown Lawrence in May. *(lawrencebuskerfest.com)*

Louisburg Ciderfest: Celebrate all things apple in late September. *(louisburgcidermill.com)*

EATING & DRINKING IN LAWRENCE: OUR PICKS

Free State Brewing: Opened in 1989 as the first brewery in Kansas since Prohibition, with pints and pub grub. The cheddar ale soup is classic. *11am-9pm* **$$**

715: Classy but laid-back Italian-influenced restaurant with a neighborhood feel on Mass St. A happy hour favorite. *3-9pm Tue & Wed, to 10pm Thu-Sat* **$$**

Barker: Out-of-this-world pastries from a James Beard–nominated chef. Go early lest they sell out. *7am-8pm Mon-Fri, 8am-2pm Sat & Sun* **$$**

John Brown's Underground: The best cocktail bar in town is named for the famed abolitionist and Kansas hero. *5pm-midnight Wed-Sat*

BEST KANSAS SMALL TOWNS

Humboldt: A brewery, a boutique hotel with a cool cocktail bar, and lakeside cabins have put tiny Humboldt on the map in a big way. *(abolderhumboldt.com)*

Lindsborg: Its Swedish heritage shines with events like Våffeldagen (Waffle Day) and a Midsummer's Festival. *(visitlindsborg.com)*

Nicodemus: Formerly enslaved people founded Nicodemus in 1877 as the first Black town west of the Mississippi. The National Park Service has restored the town hall and church. *(nps.gov/nico)*

Council Grove: Main St was the Santa Fe Trail, and historic businesses, including Hays House, the oldest continuously operating restaurant west of the Mississippi, line the route. *(councilgrove.com)*

Climb to the top of the Kansas State Capitol

The grand **Kansas State Capitol** *(kansashistory.gov/capitol; free; closed Sun)*, made of state-sourced limestone, took 37 years to complete after its cornerstone was laid in 1866. You can take a guided or self-guided tour of the building – either way, don't miss *Tragic Prelude* on the east side of the 2nd-floor rotunda. This fiery mural by Kansas-born artist John Steuart Curry depicts a raging, oversized John Brown, a famous abolitionist who was later convicted of treason, holding a Bible in one hand and a rifle in the other. Brown stands in front of sparring Union and Confederate Civil War soldiers with a tornado and a prairie fire engulfing the background. Guided tours depart on the hour between 9am and 3pm, except at noon, Monday to Friday, and 10am, 11am, 1pm and 3pm on Saturday.

The Kansas Statehouse is one of the few where you can climb up into the huge copper dome on a guided tour. Brace yourself for the 296 steps; there's no elevator. Dome tours take place at 15 minutes past the hour.

Abilene

Make like Ike in Eisenhower's childhood home

In the late 19th century, Abilene was a rowdy cow town at the end of the Chisholm Trail. Today, its compact core of historic brick buildings and well-preserved neighborhoods seems perfectly appropriate for the birthplace of Dwight D Eisenhower, the 34th president.

The **Dwight D Eisenhower Presidential Library and Museum** *(eisenhowerlibrary.gov; adult/child $20/15)* includes Ike's boyhood home, a museum and library, and his and his wife's graves. Interactive exhibits cover the Eisenhower presidential era (1953–61) and his role as the Supreme Allied Commander in Europe in WWII. Don't miss the original script for his landmark 1961 speech in which he famously warned of the military-industrial complex.

Flint Hills

Pieces of the last surviving tallgrass prairie

Prairie once covered more than 30% of North America – some 170 million acres – but was decimated by agriculture and urban development. Only a tiny sliver remains today, mostly in Kansas' Flint Hills, which were never plowed because the soil is too rocky.

Run by the National Park Service, the 11,000-acre **Tallgrass Prairie National Preserve** *(nps.gov/tapr; free; buildings 8:30am-4:30pm, trails 24hr)* protects one of the last stands of this ecosystem that's symbolic of the center of the country. Walking trails meander along gently rolling hills, including through a pasture where reintroduced bison roam, as well as to the **Lower Fox Creek School**, a one-room limestone schoolhouse that drew in students from 1882 to 1930.

Near the visitor center, the impressive 1881 **Spring Hill Ranch House** was surprisingly sophisticated for its remote

Tallgrass Prairie National Preserve

ROUTE 66 IN KANSAS

The Sunflower State holds a mere 13 miles of the Mother Road (less than 1% of the total), but it still has a lot to see. It's also the only part of Route 66 that hasn't been overwritten by the interstate.

Entering from Missouri, you pass through mine-scarred **Galena**, where a rusty old tow truck inspired Pixar animators to create the character Mater in *Cars*. Look for the original outside **Cars on the Route** *(facebook.com/ CarsOnTheRoute)*, a restored gas station.

West of Galena, stop at the red-brick **Old Riverton Store** *(oldrivertonstore. com)* and stock up on sandwiches and Route 66 memorabilia. Continue to the 1923 **Rainbow Bridge** and then to the **Kansas Route 66 Visitor Center** *(baxtersprings museum.org)* in **Baxter Springs**.

location in the rural countryside, built in Second Empire style with a mansard roof, a grand walnut staircase, and ornate woodwork and ceiling medallions. Find the preserve 2 miles northwest of tiny Strong City or 23 miles west of Emporia, a larger city that sits on I-35. A scenic way to get here is on the **Flint Hills National Scenic Byway**, where grasses and wildflowers wave you on through the timeless landscape that looks much the same as it did when the Native Kaw, Osage, Pawnee and Wichita people called it home.

If you're driving I-70 through Kansas, a closer option is the **Konza Prairie Biological Station** *(nature.org; free)* near the college town of Manhattan, home to Kansas State University. It's smaller and doesn't have bison, but its three looped hiking trails are just as evocative. Remember that these areas are grassland, so you won't find shade from trees. Sun protection and timing your hikes for cooler parts of the day are musts.

In March or April every year, prescribed burns set 2.2 million acres of the Kansas prairie on fire. This process, now started by humans instead of naturally by lightning, preserves the ecosystem and is a sight to see.

Wichita

A family-friendly, history-filled day out

The **Museums on the River** district could occupy a day or more of your time in Wichita. Note that here the name of the Arkansas River is pronounced 'OUR-Kansas,' not like the state of Arkansas.

A hit with kids and history-lovers, the **Old Cowtown Museum** *(oldcowtown.org; adult/child $12/10; closed Mon & Tue)* recreates the Wild West. This mini city is complete with dirt streets and a significant number of authentic 1800s buildings from Wichita and around Kansas, which were saved from demolition and relocated here. Don't miss the opportunity to sip a sarsaparilla in the saloon. From April to October, costumed cowboys, blacksmiths, newspaper printers and schoolmarms wander the grounds to bring history to life, and gunfights are known to break out.

Another kid favorite is **Exploration Place** *(exploration.org; adult/child from $12/10)*, an architecturally striking children's museum that has no end of cool exhibits, including a tornado chamber where you can feel 75mph winds and a sublime erosion model that shows water creating a new little Kansas. A 6-acre playground is set to open in spring 2026.

On the other side of the river, the **Mid-America All-Indian Museum** *(theindianmuseum.org; adult/child $7/3; closed Sun & Mon)* features Native art from its 3000-piece collection, particularly those of Kiowa-Comanche artist Blackbear Bosin – his 44ft-tall **Keeper of the Plains sculpture** stands outside at the river confluence. The Keeper is an icon of the city, and every night a 'ring of fire' is lit around the base of the statue for 15 minutes, starting at 9pm in spring and summer and 7pm in fall and winter.

For a dose of culture and color, head to **Botanica** *(botanica.org; adult/child $12/10)*, the city's botanical gardens including a children's area with a carousel, and the **Wichita Art Museum** *(wam.org; free; closed Mon & Tue)*, which greets you with the vibrant glasswork of Dale Chihuly.

Hutchinson

Below ground and above the atmosphere

About 50 miles northwest of Wichita, Hutchinson has two incredible sights that are worth a detour.

Possibly the most surprising sight in the state, the amazing **Cosmosphere** *(cosmo.org; adult/child $16.50/13.50)* captures the race to the Moon better than any other museum on the planet. Absorbing displays and artifacts such as the *Apollo 13* command module and entire rockets will enthrall you for hours. You'll come to realize why the museum is regularly called in to build props for Hollywood movies portraying the space race, including *Apollo 13*.

Speaking of Hollywood props, a surprising number are stored nearby at **Strataca** *(underkansas.org; adult/child from $25/18; closed Mon)*, a salt mine 650ft underground,

MORE WICHITA ATTRACTIONS

Frank Lloyd Wright's Allen House: Completed in 1918, with more than 30 pieces of Wright-designed furniture and original art glass windows. *(flwrightwichita.org; $22)*

Original Pizza Hut Museum: In 1958, two Wichita State University students borrowed $600 to start a pizza restaurant. A few exhibits are inside the tiny building. *(free)*

Kansas Aviation Museum: This museum inside the city's first airport shows off aviation artifacts and aircraft such as the 1920 Laird Swallow, the first built in Wichita. *(kansasaviationmuseum.org; adult/child $10/6)*

Hatman Jack's: Famed hat shop that's outfitted Hollywood celebrities. *(hatmanjacksict.com)*

EATING & DRINKING IN WICHITA: OUR PICKS

Doo-Dah Diner: A model for diners everywhere; regularly named Wichita's favorite restaurant. *7am-2pm Tue-Fri, from 8am Sat & Sun* $

Georges French Bistro: Wichita's first appearance on a James Beard list came in 2025 thanks to this classy spot. *11am-10pm Mon-Sat, 10am-2pm Sun* $$$

Central Standard Brewing: Our favorite brewery in town is this chilled-out spot with mid-mod furniture. *3-10pm or later Mon-Fri, noon-midnight Sat, to 5pm Sun*

Lava & Tonic: Speakeasy-style tiki bar with drinks in appropriately retro ceramicware. *5-11pm Wed & Thu, 4pm-12:30am Fri & Sat, 4-10pm Sun*

including the original camera negatives of *Gone with the Wind,* and Batman and Mr Freeze costumes. Why are they here? Stable temperatures, low humidity and the fact that salt doesn't catch on fire. Visits are by tour, which includes a tram ride through some of the 150 miles of tunnels.

Lucas

Get weird in the grassroots art capital of Kansas

Nothing is too off the wall for tiny Lucas, population 333, a hub of 'outsider' art made by self-taught creators.

If you only have time for a bathroom break, **Bowl Plaza** is the place to stop. These public restrooms have a toilet-shaped entrance and are covered in mosaics and trinkets.

Also on Main St are the **Grassroots Art Center** *(grassrootsart.net; adult/child $9/5),* an intriguing collection of 'outsider' works, and the **World's Largest Collection of the World's Smallest Versions of the World's Largest Things** *(worldslargestthings.com; free),* a museum that perfectly encapsulates the spirit of Lucas.

A few blocks east is the **Garden of Eden** *(gardenofedenlucas.org; adult/child $9/4),* the former home of Civil War veteran SP Dinsmoor, who decorated his yard with kooky concrete sculptures of bankers, politicians and biblical figures. He even prepared his own mausoleum, where you can see his moth-munched remains under a glass-topped coffin.

Dodge City

Relive the cowboy days in the 'queen of the cow towns'

Dodge City – where famous lawmen Bat Masterson and Wyatt Earp tried, sometimes successfully, to keep law and order – had a notorious reputation during the 1870s and 1880s. The **Boot Hill Museum** *(boothill.org; adult/child $20/14)* brings it roaring back to life with gunslingers and cancan dancers along reconstructed Front St, Dodge City's historic main street, with some original buildings, including the 1865 Fort Dodge jail.

Today, Dodge City is still a cow town, but of a different sort. Along with nearby Garden City and Liberal, Dodge City is home to multiple cattle slaughterhouses, which 'process' up to 5800 cows a day each. The stench might make you want to get the hell out of Dodge, but if you want a view over the enormous cattle pens, visit the **Feed Yard Overlook** off Wyatt Earp Blvd.

SIGHTS ON THE SANTA FE TRAIL IN WESTERN KANSAS

Unlike the later California and Oregon Trails, the Santa Fe Trail (1821–80) was primarily for commerce, not emigration. On this route, traveling traders moved goods between Missouri and Mexico.

Santa Fe Trail Tracks: See evidence of the thousands of 50in wooden prairie-schooner wagon wheels that carved their way through the Plains about 10 miles west of Dodge City, off US 50.

Fort Larned National Historic Site: A remarkably well-preserved 1860s fort in an evocative setting. It's well worth the trip, about 60 miles northeast of Dodge City, to learn about the turbulent history of the Indian Wars era. *(nps.gov/fols; free)*

EATING & DRINKING IN DODGE CITY: OUR PICKS

Central Station Bar & Grill: Dine on steak or Mexican food in an extension of the train station or an old railroad car. *11am-10pm Mon-Fri, from 4pm Sat* **$$**

Gollo Grande: About 65% of Dodge City's residents are of Hispanic descent, and this is one of the top Mexican joints. *10:30am-9pm or later Wed-Mon* **$**

Boot Hill Distillery: Three farmers run and supply the grains at this soil-to-sip distillery. Ask about the prickly ash bitters. *3-11pm Wed-Sat*

Dodge City Brewing: Southwest Kansas' first craft brewery serves its own excellent beers plus brick-oven pizza. *4-10pm Wed-Fri, from 11am Sat, 11am-8pm Sun*

Oklahoma

NATIVE STORIES | COWBOY LORE | COOL CITIES

Places
Tulsa p614
Pawhuska p619
Oklahoma City p620
Fort Sill p622
Wichita Mountains p623

Oklahoma gets its name from Choctaw words meaning 'brave people.' With 39 tribes located in the state – many forcibly relocated to the unwanted 'Indian Territory' in the 19th century – it remains a place of deep Native heritage that has withstood the onslaught of centuries of assimilation and erasure that the word brave hardly begins to cover.

On the other side of the Old West coin, cowboys also figure prominently in the Sooner State, and there's still a great sense of the open range, interrupted only by urban Oklahoma City and Tulsa. Both cities, but Tulsa in particular, feel as if they are on the up, with so many new attractions, restaurants, breweries and bars that you're destined to find yourself adding extra days to your itinerary.

Oklahoma's share of Route 66, the second-longest of any state, links some of the Mother Road's iconic highlights and atmospheric old towns.

☑ TOP TIP

If you're in Oklahoma to visit its hard-hitting, top-notch museums, leave your visit for later in the week. Many are closed on Mondays or Tuesdays – or both.

Tulsa

Remembering Black Wall Street

On May 30, 1921, a Black male teenager and a white female teenager were alone in an elevator in downtown Tulsa when she screamed. The how and why have never been answered, but the incident sparked three days of race riots that engulfed the neighborhood of Greenwood, nicknamed 'Black Wall Street'

GETTING AROUND

Highways crisscross the state, including Route 66 (mostly overtaken by I-40 west of OKC). Several of the US highways and interstates are toll roads that can't be paid for with cash. It's worth ordering a Pikepass *(pikepass. com)* in advance for discounts of up to 50%. Passes used for toll roads in Kansas (K-TAG; *ksturnpike.com)* and Texas (EZ TAG, TollTag, TxTag) are also valid on Oklahoma highways.

Parking is paid in downtown Tulsa and OKC. Download ParkMobile *(parkmobile.io; $1/hour)* in Tulsa and Flowbird *(flowbirdapp.com; $2/hour)* for OKC.

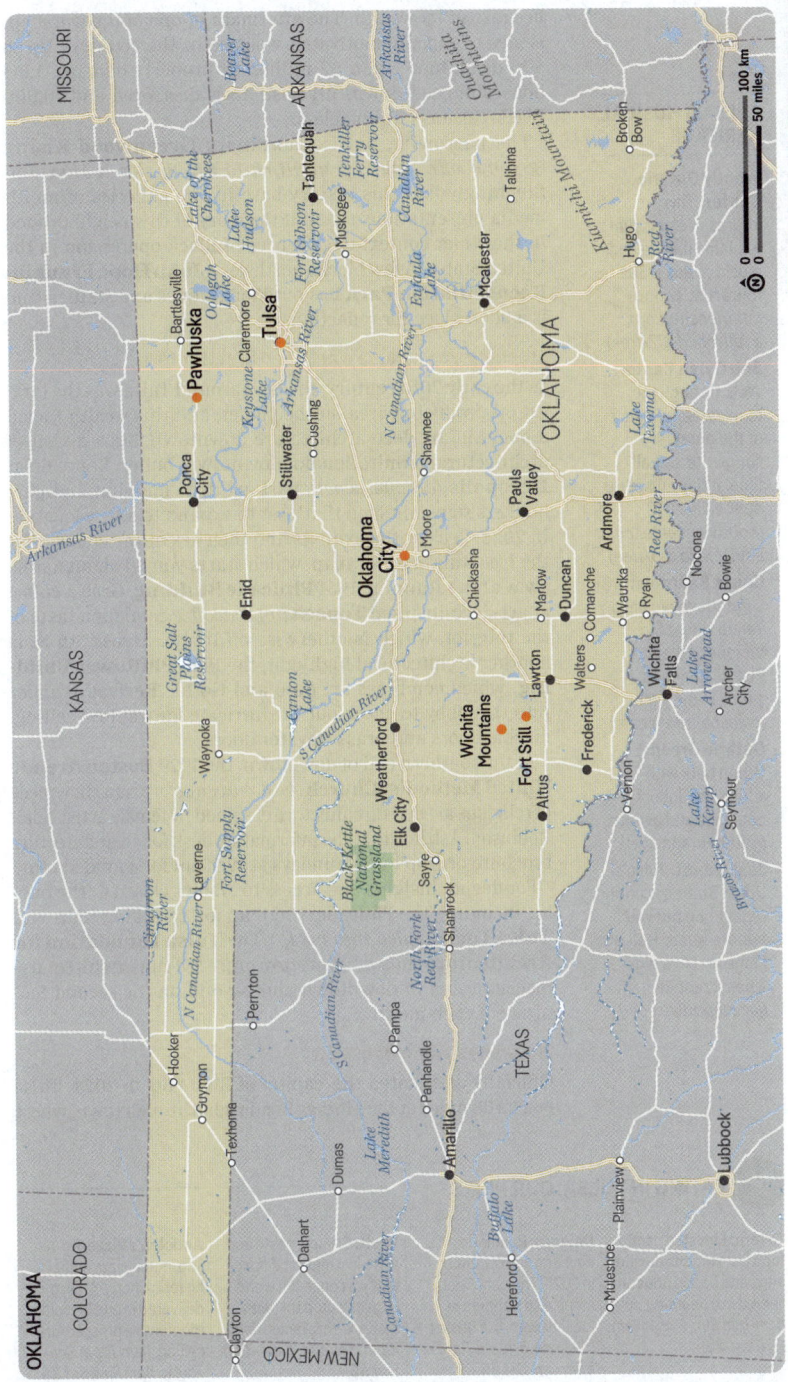

TULSA'S MUSICAL HERITAGE

Woody Guthrie Center: This impressive museum explains the life and music of this 1930s folk artist. *(woodyguthriecenter.org; adult/child $12/free)*

Bob Dylan Center: Walk through the long career of one of the greatest songwriters of all time at this museum, opened in 2022. *(bobdylancenter.com; adult/child $15/free)*

Cain's Ballroom: Legendary live music venue where Sid Vicious of the Sex Pistols punched a hole in the wall. *(cainsballroom.com)*

Guthrie Green: Urban park with a full schedule of concerts and events. *(guthriegreen.com)*

Jazz Depot: Tulsa's Union Station is under renovation but will feature a Jazz Hall of Fame and live gigs when it reopens. *(jazzdepotlive.com)*

because of its wealth. The aftermath of one of the worst episodes of racially motivated violence in the country? Up to 300 dead, more than $2 million in property damage, 1256 houses burned down, 191 businesses destroyed and 10,000 Black Tulsans left homeless.

The harrowing but extraordinary **Greenwood Rising** *(greenwoodrising.org; adult/child $15/8; closed Mon)* unflinchingly lays this history bare in five galleries of multimedia presentations that put the story of this neighborhood in the wider context of centuries of Black oppression in the United States. A few blocks northwest, **John Hope Franklin Reconciliation Park** has outdoor plaques and statues, and is a good place for reflection.

Tracking down Tulsa's art deco architecture

In the early 20th century, the land around Tulsa was the largest oil-producing area on the planet, and this wealth fueled a boom in art deco architecture downtown. Start a visit of architectural admiration not downtown, but on Route 66 at **Decopolis** *(decopolis.net)*, part art deco museum and part bonkers souvenir shop that's set to expand to a new location in 2026. Peek at the exhibits and then ask at the counter for the free walking-tour map, which starts you off about a mile away at the stunning 1931 **Philcade Building**. Grab a coffee at art-deco-inspired **Topeca** *(topecacoffee.com)* for a taste of the interior, which is otherwise off limits. Across 5th St is another architectural highlight, the 1928 **Philtower Building**, which combines art deco and Gothic Revival. Wander into the lobby to check out the intricate fan-vaulted ceiling, marble floors and brass elevator doors.

At the southern end of downtown, the 1929 **Boston Avenue United Methodist Church** *(bostonavenue.org)* is a showpiece of religious art deco architecture designed by female artist Adah Robinson. Ask inside at the information desk for an architecture brochure or stop by on Sundays at 12:15pm for a guided tour.

For deeper insights and access to lobbies closed to the public, including the Philcade's, sign up for a walking tour with **Tulsa Tours** *(tulsa.tours; $45)*. The **Tulsa Foundation for Architecture** *(tulsaarchitecture.org; $20)* runs architecture-focused tours in downtown and beyond on the second Saturday of each month.

Must-sees along Route 66

Officially designated the 'capital of Route 66' in 2024, Tulsa boasts 28 miles of the Mother Road right through town, where

EATING IN TULSA: OUR PICKS

Tavern: Elevated comfort food like sriracha devilled eggs and bacon popcorn served in a beautiful pub. *11am-1pm Sun-Thu, to 1am Fri & Sat* **$$**

Daigoro: Romantic riverside spot opened in 2025. The pan-Asian menu also peppers in local flavors, like brisket fried rice. *5-10pm Tue-Fri, from 11am Sat* **$$**

Vault: Brunch, pasta and more in a mid-mod space that was once the world's largest 'autobank' with six drive-thru lanes. *11am-10pm Mon-Sat, 10am-3pm Sun* **$$**

Andolini's Pizzeria: Top-notch pizza in the historic Cherry St District delivered in an old dining room with a pressed-tin ceiling. *11am-10pm Sun-Thu, to 11pm Fri & Sat* **$$**

TULSA

● SIGHTS
1 Bob Dylan Center
2 Center of the Universe
3 Greenwood Rising
4 Guthrie Green
5 Jazz Depot
6 John Hope Franklin Reconciliation Park
7 Meadow Gold Mack
8 Meadow Gold Sign
9 Philcade Building
10 Philtower Building
11 Woody Guthrie Center

● ACTIVITIES
12 Tulsa Foundation for Architecture
13 Tulsa Tours

● SLEEPING
14 Mayo Hotel

● EATING
15 Ike's Chili
16 Tavern
17 Vault
18 Wildflower Cafe

● DRINKING & NIGHTLIFE
19 Saturn Room
20 Soundpony Lounge
21 Topeca

● ENTERTAINMENT
22 Cain's Ballroom

● SHOPPING
23 Buck Atom's Cosmic Curios on 66
24 Decopolis

TOP ROUTE 66 STOPS IN OKLAHOMA

Oklahoma has more miles of the original alignment than any other state.

Blue Whale: One of the most photographed Route 66 landmarks is the 80ft-long Blue Whale, the centerpiece of a long-gone water park in Catoosa.

Pops 66: A 66ft LED soda bottle near Arcadia lures you into buying some of the hundreds of varieties of pop from around the world. *(pops66.com)*

Oklahoma Route 66 Museum: If you take time for just one museum, make it this engagingly designed exhibition in Clinton. *(okhistory.org/sites/route66; adult/child $7/4)*

Pony Bridge: The 38-truss, 0.75-mile-long Pony Bridge crosses the Canadian River in rhythmic style.

---

it's called 11th St. The **Meadow Gold District** *(meadowgolddistrict.com)* is one of the most interesting stretches, so called because of the 1930s neon-lit **Meadow Gold sign**. Originally a promo for a dairy company, this Route 66 landmark was saved from demolition by preservationists and moved a few blocks from its original location. It now sits atop an open brick structure built specifically for it.

Look nearby for the three 20ft-tall 'muffler men' sculptures – **Meadow Gold Mack** *(meadowgoldmack.com)*, the friendly lumberjack; and space cowboy Buck Atom and gunslinging cosmic cowgirl Stella Atom outside **Buck Atom's Cosmic Curios on 66** *(buckatomson66.com)*, a teeny former gas station turned souvenir shop.

For more neon nostalgia, the glowing beacon of the **Route 66 Neon Sign Park** *(free)* is on the way out of town if you're driving west to Oklahoma City.

Take the family to the country's favorite city park

The 66-acre **Gathering Place** *(gatheringplace.org)* is a model for parks worldwide – since it opened in 2018, it's ranked at the top of lists of the best green spaces in the USA. Multiple themed playscapes designed for different age groups include a 5-acre adventure playground and Slide Vale (which has a slide that goes underground), plus a skate park and courts for pickleball, basketball, volleyball and street soccer.

Parents, don't hold back – you can join in the fun, too. The boathouse, with views of downtown and the Arkansas River, rents out free pedal boats and canoes, and tons of events take place on the huge lawn and stage.

Accessibility is built into the park so that kids of all abilities can enjoy it. It's fully ADA-compliant and offers quiet spaces, sensory bags, and free wheelchairs to rent.

Nearby, **Discovery Lab** *(discoverylab.org; $14)*, a huge science-centric children's museum, is an ideal indoor alternative when the weather isn't cooperating for a park visit.

Arty attractions

South of town, the **Philbrook Museum of Art** *(philbrook.org; adult/child $18/8; closed Mon & Tue)* is housed in an oil magnate's converted 1920s Italianate villa that's just as much a work of art as the pieces it contains. It displays fine Native American works, and classic and contemporary international art.

Northwest of downtown, the superb **Gilcrease Museum** *(gilcrease.org)* is another gem in Tulsa's cultural crown, but it's undergoing a huge renovation and reconstruction project and is

---

 EATING IN TULSA: OUR PICKS ON ROUTE 66

Tally's Good Food Cafe: Let the neon signs lure you into this bustling chrome-and-vinyl diner dishing up Americana on a plate. *6am-11pm* $

Ike's Chili: Serving chili for more than 110 years. Get it straight, in a Frito pie (a Midwest fave), or atop a hot dog, fries or spaghetti. *10am-2:30pm Mon-Sat* $

Mother Road Market: This sprawling food hall attracts joyous groups who feast on the plethora of creative offerings. *11am-9pm Tue-Sun* $

Wildflower Cafe: A brunch staple with made-from-scratch waffles, biscuits and gravy, and a line out the door on weekends. *7am-3pm* $

Meadow Gold sign

set to open in fall 2026. It's named for Thomas Gilcrease of the Muscogee (Creek) Nation, who discovered oil on his allotment.

Pawhuska

Hear Osage stories

The Hollywood spotlight shone on the Osage Nation (Ni Okašką, 'People of the Middle Waters') in a big way with the 2023 release of *Killers of the Flower Moon*, detailing the true story of a series of murders after oil was discovered on their reservation. The town of Pawhuska was the center of the movie's production. Its historic main street, Kihekah Ave, was covered in dirt, and the old brick storefronts were restored to their original looks, traces of which remain. Stop for a 'cowboy coffee' (dark roast with sarsaparilla syrup) or a bite to eat at **Pioneer Woman Mercantile** *(themercantile.com)*, started by Food Network star Ree Drummond.

At the **Osage Nation Visitors Center** *(osageculture.com; closed Sat & Sun)*, staff can help you plan your visit, and you can browse a few history and art exhibits. The small **Osage Nation Museum** *(free; closed Sun & Mon)* is in an old stone chapel and is the country's oldest tribal museum.

Get a sense of the land's majestic sweep and what many Osage must have seen at the **Joseph H Williams Tallgrass Prairie**

BEST OKLAHOMA FESTIVALS

Red Earth Festival: A three-day celebration of Native culture in OKC, with an art market, tribal dance performances and a powwow in March. *(redearth.org)*

Paseo Arts Festival: This late-May event shows off the galleries and restaurants of its namesake neighborhood in OKC. *(thepaseo.org)*

Fried Onion Burger Day Festival: Watch the world's largest fried onion burger – 850lb – get cooked, and feast on this Depression-era classic in El Reno in May. *(facebook.com/elrenoburgerday)*

Tulsa Juneteenth Festival: Experience this federal holiday that marks the end of slavery in Greenwood (p616), Tulsa's Black Wall Street, with food trucks, vendors and games. *(tulsajuneteenth.org)*

 DRINKING IN TULSA: OUR PICKS

American Solera: Sip award-winning craft beer in this brewery's laid-back industrial-mod space. *4-9pm Mon-Thu, noon-10pm Fri & Sat, to 6pm Sun*

Soundpony Lounge: A sticker-covered dive bar par excellence with welcoming bartenders, live music and karaoke nights. *3pm-2am*

Saturn Room: Find the 'tropics of Tulsa' at this adorable tiki bar with a light-strung patio. It pours knock-out drinks with just the right amount of rum and fire. *4pm–2am*

Pump Bar: A 1960s gas station morphed into a kitschy vintage bar with great drinks and snacks like 'trashy tots.' *11am-10pm Tue-Thu & Sun, to midnight Fri & Sat*

TRAIL OF TEARS

In the 1830s, white farmers in the southeastern US wanted to expand onto land occupied by more than 125,000 Native people. President Andrew Jackson used the army to remove tribes from their homelands and forced them to walk upwards of 1000 miles to Indian Territory, present-day Oklahoma.

Tens of thousands of people from the Cherokee, Chickasaw, Choctaw, Muscogee (Creek) and Seminole nations – the 'five civilized tribes' – made the journeys. A third are thought to have died along the way. Don't miss the **Five Civilized Tribes Museum** *(fivetribes.org; adult/child $6/3)* in Muskogee or the many museums in **Tahlequah**, the capital of the Cherokee Nation since 1839.

Preserve *(nature.org; free)*, the world's largest remaining protected area of its kind that's home to 2500 free-range bison. Enthusiastic staff can talk you through the nature exhibits in the small visitor center, and you can get out into nature on three looped hiking trails, ranging from a half-mile to 2 miles.

Oklahoma City

Myths and truths about the American West

Oklahoma has the highest proportion of Native people of any state (14.2% of residents), and the **First Americans Museum** *(famok.org; adult/child $15/5; closed Tue)* tells the stories of the 39 tribes that call this place home – many because of forced government migration along the Trail of Tears. With a collection largely sourced from the storage rooms of the Smithsonian's National Museum of the American Indian in Washington, DC, this museum, opened in 2021, is perhaps the best Native cultural institution in the country. The 2nd floor shows off the Smithsonian's goods, on long-term loan and returned to Oklahoma for the first time in a century, while the ground floor details the long history of Native life on this land, moving through deceitful US government 'deals' and laws, and into the present, explaining it all from a Native perspective in evocative multimedia displays. Outside, the free-to-visit 90ft-high mound is reminiscent of Cahokia in Illinois, and one of the three daily docent-led tours heads there. Save time for a meal made with traditional ingredients, such as bison, chokecherries and hominy, at **Thirty-Nine Restaurant**, the museum's on-site eatery, helmed by Loretta Barrett Oden, a member of the Citizen Potawatomi Nation.

Native history is often overshadowed by white cowboys and romantic – and unrealistic – Westerns, but the **National Cowboy and Western Heritage Museum** *(nationalcowboymuseum.org; adult/child $20/12)* does a more multifaceted deep dive into this background. It has some displays of Native artifacts, along with an excellent collection of historic and contemporary paintings and sculptures depicting life in the West, including works by underrepresented Native and female artists. Kids love walking through the mock cow town and running amok in the huge outdoor playground with recreated Native cliff dwellings, tipis and sod houses.

Get a combination ticket to visit both museums for $30, saving $5.

Remembering the 1995 OKC bombing

The story of the United States' worst incident of domestic terrorism is laid out in sobering hour-by-hour detail at the poignant **Oklahoma City National Memorial and Museum** *(memorialmuseum.com; adult/child $18/15)*. Outside is a free-to-visit area with 168 empty chair sculptures, one for each of the people killed in the attack; the 19 small ones are for the children who perished in the daycare center.

Park at the Memorial Parking Garage at the northeast corner of 6th and Harvey for free parking with a museum ticket purchase.

OKLAHOMA CITY

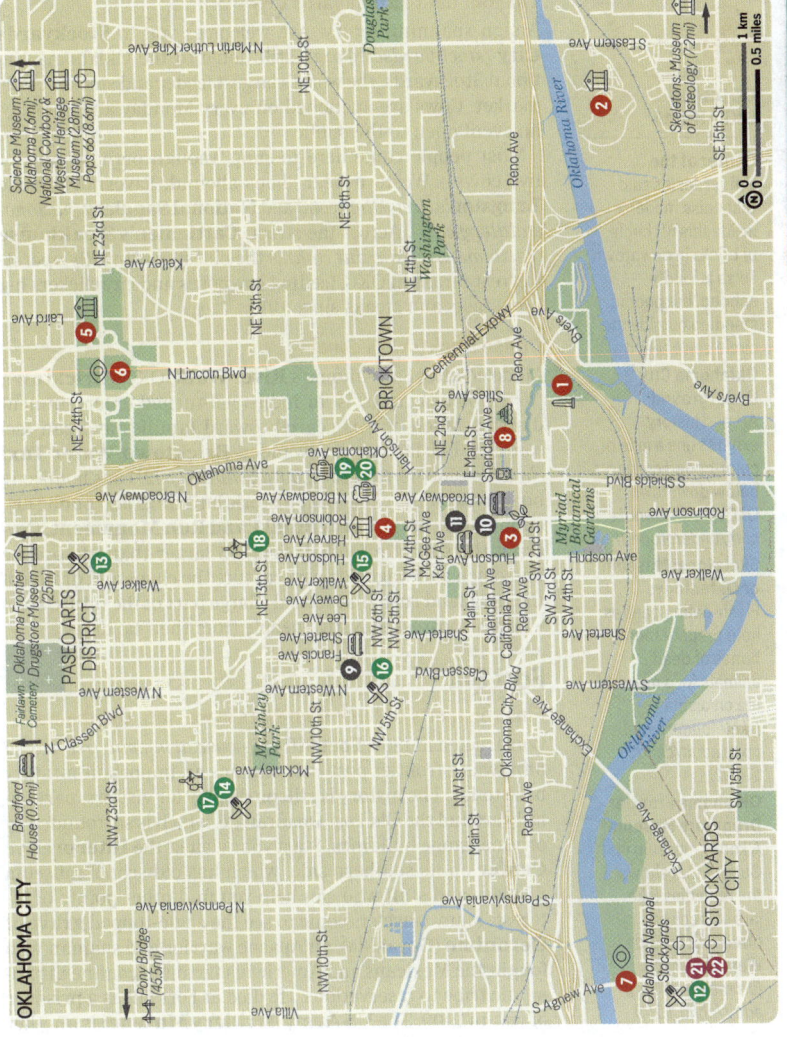

SIGHTS
1. Centennial Land Run Monument
2. First Americans Museum
3. Myriad Botanical Gardens
4. Oklahoma City National Memorial & Museum
5. Oklahoma History Center
6. Oklahoma State Capitol
7. Stockyards City

ACTIVITIES
8. Bricktown Water Taxi

SLEEPING
9. Classen Inn
10. Colcord Hotel
11. The National

EATING
12. Cattlemen's Steakhouse
13. Cheever's Cafe
14. Ma Der Lao Kitchen
15. Nonesuch
16. Sunnyside Diner

DRINKING & NIGHTLIFE
17. Good for a Few
18. Later Bye
19. Prairie Artisan Ales
20. Skydance Brewing Co

SHOPPING
21. Langston's
22. National Saddlery

ODDBALL OKLAHOMA

Center of the Universe: It's said that noise made inside this 8ft circle of bricks in downtown Tulsa is loudly echoed, but people standing outside the circle can't hear it.

Oklahoma City Underground: Art and history exhibits line a mile of color-coded corridors below downtown OKC. *(downtownokc.com/underground)*

Skeletons: Museum of Osteology: Flesh-eating beetles help prepare the bones of dead animals for a new life on display. *(skeletonmuseum.com; adult/child $14/12)*

Oklahoma Frontier Drugstore Museum: A kooky museum in Guthrie that shows the remedies (like jars of leeches) offered at an Old West pharmacy. *(drugmuseum.org; adult/child $5/4)*

Tip your hat to Stockyards City

A sign spanning Agnew Ave welcomes you to **Stockyards City** *(stockyardscity.org)*, still home to the Oklahoma National Stockyards, the world's largest feeder and stocker cattle market. Cows are auctioned off every Monday and Tuesday, an event open to the public.

Most people come here to shop, though perhaps not for live cows – Western-wear shops abound. Favorites include **Langston's** *(langstons.com)* and **National Saddlery** *(nationalsaddlery.com)*. Across the street, **Cattlemen's Steakhouse** *(cattlemensrestaurant.com)* is the oldest continually operating restaurant in OKC, feeding cowpokes and city slickers big breakfasts and steaks since 1910.

Cruise Bricktown's canal

Modeled after San Antonio's **River Walk**, OKC's **Bricktown** *(bricktownokc.com)* is an industrial-turned-entertainment district. Much of it is geared toward families and can feel touristy, but it's worth a wander. Bricktown Water Taxi *(bricktownwatertaxi.com; adult/child $15/12)* runs hour-long boat trips on the canal past historic buildings and public art, culminating at the **Centennial Land Run Monument**. Covering the size of a football field, 45 larger-than-life bronze horsemen and wagon drivers capture the chaos and drama of the 1889 land rush that settled a large part of the future state – and dispossessed Native people from their lands.

Fort Sill

Find remnants of the Indian Wars in western Oklahoma

Constructed in 1869, **Fort Sill** *(sill-www.army.mil; free; closed Sun)* was a frontier post that remains an important military base today. The history is still on display for visitors, particularly around the Old Post Quadrangle, which is surrounded by original stone buildings. Start your visit at the **Interpretive Center** on its southern side, which has old-school museum displays and staff who can help you find other points of interest. Many travelers come to see the eagle-topped **grave of Geronimo** (Goyahkla), an Apache warrior and shaman who fought the Mexicans and Americans trying to confine his nomadic tribe to reservations. He died at Fort Sill as a prisoner of war in 1909. The **US Army Artillery Museum** is another draw for those interested in historic and modern weaponry.

 EATING IN OKC: OUR PICKS

Nonesuch: Slide into one of just 22 seats for a foodie adventure in Oklahoma flavors via a multicourse tasting menu. *5:30-9pm Tue-Sat* $$$

Ma Der Lao Kitchen: A Laotian restaurant in OKC? Yes, and a damn good one, too. The crispy rice salad is a must-order. *11am-10pm Tue-Thu, to 11pm Fri & Sat* $$

Cheever's Cafe: Upscale cafe in an art deco former flower shop with excellent Southwestern-style fare. *11am-9pm Mon-Thu, to 10pm Fri-Sun* $$

Sunnyside Diner: This cheerful cheapie doles out the best breakfasts in town, from fresh blueberry pancakes to Okie poutine. *6am-2pm* $

Bison, Wichita Mountains Wildlife Refuge

Fort Sill is still an active Army base, so visitors without a Department of Defense license require a background check before entering. Speed up the process by giving your details on the Visitor Pre-Registration System online in advance. Non-US citizens aren't allowed on base unless they know someone stationed there.

Wichita Mountains
Hiking and wildlife-watching off the grid

West of Oklahoma City, the state opens into expansive prairies, nowhere as beautifully as in the Wichita Mountains. The 59,020-acre **Wichita Mountains Wildlife Refuge** *(fws.gov/refuge/wichita-mountains; free)* protects bison, elk, longhorn cattle and prairie dogs.

Displays at the **visitor center** highlight the refuge's flora and fauna, and it has large picture windows for views of prairie grasslands. For elevated views, drive to the top of **Mt Scott**, the highest peak in the refuge at 2464ft. For a short but scenic hike, try the **Kite Trail**, which climbs above the West Cache Creek and has access points to small waterfalls. Your best bet for food and accommodations is in **Medicine Park**.

MORE OKC ATTRACTIONS

Myriad Botanical Gardens: Elaborate landscapes with thousands of plants right in the city center. The IM Pei–designed conservatory holds a tropical wonderland. *(myriadgardens.org; grounds free, conservatory adult/child $10.50/5.50)*

Oklahoma State Capitol: Built in 1917, the Capitol building has stained-glass windows, rotating art exhibits and even on-site oil wells. Free walk-up tours at 11am and 1pm weekdays.

Science Museum Oklahoma: Family-friendly galleries filled with planes, dinos and a planetarium *(sciencemuseumok.org; adult/child $23/18)*.

Oklahoma History Center: Focuses on the people of the Sooner State through interactive exhibits; good Native galleries *(adult/child $12.50/9)*.

DRINKING IN OKC: OUR PICKS

Prairie Artisan Ales: Craft-beer spot run by a fourth-generation brewer in the Automobile Alley district. Bomb, a stout, is its flagship pint. *11am-10pm*

Skydance Brewing Co: Only 0.4% of craft breweries are Native-owned, and Skydance showcases Indigenous stories. *noon-10pm Sun-Thu, to midnight Fri & Sat*

Good for a Few: Magic mixologists pour incredible creations in this moody cocktail bar, semi-hidden in a burger restaurant. *4pm-midnight Wed-Sat*

Later Bye: This cozy 31-seat neighborhood cocktail bar can do no wrong. Pair drinks with Italian or Spanish small plates. *3pm-midnight Mon-Thu, to 1am Fri & Sat*

Nebraska

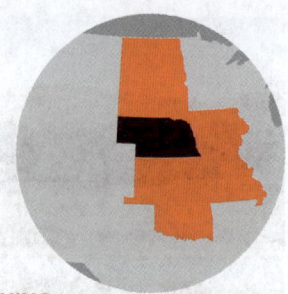

PIONEER TRAILS | FRONTIER FORTS | BIRD-WATCHING

Places

Omaha p626
Lincoln & Around p628
Grand Island & Kearney p630
Nebraska Panhandle p632
Valentine p633
Monowi p633

Travelers have traversed Nebraska for millennia: Native tribes; transcontinental settlers coming by covered wagon, railroad and automobile on the USA's first country-belting routes; thousands-strong flocks of sandhill cranes on their seasonal migration; and dinosaurs and other extinct prehistoric wildlife. You can still follow their trails, but do more than just make tire tracks through the Cornhusker State.

Alongside the state's sprinkling of cute towns, Nebraska's two main cities are culture-driven and artful. Omaha, the state's biggest urban center, is home to the brick-street Old Market district of revamped warehouses, a booming riverfront, and several museums and family-friendly attractions. Just an hour's drive away, the state capital of Lincoln is anything but stuffy, thanks to the students at the University of Nebraska who know how to have a good time.

Nature calls in the remote Nebraska Panhandle, where stark rock formations stand sentinel over the prairie, and in the lush Niobrara Valley, a federally protected scenic river.

☑ TOP TIP

Nebraska ranks second in the country (after Texas) as the state raising the most cattle, so if you're an omnivore, sampling the steak is a must. Committee Chophouse (p628) in Omaha is a top pick. Its summer-only 'steak flights' offer four perfectly prepared slabs sourced from Nebraska ranches.

GETTING AROUND

You need a car to get around Nebraska. I-80 is the state's main access point by car, and Nebraska's biggest cities are dotted along it.

The interstate allows you to zip across Nebraska for 455 miles at 75mph, but the real way to enjoy the countryside is to take the smaller roads. Some I-80 alternatives include US 6 between Omaha and Lincoln, US 30 between Omaha and Grand Island, and US 34 between Grand Island and Lincoln. US 30, the Lincoln Hwy, is particularly historic. Opened in 1913, it was the first transcontinental highway specifically for cars.

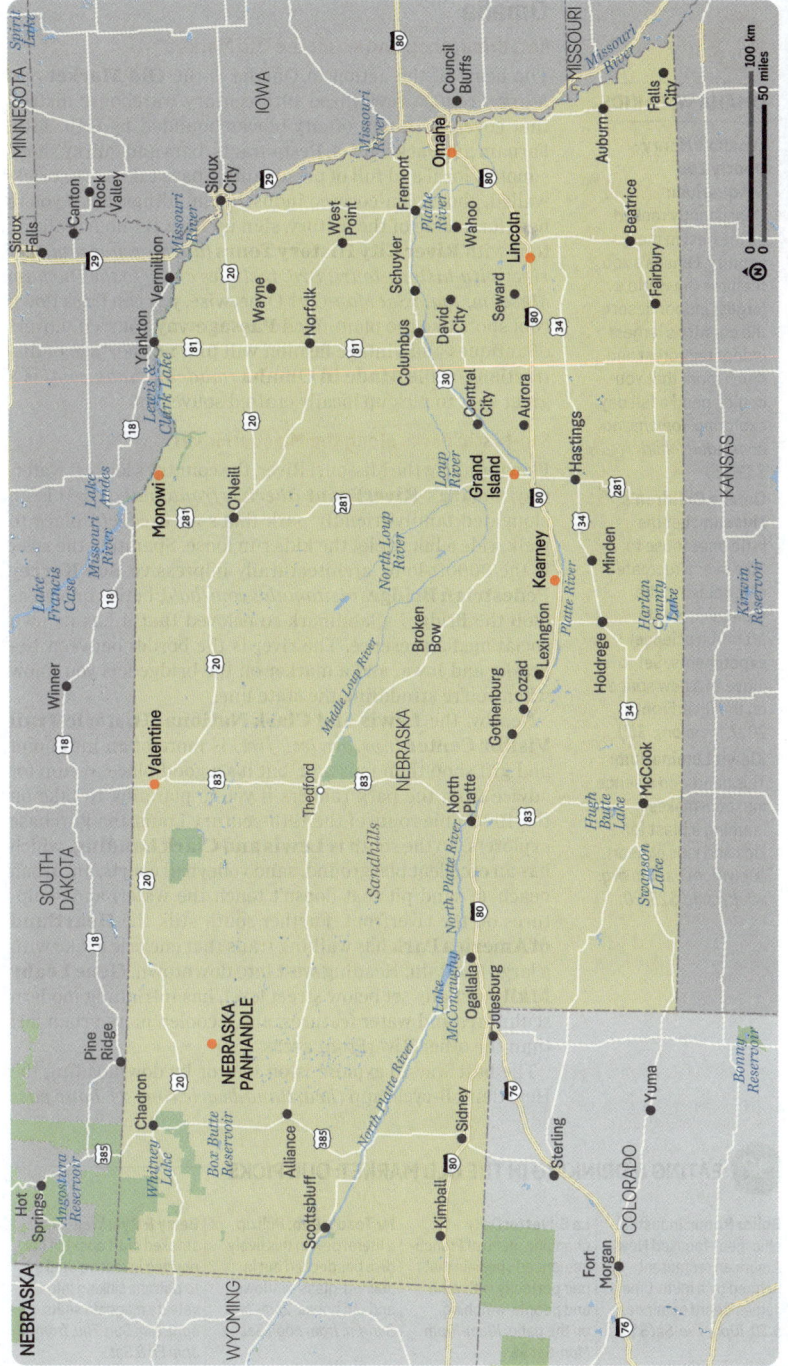

Omaha

Eat, drink, shop and stroll the Old Market

The heart of the action in Omaha is the **Old Market** *(old market.com)*, a revitalized 19th-century warehouse district that covers a square of city blocks bounded by 10th, 13th, Farnam and Jackson Sts. Restaurants, bars and quirky shops – mostly local and full of personality – have taken over brick-walled, ghost-sign-covered industrial buildings, but if you're here for a taste of the history, sign up for a 1½-hour walking tour with **River City History Tours** *(durhammuseum.org/river-city-history-tours; $26, includes entry to the Durham Museum; 10am Sat May-Oct)*. Otherwise, you can track down cool spots like the plant-filled **Passageway** yourself. Lovers of antiques and vintage fashion will find no shortage of distractions, while **Made in Omaha** *(madeinomaha.com)* is a great spot to pick up locally crafted souvenirs.

Kid-tastic parks along the Missouri River

Flowing along the Missouri River, the country's longest waterway, Omaha's **RiverFront** *(theriverfrontomaha.com)* is an elongated family-friendly park that's an excellent place to walk, ride a bike or let the kids run loose. Spanning the river is the 3000ft-long, architecturally impressive **Bob Kerrey Pedestrian Bridge** *(visitomaha.com/bob)*, better known as 'Bob the Bridge,' a landmark so beloved that it has its own social media presence. The river is the border between Nebraska and Iowa, and a marker on the bridge lets you know when you're straddling the state line.

Nearby, the **Lewis and Clark National Historic Trail Visitor Center** *(nps.gov/lecl; free)* is more of an info point and gift shop than museum, but it's a good place to stop for advice from the park rangers if you're planning to take on the 4900-mile route of the 19th-century Louisiana Purchase explorers. To the south is **Lewis and Clark Landing**, which has an excellent playground, sand volleyball courts, an 'urban beach' (a sand pit that doesn't touch the water) and sculptures on the riverfront. Further south still, the **Heartland of America Park** has walking trails that encircle a lake with a large fountain. Heading west into downtown, **Gene Leahy Mall**, partially set below street level, has intriguing modern sculptures and water features, and a cooler, more urban feel than the other RiverFront areas.

The best way to explore is on foot or by downloading the Heartland B-cycle app *(heartland.bcycle.com; 24-hour pass*

OMAHA WITH KIDS

Omaha's Henry Doorly Zoo & Aquarium: Consistently ranked as the best in the country, Omaha's zoo features the world's largest indoor desert, the country's largest indoor rainforest and much more that you could spend a full day exploring. *(omahazoo.com; adult/child $32/25)*

Omaha Children's Museum: Let the little ones loose to take over a recreated city, splash in the fountains, create art or run science experiments. Set to move to a new space on the RiverFront in 2027. *(ocm.org; $17)*

Kiewit Luminarium: This hands-on science museum makes learning a blast for kids and kids at heart. *(kiewitluminarium.org; adult/child $25/20)*

EATING & DRINKING IN THE OLD MARKET: OUR PICKS

Boiler Room: Industrial chic meat-focused New American restaurant helmed by a multi-time James Beard nominee. *5:30-10pm Tue-Sat* **$$$**

La Buvette: Daily changing menu of French-influenced specials that pair perfectly with wine and people-watching on the patio. *10am-10pm Mon-Sat* **$$**

Mr Toad's Pub: Pull up a literal pew in this lively dive bar decked out in stained-glass windows and old books. *2pm-2am Sun-Fri, from noon Sat*

Berry & Rye: Well-stocked craft cocktail bar pouring inventive drinks to patrons sinking into velvety magenta seats. *5pm-2am Sun-Thu, from 3pm Fri & Sat*

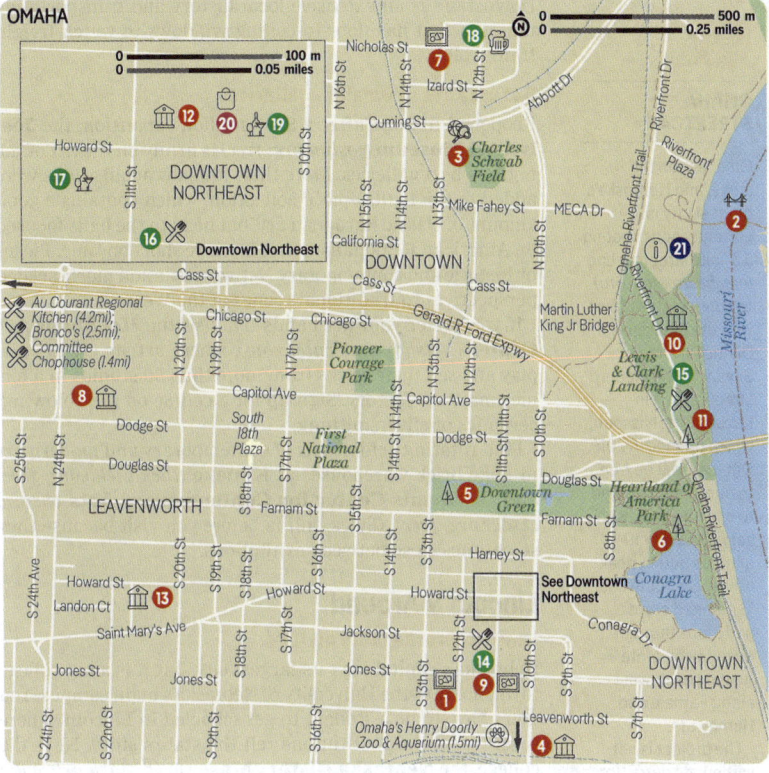

SIGHTS
1. Bemis Center for Contemporary Arts
2. Bob Kerrey Pedestrian Bridge
3. Charles Schwab Field
4. Durham Museum
5. Gene Leahy Mall
6. Heartland of America Park
7. Hot Shops Art Center
8. Joslyn Art Museum
9. Kaneko
10. Kiewit Luminarium
11. Lewis & Clark Landing
12. Old Market Passageway
13. Omaha Children's Museum

EATING
14. Boiler Room
15. Fig
16. La Buvette

DRINKING & NIGHTLIFE
17. Berry & Rye
18. Kros Strain Draft Works
19. Mr Toad's Pub

SHOPPING
20. Made in Omaha

INFORMATION
21. Lewis & Clark National Historic Trail Visitor Center

$16.05) and checking out one of the docked e-bikes. Bicycles are allowed in most RiverFront areas, while e-scooters are not. Fuel up first at **Fig** (*figomaha.com*), a sun-filled cafe overlooking the river.

All aboard for history at the Durham Museum

Though trains no longer stop here, Omaha's soaring art deco Union Station, now the **Durham Museum** (*durhammuseum. org; adult/child $15/8)*, is a sight to behold with its cathedral windows, geometric chandeliers, ornate ceilings and reliefs of railroad workers carved into the facade. Admire it from the old-school soda fountain while drinking a phosphate pop.

OMAHA STREETCAR

Omaha is on the move, and Nebraska's biggest city is currently constructing a 3-mile streetcar line *(omahastreetcar.org)* to connect downtown with the Blackstone District in Midtown. Similar to the modern streetcar line in Kansas City, Missouri, which opened in 2016, Omaha's will be free to ride. It's scheduled to open in 2028, with services every 10 minutes during peak hours. The route has 13 planned stops and loops through downtown before running east–west along Farnam and Harney Sts.

The project is not without its detractors, including Warren Buffett, Omaha's most famous resident and the fifth-richest man in the world, who said that the $306 million plan is too expensive and that residents deserved to vote on it.

Downstairs is an extensive local history and transportation museum that has floor-to-ceiling windows to watch freight trains roll by.

Get creative in Omaha's galleries

Reopened in 2024 after a $100 million expansion, the **Joslyn Art Museum** *(joslyn.org; free)* is firmly on the list of the region's best galleries. More than 100 new acquisitions were added to the 12,000-piece collection, which contains a good amount of classic European art, but head to the halls focused on American Regionalism first if you're short on time. Pieces by historic and contemporary Native artists add much-needed perspectives to traditional scenes of the West.

If you prefer your art hands-on, visit the **Hot Shops Art Center** *(hotshopsartcenter.com)*, where artists create, display and sell their works from more than 50 studios in a former mattress factory. Sign up for a course on glassblowing, ceramics or silversmithing.

Find rotating exhibitions of contemporary and modern art in huge brick warehouses at **Kaneko** *(thekaneko.org; free)* and the **Bemis Center for Contemporary Arts** *(bemiscenter.org; free)*. Check online before you visit because they sometimes close between exhibitions.

Lincoln & Around

Learn Nebraska state history

Nebraska's capital isn't its largest city, but it is a big college town, home to the University of Nebraska's main campus. You don't have to be a student to get schooled in Lincoln, where several cultural institutions tell the state's story. Near the college, the **Nebraska History Museum** *(history.nebraska.gov/museum; adult/child $5/3; closed Sun and Mon)* begins the narrative 13,000 years ago, and its three floors of displays carry on to the present.

Less than a mile south, the 400ft-high **Nebraska State Capitol** *(capitol.nebraska.gov; free)* is architectural eye candy. Completed in 1932, its art deco interiors could be mistaken for a soaring cathedral. For deeper insights, join the free guided tours that depart from the north end of the 2nd floor on the hour *(9am-4pm Mon-Fri, from 10am Sat, from 1pm Sun)*, or you can wander up on your own to the 14th-floor observation deck.

EATING & DRINKING IN OMAHA: OUR PICKS

Committee Chophouse: The summertime 'steak flight' from Nebraska ranches is an indulgent treat at this suave, low-lit steakhouse. *5-10pm* $$$

Bronco's: Classic 1950s local fast-food joint with an iconic neon sign. Burgers are made from state-sourced ground beef. *9am-10pm* $

Au Courant Regional Kitchen: Farm-fresh artful plates of New European cuisine in the Benson neighborhood west of downtown. *5-10pm Thu-Sun* $$

Kros Strain Draft Works: Sip the flagship Fairy Nectar IPA inside the industrial taproom in a former furniture warehouse or on the patio. *hours vary; closed Mon*

Nebraska State Capitol

Back to school at UNL

The University of Nebraska has its main campus in the middle of Lincoln. Nebraska doesn't have any major-league sports teams, so everyone in the state pins their hopes on the Huskers. In fall, football games kick off at **Memorial Stadium** *(huskers.com),* and the 85,000 seats often sell out.

A pigskin throw away, the **University of Nebraska State Museum** *(museum.unl.edu; adult/child $12.50/6.75; closed Mon)* has fascinating, though somewhat dated, displays of dinos, many of which were found in the Agate Fossil Beds (p631) in the Nebraska Panhandle. The museum's icon is Archie, the world's largest Columbian mammoth skeleton, which stands 15½ft tall. The newer top-floor Cherish Nebraska exhibit details the state's ecology and changing environment.

On the East Campus, agriculture majors hand-make and sell cheese and ice cream at the **UNL Dairy Store** *(dairystore. unl.edu).* Cones come in more than a dozen delicious seasonal flavors, including sweet corn and white chocolate lavender.

MORE ATTRACTIONS IN & AROUND LINCOLN

International Quilt Museum: Elevates the humble quilt to an exquisite art form. *(internationalquilt museum.org; adult/ child $8/4)*

Sunken Gardens: In the 1930s, a former neighborhood dump was transformed into this pocket park.

Lincoln Children's Museum: Kids can run free in this 23,000-sq-ft space with prairie dog–style tunnels, a three-story climbing structure and even a miniature Runza (p630). *(lincolnchildrens museum.org; adult/ child $13/16)*

Strategic Air Command & Aerospace Museum: Massive hangars contain an example of every significant US bomber, from the B-17 to the B-52. Between Lincoln and Omaha on I-80. *(sacmuseum.org; adult/child $12/6)*

 EATING & DRINKING IN LINCOLN: OUR PICKS

Dish: Lincoln's top restaurant presents inventive New American seasonal plates with locally sourced ingredients. *5-8:30pm or later Tue-Sat* $$

Hub Cafe: This creative cafe is a brunch-time favorite, best enjoyed from the sunny, park-facing seats. *7:30am-9pm Tue-Sat, to 2:30pm Sun* $

Other Room: Perhaps the best cocktail bar in the state hides behind a heavy metal door in the historic Haymarket district. *5pm-1am*

Boiler Brewing Co: A highly awarded former homebrewer now pours pints, often high-ABV, for the thirsty public. *3-10pm Mon-Thu, noon-midnight Fri & Sat, to 8pm Sun*

Pioneers on the prairie

The Homestead Act of 1862 forever altered the landscape and demographics of the western US territories, converting public land (which was Native land before the Indian Removal Act of 1830) to private ownership. Immigrants, formerly enslaved people, women and anyone else who could farm 160 acres for five years got the land cheap in exchange for back-breaking work.

The first plot of land claimed through the Homestead Act is now encompassed by **Homestead National Historical Park** *(nps.gov/home; free)*, 45 miles south of Lincoln. Start at the **Heritage Center**, which puts the Homestead Act into context, and then head outside to visit the **gravesite of Daniel Freeman**, said to have filed his homestead claim 10 minutes after midnight on the day the Act went into effect. None of the Freeman family's buildings still exist, but the 1867 **Palmer-Epard Cabin** behind the Heritage Center is from the era, originally constructed about 14 miles away. The Heritage Center closes at 5pm daily, but the trails around it through the tallgrass prairie are open until dusk.

Grand Island & Kearney

The changing face of the West

For an engaging look at the lives of the homesteaders, head to the **Stuhr Museum** *(stuhrmuseum.org; adult/child $14/12)* in Grand Island. More than 60 buildings from the 1800s were moved to this huge outdoor living-history museum, where reenactors in period dress feed the farm goats, work in the blacksmith shop and roam the wooden boardwalks. The museum gives a nod to the land's original inhabitants with a Pawnee Earth Lodge and a small bison enclosure.

Witness the sandhill crane migration

During their spring migration (mid-February to early April), more than 500,000 sandhill cranes – 80% of the world population – touch down along 80 miles of the Platte River in central Nebraska in one of the country's most spectacular wildlife events. Just off I-80 southwest of Grand Island, the **Crane Trust Nature and Visitor Center** *(cranetrust.org; closed Sun)* runs migration season tours on foot and by bus. East of Kearney, the **Iain Nicolson Audubon Center at Rowe Sanctuary** *(rowe.audubon.org; closed Sun and Mon)* also puts on guided tours. Reserve tours in advance; bookings open in January.

RUNZA

Nebraska's most iconic food is the runza, a rectangle of yeast-dough bread filled with ground beef and onions. This meaty sandwich was brought to the US by 19th-century Volga German immigrants who settled in Nebraska and Kansas (where the dish is called bierock).

The ubiquitous fast-food chain called Runza is the easiest place to try one. The first Runza opened in Lincoln in 1949, and though the original restaurant no longer exists, more than 80 other locations have popped up around the state, as well as a handful in Colorado, Iowa, Kansas and South Dakota. The classic flavor is still on the menu, but you can also order versions with mushroom and Swiss cheese, barbecue and bacon, or Southwest ranch and taco seasoning.

 EATING & DRINKING IN GRAND ISLAND & KEARNEY: OUR PICKS

Coney Island Lunch Room: Old-school diner in downtown Grand Island offering hot dogs, burgers and malts. *8:30am-5pm Mon-Fri, to 3pm Sat* $

Archives: 2024-opened speakeasy below the tourism office in a historic building in Grand Island's adorable downtown. *4-11pm Thu, 6pm-1am Fri, from 1pm Sat*

Cunningham's Journal: Laid-back spot in downtown Kearney with a lengthy menu of pub grub and local beer. *11am-1am Mon-Sat, to midnight Sun* $$

Platte Valley Taphouse: The place to go for good IPAs and pizza in Kearney. Eat, drink and play cornhole in the beer garden. *3-11pm Mon-Wed, 1pm-1am Thu-Sat*

Agate Fossil Beds National Monument

Outside migration season, both free-to-see visitor centers welcome travelers with informational displays and riverfront hiking trails to spot other waterfowl.

Converging trails around Kearney

The first outpost established to protect travelers on the California and Oregon Trails, the 1848 **Fort Kearny** *(outdoornebraska.gov/fortkearny; per vehicle $14, visitor center adult/child $5/1)* still sits among lonesome prairie about 9 miles southeast of Kearney. Today's two 1960s reconstructions are a little disappointing, but if you're here during the sandhill crane migration season, the park is a good place to see the birds.

To get a bigger-picture view of the trails under your feet, visit the **Archway** *(archway.org; adult/child $15/7)*, a museum that bends over the top of I-80 east of Kearney. An audio device leads you through hand-painted exhibits that you might think would border on hokey given the location of this attraction, but they actually do a decent job of telling colorful tales about the people who've passed this way, from pioneers in covered wagon trains to drivers zipping down the interstate.

Connect with Nebraska art

For a cultural stop in Kearney, check out the small but mighty **Museum of Nebraska Art** *(mona.unk.edu; free; closed Mon)*, the state's official art gallery. It's half set in modern premises that reopened in May 2025 after a four-year, $36.5-million expansion, and half in a neoclassical 1911 post office. Nearly two centuries of artwork, predating statehood, trace Nebraska's visual history through the creations of artists who were born, lived or worked in the state.

ROAD TRIP STOPS IN WESTERN NEBRASKA

Pony Express Station: Original log-built 1860 Pony Express stop in Gothenburg. *(ponyexpressstation.org; free)*

Buffalo Bill Ranch State Historical Park: Tour the home of Bill Cody, the father of rodeo and the famed Buffalo Bill's Wild West Show that ran for 30 years from 1883. *(park pass per vehicle $14, plus mansion tour adult/child $5/1)*

Carhenge: A faithful Stonehenge replica made of 39 wrecked cars. Kooky roadside art at its finest, 3 miles north of Alliance. *(carhenge.com; free)*

Agate Fossil Beds National Monument: Some 20 million years ago, this part of Nebraska was like the Serengeti in Africa today: a gathering place for a rich variety of creatures, now fossilized. *(nps.gov/agfo; free)*

Nebraska Panhandle

See iconic rock formations on the prairie

The remote and little-visited Nebraska Panhandle is perhaps the most evocative part of the state. Stark vistas stretch to the horizon in lands little changed in millennia, and rocky bluffs that can be seen from miles around rise out of the prairie.

At **Chimney Rock National Historic Site** *(history .nebraska.gov/rock)*, a 300ft-tall stone spire was so striking to travelers on the Oregon, California and Mormon Trails that it's estimated that 97% of pioneers mentioned it in their journals. The small **Chimney Rock Museum** *(adult/child $8/4; 9am-4pm)* has updated displays but isn't worth the admission fee. Instead, set off on the easy 2-mile loop trail *(free; dawn-dusk)* that gets closer to the base of the formation.

About 25 miles northwest, **Scotts Bluff National Monument** *(nps.gov/scbl; free)* was another important waypoint on the pioneer trails. The **visitor center** *(8am-6pm mid-May–Aug, to 4:30pm Sep–mid-May)* contains exhibits and the largest collection of original paintings and photos by William Henry Jackson, a Civil War veteran famous for his scenes of the American West. Walk in the footsteps of history on the mile-long **trail** *(dawn-dusk)* west of the visitor center, which follows the original path of the Oregon Trail and even has some swales – deep indentations in the dirt compressed by hundreds of thousands of wooden wagon wheels. Drive the **Summit Road** *(9am-5pm mid-May–Aug, to 4pm Sep–mid-May)* or hike the 3.2-mile **Saddle Rock Trail** to the top of the bluff for sweeping views.

War and peace at Fort Robinson State Park

The turbulent past of **Fort Robinson** *(outdoornebraska.gov/ location/fort-robinson; per vehicle $14)* belies its peaceful atmosphere today. Guards killed Lakota chief Crazy Horse (Tȟašúŋke Witkó) here in 1877 when it served as the Red Cloud Indian Agency, brigades of Black troops known as Buffalo Soldiers were formed for the Civil War and it was a POW camp for Germans in WWII. Understand the complex history at the **Fort Robinson Museum** *(adult/child $5/3)*. Several of the old buildings are open to wander around, and you can even stay overnight in former officers' and soldiers' quarters from 1909. Bugle wake-up call not included.

HISTORIC TRAILS THROUGH NEBRASKA

Oregon Trail (1846–69): Nearly half a million settlers traveled this 2170-mile route in the largest voluntary mass migrations in human history.

California Trail (1841–69): Few settlers took to this 1600-mile trail until 1848, when gold was discovered near Sacramento, California.

Mormon Trail (1846–69): Fleeing religious persecution, members of the Church of Jesus Christ of Latter-day Saints packed up their lives in Illinois and made the journey to Utah, then not part of the United States.

Pony Express (1860–61): Express mail on horseback cut down the time to receive a message to 10 days. Operational for only 18 months before the telegraph took over.

EATING & DRINKING IN THE NEBRASKA PANHANDLE: OUR PICKS

Mixing Bowl: This Gering cafe's specials tap into the area's German immigrant history. *6am-3pm Wed-Fri, from 7am Sat & Sun* $

Gering Bakery: Fuel a day of hiking with doughnuts from this neon-signed spot in Gering, open since 1950. *5:30am-5:30pm Mon-Fri, to 1pm Sat* $

Flyover Brewing Company: Everyone in this attractive Scottsbluff brewery is enjoying a better brew (and view) than those at 40,000ft. *11am-11pm Tue-Sun*

Mark Ferrari Specialty Coffees: Find an unexpected taste of aloha in tiny Oshkosh, population 884. *8:30am-2pm Mon-Fri, to 12:30pm Sat*

Scotts Bluff National Monument

Valentine

Raft the Niobrara National Scenic River

Kayaking, canoeing or inner-tubing down the Niobrara (pronounced nigh-oh-BRAH-rah) draws scores of people to north-central Nebraska in summer. Sheer limestone bluffs, lush forests and more than 200 spring-fed waterfalls along the banks shatter any 'flat Nebraska' stereotypes.

Most float tours start from the town of Valentine. **Brewers Canoers and Tubers** (brewerscanoers.com) is one of the original outfitters in the area and was the first to introduce tubing on the Niobrara River. You can rent canoes, kayaks or tubes with them or arrange shuttles to and from launch and landing sites.

Monowi

Eat in Nebraska's smallest town

If you don't think a ghost town can have a strong sense of community, you haven't been to Monowi. Its lone resident is nonagenarian Elsie Eiler, who runs **Monowi Tavern** (closed Mon). The bar and grill is a one-woman show, where Elsie cooks burgers, fries and steaks for a surprising number of customers. Her family has operated the tavern since 1971, and in addition to working as the cook and bartender, she's also Monowi's mayor. Farmers and people from all over the county sit down to catch up and share gossip, and travelers are welcomed just as warmly.

BEST NEBRASKA FESTIVALS

NCAA College World Series: The top Division I baseball teams head to Omaha's **Charles Schwab Field** every June. (cwsomaha.com)

Star City Pride: Lincoln turns rainbow with pride at this LGBTQ+ parade in June. (starcityprideevents.org)

Kool-Aid Days: The sugary drink was invented in Hastings in 1927, and it's celebrated with boat races and a Kool-Aid drinking contest in August. (kool-aiddays.com)

Oregon Trail Days: In Gering, the state's oldest festival includes a street dance party and a chili cook-off. (oregontraildays.com)

Nebraska Star Party: Spy on the night sky in July at Merritt Reservoir, the state's only Dark Sky Park. (nebraskastarparty.org)

Iowa

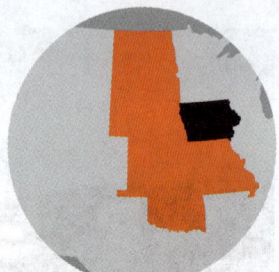

HEARTLAND BEAUTY | FANTASTIC CYCLING | INNOVATIVE ARCHITECTURE

Places

Dubuque & Around p635
Iowa City p638
Amana Colonies p638
Des Moines p640
Central Iowa p641
Mason City p642
Sioux City p644

☑ TOP TIP

Get off the interstates and spend time on Iowa's backroads, which pass the farms and fields that comprise America's heartland. The state is home to 14 national and state scenic byways *(iowadot.gov),* and you'll find at least one in every region. Slow down and soak up the pastoral beauty!

You'll come to appreciate the rumble strips that keep you alert while driving across Iowa's rural backroads, where miles and miles of fields and farmhouses cast a hypnotic spell – and stop signs pop up unexpectedly at lonely crossroads. Stretching east from the soaring Loess Hills across swaths of rolling farmland, the Hawkeye State packs in the pastoral beauty before bumping into bluffs along the Mississippi River. In the middle? The writers' town of Iowa City, the tradition-loving Amana Colonies, art-minded Des Moines and architecturally impressive Mason City. A network of biking trails link the state's picture-perfect towns.

Iowa emerges from slumber every four years as the make-or-break state for presidential hopefuls. The Iowa Caucus opens the national election battle, and wins by George W Bush in 2000 and Barack Obama in 2008 stunned many pundits and launched their victorious campaigns. Another statewide highlight is RAGBRAI, an annual multi-day bike ride that draws thousands of cyclists.

GETTING AROUND

You'll need a car to explore greater Iowa. I-80 runs east-west across the state, linking Des Moines with Chicago to the east and Omaha, NE, to the west. I-35 travels north–south, connecting Des Moines with Minneapolis to the north and Kansas City to the south. Iowa has a fantastic network of cycling trails, and they are a pretty option for exploring urban areas and beyond.

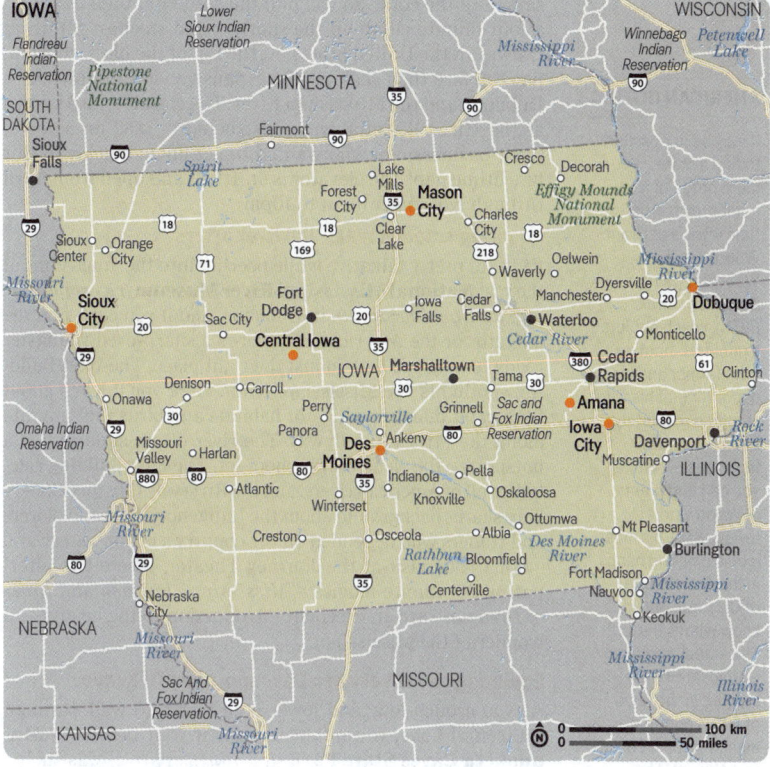

Dubuque & Around

Strolling the river cities

The historic city of **Dubuque**, with its 19th-century Victorian homes lining narrow streets between the Mississippi River and seven steep limestone hills, is a fine base for Great River Road explorations. Stroll the 9-mile path along the waterfront and explore neighborhoods in the midst of an urban revitalization that's drawing national acclaim. Don't miss the redeveloped Millwork District immediately north of downtown past 6th St. Its old wood-working factories are now home to great restaurants and nightlife. Red-brick walls are splashed with spectacular **murals** *(voicesproductions.org)* across downtown.

Davenport is the largest and most appealing of the Quad Cities about 70 miles south of Dubuque (the other three are Bettendorf in Iowa and Moline and Rock Island in Illinois). It has a grand riverfront setting with a vast network of walking and biking trails.

Ride the Fenelon Place Elevator

Stepping into Dubuque's tiny **Fenelon Place Elevator** *(fenelonplaceelevator.com; adult/child $2/1 roundtrip)* at 8:30am, especially if traveling solo, is a leap of faith. The sign

AMERICAN GOTHIC

It may be impossible to find a state more proud of a homegrown artist than Iowa is of Grant Wood. You know Wood. He painted *American Gothic* (1930), which depicts a pitchfork-holding Iowa farmer and his daughter (not his wife) standing resolutely before their tiny farmhouse. While you can find plenty of Wood works in Iowa (p638), his most iconic painting hangs in the Art Institute of Chicago. But you know what's better? The actual *American Gothic* farmhouse, located in the town of Eldon about 100 miles southeast of Des Moines. The house sits beside the **American Gothic House Center** *(americangothichouse.net; $5)*, which interprets the painting that sparked a million parodies. It even has loaner costumes so you can make your own parody selfie (for no fee) in front of the house.

says 'Pull the cord.' So you pull the cord, and then *whee!* It's a four-minute climb up the shortest and steepest funicular railway in the United States. At the top of the bluff, step out, pay the fare then soak up the expansive view of downtown Dubuque and the Mississippi River. The elevator, also known as the 4th St Elevator, was constructed in 1882 for a downtown businessman who wanted to get home quickly for his lunchtime nap! The elevator is on 4th St and open from April through November (8am to 10pm).

Aquariums, touch tanks and river otters

Kids are pretty talkative while peering into the aquariums at the vast **National Mississippi River Museum** *(rivermuseum.org; adult/child $26/20)* in Dubuque, and if you can't find the alligator or the American eel, there's a sharp-eyed youngster ready to help you look in just the right place. The West Building spotlights the Mississippi River. Here you'll learn about backwater marshes, alligator habitats and birds that migrate along the Mississippi flyway. The river otters aquarium is a hotspot for the elementary school set. The East Building celebrates all of America's rivers, and the Riverways History Gallery here shares background about the Indigenous tribes, explorers and traders who depended on the country's major waterways.

Start your visit at the Journey Theater, where two alternating 20-minute movies – *Mississippi Journey* and *River of Dreams* – are an excellent introduction to the beauty and wonder of the Mississippi.

Exploring caves between Davenport and Dubuque

As you crouch low...and lower...and lower, to walk through Dancehall Cave, you might wonder if your detour to **Maquoketa Caves State Park** *(iowadnr.gov; free)* was such a great idea. Don't worry, it was, especially if you're traveling with kids. And the ten-minute walk through the multi-room Dancehall is a highlight of a visit to this fun state park, where excited kids don headlamps before wiggling into small, marked caves. Two short loop trails, which pass 13 designated caves, link up at the vast Dancehall – where locals did indeed hold dance parties back in the day. The park is just off US 61 between Davenport and Dubuque, about 35 miles west of the Mississippi River.

Have a catch at the Field of Dreams

Several nights each week in summer the 'ghosts' of legendary baseball players step onto the **Field of Dreams** *(fieldofdreamsmoviesite.com; $20 donation)* baseball diamond from the

EATING & DRINKING AROUND DUBUQUE: OUR PICKS

Brazen Open Kitchen: Heavenly seasonal New American cuisine, plus inventive cocktails and a sizable wine list in the Millwork District. *4:30-9pm Mon-Sat* $$

L May Eatery: The creative thin crust pizzas are delicious at this chic downtown cafe. Works well for solos and celebratory couples alike. *hours vary* $$

Monk's: Every town needs a joint like Monk's: friendly folks in a creaky old house serving coffee in the morning and local beer at night. *7am-11pm most days*

Textile Brewing Co: Occupies an old sewing factory in Dyersville 30 miles west of Dubuque. Giant pretzels, fantastic flatbreads and tasty beer. *11am-9pm most days*

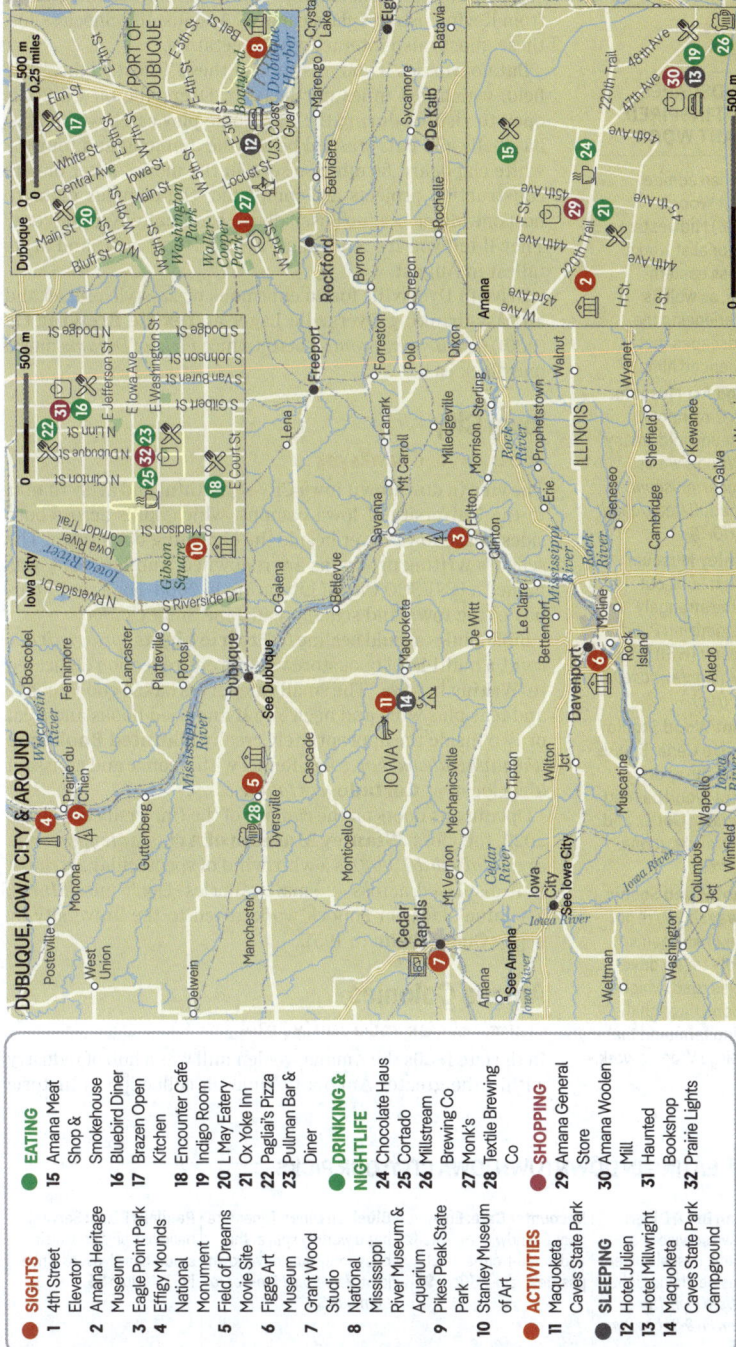

DUBUQUE, IOWA CITY & AROUND

THE GREAT PLAINS IOWA

SIGHTS
1. 4th Street Elevator
2. Amana Heritage Museum
3. Eagle Point Park
4. Effigy Mounds National Monument
5. Field of Dreams Movie Site
6. Figge Art Museum
7. Grant Wood Studio
8. National Mississippi River Museum & Aquarium
9. Pikes Peak State Park
10. Stanley Museum of Art

ACTIVITIES
11. Maquoketa Caves State Park

SLEEPING
12. Hotel Julien
13. Hotel Millwright
14. Maquoketa Caves State Park Campground

EATING
15. Amana Meat Shop & Smokehouse
16. Bluebird Diner
17. Brazen Open Kitchen
18. Encounter Cafe
19. Indigo Room
20. L May Eatery
21. Ox Yoke Inn
22. Pagliai's Pizza
23. Pullman Bar & Diner

DRINKING & NIGHTLIFE
24. Chocolate Haus
25. Cortado
26. Millstream Brewing Co
27. Monk's
28. Textile Brewing Co

SHOPPING
29. Amana General Store
30. Amana Woolen Mill
31. Haunted Bookshop
32. Prairie Lights

LANDSCAPES THAT INSPIRED GRANT WOOD

You can admire Grant Wood's (p636) Midwestern Regionalist works across eastern Iowa, as well as experiencing the landscapes that influenced him.

Figge Art Museum: This Davenport museum holds many of Wood's works. *(figgeartmuseum.org; adult/teen/child $14/10/8)*

Stanley Museum of Art: Look out for the strangely mesmerizing *Plaid Sweater* (1931) in Iowa City. *(stanleymuseum.org; free)*

Grant Wood Studio: Head to Cedar Rapids to see the spot where Wood painted *American Gothic* and other works. *(crma.org; free)*

Grant Wood Scenic Byway: If you're not a fan of museums, simply take a drive on this road, which ribbons through the rolling farmland that inspired Wood's work.

---

surrounding cornfield during a game or event, echoing a scene from Kevin Costner's classic movie. And just like Shoeless Joe, these ghosts also interact with spectators.

But no worries if you miss one of these 'Ghost Nights.' The field, which is 4 miles northeast of Dyersville off US 20, is open to visitors during the day. Come play catch with mitts, baseballs and bats stashed beside the diamond and tour the white clapboard farmhouse seen in the movie. After on-site construction projects are completed, the complex plans to host one Major League Baseball game annually. And the corn? They'll tell you it's 'knee-high by the 4th of July,' and at its tallest in August.

Drive to Dyersville for an enormous pizza-style pretzel and an easy-drinking Dyersville Lager at **Textile Brewing Co** (p601) *(textilebrews.com)*. There's a nice *Field of Dreams* mural one block east.

Iowa City

Books, art and hawkeyes

The vibe in downtown Iowa City is youthful and artsy thanks to the University of Iowa campus, which spills across both sides of the Iowa River beside the charming downtown. The school's writing programs are renowned, and Iowa City was named a UNESCO City of Literature in 2008. For a sharp parody of the town and school, read Jane Smiley's *Moo*.

Bibliophiles should beeline to **Prairie Lights** *(prairielights.com)*, a multi-level bookstore with an entire section dedicated to 'Writing in Iowa.' The small cafe serves baked goods, coffee and teas plus wine and beer. You'll find used books and a cat or two inside the appropriately creaky **Haunted Bookshop** *(thehauntedbookshop.com)*. Refuel with a coffee and croissant (delicious!) at **Cortado** *(cortadoic.com)*.

Opening its doors on the campus of the University of Iowa in 2022, the glossy **Stanley Museum of Art** *(stanleymuseum.org; adult/child $8/3)* is a whirlwind of spectacular art, most of it displayed across 12 small galleries. Don't miss *Mural*, a seminal Jackson Pollock work gifted to the university by Peggy Guggenheim in 1951.

Amana Colonies

Crafts, religion and a spiffy hotel

In the late 1800s the Amana woolen mill was a hub of industry within the greater Amana Colonies, a collection of historic

---

EATING IN DOWNTOWN IOWA CITY: OUR PICKS

Pullman Bar & Diner: Attentive service and decadent, upscale diner fare beside Prairie Lights. *8am-10pm Mon-Thu, to 10:30pm Fri & Sat, to 9pm Sun* **$$**

Encounter Cafe: Enjoy panini sandwiches, salads and made-from-scratch pastries. *7am-2:30pm* **$**

Bluebird Diner: Diner fare has a worldly spin at this busy, long-time downtown joint. *7am-9pm Mon-Sat to 8pm Sun* **$**

Pagliai's Pizza: Serving delicious pies cooked in stone-hearth ovens since 1957. *4-10pm* **$$**

Prairie Lights

German religious villages located 25 miles northwest of Iowa City. In 2020 the old mill welcomed its first guests under a brand new name and identity: the **Hotel Millwright**. An adaptive re-use project, this 66-room boutique hotel celebrates the stories and craftsmanship of the mill workers. It has also revitalized the villages, which have been a shopping and dining destination long known for its craft stores and family-style German restaurants.

If you're driving across Iowa on I-80, the colonies are a convenient stop just north of the interstate. Most attractions are located in the village of Amana, which is home to the **Amana Heritage Museum** (*amanaheritage.org; adult/child $10/5*). The museum shares a good overview of the history of the colonies. Don't skip the short introductory film.

For books, toys, gifts and a variety of preserves, stop by the **Amana General Store** (*amanaheritage.com*). Buy locally produced cheeses and smoked meats around the corner at the **Amana Meat Shop & Smokehouse** (*amanameatshop.com*). Amana-made blankets, throws and scarves catch the eye at

HISTORY OF THE AMANA COLONIES

Seven villages are stretched along a 17-mile loop just north of I-80 west of Iowa City. All were established as German religious communes between 1855 and 1861 by Inspirationists who lived a utopian life with no wages paid and all assets communally owned. Communal kitchens served daily meals to all. During the Great Depression the community voted to end the communal way of living, although the Amana Church continues. Unlike the Amish and Mennonite religions, Inspirationists embrace modern technology (and tourism).

Today the well-preserved (and discreetly tasteful) villages offer a glimpse of this unique culture, and there are lots of arts, crafts, cheeses, baked goods and wines to buy.

EATING & DRINKING IN THE AMANA COLONIES

Ox Yoke Inn: Bratwurst, schnitzels and fried chicken. Family-style meals have refillable entrees and sides for all. *11am-7pm Mon-Thu, to 8pm Fri & Sat, 9am-6pm Sun* $

Indigo Room: Bustling restaurant with a cocktail bar inside Hotel Millwright. Enjoy elevated small plates and a few mains. *4-8pm Mon, to 9pm Tue-Sun* $$

Chocolate Haus: Sells delicious artisanal truffles and fudge as well as chocolate-y coffee drinks. Wonderful frappuccinos. *10am-5pm Mon-Sun, 11am-5pm Sun*

Millstream Brewing Co: Listen to German oom-pah-pah while sipping innovative craft beer beside the mill race near Hotel Millwright. *11am-7pm most days*

TOP SIGHTS ALONG IOWA'S GREAT RIVER ROAD

Iowa's Great River Road mostly hugs the Mississippi River along the state's eastern edge. It links with numerous country byways and passes through beautiful riverfront towns.

Effigy Mounds National Monument: Hundreds of Native American burial mounds sit in the bluffs above the Mississippi in northeast Iowa.

Pikes Peak State Park: A nature reserve at the confluence of the Wisconsin and Mississippi Rivers.

National Mississippi River Museum & Aquarium: Learn about life along the length of the Mississippi in Dubuque.

Eagle Point Park: Beautiful bluff-top park in Clinton with river views and elaborate 1930s stonework.

Figge Art Museum: This glass-walled museum in Davenport sparkles above the River Road, and is now illuminated at night.

---

the **Amana Woolen Mill** *(amanawoolenmill.com),* which is located in the original weaving building beside the hotel.

Des Moines

Butter cows and fried Twinkies on a stick

Much more than just country music and butter sculpture, the **Iowa State Fair** *(iowastatefair.org; adult/child $16/10)* draws more than one million visitors over its 11-day run in early August. Fairgoers can admire award-winning farm animals, and they have their pick of more than 50 food items, from deep-fried Twinkies to bacon-cheddar pretzel dogs, that are shoved on a stick. It's the setting for the Rodgers and Hammerstein musical *State Fair* and the 1945 film version. The fairgrounds are 3.5 miles east of downtown Des Moines.

If you're not in Iowa for the fair, try instead **Des Moines' Downtown Farmers Market** *(facebook.com/downtownfarmersmarket).* Held Saturday mornings from May though October, this popular market – which began in 1975 – hosts hundreds of vendors selling produce, prepared foods, baked goods, meals, snacks and crafts.

A gold dome and top-drawer digs

You're looking pretty impressive there, **Iowa State Capitol** *(iowa.gov; free).* Perched on a hill overlooking an enormous green lawn, this is one state capitol that is worth a closer look. Topped by a sparkling gold dome, the building soars 275ft. The bling-heavy interior is also a wonder, from the stained glass in the library to the spiral staircases. While exploring the 1st floor, be sure to look up to see the interior artistry of the dome. On the first floor you'll also find an intricate model of the USS *Iowa*. The enormous *Westward* mural, completed in 1905, draws you in for a closer look – are those angels protecting a wagon train? – while climbing from the 1st to the 2nd floor.

Parking is free in front of the building, and there's a public entrance under the front steps. After you're screened by security, walk straight ahead to the information desk for a self-guided tour pamphlet, or ask when the next guided tour departs. Tours last 90 minutes, but it's okay to spin off early.

Art and architecture in Des Moines

From its nondescript name to its ho-hum entry sign, the **Des Moines Art Center** *(desmoinesartcenter.org; free)* doesn't knock it out of the park when it comes to first impressions. But don't skip it. Three of the greatest architects of the modern era – Eliel Saarinen, IM Pei and Richard Meier – designed separate buildings within the complex. For visitors, it's easy to walk between them, and the varied architectural styles complement the collection's different artistic genres in striking ways. Matisse, Hopper, Rodin, Warhol and Basquiat are a few of the names represented.

From most points downtown it's an easy walk to the museum's satellite location, the **Pappajohn Sculpture Park**, where Jaume Plensa's enormous *Nomade* is particularly compelling. Grab a coffee near the park at eco-minded **Horizon Line**, where your to-go drink is served in a recyclable jar.

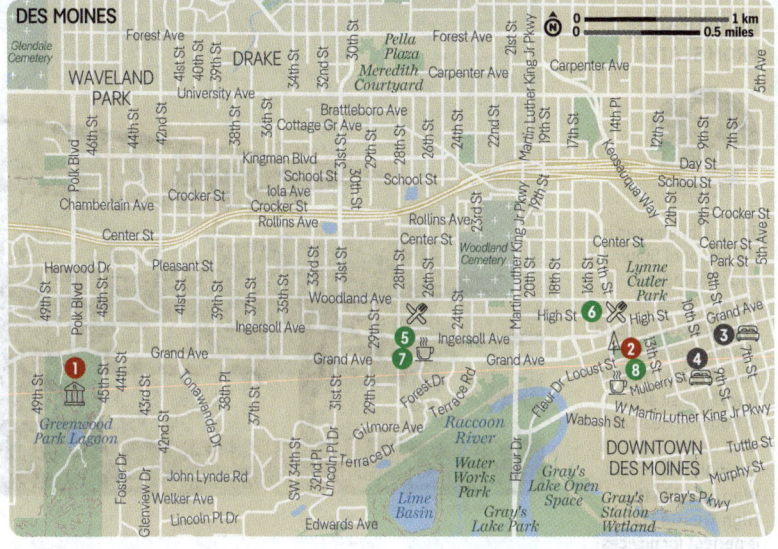

Indie shops in West Des Moines

There's not a chain store in sight in **Valley Junction** *(valley junction.com)*, a former village that has been swallowed up by West Des Moines. This five-block commercial corner unfurls along Fifth St, which is lined with locally owned shops, cafes and antique stores housed in attractive old brick buildings.

Don't miss **Bozz Prints** *(bozzprints.com)*, a print shop selling a colorful array of Iowa-promoting stickers, magnets, shirts and postcards. Prints also celebrate the Midwest and national parks. You'll find Iowa-made products a few doors down at **Heart of Iowa Marketplace** *(heartofiowamarketplace. com)*. Writers won't leave **Quill & Nib** *(valleyjunction.com)* empty-handed – it's pens and journals galore.

Central Iowa

Silos, biker bars and black dirt

It's hard to miss the **High Trestle Bridge** *(inhf.org)* at night. Forty-one steel frames, illuminated by colorful LED lights, form a tunnel over the span, which soars 13 stories above the Des Moines River Valley. With its overlooks, interpretive signage and great birdwatching, the bridge is nearly

---

● **SIGHTS**
1 Des Moines Art Center
2 Pappajohn Sculpture Park

● **SLEEPING**
3 Des Lux Hotel
4 Hotel Fort Des Moines

● **EATING**
see 5 Harbinger
5 Lachele's Fine Foods
6 Lua Brewing

● **DRINKING & NIGHTLIFE**
7 Chain & Spoke
8 Horizon Line Coffee

🍴 EATING & DRINKING IN DES MOINES: OUR PICKS

Lachele's Fine Foods: Construction workers and ladies who lunch converge at this tiny joint for delicious smash burgers. *11am-9pm Tue-Sat, 10am-3pm Sun* **$**

Harbinger: James Beard nominee Joe Tripp elevates Asian street food at this chic number. Many veggie options. *4-8pm Sun-Thu, to 9pm Fri & Sat* **$**

Lua Brewing: Nationally acclaimed brewpub has excellent beers, welcoming staff and delicious gourmet pub fare. *11am-10pm most days* **$$**

Chain & Spoke: What? A friendly bike shop? Yep, drop by for local cycling advice and fine coffee. *8am-5pm Mon-Fri, to 3pm Sat & Sun*

BICYCLE RIDES FROM SLATER

Taylor Christensen is the mayor of Slater and cofounder of Local Spokes.

Why is Slater a good starting point for a half-day bike ride in Iowa? We sit at the T of both the Heart of Iowa Nature Trail and the High Trestle Trail.

Who can ride the High Trestle Trail? It is perfect for novices or experienced cyclists. It's very clear and has a level grade – less than 2%. About every 7 miles there's a town. We will get families, with kids five to seven, to some very serious bikers.

What are some recommended stops for food and good cheer? In Madrid we have the **Flat Tire**, right on the trail. In Woodward they have the **Whistlin' Donkey**. All the bars do a great job of hosting, with live music and entertainment.

JIM PACKETT/SHUTTERSTOCK

as compelling in the daylight. It's also a fantastic final stop for cyclists pedaling the High Trestle Trail, a paved 25-mile walking and cycling path that links five small towns in central Iowa just north of Des Moines.

If you decide to take a half-day ride, you'll pass silos, fields and a few convivial trailside restaurants and bars. You'll likely see chipmunks, squirrels and rabbits, with frogs croaking songs of love (or is it hunger?) along the way. The trail, which links Ankeny and Woodward, is paved, mostly level and well marked. It's popular with families, and it links up with other long biking trails. For an e-bike rental, try **Local Spokes** (*thelocalspokes.com; half-day rental $50*) in Slater.

To see the illuminated bridge at night, you can park and hike a short distance to the span west of Madrid (*traveliowa.com/trails*).

Mason City
Frank Lloyd Wright and The Music Man

There's a lot going on in Mason City, and though it's not on the way to anywhere, this quirky place in north-central Iowa is a highly recommended stop if you are interested in

---

 EATING & DRINKING IN MASON CITY: OUR PICKS

Three on the Tree Coffee & Cafe: Wake up with a pastry and coffee downtown before checking out the architecture. *7am-3pm* $

Birdsall's Ice Cream Co: Pause beneath the red-and-strip awning for a scoop, a sundae or a malt. Around since 1931. *noon-9pm* $

LD's Filling Station: All-American breakfast and lunch fare fueling the heartland, with decor embracing classic cars. *7am-8pm Wed-Fri, to 1pm Sat & Sun* $

Northwestern Steakhouse: Renowned statewide for its Greek-style broiled steaks. Order the spaghetti as your side. *4:30-9pm Mon-Sat* $$$

Stockman House

Prairie School architecture and, well, musicals. Architectural bona fides? The only remaining hotel designed by Frank Lloyd Wright, the **Historic Park Inn Hotel** *(historicparkinn.com)*, is downtown. The hotel is open for overnight guests and for those who just want to poke around and admire his vision. Don't miss the wonderful gift shop. You can also tour the **Stockman House** *(stockmanhouse.org; tour adult/child $15/5)*, a Prairie-style home also designed by Wright.

A self-guided walking tour passes a slew of nearby Prairie School, Usonian and Arts & Crafts–style homes designed by prominent architects in the early 1900s. Pick up a free walking tour map at the downtown **visitor center** *(visitmasoncityiowa.com)*.

Mason City was also the boyhood home of Meredith Willson, who wrote the Broadway musical *The Music Man*. The play was later turned into a Warner Brothers movie of the same name. The entire **Music Man Square** *(themusicmansquare.org)*, as seen in the movie, was recreated in Mason City and often hosts music events. Theater kids, join me now... *You got trouble, right here in River City...*

And take note: Mason City's cute downtown is anchored by a festive town square. If you're not careful with your planning, you might find yourself bumping elbows with the musical masses during the **North Iowa Band Festival**, the largest free marching-band competition in the Midwest.

Bil Baird and the Sound of Music puppets

Known globally in the mid-1900s for his modernist puppets and marionettes, puppeteer Bil Baird was a native of Mason City. His puppets made numerous appearances in Broadway productions and on television variety shows. His most famous creations are probably the Lonely Goatherd puppets, which made a memorable appearance in the movie *The Sound of*

CYCLING IOWA

With more than 2500 miles of paved cycling trails, Iowa is a top destination for cyclists. Trails cater to a variety of ages and skill levels, and they are often dotted with public art, festive bars and welcoming towns. The state is known internationally for its RAGBRAI ride (p644) in July.

Recommended trails include the Cedar Valley Trails, which link Cedar Falls with Waterloo in eastern Iowa; the High Trestle Trail in Central Iowa; and the Raccoon River Valley Trail, which connects small towns with the suburbs of Des Moines. A 9-mile extension to the High Trestle Trail in 2024 linked it to the Raccoon River route, forming a 120-mile loop.

WHAT THE HECK IS RAGBRAI?

Cyclists the world over are familiar with **RAGBRAI** *(ragbrai.com)*, a one-week bike ride across the state of Iowa every July. The ride, which always starts on the western side of the state, is non-competitive, and cyclists camp at eight host communities along the way. The total distance is around 470 miles.

The event attracts about 20,000 registered riders and is the best-attended cycling tour in the world. The name is an acronym for *Register*'s Annual Great Bicycle Ride Across Iowa; two reporters for the *Des Moines Register* took the first ride for a newspaper story in 1973.

RAGBRAI riders

Music. Today, you can see the goat, one little girl in a pale pink coat, her gloating mama and the dancing couple at the **MacNider Art Museum** *(macniderart.org)* in Mason City. We're not sure where the goatherd went off to. Oh ho lay-dee odl lee o!

Sioux City

On the trail of Lewis and Clark

As they journeyed west along the Missouri River toward the Pacific Northwest, the Lewis and Clark expedition stopped near present day Sioux City. It was during this stop, on August 20, 1804, that Sgt Charles Floyd, a member of the corps, became ill and died, probably from appendicitis. He was the only person to die during the entire trek. You can learn much more about this event and other aspects of the journey at the **Lewis & Clark Interpretive Center**, which is beside the Missouri River. Inside, animatronic characters tell the story of the expedition. The information is geared toward younger visitors, but most everyone will learn something new from the exhibits, which can be fully explored in under an hour. Take exit 49 off I-29.

A bluff-top **obelisk** marks the final resting spot of Sgt Floyd, the first United States soldier to die west of the Mississippi River. A short drive from the interpretive center, his memorial is a tranquil spot to view the Missouri River and reflect on the bravery of the corps.

The iconic **Tastee Inn & Out** *(tasteeinnandout.com)* was not around when Lewis and Clark came through, but this retro drive-thru on the way to the Sergeant Floyd Monument has been around since 1955. There are two specials here: the Tastee, an Iowa loosemeat sandwich (a regional specialty that combines loose ground beef, onions and orange cheese), and onion chips, which are battered and fried.

North Dakota

BADLANDS BEAUTY | DINOSAUR FOSSILS | FARGO FUN

North Dakotans have a 'We're all in this together' charm that is pleasantly disarming after miles and miles of lonely driving. And oh, those drives. Fields of grain stretch beyond every horizon. Except for the rugged 'badlands' of the far west, geographic relief is subtle; often it's just a pond – known as a prairie pothole – creeping up against the interstate or a ruined homestead that break up the vista.

This is one of the least-visited states in the US. The lack of visitors, however, doesn't mean the state is sleepy. The Bakken oil boom (named for geologic formations beneath the surface) transformed the northwest quadrant into one vast drilling site. At night, fires burning off waste gas give the landscape hellish views. Though the boom has leveled off, once-quiet towns like Williston and Watford City have become industrial warrens.

Near the Montana border you'll find natural beauty that justifies a trip while the Missouri River is dotted with sights tied to the Lewis and Clark Expedition.

Fargo

Pose by the Woodchipper

Visitor centers can be a little ho-hum. But that's amusingly not the case in Fargo. At the engaging **Fargo-Moorhead Visitors Center** you'll find the actual **woodchipper** from the 1996 movie *Fargo*. It was used in the scene where Gaear feeds the last of Carl's body into its maw and is discovered by Marge. You can reenact the scene – although not the results – while wearing Fargo-style hats and jamming in a fake leg (both provided). There's a reproduction out front. You'll find the visitor center off exit 348 on I-94 southwest of downtown.

Celebrate like nice Vikings

Step into the enormous **Brewhalla** *(brewhalla.com)* – an indoor/outdoor beer hall and market with loads of personality. Here you'll walk past bars slinging craft beer, families

Places

Fargo p645
Theodore Roosevelt National Park p646
Bismarck p648
Medora p648

GETTING AROUND

You'll need your own vehicle to explore the state. The only interstate is I-94, which runs east-west. North Dakota's main airports are in Bismarck, Fargo and Minot. Cities served by Amtrak's *Empire Builder* train include Fargo, Grand Forks, Minot and Williston. Jefferson Lines *(jeffersonlines. com)* runs limited bus services to Bismarck, Dickinson, Fargo and Grand Forks.

☑ TOP TIP

The southwest quarter of North Dakota, including Medora, uses Mountain Time, which is one hour earlier than the rest of the state's Central Time.

TOP EXPERIENCE

Theodore Roosevelt National Park

Future president Theodore Roosevelt retreated from New York to this remote spot in his early 20s after losing both his wife and mother in a matter of hours. It's said that his time in the Dakota badlands inspired him to become an avid conservationist, and he set aside 230 million acres of federal land while in office. His North Dakota legacy is this beautiful 110-sq-mile national park.

TOP TIPS

- If escape is your goal, visit the remote, low-key Elkhorn Unit, where Roosevelt lived.

- Short on time? A quick stop at the free Painted Canyon Visitor Center off I-94 at exit 32 is recommended. View scenic badlands, hike trails and, possibly, see buffalo.

PRACTICALITIES

- nps.gov/thro
- admission $30/25 vehicle/motorcycle 7-day pass
- the park has three units: North, South and remote Elkhorn

Scenic Drives

Green prairie grasses frame rock formations streaked with red, yellow, brown, black and silver minerals in two units of the park. The colors of these badlands change with the moods of nature and time of day. The bison, elk, pronghorn and prairie dogs strutting about are clearly living their best lives. To maximize sightseeing, many visitors drive the 36-mile scenic loop (U-shaped due to construction when we visited) in the South Unit. Make the short hike up **Buck Hill** and soak up the spectacular stillness. It's also well worth the journey to the North Unit for the 14-mile one-way drive to the **Oxbow Overlook** and its wide views into the vast and colorfully striated river canyon.

Hiking & Camping

In the South Unit, the 0.4-mile **Wind Canyon Trail** leads to a dramatic viewpoint over the Little Missouri River, especially scenic at sunset. In the North Unit, the 1.5-mile **Buckhorn Trail** passes a lively Prairie Dog Town. The **Caprock-Coulee Loop** is a 4.1-mile hike across a grassy butte into the badlands. Camp at **Cottonwood Campground** in the South Unit or **Juniper Campground** in the North Unit. For a good adventure, hike or cycle the 96-mile Maah Daah Hey Trail between the two units.

chilling by fire pits and communal areas buzzing with groups playing board games. You might even muscle past a cluster of conventioneers attending the Hel's Fury Tattoo Fest. This industrially hip space is anchored by **Drekker Brewing Co**, which has a slew of innovative draft beers on tap across the market, where you'll also find food stalls selling woodfired pizzas, noodle dishes and smashburgers. Small retail shops here stay local. The vibe is welcoming and friendly – if this is the future of third places in America, we like it.

Take an art break downtown

If you're staying downtown, stroll over to the ambitious **Plains Art Museum** *(plainsart.org; free)*. Exhibits are housed in a renovated International Harvester warehouse. The permanent collection includes contemporary works by Native American and African artists. Temporary exhibits spotlight 20th- and 21st-century art.

The skybridge linking the museum with the adjacent Burgum Center for Creativity is a piece of art in its own right. Along the length of the span, a pretty screen print captures the delicate beauty of the tallgrass prairie. Look for big and little bluestems, a Harvester mouse and gray wolf tracks as you walk.

> **BIG SCULPTURES, QUIET PLAINS**
>
> Between Fargo and Theodore Roosevelt National Park on I-94, you can break up the drive by veering off the highway at exit 72. The exit marks the northern start of the **Enchanted Highway**, a 32-mile stretch that passes a series of enormous whimsical sculptures by local artist Gary Greff. The 75-ton **Geese in Flight** soars above exit 72.

 EATING & DRINKING IN FARGO: OUR PICKS

Wurst Bier Hall: German-style beer hall downtown ups the stakes with inventive sausage sandwiches, exotic meats and more than 35 beers on tap. *hours vary* $

Shack: A beloved local diner known for its pancakes and – queue Fargo accent – eggs. *6am-2pm Sat-Tue, to 8pm Wed-Fri* $

Rosewild: Elevated American fare for breakfast, lunch and dinner inside the new Hotel Jasper. Cocktails too. *7am-10pm* $$

Sky Prairie: Seasonal cocktail bar *(May-Sep)* atop Hotel Donaldson (p663) with views of downtown. *4-9pm Sat & Sun*

Bismarck

Brake for dinosaurs

Be warned. If anyone in your group is obsessed with dinosaurs and fossils, you will find yourselves hanging out at the excellent **North Dakota Heritage Center & State Museum** *(statemuseum.nd.gov; free)* far longer than originally planned. An enormous mastodon skeleton in the entranceway atrium sets the stage for the wonders to come, which include a fossilized dinosaur bone that still has its skin and soft tissue attached! This 67-million-year-old rarity was discovered in North Dakota's Hell Creek Formation, an extended rock layer southwest of Bismarck and a paleontologist's jackpot. The adjacent *Adaptation Gallery: Geologic Time* houses full-size replicas of various ancient beasts.

In addition to geology and paleontology, galleries spotlight early peoples, North Dakota history and fine art. Kids get a kick out of smelling a buffalo hide. There is a small **cafe** on-site.

Bismarck is the **state capitol**, and the museum is located on the grounds of the capitol complex. The museum is easily accessed from exit 159 on I-94.

Medora

Say 'howdy!' near the national park

As you mosey past the old wooden buildings in tiny Medora, which lounges beside the entrance to Theodore Roosevelt National Park (p646), look for the jaunty statue of the park's namesake. Roosevelt spent time in Medora and this pocket of North Dakota in the late 1800s. As the plaque here notes, Roosevelt once claimed, 'It was here that the romance of my life began.'

Today, this gateway community treads a fine line between real cowboy town and hokey modern interpretation. We'll give a nod to the former thanks to the dusty cowboy we saw who strolled into the Farmhouse Cafe with boots clomping and spurs a jingling.

For travelers, comfortable lodgings are available across all budgets and there are a handful of places to eat. Check *medora.com* for details about historic sites and family-focused activities. The much-anticipated **Theodore Roosevelt National Library** is set to open in Medora in July 2026. Note that many businesses close from October through May.

> ### BEST FOR LAST CLUB
>
> Folks who keep track of the states they've visited often leave North Dakota for last thanks to it remote location. But its status as the 50th state doesn't bother North Dakota, and they now encourage travelers to save the best for last. Visitors can celebrate this accomplishment by joining the **Best for Last Club** – just walk into the **Fargo-Moorhead Visitors Center** (p645) and tell them you've hit 50. After you sign a form, they'll take your photo in front of the Best for Last banner and hand you a certificate. There are currently 7,300 members. Does induction include North Dakota swag? You betcha.

 EATING & DRINKING IN MEDORA: OUR PICKS

| **Medora Convenience & Liquor Store:** The fresh breakfast biscuits are regional legends at this friendly gas station and store. They start selling 'em early. *5:30am-9pm* $ | **Farmhouse Cafe:** Pancakes, omelets, chicken-fried steaks and endless coffee. Nice staff. Lunch offerings too. *7am-11am* $ | **Theodore's Dining Room:** Don your cleanest shirt for bison *osso bucco* and pan-seared walleye at the fanciest joint in town. Excellent pork-belly cobb salad. *hours vary* $ | **Little Missouri Saloon:** This old-timey saloon will whip you back to the Wild West. Live music in summer. Open year-round. *11am-1am* |

South Dakota

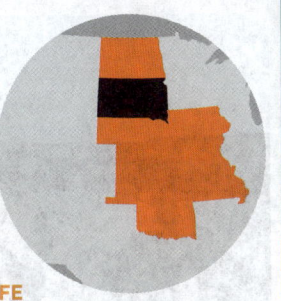

BLACK HILLS | SCENIC BYWAYS | ROAMING WILDLIFE

More than two million visitors walk the Avenue of Flags each year, squinting upward as they approach the iconic Mt Rushmore and its four presidential visages. And these attendance numbers are justified – it's a remarkable sight. But it's the unbound beauty of South Dakota that will likely stick with you. From the pine forests of the Black Hills to the ephemeral colors of the badlands to the windswept bluffs of the Missouri River, the natural beauty is rich and varied. And no one will forget their first sighting of a buffalo roaming prairie grasslands. The state's many scenic byways ribbon past these gorgeous landscapes as well as a crackerjack collection of old-school roadside attractions.

Historic and educational sites are abundant too, with mastodon fossils, old mining towns and abandoned missile silos all jostling for attention. The state is also the home of nine Native American tribes, and their stories and traditions are increasingly shared statewide.

Places
Sioux Falls p649
Wall p654
Pine Ridge Reservation p654
Black Hills p655
Deadwood p661

GETTING AROUND

Driving is the most efficient way to explore the state. I-90 links Sioux Falls in the east with Rapid City in the west. These cities have South Dakota's two main airports. Each has services to major American hubs. I-29 runs north–south and links Sioux Falls with Fargo, ND, to the north and Sioux City, IA, to the south. Jefferson Lines *(jeffersonlines.com)* buses stop in Rapid City, Wall, Mitchell and Sioux Falls along I-90.

Sioux Falls

Relax at Falls Park

It's hard to take a bad photo of the rambling waterfall that anchors **Falls Park** and the city of Sioux Falls. Paved trails frame the rocky cascades, and overlooks perch on the prettiest points. Our favorite spot? The footbridge over the Big Sioux River. The park has a perfectly placed cafe, and picnic tables are scattered about. You can also climb the five-story observation tower for high-elevation views of the action. Between mid-November and mid-January the park becomes a winter wonderland with 338,000 twinkling lights.

Continued on p653

☑ TOP TIP

Roughly the western third of South Dakota – including the Black Hills and everything west of I-90 exit 177 and west of the Missouri River north of Pierre – uses Mountain Time, which is one hour earlier than Central Time in the rest of the state.

TOP EXPERIENCE

Badlands National Park

The scenic wonders begin almost immediately along the Badlands Loop Rd, where the corrugated walls and crumbly spikes of an ancient floodplain shimmer ethereally in the afternoon light. It was understandably named *mako sica* (badland) by Native Americans, but the landscape is more secretive than bad – those geologic formations protect a motherlode of fossils. Above ground, buffalo roam the park's mixed-grass prairie.

DON'T MISS

Ben Reifel Visitor Center

Badlands Loop Rd

Big Badlands Overlook

Notch Trail

Hay Butte Overlook

Sheep Mountain Table

Park Overview

For those in a rush, the North Unit of the park is easily viewed on a one-hour drive along the **Badlands Loop Rd (Hwy 240)**. If you have an extra hour, however, several short hiking trails along the route will sling you right into the earthen wonderland here.

The park sprawls across grasslands south of I-90. The Pinnacles Entrance can be reached from exit 110, which is also the Wall Drug exit. You can access the Northeast Entrance from

PRACTICALITIES
- nps.gov/badl ● admission $15–30 for 7-day pass ● park open 24hrs
- visitor center hours vary

exit 131. The park's less accessible South Unit, also known as the Stronghold Unit, is on the Pine Ridge Indian Reservation and sees fewer visitors.

The **Ben Reifel Visitor Center** *(8am-5pm May-Aug, 9am-4pm Sep-Apr)* is located just south of the Northeast Entrance and is open year-round. Spend time here to check out the good exhibits. Don't miss the on-site **paleontology lab** *(mid-Jun–mid-Sep)* where you can watch staff prepare fossils. The **White River Visitor Center** is a small summer-only information outlet in the Stronghold Unit.

Badlands Loop Rd (Hwy 240)

The 39-mile Badlands Loop Rd stretches from the town of Cactus Flat west to the town of Wall, curving into the North Unit along a narrow ridge of rock formations known as the Badlands Wall. Carved by the White River, the wall separates the upper (to the north) and lower prairie. There are 12 overlooks and picnic areas along the way. For the best lighting and the most vibrant colors along the wall, make the drive before sunrise or sunset. The **Big Badlands Overlook** just south of the northeast entrance is particularly pretty at dawn.

Sage Creek Rim Road

This gravel road extends west from the Badlands Loop Rd, passing scenic overlooks and prairie-dog towns. Seeing buffalo is also a possibility. This drive is less traveled than the Badlands Loop Rd, and it is where most backcountry hikers and campers go to escape the crowds. There is almost no water or shade here, so don't strike out into the wilderness unprepared. For a quick introduction to scenery along the road, pull off at **Hay Butte Overlook** just west of the Badlands Loop Rd.

Hiking

Several short trails shoot into the badlands north of the Ben Reifel Visitor Center. The surreal **Door Trail** and its boardwalk lead to a scenic gap in the Badlands Wall. Take sunrise photos here. The **Notch Trail** twists through a canyon, scampers up a wooden ladder then curves along a crumbly ridge line to an expansive view of grasslands and more serrated walls. Both trailheads are accessed from the same parking lot.

Lodging & Camping

The cosy cabins at **Cedar Pass Lodge** *(mid-Apr–mid-Oct)* have air-conditioning, heat, microwaves and mini-fridges. The onsite restaurant serves breakfast, lunch and dinner. **Cedar Pass RV & Campground** *(late Mar–mid-Oct; campsites $37-47)* is the most popular place to pitch a tent in the park. Open year-round, **Sage Creek Campground** is primitive but also popular. Campsites are free.

SHEEP MOUNTAIN TABLE

For solitude and spectacular views of sweeping badlands, drive to **Sheep Mountain Table**, a plateau on the border of the North and South Units. The unpaved road to the overlook here is ideally tackled in a 4WD vehicle, but it shouldn't be too bad if the weather has been clear. The road beyond the overlook, however, is appropriate for 4WD and high-clearance vehicles only, but you can walk along the table from the overlook and soak up the otherworldly views.

TOP TIPS

● Hwy 44, which bisects the North and South Units, is a scenic route linking the Badlands and Rapid City. If you have extra time, take it to soak up the views and to avoid I-90.

● Keep at least 100ft from wildlife in the park. The animals may look approachable, but if they notice you, you are definitely too close.

● The park recommends two quarts of water per person for a two-hour hike.

● Do not collect fossils, plants, rocks or artifacts while exploring the park.

TOP EXPERIENCE

Wind Cave National Park

Home to the sixth-largest cave system in the world, Wind Cave is a sprawling treasure. But its wonders are not confined to its subterranean passages. It is also a haven for wildlife in the grasslands and forests south of Custer State Park. The namesake cave is laced with 167 miles of mapped passages. Cave tours, hikes and scenic drives are the primary activities.

TOP TIPS

- Reserve your tour before your visit. Tours are extremely popular and do sell out. You can book 30 days ahead.

- If you wing it, plan to arrive before the visitor center opens to join the line waiting to nab a ticket, particularly from March through October.

PRACTICALITIES
- nps.gov/wica
- open 24hr, tour times vary
- free admission
- tours $7-$17 at recreation.gov

Boxwork Formations

The cave's foremost feature is its collection of 'boxwork' calcite formations – 95% of all that are known to exist are here. The boxwork looks like honeycomb and dates back 60 to 100 million years.

Cave Tours

Three tours are offered year round: the easy Garden of Eden Tour, the family-friendly Natural Entrance Tour, and the strenuous Fairgrounds Tour. The unique boxwork formations can be seen on all three. The Candlelight Tour and the Wild Cave Tour are available from June through early August. Expect a lot of crawling on the Wild Cave Tour, and be aware that you will have to wriggle through a space that is 10 inches high and 3ft wide! The 30-minute Accessibility Tour is open to visitors in wheelchairs.

Hiking & Camping

More than 30 miles of trails navigate the grasslands and ponderosa pines that blanket the park. Keep watch for bison, elk, pronghorns and prairie dogs as you walk. The southern end of the 111-mile **Centennial Trail**, which links to Bear Butte State Park, begins on Hwy 87 north of the visitor center. Tucked in the pines beside the prairie, **Elk Mountain Campground** has 62 reservable spaces *($12-24 per site)*; backcountry camping *(free with permit)* is allowed in limited areas.

Continued from p549

For a fantastic meal, drive south from the park into downtown and take a seat at **MB Haskett Delicatessen** (*mbhaskett.com; hours vary*). This retro cafe serves brilliant food throughout the day.

Scramble over quartzite at Palisades State Park

Ancient quartzite formations soar above Split Rock Creek at **Palisades State Park** (*gfp.sd.gov, vehicle $10-15*), a compact state park on the prairie about 20 miles northeast of Sioux Falls. As your kids clamber at the base of the quartzite, you might see experienced climbers rappelling down the face of a nearby cliff. And geologists take note: the quartzite here is 1.2 billion years old! Swimming is allowed, but no jumping from the rocks.

Roadside attractions between Sioux Falls and Wall Drug

Roadside attractions along I-90 keep boredom at bay as you cruise west across South Dakota.

First up is the cavernous **Corn Palace** (*cornpalace.com; free*) in Mitchell. Close to 300,000 ears of corn are used annually to create new murals on the outside of the building. Head inside to learn how the facade has evolved since its creation in 1892. And please, don't eat the murals – fresh popcorn is for sale inside if you're hungry.

Continue 70 miles to the bluff-top **Lewis & Clark Interpretive Center** and rest area near exit 263 south of Chamberlain. There are worthwhile exhibits here about the intrepid duo and their voyages on the Missouri River below, but the highlight is the staggering **Dignity: of Earth & Sky** statue. Framed by sky and prairie, this 50ft-tall rendering of a Sioux woman – her magnificent quilt held against the wind – honors the Lakota and Dakota tribes. The diamond-shaped LED lights in her quilt sparkle at night.

> ### HELLO SIOUX FALLS!
>
> Parked in the southeastern corner of South Dakota, the state's largest city lives up to its name at **Falls Park** (p649), where the Big Sioux River plunges through a long series of rock faces. Just south lies a buzzing downtown district with a burgeoning foodie scene and some of the best eats in the region. You'll find more than 80 outdoor sculptures along downtown's **SculptureWalk**. Park on S Phillips Ave to start your explorations. Several hotel chains cluster downtown near the river while a slightly cheaper collection of accommodations line I-29 and I-229.

BEST SCENIC DRIVES IN SOUTHERN SOUTH DAKOTA

Spearfish Canyon Scenic Byway: Dotted with waterfalls, this curvaceous 20-mile road (US 14A) cleaves into the heart of the hills from Spearfish.

Iron Mountain Rd: Enjoy a 16-mile roller coaster of wooden bridges, tight turns, narrow tunnels and stunning vistas. Drive it north for views of Mt Rushmore.

Needles Hwy: This 14-mile drive twists past granite spires, pine trees, aspens and beautiful Sylvan Lake.

Wildlife Loop Rd: You might see bison, prairie dogs and pronghorn on this 18-mile drive in Custer State Park.

Native American National and State Scenic Byway: Drive along the Missouri River, passing through tribal lands and prairies with a dramatic pause beside *Dignity: of Earth & Sky* (p113).

Hotel Alex Johnson

About 140 miles west, the 1909 **Prairie Homestead** and its outhouse sit just a few miles from a missile silo. It's a wild juxtaposition, highlighting the rapid development of US technology in the span of 60 years. The **Minuteman Missile National Historic Site** *(nps.gov/mimi)* holds one of 1000 Minutemen II intercontinental ballistic missiles housed across the Great Plains during the Cold War (and now retired). The sod house and the Minuteman Missile site's visitor center are reached from exit 131. Tours of the Delta-01 Minuteman Missile Launch Facility *(tours adult/child $12/8)* begin off exit 127.

Shimmering mineral deposits await at Badlands National Park (p650) at exit 131. And then, at exit 110, there it is, after miles of signs: Wall Drug.

Wall

Get lost at South Dakota's wackiest roadside attraction

Only a curmudgeon could ignore all the signs along I-90 encouraging drivers to stop at **Wall Drug** *(walldrug.com)*. Fortunately this warren of kitsch, which opened in 1931, does have a few worthwhile charms behind its Old West facade: 5¢ coffee, free ice water, good doughnuts, public restrooms and loads of diversions. Amid the fudge and knickknackery is a superb bookstore with great regional titles. There's also a store selling quality cowboy boots. Out back, ride the mythical jackalope and check out the historical photos. And yes, you can still buy aspirin in the drugstore.

Pine Ridge Reservation

Exploring Lakota history and culture

Home to the Oglala Lakota Sioux, the Pine Ridge Reservation sits within beautiful prairies and badlands south of Badlands National Park. Residents face systemic hardships, from crime to unemployment, and more than half the population lives below the poverty line.

Despite being at times a jarring dose of reality, it is also a place welcoming to visitors. Tune in to KILI (90.1FM), which often plays traditional music. For an introduction to the reservation, stop by the **Red Cloud Heritage Center** *(mahpiy aluta.org; free)*. This well-curated art museum has traditional and contemporary works, and a craft shop with locally made artisan goods. The center hosts the **Red Cloud Indian Art Show** from June to early August. It's 4 miles north of the town of Pine Ridge on Hwy 18.

It helps to read up on the history before you visit the **Wounded Knee Massacre Site**, 16 miles northeast of Pine Ridge town. The mass grave sits atop the hill near a church above the massacre site. Small memorials appear daily amid the stones listing dozens of names. You can park below the hill and walk up, or tackle the rutted road to the top in your car. It's a desolate place, with sweeping views. You may encounter locals selling jewelry as well as locals looking for donations. For more details about Wounded Knee, visit nearby **Oglala Lakota College Historical Center** *(olc.edu/about-olc/historical-center; 9am-5pm Mon-Fri; free)* or the **White River Visitor Center** (p651) at Badlands National Park.

Black Hills

Presidents, artwork and shopping in downtown

An appealing capital for the Black Hills region, **Rapid City** has a cosmopolitan air best appreciated in the lively downtown where well-preserved brick buildings, filled with quality shopping and dining, make 'Rapid' a good urban base. From a shifty-eyed Nixon to a triumphant Harry Truman, lifelike **statues of America's presidents** dot street corners throughout downtown. According to lore, they are 9/10s the size of their counterparts — so they all seem just a little too small. The info center on Main St is the current home of the Trump statue.

Out back, ponder the difference between graffiti and art on a stroll through colorful **Art Alley**. For more art, step into **Prairie Edge Trading Co & Galleries**, a three-story shop with a truly mesmerizing collection of art, furniture and home goods made by members of the Northern Plains tribes. You'll find books and art supplies here too. Just across the street is **Main Street Sq**, a pleasant place to relax amid sculptures and fountains. Pop into the grand lobby at the **Hotel Alex Johnson** for its hunt-lodge vibes. Pause by the wall of photos of former celebrity guests — we see you Jerry Seinfeld!

WHAT ARE THE BLACK HILLS?

They call the Black Hills an evergreen island in a sea of high-prairie grassland. This stunning region on the Wyoming–South Dakota border lures scores of visitors with its winding canyons and wildly eroded 7000ft peaks. The region's name – the 'Black' comes from the dark ponderosa pine-covered slopes – was conferred by the Lakota Sioux. In the 1868 Fort Laramie Treaty, they were assured that the hills would be theirs for eternity, but the discovery of gold changed that and the Sioux were shoved out to low-value flatlands six years later. The 1990 film *Dances with Wolves* covers some of this period. You'll need several days to explore the byways, caves, bison herds, forests, Deadwood, and Mt Rushmore and Crazy Horse monuments.

EATING & DRINKING IN DOWNTOWN RAPID CITY: OUR PICKS

Sour: Nationally acclaimed, this slick bakery serves delicious breads and pastries, with a few daily sandwiches. *7am-2pm Wed-Sun* $

Harriet & Oak: Top-notch bakery, cafe and coffee bar with fun boho vibe. Creative sandwiches too and good draft microbrews. *7am-4pm Tue-Sat, 8am-2pm Sun* $

Tally's Silver Spoon: Savor upscale diner fare at this chic cafe and bar. Breakfasts are good; creative regional fare served nightly. *7am-2pm, 4-9pm* $$

Independent Ale House: Changing lineup of the best microbrews from the region served at the 'Indie' and its vintage-style bar. *11am-9pm most nights*

BLACK HILLS

★ HIGHLIGHTS
1. Mt Rushmore National Memorial

● SIGHTS
2. Adams Museum
3. Crazy Horse Memorial
4. Custer State Park
5. Hay Butte Overlook
6. Iron Mountain Rd
7. Mammoth Site
8. Minuteman Missile National Historic Site
9. Mount Moriah Cemetery
10. Needles Hwy
11. Peter Norbeck Scenic Byway
12. Spearfish Canyon Scenic Byway
13. Wildlife Loop Rd

● ACTIVITIES
14. Door Trail
15. Jewel Cave National Monument
16. Notch Trail

● SLEEPING
17. Blue Bell Lodge
18. Bullock Hotel
19. Cedar Pass Campground
20. Cedar Pass Lodge
21. Hotel Alex Johnson
22. Rocket Motel
23. Sage Creek Campground
24. Spearfish Canyon Lodge
25. Sylvan Lake Campground
26. Town Hall Inn

- **EATING**
- **27** Deadwood Social Club
- **28** Harriet & Oak
- **29** Hjem AM
- **30** Killian's
- **31** Skogen Kitchen
- **32** Sour
- **33** Tally's Silver Spoon
- **34** Wild Spruce Market

- **DRINKING & NIGHTLIFE**
- **35** Independent Ale House
- **36** Mt Rushmore Brewing Co
- **37** Pump House
- **see 27** Saloon No 10

- **SHOPPING**
- **38** Prairie Edge
- **39** Wall Drug

- **INFORMATION**
- **40** Ben Reifel Visitor Center
- **41** White River Visitor Center

- **TRANSPORT**
- **42** Hwy 240 Badlands Loop Rd
- **43** Sheep Mountain Table

THE STORY OF WOUNDED KNEE

In 1890 the new Ghost Dance religion became popular and Lakota followers believed it would both bring back their ancestors and eliminate the white man. This struck fear into the area's soldiers and settlers, and the frenetic circle dances were outlawed. The 7th US Cavalry rounded up a band of Lakota people under Chief Big Foot and brought them to the small village of Wounded Knee.

On December 29, as the soldiers began to search for weapons, a shot was fired (nobody knows by whom), leading to the massacre of more than 250 men, women and children, most of them unarmed. It's one of the most infamous atrocities in US history. Twenty-five soldiers also died.

Admire presidential rockstars at Mt Rushmore

Glimpses of Washington's nose from the roads leading to this popular **monument** *(nps.gov/moru, parking $10)* never cease to surprise, and they are but harbingers of the full impact of this mountainside sculpture once you're up close (and past the dreary parking area). George Washington, Thomas Jefferson, Abraham Lincoln and Theodore Roosevelt each iconically stare into the distance in 60ft-tall granite glory.

Despite the crowds, there is something inspirational about the **Avenue of Flags**. Lined with the flags of all 50 states plus six districts and territories, this corridor of patriotism frames the presidents quite photogenically. If crowds are too thick, you can escape the hoopla on the 0.6-mile **Presidential Trail**. On this loop you can pause between the pines, in relative peace, to marvel at the artistry of sculptor Gutzon Borglum and the immense labor of the workers who created the memorial between 1927 and 1941. The trail also accesses the worthwhile **Sculptor's Studio**, which conveys the drama of how the monument came to be.

The official Park Service information centers have excellent bookstores. The main museum shares the story of the creation of the monument.

Mt Rushmore is a half-hour drive southwest of Rapid City via US 16. For rock-framed views of the presidents, approach via Iron Mountain Rd. The Crazy Horse Memorial is 16 miles south via Hwy 244 and US 365.

See the Crazy Horse Memorial

The world's largest **monument** *(crazyhorsememorial.org; $15-35 admission)* is this 563ft-tall work-in-progress (with a lot of work to go). When finished it will depict the Sioux leader astride his horse, pointing to the horizon saying, 'My lands are where my dead lie buried.' No one is predicting when the sculpture will be complete (the face was dedicated in 1998). Although you can see the mountain in the distance, you need to pay another $5 for a van ride to get close.

The memorial is a huge tourist draw, attracting more than one million visitors annually, but a trip here can feel underwhelming. Exhibits about Native Americans can seem haphazard and are often poorly contextualized. The focus of the place seems to be more on its Polish-American sculptor Korczak Ziolkowski and his family than the Lakota. For these reasons and others, the sculpture has drawn controversy (p660).

A scenic drive through the Black Hills

Driving the **Peter Norbeck Scenic Byway** is like flirting with a brand new crush: always exhilarating, occasionally challenging and sometimes you get a few butterflies. Named for the South Dakota senator who pushed for its creation in 1919, the oval-shaped byway is broken into four roads linking memorable destinations in the Black Hills.

Iron Mountain Rd (Hwy 16A) is the most diverse of the four, beloved for its pig-tailing loops, Mt Rushmore–framing tunnels and one gorgeous glide through sun-dappled pines. Tackle it early to avoid caravans of cars. The 14-mile **Needles**

Bison, Custer State Park

Hwy (Hwy 87) swoops below majestic granite spires, careens past rocky overlooks and slings through a super-narrow tunnel. The other two roads within the byway are Hwys 244 and 89.

And remember, there's no right way to drive the Black Hills, and the beauty of the place is evident no matter the byway. But there can be lots of traffic, and it can be confusing figuring out where you are when driving between sites – mostly on twisty two-lane roads with intermittent cell service. Plot out your route the night before, and note that splitting your time over two or three days is better than cramming everything into one frenzied day.

Driving times are often much longer than expected due to slow-moving traffic. RV drivers: visit *custerresorts.com* for tunnel measurements.

Wildlife-watching in Custer State Park

Your first animal sighting in **Custer State Park** (*gfp.sd.gov/parks; 7-day vehicle pass $25*) will likely be a white-tailed deer loping through the ponderosa pines that blanket the surrounding Black Hills. But soon after you turn onto the 18-mile **Wildlife Loop Rd** (p654), which swoops over untouched grasslands, the animal sightings grow thrillingly diverse. Watch bison lumber beside the road. Squint at pronghorns in the misty distance. And listen for the 'chirps' of prairie dogs

SOUTH DAKOTA'S TRIBAL NATIONS

There are nine Native American tribes in South Dakota. Their members constitute 15% of the state's population, and their tribal lands, or reservations, are scattered across tallgrass prairie, rolling grasslands, pine-dotted hills and remote badlands. The US government named the Lakota tribe the Sioux in 1825, and this term has come to apply to the Lakota, Dakota and Nakota peoples and their various bands.

Learn more at the engaging **Akta Lakota Museum & Cultural Center** at St Joseph's Indian School in Chamberlain. Visitors are welcome on reservations but should always ask for permission before taking photos, sketching or making audio and video recordings. Do not remove artifacts or disturb devotional sites.

 EATING & DRINKING IN CUSTER: OUR PICKS

Skogen Kitchen: A James Beard nominee; a delicious global menu with luxury toppings like morels, caviar and sprinkles of pretension. *5–8:30pm Tue-Sat* **$$$**

Wild Spruce Market: Gourmet market with dips, specialty cheeses, produce and local bison beef. Buy drinks at the coffee and beer bar. *8:30am–6pm most days* **$**

HJEM AM: From the folks behind Skogen, HJEM serves decadent gourmet breakfasts. Reservations recommended. *8am–11am Wed-Fri, to noon Sat & Sun* **$$**

Mt Rushmore Brewing Co: The Rail Splitter Porter and other flagship beers give a nod to American history at this complex with two fine-dining restaurants. *11am–9pm*

CRAZY HORSE MEMORIAL REVISITED

Never photographed or persuaded to sign a meaningless treaty, Crazy Horse was chosen for a monument (p658) that Lakota Sioux elders hoped would balance the presidential focus of Mt Rushmore 16 miles north. In 1948 a Boston-born sculptor, Korczak Ziolkowski, started blasting granite. His family has continued the work since his death in 1982, and the monument has indeed become a counterpoint to Mt Rushmore.

On the flip side, some Lakota oppose the monument as a desecration of sacred land. Other concerns include the introductory film at the visitor center, which spotlights the Ziolkowski family with seemingly less emphasis on the stories of the Lakota. Native American exhibits and artifacts in the museums may be in need of better organization.

---

as they scamper between burrows.

To put it succinctly, this place is wonderful. The only reason this 111-sq-mile state park isn't a national park is that the state grabbed it first. What's here? One of the largest free-roaming bison herds in the world (about 1450) as well as elk, bighorn sheep, the famous 'begging burros' (donkeys seeking handouts) and more than 200 bird species.

Pick up the free Tatanka visitor guide at the entrance station for details about hiking, fishing and camping. It also includes a list of the park's daily programs. Don't miss the new **Bison Center**, where large video screens envelope you in the sights and sounds of a buffalo stampede. The corrals for the annual **buffalo round-up** are steps away. Another highlight is boulder-flanked **Sylvan Lake**; admire it from the Sylvan Lakeshore Trail.

Lodging options rival those of national parks. We're fond of the cabins and modern-rustic style of **Blue Bell Lodge**. For more information about buffalo, also known as bison, see p640.

Admire rare underground crystals

If you visit only one Black Hills cave, **Jewel Cave** (nps.gov/jeca; tours $6-45) would be a good choice. It's 13 miles west of Custer and is so named because colorful calcite crystals line many of its walls. More than 200 miles have been surveyed (about 3% of the passageway), making it the third-longest known cave in the world.

You can only enter the cave on guided tours. One unique option is the **Historic Lantern Tour**; your path is illuminated by handheld lanterns. Tours can be reserved 30 days in advance at recreation.gov. To avoid disappointment, advance reservations are highly recommended.

Mammoth-bone bonanza

Kids who love fossils – and anyone who thinks paleontology is cool – will 'dig' the **Mammoth Site** (mammothsite.com; adult/child $15/12) in the town of Hot Springs. About 26,000 years ago, hundreds of animals perished in a sinkhole here. Today you can walk around their exposed tusks and bones, which were discovered during a construction project in 1974. So far 61 mammoths – two woolly, 59 Columbian – have been found. The site is the largest left-as-found mammoth fossil display in the country and an active dig.

The self-guided tour around the bone bed pauses by a lab where assistants are happy to answer your questions. Bones of a dire wolf and giant sloth are displayed in the adjacent Great Hall.

Hot Springs is about 60 miles south of Rapid City.

Relaxing in hot springs

Empty your water bottles before heading into Hot Springs, an unhurried town south of the main Black Hills circuit. The big natural attraction here is the warm mineral springs feeding the Fall River. You can relax weary muscles in one of six outdoor pools at the stylish **Moccasin Springs Natural Mineral Spa** (moccasinsprings.com; 2hr soak pass $31.80), where the water temperature ranges from 80 to 105 degrees. The onsite **Dragonfly** restaurant serves salads, sandwiches and shareable nibbles.

The best water you'll drink in the Black Hills flows freely from Kidney Springs, just down the road from Moccasin Springs. It's not cold, but it's also not so hot you'll regret it on a sultry day. An old gazebo marks the spot along the pretty Hot Springs River Walk, across the narrow Fall River from the heart of town. Fill up your water bottles at the faucet. And you might want to stick around – downtown is home to ornate 1890s red sandstone buildings that glow at sunset.

Deadwood

Step into the past

Settled illegally by gold rushers in the 1870s, Deadwood is now a National Historic Landmark. Its atmospheric streets are lined with gold-rush-era buildings lavishly restored with gambling dollars. The lyrically foul-mouthed *Deadwood* HBO series and subsequent 2019 movie brought celebrity status.

You'll likely be greeted by a docent when stepping into the refreshingly quirky **Adams Museum** *(deadwoodhistory.com; suggested donation adult/child $5/3),* home to artifacts including a two-headed calf and a big lumpy gold nugget. These exhibits are part of a larger cabinet of curiosities originally curated by pioneer businessman WE Adams in the 1930s.

For more Wild West history, stroll casino-lined Historic Main Street. Don't miss **Saloon No 10** (p622) *(saloon10.com),* where stuffed game and old photographs recall rowdier days. Wild Bill Hickok was shot and killed while playing cards at the bar's original location across the street. Fans of *Deadwood* will recall the conflicted but upstanding sheriff Seth Bullock. He opened the **Bullock Hotel** *(historicbullock.com)* in 1895, and this creaky place still welcomes guests – and maybe a few ghosts.

A short but steep drive climbs from downtown to **Mount Moriah Cemetery** *(cityofdeadwood.com; admission $2; cash only),* where Calamity Jane, Wild Bill and Potato Creek Johnny, a colorful prospector, rest side by side.

> **WIND CAVE OR JEWEL CAVE?**
>
> Um, excuse me. A cave is not just a cave, and if you've seen one, you certainly have not seen them all. One problem for travelers in the Black Hills is that two extended cave systems, both managed by the federal park service, are open for tours. How to pick?
>
> It's win-win. Jewel Cave is a 'wet' limestone cave filled with classic formations like stalactites and stalagmites. It also has sparkling calcite crystals clustered into unusual shapes. Wind Cave (p652) is a 'dry' cave with fewer of these classic favorites. Wind Cave does, however, hold 95% of the world's known boxwork, which is a rare, honeycomb patterned calcite. Wind Cave also has outdoor hiking trails.

EATING & DRINKING AROUND DEADWOOD: OUR PICKS

Deadwood Social Club: In the historic Saloon No 10 in Deadwood, this busy restaurant offers crowd-pleasing Italian fare plus steaks. *hours vary Mon-Sat* **$$**

Saloon No 10: Legendary bar in Deadwood with dark walls, sawdust floors and knickknackery galore. *9am-2am*

Pump House: Drink a cup of locally roasted coffee or craft beer in this old Texaco gas station in Deadwood. Good sandwiches too. *7am-5pm*

Killian's: Enjoy a gouda jalapeño burger or ahi club in Spearfish before driving the Spearfish Canyon Scenic Byway. Vegan options. *11am-10pm Sun-Wed, to 11pm Fri & Sat* **$$**

Places We Love to Stay

$ Budget $$ Midrange $$$ Top End

St Louis — MAP P596

Angad Arts Hotel $$ The art-filled rooms are eye candy, as are the expansive views from the rooftop bar.

St Louis Union Station Hotel $$ The hotel lobby bar is tops, set in the 1894 barrel-vaulted train station. Good downtown location, but rooms could use a refresh.

21c Museum Hotel $$$ Our favorite hotel in St Louis has taken over a 1920s YMCA, filling it with plush rooms and an art gallery partly in the old basketball court.

Kansas City

Crossroads Hotel $$ Hip hotel with comfy rooms, excellent rooftop and lobby bars, a walkable location and an inventive Italian restaurant on the ground floor.

Hotel Kansas City $$ This downtown Gothic Revival stunner feels just as sleek as when it opened as a private members' club in the 1920s.

Truitt $$ Feel right at home at one of KC's few locally owned accommodation options. This stately 1916 converted mansion has just eight uniquely decorated rooms near the Nelson-Atkins (p601).

Branson

Ozarker Lodge $$ This reinvented roadside motel has mid-mod touches, cedar soaking tubs overlooking a creek and firepits for s'more roasting.

Tulsa — MAP P617

Campbell Hotel $ Restored to its 1927-era Route 66 splendor, this historic hotel east of downtown has 26 rooms with hardwood floors and oversized furniture.

Mayo Hotel $$ When this hotel, once Oklahoma's tallest building, opened in 1925, it was the height of luxury, and it's still one of Tulsa's top stays. Excellent choice for art deco architecture admirers.

Oklahoma City — MAP P621

Classen Inn $ Well-priced mid-century motel near downtown that's had a mod makeover.

Bradford House $$ Built in 1912 as a luxury apartment house, it's now a boutique hotel with eccentric interior design and modern, comfortable rooms.

The National $$$ Our favorite historic stay in the region is in this 1930s bank. Have a drink in the gasp-worthy lobby bar in the former banking hall with marble floors, columns and huge murals.

Omaha

Kimpton Cottonwood Hotel $$ Built as a hotel in 1915 and reimagined for modern travelers. Fantastic pool area and a knock-out **steakhouse** (p628).

Hotel Deco $$ Alice in Wonderland meets art deco detailing in this 14-story 1930s building within walking distance of the Old Market. Once you've settled into your room, track down the Wicked Rabbit, the hotel's speakeasy.

Hotel Indigo $$$ The bold accents and mismatched prints hint at the quirky personality of this modern hotel in a beautiful historic brick building downtown.

Lincoln

Kindler Hotel $$ The capital city's first indie boutique hotel is this downtown gem within walking distance of the historic Haymarket district.

Graduate by Hilton $$ Your college years never go out of fashion at this retro kitsch hotel that caters to the permanent student in every grad. It has a tiki bar, old-school pinball machines in the lobby and eclectic room decor that's part luxe, part rumpus room.

Dubuque & Around — MAP P637

Maquoketa Caves State Park Campground $ Camp beneath the pines near caves and trails at this family friendly spot between Dubuque and Davenport.

Hotel Julien $$ Built in 1915, this spiffy eight-story hotel in Dubuque was once a refuge for Al Capone. Some rooms have Mississippi River views.

Amana Colonies — MAP P637

Hotel Millwright (p639) **$$** Decor inside this historic woolen mill gives a nod to the textile industry. Rooms have smart, contemporary appeal.

Des Moines — p641

Hotel Fort Des Moines $$ A storied haunt for 20th-century powerbrokers and celebrities, this revamped number celebrates its roots with modern style.

Des Lux Hotel $$$ Luxurious downtown hotel with 51 rooms and loads of eclectic modern touches. A lavish hot breakfast is included.

Mason City

Historic Park Inn Hotel (p643) **$$** Sleep inside a work of art at the only remaining hotel designed by Frank Lloyd Wright. Beside a lovely downtown square.

North Dakota

Juniper Campground (p646) **$** Sites are first come, first served at this pleasant campground set beneath junipers in Theodore Roosevelt National Park's wildlife-filled North Unit.

Rough Riders Hotel $$ Old West meets New West at this upscale lodge in Medora, near the South Unit of Theodore Roosevelt National Park. Each room comes with a Teddy bear.

Hotel Donaldson $$ Well-appointed rooms are each decorated by a regional artist. In Fargo; don't miss the rooftop Sky Prairie for cocktails with a city view.

Sioux Falls & Around

King Campground (p609) **$** Northeast of Sioux Falls, this new campground in Palisades State Park sprawls across a scenic plain close to trails, a creek and cool quartzite formations.

Black Hills   p656

Sylvan Lake Campground $ All of the campgrounds in Custer State Park are recommended, but this one is set in the forest a short walk from a uniquely gorgeous rock-fringed lake.

Rocket Motel $ The neon sign is a jaunty welcome to this old-style motor court – a 'blast' from the past! – in Custer. Located in the center of town and well maintained.

Town Hall Inn $ Near Deadwood in Lead, this 12-room inn occupies the 1912 Town Hall and has spacious suites named and themed for their former governmental purpose.

Spearfish Canyon Lodge $$ Along a scenic byway, this Black Hills retreat sits near trails, streams and waterfalls in a gorgeous setting. Modern pine-y rooms are cozy.

Hotel Alex Johnson (p655) **$$$** The design of this 1927 classic in Rapid City magically blends Germanic Tudor architecture with traditional Lakota Sioux symbols.

Blue Bell Lodge (p660) **$$$** Chic cabins, ponderosa pines and buffalo stomping grounds in Custer State Park. Restaurant on-site and horseback trail rides nearby.

Rough Riders Hotel

Researched and curated by Regis St Louis

Texas

BIG SKIES AND OPEN ROADS

Dust off your boots and grab that cowboy hat: wide-ranging adventures in cities, mountains, deserts and beaches await in the Lone Star state.

Larger than many countries, Texas occupies a mammoth-sized footprint, both in terms of geography and the national psyche. Five of the country's 15 biggest cities are here in Texas. The state is home to the most valuable sports franchise in the world (Dallas Cowboys) and its cuisine (Tex-Mex) is known around the globe. Texas also has an astonishing diversity. Sure, there are sunny fields where the longhorn cattle roam, but this is also the land of craggy mountains and sunbaked deserts in the West, oasis-like springs in the Hill Country, and hundreds of miles of enticing Gulf Coast beaches.

Scenery aside, Texan cities and small towns alike offer a seemingly infinite array of attractions. You can explore cutting-edge art and culture, nightlife and cuisines from around the globe in Dallas, Fort Worth, Austin, San Antonio and Houston. There are atmospheric old music halls in tiny Hill Country settlements, and walkable neighborhoods bursting with creativity all across the state.

The Texas experience is about many things, from road trips across the windswept prairies to otherworldly art installations hidden on the edge of the wilderness. It's a place to create your own adventure, whether you're interested in hiking, rafting, stargazing, beach-hopping, birding, watching pro sports games or just immersing yourself in a place that's like nowhere else. Just don't try to pack in too much. You'd need a lifetime to experience it all.

THE MAIN AREAS

AUSTIN
Free-spirited city of green spaces and live music. **p670**

SAN ANTONIO & THE HILL COUNTRY
Historic missions, charming towns and wild beauty. **p680**

DALLAS & FORT WORTH
Cosmopolitan neighbors of culture and Western lore. **p690**

HOUSTON & THE GULF COAST
Multicultural epicenter and glorious beaches. **p697**

WEST TEXAS & BIG BEND
Where the mountains meet the desert. **p706**

For places to stay in Texas, see p712

THE GUIDE

TEXAS

Big Bend National Park (p708)

Find Your Way

The bigger cities in Texas are found mostly on the eastern half of the state. Beaches and seaside towns stretch down the Gulf Coast, while deserts and mountains lie in the far west.

CAR

It's tough to get far without an automobile even in major cities. Be mindful of toll roads, which are most common in Houston and Dallas. Near the border, you may be stopped by the US Border Patrol, so make sure your ID is in order.

TRAIN

Texas has 19 Amtrak stations along three routes: Sunset Limited, Heartland Flyer and Texas Eagle. This can be a slow but scenic option for long-distance travel between major cities in Texas and to surrounding states.

BUS

Some Texans may doubt the notion, but you can travel by bus to reach some places in the state. Greyhound has the most extensive network, followed by FlixBus. There are even two luxury bus lines: Vonlane and RedCoach, which connect several cities in southeast Texas.

West Texas & Big Bend National Park, p706

Craggy mountains and desert landscapes form the backdrop to dramatic state and national parks, star-filled skies, and art-loving ranch towns.

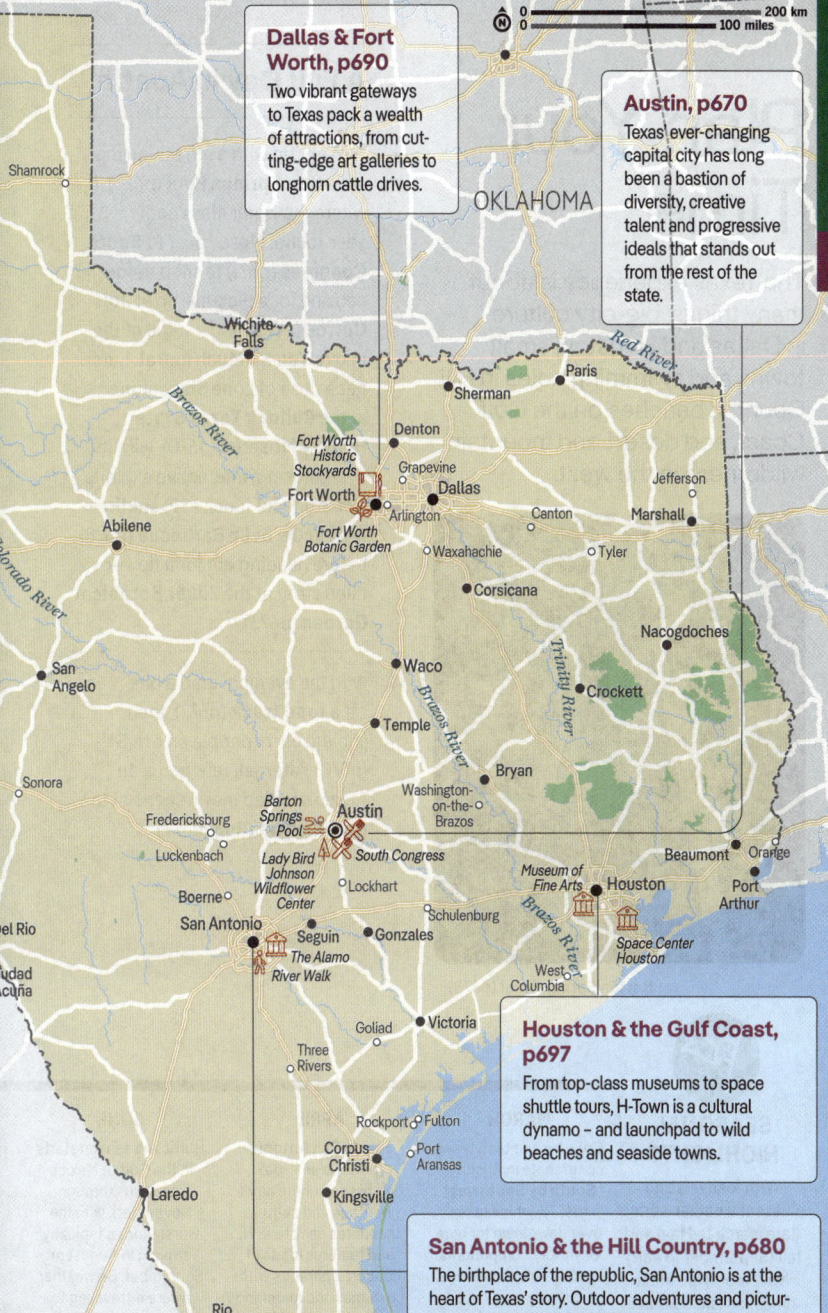

Plan Your Time

The Texas experience is about many things: big-city culture in Dallas and Houston, small towns and swimming holes in Hill Country, beaches on the Gulf Coast, and desert and mountain wilderness in the west.

Barton Springs Pool (p675)

A Full Day in Austin

● Wake up with a refreshing dip in **Barton Springs Pool** (p675), where the water stays cool year-round. Mosey over to **South Congress** (p671) to shop before pausing for a pick-me-up at **Jo's Coffee** (p673) and a selfie at the **I Love You So Much mural**. Later get a dose of Lone Star culture at the **Bullock Texas State History Museum** (p670), with its eye-catching, interactive exhibits. Get in line for lunch at **Franklin Barbecue** or **La Barbecue** (p678) before heading out for a flower-filled stroll at the **Zilker Botanical Garden** (p673).

● In the evening, grab a bite off a **food truck** (p672), then join the party people on **6th St** (p678). Alternatively, focus on Austin's fabled music scene at the **Continental Club** (p677).

SEASONAL HIGHLIGHTS

With festivals and pleasant weather, spring (late March to May) and fall (September to early November) are ideal times to visit. Summer swelters (cool off at the beach or an inland swimming spot).

MARCH

Creative and tech types congregate in Austin for **South by Southwest** (p677), which takes over downtown for nine days. Key components include film screenings, a comedy festival, art exhibitions and big concerts.

APRIL

Fiesta San Antonio (p684) is an 11-day celebration of the city's heritage and culture that dates back to 1891, and features loads of concerts, parades with costumes and marching bands, riverside events, feasting and merrymaking.

JUNE

Hurricane season starts in the Gulf of Mexico (and runs through November), with the worst storms typically arriving in August or September. Be weather aware if traveling to Houston or the Gulf Coast during these months.

Weekend in San Antonio & the Hill Country

● Start your day in San Antonio with breakfast at ultra-festive **Mi Tierra** (p684) then explore **Historic Market Square** (p684), where Mexican craft stores transport you south. Head to the **Alamo** (p680) to learn about Texas' most visited monument.

● Head up to the open-air restaurants at the **Pearl** (p684), a former brewery turned entertainment complex. Afterwards, stroll along the lovely **River Walk** (p683) and visit the impressive Latin American collections inside the **San Antonio Museum of Art** (p684).

● On your second day, hit the road for a scenic drive into Hill Country. Visit the charming town of **Boerne** (p687), followed by a hike and river swim in **Guadalupe River State Park** (p686).

Ten-Day Road Trip

● Start in Dallas at the **Sixth Floor Museum** (p690) to learn about Dallas' darkest day, then head over to **Bishop Arts District** (p692) for shopping, strolling and cafe-hopping. In neighboring Fort Worth, see cowboys in action during the daily cattle drive at **Fort Worth Stockyards** (p694), followed by boot-scootin' at **Billy Bob's Texas** (p694).

● Drive south to Houston, taking in the **Museum District** (p697) and exploring **Montrose** (p702). Admire NASA's **Space Center Houston** (p703), then head to the Gulf for beach time in **Port Aransas** (p704).

● Go northwest to San Antonio, stopping at the **missions** (p685) south of town, then veer west for experimental art in **Marfa** (p708), stargazing at the **McDonald Observatory** (p707) and exhilarating hikes in **Big Bend National Park** (p708).

SEPTEMBER
In Dallas, the **State Fair of Texas** (p694) brings ample amusement over 24 consecutive days. Carnival rides, livestock shows, concerts, fireworks and wondrous food stalls are a few draws for the 2 million-plus visitors each year.

OCTOBER
Make the journey to Marfa in West Texas to experience three days of creativity during the **Chinati Weekend** (p708). There's live music, artist talks and special exhibitions. Most events are free and open to the public.

NOVEMBER
Along the Gulf Coast, the colder months bring migrating birds passing through in huge flocks. November is a great month to see some of Texas' avian stars – endangered whooping cranes – at the **Aransas National Wildlife Reserve** (p704).

DECEMBER
Football season runs from September to January, but December is particularly exciting with NFL playoffs underway. You can also catch pro basketball. Houston is a great spot for seeing games live.

Austin

LIVE MUSIC | GREEN SPACES | BARBECUE

GETTING AROUND

The best way to get around Austin is to rent a car or use rideshare apps. Parking is expensive downtown.

Downtown Austin is laid out on a grid and best explored on foot. Bird, Lime and CapMetro rent scooters and bikes all over town, starting at $1. Download the apps to search pickup locations and to rent and return them.

It's fine to take the bus between the airport and downtown, but other routes can sometimes feel unsafe. CapMetro Rail has good service, but covers just nine stations between downtown and north Austin. Download the CapMetro app to purchase tickets.

Only a few decades ago, Austin was mostly known as a laid-back town full of slackers and no real industry besides the live music scene. Locals hopped about town in their flip-flops, cooling off at creeks under the blazing sun before emptying their pockets in dingy dive bars come dusk. Later, Austin became a safe space in the south for the queer community and for creatives honing their craft. Next came the Silicon Valley folk, lured in by tax incentives and a budding tech scene. The result has been an economic explosion and a city reimagined, which is usually what happens when a juicy secret gets out. Experience Austin's delights gastronomically through the city's blossoming food scene, during one of the capital's huge festivals like SXSW and Austin City Limits, or through the natural outdoor wonders that stretch from the outskirts right into the heart of downtown.

Capital Culture

Austin's top museums

Austin's museums might not have nationwide name recognition, but they'll surprise you. The mainstays clustered around Congress Ave satisfy an appetite for art, history and culture. The exterior walls at **The Contemporary Austin** routinely moonlight as canvases for national artists like Jenny Holzer – and outside means free viewing. Across the street, explore works by Mexican and Latino artists at the **Mexic-Arte Museum**, which also has a thoughtful gift shop. The **Bullock Texas State History Museum** takes visitors through

---

☑ TOP TIP

From March until late October, the best free show in town happens beneath the Congress Avenue Bridge. Just after sunset, vast swarms of Mexican free-tailed bats emerge into the night in a feeding frenzy. Grab a spot on the sidewalk along the bridge or on the southeast corner, close to the Austin American-Statesman building.

the state's history by way of interactive exhibits and a 4D special-effects IMAX theater.

For retro discovery, the **Museum of the Weird** carries a collection of curiosities and oddities displayed in the tradition of PT Barnum. Speaking of weird, the **Cathedral of Junk** may not qualify as a museum, but the towering sculpture fills artist Vince Hannemann's backyard with everything from dolls and car bumpers to toilets and lawn-mower tires. Just call Hannemann (512-299-7413) ahead of time to make an appointment.

Get to Know South Congress

Austin's trendiest street

South Congress, or SoCo as it's often abbreviated, is equal parts authentic charm and commercialized cool, with plenty of food, shopping and entertainment options. Austin-born favorites like **Home Slice Pizza**, **Hopdoddy Burger Bar** and **Amy's Ice Cream** whet the appetites of a daytime crowd fresh from a dip in Lady Bird Lake, while sought-after reservations at **Otoko** and **June's** give people a good reason to change into fresh clothes.

Boutiques range from vintage to contemporary and keep all tastes satisfied for hours on end, including shops to pick

HIGHLIGHTS
1. Franklin Barbecue

SIGHTS
2. Bullock Texas State History Museum
3. Cathedral of Junk
4. Red Bud Isle

SLEEPING
5. ARRIVE Austin

EATING
6. Cuantos Tacos
7. La Barbecue
8. Leroy & Lewis Barbecue
9. Micklethwait Barbecue
10. The Vegan Nom

ENTERTAINMENT
11. AFS Cinema
12. Bullock Museum IMAX Theater

EATING IN AUSTIN: FOOD TRUCKS

MAPS P672, 674

Gordough's: Take their word for it when they say these are big, fat doughnuts. One is more than enough here. *10am-midnight Mon-Fri, from 8am Sat & Sun* $

The Vegan Nom: Vegan food truck serving up delicious tacos, nachos and burritos on the east side of town. *8am-2pm & 5-10pm Mon-Fri, 8am-10pm Sat & Sun* $

Kiin Di: Fantastic Thai food along South Lamar. The Killer Noodles are a must-try. *4:30-9pm Wed-Sun* $

Cuantos Tacos: Austin's must-visit yellow truck for Mexican-style street tacos. Make sure to try the suadero. *11am-10pm Tue-Sat* $

HIGHLIGHTS
1. Barton Springs Pool
2. South Congress
3. Zilker Park

SIGHTS
4. Broken Spoke
5. I Love You So Much Mural
6. Open Room Austin
7. Pfluger Pedestrian Bridge
8. Sand Beach Park
9. Willie Nelson Mural
10. Zilker Botanical Garden

SLEEPING
11. Austin Motel
12. Carpenter Hotel
13. Hotel San José
14. South Congress Hotel

EATING
15. Amy's Ice Creams
16. Better Half Coffee & Cocktails
17. Clark's Oyster Bar
18. Dovetail Pizza
19. El Alma
20. Fresa's
21. Gordough's
22. Home Slice Pizza
23. Hopdoddy Burger Bar
24. Jo's Coffee
25. June's
26. Kiin Di
27. Loro
28. Otoko
29. Perla's
30. Polvos
31. Terry Black's BBQ
32. Uchi

DRINKING & NIGHTLIFE
33. ABGB
34. Bouldin Acres
35. Continental Club
36. Courtyard Lounge at Hotel San José
37. Donn's Depot
38. Nightcap
39. Saxon Pub
40. Tiki Tatsu-Ya

ENTERTAINMENT
41. Alamo Drafthouse Cinema
42. Austin City Limits Music Festival
43. Austin Trail of Lights
44. Eeyore's Birthday Party
45. Food & Wine Festival
46. Reggae Festival

OTHER FAVORITE OUTDOOR SPOTS

Ky Harkey, founder of The Visitor Experience and former director of interpretation at Texas Parks & Wildlife, highlights his favorite outdoor spots in Austin. *Insta: @kyharkey*

Parking is really challenging at **Red Bud Isle**, but you can also access it by paddleboard or kayak for a super-unique experience. **McKinney Falls** is the only state park within Austin's city limits. People can camp and see live music on the same day. The **Pfluger Pedestrian Bridge** (p676) is one of my favorite spots in Austin at sunrise or sunset. **Sand Beach Park** has an art installation called **Open Room Austin** (p676). It's this grand, colorful picnic table that's 24ft long. You can't reserve it – it's meant to bring different groups of people together.

---

up some cowboy boots. Cafes are well staggered along the strip, with highlights like **Jo's Coffee** and its famous **I Love You So Much mural**. Another must see/photograph is the **Willie Nelson For President mural** on Elizabeth St a few blocks away.

Zilker Park & Barton Springs Pool

Bask under the Texan sun

The beloved 358-acre **Zilker Park** is a year-round haven for humans and dogs alike in Austin. Spring is when the flowers bloom at **Zilker Botanical Garden** and when the sky is colorfully decorated by the **ABC Kite Fest**. Summer brings sunbathers and revelers armed with giant coolers, as well as the free **Blues on the Green** concert series across multiple evenings in June and July. Fall provides cooler weather for Zilker's most famous event, the **Austin City Limits Music Festival** *(aclfestival.com)*. December's lack of white powder doesn't deter the park's festive efforts, as Zilker becomes the **Austin Trail of Lights** with 2 million bulbs, 90 Christmas trees, twinkling light tunnels and a merry sleigh of displays.

 EATING IN DOWNTOWN AUSTIN: OUR PICKS — MAPS P672, 674

Better Half Coffee & Cocktails	Taqueria 10 de 10	Clark's Oyster Bar	Arlo Grey
Better Half Coffee & Cocktails: A great spot for breakfast, brunch, lunch or dinner. *8am-3pm Mon, to 10pm Tue-Thu & Sun, to 11pm Fri & Sat* **$$**	**Taqueria 10 de 10:** A taco speakeasy. Enter through ReyRey bar in the alleyway between 2nd and 3rd Sts. *11:30am-10pm Sun-Wed, to 1am Thu-Sat* **$**	**Clark's Oyster Bar:** Oysters on the half shell and other seafood options inside a beautiful space in Old West Austin. *11am-10pm Sun-Thu, to 11pm Fri & Sat* **$$**	**Arlo Grey:** Fine-dining menu from Top Chef host (and winner) Kristen Kish and a prime spot to watch the South Congress bats. *5-10pm Wed-Sun* **$$$**

DRINKING IN DOWNTOWN AUSTIN: OUR PICKS

MAPS P672, 674

Donn's Depot: A former train depot turned dive bar and go-to hang-out for many in Austin. Live music most nights. *2pm-2am Mon-Fri, 6pm-2am Sat*

Elephant Room: An underground jazz bar that's exactly what you'd want in an underground jazz bar. *5pm-2am Mon-Fri, 8pm-2am Sat, 7pm-1am Sun*

Roosevelt Room: One of Austin's top cocktail bars with a jaw-dropping menu of drinks that spans different eras. *3pm-midnight Sun-Wed, to 2am Thu-Sat*

Nightcap: Old bungalow house turned bar-restaurant with a great outdoor view of the hustle and bustle along W 6th. *5-10pm Tue & Wed, to midnight Thu-Sat*

HIGHLIGHTS
1. 6th Street
2. Red River Cultural District
3. Texas State Capitol

SIGHTS
4. Austin Public Library
5. Butterfly Bridge
6. Deep Roots Community Garden
7. Mexic-Arte Museum
8. Museum of the Weird
9. Shoal Creek Greenbelt
10. Tau Ceti
11. The Contemporary Austin
12. Waterloo Park
13. Willie Nelson Statue

ACTIVITIES
14. 9th St BMX Park
15. Ann and Roy Butler Hike-and-Bike Trail

SLEEPING
16. Firehouse Hostel
17. Hotel Van Zandt
18. The Driskill

EATING
19. Arlo Grey
20. Stubb's Bar-B-Q
21. Taqueria 10 de 10
22. Walton's Fancy & Staple

DRINKING & NIGHTLIFE
23. Barbarella's
24. Blind Pig Pub
25. Cheer Up Charlies
26. Clive Bar
27. Coconut Club
28. Elephant Room
29. Highland Lounge
30. Iron Bear
31. Jackalope
32. Kung Fu Saloon
33. Lucille
34. Neon Grotto
35. Oilcan Harry's
36. Pete's Dueling Piano Bar
37. Rain
38. Rainey Street
39. Roosevelt Room
40. Rustic Tap
41. Star Bar

ENTERTAINMENT
42. Blue Starlite Urban Drive-In
43. Creek & The Cave
44. Esther's Follies
45. Mohawk
46. Paramount Theatre
47. Pecan Street Festival
48. South By Southwest
49. Violet Crown Cinema

BEST AUSTIN FESTIVALS & EVENTS

Austin knows how to party and is much more than just SXSW and ACL.

Reggae Festival: Two days of reggae for a cause every April, raising more than $1 million for the Central Texas Food Bank in 30-plus years.

Pecan Street Festival: A free downtown music and arts festival held twice a year.

Eeyore's Birthday Party: A day-long party in late April to raise money for nonprofits in honor of Eeyore, Winnie-the-Pooh's habitually sad buddy.

Trail of Lights: Annual celebration in Zilker Park each December to ring in the holiday season.

Food & Wine Festival: The absolute best of Austin's culinary scene gets together in Zilker Park each November.

Don't miss Zilker's summer savior, **Barton Springs Pool**, a 3-acre outdoor swimming spot fed by cold-water natural springs from deep underground. The water temperature averages between 68°F and 70°F (20-21°C) all year, particularly wonderful on those brutally hot summer days when the thermostat frequently hits triple digits. In the winter, admission fees are waived for those interested in a complimentary dose of cryotherapy.

A Hike-&-Bike Trail

Skip the gym

The **Ann and Roy Butler Hike-and-Bike Trail** is Austin's outdoor gym. Whether it's a walk, run, bike ride or quality time with your pup, this is where Austin congregates to get outside and burn calories – all while taking in stunning views of downtown. The 10-mile trail loops around Lady Bird Lake, using the Roberta Crenshaw Bridge under MoPac (to the west) and Longhorn Shores (to the east) to form a circle, and features public art exhibits and a live music series in the fall.

EATING IN SOUTH AUSTIN: OUR PICKS — MAPS P672

Polvos: Delicious interior Mexican food. Now three locations, but visit the original on S 1st St for the atmosphere. *9:30am-10pm Sun-Thu, to 11pm Fri & Sat* $$

Fresa's: Another S 1st St favorite. The specialty here is wood-grilled chicken, but top it with the jalapeño crema. *11am-10pm Mon-Fri, 10am-10pm Sat & Sun* $

Dovetail Pizza: A little fancier than a normal, neighborhood pizza joint. Also located on S 1st. *11am-10pm Sun-Thu, to 11pm Fri & Sat* $$

Terry Black's BBQ: A long line on weekends, but it moves quickly. You might spend longer finding a place to park. *10:30am-9:30pm Sun-Thu, to 10pm Fri & Sat* $$

DOWNTOWN AUSTIN BIKE TOUR

Witness the best of downtown Austin on two wheels. An e-bike can be rented using the CapMetro Bikeshare app at Riverside/South Lamar Station.

START	END	LENGTH
Pfluger Pedestrian Bridge	Central Public Library	Roughly 5 miles; 50-60 minutes

Cross over the ❶ **Pfluger Pedestrian Bridge**, and circle back through Sand Beach Park to turn left on the Lance Armstrong Bikeway. Ride past ❷ **Open Room Austin**, a large picnic table slash public art installation. Turn left on West Ave and then right on 2nd St to go over the ❸ **Butterfly Bridge**. At the corner of 2nd and Lavaca, stop at the ❹ **Willie Nelson statue** at Austin City Limits Live. Keep heading east and pause for more pictures at the ❺ **Tau Ceti rainbow mural** at 2nd and Brazos. In two more blocks, turn left on Trinity St, then right on the bike path on 4th St before turning left on Red River St. Two blocks down, cross ❻ **6th Street** (p678), one of the country's most famous stretches of bars and clubs. Continue north through the ❼ **Red River Cultural District** (p679), a hub for live music. At 12th and Red River, ride through ❽ **Waterloo Park**, a new green space in downtown. Head back to 12th St and take a right up the hill toward the ❾ **State Capitol**. Ride through the grounds and exit the west gate along 12th St. At 12th and Shoal Creek Boulevard, turn left to enter the ❿ **Shoal Creek Greenbelt**. While approaching Duncan Neighborhood Park, take a slight left to avoid stairs before finding the ⓫ **9th St BMX Park**. Turn right on the trail and then a sharp left to cross the creek and pass the ⓬ **Deep Roots Community Garden**. Continue on Shoal Creek Trail until it hits the Lance Armstrong Bikeway at the ⓭ **Central Public Library**. There are stations nearby to dock your bike.

South by Southwest
Downtown Austin's March transformation

For Austin at its liveliest, visit in March during **SXSW**. Founded in 1987, the annual 10-day event features a celebration of technology, film, music, education and culture. Stop by for film premieres at the **Paramount Theatre** (p679), see hotshot new artists perform at **Mohawk** (p679), watch big-name comedians at **Esther's Follies**, and check out exhibits, panels and keynotes galore at the **Austin Convention Center**. Badge prices range from $700 to $1700, but there are also free shows for those without company budgets.

South Austin Entertainment
Where to let loose

South Austin continues to pull its weight in helping the city maintain its reputation as the Live Music Capital of the World. No visit is complete without a ticket to the **Continental Club**. Since 1955, the Continental has evolved from supper club to burlesque club to a legendary live-music stage.

Two of Austin's other most legendary live-music joints exist along a stretch of South Lamar. **Saxon Pub** is a cozy spot for happy hour or shows, and Austin mainstays like Bob Schneider and the Resentments still play regular gigs there. **Broken Spoke** is a dance hall famed for its country music and two-step lessons.

Lady Bird Johnson Wildflower Center
Bluebonnet heaven

The 284-acre **Lady Bird Johnson Wildflower Center** has been delighting generations since 1982. Every type of Texan native wildflower is represented on its grounds, with nearly 900 species of plants from the different regions of the state, which includes bluebonnets in the spring, of course. The center also offers bird-watching on the wildflower-rimmed trails, an interactive kids garden, a 1-mile tree arboretum and a quaint cafe with patio seating to rest your stems and refuel.

AUSTIN'S BEST MOVIE VENUES

Austin's film scene was born from Richard Linklater's 1990 flick *Slacker,* which acutely detailed the city's culture and vibe. Austin is now home to several film festivals and some of the best theaters in the country.

Alamo Drafthouse Cinema: Iconic Austin chain with beer and food delivery to your seat. Just don't talk or text during the movie.

Violet Crown Cinema: Small theater downtown with only a couple of rows for each screen.

AFS Cinema: Home theater of the Austin Film Society, founded by Linklater, on the city's north side.

Blue Starlite Urban Drive-In: Watch movies from your car on a downtown rooftop.

Bullock Museum IMAX Theater: The biggest screen inside the city's biggest history museum.

 EATING IN SOUTH AUSTIN: DATE NIGHT SPOTS — MAPS P672

| Uchi: One of Austin's most popular high-end restaurants. Named one of the 20 most important restaurants in the country. *4-10pm Sun-Thu, to 11pm Fri & Sat* $$$ | Loro: Asian-BBQ fusion from chefs Tyson Cole of Uchi and Aaron Franklin of Franklin Barbecue. *11am-10pm Sun-Thu, to 11pm Fri & Sat* $$ | El Alma: Authentic Mexican food in a beautiful space at the Barton Springs location. *11am-10pm Mon-Thu, 11am-11pm Fri, 10am-11pm Sat, 10am-10pm Sun* $$ | Perla's: Seafood and oysters while sitting underneath the trees on a massive patio along South Congress. *11:30am-10pm Sun-Thu, to 11pm Fri, 10:30am-11pm Sat* $$ |

TIPS FOR THE FRANKLIN LINE

Standing in line for Franklin Barbecue on a Saturday morning is a rite of passage for many Texans. **Aaron Franklin**, the pit master himself, helps you navigate the wait. *Insta: @franklinbbq)*

Show up early. I would probably get here at about 8:30am. You won't be right up front, but you won't be out in full sun.

Wear comfortable shoes. You're going to be on your feet for a while. We do have a ton of chairs as loaners, though.

Stay hydrated. You're probably gonna drink some beers later.

Make new friends. People come from all over the world to hang out, and everybody's got a reason.

Be hungry. We'll crush you. It's gonna be a great nap afterwards, though.

Neon Grotto

Austin's Barbecue Showdown
Top-notch smokers

Award-winning **Franklin Barbecue** *(franklinbbq.com)* has long been touted as the best barbecue in Austin and turned pit master Aaron Franklin into a national celebrity on the food scene. Spending a Saturday morning waiting for hours on a fold-out chair in front of the restaurant for a taste of that fatty brisket is as much an experience as the eating part.

But Franklin has plenty of legit competition for the barbecue crown these days. **La Barbecue** *(labarbecue.com)* has become one of Austin's favorite smokehouses since its opening in 2011.

Once known only for its famed food truck **Micklethwait Barbecue** *(craftmeatsaustin.com)* opened its first bricks-and-mortar location in Austin inside an old church in late 2024.

Further out, **Leroy & Lewis Barbecue** *(leroyandlewis bbq.com)* is a new-school barbecue joint that has gone from a small truck to its own, frequently sold-out store on Austin's south side.

Going Out on 6th Street
As wild or tame as you want

Any discussion of a night out in Austin likely starts with its famed **6th Street**. Locals call the portion from I-35 to roughly Congress Ave 'Dirty 6th,' and it's lined with bars and clubs that get rowdy after the sun goes down. Dirty 6th is primarily occupied by college students on the hunt for cheap-ish drinks, or bachelorette parties looking to let loose. This stretch has some fabled dive spots, including **The Jackalope**, **Blind Pig Pub** and **Pete's Dueling Piano Bar**.

The vibe changes somewhat dramatically as the party moves up to 'West 6th,' from San Antonio St to Lamar. Here, there's a slightly older crowd and establishments like **Star Bar**, **The Rustic Tap** and **Kung Fu Saloon**. Some of the city's trendiest restaurants can also be found on W 6th, such as **Walton's Fancy & Staple**, owned by Austin adoptee Sandra Bullock.

Another popular option for a night on the town is **Rainey Street**, a several-block stretch of old bungalow homes turned into bars like **Clive Bar** and **Lucille**. This area is under constant renovation with a new high-rise condo building seemingly going up every time someone turns around.

If you're looking for live performances, head to the **Red River Cultural District** along Red River St, which is home to **Mohawk**, a long-time favorite venue for smaller shows, and **The Creek & The Cave**, a stand-up comedy club. By day, **Stubb's** is a barbecue restaurant, but at night it becomes one of Austin's bigger outdoor concert stages. Street parking is easier to find here along the Red River side streets, and there are plenty of food trucks to keep your belly full.

LGBTQ+ Nightlife
Party with a rainbow crew

The thriving queer community is what distinguishes Austin from the rest of Texas. Celebrate love and acceptance on and around the 4th St Warehouse District, where colorful gay bars stand loud and proud. **Rain**, **Coconut Club**, **Neon Grotto** and **Oilcan Harry's**, the oldest of them all, are must-visits near the rainbow pedestrian crossing.

In the Red River Cultural District, **Cheer Up Charlies** has a killer dance floor, a ton of live music and a vegan food truck out back. Also on Red River, **Barbarella's** hosts the TuezGayz dance parties.

After the bars close, keep going after hours at **Highland Lounge** – and make sure to do drag brunch the next morning at **The Iron Bear**.

Paramount Theatre
Glamorous entertainment

For more than 100 years, the **Paramount Theatre** on Congress Ave in the heart of downtown Austin has entertained people within its majestic, art deco walls. The likes of Miles Davis, Katharine Hepburn, Maya Angelou and Burt Bacharach have all taken to its prestigious stage. Today the restored auditorium continues to treat crowds with music, comedy and movies.

LGBTQ+ AUSTIN

Colton Ashabranner is the marketing and communications manager at the Austin LGBT Chamber of Commerce. *Insta: @coltonashh*

Austin is very unique in that we don't actually have a gayborhood. We have 4th St, which is the unofficial LGBTQ+ district, but we're everywhere – and I would say Austin is very welcoming to our community. There are so many LGBTIQ-owned and ally businesses in Austin. Check out the Chamber events calendar *(membership.austin lgbtchamber.com/events)* or **Gay Do 512** *(gay.do512.com)*. The *Austin Chronicle* also has a section called Qmmunity *(austinchronicle.com/events/qmmunity)* where they share upcoming events. There are so many options, and there's always something to do.

DRINKING IN SOUTH AUSTIN: MUST-TRY SPOTS — MAPS P672

| **Courtyard Lounge at Hotel San Jose:** Gorgeous outdoor bar at one of the premier boutique hotels in the city. *noon-10pm Mon-Thu, to midnight Fri & Sat* | **ABGB:** Award-winning local brewery with plenty of outdoor seating, great pizza and live music. *11:30am-11pm Tue-Fri, noon-midnight Sat, noon-10pm Sun* | **Bouldin Acres:** Outdoor playground for adults (and your canine companion) with pickleball courts and other games. *11am-midnight* | **Tiki Tatsu-Ya:** Tiki bar with a wild aesthetic inside meant to take you on an immersive journey to paradise. *4pm-midnight Mon-Fri, 1pm-midnight Sat, 4-10pm Sun* |

San Antonio & the Hill Country

RIVERSIDE EXPLORING | SPANISH ARCHITECTURE | OUTDOOR ADVENTURES

GETTING AROUND

Around downtown, it's easy to walk, ride a bike or take the bus. Avoid the hassle and cost of parking and leave your car at the free lot at P+R Ellis Alley; it's a short bus ride from there to downtown (take No 25 or No 100).

Buses operated by VIA *(viainfo.net)* provide service around town. You can pay in cash ($1.30) or with the VIA goMobile+ app.

Various B-Cycle bike-share stations are scattered around downtown – as well as at the southern Missions.

You'll need a car when you're ready to head to the Hill Country.

One of Texas' most attractive major cities, San Antonio has long captivated visitors. The legendary Alamo, that iconic symbol of Texan independence, stands at the heart of the city, while the River Walk, a glorious network of waterside pathways that's tucked below street level and lined with bars and restaurants, offers leisurely strolling through downtown and beyond.

The San Antonio River has long been an integral part of life here. The headwaters were sacred to Indigenous tribes, and today the river flows past many of the city's must-see neighborhoods, including the trendy Pearl and historic King William, and reaches the edge of the historic missions south of town – part of a UNESCO World Heritage site.

San Antonio puts you in close proximity to the Hill Country, a beautiful region known for its charming small towns, refreshing swimming holes and rugged state parks. The wildflower-lined back roads are gateways to memorable scenic drives.

Exploring the Alamo

The famous battle site

The much-fabled **Alamo** *(thealamo.org)* is where Davy Crockett, James Bowie and 200 other revolutionaries died in 1836 during a battle against Mexican troops. There's much to see beyond the old church: reconstructed parts of the mission turned fort, various films that shed light on the past, and an impressive collection (admission $14) donated by Alamo enthusiast and '80s pop star Phil Collins. Admission to the church is free.

Continued on p684

☑ TOP TIP

Don't leave San Antonio without trying a puffy taco, which is a corn tortilla fired up into a puffy, crispy form that's then filled with the usual taco accouterments. It originated in San Antonio in the 1950s. **Tito's Mexican Restaurant** serves some of the best near downtown.

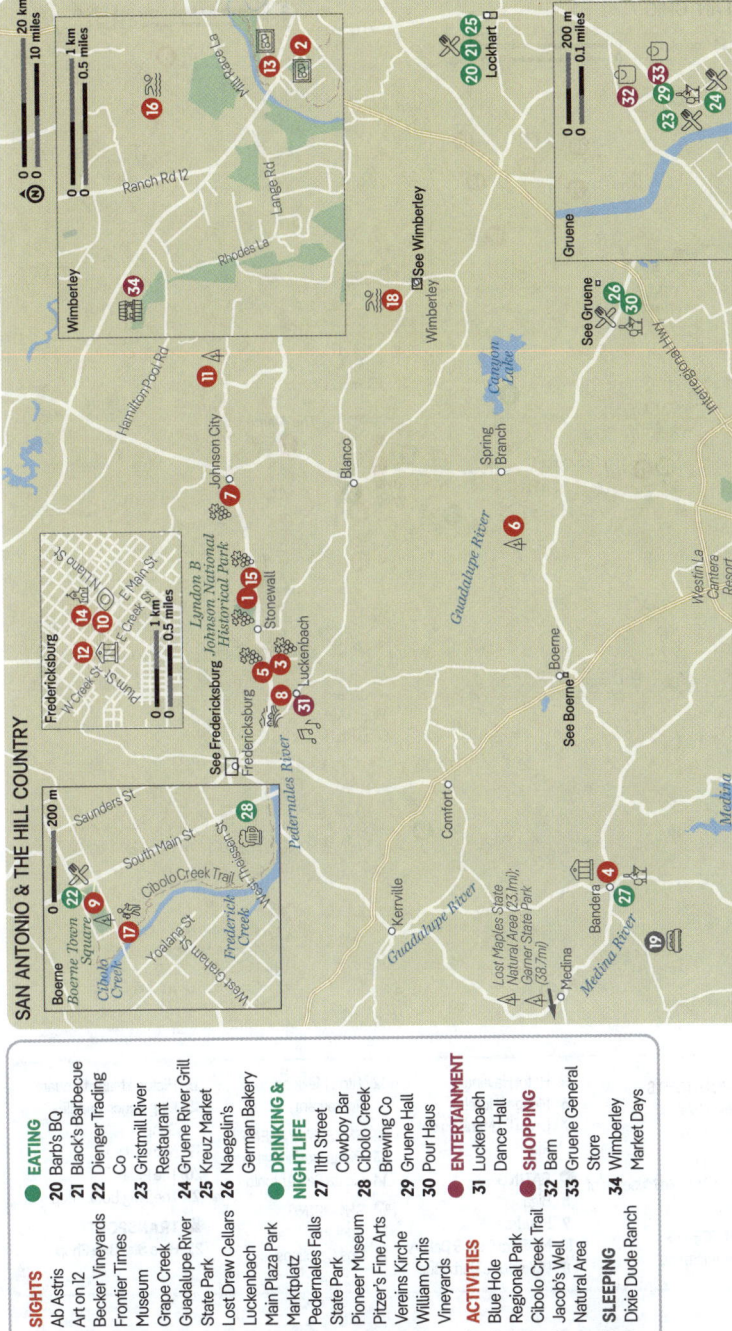

SAN ANTONIO & THE HILL COUNTRY

● SIGHTS
1. Ab Astris
2. Art on 12
3. Becker Vineyards
4. Frontier Times Museum
5. Grape Creek
6. Guadalupe River State Park
7. Lost Draw Cellars
8. Luckenbach
9. Main Plaza Park
10. Marktplatz
11. Pedernales Falls State Park
12. Pioneer Museum
13. Pitzer's Fine Arts
14. Vereins Kirche
15. William Chris Vineyards

● ACTIVITIES
16. Blue Hole Regional Park
17. Cibolo Creek Trail
18. Jacob's Well Natural Area

● SLEEPING
19. Dixie Dude Ranch

● EATING
20. Barb's BQ
21. Black's Barbecue
22. Dienger Trading Co
23. Gristmill River Restaurant
24. Gruene River Grill
25. Kreuz Market
26. Naegelin's German Bakery

● DRINKING & NIGHTLIFE
27. 11th Street Cowboy Bar
28. Cibolo Creek Brewing Co
29. Gruene Hall
30. Pour Haus

● ENTERTAINMENT
31. Luckenbach Dance Hall

● SHOPPING
32. Barn
33. Gruene General Store
34. Wimberley Market Days

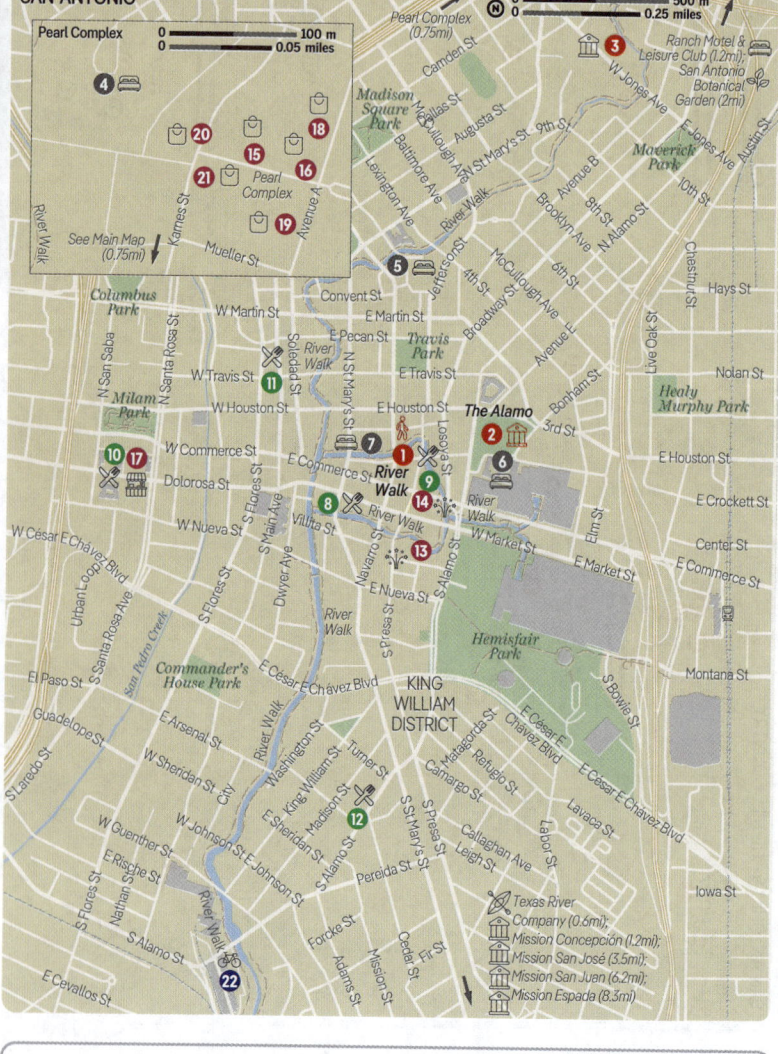

SAN ANTONIO

★ HIGHLIGHTS
1. River Walk
2. The Alamo

● SIGHTS
3. San Antonio Museum of Art

● SLEEPING
4. Hotel Emma
5. Hotel Havana
6. Menger Hotel
7. Omni La Mansión del Rio

● EATING
8. Biga
9. Boudro's
10. Mi Tierra Cafe & Bakery
11. Pinkerton's Barbecue
12. Tito's Mexican Restaurant

● ENTERTAINMENT
13. Fiesta Noche del Rio
14. Fiesta San Antonio

● SHOPPING
15. Adelante
16. Dos Carolinas
17. Historic Market Square
18. King Ranch Saddle Shop
19. Niche at Pearl
20. The Pearl
21. The Twig Book Shop

● TRANSPORT
22. Blue Star Bike Shop

TOP EXPERIENCE

The River Walk

A little slice of Europe in the heart of downtown, the 15-mile River Walk is an essential part of the San Antonio experience. Wandering this charming network of canals and pedestrian walkways, set just below the downtown streets, you can pass landscaped gardens and riverfront cafes, and linger on stone footbridges that arch gracefully across the water.

Dining & People Watching

The river makes a loop around one section of downtown, and this is the most commercial part of the River Walk. Here you'll find numerous restaurants and bars overlooking the water. It's lively day and night, with twinkling lights in the trees and music spilling out onto open terraces.

Peaceful Strolls

For a more peaceful experience, follow the river north or south of downtown. It's a memorable 1.7-mile walk from Houston St up to the Pearl District. Along the way, signposts point out unique river features – like the remains of the dam built by the visionary River Walk architect Robert Hugman in 1941. Look out for mosaics and other public artwork. Beneath the I-35 overpass, a school of larger-than-life fish floats overhead – an art installation by Donald Lipski. There's also an artificial grotto, complete with waterfall, near Newell Ave.

Boat Trips

On a fleet of of ecofriendly electric boats, **Go Rio** (*goriocruises.com*) operates narrated cruises ($16) that touch on San Antonio's history and culture. Boats depart from three different locations, including a dock below Commerce St near the Shops at Rivercenter mall. If you want to hop on and off, Go Rio runs a shuttle between downtown and the Museum Reach (north of downtown), with 15 different stops. Departures run roughly hourly between noon and 7pm (one-day pass $22).

TOP TIPS

● Rent kayaks from Texas River Company (*txrivercompany.com*), which launches from Roosevelt Park, about 2 miles south of downtown.

● The southern River Walk is great for cycling. You can hire from Blue Star Bike Shop (*bluestarbikeshop.com*) and ride down to the missions (9 miles to the furthest).

PRACTICALITIES

● Check out *thesanantonioriverwalk.com* for info on exhibits and upcoming events.

SAN ANTONIO'S BIGGEST EVENTS

Fiesta San Antonio: Over 11 days in late April, this citywide party features river and flower-filled street parades, mariachi concerts and 100 other events.

Day of the Dead: In October, San Antonio hosts one of the biggest Day of the Day celebrations with traditional altars and parades.

Battle of the Alamo: History comes to life during the commemoration of the 13-day siege, held from late February to early March.

Holiday River Parade: Gear up for the holidays with a festive parade and dazzling lights along the River Walk. It happens in late November.

Fiesta Noche del Rio: On Friday and Saturday nights in June and July catch Latin music and dancing at the Arneson River Theater.

Continued from p680

Guided tours are available throughout the day for $45 (reserve ahead). For in-depth exploration at your own pace, book a self-guided audio tour for $20.

Little Mexico

Shops, food and entertainment

About half a mile west of the River Walk, **Historic Market Square** (marketsquaresa.com) is a little piece of Mexico in downtown San Antonio. It's a fair approximation of a trip south of the border, with Mexican food, mariachi bands and more than 100 locally owned shops filled with Mexican folk art, handmade goods and clothes. A big chunk of the square is taken up by **El Mercado**, the largest Mexican marketplace outside of Mexico.

Treasures from Latin America & Beyond

5000 years of art

The **San Antonio Museum of Art** (samuseum.org; adult/child $22/free) houses an impressive trove of Latin American art, including Spanish Colonial, Mexican and pre-Columbian – one of the most comprehensive collections in the US. Beyond Latin American works, the museum holds a little of everything, from Egyptian antiquities to contemporary abstracts, as well as an impressive Asian wing with a collection of Chinese ceramics, paintings and decorative items.

Fun at the Pearl

Shopping, dining and concerts

A former brewery turned urban playground, **The Pearl** (at pearl.com) is a large complex with restaurants, shops, a boutique hotel, green spaces, a splash pad for kids and a branch of the CIA – as in Culinary Institute of America. It sits near the River Walk, and there's even a shaded amphitheater overlooking the water. The best time to visit the Pearl is on weekend mornings, when you can catch one of its captivating markets (atpearl.com/weekend-market).

Botanical Bounty

Flora from Texas and beyond

The **San Antonio Botanical Garden** (sabot.org; adult/child $22/15) is an immaculately tended, 38-acre complex with a variety of diverse environments. One area not to miss is the

---

EATING IN SAN ANTONIO: OUR PICKS

MAPS P672

Boudro's: Ideal waterfront spot for indulging in blue crab tostadas, prickly pear margaritas and other creative temptations. *11am-10:30pm* $$$

Mi Tierra Cafe y Panaderia: This festive Mexican eatery and bakery in Market Sq is a San Antonio landmark, opened in 1941. *8am-10pm* $$

Biga: A welcoming outdoor patio on the River Walk and an acclaimed menu of New American cuisine. *5-9:30pm* $$$

Pinkerton's Barbecue: Fires up some of San Antonio's best barbecue, which you can enjoy at picnic tables overlooking a small park. *11am-9pm* $$

TOP EXPERIENCE

The Mission Trail

Spain's missionary presence can best be felt at the ruins of the four missions south of town, all overseen by the National Park Service as part of the San Antonio Missions National Historical Park. The San Antonio missions were constructed in the 18th century, and Catholic services are still held in the churches, which are supported by vibrant communities.

Mission Concepción

Mission Concepción

Heading south from San Antonio, **Mission Concepción** is first mission along the Mission Trail and the oldest unrestored stone church in the country.

Mission San José

Known in its time as the Queen of the Missions, **San José** is the largest and arguably the most beautiful of the four. Because it's a little more remote and pastoral, surrounded by thick stone walls, you can really get a sense of what life was like here in the 18th and 19th centuries.

Mission San Juan

Founded in 1731, this **mission** was once self-sustaining with orchards and gardens just outside the walls and farm fields further off. Take the **Yanaguana Trail** behind the church down to the river to see some of a natural ecosystem that was common before the arrival of the Spanish.

Mission Espada

The southernmost stop on the Mission Trail is also the oldest, dating from 1690. The **church** was built between 1745 and 1756. It's the best place to check out the historic *acequias*, which were dug by the mission inhabitants in the 1700s and used to water the farm fields.

TOP TIPS

- Mission San José is home to the main park visitor center, with free tours (10am and 11am).

- You can get here by cycling an extension of the River Walk.

- Mission San José's mariachi mass at noon on Sunday (in Spanish) is a San Antonio tradition.

PRACTICALITIES

- See *nps.gov/saan* for maps, opening hours and background information.

BEST STATE PARKS & SWIMMING SPOTS IN THE HILL COUNTRY

Garner State Park *(adult/child $8/free)* Float in a tube ($10) beneath limestone cliffs and rolling green hills.

Guadalupe River State Park *(p686) (adult/child $7/free)* Straddles a 4-mile stretch of the sparkling, bald-cypress-tree-lined Guadalupe River, and it's great for water activities and hiking.

Pedernales Falls State Park *(adult/child $6/free)* Trails wind through forests, atop ridges and along the churning riverside.

Lost Maples State Natural Area *(adult/child $6/free)* Summertime swimming, hiking amid limestone canyons and grasslands, and colorful leaves in autumn.

Jacob's Well Natural Area *(adult/child $9/5; jwna.checkfront.com/reserve)* A glorious setting for a swim, though you'll need to reserve ahead.

Blue Hole Regional Park *(adult/child $12/8; wimberley parksandrec.com/blue-hole-swimming)* Leap into the spring-fed waters of Cypress Creek. Reserve ahead.

Black's Barbecue

Texas Native Trail with three separate sections devoted to South Texas, the Hill Country and the eastern Pineywoods – which has a small lake ringed with bald cypress trees.

Historic Gruene's Fabled Dance Hall
Local crafts and live music

Settled by German farmers in the mid-1800s, the welcoming and historic town of Gruene (pronounced 'green') is the musical heart of the region. Pick up a cowboy hat from the **Gruene General Store** *(gruenegeneralstore.com)* and browse ceramics made by local artists at **The Barn** *(thebarningruene.com)*. Later, head to **Gruene Hall** *(gruenehall.com)*, an 1878 dance hall with free live music every night of the week.

Tubing in New Braunfels & Gruene
Waterside adventures

During the summer, nothing beats floating on the cool and easy-flowing waters of the Guadalupe and Comal rivers. When the sun gets to be too much, you can cool off with a swim, then hop back in the tube and continue along. Dozens of local outfitters rent tubes, and at the end of your trip, you'll be bused back to your starting point. **Texas Tubes** *(texastubes.com; $25)* is a recommended outfitter in New Braunfels, while **Rockin' R River Rides** *(rockinr.com; $25)* is the best choice in Gruene.

Eating Barbecue in Lockhart
Famous food spots

Back in 2003 the Texas Legislature officially named Lockhart the 'Barbecue Capital of Texas.' You can eat well at any of its barbecue restaurants. A good place to start is **Kreuz Market** *(kreuzmarket.com)*. A local landmark since 1900, this barn-like eatery is famed for its dry rub meats – no sauce needed. Another stalwart is **Black's Barbecue** *(blacksbbq.com)*, open since 1932 – and a favorite of President LBJ. This classic barbecue spot serves up buttery rich ribs and juicy sausage.

At **Barb's BQ** *(barbsbq.com)*, the young pitmaster has turned the barbecue world on its head with her tender, delicately spiced brisket, ribs and lamb. It's open Saturday and Sunday only (11am to 3pm). Go early as they always sell out.

Strolling Boerne

Shops, restaurants and parks

Settled by German immigrants in 1849, the attractive town of Boerne (pronounced 'Bernie') has more than 140 restored historical structures.

The half-mile stretch of Main St between River Rd and Blanco St makes for some rewarding exploring. Start off the ramble at the **Main Plaza Park**. On its northeastern corner, stop in the **Dienger Trading Co** *(thediengertradingco.com)*, a bistro, bakery and boutique in an 1884 grocery-store building. A few blocks south of there, the kid-friendly **Cibolo Creek Brewing Co** *(cibolocreekbrewing.com)* is a pleasant indoor-outdoor spot for craft beers and satisfying cooking.

A pleasant add-on to Main St exploring is a walk along the **Cibolo Creek Trail**, which follows a pretty creekside some 1.7 miles all the way to City Park. Once there, you can experience more fine scenery at the **Cibolo Center for Conservation**, which has short trails through native Texan woods, marshland and along Cibolo Creek.

Cowboy Culture in Bandera

Western lore

Bandera brands itself the Cowboy Capital of the World. While touristy, with staged gunfights (Saturdays at 10am and noon) and shops selling cowboy attire, Bandera still has an air of authenticity, particularly among the cowboy bars and honky-tonks. Near town, the 725-acre **Dixie Dude Ranch** *(dixiedude ranch.com)* offers horseback riding, campfire sing-alongs and other activities.

For a little perspective on bygone days in Bandera, stop by the **Frontier Times Museum** *(frontiertimesmuseum.org; adult/child $8/4)*, which has displays of Western art and cowboy tchotchkes such as guns and branding irons.

BEST VINEYARDS OF HILL COUNTRY

Hill Country's wine destination is **Hwy 290** *(wineroad290.com)* which has over 50 wineries, many open to tastings and tours. Leave the driving to **290 Wine Shuttle** *(290wineshuttle.com; per person $50)*.

Lost Draw Cellars Produces top-quality wines that showcase the terroir of the Texas High Plains.

Becker Vineyards One of the oldest and best wineries in the region, with a tasting room that's modeled on a German barn.

Grape Creek Resembles Tuscany with its spread of vineyards and stone buildings.

Ab Astris A boutique winery that produces handcrafted vintages, with a focus on lesser-known grape varieties.

William Chris Vineyards Hill Country's most famous winery with great views and premium wines.

EATING & DRINKING IN NEW BRAUNFELS & GRUENE: OUR PICKS – MAPS P681

Gristmill River Restaurant: Get a deckside table and enjoy ribs, steak and catfish in an 1800s cotton gin behind Gruene Hall. 11am-9pm $$

Gruene River Grill: The rustic dining room in Gruene makes a relaxed setting for American and Tex-Mex comfort food. 11am-9pm $$

Naegelin's German Bakery: Pick up strudels and kolaches from this legendary New Braunfels bakery – the oldest in Texas. 6:30am-5pm Mon-Sat, 8am-2pm Sun $

Pour Haus: Take a seat in the yard, and enjoy craft brews and delicious street tacos while catching live music in New Braunfels. 4pm-midnight Mon-Fri, 1pm-midnight Sat & Sun

THE PERILOUS JOURNEY FROM GERMANY

In 1845 in Germany, overpopulation, low wages and widespread poverty inspired some to seek a better life abroad. Those that came to Texas faced a daunting journey that began with a two-month trip aboard a cramped, unsanitary ship to reach Indianola on the Gulf. Once there, the travelers discovered that war had broken out between Mexico and the US, and onward transportation was not available. This left 4000 people languishing on the beach with little shelter, impure water, contaminated food and soon-to-be-rampant disease. Over 1400 died that summer. As weeks passed, those who were able set out on foot, leaving behind many of their possessions as they trudged 200 miles through rugged lands to newly christened settlements where they would begin a new life.

Afterwards, sip a Shiner at the **11th Street Cowboy Bar** *(11thstcowboybar.com)*, billed as the 'Biggest Little Honky Tonk in Texas.'

Gallery Hopping in Wimberley
Galleries, markets and swimming spots

Small, charming Wimberley is famed as an artists' community. **Art on 12** *(arton12.com)* features works by dozens of local and regional artists. Nearby, check out the paintings and sculpture of **Pitzer's Fine Arts** *(pitzersart.com)*, another well-respected gallery. Afterwards, treat yourself to a meal at one of Wimberley's charming creekside restaurants like **The Leaning Pear**, with its elevated comfort fare, or the **Creekhouse Kitchen & Bar** with creative fare and a lovely forested backdrop.

From March to December, the first Saturday of the month is **Wimberley Market Day** *(wimberleymarketday.com)*, featuring live music, food stalls and more than 400 vendors selling arts, crafts and more.

German Roots in Fredericksburg
Pioneer architecture and schnitzel

One of the Hill Country's most vibrant towns, Fredericksburg is a former 19th-century German settlement with its history woven into the landscape. Its street signs proclaim 'Willkommen,' and you'll be welcome indeed along its main street, lined with historic buildings that house German restaurants, beer gardens, antique stores and wine-tasting rooms.

For insight into what life was like for Fredericksburg's first settlers, visit the **Pioneer Museum** *(pioneermuseum.org; adult/child $12/5)*, with its collection of restored historic buildings that you can wander through.

Music, dancing and schnitzel are on the menu every October, when Fredericksburg celebrates its German heritage with Texas' largest **Oktoberfest** *(oktoberfestinfbg.com)*. Families crowd around for oompah bands, kegs of German beer and schnitzels galore. On Saturday, join hands for the Chicken Dance!

Legendary Luckenbach
Music-loving enclave

Made up of a handful of Old West structures, tiny **Luckenbach** *(luckenbachtexas.com)* is big on Texas charm. By day, the main activity is sitting at a picnic table under an old oak tree with a cold bottle of Shiner Bock beer and listening to guitar pickers. On Friday nights, two-stepping couples whirl around the dance floor of **Luckenbach Dance Hall**.

STROLL FREDERICKSBURG'S PAST

Peer past the souvenir shops to discover Fredericksburg's immigrant past amid striking buildings from the late 19th century and early 1900s.

START	END	LENGTH
Nimitz Hotel	St Mary's Catholic Church	1 mile; 1½ hours

Start at the former ❶ **Nimitz Hotel**, an 1860 building with a curious facade (meant to emulate a steamboat) that once hosted stagecoach travelers. Today it houses one big section of the National Museum of the Pacific War. Cross the street (carefully) and continue to ❷ **249 E Main St**. The typical home, built in 1866, is the birthplace of Chester Nimitz, who would go on to command the US Naval fleet in WWII (and sign the Japanese surrender documents in Tokyo Bay). The hometown hero is the reason the museum resides in Fredericksburg.

The heart of town is ❸ **Marktplatz**, a green space and centuries-old hub of the community. The octagonal building in the square's center is a 1935 reconstruction (and 2020 remodeling) of the ❹ **Vereins Kirche**, which served as the town church, meeting hall and school.

Continue along Main St and turn down Milam. You'll soon spot one of Texas' original tiny homes. Known as a Sunday house, the ❺ **Weber House** was used by early Fredericksburgers for their stay on weekends when driving in from the country to do their shopping, attend social gatherings and go to church. Around the corner, ❻ **St Mary's Catholic Church** is one of the so-called 'painted churches' of Texas, its 1908 Gothic design replete with stained glass, artwork and stenciling.

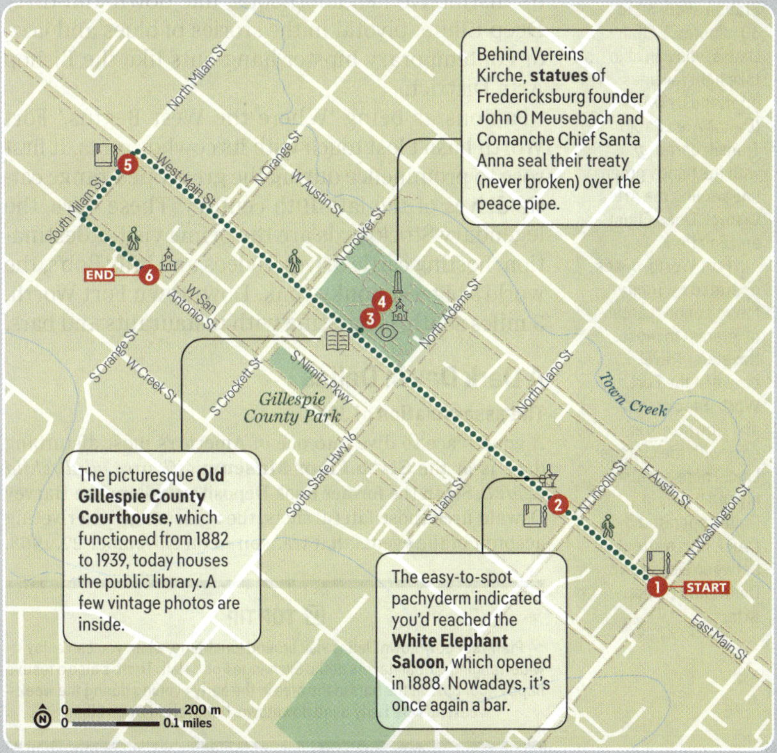
Behind Vereins Kirche, **statues** of Fredericksburg founder John O Meusebach and Comanche Chief Santa Anna seal their treaty (never broken) over the peace pipe.
The picturesque **Old Gillespie County Courthouse**, which functioned from 1882 to 1939, today houses the public library. A few vintage photos are inside.
The easy-to-spot pachyderm indicated you'd reached the **White Elephant Saloon**, which opened in 1888. Nowadays, it's once again a bar.
North Milam St
West Main St
N Orange St
W Austin St
N Crocker St
North Adams St
South Milam St
W San Antonio St
S Orange St
W Creek St
S Crockett St
S Nimitz Pkwy
Gillespie County Park
South State Hwy 16
S Llano St
North Llano St
Town Creek
N Lincoln St
E Austin St
N Washington St
East Main St
START
END
1
2
3
4
5
6
0
200 m
0
0.1 miles

Dallas & Fort Worth

ARTS & CULTURE | CATTLE DRIVES | NIGHTLIFE

GETTING AROUND

Trinity Railway Express (TRE) makes the one-hour journey between EBJ Union Station in Dallas and Fort Worth Central Station every 30 to 60 minutes. Within Dallas, you can also take light rail lines operated by DART (Dallas Area Rapid Transit; *dart.org*), with the handy green line serving the Arts District, Deep Ellum and Fair Park.

In Fort Worth, buses operated by Trinity Metro connect areas of interest to most travelers. Travel between the Fort Worth Stockyards and Downtown is easy with the Orange Line. There are also myriad buses in Dallas operated by DART, plus a streetcar between Downtown Dallas and Bishop Arts.

Dallas, the 'Big D,' is Texas' most mythologized city, rich in the stuff of which American legends are woven – including oil barons, cowboys and cheerleaders. Excellent museums in the massive, recently developed Arts District downtown offer world-class displays of art and sculpture, while unmissable sites commemorate the city's rendezvous with history in 1963, as the site of President John F Kennedy's assassination. For the quintessential Dallas experience, explore its distinctive neighborhoods, like down-and-dirty Deep Ellum, pivotal in the stories of blues and jazz, or contemporary hipster hang-outs like the Bishop Arts District.

Famous as being 'Where the West Begins,' Fort Worth hasn't lost touch with its cowboy roots. It first rose to prominence during the great open-range cattle drives of the late 19th century. These days, the legendary Stockyards are the prime visitor destination, hosting cattle drives, rodeos and Billy Bob's, the world's biggest honky-tonk. Downtown Fort Worth, 3 miles south, is bursting with restaurants and bars.

A Dark Day in Dallas

The assassination of JFK

A good place to dive into one of America's most disturbing days is at the **Sixth Floor Museum** *(jfk.org; adult/child $25/21)*. Set in the former Book Depository where Lee Harvey Oswald fired those fateful shots, the museum gives a riveting account of the events that transpired on November 22, 1963.

☑ TOP TIP

Plan your downtown Dallas visit around lunchtime, when you can enjoy wide-ranging global flavors at the Exchange Food Hall. There's also a festive happy hour buzz at the bars in the area in the early evening during the week – weekends are fairly dead downtown, but lively in Deep Ellum.

Dallas Farmers Market

Photographs, audio clips, news footage and eyewitness accounts make you feel almost as if you're experiencing it live.

Dealey Plaza, across the street from the museum, is where JFK was assassinated. The whole area is now a National Historic Landmark, with several signs detailing the day's events.

The Heart of Urban Life
Explore AT&T Discovery District

See the downtown renaissance of Dallas at the **AT&T Discovery District** (*discoverydistrictdallas.com*), which features multimedia installations, concerts and an open-air plaza that has free movie screenings and big games shown on a 104ft video wall. By day, the best reason to come here is to munch your way around the **Exchange Food Hall**, with vendors serving tacos, pizzas, sliders, Indian curries, creative salads and Mediterranean fare.

The Best Food Hall in Dallas
Food stalls and shops

Since 1941, the **Dallas Farmers Market** (*dallasfarmersmarket.org*) has been a top spot for fresh provisions. These days,

BEST SHOPPING IN DEEP ELLUM

Dated Faded Worn: A pricey but well-curated vintage shop with T-shirts, denim and shoes.

Deep Vellum: One of Dallas' best indie bookshops (and small-press publishers).

Rocket Fizz: A kaleidoscopic selection of vintage and contemporary candies and sodas.

Jade & Clover: You'll find jewelry, candles and alpaca socks, along with a much-loved plant bar.

EATING & DRINKING IN DEEP ELLUM: OUR PICKS — MAPS P693

Pecan Lodge: Dallas' best barbecue spot fires up mouthwatering brisket and smoky ribs, plus collard greens, okra and peach cobbler. *11am-8pm Tue-Sun, to 3pm Mon* $$

Velvet Taco: The taco is elevated to high art with fillings like beer-battered cauliflower and sweet chile shrimp. *11am-midnight Sun-Thu, to 4am Fri & Sat* $

AllGood Cafe: Art-filled street-corner diner with hearty breakfasts and Tex-Mex, plus a stage for live music Thursday to Saturday. *8am-3pm Sun-Wed, to 9pm Thu-Sat* $

Dot's Hop House & Courtyard: Has a charming courtyard, big beer menu and delicious comfort fare (like duck-fat fries). *4pm-1am Mon-Wed, noon-1am Thu-Sun* $$

BEST OF DALLAS' ARTS DISTRICT

The country's largest arts district stretches across some 118 acres just north of Downtown Dallas.

Perot Museum of Nature & Science *(adult/child $25/15)* A kid pleaser with five floors of interactive exhibits, plus massive dinosaur skeletons.

Dallas Museum of Art *(free)* One of Texas' best collections, with treasures that span centuries (and continents).

Klyde Warren Park Take a break between museum-hopping at this green space and community hub for outdoor yoga, movie screenings and markets. There are also food trucks and several restaurants.

Nasher Sculpture Center *(adult/child $10/free)* An impressive array of works by renowned sculptors past and present.

Crow Museum of Asian Art *(free)* Beautiful works in artfully designed exhibition halls.

---

the market has a capacious food hall where you can enjoy lattes, tacos, banh mi, sushi, thali platters, barbecue and juices.

On weekends, head to the nearby open-sided **Shed** for farm-fresh produce as well as handmade soaps, cutting boards, jewelry, and lots of other crafts and seasonal items.

Creative Deep Ellum
Music and art

Embodying the neighborhood's most creative aspect, **Deep Ellum Art Co** *(deepellumart.co)* is a spacious 5000-sq-ft multi-use venue that features an art gallery, concert stage and a backyard of art installations, murals, food trucks and yard games.

Trees *(treesdallas.com; admission from $15)* has been a mainstay in Deep Ellum since its opening back in 1990. The wide-ranging lineup leans toward indie rock, hip-hop and EDM, with concerts four or five nights a week.

Uptown's Scenic Trail
Walking, running and cycling

To enjoy some see-and-be-seen walking, running or cycling, hit the tree-lined **Katy Trail** *(katytraildallas.org)*. The former railroad line stretches for 3.5 miles from N Houston St (just above the American Airlines Center) in the south to Airline Rd in the north. Post walk or run, stop in the Katy Trail Ice House, a scenic spot with outdoor tables for barbecue and craft beers.

Exploring Bishop Arts District
Crafts, records and books

One-of-a-kind boutiques, eye-catching galleries and an array of creative eating and drinking spaces line the streets of Bishop Arts District, Dallas' most walkable neighborhood.

Start your wander along Bishop Ave at **Mosaic Makers Collective** *(mosaicmakers.co)*, featuring beautifully made jewelry, clothing, stationery and housewares, all created by female artisans and designers. Across the street, **Spinster Records** *(spinsterrecords.com)* has a brilliant selection of new and used vinyl (plus a few CDs and old-school cassettes).

Continue along N Bishop Ave to **Dolly on Bishop** *(dollypythonvintage.com)*, which is crammed full of vintage apparel and curiosities dating from the 1940s to 1980s. Book lovers should definitely make the slight detour to W 8th St for **The**

 EATING IN BISHOP ARTS: OUR PICKS ———— MAPS P693

| **Tribal All Day Cafe:** An inviting vegan-friendly spot with smoothies, seasonal vegetable bowls and breakfast burritos. *8am-5:30pm Mon-Sat, to 4pm Sun* $ | **Taco y Vino:** A delightful mashup of creative Mexican fare, tacos and good wines with a lively ambience and a spacious backyard. *11am-10pm Mon-Sat, to 3pm Sun* $$ | **The Mayor's House by Selda:** Excellent Turkish cooking in a historic building with multiple dining rooms and a breezy front porch. *noon-11pm* $$ | **Lucia:** Reserve well ahead for a table at this award-winning restaurant serving up top-notch creative Italian fare. *5-10pm Tue-Sat* $$$ |

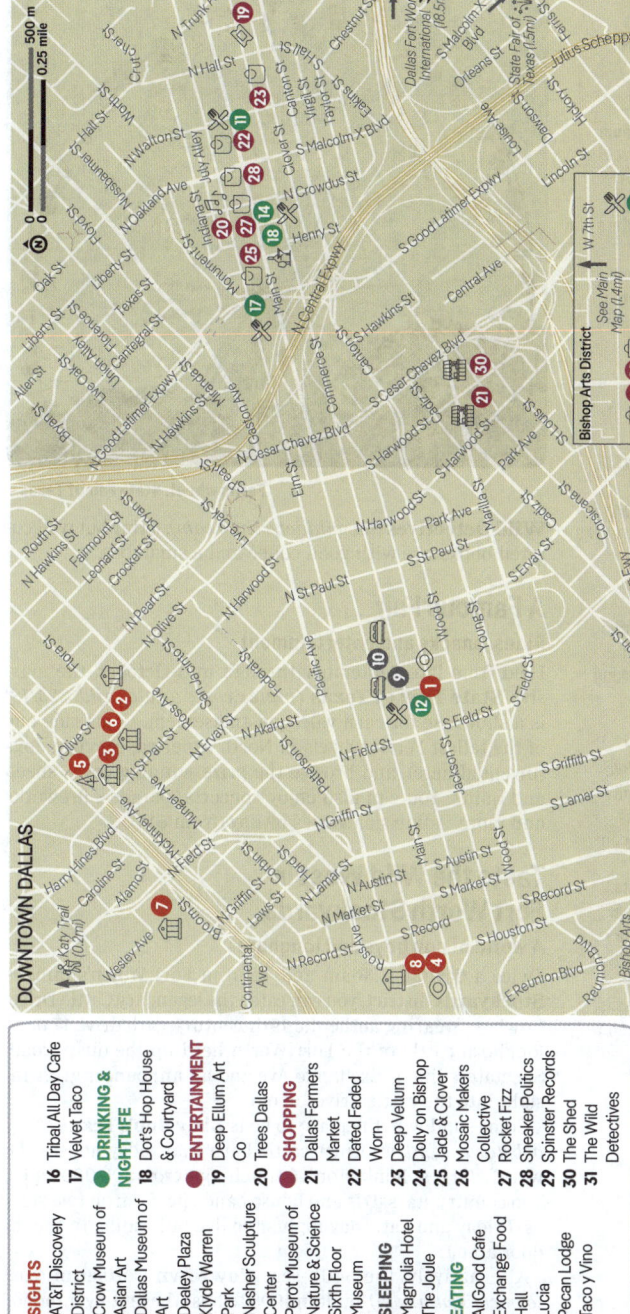

DOWNTOWN DALLAS

THE GUIDE

TEXAS DALLAS & FORT WORTH

SIGHTS
1. AT&T Discovery District
2. Crow Museum of Asian Art
3. Dallas Museum of Art
4. Dealey Plaza
5. Klyde Warren Park
6. Nasher Sculpture Center
7. Perot Museum of Nature & Science
8. Sixth Floor Museum

SLEEPING
9. Magnolia Hotel
10. The Joule

EATING
11. AllGood Cafe
12. Exchange Food Hall
13. Lucia
14. Pecan Lodge
15. Taco y Vino
16. Tribal All Day Cafe
17. Velvet Taco

DRINKING & NIGHTLIFE
18. Dot's Hop House & Courtyard

ENTERTAINMENT
19. Deep Ellum Art Co
20. Trees Dallas

SHOPPING
21. Dallas Farmers Market
22. Dated Faded Worn
23. Deep Vellum
24. Dolly on Bishop
25. Jade & Clover
26. Mosaic Makers Collective
27. Rocket Fizz
28. Sneaker Politics
29. Spinster Records
30. The Shed
31. The Wild Detectives

693

BEST MUSEUMS IN FORT WORTH CULTURAL DISTRICT

Amon Carter Museum of American Art *(free)* Showcases works by some of the nation's most famous painters and sculptors.

Kimbell Art Museum *(free)* Has a small but surprising collection that allows you to hone in on single masterpieces like Caravaggio's *The Cardsharps* or El Greco's *Portrait of Dr Francisco de Pisa*.

The Modern *(adult/child $16/free)* Inside a building that appears to float above the surrounding reflecting pools, the Modern hosts groundbreaking contemporary exhibitions.

National Cowgirl Museum *(adult/child $12/6)* Explores the myth and reality of cowgirls in American culture, with interactive exhibits.

Fort Worth Museum of Science & History *(adult/child $16/12)* Kid-friendly galleries brimming with fossils, astronomy thrills and fun things to do.

Ferris wheel, State Fair of Texas

Wild Detectives *(thewilddetectives.com)*, a tiny but well curated bookstore with good coffee and a small bar.

A Famous Fair
Rides, snacks and entertainment

Held from late September through mid-October, the massive **State Fair of Texas** *(bigtex.com; adult/child $25/18)* is a showcase for carnivalesque amusement. Come ride one of the tallest Ferris wheels in North America, eat corn dogs (invented here), and browse the prize-winning cows, sheep and quilts. You can also enjoy concerts, parades, fireworks and more. Admission varies by day (from $15).

Taste the Wild West in Fort Worth Stockyards
A world of cowboys and longhorns

Twice a day (at 11:30am and 4pm) in Fort Worth's famous **Stockyards** district, you can catch the legendary Cattle Drive. Cowboys wearing authentic 19th-century garb drive 17 or so longhorn cattle of the Fort Worth herd up the dusty road. Spectators line E Exchange Ave and an announcer gives insight into the cattle drives of old.

Come sundown, the place to be is **Billy Bob's Texas** *(billybobstexas.com)*, a former cattle barn that today houses the world's largest honky-tonk (stretching across 100,000 sq ft). Top country stars, DJs and house bands perform on two stages. Friday and Saturday nights see live bull riding in the indoor arena.

Alternatively, the 3400-seat **Cowtown Coliseum** *(cowtowncoliseum.com)*, built in 1908 to host the first-ever indoor rodeos, hosts live rodeo at 7:30pm on Friday and Saturday nights year-round.

WANDER THE HISTORIC STOCKYARDS

See why Fort Worth was the gateway to the West as you explore the hidden attractions of the Historic Stockyards.

START	END	LENGTH
Exchange Ave	Exchange Ave	3/4 mile; 1½ hours

Follow the sidewalk along brick-lined Exchange Ave past the 1 **Fort Worth Stock Yards sign** that dates from 1910. Set back from the road is the 2 **Cowtown Coliseum**, setting for weekend rodeos and other events. If the doors are open, wander inside for a look at photos and memorabilia from legendary rodeo performers of the past. Next door, the 3 **Livestock Exchange** once served as the offices for cattle traders and occasional longhorn auctions are still held (nowadays via video-satellite feed). You can freely wander the old building; a small museum in back gives insight into the people and events that shaped the Stockyards. Head over to the 4 **viewing deck** above the corral for a look at the Fort Worth herd. A signpost has pictures and descriptions of each animal. Across Exchange Ave, the 5 **Stockyards Station**, which opened in 1876, was used to ship cattle by rail to markets in Kansas City. Though it's now a mall, peek down the corridors to see old photos from the past.

Continue to shop-lined 6 **Mule Alley** and take the small lane down to 7 **Marine Creek**, a trickling waterway where you can sometimes spot herons and other wading birds. Follow the peaceful 8 **waterside path** under Exchange Ave before returning once again to the bustle of the Stockyards, with its myriad shopping and dining options.

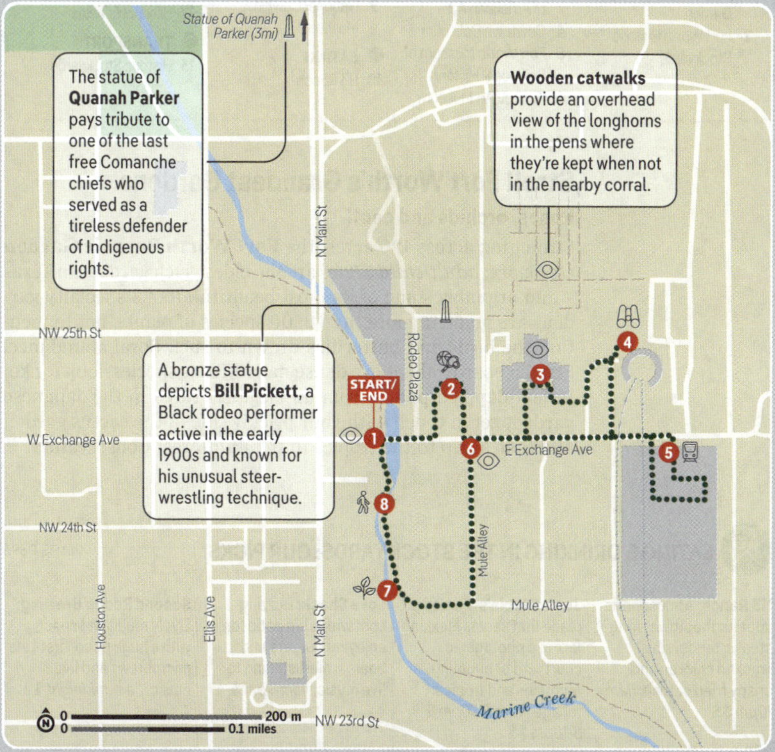

Statue of Quanah Parker (3mi)
The statue of Quanah Parker pays tribute to one of the last free Comanche chiefs who served as a tireless defender of Indigenous rights.
Wooden catwalks provide an overhead view of the longhorns in the pens where they're kept when not in the nearby corral.
A bronze statue depicts Bill Pickett, a Black rodeo performer active in the early 1900s and known for his unusual steer-wrestling technique.
START/END
N Main St
Rodeo Plaza
NW 25th St
W Exchange Ave
E Exchange Ave
NW 24th St
Mule Alley
Houston Ave
Ellis Ave
NW 23rd St
Marine Creek
0 200 m
0 0.1 miles

HIGHLIGHTS
1. Fort Worth Botanic Garden
2. Fort Worth Historic Stockyards

SIGHTS
3. Amon Carter Museum of American Art
4. Cowtown Coliseum
5. Fort Worth Museum of Science & History
6. Kimbell Art Museum
7. Modern
8. Mule Alley
9. National Cowgirl Museum

EATING
10. H3 Ranch
11. Love Shack

ENTERTAINMENT
12. Billy Bob's Texas

TRANSPORT
13. Historic Stockyards Station

Stroll Fort Worth's Grandest Gardens

Roses, orchids and cacti

Stretching across 120 acres, the **Fort Worth Botanic Garden** (*fwbg.org; adult/child $12/6*) are the oldest such gardens in Texas – and arguably some of its most beautiful. Its 23 specialty gardens are home to more than 2500 species of plants, not to mention the birds and butterflies drawn to such floral abundance. Stroll a boardwalk above dense native Texas species, look for koi in leaf-dappled ponds from an elegant bridge in the Japanese garden, get in touch with your prickly side in the cactus garden and take a trip to the tropics in the Rainforest Conservatory.

EATING & DRINKING IN THE STOCKYARDS: OUR PICKS — MAPS P696

H3 Ranch: Atmospheric spot for mouthwatering steaks, tender ribs, smoked chicken and crispy fried catfish. *11am-10pm* $$

Joe T Garcia's: Famed place that serves Mexican fare in a photogenic courtyard of bubbling fountains and tropical foliage. *11am-2:30pm & 5-10pm* $$

Love Shack: Buzzing spot with a big patio for enjoying burgers and beers while listening to live music. *11am-9pm* $

Second Rodeo Brewing: Lively multilevel space with a huge patio, first-rate microbrews and live music. *11am-midnight* $

Houston & the Gulf Coast

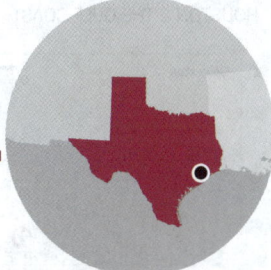

ARTS & ENTERTAINMENT | CUISINE & COCKTAILS | BEACHES

Houston's massive size places it among the top 10 US cities in both area and population, encompassing a fair bit of everything that makes Texas great. Big Oil brings in major investment in fine arts and public spaces, though you can still find cowboy boots and Texas swagger even here in the big city.

The city would take a lifetime to explore completely, but with just a few days it's easy to enjoy the highlights: downtown's revitalized Main St of bars and restaurants, the Museum District's excellent art and cultural centers, plus the indie shops and nightlife of Montrose. It's also worth setting aside a day to see NASA's Space Center Houston.

Houston makes a great starting point for a road trip down the Gulf Coast, which has hundreds of miles of beaches, historic settlements like Galveston and plenty of outdoor adventures – both on and off the water.

Modern Arts in the Museum District
Cutting-edge art and artists

The Museum District is home to a number of top-notch modern-art exhibition spaces.

If time is limited, focus on the fantastic **Museum of Fine Arts** *(mfah.org; adult/child $24/free)*, with thousands of works of art spread across three main buildings connected by underground tunnels (each a work of art itself). You could easily spend a day exploring the museum's permanent collections and special exhibitions.

GETTING AROUND

Downtown is quite compact and walkable. To travel elsewhere within the city, Houston's three METRORail train lines converge downtown around the square formed by Main, Rusk, Capitol and Fannin streets. Regular services connecting the Theater District and downtown to the Museum District, Hermann Park and NRG Stadium are convenient for travel across the limited route network. Heading down the Gulf Coast, you'll want a car. It's about a six-hour drive (370 miles) if making a straight shot from Houston to South Padre Island, though you could easily spend a few days stopping at coastal enclaves along the way.

☑ TOP TIP

Travelers exploring the Museum District in depth will benefit from the **CityPass** *(citypass.com/houston; adult/child $76/63)*, which includes entry to the Space Center Houston complex and the choice of four from the Museum of Fine Arts, Museum of Natural Science, Houston Zoo, Downtown Aquarium, Children's Museum and Kemah Boardwalk.

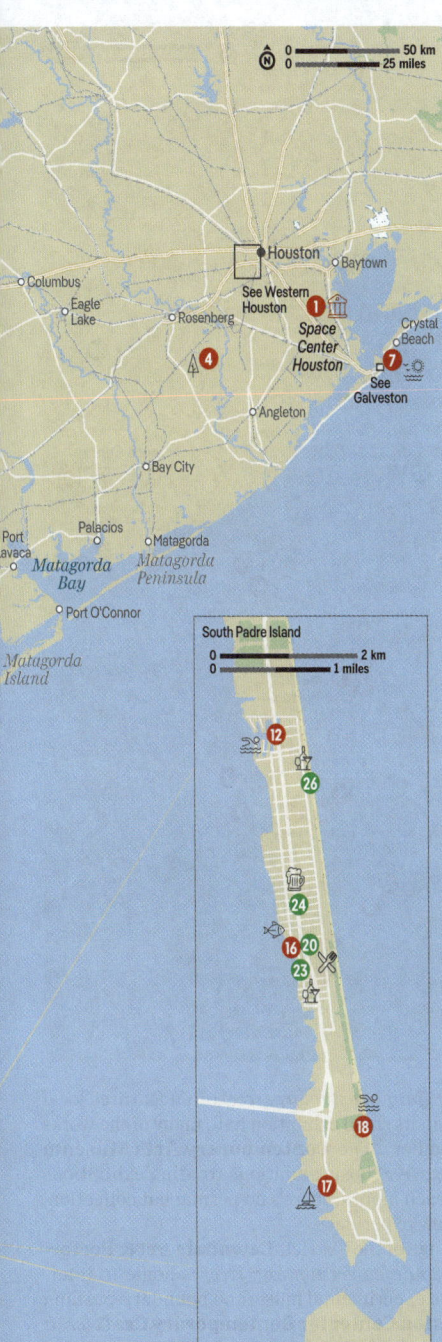

⭐ HIGHLIGHTS
1 Space Center Houston

● SIGHTS
2 Aransas National Wildlife Refuge
3 Bishop's Palace
4 Brazos Bend State Park
5 Bryan Museum
6 Buffalo Bayou Park
7 East Beach
8 IB Magee Beach Park
9 Moody Mansion
10 NRG Stadium
11 San José Island

● ACTIVITIES
12 Air Padre Kiteboarding
13 Deep Sea Headquarters
14 Fisherman's Wharf
15 Horace Caldwell Fishing Pier
16 Jim's Pier
17 The Original Dolphin Watch
18 Sonny's Beach Service

● EATING
19 Blood Bros BBQ
20 Grapevine Cafe
21 Pinkerton's Barbecue
22 Truth BBQ

● DRINKING & NIGHTLIFE
23 Louie's Backyard
24 Padre Island Brewing Company
25 Saint Arnold Brewing Company
26 Wanna Wanna Beach Bar & Grill

● ENTERTAINMENT
27 Grand 1894 Opera House

THE GUIDE

TEXAS HOUSTON & THE GULF COAST

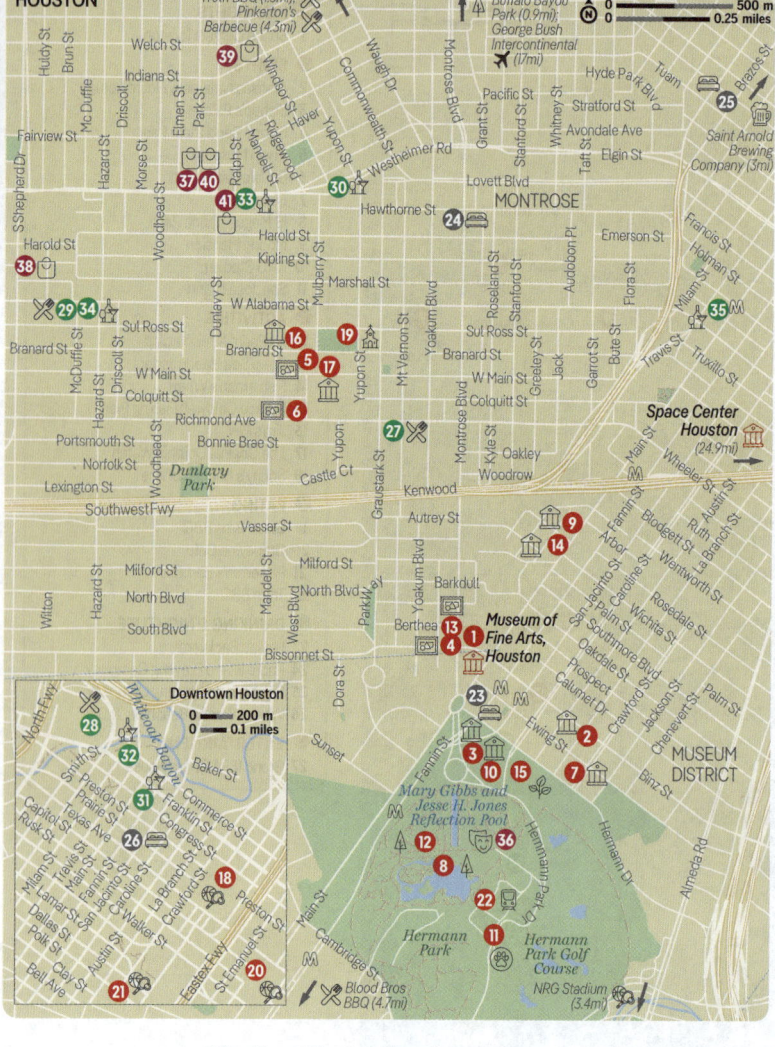

The **Jung Center** (*junghouston.org; free*) often features local and regional artists in its small exhibition hall; many of the works are for sale in the gallery. The **Contemporary Arts Museum Houston** (*camh.org; free*) hosts ambitious rotating exhibitions and several events each month; there's no permanent collection, so every visit is a new experience.

On the northern edge of the district, **Lawndale Art & Performance Center** (*lawndaleartcenter.org; free*) is home to interdisciplinary works of experimental music and boundary-pushing art. Next door, **Houston Center for Contemporary Craft** (*crafthouston.org; free*) is dedicated exclusively to crafts – the workers spaces here remain open in between rotating exhibits.

★ HIGHLIGHTS
1. Museum of Fine Arts, Houston

● SIGHTS
2. Children's Museum Houston
3. Cockrell Butterfly Center
4. Contemporary Arts Museum Houston
5. Cy Twombly Gallery
6. Dan Flavin Installation at Richmond Hall
7. Health Museum
8. Hermann Park
9. Houston Center for Contemporary Craft
10. Houston Museum of Natural Science
11. Houston Zoo
12. Japanese Garden
13. Jung Center
14. Lawndale Art & Performance Center
15. McGovern Centennial Gardens
16. Menil Collection
17. Menil Drawing Institute
18. Minute Maid Park
19. Rothko Chapel
20. Shell Energy Stadium
21. Toyota Center

● ACTIVITIES
22. Hermann Park Railroad

● SLEEPING
23. Hotel ZaZa
24. La Colombe d'Or Hotel
25. La Maison in Midtown
26. Magnolia Hotel

● EATING
27. Pit Room
28. POST Houston
29. Tacos Tierra Caliente

● DRINKING & NIGHTLIFE
30. Anvil Bar & Refuge
31. Captain Foxheart's Bad News Bar & Spirit Lodge
32. Houston Watch Company
33. Poison Girl
34. West Alabama Ice House
35. Winnie's

● ENTERTAINMENT
36. Miller Outdoor Theatre

● SHOPPING
37. BJ Oldies
38. Buffalo Exchange
39. Guild Shop
40. Old Blue House
41. Pavement

Explore Buffalo Bayou
Art-lined trails and skyscraper views

Just northwest of downtown, the 2.3-mile-long **Buffalo Bayou Park** is dotted throughout with public art, dog parks, sporting grounds, and even 250,000 Mexican free-tailed bats that depart en masse at sunset from their roosts under the Waugh Drive bridge. The most interesting section for visitors stretches along the south shore from the Sabine Street Water Works to Waugh Dr, an easy one-hour stroll that takes in the bulk of the permanent art installations and nice views of the bayou.

Dine & Dance at POST
Renovated food and events venue

On the edge of downtown, **POST Houston** (posthtx.com; 11am-9pm) is home to over 30 restaurants ranging from West African **ChòpnBlok** to a branch of beloved Austin-based Japanese street food **Eastside King** as well as tacos, fancy grilled cheese and others. Atop the building the 5-acre **Skylawn** offers superb views of the downtown skyline, and POST hosts markets, DJ nights, film screenings and other events.

A Walk in Hermann Park
Outdoor art and natural surroundings

The lawns of **Hermann Park** (hermannpark.org) make an excellent sunny-day outing. Squirrels and ducks wander freely through the 445-acre expanse, much of which is encircled by the small-gauge **Hermann Park Railroad** (full day $6) that makes a loop every 25 minutes. Stop at the meticulously planned **Japanese Garden** and the sculpture-filled spaces of the **McGovern Centennial Gardens** before checking the schedule at the **Miller Outdoor Theatre** (milleroutdoortheatre.com) for open-air performances.

BEST FESTIVALS IN HOUSTON

Houston Livestock Show & Rodeo: Join 2 million locals for rodeos, carnival rides and live music each February/March at NRG Stadium.

Art Car Parade: April's biggest bash features hundreds of mobile masterworks cruising downtown.

Art Bike Parade: A newish take on the Art Car concept now for human-powered locomotion, each May.

Pride Houston: The Pride Parade left its historic Montrose roots in 2015 for the wider streets of downtown each June.

Freedom Over Texas: Houston's biggest July 4th celebrations take place in Eleanor Tinsley Park.

Bayou City Art Festival: Enjoy October's lower temperatures at the outdoor art fest in Memorial Park.

TOP HOUSTON ATTRACTIONS FOR FAMILIES

Children's Museum Houston: Activity-filled museum, where little ones can learn how stuff works, create inventions, play games or draw in an open-air art studio.

Health Museum: More play space than museum with an oversized crawl-through colon, a 12ft-tall beating heart and brain displays.

Houston Museum of Natural Science: (HMNS) Covers archaeology to zoology and plenty in between.

Cockrell Butterfly Center: Watch winged species all around you, inside this separate-admission space in the HMNS.

Houston Zoo: Zookeeper talks, a large children's zoo with playgrounds and petting zoos, and highlights like the World of Primates (buy tickets ahead; *houstonzoo.org*) with raised wooden walkways through the animals' habitats.

Wandering Montrose
The best way to explore

A mashup of trendy and countercultural, Montrose mixes fancy cocktail bars with Texas icehouses (open-air taverns that sell cheap beer), and is one of Houston's most walkable districts. Hit the pavement for a stroll amid antique shops and colorful consignment stores, refreshing over cold drinks along the way.

The intersection of Dunlavy St and Westheimer Rd is a good starting point, where both **Old Blue House** and **BJ Oldies** are reliable sources of antiques and oddities. Surrounding here are numerous small stores of varying quality – **The Guild Shop** (*theguildshop.org*) is large enough to appeal to all sorts, while **Pavement** (*pavement.store*) and national chain **Buffalo Exchange** (*buffaloexchange.com*) focus exclusively on clothing at somewhat higher standards and corresponding prices.

After shopping, stop at local classic **Poison Girl** (*poisongirlbar.com*) for an excellent whiskey selection and generous happy hour, or **Anvil** (*anvilhouston.com*) for one of the city's best selections of cocktails – don't miss poorly hidden 'speakeasy' Refuge around back. Expect pure Texas vibes at **West Alabama Ice House** (*westalabamaicehouse.net*), where outdoor seating and good cheap beer attracts a cross-section of Montrose and Houston locals – as does excellent taco truck **Tierra Caliente** (*tacostierracalientemx.com*) across the street.

Arts in Montrose
Building on the Menils' vision

Spread across 30 acres on the southern side of Montrose, the **Menil Collection** (*menil.org*) galleries and installations are curated from the private holdings of Houston-based French philanthropists Dominique and John de Menil, who relocated here in the early 1940s. The main building – designed by Italian architect Renzo Piano – houses an eclectic collection spanning cubism and surrealism, African and Pacific tribal cultures, and far more.

Nearby, the **Dan Flavin Installation** and **Cy Twombly Gallery** both house permanent single-artist exhibitions – the latter building was custom-built for the purpose. The smaller galleries inside **Menil Drawing Institute** display regularly changing drawing exhibits. Between gallery visits, look for large-scale sculptural installations throughout the shady campus.

DRINKING IN HOUSTON: COCKTAIL BARS — MAPS P698, P700

Houston Watch Company: Dimly lit favorite off Main St with engaging bartenders and a generous happy hour. *4pm-2am Tue-Sat*

Captain Foxheart's Bad News Bar: Speakeasy with a budget-friendly happy hour and even better list of handcrafted cocktails. *5pm-2am*

Winnie's: Craft cocktails just barely edge out the excellent oysters and lunch menu for top spot here. *11am-10pm Mon-Thu, to 11pm Fri-Sun*

Saint Arnold Brewing Company: The big name in Houston brewing, straight from the source at its Fifth Ward brewpub and beer garden. *11am-10pm Sun-Thu, to 11pm Fri & Sat*

Alongside the Menil collections, **Rothko Chapel** *(rothko chapel.org)* is a nondenominational sacred space hung with 14 large-scale monotonal paintings by abstract expressionist Mark Rothko. The quiet, meditative chamber evokes strong feelings among Houstonians, particularly within the art community. In early 2024 an expansion to the site was announced to include an event plaza, meditation garden and program center to be completed in 2026.

All these galleries are free to the public; note that they're all closed Monday and Tuesday.

Journey into Outer Space
Exploring NASA's Space Center

A 30-minute drive southeast of downtown, Johnson Space Center has served as mission control for all NASA space flights to the present day starting with the Gemini 4 mission in 1965. The **Space Center Houston** *(spacecenter.org/visitor-information; adult/child $45/40)* complex showcases interactive exhibits and short films on the history of space flight, and artifacts from the US space program, including moon rocks and numerous vehicles used by NASA astronauts.

The most popular aspect for many visitors – and the only way the public can access the actual Johnson Space Center campus – are the NASA tram tours. Three separate itineraries travel to Rocket Park, Historic Mission Control tours (additional $15 surcharge) and the Astronaut Training Facility (available on a first-come, first-served basis, with reservations made at Guest Services).

You can save a few dollars (and time spent in line) by buying tickets in advance.

Gators in the Grasslands
Walking trails and wildlife in Brazos Bend

Alligators lie along the lake shores, wading birds and waterfowl calls echo through the live oak, and bird-watchers hunker behind waterfront blinds trying to capture it all at **Brazos Bend State Park** *(adult/child $7/free)*, just 45 miles south of Houston. Here 37 miles of walking trails make this a popular weekend getaway. Reserve ahead for fall and spring weekends, when the park fills to capacity.

CATCHING THE BIG GAME

During home games (baseball, basketball, football) fans flood into downtown stadiums as well as bars and restaurants in surrounding neighborhoods.

Houston Astros *(mlb.com/astros)* See baseball games at **Daikin Park**, on the edge of historic downtown, late March to early October.

Houston Rockets *(nba.com/rockets)* From October to April, basketball games take over the **Toyota Center** on the southeast edge of downtown.

Houston Dynamo *(houstondynamofc.com)* Soccer fans can get their fix at **Shell Energy Stadium** in East Downtown (EaDo) from February to October.

Houston Texans *(houstondynamofc.com)* Biggest of all are the football games happening at **NRG Stadium** from September to January. Though far from downtown, the stadium is easily reached on the Red Line METRORail.

EATING IN HOUSTON: BARBECUE

MAPS P698

Truth BBQ: Top-rated Texas barbecue joint. Expect a wait, but enjoy the views and smell of the smokers in the meantime. *hours vary* **$$$**

Pinkerton's Barbecue: Slow-smoked meat eaten at shared tables; a classic barbecue experience in the city. *11am-9pm Sun & Tue-Thu, to 10pm Fri & Sat* **$$$**

Blood Bros BBQ: Houston loves fusion; great meats here incorporate East Asian–inspired techniques and ingredients. *11am-3pm Wed-Sun, plus 6-9pm Thu-Sat* **$$**

The Pit Room: Neighborhood joint in Montrose equally popular for a lunch special or an after-hours cold one on the patio. *11am-9pm* **$$**

THE 1900 STORM

Once Texas' largest city and the nation's third-largest seaport, Galveston was dealt a devastating blow by a hurricane in 1900. Estimates show as many as one-fifth of the island's population died in the storm – making it the deadliest disaster in US history at the time – and around a quarter of the city's residents were left homeless.

In response, the city undertook massive public-works projects – raising the entire city by up to 11ft and constructing a 17ft seawall that would eventually extend 10 miles along the Gulf Coast. Galveston's economy never fully recovered, as ship traffic moved to nearby Houston and with it much of the income that made Galveston prosper.

Spoonbills, Aransas National Wildlife Refuge

Coastal Charm in Galveston
Architecture and beach-hopping

Part historic Southern town, part sunburned beach resort, Galveston Island is Houston's favorite seaside bolthole.

Self-guided tours of the **Grand 1894 Opera House** (thegrand.com; $5) offer visitors a peek behind the curtains of Texas' official opera house, though not backstage access.

The former Galveston Orphans' Home is now the **Bryan Museum** (thebryanmuseum.org; adult/child $15/free), with excellent exhibitions on Galveston and Texan history as well as an audio tour featuring residents' recollections of life in the Home.

Self-guided tours of both **Bishop's Palace** (galvestonhistory.org; adult/youth $15/12) and **Moody Mansion** (moodymansion.org; adult/youth $15/7) showcase the lifestyles of late-1800s Galveston elites, the latter boasting an excellent audioguide that adds familial context to the site.

After exploring the historic center, enjoy some downtime on the seaside. **East Beach** on the (eastern) tip of the island is party central in summer, but go west, and you'll pass miles of appealing beaches.

Hang out in Port Aransas
Texas' favorite coastal escape

On the northern tip of Mustang Island, Port Aransas is, for many lifelong Texans, the most appealing beach destination on this state's coast. The pace is relaxed, and daily life is dominated by beachgoing and sunset drinks. Connected to the mainland by a free ferry service, Port A feels like leaving real life behind.

IB Magee Beach Park and the **Horace Caldwell Fishing Pier** are great spots for swimming and fishing. Alternatively get in touch with outfitters like Texas Surf Camps (texassurfcamps.com) and Island Surf Rentals (islandsurfrentals.com) to add a bit of water-sports action to your trip. The latter has kayaks, beach bikes and paddle boards, in addition to surf gear, for rent.

Deep Sea Headquarters *(deepseaheadquarters.com)* arranges everything from half-day to offshore or overnight fishing trips. In addition, chartered trips of all sizes leave most days from **Fisherman's Wharf**, which is also home to dolphin tours, sunset cruises and the jetty boat that carries visitors across to the undeveloped **San José Island**.

Go Birding in Aransas NWR
A coastal driving tour

For bird-watchers, **Aransas National Wildlife Refuge** is a premier site on the Texas coast. More than 400 species have been documented here, and even people who don't carry binoculars and bird checklists get caught up in the frenzy. The scenery at Aransas NWR alone is spectacular. The blue Aransas Bay waters are speckled with green islets ringed with white sand. Native dune grasses blow gently in the breeze while songbirds provide background music. The easiest way to experience the refuge is by driving the 16-mile auto tour (starting on the road just past the visitor center), which features plenty of opportunities to stop and fish along piers, hike on nature trails or bird-watch from the observation tower.

Off-Shore Adventures in South Padre Island
Fun on the water

Near the southern tip of the Gulf Coast, the small resort town of South Padre Island is famed for its sparkling shoreline and clear waters. While the long beaches running through the city are built up and generally busy, miles and miles of undeveloped sand run to the Mansfield Cut channel at the north of the island.

The Laguna Madre is renowned for wind-powered water sports. You can take lessons or rent gear from **Air Padre Kiteboarding** *(airpadrekiteboarding.com)* or fly high with **Sonny's Beach Service** *(sonnysbeachservice.com)*, which offers parasailing.

For those looking for a more low-key adventure, there's kayaking and paddleboarding, along with a variety of boat trips. The **Original Dolphin Watch** *(theoriginaldolphinwatch.com)* heads out multiple times a day to get a glimpse at the pods of dolphins that call this area home.

FISHING ON SOUTH PADRE

No matter which chartered fishing guide you go with, there's a good chance you'll start and end your trip at **Jim's Pier** on the bay side of South Padre Island. This is the main dock at SPI for getting on and off boats, and it's also a fully stocked bait and tackle shop. In addition, if you need advice or help finding a guide to match what you want to do, the staff at Jim's Pier has a list of guides they can get you in contact with. They also offer fish-cleaning services after your trip. Prices vary depending on the type of fish you catch, but it's usually a couple of dollars per fish to have them fileted right there for you.

 EATING & DRINKING AT SOUTH PADRE ISLAND: OUR PICKS — MAPS P698

| **Padre Island Brewing Company:** Burgers, pizza and seafood with freshly brewed beer on tap. *11:30am-10pm Mon-Sat, to 9pm Sun* $$ | **Grapevine Cafe:** Great choice for breakfast and lunch with coffee beans roasted in-house. *7:30am-3pm* $$ | **Louie's Backyard:** Iconic SPI hang-out on the bayside with fireworks every Friday during summer (June to August). *11:30am-2am* | **Wanna Wanna Beach Bar & Grill:** Longtime favorite tiki bar steps from the sand that's known for its turbo piña coladas. *11:30am-10pm* |

West Texas & Big Bend National Park

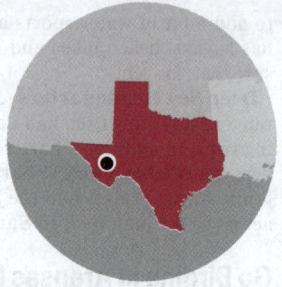

OUTDOOR ADVENTURES | DESERT LANDSCAPES | ART-LOVING TOWNS

GETTING AROUND

Public transit is limited and inconvenient beyond El Paso, and it won't get you to Big Bend National Park. Amtrak trains stop in El Paso and Alpine, while Greyhound buses connect El Paso to Fort Stockton for buses to Marfa and Alpine.

You'll need a car to experience West Texas fully. Rent a vehicle at the airport in El Paso or pick up a Jeep rental in Alpine. You'll want a high-clearance 4WD vehicle if backcountry driving is on your itinerary. Fly into El Paso International Airport to minimize your drive time to Big Bend National Park.

West Texas is home to the tallest mountains in the state, some of the darkest skies in the world, two national parks and a vast canyon that's second in size to the Grand Canyon. The only major city in the area is El Paso, which is closer to San Diego, California, than it is to Houston or Dallas.

The region's biggest attraction is Big Bend National Park, where mountain peaks soar above a vast unforgiving desert, while the Rio Grande winds its ways past steep canyons carved out of limestone. Amid this 1252-square-mile wilderness, there are ample opportunities for hiking, camping, backcountry driving, stargazing and even paddling along the Rio Grande River.

Quirky small towns fill the gaps between large swaths of unspoiled nature and sprawling ranches. Visit art galleries, shop independent boutiques, listen to small-town jam sessions or dive deep into Texas history.

The Artistry of Alpine
Mural-filled town

Set at the foot of the Davis Mountains, the railroad and ranching town of Alpine might be West Texas' best-kept secret. Independent boutiques, antique stores and lively coffee shops line streets that feel like a movie set. Murals are everywhere – even in the alleys. And when the light hits the mountains around golden hour, it's easy to see why artists are drawn to this place.

☑ TOP TIP

Big Bend is a hot desert park, and heat advisories are common, even in the fall. Avoid long hikes during the middle of the day, drink lots of water, use sunscreen and wear protective clothing, and carry extra water with you in case of an emergency.

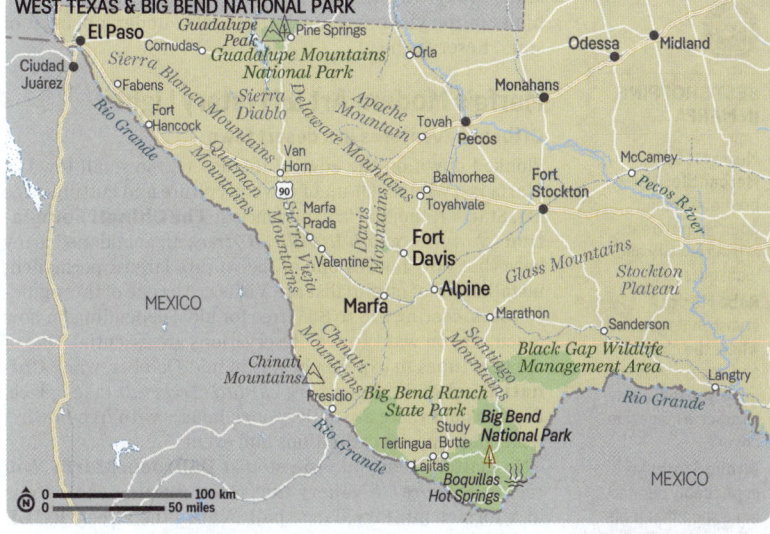

Checkout the **Welcome to Alpine** mural down the street from the historic **Holland Hotel** and the **Cattle Drive** mural across the street. Pop into the **Big Bend Gallery** (*facebook.com/bigbendartscouncil.org*) to shop for pieces from local artists that are more affordable than you might expect. Then go to the **Museum of the Big Bend** (*museumofthebigbend.com; adult/child $10/free*) for a hefty dose of West Texas–inspired fine art.

From the Springs to the Stars
Stellar highlights near Fort Davis

The **Fort Davis National Historic Site** (*nps.gov/foda; per vehicle $20*) protects a beautifully sited frontier fort established in 1854, at the northeast edge of modern Fort Davis (town). Staffed exclusively by Black soldiers between 1867 and 1881, it was abandoned in 1891, but today you can explore five of the remaining buildings set amid scores of ruins.

Thirty-three miles north of Fort Davis, **Balmorhea State Park** (*tpwd.texas.gov/state-parks/balmorhea; adult/child $7/free*) is a literal oasis in the West Texas desert. This state park is home to the world's largest spring-fed swimming pool (maximum depth 25ft), offering snorkelers and divers a chance to swim with turtles, catfish, minnows and endangered fish like the Pecos gambusia and Comanche Springs pupfish. If you're traveling during the summer, purchase day passes in advance online.

One of the best parties in West Texas starts after sunset high in the Fort Davis mountains. Here at the **McDonald Observatory** (*mcdonaldobservatory.org; adult/child $25/20*), astronomers lead visitors on a guided tour of the constellations in the night sky. Guests at these Star Parties can peek

STARGAZING IN BIG BEND

Big Bend National Park is home to some of the darkest skies in the world, and it's one of best places in North America for stargazing. National park rangers offer regular night sky programs, including moonlight walks and star parties.

For the best views of the starry skies here, give your eyes a chance to adjust to the dark. It typically take about a half-hour for eyes to acclimate to total darkness, but once they do, you'll be able to see many more stars than perhaps you thought possible. Using a phone can disrupt your night vision, so keep it in your pocket and opt for a red LED light if needed.

BEST SHOPPING IN MARFA

Marfa Mood Mercantile: A tiny boutique selling gourmet pet treats, artisan jewelry and local gifts.

Raba Marfa: A stylish vintage store where the clothes and accessories will make you feel ready to grace a magazine cover.

Wrong Store: An impeccably curated indie shop that feels more like a gallery of unique treasures.

Cactus Liquors: Obscure spirits, unique beers, fine wines and a walk-up window.

Cobra Rock: Pick up a pair of custom-made handcrafted leather boots.

Texas Rose: Shop for West Texas–inspired art, clothing and accessories.

Garza Marfa: A chic furniture and textiles store.

at the Milky Way through powerful telescopes, check out exhibits in the visitors center, or just relax under a blanket of stars. Reserve ahead.

Marfa's Modern Art & Mystery Lights
Offbeat adventures in a desert town

Plonked down on the edge of the desert, the small town of Marfa is a wild mash-up of cowboy culture and cutting-edge art. Start off the Marfa experience at **The Chinati Foundation** (chinati.org; adult/child $37/free), an abandoned army base that now houses one of the world's largest permanent installations of minimalist art. Visits are by one of three guided tours, costing $15 to $35 (free for kids) depending on how much art you want to see. Reservations are essential. One of the best times to experience it is in mid-October, when **Chinati Weekend** (chinati.org/chinati-weekend) takes place. For two days there are gallery open houses with free-flowing wine, plus special exhibitions and events.

No matter when you visit, stop at **Ballroom Marfa** (ballroommarfa.org), a gallery that hosts rotating exhibitions in a former military dance hall. Across the street, **RULE Gallery** (rulegallery.com) shows contemporary abstract and conceptual photography, sculpture and paintings in a space that's also the curator's home. For the latest information on events and exhibits, check out the Marfa Gallery Guide (marfagalleryguide.com).

After sundown, keep an eye out of the **Marfa Mystery Lights**. For more than a century, people have watched unexplained glowing orbs appear on the horizon. Stop at the **Marfa Lights Viewing Area** (on Highway 90) east of Marfa and see if you can spot them for yourself.

Adventures in Big Bend National Park
Where the mountains meet the desert

Big Bend National Park (nps.gov/bibe; per vehicle $30) boasts more than 150 miles of hiking trails. An excellent introduction to the park's varied landscapes is the 4.8-mile round-trip Lost Mine Trail. The gently sloping switchbacks climb over 1000ft through a cool, shaded forest of juniper, oak and pine trees. Take in views of Juniper Canyon and Casa Grande Peak as you approach the main viewpoint, from where cliffs, craggy peaks and lush canyons are everywhere you look.

WHERE TO EAT & DRINK IN MARFA: OUR PICKS

Para Llevar: Wood-fired sourdough pizzas, sandwiches and salads in an upscale bodega and wine shop. *11am-8pm* $$

Angel's Restaurant: A casual spot for authentic Mexican food. Try the smothered burrito, chili relleno or enchiladas. *7am-8pm Mon-Sat, 8am-2pm Sun* $

Planet Marfa: A quirky beer garden with free peanuts and a surprisingly good menu. *1-10pm, to midnight Fri & Sat* $

Marfa Spirit Co: A distillery and tasting room that feels like a favorite neighborhood bar. *3-11pm Thu-Sat, 11am-7pm Sun*

After a day on the trail, head to **Boquillas Hot Springs**, a secluded 105°F pool overlooking the Rio Grande. Be prepared: it's a half-mile (round-trip) hike to the springs, and there are no changing facilities (bathing suits required).

River trips can range from a few hours to a few days. **Angell Expeditions** *(angellexpeditions.com)* offers guided raft, canoe and kayaking trips as does **Big Bend River Tours** *(bigbendrivertours.com)*.

Climb the Highest Peak in Texas

Trails of the Guadalupe Mountains

In a remote desert setting near the border of Texas and New Mexico, **Guadalupe Mountains National Park** *(nps.gov/gumo/index; adult/child $10/free)* has jagged peaks, spires and canyons. There are more than 80 miles of trails here, though most people have their sights set on climbing Guadalupe Peak, the state's highest point at 8751ft. Spectacular views await on the strenuous ascent (3000ft elevation gain) on the 8.5-mile round-trip hike.

● SIGHTS
1. Ballroom Marfa
2. Chinati Foundation

● EATING
3. Angel's Restaurant
4. Para Llevar

● DRINKING & NIGHTLIFE
5. Marfa Spirit Co
6. Planet Marfa

● SHOPPING
7. Cactus Liquors
8. Cobra Rock
9. Garza Marfa
10. Marfa Mood Mercantile
11. Raba Marfa
12. Texas Rose
13. Wrong Store

PALO DURO ESSENTIALS

Hiking Ample water is crucial. The park recommends one quart per person per hour. Start early. You'll beat the crowds and have a better chance to see wildlife by heading out around dawn.

Food The **Trading Post** (about 2.5 miles past the visitor center) has breakfast sandwiches, burgers, fries, ice cream and other snacks. Open 9:30am to 6pm.

Camping The park has four different camping areas ($16 to $26 per site), including one spot (**Fortress Cliff** area) for tent campers only. Several first-come, first-served permits for hike-in primitive camping ($12) are also available.

Cabins and glamping Cabins range from rustic to well equipped ($50 to $160). Several have stunning views. There's also luxury glamping tents ($300).

Buddy Holly Center

The Canyons & High Plains of the Panhandle
Scenic drive through Texas' northwest

Home to wildlife-rich canyons, shortgrass prairies and empty highways stretching beneath big open skies, the Texas Panhandle makes a memorable setting for a road trip.

Start off in the sizable town of **Lubbock**. Learn about an early rock-and-roll legend on a visit to the **Buddy Holly Center** (ci.lubbock.tx.us/departments/buddy-holly-center; adult/child $10/5). Afterwards, take a journey into the past at the **Museum of Texas Tech University** (depts.ttu.edu/museumttu; admission free), which also displays textiles and pottery from some 20 different Southwest Native American tribes. Next door the **National Ranching Heritage Center** (ranchingheritage.org; free), follow a 1.5-mile path around a historical park containing 19th- and early-20th-century buildings, including an old schoolhouse, a rural church and vintage windmills.

From Lubbock, get behind the wheel for the 100-mile drive up to **Caprock Canyons State Park** (adult/child $5/free), home to 26 miles of rugged trails, plus prairie-dog towns and freely roaming bison.

Back in the car, drive 90 miles northwest to reach **Palo Duro Canyon State Park** (adult/child $8/free), home to the second-largest canyon in the United States. You'll find some impressive hiking trails including the famous 2.8-mile (one way) Lighthouse Trail, which takes you to a 312ft monolith.

End your journey in the city of **Amarillo** (25 miles northwest of the canyon). Here you can refuel at the **Big Texan** (bigtexan.com), a huge kitschy steakhouse. Nearby, you can explore some of the curious sites sprinkled along old Route 66, like the **Cadillac Ranch**, which features a row of Cadillacs, buried hood first, near a wheat field 10 miles west of Amarillo.

DISCOVER DOWNTOWN EL PASO

Visit free museums and a beautifully restored theater from the 1930, take in public art and shop for bargains in the heart of the city.

START	END	LENGTH
El Paso Museum of History	Plaza Hotel Pioneer Park	1.2 miles; 2-3 hours

Start at the ❶ **El Paso Museum of History**, in the heart of the downtown museum district, to learn how city evolved from a railroad stop into a vibrant multicultural destination. Continue along N Santa Fe St to browse the Southwestern art at the ❷ **El Paso Museum of Art** (admission free), founded in 1959 and housed in a former Greyhound station.

Next head to the nearby ❸ **Plaza Theatre**. The 1930s single-screen movie theater is an impressive example of Spanish Colonial Revival architecture and was almost demolished in the 1980s. Schedule your visit around one of the theater's free tours.

Across the street, pop into the ❹ **Hotel Paso del Norte** to admire the Tiffany Glass dome above the bar.

Check out the public art work ❺ **Bienvenido**, a giant yellow door installed in 2021; it's one of many works you'll find in downtown. While here make a detour down ❻ **El Paso St**.

Finish at the ❼ **Plaza Hotel Pioneer Park**, where you can admire the Texas decor before heading up to its La Perla rooftop bar for a drink.

El Paso Museum of Art has a small space that also pays homage to the late musical icon Selena.

Elizabeth Taylor once lived in the penthouse at **Plaza Hotel**; the bar – which offers some of the best mountain views in the city – was once her terrace.

Pop into **Dave's A Pawn Shop** while on El Paso St; it's one of the oddest retail experiences in the city. Shop for bargains while admiring well-preserved architecture.

Places We Love to Stay

$ Budget $$ Midrange $$$ Top End

Austin
MAPS P671, 672, 674

Firehouse Hostel $ Hostel with shared dorms and private suites. Find the speakeasy behind the reception's bookshelf.

The Driskill $$ Legendary hotel on 6th Street that's been in business since 1886. The site of LBJ and Lady Bird's first date – and supposedly haunted, as well.

Hotel Van Zandt $$ Enjoy in-suite record players, live music in the restaurant and a rooftop pool, with quick access to Rainey St.

ARRIVE Austin $$ This chic 2019 build along the bars, restaurants and music venues of E 6th is a local landmark thanks to its unique exterior architecture.

Austin Motel $$ This historic 1938 spot has a riot of rainbow colors in its quirky rooms – and one of the most famous neon signs in town.

Hotel San José $$ Bungalow-style hotel with roots dating back to the 1930s. Rooms surround the courtyard lounge that's a favorite hang-out spot for locals.

Carpenter Hotel $$ Prime location that's a short walk away from Zilker Park, Barton Springs and Lady Bird Lake.

South Congress Hotel $$$ A hip boutique hotel with a sexy rooftop pool and the home of Café No Sé, one of the best dessert spots in all of Austin.

San Antonio
MAP P682

Hotel Havana $$ Quiet location set apart from other River Walk hotels by Cuba-inspired, boho-chic rooms from Texas design guru and hotelier Liz Lambert.

Menger Hotel $$ You can't get closer to the Alamo than this historic hotel, built next door just 23 years after the famous battle.

Ranch Motel & Leisure Club $$ On the edge of Brackenridge Park, this 1940s motel was given a contemporary makeover without losing its vintage charm.

Omni La Mansión Del Rio $$$ Luxe property in the middle of the River Walk born out of 19th-century religious-school buildings in the Spanish-Mexican hacienda style.

Hotel Emma $$$ The epicenter of the Pearl District blends Victorian-era decor with post-industrial edge, while guest rooms evoke a stylish but understated Texas ranch.

Hill Country

Peach Tree Inn & Suites $ Less than a 10-minute walk to Fredericksburg's Main St, this homey place offers good value for its quiet rooms and spacious suites.

The Vaquero Motel $ The rooms at this well-maintained Bandera motel have a rustic, Western design with chunky wood furnishings. It's an easy walk to bars and restaurants.

The Kendall $$ This charming Southern Colonial-style inn on Cibolo Creek in Boerne has one-of-a-kind rooms, including one set in a converted chapel.

Gruene Mansion Inn $$$ This cluster of buildings in Gruene is practically its own village, with atmospheric rooms in the mansion, a former carriage house and the old barns.

Dallas
MAP P693

Magnolia Hotel $$ In a 29-story 1922 building, the Magnolia is an old classic with good prices for the no-nonsense rooms and a great location.

Canvas Hotel $$ Rooms have exposed-brick walls and big windows in this former industrial space turned boutique hotel. Rooftop pool and other inviting common areas.

The Bishop Arts Hotel by Q Resorts $$ About a half-mile north of Bishop Arts, this good-value but unstaffed place has sunny rooms and a small dip pool.

The Joule $$$ Aside from well-equipped rooms with rain showers and spa amenities, this neo-Gothic beauty has an art-filled lobby, stylish eateries and cantilevered rooftop pool.

Fort Worth

Stockyards Hotel $$ This 1907 gem has Western-themed art, handsome cowboy-inspired rooms and a grand Old West lobby.

Miss Molly's $$ The former boarding house turned bordello currently enjoys a third act as an eight-room, possibly haunted guesthouse with antique Western-style decor.

The Ashton Hotel $$ Wide range of comfy rooms (including spa suites) in a six-story building dating back to 1915 with a great location off Sundance Sq.

Hotel Drover $$$ Fort Worth's best hotel has rustic-chic rooms, beautiful outdoor spaces, and atmospheric eating and drinking options.

Houston   MAP P700

Magnolia Hotel $$ Stylish velvet- and damask-layered rooms in this 1926 downtown favorite, once home to the *Houston Post & Dispatch* printers.

La Maison in Midtown $$ One of very few excellent B&Bs in Houston, surrounded by appealing dining and nightlife.

Hotel ZaZa $$$ Hip and flamboyant, from bordello-esque colors to zebra-accent chairs, ZaZa is good fun.

La Colombe d'Or $$$ A museum-like interior and refined French dining in the heart of Montrose keep this luxury suites popular.

Gulf Coast

Manor on 17th $$ Beautifully-renovated 1890 mansion in Galveston's East End with complimentary 4pm happy hour each day and nightcaps every evening.

The Tarpon Inn $$ Rebuilt after several hurricanes, this Port Aransas island mainstay has been operating in some form since 1900.

Dancing Dunes $$ Five funky beach cabins in Port Aransas around a connecting porch have a fun, ramshackle atmosphere.

Isla Grand Beach Resort $$ Longtime South Padre Island favorite on the beach with two great pools if you don't want to get super sandy.

Big Bend & West Texas   MAP P709

Ocotillos Village $ A collection of handsomely designed A-frame cabins in Terlingua, with outdoor showers and shared indoor bathroom facilities a few steps away.

Holland Hotel (p707) **$** This historic property in the heart of Alpine has a gorgeous courtyard, freshly renovated lobby and rooms full of character.

Maverick Inn $ This southwestern-style property in Alpine looks like it came out of an old Western. It has 21 guest rooms, a pool and is pet friendly.

El Cosmico $$ Designed by famed hotelier Liz Lambert, this camp-style bohemian property in Marfa rents teepees, trailers and safari tents with outdoor showers.

Hotel Limpia $$ This charming historic hotel in Fort Davis is the ideal place to lay your head after a Star Party at McDonald Observatory. Take your pick from Victorian-style rooms, 1920s-era guest suites or budget-friendly rooms.

Gage Hotel $$$ This luxurious southwestern-style hotel in Marathon is true Texas treasure and the closest hotel to Big Bend National Park.

Hotel Emma

Researched and curated by Liza Prado

Rocky Mountains

EPIC BEAUTY MEETS OUTDOOR ADVENTURE

A four-state wonderland of mountains, rivers and alpine forests, renowned for outdoor adventuring and rich in history, arts, small-town life and urban centers.

Welcome to the Rocky Mountains, where the Great Plains meet the rugged backbone of the continent. It's a vast region, rife with towering peaks and glacial lakes, dense forests and rushing rivers. Also red-rock canyons and sand dunes, volcano-scapes and hot springs. It's a veritable playground for outdoors enthusiasts, with eight national parks and over 100 million acres of public land. World-class skiing? Check. Epic rafting and fly-fishing? Check. Hiking, climbing and mountain biking? Check, check, check. The ways and places to get an adrenaline rush are nearly endless.

But there's more to the Rockies than the outdoors. History is visible everywhere – cliff dwellings, battlefields, ghost towns and trading posts turned forts…even some of the world's best dinosaur sites. Collectively, they tell the multilayered history of the West: one of survival and conflict, fortune-seeking and possibility.

And the Rocky Mountain region continues to evolve. Today, it has a wealth of terrific cities, from Denver to Boulder, Missoula to Boise, each with engaging museums and performing arts, plus nightlife, craft breweries and culinary excellence (hello Michelin stars). Prefer something smaller? Check out historic towns turned glitzy destinations like Aspen, Jackson and Ketchum.

To visit the Rocky Mountains is to have at your fingertips spectacular landscapes, rich history, and thriving urban and small town life – the hard part is deciding where to go.

HARRY HAYASHI/SHUTTERSTOCK

THE MAIN AREAS

COLORADO
Year-round outdoors options and great cities. **p720**

WYOMING
Yellowstone, Indigenous sites and rural life. **p749**

MONTANA
Mountains, rivers and a youthful vibe. **p763**

IDAHO
Underrated destination with stunning landscapes. **p777**

For places to stay in the Rocky Mountains, see p788

Bison, Yellowstone National Park (p758)

Find Your Way

The Rocky Mountain states cover a vast and varied region, extending 1100 miles from the towering sand dunes of southern Colorado to the stunning glacial-carved peaks of northern Montana. The Rocky Mountains themselves are the backbone of it all.

Idaho, p777

A secret stash of stunning landscapes, with evocative names like Sawtooth Mountains and Craters of the Moon, plus charming towns like Boise and Ketchum.

Wyoming, p749

A place of contrasts, from the captivating beauty of Yellowstone and Grand Tetons to stark high plains, windblown towns and compelling Indigenous sites.

CAR

To fully explore the region, you'll need a car. It'll give you freedom to stop in small towns, explore national parks and forests, tour archaeological zones, and access trailheads and ski resorts, all at your own pace. In winter, consider a 4WD vehicle.

BUS

Bus service is limited. Greyhound travels between the bigger cities in the Rocky Mountain region (and beyond), while smaller companies like Bustang, Jefferson Lines and Salt Lake Express provide service to a handful of small towns in each state.

PLANE

Flying within the region cuts down your travel time tremendously – a plus if you're short on time or hate long-haul drives. Denver has the only major international airport in the Rocky Mountain region, but there are several small airports scattered around each state.

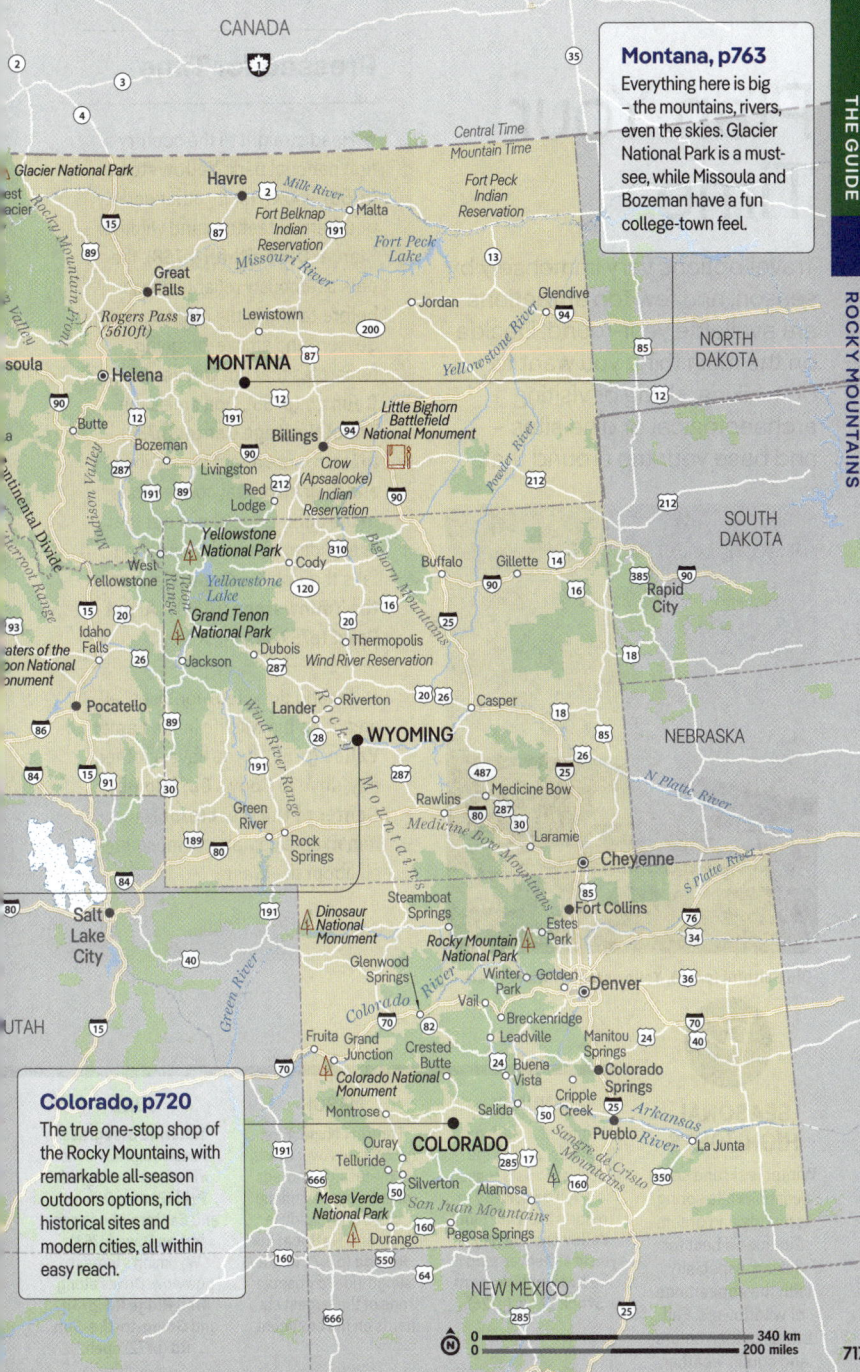

Plan Your Time

Travel options vary immensely by season, and few top attractions are available year-round. Decide on the main thing you want to do – hiking, skiing or visiting archaeological or dino sites – and base your trip around that.

Old Faithful (p758), Yellowstone National Park

Pressed for Time

● Head straight to the country's first national park: **Yellowstone** (p758), known for its otherworldly geothermal features and wildlife. Start at **Old Faithful** (p758), the park's famously reliable geyser, before taking in the other gushing geysers and smoke-belching fumaroles that dot **Geyser Country** (p758). Don't miss the **Tribal Heritage Center** (p759) to learn more about local tribes and their ancestral connections to the park. Later, check out the astounding views of thundering falls through the **Grand Canyon of the Yellowstone** (p759) – **Artist Point** (p759) is a must see.

● Around dusk, look for bison, elk and other big wildlife in the **Lamar Valley** (p759). If you have another day, drive to Cody's **Buffalo Bill Center of the West** (p756), a remarkable complex of museums all about the West.

SEASONAL HIGHLIGHTS

Winter is ski and snow season, while spring is muddy and green. Summer is best for hiking, especially with the appearance of wildflowers. Fall brings golden colors and cooler weather.

JANUARY
Winter storms dump powder across the Rockies, and ski season is in full gear. Head to resorts like **Vail**, **Sun Valley** and **Big Sky**. If you're in Denver, stop in the **National Western Stock Show** (p726).

MARCH
Treefort Music Fest (p779) takes over Boise, showcasing hundreds of indie bands and the city's artsy spirit. In Jackson's **National Elk Refuge** (p757), take a sleigh-ride to observe one of the largest elk herds on the continent.

JUNE
Telluride Bluegrass Festival (p743) kicks off summer along with **PrideFest** in Denver and **Eastern Shoshone Indian Days** (p753), Wyoming's largest powwow. Drives along **Trail Ridge Rd** (p731) and **Going-to-the-Sun Rd** (p772) open.

A Weeklong Road Trip

● With some room to breathe, start in **Mesa Verde National Park** (p740), known for its impressive cliff dwellings, and take a ranger-led tour – prepare to climb ladders and crawl through tunnels. Next drive to **Telluride** (p743), a charming mountain town tucked into a box canyon, and hike to Colorado's tallest waterfall, **Bridal Veil Falls** (p743).

● Bright and early, straight-shot it to **Black Canyon of the Gunnison National Park** (p744) for the spectacular canyon vistas along South Rim Rd. From there, drive to **Dinosaur National Monument** (p745), making sure to see the Quarry Wall, with some 1500 dino bones embedded in it. Next, spend time in **Grand Teton National Park** (p762), taking in its jagged peaks and shimmering lakes before ending your trip in **Yellowstone** (p758).

Two Weeks to Travel Around

● Begin your Rocky Mountain odyssey in **Denver** (p724), soaking in its urban energy. From there, head to **Rocky Mountain National Park** (p530) for epic hiking on alpine trails and wildflower-filled meadows. Take **Trail Ridge Rd** (p531) through the park before crossing into Wyoming.

● Continue to cowboy chic **Jackson**, making time to visit **National Museum of Wildlife Art** (p757) before exploring the majestic **Grand Teton National Park** (p762). Drive into Idaho though the gorgeous **Teton Valley** to the volcanic landscapes of **Craters of the Moon** (p786). From there, cross into Montana – big sky country – stopping at the vibrant **Missoula People's Market** (p771) before exploring **Glacier National Park** (p772) on foot, wheels or boat. Wrap up your trip at iconic **Yellowstone** (p758).

JULY
Crested Butte's **Wildflower Festival** (p738), Cheyenne's **Frontier Days** (p751) and **Sun Valley Music Festival** (p784). The mountains fill with hikers and campers, and paddlers take on the rivers.

SEPTEMBER
Cooler days begin and crowds disperse – a good time to visit national parks like **Yellowstone** (p758), **Glacier** (p772) and **Mesa Verde**. Listen for the bugling elks in **Rocky Mountain National Park** (p730).

OCTOBER
Aspen paints the region in brilliant yellows; **Grand Teton National Park** (p762) and **Million Dollar Hwy** are beautiful. **Colorado National Monument** (p746) and **Craters of the Moon** (p786) cool off, optimal for outdoor adventure.

DECEMBER
Powder hounds hit the slopes, though the snow can be hit or miss (discounted lift tickets make up for it). Hot springs like **Strawberry Park** (p733) and **Ouray** (p742) provide an easy way to warm up.

Colorado

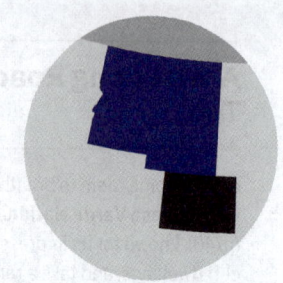

EPIC LANDSCAPES | URBAN ENERGY | SPORTS

Places
Denver p724
Boulder p728
Steamboat Springs p732
Vail p733
Leadville p734
Aspen p734
Salida p736
Crested Butte p737
Canyon of the Ancients National Monument p738
Ouray & Around p739
Telluride p743
Black Canyon of the Gunnison National Park & Around p744
Colorado Springs p747
Great Sand Dunes National Park p748
Santa Fe Trail p748

Colorado is a place of striking contrasts and seemingly endless adventure. Towering peaks, red-rock canyons, dense forests and surreal sand dunes make for a landscape that's as diverse as it is beautiful. In winter, world-renowned ski resorts like Aspen and Vail draw powder hounds from near and far, while summer brings hikers and mountain bikers to alpine trails and meadows awash in wildflowers. Off trail, you can unwind in natural hot springs or explore ancient cliff dwellings at Mesa Verde National Park. Add to all that the creative energy of cities like Denver and Boulder – with their vibrant food and craft-beer scenes, street art and museums – and the mountain chic of historic mining towns, and you've got a destination that blends outdoor adventure, layered history, cultural depth and laid-back urban cool. All that under big, bluebird skies.

☑ TOP TIP

Altitude sickness is a real thing in Colorado. Stay hydrated, take it easy and allow a few days to acclimatize. A little light-headedness, slight headaches and sluggishness are normal. But if you experience severe and continued nausea, headache and dizziness, consult a doctor and/or get to lower altitudes.

GETTING AROUND

Most visitors arrive through **Denver International Airport** (DIA) though regional airports dot Colorado. **Bustang** (ridebustang.com) provides bus service to towns along the I-70 and I-25 corridors, as well as harder-to-reach destinations like Telluride and Crested Butte. To explore further, a car is essential. City roads and highways are paved and generally well maintained; smaller mountain towns often have dirt or gravel roads. A 4WD vehicle is helpful in winter, especially on icy roads. Some mountain passes close seasonally or when driving conditions are hazardous. Before heading out, check **Colorado Department of Transportation** (codot.gov/travel) for road closures and weather warnings.

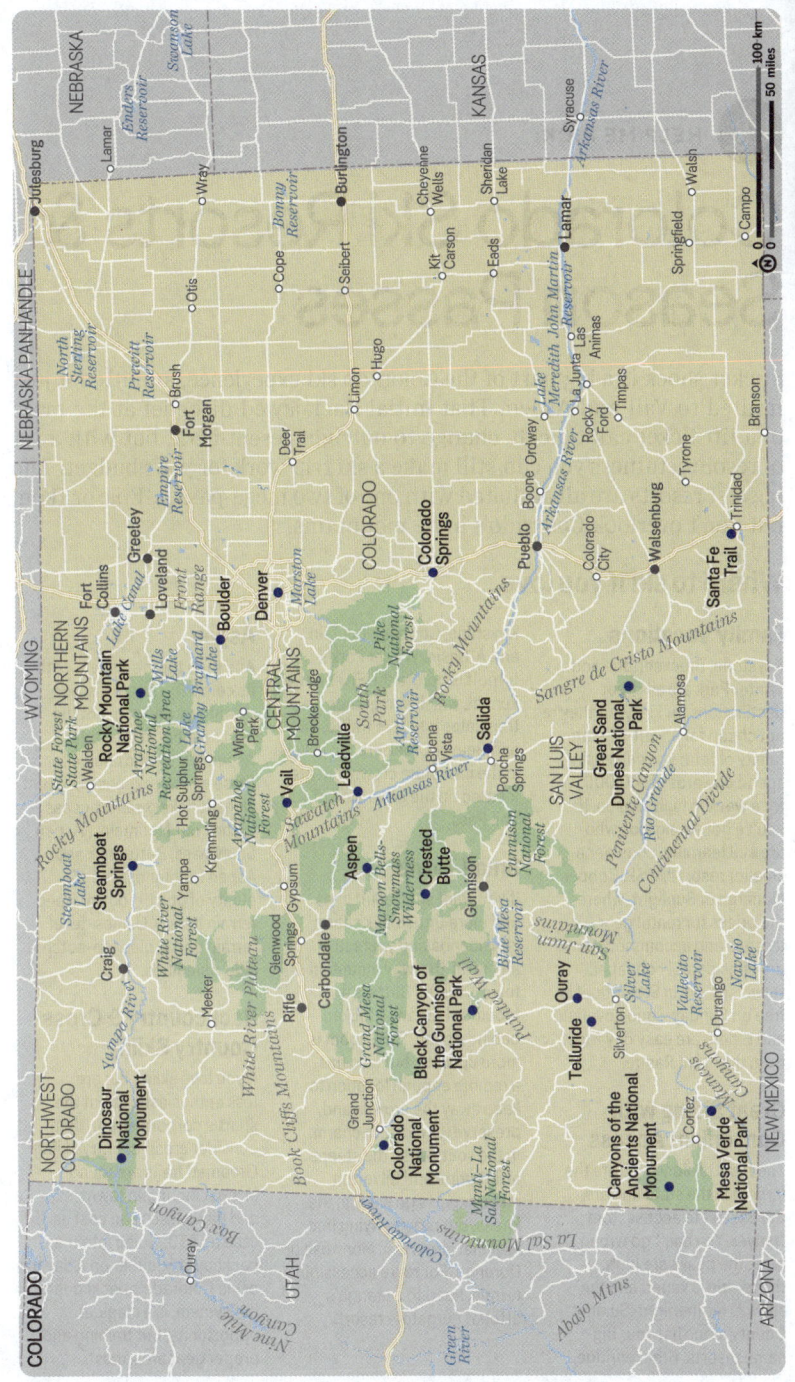

HELP ME PICK:

Colorado Ski Resorts & Season Passes

Sticker shock is a big part of the Colorado ski experience, and it's not just limited to Vail and Aspen. That initial slack-jawed disbelief at the price of a lift ticket can quickly change to outright resentment, but with a bit of resourcefulness you can still make a ski trip work for your budget. The biggest resorts are all affiliated with one of two mega-passes, Epic or Ikon, but don't overlook Colorado's indie mountains.

Where to ski if you love...

Family Vacations

Keystone, Breckenridge and Winter Park are all great destinations for kids, but they're not cheap for an out-of-state family of four: you can easily spend upwards of $10,000 for a week in high season. If you've got young kids who are still learning, consider a smaller resort like Ski Cooper, Monarch or Sunlight, where the prices for rental gear, lessons and accommodation are considerably cheaper. Howelsen Hill in Steamboat is free on Sundays, and Loveland and Eldora are easy day trips from the Front Range.

Great Skiing with Convenient Access

The resorts along I-70 are the largest in the state and are the easiest to access from Denver. You can't go wrong here: the peaks are high, the terrain is varied and the snow is featherlight. Summit County alone has four big-name resorts: Breckenridge, Keystone, Copper Mountain and A-Basin. Winter Park's turnoff is before the Eisenhower Tunnel, which sometimes translates into less traffic. Vail and Beaver Creek are the jewels in the interstate crown, but are located on the other side of Vail Pass.

Small Towns

If you want shorter lift lines and more throwback charm, consider basing yourself in an out-of-the-way mountain town. Crested Butte is a fabulous hideaway tucked behind Aspen. Steamboat is more upscale, but also has a remote enough location to keep away the crowds and preserve its Western charm. In the southwest, the steeps at Telluride and Silverton make experts go weak in the knees, but require flying into regional airports in Montrose or Durango. For more accessible terrain, head to Durango's offbeat Purgatory resort.

Aspen

And then there's Aspen. With its celebrity glitter, historic downtown and some of the best scenery in the state, Aspen is a terrific choice for those with an expense account. One lift ticket grants access to the Four Mountains: Aspen, Snowmass, Buttermilk and Aspen Highlands. There's plenty of upside-down-steep terrain here, X Games–level terrain parks, plus top-notch kids' amenities.

Backcountry & Cross-Country Skiing

If you love skiing but are less enthusiastic about the sport's corporate turn, then consider cross-country skiing. Groomed trails are found in most mountain towns, and day passes can cost as little as $30. Going into the backcountry, either on a day trip or via Colorado's backcountry hut system, is a magical opportunity, but training and proper gear are a must.

Vail (p733)

HOW TO

Don't overlook independent resorts like Telluride, Silverton, Wolf Creek, Monarch and Loveland, which also offer incredible skiing and deep powder.

Save money by packing a picnic. It sounds obvious, but the number of people who pay outrageous prices for cafeteria food is astounding.

Want first tracks in backcountry glades after a big storm? Go snowcat skiing at Purgatory, Steamboat, Shrine Pass, Jones Pass, Aspen, Monarch or Loveland.

Got the itch for steep lines and an 'I can't believe this is real' backdrop? Fork out for heli skiing in Silverton or Telluride.

Ikon Pass Versus Epic Pass

There has been a tremendous amount of corporate consolidation in the US ski industry, and the biggest names are now all affiliated with one of two season passes: Ikon or Epic. Don't get confused by the word 'season' – these passes are fully customizable, from one day to unlimited, and from a handful of local hills to the whole hog, including destinations scattered around the world. If you're headed to a big resort, getting a pass in advance – the best deals are offered in spring for the following year – will save you money and allow you the luxury of skiing in more than one place. Passes also come with perks, like discounted tickets for friends and family.

Ikon *(ikonpass.com; four-day/base/full $479/969/1359)* offers access to Winter Park, Copper, Steamboat, Eldora, A-Basin and Aspen in Colorado. Other destinations range from Big Sky (Montana) to Alta and Snowbird (Utah), and Jackson Hole (Wyoming) to Chamonix (France). The Winter Park local passes *(midweek/full $559/749)* are a cheaper option.

Epic *(epicpass.com; four-day/local/full $423/762/1025)* offers access to Vail, Breckenridge, Keystone, Beaver Creek and Crested Butte in Colorado. Other destinations include Whistler (Canada), Park City (Utah), and Heavenly, Northstar and Kirkwood at Lake Tahoe. If you're looking for a more targeted pass, consider the Summit Value Pass *(Breckenridge and Keystone $615)* or Keystone Plus *(Keystone plus five days at Crested Butte $408)*.

Denver

Tony venues and train tickets

An iconic landmark, the Beaux-Art style **Union Station** *(denverunionstation.com; free)* opened its doors in 1914 and has served as Denver's transportation hub ever since. But it's way more than that. Wander through the Great Hall, with soaring ceilings, chandeliers and cozy leather couches; lively bars and cocktail lounges line the walls alongside ice-cream shops and bookstores. Or indulge yourself at one of the swanky restaurants – including **Mercantile** *(mercantiledenver.com)* and **Ultreia** *(ultreiadenver.com),* brainchildren of James Beard Award-winning chefs. Or stay overnight at one of Denver's best hotels, **The Crawford** *(thecrawfordhotel.com).* In summer, come for its outdoor plaza, where you can peruse its popular **Saturday farmers market**, while its **pop-up fountain** entices kids (and kids at heart) to play in the urban sprinklers.

World-class performances

Come to the **Denver Performing Arts Complex** *(artscomplex.com; prices vary)*, where you can score tickets almost nightly. Across four city blocks, you'll find 10 venues connected by a sky-high glass canopy, among them the historic **Ellie Caulkins Opera House** (aka 'the Ellie'), a luxe 2200-seat theater where Opera Colorado and Colorado Ballet perform. Or head to the magnificent **Boettcher Concert Hall**, the nation's first concert-hall-in-the-round, where the **Colorado Symphony** plays classics as well as modern-day crowd-pleasers. The Arts Complex's theater wing, the similarly named **Denver Center for the Performing Arts** (called 'The DCPA'), has eight venues staging everything from experimental productions to Broadway musicals. If you're a theater junkie, take a **behind-the-scenes theater tour** *(per person $12)* with stops in dressing rooms, design studios and costume shops. Purchase tickets online for big discounts, sometimes starting at just $10 per ticket for kids, students and seniors.

Have fun in Confluence Park

Named for the meeting of the South Platte River and Cherry Creek, **Confluence Park** is a pocket of outdoorsy activity in downtown Denver. Picnic on its terraced lawns, jog along the waterfront, or just sun and splash on the park's small sandy beach. In the summer, rent inner tubes and kayaks to ride on a fun human-made stretch of white water. Rentals available at **Confluence Kayaks** *(confluencekayaks.com; per day from $55)*.

Catch a ball (game)

Coors Field *(mlb.com/rockies/ballpark)* is one of the MLB's most home-run-friendly ballparks (apparently, it's the thin air), and catching a **Rockies** game *(mlb.com/rockies; adult/child from $4/1)* is easy with 80 home games and tickets starting at just $1 in the Rockpile (aka centerfield). Theme nights include freebies like trucker hats and commemorative cups; come decked out in your purple, black and silver best to fit right in. Die-hard fan? **Stadium tours** *(adult/child $27/10)* run 70 to 80 minutes and include the field, clubhouses and mile-high seats.

THE MARADE

Denver's **Marade** – part march, part parade – is a huge, joyous, serious, welcoming, historic, and thoroughly Denver event. It's the largest Martin Luther King Jr Day celebration in the country, bringing together tens of thousands of Denverites to celebrate the life of Dr King and continue his fight for social justice. It's a massive outpouring of local people – students, elders, politicians, artists, workers, families with strollers, and activists with bullhorns – joining and chanting to manifest a better world. (Even when it's snowing, which it often does in January.) Marchers gather at the Dr King statue in City Park (p726) and march down Colfax Ave to **Civic Center Park** for rousing speeches.

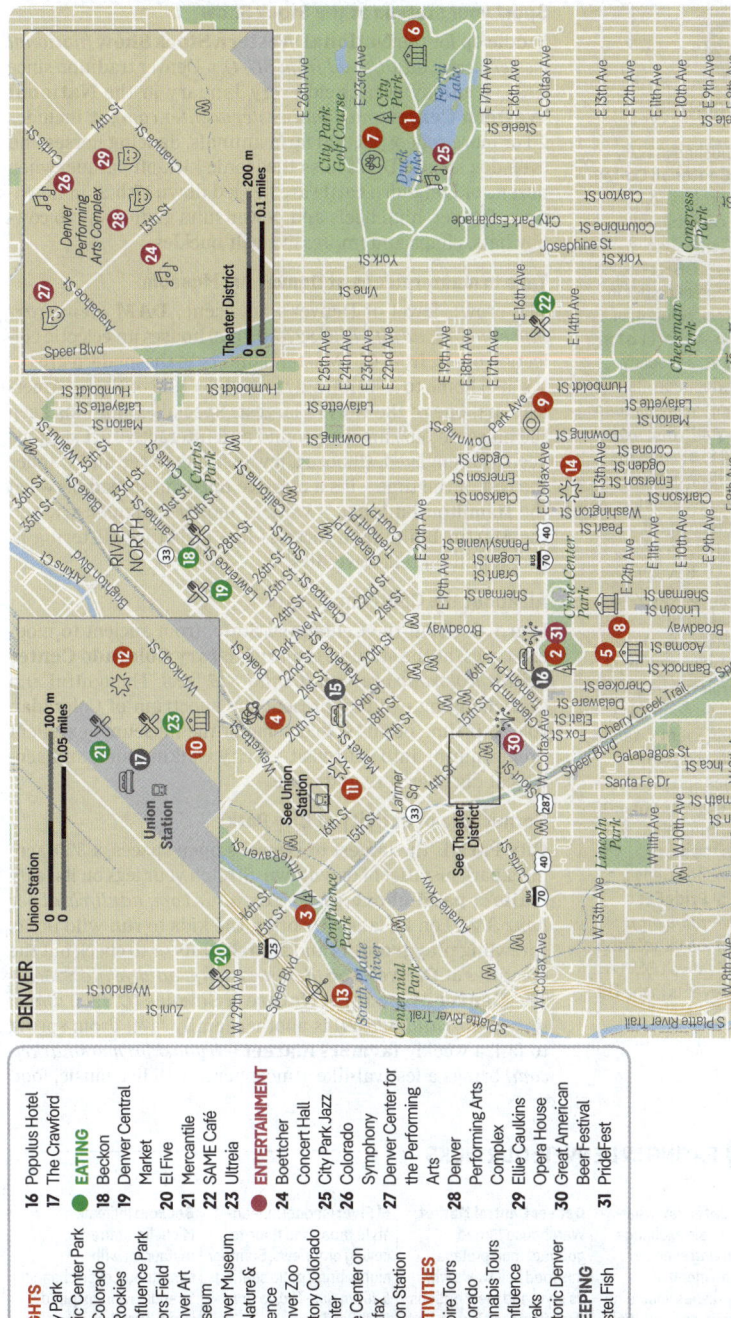

DENVER

SIGHTS
1. City Park
2. Civic Center Park
3. Colorado Rockies (see 4)
4. Confluence Park
5. Coors Field
6. Denver Art Museum
7. Denver Museum of Nature & Science
8. Denver Zoo
9. History Colorado Center
10. The Center on Colfax
11. Union Station

ACTIVITIES
12. Aspire Tours
13. Colorado Cannabis Tours
14. Confluence Kayaks
15. Historic Denver

SLEEPING
16. Hostel Fish
17. Populus Hotel
18. The Crawford

EATING
19. Beckon
20. Denver Central Market
21. El Five
22. Mercantile
23. SAME Café
24. Ultreia

ENTERTAINMENT
25. Boettcher Concert Hall
26. City Park Jazz
27. Colorado Symphony
28. Denver Center for the Performing Arts
29. Denver Performing Arts Complex
30. Ellie Caulkins Opera House
31. Great American Beer Festival
32. PrideFest

725

THE CENTER

Established in 1976, **The Center on Colfax** *(lgbtqcolorado. org)*, called simply 'the Center,' is the largest LGBTQ+ community center in the Rocky Mountain region. A vital hub for support, advocacy and education, its support services span from youth (Rainbow Alley) to elder (Sage of the Rockies) and transgender programming. It's a good resource for LGBTQ+ travelers too. Health services (including HIV testing and prevention), counseling and legal referrals are freely given. Or come for a drop-in event – watch parties, cooking classes and yoga are regularly offered. The Center also hosts the must-experience Denver's annual **PrideFest** *(denverpride.org)*, one of the largest and most festive LGBTQ+ pride events in the US.

Sport your stetson at the Stock Show

Saddle up for the **National Western Stock Show** *(nationalwestern.com; adult/child from $17/4)*, a Denver tradition since 1906. A 16-day event held every January in the **National Western Center** *(nationalwesterncenter.com)*, it includes 20 or more rodeos, 15,000 farm animals, dancing horses and even dog shows. Don't miss the iconic kick-off parade, when dozens of Longhorn cattle are herded down 17th St in downtown Denver, high heels and power suits giving way to cowboy hats, chaps and impressive belt buckles.

Take in masterpieces at Denver Art Museum

The crown jewel of Denver's art scene, **DAM** *(denverartmuseum.org; adult/child $27-30/free)* houses an eclectic collection of art, from Old Master painters to the modern greats. It's also home to a stunningly rich collection of Native American art, one of the world's largest. Special exhibitions keep the museum buzzing year-round and interactive art stations keep kids engaged. Choose a few exhibits to see and wander the rest of the time – it's a massive museum spread between the Hamilton Building, a work of modern angular art, and the Martin Building, a fortress-like structure glittering in over a million reflective tiles.

All about the Centennial State

Learn all about the Centennial State, from ancient to modern times, at the state-of the-art **History Colorado Center** *(historycolorado.org; adult/child $15/free)*. Thoughtful and ever-changing exhibits present the spectrum of Coloradan voices. If time permits, fold some of the museum's excellent programming into your visit – a city walking tour, archaeological dig, a lecture and more.

Cornucopia of activity at City Park

City Park is the largest of Denver's open spaces, a 320-acre megapark just east of downtown. Stretch your legs on its leafy **trails** or **paddleboat** *(wheelfunrentals.com; adult/child per hour $12/7)* on its lakes. Or bring the kids to run wild on its sprawling **playgrounds** and **splash pads** or to check out the creatures at **Denver Zoo** *(denverzoo.org; adult/child $25/19)*. The **Denver Museum of Nature & Science** *(DMNS, dmns.org; adult/child $26/21)* is another family fave. From spring to fall, a weekly **farmers market** *(cityparkfarmersmarket.com)* brings a festival-like atmosphere, with live music, food

 EATING IN DENVER: OUR PICKS

| SAME Café: Pay-what-you-can, fair-exchange cafe serving ever-changing menu of healthy dishes, including vegetarian options. Walk-in volunteers welcome. *11am-2:30pm Mon-Fri* $ | Denver Central Market: Warehouse turned gourmet marketplace, this food hall wows with its style and meal options. *8am-9pm Sun-Thu, to 11pm Fri & Sat* $-$$ | El Five: Mediterranean-style tapas and floor-to-ceiling city views. Summer nights bring patio seating. *5-10pm Sun-Thu, to 11pm Fri & Sat* $$ | Beckon: Intimate Michelin-starred restaurant with sumptuous, ever-changing Scandinavian-inspired menu. Prepayment required. *5-10pm Wed-Sat* $$$ |

Red Rocks Amphitheater

trucks and all manner of picnic fixin's. Summer nights also brings thousands for free **jazz concerts** *(cityparkjazz.org)*. And, that view! Skyscrapers with snowcapped mountains in the background…the icing on City Park's multilayered cake.

Experience a giant beer fest

Colorado takes its beer seriously, and with over 150 breweries in metro Denver, you certainly won't go thirsty. If you're visiting in late September/early October, try scoring tickets to the **Great American Beer Festival** *(greatamericanbeerfestival.com; from $85)*, the largest beer festival in the US. It draws over 2000 master brewers, with over 9000 beers vying for Best of Show medals in 263 categories. General admission includes unlimited 1oz tastings; pairings – small dishes created by lauded chefs – with a menu of beers are also offered. Best of all is the comradery of you and 40,000 beer buddies, all tasting outstanding brews one ounce at a time.

Be wowed by RiNo's murals

Unexpected and totally fabulous, the trendy RiNo neighborhood is draped in hundreds of murals. Bright, opinionated and ever-changing, the artwork stops you in your tracks, speaking to Denver's diversity, history and day-to-day musings. Wander the neighborhood to take them in, using **RiNo's website** *(rinoartdistrict.org/art/murals)* to find local faves. Or take a guided tour with **Denver Graffiti Tour** *(denvergraffititour.com; adult/child $30/15)*, known for its small groups and custom tours.

Catch a concert at Red Rocks Amphitheater

There's something almost primal about attending a concert at **Red Rocks Amphitheater** *(redrocksonline.com)* – the sounds of instruments enveloping you, the sight of people dancing under an umbrella of stars and the iconic 300ft-high red sandstone monoliths standing guard on either side. For many, it's reason enough for a trip to Colorado. Renowned for its natural acoustics and stunning beauty, Red Rocks is

BEST TOURS: DENVER & AROUND

Historic Denver: Denver's preservation society offers 90-minute docent-led tours *(historicdenver.org)* of the city's oldest neighborhoods.

Denver Microbrew Tours: Knowledgeable guides lead 2½-hour tours *(denvermicrobrewtour.com)* of award-winning breweries in LoDo and RiNo, tasting at least 10 brews.

Local Table Tours: Guided walking tours *(localtabletours.com)* cover some of Denver's top restaurants, integrating drink pairings and neighborhood history.

Colorado Cannabis Tours: Party-bus tours *(coloradocannabistours.com)* from two to 3½ hours, including grow operations and dispensaries.

Aspire Tours: Half- and full-day driving tours *(aspire-tours.com)* of Denver and surrounding areas, including sightseeing and hiking stops.

OPEN SPACE IS NO ACCIDENT

Boulder's unique and vast swathe of undeveloped land started back in 1898 when the city helped purchase the plot that became Chautauqua Park. In 1907 the government floated a public bond to buy Flagstaff Mountain, and in 1912 purchased 1200 more pristine mountain acres. Then, in 1967, Boulder voters legislated their love of the land by approving a sales tax specifically to buy, manage and maintain open space. This was historic. No other US city had ever voted to tax themselves specifically for open space and Boulder's Open Space and Mountain Parks *(osmp.org)* office was launched. In 1989 76% of voters increased the tax by nearly 100%; today the OSMP protects over 46,000 acres of land, criss-crossed with 155 miles of hiking trails.

synonymous with big-ticket concerts of all genres, even symphony orchestras. If a show isn't in the cards, the venue and its surrounding 816 acres are free to visit during the day. The amphitheater also regularly hosts events like early morning **yoga** *(per person $20)* and **movie nights** *(per person $20)*.

The footprints of giants

The discovery site of the first stegosaur, **Dinosaur Ridge** *(dinoridge.org; free)* also has some of the world's best preserved dinosaur tracks and fossils. Sandwiched between Hwy 470 and Red Rocks Amphitheater, the exposed rock surfaces here reveal over 250 dinosaur footprints and sandstone-encased fossils dating to the Jurassic and Cretaceous periods. A steep, paved **interpretive trail** (2.2-mile round trip) leads through the site, signage providing insight into the behavior, movement and tropical environment of the dinosaurs that once roamed here. A **self-guided audio tour** *($8)* can be downloaded at the Visitors Center. Or take a 45-minute **bus tour** *(adult/child $20/14)*, which includes three stops and a cheery guide.

Boulder

Shopping around Pearl St

Pearl Street Mall is the heart of downtown Boulder, a tree-shaded pedestrian zone filled with kids' climbing boulders and splash fountains, and lined with shops and galleries. People-watching aside, shopping is Pearl's raison d'être. Outdoor wear figures large with everybody from Italy's **La Sportiva** and Japan's **Montbell** to North American brands like **Patagonia**, **North Face** and **Black Diamond**. But it's not all ultralight puffies. Vintage shops like **Apocalypse** and **Heady Bauer** have a definite disco-hippie Boulder vibe, while trendy boutiques like **Bliss** and **Jones + Company** are a fun browse. Whatever you do, don't miss **Piece, Love & Chocolate** at the west end of Pearl St, a perfect place to relax with a decadent chocolate truffle.

Culture at Dairy Arts Center

The top cultural hub in town is the **Dairy Arts Center** *(the dairy.org)*, a historic milk-processing factory turned arts center. It's a state-of-the-art facility with three stages, four gallery spaces and a 60-seat cinema. There's always something going on, from film screenings and plays to modern dance and art exhibits. The exhibits are always free.

EATING IN BOULDER: OUR PICKS

Mountain Sun: The town's favorite brewery is as Boulder as it gets. Great burgers, chili and brews, like Annapurna Amber. *noon-11pm Wed-Sun* **$**

Rosetta Hall: A sophisticated food hall, serving everything from falafel to green papaya salad to empanadas. Rooftop bar too. *8am-11pm* **$$**

Leaf: An ethical and elegant kitchen that serves meat-free gems, using ingredients grown at the restaurant's organic farm in nearby Lafayette. *11:30am-9pm* **$$**

Frasca: James Beard, Michelin and others have all named the northern Italian cuisine here as Boulder's finest. Prix-fixe menus only; reserve well ahead. *5-9pm* **$$$**

BOULDER

SIGHTS
1 Pearl Street Mall

SLEEPING
2 St Julien Hotel & Spa

EATING
3 Boulder County Farmers Market
4 Frasca
5 Leaf
6 Mountain Sun
7 Rosetta Hall

SHOPPING
8 Apocalypse
9 Black Diamond
10 Bliss
11 Heady Bauer
12 Jones + Company
13 La Sportiva
14 Montbell
15 North Face
16 Patagonia
17 Piece, Love & Chocolate

Lake of Glass

TOP EXPERIENCE

Rocky Mountain National Park

Colorado's crown jewel, Rocky Mountain National Park (RMNP) encompasses 415 sq miles of granite mountain top, alpine lake, wildflower-filled meadow, star-filled nights, and adventures large and small. Summer brings big-time crowds, but leave the main trailheads behind and you'll quickly find your own patch of solitude, so long as you're willing to share it with the wildlife that calls this place home.

DON'T MISS

- Trail Ridge Rd
- Kawuneeche Valley
- Lake of Glass hike
- Wild Basin Trailhead
- Moraine Park Discovery Center

Bear Lake Hiking

The **Bear Lake** and **Glacier Gorge Junction** trailheads are the most popular destinations in the park, and for good reason. From here you'll have a front-row vantage point of the dramatic glacial valleys and hulking granite summits that make Rocky Mountain such a singular landscape.

Hikes range from easy jaunts to **Alberta Falls** (1.6 miles) or **Dream Lake** (2.2 miles) and **Emerald Lake** (3.6 miles)

PRACTICALITIES
- nps.gov/romo
- per vehicle $30
- 24hr

to more challenging excursions that follow the glacial valleys up to their origins. **Mills Lake** (5.6 miles) is a good choice, as is the **Loch** (6.2 miles), which can be extended to the exquisite **Lake of Glass** and **Sky Pond** (9.8 miles). And while **Flattop Mountain** (12,324ft, 8.8 miles) may not be the park's best summit, there's no denying its magnetic pull from down below. Note: in summer, the Bear Lake Corridor requires a special entry reservation between 5am and 6pm – buy early.

Wildlife Watching

RMNP is home to some 800 elk, 350 bighorn sheep, 60 moose, 20 to 30 bears, an unknown number of mountain lions and countless mule deer – and those are just the big guys. Smaller critters include beavers, marmots, pikas, porcupines, otters, foxes, coyotes and some 270 species of birds. While you probably won't spot the more elusive animals, if you pay attention, you'll likely see or hear traces of their passage. Good places to look for wildlife include **Moraine Park** (start with its excellent **Discovery Center**), **Beaver Meadows**, **Sheep Lakes**, **Trail Ridge Rd** and the marshy areas in the **Kawuneeche Valley**.

Driving Trail Ridge Road

The highest continuous paved highway in North America, Trail Ridge Rd is a remarkable 4000ft climb, offering visitors the chance to experience the Rockies' high-alpine tundra, complete with bighorn sheep, whistling marmots and eye-squinting panoramas in all directions. You can start in the east or west entrances of the park, make it a through trip or an out-and-back adventure, use it as a springboard for high-altitude hikes, or simply content yourself with a dozen superlative-worthy view points. In July, the lichen-covered boulders also light up with wildflowers. Among the can't-miss sights are the **Alpine Visitor Center** (11,796ft), which looks out over a hazy expanse of 400 sq miles, and the info-packed **Tundra Communities Trail**. Further west is the Continental Divide. Expect to spend a half-day exploring. Note: Trail Ridge Rd is only open from June through mid-October.

Rocky Mountain for Kids

The Park is an incredibly fun place for families to explore, though it may take some trial and error to find everyone's happy place. Budget time for special activities – horseback riding, a ropes course, ranger activities – to break up the monotony of driving around and posing for photos.

Don't miss the **Junior Ranger Headquarters** in Hidden Valley, which runs kids-themed programs throughout the day. A few family-friendly destinations in RMNP include Nymph and Dream Lakes (Bear Lake trailhead), Gem Lake (Lumpy Ridge Trailhead), MacGregor Ranch (adjacent to Lumpy Ridge), Eugenia Mine (Longs Peak Trailhead), Calypso Cascades (Wild Basin Trailhead), the Moraine Park Discovery Center (Bear Lake Rd), the Alpine Visitor Center (Trail Ridge Rd) and Lily Lake and Mountain (Hwy 7).

BEAR LAKE ALTERNATIVES

Couldn't score a coveted Bear Lake permit? Try these alternatives:

Fall River Area Hiking, bighorn-sheep spotting and a high-altitude drive.

Lumpy Ridge Trailhead Inspiring rambles among giant boulders and granite crags; Gem Lake (3.4 miles) is a favorite.

Wild Basin Trailhead Often overlooked, the southern corner of the park is chock-full of waterfalls.

Longs Peak Trailhead Variety of hikes from kid-friendly to the lung-busting peak.

TOP TIPS

● Timed entry tickets *(recreation.gov)* are required between late May and mid-October; buy your ticket on the first day of the month prior to your entry (ie May 1 for a June visit). Need a last-minute ticket? Reservations (40% of all available tickets) go on sale at 7pm for the following day.

● Most high-country trails are snowbound through late June; plan accordingly.

● Avoid encroaching on wildlife, for your safety and theirs. Stay at least 75ft away from elk and sheep, and 120ft away from moose and bears. And please, don't feed anything, no matter how cute it looks.

Hike in Chautauqua Park

Historic **Chautauqua Park** *(chautauqua.com)* is the gateway to Boulder's most magnificent swathe of open space: a wide-open prairie adjoining the iconic **Flatirons**, 1000ft red-rock slabs rising up out of the earth. It's a popular place for hikers, climbers and trail runners with 15 trails winding through the park.

No matter your destination, most people start on the **Chautauqua Trail** (1.5-mile loop), a relatively easy walk through a grassy meadow. If you're itching to go higher, the **Flatirons Loop Trail** (2.5 miles) leads you to the base of the First Flatiron, where climbers rope up for ascents; or do the full 700ft of elevation gain up to the top, following the trail as it zigzags up between the First and Second Flatirons. Want to go farther yet? The **Royal Arch Trail** (3.5 miles) has been a Boulder classic for over a century. This roughly 2½-hour trek leads you up to a natural arch past the Third Flatiron and has fantastic views. Expect to do some scrambling. The trails here connect to the rest of the city's open space via the long-distance **Mesa Trail**, giving you lots of options to customize your walk.

Founded in 1898 as part of the national Chautauqua Movement – an initiative aimed at adult education in rural settings – the park remains a cultural hub featuring historic cottages and dining hall as well as a 1300-seat auditorium that hosts world-class musicians, performers and speakers each summer. Plan ahead – events often sell out.

Parking is limited. On summer weekends and holidays, visitors are encouraged to take the free **Park-to-Park Shuttle** *(bouldercolorado.gov)*, which runs from downtown and satellite parking lots.

Farm fresh

The twice-weekly **Boulder County Farmers Market**, a block-long sprawl in front of the Dushanbe Teahouse, is a massive spring and summer bazaar of colorful, mostly organic 100% local food. Find flowers and herbs, as well as brain-sized mushrooms, delicate squash blossoms, crusty pretzels, vegan dips, grass-fed beef, raw granola and yogurt. Live music is as standard as the family picnics in the park along Boulder Creek. The Saturday market is a real community event, and it feels like the whole city comes out to socialize in the morning (8am-2pm). The Wednesday evening market (3:30-7:30pm) tends to be a little less busy, but it's still a notable midweek gathering place. In true Boulder style, all waste from the farmers market is recycled or composted. The market is closed in winter.

Steamboat Springs

Skiing Steamboat

Famous for its light and fluffy powder, **Steamboat Mountain Resort** *(steamboat.com; adult/child $285/230)* boasts stats that speak for themselves: 182 marked runs; 3668ft of vertical, and 3741 acres of terrain. While the summit tops out at 10,568ft, Steamboat makes up for its dearth of high-altitude steeps with super-fun tree slaloming runs. Serious skiers will also dig a number of mogul runs on the hill, and although

---

BOLDER BOULDER

Boulder's biggest party is, unsurprisingly, a 10km footrace held every Memorial Day, snow or shine. With more than 50,000 runners and pros mingling with costumed racers, live bands and sideline merrymakers, **Bolder Boulder** *(bolderboulder.com)* may be the most fun 10km run in the US. Course-side antics range from slip and slides and Elvis impersonators to red, white and blue paragliders spiraling down to the race's end at Folsom Field. Participants are divided into 100 waves, with wheelchairs going first, followed by the pros. Then come the walkers, elementary school kids and the costumed – eventually everyone makes it to the finish line. The latest addition to the race calendar is Colder Boulder, a 5km race in early December.

Strawberry Park Hot Springs

these trails are a virtual factory of Olympic skiers and snowboarders, you don't have to be world class to enjoy them. Wide, well-groomed runs are ideal cruising for intermediate skiers, making this mountain among Colorado's best all-rounders, particularly for families. Throw in the cowboy-style charm and back-of-beyond location, and you have all the makings for a winter wonderland.

Steamboat's hot springs

Just 7 miles north of Steamboat, **Strawberry Park Hot Springs** (*strawberryhotsprings.com; $20*) is an idyllic spot: a handful of natural outdoor pools set beside a cool mountain stream and nothing but acres of wilderness surrounding you. Evening visits are particularly magical: whether you're treated to a meteor shower or a full moon rising through the pines, soaking in the steaming pools – with the occasional river plunge – is a marvelously restorative experience. Note that after dark, it's adults only. In winter, you'll need AWD and snow tires to get here; if your vehicle isn't equipped, or if it's a busy weekend, take the shuttle instead.

Vail

Ski the back bowls

Vail Mountain (*vail.com; adult/child lift ticket $319/220*) is hands-down one of the best ski resorts in the world, with 5317 skiable acres, 278 trails and, ahem, some of the highest

ANCIENT ASPENS

Come late September, Colorado's roads fill with leaf peepers, out in search of the glorious golden hues that wash across the mountainsides. Aspens, of course, are well known for their quaking leaves, but there's more to this tree than meets the eye. In fact, many aspen groves are not made up of individual trees, but are instead a single interconnected organism – the aspen's most common method of reproduction is cloning, where one plant sends out identical reproductions of itself via its root system. Because of this, aspens are not only considered the world's largest organism, but also the oldest: the Pando Grove in Utah (over 40,000 'stems' strong) is considered to be at least 10,000 years old.

 EATING IN VAIL: OUR PICKS

Big Bear Bistro: An affordable fave in Vail Village, serving gourmet coffee, breakfast burritos and some damn good sandwiches at lunch. *8am-3pm* $

The Little Diner: The most popular place for a made-from-scratch breakfast is in Lionshead. No reservations. *7am-2pm* $$

Alpenrose: For the full alpine experience, get your pretzels, rösti and fondue at this Swiss German–themed restaurant. *11:30am-10pm* $$$

Sweet Basil: Vail's most celebrated restaurant: excellent seasonal, eclectic New American fare. *noon-3pm & 5-9pm Wed-Sun, 5-9pm Mon & Tue* $$$

THE VAIL DREAM

Tenth Mountain Division veteran Peter Seibert and his friend Earl Eaton climbed Vail Mountain in the winter of 1957. After one long look at those luscious back bowls, the pair knew they'd struck gold. At the time, the mountain was owned by the forest service and local ranchers. Seibert and Eaton recruited a series of investors and lawyers, eventually got a permit from the forest service and convinced nearly all of the local ranchers to sell. Much of the construction budget was raised by convincing investors to chip in $10,000 for a condo unit and a lifetime season pass. Finally, on December 15, 1962, the dream came alive. The cost of a lift ticket? $5 for nine runs.

lift-ticket prices on the continent. You can subdivide the mountain into three main zones: the front side (best for beginners and intermediate skiers), where most of the runs are groomed and the north-facing slopes offer good snow cover, even on sunny spring days; the back bowls (best for advanced skiers), with seven legendary bowls; and Blue Sky Basin (best for experts), with a more backcountry feel, including tree skiing, glades and cliffs. Distances are vast, and you'll spend a lot of time getting from one place to another, so if you have a specific destination in mind, plan carefully.

Summer adventures

All the usual suspects set up shop at Vail during the summer, from cycling to ziplining.

Bearcat Stables *(bearcatstables.com; from $80)* run one- to three-hour horseback rides, as well as longer trips like a four-day ride to Aspen. For wading and float-fishing trips, try **Gore Creek Fly Fishermen** *(gorecreekflyfisherman.com; from $345)*.

Zip Adventures *(zipadventures.com; $170)* runs six zipline tours over Alkali Canyon – followed by a cliff jump – with plenty of time to work on your primal scream.

Apex Mountain School *(apexmountainschool.com; $200-450)* offers guided climbing and mountaineering trips in both summer and winter, while **Bike Valet** *(bikevalet.com; rentals from $40)* rents cycles and runs a shuttle up to Vail Pass for the easy, scenic cruise back down.

Vail's summer amusement park, **Epic Discovery** *(vail.com; from $119)*, gets so-so reviews, though the **gondola ride** *(adult/child $59/39)* into the high country will always be impressive.

Leadville

Climb to the top of Colorado

Colorado's tallest peak and the second-highest in the continental US, **Mt Elbert** (14,433ft) is a relatively gentle giant. There are three established routes to the top, none of which are technical. The most common approach is via the northeast ridge; it's a 9-mile round trip hike with 4700ft of elevation gain, so expect to spend most of the day. The turnoff for the main trailhead is just south of Leadville on Rte 300. If you have 4WD, the South Mt Elbert Trailhead is accessed via Hwy 82, just east of Twin Lakes. It's a slightly shorter hike with only 4100ft of elevation gain.

Aspen

Skiing the four mountains

Aspen, for all its wealth, owes its current status to the surrounding slopes. Above all, this is a ski town and one of the best in America, with four mountains accessible from a **single lift ticket** *(aspensnowmass.com; adult/child lift ticket $244/164)* – each offering a different adventurous twist.

Aspen Mountain offers more than 3000ft of steep vertical right from the front door of the Little Nell. There's no

Aspen

beginner terrain here, just 800 acres of bumps, trees and World Cup–worthy runs.

Snowmass is the biggest of the four, with over 3300 acres of ridable terrain and 150 miles of trails – this is the best all-around choice. At some point make your way to the Elk Camp chairlift, which has awesome views of the Maroon Bells from the top.

Buttermilk has lots of beginner-friendly cruisers, but it also has some gnarly terrain parks: this is where you can ride the same hits and 22ft superpipe as Chloe Kim and Shaun White.

Last but not least is **Aspen Highlands**. Although there are some beginner and intermediate runs, the Highlands is all about extreme skiing in the stunning hike-to Highland Bowl: expect chutes, vertiginous drop-offs, glades and super steep lines that plunge 3600 vertical feet.

Art galleries and museums

With a handful of outstanding art venues, Aspen is the state's most culturally happening spot west of Denver. Start with **Aspen Art Museum** *(aspenartmuseum.org; free)*, with three floors of gallery space enveloped in a striking exterior designed by Pritzker Prize-winner Shigeru Ban. Lesser known is Aspen Institute's **Resnick Center for Herbert Bayer Studies** *(thebayercenter.org; free)*, with rotating exhibits related to the Austrian artist and longtime Aspen resident – a Bauhaus treat. Smaller galleries, meanwhile, are everywhere – follow

BACKCOUNTRY HUT TRIPS

For some, backcountry skiing is what it's all about: pristine snow, all-pervading quiet and the magic of waking up in the wilderness on a winter's day. If you're keen, look into the **Summit Huts Association** *(summithuts.org)*, which operates five huts that are accessible by ski and snowshoe, and usually sleep around 20 people. All have amenities such as wood-burning stoves, full kitchens and solar-powered lights; in addition, three have wood-burning saunas. The most popular hut is Francie's Cabin, a great choice for first-timers (though all groups should have at least one experienced, avalanche-trained member). Note that you need to enter a lottery by February 15 to book a hut for the following year.

EATING IN ASPEN: OUR PICKS

Big Wrap: These vaguely healthy and definitely affordable wraps have won over legions of fans. Downstairs from the main sidewalk. *10am-6pm Mon-Sat* $

Spring Cafe: Vegetarian juice bar and cafe, with tofu scrambles, tempeh burgers, seitan fajitas and plenty of greens. *7am-5pm, from 8am Sat & Sun* $$

Bosq: Chef Barclay Dodge's playful, locally sourced menu (eg bison tartare) earned him Aspen's first Michelin star. Prix-fixe menu only. *5:30-10pm* $$$

Pine Creek Cookhouse: This log-cabin restaurant is past Ashcroft's ghost town and is accessible via sleigh, skis or horseback. *lunch & dinner Dec-Mar & mid-Jun-Sep* $$$

BEST ENTERTAINMENT IN ASPEN

Belly Up: The top nightspot in town, showcasing performers from John Legend to the Chainsmokers in intimate surrounds.

Silver City Aspen: This cowpoke-themed saloon in the basement of the historic Elks Building hosts live music performances as well as a weekly karaoke night.

Wheeler Opera House: A working theater since 1889, the Wheeler still stages opera, stand-up comedy, concerts and musicals.

Theatre Aspen: The gorgeous garden complex in Rio Grande Park is the summer home of the local theater, which puts on award-winning musicals and plays.

---

your curiosity, and you're sure to turn up something unique. Longstanding studios include **Galerie Maximillian**, **Christopher Martin Gallery** (a specialist in reverse glass painting) and **Baldwin Gallery**.

Hike the Maroon Bells

If you have but one day to enjoy a slice of pristine wilderness, spend it in the shadow of Colorado's most iconic mountains: the pyramid-shaped twins of **North Maroon Peak** (14,014ft) and **South Maroon Peak** (14,156ft). Eleven miles southwest of Aspen, it all starts at **Maroon Lake**, a stunning spot backed by the towering, striated summits. The surrounding wilderness area contains nine passes over 12,000ft and six fourteeners. Some jut into jagged granite towers, others are a more generous slope and curve. You can spend an hour here or several days: the choice is yours. **Crater Lake** is only 1.8 miles one-way, but if you're hungry for a little bit more, press on to **Buckskin Pass** (12,462ft; 4.8 miles one-way) – from the narrow ledge you can see mountains erupt in all directions. This is the start of the popular **Four Pass Loop** (28 miles), a stunning multiday backpacking trip that crosses three other 12,000ft passes. Parking is extremely limited at Maroon Bells. Instead, take a shuttle from **Aspen Highlands** (p735) *(aspenchamber.org; adult/child $16/10; late May-Oct);* advanced purchase required.

Salida

Rafting the Arkansas

The headwaters of the Arkansas are Colorado's best-known stretch of white water, with everything from extreme rapids to mellow ripples. Although most rafting companies cover the river from Leadville to the Royal Gorge, the most popular trips descend through **Browns Canyon National Monument**, a 16-mile stretch that includes class-III to -IV rapids, running between Buena Vista and Salida.

If you're with young kids, Bighorn Sheep Canyon is a good bet. Those after more of an adrenaline rush can head upstream to the Numbers or downstream to the Royal Gorge (Cañon City), both of which are class IV to V. If you'd like to go solo, outfitters also rent duckies (inflatable kayaks).

Most companies are based just south of Buena Vista, close to where Hwys 24 and 285 diverge, and typically offer fullday adventure packages including zipline tours, via ferrata or horseback riding. Established outfitters include **Rocky Mountain Outdoor Center** *(rmoc.com),* **Independent Whitewater** *(raftsalida.com)* and **River Runners** *(riverrunnersltd.com).* Expect to spend from $100 to 160 for a half to a full day of rafting.

Biking Monarch Crest Trail

If you've mountain biked before, then you know: **Monarch Crest Trail** awaits. One of the most famous rides in Colorado, this is an extreme 35-mile adventure, with fabulous high-altitude views. It starts off at Monarch Pass (11,312ft), follows

Maroon Bells

RAFTING TIPS

Water flow varies by season, so time your visit for late May or early June for a wilder ride, when snowmelt has the river raging. If you've got young kids or are looking for a more relaxed experience, go in July or August when the water level is lower and warmer. Note that if you are rafting as a family, kids need to be at least six (sometimes older, depending on the trip) and weigh a minimum of 50lb. Early in the season, you'll need to wear a wetsuit (included) topped with a rain jacket, and whenever you go, take a wide-brimmed hat and sunglasses. Finally, bring a change of clothes for the end of the trip and don't forget to tip your guide.

the exposed ridge 12 miles to Marshall Pass and then either cuts down to Poncha Springs on an old railroad grade or hooks onto the Rainbow Trail. In Salida, rentals are available from **Sub-Culture Cyclery** (*subculturecyclery.com; half-day rental $70*), and **Absolute Bikes** (*absolutebikes.com; $39*) runs shuttles to the trailhead on Fridays through Sundays at 8am. **High Valley Bike Shuttle** (*monarchcrest.com; $42*) also picks up cyclists in Poncha Springs and brings them up to the trailhead twice daily, at 8am and 10am.

Explore St Elmo ghost town

An old gold-mining ghost town tucked amid the Collegiate Peaks, **St Elmo** makes for a fun excursion. The drive is gorgeous, wending its way past stands of redolent ponderosa pine, a wildlife-viewing meadow and jagged peaks before petering out at what is Colorado's best-preserved ghost town. Over 40 buildings remain, most built around 1881: the schoolhouse, an old mercantile building and a miners' exchange are among the best kept, all providing a fascinating peek into Colorado's past, when gold and silver ruled these hills. St Elmo is located on County Rd 162, which becomes dirt about half-way up. It's no problem in summer, but in winter you'll want an AWD. Try to avoid weekends here, when ATV and snowmobile enthusiasts use St Elmo as a staging point – the revving of not-too-distant engines can take away some of the charm.

Crested Butte

Brave the Teocalli Bowls

One of Colorado's best, **Crested Butte Mountain Resort** (*skicb.com; adult/child lift ticket $195/127*) is known for its stomach-lurching steeps, with infamous runs like Rambo and Banana Chute bestowing bragging rights onto survivors. The Teocalli Bowls near the summit offer more extreme lines, including a backcountry-esque 20-minute hike out at the bottom. It's not all daredevil plunges, though – the town also has

FAT-TIRE REVOLUTIONARY

In April 1998, Neil Murdoch – local CB eccentric and the founder of mountain biking as the world knows it – slipped out town with just his clothes and a bike, hours before federal marshals closed in. Murdoch, aka Richard Barrister, had settled in little-known Crested Butte in 1974 after skipping bail on a cocaine-smuggling charge in New Mexico. A consummate tinkerer, Murdoch began outfitting old Schwinn bikes to be ridden off-road, including adding low gears and wide knobby tires – thus the 'Fat-Tire Revolution' was born. When he disappeared, Crested Butte rallied behind Murdoch in absentia, even establishing a fund for his legal defense. He was eventually caught in 2001 but is still revered as the godfather of mountain biking.

a terrific **Nordic Center** (cbnordic.org; lift ticket $25) with 50km of groomed trails and a special ski-in gourmet dinner at **Magic Meadows Yurt** (reserve). The **Adaptive Sports Center** (adaptivesports.org), meanwhile, promotes mountain access for people of all abilities.

The birthplace of mountain biking

Crested Butte is one of the places that brought mountain biking to the world and it absolutely lives up to the hype. Take your pick between a fantastic **mountain bike park** (skicb.com; lift tickets from $65) or 450 miles of smooth-flowing singletrack crossing wildflower- and aspen-clad hills and meadows. The **Lupine Loop** is a great first trail, with outrageous views across the Slate River Valley. The 13-mile intermediate level ride has just enough climbing to keep you honest, interspersed with fun, flowing descents. **Big Al's Bicycle Heaven** (bigalsbicycleheaven.com) and **Alpineer** (alpineer.com) have rentals, maps and gear.

Wildflowers Everywhere

More than skiing, more than its mountain chic ethos, even more than mountain biking, Crested Butte is most famous for one thing: wildflowers. From vast hillsides of mule's ears to riverside pockets of elephant heads and shooting stars, and practically everywhere between, Crested Butte is saturated in wildflowers. Not surprisingly, the town hosts a popular **Wildflower Festival** (crestedbuttewildflowerfestival.org), typically in the second week of July. The programming is almost as varied as the flowers, from guided hikes to painting and photography classes, and even guidance on how to identify medicinal and edible flowers. One unique option is a wildflower tour with the **Rocky Mountain Biological Laboratory**, a research and educational institute in the one-time ghost town Gothic, just north of town.

Canyon of the Ancients National Monument
Explore Ancestral Puebloan ruins

Visually stunning and imbued with ineffable spiritual energy, **Canyon of the Ancients National Monument** (blm.gov/visit/canyons-ancient-national-monument; free) is home to the largest known concentration of archaeological sites in the country – more than 6000 at last count. The ruins, accessible off rough roads and remote trails, are spread over 170,000 acres of public land and span 12,000 years of human

EATING IN CRESTED BUTTE: OUR PICKS

Frank's Deli: Local fave serving hearty sandwiches and breakfast burritos perfect for the trail. Ask about the specials. *9am-6pm Mon-Sat* $

Secret Stash: Award-winning pizzeria with a boho vibe, teahouse seating and tapestries included. Cocktails pack a serious punch. *11am-9pm* $$

Sunflower: Inventive, locally sourced dishes served in a homey cabin-like setting. Menu changes with seasonal ingredients. *6-10pm Wed-Sat* $$$

Breadery: Chewy sourdough flatbreads meet shared plates (pear ricotta ravioli), and soups and salads for a family style meal. Fresh bread to go. *5-9pm Wed-Sun* $$$

Lowry Pueblo, Canyon of the Ancients National Monument

history. They range from singular hogans (traditional Navajo homes) to entire ancient pueblos – once-thriving population centers that persisted for thousands of years.

Canyon of the Ancients Visitor Center and Museum (*blm.gov/visit/canyons-ancients-national-monumentvisitor-center-and-museum; museum adult/child $6/free*) is an important first stop. A fascinating museum and research center, it has informative films and exhibits. Touch base with the rangers here; they can recommend specific sites and supply maps. A high-clearance vehicle is highly recommended. The **Southwest Colorado Canyons Alliance** (*swcocanyons.org; half/full day from $50/84*) also runs excellent tours.

The easiest ruin to visit is **Lowry Pueblo**, about 25 miles northwest of the visitors center on (mostly) paved roads. Dating to 1060 CE, the site has several stone structures and nine kivas (ceremonial enclosures), including the 47ft-wide Grand Kiva, believed to have been used for spiritual rites.

Alternatively, head to the southern entrance of Sand Canyon Trail, a relatively flat 6.5-mile (one way) trail through the breathtaking **McElmo Canyon**, with several cliff dwellings tucked into alcoves along the way. The largest, **Saddlehorn Pueblo**, is 1 mile from the trailhead.

Ouray & Around

Drive the Million Dollar Hwy

Deep in the San Juan Mountains, the **Million Dollar Hwy** connects the towns of Ouray and Silverton, and is a mind-blowingly scenic drive – one of Colorado's best. Twenty-five miles of hairpin turns and tight S-bends cut through the Uncompahgre Gorge, whose steep mountainsides loom large and close, rising into lofty, mist-shrouded peaks, while the valley floor lies far below, dotted with fir trees and wildflowers. Drive with caution – the road is formidable, even in good weather, and the lack of guardrails doesn't help. Be sure to take advantage of pullouts to see the dramatic **Bear Creek Falls** and 360-degree views from **Red Mountain Pass** (11,018ft).

WHY I LOVE CANYON OF THE ANCIENTS

Liza Prado, Lonely Planet writer.

Hiking solo through McElmo Canyon, the sky bright, the red earth dotted with yucca plants and sage brush, I can almost see them. The people who once called this red canyon home, carrying woven baskets filled with plants and berries, passing me on their way to their adobe brick homes that, remarkably, still stand in the alcoves. I can almost smell the smoke from their cooking fires and hear the sounds of their everyday life carried through the canyon – the chatter, the chopping of wood, the children playing. This place transports me, fills me with wonder and reminds me that, regardless of time or circumstance, we're all connected. For me, that's what travel is all about.

Cliff Palace

TOP EXPERIENCE

Mesa Verde National Park

Mesa Verde National Park spans 81 sq miles over two broad mesas, both rife with Ancestral Puebloan dwellings. Some are on the mesa tops, but the most compelling are built into high cliffs. While many are visible from overlooks, touring them means adventure at great heights, peering over edges, clambering up and down ladders and crawling through tunnels...all to experience these magnificent dwellings up close.

DON'T MISS

Cliff Palace

Balcony House

Step House

Petroglyph Point Trail

Mesa Top Loop Rd

Long House

Cultural Performances

Ranger Tours

Taking a ranger-led tour is one of the most rewarding ways to experience Mesa Verde. You'll deep-dive into the history and lives of the Ancestral Puebloans and have access to otherwise restricted sites such as **Cliff Palace** and **Balcony House**, plus **Long House**, a sprawling dwelling in the park's rugged backcountry. They're not for the faint of heart! Most involve walking along cliff edges, climbing up and down wooden pole ladders and crawling through tight spaces. But they're so worth it. Plan on taking two tours if you have the time; buy tickets in advance – they sell out fast.

PRACTICALITIES
● nps.gov/meve ● per vehicle $20-30 ● 24hr

Cliff Palace

Cliff Palace is the largest known cliff dwelling in the American southwest, a grand engineering achievement with 151 rooms and 23 kivas (ceremonial enclosures) that once housed 25 families. It's remarkable for its fine construction and efficient design. Walk through it on a 45-minute tour, retracing the paths taken by the enclave's original inhabitants. If you can't join a tour, check out the site from afar from the Sun Temple overlook on Mesa Top Loop Rd.

Balcony House

The **Balcony House** tour requires you to descend a 100ft staircase, climb a 32ft ladder and crawl through a 12ft tunnel...and that's just to get there. There are more ladders and steps on the way out. It's well worth the effort: the 38-room village is built in a cliffside alcove with a long arching roof, and offers views of Soda Canyon, 600ft below.

Step House

Wetherill Mesa has the park's only self-guided cliff dwelling: **Step House**. A short but steep 0.8-mile trail leads to a two-in-one village, with 7th-century pit houses standing alongside 13th-century multistoried dwellings. Information booklets are available near the trailhead; a ranger is typically at the site to answer questions.

Mesa Top Loop Rd

A complement (or alternative) to scrambling through the cliff dwellings is a 6-mile driving tour along the **Mesa Top Loop Rd**. At various pull-offs, you can enjoy magnificent overlooks of Cliff Palace and other cliff dwellings, or take short paths to a dozen different surface sites (no teetering ladders on this route). A free **audio tour** *(nps.gov/podcasts/podcasts-mtl-audiotour.htm)* guides the way.

Petroglyph Point Trail

The 2.4-mile loop **Petroglyph Point Trail** follows a leafy footpath once used by the Ancestral Puebloans. Dropping below the canyon rim, it's occasionally steep and rocky before making a short scramble back to the top of the mesa. Look for the petroglyphs at the 1.4-mile mark – a 35ft-wide wall with almost three dozen human and animal figures, spirals and handprints. A gate at the trailhead is locked in the evenings. If you arrive in the early morning, begin the trail in reverse.

Dances & Demonstrations

In summer, the park hosts cultural dances and pottery demonstrations by Native peoples with ancestral connections to Mesa Verde. Fascinating and educational, the events are a way to learn about Mesa Verde's ancient inhabitants and their modern-day descendants. Events are in the Morefield Campground (p788) amphitheater or the main visitor center, typically in the evening.

STARGAZING IN MESA VERDE

An International Dark Sky Park, Mesa Verde's remote location, high elevation and arid climate make it one of the best places in the country to enjoy the night skies. Rangers offer regular nighttime programs, from lectures and star parties to astrophotography workshops, all for free. Alternatively, stop at an overlook (or step out of your tent) to take in the sky on your own.

TOP TIPS

● Visit mid-May to mid-October. Winter and spring bring closures to several areas and amenities, and tours are suspended.

● Tickets for ranger tours can only be purchased online *(recreation.gov)* or by phone, up to 14 days in advance. Tours often sell out, so reserve early.

● Information booklets are stocked in metal bins around the park.

● Fill your tank before you arrive – you'll be driving a lot. At a pinch, there's a gas station at Morefield Campground.

● Cellphone service is limited; download audio tours and maps ahead of time.

● Except for holiday weekends, Morefield Campground almost always has walk-up availability.

THE SUN DANCE

Ricky Hayes, Weeminuche Ute tribal member.

The Sun Dance is one of the most sacred ceremonies for my people, and one I've participated in several times over the course of my life. It's performed as a deep blessing for the tribe and the earth. It takes place the third week in June in a specially made lodge on Sleeping Ute Mountain, on the north side of the reservation. For four days, we pray, dance and fast – no food or water. The ceremony is sometimes called the Thirst Dance because of it. The fasting is especially difficult, given the physical effort and the heat. Many people collapse but eventually rise and continue.

Ouray Hot Springs

Hiking high above Ouray

Forming nearly a complete loop around Ouray, the 6-mile **Perimeter Trail** is one of the most scenic ways to experience the 'Switzerland of America.' Beginning across from the **visitor center** *(visitouray.com)*, the clockwise trail charts an up-and-down path through forests and aspen groves and across creeks and meadows. Highlights include the spectacular **Cascade Falls**, **Baby Bathtubs** (a series of smooth tub-like rock divots) plus the **Ouray Via Ferrata** *(ourayviaferrata.org)* and **Ice Park** *(ourayicepark.com)*, where you can spy people clambering along sheer rock faces or climbing frozen cascades. The pièce de résistance is **Box Cañon Falls** *(visitouray.com/box-canyon-falls; adult/child $7/5)*, a thundering 285ft waterfall that drops into a spectacular quartzite canyon.

Soak in historic springs

For a healing soak or kiddish fun, try **Ouray Hot Springs** *(visitouray.com/ourayhotspringspool; adult/child $26/16)*. The springs were used and considered sacred by the Ute people before they were pushed from the region; later, miners soaked in the same waters to help their tired bodies. Today, the springs are a year-round waterpark surrounded by 13,000ft peaks. Come for the eight-lane lap pool, waterslides, a climbing wall overhanging a splash pool and several adults-only soaking areas (74°F to 106°F; 23°C to 41°C). The geothermal water is crystal clear and free of sulfur smells – a major plus.

 EATING IN OURAY: OUR PICKS

Maggie's Kitchen:	Kami's Samis:	The Smokehouse:	Brickhouse 737:
Graffiti-bombed hole-in-the-wall known for deliciously sloppy burgers and onion rings. Seating on the deck. *11am-8pm Thu-Sat, to 6pm Sun* $	Bright, modern spot with decadent breakfasts, hearty burritos and gourmet sandwiches. Loads of vegan, gluten- and dairy-free options. *7am-2pm* $$	Finger-lickin' BBQ joint serving generous portions of goodness, smoked 'low and slow.' Perfect for a post-hike meal. *8am-2pm Mon-Wed, 8am-2pm & 5-9pm Thu-Sun* $$	Cozy, upscale restaurant serving contemporary American cuisine with flair. Creative top-shelf cocktails. Reservations recommended. *5-9pm* $$$

Telluride

Telluride's past

A national historic landmark, Telluride is one of the country's most iconic Victorian-era towns, its streets lined with elegant buildings that once served as flophouses, saloons, schoolhouses and churches. Stop into the Smithsonian-affiliated **Telluride Historical Museum** (telluridemuseum.org; adult/child $9/6) to learn about Telluride's beginning as a Ute hunting ground, its mining past and its transformation into a world-class ski town. **Guided walking tours** ($15) also offered on summer and fall afternoons.

Waterfalls, lakes and panoramic views

A network of trails branch out like arteries from the heart of Telluride, crisscrossing the town's box canyon, from easy strolls along the scenic **Telluride River Trail** (4.4 miles) to the strenuous, wildflower-filled **Sneffels Highline Trail** (12.5 miles). For something in between, hike to Colorado's tallest waterfall, the 365ft **Bridal Veil Falls** (2.5 miles to the bottom, 3.4 miles to the top), along rocky switchbacks through a thick aspen forest, passing two smaller waterfalls along the way. From there, extend your hike by continuing along a narrow mining road, passing through alpine meadows and forests to the otherworldly **Blue Lake** (5.7 miles, 12,400ft).

Ski and board in style

Known for plunging runs and deep powder, those gorgeous San Juan Mountain views and a certain high-society *je ne sais quoi*, **Telluride Ski Resort** (tellurideskiresort.com; adult/child lift ticket $245/125) is a special place. Decently sized in terms of lifts and acres – it has three distinct areas served by 19 lifts – Telluride has an outsize supply of advanced and expert terrain, from steeps to trees to wide open cirques, and even more if you are willing to hike for it, including iconic Palmyra Peak. There are also ample options for beginners and intermediate cruisers, including the playful, 4.6-mile Galloping Goose run.

Banjos, hula hoops and more

Telluride Bluegrass Festival (bluegrass.com/telluride) is the town's most famous fest, a summer solstice celebration of folk music and mountain life. It draws big-name bands and over 10,000 revelers daily – many donning hula hoops as dance partners. The main stage is set in the leafy town park

TELLURIDE TOURS

Telluride Offroad Adventures: Enjoy rugged passes and stunning scenery on a variety of deluxe 4WD tours, from two-hour jaunts to full-day adventures.

Telluride Wranglers: Authentic and adventurous trail rides of various lengths and skill levels, with small groups and expert guides.

Telluride Flyfishers: Memorable all-levels fly-fishing trips on the San Miguel and Dolores rivers, or hiking to alpine lakes and streams.

Telluride Outside: One-stop shop for excellent year-round adventuring, from snowmobiling to 4WD tours to stand-up paddleboarding.

Mountain Trip: Born out of an Alaska mountaineering school; trips include rock climbing, backcountry skiing and more.

 EATING IN TELLURIDE: OUR PICKS

| **Brown Dog Pizza:** Buzzing pizza joint known for its award-winning Detroit-style pizza. Come early or prepare to wait for a table. *11:30am-9pm* $ | **Butcher & Baker:** Cute breakfast spot with generous to-go sandwiches and sides perfect for the trail. *7am-8pm Mon-Sat, 8am-2pm Sun* $$ | **Wood Ear:** Ramen meets Texas smokehouse at this inventive underground spot. Creative cocktails available to go in reusable plastic flasks. *5-9pm* $$$ | **221 South Oak:** New American cuisine by award-winning chef Eliza Gavin. Dine in the historic home or the leafy patio. *10am-1pm & 5-9:30pm Sun, from 5pm Mon-Sat* $$$ |

INTERNATIONAL DARK SKY PARK

Black Canyon of the Gunnison is an outstanding place for stargazing, thanks to its clear, dry weather and exceptionally dark skies. In 2015 the park became one of Colorado's first International Dark Sky Places (the state has 10), thanks to the park's work to limit light pollution and educate visitors on topics like astronomy and nocturnal ecosystems. Summer brings loads of **free astronomy programs** by park rangers and members of the Black Canyon Astronomical Society. In September, the park hosts **AstroFest**, with nightly telescope viewings, constellation tours, guest lectures by astronomers and info on the park's nocturnal animals.

with late-night concerts and free workshops held in smaller venues around town. Tickets sell out fast for the June event – buy early and consider a combo ticket-and-camping package for an all-in experience.

Telluride also hosts some two-dozen other festivals throughout the year. Faves include **Mountainfilm** *(mountainfilm.org)*, a documentary film festival held every Memorial Day Weekend (late May); **Telluride Mushroom Festival** *(tellurideinstitute.org/telluride-mushroom-festival)*, a celebration and education on all things fungi the third weekend in August (don't miss the parade); the internationally renowned **Telluride Film Festival** *(telluridefilmfestival.org)* over Labor Day Weekend (early September), and the season-ending **Blues & Brews Festival** *(tellurideblues.com)* in mid-September.

Black Canyon of the Gunnison National Park & Around

Views and climbing around a national park

With 2000ft-high canyon walls and colorful craggy spires, a drive along the spectacular south rim of the **Black Canyon of the Gunnison National Park** *(nps.gov/blca, per vehicle $30)* is the most popular way to experience it. For 7 miles, the flat, winding and paved **South Rim Rd** hugs the canyon's edge with a dozen overlooks offering heart-stopping views. Good pullouts include **Pulpit Rock Overlook**, a finger-like outcropping with expansive river views; **Chasm View**, the canyon's narrowest point, and **Painted Wall**, Colorado's tallest vertical cliff (2250ft), named after the magnificent pink pegmatite stripes that stretch half a mile across. Be aware there are few guardrails – keep small children close and watch your step, especially while taking selfies.

If you're an experienced climber, don't miss the lesser-traveled **North Rim**. An 80-mile drive from the South Rim (there's no bridge over the canyon), the area has 145 multipitch climbing routes rated between 5.9 and 5.13, including along the **North Chasm** and to the top of the **Painted Wall**. Wilderness permits are required, available for free at the **North Rim Ranger Station**. For guided climbing trips try **Mountain Trip** *(mountaintrip.com)* or **IRIS** *(irisalpine.com)*, an outdoors company catering to women, non-binary and trans people.

Note: in winter, South Rim Rd is only open to vehicles up to the visitor center; the remainder is open to cross-country skiers and snowshoers only. The North Rim roads are entirely closed.

Learn about the Ute

One of the few American museums dedicated to a single tribe, the **Ute Indian Museum** *(historycolorado.org/ute-indian-museum; adult/child $7/free)* in Montrose examines the many cultural and historical layers of Colorado's longest continuous residents. Artifacts, displays, videos and hands-on exhibits paint a powerful portrait of the Ute people, past and present. There are regular speaker series and film screenings, too. The museum sits on the homestead of legendary Ute Chief Ouray and his wife, Chipeta.

TOP EXPERIENCE

Dinosaur National Monument

At the end of desolate stretches of blacktop, Dinosaur National Monument is arguably Colorado's most remote destination. But for travelers fascinated by prehistoric life, it's worth every lonely mile. Spanning the Colorado–Utah border, it's one of the few places on earth where you can reach out and touch a dinosaur skeleton, snarling in its final pose, petrified eternally in rock and stone.

The Fossils

The park's indoor highlight is in Utah – the 150ft-long **Dinosaur Quarry Wall** with some 1500 dinosaur bones embedded in it. Part of an ancient riverbed where the remains of Jurassic-era dinosaurs were deposited and later fossilized, bones from allosaurus to stegosaurus can be seen.

Just outside, the **Fossil Discovery Trail** is one of the world's most spectacular open-air collections of fossils, with dinosaur bones, marine creatures and plants visible in the rocks. The moderate 1.2-mile trail has interpretive signs explaining the sights and distinct geological stages.

Panoramic Views

In Colorado, **Harpers Corner Trail** is a moderate 2-mile hike through juniper forests that eventually open to views of the park's winding canyons. At the trail's end, hikers are rewarded with spectacular views of the confluence of the Yampa and Green rivers at jutting **Steamboat Rock**. The trailhead is off Harpers Corner Rd, a scenic drive in itself.

Rafting

Rafting the Green and Yampa rivers is a popular way to experience the park. Expect class-III and -IV rapids, red-hued canyons, sandstone formations and petroglyphs. **Adrift** (adrift.com; adult/child from $120/99) and **OARS** (oars.com; from $1049) offer single and multiday trips, beginning in Utah.

TOP TIPS

● The Utah and Colorado entrances are 28 miles apart – about a 30-minute drive. Plan accordingly, especially to include a quarry visit.

● Services are few and far. Before heading out, fill your tank and be sure to carry drinks and snacks.

PRACTICALITIES
● nps.gov/dino
● per vehicle $25
● 24hr

TOP EXPERIENCE

Colorado National Monument

Colorado National Monument is a stunning natural area. Just 16 miles west of Grand Junction, it's a warren of canyons, their sheer walls painted a gorgeous cedar red and punctuated by long, rocky fins, dramatic sandstone spires and massive overhangs. It's an adventurer's (and photographer's) dream.

TOP TIPS

- Rim Rock Dr can close in winter or after storms – check the website for current conditions.
- Arrive in early morning for sightings of bighorn sheep, mule deer and golden eagles.
- Rim Rock Dr is popular with cyclists. Give them space on the narrow, curvy road.

PRACTICALITIES

- nps.gov/colm
- per vehicle $25
- 24hr

Driving Past Red Rocks

The most popular way to experience the park is driving the paved 23-mile **Rim Rock Dr**, which weaves along the cliff edges, with 19 pull-outs offering vertiginous vistas of the red sandstone cliffs, monoliths and formations carved by millions of years of erosion. Pull-outs have interpretive signage explaining the park's history, geology, flora and fauna.

Hiking Through the Park

Forty-six miles of trails make for outstanding and varied hikes, allowing visitors to appreciate the landscape close-up. Popular trails include **Devil's Kitchen** (1.9 miles round trip), a short hike and scramble to a large stone outcrop; and **Monument Canyon Trail** (11.6 miles round trip), which passes many of the park's most interesting natural features, including **Kissing Couple**, **Independence Monument** and **Coke Ovens**.

Climbing Sandstone

Colorado National Monument is a dream for experienced rock climbers, with towering sandstone spires of smooth rock interspersed with cracks, chimneys and ledges. Some favorites include **Otto's Route** on Independence Monument, the park's iconic 450ft sandstone monolith (5.9 rating); and **Sentinel Spire** with its beautiful crack routes such as West Face (5.11 rating), with steep, challenging terrain and breathtaking exposure. Head to **Gearhead Outfitters** (gearheadoutfitters.com) in Grand Junction for equipment, maps and route recommendations.

Colorado Springs

Olympic tour

The **Colorado Springs Olympic Training Center** *(usopc.org/training-centers; adult/child $16/12)* is one of just three such centers in the country. Tour the training facility (maybe spotting a few Olympic hopefuls in action), or check out the **US Olympic & Paralympic Museum** *(usopm.org; adult/child $30/17)* 2.5 miles away. The museum's spectacular and accessibly designed complex houses 12 galleries capturing Olympic history through memorabilia, athlete profiles and interactive training exhibits.

See the Garden of the Gods

This gorgeous vein of red sandstone (about 290 million years old) appears elsewhere along Colorado's Front Range, but the exquisitely thin cathedral spires and mountain backdrop of the **Garden of the Gods** *(gardenofgods.com; free)* are particularly striking. Gazing from the base of the highest rock formations on the **Perkins Central Garden Trail** inspires awe and humility. From there, numerous paved trails lead to central formations such as the **Kissing Camels**, **Three Graces** and **Montezuma's Tower**. Depending on your timing, you could easily spend an hour or two here. For more park information, stop in at the excellent visitors center. In summer, consider visiting **Rock Ledge Ranch** *(rockledgeranch.com; adult/child $8/4)*, a living history museum near the park entrance, that gives insight into the lives of the Utes and 19th-century homesteaders in the region.

Summit Pikes Peak

Pikes Peak *(coloradosprings.gov/drivepikespeak)* at 14,115ft may not be the tallest of Colorado's 54 fourteeners, but it's certainly the most popular – over 500,000 people summit it yearly. Called Mountain of the Sun by the Ute, it crowns the southern Front Range, majestically rising 7800ft from the plains. There are three ways to ascend it, all from Manitou Springs: Pikes Peak Hwy winding 19 miles to the top (three hours round trip; timed-entry reservations required late May to September); the 1891 cog railway (three hours round trip; reservations necessary), and **Barr Trail**, which most hikers split into a two-day trip due to the 7800ft elevation gain, camping at Barr Camp (10,200ft).

THE GREAT FRUITCAKE TOSS

Through the years it's been suggested that leftover fruitcakes (are there fruitcakes that are not leftover?) reincarnate as anything from doorstops to science experiments to an eco-friendly answer to street paving. Manitou has the answer: the **Great Fruitcake Toss** *(manitousprings.org)*, held each January in Memorial Park. Tosses are assessed for distance, balance, accuracy and aim, and fruitcakes are launched by mechanical devices. For staunch defenders of the edibility of fruitcakes, there's a bake-off for the best organic, non-GMO, natural fruitcake. The event supports the Manitou Springs Food Pantry and the tossed leftovers go to Jezebel the pig at Sun Mountain, so everyone is a winner.

EATING IN COLORADO SPRINGS: OUR PICKS

Birdtree Cafe: Fanciful and lively, with all-day breakfast and lunch. Veg/vegan options, rich coffee, gorgeous cocktails and a patio across from Acacia Park. *hours vary* **$$**

TAPAteria: Beautifully rendered, gluten-free Spanish tapas, with an extensive Spanish wine list. There's a 'secret' patio out back. *noon-10pm* **$$**

Uchenna: Expect homestyle cooking and a warm family atmosphere at chef Maya's Ethiopian restaurant, tucked in a shopping mall. *11:30am-2:30pm & 5-9pm Tue-Sat* **$$**

Westside Cantina: Vibrant and festive (the patio is lovely), offering cocktails and tacos with distinctive flavors and fresh ingredients. *hours vary* **$$**

THE SANTA FE TRAIL

The Santa Fe Trail linked Missouri with New Mexico (a Mexican province from 1821 to 1848), bringing manufactured goods west, and Mexican silver and Native American jewelry and blankets east. The 800-mile route took seven to eight weeks to cross in a covered wagon, and was defined by monotony and hardship. Near Dodge City in Kansas, the route divided: the southern road (Cimarron Route) cut down into New Mexico and was shorter but more dangerous, while the northern road (Mountain Route) continued through Bent's Fort and Trinidad, and was longer but safer. With the expansion of the railroad west, trade along the route eventually diminished, coming to a close in 1880.

Great Sand Dunes National Park

Great Sand Dunes National Park

Experience a natural wonder

A standout even in a state with a tapestry of exceptional beauty, **Great Sand Dunes National Park** (nps.gov/grsa; per vehicle $25) appears like an undulating sea of sand bounded by jagged peaks and scrubby plains. Home to the tallest dunes in North America, including 750ft **Star Dune**, its hikes can be challenging on the shifting sand but the rewards are otherworldly views. For a thrill, try sandboarding down the sandy slopes on special wood planks; rentals are available at **Great Sand Dunes Oasis** (greatdunes.com) near the park entrance. If you time it right, you can even enjoy a beach day alongside the dunes – in late spring, **Medano Creek** is born from snowmelt that flows from the mountains, perfect for wading and water play, disappearing by mid-summer.

Santa Fe Trail

A drive through Colorado's complicated past

Drive Hwy 350 to experience the western reaches of the Great Plains and the Santa Fe Trail. Start at **Bent's Old Fort National Historic Site** (nps.gov/beol). The beautifully restored adobe fort, used between 1833 and 1849, was once a cultural crossroads and the busiest settlement west of the Missouri.

Head northeast to Fort Lyon, where on November 29, 1864, US soldiers attacked a peaceful Cheyenne and Arapaho encampment. More than 150 people, mostly elders, women and children, were slaughtered, an event commemorated at nearby **Sand Creek Massacre National Historic Site** (nps.gov/sand).

Drive through Granada to **Amache National Historic Site** (nps.gov/amch). A WWII Japanese internment camp, it was the result of a racist response to the bombing of Pearl Harbor that forced the relocation and incarceration of people of Japanese descent, mostly US citizens. Amache once held 7567 prisoners, all brought from central California.

Wyoming

OTHERWORLDLY LANDSCAPES | COWBOY CULTURE | NATIVE HERITAGE

Wyoming is a land of extremes. Much of the state is a vast expanse of windswept plains and sagebrush hills, baking (or freezing) under brooding skies. Towns are infused with western grit and residents are content to keep this chunk of the West wild. But the country's least populated state (less than 600,000 inhabitants) is also home to one of the busiest and most recognizable natural destinations in the world, Yellowstone National Park, with its iconic geysers, unique geology and abundant wildlife. Add to that the glitzy ski destination of Jackson Hole and the truly grand Teton Range, and you'll forget Wyoming ever seemed so isolated. Wyoming also has a rich Native American history, including sites like Medicine Wheel and Devil's Tower National Monument. The Wind River Reservation hosts a remarkable regional powwow and is the final resting place of Sacajawea, the teenage mother who famously aided the Lewis and Clark expedition.

Places

Cheyenne p751

Laramie p752

Sinks Canyon State Park p753

Fort Washakie p753

Pinesdale p754

Fort Laramie p755

Devil's Tower National Monument p755

Medicine Wheel National Historic Landmark p755

Cody p756

Jackson p757

Yellowstone National Park p758

Grand Teton National Park p762

☑ TOP TIP

The weather can change quickly throughout the entire state. Be sure to wear layers and check out **Wyoming Road Conditions** *(wyoroad.info)* before setting off. If the weather gets rough, highway patrol will shut an entire interstate until it clears.

GETTING AROUND

Wyoming has several airports, **Jackson Hole Airport** being the biggest and **Laramie Regional Airport** typically the cheapest. Once here, the long distances between destinations make having your own car much preferred – the **Greyhound** *(greyhound.com)* bus is mostly limited to small towns in the south and east. While 4WD may not be essential, a high-clearance vehicle will make navigating dirt roads easier. Wyoming is notorious for its winds and fierce gusts; take special care if you are driving a recreational vehicle (RV) or pulling a trailer. Gas stations are rare, even on major highways – don't miss a chance to gas up.

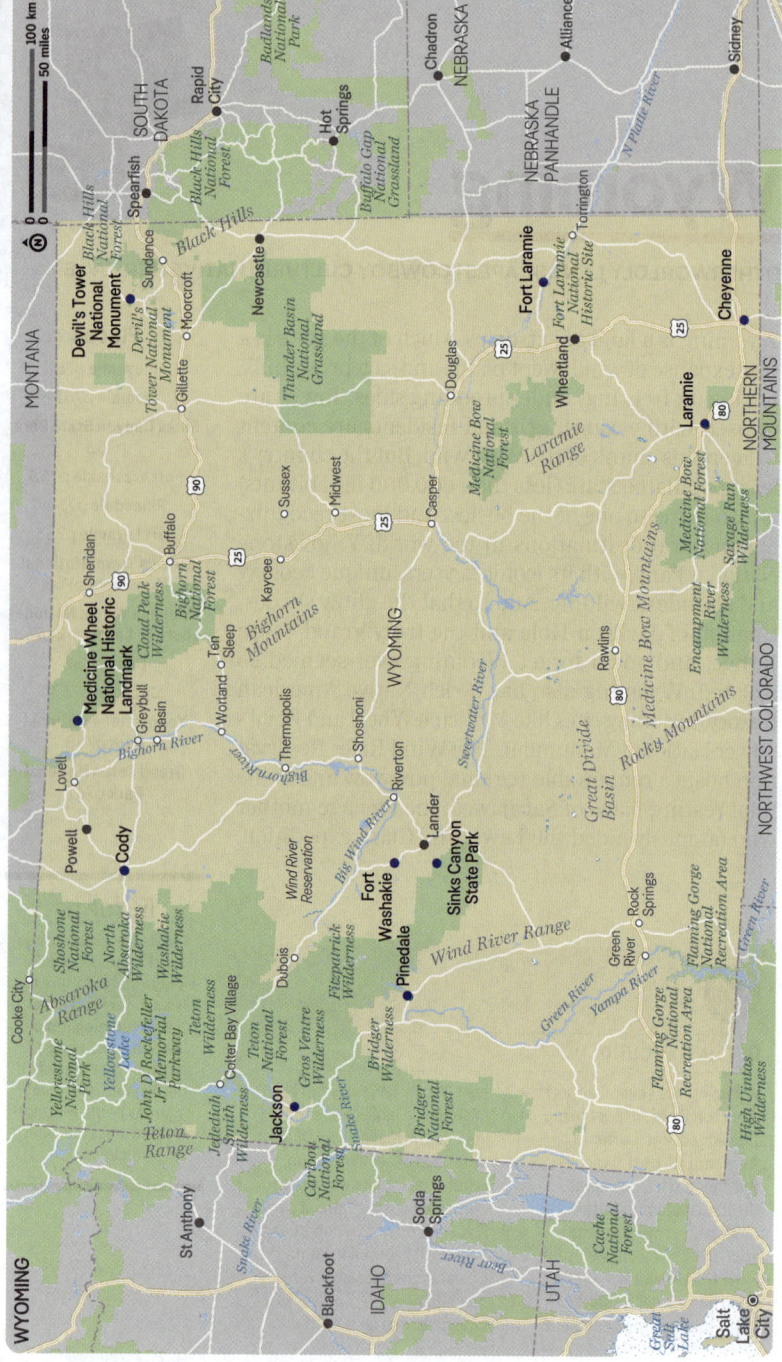

Cheyenne

Experience Cheyenne Frontier Days

Every late July since 1897, **Cheyenne Frontier Days** *(cfdrodeo.com; prices vary)* – the country's largest rodeo and celebration of all things Wyoming – has been taking over the capital city. A 10-day showcase of cowboy culture, the heart of the action is in Frontier Park, where rodeo events like bronco and bull riding, barrel racing and team roping bring top contenders and big prize money. If the events are sold out or are just too pricey, free tickets to qualifying rounds, or 'slack' rodeos, are offered too. Or check out the wildly popular Frontier Town, recreating 19th-century life with costumed characters, making sure to stop in the Indian Village, where modern-day Native dance and storytelling traditions are showcased. Evenings bring big-name music acts to Frontier Park's arena too. In town, check out the seemingly nonstop lineup of concerts, parades, air shows, carnivals and chili cook-offs that transform the typically sleepy town.

A walk through the Old West

For a deep dive into Cheyenne's pioneer past and rodeo present, visit the **Old West Museum** *(cfdrodeo.com/event/old-west-museum; adult/child $15/10)* on the Cheyenne Frontier Days rodeo grounds. It's chock-full of rodeo memorabilia, from saddles to trophies. It also displays cowboy art and photography, houses a fine collection of horse-drawn buggies, and dispenses nuggets of history – such as the story of Steamboat, the unrideable bronco who likely isn't the one depicted on Wyoming's license plates (though many will tell you he is).

All about Wyoming's history

While in Cheyenne, stop in the **Wyoming State Museum** *(wyomuseum.wyo.gov; free)* a thoughtfully curated attraction focused exclusively on the state's natural and cultural history. Spread across two floors, exhibits showcase Wyoming's dinosaur findings and modern-day wildlife, mining and national parks, plus Native American peoples and pioneers. Three to four temporary exhibits keep the museum current. If you're traveling with little ones, don't miss the hands-on area with dress-up clothes, a pint-size tipi and a recreated chuck wagon.

MARDI GRAS OF THE WEST

Sam Masoudi, Chief Investment Officer, Wyoming Retirement System.

Frontier Days in Cheyenne is a really big deal. The city gets taken over with it! People dress up for it, and there are a lot of hardcore cowboys and a decent number of bikers too. If you're going to watch rodeo, it's extraordinary, with some of the best bull riders in the country and lots of other events like women's barrel racing and cattle drives. It also has one of the biggest country-music concerts in the country. There are chuck-wagon cook-offs, too, where people prep dishes only using ingredients and tools available during pioneer days. Plus, there's a US Air Force Thunderbirds flyover. It's all really interesting, so fun. It's like the Mardi Gras of Western culture!

 EATING IN CHEYENNE: OUR PICKS

Luxury Diner: Go-to breakfast spot, set in a turn-of-the-20th-century trolley car. If in doubt, order anything with green chili. 7am-2pm Mon-Sat, to 1pm Sun $	**2 Doors Down:** Popular burger joint specializing in offbeat toppings, from teriyaki to mac 'n' cheese. Bottomless fries too. 11am-9pm Mon-Sat $	**Napoli's:** Upscale dinner spot with an art-deco ambiance. Expect mouthwatering Italian fare and attentive service. Don't miss the tiramisu. 4-9pm Tue-Sat $$	**Bunkhouse Bar & Grill:** Honky-tonk serving steaks and Rocky Mountain oyster sandwiches. Live music on weekends. 11am-8pm Wed-Thu & Sun, 11am-11pm Fri & Sat $$

SACAJAWEA

Sacajawea, the famed Shoshone interpreter on the Lewis and Clark expedition, has all but disappeared into popular myth. But this remarkable teenager embodied profound intelligence and resourcefulness. Born near Salmon, Idaho in 1788, she was kidnapped and enslaved by Hidatsa tribesmen at age 12. Two years later, a pregnant Sacajawea joined the expedition with her proclaimed husband, a French-Canadian fur trader who 'won' her gambling. Her presence proved invaluable; beyond her linguistic abilities, she helped secure horses and safe passage from the Shoshone. Though the details of her death are debated, Shoshone oral tradition holds she lived on the Wind River Reservation, dying in 1884. Her gravestone and statue sit on a quiet hillside cemetery in Fort Washakie.

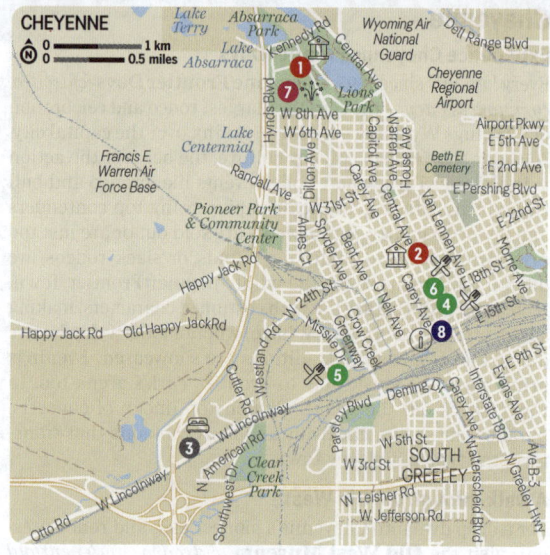

- 🔴 **SIGHTS**
  1. Old West Museum
  2. Wyoming State Museum
- ⚫ **SLEEPING**
  3. Cheyenne Guest Inn
- 🟢 **EATING**
  4. 2 Doors Down
  5. Luxury Diner
  6. Napoli's
- 🔴 **ENTERTAINMENT**
  7. Cheyenne Frontier Days
- 🔵 **INFORMATION**
  8. Cheyenne Visitor Center

Touring Cheyenne's public art

Cowboy boots are about as Wyoming as Buffalo Bill, and sculptures of colorful, larger-than-life boots add quirky charm to downtown Cheyenne. Even better, these boots can talk. Stop by the **Cheyenne Visitor Center** (*cheyenne.org*) for the brochure *These Boots are made for Talking* (or download it from the website). With the brochure in hand, follow the map to any of the 35 boot-sculptures, dial 307-316-0067, then enter the number of the boot as shown on the brochure – you'll hear the story of the boot from the artist and, in the process, learn a whole new side to the city's history.

Laramie

Spend time in prison

Stop at the impressively restored **Wyoming Territorial Prison State Historic Site** (*wyoparks.wyo.gov*; adult/child $9/4.50) to learn all about the reality of prison life in the Wild West. It is also the only prison to have held Butch Cassidy, who was in for grand larceny from 1894 to '96, only to emerge a well-connected criminal who fast became one of history's greatest robbers. His life story is told in thrilling detail in a back room, while the faces of other 'malicious and desperate outlaws' – including several women – stare hauntingly at you as you explore the main cellblocks. Outside, tour the factory where convicts produced more than 700 brooms a day – one of the prison's short-lived revenue-generating schemes. Staff members are posted throughout the site, happily answering questions; free guided tours offered May to September.

Marvel at prehistoric finds

The Morrison Formation – a vast Jurassic-era sedimentary rock layer – stretches from New Mexico to Montana, with its fossil-rich center in Wyoming. This 150-million-year-old formation has produced some of the world's most significant dinosaur discoveries in paleontology, many of which are housed in the University of Wyoming's tiny, but well-worth-a-stop, **Geological Museum** *(uwyo.edu/geomuseum; free)*. Inside, marvel at a towering 75ft apatosaurus skeleton (formerly known as the brontosaurus) as well as a rare *Diatryma gigantea*, a 7ft-tall, flightless carnivorous bird that once roamed the region's prehistoric swamps. Be sure to linger at the 'Prep Lab' observation window, where researchers liberate brittle fossils from solid rock.

Sinks Canyon State Park

See a geological phenomenon

Six miles southwest of Lander lies **Sinks Canyon State Park** *(sinkscanyonstatepark.org; free)*, a beautiful forested park nestled deep in a glacial canyon. Popular for day hikes, it's best known for a geological phenomenon involving the Middle Fork of the Popo Agie River. Here, the fast-flowing river suddenly turns into a large limestone cavern, disappearing into cracks and fissures at its back wall, known as the Sinks. The river is not seen again for nearly a quarter-mile, until it reemerges in a tranquil pool called the Rise, which is filled with enormous trout. Despite the short distance between the two, dye tests indicate that in addition to taking over two hours for the river to make the subterranean journey, it also reemerges warmer and more voluminous. The reason continues to intrigue scientists. A paved trail between the two areas makes for a scenic walk, with interpretive signs along the way explaining more about the geology, ecology and history of the park.

Fort Washakie

Wyoming's largest powwow

In late June, head to Fort Washakie on the Wind River Reservation – home of the Eastern Shoshone and Northern Arapaho peoples – where **Eastern Shoshone Indian Days** *(windriver.org; free)* is hosted. The largest and longest-running powwow in Wyoming, the three-day event is a spectacular intertribal celebration of Native identity; expect all manner of competitive dancing, drumming groups and Grand Entry ceremonies, participants of all ages decked out in magnificent regalia. Beyond the arena, artisans and food vendors line the grounds, selling

MATTHEW SHEPARD

In October 1998, Matthew Shepard, a student at University of Wyoming in Laramie, was attacked and brutally beaten, tied to a roadside fence, and left to die – all because he was gay. Shepard's murder drew national attention to hate crimes against LGBTQ+ people and spurred an outpouring of grief, outrage, activism and urgent creativity, including the critically acclaimed play *The Laramie Project*. Shepard's parents founded the **Matthew Shepard Foundation** *(matthewshepard.org)*, dedicated to promoting LGBTQ+ rights, which helped to expand federal hate-crime legislation to include sexual orientation and gender identity. A memorial bench for Shephard now sits at University of Wyoming; it bears the quiet inscription 'He continues to make a difference.'

Devil's Tower National Monument

GREEN RIVER RENDEZVOUS

In mid-July, the town of Pinedale hosts the **Green River Rendezvous Festival** (*green riverrendezvous. com*), a four-day celebration of the region's mountain man heritage. The event commemorates the annual summer 'Rendezvous' of the early 1800s where fur trappers, Native Americans and traders would gather to buy supplies, trade goods and generally party. Today, the event includes a lively parade down Main Street, historical reenactments, shooting demonstrations, craft fairs and cultural performances by Shoshone and Arapaho people. Presentations by historians are also offered at the Museum of the Mountain Man, for those looking for a deeper dive into Wyoming's frontier history.

Native goods, art and eats. While the powwow is open to the public, be mindful when taking photographs – the arena is considered a sacred place. Keep an ear out for announcements limiting photography; if in doubt, ask before snapping a pic.

Visit the Shoshone Tribal Cultural Center

Inside Fort Washakie School, learn all about the history of Wind River Reservation and its people at the **Shoshone Tribal Cultural Center** (*easternshoshone.org/cultural-center; free*). Exhibits highlight Eastern Shoshone history and contemporary tribal life as well as the legacy of Chief Washakie, renowned for his ability to navigate the changing physical and political landscapes of the West during the 1800s. There's also a display on the life of Sacajawea, Lewis and Clark's now-famous guide and interpreter. For a deeper dive in the Eastern Shoshone, ask about **guided tours of the reservation** (*by donation*); led by staff member Robyn Rofkar, tours last a few hours to multiple days, providing unique insights into the tribe's history and enduring culture.

Pinesdale

Learn about the early pioneers

Make a pitstop in Pinedale for **Museum of the Mountain Man** (*museumofthemountainman.com, adult/child $10, free*), a fascinating museum that deep-dives into the history of the

EATING NEAR FORT WASHAKIE & LANDER: OUR PICKS

| **Middle Fork:** Welcoming breakfast place with local ingredients and homemade baked goods. The eggs Benedict with cottage bacon is tops. *7am-2pm* $ | **Lander Bake Shop:** Family-owned from-scratch bakery and cafe. Sit down for brekkie and order a sandwich for the trail. *7am-4pm Mon-Fri, 8am-2pm Sat & Sun* $ | **Gannett Grill:** Casual spot known for its local grass-fed beef burgers and stone-oven pizzas. In summer, nab a seat on the leafy patio. *11am-10pm* $ | **Cowfish:** Upscale restaurant with surf-and-turf menu, perfect for date night. Order a flight of craft beer, delivered from the attached brewery. *5-10pm* $$$ |

fur trappers who came to the West during the 1820s in search of beaver pelts. An essential part of the region's development, exhibits cover everything from their food and clothing to trapping methods and marriage to Native American women.

Fort Laramie
Imagine life in a fort

In Wyoming's eastern plains, **Fort Laramie National Historic Site** *(nps.gov/fola; free)* is one of the most historically important sites in the state. Established as a fur trading post in 1834, it quickly became a place of rest and restocking for emigrants traveling on the Oregon, Mormon Pioneer and California Trails. By 1849, with surging numbers of Gold Rush fortune seekers – and increasing conflicts with Plains tribespeople – it transformed into one of the largest military forts in the West. Today, you can visit 22 original structures, including enlisted barracks, officers' quarters, a bakery and the post trader's store. Many are furnished with period artifacts. Interpretive signs provide historical context, while the visitor center has exhibits on the fort's complex role in westward expansion and the Indian Wars (don't miss the excellent film). During summer, you also can interact with staff in period dress, who talk about life in the fort and provide demonstrations in things like blacksmithing and military drills. Guided tours available from late May to early September.

Devil's Tower National Monument
Visit a sacred place

Devil's Tower National Monument *(nps.gov/deto; per car $25)*, in northeastern Wyoming, is a dramatic, nearly vertical monolith, rising 1267ft above the Belle Fourche River. Designated the first US national monument in 1906, the tower consists of striking hexagonal columns, some 20ft wide, formed over 50 million years ago. For 20 Native American tribes, the tower – often called Bear Lodge or Bear's Tipi – is a deeply spiritual site. For rock climbers, it is considered one of the best crack climbing spots in the world. Except in June, when tribes request a voluntary climbing moratorium to hold sacred ceremonies, you'll see climbers tackling the tower on over 140 routes. If you'd like to join the crowd, **Sylvan Rocks** *(sylvanrocks.com)* and **Devils Tower Climbing Guides** *(devilstowerlodge.com/Climb)* are highly recommended guides, especially for newbies. Or keep both feet on the ground, and hike the 1.3-mile **Tower Trail** circling the base, with close-up views of the tower. Keep your eyes peeled for prairie dogs.

Medicine Wheel National Historic Landmark
An ancient place of prayer

Medicine Wheel National Historic Landmark *(fs.usda.gov; free)* sits atop Medicine Mountain in Wyoming's Bighorn Range at nearly 10,000ft. A remarkable 80-ft-wide limestone circle with 28 spokes radiating from its central cairn, it is a

INFINITE OUTDOORS ACCESS GRANTED

Accessing public lands in the West is often far more difficult than maps suggest. Though these lands are publicly owned, nearly 16 million acres across the West are considered 'landlocked' – surrounded by private property, with fences and 'No Trespassing' signs blocking entry. In Wyoming alone, over 4.25 million acres of Bureau of Land Management (BLM), state and national forest lands fall into this category. To address this problem, **Infinite Outdoors Access Granted** *(infiniteoutdoorsusa.com/access-granted)* launched an app in 2025 to help outdoor enthusiasts find free entry points to private lands bordering public lands. With an increasing demand for access to public land, this seems to be a viable solution. Time will tell.

GROWING FOOD IN CAPTIVITY

The first year was particularly difficult for the Japanese-American prisoners at Heart Mountain. Torn from their homes hundreds of miles away, they suffered amid the challenging climate and isolation of remote Wyoming. The bland canned food and poor-quality meat only made things worse. James Ito, who grew up on a farm in southern California and graduated from the Berkeley College of Agriculture, organized the Japanese-American farmers among the camp and set to work. Within a year, the camp was growing most of its own food, and by 1945, they were producing a surplus – a remarkable achievement given the growing conditions of the high Wyoming desert. Ito later held a position with the US Department of Agriculture.

sacred site for several Plains tribes. For centuries, it has been used for countless ceremonies, prayers and vision quests. Today, the wheel remains an active sacred site, where cloth bundles, eagle feathers and other offerings are tied to nearby fences. Visitors are welcome to visit from mid-June through September – a well-maintained 1.5-mile trail leads there. Be aware access is occasionally restricted for ceremonies; if one takes place while you're on-site, do not take photographs. And be sure not to touch the offerings.

Cody

A dark episode in US history

Following the Japanese bombing of Pearl Harbor, more than 110,000 Japanese Americans were sent to 10 detention camps across the US. **Heart Mountain Relocation Center** *(heartmountain.org; adult/child $14/10)* in northern Wyoming was among them. Approximately 14,000 Japanese Americans were forcibly relocated from their West Coast homes to live in the 450 flimsy tar-paper barracks that once stood here. Nevertheless, they made the best of their three years of confinement, setting up a newspaper, two theaters and a high school in what quickly became Wyoming's third-largest town. Though few original structures remain – a residential barrack, hospital and root cellar – a free app allows you to point your cellphone at 16 designated stops to see real-time scenes from the internment camp, making it easier to imagine what life was once like here. Be sure to set aside plenty of time to see the powerful exhibits in the interpretive center.

Explore everything Western

Do not miss Wyoming's most impressive human-made attraction: **Buffalo Bill Center of the West** *(centerofthewest.org; adult/child $23/16)*. This sprawling complex of museums showcases everything Western, from the spectacle of Buffalo Bill's world-famous Wild West shows and galleries featuring powerful frontier-oriented artwork in **Buffalo Bill Museum** to the **Cody Firearms Museum**, with over 7000 pieces. Meanwhile, the **Draper Museum of Natural History** brilliantly explores the Yellowstone region's ecosystem; look for Teddy Roosevelt's saddle and one of the world's last buffalo tipis. Be sure to spend time in the visually absorbing **Plains Indian Museum**, an exploration of the past and present of several tribes, as well as the **Whitney Western Art Museum**, home to a world-class collection of Western art plus the recreated

EATING IN CODY: OUR PICKS

Beta Coffeehouse: Locals' favorite boho coffee shop serving baked goods, breakfast fare, and all manner of coffee drinks. *7am-2pm Tue-Fri, 8am-1pm Sat* $

Fat Racks BBQ: Food truck turned diner serving smoky Texas-style BBQ with all the fixings. Eat at outdoor picnic tables or take to go. *11am-7pm Mon-Sat* $$

Pat's Brew House: Woman-owned and -operated brewery with an eclectic menu – steamed mussels to cheeseburgers – plus craft beers on tap. *11am-9pm Wed-Sun* $$

Cody Cattle Company: Popular Western-style buffet – grilled meats, beans, cornbread and more – paired with live country music. *5-7:30pm, summer only* $$$

studio of renowned artist Frederic Remington. Entry is valid for two consecutive days – and you'll need 'em.

Jackson

See elk herds up close

If you're here in winter, head to the **National Elk Refuge & Greater Yellowstone Visitor Center** *(fws.gov/refuge/national-elk; free)*, headquarters for the 24,700-acre reserve on the northeast edge of town. Established in 1912 to protect diminishing numbers of elk herds, it's home to one of North America's largest elk populations, with numbers reaching over 7000 in the colder months. (In summer, the herds migrate into the mountains.) From mid-December to early April, **guided tours on horse-drawn sleighs** *(nersleighrides.com; adult/child $40/25)* take you into the heart of the herd for close-up views, with the snow-covered peaks of the Grand Tetons in the distance. Alternatively, take a free **audio driving tour** through 3.5 miles of the reserve, available on the website; free binoculars, as well as educational exhibits, available at the visitor center.

Mushing in the backcountry

Experience Wyoming's wintry backcountry from a dog's point of view with five-time Iditarod veteran Billy Snodgrass' **Continental Divide Dogsled Adventures** *(dogsledadventures.com; from $190)*. Excursions leave from the Togwotee Mountain Lodge in the Bridger-Teton National Forest, with one or two passengers per sled and a guide driving the team. You'll learn dogsled lore and the sport's history while teams of eight to 14 Alaskan huskies whisk you through the wilderness. Want to mush? Most guides will teach you on a safe stretch of the trail. Round-trip transportation from Jackson available too.

Admire the wild indoors

Set aside a morning in Jackson to visit the nation's only museum dedicated exclusively to wildlife art: **National Museum of Wildlife Art** *(wildlifeart.org, adult/child $18/10)*, a two-story building housing over 5000 works by traditional wildlife masters like Carl Rungius and John Audubon, and modern icons like Pablo Picasso and Andy Warhol. Wander through the collection or take a tour using the museum's excellent app, available in Spanish and English. Kid-geared activities throughout the galleries keep little ones engaged too.

Continued on p760

JACKSON'S BEST OUTDOOR OUTFITTERS

Hole Hiking Experience: Excellent hiking and snowshoeing excursions with naturalists, from two hours to overnight.

Grand Fishing Adventures: Guided fly-fishing on the Snake, Green and Salt rivers, plus exclusive access to Fish Creek.

Dave Hansen Whitewater: Reputable outfit for white-water trips on the Snake River with class II and III rapids.

Jackson Hole EcoTour Operators: Wildlife-watching tours (in vehicles) plus half-day snowshoe and cross-country ski excursions.

Teton Backcountry Guides: Backcountry ski trips including a day of climbing followed by long (3000ft) descents.

Hoback Sports: Rent mountain bikes, road bikes, e-bikes, skis and snowboards.

EATING IN JACKSON: OUR PICKS

Persephone Café Jackson: French bakery-cafe featuring artisanal breads, pastries and breakfast masterpieces. In summer, patio seating is tops. *7am-6pm Mon-Sat, 7am-3pm Sun* $$

Café Genevieve: Log-cabin cafe serving homestyle breakfast and hearty salads and sandwiches. Breakfast s'mores are good anytime. *8am-2pm Mon-Fri, to 2:30pm Sat & Sun* $$

Gather in Jackson Hole: Upscale yet laid-back restaurant featuring modern American fare with Asian and Mediterranean twists. Elk, trout and bison feature prominently. *5-9pm* $$$

Gun Barrel Steak and Game House: Jackson's best steakhouse, offering all manner of game. Set in a one-time wildlife museum; taxidermy still features large. *5-9pm* $$$

Grand Prismatic Spring

TOP EXPERIENCE

Yellowstone National Park

Teeming with wildlife, America's first national park also contains some of its wildest lands. Yellowstone is home to over 60% of the world's geysers – hot springs that periodically erupt in towering explosions of water. And while these astounding phenomena, and their neighboring Technicolor hot springs and bubbling mud pots draw in over 4.5 million visitors yearly, the surrounding canyons, mountains and forests are no less impressive.

Geyser Country

Yellowstone's **Geyser Country** holds the park's most spectacular geothermal features (over half the world's total) within the world's densest concentration of geysers (over 200 spouters in 1.5 sq miles). Many have boardwalks circling them, making it easy (and safe) to observe them up close. Don't miss **Old Faithful**, the park's poster child, spouting some 8000 gallons of water 180ft into the air every 90-ish minutes; **Black Sand Geyser Canyon** with its steaming vents and bubbling pools contrasted against rugged cliffs; and **Grand Prismatic Spring**, a 330-ft-wide shimmering hot spring, the largest in

DON'T MISS
- Old Faithful
- Grand Prismatic Spring
- Artist Point
- Yellowstone Lake
- Tribal Heritage Center

PRACTICALITIES
- nps.gov/yell
- per vehicle $35
- 24hr

the country. Most of Yellowstone's geysers line the Firehole River, whose tributaries feed 21 of the park's 110 waterfalls.

Mammoth Country

Mammoth Country is renowned for its geothermal terraces and the towering Gallatin Range to the northwest. **Mammoth Hot Springs** is the area's main attraction, a graceful collection of travertine terraces and cascading hot pools. Some terraces are bone dry; others sparkle with hundreds of minuscule pools, coral-like formations and a fabulous palette of colors. An hour's worth of boardwalks wind their way through a landscape so otherworldly it provided the backdrop for the planet Vulcan in *Star Trek* (1979).

Tower-Roosevelt Country

Ancient petrified forests, the wildlife-rich **Lamar Valley**, its tributary trout streams of Slough and Pebble Creeks, and the dramatic and craggy peaks of the Absaroka Range are the highlights in this remote, scenic and undeveloped region. Come to see one of the largest herds of bison and elk in North America.

Canyon Country

A series of scenic overlooks linked by hiking trails punctuate the cliffs, precipices and waterfalls of the **Grand Canyon of the Yellowstone**. Here the Yellowstone River continues to gouge out a fault line through an ancient geyser basin, most impressively at **Lower Falls**. South Rim Dr leads to the canyon's most spectacular overlook, at **Artist Point**, while North Rim Dr accesses the daring precipices of the Upper and Lower Falls.

Lake Country

Yellowstone Lake (7733ft) is Lake Country's shimmering centerpiece – one of the world's largest alpine lakes, with the biggest inland population of cutthroat trout in the US. Yellowstone River emerges from the north end of the lake and flows through Hayden Valley into the Grand Canyon of the Yellowstone. The lake's southern and eastern borders flank the steep Absaroka Range and the pristine Thorofare region, some of the wildest and remotest lands in the lower 48. This watery wilderness is best explored by boat; rentals available at **Bridge Bay Marina** *(yellowstonenationalparklodges.com; rowboat/motor boat from $53/76)*.

Tribal Heritage Center

Located near **Old Faithful Visitor Education Center**, the **Tribal Heritage Center** pays homage to the region's 27 associated tribal nations. From mid-May through mid-October, Indigenous artists, historians and craft makers give presentations and demonstrations in everything from beadwork and moccasin-making to storytelling and dancing. It's a great place to learn from people with a deep connection to Yellowstone.

BISON PROWESS

Despite their docile, hulking appearance, bison are surprisingly agile. They become increasingly uneasy when approached. A raised tail indicates one of two possibilities: a charge or discharge. Statistically, bison are much more dangerous than bears. Every year visitors are gored and seriously injured, sometimes even killed, by bison. Keep your distance to avoid becoming an unwilling rodeo clown, especially in August when it's rutting season.

TOP TIPS

● Visit in May or October. Services may be limited, but there will be far fewer people.

● Hit the trail. Most (95%) of visitors never set foot on a backcountry trail; only 1% camp at a backcountry site (permit required).

● Bike the park. Most campgrounds have underutilized hiker/cyclist sites, and you can slip through any traffic jam.

● Mimic the wildlife. Be active during the golden hours after dawn and before dusk.

● Pack a lunch. Eat at one of the park's many overlooked and often lovely scenic picnic areas.

● Wintertime means you'll likely have Old Faithful to yourself. Just bundle up.

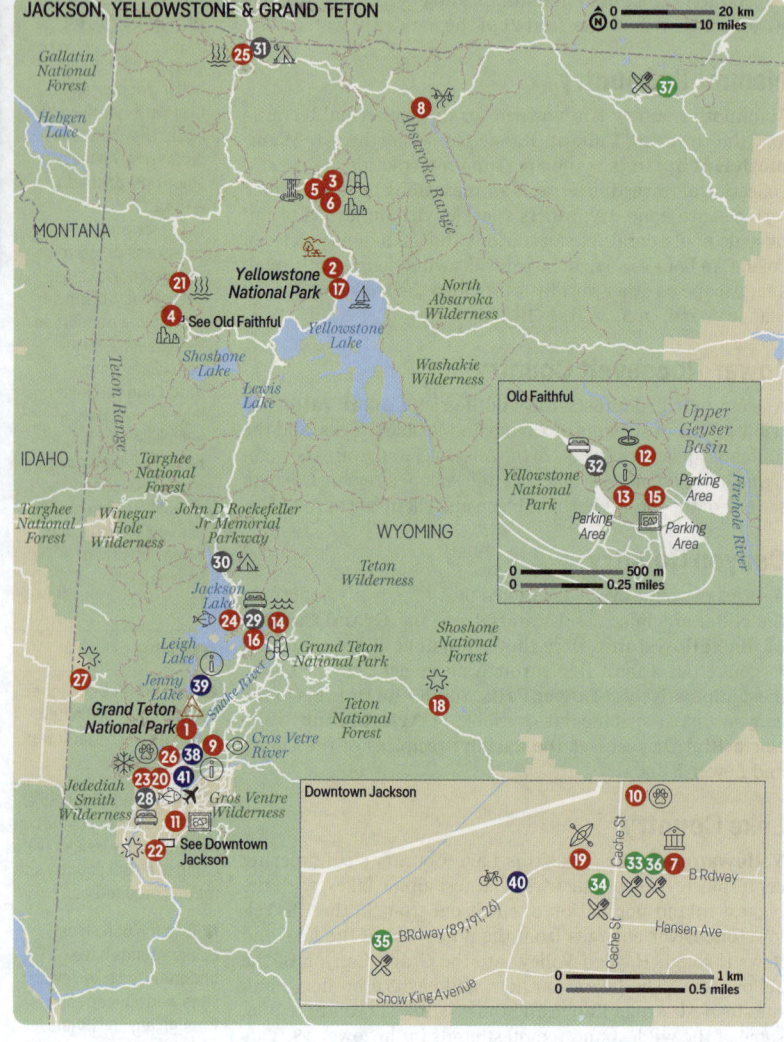

Continued from p757

Even if the museum is closed, the mile-long sculpture trail is worth visiting with works of art set into the rugged hillside, all with spectacular views over the National Elk Refuge (p757).

Examine Jackson's past

Stop at **History Jackson Hole** (*jacksonholehistory.org; adult/child $12/free*), a state-of-the-art museum chronicling over 11,000 years of regional history through interactive displays and storytelling. Open artifact drawers and watch documentaries, peruse digital photo libraries, and step inside two preserved

- **HIGHLIGHTS**
  1. Grand Teton National Park
  2. Yellowstone National Park
- **SIGHTS**
  3. Artist Point
  4. Black Sand Geyser Canyon
  5. Brink of the Lower Falls
  6. Grand Canyon of the Yellowstone
  7. History Jackson Hole
  8. Lamar Valley
  9. Mormon Row
  10. National Elk Refuge & Greater Yellowstone Visitor Center
  11. National Museum of Wildlife Art
  12. Old Faithful
  13. Old Faithful Visitor Education Center
  14. Oxbow Bend
  15. Tribal Heritage Center
  16. Willow Flats Turnout
- **ACTIVITIES**
  17. Bridge Bay Marina
  18. Continental Divide Dogsled Adventures
  19. Dave Hansen Whitewater
  20. Grand Fishing Adventures
  21. Grand Prismatic Spring
  22. Jackson Hole EcoTour Operators
  23. Jackson Hole Mountain Resort
  24. Jackson Lake
  - see 39 Jenny Lake Boating
  25. Mammoth Hot Springs
  26. Moose–Wilson Road
  27. Teton Backcountry Guides
- **SLEEPING**
  28. Hostel
  29. Jackson Lake Lodge
  30. Lizard Creek Campground
  31. Mammoth Campground
  32. Old Faithful Inn
- **EATING**
  33. Cafe Genevieve
  34. Gather in Jackson Hole
  35. Gun Barrel Steak and Game House
  36. Persephone Café Jackson
  37. Top of the World Resort
- **INFORMATION**
  38. Craig Thomas Discovery & Visitor Center
  39. Jenny Lake Visitor Center
- **TRANSPORT**
  40. Hoback Sports
  41. Jackson Hole Airport

frontier-era cabins. Biographies dot the space in a loose timeline, introducing notable Native Americans, homesteaders, ranchers and skiers. Head upstairs to check out the community-curated gallery, which explores ever-changing themes.

Skiing a winter wonderland

Nestled in the Tetons just 12 miles from downtown Jackson, **Jackson Hole Mountain Resort** *(jacksonhole.com; lift tickets from $218)* is one of the country's top mountain destinations. Spread across two mountains – **Après Vous** and **Rendezvous** – the resort is renowned for its steep, dramatic terrain, stunning alpine views and deep, consistent snowfall (over 450in annually). It also has the steepest continuous vertical drop in North America – 4139ft – offering a challenge for intermediate and expert skiers and snowboarders. While there's no doubt the resort is world-class, Jackson Hole also provides rare open access to expansive wilderness skiing. If you have avalanche training, consider venturing into the 3000 acres of unpatrolled, backcountry terrain of the Bridger-Teton National Forest. Alternatively, hire one of the **resort's backcountry guides** *(jacksonhole.com/mountain-sports-school/backcountry; per person $393-1330)* to help navigate the rugged landscape, ensuring a safer powder adventure beyond the resort boundaries.

JACKON'S ANTLERS

Jackson's Town Square is famous for its four iconic arches made entirely of elk antlers. The arches weigh several tons, each made up of 2000 to 3000 antlers collected from the National Elk Refuge (p757) by local Boy Scouts, an annual spring tradition since the mid-1960s. No animals are harmed during the collecting – the antlers are naturally dropped by elk before being gathered. The arches attract thousands of visitors yearly, each posing next to and under the antlers, hoping for a classic Jackson photo op.

TOP EXPERIENCE

Grand Teton National Park

Awe-inspiring in their grandeur, the Tetons have captivated the imagination from the moment humans laid eyes on them: 12 glacier-carved summits framing the singular Grand Teton (13,775ft). While the view is breathtaking from the valley floor, it only gets more impressive on the trail or on the water. In winter, the Tetons make a magical setting for snowshoeing and cross-country skiing.

Hidden Falls

TOP TIPS

- Stop in the **Craig Thomas Discovery & Visitor Center** for excellent exhibits and films as well as ranger help desks.

- Don't approach wildlife. Maintain at least 100yd from bears and wolves, 25yd from all others.

- Wear layers. The weather can change rapidly year-round.

PRACTICALITIES
- nps.gov/grte
- per vehicle $35
- 24hr

Scenic Drives

Cruise along **Hwy 191** and **Teton Park Rd**, stopping at staggeringly beautiful viewpoints, many with signage with interesting facts about the park. Make a slight detour to **Mormon Row**, home to the iconic Moulton Barns with the Tetons rising dramatically behind – possibly the most photographed site in the park. Or drive up **Signal Mountain Summit Rd** for sweeping mountain views.

Wildlife Watching

Head to **Oxbow Bend**, **Willow Flats** and **Moose–Wilson Rd** at dawn or dusk for your best chances of spotting moose, elk, grizzlies and bald eagles. Bring binoculars and be patient.

Hiking

Jenny Lake has a variety of breathtaking trail options. Consider hopping on a **shuttle boat** *(adult/child round trip $20/12)* to hike to **Hidden Falls** and **Inspiration Point** – a short hike with big-time views. For longer treks, head from there into **Forks of Cascade Canyon** (9.2-mile round trip) with alpine lakes and terrain.

On the Water

Rent **kayaks** *(from $35)* on **Jackson Lake** or **Jenny Lake** to experience the park from the water. Or take a **scenic rafting trip** *(adult/child from $126/74)* on the Snake River from **Jackson Lake Lodge** (p789).

Montana

MOUNTAIN ADVENTURE | COLLEGE VIBE | INDIGENOUS PRESENCE

Welcome to Big Sky Country, where the Great Plains hit the Rockies and just about anything seems possible. At Glacier National Park, known for its towering sculpted mountains and abundant grizzly bears, visitors can enjoy terrific vistas and guided boat rides in long finger-lakes formed by ancient glaciers. Montana's numerous rivers, including the Blackfoot and the Clark Fork, are famous for their rugged beauty and outstanding fishing (and for nearly stymying explorers Lewis and Clark near present-day Great Falls). Nearby, Missoula and Bozeman are lively college towns with urban energy and plenty to do, from fascinating museums to world-class skiing. And Montana's many Native American sites include a bison reserve near Flathead Lake and the Little Bighorn Battlefield National Monument, where Cheyenne, Sioux and Arapahoe warriors quashed an ill-fated attack by Lt Col George Custer. Come, explore and take in one of the most dramatically beautiful corners of the continent.

Places

Bozeman & the Gallatin Valley p765
West Yellowstone p767
Beartooth Scenic Highway p768
Billings p768
Helena p768
Missoula p769
Glacier National Park p772
CSKT Bison Range p774
Whitefish p774
Browning p774
Great Falls p774
Little Bighorn Battlefield National Monument p776

GETTING AROUND

Montana's busiest airport is **Bozeman Yellowstone International Airport**, a good starting point both for trips deeper into the state and into Yellowstone National Park. Missoula and Billings also have well-connected airports.

Greyhound *(greyhound.com)* and **Jefferson Lines** *(jeffersonlines.com)* bus passengers around the state, while **Amtrak's Empire Builder** train *(amtrak.com/empire-builder-train)* can be an attractive option for accessing Glacier National Park and other parts of northern Montana.

A private car provides much more flexibility. Just remember it's a gigantic state, with deceptively long drives between popular sites; gas up when you can to avoid getting stranded.

☑ TOP TIP

Snow can fall in Montana well into June, particularly at higher elevations and in northern regions like Glacier National Park (p782). Be sure to check forecasts and road conditions year-round. And pack layers.

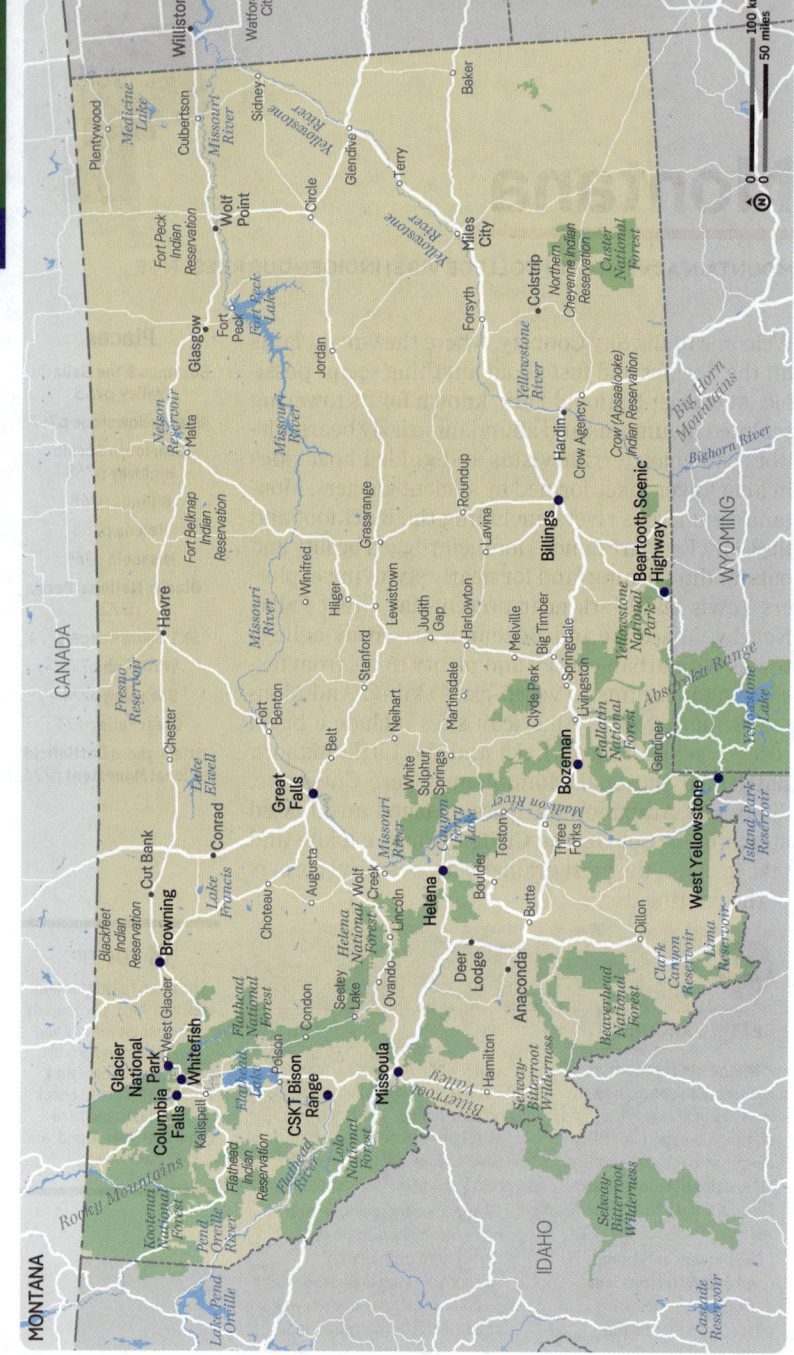

Bozeman & the Gallatin Valley

Montana's dinosaurs and peoples

One of Bozeman's most engaging museums, **Museum of the Rockies** *(museumoftherockies.org; adult/child $20/13)* focuses on the paleontological history of Montana with spectacular dinosaur exhibits that include an edmontosaurus jaw with its battery of teeth and the largest T-rex skull ever discovered. Multimedia displays include life-size dinosaur recreations that remind you that many dinosaurs were in fact clad in feathers and that sharks once swam the tropical seas covering current-day Montana. Once you've had your paleontological fill, a set of galleries focus on the cultural history of the state, including its Native American tribes, while **planetarium shows** ($5 extra) offer insight into the cosmos. In summer, don't miss the outdoor **Living History Farm**, an original 1889 homestead worked by staff in period clothing who happily engage with you, offering a glimpse into Montana's pioneer days.

The artsy side of Bozeman

A bulwark of the creative scene in Bozeman, the **Emerson Center for the Arts & Culture** *(theemerson.org; free)* is a nonprofit set in a 1918 public school building. Located a couple of blocks from Main St, here you can see – and buy – works by regional artists in the galleries and boutiques lining the 1st floor; come in the evening to take in the occasional indie film, musical performance, and open-mic night in the refurbished auditorium, the **Crawford Theater** *(prices vary)*. If you're visiting in summer, be sure to join locals for a taste of Bozeman at the free, ever-popular **Lunch on the Lawn** from 11am to 1pm on Wednesdays, with food trucks, live music and a general sense of revelry.

Hitting the trails

When it comes to hiking around Bozeman, the Gallatin Valley has a treasure trove of trails covering almost 2300 miles, much of it within **Custer Gallatin National Forest** *(fs.usda.gov/custergallatin)*. One standout is **Cinnamon Mountain Trail**, a moderately challenging 8.2-mile out-and-back trail that leads to the summit (9350ft), with spectacular 360-degree views of the surrounding peaks and valleys. For a slightly less demanding option, try **Lava Lake Trail** instead. A local favorite, the 6-mile round-trip trail winds through a

A GIANT OF PALEONTOLOGY

The former curator of the Museum of the Rockies is larger than life. Paleontologist Jack Horner is widely believed to have been the model for the character Dr Alan Grant in the book *Jurassic Park* and served as technical adviser to all the films. And yes, they did extract soft tissue from a Tyrannosaurus thigh bone, right here in Bozeman. Among scientists, Horner is perhaps best known for his discoveries related to the large herbivorous maiasaura, offering clear evidence that some dinosaurs cared for their young. Horner published over 100 research papers as well as a handful of books, including three titles about dinosaurs for children.

EATING IN BOZEMAN: OUR PICKS

Bozeman Coop Downtown: Community-owned grocery store with an array of prepared foods plus organic salad bar. *9am-8pm Mon-Sat, 11am-5pm Sun* $

Jam!: Breakfast fave, serving American classics plus offbeat international dishes. Puerco verde crêpe, anyone? Call ahead to get on the waitlist. *7am-3pm* $$

Montana Ale Works: Industrial-chic warehouse with award-winning craft brews and elevated pub grub, including wagyu, elk and bison burgers. *4-9:30pm* $$

Shan: James Beard finalist serving Chinese- and Thai-inspired dishes integrating locally sourced meats; set in a cozy *izakaya*-style dining room. *4:30-9pm Tue-Sat* $$

FLY-FISHING KNOW-HOW

Most of fly-fishing's etiquette boils down to not crowding other anglers or spooking the fish they're targeting. A few pointers:

Anglers working upstream (which will be most of them) generally have the right of way.

Avoid 'high holing' (stepping into the water directly upstream of an angler) or standing on the bank opposite someone – this can spook rising fish.

If someone is at a nice spot but not fishing, they may be 'resting the hole.' Ask if they plan to keep fishing there; if so, move on. By the same token, don't monopolize good spots. And be kind to folks who are still learning, especially kids – we've all been there once.

Fly fishing, Montana

forested canyon ending at a stunning alpine lake. Both hikes are especially beautiful in summer and early fall, when wildflowers are in bloom.

A river runs through It

Ever since Robert Redford and Brad Pitt made it look sexy in the 1992 classic *A River Runs Through It*, Montana has been closely tied to fly-fishing cool. Whether you are just learning or you're a world-class trout wrangler, the wide, fast rivers are always spectacularly beautiful and filled with fish. For DIY trout fishing, the **Gallatin River**, 8 miles southwest of Bozeman along Hwy 191, has the most accessible, consistent

DRINKING IN BOZEMAN: OUR PICKS

Bozeman Taproom: Popular sports bar with breezy rooftop seating. Order a flight from over 50 craft brews on tap. *11am-midnight Sun-Thu, to 1am Fri & Sat*

Plonk Bozeman: Stylish wine bar with an impressive selection of international bottles. Pair with a charcuterie board. *3pm-midnight Sun-Thu, to 1am Fri & Sat*

Treeline Coffee Roasters: Sit under shade trees sipping the best coffee in town, or head inside to the heady aroma of the roasting room. *6:30am-4pm*

Bridger Brewing: Friendly brewery offering a rotating selection of craft beers and mountain views. If in doubt, order the Lee Metcalfe Pale Ale. *11:30am-8:30pm*

angling spots, closely followed by the beautiful **Yellowstone River**, 25 miles east of Bozeman in Paradise Valley. If you'd like a hand, **Montana Angler** *(montanaangler.com)* and **Gallatin River Guides** *(montanaflyfishing.com)* offer guided fly-fishing trips and equipment rentals.

Year-round in Big Sky Resort

Big Sky *(bigskyresort.com; adult/child lift ticket $198/119)* is big skiing. Located between Bozeman and Yellowstone National Park, it's the fourth-largest ski hill in North America, covering 5800 acres of skiable terrain across four mountains. It's known for its steepness (4350ft vertical drop) and its surplus of advanced and expert trails; take the tram to **Lone Peak** (elevation 11,167ft) for 360-degree views and expert-only runs. Or come after the snow melts, when the resort transforms into a mountain-biking and hiking hub. You'll find over 40 miles of trails, accessible by two **scenic lifts** *(per person $25, with bicycle $40)*. Expect wildflower-filled meadows and high alpine ridges crisscrossed with all-level trails. Bike rentals available on site.

All about soul turns

Located just 16 miles north of Bozeman, **Bridger Bowl** *(bridgerbowl.com; adult/child lift ticket $84/39)* is the US's leading nonprofit ski resort. The 2000-acre, community-owned gem has a fiercely loyal following and is a true skier's mountain, with serious terrain and unpretentious mood (and affordable lift tickets to boot). Known for its 'cold smoke' – light, dry powder that blankets the slopes all winter – Bridger offers surprisingly good skiing and boarding for all levels. But its claim to fame is surely the Ridge – a massive ridgeline overlooking the entire resort, accessible only by hiking, with no official trails, and plenty of unmarked cliffs and chutes. Avalanche gear and training required.

West Yellowstone

Close encounters with apex predators

Near Yellowstone's west entrance, **Grizzly & Wolf Discovery Center** *(grizzlydiscoveryctr.org; adult/child $16.50/11.50)* is worth a stop to learn more about the region's creatures. A well-regarded refuge, it's home to grizzly bears and wolves – most removed from the wild after becoming habituated to humans and becoming a 'nuisance.' Several observation programs are offered. Among the most popular is watching one or two bears serve as 'product testers' while staffers share their backstories. Typically, they grapple with a cooler or trash can filled with treats; if they can't break in after an hour, the item earns a 'bear-proof' label. In the Naturalist Cabin, you can observe wolf packs – and even stare into the golden eyes of a wolf – through oversized windows. Staff is on hand to teach about their behavior and personality traits. If you have time, check out the sections dedicated to otters, reptiles, raptors and fish. The small on-site museum also provides fascinating and sometimes surprising insights.

BACKCOUNTRY IN BRIDGER

Wendy Bianchini, Montana State University, Instructor, Department of Health Development & Community Health.

Nothing feels better than doing a handful of Ridge hikes at Bridger Bowl. In a way, it feels more like ski mountaineering: traversing or boot packing with your skis on your back, and wearing an avalanche beacon. Hiking at Bridger opens access to some pretty spectacular mountain terrain – steep chutes, big bowls and rocky cliffs. The skiing is really fun and challenging! It's not necessarily something I'd recommend to somebody who doesn't know their way around, though. If people are passing through and want to check it out, they should talk to ski patrol and locals to get information so they can ski the Ridge...and do it safely.

Beartooth Scenic Highway

Driving the Beartooth Scenic Hwy

Take a drive along the breathtaking **Beartooth Scenic Hwy**, one of the most beautiful routes in the country and a destination in its own right. Connecting the town of Red Lodge to Yellowstone's northeast entrance, the 68-mile-long road passes through Wyoming along a twisting, turning alpine route back into Montana. It's known for its vistas: alpine lakes and dramatic canyons plus sky-high peaks like the jagged **Bear's Tooth**, **Index Peak** and **Pilot Peak**. You'll even see skiers at **Beartooth Basin** (*beartoothbasin.com; half/full-day lift ticket $40/50*), a high-altitude summer ski area. The road crests at **Beartooth Pass West Summit**, where **Top of the World Resort** (*topoftheworldresort.com*) makes a good pit stop for coffee before descending past **Beartooth Butte** to **Clarks Fork Trailhead**, a popular hiking area. The road is open May to October, taking around three hours to complete.

Billings

Crow Fair

Started as a harvest festival in 1904, **Crow Fair** (*crow-nsn.gov/crow-fair.html*) is a spectacular weeklong gathering of Plains tribes held every August in the town of Crow Agency. One of the largest Native American gatherings in the country, it draws tens of thousands to the banks of the Little Bighorn River, where attendees set up hundreds of tipis. Each day begins with a parade of families filing past tipis on horseback, in traditional regalia; afternoons bring powwows with competitive dancers in beaded dress and feathers, all-Native rodeos and death-defying relay races. Plenty of food vendors make it easy to fill up on classic Native treats (fry bread with powdered sugar, anyone?), while nearby artisans showcase handcrafted jewelry and goods. At heart a social event, the Crow Fair is a powerful expression of community, where all are welcome. Consider staying overnight in your own tipi, falling asleep to the sound of drums; **rentals available on site** (*ndnbattletours@gmail.com*).

Helena

A walk through historic Helena

Helena's historic heart beats along **Last Chance Gulch**, a winding pedestrian mall that traces the path of a gold strike made by four down-and-out prospectors in 1864. That lucky

---

POWWOW ETIQUETTE

Listen to the master of ceremonies for announcements related to protocol such as when to sit or stand, and when to refrain from taking photos or recording an event.

Do not call a Native person's outfit a 'costume'. Traditional clothing and adornments are called 'regalia,' and are often beloved family heirlooms and sources of deep pride.

Avoid touching anyone's clothing or headdress. If you're tempted, ask permission. (Prepare to be denied.)

Ask before taking photos. While it's typically acceptable to take photos of intertribal competitions, ask before taking candid photos of individuals.

Do not record drumming. Ask permission from the Head Singer if you want to record a song.

 EATING IN HELENA: OUR PICKS

| No Sweat Café: Wildly popular brunch spot with vegan and gluten-free options. Lunch menu integrates global flavors. *7am-2pm Tue-Fri, from 8am Sat & Sun* $ | Bad Betty's BBQ: Simple spot serving award-winning Southern-style BBQ, from brisket and ribs to pulled pork. *11am-3pm & 4-8pm Wed-Fri, 11am-3pm Tue & Sat* $ | Windbag Saloon & Grill: One-time brothel turned pub, serving hearty burgers and sandwiches. Twice-daily happy hour. *11am-midnight Mon-Fri, from 10am Sat & Sun* $$ | Ristorante Bella Roma: Upscale restaurant with authentic Italian flavors, homemade pastas and local ingredients. Prix-fix menu and wine pairings. *5-10pm Tue-Sun* $$$ |

Pilot and Index Peaks

find – millions in placer gold – sparked a boom that transformed the gulch into Montana's lovely state capitol. Spend a morning on the mall strolling past the grand 19th-century buildings, many of them home to boutiques and cafes; interpretive signs and public art along the way bring the town's Wild West past to life. For more historic spots, head to nearby **Reeder's Alley**, Helena's oldest surviving neighborhood. Built in the 1870s, the narrow brick road is lined with log cabins and early city dwellings; while most are filled with small businesses, informational placards offer insight into the structures and people who first inhabited them. Want more info? Take a **guided walking tour** of Helena with **The Foundation for Montana History** (mthistory.org; adult/child from $10/8).

Missoula

Wander into the past

Deep in the Garnet Range forest, **Garnet Ghost Town** (garnetghosttown.org; adult/child $10/free) is one of Montana's best-preserved mining towns. Over two dozen buildings in a state of 'arrested decay' are scattered along the mountainside – weathered cabins, saloons, general stores, a hotel from the

BRENNAN'S WAVE

Brennan's Wave is an artificial white-water feature on the Clark Fork River in downtown Missoula. On warm summer nights, crowds gather at Caras Park to watch surfers and kayakers shred and paddle in the surf, a treat in this mountain town. But the wave is more than just a playground. It's a living memorial to Brennan Guth, a Missoulian and world-class kayaker, who died while kayaking Chile's Río Palguín in 2001. It was his vision to transform the river's irrigation diversion into a training ground for white-water athletes. After his death, the community rallied around that vision, raising over $300,000 to transform the river. In 2006, Brennan's Wave debuted; it later hosted the 2010 US Freestyle Kayaking Championships. Brennan would be proud.

EATING IN MISSOULA: OUR PICKS

Bernice's Bakery: Beloved from-scratch bakery-cafe with delicious pastries and an ever-changing menu of sandwiches, soups and salads. *6am-6pm Mon-Sat, 8am-4pm Sun* **$**

Dinosaur Café: No-frills place with extraordinary Cajun food from jambalaya to po' boys. Located in Charley's Bar, a Missoula institution. *11am-9pm Mon-Fri, from noon Sat* **$**

Iron Horse Bar & Grill: Casual restaurant with an extensive international menu, from ahi tuna to BBQ. Set in a repurposed train depot. *11am-10pm* **$$**

Boxcar Bistro: Elegant European-style bistro – evocative of the dining cars of yesteryear – with a French-inspired menu. Perfect for a date night. *4-9pm Tue-Sat* **$$$**

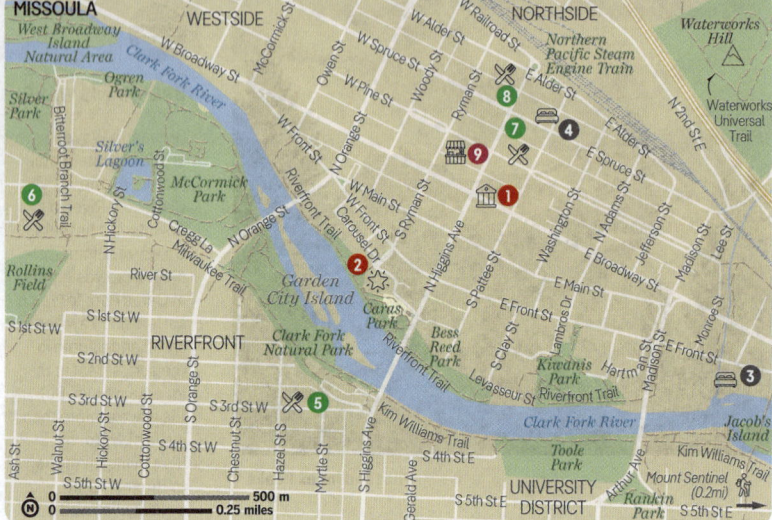

- **SIGHTS**
1 Missoula Art Museum
- **ACTIVITIES**
2 A Carousel for Missoula
- **SLEEPING**
3 Goldsmith's Riverfront Inn
4 Shady Spruce Hostel
- **EATING**
5 Bernice's Bakery
6 Boxcar Bistro
7 Dinosaur Café
8 Iron Horse Bar & Grill
- **SHOPPING**
9 Missoula People's Market

late 1800s – transporting you to gold-rush days, when mining towns were built overnight and vanished almost as quickly. It's an evocative place, where you can wander around buildings that once bustled with over 1000 people, imagining what life was once like here. Informational placards lend more info and friendly forest rangers are often present and happy to answer questions. Several hiking and biking trails make it easy to spend the day here. Or stay overnight; in winter, two **primitive cabins** with no electricity or running water are available by lottery *(per night $50)*. The rub? From January to April, the site is only accessible by snowmobile or skis/snowshoe. Located about 40 miles east of Missoula, at the end of a 6-mile-long dirt road.

Take in regional art

All hail a city that encourages free-thinking art and then displays it free of charge! Set in a renovated public library, the sleek **Missoula Art Museum** *(artsmissoula.org; free)* is a small but powerful space, showcasing works by regional and local artists, with a focus on Native American works. Head to the top floor for special exhibits.

All about smokejumpers

When you're in town, don't miss the fascinating **Missoula Smokejumper Visitor Center** *(fs.usda.gov; by donation)*. Part of an active base for the heroic men and women who parachute into forests to combat wildfires, it's the starting point for an hour-long **tour** by a smokejumper, who guides you through the facilities to see where the crew lives and trains, including areas where they painstakingly sew, inspect and test their own parachuting gear. It's a humbling tour, offering a rare glimpse into the dangerous profession. Afterwards, check out the visitor center exhibits, which explore

A Carousel for Missoula

the evolving nature of wildfire management in the face of warming climates. For deeper insight into the courage and cost of the job, pick up Norman Maclean's *Young Men and Fire* (1992), a tribute to Montana's Mann Gulch fire that took the lives of 12 smokejumpers.

Enjoy an artisanal fair

The highlight of summertime in Missoula is **Missoula People's Market** *(missoulapeoplesmarket.org; free)*, an artisanal fair held every Saturday morning from May through September. A popular community affair, the market transforms West Pine Street into a vibrant pedestrian zone filled with more than 80 stalls showcasing handmade goods by local artisans. Live music fills the air as you peruse stands filled with everything from pottery, jewelry and photography to leatherwork, wood carvings and organic skincare products. Food vendors make it that much easier to make a day of it.

Kiddie fun

If you're traveling with little ones, take a spin on **A Carousel for Missoula** *(carouselformissoula.com; adult/child $2/1)*, a beloved carousel with 40 hand-carved and individually painted horses and chariots. It was created by an army of volunteer artists who rallied around a local cabinet-maker's dream to restore a bit of whimsy to downtown. Afterwards, pop into **Dragon Hallow**, a fantastical playground next door, the product of another volunteer town effort.

Take on Mt Sentinel

The steep **Mt Sentinel** switchback trail (1.5-mile round trip) behind the University of Montana football stadium leads up to a concrete whitewashed 'M' (visible for miles around) on the 5158ft Mt Sentinel. Tackle it on a warm summer evening for glistening views of the city and its spectacular environs, including the Clark Fork River and mountains beyond. The trailhead is at Phyllis Washington Park on the eastern edge of campus.

FORT MISSOULA: ALIEN DETENTION CENTER

During WWII, Fort Missoula, originally an army post, was repurposed into an Alien Detention Center where around 1000 Japanese men were held. These lawful US residents, community leaders and successful professionals in West Coast towns were deemed 'enemy aliens' for no other reason than their Japanese heritage. Detainees lived in barracks behind barbed wire and under guard, undergoing hearings to determine whether they posed a threat to the US. None were charged with any crime. Eventually, they were transferred to Japanese internment camps like Amache (p748), Heart Mountain (p756) and Minidoka (p785). They remained unlawfully detained for the rest of the war, casualties of wartime hysteria and racial discrimination.

TOP EXPERIENCE

Glacier National Park

Few places on earth are as magnificent and pristine as Glacier National Park. Protected in 1910, the glacially carved remnants of an ancient thrust fault left behind a brilliant landscape of snowcapped pinnacles, plunging waterfalls and glassy turquoise lakes. Its dense forests are home to an abundance of bears, while smart park management has kept the place accessible and authentically wild.

> **DON'T MISS**
>
> Driving Going-to-the-Sun Rd
>
> Hiking Grinnell Glacier
>
> Wildlife-watching
>
> Paddling on Swiftcurrent Lake
>
> Blackfeet Nation exhibits and programming

Drive Going-to-the-Sun Road

Cutting through the center of Glacier National Park, **Going-to-the-Sun Rd** connects **West Glacier** with **St Mary** in the east. This epic rollercoaster ride over the Continental Divide, an engineering marvel chiseled out of raw mountainside, is considered one of the most spectacular roads in the US. Spanning 50 miles, it climbs up to Logan Pass (6646ft) and is bursting with soaring vistas, hiking opportunities, glacial melt spewing down the rocks and rushing waterfalls. Don't miss pullouts like **Bird Woman Falls Overlook**, with views

PRACTICALITIES
- nps.gov/glac
- summer/winter per vehicle $35/25
- 24hr

of the highest waterfall (492ft) on the drive; and **Jackson Glacier Overlook**, to spy one of the remaining 25 glaciers in the park on the side of Mt Jackson (10,052ft). The entire road is usually open from late June to early October.

Hike Hidden Gems

Glacier is a hiker's paradise, with over 700 miles of trails. Near **Logan Pass**, the **Highline Trail** (11.6-mile round trip) hugs cliffs and wildflower meadows with sweeping mountain views, while the **Hidden Lake Overlook** (3-mile round trip) offers a shorter, family-friendly option. In **Many Glacier**, don't miss the hike to **Grinnell Glacier** (10.6-mile round trip), one of the most dramatic treks in the park, offering up-close views of a rapidly receding glacier (or shorten the hike to 7.6 miles by taking a boat shuttle across Swiftcurrent Lake). Other must-hikes include **Avalanche Lake** (4-mile round trip) via the **Trail of the Cedars** (0.9-mile round trip), an accessible raised-boardwalk loop through a cedar forest, and the moderate loop around **Iceberg Lake** (9.6-mile round trip), where floating ice dots a turquoise basin well into summer.

Wildlife Watching

Glacier is home to an incredible variety of wildlife. Head out early or stay out late for the best chances to see animals in motion. Search the rugged **Rising Wolf Mountain** slopes for sure-footed creatures like bighorn sheep and mountain goats. Meanwhile, moose are often seen at sunset along the road into **Two Medicine**. Look out for bear tracks in prairie environments and flower fields, plus **Dawson Pass** and **Scenic Point Trail**. Be sure to carry bear spray and follow park guidelines for a safe experience.

Experience the Water

Six **historic boats** *(glacierparkboats.com; adult/child $27/13.50)* – some dating back to the 1920s – ply four of Glacier's attractive mountain lakes, and some of them combine the float with a short **guided hike** led by interpretive, often witty, guides. For more solitude (and a bit of a workout), you also can rent **rowboats** ($32.50 per hour), **kayaks** ($32.50 per hour) and **paddleboards** ($24.20 per hour) at Lake McDonald, Swiftcurrent Lake and Two Medicine Lake.

Take a Century-Old Sightseeing Tour

Glacier's vintage buses, known as the 'Rubies of the Rockies,' are emblems of the park. Introduced in 1914, the elongated Model 706s have open tops for unobstructed views, but can be covered when it rains. A dozen **Red Bus Tours** *(glaciernationalparklodges.com; adult/child from $60/30)* whizz visitors around the park, hitting the big attractions and views – they range from a few hours to nine hours and run from mid-May to late September. Tours depart from several locations on both sides of the park.

BEAR ENCOUNTERS

Running Bad idea. Bears are faster, and running may elicit an attack from a non-aggressive bear.

Bear spray If a bear charges, spray a one- to two-second blast when the bear is 30ft away.

If the bear makes contact Drop, lie flat on your stomach and cover your neck with your hands. Don't move until the bear has left.

TOP TIPS

● Visit St Mary Visitor Center to learn about the Blackfeet Nation and its deep connections to the park land, from carefully curated exhibits and ranger talks to cultural programs.

● Park rangers will give tutorials on how to properly use bear spray – be sure to ask.

● Snow can fall year-round in the park; check weather conditions before heading out.

● A free hop-on, hop-off shuttle runs along Going-to-the-Sun Rd between Apgar and St Mary visitor centers. Buses leave every 15 to 30 minutes from Apgar (every 30 to 45 minutes from St Mary). The last trips down from Logan Pass leave at 7pm.

WARRIORS OF THE FOREST

The 3000-sq-mile **Blackfeet Indian Reservation** sits east of Glacier National Park and borders Canada, spanning an area twice the size of the park. It's home to 9500 tribal members, including those from the Northern Piegan (Blackfeet), Southern Piegan and Blood tribes, who lived in the Alberta area north of the border in the 1700s. The Blackfeet were best known for their horse and gun skills and had a reputation as exceptionally formidable warriors.

This spirit continues today, exemplified by the Chief Mountain Hotshots, an elite Blackfeet firefighting crew based in Browning. Known as the 'Warriors of the Forest,' this crew works in large-scale wildland firefighting, typically working 15 to 20 large fires and traveling between 10,000 and 20,000 miles each year.

CSKT Bison Range
Meet a living legacy

Home to over 350 bison, the **CSKT Bison Range** *(bison range.org; per vehicle $20)* spans 18,500 acres of grasslands, forests and rolling hills on the Flathead Indian Reservation. The bison are direct descendants of a small herd protected in the 1800s by tribal members at a time when bison were nearly extinct, making the herd biologically and culturally significant. Two dirt roads traverse the range: the 14-mile **Prairie Dr** and 19-mile **Red Sleep Mountain Dr** (open summer only), which climbs 2000ft for sweeping views of the Mission Mountains and surrounding valleys. Along the way, keep your eyes peeled for bison grazing, calves nursing and bulls wallowing in dust. You might also see elk, bighorn sheep, pronghorn and even black bears.

Whitefish
Family-friendly winter sports

Big mountain skiing at **Whitefish Mountain Resort** *(ski whitefish.com; lift ticket adult/child $110/55)* is a laid-back affair, great for families as well as expert skiers and snowboarders willing to hike up in order to rip up off-piste double-black-diamond glades. The mountain is known for its fog, but on bluebird days, views from the summit are unsurpassed. When there's fresh powder, join locals who ditch work to make fresh tracks.

Browning
Learn all about the Plains Indians

Don't be fooled by the drab exterior of the **Museum of the Plains Indians** *(doi.gov/iacb/ourmuseums; adult/child $7/3)* on the Blackfeet Reservation – inside, you'll find rich and meticulously curated exhibits on the history and cultures of the Northern Plains tribes, including the Crow, Cree, Sioux, Cheyenne and Blackfeet. Themes range from the arts and religion to hunting and warfare; expect detailed signage alongside all manner of ceremonial regalia, art, tools, toys and more. In summer, stop into the adjacent studio to watch local Native American artists at work, giving demonstrations and selling their works, too.

Great Falls
Step into the Lewis and Clark Expedition

As you're driving through Montana, make a pit stop in Great Falls to visit **Lewis and Clark National Historic Trail Interpretive Center** *(fs.usda.gov; adult/child $8/free)*. A labyrinthine museum, it tells the fascinating story of the 2½-year, 8000-mile trek of Meriwether Lewis and William Clark, American explorers commissioned by President Jefferson to map the newly acquired lands of the Louisiana Purchase,

Whitefish Mountain Resort

establish trade with Native American tribes and find a water route to the Pacific. The exhibits deep-dive into the journey with hands-on displays, films and even a two-story diorama depicting Lewis and Clark's men hauling canoes around the waterfalls of modern-day Great Falls. Keep your eyes peeled for Seaman, a volunteer therapy dog representing Lewis' beloved Newfoundland dog, the only four-legged member of the expedition.

Marvel at C.M. Russell's Art

Another excellent stop in Great Falls is the **C.M. Russell Museum** *(cmrussell.org; adult/child $20/7)*, a sprawling complex of buildings dedicated to the art and life of Charles M Russell (1864–1926), the iconic 'cowboy artist' of the American West. Begin in the museum, home to one of the largest Russell collections in the world – over 2000 oil paintings, watercolors, sculptures and illustrated letters – which rotates through its 16 different galleries and a sculpture garden. Afterwards, head next door to Russell's log studio, built of cedar telephone poles, and his Victorian-era home, both outfitted with period furnishings and Russell's personal effects; signage provides context on his life, family and friendships.

CASINOS EVERYWHERE

As you drive through Montana, one thing stands out: casinos – over 1300 of them. Their proliferation stems from a 1972 change to the state constitution granting the legislature authority to legalize gambling on a case-by-case basis. This paved the way for small-scale gaming across the state.

Most 'casinos' are tucked into in the corners of bars, restaurants, bowling alleys or gas stations. You won't find roulette wheels or blackjack dealers – just rows of video gambling machines offering poker, keno and line games. These machines are common in rural towns and larger cities, providing convenient entertainment for passersby. For business owners, they're a financial lifeline: a single machine can generate $28,000 annually.

TOP EXPERIENCE

Little Bighorn Battlefield National Monument

The Little Bighorn Battlefield National Monument, on the Crow (Apsáalooke) Reservation, 65 miles southeast of Billings, marks General George Custer's famous 'last stand.' Here, in 1876, Lakota Sioux and Cheyenne warriors led by Crazy Horse and Sitting Bull won a major victory – briefly boosting Native American resistance before US forces crushed it, forcing most Plains tribes onto reservations within five years.

TOP TIPS

● Battlefield Tour Rd closes 30 to 45 minutes before the official park closure; arrive early enough to assure you have time to drive through the site.

● In summer, visit in the early morning for cooler temperatures and fewer people.

PRACTICALITIES

● nps.gov/libi
● per vehicle $25
● 8am-6pm Fri-Sun Jun-Sep, to 4pm Oct-May

Self-Guided Tour

Battlefield Tour Rd runs through the site, a 4.5-mile road with frequent turnouts featuring free cellphone audio guides and informative panels that bring the conflict alive. Across the fields and valleys, and within sight of the road, white tombstones indicate where US soldiers are buried, while red granite markers symbolize where Native American warriors died. Crowning the battlefield is **Last Stand Hill**, where Custer fell, and nearby **Indian Memorial** is a fascinating tribute to the Sioux and Cheyenne stories.

Apsáalooke Tours

Learn more about the battle with **Apsáalooke Tours** *(adult/child $17/10)*. Led by Crow guides, these excellent one-hour bus tours give deeper insight into the conflict from a Plains tribespeople's perspective, from precognitive dreams to war traditions. Tours run every 1½ hours from 9am to 3pm Memorial Day to Labor Day, leaving from the parking lot.

Visitor Center

The visitor center offers deeper insight on the 1876 battle with well-conceived exhibits, a 20-minute film and artifacts including Native ledger art, weapons and uniforms – plus original soldiers' grave markers made from cartridges and handwritten name slips.

Idaho

OUTDOORSY | RUGGED BEAUTY | INDEPENDENT SPIRIT

Wedged between Montana and Oregon, Idaho is one of the most underrated destinations in the western US. The oddly shaped state has nearly 4 million acres of wilderness and some of the most scenic landscapes of the lower 48. The Sawtooth National Recreation Area and remote Bitterroot Mountains offer outstanding mountain escapes, from hiking trails and alpine lakes, to thrilling mountain biking. The Salmon River, aka the River of No Return, is arguably the country's premier white-water rafting destination. On the opposite extreme, Craters of the Moon National Monument has a dramatic (and vaguely apocalyptic) char-black volcanic landscape, nearly devoid of vegetation. Meanwhile, Boise, the state capital, is an appealing place to linger, whether museum hopping or strolling along the Boise River Greenbelt, which winds through town. And of course there's Sun Valley, ski resort of the stars, home of the world's first chairlift, and still swanky after all these years.

Places
Boise p779
Idaho Panhandle p783
Ketchum & Sun Valley p783
Stanley p784
Minidoka National Historic Site p785
Craters of the Moon National Monument & Reserve p786
Blackfoot p787
Driggs p787

GETTING AROUND

Small but busy **Boise Airport** is well connected, with nonstop flights to several domestic cities. Interstate bus lines like **Greyhound** *(greyhound.com)* and **Salt Lake Express** *(saltlakeexpress.com)* will get you to and from Boise, and a handful of other cities, but service within the state is fairly limited. For that, a private vehicle is essential. You won't need 4WD to get to Craters of the Moon National Monument (p786) and other major destinations, especially in the summer. But many remote areas are only reachable by dirt road, and having a high-clearance vehicle will make travel there easier and safer.

☑ TOP TIP

Plan ahead when traveling through mountainous and rural areas: cell service can be spotty, so download offline maps. Keep your gas tank full and add cushion time between destinations – winding roads, mountain passes and unexpected gravel stretches can slow things down.

Boise

Museum-hopping in the park

In the heart of downtown Boise, the leafy **Julia Davis Park** is home to several museums, making it an easy place to spend a day – and to learn about the state – rain or shine. Start at the **Idaho State Museum** (history.idaho.gov/museum; adult/child $10/5), a state-of-the-art building that uses Idaho's spectacularly diverse landscapes as the backdrop to its development, both in people and place. Exhibits are well conceived, integrating multimedia elements as well as kid-friendly installations. The Origins Gallery, with its Native American voices, is especially rewarding. Next door, the **Idaho Black History Museum** (ibhm.org; free) is housed in the historic St Paul Baptist Church building, the first Black church in Idaho. Simple exhibits line the one-room museum, outlining Black presence and achievement in the state. Nearby, don't be fooled by the nondescript building that houses **Boise Art Museum** (boiseartmuseum.org; adult/child $9/5). Inside, the permanent collection includes masterpieces by heavy hitters like Ansel Adams and Deborah Butterfield while ever-changing temporary exhibits keep the space feeling current. Be sure to use the free cellphone audio and ASL guides.

Meandering on Boise River Greenbelt

Snaking its way through town, the **Boise River Greenbelt** is a lovely 29-mile-long riverside path with bridges, benches and shaded spots connecting a series of parks, many named after prominent Boise women. It originated as a plan in the 1960s to prevent development in the Boise River's floodplain in order to provide open space in the rapidly growing city. Today, the Greenbelt is just that: a path popular for its easy access to nature, especially known for the 150 types of birds seen year-round, from blue herons to bald eagles. Take an afternoon stroll along the river or explore further on an e-bike rental from **Sunrise Electric Bikes** (sunrise-ebikes.com; from $40). To make a day of it, stop in at one of Julia Davis Park's museums, watch surfers at Boise Whitewater Park (p781) or enjoy a riverfront tasting at Telaya Wine Co (p781) or **Payette Brewing Co** (payettebrewing.com).

Urban water play

There is no better way to spend a sunny summer day in Boise than floating down the river. Put in at **Barber Park**, where **Boise River Raft & Tube** (boiseriverraftandtube.com) rents

TREEFORT MUSIC FESTIVAL

One of Idaho's most popular events, **Treefort Music Fest** (treefortmusicfest.com) is a five-day indie music festival held every March in downtown Boise. Over 400 bands are featured at over 60 venues, from outdoor stages in Julia Davis Park to pop-ups in cafes, breweries and even shuttle buses. The fest draws tens of thousands of people showcasing Boise's vibrant, artsy spirit. Beyond music, the festival also features themed spaces or 'forts' around town like Foodfort, Filmfort, Comedyfort, Yogafort, Hackfort and Dragfort, which offer immersive experiences like food tastings, stand-up acts, wellness sessions, drag shows and more. Be sure to buy festival passes in advance – they often sell out.

EATING IN BOISE: OUR PICKS

The Warehouse: Cavernous food hall with 13 independent kitchens serving everything from burgers to fusion Vietnamese-Basque eats. *hours vary* $

Goldy's Breakfast Bistro: No-frills breakfast fave with hearty portions, scratch pancakes and hollandaise sauce. Arrive early or expect a wait. *7am-2pm* $$

Fork: Restaurant Row go-to serving a wide range of locally sourced dishes. Don't miss the asparagus fries. *hours vary* $$$

STIL: Small-batch ice-cream shop scooping creative flavors, which are paired with local beers and wines. *hours vary* $

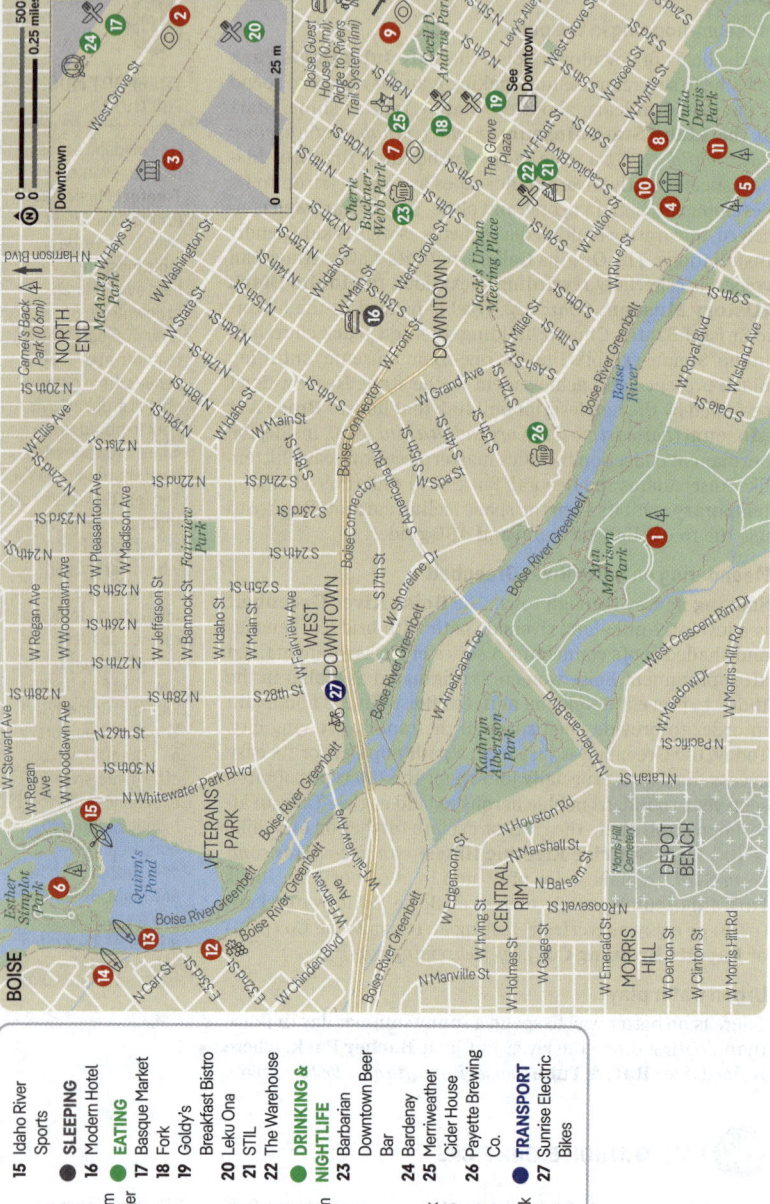

BOISE

SIGHTS
1. Ann Morrison Park
2. Basque Block
3. Basque Museum & Cultural Center
4. Boise Art Museum
5. Boise River Greenbelt
6. Esther Simplot Park
7. Freak Alley
8. Idaho Black History Museum
9. Idaho State Capitol
10. Idaho State Museum
11. Julia Davis Park
12. Telaya Wine Co

ACTIVITIES
13. Boise Whitewater Park Corridor
14.
15. Idaho River Sports

SLEEPING
16. Modern Hotel

EATING
17. Basque Market
18. Fork
19. Goldy's Breakfast Bistro
20. Leku Ona
21. STIL
22. The Warehouse

DRINKING & NIGHTLIFE
23. Barbarian Downtown Beer Bar
24. Bardenay
25. Merriweather Cider House
26. Payette Brewing Co.

TRANSPORT
27. Sunrise Electric Bikes

tubes *(single/double $18/40)*, **rafts** *(four/six-person $75/85)* and **kayaks** *($50)* for self-guided 6-mile, 1½- to three-hour floats downstream to **Ann Morrison Park**. Return your watercraft there or take a shuttle bus back to Barber. Available June through August depending on river flows.

Or if you prefer a little more action, beeline to **Boise Whitewater Park**, where hydraulically controlled waves change daily, beckoning surfers, paddleboarders and kayakers year-round. There are no lifeguards, so know your limits – the rides can be rough! For rentals, steps away **Corridor** *(surfboise.com)* rents **surfboards** *(from $20)* and **wetsuits** *(from $15)* while in adjacent **Esther Simplot Park**, **Idaho River Sports** *(idahoriversports.com)* offers **kayak** and **paddleboards** *(from $25)*.

Take in street art

You don't have to wander far in Downtown Boise to stumble upon **Freak Alley** *(freakalleyboise.com)*, one of the largest open-air public art spaces in the West. Tucked between office buildings and trendy restaurants near Bannock and 9th streets, the gallery started in 2002 with just one painted door and has grown to become a two-block-long alley draped in vibrant murals created by over 200 artists. Every summer, more are added and existing works refreshed, providing a window into Boise's independent-minded artist community. Selfies encouraged.

A window into Basque Country

Boise is home to one of the largest Basque populations outside Spain, with approximately 16,000 residing here. The original émigrés arrived in the 1910s to work as shepherds when sheep outnumbered people seven to one. Few continue that work today, but many extended families have remained, and the rich elements of their distinct culture can be seen on a small stretch of Grove Street in downtown Boise known as **Basque Block** *(thebasqueblock.com)*. A leafy block, it's anchored by the **Basque Museum & Cultural Center** *(basquemuseum.eus; adult/child $7/5)*, a well-conceived space outlining the history of the Basque in Boise through detailed multimedia exhibits; the historic **Cyrus Jacobs-Uberuaga House**, a one-time Basque boardinghouse, also sits on-site. If the museum is closed, murals, sculptures, sidewalk etchings and interpretive signs provide insight into the Boise Basque community; the street itself incorporates the symbols and colors of the Basque flag. If hunger strikes, small businesses like

ARBORGLYPHS

The trees of the Wood River Valley and Boise National Forest bear a unique and picturesque record of alpine life about a century ago. Sheepherders, mostly Basque, carved pictures and messages into soft aspen and birch trunks as they drove their flocks between grazing lands.

Known today as 'arborglyphs,' the carvings date to the early and mid-1900s – the older ones are long gone as these smooth-barked trees are relatively short-lived (even more so with climate change).

Some of the pictures are remarkably detailed – boardinghouses, horses, birds, even the occasional naked woman – while poems about missing home capture the solitary lives of Idaho's early sheepherders.

DRINKING IN BOISE: OUR PICKS

| **Barbarian Downtown Beer Bar:** Artisanal taproom known for its wide-ranging suds, from IPAs and sours to barrel-aged beers. *hours vary* | **Merriweather Cider House:** Family-owned cidery incorporating all manner of fruits. If in doubt, order the award-winning Plum Dandy. *hours vary* | **Telaya Wine Co:** Industrial-chic tasting room serving wines from Idaho and Washington. *noon-7:30pm Mon-Wed, to 8:30pm Thu-Sat, to 6:30pm Sun* | **Bardenay:** The country's first distillery-pub, pouring rum and whiskey made in-house. Located on Basque Block. *hours vary* |

IDAHO'S SHAPE

Idaho owes its unusual shape to the warping effects of greed and politics. Originally, the Idaho Territory was massive (and roughly square), including most of today's Montana and Wyoming. When the Montana Territory was proposed in 1864, the border was to be set along the Continental Divide. But behind the scenes Idaho Supreme Court Justice Sidney Edgerton quietly convinced Congress to move the border west to the Bitterroot Mountains, lopping an extra 27,500 sq miles from Idaho, leaving just that narrow panhandle. It turns out Edgerton had been paid by Montana miners to lobby for the change. He went on to lay claim to the rich Bitterroot and Deer Lodge valleys and was named Montana's first governor.

World Center for Birds of Prey

the **Basque Market** (*thebasquemarket.com*) and **Leku Ona** (*boisebasquefood.com*) offer traditional foods like braised chorizo or *croquetas*. In warmer months, their street-front patios are perfect for taking in the lineup of cultural events that are hosted outdoors, most integrating folk dancing and accordion beats.

Visiting the World Center for Birds of Prey

On Boise's south side, the **World Center for Birds of Prey** (*peregrinefund.org; adult/child $14/9*) is the headquarters of the Peregrine Fund, a nonprofit that has single-handedly brought back several species of raptors from the brink of extinction since the 1970s – from the peregrine falcon, the world's fastest bird, to the iconic California condor. Their method? A combination of captive breeding, habitat protection, local education and scientific research. Today, the center has several areas open to the public, including bird habitats, exhibit halls describing their work plus livestreams of on-site nesting areas. Knowledgeable staff members are ever-present and happy to talk raptors. Be sure to set aside time for a live raptor presentation – they are excellent!

Hiking Boise's Ridge to Rivers Trails

Easy access to some 210 miles of trails – hiking, mountain biking and horseback riding – is one of the best parts of visiting Boise. The **Ridge to Rivers** (*ridgetorivers.org*) trails meander across the city's foothills, eventually crossing grasslands, scrub slopes and tree-lined creeks on their way to the mountainous terrain of **Boise National Forest**. The options are almost endless: from short, leisurely strolls with skyscraper views to steep, challenging trails up mountainsides. For the most convenient access to the wilderness head to **Cottonwood Creek Trailhead** just east of the **capitol building**, or **Camel's Back Park** to the north. Check the Ridge to Rivers'

Idaho Panhandle

Ride an epic trail

Take a ride through the spectacularly scenic Bitterroot Mountains on the **Route of the Hiawatha** *(ridethehiawatha.com; trail pass adult/child $20/16, shuttle adult/child $20/16)*. A 15-mile gravel trail near the Idaho-Montana border, the family-friendly route follows an old rail line, starting with the 1.66-mile St Paul Pass Tunnel - damp and completely dark - requiring a headlamp, a hoodie and some nerve. From there, the trail descends gradually through thick verdant forest, passing through eight rocky tunnels and crossing seven high trestle bridges, the highest 230-ft above the valley floor. Interpretative signs explain the route's railroad history, providing places to catch your breath and take some photos too. Shuttle buses save riders the uphill ride back. Bike rentals, including lamps, are available at the trailhead by reservation only. Book early. You also can save a few bucks by booking your trail passes and shuttle tickets online. Open late May to mid-September, weather-permitting.

Ketchum & Sun Valley

Hit historic slopes

Set in the stunning Sawtooth Mountains, **Sun Valley Resort** *(sunvalley.com; adult/child lift ticket $123/242)* began as the first purpose-built ski resort in the US, a venture by the Union Pacific Railroad to boost ridership. It opened in 1936 to much fanfare, thanks to both its luxury lodge and the world's first chairlift; the resort continued to gain cachet with the presence of celebrities like Ernest Hemingway, Ingrid Bergman and Gary Cooper, who received free trips as part of a marketing plan. It worked. Sun Valley and nearby Ketchum have been synonymous with luxury skiing and swanky Hollywood clientele ever since.

Today, join snow-sports lovers who flock here for the powder (and celebrity-spotting) on its two distinct mountains: **Dollar Mountain**, a treeless hill with mellow runs and extensive terrain parks; and **Bald Mountain** (aka Baldy), a favorite for its long cruisers, steep pitches and bowls. Both sit on opposite sides of Hwy 75; free shuttles from the resort village and Ketchum get you to either.

THE GEM STATE

Although long-running nickname, 'the Gem State,' was originally a reference to the state's rugged beauty. But miners searching for gold in Idaho's rivers would regularly stumble upon sparkling garnets, agates and jaspers in their pans. Gem mining began in earnest in the late 1800s, growing alongside Idaho's gold and silver booms, and expanding to include other stones. By 1967, over 70 different precious and semiprecious stones had been found in the state. The same year, the star garnet – a deep-red gemstone showing a four- or six-pointed star – was designated the state gem. Found only in India and Idaho, these garnets cemented Idaho's unique place in the gem world, as well as the appropriateness of its nickname.

DRINKING IN KETCHUM: OUR PICKS

TNT Taproom: Historic dynamite shed turned tap room with a rotating selection of local craft beers plus biodynamic wines. *2-9pm Mon-Thu, to 10pm Fri & Sat*	Warfield Distillery and Brewer:: Classy, laid-back gastropub with a rooftop bar and creative cocktails featuring award-winning organic spirits. *11:30am-9pm*	Grumpy's: Longtime local fave, this dive bar is known for its 32oz schooners of beer, chilled-out vibe, and beer-can wall décor. *11am-9pm*	Whiskey's on Main: Upscale sports bar with live music and dancing on weekends. *11am-10pm Sun-Tue, to midnight Wed-Thu, to 1am Sat & Sun*

THE ROUNDHOUSE

Kristine Bretall, Community Engagement Manager, Wood River Museum.

I love hiking in Sun Valley! And the smell when you're outdoors. In summertime, there's this scent of sage; it's this very lovely thing. In wintertime, it's this cold-snow, wood-smoke sort of a thing. And I love getting somewhere, anywhere, I can get up high. Like the **Roundhouse** on Bald Mountain. It's this octagonal structure built by Union Pacific Railroad engineers for skiers to stop and warm up. (It resembles one of those buildings used to turn around train engines.) It's an incredibly beautiful spot where you can really get a perspective on the landscape and see what it looks like all around.

Enjoy Sun Valley Music Festival

On summer evenings from late July to early August, join the crowd at the **Sun Valley Music Festival** *(svmusicfestival.org; free)*, the country's largest privately funded classical music event. For this free series, locals and visitors alike fill the open-air **Sun Valley Pavilion** (first-come-first-served seating) or spread blankets across its lawn to hear orchestral performances by some of the world's top musicians; expect everything from major symphonic works to modern pop. The atmosphere is informal – people come in hiking clothes, picnics are laid out and kids play nearby while the sound of the orchestra floats through mountain air. Come early for pre-concert talks.

Summer nights on ice

A summer showcase featured since 1937, **Sun Valley on Ice** *(sunvalley.com; grandstand adult/child from $104/58)* blends elite figure skating with panoramic mountain views. Held at the outdoor rink next to the **Sun Valley Lodge**, the Saturday night performances run from July through early September. Each show features Olympic and world-class skaters delivering solos, duets and ensemble pieces. Seating is up-close in the grandstands – a treat – or on the terrace, with buffet dinner included. Stay afterwards for autographs or meet-and-greets with the skaters.

Deep dive into the past

Learn all about the fascinating history of Sun Valley and Ketchum at the **Wood River Museum of History and Culture** *(comlib.org/museum; free)*. An arm of the Community Library, the engaging little museum traces the region's evolution from Shoshone and Bannock homelands to glitterati ski resort and town. Interactive exhibits include displays on sheep ranching, ski heritage and local oral histories though in true Sun Valley style, the exhibit on celebrity writer Ernest Hemingway kinda steals the show.

Stanley

Out in the Sawtooths

You'll find rivers to boat, mountains to climb, more than 300 lakes to fish, and over 700 miles of trails to hike or mountain bike in the dramatic **Sawtooth National Recreation Area** *(fs.usda.gov/sawtooth)*. It protects 1170 sq miles of public lands stretching between Ketchum and Stanley, offering almost endless opportunities for exploration and recreation.

 EATING IN KETCHUM: OUR PICKS

Johnny G's Subshack: Sandwich shop serving up excellent 6in to 12in hoagies. Choose a specialty sub or build your own. *11am-4pm Mon-Fri, to 3pm Sat* $

Kneadery: Breakfast fave with a log-cabin vibe, including taxidermied creatures. Expect hearty egg dishes, French toast and freshly made pancakes. *8am-2pm* $$

Rickshaw: Cozy spot specializing in mouthwatering Southeast Asian street food. In summer, ask for a table on the leafy patio. *hours vary* $$

Fiamma: Upscale Italian with open kitchen concept highlighting its live-fire cooking. Its seasonal menu is mostly locally sourced. *4:30-10pm Wed-Sat, 10am-2pm Sun* $$$

There are several access points to the Sawtooths; among the most popular is **Galena Lodge** *(galenalodge.com)*. A community-owned spot that works in partnership with the National Forest Service, it serves as a hub to over 45 miles of well-maintained trails that crisscross the gorgeous Boulder Mountains. In the summer come for the hiking, mountain biking and wildflower-filled landscapes. In winter, it's all about cross-country skiing and snowshoeing, with groomed trails that wind through the snowy forest and alpine meadows. Friendly staffers provide trail recommendations though **snowshoeing tours** *(groups of minimum 3 people, per person $70)* and **guided mountain bike rides** *(from $175)* are a popular way to explore the area. Bike, ski and snowshoe rentals also available on-site as are hearty meals that will keep you fueled for the day.

Rafting the River of No Return

Rafting the **Middle Fork of the Salmon River** (aka River of No Return) is considered one of the greatest white-water trips in North America: a 104-mile route that winds its way through the heart of the River of No Return Wilderness Area, one of the most remote landscapes in the Lower 48. It's a clear, cold, fast-moving river – boats pass through deep canyons, alpine forest and granite gorges, and over 100 rapids, many class III and IV. Off the water, rafters can hike to waterfalls and soak in natural hot springs, spotting ancient pictographs and abandoned mining cabins along the way (not to mention bighorn sheep, bald eagles and black bear). Nights are spent camped on sandy riverbanks, eating around a campfire and sleeping under a blanket of stars.

Permits are required to ride the Middle Fork year-round; they are awarded by **lottery** *(recreation.gov)* but the competition is stiff – only about 2% of applicants receive one. Instead, most use river outfitters to access the river and to take care of all the details, from permits and shuttle service to meal prep and camp setup. Most are based in or near the sleepy towns of Salmon and Stanley, which come to life during the brief summer months. Recommended outfitters include **Solitude River Trips** *(rivertrips.com; six-day trip per person from $3250)* and **Idaho River Journeys** *(idahoriverjourneys.com; six-day trip per person from $3395)*.

Minidoka National Historic Site

Contemplate wrongful imprisonment

Located near the farming community of Jerome, **Minidoka National Historic Site** *(nps.gov/miin; free)* memorializes the incarceration of over 13,000 Japanese Americans who were forced to leave their homes by the US government to be unjustly imprisoned here during WWII. The internment camp, one of 10 in the country, was established under Executive Order 9066 as a racist reaction to the bombing of Pearl Harbor. Today, visitors can walk a 1.6-mile-long gravel **trail** past original structures like barracks, a mess hall, fire station and guard tower. Interpretive panels share personal stories

ERNEST HEMINGWAY

Ernest Hemingway's connection to Idaho ran deep, rooted in the wild, open landscapes that echoed his passion for the outdoors. He first visited Sun Valley in 1939, lured by Union Pacific's campaign to bring celebrities to the new ski resort. Captivated by the location, Hemingway returned almost yearly, hunting in the Sawtooth Mountains, fishing Silver Creek and writing prolifically. He eventually purchased a home in Ketchum, where he took his own life in 1961. Today, visitors can pay their respects at the **Hemingway Memorial** beside **Trail Creek** as well as his gravesite in **Ketchum Cemetery**. His final home, the **Hemingway House and Preserve**, is used for writer-in-residence programs, a lasting legacy.

TOP EXPERIENCE

Craters of the Moon National Monument & Reserve

This is a spectacularly vast, otherworldly place. Beginning some 15,000 years ago, a series of volcanic eruptions laid waste to the Snake River Plain, leaving a blistered land of lunar-like craters, lava-tube caves and fissures. The last eruption took place a mere 2000 years ago. The result is now a 750,000-acre national monument that's well worth a visit.

TOP TIPS

● The nearest gas station is in Cary, 25 miles away – be sure to gas up before arriving.

● From November to April, Loop Rd is closed to vehicular traffic; it's reserved for cross-country skiers and snowshoers. Plan accordingly.

PRACTICALITIES
● nps.gov/crmo
● per vehicle $20
● 24hrs

Drive Loop Road

A scenic **7-mile road** winds its way through the reserve, each turn revealing dramatic volcanic landscapes. Stop at pullouts for the views and signage, which give in-depth insight into the geology, flora, fauna and human history of the place.

Hike Volcanic Landscapes

Eight trails crisscross the reserve, offering a striking variety of features. If you're short on time, opt for the **North Crater Flow Trail** (0.3 miles), a breathtaking boardwalk suspended over young lava fields with snowcapped mountains in the distance; or take a short, steep climb to the summit of the jet-black **Inferno Cone** (0.4 miles), with 360-degree views of the reserve. For a longer hike, head to **Tree Molds Trail** (2 miles), an out-and-back trail with ancient trees preserved in hardened lava – subtle but haunting.

Enter Lava Tubes

Over **700 caves** exist in the reserve, most created by underground rivers of lava. **Indian Tunnel** is the largest and most accessible – an 800ft-long cave with a partially collapsed roof. Expect to scramble over jagged rock and uneven floors. **Cave permits** are required to enter, available for free at the visitor center.

DON MAMMOSER/SHUTTERSTOCK

and photographs that illuminate the harshness of life here – barbed wire, armed guards, extreme weather, minimal privacy...a memorial to Japanese-American resilience but also a reminder of the fragility of civil rights. The visitor center, open on weekends only, has further exhibits and a 30-minute film; ask about the excellent ranger led tours.

Blackfoot

Idaho Potato Museum

Driving through Blackfoot, you can't miss it – a statue of a gigantic baked potato (complete with sour cream and a pat of butter). It sits in front of the **Idaho Potato Museum** *(idaho potatomuseum.com; adult/child $7/3.50)*, a surprisingly engaging museum taking on the potato, from its global history and cultivation to its importance in Idaho. The exhibits are multilayered, including everything from films about McDonalds' fries to hands-on science experiments. There's also a bit of kitsch – animatronic displays, Mr. Potato Head stations, even the world's largest potato chip (25in by 14in). Don't miss the gift shop for quirky merch; and if you need a snack, the on-site cafe serves all manner of potato treats.

Driggs

Fly high at a hot-air balloon festival

For four days surrounding the July 4 holiday, the town of Driggs hosts the annual **Teton Valley Balloon Fest** *(teton valleyballoonrally.org; per vehicle $20)*, a quintessential Rocky Mountain festival, with colorful hot-air balloons soaring high above the verdant valley, the jagged, snowcapped Teton peaks in the background. It's a photographer's dream. Come at sunrise for tethered rides and the mass launch – over four dozen balloons ascending into bluebird skies. And return in the evening for the 'Rally Up and Get Down' party with live music, food-truck fare and giant balloons illuminating the Teton Valley Fairgrounds.

PERRING BRIDGE BASE JUMPERS

Standing 486ft above the Snake River, the **Perrine Bridge** in Twin Falls is the only human-made structure in the US where BASE jumping is allowed year-round without a permit. The extreme sport involves parachuting from a fixed object like a building, bridge or cliff and landing below – an especially dangerous endeavor due to low altitudes and short freefall times. At Perrine Bridge, BASE jumpers launch from platforms on the traffic-congested bridge, free-falling before deploying their parachutes to land in the canyon bottom. Nearly every day, you can see specially trained athletes from around the world preparing their parachutes in the parking lot and under nearby trees while captivated spectators line the bridge and the canyon rim.

EATING IN DRIGGS: OUR PICKS

Provisions Local Kitchen: Popular spot serving heaping plates of breakfast faves, sandwiches, salads and Mexican specialties like choriqueso. *7am-3pm* $

Captain Ron's Smokehouse: Tiny shack serving finger-licking BBQ with all the fixin's. Eat at parking-lot picnic tables. *11am-4pm Tue-Sat* $

Citizen 33: Industrial-farmhouse style taproom serving tasty craft brews and elevated pub grub. If in doubt, get the mashed potatoes. *4-9pm* $$

Forage Bistro: High-end restaurant with casual vibe; the seasonal menu focuses on locally farmed meat and veggies. Happy-hour charcuterie boards. *noon-8pm* $$$

Places We Love to Stay

$ Budget $$ Midrange $$$ Top End

Denver MAP P725

Hostel Fish $ Swanky hostel with plush dorms and cozy common areas. On-site bar plus neighborhood pub crawls bring a party feel.

Populus Hotel $$$ Luxurious carbon-forward hotel with nature-inspired features inside and out. Stunning city views. Rooms are a study in understated elegance.

Boulder MAP P729

St Julien Hotel & Spa $$$ In the heart of downtown, Boulder's finest hotel is modern and refined with Flatiron views and a spa.

Rocky Mountain National Park

Glacier Basin Campground $ Ideally located in the Bear Lake corridor and surrounded by evergreens; 73 sites.

Murphy's Resort $$ Overlooking Lake Estes, this motor lodge has plenty of family-friendly activities. Six miles from the park.

Northern Colorado

Echo Park Campground (Dinosaur National Monument) **$** Gorgeous, primitive Colorado-side campground at the confluence of the Yampa and Green rivers; 4WD highly recommended. First come, first served.

Vista Verde Guest Ranch (Steamboat Springs) **$$$** The most luxurious of Colorado's top-end guest ranches. If you have the means, this is it.

Central Colorado

Crested Butte Hostel (Crested Butte) **$** Luxurious hostel with restaurant-grade kitchen, crackling fireplace and a mix of dorms and private rooms.

Amigo Motor Lodge (Salida) **$$** This cool motel is not only Southwestern stylish, it's got five retro trailers to sleep in.

Sebastian Hotel (Vail) **$$$** Sophisticated hotel showcasing contemporary art and an impressive list of amenities, including a mountainside ski valet and luxury spa.

Mollie Aspen (Aspen) **$$$** Make like Rihanna and book a room at Aspen's coolest new digs, with understated minimalist design and rooftop pool.

Western Colorado

Morefield Campground (Mesa Verde National Park) **$** Full-service campground in a grassy canyon, 5 miles from the visitor center. General store sells basics.

South Rim Campground (Black Canyon of the Gunnison National Park) **$** Large campground in a high-altitude scrub forest. Running water available summer only.

Saddlehorn Campground (Colorado National Monument) **$** The park's only drive-up campground; potable water and flush toilets available. Open year-round.

Box Canyon Lodge & Hot Springs (Ouray) **$$** Geothermically heated motel with modern pine-board rooms and 24/7 access to spring-fed hot tubs.

Telluride

Telluride Town Park Campground $ Creekside campground in the heart of Telluride, with showers, wi-fi, a pool and tennis.

Camel's Garden $$$ Ski-in, ski-out condo-hotel at the base of the gondola. Hit the 25ft hot tub at sunset.

Southeast Colorado

Pinyon Flats Campground (Great Sand Dunes National Park) **$** Official park campground, with great location near the dune field. Reserve months ahead.

Cheyenne Mountain Resort (Colorado Springs) **$$$** Overlooking Cheyenne Mountain, this woodsy resort has an air of indulgence with golf, a spa and lake activities.

Southeast Wyoming MAP P752

Cheyenne Guest Inn (Cheyenne) **$** Older, well-maintained inn with spick-and-span rooms and a tiny indoor pool. Continental breakfast included.

Mad Carpenter Inn (Laramie) **$** Charming guesthouse with cozy, wood-trimmed rooms, a fully equipped cottage and a serious game room. Hot breakfast included.

Lander (Fort Washakie)

Mill House $$ Boutique hotel set in a beautifully renovated flour mill in downtown Lander; suites are modern with artful touches.

Northern Wyoming

The Cody (Cody) **$$** New Western chic with green credentials; there's an indoor pool and hot tub, plus free breakfast.

Devil's Tower Lodge (Devil's Tower HS) **$$** Unparalleled views and warm hospitality make this an excellent base, especially for climbers. Full breakfast included.

Yellowstone National Park MAP P760

Mammoth Campground $ Yellowstone's only campground open year-round has 85 sites set amid scattered junipers and Douglas firs.

Old Faithful Inn $$$ Variety of rooms in a historic log-walled inn with a frenetic lobby that quietens by night.

Grand Teton National Park & Around MAP P760

Lizard Creek Campground (Grand Teton NP) **$** Small campground with pleasantly shaded sites set amid spruce- and-fir forest on the shores of Jackson Lake.

The Hostel (Jackson Hole) **$$** Skiers' favorite for budget accommodations, including four-bed rooms, plus spacious lounge with pool table.

Jackson Lake Lodge (Grand Teton NP) **$$$** Attractive hotel- style rooms and cottages, some with dramatic mountain views.

Bozeman & the Gallatin Valley

Howlers Inn (Bozeman) **$$** Cozy log cabin-style B&B on a sanctuary for rescued captive- born wolves; profits support the cause.

RSVP Motel (Bozeman) **$$$** Stylish upscale motel with colorful rooms and a great little on-site cafe and restaurant.

Rainbow Ranch Lodge (Big Sky) **$$$** Rustic-chic lodge with stylish rooms, most with stone fireplaces and balconies. Located 5 miles from Big Sky turnoff.

Helena

Lamplighter Cabins & Suites $$ Cute, uniquely decorated cabins and contemporary suites, some with kitchenettes. Located steps from downtown.

Missoula MAP P770

Shady Spruce Hostel $ Centrally located hostel in a renovated Victorian home; private rooms and dorms are clean, bright and spacious. Modern guest kitchen too.

Goldsmith's Riverfront Inn $$ Charming riverfront home converted into six cheery suites and fully equipped apartments.

Glacier National Park

Bowman Lake Campground $ Spacious sites in forested grounds, and beautiful Bowman Lake is only steps away.

Many Glacier Hotel $$$ A massive, Swiss-chalet-inspired lodge in a wondrous lakefront setting in the park.

Great Falls

Hotel Arvon $$ Boutique hotel set in a beautifully renovated historic building. Rooms are modern and spacious. Breakfast and parking included.

Boise MAP P780

Modern Hotel $ Urban-chic motel with midcentury-modern rooms. A trendy on-site bar means creative cocktails by the firepit.

Boise Guest House $$ Historic home beautifully transformed into six tasteful suites with kitchenettes. There's a verdant backyard plus cruiser bikes.

Ketchum

Best Western Tyrolean Lodge $$ Chalet-themed motel with dated but comfortable rooms. Breakfast buffet included too. The best budget hotel in town.

Limelight Hotel $$$ Trendy downtown hotel with luxe rooms, some with mountain views. Outdoor pool, full breakfast and complimentary airport shuttle too.

Craters of the Moon National Park

Lava Flow Campground $ Small campsite set on volcanic landscape. Water and flush toilets available May to November only. First come, first served.

Driggs

Teton Valley Cabins $-$$ Pleasant log cabins on a forested lot, some with kitchenettes. In evenings, roast marshmallows around the communal fire pit.

Curated by
Anthony Ham

Southwest USA

ONE OF AMERICA'S GRAND EPICS

Soulful deserts and weirdly wonderful mountains. Frenetic cities and ancient stories. Las Vegas and the Grand Canyon. Welcome to America's fabulous west.

The Southwest could only happen in America. Take an astonishing landscape, the kind of place that is both cinematic in scope and part of a deeply American tradition of starring on the silver screen. Overlay that with a fascinating roll-call of civilizations, from the Ancestral Puebloans and Native American cultures like the Hopi, Navajo and Apache to the gunslingers and bandits (like Butch Cassidy or Billy the Kid) of the Wild West. And then, carrying all of this with you as you go – perhaps along Route 66 – rush headlong into the future toward places like Las Vegas or the space race of Las Cruces. Then let your mind consider the supernatural at Roswell and Area 51. And as you contemplate this remarkable collage that is America writ large, tuck into a meal laced with the green chiles of New Mexico in all their fiery manifestations.

But it's the backdrop to all of this – the landscapes that bring such gravitas to this corner of the country – that is the real star of the show. Yes, the Grand Canyon has no rivals. But the Mojave and Sonoran Deserts, the deep canyons and hallucinatory rock formations of Utah's national parks, or Monument Valley and the Petrified Forest, also combine to make a compelling case for calling the Southwest America's mostly wildly beautiful corner.

THE MAIN AREAS

LAS VEGAS
Nevada's brightly lit capital of glitz. **p796**

NEVADA
Desert landscapes and cities. **p802**

PHOENIX
Arizona's cultured gateway and capital. **p808**

GRAND CANYON NATIONAL PARK
A true wonder of the natural world. **p813**

For places to stay in Southwest USA, see p878

THE GUIDE

SOUTHWEST USA

WIRESTOCK CREATORS/SHUTTERSTOCK

Skywalk (p819), Grand Canyon West

NORTHERN ARIZONA
Mystics, natural beauty and the OK Corral.
p821

SOUTHERN ARIZONA
Tucson and Saguaro National Park. **p835**

UTAH
National parks at every turn. **p843**

NEW MEXICO
Food, stirring terrain and ancient cultures.
p863

Find Your Way

Deserts, mountains and a very far horizon make for miraculous, big-sky road-making – no wonder Route 66 sends everyone a little crazy. Getting around is easy but requires careful map-plotting. Distances are huge. Plan accordingly.

Utah, p843
Explore Mormon culture in Salt Lake City, then head for five of America's best national parks: Arches, Canyonlands, Capitol Reef, Bryce Canyon and Zion.

Nevada, p802
Reno, the Mojave Desert, Hoover Dam, Area 51... It's amazing how much Nevada packs into an area that's almost entirely (and beautifully) desert.

Las Vegas, p796
The Strip (Las Vegas Blvd) is among the most famous streets in the world. Fremont St and the Arts District are just as exciting.

Phoenix, p808
Arizona's capital, Phoenix is the epicenter of culture and cuisine in the Sonoran Desert, and luxurious resorts abound. Alfresco dining and sunsets are highlights.

Grand Canyon National Park, p813
This geologic wonder is worth the hype, with billion-year-old rocks, luminous sunsets and hiking trails that immerse you in its vast beauty.

TRAIN & BUS
Amtrak (trains) and Greyhound (buses) cross the Southwest. They're more useful for reaching the Southwest (or crossing it from one side to the other) than they are for traveling within the region.

CAR
Having your own vehicle means there are few places you can't go; consider renting a 4WD for following enticing dirt side roads. Most roads are in excellent condition, but plan for long stretches of tarmac between gas stations.

PLANE
To make the most of your time, flying a couple of legs is worth considering. Phoenix, Las Vegas, Reno, Salt Lake City, Santa Fe and Albuquerque receive flights from across the US, but you can also fly between them and other towns of the Southwest.

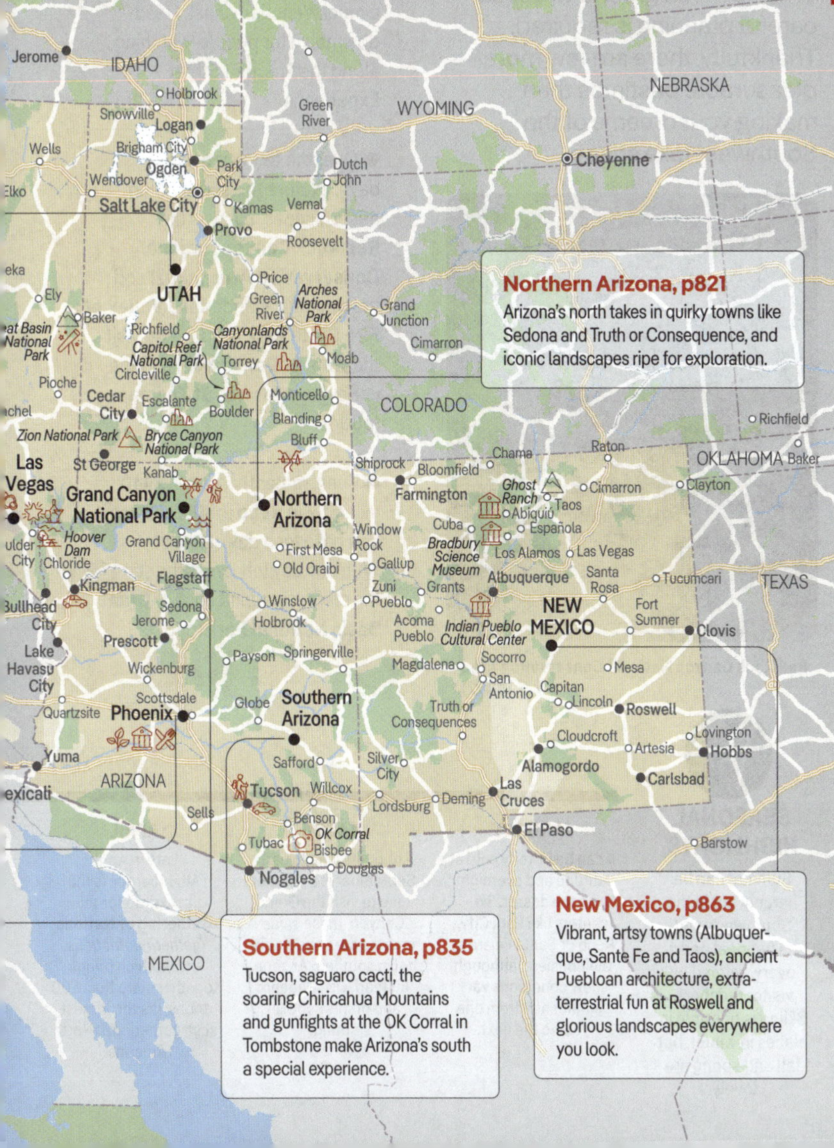

Northern Arizona, p821
Arizona's north takes in quirky towns like Sedona and Truth or Consequence, and iconic landscapes ripe for exploration.

Southern Arizona, p835
Tucson, saguaro cacti, the soaring Chiricahua Mountains and gunfights at the OK Corral in Tombstone make Arizona's south a special experience.

New Mexico, p863
Vibrant, artsy towns (Albuquerque, Sante Fe and Taos), ancient Puebloan architecture, extra-terrestrial fun at Roswell and glorious landscapes everywhere you look.

Plan Your Time

With so much ground to cover, careful planning is required. Thankfully, there are few more pleasurable pastimes than making your dreams of the Southwest take shape.

Red Rock Canyon National Conservation Area (p802)

Seven Nevada Days

● Begin two days in **Las Vegas** (p796) with a wander around the Strip, taking note of the Egyptian pyramid, summiting the Eiffel Tower and riding a gondola in a mock Venetian canal. Head downtown for people-watching along the Fremont Street Experience.

● Over the following two days, explore the surrounding desertscapes, such as the **Red Rock Canyon National Conservation Area** (p802) and the geologic wonderland **Valley of Fire State Park** (p803), and visit the **Hoover Dam** (p803) and the eerie ghost town of **St Thomas** (p804).

● Then, rather than driving 440 miles, fly to **Reno** (p804) and use it as a base for a day of exploration. With one day left, cross the state for the stirring magnificence of **Great Basin National Park** (p807).

SEASONAL HIGHLIGHTS

Summer can be fiercely hot in the Southwest, and its national parks overwhelmed by visitor numbers. Skiing is possible in places in winter, but fall and spring are lovely.

JANUARY
It can be bitterly cold at altitude and overnight in the desert. Ski centers like Park City, Reno or Santa Fe are at their busiest, although snow conditions vary significantly from one year to the next.

MARCH
Although June to early September is a popular time to visit the Grand Canyon, those same months are unbearably hot in southern Arizona. Instead, visit Phoenix and points south in spring.

APRIL
Late in April, Albuquerque is the backdrop for the **Gathering of Nations** (gatheringofnations. com), which brings together more than 500 tribes; it's the largest such gathering in North America.

Ten Arizona Days

● Head to the South Rim of the **Grand Canyon** (p816) for two days of exploring this utterly magnificent natural wonder, with at least another day around the low-key **Grand Canyon North Rim** (p818). Concentrate on following a small number of trails and seeing a handful of overlooks well, rather than racing around and trying to see everything. Allow an extra couple of days for Grand Canyon hikes.

● Loop around the crimson buttes of **Monument Valley** (p829), then start your **Route 66** (p833) retro drive in Kingman. Sip microbrews in **Flagstaff** (p827) and follow gorgeous **Oak Creek Canyon** (p825) to **Sedona** (p821) where you can try and locate your chakra. Swing through **Jerome** (p826) and **Prescott** (p826) for art and history.

Two Weeks in Utah & New Mexico

● Begin with a day spent exploring the Mormon story in multi-dimensional **Salt Lake City** (p845), followed by a couple of days each in two of Utah's best national parks where you're spoiled for choice: **Zion** (p860), **Bryce Canyon** (p858), **Arches** (p854), **Canyonlands** or **Capitol Reef** (p853). If you have the time, visit them all.

● Fly from Salt Lake City to **Albuquerque** (p865), which is worth a couple of days for its museums and opportunities to feast on feisty New Mexican dishes. **Taos** (p870) is another fun place to catch the magic of New Mexico.

● Reserve your final day for **White Sands National Park** (p877) or the little green men of **Roswell** (p874).

JUNE
Warmer temperatures in northern New Mexico are perfect for wildflower-laden hikes and rafting around Taos. Further afield, summer has yet to set the Southwest fully ablaze and summer crowds have yet to arrive en masse.

JULY
July 24 is **Pioneer Day** in Utah, a state holiday remembering the arrival of the first Mormon pioneers in 1847. Reenactors march through Salt Lake City, while non-Mormons prefer to mark it as 'Pie and Beer Day.'

OCTOBER
Neon aspen leaves, mild temperatures and so many festivals, including Albuquerque's **International Balloon Fiesta**. Apart from anything else, it's a beautiful time to be anywhere in the Southwest.

DECEMBER
Don your cowboy hat and spurs as **National Finals Rodeo** returns Las Vegas to its Western roots. On New Year's Eve, the Strip becomes a huge party as thousands turn out for headliner bands and fireworks.

Las Vegas

NON-STOP ENTERTAINMENT | SPECTATOR SPORTS | GREAT DINING

☑ TOP TIP

If you're new to gambling, or on a budget, it makes sense to try your luck Downtown rather than on the Strip. Downtown casinos offer games with slightly better odds, and minimum bets are significantly lower.

The story of Las Vegas begins in Downtown, where the city was founded in 1905. That's right: this historic core and its casinos were thriving long before the glitz of Las Vegas Blvd took the spotlight, and in recent years, Vegas' Downtown has staged a comeback. The five-block Fremont Street Experience, beneath a canopy of millions of LED lights, debuted in the mid-1990s. Then in 2012, Zappos' CEO Tony Hsieh infused $350 million into revitalizing the neighborhood.

But Las Vegas is also the Strip – a 4-mile eruption of color and possibility also known as Las Vegas Blvd. This is what happens when unchecked indulgence reigns. Love it or loathe it, this over-the-top 'playground for grown-ups' taps into the hopes and dreams of the masses. They no longer come for just the gambling, either, but for the dazzling performances, intriguing art installations, world-class restaurants and ever-popular sporting events that relentlessly infuse the Strip with new energy.

Fremont Street

The beating heart of Downtown

Streaking down the center of Vegas' historic district, the **Fremont Street Experience** *(vegasexperience.com)* is a

GETTING AROUND

Downtown is mostly walkable. Most of the action is at the Fremont Street Experience, where you'll be on foot. If you prefer exploring on two wheels, the RTC bike-share program has stations Downtown. Taxis are widely available in front of hotels, and rideshares are popular (just be sure you're at the right pick-up area). The free Downtown Loop bus stops at all the big attractions. Walking the Strip is an adventure, often involving sidewalk performances, escalators and pedestrian bridges over the highway.

'Welcome to Fabulous Las Vegas' sign

five-block pedestrian mall lined with old-school casinos and topped by an arched steel canopy. Hourly from dusk until midnight, the 1400ft-long canopy turns on a six-minute light-and-sound show. The shows are cheesy, but mesmerizing if you're drunk. It's even more exhilarating if you happen to be zooming by on the zipline cables attached to the 12-story **SlotZilla** (*vegasexperience.com/slotzilla-zip-line; from $49*), a slot-machine-themed platform at the mall's eastern end.

Welcome to Fabulous Las Vegas

Arriving on the Strip

The **'Welcome to Fabulous Las Vegas' sign**, in the center of bustling Las Vegas Blvd, makes for a great place to start your explorations. In a city famous for neon signs, this one reigns supreme, and is the unofficial beginning of the Strip.

Designed by Betty Willis at the end of the 1950s, this sign is a classic photo op and a reminder of Vegas' past. Get here by midmorning to avoid long lines of jovial, selfie-seeking tourists.

WEDDING CHAPELS

Driving along Las Vegas Blvd, it's impossible to miss the abundance of wedding chapels – a testament to how easy it is to get married here.

Near the iconic 'Welcome to Fabulous Las Vegas' sign, the **Little Church of the West** is one of the oldest of the dozens of wedding chapels in Las Vegas. Since 1941 this one has hosted the weddings of celebrities including Judy Garland and Mark Herron, Richard Gere and Cindy Crawford, and Billy Bob Thornton and Angelina Jolie. Hang around outdoors for a few minutes and you'll probably see some newlyweds posing for pictures.

 EATING ON THE STRIP: BEST RESTAURANTS

Golden Steer: The Rat Pack, Marilyn Monroe and Elvis all dined at this fabulously retro steakhouse with steer's head out front. *4:30-9:45pm* **$$$**

Joël Robuchon: In the famous chef's art deco-inspired dining room, seasonal tasting menus deliver the meal of a lifetime. *5-9:30pm* **$$$**

Peppermill: This Vegas institution is famous for its campy atmosphere, firepit-fountains and massive portions. *hours vary* **$$**

Delilah: See and be seen in this modern supper club that drips with style and regularly attracts A-list celebs. No photos. *hours vary* **$$$**

LAS VEGAS SOUTHWEST USA

THE GUIDE

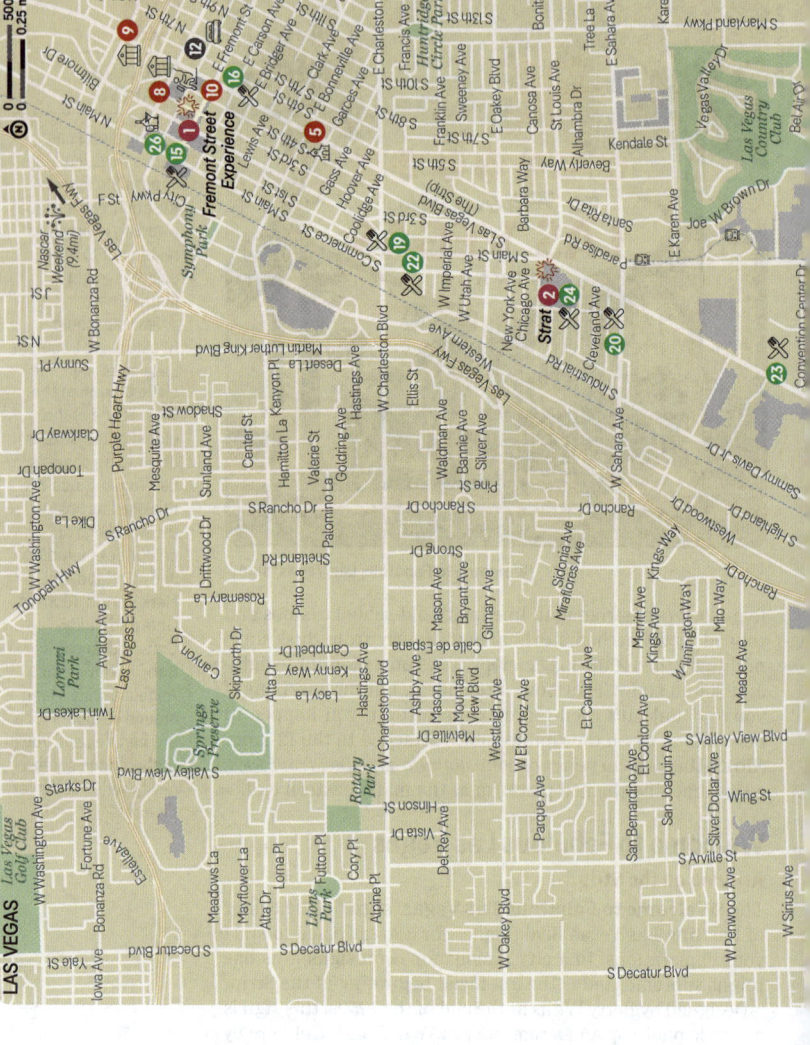

★ HIGHLIGHTS
1. Fremont Street Experience
2. Strat
3. Welcome to Las Vegas Sign

● SIGHTS
4. Eiffel Tower Experience
5. Graceland Wedding Chapel
6. High Roller
7. Little Church of the West
8. Mob Museum
9. Neon Museum

● ACTIVITIES
10. SlotZilla

● SLEEPING
11. Cosmopolitan
12. El Cortez
13. Luxor
14. Skylofts

● EATING
15. Barry's Downtown Prime
16. Carson Kitchen
17. Delilah
18. Eiffel Tower Restaurant
19. Esther's Kitchen
20. Golden Steer
21. Joël Robuchon
22. Main St Provisions
23. Peppermill
24. Top of the World

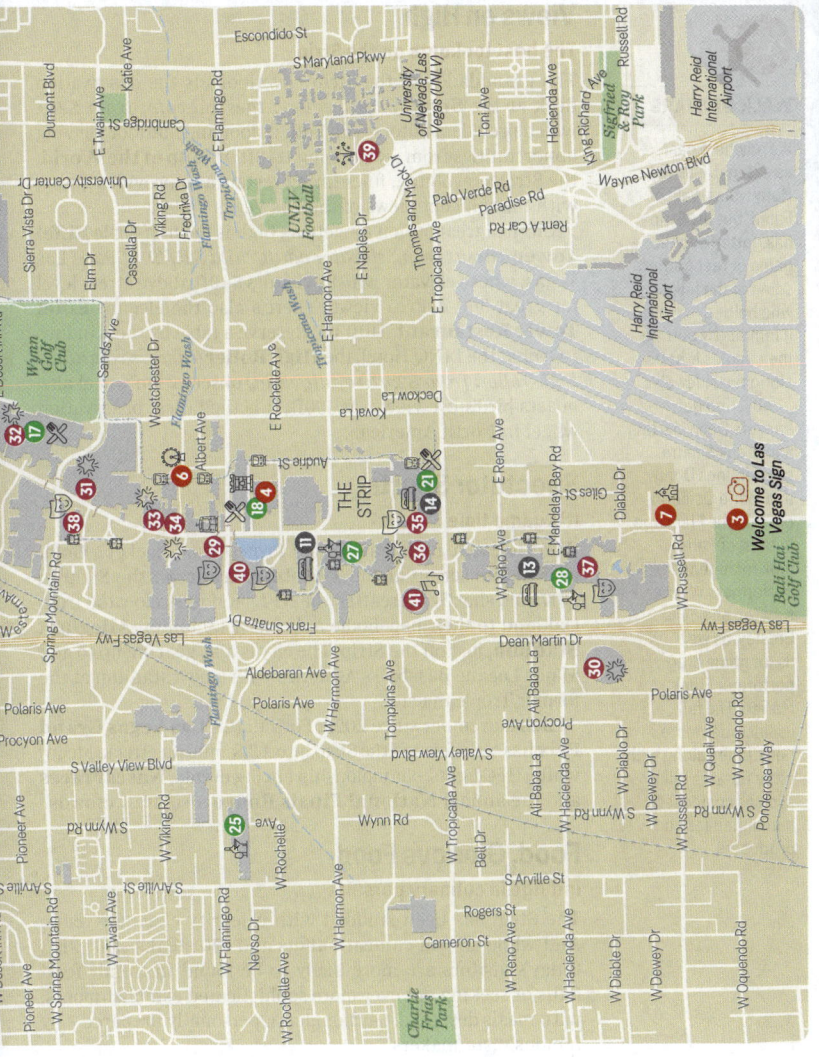

SOUTHWEST USA LAS VEGAS

● **DRINKING & NIGHTLIFE**
25 Ghostbar
26 Legacy Club
27 Skybar
28 Skyfall Lounge

● **ENTERTAINMENT**
29 Absinthe
30 Allegiant Stadium
31 Atomic Saloon Show
32 Awakening
33 Big Elvis
34 DiscoShow
35 Kà
36 Mad Apple
37 Michael Jackson ONE
38 Mystère
39 National Finals Rodeo
40 O
41 T-Mobile Arena

Views on High

The best lookouts on the Strip

The granddaddy of the Strip's overlooks is the observation deck at the **Strat** *(Stratosphere; thestrat.com; from $20)*, which provides visitors with both indoor and outdoor viewing opportunities from a whopping 1149ft up. **Top of the World**, the Strat's revolving, fine-dining restaurant, provides guests with magnificent views of the Las Vegas Valley.

Another great option for getting high is the half-scale **Eiffel Tower** *(caesars.com; elevator adult/child $25/19)* at Paris Las Vegas, whose elevator whisks visitors 540ft above street level for great 360-degree views. There's also the elegant **Eiffel Tower Restaurant**, 110ft up. Reserve a table by the window.

Over at the LINQ Hotel, the **High Roller** *(caesars.com/linq/high-roller; from $29/10 adult/child)* observation wheel also boasts bird's-eye views. At 550ft, it is the tallest observation wheel in North America.

Spectator Sports

It's game time

Want to catch a game in Vegas? Professional hockey's Golden Knights set up at the **T-Mobile Arena** on the Strip in 2017, and shortly thereafter, the NFL's Raiders relocated from Oakland to their new home at Vegas' $1.9 billion **Allegiant Stadium**, just off the Strip. The city is also gearing up to add Major League Baseball's Athletics with a new stadium at the former Tropicana site.

Each November since 2023, Formula 1's **Las Vegas Grand Prix** has transformed the Strip into a 3.8-mile racetrack. Meanwhile, UFC fights, championship boxing events, **Nascar races** and the annual **National Finals Rodeo** also draw crowds.

Food, Glorious Food

Indulge in culinary pursuits

The Strip has been studded with celebrity chefs for years. And while all-you-can-eat buffets and $10 steaks still exist, today's visitors are more likely to be found in trendy food halls or seeking out ever more sophisticated establishments, with meals designed – although not personally prepared – by famous taste-makers.

If food is your *raison d'être,* look no further than **Lip Smacking Foodie Tours** *(lipsmackingfoodietours.com)*.

WALK OF STARS

It's nowhere near as extensive as the Hollywood Walk of Fame, but the Strip has gotten into the game of recognizing some of the folks who helped to make it famous by putting their names in stars along the sidewalks.

You'll find Rat Packers Dean Martin and Frank Sinatra, plus siblings Donny and Marie Osmond, outside the Flamingo. In front of Paris, look for legendary performers Wayne Newton and Elvis Presley, as well as longtime drag performer Frank Marino. The full list includes more performers along with other notable folks such as composers, humanitarians and producers.

DRINKING ON THE STRIP: BEST ROOFTOP BARS WITH STRIP VIEWS

GhostBar: Off the Strip at Palms, this 55th-floor club with outdoor deck is reached by a private lift. Fun vibe, great DJs. *7pm-2am Wed-Sat*

Skybar: Floor-to-ceiling windows enhance the vistas from this classy 23rd-floor bar at Waldorf Astoria. Great cocktails, too. *hours vary*

Skyfall Lounge: Sophistication, creative seasonal cocktails and killer views align on the 64th floor of Delano. *5pm-midnight*

Legacy Club: Downtown penthouse lounge on Circa's 60th floor with panoramic Strip views and killer weekend parties. *4pm-2am*

Showtime on the Strip
Are you not entertained?

Las Vegas is a hub for the world's top entertainers, and the nightly performances up and down the Strip reflect this remarkable consolidation of talent.

Cirque du Soleil captivates with its five productions: **O** at the Bellagio is a mesmerizing water-based show, featuring high-flying acrobatics and surreal aquatic stunts; **Kà** at MGM Grand tells a tale of familial love and conflict on a rotating, oftentimes vertical stage; **Michael Jackson ONE** at Mandalay Bay pays tribute to the King of Pop; **Mad Apple** is a homage to New York City in (where else) New York–New York; and **Mystère** at Treasure Island combines classic circus artistry with vibrant costumes and high-energy stunts.

Absinthe at Caesars Palace blends incredible acrobatic feats with edgy humor in an intimate setting beneath a Big Top. Meanwhile, **Atomic Saloon Show** at the Venetian is a mix of burlesque, comedy and acrobatics in a rowdy, Wild West–themed saloon. **DiscoShow**, in the LINQ Hotel, is a thrilling love letter to disco that invites the audience into the dance party.

The Wynn adds its own magic with **Awakening**, an extraordinary spectacle combining innovative stage design, elaborate costumes and mind-blowing special effects in a mythical adventure story.

Then there are, of course, the residencies. Superstars perform in resort theaters seating thousands for weeks, months and even years on end. And pop icons, comedians and magicians regularly perform at the Strip's many venues. Plan ahead and look into who you might be able to catch in residence.

The Mob & Neon Lights
Learn about gangsters and see vintage signs

The highly respected **Mob Museum** (*National Museum of Organized Crime & Law Enforcement; themobmuseum.org; from $34.95*) chronicles the era when gangsters controlled Las Vegas and got rich stealing casino profits. The museum shares gangster stories alongside those of the law enforcement officers whose job it was to nail the bad guys.

While not old itself, **Neon Museum** (*neonmuseum.org; adult/child $25/12.50 day, $35/17.50 evening*) is chock-full of vintage signs that once hung on long-gone properties such as Binion's Horseshoe, the Moulin Rouge and Stardust.

FINDING ELVIS

Elvis has definitely left the building. In 1976 he ended a run of 636 shows at the International (later the Las Vegas Hilton). Now the Westgate, the hotel honors the King with a bronze statue in the lobby. Its International Theater remains, still attracting top-tier headliners.

Downtown's **Graceland Wedding Chapel** offers couples a package that includes an Elvis impersonator. And although Elvis-themed shows come and go, **Big Elvis** has been a hit in Strip lounges since 2002. Pete Vallee's voice is as rich as his jumpsuit is big. He once weighed an incredible 945lb but has since shed hundreds. He performs for free four afternoons a week at Harrah's.

EATING DOWNTOWN: BEST BITES

Carson Kitchen: Tiny eatery with an industrial vibe, a rooftop patio and excellent shared plates of creative American classics. *hours vary* **$$**

Barry's Downtown Prime: Classy steakhouse; cuts are mouthwatering and lobster mac explodes from the shell. *hours vary* **$$$**

Esther's Kitchen: A cozy, popular restaurant with excellent Italian cuisine at commendable prices. *hours vary* **$$**

Main St Provisions: Delicious modern American place, it feels like a neighborhood staple while still offering foie gras add-ons. *hours vary* **$$**

Nevada

SCENIC LANDSCAPES | OUTDOOR ADVENTURE | URBAN CULTURE

Places

Mojave Desert p802
Hoover Dam p803
Reno p804
Great Basin National Park p807

Nevada has soul to go with the glitz and glamor of Las Vegas. Much of that comes from the Mojave Desert, which is a destination in itself, perhaps even the necessary counterpoint to the bright lights of Vegas. All across the Mojave, stunning natural wonders – the wind- and water-carved landscapes of Red Rock Canyon and the Valley of Fire, for example – rise from the desert floor. Even the human footprint can be seen on a grand scale, such as at the Hoover Dam, while the haunting ruins of St Thomas are a reminder of how fragile the human presence can be out here.

Ranging further afield, Reno, with its echoes of the Burning Man Festival, is like a more manageable Vegas but with history and art instead of nonstop show business. It's also an emerging adventure hub. In other words, there are good reasons why Nevada draws tens of millions of visitors each year.

☑ TOP TIP

The Mojave Desert is the driest desert in North America, and visitors often don't realize that just because they don't feel sweaty, they're still perspiring; it instantly evaporates in the hot and dry conditions. Dehydration can be deadly, so carry and consume lots of water.

Mojave Desert
Exploring the unspoiled desert

Drive just about any direction from Las Vegas and before long you'll be at one of Southern Nevada's wonderful natural resources that are light-years away from the neon of the Strip. Just 20 miles from the resorts, **Red Rock Canyon National Conservation Area** *(redrockcanyonlv.org; vehicle/bicycle $20/10; reservations required 8am-5pm Oct-May)* welcomes

GETTING AROUND

If you're short on time, tours out of Vegas can get you to highlights such as Hoover Dam, Red Rock Canyon and Valley of Fire, and coaches travel as far as the Grand Canyon. But given the state's great distances and the remoteness of popular destinations, to fully soak in the delights, a car – or better yet, a high-clearance SUV – is required. It's the only way you can reach off-the-beaten-path places. Rental cars are available at airports and some hotels. If you're sticking to the cities, several airlines (including Southwest and Spirit) connect Las Vegas and Reno.

A CITY WITHOUT CASINOS

In all Nevada, there are only two communities where gambling remains illegal. The small Lincoln County town of Panaca is one and Boulder City is the other.

Built during the Great Depression to house dam builders, **Boulder City** was under control of the federal government, which saw gambling as a costly vice that should be discouraged. In 1931, after gambling had been legalized elsewhere in Nevada, the highway between Boulder City and Las Vegas became a busy thoroughfare as workers flocked to Downtown gambling halls in search of fortune – or at least an escape from the drudgery of their jobs. Now, there are casinos a few miles to the east and west of Boulder City.

more than two million visitors each year. There's a visitor center and a 13-mile paved road that winds through multicolored formations of sandstone. Visitors can hike or bike the paved road.

For a much less crowded desert park with great trails and petroglyphs, head south from Las Vegas to **Sloan Canyon National Conservation Area** *(blm.gov)*.

Travelers willing to venture further afield will relish their drive or hike through spectacular **Valley of Fire State Park** *(parks.nv.gov/parks/valley-of-fire; Nevada/non-Nevada vehicles $10/15)*. About an hour from Las Vegas, the park is home to mile after mile of awe-inspiring, otherworldly geologic curiosities, some with pastel hues and others rust-colored.

Hoover Dam

Hoover Dam and a Lake Mead ghost town

About 35 miles east of Las Vegas, Hoover Dam is an engineering marvel built in the 1930s to harness the Colorado River while providing a dependable water supply to Southern California and generating hydroelectric power. Although the dam's hydroelectric output has been significantly reduced due to drought in recent years, the towering 726ft structure still controls the flooding of the Colorado River, helps to irrigate more than 1.5 million acres of land and provides water to 25 million people.

Visit to learn about how 21,000 men built the dam during the height of the Great Depression – and how climate change threatens to diminish its functionality. First, though, you'll want to drive across the top of the dam into Arizona for the best views of the hulking construction. Another remarkable view can be found back in Nevada, where an accessible, albeit uphill, walkway leads to the sidewalk along the Mike O'Callaghan–Pat Tillman Memorial Bridge. Hold the railing when it's windy – this isn't for anyone with a fear of heights.

History buffs can delve deeper on a guided tour. They begin at the **Hoover Dam Parking Garage & Visitor Center** (which got a fancy new exhibition center in 2025). The one-hour dam tour ($30) explores historic tunnels, takes in the Colorado River through a ventilation shaft and rides an elevator to the top.

Hoover Dam created the enormous **Lake Mead**, which is actually a reservoir, in the 1930s. The lake is bisected by the Nevada–Arizona state line. The highlight of visiting Lake Mead is **St Thomas Ghost Town**. Navigate the deeply rutted road for roughly 3 miles to the end. From the history-filled kiosks, there's a 2.5-mile desert trail leading to the remains of the town flooded by the creation of Lake Mead following the construction of Hoover Dam. Submerged under 60ft of water for nearly eight decades, the foundations and walls of some of St Thomas' buildings have eerily re-emerged during the drought.

Reno

Learn Reno's historical story

Driving in beneath the downtown arch that proclaims Reno 'the Biggest Little City in the World,' and eyeballing its gaudy casinos and mid-century modern architecture, you may be tempted to label it a smaller Las Vegas. But once you've strolled through the Riverwalk District along the alpine-fed Truckee River, grabbed brunch and cocktails at a hip bistro in Midtown and been intrigued by public art at every turn, the truth becomes clear: Reno has a fascinating story and has come into its own.

The **Nevada Museum of Art** (*nevadaart.org; adult/child $15/3*) building was inspired by the geological formations of the Black Rock Desert to the north, and inside, a floating staircase leads to galleries showcasing its temporary exhibits and eclectic collection. Visitors are free to explore the Sky Room on the 4th floor, essentially a rooftop penthouse and patio with killer views, and a 50,000-sq-ft wing that opened in 2025.

RENO'S BEST EVENTS

Reno River Festival: The world's top freestyle kayakers compete in a mad paddling dash through Whitewater Park in mid-May.

Hot August Nights: Celebration of hot rods and rock 'n' roll in early August in various locations around Reno and beyond.

Great Reno Balloon Race: In one of Reno's most inspiring spectacles, more than 100 hot-air balloons race across the desert over three days every September.

Artown: Throughout July, this Riverwalk District celebration centers on art and culture, with hundreds of events, workshops and performances.

Reno Rodeo: Each June, roping and bull-riding action takes place at the Livestock Events Center, with a five-day cattle drive across the high desert.

EATING IN RENO: OUR PICKS

| **Beline Carniceria & Deli:** Reno's best Mexican at this market counter and restaurant north of town. Don't miss the tortas. *9am-7pm* $ | **Perenn:** Locals are obsessed with the boules and baguettes at this hip bakery. *7am-noon Midtown, to 2:30pm Village at Rancharrah* $ | **Brasserie Saint James:** Eclectic menu, plus beers made using water from an aquifer underneath it. Great patio. *11am-9pm Tue-Sun* $$ | **Atlantis Steakhouse:** Highly rated place serving premium Allen Brothers and Wagyu beef. Special-occasion vibes. *5-10pm Wed-Sun* $$$ |

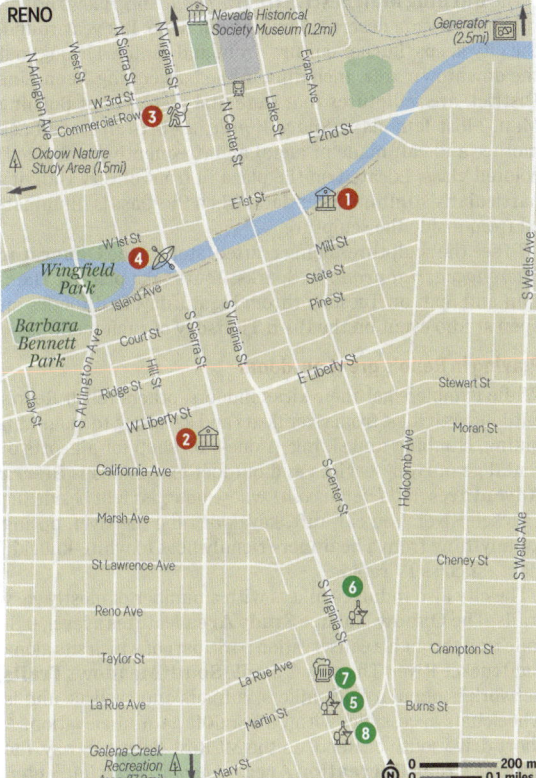

SIGHTS
1. National Automobile Museum
2. Nevada Museum of Art

ACTIVITIES
3. BaseCamp
4. Sierra Adventures

DRINKING & NIGHTLIFE
5. Craft Wine & Beer
6. Death & Taxes
7. Local Beer Works
8. Rum Sugar Lime

RENO'S QUICKIE DIVORCES

Long before Las Vegas developed the moniker of 'Wedding Capital,' Reno's reputation focused on 'quickie' divorces. The process, also known as 'migratory divorce,' took six weeks, but that was quick compared to the long, drawn-out procedures elsewhere, which typically assigned marital property to husbands. In Reno, owners of everything from private homes to dude ranches to luxury hotels got in on the act of offering short-term rentals to women who, once they had lived in Nevada for six weeks, could get a divorce decree citing just about any circumstance. Thousands flocked to Reno from the 1930s to the '60s, but when divorce laws were relaxed in other states, the 'quickie divorce' industry fell into a steady decline.

Get an understanding of the region's vibrant past with a visit to the **Nevada Historical Society Museum** (*nvculture.org/historicalsociety; adult/child $6/free*). Opened in 1904, it's the state's oldest museum. Just beyond the entrance is its pride and joy: a collection of priceless, 19th-century baskets woven by Dat-So-La-Lee, a Washoe woman who lived in the area. Another exhibit explores the rich history of mining, and there's also a section devoted specifically to Reno's history.

The **National Automobile Museum** (*automuseum.org; adult/child $15/10*) has casino pioneer Bill Harrah to thank for its existence. While building resorts across the state, Harrah also amassed a mind-boggling collection of 1400 vintage cars, many of which used to be kept in warehouses in neighboring Sparks. The museum's gems include a 1907 Thomas Flyer 35, a 1937 Cord 812 and an original Batmobile from the 1960s.

Burning brightly year-round

Each August, 'Burners' from around the world descend on the Black Rock Desert to build Black Rock City, tear it down, and set fire to an effigy of 'the man,' with plenty of peace, love, music, art, nakedness, drugs, sex and frivolity thrown in.

The **Burning Man Festival** (*burningman.org*) glows brightly in the Nevada desert 115 miles from Reno. But year-round, the city keeps 'Burner culture' front and center. Throughout the downtown area, including in the burgeoning Neon Line District, are sculptures that were first displayed at Burning Man. Most famous is *Space Whale,* a 40ft-tall humpback mother and calf made of metal and (frequently vandalized) colored glass. Located on the plaza in front of City Hall, it's particularly stunning after dark, when the glass is illuminated from inside the sculpture.

To see the sculptures being crafted, stop by the **Generator** (*therenogenerator.com*) in Sparks. Tours take place at 11am, 1pm and 5pm on Tuesday through Saturday, and there's an open studio event on the third Thursday of each month.

Playing in Reno's great outdoors

While gamblers get their kicks indoors, others relish Reno's outdoor activities, from river floats and kayaking to mountain biking, climbing and skiing. A one-stop shop for all sorts of rental gear, river services and outdoor excursions is **Sierra Adventures** (*wildsierra.com*), whose office is right beside the Truckee River. You can raft, kayak or tube the river, opting for anything from a beginner-friendly float to white-knuckle rides on class IV rapids.

The city also indulges hikers with a number of mostly easy trails. The **Oxbow Nature Study Area** features a level, 0.8-mile trail through a conservation park, part of which sits along the Truckee River. The paved, 5-mile **South Meadows Trails** network is popular with hikers, runners and cyclists, and is wheelchair-accessible, with only a 60ft gain in elevation. A short drive south of Reno, on the Mt Rose Scenic Byway, the **Galena Creek Recreation Area** (*galenacreekvisitorcenter.org*) has a great visitor center and a paved interpretive trail out back, plus a few longer trails. Two other recommended hikes just outside the city include **Hunter Creek Trail** (to a 30ft waterfall) and **Tom Cooke Trail** (along a scenic river).

A non-gaming property downtown, the Whitney Peak Hotel is known for **BaseCamp** (*basecampreno.com*). Along with a state-of-the-art indoor bouldering gym, BaseCamp includes outdoor climbing challenges on the hotel's east wall. The Big Wall, which holds a Guinness World Record as the planet's largest outdoor climbing wall, sends thrill-seekers on a 164ft ascent to the roof. BaseCamp also offers climbs and climbing classes for every skill level, from beginner to world-class professional athlete.

AREA 51

After years of refusing to acknowledge that Area 51 existed, in 2013 the US government admitted that the desert site was used to develop specialized aircraft. Skeptics, however, believe that aliens from a UFO crash site near Roswell (p334), New Mexico, were brought to Area 51 in 1947. The unconfirmed legends continue to lure believers to the nearby Extraterrestrial Highway (NV375) and its alien-themed attractions.

From Ash Springs, it's a five-minute drive north on US 93 to the turnoff for NV 375, the road that runs tantalizingly close to Area 51. The junction is marked by the **ET Fresh Jerky** shop, which sells alien-themed merchandise and a wide variety of jerky flavors supposedly made from cows surrounding Area 51.

DRINKING IN RENO: OUR PICKS

Local Beer Works: Solid craft beers and fun seasonal specials. Don't miss the Irish Stout aged in Frey Ranch bourbon bottles. *hours vary*	**Craft Wine & Beer:** A bottle shop with products from small local brewers and growers, a cute little bar, a good crowd and tastings. *hours vary*	**Death & Taxes:** Perch on a Victorian barstool and sip delicious cocktails like works of art at this all-black, death-themed tavern. *hours vary*	**Rum Sugar Lime:** A bright and chic tropical cocktail bar in Midtown; killer rum drinks, strong list of non-alcoholic libations. *4pm-midnight Tue-Sun*

TOP EXPERIENCE

Great Basin National Park

One of the least-visited national parks, Great Basin National Park is a must for people in search of solitude and natural beauty. The free-to-visit park is lorded over by Wheeler Peak, a 13,063ft ice-sculpted horn, which shelters a shrinking but still-visible glacier. Hiking and camping opportunities abound, and the park is a designated International Dark Sky Park.

Wheeler Peak

Wheeler Peak Scenic Drive

Ascending 3000ft over 12 miles, this out-and-back scenic drive rises steeply through several distinct eco-regions. It winds first through low-lying sagebrush, then up past pinyon pines, a mountain mahogany wilderness, a mixed-conifer forest peppered with aspens and, finally, a zone of subalpine forest, at which point astonishing views of Wheeler come into sight.

Hitting the Trails

Great Basin is a hiker's wonderland, with over 60 miles of trails. The 26 trails traverse mountains studded with ancient forests and meander around glacier-fed lakes, and one even leads to Nevada's only glacier. Hikers of all levels will find plenty of options.

The **Glacier Trail** is one of the park's best. It culminates at the rock glacier ensconced beneath Wheeler Peak, and the 8.4-mile round trip also brings you to a grove of ancient bristlecone pines, the world's oldest non-cloned organisms.

Lehman Caves

A colossal marble cavern, Lehman Caves has a staggering collection of formations including stalactites, stalagmites, helictites, flowstone, popcorn and rare shields. They are a fragile resource, accessible only by guided tour.

TOP TIPS

● Baker (population 36), less than 5 miles from the park, has lodgings and food.

● The park has five developed campgrounds ($20 per night).

● Book your Lehman Caves tour two weeks in advance; spots fill quickly.

● Don't miss the evening astronomy ranger program – it's excellent.

PRACTICALITIES
● nps.gov/grba

Phoenix

ENDLESS SUNSHINE | SOUTHWEST CULTURE | OUTDOOR ADVENTURES

☑ TOP TIP

Consider the weather before booking. From January to March, warm desert temps make Phoenix a popular winter retreat for snowbirds. June to August is scorching hot, but you can score incredible deals on upscale resorts. Temps are nearly perfect in October and November, before winter's peak rates arrive.

A thriving desert metropolis, Phoenix is the cultural and economic heart of Arizona. The city is also a convenient base for desert and red-rock wanderings. Southwestern and Mexican restaurants abound and swanky resorts stand ready to pamper. With more than 300 days of sunshine a year, exploring, eating and relaxing should be on your agenda – except in the searing heat from June to August.

The city offers an opera, ballet, several theaters and three of the state's finest museums – the Heard, Phoenix Art and Musical Instrument museums – while the Desert Botanical Garden is a stunning introduction to the region's ecology. There are plenty of options to hike, mountain bike and climb in the regional parks, all easily accessible. Golf may as well be the official sport of the area, with nearly 200 courses covering Greater Phoenix. So slather on the sunscreen and get outside.

Visit the Heard Museum

Native American art and culture

A 30ft-long fence of blown-glass cactus ribs and small sculptures of desert animals is an evocative portal into the Home

GETTING AROUND

To hop around Greater Phoenix, a car is a must in this colossal urban sprawl. Rent one on arrival at Sky Harbor International, Phoenix's major airport. The much smaller Phoenix-Mesa Gateway Airport on the easternmost edge of the Valley of the Sun only serves Allegiant Air and Sun Country Airlines. Phoenix public transportation is not as expansive as other major US cities, but the reliable Valley Metro light rail covers Phoenix proper, Tempe and Mesa. If you stay in one general part of town, Uber and Lyft rideshare will be sufficient for your stay.

PHOENIX

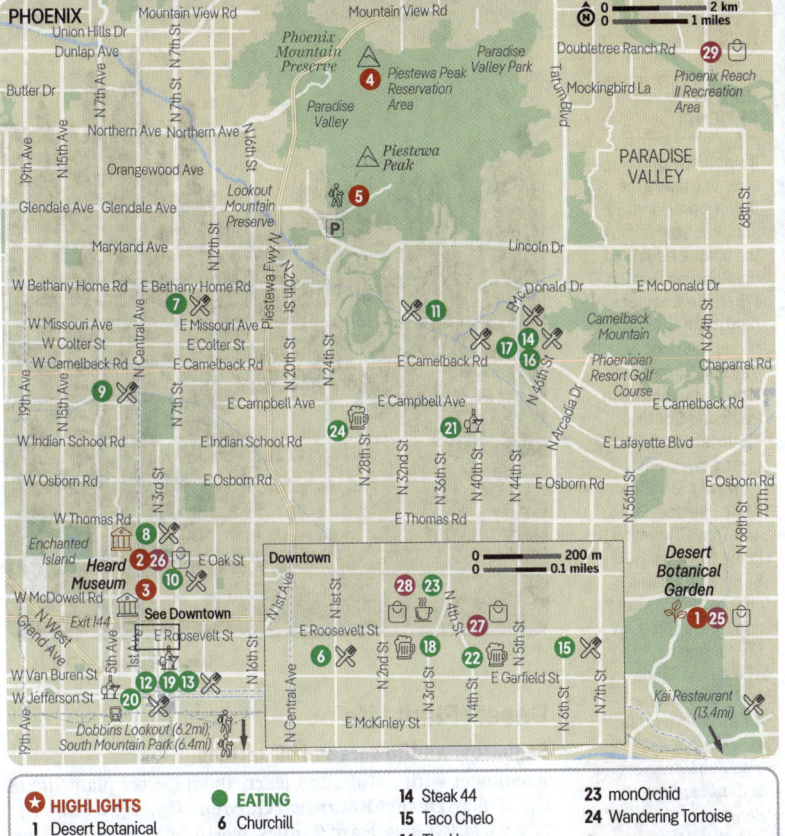

- ★ **HIGHLIGHTS**
  1. Desert Botanical Garden
  2. Heard Museum
- ● **SIGHTS**
  3. Phoenix Art Museum
- ● **ACTIVITIES**
  4. Phoenix Mountains Preserve
  5. Piestewa Peak
- ● **EATING**
  6. Churchill
  7. Culinary Dropout at the Yard
  8. Durant's
  9. Fry Bread House
  10. Green New American Vegetarian
  11. LON's at the Hermosa Inn
  12. Pa'la
  13. Pizzeria Bianco
  14. Steak 44
  15. Taco Chelo
  16. The Henry
  17. théa
- ● **DRINKING & NIGHTLIFE**
  18. Arizona Wilderness DTPHX
  19. Bar Bianco
  20. Bitter & Twisted
  21. Century Grand
  22. Greenwood Brewing
  23. monOrchid
  24. Wandering Tortoise
- ● **SHOPPING**
  25. Garden Shop at the Desert Botanical Garden
  26. Heard Museum Shop & Bookstore
  27. MADE Art Boutique
  28. Phoenix General
  29. Soleri Studios at Cosanti

Gallery, the heart of the **Heard Museum** (heard.org; adult/child $26/10) and a showcase for the art and culture of the 22 sovereign tribes in Arizona. Poems, quotes and videos supplement the baskets, ceramics, jewelry, textiles and Hopi kachinas (spirit dolls) on display.

The Heard is one of the best museums of its kind in the US. Annual events enliven the grounds, including competitions of mesmerizing hoop dancing in February and the Indian Fair & Market in March.

Desert Botanical Garden

HIKING IN PHOENIX

It's actually pretty easy to escape the urban jungle and immerse yourself in the unique beauty of the Sonoran Desert. When the weather's right, enthusiastic hikers flood the trails on **Camelback Mountain**, **Piestewa Peak** and **South Mountain Park** for the sweeping views of the Valley, while Pinnacle Peak and Tom's Thumb in the McDowell Sonoran Preserve are challenging but can't-miss climbs in Scottsdale.

Find maps and trail descriptions for the above from *@arizonahikers guide* on Instagram or at *phoenix.gov*. Remember to carry lots of water as you'll be hiking in the harsh Arizona sun. If you want a more remote experience, try the East Valley's Superstition Mountains.

Desert Plant Life

Saguaros, wildflowers and butterflies

Reconnect with nature and learn about desert plant life at the 55-acre **Desert Botanical Garden** *(dbg.org; adult/child $32.95/14.95)*. There are 2 miles' worth of looping trails arranged by theme, including a Sonoran Desert nature loop and an edible desert garden. The showstopping Desert Wildflower Loop trail showcases bluebells and Mexican gold poppies blooming from March to May. It's stunning year-round, but busiest and most colorful in the flowering spring season.

Ramble Down Roosevelt Row

Downtown arts and beer gardens

The *Welcome to Roosevelt Row* mural on the corner of Roosevelt and N 7th Sts is a launchpad for downtown's most vibrant neighborhood.

First, for a good craft beer, pop into the stylish indoor-outdoor digs at **Greenwood Brewing** *(greenwoodbrews.com)* or snag a table in the beer garden at the welcoming **Arizona Wilderness DTPHX** *(p812; azwbeer.com)*. Snack on the tacos, duck-fat fries and churro bites. Dinner options range from tacos and tortas at trendy **Taco Chelo** *(instagram.com/tacochelo)* to elite burgers and pizza at the **Churchill** *(thechurchillphx.com)*, a shaded courtyard housing multiple food stands, bars and locally owned shops. The **monOrchid** *(monorchid.com)* is a coffee shop, gallery, gift shop, brewery and event space rolled into one. On the first Friday of the month, 70 or so galleries open for mingling and art viewing (6pm to 10pm).

Sample Native American Tastes
Award-winning indigenous menus

For a rewarding culinary tour through locally sourced native dishes, drive to **Kai Restaurant** *(kairestaurant.com)*. Here, Native American cuisine – based on traditional crops grown along the Gila River – includes creations such as grilled buffalo tenderloin with smoked corn puree and cholla buds, or wild scallops with beef tongue pastrami and tepary-bean crackling. Kai is located at the **Sheraton Grand at Wild Horse Pass** *(wildhorsepass.com)* on the Gila River Indian Reservation in Chandler. Book ahead and dress nicely.

Back in Phoenix, try the **Fry Bread House** *(frybreadhouse az.com)*. Known as an elephant ear or Navajo taco, frybread is a flat piece of fried dough topped with meat, beans and veggies, or, for dessert, smeared with honey.

Hiking Piestewa Peak & Phoenix Mountains Preserve
Steep hike to city views

Covered in saguaros, ocotillos and teddy-bear cholla, the picturesque summit of **Piestewa Peak** *(phoenix.gov/parks)* was previously known as Squaw Peak. It was renamed for a local soldier, Lori Piestewa, who was killed in Iraq in 2003. Be warned: the 1.2-mile trek to the 2608ft peak is difficult but hugely popular for the south-facing views of downtown Phoenix. The surrounding **Phoenix Mountains Preserve** *(phoenix.gov/parks)* has nearly 70 trails and typically gets jammed on winter weekends.

For an easier hike, follow the Freedom Trail around the base of the peak. Look for parking lots along Piestewa Peak Dr within the park.

ORIENTATION

The Valley of the Sun is ringed by mountains that encompass a hot pancake, otherwise known as Greater Phoenix. A few important east–west roads cut across town: beginning in the south, these are Washington St, Van Buren St, Roosevelt St, McDowell Rd, Indian School Rd and Camelback Rd.

Phoenix is Arizona's largest city and houses the state capitol, the oldest buildings, several important museums and pro sports facilities. Scottsdale starts at around 56th St, east of Phoenix. The main drag, Scottsdale Rd, is technically 72nd St. Southeast of Phoenix is Tempe ('tem-*pee*'), home of Arizona State University, which is anchored around Mill Ave and University Rd.

 EATING IN PHOENIX: OUR PICKS

théa: Order pasta, seafood and skewers for the table at the Global Ambassador hotel rooftop. *4-10pm Mon-Fri, from noon Sat & Sun* $$$	**Steak 44:** Top-tier steaks and seafood in a stunning setting. Check online for the dress code. *4-10pm Sun-Thu, to 11pm Fri & Sat* $$$	**Pa'la:** Seasonal veg and sustainably sourced seafood served hot off the grill. Two locations. *5-10pm Tue-Sat, to 9pm Sun* $$	**The Henry:** A cozy, elegant stop. Short rib, seafood and salad options and a deep wine list. *7am-9pm Sun-Thu, to 10pm Fri & Sat* $$$
Durant's: A gloriously old-school steakhouse with cozy red-velvet booths, juicy steaks and effortless cool. *4-8:30pm Wed-Sun* $$$	**Culinary Dropout at the Yard:** Next-level pub food between games of cornhole and ping-pong in this open-air space. *hours vary* $$	**Green New American Vegetarian:** Mock meats as good as, if not better than, their carnivorous counterparts. *11am-9pm Mon-Sat* $	**LON's at the Hermosa Inn:** Quaint hacienda where Phoenicians bring guests for fine dining and glorious sunsets. *7am-9pm* $$$

Chris Bianco: 35+ Years of Pizza Wizardry
Wood-fired pizzas and gourmet sandwiches

Awarded the Outstanding Restaurateur award by the James Beard Foundation in 2022, Chris Bianco has been crafting thin-crusted wood-fired pizzas in Phoenix since 1988. In the process, he pioneered an 'artisanal pizza revolution' nationwide and expanded from his downtown mothership to a half-dozen successful ventures. The tiny **Pizzeria Bianco** (*pizzeriabianco.com*) is the original restaurant – a convenient stop for travelers exploring Heritage Square. Pro tip: there is almost always a wait, so put your name on the list before exploring the square, or pop next door to **Bar Bianco** for a glass of waiting wine.

Get Inspired at the Phoenix Art Museum
Western, contemporary and totally immersive art

Make a beeline for the **Phoenix Art Museum** (*phxart.org; adult/child $28/18*) to see how the Arizona landscape has inspired everyone from early pioneers to modernists. From here, Arizona's premier repository of fine art only gets more interesting, with works by Claude Monet, Frida Kahlo, Georgia O'Keeffe and Kehinde Wiley. Navigate to the far-back reaches of the museum for a trippy moment inside Yayoi Kusama's infinity mirror room, *You Who Are Getting Obliterated in the Dancing Swarm of Fireflies*.

Explore South Mountain Park
Morning hikes and petroglyphs

Pima Canyon is just one of many hiking destinations at the enormous **South Mountain Park** (*phoenix.gov/parks*), where a 51-mile network of trails (leashed dogs allowed) dips through canyons, over cacti-studded hills and past granite walls. Hike or drive to **Dobbins Lookout** for valley views at sunset.

The main entrance is at 10211 S Central Ave; the Pima Canyon entrance is at 4771 E Pima Canyon Rd.

BEST PLACES TO SHOP IN PHOENIX

Soleri Studios at Cosanti: Studio of Frank Lloyd Wright student Paolo Soleri, whose signature bronze and ceramic bells are crafted and sold here.

MADE Art Boutique: Jewelry, ceramics, art prints, candles and more from mostly local artists. On Roosevelt Row in downtown Phoenix.

Garden Shop at the Desert Botanical Garden: Plant your own desert garden with a starter cactus kit, plus Southwestern cards and cactus jellies.

Phoenix General: Bring the smell of desert rain to your shower with one of the sustainably harvested creosote bundles.

Heard Museum Shop & Bookstore: Top-notch collection of American Indian original arts and crafts.

DRINKING IN PHOENIX: OUR PICKS

Wandering Tortoise: Unpretentious hangout with 20+ draft beers and a fridge full of cans. Food truck on-site, with outside food welcome. Dog-friendly. *hours vary*	Arizona Wilderness DTPHX: Environmentally conscious beers with some of the best brewery food around. Duck-fat fries are a must. *11am-11pm Mon-Thu, to midnight Fri & Sat, to 10pm Sun*	Century Grand: With three different bar concepts under one roof, this place consistently lands on lists for the best cocktail bars in the US. *4pm-midnight Tue-Thu, from 2:30pm Fri-Sun*	Bitter & Twisted: Sip a playful Bear Witness out of a honey bear bottle, or let the expert bar staff surprise you. *4pm-midnight Tue-Thu, to 1am Fri & Sat*

Grand Canyon National Park

SPECTACULAR SCENERY I MEMORABLE TRAILS I FASCINATING GEOLOGY

The Grand Canyon lives up to the hype: its immensity, its grandeur, its beauty and its very age all scream for superlatives. At about two billion years old, the layer of Vishnu schist at the bottom of the canyon is some of the oldest exposed rock on the planet. It was exposed by the Colorado River, which continues to carve its way 277 miles through the canyon – as it has for the past six million years.

At Grand Canyon National Park, you can descend into the canyon depths, stroll the rim or relax at an outcrop at either the North or South Rims. Though views from both rims are equally stunning, the South Rim boasts many more official and dramatic overlooks. One of the most beautiful, however, was the view that whispered from the Grand Canyon Lodge's patio on the canyon's quieter north side; the lodge burned to the ground in mid-2025, but there are other views nearby.

A 215-mile drive, or a strenuous day hike, connects the two rims.

Rock Out at the Geology Museum

Rock layers and the Trail of Time

Take a moment to find the Colorado River while gazing through the large windows that overlook the canyon from the small **Yavapai Geology Museum** *(nps.gov/grca; free),* where interpretive panels explain the formations below. Behind you, a topographic relief map highlights the canyon's multilayered geologic history. From here, walk west along the Trail of Time about 1.5 miles to the **Grand Canyon Village Historic District**. The trail traces the history of the canyon's formation – each meter equals one million years of geologic history. Stop by for a ranger geology talk at the museum at 11am daily.

GETTING AROUND

The South Rim is an easy 60-mile drive north of I-40 at Williams. Hwy 67 is the only road to the North Rim, closed December 1 to mid-May. Although the North Rim is only 11 miles from the South as the crow flies, it's a 215-mile, four- to five-hour drive.

Grand Canyon Village is congested March to September. Park at one of the four visitor center lots and catch a free shuttle bus. There are smaller lots at Shrine of the Ages, Market Plaza, Yavapai Geology Museum and Backcountry Information Center.

☑ TOP TIP

The park is an International Dark Sky Park, so evening light pollution is minimal and stargazing is superb. Bring a flashlight to dinner at the North Rim – the walk to your room is dark!

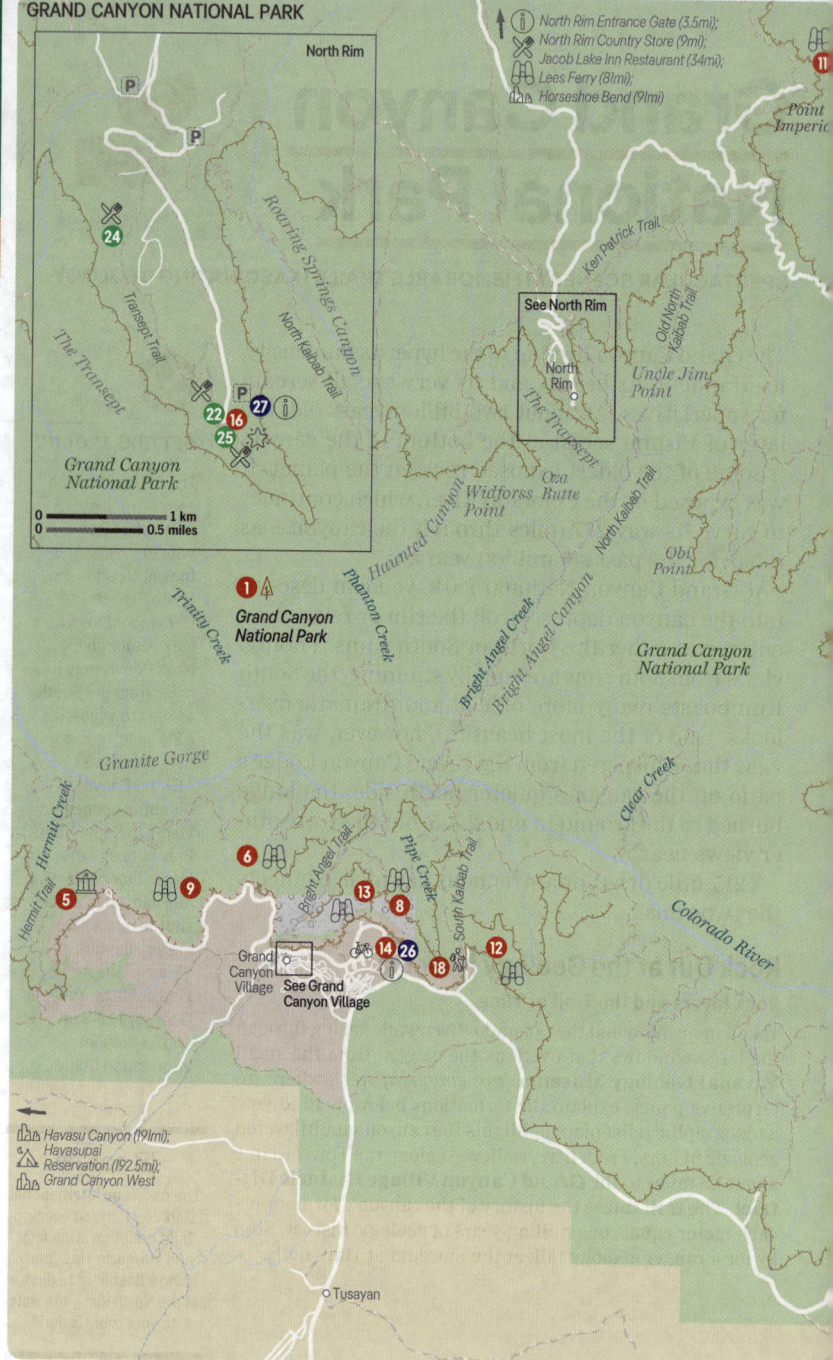

- ★ **HIGHLIGHTS**
  1. Grand Canyon National Park

- ● **SIGHTS**
  2. Angels Window
  3. Cape Royal Point
  4. Grand Canyon Village Historic District
  5. Hermits Rest
  6. Hopi Point
  7. Lipan Point
  8. Mather Point
  9. Mohave Point
  10. Moran Point
  11. Point Imperial
  12. Yaki Point
  13. Yavapai Geology Museum

- ● **ACTIVITIES**
  14. Bright Angel Bicycles
  15. Bright Angel Trail
  16. Canyon Trail Rides
  17. Grand Canyon Mule Rides
  18. South Kaibab Trail

- ● **SLEEPING**
  19. Bright Angel Lodge
  20. El Tovar

- ● **EATING**
  21. Arizona Steakhouse
  22. Deli in the Pines
  see 20 El Tovar Dining Room
  23. Harvey House Cafe
  24. North Rim General Store
  25. Rough Rider Saloon

- ● **INFORMATION**
  26. Grand Canyon Visitor Center
  27. Old North Rim Visitor Center site

South Rim

TOP EXPERIENCE

Grand Canyon

Welcome to one of the greatest natural shows on earth. Whatever you've heard about the Grand Canyon, it never disappoints, as beloved by veterans of this remarkable place as by first-time visitors. If you are among the latter, we envy you: nothing can compare with the first time you lay eyes on this beauty, and you've so much to look forward to.

DON'T MISS

- Mather Point
- Grand Canyon Visitor Center
- Bright Angel Trail
- South Kaibab Trail
- Rafting the Colorado River

Big View

If you're a first-time visitor, there's one requirement after entering from the South Rim: park your car at the **Grand Canyon Visitor Center** *(nps.gov/grca)* then dash to **Mather Point** to gaze upon the canyon in all its glory. It's a time-honored tradition and one you'll likely never forget.

PRACTICALITIES

● nps.gov/grca ● Admission to Grand Canyon National Park is $35/30 per vehicle/motorcycle and $20 per individual (under-15 free) arriving by foot, bicycle, bus, trail or raft, and is valid for seven days at both rims.

After that first mad glimpse, however, it's worth spending time at the visitor center itself. On the visitor-center plaza, bulletin boards and kiosks display information about ranger programs, the weather and tours. You'll also find helpful trail summaries. Inside is a ranger-staffed information desk, a lecture hall and a theater screening *Grand Canyon: A Journey of Wonder* – an introduction to the park's geology, history, and plant and animal life – and *We Are Grand Canyon,* a welcome from the 11 regional tribal communities. Each film is 24 minutes. The visitor center is also a stop on several shuttle routes.

Hike into the Canyon

As you'll quickly discover, the **Bright Angel Trail** is spectacularly scenic as it makes a 7.8-mile descent to the Colorado River. Though steep, long stretches near the start of this trail are not overly precarious, making this an excellent choice for families. Day hikers should turn around at one of the two rest houses (3- or 6-mile round trip) or hit the trail at dawn for longer hikes to Indian Garden and Plateau Point (9.2- and 12.2-mile round trip).

The **South Kaibab Trail** combines stunning scenery and unobstructed 360-degree views. Steep, rough and wholly exposed, this ridgeline descent plummets 4470ft along 6.4 miles to the Colorado River. You'll twist down tight switchbacks – flanked by a wall of Kaibab Limestone – before reaching Ooh Aah Point, a popular marked turnaround, at 0.9 miles. If you have more time, continue to Cedar Ridge at 1.4 miles. In addition to expansive views of the canyon, you'll find pit toilets here and a large, red-dirt overlook – mostly without shade – for a picnic.

Rafting the Grand Canyon

As you push off from **Lees Ferry** and float toward the soaring red walls of Marble Canyon, the sense of anticipation is something you won't soon forget. To come? More than 160 sets of rapids, camping under the stars, a float down the turquoise waters of the Little Colorado, hikes into mysterious slot canyons and a sense of camaraderie born from shared adventure – and no outside communications. Yep, a weeklong rafting trip on the Colorado River is a worthy bucket-list adventure, and one that is totally doable by the average traveler.

Consider the following before booking a trip: the number of days you want to be on the river, where you want to begin and end, and the type of boat – dory, oar-powered raft, paddle-steered raft or a motorized pontoon raft. The latter are the only ones that can travel the canyon's 277-mile course in a week. The national park *(nps.gov/grca)* has approved 15 commercial outfitters, listed on its website.

GAS & GARAGES AT THE GRAND CANYON

The **Desert View Chevron Service Station** is the only gas station on the South Rim, but gas stations in Tusayan are about 7 miles south of Grand Canyon Village. There is one gas station in the park on the North Rim, near the campground. You can also fill up in Jacob Lake or on Rte 67 at the **North Rim Country Store**.

TOP TIPS

● No cash is accepted at either the South or North entrance gates – credit/debit cards only.

● From the South Entrance it's 5 miles to the Grand Canyon Visitor Center, the primary informational hub.

● Transportation desks at Bright Angel, Maswik and Yavapai Lodges book bus tours.

● The Bright Angel desk also assists with Phantom Ranch and mule-ride reservations.

● The Backcountry Information Center supplies maps and backcountry permits.

● Cars are not allowed on the road to the South Kaibab Trailhead and Yaki Point nor, from March through November, on Hermit Rd.

Angels Window

BEST OVERLOOKS

Mohave Point: For a look at the river and three rapids. With multiple viewing spots, Mohave is particularly good for sunrise and sunset in high season.

Hopi Point: Magnificent east–west views, making it an excellent choice for dawn and dusk.

Lipan Point: Geology buffs: you can clearly see the tilting layered rocks of the Grand Canyon Supergroup here.

Moran Point: River views and excellent panorama of the canyon's geologic history. Named after Thomas Moran, the landscape painter who spent many winters at the canyon from 1899 to 1920.

Yaki Point: A favorite spot to watch the sunrise warm the canyon's features.

Shake the Crowds along Hermit Road
Hike, bike or ride the shuttle

Dotted with nine incredible canyon overlooks and roughly paralleling the rim, the 7-mile Hermit Rd stretches west from Grand Canyon Village Historic District to **Hermits Rest**. Designed by Mary Colter in 1913, the low-slung stone building at Hermits Rest is the South Rim's westernmost scenic overlook. The road is accessible year-round by bike, bus tour and by hiking the Rim Trail. Private vehicles can drive it December through February only. From March 1 through November 30, a park shuttle services all overlooks.

One of the best ways to experience Hermit Rd is by bike; rent one at **Bright Angel Bicycles**. You can also hike between shuttle stops via the Rim Trail.

Ride a Mule on the North or South Rim
Epic views and private cabins

If you take a mule ride, you're going to be sore – even if the ride lasts just an hour or two. But weary muscles have not scared away riders – they've been clip-clopping to the bottom

---

EATING ON THE SOUTH RIM: OUR PICKS

Harvey House Cafe: Savor a double-bacon cheeseburger and other American fare with canyon views. *6:30-10:30am, 11am-3pm & 4-9:30pm* $$

Arizona Steakhouse: Not just steaks – salads, sandwiches and burgers are on the menu, steps from South Rim. *11:30am-3pm & 4:30-9pm* $$

El Tovar Dining Room: Park dining at its best; windows frame the Rim Trail and canyon. Reserve. *6-10am, 11am-2:30pm & 4:30-9:30pm* $$$

of the Grand Canyon for more than 100 years. On the South Rim, **mule rides** *(grandcanyonlodges.com; from $1231)* follow the Bright Angel Trail – a bumpy, 10-mile trip with big views – to Phantom Ranch, which sits just north of the Colorado River. After one or two nights, they saddle up for an 8-mile ascent on the South Kaibab Trail. All meals are included in the ticket price. Make your reservation 15 months in advance.

Family-run **Canyon Trail Rides** *(canyonriders.com; 1/3hr $60/120)* offers one- and three-hour trips on the North Rim- from mid-May through mid-October.

Drive the Scenic Cape Royal Road
North Rim ponderosas and canyon views

Cape Royal Rd is a scenic must-do for any North Rim visitor. And your payoff after driving it is the chance to stand upon **Angels Window**, a natural arch that juts into the canyon, dropping dramatically on three sides. A place for awe and plenty of photos.

Descending gradually from the trailhead at 8200ft to 7865ft at Cape Royal, Cape Royal Rd ribbons scenically for 15 miles through evergreens and ponderosas. Along the way you can take the spur road to 8803ft-tall **Point Imperial**, the highest viewpoint in the park, for a look at Marble Canyon.

At the end of the drive, a 0.6-mile paved path, lined with pinyon, cliffrose and interpretive signs, leads to the arch and to **Cape Royal Point**, arguably the best view from this side of the canyon.

Peer Through a Glass Skywalk
A transparent overlook

The glass-bottomed **Skywalk**, perched 4000ft above the floor of the Grand Canyon, is not for the faint of heart. But it is pretty darn cool. The Skywalk is one of several attractions at **Grand Canyon West** *(grandcanyonwest.com; general admission & Skywalk $68)*, a commercial venture managed by the Hualapai Nation.

Also be aware that Grand Canyon West is not part of the Grand Canyon National Park, which is 240 miles east. But it is a convenient, if pricey, place to see the canyon if you're staying in Las Vegas.

TIPS FOR THE GRAND CANYON

Avoid the temptation to run from overlook to overlook, snapping photos, looking for that perfect view and determined to see them all. A few hours sitting on a rock, the sun on your face and miles of layered canyon expanding in panorama around you, may just be the perfect canyon experience.

The canyon is best appreciated slowly, with patience, humility and respect.

Never hike to the river and back in one day.

Bring a cooler and snacks. Park food is notoriously bad and expensive.

Stay hydrated; dehydration and altitude sickness can ruin a canyon visit.

Spend at least three nights in the park, and let the park reveal itself slowly.

EATING ON THE NORTH RIM: OUR PICKS

North Rim General Store: Beside the campground, this market sells basic grocery items, plus snacks and ice cream. *7am-9pm* $

Deli in the Pines: Takeaway salads and sandwiches for a picnic, plus pizza, soft-serve ice cream. Elk chili is the winner. *10am-8pm* $

Rough Rider Saloon: Grab morning pastries and breakfast burritos at the counter; slices of pizza in the evening. *11am-11pm* $

Jacob Lake Inn Restaurant: Welcoming spot for breakfast, lunch or dinner 45 miles north of the North Rim. Great cookies! *7am-9pm* $$

Havasu Falls

Swimming Holes & Blue-Green Waterfalls
Get in the water

The blue-green waterfalls of **Havasu Canyon** are among the Grand Canyon region's greatest treasures. Tucked away in a hidden valley, the five stunning, spring-fed waterfalls – and their inviting azure swimming holes – sit in the heart of the 185,000-acre **Havasupai Reservation** *(havasupai reservations.com)*, which can only be accessed by trail.

The Havasupai Reservation is located south of the Colorado River and four hours west of Grand Canyon National Park's South Rim, off Route 66.

Hike or Paddle at Horseshoe Bend
Views and kayaks

Calling the view dramatic at **Horseshoe Bend** *(horseshoe bend.co; car/motorcycle parking $10/5)* is a wild understatement. The scenic overlook here sits on sheer cliffs that drop 1000ft to the river below, which carves a perfect horseshoe through the Navajo sandstone. And guardrails are few.

The trailhead is south of Page off Hwy 89, just past Mile 545. It's a 1.2-mile round-trip walk from the parking lot.

You can also **kayak** *(kayakhorsehoebend.com or kayakthe colorado.com; from $115)* the Colorado River through Horseshoe Bend and admire its soaring grandeur from below. **Horseshoe Bend Slot Canyon Tours** takes you to views from the south.

GETTING STARTED AT THE NORTH RIM

The **North Rim Entrance Gate**, 31 miles south of Jacob Lake, does not accept cash; only credit and debit cards. The entrance is open 24 hours; a pass is valid for seven days.

From here, it's another 13 miles to where the visitor center and **Grand Canyon Lodge** were located, until a fire in 2025 destroyed them. Check the National Park Service website *(nps.gov)* for updates. Without the Grand Canyon Lodge, which was the only lodging inside the park on the North Rim, the nearest accommodations are in Jacobs Lake.

Full services are available on the North Rim from mid-May through mid-October. From December 1 to May 14, North Rim roads are closed to all vehicles.

Northern Arizona

ANCIENT CULTURES | SPIRITUAL JOURNEYS | DESERT LANDSCAPES

If you broaden your horizons beyond Phoenix and the Grand Canyon, you'll move through the heartland of the American West. This is a world where crimson buttes, saguaros and ponderosa pines are the backdrop for outdoor adventures. Elsewhere, mountain towns and cliff dwellings offer introductions to a fascinating past.

Grand Canyon National Park may be Arizona's biggest draw, but it's also a launchpad for visits to nearby sites that delve into the culture and history of 11 tribal nations. Much of the area in the north and center of the state lies on, or just below, the Colorado Plateau, a high-desert playground that is cool, wooded and mountainous. Anchored by Flagstaff, this region is blessed with the state's most diverse and scenic sites. As a starting point, you can explore a vortex in Sedona, camp beside Oak Creek Canyon, or admire the 1000-year-old dwellings of the Ancestral Puebloans. Stargazing is amazing everywhere.

Sedona & Around

Good vibes and vortexes

It's hard to have a bad day in Sedona. Red rock buttes, forested canyons and lush creek sides – it's a spectacular backdrop that has long attracted spiritual seekers, artists and healers. Over

Places

Sedona & Around p821
Jerome p826
Prescott p826
Flagstaff p827
Monument Valley Navajo Tribal Park p829
Canyon de Chelly p830
Navajo National Monument p832
Petrified Forest National Park p832
Homolovi State Park p833
Kingman & Route 66 p833

☑ TOP TIP

A Red Rock Pass ($5/15 day/week) covers everything from parking to spending time exploring National Forest land around Sedona, Oak Creek Canyon, Flagstaff and surrounds. It's available at ranger stations, visitor centers, most trailheads and *recreation.gov*.

GETTING AROUND

The sixth-largest state in the US, Arizona rewards those who explore by car; rentals are available from airports, but you'll find a better deal closer to your hotel. The main airports are at Phoenix, Flagstaff and, in the south, Tucson, with regular flights between the three. And if you prefer to ride the rails, Amtrak connects Los Angeles with Kingman, Flagstaff and Winslow on the daily *Southwest Chief*, which continues east to Albuquerque, NM. The daily scenic Grand Canyon Railway runs between Williams and Grand Canyon Village.

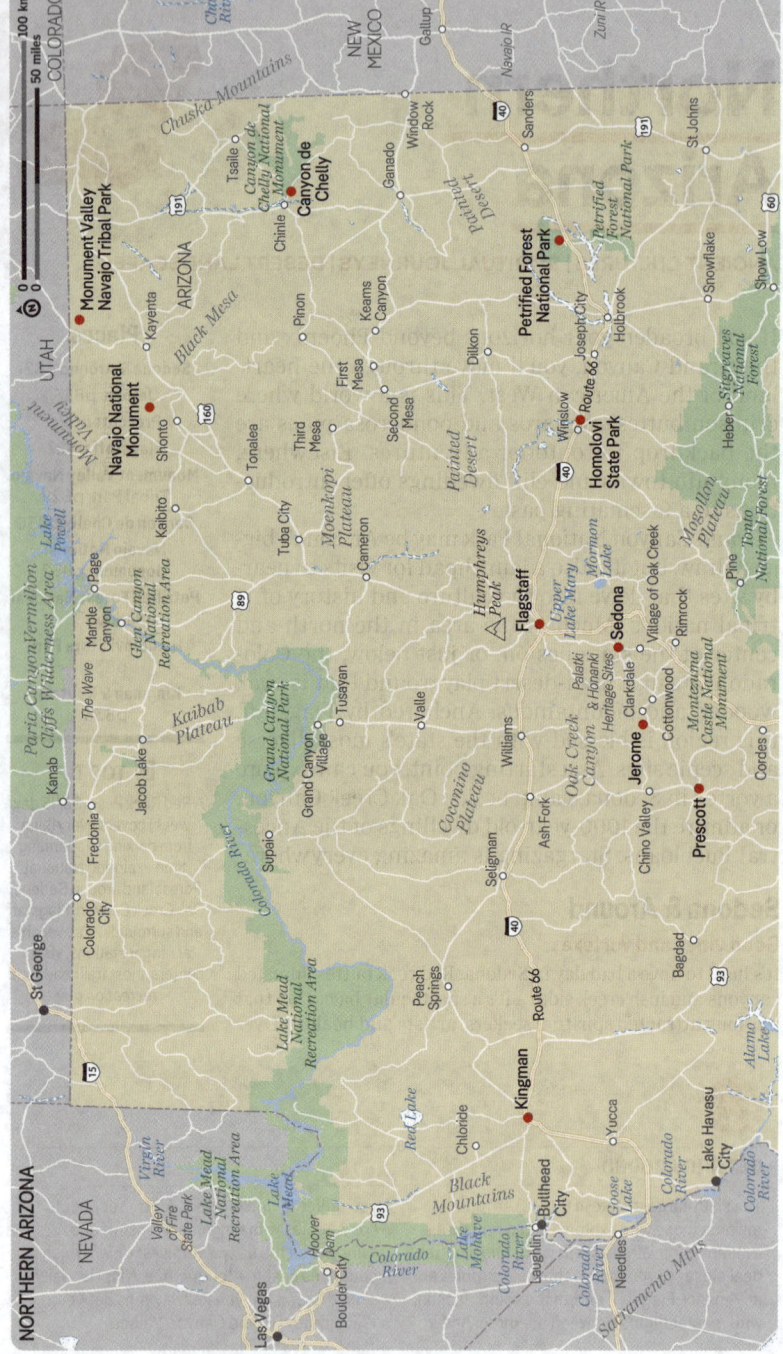

the years Sedona has developed into an extremely popular New Age destination. The reason? Spiritual-minded folks believe that the sandstone formations here hold vortexes, which vibrate to the frequencies of the deepest earth energies. Many believe this energy encourages healing and spiritual well-being.

To learn more, step inside the **Center for the New Age** *(sedonanewagestore.com)*, the big purple building on Hwy 179 south of Uptown. Shelves of this metaphysical superstore are crammed with crystals, spirituality books and vortex guides. Similar shops are scattered across town. The best-known vortexes are **Bell Rock** (near the Village of Oak Creek), **Cathedral Rock** (near Red Rock Crossing), **Airport Mesa** (Airport Rd) and **Boynton Canyon**.

Airport Mesa is the closest to town, and the drive up Airport Rd opens up to panoramic views of the valley. It's a half-mile walk from the mesa-top parking lot ($3) to the best viewpoint: a red rock hilltop with astounding 360-degree views.

Red rocks encourage deep thoughts at two beloved spots in Sedona. The better known of the two is the **Chapel of the Holy Cross** *(chapeloftheholycross.com; free)*, a small 1956 Roman Catholic chapel that soars from the surrounding rock like a slice of the majestic land itself.

A consecrated Buddhist shrine is set quite stunningly amid pinyon and juniper pine and the ubiquitous rocks at the low-key **Amitabha Stupa & Peace Park** *(tara.org/amitabha-stupa; free)* in West Sedona. Trails meander past colorful prayer flags, leading to a labyrinth and more red rock views.

Petroglyphs and cliff dwellings

The more than 1000 images (deer, turtles, birds, an embracing couple) carved into the sandstone panels at **Crane Petroglyph Heritage Site** *(fs.usda.gov; 9:30am-3pm Fri-Mon)* were created by the Sinagua people between 1150 and 1400 CE.

Seven miles of dirt road in northwestern Sedona lead to 1000-year-old Sinaguan cliff dwellings and rock art at the **Palatki Heritage Site** *(fs.usda.gov; reservations required)*, which is perched enchantingly on the edge of the wilderness. You can view more Sinaguan ruins 3 miles north at sister site **Honanki**. Both are open from 9:30am to 3pm Thursday to Tuesday and to noon Wednesday.

Red Rock ($5 per vehicle) and National Park passes (price varies) grant admission to all three sites, which are located in the Coconino National Forest.

BEST HIKES IN SEDONA & OAK CREEK CANYON

Bell Rock & Courthouse Butte: Easy 4-mile loop; follows multiuse Bell Rock Pathway around the immense Bell Rock then circles Courthouse Butte.

Boynton Canyon: Pretty 6-mile round-trip hike with shaded stretches, petroglyphs and Sinaguan ruins. Look for the side trail to Kachina Woman rock formation.

Devil's Bridge: Crowded, but the namesake arch is a photogenic prize on this 4-mile round-trip hike from Mescal Trailhead.

West Fork Trail: A 6½-mile round-trip Oak Creek Canyon hike with 13 creek crossings; red rock walls soar more than 200ft in some places. Gorgeous October foliage.

EATING IN SEDONA & AROUND: OUR PICKS

Sedonuts: Apple fritter is the top seller, but we dig the Red Rock Oreo at this decadent West Sedona doughnut shop. *6am-noon* $

Indian Gardens Cafe & Market: The breakfast sandwich is a delicious mess of eggs, chimichurri, cheddar; in Oak Creek Canyon. *8am-4pm Sat-Thu, to 8pm Fri* $$

Hudson: Prickly pear ribs, smoked-salmon bruschetta and fireball chicken wings infuse Sedona with urban cool. Great red-rock views. *11:30am-9pm* $$$

Mariposa: Stunning red-rock views and divine Latin-inspired food from the grill are the hallmarks of this upmarket option. *11am-2pm & 4-9pm* $$$

Hike Oak Creek Canyon

From the soaring overlook at **Oak Creek Vista**, 14 miles south of Flagstaff, the pine-draped glory of Oak Creek Canyon swoops south to the horizon like an unruly child just released from Nature's time-out. From the overlook, you'll corkscrew down Hwy 89A into the 13-mile canyon, where russet and vermilion cliffs soar above the creek and the highway. Giant cottonwoods clump along the waterway, providing a scenic, shady backdrop for trout fishing and swimming. If hiking is on your agenda, pull over for the popular **West Fork Trail**, which crosses Oak Creek 13 times as it winds through the canyon. Its imposing walls can soar more than 200ft.

A few miles south, an 80ft sandstone chute whisks swimmers through Oak Creek at **Slide Rock State Park** *(azstateparks.com; $10-30 per vehicle)*. The chute and the rock slides here are a blast but they can get oppressively crowded in summer, particularly between 10am and 3pm.

Drive the Red Rock scenic routes

The easiest scenic drive is also one of the best: the **Red Rock Scenic Byway** *(redrockscenicbyway.org)*. This National Scenic Byway and All-American Road tracks Hwy 179 from I-17 (exit 298) north of Phoenix for 7.5 miles, passing red hills and the Red Rock Ranger District Visitor Center before ending just north of the Village of Oak Creek in a pull-over, grab-your-camera explosion of red-rock impressiveness that includes Bell Rock and Courthouse Butte.

Any time is a good time to drive the winding 7-mile **Red Rock Loop Road**, which can be accessed via Upper Red Rock Loop Rd off Hwy 89A, 4 miles west of the Y intersection in Sedona. First up is the **Crescent Moon Picnic Site** *(vehicle/pedestrian $12/3)*, where a small army of photographers usually gathers at sunset at Red Rock Crossing to record the dramatic light show unfolding on iconic **Cathedral Rock**, a vortex.

Taste Verde Valley wines

The **Merkin Vineyards Hilltop Winery & Trattoria** *(merkintrattoria.com)* in Old Town Cottonwood – a 25-minute drive from Sedona – has a grand patio with sweeping views of the Verde Valley, where you can sip some darn good wines while nibbling on bruschetta and lasagna 'cupcakes.'

Merkin is one of two dozen or so vineyards, wineries and tasting rooms in the well-watered valley of the Verde River. Bringing star power to the **wine trail** *(vvwinetrail.com)* is Maynard James Keenan, lead singer of the band Tool and owner of Merkin Vineyards and **Caduceus Cellars** *(caduceus.org)*. His 2010 documentary *Blood into Vine* takes a no-holds-barred look at the northern Arizona wine industry.

Another good stop in Old Town Cottonwood is the tasting room at **Arizona Stronghold** *(azstronghold.com)*. Three wineries with tasting rooms hug a scrubby stretch of Page Springs Rd between Sedona and Cottonwood, near Cornville: bistro-housing **Page Springs Cellars** *(pagespringscelllars.com)*, the welcoming **Oak Creek Vineyards** *(oakcreekvineyards,net)* and the mellow-rock-playing **Javelina Leap Vineyard & Winery** *(javelinaleapwinery.com)*.

SEDONA SHUTTLES

Several helpful **shuttles** *(sedonashuttle.com)* crisscross the city.

Free **hiker shuttles** run to the most popular trailheads Thursday to Sunday, 7am to 5:30pm, with extra days when it's busy. These shuttles pick up passengers from three park-and-ride lots and run to Cathedral Rock/Little Horse, Dry Creek Vista/Mescal and Soldier Pass. Be aware that the Cathedral Rock and Soldier Pass Trailhead lots are closed to cars on the days the shuttle is running.

The new **Sedona Shuttle Connect** *(6:30am-6pm Thu-Sun; one way $2)* is an on-demand, app-driven service with stops in a defined area. **Verde Shuttle** *(6am-10pm; one way $2)* connects Sedona with Cottonwood, with stops along the way.

ARIZONA TIME ZONES

Arizona is on Mountain Time (seven hours behind GMT). It is the only Western state not to observe daylight saving time from spring to fall. The exception is the Navajo Reservation, which – in keeping with those parts of the reservation located in Utah and New Mexico – does observe daylight saving time. Confusingly, the small Hopi Reservation, which it surrounds, follows Arizona. The varying time zones come into play in Page and Monument Valley, which straddle the Arizona/Utah state line, during daylight saving time. Many hotels have two clocks on the wall, so you'll know what the times are. Keep the discrepancy in mind when scheduling tours in the region or your hotel check-in.

Jerome
Galleries, saloons and old hotels

Jerome can really mess with your mind: it can be hard to tell whether the buildings are winning or losing their battle with gravity. The **Sliding Jail**, lodged in the dirt southeast of the **Chamber of Commerce** visitor center, has moved 225ft from its original 1927 location. It isn't surprising, considering that there are 88 miles of tunnels, many of which were frequently dynamited and cut into steep hills, under your feet.

Main St is home to the engaging **Mine Museum** *(jerome historicalsociety.com; $2)*, which spotlights local characters and stories. Just north, the allegedly haunted 1898 **Connor Hotel** (p878; *connorhotel.com*) was the town's first solid-stone lodging – don't miss the **Spirit Room**, the fun in-house saloon with murals sporting bordello scenes. From here, a climb leads to **Jerome Grand Hotel** (p878; *jeromegrand hotel.com*), the one-time home of the United Verde Hospital. Known for its ghosts and the venerable **Asylum Restaurant** *(asylumrestaurant.com)*, it's a cool place to enjoy expansive views of the crimson-gold rocks of Sedona and the Verde Valley.

Prescott
Have a beer on Whiskey Row

Montezuma St, west of the plaza, was the infamous **Whiskey Row**, where 40 drinking establishments supplied suds to rough-hewn cowboys and miners. In 1900 a devastating fire destroyed 25 saloons, five hotels and the red-light district, although several early buildings remain. Many are still bars to this day, mixed with boutiques, galleries and restaurants.

Push through the swinging doors to enter the historic **Palace Saloon** *(whiskeyrowpalace.com)*. It can be hard to tell if the men in cowboy hats are costumed waiters or actual cowboys. But no mind. This bar was once frequented by Wyatt Earp and Doc Holliday, so Old West duds come with the territory. Rebuilt in 1901 after the fire, it displays a museum's worth of Old West photos and artifacts. A scene from the 1972 Steve McQueen movie *Junior Bonner* was filmed here, and a mural honoring the film covers an inside wall.

Art, history, booze and good eats collide in the saloon and other century-old buildings surrounding **Yavapai County Courthouse**, which anchors an elm-shaded plaza in the heart of Prescott. Pause for breakfast or lunch at the cafe inside historic Hotel St Michael (p878).

EATING IN JEROME & PRESCOTT: OUR PICKS

Haunted Hamburger: Perched high on a Jerome hill, this beloved hamburger joint also serves big views and tasty margaritas. *11am-9pm* **$**

Clinkscale: Hot new kid in Jerome serving New American fare in stylish digs. *8:30am-8:30pm* **$$**

Farm Provisions: Farm-to-table Prescott favorite with gourmet options like deep-fried deviled eggs or kicky tacos with cilantro aioli. *11am-9pm Wed-Sun* **$$**

El Gato Azul: Creative Southwest and Spanish dishes that all sound good, including green-chile mac and cheese in Prescott. *11am-8pm most days* **$$**

Mt Elden

Buildings east and south of the plaza escaped the fire. The three-story Burmister Building houses a snazzy gift shop as well as **Superstition Meadery** *(superstitionmeadery.com)* and the **County Seat** *(countyseataz.com)* restaurant.

The **Chamber of Commerce Visitor Center** leads free guided walking tours (10am, Friday to Sunday from May to October).

Flagstaff

Flagstaff at all hours

Begin your Flagstaff day with chilaquiles and banana-split French toast at the now-legendary downtown **MartAnne's bistro** *(martannes.com)*. Come hungry for this one. Red walls, black booths and a bevy of oil paintings convey a unique, salon-like feel, and this Day of the Dead vibe is part of the quirky charm. And it ultimately plays well with the wonderfully messy creations on the menu. Of these, the Jerry el Mujeriego (Jerry the Womanizer; a green-chile pork enchilada topped with cheese, sour cream and two eggs) takes the top honors. Just don't plan on doing anything too strenuous immediately afterward. It's open 8:30am to 8pm most days.

Once you've recovered, it's time for a museum. Housed in an arts-and-crafts-style stone building, the small but excellent **Museum of Northern Arizona** *(musnaz.org; adult/ Native American/child $15/10/10)* spotlights regional Native American archaeology, history and culture, as well as geology, biology and the arts. Representatives from 10 regional tribes worked with museum curators to select items displayed in the 'Native Peoples of the Colorado Plateau' ethnological exhibit, where you'll see baskets, pottery, jewelry and even a skateboard. Video messages from tribal members enhance the experience. On the way to the Grand Canyon, the museum makes a wonderful introduction to the human and natural history of the region.

TOP HIKES IN FLAGSTAFF

Fatman's Loop: Moderate 2-mile loop with volcanic rock formations, city views, varied trees and one tight squeeze. Begins 5 miles northeast of downtown.

Elden Lookout: Six-mile round-trip hike with a steep 2300ft climb to the summit of Mt Elden, a lava dome. End at a historic fire tower with views of Flagstaff, Sunset Crater and the San Francisco Peaks.

Aspen Nature Loop Trail: On the slopes of Mt Humphreys, this 2.5-mile trail loops past wildflowers, meadows and a forest thick with aspen, spruce and pine.

Kachina Trail: Aspens glow a luminous yellow in fall on this moderate forest-and-meadows trail on Mt Humphreys. It's a 10-mile round trip.

DISCOVER ROUTE 66 & HISTORIC HOTELS

Enjoy a mix of culture and history on this easy downtown walk that takes in public art, a gallery and Old West hotels.

START	END	LENGTH
Flagstaff Visitor Center	Flagstaff Visitor Center	0.5 miles; 30 minutes

Exploring downtown Flagstaff is an agreeable experience – just don't get hit by a passing train. Daily, more than 100 of them whizz past the ❶ **Flagstaff Visitor Center**, which shares space with Amtrak inside a Tudor Revival station house. For details about the city's 40 murals, pick up the Flagstaff Public Art Map. Across San Francisco St, the bronze ❷ **Gandy Dancer** statue depicts a hardworking railroad man. Cross Route 66 and stroll into downtown, where Old West heritage looms large. Pop into the ❸ **Artists' Gallery** for locally made art, jewelry and ceramics. A neon sign towers over the ❹ **Hotel Monte Vista**, which opened in 1927. Past guests include John Wayne, Clark Gable and Humphrey Bogart.

Built in 1888 by the Babbitt family on the northwest corner of Aspen Ave and San Francisco St, the sandstone ❺ **Babbitt Building** was the first two-story structure in town. A long-running department store, it now houses an outdoor gear and apparel shop. In summer, ❻ **Heritage Square** is a hub for festivals, movies and live music. Home to three separate bars, the 1900 ❼ **Weatherford Hotel** (p878) is the coolest building in town. Two icons of the west, artist Thomas Moran and author Zane Grey, are former guests. Open since 1917, the ❽ **Orpheum** hosts live music, films and community events. Cross Route 66 again and return to the visitor center.

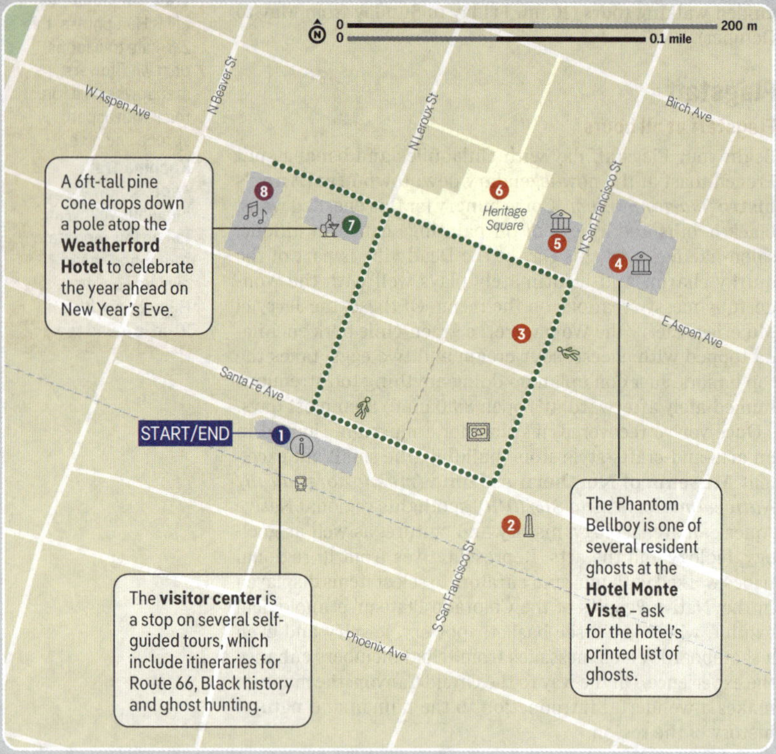

A 6ft-tall pine cone drops down a pole atop the **Weatherford Hotel** to celebrate the year ahead on New Year's Eve.

The **visitor center** is a stop on several self-guided tours, which include itineraries for Route 66, Black history and ghost hunting.

The Phantom Bellboy is one of several resident ghosts at the **Hotel Monte Vista** – ask for the hotel's printed list of ghosts.

As darkness falls, the **Museum Club** *(museumclub.net)*, an enormous log cabin perched right beside Route 66, comes into its own. To appreciate fully the kitschy appeal of this country-music roadhouse, sometimes called the Zoo, step inside to the large wooden dance floor, animal mounts and a sumptuous elixir-filled mahogany bar. Stick around for the band to fully immerse in the fun. Check its website for the live-music schedule and free line-dancing lessons.

Then when it's *really* dark, it's time for some stargazing. Flagstaff became an official Dark Sky City in 2001 – the very first community in the world to earn this designation from the International Dark-Sky Association. Cherished by astronomers for its dark and cloud-free night skies, Flagstaff is home to **Lowell Observatory** *(lowell.edu; adult/child/senior $35/20/30)* where you can check the marquee for details about daily talks and tours. At night, the Giovale building slides back to expose its telescopes – and budding astronomers – to a jaw-dropping view of the night sky. Evening constellation tours start nearby. For information about star parties and celebrations visit flagstaffdarkskies.org.

Monument Valley Navajo Tribal Park

Explore Monument Valley and Navajo history

If you drive south from Utah on Hwy 163, the rugged sandstone formations of **Monument Valley Navajo Tribal Park** *(navajonationparks.org; $8 per person)* initially rise into view like the ramparts of a prehistoric fortress, a huddled collection of red and gold defenses protecting ancient secrets.

Up close they're hypnotic, an alluring mix of familiar and elusive. Yes, we've seen them in the John Ford Westerns, but the big screen doesn't capture the changing patterns of light, the imposing height, or the strangeness of the angles and forms. You'll see the most striking formations from the rough **17-mile dirt road** *(7am-7pm; shorter hours in winter)* that loops through the park.

The **Wildcat Trail** is a 3.8-mile loop trail around the West Mitten formation that begins at the entrance to the 17-mile drive.

Rounding out your experience (and understanding) of these Navajo lands, it's time to listen to revisit the past. The Navajo Nation became the new owners of **Goulding's Lodge** *(gouldings.com)*, a storied trading post and hotel near the tribal park, in 2023. Harry Goulding and his wife Leone (better known as 'Mike') established the trading post in 1925. In

GUIDED TOURS

Tour guides at Monument Valley shower you with details about the reservation, movie trivia and whatever else comes to mind. They can also take you into the backcountry.

Navajo guides set up kiosks in the parking lot at the visitor center. They are pretty easygoing, so don't worry about high-pressure sales. Tours leave frequently in summer, less so in winter.

Outfits in Kayenta and at Goulding's Lodge also offer tours. To reserve in advance, check out the list of guides on the tribal park's website *(navajonationparks.org)*. Rates start at about $70 for a 2½-hour motorized trip, and may require a two-person minimum. You do not need a guide to hike the Wildcat Trail.

 EATING IN FLAGSTAFF: OUR PICKS

Karma Sushi Bar: Delicious sushi, but the tonkotsu ramen is legendary. On Route 66. *11am-9pm Sun-Thu, to 10pm Fri & Sat* **$**

Pizzicletta: Come here for gourmet toppings heaped on wood-fired pizzas. *noon-9pm Fri-Mon, 5-9pm Tue-Thu* **$$**

Josephine's: New American fare in a 1911 arts-and-crafts bungalow. Good for Saturday breakfast. *5-8:30pm Mon-Sat, 9am-2pm Sat* **$$**

Tinderbox Kitchen: Casual sophistication, chef-driven fare. Annex Cocktail Lounge for drinks. *3-10pm Mon-Thu, to midnight Fri & Sat* **$$$**

GHOST TOWNS

The discovery of gold, silver and copper brought fortune seekers to Arizona from the 1860s. New towns mushroomed overnight near the richest mines, and they were notoriously wild and dangerous places. Abandoned mining towns are scattered across the state's scrub-covered mountains and deserts. Typically there is not much to see at these sites unless you're into rusty equipment and weathered wooden shacks, but they can be cool for photos and for understanding the harshness of mining-town life.

For a list of sites across Arizona and the Southwest, visit americansouthwest.net/ghost-towns.html. For an atmospheric introduction, visit **Vulture City & Mine** (vulturecityghosttown.com; adult/child $18/10), 12 miles west of Wickenburg.

the ensuing years, Goulding convinced director John Ford to film his Westerns in the butte-dotted valley. Today Goulding's is home to the lodge as well as a restaurant, a campground and a free museum inside the old trading post. Step inside the museum to see a replica of the store, a room dedicated to the movies shot here, the couple's upstairs living quarters and a collection of black-and-white photos of Navajos and the surrounding landscape.

Canyon de Chelly

Embrace the silence at Spider Rock

If you drive to the **Spider Rock Overlook** at Canyon de Chelly in the late afternoon, you might just have the place to yourself. And the empty silence is strangely invigorating as you gaze down at **Spider Rock**, a 800ft bifurcated sandstone spire guarding the place where **Canyon de Chelly National Monument** (nps.gov/cach; free) meets Monument Canyon. The overlook is the fifth and final stop on the 16-mile **South Rim Drive**, which runs along the main canyon and shares dramatic vistas.

EATING IN MONUMENT VALLEY & KAYENTA: OUR PICKS

Blue Coffee Pot: So this is where everybody is. This busy spot in Kayenta serves Navajo tacos and diner fare. 7am-9pm Mon-Fri $

Amigo Cafe & Coffee Bar: Huevos rancheros, burgers with chipotle aioli, mutton tostadas on this tasty menu in Kayenta. 8am-8pm Tue-Sat $

Stagecoach Restaurant: Impressive views in Goulding's Lodge. So-so American and Navajo fare and can swarm with tourists. 7am-9pm $$

View Restaurant: The Navajo food doesn't always shine, but whoa, that view of the monuments is sublime. 7-11am & 5-9:30pm $$

Spider Rock, Canyon de Chelly

For the most part, **North Rim Drive** follows a side canyon called Canyon del Muerto, which has four overlooks. At the first, **Antelope House Overlook**, a short walk ends at stunning cliff-top views of a natural rock fortress and cliff dwellings. To see the latter, walk to your right from the walled **Navajo Fortress Viewpoint** to a second walled overlook.

If you have a 4WD, you could go a little further. Past the mouth of Canyon de Chelly, heading deeper into the valley, the canyon's sandstone walls soar ever higher, narrowing your views of the sky. But the view ahead? It grows lush, filling with crops, livestock and cottonwood trees, all hugging a growing stream. Petroglyphs and cliff dwellings here are portals to the past, while hogans (homes) and fences give a nod to the vibrant present.

Check the **Navajo Nation Parks & Recreation** website *(navajonationsparks.org)* or stop by the national monument visitor center for a list of tour guides. Guided trips with **Beauty Way Jeep Tours** *(beautywaytours.com; 3hr tour $95.40)* travel all the way to White House Ruin deep in the canyon.

Navajo Code Talkers

WWII prompted the first large exodus of Native Americans from the reservations, when they joined the US war effort. The most famous were the Navajo code talkers – 420 US marines who used a code based on their language for vital messages in the Pacific Theater. Navajo is a notoriously complex Athabascan language, and Japan never broke the code. Code talkers were considered essential to US victory. You'll find code-talker exhibits at the Burger King in Kayenta and the **Explore Navajo Interactive Museum** in Tuba City. The work of the code talkers was kept classified until 1968, and they were granted Congressional Gold Medals in 2001.

STANDING ON THE CORNER IN WINSLOW

Thanks to the lyrics of the Eagles' catchy '70s tune 'Take It Easy,' tiny Winslow is now a popular roadside spot. At the small **Standin' on the Corner Park** on Route 66 you can pose with a life-size bronze statue of a hitchhiker backed by a charmingly hokey trompe l'oeil mural of that famous girl – my Lord! – in the song's famous flatbed Ford. Above, a painted eagle keeps an eye on the action.

For information about Winslow and historic exhibits, stop by the town **visitor center**, which is tucked inside the renovated Lorenzo Hubbell Trading Post five blocks west of the park.

WHAT IS A PETRIFIED LOG?

The Painted Desert at Petrified Forest National Park is strewn with fossilized logs predating the dinosaurs. The 'trees' are fragmented, fossilized 225-million-year-old logs scattered over a vast area of semidesert grassland. Many are huge – up to 6ft in diameter – and at least one spans a ravine to form a natural bridge. The trees arrived via major floods, only to be buried beneath silica-rich volcanic ash before they could decompose. Groundwater dissolved the silica, carried it through the logs and crystallized it into solid, sparkly quartz mashed up with iron, carbon, manganese and other minerals. Uplift and erosion eventually exposed the logs.

Navajo National Monument
Solitude and cliff dwellings

Hikers who love history, beauty and a bit of a challenge should detour to the serene **Navajo National Monument** *(nps.gov/nava; free)*, which is anchored by two sublimely well-preserved cliff dwellings. But plan ahead. The monument sits in a remote corner of the Navajo Reservation between Monument Valley and Tuba City, and the guided cliff-dwelling hikes are only offered on certain days.

You'll reach **Betatakin**, which translates as 'ledge house,' on a strenuous, ranger-led, 5-mile round-trip hike (late May to early September) that leaves the visitor center early on Saturdays and Sundays. This hike is first come, first served. For a distant glimpse of Betatakin, follow the easy **Sandal Trail** about half a mile from the visitor center.

The trail to the astonishingly beautiful **Keet Seel**, the largest Ancestral Puebloan structure in Arizona, is a challenging two-day guided hike (17 miles round trip; May to September) with one night of backcountry camping – and possibly quicksand! This trip is capped at 20 people. Register and confirm dates in March.

Petrified Forest National Park
Crystallized logs, petroglyphs and badlands

The 28-mile scenic drive through the **Petrified Forest National Park** *(nps.gov/pefo; car/motorcycle/bicycle/pedestrian $25/20/15/15)* has more than a dozen pullouts with interpretive signs and short trails. Several trails near the southern entrance provide the best access for close-ups of the petrified logs: the 0.4-mile **Giant Logs Trail** (with the park's largest log behind the Rainbow Forest Museum), the 1.6-mile **Long Logs Trail**, the 0.75-mile **Crystal Forest Loop** and the **Jasper Forest lookout**.

A highlight in the center section is a 3-mile loop drive to **Blue Mesa**, where you'll be treated to 360-degree views of spectacular badlands, log falls and logs balancing atop hills with the leathery texture of elephant skin. The 0.9-mile **Blue Mesa Trail** drops scenically into the badlands. Nearby, at the bottom of a ravine, hundreds of petroglyphs are splashed across **Newspaper Rock** like some prehistoric bulletin board. You'll find more petroglyphs and Ancestral Puebloan ruins at **Puerco Pueblo**.

North of I-40 lies a Route 66 interpretive marker and an especially brilliant section of the **Painted Desert**. Nature puts on a kaleidoscopic show here at sunset: the most mesmerizing views are from **Kachina Point** behind the historic **Painted Desert Inn**. The Painted Desert is a beautiful place to camp. A free permit is required. Pick one up at the **Painted Desert Visitor Center** at the north entrance before 4:30pm.

Videos describing how the logs were fossilized run regularly at Painted Desert Visitor Center and the visitor center at **Rainbow Forest Museum** near the south entrance. Both visitor centers have park exhibits, maps and gift shops.

Petrified Forest National Park

Homolovi State Park
Petroglyphs and ancient pueblos

A grasslands park beside the Little Colorado River, **Homolovi State Park** *(azstateparks.com; vehicle/pedestrian/bicycle $7/3/3)* protects artifacts and archaeological sites within the sacred Hopi homeland. Short hikes lead to petroglyphs and partly excavated pueblos, most likely built by the Ancestral Hopi. The trail to the **Homolovi II ruins** is paved and wheelchair accessible. Before the area was converted into a park in 1993, bold thieves used backhoes to remove artifacts.

There's a **campground** with electric hookups, water and showers near the excavated pueblos. The park is 3 miles northeast of Winslow via Hwy 87.

Kingman & Route 66
Celebrate Route 66 – and some new stuff!

The best attractions along Route 66 are eye-catching and enormous, and the drive-thru Route 66 sign at the **Kingman Visitor Center** *(explorekingman.com)* is no exception. Park your ride beneath the sign, then, if you're alone, ask a kind-hearted stranger to take your photo. The visitor center, tucked inside the 1907 Powerhouse, stocks the requisite free brochures, but the big draw is the engaging **Route 66 Museum** *(mohavemusuem.org; adult/child $10/free),* which shares an informative historical overview of travel along the Mother Road.

From here, it's a short drive to Beale St, the axis of the historic downtown. After sunset, cruise Route 66 and immerse yourself in its neon glory. The next morning, breakfast is served with a side of kitsch at **Mr D'z Route 66 Diner**, a roadside vision in turquoise and 1950s nostalgia.

PETRIFIED FOREST ORIENTATION

Straddling I-40, Petrified Forest National Park has an entrance at exit 311 off I-40 in the north, and another off Hwy 180 in the south. These are the only two entrances, and a 28-mile paved scenic road within the park links them. Note that the south entrance has the highest concentration of petrified wood and so is the most interesting part of this park.

To reach the south entrance from I-40, without following the park scenic road, you will need to leave the interstate at exit 285 and follow signs to Hwy 180 and the national park. The south entrance is 18 miles from I-40, so you can't simply pull over for a quick look if you're on I-40.

Kingman (p833)

ROUTE 66, UNINTERRUPTED

North of Kingman, Route 66 arcs north away from I-40 for 115 dusty miles through the high desert. It merges with I-40 near Seligman then reappears briefly as Main St in Williams. Cell service is unreliable and gas stations are rare, so make sure you have enough fuel. The road is not heavily traveled, and you'll likely find that your car is the only vehicle on the road for miles at a time. The total distance to Williams is 130 miles.

Nicknamed the 'Mother Road' by novelist John Steinbeck and completed in 1926, Route 66 travels through eight states, linking a series of small towns between Chicago and Los Angeles.

Leaving Kingman, 9 miles east of Peach Springs, a plaster dinosaur marks your arrival at **Grand Canyon Caverns** *(gccaverns.com; per person $69.95)*. Tours of this fascinating cave complex deep underground run regularly. Above ground, you'll find a campground, motel and restaurant. The complex is now owned by the Havasupai Tribe, and the motel doubles as the check-in point for tours.

Further along, look for red-and-white Burma Shave signs on the 23 miles of road slicing through the rolling hills to **Seligman**, the inspiration for Radiator Springs in Pixar's *Cars*. Angel Delgadillo retired from **Angel's Barbershop** *(route66gift shop.com; 9am-5pm)* in roadside Seligman in 2022 at age 95 – but his barber's chair is still there. Today the barbershop is a museum and souvenir store. Angel's madcap brother Juan, who died in 2004, ruled prankishly supreme over the nearby **Delgadillo's Snow Cap** – a Route 66 institution still serving burgers and ice cream. Beware the fake mustard bottle! For a full-service meal, try the German and American dishes at **Westside Lilo's Cafe** *(westsidelilos.com)*.

From Seligman, one of the last sets of **Burma Shave signs** reads: 'Passing cars… When you can't see… May get you a glimpse… Of eternity.'

DRINKING IN KINGMAN: OUR PICKS

Cellar Door: Downtown wine bar with more than 120 wines and dozens of beers, live music and trivia nights. *varies 3-9pm Wed-Sat*

Rickety Cricket: Creative beer selections – we're looking at you Snoszberry – plus pizza, nachos and tiramisu. *varies 11am-9pm*

Liquid Bistro & Coffee Shop: Low-key coffee shop with mid-century cool, but no kitsch. Distinctive turquoise-and-white digs. *7am-3pm*

Desert Diamond Distillery: Sample whiskey and rum at this small distillery near Kingman airport. *10am-5pm Sun-Thu, to 6pm Fri & Sat*

Southern Arizona

VIBRANT CITY | OLD WEST | SCENIC DRIVES

Arizona's deep south concentrates some of the state's most rewarding attractions. Tucson is one of the most engaging towns in the entire West, a cultural powerhouse, not to mention an emerging culinary superstar. It has so much to offer, both as an underrated destination in its own right and as gateway to a region that can seem like a stereotype of the Old West. You barely need to leave Tucson before Saguaro National Park and the Sonoran Desert offer up classic landscapes and the world's most recognizable cactus. A little further afield, it's the old mining town of Bisbee and gunfights at the OK Corral in Tombstone; the latter is one of the must-see places if you're eager to immerse yourself in the legends of the storied West. Crowning this beautiful region are the Santa Catalina Mountains, which are the perfect place to explore on a series of scenic drives.

Places
Tucson p835
Bisbee p839
Saguaro National Park p840
Tombstone p841
Chiricahua National Monument p841

☑ TOP TIP
Don't be fooled by how close the attractions of southern Arizona can appear: it's only by comparison to the rest of the state. Plan to spend longer than you expect, and add a day or two to your plans to allow you to follow curiosity down quiet back roads.

Tucson
Explore an Arizona desert city

Set in a flat valley hemmed in by snaggle-toothed mountains and swaths of saguaro, Arizona's second-largest city smoothly blends Native American, Spanish, Mexican and Anglo traditions. Distinct neighborhoods and 19th-century buildings

GETTING AROUND

As ever out here in the West, having your own vehicle will greatly enhance your experience: many attractions in these parts can only be reached in your own SUV or 4WD. Rental is easy (book ahead to ensure the best rates) at Tucson airport or downtown. Tucson International Airport serves southern Arizona, with regular flights around the Southwest. Part of the mix for getting to Tucson from beyond the region includes train: Amtrak's thrice-weekly *Sunset Limited* links Tucson with LA, Houston and New Orleans.

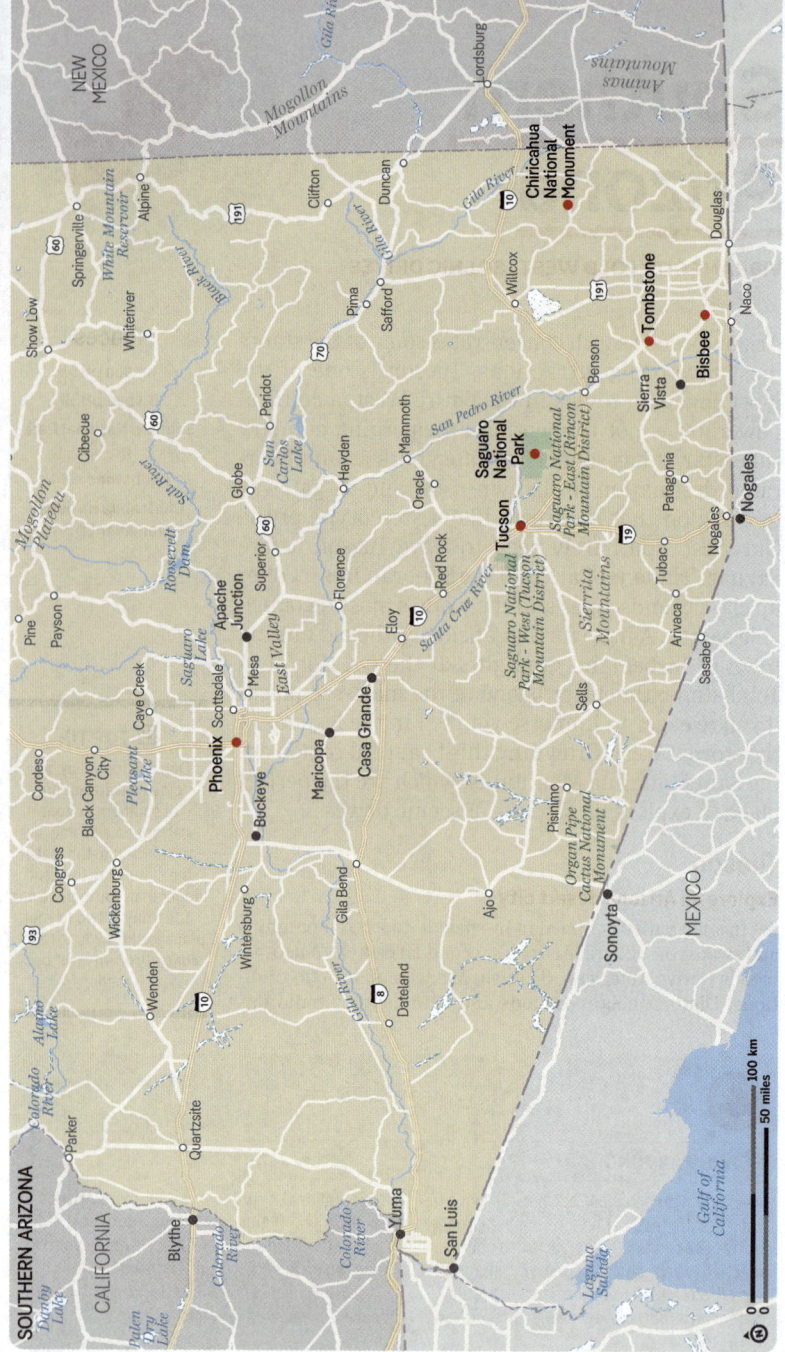

give a rich sense of community and history not found in more modern, sprawling Phoenix. The eclectic shopping, affordable restaurants, whimsical murals and fun-loving dive bars don't let you forget Tucson is a college town at heart, home turf to the 50,000-strong University of Arizona (U of A).

The **Tucson Museum of Art** *(tucsonmuseumofart.org; adult/child $15/free)* is part of the low-key **Presidio Historic District** and embraces the site of the community's original Spanish fort and upmarket 'Snob Hollow.' This is one of the oldest continually inhabited places in North America: the **Spanish Presidio de San Augustín del Tucson** *(tucson presidio.com; adult/child $9/6)* dates back to 1775, but the fort itself was built over a Hohokam site that has been dated to between 700 and 900 CE. The district teems with adobe townhouses and restored 19th-century mansions. **Old Town Artisans** *(oldtownartisanstucson.com)* is the place for Mexican and Southwestern art and crafts.

When it's time to eat, tucked in a rambling downtown hacienda, the buzzing **El Charro Café** (p839; *elcharrocafe.com*) celebrated its centennial in 2022. Overseen by chef-owner Carlotta Flores, it's famous for its *carne seca*, sundried lean beef that's been reconstituted, shredded and grilled with green chile and onions. The fabulous margaritas also pack a serious punch. The restaurant's original matriarch, Monica Flin, is said to have invented the chimichanga after accidentally dropping a burrito into a deep fryer.

Elsewhere, Tucson's signature dish is the Sonoran dog, a bacon-wrapped hot dog layered with tomatillo salsa, pinto beans, shredded cheese, mayo ketchup, mustard, chopped tomatoes and onions. Dig into one at one of two **BK Carne Asada & Hot Dogs** *(bktacos.com)* locations.

And as the day draws to a close, you have a couple of great options for watching the sunset in west Tucson. The **Brown Mountain Trail** *(pima.gov)* climbs past saguaros, cholla and other desert vegetation to sweeping ridgeline views of the Tucson Mountains, the Tohono O'odham Reservation, the Santa Rosa Mountains and the Aguirre Valley. This view is awash in luminous color at sunset. If you don't want to hike, drive to the **Gates Pass Scenic Lookout** *(nps.gov)* on West Gates Pass Rd for a splendid, expansive sunset view of the saguaro-dotted mountain pass.

Drive the Mt Lemmon Scenic Byway

Generations of Tucsonans have escaped the summer heat by driving up Mt Lemmon in the Santa Catalina Mountains. You

BEST UNIQUE TUCSON MUSEUMS

Ignite Sign Art Museum: More than 900 old neon signs, primarily from Tucson, light up the museum. Watch a neon bending demo or take a class.

Mini Time Machine Museum of Miniatures: Delightful museum with intriguing dioramas that are fantastical and historical.

Pima Air & Space Museum: An SR-71 Blackbird spy plane and B-52 bomber are among the stars of this extraordinary private aircraft museum.

Center for Creative Photography: Ever-changing, high-caliber exhibits. Administers the archives of Ansel Adams.

Coit Museum (formerly the History of Pharmacy Museum): Old-timey tinctures and a full-size pharmacy replica once found on Disneyland's Main Street, USA.

EATING IN TUCSON: OUR PICKS

Charro Steak & Del Rey: Scrumptious steaks, seafood and libations in a modern rustic space. *3-9pm* $$$

Beyond Bread: Daily breads and a mouthwatering array of sandwiches. Several locations. *7am-7pm* $

HUB Restaurant & Ice Creamery: Upscale comfort food in exposed-brick digs on Congress St. Save room for ice cream. *11am-9pm Sun-Thu, to 11pm Fri & Sat* $$

Maynards: Regionally sourced and seasonal American fare in the Historic Depot downtown. *5-9pm Wed-Sun* $$

TUCSON

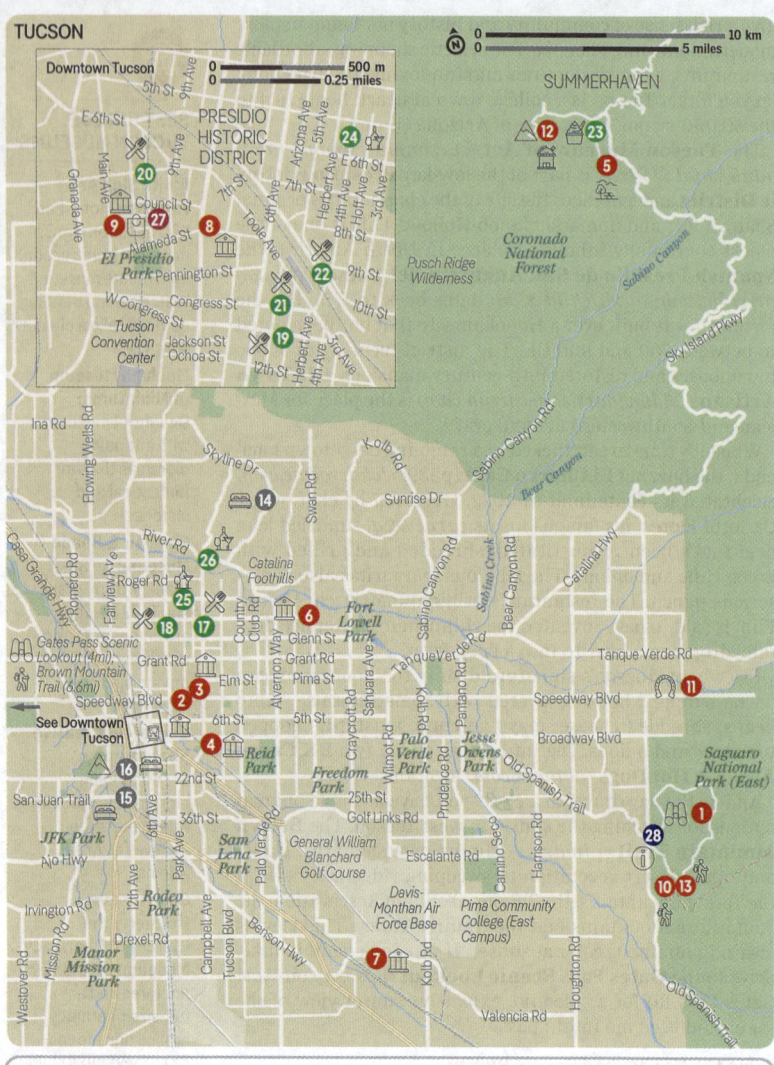

SIGHTS
1. Cactus Forest Loop Drive
2. Center for Creative Photography
3. Coit Museum
4. Ignite Sign Art Museum
5. Marshall Gulch Picnic Area
6. Mini Time Machine Museum of Miniatures
7. Pima Air & Space Museum
8. Spanish Presidio de San Augustín del Tucson
9. Tucson Museum of Art

ACTIVITIES
10. Freeman Homestead Trailhead
11. Houston's Horseback Riding
12. Mt Lemmon SkyCenter Observatory
13. Tanque Verde Ridge

SLEEPING
14. Hacienda del Sol Guest Ranch Resort
15. Hotel McCoy
16. Tuxon

EATING
17. Beyond Bread
18. BK Carne Asada & Hot Dogs
19. Charro Steak & Del Rey
20. El Charro Café
21. HUB Restaurant & Ice Creamery
22. Maynards
23. Mt Lemmon Cookie Cabin

DRINKING & NIGHTLIFE
24. BOCA by Chef Maria Mazon
25. Guadalajara Original Grill
26. Reforma Modern Mexican

SHOPPING
27. Old Town Artisans

INFORMATION
28. Rincon Mountain Visitor Center

can follow their tracks on the very picturesque **Mt Lemmon Scenic Byway** (also called the Catalina Hwy Scenic Drive), which meanders 27 miles from saguaro-dappled desert to pine-covered forest near the summit (9157ft). Allow at least three hours for the round trip and watch for cyclists.

Of the vista points, Babad Do'ag, Windy Point and Aspen are the most rewarding. In lofty Summerhaven, everybody stops for ice cream and cookies the size of your face at the **Mt Lemmon Cookie Cabin** (*thecookiecabin.org*). Nearby, the loop connecting the **Marshall Gulch Trail & Aspen Trail** (*fs.usda.gov; day pass per vehicle $8*) is a recommended 4-mile hike through ponderosas, aspens and firs.

You can attend an evening SkyNights StarGazing Program at the **Mt Lemmon SkyCenter Observatory** (*skycenter.arizona.edu; adult/child $85/60*). Reserve a spot at least one week in advance.

Bisbee

Mining museum and mine tour

Bisbee built its fortune on ore discovered in the surrounding Mule Mountains. In their 19th- and 20th-century heyday, the underground and open-pit mines here coughed up copper worth more than $6 billion.

Start your day with huevos rancheros at the **Bisbee Breakfast Club**, followed by a stroll along adjacent Erie St. Lined with vintage cars and pickup trucks, as well as storefronts from an earlier era, the street is an eerily accurate model of a mid-century downtown.

Now it's time to go underground. You'll don a hard hat and a safety vest during the pre-trip orientation at the **Queen Mine** (*copperqueenmine.com; adult/child $16/8*) south of downtown. Today, visitors ride 1500ft into the mountain on a subterranean mine train, often guided by the mountain's last miners or their offspring.

In the 1897 former headquarters of the Copper Queen Consolidated Mining Company, the **Bisbee Mining & Historical Museum** (*bisbeemuseum.org; adult/child $10/free*) traces the town's past.

Echoes of Bisbee ripple out across the surrounding countryside. A former mining community southeast of Bisbee, Lowell was mostly consumed by the adjacent Lavender Pit mine. Today, this short strip of Americana – mostly abandoned

MT LEMMON: NEED TO KNOW

There is no cost for the drive or for stopping at the vista points, but to explore the forest you must get the **Coronado Recreation Pass** (*fs.usda.gov; per day/week $8/10*). Buy it online, at trailside kiosks or at the Palisades Visitor Center (Mile 19.6).

For an audio tour explaining the science behind the sights you'll see along the 27-mile drive, download the free Mt Lemmon Audio Tour app on your smartphone (see visittucson.org).

Several campsites line the drive, with overnight rates ranging from $20 to $28. Call the Pima County Sheriff's Road Conditions hotline at 520-547-7510 for road conditions.

 DRINKING IN TUCSON: WHERE TO GET A MARGARITA

| **El Charro Café:** There are 18 delicious margaritas on the menu, and all of them pack a punch. *11am-9pm Wed-Sat, to 8pm Sun* | **Guadalajara Original Grill:** The frozen Bandera margarita is stacked with three colorful layers – green, white and red – to resemble the Mexican flag. *11am-10pm Sun-Thu, to 11pm Fri & Sat* | **BOCA by Chef Maria Mazon:** They serve them by the carafe, and at happy hour the house margaritas are $8. *noon-9pm Mon & Tue, to 10pm Fri & Sat, to 8pm Sun* | **Reforma Modern Mexican:** Mango habanero, blueberry basil, blood orange, prickly pear are among Reforma's elevated options. Kick back and sip away on its beautiful patio. *hours vary* |

TOP EXPERIENCE

Saguaro National Park

Saguaros are icons of the American Southwest, and an entire cactus army of these majestic, ribbed sentinels is protected in Saguaro National Park. Exploring these strange life forms - they can really mess with your mind on a moonlit night - is the main reason to visit this beautiful park.

Go for a Drive or Ride

The 8-mile **Cactus Forest Loop Drive** *(nps.gov/sagu)* in the Rincon Mountain District is special, and its beauty is open to drivers and cyclists alike. The scrubby desert scenery here also evokes the Old West. To embrace the John Wayne vibe, saddle up for a horseback ride with family-run **Houston's Horseback Riding** *(tucsonhorsebackriding.com)*.

Hike Saguaro Trails

Hikers pressed for time can follow the 1-mile round-trip **Freeman Homestead Trail** *(nps.gov/sagu)* to a grove of massive saguaros. For a full-fledged desert adventure with high-elevation views, head out on the steep and rocky **Tanque Verde Ridge Trail** *(nps.gov/sagu)*, which climbs to the summit of Tanque Verde Peak and back in 18 miles. An $8 backcountry camping permit is required for overnight use. The **Rincon Mountain Visitor Center** *(nps.gov/sagu)* has information about day hikes, horseback riding and backcountry camping. Seven-day passes per vehicle/motorcycle/bicycle cost $25/20/15. Cash is not accepted.

Learn about Saguaros

Saguaros (suh-*wah*-ros) only grow in the Sonoran Desert and they do so slowly, taking about 15 years to reach a foot in height, 50 years to reach 7ft and almost a century before they begin to take on their typical many-armed appearance. In April each year, the cacti begin blossoming with lovely white blooms – Arizona's state flower. By June and July the flowers give way to ripe red fruit that local Native Americans use for food. It is illegal to damage or remove saguaros.

TOP TIPS

● The national park is divided into east and west, separated by 30 miles and Tucson itself.

● Each section distributes its own hiking guide with maps and trail summaries.

● The busy season runs November through March; temperatures range from the high 50°Fs to mid-70°Fs (around 14°C to 24°C).

– gives a nostalgic nod to the 1950s. Just north on Hwy 80, look for the not-so-truthful 'Scenic View' sign. It's pointing toward the Lavender Pit, an immense stair-stepped gash in the ground that produced about 600,000 tons of copper between 1950 and 1974.

Tombstone
OK Corral and Old West museums

If you were to visit one town to capture the essence of the Wild West, we'd make it Tombstone.

Like death and taxes, the daily reenactment of the gunfight at the **OK Corral** *(ok-corral.com)* is a sure thing. Before the show, you'll see Doc Holliday and the Earp brothers silently stroll down dusty Allen St. The thrice-daily performance ($10) takes place inside the corral, which is the heart of both historic and touristic Tombstone.

From here, plank sidewalks and dirt roads are portals to the Old West, with wooden storefronts and a horse-drawn stagecoach setting the scene. It's hokey, but also fun, and it's easy to imagine cowboys, gunslingers and miners roaming the streets.

The **Bird Cage Theatre** *(tombstonebirdcage.com)* was a one-stop sin-o-rama, with onstage shows as well as a saloon, dance hall, gambling parlor and a home for 'negotiable affections.' Today, with its dusty knickknacks, illicit history and ghost tours, it's ground zero for kitschy deliciousness – a place for which road trips are made.

And the epitaphs at **Boothill Graveyard** *(discoverboothill.com; $6)* tell you everything you need to know about living – and dying – in Tombstone in the late 1800s. 'Murdered.' 'Shot.' 'Suicide.' They spotlight the violence of the place, where life was hard and often short. The graves of Billy Clanton and Tom and Frank McLaury, all killed at the shoot-out at the OK Corral, are in Row 2. Some headstones are twistedly poetic: the oft-quoted epitaph for Lester Moore, a Wells Fargo agent, may be the most famous: 'Here lies Lester Moore, Four slugs from a .44, No Les, no More.'

Chiricahua National Monument
Volcanic rocks and Apache history

From the viewing area at Massai Point, the rhyolite rock pinnacles at the remote **Chiricahua National Monument** *(nps.gov/chir)* resemble a goblin army, a vast force ready to march down the mountain and do battle for their goblin king. This rugged yet whimsical wonderland, covering nearly 19 sq miles across a desert sky island in the Chiricahua Mountains, is one of Arizona's most evocative landscapes, a wind-chiseled volcanic landscape of fluted pinnacles, natural bridges, balancing boulders and soaring spires. The remoteness made Chiricahua (cheery-*cow*-wha) a favorite hiding place of Apache warrior Cochise and his men in the 1800s. The park is a two-hour drive from Tucson.

GUNFIGHT AT THE OK CORRAL

Tombstone is the location of the infamous 1881 gunfight at the OK Corral, when Wyatt Earp, his brothers Virgil and Morgan, and their friend Doc Holliday gunned down outlaws Billy Clanton and Tom and Frank McLaury, who belonged to a loose association of rustlers and thieves called the Cowboys. On the day of the shoot-out, the Cowboys had come to Tombstone and were in apparent violation of the law, requiring them to check their weapons. The ensuing gunfight only lasted about 30 seconds but so caught people's imaginations that it not only made it into the history books, but also onto the silver screen – many times – including the 1993 flick *Tombstone*, starring Kurt Russell and Val Kilmer.

APACHE CONFLICTS

For decades, US forces pushed west across the continent, killing or forcibly moving tribes of Native Americans who were in their way. The last serious conflicts were between US troops and the Apache, partly because raiding was the essential path to manhood for the tribe. US forces and settlers moving into Apache land became obvious targets for the raids that were part of the Apache way of life. This continued under the leadership of Mangas Coloradas, Cochise, Victorio and Geronimo.

Geronimo surrendered in 1886 after being promised that he and the Apache would be imprisoned for two years, then allowed to return to their homeland. As with many promises made during those years, this one was broken.

Chiricahua National Monument (p309)

Past the entrance, the paved **Bonita Canyon Scenic Drive** climbs 8 miles to **Massai Point** at 6870ft, passing several scenic pullouts and trailheads. If you're short on time, hit the **Massai Point Nature Trail** (0.5 miles round trip), the most common stop for photos, or hike the **Echo Canyon Trail** at least half a mile to the **Grottoes**, an amazing 'cathedral' of giant boulders where you can lie still and enjoy the wind-brushed silence. The most striking formations cluster in the **Heart of Rocks**, reached via several linking trails on a 7.3-mile round-trip hike. A free hiker shuttle runs from Faraway Ranch and Bonita Campground to the Echo Canyon and Massai Point trailheads from September to May. Reserve ahead.

Chiricahua is one of 127 designated Dark Sky Parks worldwide, making it an increasingly popular destination for astrophotography. Depending on the time of year, you'll have clear views of the Milky Way, Orion, Big Dipper and comets at night. There is no cell-phone service in the park and very limited service in the surrounding area. Water is available only at the visitor center. The closest gas station is 27 miles away in Sunizona. The nearest community, Willcox, is 37 miles away.

Utah

STIRRING LANDSCAPES | NATIONAL PARKS | MORMON HEARTLAND

Before Native people and Mormon pioneers, dinosaurs once roamed this land, and remnants of all three collide in the 45th state. Utah's incredible diversity of geological formations were shaped by millions of years of erosion, despite there being so little water in sight. Utah boasts five national parks – the densest concentration of any state, with Arches, Canyonlands, Capitol Reef, Bryce Canyon and Zion – that rank among the big hitters of the American wild. And with dozens more national monuments, recreation areas and state parks, everything in this state feels ready-made for big adventures. Towns like Moab and Park City can seem like they're set up for getting you out and into nature on a mountain bike, skis or a white-water raft. In the midst of it all, Salt Lake City, the heartbeat of Mormon belief and governance, is one of the most intriguing urban experiences anywhere in the US.

Places

Salt Lake City p845
Park City p847
Moab p848
Bears Ears National Monument p851
Capitol Reef National Park p853
Arches National Park p854
Canyonlands National Park p856
Bryce Canyon National Park p858
Zion National Park p860

☑ TOP TIP

Distances in Utah are longer than they look and each national park is worth exploring in depth. You'd need *at least* a couple of weeks to do them all well. If you're here for a shorter period, plan to see one or two parks well, rather than trying to do too much.

GETTING AROUND

As is so often true out in the West, unless your itinerary is limited to a few locations, having your own set of wheels is essential for getting around Utah. Rent a car in Salt Lake City or even Las Vegas, Nevada. If you're staying in a town like Salt Lake City, Moab or Park City, shuttle and other buses sometimes connect you with nearby ski stations or hiking trailheads. Amtrak has five stations in Utah on the *California Zephyr* line, but the daily departures mean the train is not a viable option for most travelers.

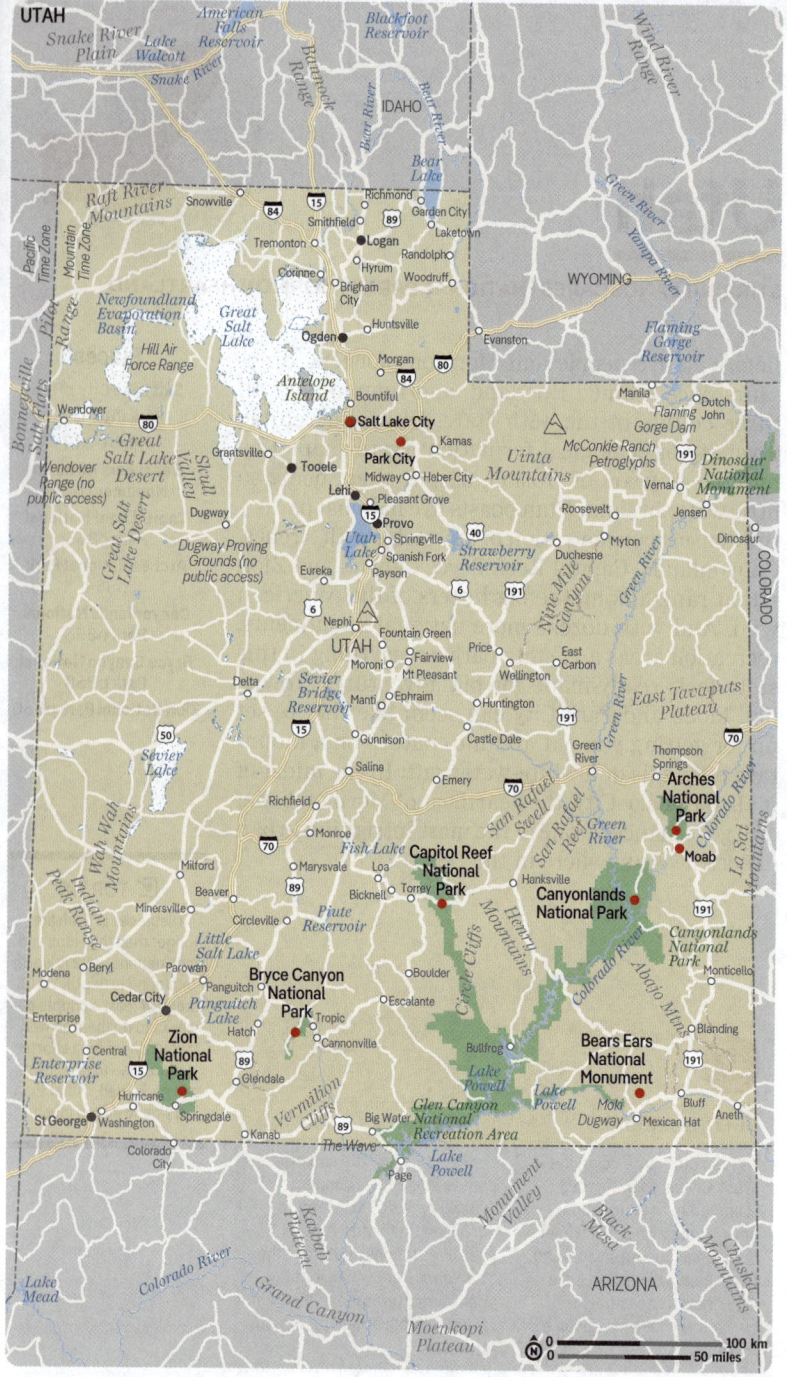

Salt Lake City
Explore Mormon SLC

Founded in 1847 by Mormon pioneers in what was then Mexican territory outside the boundaries of the US, Salt Lake City (SLC) remains the headquarters of the Church of Jesus Christ of Latter-day Saints; it's the Mormon equivalent of Vatican City for Catholics.

The epicenter of the Church of Jesus Christ of Latter-day Saints (LDS) is **Temple Square** *(churchofjesuschrist.org; free)* in the heart of downtown Salt Lake City. Members of the church, wearing name badges and modest clothing, happily assist with questions and directions. (Don't worry, they won't try to convert you unless you express interest.)

Start your visit at the **Conference Center**, which is serving as a visitor center during ongoing renovations. Join a tour or poke around the grand 21,000-seat auditorium yourself. Don't miss the rooftop garden with expansive views of the Salt Lake Valley.

Lording over Temple Square is the impressive **Salt Lake Temple**, the largest LDS temple in the world, completed in 1893 after more than 40 years of construction. The interior is open only to church members in good standing. Six spires, the tallest measuring 210ft, reach into the heavens. Home to the world-famous Tabernacle Choir, the **Salt Lake Tabernacle** is a domed 1867 auditorium with an 11,623-pipe organ and incredible acoustics – wait for the demonstration of a pin being dropped, which can be heard almost 200ft away.

Time your visit for noon Monday to Saturday or 2pm Sunday for a free organ recital (without the choir). The choir rehearses on Thursday evenings (7:30pm to 9:30pm) and Sunday mornings (8:15am to 9:30am) but is sometimes on tour elsewhere; check *thetabernaclechoir.org/upcoming-events*.

West of Temple Square, the **Church History Museum** gets into the nitty-gritty of the church's foundations. About a 5-mile drive east of Temple Square, the 450-acre **This Is The Place Heritage Park** *(thisistheplace.org; adult/child $18.95/14.95)* is dedicated to the 1847 arrival of the Mormons in Utah. Buy tickets at the Pioneer Center and then head into the living history village, which has several streets of original and replica pioneer buildings. Inside, costumed docents recount mid-19th-century life.

HIP 'HOODS

Get under the skin of Salt Lake by exploring the neighborhoods beyond downtown.

9th & 9th (900 South & 900 East): Several spots fly Pride flags in this mini 'gayborhood.' In 2016, 900 South was renamed Harvey Milk Blvd in honor of the gay-rights activist.

Sugar House: Walkable neighborhood with restaurants, coffee shops, breweries and a beloved urban park.

15th & 15th (1500 South & 1500 East): Enclave of excellent international restaurants and an indie bookstore.

Marmalade: This historic district west of the capitol is ideal for architecture lovers, so called because it was an orchard for early Mormon settlers.

EATING IN SALT LAKE CITY: OUR PICKS

Copper Onion: Elevated American food served brasserie style: think ricotta dumplings and Wagyu stroganoff. *11:30am-10pm or later Mon-Fri, from 10:30am Sat & Sun* **$$**

Lucky 13: Divey bar with the best burgers in the capital. The Nutter Butter Burger with peanut butter is a divine, delicious mess. *10am-2am* **$**

Red Iguana: Mexican food that's worth the inevitable wait. Get the mole sampler to try all its famous sauces. *11am-9pm or later* **$$**

Pago: Beautifully plated farm-to-table New American dishes pair perfectly with the acclaimed wine list. *5-9pm* **$$$**

SIGHTS	5 Red Butte Garden	ACTIVITIES	15 Red Iguana
1 Church History Museum	6 Salt Lake Tabernacle	11 FamilySearch Library	DRINKING & NIGHTLIFE
2 Conference Center	7 Salt Lake Temple	EATING	16 Fisher Brewing Company
3 Delta Center	8 Temple Square	12 Copper Onion	17 Water Witch
4 Natural History Museum of Utah	9 This Is the Place Heritage Park	13 Lucky 13	
	10 Utah State Capitol	14 Pago	

Trace your family tree

Mormons believe that families can be united in heaven for eternity, and since 1894 the church has collected genealogical records. Open to all, the church-sponsored **FamilySearch Library** (*familysearch.org/en/library; free*) houses the largest repository of family history on the planet, with information on more than three billion deceased people from around the world.

Friendly researchers can help you track down records of your family and will even print out a free 3ft-by-2ft full-color poster of the lineage documented during your visit for you to take home.

Tour the Utah State Capitol

Completed in 1916, the neoclassical-style **Utah State Capitol** (*utahstatecapitol.utah.gov; free*) is where state laws have been made for more than a century. You're free to wander around

 DRINKING IN SALT LAKE CITY: OUR PICKS

Fisher Brewing Company: Known for its experimental brews made in a former auto shop. *11am-10pm or later*	Emigration Brewing Co: 'Mountain minimalist' brewery in a scenic canyon setting. *5-9pm Mon-Fri, from 10am Sat, 10am-2pm Sun*	SaltFire Brewing Co: Sociable taproom with friendly bartenders. Don't miss the chai stout. *3-9pm Mon-Thu, to 11pm Fri, noon-11pm Sat, to 8pm Sun*	Water Witch: Go 'roulette' and allow the mixologists to pour perfection from the cocktail shaker. *3pm-1am Mon-Wed, from noon Thu-Sun*

the five floors yourself or join a guided tour, which run on the hour between 10am and 3pm Monday to Friday. Guided tours give access to the basement, where you can see the base isolators that can move up to 2ft to protect the building from earthquakes. The capitol's interior dome, which reaches 165ft above the rotunda floor, steals the show.

Culture on campus

Established in 1850, the University of Utah, often shortened to 'the U,' provides lessons in history, botany and art for all, no matter your enrollment status.

The **Natural History Museum of Utah** (nhmu.utah.edu; adult/child $22.95/17.95) is housed in the sleek, modern Rio Tinto Center in the foothills of the Wasatch Mountains. The five-floor building showcases a dozen permanent exhibits, including displays on Utah's Native tribes, the Great Salt Lake and dinosaurs. Put on your hiking shoes before you head next door to **Red Butte Garden** (redbuttegarden.org; adult/child $16/8), which has 5 miles of trails in addition to 21 acres of beautifully tended display gardens, originally cultivated by a botany professor.

Park City

Activities for all seasons

From boarder dudes to families with tots, everyone is on the slopes at **Park City Mountain Resort** (parkcitymountain.com; day lift ticket adult/child from $140/73). The awesome terrain – 7300 acres of skiable slopes rising above the Old Town – couldn't be more family friendly or more accessible, with ski-in-ski-out access to Park City's Main St via the **Town Lift**. This area offers 344 runs (8% beginner, 44% intermediate, 48% advanced) and is a particular favorite for snowboarders – it hosted snowboarding and skiing half-pipe events in the 2002 Winter Games and is putting them on again in 2034. The first ski area you reach when visiting Park City from Salt Lake City, **Canyons Village** is part of Park City Mountain Resort and is known for having the first heated-seat chairlift in North America, the Orange Bubble Express.

On Park City's southern side, **Deer Valley** (deervalley.com; day lift ticket adult/child from $229/142) is a skiers-only resort of superlatives: superb dining, a complimentary ski valet so you can drop them off like a coat check and even tissue boxes at the base of the slopes. Deer Valley has 123 runs (25% beginner, 43% intermediate, 32% advanced) and a vertical

SALT LAKE CITY PRACTICALITIES

SLC is a car-centric city, but TRAX, the light-rail system, is a great way to get around. Buy tickets (one way/24hr $2.50/5) from machines at station platforms or on the **Transit app** (transitapp.com). Cycle lanes abound. Grab a set of wheels from **Greenbike** (greenbikeutah.org), SLC's bike-share system. For parking, download the **Park SLC app** (parkslc.com). Spaces are often limited to two hours on weekdays ($2.25 per hour).

Attraction costs add up quickly, so check whether buying the **Salt Lake Connect Pass** (visitsaltlake.com) makes sense. It's valid for one, two or 365 days and also includes places in Park City and Snowbird.

EATING IN PARK CITY: OUR PICKS

Davanza's: Crowd into the small space to carb load for another day on the slopes with burgers, sandwiches and pizzas. 11am-9pm $

Farm: Slope-side bistro-style dining room in Park City that uses seasonal local ingredients. 11:30am-10pm Dec-Apr $$$

Five5eeds: Australian cafe serving strong coffee and all-day breakfasts of smashed avo toast and pulled pork Benedict. 7:30am-3pm $$

Top of Main Brew Pub: Utah's first craft brewery still serves pints and pub grub. 11:30am-9pm Mon-Fri, from 10:30am Sat & Sun $$

BEST MOAB BIKE SHOPS

Moab Cyclery: High-performance bike shop offering tours and rentals. Offers shuttles and good half-day, full-day, multiday and multisport tours.

Bike Fiend: Specialists in desert bikepacking, with everything you need for your overnight trip, including bags.

Poison Spider Bicycles: Shuttles to Bar M, Whole Enchilada and more, allowing you to have more riding time and fun.

Chile Pepper Bike Shop: Rent, service or buy a bike to explore the nearby desert at this friendly shop.

E-Bike Moab: The place to pick up bikes to cover longer distances quickly.

Rim Cyclery: Moab's longest-running family-owned bike shop offers tours, rentals and repairs.

---

drop of 3000ft. Its East Village expansion will nearly triple Deer Valley in size.

Fun in Park City doesn't stop when the snow melts. More than 300 miles of hiking and mountain-biking trails criss-cross the mountains, and you'll feel on top of the world in the peaks over the town. Pick up summer trail maps at the resorts or the **Park City Visitors Center** (visitparkcity.com). The ski resorts and outdoor outfitters around town rent mountain bikes.

Watch Olympians

Built for the 2002 Winter Games, **Utah Olympic Park** (utaholympiclegacy.org) was the site of the Games' ski jumping, bobsleigh, skeleton and luge events, and it will host many events again for the 2034 Games. The US Ski Team practices here year-round, and when there's no snow on the slopes, you can watch freestyle jumpers land in a bubble-filled jetted pool.

Not content to sit on the sidelines? Pretend to be an Olympian for the day by taking a 60mph **bobsleigh ride** (per person winter/summer $225/100) with up to 5Gs of centrifugal force. **Guided tours of the park** (adult/child $20/15) are available at 11am, 1pm and 3pm daily – even just peering over the edge of the ski jump is an adrenaline rush.

Moab

Scenic off-road drives

Moab's hundreds of miles of primitive back roads are coveted by 4WD enthusiasts. **Hell's Revenge** (blm.gov/visit/hells-revenge-trailhead) is the best-known 4WD road in Moab, but the extreme terrain mandates solid driving experience. It's in the BLM-administered area east of town and follows an 8.2-mile route up and down shockingly steep slickrock.

The 33-mile **Hurrah Pass** offers jaw-dropping vistas of the Colorado River, Dead Horse Point and **Grand View Point** in Canyonlands National Park, while on the other side of the Colorado River, the 15-mile scenic desert drive on **Potash Road** passes mining remnants on the way into dry country with soaring rock walls and solitude.

Outfitters such as **Cliffhanger Jeep Rental** (cliffhangerjeeprental.com) and **Twisted Jeeps** (twistedjeeps.com) rent Rubicons and Wranglers. If you'd rather someone else does the driving, join a group 4WD tour, dubbed 'land safaris,' in modified six- to eight-person Humvee-like vehicles. **Dan Mick's Jeep Tours** (danmick.com) is a highly regarded local operation that visits some 25 trails, including Hell's Revenge.

 DRINKING IN MOAB: OUR PICKS

Proper Burger & Brewing Co: Southerly outpost of the SLC brewery; heaven for hopheads. *11:30am-9pm or later Wed-Mon*

Moab Brewery: The hometown brewery makes nearly a dozen beers in the vats just behind the bar area. *11:30am-8pm*

Woody's Tavern: 'World famous' neighborhood bar open for 60-plus years; live music on Fridays and Saturdays. *2pm-1am*

Moab Coffee Roasters: Low-key downtown spot to kick back with coffee, gelato and affogato. *7am-7pm Mar-Oct, to 5pm Nov-Feb*

Utah Olympic Park

The country's mountain-biking capital

Moab's mountain biking is world famous. Challenging trails ascend steep slickrock and wind through woods and up 4WD roads outside of town in every direction. Bike-shop websites and **Discover Moab** *(discovermoab.com/mountainbiking)* are good trail resources.

East of town in the Sand Flats Recreation Area, Moab's legendary **Slickrock Trail** *(blm.gov/visit/slickrock-national-recreation-trail; 1-/7-/365-day pass $5/10/20)* will kick your butt. The physically and technically difficult 12-mile round-trip route is for experts only, as is the practice loop. Plan on half a day.

Beat the heat on the **Moonlight Meadow Trail**, a 10.8-mile loop among aspens and pines that reaches a 10,500ft altitude in the La Sal Mountains south of Moab. The nearby **Whole Enchilada** trail system combines six routes that offer everything from high-mountain descents to slickrock. It's a full-day affair for advanced riders, with 7500ft of vertical drop and 34 miles of trails.

White waters of the Colorado and canyons

Rafting might be the highlight of your visit to Moab. Choose from full-day floats, white-water trips, multiday excursions and jet-boat trips.

Half- and full-day trips stick to the Colorado River, northeast of Moab. With class I to II rapids, the most popular stretch of

MOAB'S MOVIE HISTORY

Even if you haven't been to the countryside around Moab before, you've almost certainly seen it. This stunning scenery has starred as the background of major movies for nearly a century. The **Moab Museum of Film & Western Heritage** *(redcliffslodge.com/the-lodge/moab-museum-of-film-and-western-heritage; free)*, based at Red Cliffs Lodge on Hwy 128, has memorabilia from locally shot movies, and the ranch itself was the filming location for many of the first films set around Moab, such as *Wagon Master* and *Rio Grande*.

Movies as diverse as *Austin Powers*, *Thelma & Louise* and *Mission Impossible II* have been filmed here. Actor and director Kevin Costner premiered his locally shot passion project *Horizon: An American Saga* in 2024.

EATING IN MOAB: OUR PICKS

Desert Bistro: Southeastern Utah's top restaurant, serving perfectly plated game and seafood in an 1892 dance hall. *5-9pm* $$$

Moab Food Truck Park: A dozen-plus trucks dishing up crowd-pleasing Chinese dishes, pizza, hot dogs, sushi and more. *11am-9pm* $

Milt's Stop & Eat: Moab's oldest restaurant (established 1954), with classic diner grub: burgers, fries and milkshakes. *11am-8pm* $

Birdy's Finer Diner: Elevated comfort food in an Insta-worthy former Denny's covered in bold wallpaper and mod furnishings. *5:30-9:30pm Wed-Sun* $$$

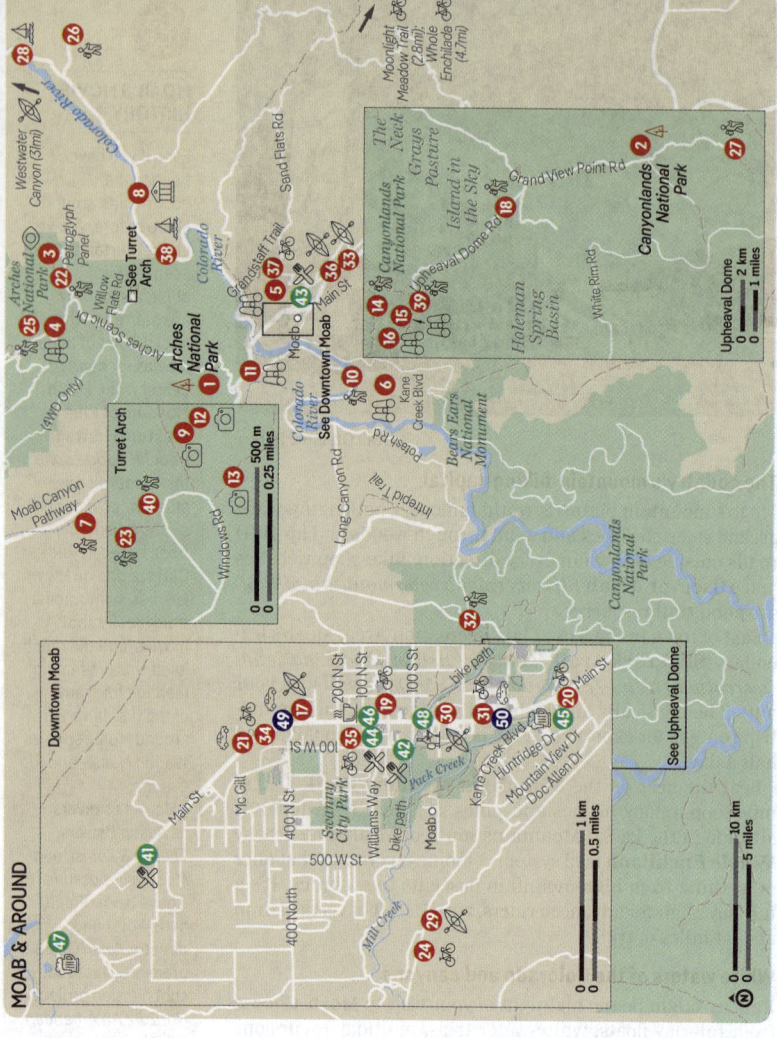

river near Moab is from **Hittle Bottom** to **Takeout Beach**, perfect for first-timers.

Longer multiday expeditions head to Cataract Canyon, Westwater Canyon and Desolation Canyon. The legendary class V rapids of **Cataract Canyon** are Utah's most intense stretch of white water. Outfitters run excursions lasting two to six days.

Find serious white water at **Westwater Canyon**, which boasts class III and IV rapids squeezed by 1200ft rock walls. Over on the Green River, **Desolation Canyon** is an epic four- to six-day adventure that starts with a scenic flight from Moab to the launch point.

- ⭐ **HIGHLIGHTS**
- 1 Arches National Park
- 2 Canyonlands National Park
- 🔴 **SIGHTS**
- 3 Delicate Arch
- 4 Fiery Furnace Viewpoint
- 5 Hell's Revenge
- 6 Hurrah Pass
- 7 Mill Canyon Dinosaur Tracksite
- 8 Moab Museum of Film & Western Heritage
- 9 North Window
- 10 Poison Spider Trailhead
- 11 Potash Road
- 12 South Window
- 13 Turret Arch
- 14 Upheaval Dome
- 15 Upheaval Dome First Overlook
- 16 Upheaval Dome Second Overlook
- 🔴 **ACTIVITIES**
- 17 Adrift Adventures
- 18 Aztec Butte Trail
- 19 Bike Fiend
- 20 Chile Pepper Bike Shop
- 21 Dan Mick's Jeep Tours
- 22 Delicate Arch Trailhead
- 23 Double Arch Trail
- 24 E-Bike Moab
- 25 Fiery Furnace
- 26 Fisher Towers Trail
- 27 Grand View Point Trail
- 28 Hittle Bottom
- 29 Mild to Wild
- 30 Moab Adventure Center
- 31 Moab Cyclery
- 32 Neck Spring Trail
- 33 OARS
- 34 Poison Spider Bicycles
- 35 Rim Cyclery
- 36 Sheri Griffith River Expeditions
- 37 Slickrock Trail
- 38 Takeout Beach
- 39 Upheaval Dome Trailhead
- 40 Windows Trailhead
- 🟢 **EATING**
- 41 Birdy's Finer Diner
- 42 Desert Bistro
- 43 Milt's Stop & Eat
- 44 Moab Food Truck Park
- 🟢 **DRINKING & NIGHTLIFE**
- 45 Moab Brewery
- 46 Moab Coffee Roasters
- 47 Proper Burger & Brewing Co
- 48 Woody's Tavern
- 🔵 **TRANSPORT**
- 49 Cliffhanger Jeep Rental
- 50 Twisted Jeeps

BEST RAFTING COMPANIES

Mild to Wild: Excellent rafting trips for any amount of time, including half-day sessions. *(mild2wildrafting.com)*

Adrift Adventures: Combine a trip on the river with a Jeep tour. *(adrift.net)*

OARS: Has a permit for Canyonlands and runs epic weeklong expeditions that raft and hike to tough-to-reach parts of the national park. *(oars.com)*

Sheri Griffith River Expeditions: Operating since 1971, this rafting specialist offers a great selection of activities, from family floats to rapids. *(griffithexp.com)*

Moab Adventure Center: Tons of boat tours for every level of adrenaline, including thrilling jet boats. *(moabadventurecenter.com)*

Rafting season runs from April to September; the jet-boating season lasts longer. Water levels crest in May and June.

Discover dinosaur tracks near Moab

The first fossils found in the western US were discovered near Moab in 1859. Just off Potash Rd (Hwy 279), the **Poison Spider Dinosaur Tracksite** *(free)* has prints from at least 10 three-toed meat-eating theropods walking along the edge of a lake.

At the **Mill Canyon Dinosaur Tracksite** *(blm.gov/visit/mill-canyon-dinosaur-trailhead-interpretive-site; free)* north of Moab, a raised boardwalk leads travelers above prints from at least 10 species of dinosaur. They include sickle-clawed raptors and long-necked herbivores as well as crocodile ancestors, giving it the most diversity of any site in North America, with 200 individual tracks.

Copper Ridge Dinosaur Tracksite *(blm.gov/visit/copper-ridge-dinosaur-tracks-interpretive-site; free)* is the first place in Utah where the prints of a Jurassic-period sauropod (a herbivore with a long neck) were discovered.

Bears Ears National Monument

Hike through ancient landscapes and cultures

The first national monument created at the request of Native tribes, **Bears Ears** *(blm.gov/visit/bears-ears-national-monument)* covers more than 2100 sq miles and is named for a pair of reddish, nearly symmetrical buttes. The huge area protects sites of cultural significance to Native people, with ancient rock art, cliff dwellings, ceremonial sites and granaries. Bears Ears has been the focus of political ping-pong

VISIT WITH RESPECT

Bears Ears is a delicate environment, in terms of both the environment and archaeology. Keep the impact of your visit to a minimum by following these guidelines.

Leave fossils and cultural artifacts undisturbed: This includes pieces of pottery, corn cobs, animal tracks and bones.

Steer clear of ancient structures: Do not touch, climb or stand on historic buildings or lean on their walls.

Stay on established trails and roads: Protect cryptobiotic soil by walking and driving on durable surfaces.

Use rubber-tipped hiking poles: Sharp tips scratch the rocks.

Pay your fees: This money ensures that sites are monitored and facilities are maintained.

---

for several years. In one of his final acts as president, Barack Obama designated the land as a national monument in 2016, but when Donald Trump took over the White House, he cut the monument's size by 85%. Biden later issued a proclamation that restored Bears Ears to its original size.

Given its recent establishment and back-and-forth status, Bears Ears can be confusing to visit. The monument doesn't have clear entrances, and signage on the ground is minimal, so you might not even know when you're in it. Start your visit at the **Kane Gulch Ranger Station** (blm.gov/visit/kane-gulch-ranger-station; open spring & fall only) on Hwy 261 or the **Bears Ears Education Center** (bearsearspartnership.org/education-center) in Bluff, a community-run information center with interpretative displays. At either spot, pick up maps and ask for advice on exploring the area.

Bears Ears is divided into three sections: Indian Creek, Cedar Mesa and the San Juan River. Cedar Mesa is the most easily accessible area, mostly along Hwy 95. Some sites, such as the 700-year-old **Mule Canyon Kiva**, are short and easy roadside stops. The 1-mile round-trip **Butler Wash Trail** crosses slickrock to reach a viewpoint looking toward a cliff dwelling across the chasm. An easy 2-mile hike along the South Fork creek of Mule Canyon leads to small Ancestral Puebloan granaries known as **House on Fire**, so named because one of the small dwellings appears to be engulfed in flames due to an unusual gold-orange sandstone overhang.

One of the largest and most evocative archaeological sites is **Moon House**, which has 49 rooms across three well-preserved dwellings. Its name comes from pictographs that show the lunar phases. Access to Moon House is limited to 20 people per day, doled out by permit on recreation.gov for $5 per person, plus a $6 reservation fee. Permits often sell out several days in advance, and in spring and fall they must be validated in person at the Kane Gulch Ranger Station or the **BLM Monticello Field Office** (blm.gov/office/monticello-field-office), a 1½-hour drive from the trail. The road to the trailhead requires a high-clearance 4WD vehicle.

Hiking in the canyons of Cedar Mesa, including to House on Fire, requires day-use permits (per person per day/week $5/10), which you can purchase on recreation.gov (cell signal is poor, so do this in advance) or by using the fee envelopes at trailheads. Backpackers also need permits to camp overnight.

The land protected by Bears Ears National Monument remains sacred to five Native tribes – the Hopi, Navajo, Ute Mountain Ute, Zuni and Ute – who formed a coalition in 2015 to appeal for its preservation. Louis Williams, a member of Diné Bikéyah (the Navajo Nation), founded tour company **Ancient Wayves** (tourancientwayves.com) to enrich visitors' experience of hiking in Shash Jaa' (Bears Ears in Diné) with a Native perspective. Hikes head to trailheads around Cedar Mesa, Butler Wash and other locations for half-day, full-day and multiday excursions.

In addition to hikes, Williams, a longtime river runner, also operates rafting trips on the San Juan, the northern boundary of Diné Bikéyah.

TOP EXPERIENCE

Capitol Reef National Park

In a forgotten fold of the Colorado Plateau, slot canyons appear as cathedrals cut from the earth, and giant cream-colored domes arc into perfectly blue skies. Capitol Reef National Park doesn't always make it onto travelers' itineraries. Discover petroglyphs and early Mormon settlements, sandstone streaks and hidden arches, as you hike a labyrinth of canyons stretching back millions of years.

Cassidy Arch

Grand Wash

Grand Wash, Capitol Reef's most captivating canyon off Scenic Dr, is worth visiting just to walk between the Narrows' sheer walls. This flat, easy hike with just 200ft of elevation change is sandwiched between the sides of a Navajo sandstone canyon that at one point tower 80 stories high but are only 15ft apart.

Cassidy Arch

A 3.3-mile round-trip side trail from Grand Wash leads to Cassidy Arch, a natural red-rock formation. With 670ft of elevation change, this hike is more difficult than Grand Wash, switchbacking up the cliffside and traversing some sheer drops, but the views en route are worth it. The arch is named after Utah-born Butch Cassidy, who, according to legend, hid from the law high on these cliffs.

Hickman Bridge Trail

Hickman Bridge Trail, Capitol Reef's most popular trail, is diverse, offering a canyon and desert-wash walk to a natural bridge, plus big-sky views and spring wildflowers. This hike is easy enough for anyone to enjoy. Because the route is largely exposed, it's best to hike in the early morning.

TOP TIPS

● Capitol Reef's gateway town is tiny Torrey, population 257, 11 miles west, where you'll find restaurants, gas stations and accommodations.

● Torrey doesn't have a full-sized grocery store; if you need specific items, Loa lies 17 miles west.

PRACTICALITIES

● nps.gov/care
● 7-day pass per vehicle $20
● national parks pass accepted

Delicate Arch

TOP EXPERIENCE

Arches National Park

Giant sandstone arcs frame snowy peaks and desert landscapes at Arches National Park, home to 2000 rock arches, the highest density of them anywhere on earth. You'll lose all perspective on size at some, and a scenic drive through the park makes the spectacular arches accessible to all. Arches has many short trails, with most of the main sights close to paved roads.

DON'T MISS

- Windows Trail
- Turret Arch
- Double Arch Trail
- Delicate Arch
- Fiery Furnace
- Fiery Furnace Viewpoint
- Baby Arch

The Windows Trail

The Windows Trail is an easy 1-mile loop trail that gently climbs to three massive photogenic arches: North Window, South Window and Turret Arch. It's hard to grasp the immensity of these gigantic marvels until you're beside them. This hike is one of the busiest in the park, but you can leave some of the crowds behind by returning on the longer **Windows Primitive Loop**, with a beautiful back view of the two

PRACTICALITIES
- nps.gov/arch
- 7-day pass per vehicle $30
- national parks pass accepted

windows. The primitive trail is less obvious and doesn't have as many trail markers.

The trail forks about 500ft from the parking lot. Take the left fork and head to the **North Window**, which measures 51ft high and 93ft wide and frames the distant desert. A spur trail (part of the Windows Primitive Loop) heads to the **South Window**, sitting higher from the ground than the North Window. The main Windows Loop trail then circles to the castle-like **Turret Arch**.

For a bonus arch, head back to the parking lot and set off on the 0.6-mile **Double Arch Trail**. Double Arch is the tallest in the park at 112ft, and you're allowed to walk and scramble underneath it (but not on the arch itself).

Delicate Arch

You've seen Delicate Arch before: it's the unofficial state symbol, stamping nearly every Utah tourist brochure and gracing license plates. While two viewpoints provide perspective (and an easier hike) from below, the best way to experience the arch is close up.

The trail to Delicate Arch may seem interminable on the way up, but the rewards are so great that you'll quickly forget the toil, provided you wear rubber-soled hiking shoes and drink a quart of water along the way – there is zero shade. This hike is best tackled early in the day when you'll feel less like an ant under a magnifying glass.

Fiery Furnace

So named because of its spectacular rock formations that glow red and orange in the sunset, the narrow sandstone maze of Fiery Furnace has no marked trails and provides an extra level of adventure for hikers. Because of the extreme nature of wayfinding here (online maps and GPS do not work well because of the high canyon walls), as well as sections that require jumping across ledges and shimmying through crevices, permits are required – the only hike in Arches where they are mandatory.

Permits come in two flavors: ranger-led ($16 per person) or self-guided ($10 per person). Purchase them on recreation.gov a week in advance.

The National Park Service recommends that people hiking Fiery Furnace for the first time go on a ranger-guided tour. Permits must be picked up the day before or the day of the hike at the Arches National Park Visitor Center, which opens at 7:30am.

If you don't manage to snag a hiking permit, still survey the scene from the **Fiery Furnace viewpoint**.

OUTSTANDING ARCHES

Karen Henker has worked at the national park for more than a decade.

Double Arch
More than 100ft high, this arch in the Windows section is the park's tallest.

Baby Arch
Not marked on the park map, this one near the Courthouse Towers is a hidden treasure.

Delicate Arch
I recommend the easy Lower Viewpoint walk; the long hike up is like climbing 50 flights of stairs.

TOP TIPS

● If you're planning to visit between 7am and 4pm from April through October, you must reserve an hour-long entry window on recreation.gov, which costs $2 and doesn't include the park entry fee.

● Driving is the best way to get around. There's no shuttle or public transportation. Some companies in Moab run bus tours through the park.

● Cyclists beware: it's a steep climb right after the visitor center and about 17 miles one way to the end of the scenic drive.

● The park has no non-camping accommodations or anywhere to buy food.

● Usually no cell-phone service. Download maps and apps before you arrive.

Aztec Butte

TOP EXPERIENCE

Canyonlands National Park

A 527-sq-mile vision of ancient earth, Canyonlands National Park is Utah's largest – and least-visited – national park. Vast serpentine canyons tipped with white cliffs loom 1000ft over the Colorado and Green Rivers. Skyward-reaching needles and spires, deep craters, swirling tie-dye mesas and majestic buttes dot the landscape. The 6000ft-high Island in the Sky promises some of the most enthralling vistas in Utah.

DON'T MISS

- Island in the Sky
- Neck Spring
- Aztec Butte
- Upheaval Dome Trail
- Needles District
- Slickrock Trail
- Chesler Park Loop

Neck Spring

One of Canyonlands' few loop trails, Neck Spring (5.6 miles, moderately challenging) is good for solitude seekers. Despite its proximity to the visitor center, this trail attracts few hikers, perhaps because it doesn't take in the panoramic vistas that are the signature of **Island in the Sky**, but this stream canyon is a magnet for wildlife and fills with wildflowers in springtime as one of the plateau's rare water sources.

PRACTICALITIES

- nps.gov/cany
- 7-day pass per vehicle $30
- national parks pass accepted

Aztec Butte

Shortly after the turnoff on Upheaval Dome Rd, the moderately challenging 1.4-mile round-trip Aztec Butte Trail climbs to the only archaeological site at Island in the Sky. The short ascent of a Navajo sandstone dome yields stellar views; it's a steep hike over slickrock to the top.

A little more than a quarter mile from the parking area, a spur trail leads to a granary built around 1200 to 1300 CE, tucked below an overhang on the butte's northern side. (Despite the name, the structure was built by Ancestral Puebloans, not the Aztecs.) Use the cairns and switchbacks to follow the route up to the butte, which levels off at the top, revealing panoramic views and endless sky.

Upheaval Dome

Was Upheaval Dome created by salt or something from outer space? Scientists disagree over how the feature formed. Some suggest it's a collapsed salt dome, while more recent research posits that it was the site of a meteorite strike some 60 million years ago. Scope out the geological drama on the moderately challenging **Upheaval Dome Trail**, which leads to two overlooks that gaze out at the 3-mile-wide crater.

It's an easy 0.3 miles one way to the **first overlook**. To reach the **second overlook**, return to the fork in the trail and bear right, descending over slickrock before clambering to a final steep ascent. From here, you have a broader panorama of the surrounding landscape. The afternoon light is magnificent, and this viewpoint adds only 1 mile to the trip.

Slickrock Trail

Over in the Canyonlands' Needles District, the ridgeline Slickrock Trail (2.4 miles, easy) is high above the canyons with views below, almost entirely on its namesake type of stone. Keep an eye out during your hike – bighorn sheep are occasionally seen here.

If you're short on time, at least visit **Viewpoint 1** for a panorama where giant red cliffs hang like curtains below high buttes and mesas, the district's namesake needles touch the sky, and the La Sal and Abajo Mountains lord over the whole scene.

Chesler Park Loop

Get among the namesake 'needles' formations on the Chesler Park Loop, an awesome 11-mile route across desert grasslands, past towering red-and-white-striped pinnacles, and between deep, narrow slot canyons, some only 2ft across. Elevation changes are mild, but the distance makes it a challenging day hike. Make sure you plan your route and download maps in advance, as this area has a number of intersecting circular trails.

WHO WERE THE ANCESTRAL PUEBLOANS?

The Ancestral Puebloans were a Native people who lived across the Four Corners region (modern-day Utah, Colorado, New Mexico and Arizona) from as far back as the 12th century BCE. Prime examples of their impressive architecture can be found at Mesa Verde National Park (p740) in southwestern Colorado. Their modern descendants include the Pueblo, Hopi and Zuni.

TOP TIPS

● The park's two rivers form a Y that divides the park into four separate districts, inaccessible to one another from within the park.

● Cradled atop the Y, Island in the Sky is the most developed and visited district because of its proximity to Moab and Arches National Park's entrance, both about 30 miles from the visitor center.

● The easiest way to visit Canyonlands' Island in the Sky district is by car. There is no shuttle system or public transportation.

● Some companies in Moab run bus tours through the park.

● From Island in the Sky, it's a two-hour drive south to the Needles.

Fairyland Loop

TOP EXPERIENCE

Bryce Canyon National Park

You never forget your first sight of otherworldly Bryce Canyon National Park. Yes, you're still in the desert, but it's the wonderful power of water that sculpted this soft sandstone and limestone into alien formations that tickle the imagination. Though it's the smallest of Utah's national parks, Bryce Canyon stands among the most prized. In Utah, that's quite a claim.

DON'T MISS
- Rim Trail
- Silent City
- Thor's Hammer
- Fairyland Loop
- Tower Bridge
- Peekaboo Loop Trail

Rim Trail

The easiest hike in the national park, the 0.5- to 5.5-mile (one-way) Rim Trail outlines Bryce Amphitheater from Fairyland Point to Bryce Point, promising a journey of incredible views. From Bryce Point to **Inspiration Point**, the trail skirts the canyon rim atop white cliffs, revealing gorgeous formations, including the Wall of Windows. After passing briefly through trees, it continues along the ridge top to the uppermost level of Inspiration Point, 1.3 miles from Bryce Point. The leg to

PRACTICALITIES
- nps.gov/brca
- 7-day pass per vehicle $35
- national parks pass accepted

Sunset Point drops 200ft in 0.75 miles, winding its way along limestone-capped cliffs. Below the rim, **Silent City** rises in all its hoodoo glory.

Stay the course and look for **Thor's Hammer** as you continue the 0.5-mile stroll along a paved path to **Sunrise Point**, the most crowded stretch of trail in the entire park. The views are worth it. Past Sunrise Point the crowds thin as the trail climbs 150ft toward North Campground. Topping out near North Campground, the path ambles across gently rolling hills on the forested plateau before rejoining the canyon rim at Fairyland Point, 2.5 miles from Sunrise Point.

Fairyland Loop

Fairyland Loop is a great 8-mile day hike and a good workout, with 1900ft of elevation gain. Unlike Bryce Amphitheater, Fairyland is spared the crowds. This trail is difficult primarily because it meanders in and out of the hoodoos, down into washes, and up and over saddles.

This trail begins at **Fairyland Point** and circles the majestic cliffs of flat-topped, 8076ft Boat Mesa, emerging on the rim near Sunrise Point. The last 2.5 miles of the loop follow the Rim Trail back to the trailhead.

From Fairyland Point, the trail dips gradually below the rim. At Fairyland Canyon, 600ft below your starting point, towers of deep-orange stone stand like giant totem poles. Zigzagging up and down, the trail eventually reaches a seasonal wash on the floor of Campbell Canyon. Keep an eye out for **Tower Bridge**, which connects three spires to two windows. To reach the base of the formation, take the clearly marked dead-end spur from the wash. From Tower Bridge it's a 950ft climb over 1.5 miles to the Rim Trail.

Peekaboo Loop Trail

An ideal half-day hike, the Peekaboo Loop Trail sees the most variety of terrain and scenery in Bryce, with 1560ft of elevation change.

From Bryce Point, follow signs to the Peekaboo Connecting Trail east of the parking area. Just over a mile down the trail, past where hoodoo columns take on a bright orange hue, work your way down the switchbacks, watching for the **Wall of Windows**, which juts above the hoodoos atop a sheer vertical cliff face perpendicular to the canyon rim.

As you continue, you'll pass ancient bristlecone pines, some of whose roots are over 1000 years old; an inch of these trees' trunks represents a century of growth. Other highlights include the cluster of delicate red spires at Fairy Castle, spectacular views of Silent City, and the Cathedral, a majestic wall of buttress-like hoodoos.

SEEING STARS IN BRYCE CANYON

Amateur astronomers are in for a treat at Bryce Canyon. The National Park Service puts on some 100 astronomy programs a year, including an **Astronomy Festival** in June, full-moon hikes and regular ranger talks. Check the park's calendar online (nps.gov/brca/planyourvisit/calendar.htm) and stop by the visitor center when you arrive to see what's happening while you're here.

TOP TIPS

● When the free park shuttle is running, you can take it to any one point and return from another, instead of backtracking to your car.

● You can join the Rim Trail anywhere along its 5.5-mile route. Note that shuttle buses don't stop at Fairyland.

● If you time your visit for the new moon, when the skies are darkest, watch as the Milky Way shimmers all the way to the horizon.

● At full moon, see the hoodoos take on spooky personalities when rangers lead 1- to 2-mile walks (taking about two hours) among the formations in the moonlight. Reserve a spot ($1) on *recreation.gov*.

The Narrows

TOP EXPERIENCE

Zion National Park

Visiting heavenly Zion National Park can feel like a religious experience. The park's soaring red and white cliffs, one of Utah's most dramatic natural wonders, rise high over the Virgin River. From the canyon floor to Zion's highest peak there is nearly 5000ft of elevation change, resulting in a fabulous range of ecozones and experiences.

Riverside Walk

The easy 2-mile out-and-back Riverside Walk is the dry and paved part of the experience, for those who like an easy adventure. Shadowed from the sun by lofty canyon walls, this fun path parallels the Virgin River's slippery cobblestones and rambles by seeps, hanging gardens and wading spots. Points along the way give access to the riverbank and water, making it a family favorite.

The Narrows: Zion's Classic Hike

At the end of the Riverside Walk, stairs descend to the water and the adventure begins. Hiking through a rocky river in

DON'T MISS

Riverside Walk

The Narrows

Emerald Pools Trails

Canyon Overlook Trail

Observation Point

PRACTICALITIES
- nps.gov/zion
- 7-day pass per vehicle $35
- national parks pass accepted

ankle- to chest-deep water as the canyon walls rise up to 1000ft tall and press in to just 20ft wide: the Narrows is quintessential Zion.

The best part about hiking the Narrows is that you can walk for as little or as long as you'd like and still have a great time; the further you go, the smaller the crowds. This out-and-back route is not about reaching a specific spot, but simply soaking up the scene. Day hikers are allowed to go as far as **Big Spring**. Don't underestimate the difficulty or distance (9.4 miles return, about eight hours).

You'll want a sturdy hiking stick to avoid falling in the water, plus quick-drying fabrics, layers and proper footwear. In cooler months, bring waterproof bags and warm, waterproof gear, which you can rent from outfitters near the park entrance like **Zion Outfitter** (zionoutfitter.com/narrows-rentals).

Emerald Pools

Short and sweet, the Emerald Pools trails are a superb introduction to Zion's unique ecology and microhabitats. The paved **Lower Emerald Pool Trail**, the easiest of the three, gradually rises and falls for 0.6 miles before reaching the first pool. Waterfalls cascade down a multicolored, mineral-stained overhang, misting the trail (and you) as you pass beneath. A dirt trail ascends 150ft to the less dramatic **Middle Emerald Pool** feeding the waterfalls below. From here a steep 0.5-mile spur leads to the **Upper Emerald Pool**. It's the loveliest grotto of all, surrounded by Lady Mountain's sheer-walled skirts.

Canyon Overlook Trail

A convenient stop off Hwy 9, the 1-mile out-and-back Canyon Overlook Trail is a relatively quick hike with a much photographed panoramic vista. Although it's not a particularly strenuous hike, the slickrock terrain is somewhat rugged. The final sweeping Canyon Overlook has lower Zion Canyon views. The hike's most challenging part might be finding somewhere to park. If the small lot near the trailhead is full or if you're coming from Mt Carmel, park in the overflow lots 300ft east of the **Zion–Mt Carmel Tunnel**.

Observation Point

It feels deliciously like cheating to wander along a mostly flat woodland path and then descend to Observation Point, which towers more than 700ft above **Angels Landing** – you get all of the rewards with hardly any of the work. If you're planning to hike Angels Landing, know that you can't just show up and hike it; you have to apply for a permit.

The **trailhead** is at the end of a small parking area off a 4WD road in East Zion. The parking lot fills early, and the road is often too rough for standard sedans. Instead, book a spot on a shuttle run by **East Zion Adventures** (eastzion adventures.com; round trip per person $7), which leaves from nearby Zion Ponderosa Ranch Resort (p879).

CAUTION

Preparation and timing are the keys to a successful Narrows adventure. *Always* check conditions and the flash-flood forecast with rangers before setting off. A sudden rainstorm miles away can send down a surge of rock- and log-filled water that sweeps away everything in its path. Some years there's little change in water levels, but the Narrows could be closed in April, May or June.

TOP TIPS

- Avoid visiting in summer if you can: this is the third most-visited national park in the country and summers can feel claustrophobic.

- For most of the year, private vehicles are not allowed on Zion Canyon Scenic Drive. Instead, you must ride the Zion Park Shuttle, which makes nine stops between the visitor center and the Temple of Sinawava.

- Limited free parking is available inside the park; arrive as early as possible.

DRIVING THE COLORADO RIVER SCENIC BYWAY

The curvy Colorado River Scenic Byway (Hwy 128) follows the winding waters through gorgeous red-rock country of high cliffs, alfalfa fields and sagebrush.

START	END	LENGTH
Matrimony Spring	Dewey Bridge	30 miles; 1½ hours

The Colorado River forms Arches National Park's southern boundary for the first 15 miles of this journey. Near the start of the 'river road' just east of Hwy 191, ❶ **Matrimony Spring** is said to have magical properties, and couples who drink from it might soon hear wedding bells. After the first major bend is the ❷ **Grandstaff Canyon Trailhead**, which leads to a beautiful arch.

At the head of the next bend (6 miles from Hwy 191), spot boulderers on the rocks at ❸ **Big Bend Recreation Site**, where you can picnic by the river. As you round the mesa near Red Cliffs Lodge, look on the right for ❹ **Castleton Tower**, a narrow 400ft sandstone spire that rises above Castle Valley and is one of the area's most iconic rock climbs. In the 1960s and '70s, Chevrolet filmed TV commercials here, helicoptering a car to the summit. Carry on to the turnoff for ❺ **Fisher Towers**. The 900ft-high Titan, standing solemnly at the end of the formation, is the country's tallest freestanding natural tower.

The road finally crosses the river at ❻ **Dewey Bridge**, where you might spot rafters drifting by. The scenic byway soon ends at a three-way intersection. Return to Moab or double back to the La Sal Mountain Loop Rd. You're also less than 10 miles from I-70.

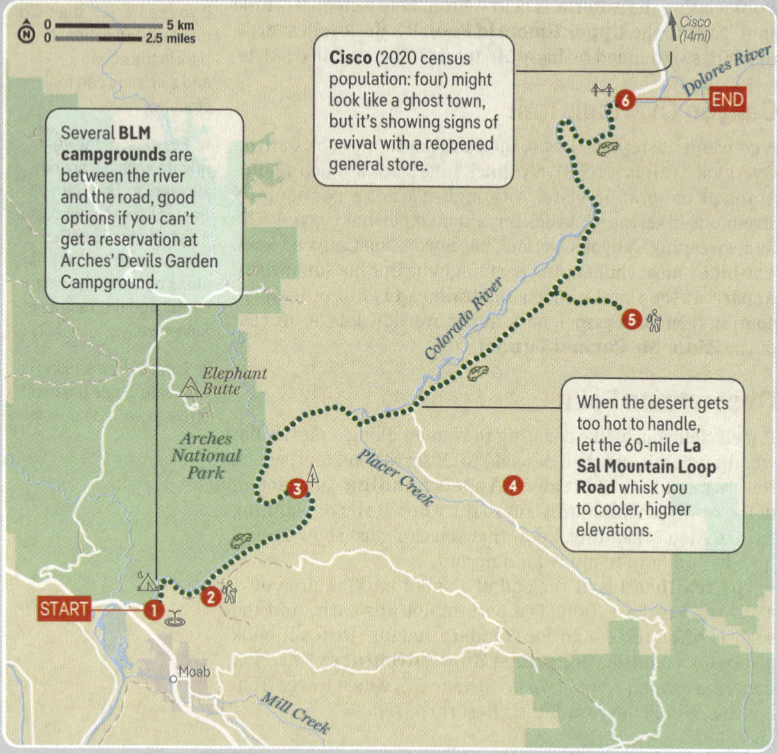

Cisco (2020 census population: four) might look like a ghost town, but it's showing signs of revival with a reopened general store.

Several **BLM campgrounds** are between the river and the road, good options if you can't get a reservation at Arches' Devils Garden Campground.

When the desert gets too hot to handle, let the 60-mile **La Sal Mountain Loop Road** whisk you to cooler, higher elevations.

New Mexico

FASCINATING HISTORY | UFO MYSTERIES | SPACE RACE

Traveling in New Mexico is a journey through time and space. It's one big living museum, home to 1000-year-old Indigenous dwellings and some of the longest continuously inhabited communities in the US. It's also the setting for the most famous alleged UFO sighting, it's where the Space Race began, and the state now has the first airport serving trips beyond earth's orbit.

New Mexico doesn't have a single standout city or site – Santa Fe, Taos, Albuquerque and its phenomenal national parks all top the list. The best way to visit is with a road trip along one of many scenic byways or retro Route 66, where neon signs and dry shrubs transform into ghost towns and high-mountain forests.

The best way to fuel any New Mexico adventure? With chili (or chile, as it's spelled here) – practically everything is smothered with the delicious spicy fruit and the chance to explore New Mexico's unique culinary culture is yet another very good reason to visit.

Places

Albuquerque p865
Santa Fe p867
Abiquiú p869
Bandelier National Monument p870
Los Alamos p870
Taos p870
Roswell p874
Las Cruces p875
Truth or Consequences p876
White Sands National Park p877

☑ TOP TIP

Don't make too many UFO jokes around New Mexicans. There's a good chance they've seen something in the sky that they can't explain. Despite its small population, New Mexico often ranks near the top when it comes to UFO sightings compared to other states.

GETTING AROUND

Renting a car is your best bet if you want to travel beyond Albuquerque and Santa Fe. Both cities have plenty of rental offices. A 4WD drive is desirable, especially in the Four Corners Region, but most cars with high clearance should do. Between cities, you can take the Rail Runner Express commuter train from Albuquerque to Santa Fe. Albuquerque and Santa Fe have internal bus services. Greyhound serves some cities and towns, though they're usually best for getting to and from New Mexico rather than around the state.

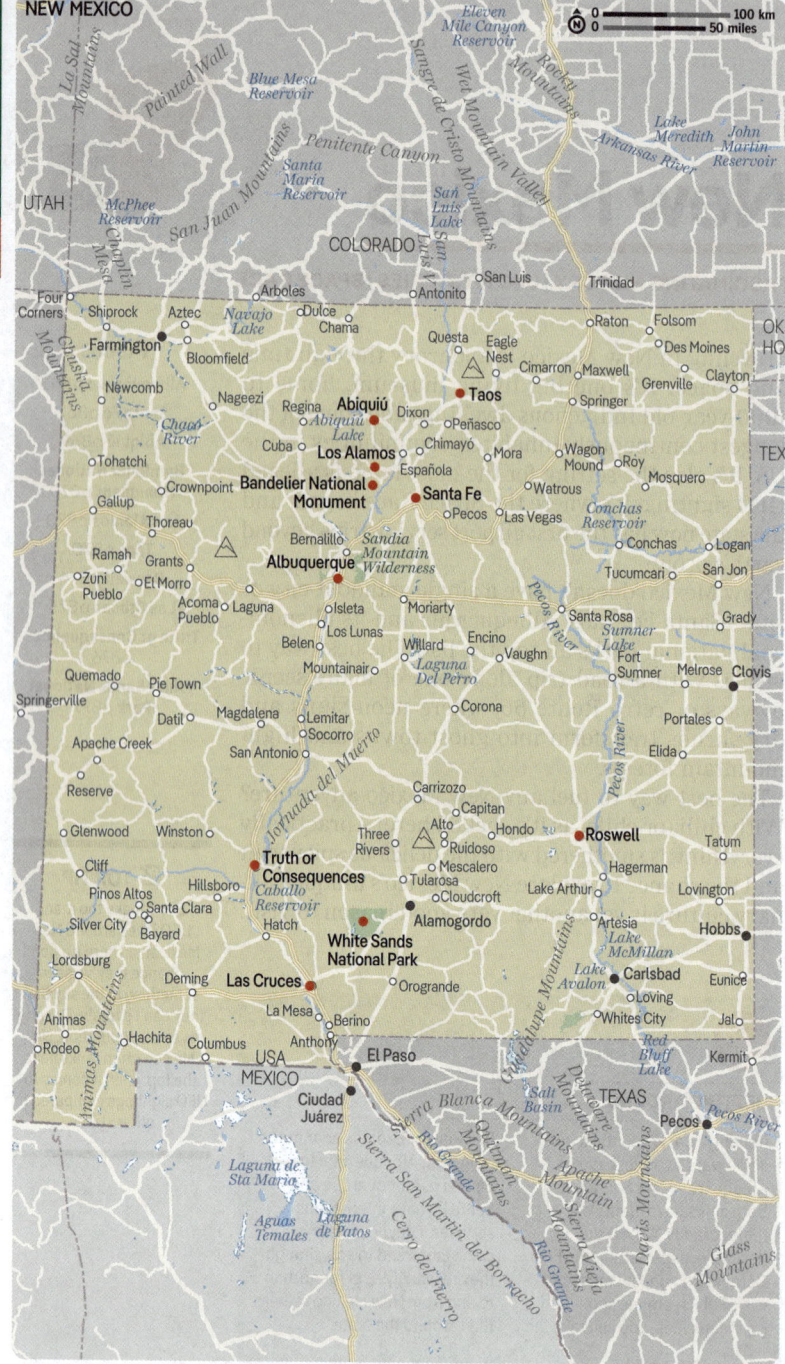

Albuquerque

Wander the century-old adobe houses

Once a homeland for the Tiwa people, starting around 1250, 'Alburquerque' was taken over by Spain in the 1680 Pueblo Revolt, and in 1706, 15 Spanish families settled here in Old Town. The neighborhood's plaza and **San Felipe de Neri Church** *(sanfelipedeneri.org; free entry)* – look out for the Virgen de Guadalupe carved inside a tree trunk outside the church – were the hub of daily life and a major rest stop for those passing through. Outlaw Billy the Kid allegedly frequented a brothel or two here in the 1870s.

The plaza graciously remains, and Old Town is starting to evolve, especially since the COVID-19 pandemic, with quality shops and galleries promoting New Mexican artisans hoping to revamp the historic core.

When your feet get tired, have a Southwestern lunch at **Church Street Cafe** *(churchstreetcafe.com),* before tasting chile wine at **Noisy Water Winery** *(noisywaterwinery.com)* and pondering the cool art in the adjacent **Lapis Room** *(lapisroom.com).*

The world's largest balloon festival

What started as a shopping mall in 1972 has ballooned, quite literally, into one of America's largest festivals, attracting nearly one million people every year to **Balloon Fiesta Park** *(balloonfiesta.com; free park entry; Balloon Fiesta tickets $15)* on the northern edge of Albuquerque city limits for nine days in early October. Standing beneath so many balloons is a surreal experience; the 2022 fest reported a record 648.

You arrive at the grounds before sunrise and are ushered into parking lots (shuttles can get you to the grounds and an app tracks where you parked). Then you're greeted by dozens of vendors offering everything from loaded ribbon fries to hot coffee and, of course, breakfast burritos. At dawn, referees in striped uniforms clear the hordes as balloons are laid out flat before being launched one by one. Besides sunrise flights, events throughout the day include drone shows, chainsaw exhibitions, a sunset flight and fireworks.

Riding in a balloon is typically reserved for local crews, though **Rainbow Ryders** *(rainbowryders.com; prices vary)* offers a handful of visitor spots. You'll have a better chance of booking sunrise flights throughout the year.

Balloon Fiesta Park is also home to the **Anderson-Abruzzo Albuquerque International Balloon Museum**

GREEN OR RED CHILE?

New Mexico is not the same as south of the border or even Texas. It has its own distinct flavors, influenced by Pueblo and other Indigenous groups, Spain, Mexico and Hispanic or Mexican Americans.

The dominant ingredient in New Mexican food is chile (spelled like the country, not the meat stew), a spicy bell pepper infused into everything from chocolate to wine, though you'll find it most often as a sauce. Red or green? That's a question you'll hear in New Mexico, asking you to choose your type of chile sauce. Green chiles ripen first and tend to be spicier. Undecided? Ask for Christmas, which means half and half.

Vegetarians beware that chile sauces are usually made with pork.

EATING IN ALBUQUERQUE: BEST NEW MEXICAN FOOD

Sadie's: Gigantic portions of New Mexican food. Seriously, do not tackle the large nachos alone. *10:30am-10pm* **$**

El Pinto: Delicious plates in a Southwestern-themed dining room in an old hacienda. Try red-chile ribs. *11am-9pm Sun-Thu, to 10pm Fri & Sat* **$**

Los Cuates: Our favorite branch on Lomas Blvd has a low-key retro dining room and good red- or green-chile rellenos. Try the cucumber jalapeño margaritas. *11am-9pm* **$**

Los Compadres: Route 66 spot with a huge menu (and lineup) and classics like saucy carne adovada. *9am-8pm Tue-Sat, to 2pm Sun* **$**

SIGHTS
1. Anderson-Abruzzo Albuquerque International Balloon Museum
2. Indian Pueblo Cultural Center
3. Lapis Room
4. San Felipe de Neri Church

ACTIVITIES
5. Rainbow Ryders

SLEEPING
6. Hotel Chaco
7. Monterey Motel
8. Painted Lady

EATING
9. Church Street Cafe
10. El Pinto
11. Indian Pueblo Kitchen
12. Los Compadres
13. Los Cuates
14. Sadie's

DRINKING & NIGHTLIFE
15. High Noon Saloon
16. Noisy Water Winery

ENTERTAINMENT
17. Gathering of Nations Powwow
18. International Balloon Fiesta

(balloonmuseum.com; adult/child/under 5 $6/3/free), which details the history of hot-air balloon flights dating to 1783 with interactive exhibits and games for kids.

Find out about Pueblo culture

North of I-40 on 12th St was the site of one of America's first 'Indian' schools, where Indigenous children were forcibly assimilated and punished for speaking their language or practicing their culture. The land has since been reclaimed by 19 of New Mexico's Pueblo tribes and transformed into the fascinating **Indian Pueblo Cultural Center** (indianpueblo.org; adult/child/under 5 $12/8/free). Learn about the knowledge of agriculture and the stars that allowed thousands of Indigenous groups to thrive in the Southwest through artifacts, interactive videos and exhibits. Guided tours are offered at noon on Thursdays and Fridays.

The center is also home to one of Albuquerque's best places to try New Mexican cuisine, **Indian Pueblo Kitchen** (indianpueblokitchen.org), which serves fry-bread tacos, housemade stews served with Pueblo oven bread and red- or green-chile-smothered enchiladas alongside the Three Sisters (corn, beans and squash).

At the end of April, Albuquerque hosts North America's biggest powwow, **Gathering of Nations** (gatheringofnations.

EATING IN SANTA FE: BEST NEW MEXICAN FOOD

Tia Sophia's: The first to put breakfast burritos on a menu and to offer Christmas sauces. *7am-2pm Mon-Sat, 8am-1pm Sun* $

La Choza: Local favorite, often with a line; blue-corn versions of the specialties and cocktails. *11am-2:30pm & 4:30-9pm Mon-Sat* $$

Cafe Pasqual's: Cozy space with New Mexico classics and dishes that lean south of the border. *8am-9:30pm Wed-Mon* $$

Coyote Cafe: Credited with putting upscale Southwest cuisine on the culinary map. *11:30am-9pm Sun-Thu, to 9:30pm Fri & Sat* $$$

com; entry from $25 per person), which attracts more than 500 tribes from across the Americas and beyond.

Santa Fe

Roam the historic city center

New Mexico's state capital feels culturally, aesthetically and geographically different to others in the US. There are many reasons for this. One of the biggest reasons is that, founded in 1607, it's the oldest capital in the nation and was one of the earliest European settlements – this is reflected in Santa Fe's distinctive architecture. Pueblo Revival style dominates the landscape with low-slung, earth-colored adobe houses inspired by pueblos – built with mud, earth and straw – plus striking old churches, chapels and missions.

Santa Fe is easily walkable and peppered with memorable sites. Start from the **Plaza**, which has stood as the heart of the city for 400 years. The close-by **St Francis Cathedral** *(cbsfa.org; free)* with its dramatic facade in Romanesque Revival style looks more suited to Europe than the Wild West, but inside it's New Mexican in appearance with a Hispanic altarpiece and folk art.

Two minutes by foot south is the **Loretto Chapel** *(loretto chapel.com; adult/child/under 5 $5/3/free)*, the first Gothic-style building west of the Mississippi. The chapel was built by French and Italian architects in 1878, but its unsupported wooden staircase, St Joseph's Miraculous Staircase, is what draws the crowds, spiraling upward without center or side supports.

Up Old Santa Fe Trail, **San Miguel Mission** *(sanmiguel chapel.org; free)* is considered the oldest Catholic Church in the US. Next to the mission, the blue-doored **Casa Vieja** (1646) is considered the oldest house in the US.

NEW MEXICO CULTURAL FESTIVALS

San Ildefenso Feast Day: Traditional dances and Taos Pueblo's famous pottery; January 23.

Taos Fall Arts Festival: Celebrating the creativity of the area; October.

1680 Pueblo Revolt Anniversary: Picuris Pueblo, 20 miles south of Taos, celebrates with a ceremonial foot race, pole climb, dances; August 10.

Fiestas de Taos: Dance and music pours onto the streets in this celebration of Spanish culture; July.

● **SIGHTS**
1 Casa Vieja
2 Georgia O'Keeffe Museum
3 Loretto Chapel
4 San Miguel Mission
5 St Francis Cathedral

● **ACTIVITIES**
6 Santa Fe School of Cooking

● **SLEEPING**
7 La Fonda

● **EATING**
8 Cafe Pasqual's
9 Coyote Cafe
10 Five & Dime
11 Horno
12 Sazón
13 Tia Sophia's

● **DRINKING & NIGHTLIFE**
14 Anasazi
15 Cowgirl

● **INFORMATION**
16 Santa Fe Plaza Visitor Center

Ski, hike and bike

Sitting at more than 7000ft above sea level, Santa Fe is the USA's highest state capital, bordered by the imposing Sangre de Cristo Mountains (part of the Rocky Mountains). It never feels claustrophobic, thanks to easy access to nature and outdoor pursuits like hikes and skiing.

Just 16 miles from town, **Ski Santa Fe** *(skisantafe.com; ski passes $48-90 depending on ability)* in the Sangre de Cristo Mountains offers dry powder like its more famous cousin, Taos Ski Valley, with a higher base elevation (10,350ft). It includes seven lifts and 86 runs. **North Central Regional District** *(ncrtd.org/ski-bus)* offers free buses to the top, stopping along trailheads on the way up the mountain.

Trails here range from all-day adventures to short strolls. From the ski basin parking lot, the challenging 10.8-mile **Raven's Ridge** loop cuts east along the **Upper Winsor Trail** after the first steep mile of switchbacks to follow the Pecos Wilderness boundary high above the tree line to the top of **Lake Peak** (12,409ft).

Aspen Vista, the premier path for immersing yourself in the magical bright-yellow fall foliage, lives up to its name. The first mile of the 11.5-mile full-day trail is easy, gaining little elevation and following an old dirt road.

Learn to cook like a New Mexican

Once you've eaten plenty of breakfast burritos, enchiladas and gallons of green chile, you can learn how to make New Mexican food at home with a specialty cooking class. Family-run **Santa Fe School of Cooking** *(santafeschoolofcooking.com; 3hr class from $100)* has been teaching New Mexican cuisine for more than three decades and offers a number of different kinds of classes in a beautiful space west of the Plaza.

On Fridays, the cooking school leads restaurant tours where you walk around town and meet with top chefs who give a presentation as well as tastings of their dishes and drinks.

Drive from Santa Fe to Taos

Leave Santa Fe northbound and watch shrubby desert transform into lush forest on the 58-mile **High Road to Taos**. The winding road zigzags up past artsy villages and adobe homes, 18th- and 19th- century churches and truly spectacular views. Leave at least four hours to experience all the road has to offer, including stops.

Shortly after leaving Santa Fe, turn into the Hispanic village of **Chimayó**, which was founded in 1598 on a pueblo that had

---

MARGARITA TRAIL

Get a Margarita Trail booklet at the **Santa Fe Visitor Center** or download the app ($2.99) for the ultimate Santa Fe booze crawl. More than 50 restaurants and bars offer jazzed-up margaritas that are $1 off with the booklet or app. Drinks include the **Meow Wolf** Meowgarita (reposado tequila, Cointreau, agave, fresh lime juice, butterfly-pea-flower tea topped with a puffy colorful cloud); the **Cowgirl** Cadillac Margarita (Dulce Vida tequila, Grand Marnier, sweet and sour mix, lime and orange juice); and the **Anasazi** Sandia y Pepino Margarita (Mi Campo tequila, agave, watermelon and cucumber juice, tajin-lime salt rim). Get a stamp at each bar to win prizes, including a T-shirt. You can only earn two stamps per 12 hours.

 EATING IN SANTA FE: OUR PICKS

Five & Dime General Store: Try a Frito Pie – chile, beans, beef, onions and cheese in a bag of Fritos. *9am-9pm* $

Horno: Try the squid-ink capellini at this upscale street-food restaurant a block from the Plaza. *5-9pm Mon-Sat* $$

Sazón: Mexican chef Fernando Olea's delicious, surprising creations put a grin on every patron's face. *5-9pm Mon-Sat* $$$

Sweetwater Harvest Kitchen: Salads and smoothies here use farmers market produce. *10am-3pm Mon-Fri, 9am-3pm Sat & Sun* $$

El Santuario de Chimayó

been abandoned 200 years prior and holds major significance for Catholics. **El Santuario de Chimayó** (*holychimayo.us; free*) was built in 1816 atop a spot of 'holy dirt' said to be miraculous and to hold curative powers. During Holy Week (mid-April) some 30,000 pilgrims walk to Chimayó from Santa Fe in the largest Catholic pilgrimage in the US.

Up the road, turn off into **Truchas**, an 18th-century Spanish town with century-old adobe buildings and a couple of galleries. In **Peñasco**, the **Peñasco Theatre** (*facebook.com/penascotheatre; prices vary*) bills itself as the area's only solar-powered hand-built adobe theatre. Continue northbound by making a U-turn at Hwy 518 to the most forested part of the road to Taos (p870).

Abiquiú
Hike in Georgia O'Keeffe's footsteps

Iconic artist Georgia O'Keeffe spent summers on mesmerizing **Ghost Ranch** (*ghostranch.org; adult/child $10/free*) with its multicolored bluffs, gorgeous canyons, plains and grasslands filled with spectacular trails. O'Keeffe painted more than 100 paintings on these grounds.

Many visit to do the 3-mile climb up to **Chimney Rock**, an enormous pillar that breaks off from the mesa top with breathtaking views.

O'Keeffe's main **home** and studio, where she lived from 1949 to 1984, sits 12 miles south of Ghost Ranch in Abiquiú. It has Native American and Spanish Colonial building styles, and some rooms date to 1744. It was given National Historic Landmark status in 1998 and is now part of Santa Fe's **Georgia O'Keeffe Museum** (*okeeffemuseum.org; adult/child/under 5 $22/12/free*). There's also a nearby **O'Keeffe Welcome Center** next to the Abiquiu Inn, with a gift shop and some of her personal effects.

CONTINENTAL DIVIDE TRAIL

Hundreds of thru-hikers brave the 3100-mile Continental Divide Trail each year, which crosses into New Mexico's **San Pedro Parks Wilderness** northwest of Santa Fe. The trail is less popular but no less extraordinary than some of the US' 11 other National Scenic Trails, including the Appalachian and Pacific Crest trails. Many begin the trail on the US border with Chihuahua in Mexico and wind all the way to Alberta, Canada. It takes six months if you hike 17 miles a day.

In New Mexico, the trail stretches 820 miles from the Southwestern desert through Silver City and Gila National Forest to Grants, Jemez Mountains and the Chama Wilderness before hitting the Colorado Rockies. It can also be hiked in shorter segments.

OPPENHEIMER'S DOWNFALL

J Robert Oppenheimer was born in New York in 1904, visited New Mexico as a teen, then studied at Harvard, Cambridge and Göttingen in Germany before being selected as the physicist in charge of the Manhattan Project. After the bombs were dropped on Japan in 1945, Oppenheimer opposed continued development of nuclear weapons. FBI Director J Edgar Hoover began to investigate Oppenheimer for Communist Party links and while none were found, he was stripped of his security clearance in 1954 during the Red Scare, and dismissed for opposing the arms race.

The US went on to do more than 1000 nuclear tests until 1992. *Oppenheimer*, a film directed by Christopher Nolan, was released in 2023.

Bandelier National Monument
Ancient Indigenous caves and petroglyphs

Ancestors of Navajo and current Pueblo people lived in this 33,000-acre area now run by the National Park Service. Some 3000 settlements have been discovered in **Bandelier National Monument** *(nps.gov/band; $25 per vehicle)*.

You can visit some of the cave dwellings, just 400yd from the visitor center, by climbing ladders on the 1.4-mile **Pueblo Loop Trail**. There are also remains of adobe-brick buildings and petroglyphs on the cliff face. If you're up for a bigger day of hiking, Bandelier is 70% wilderness with 70 miles of backcountry trails. Get a backcountry permit at the visitor center.

Los Alamos
Where the atomic bomb was born

Los Alamos occupies a special place in US history as one of the creation places of the atomic bomb, and its excellent **Bradbury Science Museum** *(lanl.gov/engage/bradbury; free)* is worth making a trip for. Learn about the history and people behind the Manhattan Project, see a replica of the bomb dropped on Nagasaki and learn about the government research that continues today, including nanoscience, sustainable technology and preventing infectious diseases.

The story here doesn't flinch from the truth. It was here, in 1942 at the height of WWII, that Franklin D Roosevelt called on Lieutenant General Leslie Richard Groves Jr and physicist J Robert Oppenheimer to assemble a secret lab to develop a weapon unlike anything the world had ever seen. The result was the world's first atomic bomb detonation, on July 16, 1945, at the Trinity Site in southern New Mexico. The nuclear bombs designed by the Manhattan Project killed an estimated 135,000 to 215,000 people.

Taos
See where Pueblo culture thrives

A magical spot even by the standards of this Land of Enchantment, Taos is a beautiful town in northern New Mexico surrounded by 12,300ft snowcapped peaks that hit a sage-speckled plateau before plummeting 800ft into the Rio Grande Gorge.

One of the oldest continuously inhabited communities in the US and both a UNESCO World Heritage Site and US National Historic Landmark, **Taos Pueblo** *(taospueblo.com; adult/child under 10 $25/free)* is an extraordinary place to

EATING IN TAOS: OUR PICKS

La Cueva Cafe: Probably Taos' most popular restaurant. New Mexican classics from breakfast to close. *10am-8pm Mon-Fri, to 5pm Sat* $

ACEQ: Pronounced 'ah-sec,' this popular Arroyo Seco spot has great food and is Guy Fieri-approved. *5-10pm* $$

Love Apple: Romantic candlelit restaurant in a 19th-century chapel serving seasonal fare and funky wines. Cash only. *5-9pm Wed-Sun* $$

Chokola: Fair-trade and organic bean-to-bar chocolate tasting room in the Plaza for six kinds of mousse, ice cream, cakes and bars. *11am-6pm* $

TAOS

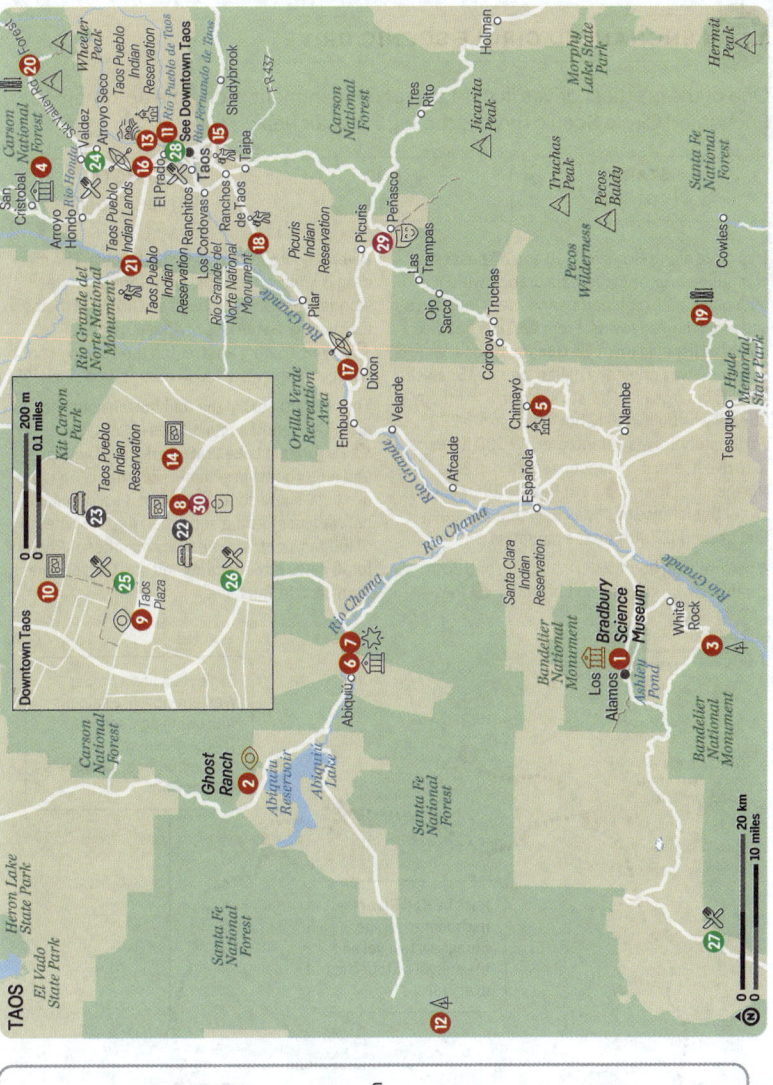

★ HIGHLIGHTS
1 Bradbury Science Museum
2 Ghost Ranch

◉ SIGHTS
3 Bandelier National Monument
4 DH Lawrence Ranch & Memorial
5 El Santuario de Chimayó
6 Georgia O'Keeffe Home
7 O'Keeffe Welcome Center
8 Parsons Gallery of the West
9 Plaza
10 Robert L Parsons Fine Art Gallery
11 San Geronimo Church
12 San Pedro Parks Wilderness
13 Taos Pueblo
14 Wilder Nightingale Fine Art

◉ ACTIVITIES
15 Devisadero Loop Trail
16 Far Flung Adventures
17 New Mexico River Adventures
18 Rift Valley
19 Ski Santa Fe
see 15 South Boundary
20 Taos Ski Valley
21 West Rim

● SLEEPING
22 Doña Luz Inn
23 Historic Taos Inn

● EATING
24 ACEQ
25 Chokola
26 La Cueva Cafe
27 Los Ojos Restaurant & Saloon
28 Love Apple

● ENTERTAINMENT
29 Peñasco Theatre

● SHOPPING
30 El Rincón Trading Post

ENCHANTED CIRCLE SCENIC DRIVE

One of the prettiest drives in this Land of Enchantment, along the aptly named Enchanted Circle Scenic Byway, circling Wheeler Peak.

START	END	LENGTH
Taos	Taos	90 miles; 3–6 hours

This drive along Hwys 522, 38 and 64 passes crystalline lakes, pine forests draped with feldspar, alpine highlands, windswept meadows and old-timey ski towns. From ❶ **Taos** head north to Hispanic town ❷ **Questa**, whose name is a typo – it was originally called 'cuesta,' Spanish for cliff or large hill. Questa's adobe St Anthony's Church was built in 1842 but collapsed in 2008. Fortunately, locals volunteered 49,000 hours to revive it, and it was reconsecrated in 2016. Northeast of town, ❸ **Latir Peak Wilderness** has sweet but intense multiday backpacking trails that ascend 12,708ft up the mountain.

A gold-mining boomtown in the 19th and 20th centuries with saloons and brothels, ❹ **Red River** is now a family-friendly ski town. The main drag is lined with shops, with German-style wooden lodges mixed with an Old West theme. On summer Saturdays at 4pm outside ❺ **Frye's Trading Post**, catch the cowboy shoot-out reenactment, a Red River tradition since 1950.

The western part of the trail flattens out and mountain runoff accumulates in 2400-acre ❻ **Eagle Nest Lake State Park**, filled with pike and motorboats in summer. ❼ **Angel Fire** looks like time-share condo land, but it's a popular ski hill with mostly blue and green runs and plenty of lodges. Loop around the remainder of Rte 64 for 18 miles through farmland and Carson forest, then back to Taos.

Pass by **Red River** in midsummer for the Bluegrass festival and the annual Oktoberfest every fall.

Eagle Nest has a proper Western vibe, like saloons with swinging doors. Try the green-chile cheeseburger at **Cowboy's Corner Cafe**.

In winter, there's ice fishing on the **Eagle Nest Lake** and elk outnumber residents of the neighboring town five to one.

Eagle Nest Lake State Park

see New Mexican Pueblo culture thriving in the present day. Three miles northeast of Taos Plaza, the Pueblo's multistory mud-and-straw adobe apartments stand tall and proud under the backdrop of the Sangre de Cristo Mountains, as they've done for 1000 years.

Taos Pueblo welcomes visitors for guided tours. Visitors are taught about Pueblo ways of life, adobe architecture and history, including the 1680 Pueblo Revolt that tossed out the Spanish. You can also visit Taos Pueblo's unique **San Geronimo Church** *(ologtaos.com; free)*, which highlights Mary rather than Jesus at the pulpit.

Taos Pueblo is closed from late winter (usually end of January) to the third week of March.

The art of Taos

Taos went on to become a trading post on the Santa Fe Trail and later an attraction for early-20th-century artist transplants from New York and California, who came to visit and couldn't leave after witnessing the sapphire-blue skies and paint-stroke sunsets.

Taos centers on its atmospheric **Plaza**, with a green park and benches in the middle of a square of adobe homes, the old courthouse and Taos jail on the north side of the Plaza, and buildings dating to 1796. The nearby **Robert L Parsons Fine Art Gallery** *(parsonsart.com)* on Bent St sells works from Taos Society of Artists painters. Its sister, **Parsons Gallery of the West** *(parsonsart.com/parsonswest)* on Kit Carson Rd, features 20 different artists, mostly from Taos, in a beautiful hacienda built in 1803. Across the road, **Wilder Nightingale Fine Art** *(wnightingale.com)* has been selling an eclectic collection of contemporary Taos art for more than 30 years from its huge gallery. For Indigenous art and jewelry, pop into the dusty museum-like **El Rincón Trading Post** *(instagram.com/elrincontradingpost)*, which has been open since 1909 and hasn't changed much.

BEST MOUNTAIN-BIKING TRAILS AROUND TAOS

Taos Ski Valley & Angel Fire: Ride the lifts and zoom down the mountain.

Rift Valley: Mostly flat, winding single-track trail suitable for intermediate cyclists and fun for advanced riders.

South Boundary: Twenty-eight-mile ride considered one of the nation's best mountain-bike trails. Experienced cyclists only.

West Rim: Easy 9-mile trail in Rio Grande del Norte with great views of the Rio Grande Gorge.

Devisadero: Steep and difficult trail with plenty of rocks. Watch out for rattlesnakes.

Tackle the rivers

From April through October, sections of the Rio Grande near Taos are the best places in New Mexico to go white-water rafting. Guides lead trips into the turbulent **Taos Box** north of town, which has lots of class IV and sometimes class V rapids. Boats do tend to flip, and the remoteness of this area makes it extra scary – and thrilling. If Taos Box intimidates you, the **Racecourse** and **Lower Gorge** downriver near Pilar are popular family-friendly spots with gentler waves.

You can book half-, full- or multiday rafting trips with the reputable and knowledgeable **New Mexico River Adventures** (newmexicoriveradventures.com; rafting $40-450) and **Far Flung Adventures** (farflung.com; rafting $54-400), which has been in the business since 1976 and has permits from the Forest Service and local tribes. Rock climbing, horseback riding and fly-fishing tours are also available.

Taos and DH Lawrence

British poet and novelist David Herbert Lawrence might have only spent two years (1924–26) on the 160-acre ranch he owned here with his wife Frieda, but it was enough to declare that New Mexico 'changed me forever.' Fans of the author who wrote such classics as *Lady Chatterley's Lover* can visit **DH Lawrence Ranch** (dhlawrenceranch.unm.edu; free but donations welcome; 9:30am-3:30pm Tue-Thu), 20 miles north of Taos, now administered by the University of New Mexico. If you manage to make the narrow opening window, you can visit the famous Lawrence Tree painted by Georgia O'Keeffe, the cabin Dorothy Brett stayed in when Lawrence invited her to start a utopian society and the 19th-century homesteader's cabin where the writer worked on *St Mawr*, *David* and *The Plumed Serpent*.

Roswell

Put on your tinfoil hat

In July 1947, two years after the first atomic bomb test in Trinity, 350 people say they witnessed an unidentified flying object crash in the desert outside Roswell. More than 75 years later, questions remain about the crash. Was it a flying saucer, as UFO fanatics believe? Or was it a weather balloon as the US government argued? Or was it something else?

Put on a tinfoil hat and investigate the answer at Roswell's **International UFO Museum & Research Center** (roswellufomuseum.com; adult/child $7/4). The museum

---

BEST SALOONS IN NEW MEXICO

Melody Groves, author of *Hoist a Cold One! Historic Bars of the Southwest*, shares New Mexico's best Old West saloons.

No Scum Allowed: Funky White Oaks bar in an 1884 building – the best part is the name.

Double Eagle: During the Civil War, Confederate officers used the back room of this Mesilla bar as a ballroom.

High Noon Saloon: Albuquerque Old Town saloon bar dating to 1785. It's now a steakhouse and apparently haunted.

Buckhorn Saloon: This Pinos Altos saloon north of Silver City is old, as is the bar itself.

Los Ojos: This Jemez Springs place is 100 years old and cool, too. Stop for beer or food.

EATING IN ROSWELL: OUR PICKS

El Coco Pirata: Probably your best meal in southeast New Mexico. All about seafood, with fresh ceviche and shrimp platters. *10am-9pm* $

Cowboy Cafe: Beloved of locals, this breakfast joint serves hearty New Mexican specialties and burgers. *6am-2pm* $

Martin's Capitol Cafe: Adobe building with Moorish arches. New Mexico classics like burritos, stuffed sopaipillas. *6am-8:30pm Mon-Sat* $

Antigua Cocina: Mexican specialties like *cochinita pibil*, *chile en nogada* and steak with a big tequila list. *11am-10pm Mon-Thu* $$

International UFO Museum & Research Center

details accounts of the Roswell incident and what happened in the aftermath.

Continue your investigation around the corner at **Spaceport Roswell** *(spaceportroswellnm.com; adult/child $14.40/9.50),* where you can put on VR glasses to experience what it might've been like to be on board the flying saucer that crashed outside Roswell, or join Neil Armstrong on the *Apollo 11* mission to the Moon. Across the street, walk beside aliens and try not to get abducted at **Roswell UFO Spacewalk** *(roswellspacewalk.com; $6),* an immersive room filled with creepy dayglow decor and lights.

Las Cruces

Feel the downtown vibe

Las Cruces and its older and smaller sister city Mesilla sit in a broad desert basin beneath the striking eastern peaks of the Organ Mountains. There's something special about the combination of bright, white sunlight, glassy blue skies, flowering cacti, rippling red mountains and desert lowland landscape found here. It's worth stopping by to experience New Mexico's most Hispanic/Latinx-influenced city (60% identify as such), and explore Mesilla's cute adobe homes.

Start by walking along Main St in downtown Las Cruces on a Saturday morning and you'll see this sleepy city come to life. From 8:30am to 1pm, vendors at the **Farmers & Crafts**

CONFEDERATE CAPITAL

In July 1861, a small Confederate force from Texas humiliated a force of Union soldiers more than three times its size, between Fort Fillmore (near Mesilla) and San Augustin Pass. Mesilla went on to briefly become the capital of the Confederate Territory of Arizona, but Confederate control only lasted five weeks before soldiers fled the city and then the state.

The Civil War–era **Fort Selden Historic Site** *(museumfoundation.org; adult/child $5/free),* 20 minutes from downtown Las Cruces, had about 1800 soldiers at its prime, including more than 400 African Americans. Inside is a detailed one-room exhibit, and outside are the fort ruins, including its jail, bakery and barracks. Entry is free with a **New Mexico Culture Pass**.

EATING IN LAS CRUCES: OUR PICKS

!Andele!: Mesilla New Mexican place with a salsa bar, homemade nachos, loaded hot dogs. *8am-9pm Tue-Sun, to 2:30pm Mon* $

La Nueva Casita: Bargain Mexican and New Mexican food, primarily for breakfast. Try the *machaca* scrambled eggs. *9am-3pm Wed-Mon* $

Chala's Wood-Fired Grill: New Mexican done right in Mesilla. Try house-smoked pulled pork. *8am-9pm Mon-Thu, to 9:30pm Fri & Sat, to 2pm Sun* $

Spotted Dog Brewery: Green-chile pesto wings, burgers, cheese, craft beer. *11:30am-10:30pm Mon-Thu, to midnight Fri & Sat, noon-8:30pm Sun* $$

BORDER PATROL

Along I-25, some 22 or so miles north of Las Cruces, signs will tell you to slow down to pass through a US border checkpoint. These types of government checkpoints are common in the southern part of the state, being so close to the border, and you're nearly guaranteed to see one if you're driving. If waved over, you'll have to answer a few questions, or you might not have to do anything at all as a green light flashes you through. Always carry ID, including a valid tourist visa if you're a foreign citizen, as well as car registration or the rental agreement. Be polite and allow them to search inside the trunk if they ask.

Market *(farmersandcraftsmarketoflascruces.com; free)* show off their hauls of local pecans and Hatch chiles, while food trucks sling tacos and churros. Local artisans are here, too, selling pottery, jewelry, fun shirts and the like. Someone might be jamming at **Downtown Blues Coffee** *(downtownbluescoffee.com)*, a cafe, record store and hub of cultural life.

Range a little further and **Mesilla**, technically its own distinct town 4 miles south of downtown, is Las Cruces' most historic neighborhood, and walking around here feels like being in 19th-century Mexico; the trial of outlaw Billy the Kid happened here in 1881. Today Mesilla is a beautifully preserved slice of history with cute adobe houses and a beautiful historic plaza with its 1855 **Basilica of San Albino** *(sanalbino.org; free)*.

The birthplace of the Space Race

Being a high-elevation desert, southern New Mexico is a great place to see the stars – and to launch spaceships.

In Alamogordo, a dusty town at the base of Lincoln National Forest's mountains an hour east of Las Cruces, is the **New Mexico Museum of Space History** *(nmspacemuseum.org; adult/child $8/6)*. Built like a space shuttle, this four-floor museum has interesting exhibits that take you from the history of Indigenous awareness of the stars to Robert H Goddard's liquid fuel rocket test in 1926 to the atomic bomb and modern space tourism.

The tradition continues at Virgin Galactic's **Spaceport America** *(spaceportamerica.com)*, the world's first commercial spaceport and an active rocket test facility, one hour north of Las Cruces. While not open for pop-ins, you can visit by booking a private tour with **Final Frontier Tours** *(spaceportamerica.com/visit; adult/child $49.99/29.99)*. Inside the facility, you'll visit mission control, speak with firefighters about potential crashes, ride the runway and test out the Multi-Axis Trainer (MAT), which prepares astronauts for zero gravity.

Truth or Consequences

Hippies and hot springs

Vying for the title of New Mexico's quirkiest town (the competition is admittedly stiff) is Truth or Consequences (also called T or C), 75 miles north of Las Cruces. Formerly known as Hot Springs, the municipality changed its name in 1950 when the then-host of a radio show called Truth or Consequences promised to air the 10th-anniversary program in the town that changed its name to the title of the show.

Today, Truth or Consequences has an artsy, transient, end-of-the-world vibe, like Joshua Tree 30 years ago. Its small downtown is packed with art galleries and eclectic gift shops. But the main reason to come to Truth or Consequences is to soak in its hot springs. Most hotels and private dwellings have them – all they need to do is dig – but the best are at **Riverbend Hot Springs** *(riverbendhotsprings.com; common pools from $25, private from $35 per 50min)*.

TOP EXPERIENCE

White Sands National Park

Fifty miles east of Las Cruces, ethereal snow-white sand dunes roll on as far as the eye can see like something out of a dream. The phenomenal 275-sq-mile White Sands National Park is nowhere near the ocean; the dunes are actually made from powdered gypsum crystals that blew from an ancient sea over the San Andres and Sacramento Mountains 4000 to 7000 years ago.

Drive

From the visitor center, drive the 16-mile scenic sandy loop (fine for cars and RVs) and stop along the way to sink your toes in the dunes. The temperature can change by 50°F in a day. Bring lots of water (1 gallon per day per person). Picnic areas along the drive offer shaded benches for lunch.

Walk (or Slide)

Walking in the silence and solitude of the dunes is almost a spiritual experience, especially at sunrise or sunset when the sea of sand sparkles. Escape the crowds on the **Alkali Flat**, a 5-mile round-trip backcountry trail through the heart of White Sands (follow the markers as it's easy to get lost). It's really a winter trail but possible to hike if you come early before it's hot. Or try the simple 1-mile loop **Dune Life Nature Trail**, which climbs two steep dunes rich with desert plant life.

Tumble down the dune or slide down on a sled or sandbar of your choice. You can buy/rent a plastic saucer ($24.99/15) at the visitor-center gift shop. You can rent a board for $25 to surf the dunes. Buy wax to make it a faster experience.

Camp

You can camp in the vast desert on the 2-mile round-trip **Backcountry Camping Loop Trail** (no water, shade or toilets). When darkness falls, the dunes mirror the night sky for ultimate blackness – the Milky Way is visible on a moonless night. At the time of research, camping was unavailable due to maintenance – check before a visit.

TOP TIPS

● Map GPS points on your trail, including where your car is. It's easy to get lost.

● The dunes get more impressive further into the park, so go to the furthest point first.

● Bring sunglasses and sunscreen – reflection can cause sunburn under your chin.

● Note that the park can close during nearby missile tests.

PRACTICALITIES

● nps.gov/whsa
● $25 per vehicle

Places We Love to Stay

$ Budget $$ Midrange $$$ Top End

Las Vegas
MAP P798

Luxor $ A pyramid-shaped, Egyptian-themed resort with cutting-edge entertainment and comfy rooms.

El Cortez $ A Fremont St icon since 1941, when the mob ran the joint. Recently revamped and adults only.

Cosmopolitan $$ These digs are the hippest on the Strip, with rooms featuring balconies, Japanese tubs and plush furnishings.

Skylofts $$$ Inside the MGM Grand, these glamorous two-story apartments have every indulgence, from spa tubs to gourmet kitchens. Butler included.

Southern Nevada

Baker Creek Campground $ Unfurl your tent next to an alpine stream under a canopy of aspens in Great Basin National Park.

Atlatl Rock Campground $ Gorgeous sites among sandstone formations at the heart of jaw-dropping Valley of Fire State Park.

Hidden Canyon Retreat $$ A breathtaking and historic resort tucked into a vast canyon and stretching over 375 acres near Great Basin National Park.

Grand Canyon National Park
MAP P815

Bright Angel Lodge $ Simple lodge rooms and rustic cabins on the canyon edge are excellent budget accommodations.

El Tovar $$$ Public spaces in this wooden lodge ooze old-world national-park glamor, but room aesthetics vary in appeal.

Sedona & Around

Wigwam Motel $ Each room at this 1937 motel on Route 66 in Holbrook is a self-contained concrete tipi.

La Posada $$ An impressively restored 1930s hacienda in Winslow with artistic, period-styled rooms named for illustrious former guests.

Jerome

Connor Hotel (p826) **$** Twelve restored rooms capture the Victorian period, with pedestal sinks, flower wallpaper and pressed-tin ceilings.

Jerome Grand (p826) **$$$** Built in 1926 as a hospital, the sturdy fortress plays up its unusual history with halls filled with relics of the past.

Prescott

Hotel St Michael (p826) **$$** Gargoyles, ghosts and a 1925 elevator keep things offbeat at this Victorian-era hotel on Whiskey Row.

Hotel Vendome $$ This dapper inn, dating from 1917, blends up-to-date style with period touches. Ask about the ghost (Abby) in room 16.

Flagstaff

Americana Motor Hotel $ Revamped rooms celebrate the '70s with disco balls and space-age decor. Fun vibe and two free drinks at check-in.

Weatherford Hotel (p828) **$** It's not for everyone – and potentially loud – but this historic hotel in the thick of the action downtown maintains turn-of-the-20th-century authenticity.

Canyon de Chelly

Thunderbird Lodge $ This ranch-style hotel with modern rooms is the only lodging in the park. Offers canyon tours.

Spider Rock Campground $ Peaceful Navajo-run campground surrounded by pinyon and juniper trees.

Tucson
MAP P838

Tuxon $ Former Motel 6 converted into a minimalist-chic dream. Immediately west of downtown off I-10.

Hotel McCoy $$ Welcoming guests with genuine friendliness and emblazoned with murals, this is our local favorite. Enjoy local craft beer at night and an oatmeal bar in the morning.

Hacienda del Sol Guest Ranch Resort $$$ This relaxing refuge has artist-designed Southwest-style rooms and teems with unique touches.

Bisbee

Shady Dell $ Vintage Airstreams feature mid-century decor at this retro-minded trailer park in Bisbee.

Copper Queen Hotel $$ Older than the state of Arizona itself, Copper Queen Hotel opened in 1902 and was John Wayne's Bisbee hotel of choice. Most of the original decor remains.

Torrey

Torrey Schoolhouse B&B $$ Sleep in the now-cozy former classrooms of this 1917 schoolhouse.

Skyview $$$ Reach the rooms, some with private hot tubs, through a 'slot canyon' art installation, or spend a starry night in a geodesic dome.

Bryce Canyon National Park & City

Lodge at Bryce Canyon $$ Charmingly rustic 1920s lodge; the cabins are a better pick than the generic motel-style rooms.

Bryce Canyon Grand Hotel $$ The large, clean rooms here are a step up from other hotels clustered outside the park entrance.

East Zion

Zion Ponderosa Ranch Resort (p861) **$$** Families love this activity-rich ranch on 6.25 sq miles with swimming pools, climbing walls and mini-golf.

Zion Mountain Ranch $$$ A luxury ranch with six types of cabins, larger lodges and its own herd of roaming bison.

Albuquerque MAP P866

Monterey Motel $ Revived Route 66 motel near Old Town with Tempur-Pedic mattresses, color-changing pool and bar.

Painted Lady $$ Former 19th-century brothel transformed into a bed and brew (beer) and backyard trolley taproom.

Hotel Chaco $$$ Modern Pueblo-style boutique hotel beautifully decorated with precious art; great rooftop bar.

Santa Fe MAP P867

Silver Saddle Motel $ A 1958 Route 66 motel revived in 2022 with a hip California vibe and sleek modern bathrooms.

El Rey Court $$ Revived 1936 auto court with 85 stylish rooms, saltwater pool and bar with live music every Wednesday.

La Fonda $$$ Former end to Santa Fe Trail, then a Harvey House designed by John Gaw Meem and now a luxury hotel on the Plaza.

Taos MAP P871

Doña Luz Inn $$ Each of the eight rooms in this joyful B&B is a work of Southwestern art.

Historic Taos Inn $$ Old inn with wooden furnishings, adobe fireplaces, lots of Southwest charm and a good restaurant.

Roswell Area

Roswell Inn $ Rare independent motel updated in 2015 with bargain prices and continental breakfast.

Home2 Suites by Hilton $$ Fresh four-floor Hilton with a pool, gym and buffet breakfast. Roswell's nicest option.

Las Cruces

Best Western Mission Inn $ Prettier than your typical chain hotel. Adobe walls and Hispanic art at reception.

Lundeen Inn of the Arts $ Cozy, seven-room family-run alternative to chains. Also hosts a gallery with Southwestern art.

Chandelier Bar, Cosmopolitan

Researched and curated by Helena Smith

California

THE LEISURELY LEFT COAST

Epic national parks, wild coastlines, spectacular cities and a progressive vibe. What's not to like, California?

From misty Northern California redwood forests to sun-kissed Southern California beaches, the enchanted Golden State makes Disneyland seem normal. Combining bohemian spirit and high-tech savvy, California embraces contrast and contradictions. It is home to both vibrant metropolises and rugged wilderness, snowy mountains and desert expanses, and miles and miles of spectacular coastline.

It was here that the hurly-burly Gold Rush kicked off in the mid-19th century, where poet and naturalist John Muir rhapsodized about the Sierra Nevada's 'range of light,' where Jack Kerouac and the Beat Generation defined what it meant to hit the road, and where the twin dream factories of tech and entertainment flourished.

Above all, this is a state that celebrates the good life – whether that means cracking open a bottle of old-vine zinfandel, climbing a 14,000ft peak or surfing the Pacific. The Golden State has surged ahead of France to become the world's sixth-largest economy. But like a kid that's grown too fast, California still hasn't figured out how to handle the hassles that come along with such rapid growth, including housing shortages, traffic gridlock and rising costs of living.

Escapism is always an option here, thanks to Hollywood blockbusters and legalized marijuana dispensaries. But California is coming to grips with its international status and taking leading roles in such global issues as environmental standards, online privacy, marriage equality and immigrant rights.

MICHAEL RUNKEL/GETTY IMAGES

THE MAIN AREAS

SAN FRANCISCO & THE BAY AREA
Vertiginous streetscapes and a beautiful bay. **p886**

NORTHERN CALIFORNIA: REDWOODS & WINE COUNTRY
Giant trees and tasty vintages. **p911**

YOSEMITE, LAKE TAHOE & GOLD COUNTRY
Towering rock faces and historic towns. **p925**

For places to stay in California, see p977

Hiker, Joshua Tree National Park (p963)

CENTRAL CALIFORNIA: THE COAST & SACRAMENTO
Wild coast and the green Cali capital. **p937**

LOS ANGELES & THE DESERTS
City of stars fringed by desert.
p949

SOUTHERN CALIFORNIA: DISNEYLAND TO SAN DIEGO
Find Mickey on the route south.
p967

THE GUIDE

CALIFORNIA

Northern California: Redwoods & Wine Country, p911

California's redwoods will stop you in your tracks. Or possibly send you to the nearest vineyard for fine local vintages.

Yosemite, Lake Tahoe & Gold Country, p925

Yosemite's improbable sheer rocks are nature at its most imposing, Lake Tahoe lures hikers and skiers, and the Gold Country's pretty cities entice.

San Francisco & the Bay Area, p886

Grab your coat and a handful of glitter, and enter a wonderland of fog and fabulousness. So long, inhibitions; hello, San Francisco!

Central California: The Coast & Sacramento, p937

Cali's capital features a wealth of historic buildings, its streets overarched with trees, while coastal California is romantically windswept.

Los Angeles & the Deserts, p949

LA's life-affirming moments: a cracked-ice cocktail, a hike into Griffith Park, a pink-washed sunset over Venice Beach, the perfect taco...

Southern California: Disneyland to San Diego, p967

Sunny San Diego is a collection of villages tied into a laid-back city with 60 beaches. Disneyland represents the ultimate escape from reality.

Find Your Way

California crams incredible geographic diversity into 163,696 sq miles: the mighty Sierras, the fertile Central Valley, a craggy coastline and arid deserts. From lofty Mt Whitney to the depths of Death Valley, there's a lot of ground to cover.

TRAIN
The California coast provides superb scenery for the north-south *Coast Starlight* and *Pacific Surfliner* trains; the Capitol Corridor route cuts east-west across the north of the state; while the *San Joaquins* trains cross the Central Valley and Sacramento, with connections to Yosemite.

CAR
Between LA, San Francisco and Northern California, the fastest route is I-5 through the San Joaquin Valley. Hwy 101 is slower but more picturesque. The most scenic – and slowest – route is Hwy 1 (Pacific Coast Hwy), but check first to see if there are closures.

BUS
Greyhound and Amtrak Thruway buses connect destinations across the state, providing an affordable alternative to car travel. You can speed up your trip by combining rail travel with bus trips to more out-of-the-way places.

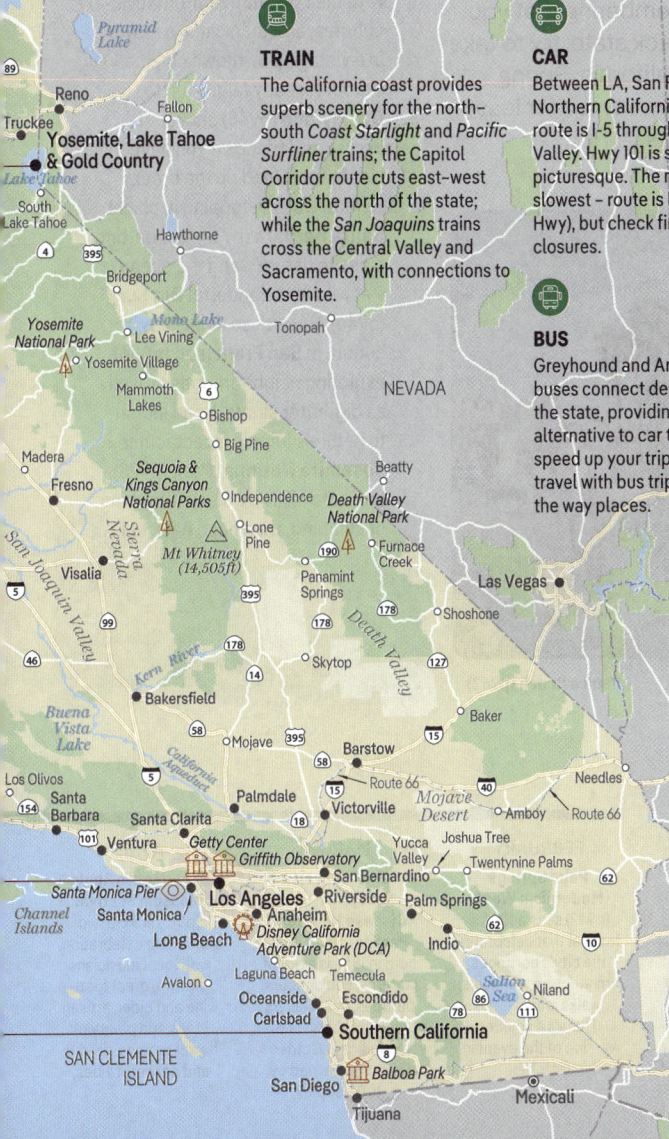

Plan Your Time

It's worth remembering that you are in a laid-back state: try to take your time in California. Spring and fall are prime times for less-pressured visits.

Venice Beach (p962)

One Week to Explore

● Trying to capture California in a nutshell you can start with the superlative galleries and sweeping beaches of **Los Angeles** (p949), with their distinctive alternative cultures, and then catch a movie in a vintage Downtown cinema. Detour for zany family fun to **Disneyland** (p968) and meet Mickey and friends if you have kids in tow. Head up the breezy Central Coast, stopping in chichi **Santa Barbara** (p937) and getting close to nature – and the ocean – at wild and wonderful **Big Sur** (p944). Get a dose of big-city culture in **San Francisco** (p886), exploring neighborhoods as well as big-hitter sights. Head inland to nature's temple, spectacular **Yosemite National Park** (p928), for some hiking, waterfall-bathing or climbing, then head back to LA.

SEASONAL HIGHLIGHTS

Californians know how to have fun, and you'll never be far from a festival or event. In a food-loving state, many of these are focused on celebrating fine seasonal produce.

FEBRUARY

Palm Springs Modernism Week (p942) sees a 10-day festival that celebrates the city's gorgeous architecture with talks, walks and events. There's a smaller version of the event in October.

MARCH

In February or March, San Francisco's **Chinese New Year Parade** (p897), first held in 1851, is a riot of lanterns, lion dancers, parades, stilt walkers and acrobats. The magnificent Golden Dragon is carried by 100 people.

APRIL

Sebastapol's **Apple Blossom Festival** (p815) is a classic springtime celebration, with local musicians playing, great food, wine and cider, artisan stalls and plenty of flower crowns, tie-dye and peaceful vibes.

Two Weeks in the Golden State

● Follow the earlier one-week itinerary, but at a less frenetic pace, taking time for more ocean stops at destinations such as **Carmel-by-the-Sea** (p943). Add side trips to NorCal's **Wine Country** (p911) for leisurely vineyard visits and farm-to-fork eating, with excursions to see some big trees, or head to magnificent **Lake Tahoe** (p925), perched high up in the Sierra Nevada, which draws hikers and water-sports fans as well as skiers and snowboarders in the winter months.

● In Southern California, laid-back **San Diego** (p973) takes you off the usual city trail and offers a multitude of beaches for dipping and dreaming, while **Joshua Tree National Park** (p963), near the chic desert resort of **Palm Springs** (p962), features some truly arresting plant life and vistas.

California for a Month

● Do everything described in the earlier itineraries, and then some. From San Francisco, head up the foggy north coast, starting in Marin County at **Point Reyes** (p907). Stroll Victorian-era **Mendocino** (p916) and **Eureka** (p920), find yourself on the **Lost Coast** (p919) and ramble through fern-filled **Redwood National & State Parks** (p921), whose lofty trees will keep you gazing upwards.

● Inland, snap a perfect photo of **Mt Shasta** (p922), drive through **Lassen Volcanic National Park** (p924) with its sulfur ponds and bubbling mud pools, and visit California's historic and enchanting **Gold Country** (p925), with time to absorb alternative culture and pine-cloaked hills in picturesque **Nevada City** (p935). Trace the backbone of the Eastern Sierra before winding down into **Death Valley** (p964).

JUNE
Art at the Source (p815) in Sonoma sees artist studios opening around town and across the area, with printmaking, painting, sculpture, jewelry-making and more. It's a great time to buy unique local gifts.

JULY
July 4th celebrations usher in **high summer** in California. While temperatures and visitor numbers are often high, it is nonetheless an action-packed time to visit. Be sure to book accommodations in advance.

SEPTEMBER
The ultimate small town event and celebration of seasonal fare, the **Kelseyville Pear Festival** (p819) sees three stages crammed with musicians and dancers, plus over 100 craft and food vendors.

OCTOBER
In late October and early November, the **Paderewski Festival** (p942) in Paso Robles comprises concerts showcasing the work of Polish musician turned rancher Ignacy Paderewski.

San Francisco & the Bay Area

RADICAL THINKING | ARCHITECTURAL GLORY | WILD BAY

GETTING AROUND

Muni buses connect the Wharf, Marina and Presidio with points beyond; Golden Gate Transit crosses the bridge; and Presidio GO shuttles cover Presidio parks. Download maps and schedules – especially if you're headed to the Presidio, where cell signal is variable. The best way to see Fisherman's Wharf and Presidio nature trails is at your own pace, with frequent stops for entertainment and photos. Cover the waterfront on rental bikes with pickups at the Presidio and/or Wharf, but book ahead on weekends.

Adventurous food, wild entertainment, trippy tech: a weekend in San Francisco can seem like a quick trip into the future, except that you're surrounded by bedazzling Victorian architecture. Gold found in nearby Sierra Nevada foothills turned a sleepy 800-person village into a port city of 100,000 freewheeling prospectors, opera divas, con artists and laborers from across the globe. The psychedelic '60s took off here, and the Summer of Love brought free food, love and music to the Haight. As in San Francisco's early days, new ideas keep arriving here. So come on in: you're just in time for its next act. In the Bay Area, visit wizened ancient redwoods body-blocking the sun, and herds of elephant seals on the sands of Point Reyes. Oakland is the diverse, radically proud place San Francisco once was, while Berkeley, with its long-standing university, continues at the forefront of left-leaning political causes.

R&R in the Presidio

MAP P892

Play in an ex-army outpost

'Presidio' means fort in Spanish – but in San Francisco, it's a playground for the people. It started in 1776 as a Spanish military post built by conscripted Ohlone people, and was officially retired from its military duties in 1996. To the obvious delight of shorebirds, puppies, locals and visitors, the **Presidio of San Francisco** is now a national park. To allow wildlife to thrive in the park, commuter traffic was rerouted underground – revealing glorious views clear across the bay from driftwood-shaped picnic benches at **Tunnel Tops** park, with the nature-themed **Outpost Playground** downhill. This is wildly popular for its nature-themed play structures, water features, nearby food trucks, picnic facilities and clean bathrooms.

On hot days, race the crowds to **Baker Beach**, the sandy Presidio cove with spectacular views of the Golden Gate framed by wind-sculpted pines – plus nude sunbathing behind the

SAN FRANCISCO & THE BAY AREA

rocks on the clothing-optional, gay-friendly, no-photography-allowed north end. Picnickers and sand-castle architects stick to the sandy south end, near the parking.

Other rest and recreation opportunities abound here. Civilians can now throw strikes at the post's **Presidio Bowl bowling alley** *(presidiobowl.com; per lane up to 6 people before 6pm weekdays/weekends $55/75, after 6pm weekdays/weekends $75/85, shoe rental $7.50)* or bounce off walls inside an ex-airplane hangar lined with trampolines called the **House of Air** *(houseofair.com; adult/child 1hr $20-28)*. The post's former PX (provisions warehouse) is now a **Sports Basement** *(sportsbasement.com)* that stocks bikes, wetsuits and other sporting equipment to rent, buy or trade.

☑ TOP TIP

Plan outfits strategically, as coastal weather shifts suddenly. Dress in layers: windbreaker for Golden Gate Bridge hikes, cozy sweater for panoramic Presidio picnics and nice (but washable) shirt for seafood feasts at the Wharf or Marina.

EATING IN THE PRESIDIO: FOOD TRUCKS TO CHASE — MAP P892

Borsch Mobile: Ukrainian comfort food like borscht and potato dumplings warm the belly on a blustery day. *hours vary* $

Señor Sigsig: Filipino-style saucy, succulent meats and adobo garlic rice folded into a burrito – lunch is a wrap. *hours vary* $

Fort Point Beer: Brews crafted just uphill go down even easier on sunny Presidio Parade Grounds with Dungeness crab rolls. *hours vary* $

Kabob Trolley: Get your pick of Afghani-spiced meats described as 'hella Halal' packed into sliders, wrapped into 'gyrritos,' or piled on fries to share... maybe. *hours vary* $

SAN FRANCISCO & THE BAY AREA CALIFORNIA

THE GUIDE

DOWNTOWN SAN FRANCISCO

HIGHLIGHTS
1. San Francisco Museum of Modern Art (SFMOMA)

SIGHTS
2. Cartoon Art Museum
3. Chinese Historical Society of America
4. City Hall
5. Civic Center
6. Filbert Street Steps
7. Francisco Street Steps
8. Jack Kerouac Alley
9. Musée Mécanique
10. Pier 39
11. San Francisco Carousel
12. San Francisco Main Library
13. Tenderloin Museum

ACTIVITIES
14. Adventure Cat
15. Red & White Fleet
16. Tenderloin Museum Walking Tours

SLEEPING
17. Fairmont San Francisco
18. Green Tortoise Hostel
19. Hotel Bohème
20. Orchard Garden Hotel
21. Pacific Tradewinds Hostel

EATING
22. Bini's Kitchen
23. Dim Sum Bistro
24. Dragon Horse
25. Estrellita's Snacks
26. Fairuz Eatery
27. Golden Boy
28. Good Mong Kok
29. Hang Ah Tea Room
30. Hinodeya Ramen Union Square
31. Mario's Bohemian Cigar Store Cafe
32. Molinari
33. Moya
34. Palermo II Delicatessen
35. Pinecrest Diner
36. Tempest Bar & Box Kitchen
37. Today Food
38. Yank Sing

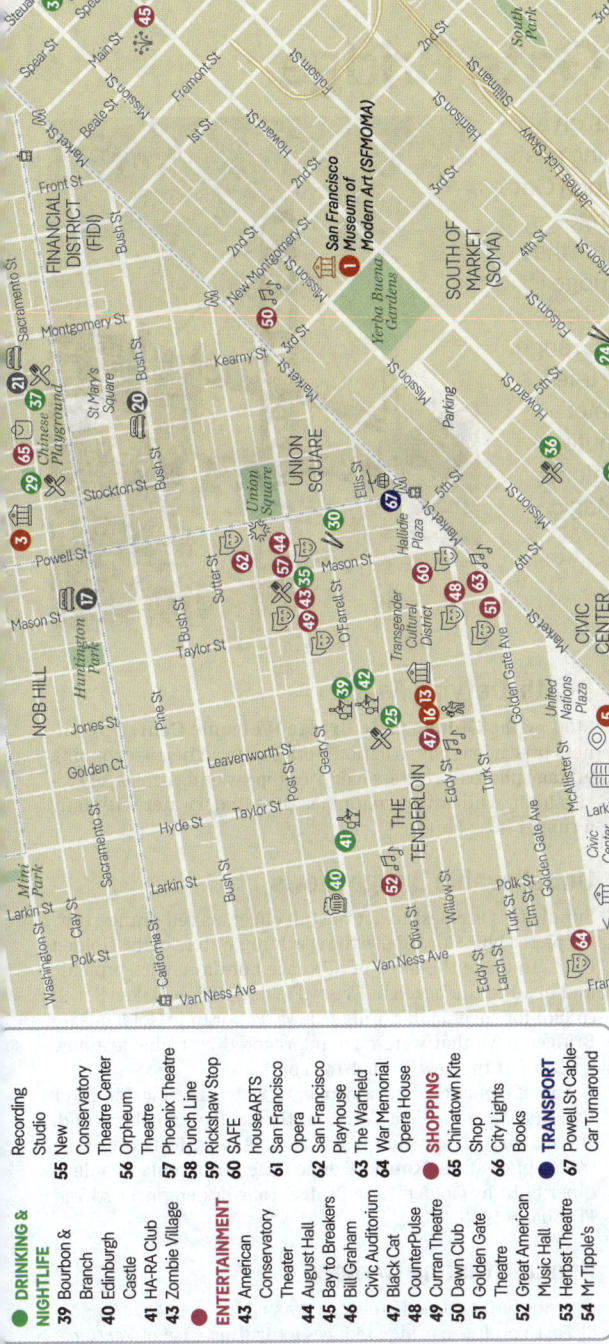

● DRINKING & NIGHTLIFE
- 39 Bourbon & Branch
- 40 Edinburgh Castle
- 41 HA-RA Club
- 43 Zombie Village

● ENTERTAINMENT
- 43 American Conservatory Theater
- 44 August Hall
- 45 Bay to Breakers
- 46 Bill Graham Civic Auditorium
- 47 Black Cat
- 48 CounterPulse
- 49 Curran Theatre
- 50 Dawn Club
- 51 Golden Gate Theatre
- 52 Great American Music Hall
- 53 Herbst Theatre
- 54 Mr Tipple's
- 55 New Conservatory Theatre Center
- 56 Orpheum Theatre
- 57 Phoenix Theatre
- 58 Punch Line
- 59 Rickshaw Stop
- 60 SAFE
- 61 houseARTS San Francisco Opera
- 62 San Francisco Playhouse
- 63 The Warfield
- 64 War Memorial Opera House

● SHOPPING
- 65 Chinatown Kite Shop
- 66 City Lights Books

● TRANSPORT
- 67 Powell St Cable-Car Turnaround

889

CALIFORNIA SAN FRANCISCO & THE BAY AREA

TOP EXPERIENCE

Golden Gate Bridge

No other bridge puts on a show like this. Morning mists lift to reveal the Golden Gate Bridge, glowing orange-red against blue skies: the sleek suspension bridge is painted a signature shade called International Orange. Stick around for the late-afternoon grand finale: as fog swallows commute traffic, deco towers float above the clouds. Magic.

CANADASTOCK/SHUTTERSTOCK

TOP TIPS

● Always wear a water-resistant outer layer.

● Bicycles and e-bikes are allowed on bridge sidewalks, but not skateboards, electric scooters or skates.

● Volunteer City Guides lead free bridge tours ($20 donation suggested) most Sundays and Thursdays at 11am, departing from outside the Welcome Center.

PRACTICALITIES

● goldengate.org
● vehicle toll: northbound free, southbound $9.50
● Welcome Center: 9am-6pm

Death-Defying Feats

Stop by the **Golden Gate Bridge Welcome Center** to witness precarious construction work captured in jaw-dropping vintage photos – riveters balance atop swaying cables 80 stories high, while divers plummet 110ft underwater with only a rubber hose for air.

Unbelievable Bridge Views

Sunny days are best to get the full effect, as red-orange towers pierce blue skies above the sparkling waters of the Golden Gate. To make the most of SF's rare hot days, pack a picnic and head to the beach at Crissy Field (p893) or Baker Beach (p886) for spectacular bridge views. Panoramic Golden Gate Bridge views that were once interrupted by traffic are now revealed at the new Tunnel Tops park.

Fog aficionados don raincoats to watch the marine layer roll past Marin's Vista Point, on the bridge's northern end. Or you can stay dry and watch acrobatic fog feats over fair-trade coffee at the **Round House Café**, the circular art deco diner built by Golden Gate Bridge ironwork engineer Alfred Finnila in 1938.

Scene-Stealing Cameos

Cinema buffs know Hitchcock was right: seen from below at Fort Point, the bridge induces a thrilling case of *Vertigo*.

TOP EXPERIENCE
Golden Gate Park

When San Franciscans refer to 'the park,' there's only one that gets the definite article: Golden Gate Park. Everything SF holds dear is here: free spirits and free music, butterfly domes and underground art, chatty penguins and hushed redwood groves, tenacious bonsai and massive, mellow bison. Landmark venues celebrating nature, music, art and science are dotted across the park's 1017 acres.

Japanese Tea Garden

Art in the Park

There's no denying the park's all-star art attraction: the **de Young Museum** (*famsf.org; adult/youth $20/free*). The cross-cultural collection featuring Olmec stone heads and Turkish kilims alongside California crafts and avant-garde American art has been broadening artistic horizons for a century.

Park Music Events

Golden Gate Park has hosted epic festivals ever since the 1967 Human Be-In, when free spirits gathered to 'tune in, turn on, drop out.' Today, multistage festivals are held around Polo Fields – notably free **Hardly Strictly Bluegrass** (*hardlystrictlybluegrass.com*), held in the first weekend in October.

Natural Wonders

At the east entrance to the park, you can't miss the grandly elegant **Conservatory of Flowers** (*gggp.org; adult/youth & senior/child $17/7/3*). This gloriously restored 1878 Victorian greenhouse is home to freaky outer-space orchids and serene floating lilies. **San Francisco Botanical Garden** (*gggp.org; adult/youth & senior/child $17/7/3*) covers a world of vegetation, from South African savanna to New Zealand cloud forest.

Since 1894 the 5-acre **Japanese Tea Garden** (*gggp.org; adult/youth & senior/child $15/7/3; first hour free*) has blushed pink with cherry blossoms in spring and turned flaming red with maple leaves in fall.

TOP TIPS

● John F Kennedy Dr is pedestrian-only starting at 9th Ave – a weekend hot spot with roller disco and free Lindy Hop dance lessons.

● Volunteer docents lead free tours covering park history; for times, see sfcityguides.org.

PRACTICALITIES

● sfrecpark.org
● 24hr
● free

Happy Trails

MAP P892

Walk on San Fran's wild side

Hiking adventures begin at the **Presidio Visitors Center**, well-supplied with trail maps. For a moderately challenging, inspirational 1.4-mile hike, follow the **Ecology Trail** through redwood groves and spring wildflower meadows to **Inspiration Point** for bird's-eye bay views, then push onward to reach the Presidio's artistic pinnacle: Andy Goldsworthy's **Spire**, made from reclaimed cypress trees. Adventurous hikers take on the 2.7-mile **Batteries to Bluffs Trail**, heading uphill above Baker Beach (p886) to splendid Golden Gate Bridge vistas.

HIGHLIGHTS
1. Golden Gate Bridge
2. Golden Gate Park
3. Ocean Beach
4. Presidio of San Francisco

SIGHTS
5. Arion Press
6. Baker Beach
7. Bay Area Discovery Museum
8. Conservatory of Flowers
9. Crissy Field
10. de Young Museum
11. Fort Baker
12. Fort Mason Center
13. Fort Point
14. Haines Gallery
15. Japanese Tea Garden
16. Lands End
17. Palace of Fine Arts
18. San Francisco Botanical Garden
19. SF Camerawork
20. Spire
21. St John Coltrane Church
22. Tunnel Tops
23. Wave Organ

ACTIVITIES
24. Batteries to Bluffs Trail
25. Coastal Trail
26. House of Air
27. Oceanic Society
28. Presidio Bowl

SLEEPING
29. Cavallo Point Lodge
30. HI San Francisco Fisherman's Wharf
31. Hotel del Sol
32. Lodge at the Presidio
33. Parsonage
34. Union Street Inn

EATING
35. Al6
36. Atelier Crenn
37. Borsch Mobile
38. Dalida
39. Greens
40. Izzy's Steakhouse
41. Kabob Trolley
42. Komeya No Bento
43. La Fromagerie
44. Lucca Delicatessen
45. Señor Sigsig
46. Warming Hut

DRINKING & NIGHTLIFE
47. Beach Chalet
48. Fort Point Beer
49. Round House Café
50. Travis Marina

ENTERTAINMENT
51. BATS Improv
52. Hardly Strictly Bluegrass
53. Magic Theatre
54. San Francisco Art Fair

SHOPPING
55. Fort Mason Outdoor Markets
56. Sports Basement

INFORMATION
57. Golden Gate Bridge Welcome Center
58. Presidio Visitors Center

BEST WAYS TO SAIL AWAY

When the fog lifts and the sun shines, only one thing tops waterfront strolls: boating on the bay. These are our top picks for setting sail in San Francisco.

Oceanic Society: Naturalist-led Pacific whale-watching expeditions run during migration seasons. *(oceanicsociety. org; 7½hr; per person $300)*

Adventure Cat: Skim across the bay with the wind in your hair on catamaran trips, including 'Sail and Jail' getaways to/from Alcatraz. *(adventurecat.com; 90min cruise adult/child $75/35, Sail and Jail $125)*

Red & White Fleet: SF's original sunset bay cruises since 1892 – ring boxes keep popping. New triple-decker boats offer full bars and snacks. *(redandwhite. com; 1hr cruise adult/child $39/29, 2hr sunset cruise $58/38)*

Follow San Franciscan regulars to **Crissy Field** to stroll, jog, bike, skate or roll along scenic, flat, wheelchair-accessible paths. The strip where military planes once landed is now a reclaimed tidal marsh, where birders perch on strategically positioned benches. Puppies chase kite-fliers across Crissy Field's grassy lawn, and windsurfers skim bay waters along **East Beach**. Pick up the Bay Trail to reach **Fort Point** (1.6 miles from East Beach) and head over the Golden Gate Bridge (p890), or stop at certified-green cafe **Warming Hut** to browse California field guides and warm up with fair-trade coffee.

Showtime at Fort Mason Center
MAP P892

Watch talents launch in waterfront waterhouses

San Francisco takes subversive glee in turning military installations into civilian playgrounds. **Fort Mason** *(fort mason.org; free)* was an embarkation point for WWII troops, but today it launches cutting-edge theater and comedy. Pushing boundaries since 1967, **Magic Theatre** *(magictheatre. org; tickets sliding scale $35-75)* stages breakthrough works by provocative playwrights. The Magic houses stunning new murals and artistic residencies plus freeform jazz worship services for SF's legendary St John Coltrane Church.

Next door, Bay Area Theater Sports, aka **BATS Improv** *(improv.org; tickets adult/student $25/20)* dares you to suggest plot twists for raucous improvised comedy shows. Take center stage at improv workshops or weekend intensives

ST JOHN COLTRANE

'There's music in his name,' proclaims the reverend at the African Orthodox **St John Coltrane Church**, a place of worship founded by passionate Bird fans and social activists Franzo and Marina King: Coltrane was posthumously made patron saint of the church in 1982. Mass kicks off with a joyous jam session Sundays at 11am in the Magic Theatre, and all are invited to participate – if you have an instrument to play or a groove in your soul, bring it. Over sessions that can run for five hours, liturgy is intermingled with fellowship and jamming. There's also a monthly meditation based around *A Love Supreme*, Coltrane's masterful 1964 album, which was recorded in one session. Even nonbelievers leave the church feeling Bird's sprit.

like improvised Shakespeare. Book in advance: classes fill quickly.

Make Art, Not War
Find artistic inspiration in military storehouses

MAP P892

During WWII, Fort Mason shipped out 23 million tons of wartime supplies – but now its storehouses supply artistic inspiration to 1.4 million visitors annually. Dockside nonprofit **SF Camerawork** (sfcamerawork.org; free) has showcased next-wave photographers since 1974, while **Haines Gallery** (hainesgallery.com; free) represents leading global contemporary artists like Andy Goldsworthy and Ai Weiwei. **Arion Press** (arionpress.com; free) showcases limited edition, letterpress art books featuring collaborations by leading poets and artists. The former pier warehouse, now known as Herbst Pavilion, includes arts-and-craft fairs among its arsenal of events, with annual highlights including spring's **San Francisco Art Fair**.

Brunch with Bridge Views
Chew the scenery at Greens

MAP P892

Since 1979, Fort Mason's ex-army mess hall has been commandeered by female star chefs, inventing flavor-bomb vegetarian dishes with organic ingredients from Marin's Buddhist Green Gulch Farm. Reserve ahead for bayfront tables at **Greens** (greensrestaurant.com) with breathtaking Golden Gate Bridge views, savor bar bites with Buddha-hand-infused cocktails at JB Blunk's reclaimed-redwood-stump tables, or get boxed lunches to enjoy on the docks of the bay.

Strike Poses at Palace of Fine Arts
Photobomb prom photos at SF's best backdrop

MAP P892

Like many a fine romance, the **Palace of Fine Arts** (palaceoffinearts.com; free) was a folly that wasn't expected to last. The California Arts and Crafts movement's leading architect Bernard Maybeck originally built this Greco-Roman ruin in plaster for the 1915 Panama-Pacific International Expo, but San Francisco decided to keep the palace after the fair, and eventually recast it in concrete. Join shy prom dates and shivering brides posing for photos under the Rotunda frieze, which shows art under attack by materialists.

 EATING IN THE MARINA: FIVE-STAR PICNIC SUPPLIES — MAP P892

Lucca Delicatessen: Leave picnics to the pros at Lucca, makers of Italian deli classics since 1929. *9am-6pm* $

Komeya No Bento: Proper Japanese bento: sustainable salmon or duck breast, sushi rice, dashi broth and side salads. *11:30am-2:30pm & 5-6:30pm Tue-Sat* $

La Fromagerie: This sandwich board spoils you for choice – you can't lose with Toulouse, piled with duck, manchego and fig jam. *11am-6pm Mon & Tue, from 10am Wed-Sun* $

Fort Mason Outdoor Markets: Ex-shipyards host Sunday farmers markets, plus monthly (last Friday) night markets. *9:30am-1:30pm Sun & 4-9pm Fri* $

Musée Mécanique

Listen to the Wave Organ
MAP P892
Hum along with the bay

Follow a trail past yacht-club docks along a jetty poking into the bay, and you'll discover an aural oddity: the **Wave Organ** (*exploratorium.edu; free*). Eerie sounds wheeze from repurposed SF cemetery marble statues and PVC plumbing parts, ingeniously reconfigured into acoustic sculpture by Exploratorium artists Peter Richards and George Gonzalez.

Game on at Fisherman's Wharf
MAP P892
Play vintage games at SF's Wild West arcade

The massive boatshed at Pier 45 can scarcely contain this sprawling, mind-blowing collection of 300-plus vintage mechanical amusements. Giant, freckle-faced Laughing Sal has freaked out kids for over a century, but don't let this deter you from the **Musée Mécanique** (*museemecanique.com; free*). For less than a buck, you can battle Space Invaders, get your fortune told by an all-seeing wizard, peep at belly dancers through a vintage Mutoscope, or get hypnotized by a Ferris wheel made entirely from toothpicks.

PARTY OF THE CENTURY

San Francisco rebuilt from the ground up after the 1906 earthquake leveled almost everything – the city celebrated its comeback with an epic party in 1915: the **Panama-Pacific International Expo**. The northern shoreline was extended with landfill, then topped with a vast fairground. Across almost 400 square city blocks, the PPIE had it all: fanciful architecture crowned with the 435ft Tower of Jewels, glittering with 100,000 cut-glass gems; flashy technology, including a giant 14-ton Underwood typewriter; a huge Palace of Fine Arts lined with modern painting and sculpture; and forward-thinking events such as the International Conference of Women Workers to Promote Peace. The party was a smash – and technology, art and peace remain works in perpetual progress in San Francisco.

 EATING IN MARINA: BEST FOR DINNER DATES — MAP P892

Dalida: Mediterranean flavors: Istanbul stuffed mussels, Aleppo roast chicken, Yemeni lamb stew, mmmm. *11:30-2pm & 5-9pm Fri-Wed, 11am-2pm Thu* $$	**Atelier Crenn:** Triple-Michelin-starred chef creates edible art inspired by SF's seafaring legends and her own farmstead. Reserve two months ahead. *5-9pm Tue-Sat* $$$	**A16:** Romance is assisted by award-winning wood-fired pizzas, house-cured salami and a deep Italian wine list. *5-9pm Mon-Thu, noon-9:30pm Fri & Sat, noon-9pm Sun* $$	**Izzy's Steakhouse:** SF's surest sign of commitment is sharing the Gomez, Izzy's plump prime rib with gooey au gratin potatoes. *5-9:30pm Mon-Fri, from 4pm Sat & Sun* $$$

SAN FRANCISCO'S FAVORITE SEA-LEBRITIES

Sea lions started taking over San Francisco's most coveted waterfront real estate in 1989 following the Loma Prieta earthquake, and have been making a glorious public display of themselves ever since. Night and day they canoodle, belch, noisily bark, scratch and gleefully shove one another off the docks, protected from predators and with plenty of herring and other bay fish to keep them full. Up to 2100 sea lions at a time converge on Pier 39's K dock between January and July, and whenever else they feel like sunbathing – California law requires yacht owners to relinquish valuable dock slips to accommodate them. Move aside, billionaires: San Francisco's sea mammal mascots are here to stay.

Seals, Pier 39

Meet Superheroes MAP P888
Get up close and personal with comic legends

Founded with a grant from Bay Area cartoon legend Charles M Schultz of *Peanuts* fame, the **Cartoon Art Museum** (*cartoonart.org; adult/child $10/4*) showcases cartoon classics from Batman blockbusters to Calvin & Hobbes strips. But these curators aren't afraid of serious subjects either, showcasing Ukrainian political cartoons, SF feminist comics trailblazer Trina Robbins and Wahab Algarmi's stories of growing up Muslim by the Bay.

Family Fun on Pier 39 MAP P888
Choose your own bayside adventure

Sea lions aren't the only ones who enjoy sunny days out at **Pier 39** (*pier39.com; free*). Families flock to this boardwalk for amusement-park atmosphere without the prohibitive entry fees. On the pier's bayside end, your chariot awaits at the antique **San Francisco Carousel** (*10am-8pm; $6 per ride*), twinkling with 1800 lights and hand-painted with local landmarks.

 EATING IN CHINATOWN: FAMILY-STYLE FEASTS MAP P888

Good Mong Kok: Plump dumplings whisked from vast steamers into takeout containers. Takeout only. *7am-6pm* $

Hang Ah Tea Room: Families have converged here for generations – classics include spicy purse dumplings and creamy thousand-year-egg custard *bao*. *10:30am-8pm* $$

Dim Sum Bistro: Fresh, high-quality dim sum, including tender shrimp and chive dumplings, juicy pork and shrimp *siu mai*, and perfectly toasted sesame balls. Takeout only. *8am-3pm* $

Today Food: Watch pros rolling dough until translucent, loading in fresh veggies, shrimp and organic chicken to peak plumpness, then promptly pan-frying or steaming your meal. *8am-8pm* $

Celebrate Lunar New Year

MAP P888

Brighten winter nights with celebrations

Chase the 200ft dragon, legions of lion dancers, and local politicians on floats tossing lucky chocolate coins in red envelopes. The **Chinese New Year Parade** *(chineseparade.com)* is the highlight of San Francisco winters, complete with fireworks, drumlines and fierce troops of tiny-tot martial artists. By the end of the night, everyone's happy and hoarse from exchanging best wishes for prosperity.

Every 12 years or so, the lunar year's animal zodiac sign coincides with the animal zodiac sign of your birth year – which means you have an extra excuse to party. If you're not sure what your sign is, the red envelope-covered Chinese Zodiac Wall on **Jack Kerouac Alley** provides a handy summary of the animals, elements and character traits associated with your birth year.

Chinatown celebrates for a month, with special **night markets** *(bechinatown.weebly.com)* on lantern-lit Grant Ave supplying essential goods for an auspicious year ahead – including lucky bamboo, red envelopes and miniature mandarin trees. **Chinatown Kite Shop** *(chinatownkite.com)* sells two-person, papier-mâché lion-dance costumes.

Time-Travel at the Chinese Historical Society of America

MAP P888

Follow epic tales inside a living landmark

Built as Chinatown's YWCA in 1932 by Hearst Castle architect Julia Morgan, the **Chinese Historical Society of America** *(chsa.org; adult/student/child $12/10/5)* displays WWII Chinatown nightclub posters, Frank Wong's Chinatown miniatures, and Bruce Lee's martial arts costumes and extensive philosophy library. Exhibits trace anti-Asian hate speech from the Chinese Exclusion Act (1882–1943) to today, alongside 175-plus years of history-changing civil-rights activism.

Turn on the City Lights

MAP P888

Browse one of the world's most famous bookstores

Free spirits and free speech have found refuge at **City Lights Books** *(citylights.com)* since poet Lawrence Ferlinghetti founded the store in 1957. Wax poetic in the upstairs Poetry Room, load up on zines on the mezzanine and entertain radical ideas downstairs in the Pedagogies of Resistance section. On the main floor, City Lights publications include titles by Angela Davis, Diane di Prima and Noam Chomsky, proving the point on another of Ferlinghetti's signs: 'Printer's Ink Is the Greater Explosive.'

Telegraph Hill Stairway Hikes

MAP P888

Earn panoramic, romantic city views

In the 19th century, a ruthless entrepreneur began quarrying on the side of Telegraph Hill. City Hall eventually stopped the quarrying, but the view of the bay from the **Filbert Street**

CHINATOWN'S TECH TRAILBLAZERS

California's earliest high-tech adopters weren't 1970s Silicon Valley programmers – they were Chinatown switchboard operators c 1887 at the **Chinese Telephone Exchange** (today a bank at the corner of Washington and Grant Sts). Operators spoke six languages and memorized thousands of Chinatown residents by name, residence and occupation. Since people born in China were prohibited from entering the US during the 1882–1943 Chinese Exclusion era, the exchange provided Chinatown residents with their only family contact for over 60 years. A crew of women operators operated the switchboard seven days a week, with no holidays – until they unionized in 1943, and won a landmark victory for overtime back pay. Eventually private phone lines were installed citywide, and the exchange quietly closed in 1949.

EXPLORE THE WHARF'S WILD SIDE

Take photos of sea lions, stare down sharks, hop a submarine and swap stories with sailors.

START	END	LENGTH
Pier 39	Musée Méchanique	0.5 mile; 45 minutes

Take a selfie with the ❶ **sea lions at Pier 39** but keep a safe distance – they may be adorable, but sea mammals can get territorial. Cross over to the east side of Pier 39 and head for dry land. Just before you reach it, your next stop is on the right-hand side. The sea lions were just a preview of what's ahead at the ❷ **Aquarium of the Bay** – descend into underwater chambers lined with glowing jellyfish tanks, then step into glass tubes jutting deep into San Francisco Bay. Emerge from the deep and return to dry land. Head away from the tides of tourists strolling the Embarcadero and turn onto North Point.

❸ **Bill Chester Longshoremen's Union Hall** is named for SF's trailblazing 1930s Black union leader. Behind the hall at the edge of the parking lot – the spot where the '60s psychedelic movement started – you'll spot Beniamino Bufano's serene statue of the city's patron St Francis. Turn right here.

Keeping a low profile on the east side of Pier 45 is the ❹ **USS Pampanito**, a 1943 submarine that survived WWII to tell hair-raising tales of torpedo battles and deep dives in riveting onboard audio tours. Then head into the Pier 45 boatshed right next to the *Pampanito* for ❺ **Musée Méchanique**, with its fully functional vintage games.

Head below deck at the **USS Pampanito** to inspect immaculately polished instruments and impossibly close quarters.

At the **Aquarium of the Bay** you're surrounded by marine life – sharks circle overhead, while manta rays seem to be practicing ballet moves.

Bill Chester Longshoremen's Union Hall was the site of one epic party: the 1966 Trips Festival where novelist Ken Kesey spiked Kool-Aid with LSD.

Steps is still (wait for it) dynamite. Climbing the steps to Coit Tower you'll have sweeping Bay Bridge vistas, and can peek at hidden cottages along Napier Lane's wooden boardwalk, and sculpture-dotted gardens in bloom year-round.

For more well-earned views, find the urban trailhead between 150 and 155 Francisco St to the **Francisco Street Steps**. Cross the courtyard, ascend to Grant Ave, and turn left to reach Jack Early Park, where you'll find scenic seats for two. Climb higher for Golden-Gate-to-Bay-Bridge panoramas, then descend via Grant Ave for a well-earned slice of pizza at **Golden Boy**.

Tarry in Union Square
Watch the cable cars turn
MAP P888

Union Square's image as a main tourist hub with shopping and hotels galore had been challenged by the pandemic, with major retailers and companies leaving the area. However, it's still a top place to stay while visiting – a great location for sights such as the San Francisco Museum of Modern Art (SFMOMA; p903) – and it's still home to the main cable-car turnaround – a part of classic San Francisco that remains steadfast.

Ride All Three Cable-Car Lines
Old-school San Fran
MAP P888

Cable cars almost disappeared in 1947, but the city came to its senses and eventually designated the system a National Landmark in 1964. Part of the city's **Muni system** (*sfmta .com/getting-around/muni/cable-cars; single $8, $13 1-day Muni passport recommended*) since 1944 (but here since 1873), SF's cable cars are the only operating cable-car system in the world, with more than 254,000 passenger trips per month. Ride north–south up and down the hills on both the Powell/Hyde and Powell/Mason lines, starting at the **Powell Street Cable-Car Turnaround**, which take riders between Downtown's skyscrapers, through culture-filled **Chinatown**, past Nob Hill's Fairmont Hotel and Grace Cathedral, ending at the tourist attractions of Fisherman's Wharf (p895). Most visitors stick to these lines, but there's a third line that tends to be less crowded – the east–west California line that runs between Van Ness Ave in Nob Hill and Davis St in FiDi. It passes many of the same landmarks, with the addition of Polk Gulch and more of FiDi.

THE TATTOOED LADIES OF NORTH BEACH

Back in the 1950s, Ringling Brothers Circus drew crowds just to see a 'tattooed lady' – meanwhile in San Francisco, Lyle Tuttle quietly opened a tattoo parlor that would inspire women worldwide to get tattoos. Over his 60-year career, Tuttle inked women across six continents and attracted celebrities to his shop – including Jane Fonda, Joan Baez, Janis Joplin and Cher. Tuttle credited his success to women's liberation, and was proud to assist women taking control over their own bodies and self-expression at his North Beach shop – and he made the process safer for everyone, championing sanitary tattooing practices with SF's Health Department. Tuttle has gone on to that great ink cloud in the sky, but you'll spot his Western Traditional designs around North Beach.

 EATING IN NORTH BEACH: PANINI PICKS — MAP P888

Molinari: Massive panini loaded with buffalo mozzarella, sun-dried tomatoes, prosciutto and slabs of house-cured salami. *9am-5:30pm Mon-Fri, 9am-9pm Sat, 11am-3:30pm Sun* $	**Palermo II Delicatessen:** Try the irresistible signature sandwich: eggplant parmigiana with their own marinara and fresh mozzarella. *10am-5pm Tue-Sun* $	**Fairuz Eatery:** North Beach *nonnas* line up for falafel perfected over 20 years: crunchy yet fluffy, with nutty tahini and citrusy sumac in warm pita. *11am-8pm Sun-Thu, to 10pm Fri & Sat* $	**Mario's Bohemian Cigar Store Cafe:** Enjoy onion focaccia with meatballs, eggplant or grilled chicken, plus Chianti by the carafe and prime people-watching. *11am-9pm* $

AFFORDABLE OPERA

Yes, super cheap tickets for the **San Francisco Opera** *(sfopera.com)* still exist! For certain performances, they're available to everyone who creates an SF Opera account online and registers. The tickets are usually available from 11am to midnight the day before a performance, or until they're sold out. Check your email for notifications about ticket availability. There are also 200 standing-room tickets for most main-stage opera performances, which are for the rear orchestra or rear balcony. Tickets are only $10 each, but are cash only. They go on sale on the day of each performance, with a limit of two per person. Starting from 10am on the day, 150 tickets become available, whereas the remaining 50 are released two hours prior to the performance.

● **ACTIVITIES**
1 Mission Cultural Center for Latino Arts
2 Potrero del Sol/La Raza Skatepark

● **DRINKING & NIGHTLIFE**
3 El Rio
4 Jolene's
5 Mother
6 Wild Side West

● **ENTERTAINMENT**
7 Bissap Baobab
8 Bottom of the Hill
9 Carnaval
10 Chapel
11 Red Poppy Art House
12 Verdi Club

Visiting a Storied Neighborhood

MAP P888

The Tenderloin Museum and its walking tours

In the **Tenderloin**, Muhammad Ali boxed, Billie Holiday sang, and LGBTQ+ activists fought for their right to be served in cafeterias – and established America's first Transgender Cultural District. Historians from the Tenderloin Museum lead visitors on **tours** past these and other groundbreaking locales. You'll see the site of the Compton's Cafeteria Riot, plus some of the area's most iconic murals and public artworks. The museum also has robust programming, like a Compton's Cafeteria Riot play twice weekly at the annex space at 835 Larkin St.

The **Tenderloin Museum** *(tenderloinmuseum.org; adult/senior & student/12 & under $10/6/free)* itself takes about 45 minutes to peruse, showing visitors through photographs and

EATING NEAR DOWNTOWN MUSEUMS: OUR PICKS

MAP P900

Bini's Kitchen: Chef Bini Pradhan was the first in SF to serve Nepalese *momos* (dumplings). The turkey ones pop with a tomato-cilantro sauce. *11am-3pm* $$

Moya: This unassuming SoMa corner Ethiopian spot is known for mushroom and tofu *tib* (stew). *11am-2pm & 5:30-8:30pm Mon-Fri, 5:30-8:30pm Sat* $$

Estrellita's Snacks: A favorite La Cocina incubator alum brick-and-mortar spot dishing up huge Salvadorean pupusas. *10am-8pm Mon-Fri* $

Yank Sing: Upscale dim sum place with a daily rolling cart service – a rarity these days. *11am-3pm Tue-Fri, from 10am Sat & Sun* $$$

other information and ephemera covering the Tenderloin's long history, from the hopping nightclubs and brothels to an immigrant hub with affordable housing, to the fact that present-day Tenderloin has nearly more than 3500 children – the highest density of children in the city.

Municipal Magic
Astounding edifices

MAP P888

The **Civic Center** is anchored by the gold-accented dome of the beaux-arts **City Hall**. It's been the site of historic happenings, from the assassination of supervisor Harvey Milk and mayor George Moscone, to the first same-sex marriages. Neighboring the City Hall is the **San Francisco Main Library**, whose Larkin St entrance features a new Maya Angelou sculpture, *Portrait of a Phenomenal Woman,* by Berkeley artist Lava Thomas.

Experience the Theater District
Delve into musicals, plays, live music and more

MAP P888

SF's Theater District bursts with culture, from majestic old theaters to big concert venues to hoppin' new jazz clubs. For nationally touring smash-hit musicals like *Wicked* and *Hamilton,* look at the grand old **Curran** *(broadwaysf.com),* **Golden Gate** *(goldengatetheatresf.com)* and **Orpheum** *(orpheumsanfrancisco.com)* theaters. The **Herbst Theatre** *(sfwarmemorial.org/herbst-theatre)* is a smaller, 900-seat venue inside the **War Memorial Opera House** that hosts performances such as string quartets and solo guitarists.

Go to the **American Conservatory Theater** *(act-sf.org)* for breakthrough shows that launch at this turn-of-the-century landmark. There are also smaller or experimental companies like **San Francisco Playhouse** *(sfplayhouse.org),* **New Conservatory Theatre Center** *(nctcsf.org),* **CounterPulse** *(counterpulse.org),* **SAFEhouseARTS** *(safehousearts.org)* and **Phoenix Theatre** *(phoenixtheatresf.org).*

Several jazz clubs pay tribute to past venues, where Miles Davis, Billie Holiday and Charlie Parker played underground. **Black Cat** *(blackcatsf.com)* is out to restore the laid-back, lowdown glory of the capital of West Coast cool with both a basement club and street-level bar. **Mr Tipple's Recording Studio** *(mrtipplessf.com)* hosts top local talent, plus a decent dumpling menu. The newest **Dawn Club** *(dawnclub.com)* revives a 1946 jazz venue, with top-rated cocktails.

FROM BAWDY TO BROADWAY

While the historic theaters of San Francisco all have rich history, the Golden Gate theatre on Taylor near Market St may have the most fun origin. It was originally built as a vaudeville house in 1922, hosting up to seven acts a night. As the theater evolved into a concert hall, stars like Frank Sinatra, Judy Garland and Nat King Cole graced its stage. During the theater's evolution, much of the gorgeous interior was torn down in favor of a more modern appearance. However, the late 1970s saw the Golden Gate restored to its art deco roots and it was reopened as a performing arts venue. The Golden Gate was added to the National Register of Historic Places in 1986.

TENDERLOIN BARS: OUR PICKS

MAP P888

HA-RA Club: Open since 1947, this classic dive with its iconic neon sign still has its original phone booth. *3pm-2am Mon & Tue, from noon Wed-Fri & Sun, from 3pm Sat*

Edinburgh Castle: Bagpiper murals on the walls, the *Trainspotting* soundtrack blaring and vinegary fish and chips until 9pm. *6pm-2am*

Bourbon & Branch: For award-winning cocktails in the liquored-up library, whisper the password ('books'). *6pm-midnight Sun-Wed, to 2am Thu-Sat*

Zombie Village: This reincarnation of a 1942 tiki bar is irresistible – the skull-lined bar serves potent rum. *5pm-midnight Wed, to 12:30am Thu, to 2am Fri & Sat*

BEST MISSION LIVE MUSIC VENUES

Chapel: Musical prayers are answered in a 1914 California arts-and-crafts landmark with heavenly acoustics for folk, indie artists and performance-art mayhem.

Bissap Baobab: Come for shareable Senegalese food, stick around for live acts and DJs after 9pm – bachata, Cuban jazz, Afrobeats, flamenco and jam sessions.

Red Poppy Art House: A snug Mission storefront doubles as a concert hall for international artists-in-residence, ranging from Armenian duduk virtuosos to Argentine tango quartets.

Verdi Club: Throwing swanky soirees since 1916 – check the calendar for bachata, queer two-stepping, Brazilian zouk and swing-dance nights preceded by lessons – and bring cash for the speakeasy bar.

For other live music, **Rickshaw Stop** (rickshawstop.com) and **Bottom of the Hill** (bottomofthehill.com) are great small- to mid-size clubs for indie and underground acts. Larger concert halls like **Great American Music Hall** (gamh.com), **Bill Graham Civic Auditorium** (billgrahamcivic.com), **The Warfield** (thewarfieldtheatre.com), **August Hall** (augusthallsf.com), the Masonic and Regency Ballroom bring big touring acts. Don't forget the long-standing comedy club **Punch Line** (punchlinecomedyclub.com) in the Embarcadero, which local comedian Ali Wong graced during her rise to fame.

Toast Herstory at Lesbian Landmarks   MAP P900
Welcome home to Mission's legacy lesbian bars

Women have been making herstory in the Mission since the 1970s. After all that work, lesbians deserve somewhere to unwind – and the Mission provides lots of options.

Lesbian-owned since 1962, **Wild Side West** (wildsidewest.com) has stayed busy making herstory in the beer garden and making out on the pool table (Janis Joplin started it). You'll recognize femme-forward, cash-only corner bar **Mother** (mothersf.com) by its purple exterior and punk vibes. At women's watering hole **Jolene's** (jolenessf.com), the neon sign announcing 'you are safe here' makes room for lesbian, trans, nonbinary and questioning partiers. Legendary lesbian-owned club **El Rio** (elriosf.com) started as a Brazilian gay bar, and today the full rainbow spectrum of colorful SF characters comes here to party.

Join Mission Cultural Festivals   MAP P900
Celebrate life to the fullest

SF is far from Rio, but you'd never know it during **Carnaval** (carnavalsanfrancisco.org), when everyone shakes their tail feathers in Mission streets. On **Día de los Muertos** (dayofthedeadsf.org), brass bands, dancing skeletons and Fridas galore meet in the Mission. Offerings line the processional route along Calle 24, culminating in moving outdoor community altars at **Potrero del Sol/La Raza Skatepark** (sfrecpark.org).

Don't miss Día de los Muertos altar displays and epic mole tastings at **Mission Cultural Center for Latino Arts** (MCCLA; missionculturalcenter.org), where celebrations of Latin culture range from gallery openings to documentary screenings.

 EATING IN DOWNTOWN: POST-SHOW LATE-NIGHT EATS   MAP P888

Hinodeya Ramen Union Square: Wholegrain ramen in a light dashi-style broth made with bonito, kombu and scallops, and topped with *chashu* and soft egg. *10am-1:30am* **$$**

Tempest Bar & Box Kitchen: This favorite SoMa dive bar has a pool table, decades' worth of graffiti and satisfying bar food. *11am-2am Mon-Fri, from noon Sat & Sun* **$**

Pinecrest Diner: A (now mostly) 24-hour diner, family owned and operated since 1969. Dig into eggy breakfasts and big burgers anytime. *7am-11pm Sun-Tue, 24hr Wed-Sat* **$**

Dragon Horse: Cocktails, sushi, karaoke: say no more. *4-11pm Sun-Wed, to midnight Thu-Sat* **$$**

TOP EXPERIENCE
SFMOMA

At **San Francisco Museum of Modern Art** (SFMOMA), boundary-pushing modern and contemporary master works sprawl over seven floors. See the world-class photography collection, get an eyeful of Warhol's pop art and immerse yourself in cutting-edge contemporary installations. And see how SFMOMA began, with colorful characters worthy of SF by Frida Kahlo, Diego Rivera, Paul Klee and Henri Matisse.

Alexander Calder: Dissonant Harmony

The crowd-pleasing mobiles and metal sculptures of abstract artist Alexander Calder occupy part of the 3rd floor. Kinetic and whimsical, Calder's elements were actually always painstakingly thought-out. SFMOMA's collection includes the multicolored *Lone Yellow* and the spellbinding movements of *Quatrro Pendulati*. Outside the Calder gallery is the impressive *Living Wall*.

Afterimages: Echoes of the 1960s

The 5th-floor collection presents some of the greatest hits of pop art, including Andy Warhol's electrically colored prints of celebrities to Ellsworth Kelly's joined canvases of unevenly shaped, bold colors. The pieces push the idea that the consciousness-shifting art movements of the 1960s are still relevant today.

1900 to Now: SFMOMA's Collection

Rotating experimental works and masterpieces from its massive collection, SFMOMA encourages viewers to constantly re-examine the contradictions and interpretations of some of the greatest works of our time. Ponder the evolution of Diego Rivera's boldly colored works from cubist to postimpressionist and beyond, and Georgia O'Keefe's interpretations of nature and the feminine through her genre of combining fine charcoal lines with paint.

TOP TIPS

● Check your coat and bag for free.

● Up the stairs on the 2nd floor are the ticket booth and STEPS cafe, plus most of the free art on the walls, ceilings and floor below.

PRACTICALITIES

● sfmoma.org
● adult/senior/student/18 & under $30/25/23/free (special exhibits $10 extra)
● free first Thursday
● 10am-5pm Fri-Tue, noon-8pm Thu

TOP EXPERIENCE

Ocean Beach

At this blustery, atmospheric city beach, the sun sets over the Pacific – though fog banks may swallow it first. But fog doesn't keep hardy beachcombers, power-walkers and determined sandcastle architects away from this vast, serene stretch of pale golden sand. Standing at the water's edge you can watch the Pacific ebb and flow, with only a few surfers to remind you what century you're in.

Lands End

TOP TIPS

● Break out your favorite costume or your most comfortable glitter thong for May's **Bay to Breakers** (baytobreakers.com), a truly fun 7.5-mile run from the Embarcadero to Ocean Beach.

● The restaurant out back of Beach Chalet hosts raucous weekday happy hours, plus lazy brunches and live music at weekends.

PRACTICALITIES

● parksconservancy.org
● 24hr; parking lot closes at 10pm
● free

Walking Wild

San Francisco's 3.5 mile beach is not like the ones in Hollywood movies. Except for sunny spells in September and October, most days are too chilly for bikinis and clambakes here, and much better suited to meditative, windblown walks. Swimmers, beware riptides; walkers, mind sneaker waves. Keep an eye on the Pacific and you might spot brave surfers, passing ships and sea lions bobbing in the waves.

Sunset Dunes

By popular vote in 2024, San Francisco converted this section of highway to park trails for joggers, cyclists, skaters and walkers to enjoy. This section of the **Coastal Trail** connects **Fort Funston** to Ocean Beach and **Lands End**; stick to paths in areas undergoing habitat restoration, and keep dogs on leashes to protect wildlife. The dunes offer shelter for birdwatching – you might spot skittish snowy plover shorebirds taking cover here in winter.

Break for Art & Beer at the Beach Chalet

Take a break for food, drink, bathrooms and inspiration at an SF landmark. The Beach Chalet entryway is lined with splendid 1930s Works Project Administration (WPA) frescoes by Lucien Labaudt that celebrate the building of Golden Gate Park.

The Heart of Oakland
Downtown Oakland and Chinatown

Pedestrianized **City Center**, between Broadway and Clay St, 12th and 14th Sts, forms the heart of downtown Oakland. Enjoy a free noontime concert. Nearby **Oakland City Hall** is a beautifully refurbished 1914 beaux-arts masterpiece. Walking the streets, look for old gems such as the 1914 **Cathedral Building**, a Gothic Revival wonder on a triangular plot. It was a setting for Boots Riley's 2018 sublime dark comedy *Sorry to Bother You*.

Old Oakland, west of Broadway between 8th and 10th Sts, is lined with restored historical buildings dating from the late 19th century. The area has a lively restaurant and after-work scene.

East of Broadway and bustling with commerce, Oakland's workaday **Chinatown** centers on 8th and Webster Sts, as it has since the 1850s. Wholesale markets spill into the streets; check out the changing exhibits at the **Oakland Asian Cultural Center** (*oacc.cc; free*).

California's Museum
Dive into Oakland's history

The top draw is the **Oakland Museum of California** (*museumca.org; adult/child $19/free*). Dedicated to the state, its permanent galleries range from California's diverse ecology and history to art – from traditional landscapes to reimagined cartography. Watch for blockbuster temporary exhibitions. It's open 11am to 5pm Wednesday to Sunday.

Visit the UC Berkeley Campus
Go Bears!

The Berkeley campus of the **University of California** (*berkeley.edu*), called 'Cal' by both students and locals, is home to the oldest university in the state. It was founded in 1866, with the first students arriving in 1873. Today, Cal has more than 40,000 students, over 1500 professors and more Nobel laureates than you could point a particle accelerator at.

Officially called Sather Tower, the **Campanile** – as it is widely known – was modeled on St Mark's Basilica in Venice. The 307ft spire offers fine views of the Bay Area, and at the top you can stare up into the carillon of 61 bells. The Campanile is open from 10am to 4pm.

HISTORIC FORT BAKER

Fort Baker (*nps.gov/goga; free*), the 1905 army base with one of the world's best views, helped guard the entrance to the San Francisco Bay along with the better-known Fort Point on the south side. It was one of the last major forts built on the bay, and the army tried to stem its perennial problem of desertion by making the facilities here better than average. As you'll see from the buildings that still surround the parade grounds, there were porches, large windows and even indoor toilets.

Today the decommissioned fort fronts Horseshoe Cove, where there's still a Coast Guard station. Trails extend along the coast and you can spend the night in former officers' quarters at the luxe **Cavallo Point Lodge**.

EATING IN OAKLAND & BERKELEY: CASUAL DINING

Fentons Creamery: Everyone wants a scoop of luscious ice cream at this old-school Oakland parlor. Also old-fashioned lunches and snacks. A beloved classic. *11am-10pm* **$**

Arizmendi Bakery: Great for breakfast or lunch near Lake Merritt in Oakland. Bakery co-op not for the weak-willed: gourmet vegetarian pizza, chewy breads and gigantic scones. *8am-8pm* **$**

Acme Bread: Berkeley has one of the region's best bakeries, beloved for its take on classic sourdough bread. Memorable snacks like the ham and cheese croissant. *8am-4pm* **$**

La Note: Casual Berkeley cafe with a strong French accent. Popular at breakfast (goat cheese is an option); lunch brings salads and sandwiches. Sunny garden. *8am-2pm* **$$**

BERKELEY'S BEST BOOKSTORES

Moe's Books: New and used books in a vast store south of campus. Renowned for its knowledgeable staff; enjoy browsing across four floors.

Dark Carnival Imaginative Fiction Bookstore: One of the oldest science-fiction, fantasy and horror bookstores west of the Mississippi. It's all controlled chaos; lose yourself in the stacks.

Pegasus Books: Right on the Shattuck Ave commercial strip, Pegasus has great staff recommendations and daily specials on new and used titles.

Book Society: Browsing for books in this cozy, comfy space is all the better given the machines in back that dispense wine by the glass.

Sleepy Cat Books: You'll find the namesake felines dozing away as you browse the carefully curated selection of offbeat fiction and hard-to-find non-fiction. Also sells intriguing postcards.

● SIGHTS
1. BAMPFA
2. Bancroft Library
3. Campanile
4. Cathedral Building
5. Chinatown
6. City Center
7. Oakland Asian Cultural Center
8. Oakland City Hall
9. Oakland Museum of California
10. Old Oakland
11. University of California – Berkeley

● EATING
12. Acme Bread
13. Arizmendi Bakery
14. Chez Panisse
15. Fentons Creamery
16. La Note

● SHOPPING
17. Book Society
18. Dark Carnival Imaginative Fiction Bookstore
19. Moe's Books
20. Pegasus Books
21. Sleepy Cat Books

Inside a stainless-steel exterior, **BAMPFA** (Berkeley Art Museum and Pacific Film Archive; bampfa.org; adult/child $18/free) holds galleries showcasing artworks, from ancient Chinese to cutting-edge contemporary.

The **Bancroft Library** houses, among other gems, the papers of Mark Twain, a copy of Shakespeare's folios and a diary from the Donner Party. Public exhibits include the surprisingly small gold nugget that sparked the 1849 Gold Rush.

Berkeley's World-Famous Restaurant
Chez Panisse changed dining globally

California cuisine, farm-to-table, seasonal fare, sustainably sourced. These are just some of the food trends that **Chez Panisse** *(chezpanisse.com),* open 5:30pm to 8:45pm Monday to Saturday, and its superstar proprietor Alice Waters can take at least some of the credit for. Pull out all the stops with a prix-fixe meal at the restaurant downstairs, which first opened in 1971. As always, the menu changes daily and is as good and popular as ever.

Walking Sausalito & the Golden Gate Bridge
Take a trip across the Golden Gate Bridge

One of the Bay Area's best walks begins and ends in San Francisco and features some of the region's best scenery.

Catch a mid-morning ferry to Sausalito, enjoying the views of Alcatraz and Angel Island. Stroll the town and get refreshments and a picnic. Follow East Rd south along the beautiful shoreline until you reach Fort Baker. Walk under the Golden Gate Bridge (p890) – which looms large and red overhead – and curve up the access road until you reach the popular viewpoint. Cross the bridge on the eastern walkway (the west side is for cyclists). Dress warmly! It's 1.7 miles across – take your time for the stellar views. It's 5 miles from Sausalito to the San Francisco side of the bridge, where you can stroll onwards to the Presidio and the Marina.

Enticing Fort, Seafront & Museum
Crab fishers and Bay ecology

Below the north tower of the Golden Gate Bridge, surprisingly uncrowded Fort Baker (p905) hides in plain sight. Stroll Horseshoe Bay, watch the winter-time crab fishers, and get a snack or lunch from one of several good outlets.

A highlight is the **Bay Area Discovery Museum** *(bayareadiscoverymuseum.org; $20),* a child-centric, indoor-outdoor facility that introduces kids to the ecology of the bay.

Hit the Beaches at Point Reyes
Point Reyes' world-class coast

Virtually every strip of sand is a long drive from anywhere at Point Reyes, but every one is worth the effort. **Limantour Beach** is a great all-arounder with an array of wilderness

POINT REYES WILDLIFE

Point Reyes has an extraordinary range of wildlife, including 80 species of mammals and nearly 30 species of reptiles and amphibians. The largest animals here are the **elephant seals**, which number upward of 2000 on shore during late winter and early spring. As they rest after months of feeding non-stop at sea, you can see the adult males snoozing on the sand. Each weighs from 4400lb to 6000lb. Look for pups from January to March; August is the only month when you're unlikely to find any elephant seals at Point Reyes. Offshore, late December through mid-April is migration season for **gray whales**. You can often spot these behemoths from shore.

 EATING & DRINKING IN SAUSALITO: OUR PICKS

| **Scoma's:** Classics such as *cioppino* (a piquant seafood stew) and Crab Louie salad served on a pier. Sustainable seafood lineup changes daily. *11:30am-9:30pm $$$* | **Venice Gourmet Delicatessen & Pizzeria:** In the center; build a picnic with Italian sandwiches, prepared foods and baked goods or a crispy pizza. *9am-5pm $* | **Barrel House Tavern:** Waterfront tavern serving California cuisine like local cheeses and charcuterie. Good list of regional beer, wine and spirits. Book ahead. *11am-9pm $$* | **Travis Marina:** Fort Baker's near-secret bar welcomes everyone with incredible bay and bridge views. Regular live music. *4-8pm Fri, noon-8pm Sat, noon-6pm Sun* |

BEST HIKES NEAR PALO ALTO

Stanford Dish Loop: The hilly 3.7-mile paved path is popular with runners, walkers and science nerds who want to see the 150ft-diameter radio telescope ('the Dish') that once communicated with NASA's *Voyager* spacecraft.

Baylands Observation Deck & Boardwalk: A hub for hiking trails that follow the bay shoreline through parks and wildlife-filled estuaries.

San Andreas Fault Trail: Learn all about earthquake geology on this gentle 1.5-mile self-guided path inside the Los Trancos Open Space Preserve.

Wunderlich County Park: Trails follow hillsides, gulches and streams under shady redwoods and oaks.

Windy Hill Preserve: Head west into the Santa Cruz Mountains. From this grass-covered hilltop trails radiate out into the redwoods.

hikes and stunning sunsets. **Drakes Beach** is backed by white sandstone cliffs and is arguably the most gorgeous of the main beaches. There's also the seasonal **Kenneth C Patrick Visitor Center**, which offers information, especially in elephant-seal mating season. West-facing **Point Reyes Beach** offers 11 miles of solitude. On many days – especially from late fall to spring – the sky turns an iridescent vermilion at sunset. Bring a blanket and enjoy the show.

Trails, Seabirds & Elk Reserve

Hiking the Point Reyes wilderness

Alluring trails crisscross Point Reyes over hillsides and along the shoreline. For views, the **Inverness Ridge Trail** heads for around 3 miles up to **Point Reyes Hill** (1339ft), affording spectacular vistas of the entire national seashore.

For wildlife, **Pierce Point Road** continues to the huge windswept sand dunes at **Abbotts Lagoon**, full of peeping killdeer and other shorebirds. At the end of the road is historical **Pierce Point Ranch**, the trailhead for the 9.4-mile roundtrip **Tomales Point Trail** through the **Tule Elk Reserve**. The many elk are an amazing sight, standing with their huge horns against the backdrop of **Tomales Point**. The herd is one of the last in the lower 48 states of the US.

Exploring Stanford

An art and architecture tour

Stanford University (*stanford.edu*) is one of America's top universities academically, and among the most expensive. The faux California Mission Revival–style campus is a genteel place to stroll, with public artwork and murals. (Note: the rivalry with publicly funded UC Berkeley is intense.) Having been built on the site of the Stanford family's horse farm, the university maintains the humble-brag nickname The Farm.

Stop by the **Stanford Visitor Center** (*visit.stanford.edu*) off Galvez St for self-guided-tour info and maps. Many cover the multitudes of public art around campus. Download the Stanford Mobile app, which has walking tours.

Auguste Rodin's *Burghers of Calais* bronze sculpture marks the entrance to the **Main Quad** (begun 1887), an open plaza where the original 12 campus buildings – a mix of Romanesque and Mission Revival styles – are joined by the **Memorial Church** (1903). The church is noted for its beautiful

---

EATING NEAR POINT REYES: OUR PICKS

Saltwater Oyster Depot: Appealing chef-run bistro in Inverness with a sophisticated local seafood menu. Seasonal offerings include the famous oysters. *5-8pm Fri-Mon* $$

Tap Room: Inverness spot for sandwiches, burgers and noodle bowls alongside microbrews and top regional wines. A convivial mix of residents and visitors. *4-9pm Mon-Sat* $$

Bovine Bakery: The place to get breakfast and/or a picnic near the entrance to the peninsula. Organic treats, sandwiches, breads and good coffee. *7am-4pm* $

Cafe Reyes: Enjoy wood-fired pizza inside, on the patio or to go at this Point Reyes Station favorite. Great range of toppings. *noon-8pm* $$

Memorial Church

mosaic-tiled frontage, stained-glass windows and five organs with more than 8000 pipes.

Think Rodin
Stanford's masterpiece of a museum

Fronted by Ionic columns, the **Cantor Arts Center** *(museum. stanford.edu; free)* includes works from ancient civilizations to contemporary art, spanning the globe. The museum is renowned for its Rodin collection of over 200 works displayed both inside and out in a garden, including *The Thinker*. Rotating shows are eclectic in scope and include well-curated photography exhibitions.

Fun at Half Moon Bay
Get lost in the surf, sun and fog

Home to a long coastline, mild albeit foggy weather (bring layers!) and Mavericks, one of the biggest and gnarliest surf breaks on the planet, Half Moon Bay and neighboring Miramar and El Granada are prime real estate.

Although the shallowness of the bay means it should be called Quarter Moon Bay, the long stretches of sandy beach and coastal bluffs attract surfers, hikers and active-minded weekenders. The small downtown is architecturally historic and good for a stroll.

GREAT PUMPKINS

It's not just brussels sprouts and houseplants (that's what's in all those greenhouses) growing in Half Moon Bay. Starting early in the fall, fields are dotted with bright, nearly radiant pumpkins. The spectacle of rolling fields tightly speckled with orange stretching into the distance provides some of the only competition for attention with the views on the ocean side of the road. The best fields for the spectacle are south of Half Moon Bay.

Leading up to Halloween, pumpkin vendors line Hwy 1. The two-day **Half Moon Bay Art & Pumpkin Festival** *(hmbpumpkinfest. com)* in mid-October is famous for its pumpkin weigh-off, where beasts grown by fanatical cultivators (who zealously guard their secrets) can weigh more than 2500lb.

EATING & DRINKING IN PALO ALTO: OUR PICKS

Camper: In Palo Alto's symbiotic twin Menlo Park, a classic NorCal menu of locally sourced food prepared creatively. *10am-1pm Sat & Sun, 5-8:45pm Mon-Sat* **$$$**

Tamarine Restaurant & Gallery: Exquisite Vietnamese food in artful surrounds. Cocktails pair with small and large plates. *11:30am-2:30pm & 5-9pm* **$$$**

Palo Alto Creamery: A downtown institution, with sparkling chrome-and-red booths and a 1920s look; famous for breakfasts, milkshakes and pies. *8am-9pm* **$$**

Vino Locale: A wine bar in a Victorian house with an inviting terrace. Unpretentious by local standards, with a focus on regional foods and tasty bites. *3-9pm*

Half Moon Bay State Beach

Crescent-shaped and over 4 miles long, **Half Moon Bay State Beach** (*parks.ca.gov*) is a beautiful ribbon of sand along the Pacific. Much of it is nearly untrodden and it's easy to leave other visitors behind as you walk along the sandstone cliffs and dunes.

The 7.2-mile **Coastside Trail** runs the length of Half Moon Bay from the bluff above Manhattan Beach north to Pillar Point Harbor. Look for driftwood after storms and watch for whales offshore. When the bay is calm, get out and cruise water with **Half Moon Bay Kayak Co** (*hmbkayak.com; per hour from $30*), which rents kayaks and SUP sets.

Wander the Town

Strolling downtown

Half Moon Bay's old **downtown** comprises six blocks of early-20th-century buildings dotted with cafes, boutiques, bookstores and more. It's good for an hour's stroll or more. Stop into the renovated **Half Moon Bay Coastside History Museum** (*halfmoonbayhistory.org; free*) for exhibits on local history, including surfing, and for a look inside the restored 1919 town jail.

 EAT & DRINKING IN HALF MOON BAY: OUR PICKS

Jettywave Distillery: One of many fine choices near Pillar Point Harbor, serving locally caught seafood with Med and Thai accents. Welcoming patio. *noon-8pm Fri-Sun* $$

Old Princeton Landing Public House & Grill: Half Moon Bay's top venue for live music; an all-day bar near Pillar Point Harbor with elevated bar chow. *9am-11pm* $$

Ciya Mediterranean Cuisine: Superb uses of local ingredients and produce for dishes that capture flavors from around the Eastern Med, from Greece to Türkiye. *11am-9pm* $$

Hop Dogma Brewing Co: Top NorCal brewery serving hop-forward beers. Esoteric choices include Nintai, a Japanese-style rice lager, and their West Coast IPA 'Sincerely, Simcoe.' *2-8pm*

Northern California: Redwoods & Wine Country

WINE SIPPING | GIANT TREES | MOUNTAIN HIKES

California's wine valleys sparkle with a constellation of cool communities. In the Napa Valley, organic family wineries dare to make wines besides classic cabernets, while cyclists wave hello to sous-chefs weeding kitchen gardens. Head west to Sonoma County to wander thousand-year-old redwoods, pop open a bottle of bubbly with a saber in Healdsburg and visit farm-to-spliff dispensaries in Sebastopol. 'Wild' is the word that springs to mind when visiting the north coast and redwoods. The beaches are notably untamed, and the forests are called 'the redwood curtain' because the trees grow so tall and dense. In Eureka they've preserved a town's worth of Victorian-era architecture. In the northeastern corner of the state there are vast expanses of wilderness – some 24,000 protected acres – divided by rivers and dotted with cobalt lakes, horse ranches and alpine peaks. Even the two principal attractions, Mt Shasta and Lassen Volcanic National Park, remain relatively uncrowded.

GETTING AROUND

Napa and Sonoma Counties and their myriad valleys are surprisingly vast. They're easiest seen with your own wheels, but transit.511.org is a helpful resource to see the interlocking transit networks. Exploring the area around Mendocino means driving both north and south on Hwy 1, where rideshare services are scarce. I-5 divides the better-known mountain areas to the east from the lesser-visited forests, small towns and lakes to the west. Hwy 89 is the principal route to get around Mt Lassen.

☑ TOP TIP

Wine tasting in California can be a pricey undertaking, especially in the Napa Valley. Keep in mind that some tasting fees are waived with a set bottle purchase. If Napa's fees are exorbitant for you, consider more reasonably priced wineries in the Russian River, Healdsburg and Alexander Valley regions, which also sometimes accept walk-ins.

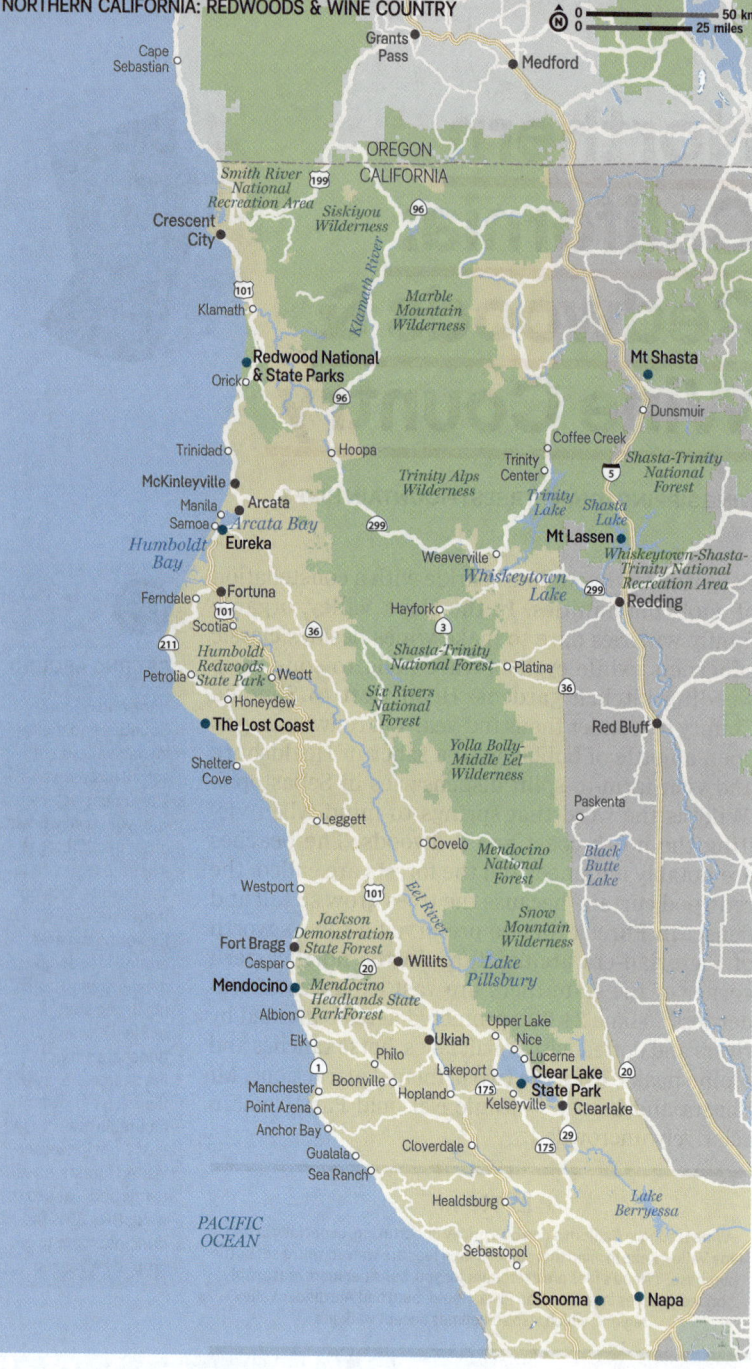

Napa Valley Wine Train

Napa's Historic Streets & Tasting Rooms
Sample wines in the central city

Napa's buzzy 1st St is lined with indie wine-tasting rooms in historic storefronts. The most punk-rock tasting room is **Gamling & McDuck** (gamlingandmcduck.com; tasting $35).

At **Brown Downtown** (brownestate.com; tastings from $50) find liquid courage with Duppy Conqueror, Jamaican folklore hero of Bob Marley songs. **Vintner's Collective** (vintnerscollective.com; tastings from $50), housed in an 1875 former saloon, specializes in super small-batch wines. Or hit **Rebel Vinters** (rebelvintners.com; tastings from $30), with board games and indie wines lining the bar.

Napa by Train or Gondola
Kick back, take it all in

Chug along in the **Napa Valley Wine Train** (winetrain.com; ticket including dining from $223) from downtown Napa to St Helena and back in a plush vintage dining car. If floating is more your speed, glide downstream with **Napa Valley Gondola** (napavalleygondola.com; from $175).

NAPA WINE-MAKING HISTORY

Grapes have been grown on this 5-by-35-mile strip of farmland since the Gold Rush. But earthquakes and juice-sucking phylloxera bugs struck, followed by Prohibition and the Great Depression. Napa had 140 wineries in the 1890s, but by the 1960s only around 25 remained. In 1976 winemakers entered a few bottles into a blind tasting competition in Paris – and to much surprise, Napa wines took top honors. As Napa's reputation grew, global wine conglomerates moved in. With land now priced at up to $1 million an acre, independent, family-owned wineries work hard to stand their ground. Today, Napa wine tasting is not just famous, it allows you to get hold of many vintages only available on-site.

EATING IN NAPA: FINE DINING

Kenzo: Napa Michelin-starred Japanese magic paired with top wine and sake in chic minimalist harmony. Book ahead. *5:30-8:30pm Wed-Sun* $$$

Compline: This cozy, unpretentious bistro/wine bar offers a short, seasonal menu of hearty dishes. *5-11pm Wed & Thu, 11:30am-11pm Fri-Sun* $$$

Bistro Don Giovanni: With copper pans, garden fountains and black-vested waiters, the Don ladles on Italian charm. Weekends get packed and loud. *11:30am-9pm* $$$

Bear: Stanly Ranch's creative Californian fare spans Asian-dressed oysters to delicate handmade pastas. *7am-10pm* $$$

Mission San Francisco Solano

WINE TASTE LIKE A PRO

Swirl, sniff and swish Swirl your wine in the glass to release aromas, then have a good sniff to excite your salivary glands. Take a small sip and swish it around your mouth so all your taste buds get in on the action.

Sip and spit If you love what you're tasting, you'll want to try plenty – and that means pacing yourself. It's fair game to spit out your last sip, or even pour leftovers into the spittoon (aka 'chuck bucket').

Remember to eat Some wineries serve bites; otherwise snack in between.

Consider joining wine clubs carefully Your pourer may suggest joining their wine club (to buy discounted bottles annually). Don't feel pressured, especially if you're tipsy and fuzzy on the details.

Sonoma's Plaza, Ringed by Monuments
Amble through California history

Sonoma's pride and joy is the plaza, with its venerable old theater, food and oh, yes, drinking options. **Tuesday night markets** are a tradition, May to November, with live music, food and artisan's wares. Bring a picnic for the free **jazz concerts** *(sonomavalleyjazzsociety.org)* from 6pm to 8:30pm every second Tuesday from June to September. Anchored by adobe **Mission San Francisco Solano** *(sonomaparks.org)*, the plaza's sights allow you to time travel across 200 years of California history.

Pair Local Art & Libations
Creativity for all the senses

Sonoma remains staunchly independent and proud of its creativity, which is on display at **Sonoma Valley Museum of Art** *(svma.org; adult/child/family $10/free/$15)* and the **Arts**

EATING IN SONOMA TOWN: RELAXED & DELICIOUS

Valley: Smack on Sonoma Plaza, this welcoming wine bar dishes up creative, seasonal offerings. *9am-3pm & 5-9pm Thu-Mon* **$$**

El Molino Central: Unforgettable Wine Country meals combine homegrown ingredients and Mexican culinary traditions. *11am-8pm Mon-Thu, from 9am Fri-Sun* **$**

Delicious Dish: Succulent burgers, fresh-catch fish sandwiches and salads with fries at a field-side diner with a patio. *10:30am-6:30pm Mon-Thu, to 2:30pm Fri* **$**

Sunflower Caffé & Wine Bar: The big back garden at this local hangout is a great spot for breakfast, a no-fuss lunch or an afternoon wine. *8am-3pm* **$$**

Guild of Sonoma (artsguildofsonoma.org; free). Make an appointment to visit collective **La Haye Art Center** (lahaye artcenter.com; free), located in a converted foundry, where you can tour its gallery and meet the artists.

In June join **Art at the Source** (artatthesource.org; free) and in October **Sonoma County Art Trails** (sonomacounty arttrails.org; free), each two-week events that give you a chance to travel from studio to studio. Maps of the ateliers are available year-round.

Fantastical Sebastopol Sculptures
Art for art's sake

A cow rides a tractor, a rocket blasts off the lawn and a dinosaur grabs a red convertible for lunch: it's all happening on Florence Ave, in dozens of sculptures by **Patrick Amiot** (patrickamiot.com), which are painted by Brigitte Laurent and made for neighbors' yards from recycled junk.

Around the corner at **Sebastopol Center for the Arts** (seb arts.org; free), see the world from the perspective of Sonoma County's boundary-pushing artists. They organize excellent open-studio weekends county-wide, with Sonoma County Art Trails in October and Art at the Source in June.

Apples, Daisies & Good Times
Hearty horticulture and hard cider

Sebastopol had a reputation for boozy shenanigans long before Sonoma County's wine industry took off, because the heirloom-apple orchards that thrived here weren't originally intended for roadside bakery **Mom's Apple Pie** (momsapple pieusa.com). They were used to make hard cider – a tradition upheld today at **Hopmonk Tavern** (hopmonk.com) and tasting room **Horse & Plow** (horseandplow.com), and celebrated twice annually at the **Apple Blossom Festival** (appleblossomfest.com) in April and **Gravenstein Apple Fair** (gravensteinapplefair.com) in August.

About 150 years ago horticulturalist Luther Burbank cultivated fruit trees and daisies (like popular Shasta daisies) at **Luther Burbank's Gold Ridge Experiment Farm** (wschs.org/farm; free), which is open to the public. You can also reserve ahead to taste namesake Gold Ridge Farms' organic apple and olive-oil products.

HOMEGROWN BOUNTY

Nicholas Izzarelli, Sebastopol native and owner-operator of **Goldfinch**, tells us his favorite ways to eat local. *goldfinch sebastopol.com*

We are lucky to be surrounded by farmers, ranchers, wineries, cheesemakers, foragers and fishermen and women, producing some of the best bounty available anywhere. Check out a farmers' market or winery (**Iron Horse** is my go-to), and meet incredibly talented and hardworking people showcasing what this county has to offer. As for restaurants, I *love* **Terrapin Creek** in Bodega Bay. Every dish is thoughtful, delicious and perfectly executed. **Khom Loi** offers locally sourced dishes with amazing Thai street-food flavors. On the coast, stop by **Hog Island Oyster Co** or the **Marshall Store** for the freshest seafood, beautiful scenery and chill Sonoma County vibes.

 EATING & DRINKING IN SEBASTOPOL: INDIE FOODS & SWEET TREATS

| **Barlow:** Two-acre village of indie food producers, ice cream makers, artists, winemakers, coffee roasters and distillers. *hours & prices vary* | **Screamin' Mimi's:** Luscious homemade ice cream served by the ounce. Choose from a seasonal lineup of flavors. *11am-9:30pm Sun-Thu, to 10pm Fri & Sat* $ | **Sebastopol Cookie Co:** Aromas entice at this indie bakery making restorative triple-chocolate cookies, snickerdoodles and more. *8:30am-5pm Tue-Sat, 9am-3pm Sun* $ | **Hardcore Espresso:** Shambolic spot with quirky art around gardens and patios and crammed inside, plus top coffee and baked goods. *5:30am-5:30pm* |

Sparkling Healdsburg
Parade of sensations

A stroll around Healdsburg's verdant central plaza, lined with cool boutiques, bookstores and tasting rooms, will quickly reveal why it's regularly listed among the top small towns in America.

Drink all along Northern California's coast from the comfort of your lounge seat at **Lioco** (liocowine.com; tastings from $30), specialist in coastal chardonnays and pinot noirs. At **Idlewild** (idlewildwines.com; tastings $30), especially fascinating Piedmontese wines are quietly made by fourth-generation winemaker Sam Bilbro. Also of Italian origin, the wines at **Portalupi** (portalupiwine.com; tastings from $20) include unexpected sparkling barbera. For eating, you can splash out at a gastronomic temple like **SingleThread** (singlethread farms.com), where edible Sonoma landscape is the first of 11 sensational seasonal courses. **Little Saint** (littlesainthealds burg.com), with a delicious plant-based menu, lights up on its free music Thursdays. And what's not to love about **Noble Folk Ice Cream & Pie Bar** (thenoblefolk.com)?

Produce & Live Music Market Days
Tuesday and Saturday certified farmers markets

On sunny Tuesdays from May to September, Healdsburg's **farmers market** (healdsburgfarmersmarket.org) on the plaza begins with warm hellos from Sonoma County farmers and rolls into inspiring cooking demos and live music, plus seasonal events. Graze regional delicacies, such as Dry Creek peaches, steaming hot samosas, bean-to-bar chocolate, award-winning cheeses and organic Preston olive oil. On Saturdays (8:30am to 9pm from April to December) the **market** sets up in the West Plaza Parking Lot at North and Vine Sts, one block west of the plaza.

Mendocino: Timber Town
Step inside an 1860s house

Mendocino is the ultimate historic timber town. Transplants from New England founded the village along with a mill in 1852, bringing architectural influences that can be seen in the area's Victorian buildings today. The area's lumber industry thrived through the turn of the century, but when the mill closed in the 1930s the town's population and economic

---

HEALDSBURG'S ENTERTAINMENT & FESTIVALS

Tuesdays in the Plaza Concerts: In summer, join free Tuesday concerts; food vendors set up at 5pm, music plays from 6pm to 8pm. *(healdsburg.gov)*

Farmers Market Concerts: Check the website to see what's playing at Tuesday's market. *(healdsburg farmersmarket.org)*

Healdsburg Jazz Festival: Jazz venues in June include wine-tasting courtyard Bacchus Landing. *(healdsburgjazz.org)*

Wine Road Barrel Tasting: In March, wineries throw open wine-cave doors to sample wine from the barrel. *(wineroad.com)*

Healdsburg Wine & Food Experience: In May, revel in local and international wine and farm-to-table food. *(healdsburgwineand food.com)*

Wine & Food Affair: In November, 100 Sonoma County wineries offer a featured dish and wine pairing. *(wineroad.com)*

 EATING IN HEALDSBURG: COOL BAKERIES & CAFES

Quail & Condor: The hot new kid on the block, with bakers from SingleThread making superb French-style pastries and bread. *8am-3pm Wed-Mon* $

Costeaux French Bakery & Cafe: Serving breakfasts since 1923, this bakery-cafe crafts quiches, omelets and pastries. *7am-3pm Sat-Tue, to 8pm Wed-Fri* $

Acorn Cafe: Stop in for coffee and breakfast or gourmet sandwiches, and end up people-watching on the plaza patio. *8am-3pm Mon-Fri, to 5pm Sat & Sun* $$

Troubadour Bread & Bistro: Classic boulangerie: sandwiches by day, pricey bistro with a set menu by night. *7am-4:30pm Tue-Sat, 8am-3pm Sun* $$$

CRUISING THE SONOMA COUNTY COAST TO MENDOCINO

Celebrate an uninterrupted stretch of coastal highway that skirts rocky shores, secluded coves and wind-sculpted beaches.

START	END	LENGTH
Bodega Bay	Mendocino	110 miles; 5 hours

Start alongside the fishing fleets of **1 Bodega Bay**, cruising past the brilliant NorCal Pacific Coast scenery of Sonoma County State Park to the seal colony at the mouth of the Russian River at Goat Rock in **2 Jenner**. As you cruise north again, you'll pass Jenner Headlands Preserve, which offers more walks, or continue straight to **3 Fort Ross State Historic Park**, a reconstruction of a 19th-century Russian fur-trading fort.

From here, the road twists past the free **4 Kruse Rhododendron State Natural Reserve**, with its rhododendron groves. One of the best reasons to spend the night around these parts is **5 Salt Point State Park**, a 6000-acre stunner with sandstone cliffs dropping into a kelp-strewn sea and hiking trails crisscrossing windswept prairies and wooded hills. It's especially popular with mushroom foragers.

Weather-beaten but ritzy private community **6 Sea Ranch** lines an ocean bluff, with five beaches open to the public. **7 Gualala** is a hub for weekend getaways and sunny weather, with its arts center. Another half-hour up the coast, climb the **8 Point Arena Lighthouse**, which has guarded the windy point since 1908. Slip a little further north to **9 Elk**, a hamlet famous for its stunning clifftop views of towering rock formations. Wrap up by arriving at **10 Mendocino** for an idyllic weekend.

> Look for the unique, redwood swirl of **Sea Ranch Chapel**. Pop in from dawn to dusk, as long as there's no ceremony going on.

> At Sea Ranch, **Stengel Beach** has a large, free parking lot and a short cypress-lined trail to a wooden staircase to the beach.

> The road plunges down a canyon to **Russian Gulch State Beach**, a windswept arc of creamy sand, then switchbacks up to the bluff top.

WRECK OF THE FROLIC

In 1850 a ship retired from the opium trade – the *Frolic* – struck a reef near **Point Cabrillo**, about 3 miles north of Mendocino, and ran aground. Jerome Ford, who came from San Francisco to salvage the cargo, was too late as the Native Pomo (who had inhabited the region for some 10,000 years) had already recovered the Chinese luxury goods on board. But Ford took notice of the coast's real treasure: the enormous redwoods. He teamed up with entrepreneur Henry Meiggs, who bought a sawmill and had it transported to Big River. During the mill's 50-year run, it yielded a billion board feet of timber, used to build San Francisco and to rebuild it after the 1906 earthquake.

stability took a hit. Things turned around with the establishment of the Mendocino Art Center in 1959, revitalizing the town and infusing it with artistic charm: nearly two million travelers make a pilgrimage each year to shop at exquisite art galleries, dine at top-tier restaurants and soak up the views offered by a tiny town perched atop Pacific-kissed bluffs.

To get up close and personal with life in a 19th-century logging town, head to the **Kelley House Museum** *(kelley housemuseum.org; suggested $5 donation)*. William Kelley, a businessman who once owned almost all the land that would become Mendocino, built the historic house in 1861. Today, visitors can wander its bedrooms and see period furnishings and personal effects.

A Diamond in the Bluff
Stroll an extraordinary oceanside trail

If hiking trails were judged by ocean views, the path at **Mendocino Headlands State Park** *(parks.ca.gov)* would score an uncontested 10/10. For over 2 miles in one direction, the trail follows the edge of 70ft bluffs, meandering through wildflowers on land and past rock formations and dramatic arches in the water.

Experience Clear Lake State Park
Hiking trails and history

First things first: 'Clear Lake' is the body of water and 'Clearlake' is a town on its southeastern side. It's considered the oldest lake in North America, dating back one to two million years.

Dip your toe into Clear Lake, both metaphorically and literally, at **Clear Lake State Park** *(parks.ca.gov)*. Swim, fish, hike and bike, and get a feel for the lake's Indigenous history by hitting the half-mile **Indian Nature Trail**, which passes through what was once a Pomo village.

Summiting a Volcano
Hike Mt Konocti

The fact that Mt Konocti is a dormant volcano is only part of what makes hiking it so intriguing. Follow the 6-mile Wright Peak Summit Trail and you'll also spot an early 1900s cabin as well as the wreckage from a tragic 1970 plane crash.

The hike begins at the trailhead for **Mt Konocti County Park**. From here it's a steep climb to the top, gaining 1800ft

EATING IN MENDOCINO: OUR PICKS

GoodLife Cafe & Bakery: Starting the day with a blackberry Danish or biscuits smothered in sausage gravy – both served here – really is the good life. *7:30am-2pm* $

Mendocino Cafe: The eclectic menu at this lunch and dinner spot includes a Thai burrito, Indian-style curry and locally caught rockfish. *11am-4pm & 5-9pm* $$

Trillium Cafe: Swing by for fine dining focused on organic seasonal ingredients, or order a picnic basket to go. *11:30am-2:15pm & 5-8:30pm Fri-Tue* $$$

Fog Eater Cafe: This cozy vegetarian spot serves Southern-inspired recipes for dinner and a full brunch menu on Sundays. *4-8pm Wed-Sat, 10am-2pm Sun* $$

Mt Konocti

of elevation. You'll pass Downen Cabin, where the intrepid and peace-seeking Mary Downen lived solo in the early 1900s, about 2 miles into the hike. The mangled pieces of the white-and-turquoise Navion A aircraft, visible just to the right of the trail, sit just before the summit. At the top you'll get an eyeful of Clear Lake below, and on a good day you can also spot Mt Lassen and Mt Diablo. The downhill return is much easier on the muscles.

Panoramic Picnics on the Lost Coast
Enjoy a DIY outdoor meal

On your way into Shelter Cove, stop off at the **Shelter Cove General Store** *(sheltercovegeneralstore.com)* to grab sandwich supplies, snacks, locally brewed beer or a bottle of wine. Then, take your supplies to either **Abalone Point** or **Seal Rock** for a Pacific-view picnic. Both spots sit on a bluff overlooking the ocean and have picnic tables.

Urchins & Abalone Galore
Tide-pooling in Shelter Cove

Probably the most fascinating (and free!) Lost Coast activity for kids is to discover the diverse and wonderfully weird creatures living in the tide pools.

KELSEYVILLE PEAR FESTIVAL

Held on the last Saturday in September, Lake County's largest one-day event – the Kelseyville Pear Festival – is a real hoot and a showcase of the region's agricultural heritage, including the almighty pear. There are parades, live music and dancing on three stages, a giant decorative pear, a pie-eating contest, a scarecrow contest and plenty of street vendors. There are also special exhibits held all over town; for example, a tractor and engine show, or a display on the history of Kelseyville farming within the Pear Pavilion.

The event has grown from just 1500 attendees in 1993 to more than 10,000 in recent years. The festival's highly appropriate slogan? 'Catch the small-town magic.'

 EATING AROUND CLEAR LAKE: OUR PICKS

Saw Shop Public House: A laid-back Kelseyville restaurant with superior farm-to-table California cuisine and delicious cocktails. *noon-8pm Tue-Sat, 11am-8pm Sun* $$

Park Place Restaurant: Lakeport's premier dining venue offers classic Italian and American dishes and lake views. *11am-7pm Sun-Thu, 11am-8pm Fri & Sat* $$

Blue Wing Saloon: Cozy up on the heated veranda with casual American fare and live music at this upper lake restaurant in the Tallman Hotel. *hours vary* $$

Catfish Coffee House: With a convenient drive-through window, this is the spot to grab coffee and bagels. *5:30am-6pm Mon-Fri, 6am-6pm Sat, 6:30am-6pm Sun* $

Start your tide-pooling adventure by parking at **Mal Coombs Park**, where you can't miss the **Cape Mendocino Lighthouse** *(capemendocinolighthouse.org; free)*. Originally located about 60 miles north of here, the lighthouse was moved in 1998 for preservation purposes. Today, it's maintained by the Cape Mendocino Lighthouse Preservation Society, who open it to the public as a museum each summer, from Memorial Day to Labor Day.

After giving the historic lighthouse a look, head down the set of stairs to the beach. At low tide, the area looks otherworldly, with rugged black rocks exposed. You may find treasures in the sand, like pieces of petrified wood or dried urchin shells, but climb the rock formations (always keeping an eye on the tide, of course), and peer into the puddles to an entire world of living aquatic critters.

Historic Crafts in Eureka
Get hands-on with historic traditional crafts

The word 'Eureka' expresses joyous discovery. It's also California's official state motto and the name of Humboldt County's capital – both fitting applications. In the city of Eureka, you're likely to find plenty of moments of joyful discovery.

Part museum, part professional woodworking studio, part center for learning traditional crafts, the **Blue Ox Historic Village** *(blueoxhistoricvillage.com)* houses a massive collection of Victorian-era woodworking machinery (still used today), a print shop, a craftsman's apothecary (for mixing stains, varnishes, paints and glues) and a textile atelier. And that's only what's inside the main building. Outside, guests can explore a skid camp – complete with a bunk house, cook shack and theater – and imagine what it was like to live in the area as a logger in the early 1900s. Keep walking the grounds and you'll also come upon working blacksmithing and ceramics studios. For the ultimate experience, book a **Blue Ox class** *(adult/child from $120/90)*, with activities such as blacksmithing, ceramics or stained-glass making.

Hiking 100 Feet High
Stroll the redwood canopy

At the **Redwood Sky Walk** *(redwoodskywalk.com)* inside Eureka's **Sequoia Park Zoo** *(redwoodzoo.org; adult/child $25/13)*, you can stroll up into a redwood grove and explore

EUREKA'S BEST SHOPS

Humboldt Mercantile: Snag redwoods tees, hemp hand soap and locally made hot sauce at this souvenir hot spot.

Many Hands Gallery: Like visiting a few dozen artists' studios in one fell swoop; the gallery stocks ceramics, jewelry and particularly pretty leather journals.

Land of Lovely: Consider a visit here your personal invitation to luxuriate and pick up a new robe, bath soaks and botanical candles.

Eureka Books: Browse new, used and rare books, then have the Zoltar machine in front read your fortune.

Little Shop of Hers: Find an expertly curated collection of vintage clothes and accessories here for both him and her.

EATING IN SHELTER COVE: OUR PICKS

Surf Point Coffee House: Find coffee, housemade pastries and wine pours to pair with lunch at this bistro with breathtaking views. *7:30am-4pm Fri-Wed, 7:30am-4:30pm Thu* $

Mi Mochima: From out of nowhere comes delicious and authentic Venezuelan cuisine: empanadas, arepas, *patacón* sandwiches. *hours vary* $$

Gyppo Ale Mill: California's most remote brewery serves its own lagers, pilsners and blondes, and knocks burgers and wings out of the park, too. *5-9pm Mon-Thu, noon-9pm Fri-Sun* $$

Mario's Marina Bar: This local hangout has killer ocean views from its patio and frequent live music. *hours vary* $$

the ancient giants from 100ft above the forest floor. The elevated trail is the longest of its kind in the western United States, with an ascent ramp, launch deck, accessible main loop, nine viewing platforms and an optional hanging bridge.

Discover Redwood National & State Parks
Unforgettable hiking and natural wonders

Waterfalls, fern-covered canyons, rugged ocean coastline and, oh yes, the world's tallest trees... In the upper reaches of California's Pacific Coast, the area is maintained by the National Park Service and California State Parks. In addition to **Redwood National Park**, this northern natural wonderland includes three state parks: **Prairie Creek Redwoods State Park**, **Del Norte Coast Redwoods State Park** and **Jedediah Smith Redwoods State Par**k. There isn't one main entrance to the area: the parks sit along a 50-mile driving route on Hwy 101.

For a quick hike, take the **Fern Canyon Loop** (southern): there's nothing quite like this 1-mile Prairie Creek canyon trail, which follows a stream surrounded by towering fern-covered walls (it served as a backdrop for *The Lost World: Jurassic Park*). Another option is **Simpson-Reed & Peterson Loop** (northern): hike two trails in under an hour at Jedediah Smith Redwoods. Combining these two short loop trails creates a 0.8-mile hike through a redwood grove that's suitable for just about any ability level.

If you have kids in tow, the **Lady Bird Johnson Grove** (southern), a 1.4-mile hike in Redwood National Park, is the ideal length for little ones, plus you'll find a number of benches for moments of rest. Another hike for kids is the **Stout Grove Loop** (northern): first-time hikers will feel a major sense of accomplishment when they dominate this 0.6-mile loop in Jedediah Smith Redwoods. The redwoods soaring above a lush forest floor will have kids hooked on the great outdoors.

For those hoping to see a waterfall, there's the **Trillium Falls Loop** (southern): at only 2.7 miles and with a trailhead that's right off Hwy 101, this Prairie Creek path could also qualify for the quick and kid-friendly categories. The scenic and soothing falls are located within the first half-mile of the walk. There's also the **Boy Scout Tree Trail** (northern): you'll have to put in a little more work to see the falls along this trail, located in Jedediah Smith Redwoods, but it's worth it. The total out-and-back hike is 5.6 miles and the waterfall, called Fern Falls, is the turnaround point.

YUROK COUNTRY

With 6500 enrolled members, the Yurok ('downriver people') comprise California's largest Native American tribe. Historically, they've been celebrated as expert basket weavers, canoe makers and fishers, and traditions continue to this day, including the **Klamath Salmon Festival** each August. In addition to supporting the tribe by hiring Yurok people as outdoor guides, consider purchasing their locally made handicrafts, especially the jewelry. You'll find dangly earrings made from pieces of abalone shell, and long beaded necklaces strung with pine nuts and white, tubular dentalium shells. Resembling miniature elephant tusks, dentalium shells were once used by the Yurok as currency. One great place to shop is the **Yurok Country Visitor Center** in Klamath, which has jewelry, in addition to T-shirts and hand-knit hats featuring tribal symbolism.

DRINKING IN EUREKA: BEST FOR BEER & COCKTAILS

The Shanty: Popular with young hipsters for its pinball, pool and sweet back patio, this is the coolest bar in town. *noon-2am*

Lost Coast Brewery & Cafe: Head to its restaurant on Fourth St for craft beers and burgers, or visit the brewery for a tour. *11:30am-9pm Wed-Sun*

Phatsy Kline's Parlor Lounge: Located inside the historic Eagle house, Phatsy's is the place for a fancy cocktail. *4-9pm Wed & Thu, 4-11pm Fri & Sat*

The Speakeasy: Squeeze in with the locals at this New Orleans–inspired bar with live blues and a convivial atmosphere. *4-11pm Sun-Thu, 4pm-2am Fri & Sat*

THE DAM AT SHASTA LAKE

On scale with the enormous natural features of the area, the colossal 15-million-ton **Shasta Dam** is second in size only to Grand Coolie Dam in Washington state and second in height only to Hoover Dam in Nevada. It was built between 1937 and 1949, with its 487ft spillway nearly three times as high as Niagara Falls. Woody Guthrie wrote 'This Land Is Your Land' here while he was entertaining dam workers. The **Shasta Dam Visitors Center** offers a 21-minute video shown on request, and self-guided walking tours across the vertiginous top of the dam are available from 6am to 10pm daily. It's located at the south end of the lake on Shasta Dam Blvd.

Hiking Mt Shasta
Woodland strolls, ambitious summit

At 14,179ft, Mt Shasta is only the fifth-highest mountain in California, but its beauty is unrivaled. The mountain has two cones: the younger, shorter cone on the western flank, called Shastina, has a crater about half a mile wide.

The moderate 3.5-mile out-and-back hike to the beautiful stone 1922 **Sierra Club Horse Camp hut** leaves from **Bunny Flat** (6940ft) and is open year-round, though you'll want snowshoes in winter. Bunny Flat is the starting place of the challenging **Avalanche Gulch**, the easiest route to the summit, best done between May and September. Although it's only about 10 miles round-trip, the vertical climb is more than 7000ft, so acclimatizing to the elevation is critical – many hikers overnight at **Helen Lake** (10,443ft). This route requires crampons, an ice axe and a helmet, all of which can be rented locally.

Crystal Shops & Vortex Tours
A mystical energy center

Mt Shasta is considered a power center, where mythical ley lines cross, producing a high concentration of electromagnetic energy. Within the town's tiny grid of streets you'll find six crystal shops, each different from the next. Our favorite is **Crystal Matrix** (*crystalmatrixgallery.com*), open 10am to 6pm Wednesday to Monday, which feels more like a rockhound shop with a kind and intuitive owner who knows his stuff. Crystals in hand, sign up for a Vortex Tour. Ashalyn with **Shasta Vortex Adventures** was the first to introduce these types of tours but there are several operators around town.

Houseboating on Shasta Lake
Cruise a forested coastline

Shasta Lake is known as the 'houseboat capital of the world,' and with good reason: the water reaches 78°F (26°C) in summer and there are 365 miles of shoreline to putter along. All you need is a driver's license to rent a boat, and you'll get to pilot one of the many vessels gliding through the water at a reasonable 15mph. Pack your own supplies and enjoy lazy evenings cooking for yourself beneath the star-filled sky.

While some will be happy to float and swim at leisure, there are also several destinations to explore, including the famous

EATING IN THE MT SHASTA REGION: OUR PICKS

Bistro 107: Get excellent burgers and hearty hot sandwiches at this homey yet classy little joint. *11:30am-9pm Fri-Tue* $$

Hari On Shri Ram Indian Cuisine: The most authentic and delicious Indian food for hundreds of miles, served with a smile. *noon-3pm & 5-9pm Wed-Mon* $$

Lily's: Great American breakfasts plus Asian or Mediterranean-touched salads, fresh sandwiches and good, square meals. *8am-2pm & 4-8pm Wed-Sun* $$

Crave: Street tacos, sandwiches, barbecue, vegetarian...it's all good. The setting is basic but comfy and friendly. *11:30am-8pm Tue-Sat* $$

Mt Shasta

Lake Shasta Caverns, waterfalls like **Little Backbone Creek** (don't miss the natural waterslide), the Shasta Dam and any number of hiking trails.

This massive lake hosts the largest reservoir populations of ospreys and bald eagles in California. Ospreys are best seen between May and June, which is their nesting season. Look for bald eagles year-round.

Get Deep at Shasta Caverns
Underground geological wonderland

Located high in the limestone megaliths at the north end of Shasta Lake are the impressive **Lake Shasta Caverns** *(lake shastacaverns.com; 2hr tours adult/child $44/26).* Tours operate daily and include a boat ride across Shasta Lake. Once inside, it's a one-hour meander along lighted trails and some 600 steps, passing a wondrous array of formations, including waterfall-like curtains of limestone, impressively large stalactites and stalagmites, Jurassic fossils and coral-like helictites.

MT SHASTA'S BEST CAMPING

Lower Panther Meadows: Fifteen walk-in, summer-season tent sites are the highest on the mountain and have spectacular views.

Castle Lake Campground: Only six primitive, summer campsites are found here, about a quarter mile below the lake, but they are very special indeed.

Lake Siskiyou Beach & Camp: On the shore of Lake Siskiyou, this sprawling, family-friendly place has a summer-camp feel, with swimming and boat rentals.

Castle Crags State Park Campground: The campsites here are shady, pretty and have plenty of amenities.

McCloud Dance Country RV Park: With campsites under the trees and a small creek, this is a good option for families. The view of the mountain is breathtaking.

 DRINKING IN REDDING: OUR PICKS

Fall River Brewing: Best beers around. Bring your kids if you have them and expect to mingle with locals. *noon-8pm*

Woody's Brewing Co: Open since 2015, with great beers plus a food menu – from burgers and salads to crunchy Tater Tots. *11am-9pm Tue-Sun*

Final Draft Brewing Company: Industrial-style brewpub with vats on display. Try beer styles you won't find elsewhere in Redding. *11am-9pm*

Westside Tap & Cork: Several wineries have tasting rooms in Redding but this is a good stop to sample a variety of them plus local beers. *4-9pm Tue-Sun*

A DRIVING TOUR OF LASSEN VOLCANIC NATIONAL PARK

This fiery landscape features roiling hot springs and crater lakes. Hiking stops can make it a multiday trip, but otherwise it takes a few hours.

START	END	LENGTH
Visitor Center	Manzanita Lake	28 miles; 3+ hours

Near the park's southwest entrance, the handsome ❶ **Kohm Yah-mah-nee Visitor Center** is the perfect starting place, with educational exhibits, a gift shop, cafe and toilets. Turn north out of the parking lot and drive 1 mile. The best roadside place to see geothermal action, the ❷ **Sulfur Works Hydrothermal Area** has bubbling mud pots, hissing steam vents, fountains and fumaroles. You can hike 1 mile to the Ridge Lakes from here.

The next 5 miles winds through some of the best vistas in the park. The big parking lot at the ❸ **Brokeoff Volcano Scenic Vista** hosts a beautiful view of Brokeoff Volcano, Mt Conard and Diamond Peak.

In just over a mile turn into a parking lot for the ❹ **Lassen Peak Scenic Vista**: the sight of the rocky slopes up close is awe inspiring. ❺ **Hat Creek Meadow** is one of the best stops for fall foliage. It's a quick half-mile to your next stop on the right, the ❻ **Devastated Area**, with a quarter-mile interpretive loop through a former eruption zone. The scenery becomes lusher over the next 7.5 miles.

❼ **Chaos Crags** is a giant field of rock rubble, the result of a massive slide in the 1660s. It's about a mile through light forest to your final stop, ❽ **Manzanita Lake**, where there are kayak rentals in summer.

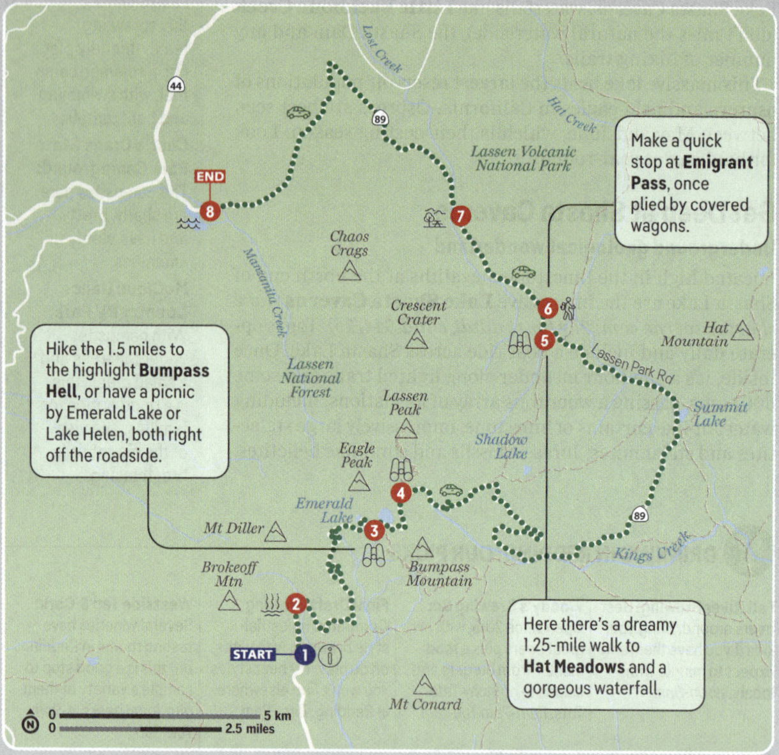

Make a quick stop at **Emigrant Pass**, once plied by covered wagons.

Hike the 1.5 miles to the highlight **Bumpass Hell**, or have a picnic by Emerald Lake or Lake Helen, both right off the roadside.

Here there's a dreamy 1.25-mile walk to **Hat Meadows** and a gorgeous waterfall.

Yosemite, Lake Tahoe & Gold Country

MAJESTIC DOMES | TURQUOISE WATERS | SPARKLING TOWNS

Yosemite, crown jewel of California's national parks, is defined by its plunging waterfalls, soaring trees, wildflower-dotted valleys and majestic domes. Carved by ancient glaciers, these stunning granite features have been gazed upon by devoted humans for some 8000 years.

Lake Tahoe sits more than 6000ft above sea level, straddling the California–Nevada border. The lake's almost unreal shades of blue and turquoise aren't found anywhere else in California, and the surrounding Sierra Nevada mountains frame the lake with dramatic peaks and dense pine forests. Winter brings deep snow and a flurry of activity at ski resorts.

A visit to Gold Country feels like traveling back in time. Historic buildings in their original glory, clapboard saloons, oak-lined byways and even the clip-clopping of horses all nod to the rich history of the area, famously known as the home of the Gold Rush of 1849.

Time Travel in Mariposa
Make a Gold Rush stop on your way to Yosemite

En route to Yosemite, this former Gold Rush town packs quite the cultural punch. The **Mariposa Museum & History Center** *(mariposamuseum.com; adult/child $10/5)* displays old menus, train tickets, photos and the like, and a Miwuk exhibit features expertly woven baskets, jewelry, arrowheads and

GETTING AROUND

Driving is the most popular way to get around: in Yosemite this means traffic, smog and frustrating battles for spaces during summer. Tahoe Transportation District serves the south lake shore, and bike-rack-equipped Tahoe Area Regional Transit (TART) serves Truckee, the north shore and the Tahoe City area. The Gold Country is best enjoyed with your own vehicle, especially up Hwy 49. Distances are short, so fuel needs will be minimal (or do it all with only one charge).

☑ TOP TIP

Before driving to Yosemite, find out if you'll need a reservation for your visit and secure it through recreation.gov. If reservations are sold out, you can enter by booking lodgings within the park, taking a guided tour, obtaining a wilderness permit or Half Dome permit, or riding a YARTS bus.

Lake Tahoe

more. Over at the county fairgrounds, rock hounds will dig the **California State Mining & Mineral Museum** *(parks.ca.gov; adult/child $4/free)*, where the 13lb 'Fricot Nugget' (the largest crystalized gold specimen from the California Gold Rush era) is proudly displayed.

Bouldering & River Rafting
River deep, mountain high

Climbing enthusiasts should pop over to the **Yosemite Climbing Museum** *(yosemiteclimbing.org/museum; suggested donation $5)*, which contains memorabilia stretching back to when the sport's pioneers were making their own gear. There's also the **Yosemite Boulder Farm**, a B&B with climbing and disc-golf on the town's outskirts. The property offers 6 acres of granite, with 20 boulders and climbs for every level. The owners spent three years clearing brush, leveling landings and power washing the boulders, and they operate the super-convivial B&B.

Declared a Wild and Scenic River by Congress in 1987, the **Merced** has twisting and tumbling white water that's best experienced on a raft. In spring, the exhilarating trip takes you down class III and IV rapids, whereas things get a lot more relaxed in summer after most of the snowmelt has run its course. **Zephyr Whitewater Expeditions** *(zrafting.com)* has been running trips on the Merced since 1973, and the large, reputable company has experienced guides and a seasonal office across from Yosemite Bug near Briceburg. Half-day trips cost $113 to $128; full-day trips range from $176 to $191 and include lunch.

If white water feels too extreme, head up the road to the **Merced River Recreation Management Area** *(blm.gov/visit/merced-river)* in Briceburg, where there's a **visitor center**, a picnic area, an extension bridge over the river, some campgrounds and a trail system. Depending on the time of year, it's an ideal spot for fishing, camping, hiking or just watching the rafts drift by.

BEST DAY TRIPS FOR HISTORY BUFFS

Hornitos: An old gold-mining settlement 30 minutes' drive west of Mariposa, with a still-operational bar, objects of intrigue and possibly ghosts.

Coulterville: Historic buildings line the streets of this charming former Gold Rush supply town 25 miles north of Mariposa.

Columbia State Historic Park: A mini Gold Rush theme park where volunteers dress in 19th-century garb and parade around blacksmith shops, theaters and saloons.

Hite Cove: Hike to a true ghost town on this 4.5-mile trail (one way) along the Merced River. Rock walls and heavy machinery remain.

Gold-Panning with Ira Estin: This longtime local (209-966-7262) takes you gold-panning along the Merced, teaching about the history and tools of the Gold Rush.

TOP EXPERIENCE

Yosemite National Park

Show-stopping Yosemite National Park is a UNESCO World Heritage Site, visited by millions of people each year. The original caretakers, the Ahwahneechee people, were violently displaced in the mid-1800s by white settlers. In 1864 President Abraham Lincoln ceded the land to California as a state park. This, paired with the efforts of conservationist John Muir, led to a congressional act in 1890 creating the national park.

Mariposa Grove

TOP TIPS

- Yosemite Village hosts the main visitor center, a museum, eateries and services.

- Curry Village is another valley hub with rooms, cabins, dining options and trailheads for popular hikes.

- Glacier Point can be reached on foot or with wheels and offers the park's most spectacular views.

PRACTICALITIES

- nps.gov/yose
- $20 per person, $35 per car to enter the park for three consecutive days

Touring Yosemite Valley

The **Yosemite Valley Loop Trail** generally follows Northside and Southside Drs, with some sections tracing the routes of former wagon roads. The most famous features you'll see are monumental 7569ft **El Capitan** (El Cap), one of the world's largest granite monoliths and a magnet for rock climbers, and 8842ft **Half Dome**, the park's spiritual centerpiece – its rounded granite pate forms an unmistakable silhouette. Meanwhile, Yosemite's waterfalls mesmerize even the most jaded traveler.

Climbing Half Dome

Just hold on, don't forget to breathe and – whatever you do – don't look down. A pinnacle so popular hikers need a permit to scale it, Half Dome is Yosemite Valley's coveted cocked-top jewel. The hike takes longer than an average work day, with an elevation gain equivalent to 480 flights of stairs and a near-vertical final stretch.

Mariposa Grove

In this cathedral of ancient trees, almost 500 hardy sequoias rocket to the sky. Early in the morning, explore Mariposa Grove in solitude and contemplate the thousands of years the trees have witnessed. Other highlights include walking through the heart of the still-living California Tunnel Tree and witnessing the girth of the Grizzly Giant.

YOSEMITE NATIONAL PARK

HIGHLIGHTS
1 Yosemite National Park

SIGHTS
2 California State Mining & Mineral Museum
3 Columbia State Historic Park
4 Coulterville
5 El Capitan
6 Half Dome
7 Hite Cove
8 Hornitos
9 Mariposa Grove
10 Mariposa Museum & History Center
11 Tuolumne County Museum
12 Yosemite Climbing Museum

ACTIVITIES
13 Yosemite Mountain Sugar Pine Railroad
14 Zephyr Whitewater Expeditions

SLEEPING
15 Sonora Inn
16 Yosemite Basecamp
17 Yosemite Bug Rustic Mountain Resort

INFORMATION
18 Briceburg Visitor Center

Riding the Sugar Pine Railroad
Steam train adventure

From mid-March through late November, the historic steam train of the **Yosemite Mountain Sugar Pine Railroad** *(ymsprr.com; per person from $31.80)* chugs from Fish Camp through Sierra National Forest on a 4-mile loop used for lugging lumber at the turn of the 20th century. It's a classic family adventure with some good history woven in. There's also a small museum, a gift store and a sandwich shop, plus gold-panning tours ($10/15 per person online/on-site) with a prospector.

TOP EXPERIENCE

Sequoia & Kings Canyon National Parks

Far from the hubbub of Yosemite Valley, in the side-by-side parks of Sequoia and Kings Canyon, it's easy to find solitude in wildflower-strewn meadows or by an alpine lake, to unwind before a gushing waterfall or pull off a deserted highway and gaze into a dramatic gorge. People mainly visit, however, for the parks' forests, featuring some of the planet's largest giant sequoias.

Giant Forest

Superlative Sequoias

Build your big tree anticipation with a primer on their intriguing ecology and history at the **Giant Forest Museum**, housed in a historic 1920s building. Jump on the shuttle up the highway to **Giant Forest**, a 3-sq-mile grove that protects around half of the world's most gargantuan tree specimens. Among them is the world's biggest by volume, the **General Sherman Tree**, rocketing 275ft into the sky.

Hit the Trails

Moro Rock, just south of the Giant Forest, offers a quick ascent to the tippy-top of a granite dome and panoramic views, while Mineral King's Eagle Lake is a more secluded jaunt to a glacially carved tarn. The **High Sierra Trail**, a 49-mile stunner along a dramatic ridge, offers epic views and river crossings, concluding at Mt Whitney.

Spelunking

Crystal Cave (visitsequoia.com/sequoia-national-park-attractions/crystal-cave; tour adult/child $20/10) was carved over millennia by an underground river with marble formations estimated to be up to 100,000 years old. Stalactites hang like daggers from the cave ceiling, and milky-white formations take the shape of ethereal curtains, domes, columns and shields. Tickets for the 50-minute tour are only sold online in advance.

TOP TIPS

- From late May to early September, Sequoia Shuttle runs buses four times daily between Visalia, Three Rivers and the Giant Forest Museum in Sequoia National Park.

- Campsites and wilderness permits must be booked on recreation.gov.

- Park-approved, bear-proof food canisters are mandatory for wilderness trips.

PRACTICALITIES

- nps.gov/seki
- $20 per person, $35 per car
- wilderness permit required for overnight backpacking

Skiing in Heavenly, Tahoe
Hit the slopes at Heavenly Resort

Tahoe is a year-round destination, with slow seasons a thing of the past. Winter brings deep snow at ski resorts like **Heavenly Mountain Resort** *(epicpass.com; Epic Pass single-day ticket adult/child from $94/48)* is perhaps the most well-known in California. It sits steps from the Lake Tahoe shoreline, with flabbergasting views plus trails that look like you're about to ski into the lake. With a base area at 6200ft above sea level and a summit above 10,000ft, it has the most skiable vert (vertical feet top-to-bottom) in Tahoe.

Follow the sun by skiing on the Nevada side in the morning for desert views, then moving to the California side in the afternoon. Snowboarders will want to carry speed on some flats to avoid hopping between states. Buy an Epic single-day ticket, rather than buying day-of at the ticket window, to save some dough.

High-Elevation Family Fun
Heavenly isn't just for winter

The **Heavenly Gondola** *(skiheavenly.com; adult/child from $79/39)* soars guests from the Heavenly Village in Stateline to Tamarack Lodge at more than 10,000ft above sea level. There's an observation deck at the halfway point with panoramic views of the entire Tahoe Basin, with summer activities like a zipline, a mountain coaster, tubing and hiking trails at the top. The gondola runs year-round for sightseeing, though the mountain may limit capacity for non-skiers on busy weekends.

Venture into Desolation Wilderness
Explore Tahoe's backcountry

Sculpted by powerful glaciers aeons ago, **Desolation Wilderness** *(fs.usda.gov)* covers 100 sq miles of high-elevation forest spread between the south and west shores. With no roads, the only way to visit is on foot, with dozens of hiking trails passing polished granite peaks and leading to deep-blue alpine lakes, glacier-carved valleys and resplendent pine forests that thin quickly at the higher elevations. It has exceptional wildflower hiking well into July.

Permits are required year-round for both day and overnight explorations, though day hikers can get them from self-issue stations at trailheads. Backpacking permits are available in

> **SEE ENVIRONMENTAL PROTECTION IN ACTION**
>
> **Caroline Waldman**, local expert and South Lake Tahoe resident, works for the Tahoe Fund, a nonprofit working to improve and protect Tahoe's environmental resources. *tahoefund.org*
>
> The first stop on any sustainability success tour should be **Taylor Creek**. Walk along the interpretive trail to the viewing platforms and you may spot wildlife in action: kokanee salmon swimming, black bears napping or bald eagles soaring overhead. Next, head to Ski Run Blvd, where you'll find an empty lot transformed into the new **Ski Run Community Park**, complete with a climbing boulder. Head to Stateline, and in front of the **Tahoe Blue Event Center** you'll see a sculpture of a bald eagle holding a Lahontan cutthroat trout, crafted entirely from litter removed from Lake Tahoe by scuba divers.

EATING ON TAHOE'S SOUTH SHORE: ROMANTIC RESTAURANTS

Chart House: White-tablecloth dining a few miles from the tourist strip; lake views, and wildlife sightings aren't uncommon. *4-9:30pm Mon-Sat, to 9pm Sun* $$$

Edge Restaurant & Lounge: Tables are next to floor-to-ceiling windows. Check what time sunset is and reserve for 30 minutes beforehand. *hours vary* $$$

Wolf by Vanderpump: Arguably the most chichi casino restaurant in the area, with over-the-top decor and cocktails. *5-10pm Sun-Thu, from 4pm Fri & Sat* $$$

Evans American Gourmet Café: Reliably delicious and non-pretentious, with creative daily specials. *5-9pm Tue-Sat* $$$

YOSEMITE, LAKE TAHOE & GOLD COUNTRY CALIFORNIA

THE GUIDE

LAKE TAHOE & AROUND

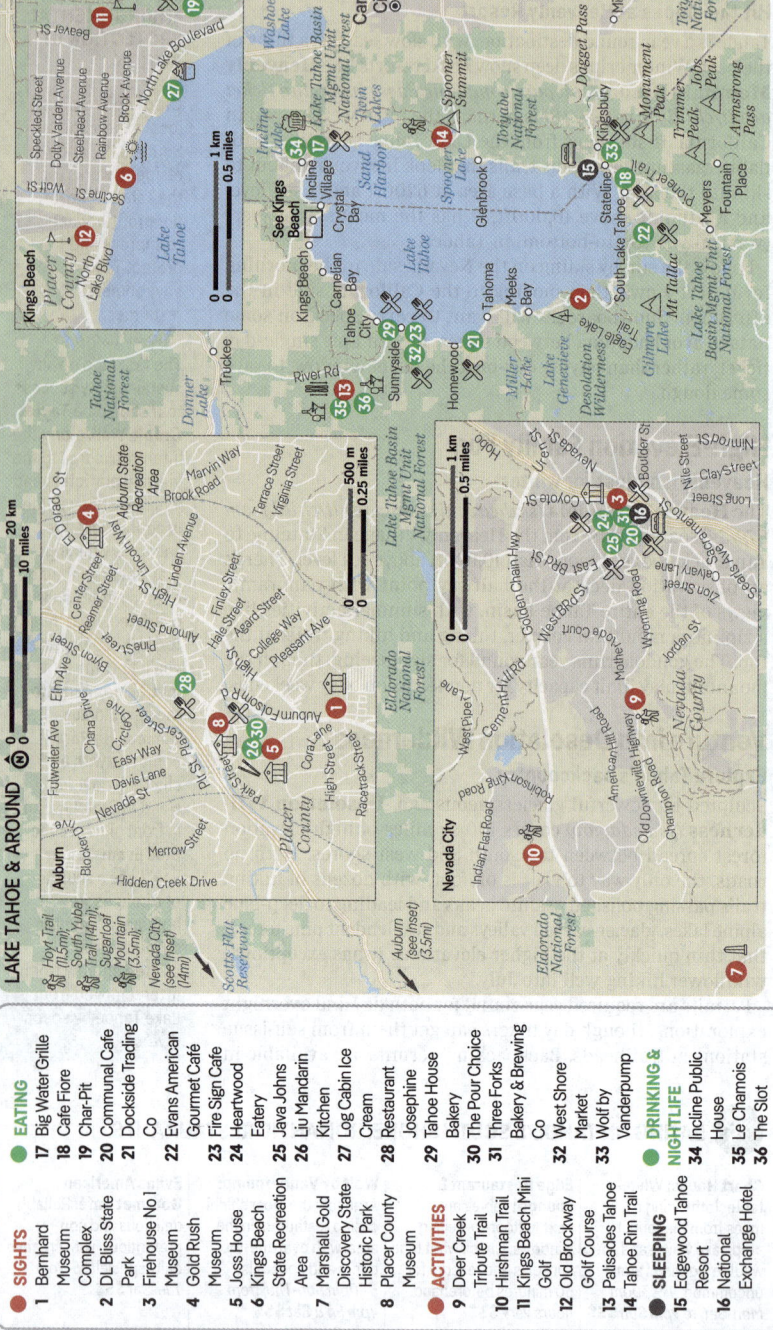

● SIGHTS
1. Bernhard Museum Complex
2. DL Bliss State Park
3. Firehouse No 1 Museum
4. Gold Rush Museum
5. Joss House
6. Kings Beach State Recreation Area
7. Marshall Gold Discovery State Historic Park
8. Placer County Museum

● ACTIVITIES
9. Deer Creek Tribute Trail
10. Hirshman Trail
11. Kings Beach Mini Golf
12. Old Brockway Golf Course
13. Palisades Tahoe
14. Tahoe Rim Trail

● SLEEPING
15. Edgewood Tahoe Resort
16. National Exchange Hotel

● EATING
17. Big Water Grille
18. Cafe Fiore
19. Char-Pit
20. Communal Cafe
21. Dockside Trading Co
22. Evans American Gourmet Café
23. Fire Sign Cafe
24. Heartwood Eatery
25. Java Johns
26. Liu Mandarin Kitchen
27. Log Cabin Ice Cream
28. Restaurant Josephine
29. Tahoe House Bakery
30. The Pour Choice
31. Three Forks Bakery & Brewing Co
32. West Shore Market
33. Wolf by Vanderpump

● DRINKING & NIGHTLIFE
34. Incline Public House
35. Le Chamois
36. The Slot

DL Bliss State Park

advance online. Be prepared to face hefty fines if you're not fire and bear aware.

The West Shore's Best Beaches
Spend the day in Bliss

Just a few miles north of Emerald Bay State Park is **DL Bliss State Park** *(parks.ca.gov; parking $10),* and while it's named for an early Tahoe tourism magnet, it could also be in honor of how you'll feel when you relax on its picture-perfect beaches. The park's Lester Beach and Calawee Cove are walk-in-only beaches tucked into small coves that somehow never seem too crowded. The park's Balancing Rock Trail goes past an oddity of nature that time seems to ignore, while the Lighthouse Trail heads to a historic lighthouse built by the Coast Guard in 1916. At 8600ft above sea level, it's the country's highest-elevation public lighthouse.

Romping Around Vintage Kings Beach
Hit the beach, 1960s-style

Few places in Tahoe are as untouched by recent development as Kings Beach. The humble and walkable town has a smattering of modest retro motels and a host of old-school dining establishments, from the vintage **Char-Pit** *(charpit.shop)* for burgers to family-owned **Log Cabin Ice Cream** *(logcabin icecream.squarespace.com).*

YOU'RE IN THEIR HOME: BE BEAR AWARE

Black bears are cute from a distance, but leaving food and other items out brings them close to people – and when bears get too close to people, they face severe penalties. Help keep bears alive by following basic bear safety rules: never leave scented items unattended (or in your car), close kitchen doors and windows at night, and never leave trash outside next to a full dumpster. Bear canisters are mandatory for all overnight camping in the Tahoe basin. You can rent them from the Taylor Creek Visitor Center in South Lake Tahoe between June and October. If you see a bear in need of help, inform the **Tahoe Bear League** *(savebears.org).*

 EATING ON TAHOE'S WEST SHORE: CHEAPER PICKS

Tahoe House Bakery: A Swiss-style bakery and deli plus to-go breads, cheese and chocolate. *6am-3pm* $

West Shore Market: Fresh sandwiches and gelatos scooped lakeside at the deli. *7am-8pm, deli 10am-3pm or 3:30pm* $$

Fire Sign Cafe: A west-shore institution with constant crowds and wildly fluffy pancake stacks. *7:30am-2:30pm* $$

Dockside Trading Co: Grilled items, plus grab-and-go sandwiches and cheese-tastic burritos. *7am-7pm* $$

THE IMPRESSIVE TAHOE RIM TRAIL

The 165-mile-long **Tahoe Rim Trail** (tahoerimtrail.org), or TRT, was first envisioned in the early 1980s, but wasn't completed until 2001. It encircles the lake, traversing its summits with an elevation gain/loss of about 24,000ft. In one go, it'll take an experienced hiker about 12 days to finish. Fortunately, there are 12 official trailheads throughout the basin, allowing hikers to explore select segments as day hikes or overnight trips. Mountain bikes are banned in designated wilderness areas and on sections that overlap with the Pacific Crest Trail. Bike-friendly segments include Brockway Summit to Watson Lake, Kingsbury Grade to Armstrong Pass, and Tahoe Meadows to Spooner Summit (allowed on even-numbered days). Be aware of wildlife and altitude risks while on the trail.

Kings Beach State Recreation Area

In summer, all eyes are on **Kings Beach State Recreation Area**, a seductive 700ft-long beach that often gets deluged with sunseekers. The nostalgic 1920s **Old Brockway Golf Course** (oldbrockway.com; green fees adult/child from $60/50) will please golfers with its peekaboo lake views and a popular lakeview bar. Less-serious golfers can enjoy **Kings Beach Mini Golf** (kingsbeachminiaturegolf.com; $15).

Winter at Palisades Tahoe

A hub for big-mountain winter sports

Combined, **Palisades Tahoe** (palisadestahoe.com) and Alpine Meadows (connected by lift and sharing one lift ticket) have 6000 skiable acres, making it the biggest ski resort in California. Though known for its expert runs and chutes, it has an expansive beginner area with a unique feature: it's near the top. That means beginners get expert-level views, even on their first day. Lift tickets are expensive, pushing $300 per day on winter weekends, so an all-season Epic Pass may be a better deal for repeat skiers. Parking reservations are required on winter weekends and holidays. If skiing isn't your thing, other winter draws include an all-ages snow-tubing area, a year-round sightseeing gondola, and the 'Cushing Crossing' pond skim each May.

 DRINKING ON TAHOE'S NORTH SHORE: BEST APRÈS-SKI

Big Water Grille: This lake-view restaurant near Diamond Peak is popular for sunset happy hours for deep-pocketed locals. *hours vary*

Incline Public House: Alibi Brewing's large location in Incline Village is a year-round favorite, with about a dozen local beers. *hours vary*

The Slot: An institution for cheap beer, loud music and '80s ski movies on repeat. *hours vary*

Le Chamois: Ski-in bar at Palisades Tahoe with Adirondack chairs, pizzas, an outdoor bar and plenty of post-ski sun in spring. *hours vary*

Touring Gold Country History in Auburn
History-rich museums

Often considered the heart of Gold Country, Auburn is the region's largest town and is steeped in Gold Rush charm. Stroll the Old Town for buildings dating to the 1850s – all with free admission. On the south side, the **Bernhard Museum Complex** *(placer.ca.gov)*, built in 1851 as the Traveler's Rest Hotel and later serving as the home of the Bernhard family, reflects 19th-century farm life.

Rebuilt by the Yue family in the 1920s after a mysterious fire, the clapboard **Joss House** *(auburnjosshouse.org)* stands on 'Chinese Hill,' one of many Chinese communities established during the Gold Rush, and gives an intimate look at what life was like for Chinese laborers back then. Tours run every Saturday between 10:30am and 2:30pm.

The 1st floor of the historic courthouse is home to the **Placer County Museum** *(placer.ca.gov)* and displays Native American artifacts, an 1877 stagecoach and huge unrefined gold nuggets. In the old Auburn train station, the kid-friendly interactive **Gold Rush Museum** *(placer.ca.gov)* includes a reconstructed mine and gold panning.

Gold Rush at Marshall Gold Discovery State Historic Park
Where the rush began

The **Marshall Gold Discovery State Historic Park** *(parks.ca.gov)* comprises a fascinating collection of buildings in a lovely riverside setting at the site of James Marshall's discovery. The museum tells the stories of some early settlers here, such as a group of African Americans who were once enslaved. Follow a short path along the south fork of the American River to the place where James Marshall made his fateful discovery and kickstarted the birth of the 'Golden State,' with its horrific consequences for the state's Indigenous people.

Gold Country's Star Town
Walking Nevada City

You can stroll around this charming town in just an hour if you're in a hurry, but it's best to take a leisurely stroll, stopping to eat, drink and shop along the way. Begin at **Firehouse No 1 Museum** *(nevadacountyhistory.org)*, a stately 1861 building and home to a small exhibit featuring curated

> ### ALL THAT GLITTERS IS TRAGIC
>
> John Sutter, who had a fort in Sacramento, partnered with James Marshall to build a sawmill on the swift stretch of the American River at Coloma in 1847. It was Marshall who discovered gold here on January 24, 1848, and though the men tried to keep their findings secret, prospectors from around the world stampeded into town. In one of the ironies of the Gold Rush, the men who made this discovery died nearly penniless. Many of the new immigrants who arrived seeking fortune were indentured, taxed and bamboozled out of anything they found. Meanwhile, the world of the local Native American Nisenan people was collapsing due to disease and displacement.

EATING & DRINKING IN AUBURN: OUR PICKS

The Pour Choice: Downtown coffee shop that also serves top-notch pastries, sandwiches and even cocktails. *7am-7pm Sun-Wed, to 9pm Thu & Sat* **$$**

Liu Mandarin Kitchen: Homemade dumplings and other northern Mandarin dishes tantalize the taste buds. *11am-9pm Thu-Tue* **$$**

Restaurant Josephine: A local go-to for a special occasion; dine on seasonal French cuisine in a handsome brick building. *5-9pm Tue-Thu, 4-10pm Fri & Sat* **$$$**

Maria's Mexican Tacos: Indulge in Maria's authentic tacos, burritos, tortas and fajitas right off the 80 at this local favorite. *Tue-Sat 10am-8pm* **$$**

Deer Creek Tribute Trail

NEVADA CITY'S BEST HIKES

Deer Creek Tribute Trail: Popular hike that starts in downtown and leads into the woods. Listen for rushing water and follow signs to the Angkula Seo Suspension Bridge or the Chinese Tribute Bridge.

Hirschman Trail: Tranquil 4.1-mile round-trip walk through wooded scenery leading to Hirschman's Pond. Especially stunning in the fall when the foliage changes colors.

Sugarloaf Mountain: Short 1.8-mile round-trip trail that offers stunning views of the town and surrounding landscape.

Hoyt Trail: Moderate 1.6-mile scenic river walk that leads to swimming holes along the South Yuba River and Hoyt Crossing.

South Yuba Trail: For the adventurous hiker or mountain biker, a portion of this quiet 20-mile trail takes you along the South Yuba River. Cell service is spotty.

items that tell the story of the local people, from stunning Nisenan baskets to preserved Victorian bridal wear. The prize exhibits are relics from the Chinese settlers who often built but seldom profited from the mines. It's open Wednesday to Sunday from May to October.

Follow Commercial St to numbers 309 to 316, the tiny survivors of the 19th-century Chinese Quarter. The South Yuba Canal Building (1855) is among the town's oldest. The renovated **National Exchange Hotel** (thenationalexchangehotel.com) welcomed its first guest in 1854 and is still the best place to stay in town – and to grab a craft cocktail. Take a break at Three Forks Bakery & Brewing Co, which serves beers and coffee, luscious baked goods and artisanal pizzas.

Untold Stories in Sonora

Historic nuggets

In the former 1857 Tuolumne County Jail, you'll find the great little **Tuolumne County Museum** (tchistory.org; free), with a fortune's worth of gold displayed in the form of nuggets and gold-bearing quartz. Each of the former jail cells spotlights a different theme, one of which is the little-told story of African Americans during the Gold Rush. You can learn about former enslaved man William Suggs, who set up a leather harness business and successfully campaigned to overturn segregation in local schools.

 EATING & DRINKING IN NEVADA CITY: COZY COFFEE SPOTS

Three Forks Bakery & Brewing Co: Come for the organic and fair-trade coffee, stay for the freshly baked pastries. *8am-8pm Mon-Thu, to 9pm Fri & Sat* $$

Communal Cafe: Hipster menu items like mushroom coffee and a vibrant butterfly pea matcha pair well with their farm-to-table fare. *7am-6pm* $

Heartwood Eatery: Signature latte, like their fragrant rose cardamom latte, nourishing bowls and farm-fresh salads make this a local go-to. *10am-4pm* $$

Java Johns: Homey family joint with an extensive coffee and tea menu. Prepare to wait during the weekends. *7am-2pm Mon-Fri, to 4pm Sat & Sun* $

Central California: The Coast & Sacramento

WILD SEAS | GREEN CAPITAL | VALLEY TOWNS

Santa Barbara has long been a weekend getaway for Angelenos, cozily nestled between the picturesque Santa Ynez Mountains and the Pacific Ocean, graced with Spanish Colonial architecture and chill, beach-town vibes. Along the coast from San Luis Obispo to Santa Cruz, savage landscapes are everywhere. Cliffs and sea stacks are smashed by the waves, redwood forests reach skyward and volcanic peaks defy all sense of time. With wind-buffeted hikes, white-knuckle road trips and a taste of the truly remote, nothing beats this coastline. The scent of sagebrush and salty sea air make you feel bracingly alive, while fog-diffused light adds an ethereal glow. Inland, attractive state capital Sacramento mixes history and culture with great food and drink, and every non-glitzy aspect of California is celebrated at the annual California State Fair. Wine is foundational to the valley's produce, and you can enjoy that and excellent craft beer at enticing university towns such as Davis and Chico.

Classic Santa Barbara Landmarks
Architecture, gardens and natural history

Once you see the **Santa Barbara County Courthouse** (*sbcourthouse.org; free*), you'll understand why couples plan weddings here. Taking up an entire city block, the Spanish Colonial Revival stunner is surrounded by inviting lawn and sunken garden. **Docent-led tours** (*weekdays at 10:30am, except for court holidays*) give details on the Moorish-style tile work and intricately painted Mural Room.

Founded in 1786, **Old Mission Santa Barbara** (*santabarbaramission.org; adult/youth $17/12*) is only one of two California missions that have continuously operated since their

GETTING AROUND

Though it's not the most scenic part of the route, the *Coast Starlight* train connects the Bay Area (Oakland and San Jose) with Salinas (near Monterey), Paso Robles, San Luis Obispo and Santa Barbara. Smaller towns can often be reached by bus but schedules are patchy; plan ahead. The Central Valley has an excellent train service. All the main cities of the San Joaquin Valley are linked to Sacramento and the Bay Area by fast and frequent Amtrak trains.

☑ **TOP TIP**

Check your feet after beach visits, as Santa Barbara shores have naturally occurring tar seeps that ooze up through the sand. If you've been tarred, give it a good dab of sunscreen and wipe with a paper towel.

establishment. If you're here during Memorial Day weekend, be sure to check out the chalk-painting festival **I Madonnari** (@imadonnari) as it transforms the Mission sidewalk into art.

Head a little further toward the foothills to the **Santa Barbara Museum of Natural History** (sbnature.org; adult/child $19/14) in its creekside nook amid oak habitat. Find natural context in exhibits ranging from Chumash culture, indigenous wildlife and geology, then complement it with forest bathing at the nearby **Santa Barbara Botanic Garden** (sbbotanicgarden.org; adult/child $20/12) – reservations required. The Channel Islands section offers spectacular views and native island flora.

Pacific Ocean Pleasures
Swim, surf, paddle, whale-watch

You could visit Santa Barbara without dipping a toe in the ocean...but why would you? Buffered from open ocean by the Channel Islands, the south-facing coastline offers a string of beautiful protected beaches. Novice surfers will appreciate the smaller swell of summer; most surf spots are best during the winter. **Leadbetter Beach** has a slow-rolling wave that makes it popular for lessons and beginners. Book surf lessons with **Santa Barbara Surf School** (santabarbarasurfschool.com) or **Surf Happens** (surfhappens.com).

At the harbor, rent an SUP or a kayak at **Paddle Sports Center** (paddlesportsca.com). Even within the breakwater, you'll encounter harbor seals, pelicans and rays on your paddle. Wildlife-watchers can book a whale-watching tour on the *Double Dolphin* of the **Santa Barbara Sailing Center** (sbsail.com) or with **Condor Express** (condorexpress.com), to cruise the Santa Barbara Channel in search of over 30 species of cetaceans, including migrating humpbacks, blue or gray whales and orcas (depending on the season).

Spanish San Luis Obispo
On a mission

People who know San Luis Obispo can't utter its name without a faraway smile. SLO (pronounced 'slow') captures California's many charms in a petite package. Snuggled among volcanic peaks, the city is in easy reach of hiking trails, wine country and beach towns. Local architecture has a strong Spanish accent. SLO was founded by Spanish colonists in 1772 when the **mission** was built under orders of Junípero Serra, a key

---

BUILDING A CHUMASH CANOE

Alan Salazar, Ventureño Chumash and Tataviam Tribal Elder.

We established the Chumash Maritime Association in January 1997 to oversee construction of a *tomol* (plank canoe) for the Chumash community. We had to relearn the skills of building, paddling and navigating. In 1912 Fernando Librado Kitsepawit, whose family was of the *tomol* brotherhood, built one as a demonstration; our research relied on extensive notes taken by anthropologist JP Harrington from interviews with Librado.

In 1997 we built the first working *tomol* in modern times, with the help of the Santa Barbara Maritime Museum, and paddled it across the Santa Barbara Channel in 2001. Our goal was to revitalize the Chumash maritime culture, especially to involve our young people. Conditions permitting, we now do the channel crossing annually.

 EATING IN SLO: BEST OUTDOOR DINING

Ebony: Sop up lentil stew with *injera* (teff flour bread) at this vegan counter-serve Ethiopian spot. 11am-8pm Thu-Sat, 10am-3pm Sun $

Kiko: Tucked in the Central Market arcade, this colorful Peruvian place has a patio that is perfect for tangy ceviche and slow-cooked beef with a view. 5-9pm $$

Novo: The tree-shaded patio is a place to fall in love...with your companion, or with pork carnitas and lamb shank. 11am-9pm Mon-Sat, from 10am Sun $$$

Luna Red: Buzzing outdoor terrace. The menu travels from Mexico to Spain via mole tacos and seafood paella. 11am-9pm Sun-Thu, to 10pm Fri & Sat $$

Madonna Inn, San Luis Obispo

UNIQUE SHOPS & SOUVENIRS IN SLO

Blackwater: Nothing you need but everything you want: shirts, sarcastic greetings cards, needlepoint cushions and vintage signs.

Buen Dia Market: Grocery store or art gallery? Be amazed by meticulously curated delicacies, then shop for art prints at its sister store at 790 Higuera St.

Bizarre Antiques & Oddities: Rummage crystals and curios here.

Hands Gallery: Upscale boutique selling mosaic art, locally made jewelry and novelty socks.

Mama Ganache: Ethically sourced small-batch chocolate, including vegan truffles and cashew chews. Chocolate bark is durable enough for your journey home.

player in the Spanish Empire's expansion. Exploring the city's mosaic of Spanish Mission style, art deco and the rosy-pink confection of the **Madonna Inn** is a sweet experience.

SLO's Highest Point

Hike to panoramic views at Bishop Peak

San Luis Obispo County's craggy beauty is a gift of the 'Nine Sisters,' a daisy chain of volcanic peaks stretching from Islay Hill, southeast of SLO, northwest to the coast at Morro Bay. The tallest is **Bishop Peak** (1559ft) and trails switchbacking up this volcanic plug start 2.5 miles northwest of downtown SLO.

To hike the **Summit Trail** (4 miles return; intermediate to advanced; 1180ft elevation) get over to Patricia Dr. There's a gentle incline after the **trailhead gate**, then take the left fork to follow the Summit Trail. Make your way up to the rocky summit for expansive views of SLO and the Santa Lucia Mountains beyond. Extend your ramble by adding the **Felsman Loop** (1.6 miles; easy to intermediate; 580ft elevation).

Cambria's Gem-Studded Moonstone Beach

Mosey along Cambria's multicolor shore

The jewel in Cambria's crown, Moonstone Beach glitters with colored pebbles. Walk down to the beach to admire smooth colorful gems washing ashore (look, don't take). The boardwalk

EATING & DRINKING IN CAMBRIA & CAYUCOS: LOCAL FAVORITES

| **French Corner Bakery:** Cambria's croissant enthusiasts rave about the golden buttery goodies prepared at this casual cafe. *6:30am-6pm* $ | **Schooners:** For sea dogs with discerning tastes (halibut with peanut slaw, rare ahi tuna), this friendly nautical boozer in Cayucos delivers. *11am-10pm Sun-Thu, to 11pm Fri & Sat* $$ | **Lunada Garden Bistro:** Cayucos' enchanting garden sets the stage for elevated bistro dishes, from French-style duck to coffee-glazed pork. *11am-1:45pm & 5-8pm Tue-Sun* $$$ | **Salty Tiger:** A secret speakeasy tucked into an upscale motel? We're in. Ask at Cayucos' Pacific Motel about its jauntily decorated one-room bar. *hours vary* |

follows the shore for roughly 1.5 miles through coastal prairies. You'll see ground squirrels racing past and enjoy exhilarating views of the bluffs. Time your walk for late afternoon, when the sun casts a coppery glaze across the pebble beaches. Then you're just in time for dinner at the nautical-themed **Sea Chest Oyster Bar** *(seachestoysterbar.com; cash only; 5:30-9pm Wed-Mon)*, perhaps *cioppino* with a glass from their local-leaning wine list.

Improbable Hearst Castle
Venetian balconies and zebras

With a celestial hilltop setting and artworks to rival the Louvre, San Simeon's **Hearst Castle** *(hearstcastle.org; adult/child from $35/18)* is the jaw-droppingly opulent passion project of media mogul William Randolph Hearst (1863–1951). No expense was spared to build this 165-room hilltop estate, from Rapunzel-like towers to Italian marble monuments to a library crammed with priceless Greek urns. A menu of different guided tours lead you through the labyrinthine palace and its hidden corners. Ask staff where the zebras, descendants of Hearst's originals, were last spotted. The **Grand Rooms Tour** is ideal for first-time visitors but we love the **Upstairs Suites Tour**, which climbs to ornate guest rooms like the tower-top 'Celestial Bedroom' (there are 367 steps in total).

Art Until Sundown in Paso Robles
Immerse yourself in Paso Robles' art scene

Mission and now winery town Paso Robles has all the ingredients for an eclectic art scene: rolling hills that beg to be captured in watercolors and a collision of Native American, Spanish and cowboy aesthetics. **Studios on the Park** *(studiosonthepark.org; free; noon-4pm Sun-Thu, to 9pm Fri & Sat)* is an excellent porthole into the multifaceted scene. Step inside to muse at photography, pottery and glass art.

As the sun dips, see the hills sparkle at **Sensorio** *(sensorio paso.com; adult/child $45/22)*, an outdoor art hub where Bruce Munro's *Field of Light* installation is in indefinite residence. Entranced by the light of more than 100,000 bulbs, you'll meander around fields turned multicolor. It's 5 miles northeast of Paso (Rte 46); book ahead. It's open 6:30pm to 10:30pm Thursday to Sunday from May through August, and 6pm to 10pm Thursday to Sunday in April.

NORTHERN CHUMASH MARINE PROTECTED AREA

When 156 miles of California's coast were designated a marine protected area in October 2024, there were many reasons to celebrate. The protected status of 4543 sq miles (south of Morro Bay to the northern edge of the Channel Islands) would allow whales, turtles, seabirds and more to thrive without the threats of pollution or natural gas extraction. It was also a victory for Northern Chumash Tribes, who comanage the reserve. They campaigned for decades for community control over the area's ocean management. The **Northern Chumash Heritage National Marine Sanctuary** *(sanctuaries.noaa.gov/chumash-heritage)* is also good news for visitors, who flock to these shores to witness the abundant marine life.

 EATING IN PASO ROBLES: BUDGET OPTIONS

Paso Market Walk: Our picks at this mini food court: coffee from Common Grounds, vegan cheeses from the Vreamery and mini cupcakes from Just Baked. *hours vary* $

Paso Robles Farmers Market: Behold the local bounty! Grab-and-go food from tacos to gluten-free doughnuts, along with seasonal fruits and veggies. *9am-1pm Sat* $

Jeffry's Wine Country BBQ: Dry-rubbed and wood-fire smoked, the tri-tip and chicken are moreish. Veggie burgers and garlic mac 'n' cheese too. *11am-8pm Thu-Mon* $$

Aliyah's Kitchen: Want to feel full? Try seafood towers, heaped combo plates and $2 taco Tuesday. *10am-9pm Mon-Thu, to 1am Fri & Sat, 8am-9pm Sun* $

BEST FESTIVALS AROUND PASO ROBLES

Spring Release Month: March is for wine-lovers. A month-long program of winemaker dinners, talks, tours and more. *(pasowine.com)*

Art in the Park: Artists assemble in Paso's Downtown Sq to showcase their wares for a weekend (April and November). *(pasoroblesartinthepark.com)*

Paso Wine Fest: Let wine and live DJ sets wash over you at this mid-May celebration of good wine and good living. *(pasowine.com/winefest)*

Atascadero Lakeside WineFest: Wine, craft beer, live music and family-friendly fun at Atascadero's Lake Park in mid-June. *(atascaderolakesidewinefestival.com)*

Paderewski Festival: Concerts from late October to early November celebrate visionary composer Ignacy Paderewski (1860–1941), a Polish musician turned Paso rancher. *(paderewskifest.com)*

Urban Wine Tasting
Sip your way around Tin City

Less than 10 minutes by rideshare along Hwy 101 from Paso Robles, Tin City is a post-industrial cluster of friendly tasting rooms and distilleries. Start at **Union Sacré Winery** *(unionsacre.com; tastings $20)* where they have managed to make riesling cool again. Around the corner is **Field Recordings** *(fieldrecordingswine.com; tastings $25)*, which prides itself on sourcing exceptional grapes from underrated vineyards. At **ONX Wines** *(onxwines.com; tastings $25)*, the fruit-forward zinfandels slip down very easily at their terrace with a babbling fountain. All wine'd out? Close out the experience at **Tin City Cider Co** *(tincitycider.com; tasting paddle $20)*, where hand-harvested apples yield silky, not-too-sweet ciders.

The Life of Monterey's Marine Mammals
Spot sealife right from the shore

Some of Monterey's best beaches are VIP-only, and those VIPs are harbor seals. Just half a mile north of Monterey's famous aquarium is the **Harbor Seal Viewing Point**, where plump seals loll on a protected arc of pristine white sand. Further south, spy on sea lions from the pier at **San Carlos Beach** and **Old Fisherman's Wharf**. Along the way you'll spy playful sea otters and sea lions that belly-flop from the rocks.

Historic Cannery Row
Amble from overfishing to ocean conservation

On Monterey's Cannery Row, cacophonous fish factories have been replaced by a different kind of chaos: merry-making tourists! Formerly Ocean View Ave, the street was renamed in 1958 after author John Steinbeck captured this gritty neighborhood in his masterpiece *Cannery Row* (1945). Meandering along Cannery Row combines industrial history with the innocent pleasures of present-day Monterey. Make sure you idle through a souvenir store or slurp soft-serve along the way

Start a block northwest of the aquarium at the 1926 **American Tin Cannery** (when we passed through, it was destined to transform into a hotel). This powerhouse factory was one of the big players on Cannery Row in the 1930s and '40s, when the pungent tang of fish was heavy in the air.

Factories operated day and night, processing 250,000 tons of sardines annually. The Norwegian founder of Hovden Cannery

EATING IN MONTEREY: ECOFRIENDLY PICKS

Happy Girl Kitchen: An ecoconscious one-stop shop for coffee, every-grain avocado toast and deli food, just two blocks from Ocean View Blvd. *7am-5pm* $

Passionfish: Sustainably harvested seafood and local ingredients, from tomato-truffle scallops to 12-hour lamb. Beautifully presented with small-batch wine. *5-9pm* $$$

Fish Hopper: Dishing up sustainable fish since 1950, this bustling place has splendid views to accompany pasta, seared tuna or ribeye. *10:30am-9:30pm* $$$

Revival Ice Cream: Cold-brew coffee, honey and passion-fruit-mango are among the plant-based scoops. Dairy options too. *noon-9pm Sun-Thu, to 10pm Fri & Sat* $

Monterey Bay Aquarium

pioneered undersea pipes to vacuum tons of fish into his factory every minute. But cosmic balance has been restored: this site of voracious overfishing is now a bastion of ocean conservation, home to the **Monterey Bay Aquarium**.

A few steps south and across the street is the former **Wing Chong Company Grocery** (1918). Monterey's fishing industry was developed in the 1850s by Chinese fishers who established themselves at Point Alhones. Wing Chong was also the inspiration for a similarly named grocery in Steinbeck's *Cannery Row*.

Surf's Up in Santa Cruz!
Learn to catch waves on Cowell's Beach
Between Silicon Valley and Monterey, the city of Santa Cruz is where students, dropouts and tech royalty all compete for the best surf breaks.

Even if your surfing experience goes no further than clinging to a bodyboard for dear life, that can all change in the gentle, predictable waves lapping **Cowell's Beach**. This sheltered cove on the west side of the **Santa Cruz Wharf** has excellent conditions for first-timers to stand up on a board, especially during the spring. Book a class with the venerable **Richard Schmidt Surf School** *(richardschmidt.com)*, teaching first-timers and improvers since 1978 (all equipment is included).

CARMEL'S REAL-LIFE DOLLHOUSES

There's a reason why **Carmel-by-the-Sea**, 9 miles south of Monterey, looks like it's from the pages of a fairy tale. More than two dozen buildings have steep gabled roofs, undulating lines and craggy stone chimneys, the design hallmarks of self-taught architect Hugh W Comstock (1893–1950). Their whimsical appearance was inspired by Hugh's wife, Mayotta Browne Comstock, who operated a successful business selling 'Otsy-Totsy' dolls. Mayotta wanted to create a suitably magical home for her rosy-cheeked ragdolls, and Hugh quickly went to work. First came the charming 'Hansel and Gretel Cottages,' then the 'Snow White Summer Palace.' Local demand for these quaint abodes boomed and the candy-colored houses remain some of the most coveted real estate in Carmel.

 EATING IN SANTA CRUZ: OUR PICKS

Hanloh: Outstanding bar-restaurant with a short menu of well-spiced and slow-cooked Thai meals. Inside the Bad Animal bookstore. *5–9pm Wed–Sun* $$$	**Abbott Square Market:** Counter-serve choices galore: coffee, sushi, Venezuelan arepas and West African vegan stews. *8am–10pm Sun–Thu, to 11pm Fri & Sat* $	**Chocolat:** Eat more chocolate! Start with three types of mole, chocolate-BBQ pork and chocolate mezcal martinis. *noon–4pm Fri–Sun & 5–9pm Thu–Mon* $$	**Penny Ice Creamery:** Cult favorite for classic and outlandish flavors (blood-orange creamsicle, butter caramel). We're here for toasted marshmallow topping. *noon–11pm* $

ROAD TRIP

Big Sur Road Trip

Surreally beautiful, Hwy 1 from Point Lobos to Ragged Point dances along fearsome cliffs and through forest groves. Don't rush: a day is doable but stay overnight to marinate in Big Sur's magic. Download maps (there's no cell service) and research online: when we last cruised through, a section of road south of Lime Creek Bridge remained closed due to a rock slide.

❶ Painters Point

This cliff lookout is a breathtaking introduction to Big Sur. Prolong the views on a 1.5-mile return hike to inspiring Soberanes Point just south.

The Drive: Visitors are dazzled by their first views of Big Sur, so this section gets hectic with distracted drivers. Watch the road!

❷ Garrapata Beach

Stroll the trail above the attractively rock-studded Garrapata Beach. It crosses a creek where white calla lilies burst into bloom (mid-February to mid-April).

The Drive: Along the next 4 miles to Bixby Bridge, you'll cross bridges and skirt bumpy headlands. Parking is a circus; only stop for photos if it's safe.

❸ Bixby Bridge

This 1932 bridge clasps the devilishly steep Bixby Canyon, looping 260ft over the golden beach below. Castle Rock Viewpoint offers a picture-perfect vantage point.

The Drive: Ocean views are on show throughout this meandering, 8-mile stretch to Andrew Molera State Park.

❹ Andrew Molera State Park

Meadows, beaches and bluffs make this tranquil state park a joy to explore. For big views of the rolling surf, take the Bluffs Trail (1.7 miles one way).

Garrapata Beach

The Drive: The road nudges inland and the next 4.5 miles are lined with redwoods, a precursor to rambles in the state park.

5 Big Sur Lodge

This lodge in Pfeiffer Big Sur State Park is a convivial place to grab coffee and baked goods before a heavenly forest hike; head high to Valley View (2 miles round trip; 200ft elevation).

The Drive: After 1.5 miles, take a sharp right (Sycamore Canyon Rd) to Pfeiffer Beach.

6 Pfeiffer Beach

This beach is renowned for sand that appears purplish when the light hits just right, the gift of manganese garnet from crumbling hills nearby. In winter you can catch sunset through Keyhole Arch... otherworldly.

The Drive: Rejoin Hwy 1: it twists and turns for 10 miles through forest and then along a serpentine stretch with Pacific views.

7 McWay Falls

Julia Pfeiffer Burns State Park is a beloved stop for 80ft McWay Falls, which cascades onto the beach. If the overlook trail is closed, viewpoints from Hwy 1 are signed from the road.

The Drive: If the road's open, 33 ocean-view miles extend to Ragged Point. In 2025, travelers had to turn around at Lime Creek, 4 miles south of McWay Falls.

8 Ragged Point

At this headland, toothy cliffs drop to deep-blue ocean. A short but steep walk descends to an ashen beach and the variable trickle of Black Swift Waterfalls. Celebrate journey's end at Ragged Point's inn-restaurant.

STORM-TOSSED SANTA CRUZ WHARF

Jutting out into the Pacific from the southern end of the beach boardwalk, Santa Cruz Wharf (p943) morphed from a potato-shipping outpost in 1914 into a big cog in Monterey Bay's sardine-canning machine, until the industry collapsed in the 1950s. It found a new identity for holidaymakers, who continue to pile into its bars and restaurants, or just peer through the portholes at sea lions, which can grow up to 8ft long. It lost its crown as the longest pier on the West Coast when violent waves in December 2024 caused an 150ft section to collapse, though you can't keep this venerable wharf down: the remainder was up and running again just two weeks later.

Beach Boardwalk Thrills

Get playful on roller coasters and a popular beach

Yelps of delight ring out from the Giant Dipper as it rattles along its tracks. Sugary air wafts from stalls selling funnel cakes and cumulonimbus-sized puffs of cotton candy. Families, groups of teens and wide-eyed visitors all pile onto the **Santa Cruz Beach Boardwalk** *(beachboardwalk.com; hours vary)*.

Founded in 1907, this palace of amusements, sprawled along a wooden boardwalk lining Santa Cruz Beach, is the oldest of its kind in the US. Don't skip a spin on the **Looff Carousel** (1911), with its original 1894 pipe organ, and the wildly popular landmark **Giant Dipper** (1924) wooden roller coaster. Tip: get garlic fries after the fast-rotating **Cyclone** and 125ft **Double Shot**, not before.

Explore Old Sacramento

Historic center with fascinating museums

The historic river port next to downtown, **Old Sacramento** *(oldsacramento.com; free)* is the city's top visitor draw: if you're walking here from town, enter the area on K St to avoid the deafening spaghetti junction of roads. The kitschy Gold Rush–era atmosphere makes it great for a stroll.

Join the underground tour run by the on-site **Sacramento History Museum** *(sachistorymuseum.org; adult/child $12/6, underground tour $30/25)*, which explores the tunnels that date from the time before everything was raised 18ft due to floods. The top sight is the **California State Railroad Museum** *(csrmf.org; adult/child $12/6)*, which has a huge collection of restored and notable locomotives and cars.

Sacramento's Colonial Origins

Dig into John Sutter's historic fort

Originally built by Swiss immigrant John Sutter, the mostly reconstructed site of **Sutter's Fort State Historic Park** *(suttersfort.org; adult/child $5/3)* was once the only white settlement for hundreds of miles. It was established in 1840 as part of the Mexican province of Alta California; today you can stroll within the fort's whitewashed adobe walls, where displays including furniture, medical equipment and a working blacksmith shop recreate life in the 1850s. A replica wagon illustrates the hardiness of pioneer families, who would load up their vehicles with belongings, then walk alongside, often for hundreds of miles.

EATING IN SACRAMENTO: OUR PICKS

Localis: A relaxed Midtown temple to Central Valley produce and California cuisine. Book ahead, especially for patio tables. *5-8:15pm Wed-Sat* **$**

Aioli Bodega Espanola: Spanish tapas in a garden near the capitol, plus a long wine list. *11am-10pm Mon-Sat, 3-9pm Sun* **$$**

Veg Café & Bar: Veg enchants with a modern space, and beautifully presented vegan dishes like cauliflower momo. *11:30am-9pm Tue-Sat, 11am-3pm Sun* **$$**

Tower Café: Best bet for big breakfasts, next to the iconic art deco movie theater. *8am-3pm Mon & Tue, 8am-8pm Wed, Thu & Sun, to 9pm Fri & Sat* **$$**

Sutter was an entrepreneur, con artist and itinerant debtor who enslaved the local Native American population to create his fortune, which was lost after gold-seekers swamped his lands. Visit the neighboring **State Indian Museum** *(parks. ca.gov; adult/child $5/3)* to learn about the culture that Sutter helped destroy.

Get Down in Davis
Bookstores, bikes, galleries and tree-lined streets

Much of Davis' energy comes from the free-spirited students who flock to the University of California, Davis (UC Davis), which boasts one of the nation's leading viticulture departments. Bikes outnumber cars two-to-one, and students make up half the population. Strolling the shady downtown, you'll pass family-operated businesses including some great book and thrift stores (the city council has forbidden any store over 50,000 sq ft – sorry, Walmart) plus public art projects.

The university is all about agriculture, and new types of produce that end up in your supermarket are developed here. The 100-acre **UC Davis Arboretum** *(arboretum.ucdavis.edu; free)* is a must-see for its well-marked botanical collections.

The campus has two notable cultural centers. The **Jan Shrem & Maria Manetti Shrem Museum of Art** *(manetti shremmuseum.ucdavis.edu; free)* features contemporary artists working across a wide range of mediums in a dreamy modern space. The **John Natsoulas Center for the Arts** *(natsoulas.com; free)* is marked by an outsize mosaic cat on the way into town; the ceramic calico guards one of the state's most vibrant small contemporary art galleries.

The Original Farmers Market
Eat, drink and be merry

The **Davis Farmers Market** *(davisfarmersmarket.org)* is renowned for being one of the best in the country, and features over 150 food vendors; on Wednesday evenings bands play in the adjacent park.

Wander an Oak-Shaded Student Town
Good times in Chico

With its huge student population, **Chico** has the wild energy of a college kegger during the school year, and a lethargic hangover during summer. The oak-shaded downtown and lively

LIVE MUSIC IN SACRAMENTO

Jen Moore, owner of *@rivercitymarket place*, introduces the city's music scene.

Midtown's vibrant, eclectic music scene pulses with creativity and community. From soulful acoustic sets and indie rock to energetic funk, jazz and hip-hop, every genre finds a home in this lively urban hub. On any given night, music spills from cozy clubs, open-air patios and bustling taprooms, creating a rich tapestry of sound that reflects the city's diversity. The neighborhood's walkability makes it easy to explore multiple shows in one evening, whether you're catching a rising local artist or a surprise touring act. With events ranging from intimate performances to full-blown music festivals, the area offers an inclusive, ever-evolving experience that celebrates artistry and connection. It's more than music – it's the heartbeat of Sacramento.

DRINKING IN DAVIS: CRAFT BEER & COFFEE

Delta of Venus Cafe & Pub: Converted bungalow with a social, shaded patio, tons of veggie/vegan options, a bar and live music. *hours vary*

Davis Beer Shoppe: Mellow Davis beer hall with 650 varieties of craft beer, bottled and on tap. *11am-10pm Mon-Sat, to 8pm Sun*

Miskha's Cafe: A quintessential university cafe with a homey twist – the rose and lavender infused lattes are house favorites. *7:30am-6pm*

Three Mile Brewing Company: Microbrewery with a fantastic flight of crisp, hoppy beer made from local ingredients. *3-10pm Mon-Thu, from noon Fri-Sun*

Bidwell Park, Chico

WILD CHICO

It's not just the student parties that are wild in Chico. From the dense trees arcing over the streets to the rushing waters of Chico Creek, this city is intertwined with nature. Growing out of downtown, Bidwell Park stretches for 10 glorious miles northwest along the creek. Several classic movie scenes have been shot here, including from *Gone with the Wind* and *The Adventures of Robin Hood*.

The upper park is an untamed oasis, with miles of trails weaving along creek banks, between basalt rock formations and across meadows dusted in spring wildflowers. Bidwell is also full of swimming spots for hot Chico days. You'll find pools at One-Mile and Five-Mile recreation areas, and swimming holes in Upper Bidwell Park, north of Manzanita Ave.

California State University, Chico make it one of Sacramento Valley's most attractive hubs. Folks mingle late here in the restaurants and bars, which open onto patios when it's warm.

All ages will delight in **Shubert's Ice Cream & Candy** (shuberts.com), a beloved old-time shop where five generations of Shuberts have produced delicious homemade ice cream, chocolates and confections.

Though the city – like the rest of the valley – wilts in the summer heat, the swimming holes in impressive **Bidwell Park** (chico.ca.us) offer an escape, as does floating down the gentle Sacramento River. The park stretches 10 miles northwest of downtown with lush groves and miles of trails.

Tour with a Brewmaster

Chico's iconic brewery

For many, Chico's top attraction has pilgrimage status: this is the home of the legendary **Sierra Nevada Brewing Company** (sierranevada.com). Founded in 1979, the brewery was one of the pioneers of the craft-beer revolution. Today Sierra Nevada continues to try out new styles of beer at the various taprooms at its huge brewery complex near Hwy 99. Take a self-guided tour or go for one of the deep-immersion (not literally) sessions with a brewmaster. Soak up the suds in the excellent restaurant.

DRINKING IN CHICO: OUR PICKS

Secret Trail Brewing: Unassuming brewery away from downtown with a small, energetic taproom, live music Fridays and food trucks outside. *3-7pm Tue-Thu, noon-7pm Fri-Sun*

Roselle Bar & Lounge: Elegant cocktail bar in a nightlife area east of the center. Classy bar food and DJ nights. *4-10pm Wed-Fri, 11am-midnight Sat, 11am-4pm Sun*

Tender Loving Coffee: Craft-roasted coffee and big vegan breakfasts from this community hub near radical Pageant Theatre. *8am-2pm Tue-Sun*

Sierra Nevada Brewing Company: Hordes of fans gather at the birthplace of Sierra Nevada Pale Ale and Schwarber, a Chico-only black ale. *11am-4pm Sun-Thu, to 5:30pm Fri & Sat*

Los Angeles & the Deserts

CINEMATIC CITY | OUTSTANDING ART | DESERT DREAMS

Los Angeles means many things to many people. It is a city of dreams but has too much traffic. It enjoys perfect weather but there are so many mountain fires. It has the best golden-hour sunsets but the smog is terrible. All these things ring true about this enormous city in Southern California, and one thing is absolutely for sure – nothing beats the pulsating, vivacious flair of Los Angeles. LA is also a kaleidoscope of cultures from around 140 countries, with nearly 220 languages spoken, creating an intricate web of diversity that connects deep beneath the surface. It is a place of acceptance, and what makes LA truly shine is the diversity of its people, who uniquely come together as one. Beyond the City of Angels, California's vast desert landscapes await adventurous souls with geologically diverse trails, environmental art, dark starry skies and the ever-sunny culture of Palm Springs.

GETTING AROUND

Los Angeles is vast and not walking-friendly, so traveling by car or public transportation – Metro buses, DASH buses and Metro Rail trains – is recommended, though avoid the freeways between 5pm and 7pm. Dockless scooters with Lime and Bird are also a great way to buzz around. A car or recreational vehicle (RV) is the best way for getting around the deserts; the parks encompass thousands of square miles and are not served by public transportation.

Hollywood's Galaxy of Stars

MAP P952

Follow the Walk of Fame

Jennifer Lopez, Bob Hope, Marilyn Monroe and Aretha Franklin are among stars being sought out, worshipped, photographed and stepped on along the **Hollywood Walk of Fame** (walkoffame.com). Or, in the case of many names, pondered over, since production staff and writers are also honored. They've been adding the brass and pink-terrazzo stars since 1960.

Follow the galaxy along Hollywood Blvd between La Brea Ave and Gower St, and on Vine St between Yucca St and Sunset Blvd. At least 30 new stars are added a year and the ceremonies often draw famous faces. Check the website for the schedule.

☑ TOP TIP

Los Angeles is known for perpetual sunshine. But come the evenings the temperatures can dip dramatically. Pack a pullover for your nocturnal LA adventures.

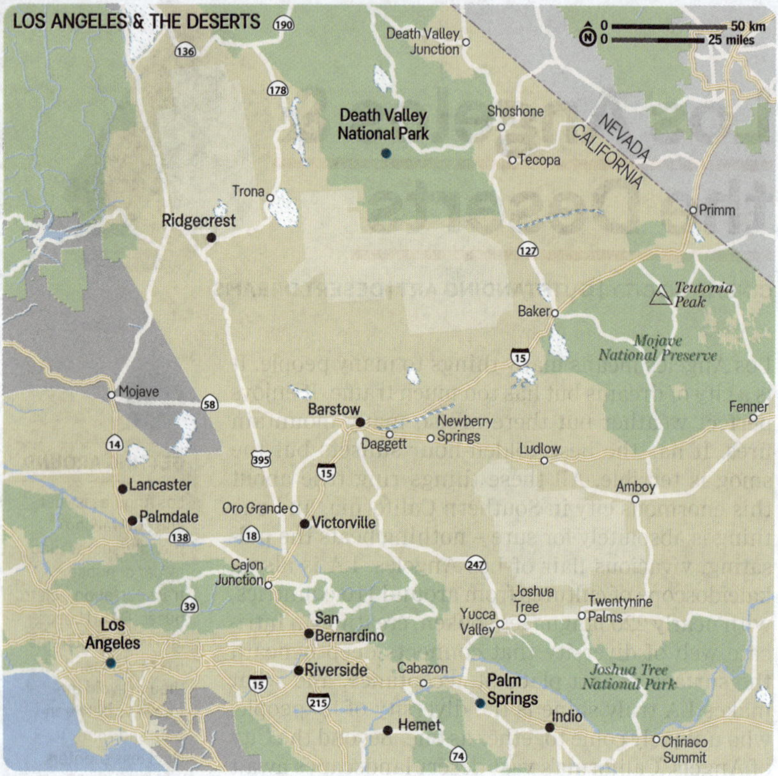

LOS ANGELES & THE DESERTS

An Icon Was Born

Spot the Hollywood Sign

Perched at the top of Mt Lee in the Hollywood Hills is the iconic **Hollywood Sign** (*hollywoodsign.org*). The story goes that *Los Angeles Times* publisher and real estate developer Harry Chandler erected the sign in 1923 (back then it said 'Hollywoodland') as a way to advertise luxury homes in the hills. What was only supposed to be there for 18 months became a permanent landmark that has come to symbolize a place, an industry and a mythology.

Three hiking trails lead to the sign: Brush Canyon Trail, Mt Hollywood Trail and Cahuenga Peak Trail.

DRINKING IN HOLLYWOOD: OUR PICKS

MAP P952

Frolic Room: Anything goes at this dive that's served everyone from Judy Garland to Charles Bukowski. Toast the fabulous cartoon mural. *11am–2am*

Harvard & Stone: Lures partiers with bands, DJs and burlesque troops working their saucy magic. It's ski lodge meets steampunk factory, with a rockabilly soul. *9pm–2am*

Bar Lis: Hollywood's all around the rooftop lounge of the hip Thompson Hollywood. There's a bit of a posh Med vibe (Cannes, anyone?). *6pm–midnight*

Tabula Rasa Bar: Away from the glitz, this unpretentious wine bar gets everything right with well-picked tunes and regular live gigs. Rear terrace. *2pm–midnight*

Hollywood's Last Great Studio MAP P952
Tour Paramount Studios

Indiana Jones, *The Godfather* and the *Ironman* series are among the blockbusters that originated at **Paramount Pictures**, the country's second-oldest movie studio (1914) and the only major one still in Hollywood proper. Two-hour **golf-cart tours** *(paramountstudiotour.com; from $69)* of the studio complex are offered year-round, taking in the back lots and sound stages. Passionate, knowledgeable guides offer fascinating insights into the studio's history and the moviemaking process in general.

Observe LA!
And the universe from the Griffith Observatory MAP P952

The universe aside, the rooftop viewing platform of the **Griffith Observatory** *(griffithobservatory.org; free)* offers unparalleled views of LA and the Hollywood Hills. The art deco observatory has made cameos in numerous movies and TV shows, among them *La La Land*, *Terminator*, *24* and *Alias*. The film it's most associated with, however, remains *Rebel Without a Cause*, commemorated with a bust of James Dean on the west side of the observatory lawn. Inside, there's a planetarium and all sorts of unmissable exhibits on the cosmos.

Finding parking can be akin to finding life on another planet. It's best to arrive on a weekday before noon. Otherwise, especially on weekends, try hiking up the hillside from Los Feliz (it *is* a great trail). Or, take the DASH Observatory/Los Feliz shuttle bus from the Vermont/Sunset metro station.

Famed Film Locations in Griffith Park MAP P952
Hike to Bronson Caves

With more than 50 miles of trails, Griffith Park is LA's great hub of hiking, accessible from all directions and offering all types of experiences. A good start is the family-friendly short (0.7 miles one way) jaunt up **Bronson Canyon** off Canyon Dr to **Bronson Caves**. The latter are legit stars: among many appearances, they were the Bat Cave in the old *Batman* TV series and were the climactic location in the still-relevant *Invasion of the Body Snatchers* (1956). From here, more challenging trails lead to sights like the Hollywood Sign.

BEST FILMS ABOUT HOLLYWOOD

Sunset Boulevard (1950): Director and screenwriter Billy Wilder at his best, plumbing the dark side of fame and Hollywood's delusions.

The Player (1992): Robert Altman brings decades of experience on the front lines to this biting satire about the moral rot at the heart of studio execs.

La La Land (2016): Timeless musical of plucky kids hoping to make it big in Hollywood.

The Artist (2011): Won the Oscar for Best Picture for its story of the often-brutal late-1920s transition from silent pictures to talkies.

A Star Is Born: Pick your version (1937, 1954, 1976, 2018) of the classic drama about fame and tragedy.

EATING & DRINKING IN LOS FELIZ: OUR PICKS MAP P952

Figaro Bistrot: A culinary ménage à trois involving a boulangerie, bistro and lounge, Figaro channels Paris with heavy mirrors, sidewalk tables and Gallic-inspired fare. *8am-midnight* $$

House of Pies: Indomitable survivor of a chain that once swept California, the House serves top diner fare plus its namesake desserts in myriad flavors. *7am-1am* $$

Covell: Over 150 wines by the glass, showcasing interesting producers, unusual grapes and lesser-known regions. Barkeeps are generous with tastings. *4pm-midnight*

Tiki-Ti: Channeling Waikiki since 1961, this tiny tropical tavern packs in everyone from stylish slummers to 'non-ironic' partiers in Hawaiian shirts. *6pm-midnight Wed-Sat*

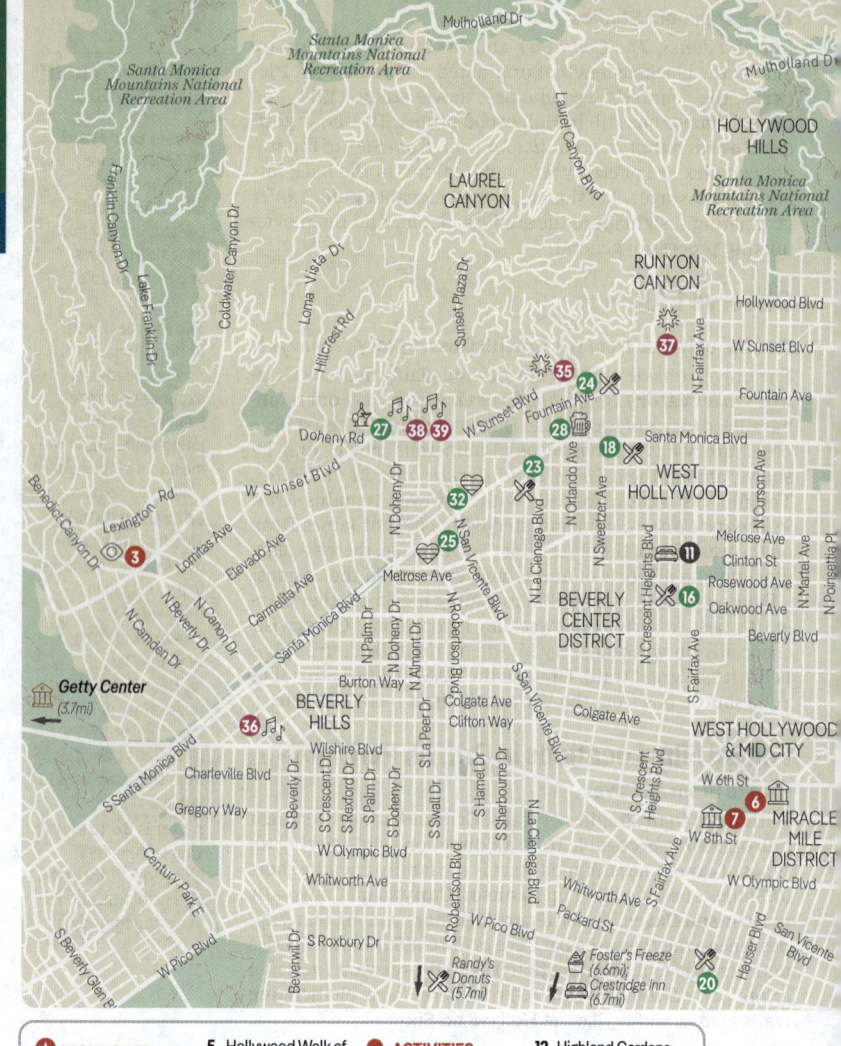

GREATER LOS ANGELES

- **HIGHLIGHTS**
  1. Griffith Observatory
  2. Paramount Pictures
- **SIGHTS**
  3. Beverly Hills Hotel
  4. Disney's First Studio
  5. Hollywood Walk of Fame
  6. La Brea Tar Pits & Museum
  7. LACMA
  8. Snow White Cottages
- **ACTIVITIES**
  9. Bronson Canyon
  10. Bronson Caves
- **SLEEPING**
  11. Banana Bungalows Hotel & Hostel West Hollywood
  12. Highland Gardens Hotel
  13. Hollywood Roosevelt
  14. Hotel Normandie LA
  15. Silver Lake Pool & Inn

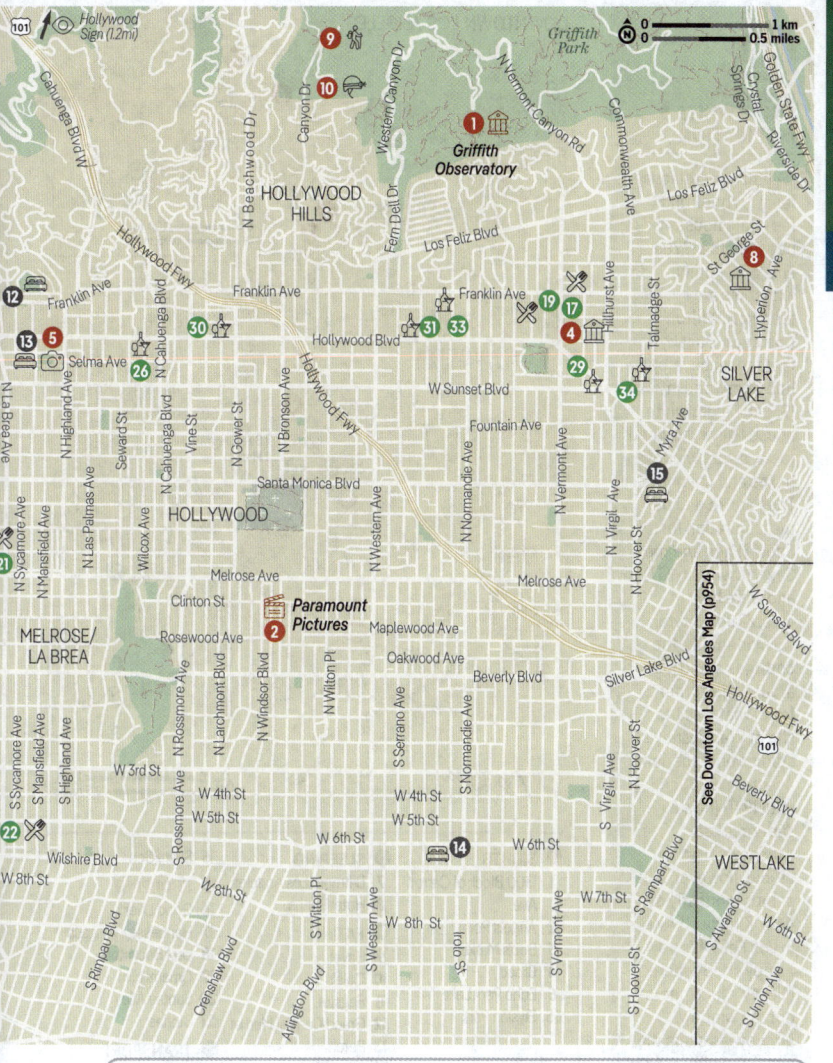

● **EATING**	27 Bar Next Door
16 Canter's	28 Barney's Beanery
17 Figaro Bistrot	29 Covell
18 Hamburger Mary's	30 Frolic Room
19 House of Pies	31 Harvard & Stone
20 My 2 Cents LA	32 Micky's WeHo
21 Pink's Hot Dogs	33 Tabula Rasa Bar
22 République	34 Tiki-Ti
23 Tail O' the Pup	
24 Tower Bar	● **ENTERTAINMENT**
	35 Comedy Store
● **DRINKING &**	36 Jazz Café at Cipriani
NIGHTLIFE	Beverly Hills
25 Abbey	37 Laugh Factory
26 Bar Lis	38 Roxy Theatre
	39 Whisky-a-Go-Go

THE GUIDE

CALIFORNIA LOS ANGELES & THE DESERTS

SNOW WHITE'S INSPIRATION

LA had a secret love for storybook and fairy-tale houses between the 1920s and '30s – prime examples are the **Snow White Cottages**. Built by fantastical developer Ben Sherwood in 1931, the eight white houses have thatched roofs, sweet window boxes and chimneys. They are said to be the inspiration for *Snow White and the Seven Dwarfs* (1937) and were built in ersatz Tudor style. Coincidentally, the cottages stand just around the corner from what was the site of Walt Disney's studios on Hyperion Ave from 1926 until 1940 (now a supermarket).

Disney's first studio, however, still stands modestly at 4647 Kingswell Ave in Los Feliz. It's now a copy shop, where Mickey's face peers out the window. Employees claim they sense the ghost of Walt every day.

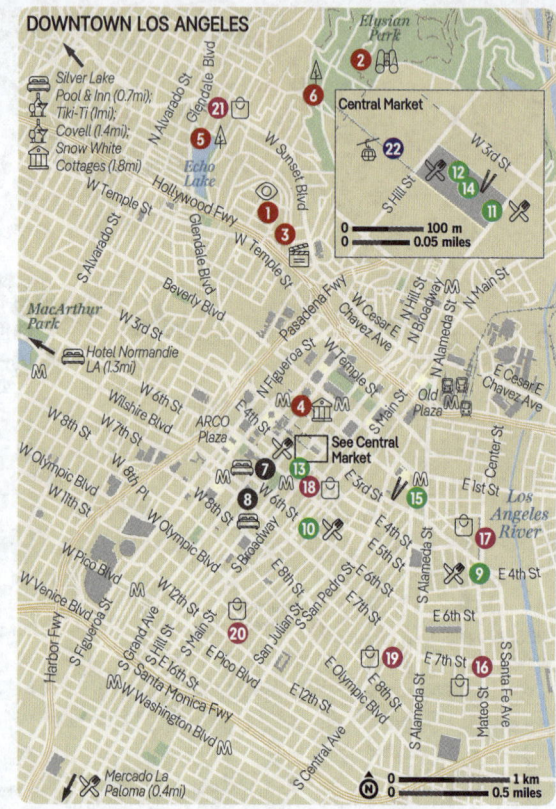

● **SIGHTS**
1 1300 Block of Carroll Ave
2 Angels Point
3 Bob's Market
4 Broad
5 Echo Park Lake
65 Elysian Park

● **SLEEPING**
7 Biltmore Los Angeles
8 Hotel Per La

● **EATING**
9 Bavel
10 Cole's
11 Eggslut
12 Grand Central Market
13 Perch
14 Sticky Rice
15 Sushi Gen

● **SHOPPING**
16 Good Liver
17 Hennessey + Ingalls
18 Last Bookstore
19 Omami Mini
20 Santee Alley
21 Stories

● **TRANSPORT**
22 Angels Flight

 EATING IN DOWNTOWN: BEST HIGHER-END PLACES  MAP P954

Sushi Gen: Grab a lunch seat in Little Tokyo; chefs carve slabs of the freshest fish. Dinner is less frenetic. *11am-2pm & 5-8:30pm Tue-Sat* $$

Perch: Two elevators get you to this French rooftop bar-restaurant on the vintage Pershing Square Building. Bewitching Manhattan-esque views. *4pm-1am* $$

Bavel: Sleek, loud and showered in cascading vines, come here for phenomenal, modern takes on Middle Eastern classics. Fine cocktails. *5-11pm* $$$

Cole's: Dark, time-warped tavern, claims progeny (with Philippe) of the French dip sandwich. Great time-warp bar area and cocktails. *3pm-midnight* $$

Downtown's Striking Museum
Be dazzled at the Broad

MAP P954

Rapidly evolving, DTLA (Downtown LA's preferred moniker) is the city's most intriguing patch, where cutting-edge architecture and killer modern-art museums contrast sharply with blaring mariachi tunes. The **Broad** (thebroad.org; free) is a must-visit for contemporary-art fans ('Broad' rhymes with 'road'). It houses the world-class collection of local philanthropist and billionaire Eli Broad and his wife, Edythe, with more than 2000 postwar pieces by dozens of heavy hitters, including Cindy Sherman, Jeff Koons, Andy Warhol, Roy Lichtenstein, Robert Rauschenberg, Keith Haring and Kara Walker. The striking museum is popular, so secure your free entrance time online.

Taste Grand Central Market
A global culinary feast

MAP P954

Designed by prolific architect John Parkinson and once home to an office occupied by Frank Lloyd Wright, LA's beaux-arts **Grand Central Market** (grandcentralmarket.com) has been satisfying appetites since 1917 and today is DTLA's always-busy hub of food culture (opening hours vary). Lose yourself in its bustle of neon signs, stalls and counters, peddling everything from fresh produce and nuts, to sizzling Thai street food at **Sticky Rice**, hipster breakfasts at **Eggslut** and modern deli classics, artisanal pasta and specialty coffee.

For a digestive interlude, exit and cross S Hill St for a quick ride on **Angels Flight** (angelsflight.org; $1), the famous, short funicular up to Bunker Hill and yet another local star of many a production.

Soaring Folk Art
Marvel at the Watts Towers

The three 'Gothic' (or is it Gaudí-esque?) spires of the fabulous **Watts Towers** (wattstowers.org; tour adult/child $7/3) rank among the world's greatest monuments of folk art. In 1921, Italian immigrant Simon Rodia set out to 'make something big' and then spent 33 years cobbling together this whimsical free-form sculpture from concrete, steel and a motley assortment of found objects: from green 7Up bottles to seashells, tiles, rocks and pottery. The towers reach up to 99.5ft in height, just below the city's legal limit of 100ft.

DOWNTOWN'S BEST SHOPPING

Last Bookstore: LA's largest new-and-used bookstore. Rare tomes, terrific vinyl, good prices and staff recs. (lastbookstorela.com)

Omami Mini: In Row DTLA, fashion-forward clothing for under-12s (though it's really aimed at parents). Lots of comfy cottonwear. (omamimini.com)

Hennessey + Ingalls: Arts District new-and-used bookstore focusing on design, from architecture and landscaping to photography and fashion. Good set design section. (hennesseyingalls.com)

Good Liver: Carefully curated space with beautiful objects you're unlikely to find elsewhere, each displayed with its story. (good-liver.com)

Santee Alley: Scores of alley vendors with bargains in clothing and eyewear between Santee St and Maple Ave from Olympic Blvd to 12th St.

 EATING IN SOUTH LA: TOP CHOICES FOR A QUICK BITE — MAP P961

Mercado La Paloma:	**Patria Coffee Roasters:**	**Foster's Freeze:**	**Randy's Donuts:**
A quick walk under I-110 from Expo Park, fabulous food hall has everything from Yucatan cuisine to Thai. 9am-9pm $	Only a block from Compton's City Hall, this art-filled coffeehouse is a standout for top-end coffee drinks. Next to a park. 8am-3pm $	Time-warp Inglewood ice cream emporium that hasn't changed in decades. Order a hot fudge sundae and enjoy it at a picnic table. 10am-8pm $	Famously excellent doughnuts are your first or last memory of LA going to/from LAX. Simplest flavors, like glazed old-fashioned, are best. 24hr $

DISPLAYING ART IN A NEW WAY

LACMA's new building is the bold vision of Swiss architect Peter Zumthor, who is known for his works on cultural and social service institutions. The curvaceous, airy, cantilevered galleries straddle Wilshire Blvd. Floor-to-ceiling windows will make the most of LA's natural beauty, highlighting its hills and celebrated natural light.

Inside, LACMA's curators have challenged themselves to utterly rethink how their huge and rich collection is displayed. They want to dispense with the Eurocentric and chronological narrative that dominates art museums and instead show how works spanning mediums, cultures and time interrelate. As they readily admit in interviews, this new paradigm is a 'challenge.' Debate about their efforts will undoubtedly be vigorous, beginning with the new building's opening in 2026.

Compton's Anthem
See the site of 'Not Like Us'

West Coast rap and hip-hop have been part of Southern California since NWA's 1988 album *Straight Outta Compton* launched the careers of Eazy E, Ice Cube and Dr Dre, and established gangsta rap.

Jump ahead and Compton remains relevant as megastar Kendrick Lamar showed in 2024 with his music video for 'Not Like Us.' Viewed millions of times, it features scenes shot at the striking modernist **Martin Luther King Memorial** on the wide open plaza at **Compton City Hall**.

Lamar invited Compton to show up for the shoot and they did. The results are joyous, vivacious. It's worth visiting the location while watching the video on your phone. After, cross S Acacia Ave and see what's on at the **Compton Art & History Museum** (comptonmuseum.org; adult/child $5/3).

A Stunning New Home for Art
Take in the wealth at LACMA

MAP P954

Soaring across Wilshire Blvd, the new **LACMA** (*Los Angeles County Museum of Art; lacma.org; adult/child $28/13*) is set to open for visitors by mid-2026. The $720 million David Geffen Galleries will replace the museum's four aging buildings.

As well as millennia worth of stunning global treasures, permanent collection highlights include Chris Burden's outdoor installation *Urban Light* (a surreal selfie backdrop of hundreds of vintage LA streetlamps). Two other works are iconic LA: *Mulholland Drive* by David Hockney and *105 Freeway* by Catherine Opie.

LACMA's Zen-like Pavilion for Japanese Art houses pieces ranging in origin from 3000 BCE to the 21st century.

Smell the Ice Age
Get stuck on the La Brea Tar Pits

MAP P954

Mammoths, saber-toothed cats and other critters roamed LA's savanna in prehistoric times. The **La Brea Tar Pits & Museum** (*tarpits.org; adult/child $18/7*) preserve a trove of skulls and bones and are one of the world's most famous fossil sites. Generations of young dino hunters have come to learn about paleontology in the museum.

Outside, the smell of asphalt permeates the air as the tar pits still bubble away, and beloved models show mammoths stuck in the gooey crude oil bubbling up from deep below

EATING IN MIRACLE MILE & FAIRFAX: OUR PICKS

MAP P952

République: Artisan bakery, light-filled cafe and buzzing bistro with daily-changing French-accented dishes. Great desserts. *8am-2pm & 5:30-10pm* $$

Canter's: This veteran deli isn't closed despite appearances. Legendary pastrami and other standards. Comfy booths, knowing servers and parking. *6am-11:30pm* $$

My 2 Cents LA: The acclaimed restaurant of TV chef Alisa Reynolds has a loyal, A-lister following for Southern fusion fare. Book ahead. *11:30am-9:30pm Thu-Sun* $$$

Pink's Hot Dogs: Famous doggeria (since 1939) with slow-moving lines thanks to the droves who descend for garlicky all-beef frankfurters drenched in chili. *9:30am-midnight* $

SEEING ECHO PARK

From old Victorians to an iconic lake, Echo Park is a star on screen and off. Its shops and views are bonuses.

START	END	LENGTH
Bob's Market	Angels Point	3.1 miles; 3 hours

Begin at **1 Bob's Market** (1913), aka Toretto's Market & Deli, owned by Vin Diesel's character in the *Fast & Furious* franchise. Look for the shelf of merch. It was also in *LA Confidential*.

Walk uphill to Angelino Heights, established in the mid-1880s as one of LA's first suburbs. Its most charming street is **2 1300 Block of Carroll Ave**, home to the city's largest concentration of Victorian-era homes. A few house numbers of note: 1300 is the grandest on the block; 1316 captures the look of the 1880s with its old-style drapes; 1329 is the most original and was Halliwell Manor in the TV series *Charmed*; 1330 has Asian details like the lion dogs below the arch; and 1337 is the oldest house on the block (1872).

Walk down via Bellevue Ave to **3 Echo Park Lake**, anchor of the lovely, namesake park. Rent a swan-shaped pedal boat. One block of Sunset Blvd has a thicket of cool retail like the literature-rich **4 Stories** and the indescribable Time Travel Mart. You won't regret a minute you spend inside.

Walk north up Portia St and use your map app to wander through leafy **5 Elysian Park** and up to **6 Angels Point**. Under towering public art, you'll enjoy uncommon views of LA, including Dodger Stadium, Downtown and Hollywood.

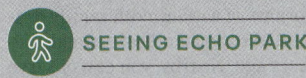

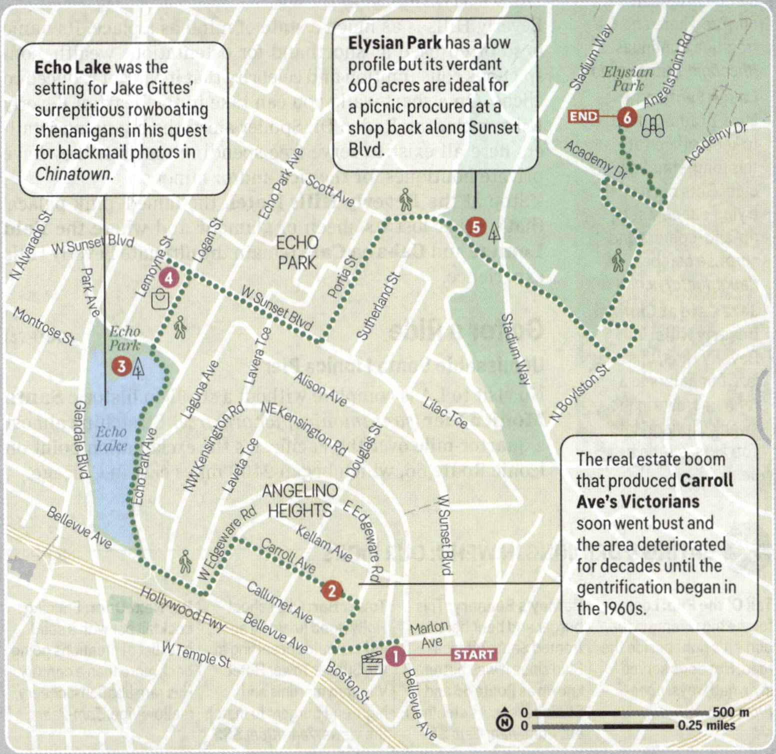

Echo Lake was the setting for Jake Gittes' surreptitious rowboating shenanigans in his quest for blackmail photos in *Chinatown*.

Elysian Park has a low profile but its verdant 600 acres are ideal for a picnic procured at a shop back along Sunset Blvd.

The real estate boom that produced **Carroll Ave's Victorians** soon went bust and the area deteriorated for decades until the gentrification began in the 1960s.

WEHO'S BEST LIVE PERFORMANCES

Whisky-a-Go-Go: The Whisky trades on its legend status when the Doors were the house band and go-go dancing was invented here back in the '60s. *(whiskyagogo.com)*

Roxy Theatre: A Sunset Strip fixture since 1973, this small venue puts you close to the bands. The lineup varies, with some big-names. *(theroxy.com)*

Comedy Store: The club with cred. Richard Pryor, George Carlin, Eddie Murphy, Robin Williams and David Letterman were nurtured here and the tradition continues. *(thecomedystore.com)*

Laugh Factory: The Marx Brothers used to keep offices at this long-standing club. Gets big names trying out new sets, up-and-comers and surprise celebs. *(laughfactory.com)*

Jazz Café at Cipriani Beverly Hills: In Beverly Hills, this luxe jazz bar caters to a refined crowd in the swank Cipriani Hotel. Top acts. *(cipriani.com)*

Wilshire Blvd. A life-size diorama of a mammoth family dramatizes the cruel fate of countless thousands of animals between 50,000 and 10,000 years ago. Nearby, you can observe pits where fossils are still being discovered.

Do the West Hollywood Walk   MAP P954
A neighborhood like no other

Santa Monica Boulevard is the main drag of West Hollywood (WeHo) and bar-hopping its length is one of the LA region's great joys. The LGBTQ+-centric bars and clubs heave through the weekends, with Sunday brunch being a must, while weeknights are busy as well.

Central to WeHo is one of the most iconic gay nightclubs on the West Coast today, the **Abbey**, which serves the community as much as a cultural center as a bar and nightclub. With over three decades in the game, it's been called the best gay bar in the world. It's open from 11am to 2am daily.

The boulevard abounds with choices like the iconic **Micky's Weho**, with long-running drag shows. It's open noon to 2am. **Hamburger Mary's** is the Sunday afternoon brunch go-to; it's open from 11am to 10pm.

If You Were Rich & Famous   MAP P954
The Beverly Hills experience

Beverly Hills is as much a state of mind as a place. Its name is so often used as shorthand for ostentatious wealth, conspicuous consumption and celebrity that it can get reduced to cliché. On a short walk, you can take in the heart of Beverly Hills, including Rodeo Dr. Spoiler alert: the big-name retailers here all exist to serve free-spending tourists; they have private boutiques for the rich and/or famous.

Stop at the **Beverly Hills Hotel**, the famed 'pink palace' that's never lost its sheen of glamour and where the **Polo Lounge** and **Cabana Cafe** remain the ultimate Beverly Hills experience.

Go for a Ride   MAP P961
Unmissable Santa Monica Pier

No visit to LA is complete without a stroll on historic **Santa Monica Pier** *(santamonicapier.org; free)*. Stretching almost a quarter-mile over the Pacific, it's the exclamation point on iconic Route 66, which began 2400 miles east in Chicago.

 EATING & DRINKING IN WEHO: OUR PICKS   MAP P952

Tail O' the Pup: Look for the big weenie in the bun – it's right beside the road. Hot dogs served in myriad ways. *noon-10pm* $

Barney's Beanery: This burger and beer bar has fronted Santa Monica Blvd since it was better known as Route 66 and Studebaker cars steamed out front. *11am-2am* $$

Tower Bar: Old-school Hollywood luxury in an indoor-outdoor setting at the Sunset Tower Hotel. Vaunted martinis and high-end burgers to match the views. *7am-10pm* $$$

Bar Next Door: Enticing cocktail bar with a solid backlist of creations going back more than a century. Has rare libations; cheery, mellow vibe. *5pm-2am*

Venice Boardwalk

Dating to 1908, the pier is the city's most compelling landmark. Every angle is dominated by **Pacific Park** *(pacpark.com; rides from $8)* amusement park and its family-friendly arcades, carnival games, soaring Ferris wheel and tame roller coaster. Nearby is a vintage 1922 carousel and an aquarium. The pier is most photogenic when framed by California sunsets and when it comes alive with free concerts and outdoor movies in the summertime.

Living Life on the Sand

MAP P961

Venice's beach and boardwalk

Prepare for a sensory overload on the **Venice Boardwalk**, one of LA's essential experiences. Buff bodybuilders brush elbows with street performers and sellers of sunglasses, ribald underwear, Mexican ponchos and cannabis, while cyclists and in-line skaters whiz by on the bike path, and skateboarders and graffiti sprayers get their own domains.

BEACHES FROM SANTA MONICA TO MALIBU

El Matador State Beach: Park on the bluffs and stroll down to sandstone towers rising from emerald coves. Dolphins breach the surface beyond the waves.

Zuma Beach: Easily accessed from the PCH (and Metro bus), with parking and long stretches of sand. Find privacy in the southeast at Pirate's Cove.

Malibu Lagoon State Beach: Where Malibu Creek meets the ocean, migratory birds proliferate, attracting human spotters. To the north are popular surf breaks.

Will Rogers State Beach: The quiet alternative to the famous strands to the south. This is the beach used for *Baywatch* and dozens of other productions.

Santa Monica State Beach: There are endless ways (volleyball's big!) to enjoy this 3.5-mile stretch of sand, running seamlessly into Venice Beach in the south.

EATING IN SANTA MONICA & VENICE: OUR PICKS

MAP P961

Bay Cities Italian Deli & Bakery: In Santa Monica, this is LA's best Italian deli, period. Signature sandwich: the spicy Godmother. *9am-6pm Wed-Sun* $

Santa Monica Farmers Markets: Explore one of Santa Monica's outdoor farmers markets stocked with a vast bounty. *8am-1pm Wed & Sat* $

Café Gratitude: Cutting-edge Venice vegan dishes are paired with an open patio and sea breezes. It's sustainable, locavore, organic and always surprising. *10am-9pm* $$

Gjusta: A very local bakery, cafe and deli behind a nondescript storefront on a hidden Venice side street. Great patio. Food to go is ideal for picnics. *7am-4pm* $$

TOP EXPERIENCE

Getty Center

Straddling a hilltop in the Santa Monica Mountains off the 405, the palatial Getty Center offers an irresistible feast of art, design and botanical beauty. Ponder the myths and landscapes of Dossi, Van Gogh and Cézanne, gaze out over the City of Angels and kick back in a verdant wonderland of gurgling water, lush lawns and world-famous sculptures.

TOP TIPS

● Visit early morning or mid-afternoon. Sunsets create a remarkable alchemy of light and shadow. Saturday nights are usually less crowded.

● Get the essential GettyGuide app. Free audioguides are available in the lobby. Bring photo ID.

● Consider bringing a picnic lunch to enjoy on the beautiful grounds.

PRACTICALITIES

● getty.edu
● free, timed entry reservation
● parking $25

Artistic Highlights

The Getty's collections focus on European art, with a concentration on works from the 19th and 20th centuries. There are genuine treasures here. In the east pavilion, seek out Gentileschi's *Danaë and the Shower of Gold* and Rembrandt's self-portrait, *Rembrandt Laughing*. In the west pavilion, look for Van Gogh's *Irises*, Monet's *Wheatstacks, Snow Effect, Morning*, Manet's *Jeanne (Spring)* and Turner's *Modern Rome – Campo Vaccino*. The south pavilion's outdoor terrace is home to Marino Marini's excitable bronze *Angel of the Citadel*, while the grounds themselves are studded with prized sculptures, including three works by Henry Moore.

Fossils & Gardens

The 16,000 tons of travertine cladding the Getty came from the same Italian quarry used for Rome's ancient Colosseum. Look closely to spot fossilized shells, fish and foliage. Don't miss the lovely Cactus Garden on the remote South Promontory for breathtaking city views.

Unmissable Events

Concerts, lectures, films and other cultural events for grown-ups keep the space buzzing with locals. Most are free, but some require reservations (or try standby). On Saturday evenings in summer, the center hosts Off the 405, a popular series featuring top progressive pop and world-music acts in the Getty courtyard.

VENICE & SOUTH COAST BEACHES

- ★ **HIGHLIGHTS**
  1. Santa Monica Pier
- ● **SIGHTS**
  2. Santa Monica State Beach
  3. Venice Beach
  4. Venice Beach Art Walls
  5. Venice Boardwalk
- ● **SLEEPING**
  6. Crestridge Inn
  7. Georgian Hotel
  8. HI Los Angeles Santa Monica Hostel
  9. Samesun Venice Beach
- ● **EATING**
  10. Bay Cities Italian Deli & Bakery
  11. Café Gratitude
  12. Foster's Freeze
  13. Gjusta
  14. Randy's Donuts
  15. Santa Monica Farmers Markets
- ● **ENTERTAINMENT**
  16. Pacific Park

Agua Caliente Cultural Museum

PALM SPRINGS ARCHITECTURE TOURS

The Modern Tour: This long-running agency arranges intimate looks into the interiors of notable architectural gems, in their comfortable vehicles or your own.

Palm Springs Mod Squad: Admire from outside, and get a peek at the interiors of meticulously designed mid-century-modern homes.

PS Architecture Tours: Insightful, insider tours guided by bike or car; it's best to book well ahead.

Palm Springs Historical Society: Themed tours featuring celebrity homes (Sinatra, Elvis, Elizabeth Taylor), and guided driving, biking and walking architectural tours.

Desert Tasty Tours: Get a taste of local history and architecture with a side of Palm Springs cuisine.

Venice Beach has long been associated with street art. The free-standing concrete wall of the **Venice Beach Art Walls** (*veniceartwalls.com*), right on the beach, has been covered by graffitists from 1961 to the present. Gym rats with an exhibitionist streak can get a tan and a workout at the famous outdoor gym right on the Venice Boardwalk, where Arnold Schwarzenegger and Franco Columbu once bulked up.

Palm Springs' Modernism Week
Revel in desert modern style

Desert retreat Palm Springs prides itself not only on its queer culture but also on its mid-century-modern identity, which remains intrinsic to the Palm Springs aesthetic.

Mid-mod fever seizes the town during February's 10-day **Modernism Week** (*modernismweek.com*). In addition to talks, book signings and art openings, the fun includes double-decker bus tours of notable architecture sights, rare tours of significant homes and countless soirees. A mini Modernism Week pops up in October over a long weekend.

EATING IN PALM SPRINGS: OUR PICKS

Farm: Buzzy, relaxed, French-style simplicity. Breakfast and lunch are walk-in only; expect a wait. Reserve a table for prix-fixe dinner. *8am-2pm daily & 5:30-9:30pm Fri-Tue* **$$**

Rooster & the Pig: No reservations; arrive before opening and come hungry for Vietnamese fusion. Cocktails incorporating Asian twists perfectly complement the cuisine. *5-9pm Wed-Sun* **$$**

El Mirasol: Family-run Mexican restaurant whose mole and *pipián* make a spicy change of pace from your favorite standbys. *9am-9pm* **$$**

Barn Kitchen: Locally sourced ingredients prepared beautifully for fresh American cuisine, enjoyed in open-air elegance. *11am-9pm* **$$**

Otherwise, look out for the cantilever-roofed **Palm Springs Visitors Center**, the Mountain Station of the **Palm Springs Aerial Tramway** and the **Palm Springs Art Museum**.

Agua Caliente Cahuilla Culture
Explore Agua Caliente Cultural Museum

A wonderful way to learn about the history and culture of the Agua Caliente Band of Cahuilla Indians is at the **Agua Caliente Cultural Museum** *(accmuseum.org; adult/senior $10/5)* on North Indian Canyon Dr. Historical photographs, interactive displays and audio components bring to life the Indigenous experience of colonialism and its effect on the culture, but also spotlight living traditions and the natural history of the area.

The 'Agua Caliente' in the tribe's name speaks to one of its ancestral land's sacred treasures: the mineral hot springs known as Séc-he. In the larger plaza complex, the **Spa at Séc-he** *(thespaatseche.com)* welcomes guests to partake in these thermal waters. Book ahead for luxury spa treatments or relax with a day pass that includes a 15-minute private soak.

Remnants of Joshua Tree's Human History
Rock art and ruins

At the **Joshua Tree National Park** *(nps.gov/jotr; 7-day pass per car $30)*, the mostly flat, rewardingly varied **Barker Dam Loop Trail** journeys into this wonderful park's natural history: a little spur leads to a shallow cave full of petroglyphs.

An easy walk takes you to the well-preserved **Wall Street Mill**, passing ore-crushing ruins, the headstone of the unfortunate loser of a shootout and the **Desert Queen Well**, and continues to the crumbling pink ruins of **Wonderland Ranch**.

The ruins of **Ryan Ranch**, an easy half-mile walk from the road, are worth a look as the Ryan brothers incorporated gold dust into the adobe. At the park's southern end, it's a quarter-mile walk beyond the coolness of **Cottonwood Spring** to some trailside *metates* (grinding stones) left by the Cahuilla.

Hiking Joshua Tree's Varied Terrain
Follow classic JTree trails

If you're hiking with children, the **Discovery Trail** offers a bit of scrambling and informative interpretive signs and is a great park intro for grown-up kids as well. For

PLAN & PREPARE

All of the principles of **Leave No Trace** *(lnt.org/why/7-principles)* apply when visiting Joshua Tree National Park, but it's particularly important to plan ahead and prepare. Once you enter the park, there are zero services aside from vault toilets at trailheads and campgrounds, and running water only at the park entry points. Cell-phone service is nonexistent inside the park. Bring everything you'll need: plenty of water (at least a gallon per person for the day), salty snacks to keep your electrolytes balanced and layers so you can adjust to sudden weather changes. Have all of the survival basics so you can fully enjoy the spectacular desert environment.

EATING IN JTREE: PICNIC PROVISIONS

Campbell Hill Bakery: Superb pastries, soups, pizza and a line out the door in Twentynine Palms; check IG for current hours and arrive early. *6-9pm Thu-Sat* $

The Dez: Grab-and-go sandwiches, salads, charcuterie and coffee in Joshua Tree for your national park picnic. *6:30am-4pm* $

Desierto Alto: An excellent bottle shop with a well-rounded selection of picnic goodies and gift-worthy edibles. *7am-7pm* $

Joshua Tree Farmers Market: Both Twentynine Palms and Joshua Tree hold Saturday farmers markets. *8am-1pm* $

THE FIRST PEOPLE OF DEATH VALLEY

Timbisha Shoshone people lived in the Panamint Range for centuries, visiting the valley every winter to gather acorns, hunt waterfowl, catch pupfish in marshes and cultivate small areas of corn, squash and beans. After the federal government created Death Valley National Monument in 1933, the tribe was forced to move several times and was eventually restricted to a 40-acre village site. Years of protests and lobbying by tribal activists resulted in President Clinton signing the Timbisha Shoshone Homeland Act in 2000, transferring 7500 acres of land back to the tribe and creating the first Native American reservation inside a US national park. Today, a few dozen Timbisha live in the **Indian Village** near Furnace Creek.

classic bouldery Joshua Tree scenery, the 2.5-mile **Split Rock Loop** is another easy one, with a short spur leading to **Face Rock**.

Hikers wanting to gain elevation can head to the lesser-trafficked northwestern corner of the park, where the 6.5-mile **Panorama Loop** takes you through Joshua trees before rising into piñon-and-juniper forest atypical to most of the park. You'll find panoramic views of the Coachella and Yucca Valleys along the 1200ft climb.

Rambling & Scrambling in Death Valley

Day hiking in Death Valley

True, it's the lowest place in North America, at 282ft below sea level, the hottest place in the world, when it hit 128°F (53°C) in the summer of 2022, and the driest of the US national parks – but **Death Valley National Park** *(nps.gov/deva; 7-day pass per car $30)* is an amazing place to hike. Because of its brain-melting extremes, it's best to hike before 10am and after 4pm during the hottest seasons.

Flash floods are the reason that sinuously winding slot canyons like **Mosaic Canyon** even exist, and hikers have them to thank for this canyon's beautifully exposed layers of juxtaposed Noonday dolomite and Mosaic Canyon breccia (mudflow carbonates studded with inclusions of rock fragments).

A quite differently spectacular gallery of wondrous geology is **Golden Canyon**, off the northern end of Badwater Rd. Take the Golden Canyon–Gower Gulch loop that starts in a narrow slot and climbs along a towering golden wall before dropping you into the badlands visible from **Zabriskie Point**.

Desolation Canyon is another stunner, with splashes of pink, green and purple from iron oxides and chlorite, and the payoff of a beautiful view at the end. Some minor scrambling is involved. Finally, at **Ubehebe Crater**, a 1.5-mile hike around the rim gives you a fascinating look at the remains of a maar volcano, in which the meeting of magma and groundwater causes a steam explosion. In spring, desert flowers bloom in the pyroclastic pebbles.

Hiking Anza-Borrego Desert State Park

Nature trails and route-finding adventures

Many visitors to Anza-Borrego Desert State Park wind up hiking the **Borrego Palm Canyon Nature Trail** *(day use $10)*, but it's popular for good reason. The fun, easy trail ends

---

EATING IN DEATH VALLEY: OUR PICKS

Panamint Springs Resort: An inclusive, sunny saloon ambience and good food; this spot is a welcome stop on the park's western end. *7am-9pm* $$

Toll Road Restaurant: Buffet breakfasts and square meals at Stovepipe Wells, with a bar next door and a convenience store across the road. *7-10am & 11:30am-9pm* $$

Ranch 1849 Buffet: At the Ranch plaza in Furnace Creek, the buffet spread won't wow you, but the plentitude will satisfy. *6-10am, 11am-2pm & 5-9pm* $$

Last Kind Words Saloon: Burgers and pasta in Wild West–bedecked environs, complete with taxidermied critters and hammered-tin ceilings. *5-9pm* $$

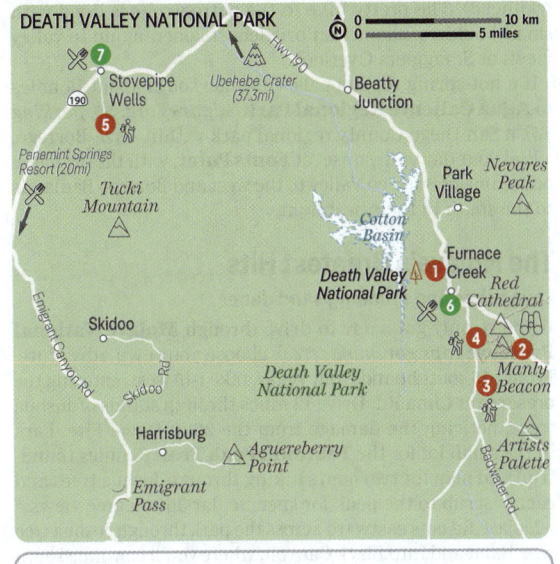

HIGHLIGHTS
1. Death Valley National Park

SIGHTS
2. Zabriskie Point

ACTIVITIES
3. Desolation Canyon
4. Golden Canyon
5. Mosaic Canyon Trail

EATING
see 6 Last Kind Words Saloon
6. Ranch 1849 Buffet
7. Toll Road Restaurant

at the Borrego Palm Canyon Oasis, named after its native California fan palms.

A longer alternative to Borrego Palm Canyon is the nearby 5-mile **Hellhole Canyon Trail**, taking you from the open desert to lush oases with little waterfalls and maidenhair ferns.

Anza-Borrego South to North

Petroglyphs, hot springs and diverse landscapes

Pack a lunch and start early for your drive south, through the park's Pinyon Mountains and beautiful higher-elevation piñon and juniper country. From the junction of Hwy 78 and County Rd S2, drive 6 miles to the Blair Valley turnoff, a dirt road at Mile 22.9. A map there shows the way to the **Pictograph Trail** (a high-clearance vehicle recommended to the

---

GREAT HIKES NEAR BORREGO SPRINGS

Robin Halford, author of *Hiking in Anza-Borrego Desert, Volumes 1–3*, suggests hikes located within 25 minutes of Borrego Springs.

Cannonball Run
In addition to the cannonball formations embedded in the mudstone here, you can also see the uplifting that occurred eons ago that's almost like natural rock art.

Cool Canyon
A wonderful meandering canyon at a higher elevation, with different vegetation and cooler temperatures than on the desert floor.

Bill Kenyon Trail
This out-and-back isn't difficult, with wonderful cacti and other desert flora along the trail. You end up with a really nice view across Hwy 78 to a *bajada*, where several alluvial fans come together.

 EATING & DRINKING IN BORREGO SPRINGS: OUR PICKS

Kendall's Café: Friendly, relaxed, nostalgic little diner with a patio on the strip mall, serving typical American breakfast and Mexican options at lunch. *7am-2pm* $

Carmelita's Mexican Grill & Cantina: Down-home Mexican favorites tucked away in a corner of the mall, with shaded patio seating. *10am-8pm* $

Red Ocotillo: Crab-cake eggs Benedict for breakfast, lamb shanks for dinner. A lovely garden spot with a cute patio. *7:30am-8:30pm* $$

Carlee's: With hearty American food, a wraparound bar (open later) and pool tables after food service has ended, this is the best evening hang in town. *11am-9pm* $$

DESERT TORTOISES

The desert tortoise is a threatened species found in the Mojave Desert Preserve as well as California's larger desert regions. Though the species has been around for millions of years, its populations have declined over the past several decades. Stressors include rising temperatures from climate change, disease, human encroachment on desert habitats and even ravens, which prey on baby tortoises. Consider it a blessing if you see a desert tortoise in the wild. In fact, always check under your parked car before driving away, and watch out for tortoises trundling across roads.

trailhead). The pretty hike to the petroglyphs is lined with small boulders, cholla and brittlebush, opening up to valley views at Smugglers Overlook.

If a hot-spring dip appeals, continue south about 15 miles to **Agua Caliente Regional Park** *(sdparks.org; $5, parking $5)*, a San Diego County regional park within Anza-Borrego.

End your day with sunset at **Fonts Point**, with the dramatic panorama of Borrego Valley to the west and Borrego Badlands to the south in their best light.

The Mojave's Greatest Hits
Lava tubes and stunning sand dunes

If you've only got a day to drive through **Mojave National Preserve** *(nps.gov/moja; free)*, choose your own adventure. From I-15 southbound from Vegas, take I-15 west, entering the preserve at Cima Rd. Drive 12 miles through stands of Joshua trees, noticing the damage from the 2020 Dome Fire. Park in the small lot for the **Teutonia Peak Trail** (3 miles round-trip) and plan for two hours hiking through Joshua trees and cactus scrub to the peak for spectacular 360-degree views.

Mojave Rd cuts eastward across the park through Joshua tree woodland and into Black Canyon, where you'll continue south again through remote ranchlands between Mojave mountain ranges. About 10 miles south along Black Canyon Rd, stop at **Hole-in-the-Wall Visitor Center** and walk the flat, one-mile **Rings Loop Trail** clockwise (south from the parking lot). The walls on this fun hike include steep sections featuring bolted rings for handholds. Exit to I-40 along Essex Rd.

Alternatively, head 24 more miles westward along I-15 to Baker to take Kelbaker Rd south into the park. At the Aiken Mine Rd turnoff 19 miles in, drive another 5 miles through lava-bed landscape to the hilltop **lava tube** spotlit on one end by natural skylights. Look for the ladder descending into the cave.

Continue south on Kelbaker Rd, stopping at the **Kelso Depot Visitor Center** to learn a bit of preserve history. Around 7 miles further south, turn off toward the magnificent **Kelso Dunes**. Allow two to three hours for the round-trip hike, then onward to I-40.

Mitchell Caverns Detour
Geological salons of Mojave history

A little pocket of a California state park surrounded by Mojave National Preserve, **Providence Mountains State Recreation Area** *(parks.ca.gov; $10)* is a high-altitude encapsulation of the Mojave. The isolated mountains here support distinct species like rock squirrels. The main draw is **Mitchell Caverns** *(reservecalifornia.com; tour including day-use fee $20)*, a protected chain of stalactite- and stalagmite-laden chambers.

Southern California: Disneyland to San Diego

DISNEY MAGIC | WINERY-HOPPING | LAID-BACK CITY

Today, Disneyland Resort®, which comprises the Disneyland Park and newer Disney California Adventure theme park, remains a magical experience for the more than 14 million kids, grandparents, honeymooners and international tourists who visit every year. At alluring Newport Beach you'll find the largest recreational harbor on the West Coast, with 10 miles of waterfront offering boating and fishing, water sports and endless views. En route to San Diego, Temecula features fine wineries, while small beach communities like La Jolla have cultures uniquely their own.

San Diego is a city unlike any other in California. The second-largest in the state by population, it has everything you could ask for in a metropolis: vibrant arts and culture, diverse and varied neighborhoods, incredible food and more entertainment than you could ever see yourself. But even with all that, the city manages to always feel relaxed. Chill coastal vibes are ingrained in every corner of this Southern California paradise.

☑ **TOP TIP**

San Diego shares an international border with Tijuana, and it's easy for US citizens with passports to head south and explore one of the world's most-visited cities. There's even a Cross Border Xpress skybridge connecting the Tijuana International Airport to San Diego.

GETTING AROUND

Newport Beach lies an hour's drive south of Downtown LA. Amtrak or Metrolink trains from LA are fast and scenic and stop at Anaheim's ARTIC transit center, a short shuttle ride to Disneyland by bus (routes 14 or 15). For San Diego, take Amtrak's *Pacific Surfliner* train, which travels daily between Santa Barbara, Los Angeles and the city, with stops in between.

Disney California Adventure Park

TOP EXPERIENCE

Disneyland Resort®

Walt Disney's creation is the self-dubbed 'Happiest Place on Earth.' The streets of the Disneyland Resort are always clean, employees always upbeat and parades happen daily. Since opening in 1955 Disneyland has delighted hundreds of millions. Disneyland Park is the original and most famous area, Disney California Adventure Park (DCA) the newer theme park, and Downtown Disney District comprises an outdoor pedestrian mall with restaurants.

DON'T MISS

- Star Wars: Rise of the Resistance
- Space Mountain roller coaster
- New Orleans Square
- Indiana Jones Adventure
- Grizzly River Run
- World of Color fireworks

Disneyland Park

From the entrance of Disneyland Park, you leave SoCal behind and enter **Main Street USA**, an idealized turn-of-the-20th-century town fashioned after Walt's hometown of Marceline, Missouri. Hop the steam **Disneyland Railroad** for a great intro to the park as it circles the perimeter. Controversially in 2025, *Great Moments with Mr Lincoln*, the 15-minute audio-animatronic show with Honest Abe spouting bromides, has been partially replaced by *Walt Disney – A Magical Life*, in which a robotic Walt (who died in 1966) talks about his vision for Disneyland and sings a song.

PRACTICALITIES

- disneyland.disney.go.com

Star Wars: Galaxy's Edge

Inside Disneyland's largest 'land' (14 acres), the mega-popular **Star Wars: Rise of the Resistance** puts you in an immersive adventure where you must escape from a Star Destroyer. Nearby are opportunities to make your own lightsaber or droid, or drink adult beverages or blue milk at Oga's Cantina, modeled after the inside of Jabba's Palace. Fans of the movies will enjoy just wandering around, marveling at Disney's fanatical attention to detail.

Tomorrowland

The 1950s Imagineers' vision of the future could now be called Mid-Century Land. Venerable **Space Mountain** remains one of the USA's best roller coasters, hurtling you into complete darkness at great speed. For retro high-tech, the **monorail** glides from Downtown Disney and the hotels to its stop in Tomorrowland.

Fantasyland & Frontierland

Fantasyland is best known for 'It's a Small World,' a boat ride past hundreds of audio-animatronic international children singing an earworm of a theme song. After a revamp, it reopened in 2025 with even more tiny characters, including ones from *Coco*.

Thrills are provided by **Big Thunder Mountain Railroad**, a mining-themed roller coaster.

New Orleans Square & Bayou Country

Honoring Walt's favorite city, New Orleans Square captures a slice of French Quarter charm. The ever-wonderful **Pirates of the Caribbean** is the second-longest ride in Disneyland (17 minutes) and provided inspiration for the popular movies. The water ride **Tiana's Bayou Adventure**, inspired by *The Princess and the Frog*, opened in 2024. **Tiana's Palace** is popular for its authentic New Orleans cuisine.

Adventureland

Among the attractions here, the hands-down highlight is the safari-style **Indiana Jones Adventure**. Cool down on the purposely hokey **Jungle Cruise**. The classic **Enchanted Tiki Room** features a campy show of singing, dancing birds and flowers. Skip the overhyped Dole Whips.

Disney California Adventure Park

Across the plaza from Disneyland, DCA is an ode to the state with an overlay of Disney intellectual property. It feels less crowded than Disneyland Park and has excellent rides and attractions. The superb **Grizzly River Run** takes you 'rafting' down a faux Sierra Nevada river – you will get wet. Kids can tackle the **Redwood Creek Challenge Trail**, with its 'Big Sir' redwoods. If you're hungry, the **Corn Dog Castle** has a grab-and-go hot link corn dog that's the best in the parks.

PARADES, FIREWORKS & LIVE ENTERTAINMENT

There are daily parades in Disneyland and DCA, with floats accompanied by Disney tunes and costumed characters. Don't miss DCA's premier show, the 22-minute **World of Color** nighttime spectacular, with fireworks over the lagoon.

TOP TIPS

● Buy your tickets in advance online at disneyland.disney.go.com. Many Disney vacation planning sites offer discounted tickets.

● On busy days, waits for the most in-demand rides can range from one to two hours, but the Lightning Lane Multi-Pass ($35 per day per person) allows priority access on many rides. For the most popular rides there's an additional Individual Lightning Lane cost per ride – you can purchase these without having to buy a Multi-Pass.

● Bring a power bank for your smartphone. The Disneyland app is a must-have to keep track of wait times, book Lightning Lane passes, order food, make dining reservations and lots more.

SOUTHERN CALIFORNIA: DISNEYLAND TO SAN DIEGO

Make a Splash at Newport Beach

If you don't get on the water, you didn't visit Newport

For an adventure by sea – or just to see the superyachts docked nearby – head to Mariner's Mile. This is where you'll disembark for water excursions like harbor tours, gondola rides and sailing lessons. Or rent your own **Duffy boat** *(duffyof newportbeach.com)* and cruise around the harbor on your own. There are even **sunset dinner cruises** *(citycruises. com)* where you can enjoy dinner and drinks as you take in Orange County's singular sunset.

EATING IN NEWPORT BEACH: WATERFRONT RESTAURANTS

| **21 Oceanfront:** In Doryman's Oceanfront Inn, this fine-dining seafood and steak restaurant serves up unparalleled beach views. *4pm-late* $$$ | **Nobu Newport Beach:** Outpost of the legendary Japanese with two floors of water views. *noon-3pm Fri-Sun, Tanoshi 5-7pm Mon-Thu, dinner from 5pm* $$$ | **Rusty Pelican:** An institution in Mariner's Mile since 1972, this harborside restaurant serves creative fish preparations with a robust wine list. *11am-10pm* $$$ | **Crystal Cove Shake Shack:** Serving burgers and shakes on the beach since 1945; eat them on picnic tables and head straight back to the sand. *7am-9pm* $$ |

To enjoy the water from land, head to **Lido Marina Village** *(lidomarinavillage.com)*, a waterfront shopping and dining area with its own cinema, boutiques and an array of restaurants from casual to fine dining. Mariner's Mile and Lido Marina are also where you'll see boats decorated for the holidays.

Fun on Four Wheels

Moke Cruising

A quintessentially SoCal experience is cruising around in a Moke. It looks a bit like a miniature Jeep, with an open top and a roll bar, but it's an electric vehicle that tops out at 25mph. It's perfect for cruising along the shore or any low-speed road, especially on a sunny day. Rent one from **Newport Beach Moke** *(newportbeachmoke.com)*, or **Adventure OC** *(adventureoc.com)* in Huntington Beach. Rentals are available by the hour, day or week.

Wandering Old Town Temecula

Step into the past

The heart of Temecula Valley was an important location in the Old West: after Mexico ceded California to the United States, Temecula served as a stagecoach stop and was also home to California's second-ever post office, after San Francisco. Following the Civil War, the town saw an influx of settlers from the East. In 1882 the area saw the establishment of the Pechanga Reservation and the construction of a train station. The **Temecula Valley Museum** *(temeculavalleymuseum.org)* explores local history, from the Native Luiseno tribe to Mission San Luis Rey (1798), with a miniature street scene for kids to play in.

Walking into Temecula's Old Town today recalls the late 1800s: there are still plenty of historic Old West buildings along Front St, but now they're home to antiques stores, boutiques, craft breweries and restaurants. **Temecula Olive Oil Company** *(temeculaoliveoil.com)* grows its own olives and presses them into robust olive oils; tastings are free in the shop. **Old Town Spice & Tea Merchants** *(spiceandteamerchants.com)* sells 350 spices and 100 loose-leaf teas. **Temecula Lavender Co** *(temeculalavernderco.com)* sells products made from flowers grown on its own local lavender farm. One block on Fourth St holds several antiques shops, like **Old Town Antique Faire** and **RECLAIMED @ Main St Market**,

NEWPORT BEACH'S BEST BEACHES

Crystal Cove State Park: Unique destination with three beaches, campsites, cabins and an underwater park for snorkeling and diving.

Corona del Mar State Beach: Known as Big Corona, this beach is family- and pet-friendly. If it looks familiar, you might recognize the beach from *Gilligan's Island*.

Newport Beach Pier: The stretch of sand on Balboa Peninsula around the Newport Beach Pier has fine sand and views, and proximity to many shops and cafes.

Little Corona del Mar Beach: Calm beach known for snorkeling and tide pools, with no steps down to the sand.

The Wedge: This scenic beach's waves make it popular with surfers. In the summer, boards are prohibited between 10am and 5pm.

DINING IN TEMECULA: OUR PICKS

Bolero Restaurante: Serves Spanish tapas with a gourmet sensibility. Chef Hany Ali trained and cooked throughout Europe before arriving in California. *8am-9pm* $$

Small Barn: This farm-to-table restaurant and boutique winery evolved from the owners' backyard winemaking operation. *5-9pm Tue-Thu, 11am-10pm Fri, 10am-10pm Sat, 10am-8pm Sun* $$

Espadín Mezcal + Cocina: When you need a break from wine, this spot serves inspired regional Mexican food with agave-based cocktails. *11am-9pm Sun-Thu, 11am-10pm Fri & Sat* $$

The Goat & Vine: This stone-hearth kitchen might be casual, but its approach to food is not: everything (pizza dough, sauces etc) is made in-house daily. *11am-9pm* $$

PECHANGA RESORT CASINO

One of the largest casinos in the country is in Temecula, just minutes from Old Town. Pechanga, owned by the Pechanga Band of Indians, has 200,000 sq ft of gaming – and a lot of reasons to visit, even if gambling isn't your thing. The AAA Four Diamond property (named the best casino in the country by *USA Today*) has a large luxury hotel with an enormous pool complex and spa, a concert venue that brings in acts like the Beach Boys and comedian Kevin James, and more than a dozen restaurants including a fine-dining steakhouse and an upscale sushi bar.

EKAM/SHUTTERSTOCK

which refurbishes vintage furniture. The largest country music venue on the West Coast, the **Stampede** *(thetemecula stampede.com)* has line dancing, bull riding and live music every weekend. It's located in the Old Town.

Winery-Hopping in the Temecula Valley
Enjoying wineries and much more

Because the weather is dry and hot, similar to a Mediterranean climate, Temecula is especially well-suited to growing Spanish, French and Italian grape varietals. Expect to sip sangiovese and syrah – though vineyards farm more than two dozen different grapes locally. At **Doffo Winery**, Marcelo Doffo channels his Argentine and Italian heritage to make outstanding zinfandel and red blends, and also has a collection of vintage motorcycles at the winery. **Miramonte Winery**, another standout, focuses on Spanish- and Portuguese-influenced styles like tempranillo and medium-bodied red blends.

La Jolla's Public Art
Natural beauty and creative vibes

The natural beauty of the hilly coastal city isn't the only thing worth looking at in La Jolla. A massive public-art program has been working on beautifying the city since 2010. Today, there are 15 large-scale murals on display, and more than 40 total pieces of public art, which are always a pleasant surprise to stumble on in your explorations.

Grape vines, Temecula Valley

The **Murals of La Jolla website** *(muralsoflajolla.com)* details the art and the artists, includes YouTube videos, and offers a self-guided walking tour to see them for yourself. If you can't get enough of the vibrant works, take them home with you in *The Murals of La Jolla* coffee-table book, a work of art in itself that supports the project.

Fine Art in La Jolla

Art walk and galleries

The city has a robust art scene, especially in the number of nationally renowned artists whose works are on display in galleries. On the **La Jolla Village Art Walk** *(lajollabythesea.com)*, find Martin Lawrence Galleries as well as LIK Fine Art, the showroom of the artist who sold the world's most expensive photograph: Peter Lik's *Phantom* sold for $6.5 million in 2014. The Museum of Contemporary Art San Diego, which also has a location in downtown San Diego, showcases works created since 1950 and has strong collections of pop art, Latin American art and works by San Diego and Tijuana artists.

Exploring the Heart of San Diego

Downtown, the Gaslamp District and the Embarcadero

San Diego is a large city, packed with so many fascinating sights that you'll want to give yourself a good amount of time to explore. The Gaslamp District downtown was named for the gas streetlights installed in the area in the late 1800s.

BEST BEACHES OF LA JOLLA

Directly below Scripps Park in La Jolla Village is **La Jolla Cove**, one of the most famous beaches in Southern California. The cove is great for swimming or just lounging in the sand. This is also the beach where you're almost guaranteed to spot sea lions. Remember to keep your distance; some days there are ropes in place to ensure the sea lions have enough space on the beach.

Families love **La Jolla Shores**, **Windansea Beach** and **Torrey Pines State Beach** for their mild surf and expansive sand. Surfers love **Black's Beach** and **Tourmaline Surf Park**, which is better for beginners because of its milder surf.

SAN DIEGO

HIGHLIGHTS
1. Balboa Park

SIGHTS
2. Centro Cultural de la Raza
3. Fleet Science Center
4. Gaslamp Museum at the Davis-Horton House
5. Maritime Museum
6. Museum of Photographic Arts
7. Museum of Us
8. San Diego Air & Space Museum
9. San Diego Museum of Art
10. San Diego Natural History Museum
11. San Diego Zoo
12. Spanish Village Arts Center
13. Timken Museum of Art
14. USS Midway Museum
15. Civico 1845
16. Civico 1845
17. Fish Market
18. Headquarters at Seaport
19. Juniper & Ivy
20. Mona Lisa Italian Foods
21. Morning Glory
22. Werewolf

EATING
15. Animae

EATING IN SAN DIEGO: LITTLE ITALY

Juniper & Ivy: One of the most decorated restaurants in San Diego, with a seasonally driven fine-dining menu. *5-9pm Sun-Thu, to 10pm Fri & Sat* $$$

Mona Lisa Italian Foods: This grocery and restaurant is like the local version of Eataly. *deli 9am-10pm, restaurant 11am-9:30pm Mon-Sat, from noon Sun* $$

Civico 1845: In addition to freshly made pasta and Calabrian cuisine, this restaurant has a full slate of vegan offerings. *4-9pm Sun-Thu, to 10pm Fri, noon-10pm Sat & Sun* $$

Morning Glory: Whimsical brunch restaurant with a roving Bloody Mary cart and breakfast carbonara and chilaquiles. *8am-3pm Mon-Fri, to 4pm Sat & Sun* $$

There are more than 100 places to eat, drink, shop and dance in Gaslamp's 16 square blocks. This is where to head if you're looking for nightlife in San Diego, or to have a cocktail on a rooftop lounge. Rumors of ghost sightings swirl throughout the neighborhood, especially at the **Gaslamp Museum at the Davis-Horton House** (gaslampfoundation.org; entry $8), which offers ghostly walking tours.

At the waterfront area of downtown San Diego, Embarcadero, tour the **USS Midway Museum** (midway.org; adult/child $39/26), a decommissioned aircraft carrier that served for 47 years, and explore the **Maritime Museum** (sdmaritime.org; adult/child $24/from $12), a collection of historic ships that includes the 150-year-old *Star of India*, the oldest active sailing ship.

Discover Old Town San Diego
A true step back in time

Old Town San Diego State Historic Park (oldtownmarketsandiego.com) is a stretch of 19th-century buildings where people lived and worked nearly 200 years ago. Tour an old schoolhouse, or see the spot where the first American flag was raised in San Diego, in 1846. Shops in the park represent a simpler way of life. You can make your own candles or buy penny candy. Bazaar del Mundo, in the center of the historic area, translates to 'marketplace of the world' and brings together merchants selling everything from jewelry to pottery.

Arguably the most iconic of Old Town's historic buildings is the **Whaley House Museum** (whaleyhousesandiego.com; adult/child $13.30/9.50), constructed in 1856 on the site where public hangings once took place. Today, it's rumored to be so haunted that it's been featured on many ghost-hunting TV shows. At night it offers ghost tours and after-hours paranormal investigations.

Cruising the Coast
San Diego's varied coastal communities

The sparkling beach on **Coronado Island** is praised as one of the best in the country, while the southernmost beach town in California is in **South Bay**, only a few miles from the Mexico border. **Imperial Beach** is popular for fishing, surfing, bird-watching and cycling. **Mission Bay Park** is the place to go for water sports, or to charter a fishing or sailing excursion.

SAN DIEGO'S BEST BIKE PATHS

San Diego has over 1800 miles of bikeways – use the **San Diego Regional Bike Map** (sandag.org) to find your route.

Bayshore Bikeway: A 24-mile loop from Coronado to Chula Vista, but you can stick to the beachside **Silver Strand** for a bike-path-only route.

Mission Bay Bike Loop: Mission Bay, between SD and La Jolla, has a flat 12-mile bike path with gorgeous views.

Balboa Park Loop: Cruising around the park on two wheels offers a new perspective.

San Diego River Bike Path: This 20-mile car-free path follows the San Diego River from Mission Valley to Ocean Beach.

Los Peñasquitos Canyon: This mountainous area has hiking and biking paths for all levels.

 EATING IN SAN DIEGO: GASLAMP & EMBARCADERO

| **Headquarters at Seaport:** Village San Diego's old police HQ now houses with food stalls, fine dining and shopping. *10am-9pm Mon-Sat, to 8pm Sun* $$ | **The Fish Market:** Freshly caught fish goes straight from the sea to your plate at this Embarcadero restaurant. *11am-8:30pm Sun-Thu, to 9pm Fri & Sat* $$ | **Animae:** Steakhouse infused with Japanese and Filipino influences from chef Tara Monsod. Chic, art-filled dining room. *5-9pm Sun-Thu, to 9:30pm Fri & Sat* $$$ | **Werewolf:** This lively brewpub in the Gaslamp is a high-energy destination serving brunch and elevated bar food. Nightly karaoke. *8am-2am* $$ |

Flamingos, San Diego Zoo

VISITING MEXICO

As San Diego shares an international border with Tijuana, US citizens with passports can easily travel south to explore the Mexican border town. A Cross Border Xpress skybridge connects the Tijuana International Airport to San Diego. International visitors can also cross the border, but need a valid passport as well as a valid I-94 form or multiple entry visa or visa waiver, which can be managed through the US Customs & Border Patrol's CBP One app.

In TJ, as locals call it, you can shop duty free, eat Mexican food and explore the city's sights, like the Tijuana Cultural Center, which combines art galleries with a botanical garden, performance stages and an aquarium.

Museum-Hopping in Balboa Park
Art, history and science museums

The nickname for **Balboa Park** *(balboapark.org)*, 'the Smithsonian of the West,' isn't hyperbole. San Diego's version of New York's Central Park is home to 17 museums and performance venues, Spanish Renaissance architecture and the **San Diego Zoo** *(sandiegozoo.org; adult/child $76/66)*.

For fine-arts appreciation, try the **Museum of Photographic Arts** *(mopa.org; entry by donation)* for its vast photography collection, the **San Diego Museum of Art** *(sdma.org; adult/child $20/free)* for its rotating international exhibits and the **Timken Museum of Art** *(timkenmuseum.org; free)* for works by European Old Masters.

The **Centro Cultural de la Raza** *(centrodelaraza.com; free)* is an arts center highlighting Mexican, Indigenous and Latino culture; at the **Spanish Village Arts Center** *(village artscenter.org)* a community of more than 200 artisans show their works.

To learn about the world, try the **Museum of Us** *(museumofus.org; adult/child $19.95/16.95)*, dedicated to human history. The **San Diego Air & Space Museum** *(sandiegoairandspace.org; adult/child $35/22)* has the real Apollo 9 Command Module and artifacts from Amelia Earhart and Charles Lindbergh. The **Fleet Science Center** *(fleetscience.org; adult/child $24.95/19.95)* features 100 interactive science exhibits and the **San Diego Natural History Museum** *(sdnhm.org; adult/child $24/14)* displays a T rex skeleton.

Places We Love to Stay

$ Budget $$ Midrange $$$ Top End

San Francisco   MAPS P888, P892

HI San Francisco Fisherman's Wharf $ Get million-dollar waterfront views in an ex-army barracks that's now SF's top hostel. Choose private rooms or dorms (some co-ed), all with shared bathrooms and a communal kitchen offering free breakfasts.

Green Tortoise Hostel $ North Beach's hostel encourages bonding with pool, ping-pong, games, co-working stations and weekly live music shows in the sunny ballroom. Perks include a sauna, free breakfast, good wi-fi, on-site laundry and communal kitchen. Dorm rooms have generous lockers.

Pacific Tradewinds Hostel $ San Francisco's smartest all-dorm hostel has a fully equipped kitchen (free coffee, tea and PB&J sandwiches), spotless showers, sturdy bunk beds, laundry (free sock wash), luggage storage, no lockout time and, best of all, fun staff. No elevator.

Hotel del Sol $$ With splashy beach-ball color schemes, a palm-lined courtyard and heated outdoor pool, the Marina's mid-century motor lodge is SF's top choice for families.

Lodge at the Presidio $$ The officers' post turned ecolodge has dashingly handsome guest rooms with pillowtop beds, historic photos and commanding views – request a room overlooking the Golden Gate Bridge.

Orchard Garden Hotel $$ SF's first LEED-certified green hotel is surprisingly affordable and conveniently located just outside Chinatown, with a gym, rooftop deck and optional breakfast at the sustainable Roots restaurant.

Hotel Bohème $$ The quintessential North Beach inn has smallish rooms named after Beat writers, with wrought-iron beds, original artwork and small bathrooms. Some rooms face noisy Columbus Ave and there's no elevator – but novels practically write themselves here.

Union Street Inn $$$ Live like a Victorian socialite at this grand B&B with six antique-filled guest rooms, afternoon tea in lush gardens and generous breakfasts in the parlor.

Fairmont San Francisco $$$ Magnificent marble lobby, opulent mosaic penthouse suite – plus San Francisco eccentricity, including the tiki Tonga Room and the circus-mural Cirque Bar. Guest rooms have business-class comfort. For historic appeal, reserve in the original 1906 building; for jaw-dropping views, go for the tower.

Parsonage $$$ At this 1883 Italianate Victorian, with original Carrara-marble fireplaces, rose-brass chandeliers and period furnishings, the antique-adorned rooms are named after San Francisco's grand dames. Architect Julia Morgan gets the best views. Two-night minimum.

Bay Area

B-Love's Guest House $ Artist Traci 'B-Love' Bartlow rents out rooms in her West Oakland house, which includes a garden. The shared bathroom has Bartlow's photography on the walls.

Dinah's Garden Hotel $ South of the university campus and downtown in Palo Alto, with great rates, oversized rooms, balconies and garden-filled grounds and an outdoor pool.

Graduate Berkeley $$ Only a block from campus at Berkeley, this seven-story 1928 hotel plays up its ties to the university. Collegiate-inspired details throughout.

Gables Inn Sausalito $$ Tranquility, style and peace in Sausalito. The inn includes a historical 1869 home, and has 13 rooms, four cottages and three apartments, some with grand views.

Mill Rose Inn $$ Right near the center of Half Moon Bay on a large plot with private gardens filled with flowers. Traditional style with luxe details.

North Coast & Redwoods

Mattole Campground $ At the northern point of the Lost Coast Trail, this campground is just steps from the beach and has 27 sites.

Jedediah Smith Redwoods Campground $ Stay in the main loop, outer loop or redwoods cabin area, with cabins that sleep up to six.

Inn at 2nd & C $$ This glorious historic hotel in Eureka has been tastefully restored to combine Victorian-era decor with every possible modern amenity.

Historic Requa Inn $$ Every room at this 100-year-old inn has a Klamath River view – and one room is the town's former post office.

Mendocino Grove $$ This glamping gem by the sea in Mendocino has safari-style tents and elegant bathhouses.

Camellia Inn $$$ Cheery pink 1871 mansion in Healdsburg, with camellia-filled gardens, sociable parlors and upbeat, helpful innkeepers.

Napa & Sonoma

Sonoma Creek Inn $ Quirky 16-room motel in Sonoma with retro-Americana decor, including vintage California travel posters and postcard lamps.

An Inn 2 Remember $$ Steps from Sonoma Plaza, this vintage 1910 charmer offers warm welcomes and private, comfortable lodgings.

Inn at Occidental $$ Escape the ordinary at this 16-room Victorian inn in Occidental, with heirloom quilts for getting cozy in the redwoods.

Blackbird Inn $$$ In Napa, relax in a ruggedly handsome 1902 California Craftsman cottage with eight plush rooms.

Mt Shasta

LOGE Mt Shasta $$ Dorms, gear lockers, shared bathrooms and covered campsites geared toward social, active folks.

Bidwell House B&B $$ Near Mt Lassen, the historic summer home of pioneers John and Annie Bidwell has classic accommodations that come with all the modern amenities.

Sequoia, Yosemite & Lake Tahoe   MAP P929

evo Tahoe City Hotel $ An adventure-focused hotel in Tahoe City with modern rooms and lots of communal social spaces, plus a sauna and cold plunge.

Yosemite Bug Rustic Mountain Resort $ Budget-friendly oasis with eclectic accommodations, a beloved restaurant and a spa. Near Mariposa.

Yosemite Basecamp $$ An 'adventure loft' and 'basecamp bunkhouse' in Groveland with boot dryers and soaking tubs.

John Muir Lodge $$ A stone-and-timber retreat in Grant Grove Village with homespun rooms, a cozy fireplace and tent cabins (Sequoia and Kings Canyon National Parks).

Granlibakken Resort $$ A 74-acre historical resort at Tahoe City with on-site activities, where vintage cabin meets modern wilderness lodge.

Village at Palisades Tahoe $$ Hotel rooms up to multiroom condos lofted above the shops of the Palisades Village.

Gold Country   MAP P929

Foothills Motel $ Good-value retro-modern motel in Auburn with an on-site bowling alley with 24 lanes, a bar, and a diner. It's a five-minute drive to Old Town.

Two Room Inn $$ Sweet two-room Victorian cottage with stained-glass lattice windows and a prime spot on Broad St, Nevada City, just steps away from all the action.

Sonora Inn $$ A historic 1896 hotel in Sonora, redone for modern times. Rooms and suites are pet-friendly for an added fee. The rooftop pool is a beloved respite on hot days.

The Central Coast

Apple Farm Inn $ A whimsical tree-shaded complex surrounding a century-old millhouse in San Luis Obispo.

Fogcatcher Inn $$ Elegant and plush, the design is all earth tones and driftwood at this inn on Cambria's Moonstone Beach.

Fernwood Resort $$ Stay in woodsy rooms with outdoor hot tubs or snug glamping tents at this friendly, few-frills resort with a cozy tavern in Big Sur.

Martine Inn $$ Old-fashioned elegance in Pacific Grove, Monterey, with 25 antique-dotted rooms filling an early-20th-century estate.

Pine Inn $$$ Leaning into its 1889 origins, this elegant hotel in Carmel-by-the-Sea has rooms with baroque prints and barrel armchairs. Splurge on an ocean-view room.

Pacific Blue Inn $$$ Between downtown and the boardwalk in Santa Cruz, this courtyard B&B with earth-tone rooms prides itself on a light carbon footprint.

El Encanto $$$ An enchanting 1920s classic in the Riviera neighborhood looks out over the city from its foothill perch, a real Santa Barbara refuge.

Allegretto Vineyard Resort $$$ Old-world elegance, on-site wine tasting and spa treatments in Paso Robles. The rooms are adorned with velvet and chandeliers.

Sacramento

HI Sacramento Hostel $ This hostel in a magnificent Victorian mansion offers good trimmings at rock-bottom prices. It's within walking distance of Old Sac.

Family Laundry & Spa $ Named for its neon sign, this B&B is located in a 1920s Craftsman-style home with three comfortable suites.

Delta King $$ It's a kitschy treat to sleep aboard the *Delta King*, a 1927 paddle wheeler docked on the river in Old Sacramento.

Citizen Hotel $$ This 1924 beaux-arts tower features luxe linens, an atmospheric reception and an upscale farm-to-fork restaurant on the ground floor.

Davis & Chico

Vine Inn $$ Located right in the beating heart of Davis, this modern motel-style inn has simple, comfortable rooms.

Goodman House $$ Delightful B&B in a 1906 home on a tree-lined Chico esplanade. Features include claw-foot baths, French antique beds and a Viennese grand piano.

Hotel Diamond $$$ This 1904 building is the most luxurious place to lay your head in Chico, with a high-thread count, a swanky bar and a top-notch restaurant.

Los Angeles

MAPS P952, P954, P961

HI Los Angeles Santa Monica Hostel $ Near the beach and promenade, budget-friendly digs that rival facilities at properties costing many times more. Single-sex dorms and private rooms.

Highland Gardens Hotel $ Famous landing spot for future celebs. Motel-style accommodations are only one block from the first star on the Walk of Fame.

Banana Bungalows Hotel & Hostel West Hollywood $ Budget digs in a primo location. Private rooms are a great deal, especially those with full kitchens.

Crestridge Inn $ A good indie motel in Inglewood that's convenient to the SoFi Stadium area and LAX. Basic, budget-friendly rooms.

Samesun Venice Beach $ In a refurbished 1904 building with spectacular rooftop views of Venice Beach. Dorms, private rooms and a cool travelers' vibe.

Hollywood Roosevelt $$ Hollywood lore lives large at its most famous hotel (tip: get a pool room). Celebrity stories abound.

Biltmore Los Angeles $$ Grand old dame awash with history, grandeur and legend. The Academy Awards were founded in the Crystal Ballroom in 1927.

Hotel Normandie LA $$ Dating to 1926, the Normandie has vintage luxuries and a famous bar.

Hotel Per La $$$ Vintage interiors and a rooftop pool in a restored Downtown palazzo that was once the grand digs of the Bank of Italy. Plush rooms.

Silver Lake Pool & Inn $$$ Channeling Palm Springs, effortlessly hip, chilled and awash in SoCal light; the design credentials include locally produced art and bright rooms.

Georgian Hotel $$$ Across the street from Palisades Park and the Pacific beyond, this eye-catching 1933 art deco landmark has a snug ocean-view veranda.

Palm Springs & the Deserts

MAP P965

Jumbo Rocks Campground $ There's classic bouldery JTree landscape at this popular campground with over 100 sites.

Panamint Springs Resort $ A spacious, family-run campground and rustic motel rooms at Death Valley National Park's western end, with sweeping views across the Panamint Valley.

Mid Hills Campground $ This tranquil campground in Mojave National Preserve is set amid trees.

Drift Palm Springs $$$ The airy rooms and suites have a spare, desert-inspired design; located in downtown Palm Springs on Indian Canyon Dr.

Southern California

MAP P974

Resort at Pelican Hill $$$ This sprawling Newport Beach oceanside resort has five restaurants and two golf courses. Accommodations go up to four-bedroom villas.

Orli La Jolla $$$ In a historic building in La Jolla, this 13-room boutique hotel has thoughtful touches and a fun vibe.

San Diego

Wayfarer San Diego $$ On Pacific Beach, this newly renovated hotel has suites and rooms with gorgeous ocean views.

Kona Kai Resort & Spa $$ A Shelter Island hotel with a private beach – a rarity in San Diego – and a tropical island feel.

Guild Hotel $$$ A boutique hotel in a century-old building that was once a YMCA, with original architectural details.

Hotel del Coronado $$$ One of the most historically significant and beautiful hotels in California, located directly on the beach.

THE GUIDE

Researched and curated by Sarah Etinas

Pacific Northwest

AN UNBEATABLE NATURE ESCAPE

Innovative cities and gorgeous natural landscapes come together in the Pacific Northwest.

As much a state of mind as a geographical region, the northwest corner of the US is a land of subcultures and new trends, where evergreen trees frame snow-dusted volcanoes and inspired ideas scribbled on the back of napkins become tomorrow's start-ups. You can't peel off the history in layers here, but you can gaze wistfully into the future in fast-moving, innovative cities such as Seattle and Portland, which are sprinkled with food carts, streetcars, microbreweries, green belts, coffee connoisseurs and quirky urban sculptures.

Before the Pacific Northwest (PNW) became the unconventional, tech-forward region that we know today, it was home to several long-established Native American communities, including the Chinook, the Salish, the Nez Percé and the Yakama, to name just a few. Western contact didn't occur until the 18th century, and from there, it was a snowball effect of changes – native populations were wiped out, city infrastructure began to develop, and the landscape was transformed by new industries like logging and mining.

These changes formed the basis for what is now the modern-day Pacific Northwest – a region more diverse than its regional generalizations depict. The urban hubs of Seattle and Portland serve as emblematic cities, with their progressive politics and tech industries, but head east into the region's drier and less verdant interior, where the cultural affiliations become increasingly more traditional and where raucous rodeos, peaceful fly-fishing and small-town values are still very much alive.

DANITA DELIMONT/SHUTTERSTOCK

THE MAIN AREAS

SEATTLE
A city surrounded by natural beauty.
p986

WASHINGTON
Stunning landscapes, fresh seafood, picturesque wineries.
p996

PORTLAND
Unconventional and quirky from the start.
p1011

OREGON
Beaches, waterfalls, and snowcapped mountains.
p1021

Multnomah Falls (p1026), Oregon

Find Your Way

Washington and Oregon are the two states at the heart of the Pacific Northwest. The major cities of Seattle and Portland are west of the Cascade Mountains but they're still a couple of hours' drive from the Pacific Ocean.

CAR
Like much of the US, traveling around the greater Pacific Northwest region requires a car. Parking can sometimes be tricky and pricey in big cities, but overall, a car is still the most convenient transportation option.

Seattle, p986
Incredible museums, sprawling parks and a global dining scene are just some of the things to experience in this lively city.

LIGHT-RAIL
Portland, Oregon; Seattle, Washington; and Tacoma, Washington, all have convenient light-rail systems that make it easy to get around the main metro areas sustainably. These light-rail routes don't currently expand beyond the major cities.

Portland, p1011
Flavorful restaurants and gorgeous parks will compete for your attention in Oregon's unabashedly quirky big city.

BUS
Buses offer affordable intracity and intercity transportation options. While not typically the speediest option, they can be great for travelers on a budget or looking to travel more sustainably.

Oregon, p1021
Wineries, waterfalls, mountains and beaches are just the beginning of the classic Pacific Northwest beauty found in greater Oregon.

Washington, p996

From peaceful islands in the west to wine regions in the east, greater Washington State is fantastic for a calm, nature-filled escape.

THE GUIDE

PACIFIC NORTHWEST

Plan Your Time

The Pacific Northwest covers a lot of ground. You'll want to prioritize what's most important to you – whether it's bustling city life, hiking adventures or peaceful winery visits.

A Weekend Getaway

● Start at Seattle's **Pike Place Market** (p990), getting lost, browsing, tasting and bantering with the producers. Don't miss the gum wall or the salmon tossing. Take the monorail to Seattle Center, where you'll spend the afternoon admiring the views at the top of the **Space Needle** (p986) and the art at **Chihuly Garden and Glass** (p987).

● Explore the best of North Seattle, with a kayaking adventure at the **Washington Park Arboretum** (p994) or a few hours at the **Ballard Locks** (p994). Dive into Belltown's nightlife scene, catching a performance at the **Pacific Northwest Ballet** (p992) or a jazz act at **Dimitriou's Jazz Alley** (p992). If time allows, watch the Seattle Kraken taking to the ice of the **Climate Pledge Arena** (p991) or the Seahawks racing down the lengths of **Lumen Field** (p995).

Lumen Field (p995)

SEASONAL HIGHLIGHTS

There's always something new happening in the Pacific Northwest. Plan your visit around the seasonal activities that catch your eye or be surprised by the festivities on arrival.

MARCH
Much of the region is still overcast. Lower-elevation hikes have thawed from winter snow, while higher elevations still have prime snowshoeing conditions. The **Penn Cove Musselfest** (p1001) takes place on Whidbey Island.

APRIL
With April showers, the US' largest tulip festival comes to life. Tiptoe through a rainbow of beautiful blooms at the **Skagit Valley Tulip Festival** (p1003) in Mt Vernon, Washington. Stick around the region for rummage sales and locally made ice cream.

MAY
In McMinnville, Oregon, the **UFO Fest** (p1024) puts on a whole weekend of alien-themed events, with the highlights being the Alien Pet Costume Contest and the Alien Costume Parade.

A Weeklong Trip

● Experience the best of Western Oregon, starting with the Portland highlights, like **Washington Park** (p1017) and **Powell's City of Books** (p1011). From there, buckle in and get ready to hit a few noteworthy Oregon towns: **Astoria** (p1030), a beautiful coastal city where *The Goonies* was filmed; **McMinnville** (p1021), for charming wineries and a space-themed water park; and **Eugene** (p1025), for its hippie-esque atmosphere and lively Saturday market.

● Round out your week in Oregon with a visit to **Crater Lake National Park** (p1022), the only national park in Oregon and home to the deepest, bluest lake in the US. Drive around to stop at the many viewpoints, or lace up your hiking shoes to tackle the challenging but rewarding 3.5-mile **Garfield Peak** hike.

Two Weeks to Explore

● With two weeks, you have time to tackle the aforementioned Oregon road trip, journey up to Seattle to hit the previously noted highlights and add Washington's best national parks to the itinerary too. Start with **Mt Rainier National Park** (p998), where you can take in the awe-inspiring mountain views from **Ricksecker Point** and tackle the beloved **Sourdough Ridge Trail**.

● Once you've got your fill of one national park, venture to the next: **Olympic National Park** (p999), where the diverse array of landscapes serves as a playground for nature-lovers. Hike around the accessible **Hurricane Ridge**, soak in the healing mineral waters of **Sol Duc Hot Springs**, admire the sea stacks at Rialto Beach and bask in the greenery of the **Hoh Forest**, just to start.

THE GUIDE

PACIFIC NORTHWEST

JUNE
The popular **Portland Rose Festival** (p1017) harkens in summer with carnival rides, live entertainment, dragon boat races, and daytime and after-dark parades. June is also when several types of salmon will start 'running' from saltwater to freshwater.

JULY
July is peak season in the region, thanks to the ideal temperatures and sunshine-filled skies. It's when hikes are at their greenest, wild berry bushes are at their fullest and waterways come alive with kayakers and paddleboarders.

SEPTEMBER
There are quite a few annual events that take place in the PNW each September, but **Bumbershoot** (p990), Seattle's premier arts and music festival, may be the best of the bunch.

OCTOBER
While you can forage at every time of year, October is a favorite, thanks to the abundance of mushrooms that pop up. (Be sure to go only with an experienced forager.)

Seattle

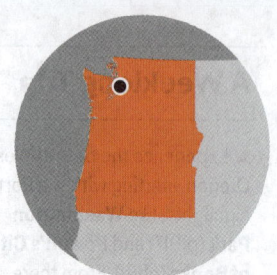

STUNNING VIEWPOINTS | LGBTQ+ HANGOUTS | ELECTRIC SPORTS GAMES

GETTING AROUND

The layout of Seattle is fairly straightforward, tucked between Puget Sound on one side and Lake Washington on the other, with I-5 running straight down the middle. Most of the main neighborhoods are reachable by the city's Link light-rail train. Otherwise, buses, cars, streetcars or bikes – depending on where you're staying – are options.

As the home of big-name technology giants like Microsoft and Amazon, Seattle is often thought of as the height of innovation. Each of the city's approximately 1500 tech start-ups – from pioneers of advanced artificial intelligence to innovators working on sustainable space travel – seems on the verge of its big breakthrough.

And while much of the city is now filled with towering glass skyscrapers to house these innovators, the surrounding nature serves as a beloved juxtaposition. With sparkling Puget Sound to the west, the snowcapped Cascade Mountains to the east and urban green spaces dotted all throughout town, it's easy enough for Seattleites to escape the urban hustle.

All of that said, at its core, Seattle is a city of kindness and acceptance. Cultural communities share the flavors of their ancestry in family-owned restaurants, rainbow flags fly proudly over LGBTIQ-owned businesses and local bookstores stock their shelves with accessible titles. It's safe to say, Seattle is a city more than worth exploring.

To the Top of the Space Needle
Views from a UFO-inspired landmark

If there's one attraction that comes to mind when you think of Seattle, it's undoubtedly the **Space Needle** *(spaceneedle. com; adult/child from $35/30)*. Standing proudly in Seattle Center at 605ft tall, this UFO-inspired tower was originally built for the 1962 World's Fair and continues to welcome about a million visitors every year. Head to the upper observation deck for an open-air deck showcasing some of the best views of the city, Puget Sound and Mt Rainier. Then, venture to the lower Loupe Level, where a revolving deck spins guests around during a leisurely 30-minute circumnavigation.

☑ TOP TIP

To ride the easy-access Link light-rail system, opt to use either the Transit Go app or an ORCA card to make your experience as seamless as possible.

Space Needle

Feel Inspired by Whimsical Glass Art
Visit Chihuly Garden and Glass

An exquisite exposition of the life and work of dynamic local sculptor Dale Chihuly, **Chihuly Garden and Glass** *(chihulygardenandglass.com; adult/child $32/free)* is possibly the finest collection of curated glass art you'll ever see. It shows off Chihuly's creative designs in a suite of interconnected rooms and an adjacent garden in the shadow of the Space Needle.

Dive into Pop Culture
Architecture meets entertainment

The **Museum of Pop Culture** *(mopop.org; adult/child from $25/19)* – or MoPOP – is an inspired marriage between supermodern architecture and legendary rock-and-roll history. Inside its avant-garde frame, you can tune in to the famous sounds of Seattle or attempt to imitate the rock masters in an interactive 'Sound Lab.'

EATING NEAR THE SPACE NEEDLE: OUR PICKS

Maiz Molino: Get your Mexican food fix at Maiz Molino, where the brunch chilaquiles and dinner duck mole chalupas are both sure to please. *hours vary* **$$**

Paju: A small and simple space that serves modern takes on beloved Korean dishes. *hours vary* **$$**

Toulouse Petit: Cajun-Creole restaurant with New Orleans–inspired food, decor and ambience. Get the perfectly puffy buttermilk beignets. *hours vary* **$$**

Tilikum Place Cafe: Savor French onion soup and Dutch baby pancakes at this seasonal, European-style cafe. Make reservations. *hours vary* **$$**

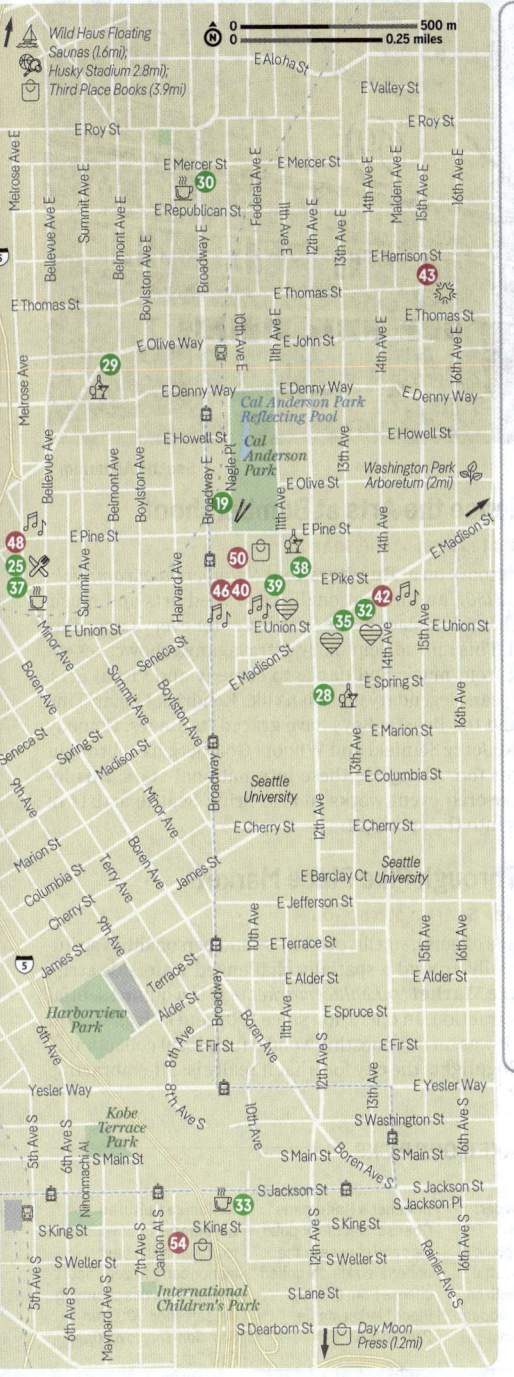

PACIFIC NORTHWEST SEATTLE

★ HIGHLIGHTS
1. Space Needle

● SIGHTS
2. Center for Wooden Boats
3. Chihuly Garden and Glass
4. Gum Wall
5. Lumen Field
6. Museum of Pop Culture
7. Public Market Sign
8. Seattle Aquarium
9. Seattle Art Museum

● ACTIVITIES
10. Argosy Cruises
11. Bill Speidel's Underground Tour
12. Climate Pledge Arena

● SLEEPING
13. Edgewater
14. Green Tortoise Seattle Hostel
15. Hotel Crocodile
16. Inn at the Market

● EATING
17. Beecher's Handmade Cheese
18. Hellenika Cultured Creamery
19. Ltd Edition Sushi
20. Maiz Molino
21. Matt's in the Market
22. Paju
23. Pike Place Chowder
24. Pike Place Fish Market
25. Taylor Shellfish Oyster Bar
26. Tilikum Place Cafe
27. Toulouse Petit

● DRINKING & NIGHTLIFE
28. Canon
29. Doctor's Office
30. Espresso Vivace
31. Futurebean by Storyville Coffee
32. Madison Pub
33. Phin
34. Phocific Standard Time
35. Pony
36. Rachel's Ginger Beer
37. Starbucks Reserve Roastery
38. Unicorn
39. Wildrose

● ENTERTAINMENT
40. Barboza
41. Bumbershoot
42. Chop Suey
43. Club Comedy Seattle
44. Crocodile
45. Dimitriou's Jazz Alley
46. Neumos
47. Pacific Northwest Ballet
48. Vice Seattle

● SHOPPING
49. Eighth Generation
50. Elliott Bay Book Company
51. Metsker Maps
52. Pike Place Market
53. Seattle Waterfront Market
54. Tsue Chong Retail Store

Seattle Aquarium

MAKE A REAL CHANGE

As of 2024, it was estimated that around 16,000 people were experiencing homelessness in Seattle. And while the city's large population of unhoused people may give some visitors pause, it's important to keep in mind that they are citizens of the neighborhood the same as anyone else, and pose no more a threat than their housed neighbors. One way to contribute to the solution is by buying the weekly newspaper *Real Change*. You'll see vendors, many of them unhoused people, selling it on the street for $2 (vendors buy the paper for $0.60 a copy and keep the profit). The paper, founded in 1994, generates over $1 million a year for homeless causes.

Experience the Arts at Bumbershoot

The music festival of the season

Get your groove on at **Bumbershoot** *(bumbershoot.com; tickets from $150)*, an internationally renowned arts and music festival that takes place at the Seattle Center every Labor Day weekend. This multidisciplinary extravaganza showcases everything from music and dance to comedy and visual arts. Over the years, legendary musicians like Kendrick Lamar, Tina Turner and the Beastie Boys have graced its stages. Comedy giants like Jerry Seinfeld and Whoopi Goldberg have brought the laughs too. Alongside these international stars, this locally sponsored event works to also bring Seattle artists of all kinds into the spotlight.

Shop Through Pike Place Market

A must-see Seattle attraction

A cavalcade of noise, smells, quirkiness and personalities sprinkled liberally around a spatially challenged waterside strip, **Pike Place Market** *(pikeplacemarket.org)* is a quintessential Seattle attraction. In operation since 1907 and still as soulful today as it was on day one, this wonderfully local collection of vendors highlights the city for what it really is: all-embracing,

 EATING IN PIKE PLACE MARKET: OUR PICKS

Matt's in the Market: The menu at Matt's features ingredients that come from the famed market down below. *11:30am-2:30pm & 5:30-10pm Mon-Sat* $$$

Pike Place Chowder: This counter-serve restaurant is the place to get some fresh Seattle clam chowder – with an optional fresh sourdough bread bowl too. *11am-5pm* $

Beecher's Handmade Cheese: Get the popular mac and cheese or the underrated kimchi grilled cheese from this Pike Place Market staple. *9am-7pm* $

Hellenika Cultured Creamery: Treat yourself to arguably the best marionberry frozen yogurt around from this charming dessert shop. *10:30am-6pm Sun-Thu, to 6:30pm Fri & Sat* $

eclectic and proudly unique. Be sure to snap a picture with the neon **Public Market sign**, watch the fishmongers at the **Pike Place Fish Market** stall toss massive salmon around, press your own sticky addition to the **Gum Wall**, pick up a blooming flower bouquet, and snack on a cheesy meal from **Beecher's Handmade Cheese**, just to start.

Make Marine Animal Friends
The new and improved Seattle Aquarium

More than 10,000 underwater creatures call the **Seattle Aquarium** *(seattleaquarium.org; adult/child from $34/22)* home, including otters, seahorses, rays and even a giant Pacific octopus. Most recently, the aquarium has added a state-of-the-art Ocean Pavilion, which includes a 360,000-gallon tank housing animals from the Indo-Pacific.

Sail Puget Sound
Stunning water views await

The stunning Puget Sound is a highlight of any visit to Downtown Seattle. Want to experience it firsthand? **Argosy Cruises** *(argosycruises.com; adult/child $45/29)* provides the perfect opportunity with multiple daily cruises departing from Pier 55. The popular Harbor Cruise is one hour of delightfully informative narration and lovely city skyline views.

Stroll Through the Seattle Art Museum
Spotlighting Native art

The collection at the **Seattle Art Museum** *(seattleartmuseum.org; adult/child from $30/free)* feels uncommon, intimate and extraordinary. Its sterling selection of contemporary and antique art of the Indigenous peoples of the Pacific Northwest alone makes this a required stop on any city getaway.

Catch a Game at Climate Pledge Arena
Sustainability meets sports

The **Climate Pledge Arena** *(climatepledgearena.com)* is an incredibly cool venue, in more ways than one. First off, the arena officially became zero carbon-certified in October 2023 – and it required a whole lot of sustainable plans to get there. It's powered by 100% renewable energy, implements on-site

BEST LITERARY FINDS IN SEATTLE

Elliott Bay Book Company: Pop into arguably the best-known bookstore in the city. Located in Capitol Hill, this literary haven has over 150,000 titles and an incredibly inclusive selection.

Third Place Books: Find your next read – new or used – at Third Place Books. Then, settle in to read it at the on-site cafe or pub.

Day Moon Press: A cozy, family-owned letterpress print shop with loads of old-school printmaking gear and a small retail section.

Book Larder: Experience the best of books and bites at Book Larder, a North Seattle gem with shelves stocked to the brim with cookbooks.

Metsker Maps: Get equipped for your next travel adventure at Metsker Maps. This nearly century-old shop is filled with maps, globes and travel guidebooks.

 DRINKING IN SEATTLE: BEST COFFEE SHOPS

Futurebean by Storyville Coffee: The cozy yet modern coffee shop serves impeccable breakfast sandwiches, cinnamon rolls, salted caramel cookies and, of course, coffee. *8am-2pm*

Espresso Vivace: Widely regarded as the best espresso in the city. The founder David Schomer is also credited with bringing latte art to the US. *6am-7pm*

Milstead & Co: This fabulous Fremont coffee bar meticulously selects its beans with sommelier-level skill and has a 'bean menu' that changes daily. *7am-4pm*

Phin: Venture to Little Saigon in the International District, where the baristas at Phin brew fantastic condensed milk-drizzled Vietnamese coffee drinks. *8am-3pm Mon & Wed-Fri, to 5pm Sat & Sun*

SEATTLE: THE BIRTHPLACE OF GRUNGE

Grunge emerged in Seattle in the 1980s as a reaction against the perceived excesses of 1980s hair metal and mainstream rock. Bands like Green River, Mudhoney and the Melvins blended the raw energy of punk rock with the heavy, distorted sounds of metal, often played at a slower tempo, creating the gritty, sludgy sound that grunge is known for. Initially many artists disliked the 'grunge' label, (accurately) viewing it as a marketing term. However, as the genre gained mainstream popularity in the early 1990s with bands like Nirvana, Pearl Jam, Soundgarden and Alice in Chains, the term became widely accepted, even if begrudgingly by some, as a descriptor for this unique 'Seattle Sound'.

waste sorting to prioritize zero waste initiatives and uses captured rainwater to make the Kraken's ice rink, just to start.

While these sustainable features are fantastic in their own right, the venue's two sports teams bring even more excitement. First, there's the Seattle Kraken, a pro hockey team that officially joined the NHL in 2021 and soon after qualified for the Stanley Cup playoffs in 2023. Then, there's the Seattle Storm, a legendary WNBA team that has garnered 16 playoff appearances and four championships under their belt since their establishment in 2000. Both teams have amassed thousands of die-hard fans, making the game atmosphere absolutely electric.

Visit the Birthplace of Grunge Music
Welcome to the Crocodile

Seattle is considered the birthplace of grunge music, and the **Crocodile** *(thecrocodile.com)* is one of the main venues that made that musical renaissance happen. Grunge greats like Nirvana, Pearl Jam, Soundgarden, Alice in Chains and Mudhoney have all performed at the Crocodile, and to this day, you can still see incredible live music acts – grunge or otherwise – at this legendary Seattle institution.

Listen to Live Music at Dimitriou's Jazz Alley
A legacied jazz hub

Not a lot of people know it, but Seattle was a hive of jazzy creativity in the 1940s and '50s. Some of the legacy remains at **Dimitriou's Jazz Alley** *(jazzalley.com/www-home)*, where national and international jazz acts take the stage. It's a holdout in the face of the area's gentrification and a local institution for more than four decades. It's worth noting that this intimate space is a seated venue, but dining is optional.

Spend an Evening at the Ballet
A dance performance to remember

Founded in Seattle in 1972, the **Pacific Northwest Ballet** *(pnb.org; tickets from $5)* is a leading American ballet company. Under the artistic direction of Peter Boal since 2005, the PNB presents over 100 annual performances at McCaw Hall, featuring a diverse repertoire of classical and contemporary works including their renowned *Nutcracker*. Even better, they're forward thinking regarding who can be a ballet

EATING IN SEATTLE: BEST SEAFOOD

Taylor Shellfish Oyster Bar: Arguably Seattle's best oyster spot, with several locations around the city. Capitol Hill is the flagship. *noon-8pm Sun-Thu, to 9pm Fri & Sat* **$$**

Ltd Edition Sushi: Splurge on a seasonally inspired omakase (chef's choice) experience at this Michelin-worthy restaurant. *5-9:30pm Mon-Fri* **$$$**

Pacific Inn Pub: Amidst all the competition, Pacific Inn Pub's expertly spiced, panko-crusted fish and chips are some of the best in town. *11am-2am* **$$**

Little Chinook's: This casual eatery is known for its fish and chips, with both crisp panko-breaded and lighter tempura options. *11:30am-6pm* **$**

Red panda, Woodland Park Zoo

dancer, with exceptionally talented BIPOC, nonbinary and transgender dancers taking to their stage.

Swap Tailgating for Sailgating
At UW's Husky Stadium

You've heard of tailgating, but what about sailgating? Since the University of Washington's **Husky Stadium** *(gohuskies. com)* is right on Lake Washington, the most avid football fans charter boats, join sailgating cruises, or even take out their own vessels, dropping anchor a little ways away from the shore and reveling in pregame food, drinks and fun. To reach the stadium, flag down the shuttle boat service – they start getting crowded an hour before kickoff – and they'll get you where you need to go.

Find the Fremont Troll
Aptly hidden under the bridge

Beneath the Aurora Bridge sprouts the *Fremont Troll*, a 13,000lb steel and concrete sculpture of a troll crushing a Volkswagen Beetle. It was made by four artists – Steve Badanes, Will Martin, Donna Walter and Ross Whitehead – and was the winner of a 1989 competition to design thought-provoking public art.

Meet the Animals at Woodland Park Zoo
Running semi-free

The **Woodland Park Zoo** *(zoo.org; adult/child from $27/16)* is consistently rated as one of the top 10 zoos in the country. It was one of the first in the nation to free animals from their restrictive cages in favor of ecosystem enclosures, where animals from similar environments share large spaces designed to replicate their natural surroundings. Say hello to the beloved red pandas and Humboldt penguins!

WHERE TO SHOP LOCAL IN SEATTLE

Ballard Farmers Market: Experience the local tradition of a weekend farmers market visit with a trip to Ballard Farmers Market, home to more than 100 vendors.

Eighth Generation: Admire Native American artistry first-hand at Eighth Generation, a new addition to Seattle's downtown owned by the Snoqualmie Tribe.

Seattle Waterfront Market: Support local artists at this collective selling everything from watercolor paintings to floral soaps.

Tsue Chong Retail Store: Get yourself some 'unfortunate' (misshapen) fortune cookies from the family-owned Tsue Chong Retail Store.

Easy Street Records & Cafe: Purchase a record from a new-to-you artist at arguably the city's most multifarious record store.

SEATTLE ON THE WATER

Washington Park Arboretum: Kayak your way around Washington Park Arboretum for beautiful blooms and unbeatable water views.

Wild Haus Floating Saunas: Heat your worries away as you sail on Lake Union via a wood-fired sauna boat, courtesy of Wild Haus Floating Saunas.

Center for Wooden Boats: Enjoy a completely free boat ride on Lake Union each Sunday with the Center for Wooden Boats, departing from Lake Union Park.

Kenmore Air: Take to the water and to the skies with Kenmore Air's Seattle Scenic Seaplane Tour.

Alki Beach Park: Soak up the sun on Seattle's most popular shoreline, tucked away from the hustle and bustle in West Seattle.

Starbucks Reserve Roastery

Experience the Ballard Locks
A feat of engineering

The **Ballard Locks** *(ballardlocks.org)*, a popular attraction that allows boats to move between the Puget Sound and the Ship Canal, travel a 22ft rise from saltwater to fresh. The fish ladder here is open to the public and offers a unique opportunity to watch salmon migrate upstream.

Tour the Starbucks Reserve Roastery
Behind the coffee curtain

While most Starbucks fans will venture to the first Starbucks in Pike Place (p990), the **Starbucks Reserve Roastery** *(starbucksreserve.com/locations/seattle-roastery)* in Capitol Hill may be time better spent. At the roastery of this Seattle-grown chain, you can sip on coffee-tasting flights ($13 to $19), take a behind-the-scenes look at the roasting area ($45) or take an espresso martini-making class ($95), just to start.

Experience Capitol Hill's Nightlife Scene
Bars, clubs and comedy

Capitol Hill comes to life after dark. Looking to dance the night away to DJ sets or live music performances? Pick your venue based on music genre. **Vice Seattle** *(viceseattle.com)* is known for EDM, **Neumos** *(neumos.com)* leans toward punk and hip-hop, **Barboza** *(thebarboza.com)* has an eclectic but pop-heavy line-up, and **Chop Suey**'s *(chopsuey.com)* bookings are as mixed as the dish it's named after.

Still yet, there are loads of LGBTQ+ hot spots. **Pony** *(ponyseattle.com)* has reached a level of popularity where most denizens either love or loathe it, while circus-themed **Unicorn** *(unicornseattle.com)* has made its mark with jello shots and pinball games. Let's not forget **Madison Pub** *(madisonpub.com)*, a gay sports bar, and **Wildrose** *(thewildrosebar.com)*, a longtime lesbian bar.

Alternatively, swap bass drops for punch lines with a show at **Club Comedy Seattle** *(clubcomedyseattle.com)*, which features both national headliners and up-and-coming local artists.

Catch a Game at Lumen Field
Feel the energy of the crowd

While **Lumen Field** *(lumenfield.com)* is best known as the home of the Seattle Seahawks (NFL), this iconic sports arena also lays claim to the Seattle Reign (NWSL) and the Seattle Sounders (MLS). All of these teams have won multiple titles in their respective sports and divisions. Even better, they boast some of the most enthusiastic fan bases in the country; book tickets far in advance – especially for Seahawks games – as they often sell out quickly.

Explore Seattle's Hidden City: the Underground
A subterranean adventure

Believe it or not, the original 1800s Seattle was built on unstable, sandy ground. Over time those buildings began to sink. When the Great Seattle Fire of 1889 decimated a 30-block radius, much of the city needed to be rebuilt. Today, visitors can explore these sunken streets and structures – reminiscent of an abandoned construction site crossed with a Hollywood movie set – through **Bill Speidel's Underground Tour** *(undergroundtour.com; adult/child $22/10)*. Mix in a little humor and history and you have a recipe for a fun and educational activity.

LOOKING FOR MORE TROLLS?

If you thought the greater Seattle area could only have one troll sculpture, well, you'd be wrong. Besides the Fremont Troll, there are a handful of others spread around, all made by Danish environmental artist Thomas Dambo. Find these trolls in Ballard, West Seattle, Bainbridge Island, Vashon Island and Issaquah (with the final one in the Pacific Northwest series in Portland, Oregon; p918), tucked amidst the trees or standing proudly in front of museums. Learn more about these incredible sculptures and the artist behind them at *nwtrolls.org*.

DRINKING IN SEATTLE: OUR PICKS

Letterpress Distilling: Travel to Italy at Letterpress Distilling for liqueurs like amaro and limoncello. *noon-6pm Sat, to 4pm Sun*	**Westland Distillery:** Sip on some of the finest whiskey in town – straight or in cocktails – at Westland Distillery. *hours vary*	**Lucky Envelope Brewing:** Sample beers with fun flavor notes, from gingerbread to citrus, at Lucky Envelope Brewing. *hours vary*	**Schilling Cider House:** Enjoy the crispness of Pacific Northwest apples in drink form. *3-9pm Wed & Thu, 1-10pm Fri, noon-10pm Sat, to 8pm Sun*
Phocific Standard Time: Chase a pho-fat-washed shot of Jameson with pho broth at this Vietnamese-inspired speakeasy. *5-11pm Tue-Thu, to midnight Fri & Sat*	**Rachel's Ginger Beer:** The zingy, ginger-based drinks pack a punch – both in the original non-alcoholic form and mixed into fun cocktails. *11:30am-8pm Mon-Sat*	**Canon:** Frequently listed as one of the best bars in the world, with innovative cocktails as tasty as they are artful. *5pm-1am Sun, Wed & Thu, to 2am Fri & Sat*	**Doctor's Office:** Way more fun than your usual doctor's visit, here your 'prescription' is a masterfully crafted cocktail of your choice. *4pm-1am*

Washington

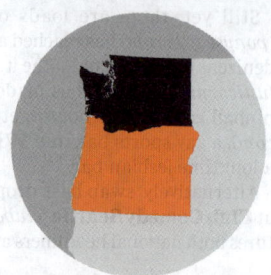

STUNNING LANDSCAPES | FRESH SEAFOOD | PICTURESQUE WINERIES

Places

Bellingham & Around p1001
Whidbey & Fidalgo Islands p1001
Mt Baker p1002
Skagit Valley p1003
San Juan Islands p1004
Bainbridge Island 1005
Sequim p1005
Olympia p1005
Seaview p1005
Washington Cascades p1006
Yakima Valley p1008
Walla Walla p1008
Palouse Falls State Park p1009
Spokane p1100
Grand Coulee Dam p1100

☑ TOP TIP

Make time for Washington's beautiful national parks. While this may require planning ahead (timed entry passes, transportation logistics etc), these landscapes are more than worth the extra effort.

Aptly nicknamed the 'Evergreen State,' Washington is arguably the heart of the Pacific Northwest. With that title comes everything you'd hope for, from the lush, green Olympic Peninsula to the wild, white peaks of the Cascade Mountains and the relaxed, kayaker-friendly San Juan Islands. Head east and you'll see another side of the state: aridly beautiful, with upscale wineries and cowboy-style breakfasts in equal measure, plus orchards, wheat fields and pioneer history.

Outside of the big urban jolt of Seattle, there are a few other main population centers – Spokane, Bellingham, Olympia – each with its own sort of charm. Still, to get the most out of visiting Washington, you'll want to leave the cities behind and lose yourself in the mountains and the woods, along the coast or on the islands. The state's three national parks are incredible in their own rights, while the lesser-known nature spots offer equally rewarding experiences. Safe to say, the best experiences here are mostly unmediated.

GETTING AROUND

To keep it simple, a car is by far the best option for getting around Washington. There are bus routes and Amtrak train routes crisscrossing the Evergreen State, but they're not the most convenient for traveling lengthy distances. Ferries are also an important part of Washington's transportation infrastructure, shuttling people and cars across the Puget Sound; when taking a vehicle aboard a ferry, be sure to give yourself quite a bit of buffer time, as the ferries often get filled to capacity, meaning you'll have to wait for the next sailing.

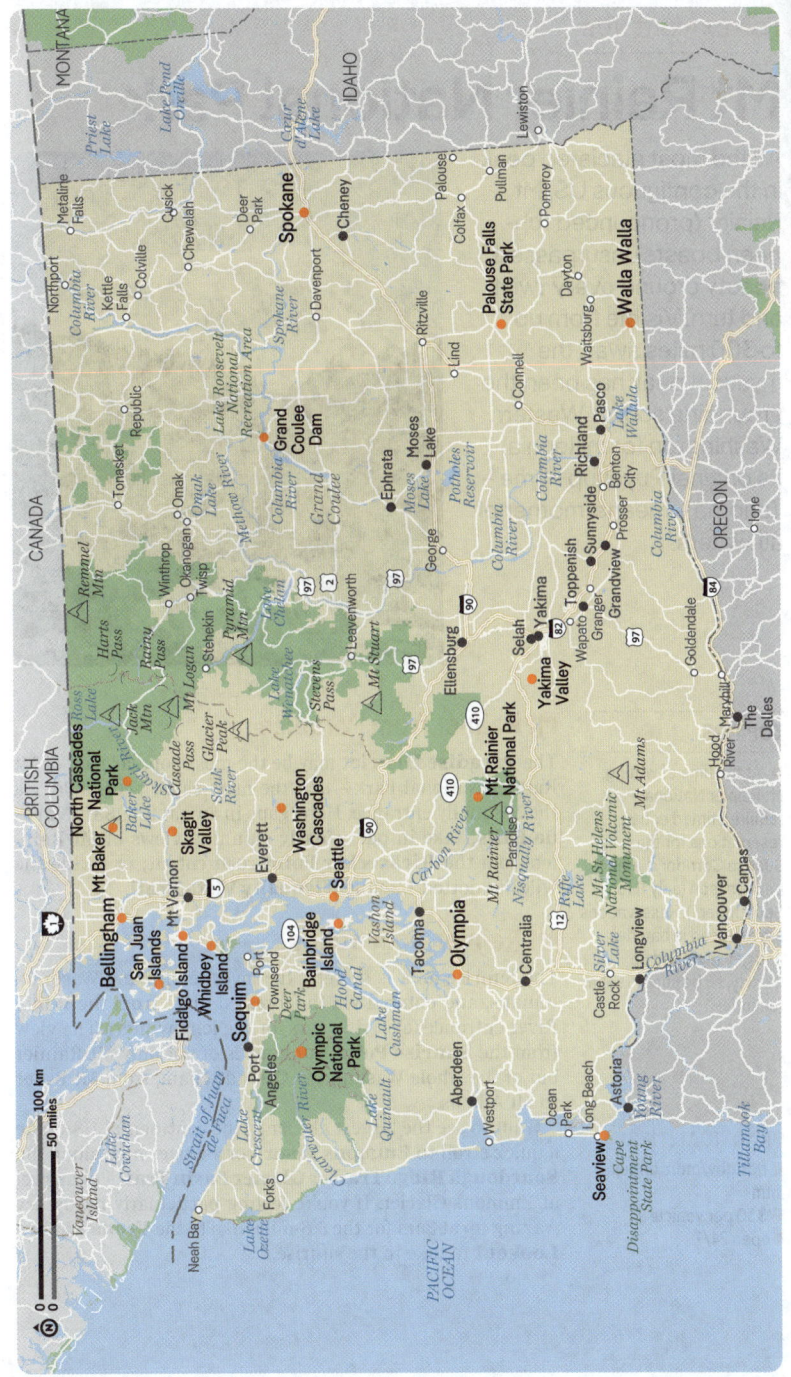

TOP EXPERIENCE

Mt Rainier National Park

As the most glaciated peak in the contiguous US, Mt Rainier (pronounced ruh-*neer*) boasts unsurpassed beauty around every twist and turn. Visible from up to 300 miles away, the mystical peak has been the grounding soul of Western Washington for millennia. Its original Puyallup name – Tahoma – means 'mother of all waters.'

TOP TIPS

- At the time of writing, Mt Rainier National Park required timed entry reservations for the Sunrise Corridor during peak season (July 11 to September 1). Reservations are released in batches and get snatched up quickly, so be sure to set a reminder.

PRACTICALITIES

- nps.gov/mora/index.htm
- $30 per vehicle
- open 24/7

Mt Rainier from Paradise

The **Paradise District** may be the most popular part of Mt Rainier National Park – and the most easily accessible, via the Nisqually entrance. Here, gape in awe at the 188ft **Narada Falls**; take in particularly stunning views of Mt Rainier from the **Ricksecker Point** road cutout; or tackle the wildlife-dotted 1.2-mile **Nisqually Vista Trail**.

Mt Rainier from Sunrise

The Sunrise area is secretly the favorite of many Washingtonians, and entered via the forested drive from the White River entrance (closed to cars for the long winter). The view from the **Sunrise Point Lookout** is of not only Mt Rainier but of the whole Washington Cascade chain, from Mt Baker to Mt Adams.

Want to see the largest glacier in the continental US? Take a quick stroll to **Emmons Vista** – or a longer hike along the **Sourdough Ridge Trail** or **Glacier Basin Trail** – to marvel at Emmons Glacier. If you're feeling particularly hardy, try waking up at 3am for the 5.6-mile hike to the **Fremont Fire Lookout** to take in the sunrise.

TOP EXPERIENCE

Olympic National Park

Olympic National Park is one of the most ecologically diverse places on earth. The terrain gets in your bones (and that's not just the dampness). You could wander the moss-draped trails of the Hoh Rainforest, discover the Pacific Ocean in a colorful tide pool, ski on one of the National Park System's only ski lifts, and camp under stars you haven't seen in decades.

Hurricane Ridge

In the winter, the 10-mile drive to the top of the accessible Hurricane Ridge leads to a wintertime ski treat, where snow-shoeing, tubing, cross-country skiing, downhill skiing and snowboarding opportunities abound. (Note: bring your own food, supplies and rental gear.) In the summer months, wildflowers, hiking and stargazing are at their peak.

Sol Duc Hot Springs

Three healing mineral water pools are fed by a constant stream of the Sol Duc hot springs (there's also a conventional pool). Plus, just across the way, there's a delightful 0.8-mile trail to **Sol Duc Falls**.

Rialto Beach

Rialto Beach's coastline is wild and cinematic, filled with crashing waves, timeless driftwood and a raft of offshore sea stacks. Seals, bald eagles and gray whales make appearances, and in low tide, tide pools reveal starfish, anemone and urchins.

Hoh Rainforest

After years of listening to nature, sound recording expert Gordon Hempton found the quietest place in the lower 48: a mossy log in the Hoh Rainforest. While the secret is out and the forest isn't quite as quiet, admire the Tolkien-like magic of the details: old-growth cedar and spruce, Jurassic ferns and noise-swallowing moss, lichens and fungi.

TOP TIPS

- Download the National Park Service app before you go for maps. Internet coverage is spotty (at best).

- Gas up and load up on supplies in Port Angeles.

- With only five restaurants in the entire park, plan ahead or dine in Forks or Neah Bay.

PRACTICALITIES
- nps.gov/olym/index.htm
- $30 per vehicle
- open 24/7

TOP EXPERIENCE

North Cascades National Park

Protected by sharp mountain peaks with frightening names – Mt Fury, Mt Terror and Desolation Peak – North Cascades National Park has only one access road (Hwy 20, aka the North Cascades Scenic Hwy), which is closed in winter. But once you make it inside, there's a whole host of breathtaking nature sights: 300 glaciers, 200 types of birds and countless hikes are just the beginning.

Diablo Lake

Glacial Waters Run Deep

One of the few sights in North Cascades National Park that's generally accessible year-round, **Diablo Lake** is also among the most stunning. Its shocking turquoise color comes from reflective 'glacial flour' in the water. Though glacier-fed, the lake is actually an artificial reservoir, a result of the 1920s-era Skagit River Hydroelectric Project. You can easily gaze upon Diablo Lake from your car at a viewpoint along Hwy 20, but it's worth taking time for a closer look. Kayaking the lake is otherworldly; if you didn't bring your kayak, the educational **North Cascades Institute** *(ncascades.org; adult/child $50/30)* offers informative three-hour boat tours.

Stay in Stehekin

What, no road access? Cut off from the rest of Washington's highway network by craggy mountains, Stehekin is that rarest of modern American settlements: it's unreachable by car. Getting here is largely the point of a visit, although being here is also wonderful, as the remoteness makes the village impossibly peaceful and quiet. The only thing resembling stress here is making sure you get to the **bakery** on time.

TOP TIPS

- To reach Stehekin, take the **Lady of the Lake ferry** *(ladyofthelake.com; one way $25-45)* across Lake Chelan, either as a day trip or for an overnight stay (book well ahead for both ferry and lodgings).

PRACTICALITIES

- nps.gov/noca/index.htm
- free
- open 24/7

Bellingham & Around

Saltwater adventures in Fairhaven

Perched above Bellingham Bay, the southside district of Fairhaven is Bellingham's unofficial outdoor adventure hub – and an epicenter for bioluminescent activity. Both the **Community Boating Center** *(boatingcenter.org; $100)* and **Moondance Sea Kayak Adventures** *(moondancekayak.com; $105)* offer summer bioluminescence paddles to see this neon-colored phenomenon, and should be booked well in advance.

Wind down Chuckanut Drive

This 24-mile road winds along the coastline from Bellingham to Skagit County's **Bow**, with the Cascade Mountains and Bellingham Bay framing each side. Be sure to stop at **Larrabee State Park** *(parks.wa.gov/find-parks/state-parks/larrabee-state-park; $10)* along the way for gorgeous hikes and marine-creature-filled tide pools. Need to refuel? **Taylor Shellfish Farm** *(taylorshellfishfarms.com)* isn't far, and the salty, fresh oysters make for a particularly delicious waterside meal.

Whidbey & Fidalgo Islands

Connecting the islands

Linked by the iconic Deception Pass bridge, Fidalgo and Whidbey islands are home to the sprawling **Deception Pass State Park** *(parks.wa.gov/find-parks/state-parks/deception-pass-state-park; $10)*. On the Fidalgo (Anacortes) side, stop by **Rosario Head** for a short walk to epic sea cliffs. Hike or drive from Rosario to the busy boat launch and sprawling lawn at **Bowman Bay**. Trekking south from Bowman Bay leads to **Lottie Point** and **Lighthouse Point** – scenic sea bluff trails through evergreen forest and Pacific madrone.

Sustainable seafood in Coupeville

Whidbey Island's Coupeville is home to **Penn Cove Shellfish** *(penncoveshellfish.com)*, a sustainable seafood farm famous for its mussels. Countless island restaurants serve Penn Cove mussels, clams and oysters, and you can see the beds just west of town along Madrona Way. Stop by local grocery stores (like Prairie Center Market) to purchase and cook your own, or attend **Penn Cove Musselfest** (March) to tour and dine on the property.

ANACORTES' BEST TOURS

Outer Island Excursions: Whale-watching tours (May to September) launch from Anacortes' Skyline Marina. *(outerislandx.com)*

Anacortes Kayak Tours: Kayak outings from 1½ to five hours, plus bioluminescence tours and multiday trips. *(anacorteskayaktours.com)*

Maritime Heritage Center: Free museum detailing Anacortes' maritime history. Take a self-guided tour of the WT *Preston* sternwheeler. *(anacorteswa.gov/422/Maritime-Heritage-Center)*

Skagit Guided Adventures: Walking and hiking tours from a six-hour ecotour to a three-hour guided hike. Both include transportation. *(skagitguidedadventures.com)*

Self-guided tours: Anacortes offers free self-guided tours on its website. *(anacorteswa.gov)*

 DRINKING IN NORTHWESTERN WASHINGTON: BREWERIES

Chuckanut Brewery: This celebrated lager brewer operates a barn-red production facility and sunny beer garden at the Port of Skagit. *1-8pm Mon-Thu, noon-8pm Fri-Sun*

Terramar Brewstillery: Sip Skagit-made beer, spirits and non-alcoholic options from Terramar's sprawling beer garden with views of the Chuckanut Mountains. *11:30am-9pm*

El Sueñito Brewing: Super-satisfying tamales and tacos complement sessionable brews at this LGBTIQ- and Mexican-owned brewery. *11am-10pm*

Anacortes Brewery: One of the oldest breweries in Washington (established in 1994) with time-tested beers, a robust food menu and live music. *11am-8pm Sun-Thu, to 10pm Fri & Sat*

Picture Lake

ANNUAL EVENTS AT MT BAKER

Mt Baker hosts two big annual events during the snow season. In January or February, snowsports enthusiasts flock to the ski area to witness the **Legendary Banked Slalom** race. Started by 16 snowboarders in 1985, it's one of the sport's longest-running events and draws world-class competitors.

Every Memorial Day Weekend in May, the **Ski to Sea** race – a multisport team relay – begins at **Mt Baker Ski Area** and ends 93 miles away at Bellingham Bay. Racers compete in cross-country skiing and downhill ski/snowboard legs at Mt Baker before running and road biking down Mt Baker Hwy. First run in 1973, Ski to Sea is the largest one-day event in Whatcom County.

Mt Baker

A scenic drive to Mt Baker's Artist Point

Summer at the 10,781ft Mt Baker is spectacular. Subalpine trails lead through forests and wildflower meadows to glacier-clad mountain views. The 57-mile **Mt Baker Scenic Byway** (bellingham.org/drive-and-hike-mt-baker-scenic-byway) is ideal for road-trippers, quickly leaving the city behind and transitioning from blueberry fields to old-growth forests.

Most visitors make a beeline for **Picture Lake** – and for good reason. Pull off the road for an iconic shot of 9131ft **Mt Shuksan** reflected in the waters. Sometimes called the most photographed mountain in North America, Shuksan's rugged appeal is undeniable.

The first 55 miles of Mt Baker Hwy are open year-round. To drive the final 2.5 miles from Heather Meadows to **Artist Point** – by far the road's most spectacular stretch – visit between July and September.

The road ends at Artist Point. There's no road through these mountains – just miles of national forest and the Mt Baker

EATING & DRINKING ALONG MT BAKER HWY

Wake 'N Bakery: 'Get sconed' at the go-to spot for baked goods, breakfast burritos, coffee and trail snacks in Glacier. *7am-5pm* $

The North Fork Brewery: Locals drive from Bellingham for the North Fork's pizza and beer in Deming. Always packed, but worth the wait. *noon-9pm* $$

Chair 9: Unpretentious, all-ages après-ski bar and pizza place boasting the 'first cocktail' on the way back from Baker. *hours vary* $$

Graham's Bar & Restaurant: Old-fashioned pub in a 1906 building, serving Glacier off-and-on since the 1970s. *hours vary* $$

Wilderness. Walk south on the short, paved Artist Ridge Trail, where Mt Baker dominates the western skyline and Mt Shuksan rises to the east. Stay after dark for incredible stargazing.

Heaven for hikers

Hikers can experience everything from a joyous jaunt to epic, multiday backpacking trips during summer hiking season at **Mt Baker** *(fs.usda.gov/r06/mbs/recreation; $5)*. **Horseshoe Bend Trail** is a forested, 3-mile round-trip trek along the Nooksack River. At the end of Mt Baker Hwy, the 1-mile round-trip **Artist Ridge Trail** is the most popular hike on the mountain, climbing gently to Huntoon Point for incredible views of Mts Baker and Shuksan.

Then there's the moderate **Chain Lakes Loop**, which gains 1800ft of elevation and showcases a series of picturesque lakes along its 6.5-mile route. The nearby, strenuous **Lake Ann Trail** (8.2 miles round-trip, 2100ft elevation gain) leads to a stunning lake and close-up views of Mt Shuksan.

Trails around Mt Baker are typically accessible between July and early October. Check with the **Forest Service** *(fs.usda.gov/mbs)* for road and trail conditions before setting out. Always dress in layers, check the forecast and plan accordingly. A Northwest Forest Pass is required for parking at national forest trailheads.

Skagit Valley

Farms, food and flowers

Between La Conner and Mt Vernon, the lower **Skagit River Valley** *(visitskagitvalley.com)* thrives in every season, especially spring and summer. During the former, flowers reign supreme in Skagit Valley. The season kicks off in March with **La Conner Daffodil Festival**, a celebration of bright yellow blooms. In April, the famous **Skagit Valley Tulip Festival** draws massive crowds. The ticketed **Roozengaarde** and **Tulip Town** experiences burst with colorful tulip fields and offer endless photo opportunities.

And during the latter, Skagit Valley farms produce abundant fruits and veggies, with over 90 different crops grown in the region. Taste your way across the valley with farm visits – from produce stands to pumpkin fields. Don't miss an essential stop at **Snow Goose Produce** *(snowgooseproducemarket.com)*, an open-air country market overflowing with local produce, flowers and 'immodest' ice-cream cones.

WHY I LOVE THE SKAGIT VALLEY TULIP FESTIVAL

Sarah Etinas, Lonely Planet writer

When I first heard about the Skagit Valley Tulip Festival, I wasn't sure what to make of it. I wasn't sure if there were really fields of colorful tulips stretching on and on, or if the photos I was seeing were all camera angles primed to perfection. So I bought my ticket and drove my way up.

A bit of traffic later, and my doubts were proven gloriously wrong. At just one of the farms, colorful rows of tulips in a dozen shades spread far and wide, with the snowcapped Cascade Mountains providing an even more beautiful backdrop. Cozy swings, tucked-away daffodils and an adorable gift shop completed the visit – one that I hope I get to repeat sometime soon.

 EATING IN WASHINGTON: WORKING OYSTER FARMS

Goose Point: Right on Willapa Bay, Goose Point has been family-run since 1975. Enjoy oysters at a rustic picnic table or take oyster shooters to go. *9am-5pm* $

Taylor Shellfish Farms Shellfish Market: With three restaurants in Seattle, Taylor Shellfish Farms' market next to its Hood Canal processing plant offers fresher-than-fresh oysters. *10am-6pm* $

Brady's Oysters: A family-run oyster farm just west of Aberdeen with a couple of picnic tables, an authentic Pacific Northwest vibe, and oysters harvested feet away. *9am-6pm* $$

Oysterville Sea Farms: The most 'full service' of the bunch, with elegant picnic tables and a dozen menu options. *11am-6pm Thu-Mon* $

Billy Frank Jr Nisqually National Wildlife Refuge

ROCHE HARBOR HISTORY

At the north end of San Juan Island, seaside Roche Harbor was once the largest lime producer in the Pacific Northwest. The company town was built by Tacoma and Roche Harbor Lime Company founder John S McMillin in 1886 to support his enterprise. The lime kilns, hotel, and historic structures still stand today, restored and transformed into the stylish **Roche Harbor Resort**. Brick-lined paths lead to three unique eateries – from casual, dockside Lime Kiln Cafe to formal McMillin's Dining Room.

The McMillin family is memorialized north of Roche Harbor at the **McMillin Memorial Mausoleum** (also known as Afterglow Vista). This otherworldly open-air rotunda features six chairs surrounding a limestone table, each containing the remains of a McMillin.

San Juan Islands

Whale-watching by land and sea

Near the top of every Pacific Northwest bucket list are the San Juan Islands, an emerald archipelago made up of 172 named isles and reefs. The most populous and developed of the islands, **San Juan Island** *(visitsanjuans.com/san-juan-island)* is ground zero for whale-watching.

The most environmentally friendly way to see whales and other sea mammals is from land. **Lime Kiln Point State Park** *(parks.wa.gov/find-parks/state-parks/lime-kiln-point-state-park; $10)*, also known as 'Whale Watch Park,' is one of the best places in the world to view orcas from land. Though sightings are never guaranteed, visiting between May and September (and bringing binoculars) increases your chances of seeing southern resident orcas offshore.

Consider joining a responsible whale-watching tour to significantly increase your orca-spotting odds. **Western Prince Whale & Wildlife Tours** *(orcawhalewatch.com; adult/child $155/145)*, the San Juans' oldest whale-watching company, specializes in adventurous open-air excursions.

Take a hike on Orcas Island

The largest and most mountainous of the San Juan Islands, rugged **Orcas Island** *(visitsanjuans.com/orcas-island)* is beloved for its natural beauty. Rural roads connect seaside hamlets, with parks and preserves taking up much of the island's 57 sq miles. **Moran State Park** *(moranstatepark.com)* alone is home to over 30 miles of forested trails leading to lakes, waterfalls, and island views that will leave you gaping in awe.

Bainbridge Island

Visit the Bloedel Reserve

A poetic juxtaposition of untamed Pacific Northwest forest and manicured English gardens, **Bloedel Reserve** *(bloedelreserve.org; adult/child $26/9)* is a 140-acre sanctuary at the north end of Bainbridge Island. It includes meadows, reflection pools and the original Bloedel family's French-style home. In summer, Bainbridge Performing Arts puts on a not-to-be-missed Shakespeare performance. Reserve timed tickets online.

Sequim

Looooong walks on Dungeness Spit

The longest sand spit in the US at 5.5 miles long, **Dungeness** *(fws.gov/refuge/dungeness; $3)* is also the namesake of the famous crab. . Washingtonians consider walking this Sequim trail a rite of passage. Brave souls kayak to the lighthouse, and adventurers can spend a week there as volunteer keepers. (Thankfully, you get driven.)

Olympia

Boardwalk stroll through wildlife

Stroll below bald eagles, hummingbirds and kestrels in the **Billy Frank Jr Nisqually National Wildlife Refuge** *(fws.gov/nisqually; $3)* in Olympia. The peaceful and picturesque estuary park was established in 1974, and is the protective home of hundreds of migratory birds, steelhead trout and salmon and seals. As you traverse the accessible 4 miles of boardwalk and gravel path, keep an eye out for mammals, too, including beaver, mink, muskrat and coyote. (You can even rent binoculars from the visitors center.) Arrive early, as parking fills up quickly.

Seaview

Digging razor clams

Razor clamming on **Long Beach** is just about the most Washingtonian activity imaginable. All you need to razor clam are three things: a shellfish license, a clam gun or small shovel and to go during razor-clam season. (Many hotels and guesthouses offer shovels and clam guns to guests, or you can buy one locally.) Show up about an hour before low tide and look for 'clam shows': dimples, doughnuts or keyholes in the wet

TWILIGHT TIME IN FORKS

When *Twilight* series author Stephenie Meyer searched for the rainiest, grayest town to set her vampire novel, she landed on Forks, WA, sight unseen. Several books and movies later, this remote Olympic peninsula logging town has become a global *Twilight* pilgrimage site. While the movies weren't filmed there, there are now *Twilight* tours, *Twilight*-themed shops and the Forever Twilight Festival (annually in September).

Bonus: Forks has many affordable motels, and is perfectly situated for a night's rest between the northern highlights and the western beaches.

EATING & DRINKING IN LONG BEACH

Seaview Biscuit Company: Flaky, airy biscuit perfection with Southern classics like fried chicken, pimento cheese and homemade jam. *7am-1pm, Thu-Tue* $

The Pub at Shelburne Hotel: Inside a 100-year-old hotel, a cozy, wood-paneled spot serves pub fare with charm and local flair. *noon-10pm Sun-Thu, to 11pm Fri & Sat* $$

Adrift Distillers: Celebrate the region's signature cranberry with a sweet-tart liqueur at this relaxing beachside tasting room. *10am-5pm Mon & Tue, 11am-7pm Wed-Sun*

Ilwaco Cider Company: Rustic wood tables, small-batch ciders, Nordic-leaning flavors like elderberry and cardamom – and, of course, local cranberries. *noon-8pm*

THE SALMON'S IMPOSSIBLE JOURNEY

Every year, salmon return from the open Pacific Ocean to the exact river where they were born – often making impossible leaps to complete their mind-boggling journey. Scientists still don't fully understand these feats, but the salmon seem to rely on chemical cues and magnetism. Their lifecycle is brutal: many fish die mid-jump, battered by rocks or snatched by bears, eagles or mountain lions. If they 'succeed,' they spawn (laying or fertilizing eggs), then die, nourishing their native forested ecosystems. You can spot these salmon doing these death-defying stunts in waterways throughout the Pacific Northwest between July and November.

sand. Center the clam gun, twist, pull the plug, and grab fast – razor clams are shockingly speedy for mollusks and can dig up to 1ft per minute.

Check wdfw.wa.gov for dates and locations, typically announced a few days or weeks in advance. Fall season runs September to December; spring is March through May. Open dates depend on tides, toxins, algae and clam population health.

Follow in Lewis and Clark's windswept footprints

Cape Disappointment State Park *(parks.wa.gov/find-parks/state-parks/cape-disappointment-state-park; $10)* feels like an Olympic National Park in miniature, with dramatic coastlines, isolated beaches and grand lighthouses (with a fraction of the tourists). The rugged headland marks the end of Lewis and Clark's journey, as well as the confluence of the Columbia River and Pacific Ocean (also known as the Graveyard of the Pacific, with over 200 shipwrecks in its churning waters).

The fortress-like **Lewis & Clark Interpretive Center** *(parks.wa.gov; adult/child $5/2.50)* was built to withstand the same battering weather the explorers faced. From the center, you can see (or walk to) the **Cape Disappointment Lighthouse**, the Pacific Northwest's first, built in 1856. For dramatic, misty cliffs, head to **North Head Lighthouse**.

Kite condition perfection

With wide beaches and steady winds, Long Beach is now home to one of the US' largest concentrations of world-class kite fliers. The **World Kite Museum** *(worldkitemuseum.com; adult/child $6/4)* celebrates this heritage with kites from around the globe, including traditional designs from Asia, as well as military kite history. The museum sponsors the annual Washington State International Kite Festival in the third full week of August. Want to try it yourself? Its shop sells kites, conveniently across the street from one of the best kiting beaches in the world.

Washington Cascades

Brats, brews and music

It's hard to resist the Bavarian act put on by **Leavenworth** *(leavenworth.org)*, even if it's a little over the top. The town is small (about 2400 people) but crammed with shops, restaurants and hotels – every last one decorated like something out of a community theater production of *The Sound of Music*. Leavenworth's cute schtick goes down smoother with beer and sausages – easy to find in this pedestrian-friendly town. As you stroll along Front St, consider **Gustav's Grill & Beer Garden** *(gustavsleavenworth.com)* for the faux-Alpine facade, or **München Haus** *(munchenhaus.com)* for outdoor seating and Icicle Brewing Company beer. Suitably primed, make your way to the gazebo at Front St Park, where most days you'll find a Bavarian-themed event going on: an expansive Christmas market, accordion concert or the annual **Leavenworth International Alphorn Festival** *(leavenworthalphorns.org/alphorn-festival)*.

Mt St Helens National Volcanic Monument

Volcanic adventures

On May 18, 1980, at 8:32am, Mt St Helens erupted with a violence that blew off the mountain's entire north face and melted several glaciers. It was the most destructive volcanic eruption in US history. Hundreds of sq miles of surrounding forest and thousands of wild animals were obliterated in its wake, and 57 people died.

The volcano and the zone of devastation around it are now preserved as **Mt St Helens National Volcanic Monument** *(fs.usda.gov/visit/national-monuments/mount-st-helens)*, dotted with viewpoints and visitor centers that offer an up-close way to witness both the destructive and the restorative forces of nature. You can peer at the blast zone from access roads, paddle a lake formed in the eruption, hike through millennia-old lava tubes, or even trek all the way to the summit.

Hike hundreds of miles of trails

There are literally hundreds of miles of hiking trails crisscrossing the **North Cascades**. Even just covering the best-known routes would take years. (We speak from experience.) So how do you decide where to go? The good news is, there are no bad choices.

Icicle Ridge Trail *(wta.org/go-hiking/hikes/icicle-ridge-1)* is a 6-mile round-trip trek with epic views over Leavenworth. **Lake Valhalla** via the Smithbrook Trail *(wta.org/go-hiking/hikes/lake-valhalla)* is a 7-mile round trip that would be a good first backpacking trip for kids or beginners. The pretty lake has a sandy beach, and a short side trip to Mt McCausland offers views of Glacier Peak. And **Cascade Pass and Sahale Arm** *(wta.org/go-hiking/hikes/sahale-arm)* is one of the top hikes in the North Cascades National Park area for good reason. You'll see carpets of blueberry bushes in the meadows, friendly marmots sunbathing, outrageous fall colors and maybe a bear.

MAKING A HIKING PLAN

Planning a few months in advance will help you get the most out of any hike in the North Cascades. Some popular trails require permits, so that's step one: make sure they're available for the area you want to visit on the dates you want to go. If permits aren't an issue, you have greater flexibility.

For the most up-to-date information, seek out recent trip reports for the places you want to hike. Start with the Washington Trails Association's excellent database *(wta.org)*. As your trip gets closer, contact the land manager responsible for that area, usually National Park headquarters or a US Forest Service ranger station. They'll have details on trail conditions, road closures, weather and any unexpected concerns, like fire danger.

Yakima Valley

Floating the Yakima River

It's hard to beat a lazy summer day floating along the mellow **Yakima River**. The water is calm enough to be beginner-friendly (class I-II), and there are multiple road-access points and campsites along the 27-mile stretch through the Yakima River Canyon, so you can customize the length of your trip. It's perfect for zero-stress river camping. You can rent rafts and arrange a car-shuttle service through **Red's Fly Shop** *(redsflyfishing.com; from $129)*.

Unpretentious wine tasting

The Yakima Valley is home to more than 90 wineries and encompasses five AVAs (American Viticultural Areas) in a compact area. These vineyards grow more than half the wine grapes produced in Washington State. The broad range of different wines, plus the famous lack of stuffiness in these farm-country vineyards, makes this an ideal place to learn about wine tasting or to introduce a hesitant friend to its pleasures.

A few places to seek out include the fifth-generation **Gilbert Cellars** *(gilbertcellars.com; tastings $20)*; **Treveri Cellars** *(trevericellars.com; tasting prices vary)* for its sparkling wines and Sunday brunch; **Bonair** *(bonairwine.com; tastings $10)*, one of the valley's oldest winemakers; and **Terra Blanca** *(terrablanca.com; tastings $20)*, whose Red Mountain tasting room looks like a Tuscan villa.

Walla Walla

Tour the local tasting rooms

The Walla Walla Valley became Washington's second AVA in 1984. Today there are nearly 3000 acres of vineyards in the AVA and more than 120 wineries. Conveniently, around 30 of these wineries have tasting rooms right downtown, so you can visit several at once without needing a designated driver. For star-powered sips, don't miss **Pursued by Bear** *(pursuedbybearwine.com; tastings $25)*, the winery owned by *Twin Peaks* actor Kyle MacLachlan, a Yakima local. Other downtown stops to seek out include the friendly, family-owned **Kontos** *(kontoscellars.com)*; locally recommended **Time & Direction** *(timeanddirectionwines.com)*; and **Seven Hills** *(sevenhillswinery.com)*, one of the first wineries in the area.

TRACKS IN TIME

Visitors to Yakima might be surprised to see a rolling anachronism on the city's streets: trolley cars from the early 1900s, still in operation. The cars are part of the Yakima Valley Transportation Company's interurban electric railroad, which originally stretched for 44 miles. Trains have operated on the rail line every year since 1907. Today, 5 miles of track between Yakima and Selah are kept running as a tourist attraction, using the original powerhouse and the 'car barn' built in 1910 to store the trolleys. Trolleys run north along 6th Ave; learn more at **Yakima Valley Trolleys** *(yakimavalleytrolleys.org)*.

 EATING IN THE YAKIMA VALLEY: OUR PICKS

Red Pickle: This fun place inside an old filling station in Ellensburg serves creative tacos and fried chicken. *3-9pm Tue, 11:30am-9pm Wed-Sat, to 7pm Sun* $

Los Hernandez: It's not every day a tamale place wins a James Beard award, but this one in Yakima has. *11am-6pm* $

Essencia Artisan Bakery: Head to this homey bakery for creative sandwiches (think ginger roast beef), soups, salads and panini. *6am-4pm Tue-Fri, 7am-1pm Sat* $

Crafted: A farm-to-table restaurant in Yakima that makes the most of the surrounding agricultural bounty with an ever-changing menu. *5-9pm Thu-Mon* $$$

Yakima River

A dark chapter in history

With several paved walking trails and an informative museum, the **Whitman Mission National Historic Site** *(nps.gov/whmi/index.htm; free)* commemorates a grim event known as the Whitman Massacre, the result of a conflict in 1847 between white missionaries led by Marcus Whitman and the local people of the Cayuse Nation. Part of the complicated story of the Oregon Trail, the 138-acre park is best explored with the 90-minute self-guided audio tour available on the National Park Service app.

Palouse Falls State Park

A waterfall wonder

An hour north of Walla Walla, the thunderous 198ft **Palouse Falls** *($10)* is the kind of natural wonder that seems to appear out of nowhere. Since 2014, it has been the official state waterfall of Washington.

For the most dramatic experience, visit in spring when the water level is highest. The park offers several good viewpoints overlooking the falls. For safety, all trails to the base of the falls have been closed. Warning signs along the edge of the cliffs are very emphatic, for good reason – people have fallen to their deaths, so stay alert and obey posted closures.

HOORAY FOR HOPS

The Yakima Valley grows about 75% of the hops in the US. You'll see them as you drive around – tall green walls of climbing vines. (No wonder the air smells vaguely like a hazy IPA.) It's the female hop cone that's used in brewing; the flavor in its oils and acids balances out the malty taste and helps preserve the beer. Hops are harvested toward the end of August and into September. In October, keep your eyes peeled for local fresh-hop beers on tap. Harvesting and stripping out the cones from the hop plants is an intense, complicated process. Then they're dried, baled and sent on their way to be distributed to breweries, where, through science and magic, they reach their final form.

DRINKING IN WALLA WALLA: OUR PICKS

Coffee Perk: A comfy hangout with friendly service, good lattes and drip coffee, croissant sandwiches and free wi-fi. *7am-5pm Mon-Sat, to 3pm Sun*

Sleight of Hand Cellars: One of the most fun wineries to visit in the valley, with rock and roll on vinyl and a laid-back atmosphere. *11am-5pm*

Public House 124: Balance out all the wine with a craft cocktail or microbrewed beer at this upscale pub. *4-10pm Tue-Thu, 3-10pm Fri & Sat*

Marc Bar: Sleek cocktail lounge inside the landmark historic Marcus Whitman Hotel. *4-11pm*

SMOKEJUMPING & WILDFIRE AWARENESS

The wildfire-fighting technique known as 'smokejumping' was invented in the Methow Valley. In 1939 the Forest Service started training firefighters to jump out of planes as a way of getting them to otherwise inaccessible areas quickly. It turned out to be both effective and efficient. In 1945, the Forest Service established a base outside Winthrop, which still operates today as the **North Cascades Smokejumper Base**. The location is no accident: wildfire activity is on the rise in the region and across the state. Fires can cause sudden closures and unexpected changes to travel plans. Keep tabs on your planned routes with the Watch Duty app, the WTA Trailblazer app, recent trip reports and the Washington Department of Transportation's road status updates.

Grand Coulee Dam

Spokane

An education in regional art

Spokane's **Northwest Museum of Arts & Culture** *(north westmuseum.org; adult/child $15/9)* occupies a sleek building in the beautiful Browne's Addition neighborhood, the oldest part of town. It has a fantastic collection of art, artifacts and historical documents from around the Pacific Northwest, including Vanessa Helder's watercolor series on the Grand Coulee Dam, and a particularly good collection of Native American artwork.

Grand Coulee Dam

An engineering masterpiece

While the more famous Hoover Dam (p803) gets around 1.6 million visitors per year, the four-times-larger and arguably more significant **Grand Coulee Dam** *(usbr.gov/pn/grandcoulee/visit/index.html)*, inconveniently located far from everything, gets only a trickle of tourism. If you're in the area, don't miss it – it's one of the country's most spectacular displays of engineering and you'll get to enjoy it crowd-free.

The **Grand Coulee Dam Visitor Center** details the history of the dam and surrounding area with movies, photos and interactive exhibits. Free guided tours of the facility run regularly in summer, leaving from the visitor center, and involve taking a glass-walled elevator 465ft down into the Third Power Plant, where you can view the generators from an observation deck. Laser light shows on summer evenings tell the story of the dam's construction.

Portland

QUIRKY ART | FABULOUS FOOD | URBAN GREENSPACES

Portland started out as a port city, but its name has nothing to do with its position on the Willamette River and everything to do with a coin toss. The city's two founders wanted to name the city after their respective hometowns. While the man from Maine won, Portland could have just as easily been called Boston. This 1843 penny toss was just the beginning of an unconventional way of doing things.

In the early 2000s, people caught wind of a little city in the Pacific Northwest where housing was affordable, beer was good and nature was everywhere. What once felt like a small town in disguise emerged as a destination in its own right. The culinary scene boomed and Portland began showing up on 'best places to live' lists. Portlanders no longer had to clarify that they were from Oregon, not Maine, when on vacation elsewhere in the US. While growth has slowed recently, Portland has managed to hold onto its reputation as a bastion for hipsterism, natural beauty and exceptionally tasty food.

Explore One of the World's Largest Bookstores

A block of books

If you're big on books, the chance to visit **Powell's City of Books** *(powells.com)* may have played a role in your decision to visit Portland. Occupying three floors and a full city block, Powell's touts itself as the largest independent new-and-used bookstore in the world. Books (and a smattering of gifts) are
Continued on p1014

GETTING AROUND

Portland is compact and well planned. It's divided on an east–west axis by the Willamette River and between north and south by Burnside St. Street names are preceded by cardinal and intercardinal prefixes (eg N, S, NW, SE), making it easy to orient yourself.

The city has a robust and bicycle-friendly public transportation network that includes buses, a light-rail network known as the MAX and modern streetcars (trams). The MAX is a convenient way to get between Portland International Airport (PDX) and Downtown. You can also drive around the city, and you'll need a car for most day trips.

☑ TOP TIP

Portland is one of the most sustainability-focused cities in the US. Do your part during your visit by using public transportation, carrying a reusable water bottle and tote, and shopping local or secondhand.

HIGHLIGHTS
1. Portland Japanese Garden
2. Powell's City of Books

SIGHTS
3. Council Crest Park
4. Forest Park
5. Governor Tom McCall Waterfront Park
6. Hoyt Arboretum
7. International Rose Test Garden
8. Mt Tabor Park
9. OMSI
10. Oregon Zoo
11. Pittock Mansion
12. Skidmore Fountain
13. Vietnam Veterans of Oregon Memorial
14. Washington Park
15. Wishing Tree
16. Witch's Castle
17. World Forestry Center

ACTIVITIES
18. Cascada Thermal Springs + Hotel
19. Last Thursday on Alberta

SLEEPING
20. Heathman Hotel
21. Hotel deLuxe
22. Inn at Northrup Station
23. McMenamins Kennedy School

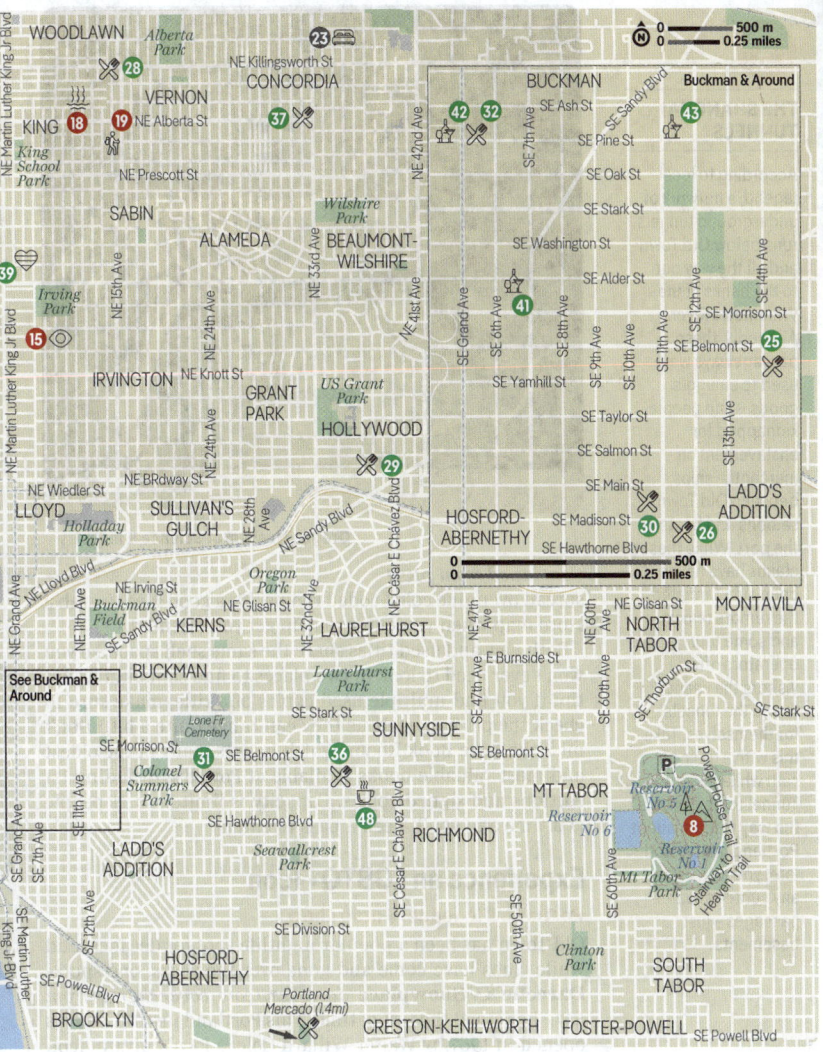

● **EATING**	**34** Langbaan
24 Andina	**35** Mediterranean Exploration Company
25 Astera	**36** Paradox Cafe
26 Cartopia	**see 26** Potato Champion
27 Escape from NY Pizza	**37** Urdaneta
28 Feral	**38** Voodoo Doughnut
29 Gado Gado	● **DRINKING & NIGHTLIFE**
30 Hawthorne Asylum	**39** Back2Earth
31 Jade Rabbit	
32 Kann	
33 Kayo's Ramen Bar	

40 CC Slaughters	● **ENTERTAINMENT**
41 Creepy's	**49** Darcelle XV Showplace
42 Doc Marie's	● **SHOPPING**
43 Hungry Tiger	**50** Always Here Bookstore
44 Kell's Irish Pub	**51** Portland Saturday Market
see 25 Nectaris	**52** Portland Skidmore Market
45 Raven's Manor	
46 River	
47 Shanghai Tunnel Bar	
see 32 Sousòl	
48 Tōv Coffee II	

1013

THE SHANGHAI TUNNELS

According to local legend, a network of underground tunnels runs below Old Town and all the way out to the banks of the Willamette River. Allegedly, these passageways were used to smuggle goods – and people kidnapped for enslavement on mercantile ships – between Old Town saloons and boats in the port. While these claims have never been substantiated, the rumors remain, and some tour operators offer visitors the chance to see the tunnels for themselves. Take this with a grain of salt: while Shanghai Tunnel tours can be a fun way to learn about Portland history and lore, you won't see any subterranean passages – just basements.

Oregon Museum of Science & Industry

Continued from p1011

spread over nine color-coded rooms. It's a good idea to grab a store map when you enter to help get you oriented.

Both new and used titles share the same shelf space, so you won't ever need to look in two places to find something. (Pro tip: if you find multiple used copies of a title, make sure to check the price of each, as they can range quite a bit.) Don't miss the Rare Book Room, which houses many of the oldest and most valuable books available at Powell's, including 1st editions and signed copies. Capacity is limited to 14 people at a time and you'll need a pass to enter.

Experience an LGBTQ+ Icon

Portland's legendary drag show

Old Town has been a popular nightlife spot for decades, and while clubs have come and gone over the years, one spot – **Darcelle XV Showplace** *(darcellexv.com; cover charges from $5)* – has stood the test of time. This Portland institution was opened in 1967 by Walter Willard Cole, a local cultural icon and LGBTQ+ rights activist who performed as Darcelle. At the time of his death in 2023, Cole was the Guinness World

DRINKING IN OLD TOWN: OUR PICKS

Raven's Manor: Celebrate the macabre at this spooky spot offering Halloweenesque cocktails and interactive experiences. *hours vary*

River: Laid-back sports bar with video poker, pool tables and TVs playing sports games. *noon-2:30am*

Shanghai Tunnel Bar: Descend into this subterranean bar with pinball and pool tables, cocktails and beer on tap. *5pm-2am Wed-Fri, noon-2am Sat, 5pm-midnight Sun-Tue*

Kell's Irish Pub: This brewpub offers a solid whiskey list plus a cigar lounge (a rarity in Portland). *4-10pm Wed & Thu, noon-midnight Fri & Sat*

Records-certified oldest drag performer in the world. Although Darcelle is no longer with us, her memory is kept alive at the club through multiple drag performances per week – including a Sunday drag brunch.

Visit OMSI
Science is for everyone

Oregon Museum of Science & Industry (omsi.edu; adult/child $20/15) is a spacious science and technology museum that offers hands-on permanent and special exhibits designed to get visitors of all ages excited about science. Check out the interactive labs focused on physics, chemistry, paleontology and insects or head to the **Natural Sciences Hall** to see displays on everything from geology to climate science. Visitors of all ages love the **Turbine Hall**, where an earthquake simulator allows you to experience the quake sensation, while young'uns can head to the **Curium**, a special area for those eight and under. Don't miss a tour of the decommissioned **USS Blueback Submarine**, the US Navy's final diesel-electric submarine, or take a trip into the night sky through a **Kendall Planetarium** show.

While children certainly are OMSI's target audience, visitors of all ages are welcome. If you feel awkward being the biggest kid around and you just want to enjoy the exhibits without worrying about stepping on tiny toes – and maybe have a drink – you can check out one of the themed monthly **OMSI After Dark** sessions, exclusively for the 21-and-over crowd.

Portland's Doughnut Obsession
Good things come in pink boxes

If you see a late-night line around the block in most cities, you'll probably assume that people are waiting to get into an exclusive nightclub. In Portland, when people line up it's almost always for food, especially at hot spots such as **Voodoo Doughnut**. Founded in the early noughties, Voodoo gained early notoriety for selling doughnuts laced with NyQuil and Pepto-Bismol, and although health authorities put a quick stop to their shenanigans, many of the doughnuts are still far from conventional. Try the Voodoo Doll – a vaguely human-shaped jelly doughnut with a pretzel stake driven where its little heart would be – or the Diablos Rex, a simple chocolate-cake doughnut adorned with a frosted pentagram.

THE BEST PARKS IN PORTLAND

Fernhill Park: Sprawling park with a splash pad and a mix of grassy lawns and forested areas.

Forest Park: Gargantuan 5200-acre wooded park with over 80 miles of trails.

Laurelhurst Park: Grassy park with paved paths for walking and jogging, picnic tables and plenty of green space.

Mt Tabor Park: Take in sunset views from the summit of this dormant, wooded cinder cone.

Oaks Bottom Wildlife Refuge: This 163-acre park near the Willamette River provides a safe haven for birds and aquatic creatures.

Washington Park: Perched above Downtown Portland, this huge park is home to the Portland Japanese Garden.

EATING IN NORTHWEST PORTLAND

Andina: This long-standing spot in the Pearl District is known for offering seasonally inspired Peruvian fare and tasty pisco sours. *5-9pm* $$$

Langbaan: This intimate Nob Hill restaurant serves Thai tasting menus crafted from seasonally available ingredients. *5:30-8:15pm Wed-Sun* $$$

Escape from NY Pizza: Order New York–style pizza by the slice at this no-frills favorite on 23rd Ave in Nob Hill. *11:30am-11pm* $

Mediterranean Exploration Company: Pearl District spot with outdoor seating showcases flavors of Greece and the Levant through meze and grilled-meat dishes. *4-10pm* $$

Portland Japanese Garden

JAPANESE GARDEN DESIGN 101

Hugo Torii, garden curator at Portland Japanese Garden, introduces Japanese garden design.

Japanese gardens have evolved over the course of 1000 years, with each iteration reflecting the needs of a given time. This evolution has created a rich diversity of garden styles, all of which offer something unique to be appreciated. However, the quintessential factor that elevates landscapes such as Portland Japanese Garden is that they allow the visitor to experience Japanese culture and its emphasis on respecting nature and being in harmony with it. Whether a space is decorative like a raked gravel garden or more rustic like a tea garden, it provides a place to confirm our connection and find our distance with nature, and in this, the opportunity to heal.

Street Food Central

Outdoor dining at food-cart pods

While Portland has plenty of great restaurants, the city is equally known for its food carts (aka food trucks). Most can be found in food-cart 'pods,' converted parking lots with common picnic-table dining spaces that house anywhere from four to upwards of 20 carts. While you'll find food-cart pods all over Portland, Southeast has a particularly high concentration. Two of the largest are **Cartopia** – famous for the poutine at long-standing food cart **Potato Champion** – and **Hawthorne Asylum**, a couple of blocks away. Just up the road, **Tōv Coffee II** serves up Egyptian-style coffee, tea and sweets in a converted double-decker London bus. If you want to try food from across Latin America, head to the **Portland Mercado**, a hybrid market and food-cart pod that showcases food from across the region.

EATING IN SOUTHWEST PORTLAND

Chart House: Take in some of the best views in Portland from the massive windows at this long-standing steak and seafood restaurant. *hours vary* $$$

Salvador Molly's: See just how much heat you can handle by trying the famed Great Balls of Fire (habanero cheese fritters). *11:30am-9pm Sun & Tue-Thu, to 10pm Fri & Sat* $$

Seasons & Regions: Head to this neighborhood seafood spot to try out fresh seafood cooked in a range of styles. *4-9pm* $$

Verde Cocina: This suburban spot blends Mexican and Pacific Northwest ingredients and flavors with excellent results. *11am-9pm Mon-Fri, from 10am Sat & Sun* $$

Down by the River
Walk along the Willamette

Stretching for 1.5 miles along the western banks of the Willamette River, **Governor Tom McCall Waterfront Park** (referred to simply as 'Waterfront' by most locals) is a great place to stroll if you want to experience Portland's greenery without having to leave Downtown. It hosts some of the city's biggest spring and summer events in the city, including the Portland Cinco de Mayo Fiesta, the **Waterfront Blues Festival** and **Portland Pride**.

It's also one of the main venues of the **Portland Rose Festival**, an annual community celebration that features multiple parades and a carnival – known as the CityFair – which takes over a section of the park for roughly two weeks.

Explore Washington Park
A park of many gardens

Just west of Downtown Portland (and a short MAX ride away), sits Washington Park, a hilly, 410-acre park characterized by tree-lined trails, grassy open spaces and some of Portland's top attractions. If you come by light-rail, you'll end up at the southwestern corner of the park where three popular sights – the **Oregon Zoo** *(oregonzoo.org; adult/child $26/21)*, **Vietnam Veterans of Oregon Memorial** and **World Forestry Center** *(worldforestry.org; adult/child $8/5)* – are located. If you have to pick one, make it the Forestry Center, which features two floors of exhibits that cover topics ranging from the future of forests to forest fires to the logging industry.

A short walk (or a one-stop ride on the park's free shuttle) will take you to the **Hoyt Arboretum**, a 'living museum' with around 2300 species of trees from around the world. From the arboretum, you can take a shuttle ride or hike along the Wildwood Trail to the **International Rose Test Garden**, where you'll have the chance to wander among over 10,000 blooming rose bushes representing more than 600 varieties, all while taking in fabulous views of the city. Up a small hill from this floral delight, the **Portland Japanese Garden** *(japanesegarden.org; adult/child $22.50/16.50)* is considered one of the most authentic Japanese gardens outside of Japan and features bridge-crossed ponds, a teahouse, numerous stone features and lots of beautiful foliage – including cherry trees.

MAY YOUR WISHES COME TRUE

Portlanders love to set up whimsical displays in their front lawns. Some tether toy horses to sidewalk horse rings (loops found in sidewalks throughout town that were used in the pre-car era to hitch horses). Others build fairy gardens, or free libraries. However, the most enchanting of Portland's sidewalk treasures is the **Wishing Tree** on the corner of NE 7th and Morris. At this interactive display, pedestrians are invited to write their wishes on tags (provided) and tie them to the tree. For an extra dose of magic, anyone making a wish should also read someone else's and hope that it comes true.

EATING IN SOUTHEAST PORTLAND: OUR PICKS

Astera: Locally foraged and farmed dishes steal the show at this upscale plant-based restaurant that strives to keep waste to a minimum. *hours vary Thu-Sun* **$$$**

Jade Rabbit: Dine on dim-sum classics and hearty Filipino dishes, or try a cocktail (come with tiny plastic bunnies instead of umbrellas). *hours vary Wed-Sun* **$$**

Kann: See what the fuss is about at Kann, a wood-fired Haitian restaurant under the helm of celebrity chef Gregory Gourdet. *4-10pm Tue-Thu, to 11pm Fri & Sat* **$$$**

Paradox Cafe: This old-school diner on Belmont St has been serving up huge breakfasts and sandwiches for decades. *9am-2:30pm Thu-Mon* **$**

Stroll Through Alberta Arts District
Celebrate Last Thursday

The stretch of NE Alberta St between NE 12th and 32nd Avenues known as the Alberta Arts District is one of Northeast Portland's biggest draws, and for good reason. This walkable stretch is loaded with cute boutiques, bars, restaurants and galleries, and is home to **Cascada**, a hotel and thermal-spa complex with a glorious subterranean soaking circuit. Black heritage markers tell an important piece of the story of this historically African American neighborhood and many businesses are decorated with colorful large-scale murals.

While the Alberta Arts District attracts crowds pretty consistently, its biggest draw is the monthly **Last Thursday on Alberta** celebration, which emerged in the late 1990s as a countercultural alternative to the long-running First Thursday art walk in the Pearl District. During this monthly event, artists and other vendors set up street-side tables to hawk their wares, street performers entertain the masses and local businesses keep their doors open late. Although Last Thursday happens throughout the year, it's far busier in the summer, when the street is also closed from traffic.

Don't Feed the Troll
A visit to Ole Bolle

Head to the wooded gardens of **Nordic Northwest** (*nordicnorthwest.org; free*) cultural center in Southwest Portland's Garden Home neighborhood to find one of the city's largest residents: **Ole Bolle**. This 19ft troll was fashioned by Danish artist Thomas Dambo, who's celebrated for using upcycled materials to create massive trolls around the world. Ole Bolle is one of six of his kind found across the Pacific Northwest as part of Dambo's *Northwest Trolls: Way of the Bird King* project. After spending time with Ole Bolle, it's worth stopping inside the cultural center's main building, **Nordia House**, to grab a Swedish snack at on-site cafe **Broder Söder** or do a bit of shopping at its gift shop.

City Viticulture
Urban wine culture

Portland's proximity to Oregon's celebrated Willamette Valley wine country makes it tempting to take a day out of your schedule for a bit of wine tasting, but thanks to **Amaterra**

LGBTQ+ PORTLAND

Always Here Bookstore: A NE Portland bookstore that focuses on books written by LGBTQ+ authors and with LGBTQ+ themes.

Back2Earth: Welcoming Northeast Portland bar with a solid sound system, dance floor areas and a few arcade games.

CC Slaughters: An Old Town LGBTQ+ nightclub and lounge with karaoke nights, dance parties and drag shows that's been around since the 1980s.

Darcelle XV Showplace: (p1014) A Vegas-style drag cabaret that was launched in 1967 by Portland's beloved drag queen, the late Walter Cole (aka Darcelle).

Doc Marie's: Billing itself as a 'lesbian bar for everyone,' this Southeast Portland spot offers regular trivia nights, karaoke and dance parties.

DRINKING IN SOUTHEAST PORTLAND: OUR PICKS

Creepy's: If you're scared of clowns, this harrowing bar will give you the ick...or have you in a fit of nervous laughter. *4pm-1am Sun-Thu, to 2:30am Fri-Sat*

Hungry Tiger: Punk-rock music and vintage tiger-themed decor add to the DIY aesthetic of this hip dive bar with pool, pinball and stiff drinks. *hours vary*

Sousòl: The subterranean sister bar of Kann serves tropical cocktails, mocktails and some seriously tasty cuisine inspired by Caribbean flavors. *4-1pm Thu-Sat*

Nectaris: Sample a wide range of wines from Oregon and around the world at this cozy neighborhood wine spot. *hours vary Thu-Sun*

Portland Saturday Market

(amaterra.com), you can get a sense of the wine country experience without venturing far. Straddling a vine-covered hillock in the West Hills, this winery feels very much like it's in the countryside, despite being less than 5 miles from Downtown. Drive up to the top of the hill where you'll have the option to dine on Pacific Northwest fare at the restaurant or do a wine tasting on a lower-level patio. Both spots offer fantastic views for miles. There's just one catch – you'll have to purchase a 'social membership' for $25, which you can apply to the purchase of two or more bottles of wine during your visit.

Getting Crafty
The hippiest markets in the land

Before farmers markets were all the rage, many Portlanders would spend their Saturdays checking out the handicrafts and food booths at the **Portland Saturday Market**

PORTLAND'S BEST VIEWS

Council Crest Park: A quick drive from Downtown via the posh West Hills will take you up to this small park. At 1073ft above sea level, it's the highest point in the city.

George Himes City Park: This wooded park is just one of many spots along SW Terwilliger Blvd where you can get great views of Portland.

International Rose Test Garden: Head to this bloom-filled spot and take in quintessential postcard views of the Portland skyline, with Mt Hood in the distance.

Mt Tabor: Stand atop Southeast Portland's own active volcano to take in Portland views for miles.

Pittock Mansion: Hike (or drive) up to this historic home on the edge of Forest Park for fantastic views of Downtown and beyond.

EATING IN NORTH & NORTHEAST PORTLAND: OUR PICKS

Gado Gado: James Beard Award–nominated spot serving Indonesian-inspired dishes, including a chili crab dinner on Sundays and Mondays. *5pm-9pm* $$$

Feral: Upscale plant-based restaurant with inventive dishes made primarily from locally farmed and foraged ingredients. *5-9pm Wed & Thu, to 10pm Fri & Sat* $$

Kayo's Ramen Bar: This spot serves hearty bowls of clear-broth ramen (rather than the better-known tonkotsu-style). *hours vary* $$

Urdaneta: Come to this intimate spot for tasty tapas and other Spanish classics and an excellent wine and vermouth menu. *5-10pm Tue-Sun* $$$

Forest Park

(*portlandsaturdaymarket.com*). Founded in 1974, it's the largest continuously operating open-air craft market in the United States, with booths extending from just next to the circa-1888 Skidmore Fountain on SW 1st and Ankeny all the way across to Governor Tom McCall Waterfront Park where live music performances are frequently staged. A second market, the **Portland Skidmore Market** (*portlandskidmoremarket.com*) occupies an entire city block east of the **Skidmore Fountain**. While everything sold at the Saturday Market must be handcrafted, vendors at the Skidmore Market have a bit more liberty – and many sell imported goods from Central America and South Asia.

A Nature Escape in the City
Portland's urban forest

If you want to experience the grandeur of Oregon's forests but don't want to drive out to the nearby Columbia Gorge (p1026), you're in luck: Portland has its own urban forest, just a few minutes' drive from the Pearl District. With over 80 miles of trails spread out over 5200 acres, **Forest Park** is big enough to rarely feel crowded, even if you hit up the popular **Wildwood Trail**, a 30-mile footpath that runs the entire length of the park, past an abandoned stone structure known as the **Witch's Castle** and into nearby Washington Park. While ambitious hikers and runners might brave the entire trail, most people just hike shorter segments.

Oregon

CRAFT BREWERIES | PEACEFUL WINERIES | WATERFALL WONDERS

It's hard to slap a single characterization onto Oregon's geography and people. Its landscape ranges from rugged coastline and thick evergreen forests to barren, fossil-strewn deserts, volcanoes and glaciers. As for its denizens, you name it – Oregonians run the gamut from pro-logging conservatives to tree-hugging liberals. What they have in common is an independent spirit, a love of the outdoors and a fierce devotion to where they live.

It doesn't usually take long for visitors to feel a similar devotion. Who wouldn't fall in love with the spectacle of glittering Crater Lake, the breathtaking colors of the Painted Hills in John Day or the hiking trails through deep forests and over stunning mountain passes? And then there are the towns: you can eat like royalty in McMinnville, go Saturday-market shopping in Eugene or sample an astounding number of brewpubs in Bend.

Places
McMinnville p1024
Silver Falls State Park p1025
Eugene p1025
Springfield p1025
Hood River p1026
Columbia River Gorge p1026
Mt Hood p1027
Bend p1028
Sisters p1030
Astoria p1030
Cannon Beach p1031
Tillamook p1032
Oregon Dunes National Recreation Area p1032
Brookings p1032
Rogue-Umpqua Scenic Byway p1033
Pendleton p1033

GETTING AROUND

Like much of the US, a car is by far the best option for getting around Oregon. If for whatever reason a car isn't feasible, there are bus routes and train routes winding their way through the state. POINT, Oregon's public intercity bus service, has routes between popular towns and cities, like Portland, Eugene, Bend and Astoria. Alternatively, Amtrak's train network nearly exclusively runs through the Cascades, with Eugene, Salem and Portland all along the way. Do note that both buses and trains have limited frequency and routes.

☑ TOP TIP

Much of the appeal of Oregon is its natural beauty. Do your part to keep the landscapes as stunning as they are by picking up after yourself, following fire-use restrictions, and making sustainable choices.

TOP EXPERIENCE

Crater Lake National Park

The only national park in Oregon, Crater Lake National Park was created by a cataclysmic volcanic eruption 7700 years ago. The collapsed caldera then filled with glacial melt and rainwater to form the deepest, bluest lake in the US. The resulting landscape is wondrous to behold – from the old-growth forests to the lake itself.

TOP TIPS

- Rim Drive, the 33-mile road circumnavigating Crater Lake with dozens of viewpoints and trailheads along the way, is getting some upgrades. The five-year project began in 2023, closing portions of the road each year. Most of the road will remain drivable, but check for closed sections before departing.

PRACTICALITIES

- nps.gov/crla/index.htm
- per car $20-30 (varies by season)
- open 24/7

An Iconic Hike

To fully grasp the size, colors, and surrounding landscape of the otherworldly Crater Lake, most visitors will hike up to higher elevations on multiple trails. Head to the east end of Rim Village and follow the paved path to the trailhead for **Garfield Peak**, a moderately challenging 3.5-mile hike up switchbacks with excellent valley views. You'll pass patches of snow almost year-round as you gaze at the jewel-blue water in one direction and mountains and valley in the other. It packs a great reward for just a two- to three-hour adventure.

Family-Friendly Trails

For a shorter but still substantial jaunt, the **Watchman Peak Trail** is short and steep, leading you to a fire tower with panoramic views. For a quick loop, check out **Sun Notch Trail**, just off Rim Drive. This family-friendly trail is just 0.8 miles, with a great view of Phantom Ship. In the winter, this is a popular spot for snow-shoeing. Remember that the temperature can change quickly with elevation changes so pack layers and plenty of water for all your hikes. Dogs are not allowed on most trails in the park.

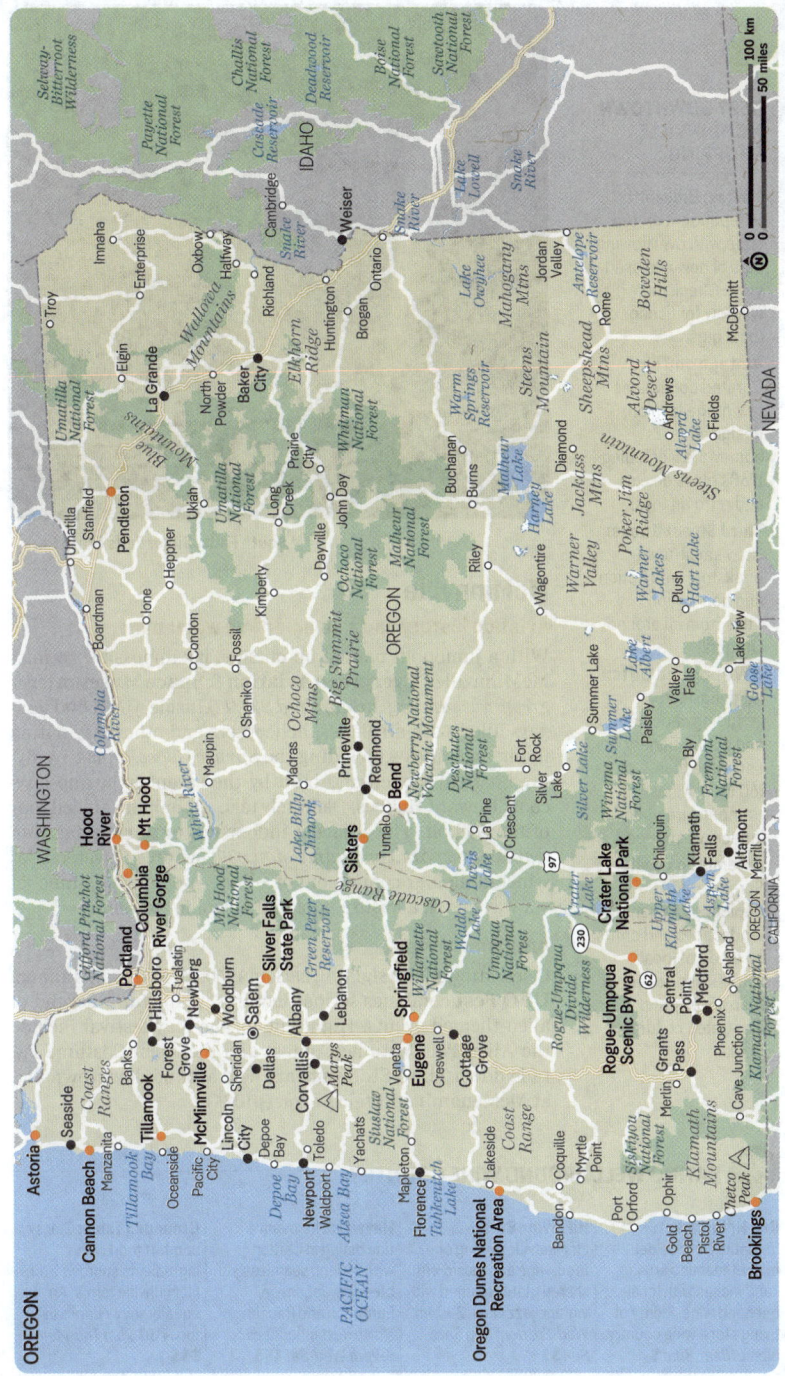

South Falls, Silver Falls State Park

BEST DOWNTOWN MCMINNVILLE SHOPPING

Vortex: Brilliant independent record shop with overflowing bins of new and used vinyl. Check the window for listings of local gigs.

Vintage on Third: Curated collections of vintage fashion, design and homewares including 1960s glass design and retro tin toys.

Third Street Books: Cozy small-town bookstore with fiction and non-fiction titles from all around Oregon.

NW Food and Gifts: All things edible including chocolate and confectionery, and more than 160 local wines. Hampers are good for indecisive shoppers.

Artemis Fox Gallery: Screen prints depicting Oregon landscapes and prints on wood of local wildlife and scenery. Also jewelry and illustrated children's books.

McMinnville

Aviation history and a summertime water park

With a jumbo jet parked up outside, it's impossible to miss McMinnville's **Evergreen Aviation & Space Museum** *(evergreenmuseum.org; adult/child $24/14).* Inside, you'll find hangars filled with airplanes, helicopters and other fascinating flying machines – including the *Spruce Goose*, a massive flying boat envisioned and built by the eccentric business tycoon, Howard Hughes. Definitely take a 15-minute guided tour of the cockpit. The adjacent indoor **water park** *(wingsandwaveswaterpark.com; admission $39)* features 10 waterslides – including four coming out of another Boeing 747 jumbo jet – a wave pool, a leisure pool and a pool for toddlers.

An alien invasion

Celebrating a UFO sighting back in 1950, McMinnville's annual **UFO Fest** combines serious lectures with a fun weekend of alien-themed events. Highlights of the May festival include the Alien Pet Costume Contest and the Alien Costume Parade down Third St. Events are held around downtown and at McMenamins Hotel Oregon (p1035).

EATING WELL AROUND WINE COUNTRY

Red Hills Market: Versatile Dundee deli-market teaming artisan sandwiches with local beer and wine. Plenty of fixings for a wine country picnic. *8am-8pm* $

HiFi Wine Bar: McMinnville pairing of food, wine and music with shared plates teamed with vintage jazz vinyl. *2-10pm Wed-Fri, from 1pm Sat & Sun* $$

Hayward: Innovative fine dining in Carlton with a menu seamlessly blending Japanese, European and Pacific Northwest influences. *5-9pm Wed-Sat* $$$

Grounded Table: Classy comfort food with ingredients sourced from McMinnville farms. An equally savvy drinks list, too. *4:30-9pm Thu-Mon* $$$

Willamette Valley wineries

Fostering delicate pinot noir grapes as well as pinot gris, chardonnay and riesling, the climate of the northern Willamette Valley make the region Oregon's most bountiful wine-growing area. Centered on McMinnville and nearby towns including Dayton, Carlton, Newberg and Dundee, the broader Willamette Valley AVA incorporates more than 700 wineries across 11 different sub-region AVAs.

Among the hundreds of wineries, some stand out. **Ken Wright Cellars** is a well-established winery with impeccable pinot noir credentials. **Soter Vineyards** serves seven-course lunch tasting menus with biodynamic pinot noir and chardonnay. Reservations are essential. **Stoller Family Estate** is the world's first LEED-Gold Certified winery guaranteeing sustainability and eco-friendly design, and it features a spectacular hilltop tasting room. **Remy Wines** – founded by a former McMinnville mayor – is known for its single-vineyard, single-varietal Italian-style wines crafted from sangiovese, dolcetto and nebbiolo.

Silver Falls State Park
Short walks for stunning views

Just east of Oregon's capital city of Salem, find the cascade-filled **Silver Falls State Park** *(stateparks.oregon.gov; $10)*. This 9000-acre escape is filled with countless waterfalls, many of which are accessible by easy to moderate hikes. The **North Falls Lookout trail** is a 1-mile return walk for views of the 136ft-high waterfall. Don't miss continuing behind the falls. At the even more spectacular **South Falls**, water thunders over a mossy ledge to a rocky pool 177ft below. The best view is on the gentle trail, down which also continues behind the falls. Last but certainly not least, the popular **Trail of Ten Falls** is a spectacular 7.2-mile moderate loop trail with natural swimming pools and, as its name implies, nearly a dozen waterfalls.

Eugene
Great weekend market and colorful street art

Primarily known as a hippie-esque college town, downtown Eugene is easily explored on foot – particularly during the popular **Saturday Market** *(eugenesaturdaymarket.org)*. Folk from around the Willamette Valley sell locally made products from food and drink to arts and crafts, and there's live music from Americana and country to jazz and classic rock. Food-cart flavors straddle the globe.

Springfield
Hang with everyone's favorite cartoon family

Oregon-born Matt Groening, creator of *The Simpsons*, confirmed in 2012 that Homer's hometown was indeed named after Springfield, Oregon. Visit the **Emerald Art Center** for a photo op with the yellow-hued clan on the famous couch, a promotional prop from 2007's *The Simpsons Movie*. Ask for a free map showing the location of more than 40 other Simpsons murals and street-art locations around downtown Springfield and the greater Eugene-Springfield area.

GETTING ACTIVE IN EUGENE

Gary Tepfer, a Eugene-based photographer, shares his favorite ways to stay active in Eugene. *(@garytepfer.com)*

Eugene's foresighted city planners preserved natural areas that can now be accessed on foot or by bike. To the east, the **Howard Buford Recreation Area** offers hiking and horseback-riding trails, and its hillsides burst with wildflowers in spring. Northwest of Eugene is **Fern Ridge Reservoir**, a large lake and marshland with the region's richest bird habitat. There are also running trails through city parks and along the river, a basalt climbing cliff on **Skinner Butte**, and a canoe path near the Willamette River. Definitely not to be overlooked is **Spencer Butte** for hiking. From the top it has unsurpassed views of the High Cascades to the east, and miles of trails and acres of old-growth forests.

BEST HOT SPRINGS IN THE CASCADE MOUNTAINS

Bagby Hot Springs: Ninety miles east of Salem. Clothing-optional hot springs with wooden tubs in semi-private bathhouses. Accessible via a 1.5-mile forest trail.

Terwilliger Hot Springs: Located 55 miles east of Eugene. Terraced outdoor pools framed by large rocks, accessed via a 500yd walk.

Breitenbush Hot Springs: More developed with spa and massage services on offer; 70 miles east of Salem.

Belknap Hot Springs: Spring-fed pools located 5 miles east of McKenzie Bridge. Also camping and a lodge.

McCredie Hot Springs: Eight miles east of Oakridge in the Willamette State Forest. Natural, undeveloped and clothing-optional.

Hood River

Brilliant display of aviation and automotive history

For fans of classic airplanes, cars and motorcycles, a visit to the **Western Antique Aeroplane & Automobile Museum** (WAAAM; waaamuseum.org; adult/child $23/12) on Hood River's south side is highly recommended. Most of the airplanes can still fly, and many are from pioneering American manufacturers now lost to the mists of time. In early September, the museum's annual **Fly-in** sees pilots arrive in their lovingly preserved aircraft. To fully appreciate the collection of more than 300 planes and vehicles, allow at least two hours.

Riding the rails on the Mt Hood Railroad

The scenic **Mt Hood Railroad** (mthoodrr.com; adult/child $37/27) is a family favorite. The railroad once transported timber and fruit from the Upper Hood River Valley, but now shuttles visitors past rivers and through fragrant orchards. Look forward to Mt Hood views en route. After 45 minutes, there's an hour-long stop at the **Fruit Company**, a gift store, orchard and heritage museum, before trundling back to Hood River. Runs from April to October. Book ahead online.

A spirited brace of tasting rooms

In a city famous for brewing beer, two Hood River tasting rooms are presenting a spin on distilling, Columbia Gorge-style. Highlights of **Hood River Distillers'** tasting room are mini-cocktails and curated flights of the award-winning gin, whiskey, vodka and bourbon, while the focus at **Wilderton Aperitivo Co** is on non-alcoholic versions of traditional Italian *aperitivo* spirits.

Columbia River Gorge

Experience Multnomah Falls

At 620ft, **Multnomah Falls** is the tallest waterfall in Oregon. A 1-mile trail leads to the top with a stop at picturesque **Benson Bridge** along the way. Since the falls are such a major attraction, you'll need to buy a timed-use permit ($2) online at recreation.gov for visits between from late May to early September. Want to continue the adventure? From the top of Multnomah Falls, trail 420 is a loop route continuing to **Wahkeena Falls**.

DRINKING IN HOOD RIVER: CRAFT BEER FAVORITES

pFriem Family Brewers: Superb beers, including barrel-aged specials, at a waterfront location. The upscale pub dining menu showcases ingredients from around the gorge. *11:30am-9pm*

Ferment Brewing Company: Ferment's sleek taproom combines gorge views with precisely crafted beers, cocktails and non-alcoholic tipples. *11am-9pm Mon-Fri, from 10am Sat & Sun*

Spinning Wheels Brewing Project: A perfect Pacific Northwest mashup of vinyl listening bar and neighborhood nano-brewery. *4-9pm Mon-Fri, from 2pm Sat & Sun*

Full Sail Brewing Company: Hood River's pioneering brewpub partners salads, sandwiches and burgers with river views. An outdoor patio is a bonus on sunny days. *11am-9pm*

Multnomah Falls

Visit the Bonneville Dam

On the Columbia River lies a powerful 20th-century feat of engineering: the Bonneville Dam. This Depression-era project generates enough electricity for 900,000 homes. After passing through security, drive slowly into the massive site – soundtracked by the spillway's thundering waters – and visit the **Bradford Island Visitor Center** *(nwp.usace.army.mil/bonneville)*. Ascend to the roof terrace for spectacular views. Downstairs is a fish ladder where lamprey and salmon journey past the dam from August to October. Just west of the dam, massive sturgeon – including Herman, a hulking 500lb octogenarian – can be seen amid the leafy grounds of the **Bonneville Fish Hatchery** *(myodfw.com)*. Visit in September and October to see spawning Chinook and Coho salmon.

Mt Hood

Snow sports on the mountain

Mt Hood offers the longest snow-sports season in the US, with the **Timberline Lodge Ski Area** *(timberlinelodge.com; day passes from $95)* usually opening early to mid-November, and sometimes staying open until late May. To the east, **Mt Hood**

HOOD RIVER'S CENTENARIAN BRIDGE

Celebrating its centenary in 2024, the 4418ft-long Hood River–White Salmon Interstate Bridge could be the gorge's least-loved thoroughfare. Each of the two lanes is just 9.5ft wide – there's no room for bicycles or pedestrians – and the surface is a vehicle-shaking iron grid. Planning to replace the bridge is ongoing (Washington State committed $50 million in May 2025), and in April 2025 payment for the bridge ($3.50) went strictly electronic. Locals can sign up for a transponder giving a discounted rate of $1.75, and if you're driving a rental car, the toll will probably be added to your hire costs. Otherwise, you have 14 days to pay online *(portofhoodriver.com)* before getting charged an additional $3 administration fee.

EATING IN HOOD RIVER: CAFES TO FINE DINING

Broder Øst: A cozy option adjacent to the Hood River Hotel with Scandinavian-inspired breakfast dishes. Try the Pytt i Panna (Swedish-style hash). *8am-3pm* **$**

Solstice Woodfire Cafe: Wood-fired pizzas, cocktails and good beer near the waterfront. Order the Coho Salmon pizza with local gorge salmon. *11.30am-8pm Wed-Sun* **$$**

Votum: Hood River's fine dining frontrunner combines a hushed space with a seafood-focused degustation menu often including salmon, oysters and king crab. *5-10pm Thu-Mon* **$$$**

Celilo Restaurant & Bar: Tender steaks and perfectly cooked fish dishes partner with a wine list featuring Oregon and Washington varietals. *5-9.30pm Tue-Sat* **$$$**

BEST TRAILS NEAR BEND

Phil's Trail: On Bend's west side, this is one of Oregon's best networks of mountain-biking trails. Young riders will love the skills course.

Pilot Butte: A 1.8-mile out-and-back trail ascends the 4142ft-high peak of this volcanic cone just east of downtown.

Tumalo Falls: Central Oregon's most photographed waterfall (97ft) has trails leading to several smaller cascades upstream.

Shevlin Park: A locals' favorite spot for hikes along Tumalo Creek. Trails of up to 6 miles explore old-growth ponderosa forest.

Deschutes River: South of town, start at **Lava Island Falls** from where it's 2.5 miles to **Dillon Falls**, a great spot for a picnic.

Meadows *(skihood.com; day passes from $99)* also opens early November and closes around early May. Courtesy of the Palmer Snowfield, it's even possible to tackle the Timberline Lodge Ski Area in summer, an alpine thrill mainly reserved for experienced and professional skiers.

Near Government Camp, **Mt Hood Skibowl** *(skibowl.com; day passes from $72)* is the closest ski area to Portland, and it's popular for night-skiing with Portlanders driving out for an evening on the slopes. On the northeastern slopes of the mountain, **Cooper Spur Ski Area** *(day passes from $52)* caters mainly to beginners and families.

Cross-country skiers and snowshoers can try **Trillium Sno Park** or the **White River West Sno Park**, while just off Hwy 35, **Teacup Nordic** has around 15 miles of groomed trails.

A Sno-Park **parking permit** *(1 day/3 days/annual $4/9/25)* is required for most Mt Hood snow sports areas from November to April.

Hiking around Oregon's highest peak

While Mt Hood is great for winter sports when the temps are chilly, it's equally as fantastic for hiking during the warmer months with its miles of trails ($5). The 7-mile loop trail passing by the 120ft **Ramona Falls** may be the most popular of the bunch, though the shorter, 4.2-mile trail to pretty **Mirror Lake** draws its fair share of crowds too. Another kid-friendly trail is the **Old Salmon River Trail**, which is 4 miles, out and back. Look forward to towering trees draped in moss and a shimmering pool that's perfect for a dip on a hot day.

For a more rigorous challenge, the **Timberline Trail** is a 42-mile trail circumnavigating Mt Hood, and passing by waterfalls and alpine meadows. Check ranger stations on track conditions, as parts of the trail get washed out.

Bend

Tubing the Deschutes River

Floating along the Deschutes River through town is the quintessential Bend experience. From mid-June through Labor Day, **Tumalo Creek Kayak & Canoe** *(tumalocreek.com; 2hr including shuttle $27)* operates a tube rental and shuttle service that is bookable online. Book well ahead.

Beginning at **Riverbend Park** in the Old Mill District and ending in Drake Park near downtown, the float route – plan on 60 to 90 minutes – is gentle most of the way except for a

---

EATING & DRINKING AROUND MT HOOD: OUR PICKS

Glacier Public House: In Government Camp with menu options including salmon cakes and a warming cheese fondue. Definitely a good option in cooler weather. *9am-9pm* **$$**

Mt Hood Brewing Co: Government Camp's brewpub combines a relaxed ambience with hearty fare including pizzas, sandwiches and short ribs. *11am-9pm* **$$**

Barlow Trail Roadhouse: Century-old rustic and unpretentious restaurant and bar near Zigzag. Serves big-portioned diner-style meals. *8am-8pm Thu-Sat, to 4pm Sun* **$$**

Blue Ox Bar: The coziest of the eating and drinking options at Timberline Lodge (p1035). Mt Hood Brewing beers, mountain-inspired cocktails and flatbread pizza feature. *11am-8pm* **$$**

Deschutes River, Bend

short stretch of rapids dubbed the Fish Ladder. If you're tubing with younger family members, it's possible to bypass these rapids with a short on-the-land portage detour. Sunblock, a hat and river shoes are all essential.

The last Blockbuster

In Bend, you don't need a DeLorean to travel back in time 30 years. Just visit the corner of Revere Ave and Third St where you'll find the world's last **Blockbuster** *(bendblockbuster.com)* video store. Inside, the DVD racks, blue-shirted employees and packages of microwave popcorn will instantly transport you back to the '90s. There are also racks of VHS tapes for sale.

Visit Newberry National Volcanic Monument

South of Bend, the Newberry National Volcanic Monument is a sprawling landscape of lava flows, tubes and dormant craters. Stop at the visitor center to get the lay of the land, before continuing to the **Lava River Cave**, a mile-long lava tube under the forest. Tours are self-guided, but timed permits from recreation.gov are mandatory.

Don't miss the **Newberry Caldera**, a massive crater 5 miles in diameter. Both **Paulina Lake** and **East Lake** are located inside the caldera. Most visitors start their exploration at **Paulina Falls** (80ft), where a short trail (150yd) leads from the parking lot to the top of a twin waterfall, before heading back to the lakes for fishing, hiking, campgrounds and hot

HIKING PERMITS IN THE CASCADES

Central Cascades Wilderness Permits *(per person $1)* are required on 19 of the 79 trailheads in the Mt Jefferson, Mt Washington and Three Sisters wilderness areas from June 15 to October 15. A Forest Service employee is usually at the trailhead to check permits and provide trail information. The permits are also needed for overnight stays (per group $6) in all three wilderness areas. In addition to the hiking permits it's also a good idea to have a Northwest Forest Pass, which allows parking in the national forest parking areas. Printable day passes ($5) are available online. Several retailers in Bend also sell the passes. Some (but not all) trailheads have parking ticket machines.

DRINKING IN BEND: CRAFT BEER

Deschutes Brewery & Public House: Est. 1988 as Bend's first craft brewery; classics are Black Butte porter and Mirror Pond pale ale. *11am-9pm Sun-Thu, to 9:30pm Fri & Sat*

Crux Fermentation Project: A five-beer tasting flight is the best way to experience this Bend favorite with beautiful Cascade views. *11am-9pm Sun-Thu, to 10pm Fri & Sat*

Boss Rambler Beer Club: There's a quirky, aprés ski ambience at this Westside taproom with refreshing hazy IPAs. *noon-8pm Sun-Thu, to 9pm Fri & Sat*

Ale Apothecary: Wild-fermented, sour and spontaneously fermented beers are the fascinating highlights of this rustic taproom. *2-8pm Wed-Sat, to 6pm Sun*

springs. Alternatively, there's the **Paulina Lakeshore Trail**, a 7.5-mile loop trail that takes around 2½ hours, while mountain bikers can tackle the 21-mile-long **Crater Rim Trail** encircling both lakes.

Sisters

Take advantage of Central Oregon's dark skies

With more than 300 days of clear skies per year, minimal pollution and higher elevations, Central Oregon is ideal for stargazing. In 2025 the town of Sisters was awarded International Dark Sky Place status. A good pair of binoculars and a stargazing app like SkySafari makes a fine combo for a DIY night sky encounter. Alternatively, visit the Hopservatory at **Worthy Brewing** *(worthygardenclub.org; donation $5)* and observe the heavens through the research-grade telescope. **Wanderlust Tours** *(wanderlusttours.com; $130)* also offers stargazing experiences at Fort Rock on selected nights from late May to October. Book well ahead.

Drive the Cascade Lakes Scenic Byway

Usually open from late May to October, the 66-mile Cascade Lakes Scenic Byway begins in Bend and travels south through volcanic highlands and the Deschutes National Forest. Day trips visiting spring-fed lakes surrounded by snowcapped peaks are possible, but campsites and resorts make overnighting easy.

Start with the 9065ft **Mt Bachelor**, a ski resort on a dormant stratovolcano that has epic summer hiking, mountain biking and zip-line opportunities. Past Mt Bachelor, the highway only opens in late May, after the worst of winter. Four miles on is the **Todd Lake Trailhead** (permit required), offering a family-friendly 1.7-mile hike around **Todd Lake**. Experienced hikers should consider venturing to spectacular glacier-fed **No Name Lake** (permit required), only thawing in late July to reveal its turquoise-green color.

Continue 6 miles southwest to **Elk Lake**, a family destination with a rustic resort, while the twisting shoreline of nearby **Hosmer Lake** is popular with kayakers. Atlantic salmon, rainbow trout and brook trout are easily spotted (fly-fishing only). Round out the drive with a few more stunning lakes, including **Lava Lake**, **Cultus Lake** and **Twin Lakes**.

Astoria

In the footsteps of Lewis and Clark

Although the land now known as Astoria has been inhabited for millennia, its current incarnation started at the turn of the 19th century, when explorers and fur traders began taking an interest in the region. Among them were Captain Meriwether Lewis and Second Lieutenant William Clark who, under the auspices of the US Army's Corps of Discovery, journeyed to the West, ultimately ending their journey just 6 miles south of downtown Astoria. It was here that the Corps built **Fort Clatsop**, where they lived from December 1805 until March 1806.

MINDFUL TIDE-POOLING

Marine Science educator **Alanna Kieffer**, who runs foraging, clamming and coastal explorations through her company Shifting Tides, shares advice on responsible tide-pooling. *(@shifting_tides_nw)*

It's important to be careful about walking on rocks. When the tide goes out, you'll see rocks covered in species that aren't moving. While these species don't appear to be alive, they often are. So it's best to walk on bare rocks or stick to the sand. While one person stepping on things that may be alive might not be that harmful, when everyone at the beach does it – which happens in the spring and summer – there's a big impact.

Todd Lake

Today, the Fort Clatsop area is protected as part of the **Lewis & Clark National State and Historical Park** *(nps.gov/lewi/index.htm; free)*, which has a collection of 12 different spots across Oregon and Washington related to the Lewis and Clark expedition. Although the original fort is no longer standing, there's a fully furnished replica in its place. When you're done exploring the compact fort, head to the visitor center's exhibit hall to check out displays featuring everything from old weapons to a model canoe.

The Hollywood of Oregon

If you've ever watched the 1985 kids' film *The Goonies*, then you've seen Astoria, at least on a screen. Start your *Goonies*-themed adventure with a visit to Mikey's house, known locally simply as the Goonies House, located at 368 38th St – just note that you can only see it from the outside. From here, it's a 2-mile drive to the **Flavel House Museum** *(astoriamuseums.org/explore/flavel-house-museum; 20adult/child $7/2)*, where Mr Walsh (Mikey's dad) worked in the movie.

Cannon Beach
Picture-perfect

The coastal town of Cannon Beach is a popular day trip amongst Portlanders, especially in the summer. Start at the main thoroughfare, **Hemlock St**, a boutique-dotted drag

WILDFIRE AWARENESS

Southern Oregon has seen devastating wildfires become stronger and more frequent in recent years, largely due to climate change. In 2020, record-breaking wildfires across the state burned over a million acres and killed 11 people. You'll see evidence of that fire and more recent ones as you drive around the region. As dry summer months and ongoing drought persist, visitors should be aware that wildfires can impact travel plans. If you are camping in the summer, check on fire restrictions at ranger stations – by late summer, campfires are typically banned. Check Southern Oregon air quality at aqi.oregon.gov if smoke is a concern. An AQI over 100 is considered unhealthy, and you may want to reconsider outdoor activities.

 EATING IN ASTORIA: OUR PICKS

| **Bowpicker Fish & Chips:** A converted boat turned food cart serving breaded albacore and British-style fries. *11am-6pm Tue-Sat, to 4pm Sun* $ | **Daphne:** High-end farm-to-table spot with an extensive wine list and menu that evolves with the season. *5-9pm Tue-Sat* $$$ | **Fedé Trattoria:** Upscale Italian spot with hearty meals made mostly from locally sourced ingredients, including seafood. *3:30-9pm Tue-Sat* $$$ | **Himani Indian Cuisine:** No-frills North Indian restaurant with large portions and an even larger selection. *noon-8pm Sun-Thu, 9am-4pm Fri* $$ |

that is among the best places in the region to pick up fine art and higher-end souvenirs. Book-lovers can easily spend hours poring over the tomes in the **Cannon Beach Book Company** *(cannonbeachbooks.com)*. Once you've had your retail fix, head to the beach to see **Haystack Rock**, a 17-million-year-old Oregon icon. If you've got binoculars, bring them: this frequent star of Oregon Coast postcards is around 235ft tall and provides refuge to all sorts of seabirds, including fluffy tufted puffins. The area around the monolith is particularly fun during low tide, when the waves recede to reveal lots of little tide pools.

Tillamook
A different type of tasting room

The city of Tillamook is a very cheesy place – literally. The city's biggest draw is the **Tillamook Creamery** *(tillamook.com/visit-us/creamery; free)*, where you can take a self-guided walk through Oregon's best-known cheese-and-dairy-product factory or get a closer look at what goes into making Tillamook products with a guided cheese or ice-cream tour. Expect plenty of free samples.

Oregon Dunes National Recreation Area
The dunes that inspired Dune

Extending for around 40 miles from just south of Florence all the way to Coos Bay, the **Oregon Dunes National Recreation Area** *($5)* is the largest expanse of coastal sand dunes on the continent. It was these very dunes that provided the inspiration for Pacific Northwest author Frank Herbert's eco-sci-fi novel *Dune,* which was later adapted into film versions.

The dunes are popular for off-highway vehicle adventures, though if you'd rather approach the sands with a little less adrenaline, take a hike along the **Oregon Dunes Loop Trail**.

Brookings
A gorgeous stretch of coastline

The **Samuel H Boardman State Scenic Corridor** might just be the prettiest stretch of an already gorgeous coastline. Start your sightseeing at **Arch Rock**, where a small path leads to a couple of benches that look out over gorgeous sea stacks, including the aptly named Arch Rock itself. From here, continue south to the not-so-secret **Secret Beach** and **Thunder Rock Cove**. Take in views from the parking lot or head down a ¾-mile trail to the beach – just don't attempt this during high tide when most of the beach is submerged. Make **Natural Bridges** your next stop to see bridge-like rock formations as they're lapped by frothy sea spray. By now, you've probably spent enough time looking at the beach that you'll actually want to head down to the seashore. Continue south over the **Thomas Creek Bridge** until you reach **Whaleshead Beach**. Drive right down to the beach or park at the **Whaleshead Viewpoint** and follow a steep trail down to the shore.

FINDERS KEEPERS

If you spend much time browsing antique shops on the Oregon Coast, you'll probably notice round glass balls of all sizes in shades of soda-bottle green. While there are some replicas out there, many of these balls are Japanese fishing floats that were traditionally used to keep fishing nets afloat. They used to be a common beachcomber's find on the Oregon Coast; today, you'll mostly find the floats in local shops.

These floats were also the inspiration for Lincoln City's Finders Keepers in which around 3000 blown glass floats per year are hidden on the beach for lucky visitors to find. If you find one of the colorful baubles, it's yours to keep – you can even register it online for a certificate of authenticity.

Umpqua Hot Springs

Rogue-Umpqua Scenic Byway

Chasing eye-catching cascades

The second half of the Rogue-Umpqua Scenic Byway heads south, past Crater Lake, to follow the waterfall-dotted Rogue River. The 1.5-mile **Susan Creek Falls Trail** is a good place to start; it offers informational placards to get you acquainted with the local flora, including vine maples, Pacific dogwoods and grand firs.

Further down Hwy 138, **Fall Creek Falls** is a sparkling cascade over a rock wall into a shallow pool that's great for swimming on hot days. **Toketee Falls** is a popular stop where the parking lot is often full, but people move in and out quickly as the trail is only 0.8 miles long. Keep driving past Toketee Falls to **Umpqua Hot Springs**, an iconic Oregon spot to soak where cascading pools invite you to soak and relax in the mossy forest. Unfortunately, it's also well known for being overused and attracting litterbugs. Hopefully, those before you will leave it better than they found it, and you can do the same.

Pendleton

A spectacle of Western culture

For the second full week of September, the Eastern Oregon town of Pendleton is transformed into a rollicking Western celebration. The very first round-up took place in 1910 and exceeded all expectations for attendance and festivity – and the enthusiasm has held strong since. From bull riding and Indian relay racing to the Happy Canyon Pageant, a dramatic enactment of the settling of the American West, every day is action-packed. The nightlife can get a little rowdy, but there are plenty of activities for families, too. Plans for the round-up should be made well in advance.

DARK SKY SANCTUARY

Have you met ALAN? (You definitely have.) Artificial light at night (ALAN) is pervasive in most places thanks to lightbulbs, traffic lights, glowing screens and all the ways humans have found to illuminate darkness. ALAN impacts navigation, hunting and sleep patterns for many animals, including humans. DarkSky International is a leading organization in promoting natural darkness by encouraging the reduction in ALAN and designating certain places as distinctly dark – making them destinations for stargazing. In 2024 the Oregon Outback was named a Dark Sky Sanctuary. Thanks to the vast desert and low population of this 1.5-million-acre swath of Lake County – along with collaboration and public education on reducing light pollution – Oregon is now home to the largest Dark Sky Sanctuary in the world.

Places We Love to Stay

$ Budget $$ Midrange $$$ Top End

Seattle
MAP P988

Green Tortoise Seattle Hostel $ Meet new people and make easy trips to Pike Place Market when staying at this affordable hostel.

Hotel Crocodile $$ Settled above the city's famed grunge venue, the Crocodile, this boutique hotel has 17 rooms, each with a unique mural from a local artist.

Inn at the Market $$$ Located within Pike Place Market, this boutique hotel is in the middle of the excitement but still manages to be surprisingly quiet within the rooms.

The Edgewater $$$ This high-end, over-water hotel balances classy and rustic design styles – and has epic Puget Sound views.

Olympic Peninsula & Washington Coast

Sol Duc Campground $ Reserve early on recreation. gov for the best campsites, including quiet Sol Duc, or check out mossy Hoh Rainforest, seafront forested Mora, or the isolated vistas of Deer Park.

Sol Duc Hot Springs Resort (p999) $$$ Cozy cabins surround the lodge and hot springs. Guests can soak an hour before the public. Kitchenettes available.

Northwestern Washington & the San Juan Islands

Deception Pass State Park $ Even with over 300 camping spaces across several wooded loops, the views mean you need to book now. Mix of tent and RV sites with hookups.

San Juan County Park Campground $ Situated on San Juan's western shoreline, these 20 campsites are in high demand. Reserve in advance.

Doe Bay Resort $$ A true wellness retreat, serene Doe Bay offers camping, yurts and cabins, plus outdoor soaking tubs. On-site Doe Bay Cafe grows organic ingredients and serves elevated locavore food.

Hotel Bellwether $$$ Bellingham's premier waterfront hotel, located in a park-like marina setting. Its bay-view suites offer touches of luxury, including jetted tubs and fireplaces.

Washington Cascades

Stehekin Valley Ranch $$ All kinds of activities, including cycling, horseback riding, kayaking and hiking, go on at this well-organized place in North Cascades National Park.

Paradise Inn $$ Designed to blend in with the environment and constructed almost entirely of local materials, the historic (1916) Paradise Inn was an early blueprint for National Park–rustic architecture.

Ross Lake Resort $$$ The floating cabins at this secluded resort in Stehekin (near North Cascades National Park) were built in the 1930s. Reached by ferry from the parking area near Diablo Dam.

Walla Walla

Columbia River Inn $$ Opposite the visitor center in Grand Coulee is this clean, comfortable inn, with some hot-tub rooms, a fitness center and a sauna. It's the best place in town.

Freehand Cellars $$$ If staying *near* wine country isn't good enough, you can book one of two apartments or the luxury Airstream trailer right on the grounds of this Wapato vineyard.

The Inn at Abeja $$$ Historic farmhouse and winery set in the foothills of the Blue Mountains, 4 miles east of Walla Walla. Luxury accommodations are in impeccably restored self-contained houses that played a historical role at the farm (hayloft, mechanic's shed etc).

Portland
MAP P1012

Hotel deLuxe $ Longtime hotel just west of Downtown near the Goose Hollow neighborhood featuring vintage Hollywood-inspired decor and elegant brunches at on-site restaurant Gracie's, a long-time Portland institution.

Heathman Hotel $$ A classic Portland hotel with elegant rooms, great on-site dining and a library full of books signed by past-guest authors.

Inn at Northrup Station $$ Colorful, all-suites hotel within a short jaunt of the shops and restaurants on NW 23rd Ave.

McMenamins Kennedy School $$$ Sprawling concept hotel occupying a converted elementary school, complete with rooms that were once classrooms (with the cloakrooms and chalkboards to show for it), multiple pubs and a hot soaking pool.

Willamette Valley

Timbers Inn $ This recently renovated 1958 motel celebrates a super-convenient downtown Eugene location. Retro design touches partner with modern rooms.

McMenamins Hotel Oregon $$ Eclectic artwork enlivens this McMinnville outpost of McMenamins' Pacific Northwest hospitality empire. In warmer months, don't miss drinks at the rooftop bar.

Atticus Hotel $$$ Luxurious downtown McMinnville hotel with ultra-modern decor and large rooms. Bikes are available for guest use, while the hotel's Cypress restaurant channels the best of the Mediterranean.

Gordon Hotel $$$ Downtown Eugene boutique hotel with bars and restaurants including a Prohibition-style speakeasy, a Mexican-themed rooftop bar and a modern American tavern.

Columbia River Gorge

Hood River Hotel $$ This characterful and historic hotel was built in 1912 and retains its early-20th-century character. Eclectic design touches abound and the downtown location is very convenient.

Timberline Lodge (p1027) **$$$** A gorgeous lodge oozing with history and charm, Timberline offers a variety of cozy rooms from dorms to deluxe. Ski-field access in winter, and elevated alpine hiking in spring and summer.

Columbia Gorge Hotel & Spa $$$ A historic Spanish Mission–style hotel set amid lush gardens with its own natural waterfall. The hotel's lounge bar is exceptionally cozy on a cooler day. Around 2 miles west of downtown Hood River.

Central Oregon & the Cascades

Bunk + Brew Hostel $ In a historic house near downtown Bend, this social hostel with mixed dorms and private rooms also features a sauna and regular events including live music.

Oxford Hotel $$$ The most upscale accommodation in Bend with super-spacious rooms, an understated and elegant ambience, and Modern American fine-dining onsite at ROAM restaurant.

The Oregon Coast

Norblad $ Hip, century-old hotel offering budget-friendly rooms in Astoria's city center.

Crater Lake Lodge $$ Sleep next to Crater Lake in this historic lodge whose exterior is featured in 1980 horror film *The Shining*. Amenities are basic but the location makes up for any shortcomings.

Stephanie Inn $$$ Romantic, upscale inn with close-up Haystack Rock views plus a spa and a fine-dining restaurant with great wine.

Bowline Hotel $$$ Astoria boutique hotel in a former fish-processing plant with maritime-themed rooms, many overlooking the Columbia River.

Eastern Oregon

Pendleton House Historic Inn $$ A pink 1917 mansion built in the Italian Renaissance style with beautiful vintage decor.

The Lodge at Hot Lake Springs $$$ Soak in the natural hot springs right outside a historic lodge. Pub and movie theater make it hard to leave this La Grande accommodation.

Portland streetscape, including the Heathman Hotel

THE GUIDE

ALASKA

For places to stay in Alaska, see p1057

CAVAN IMAGES/BRENT DOSCHER/GETTY IMAGES

Above: Kayaking, Glacier Bay National Park (p1043); Right: Humpback whale, Kenai Peninsula (p1052)

THE MAIN AREAS

JUNEAU & THE ALEXANDER ARCHIPELAGO
Rainforests, glaciers, totem poles. **p1040**

ANCHORAGE
Urban playground; incredible natural surrounds. **p1046**

DENALI NATIONAL PARK & PRESERVE
Enormous mountain and vast wilderness. **p1054**

Researched by Kevin Raub

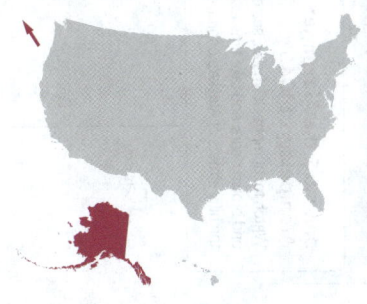

Alaska

NATURE, WILDLIFE AND MONUMENTAL ADVENTURES

Nation-sized national parks, glaciers bigger than Tokyo, brown bears more stout than bison – Alaska is a Great Land of marvelous superlatives. In a word: epic.

Since the first arrival of humans to Alaska via the Bering Land Bridge, connections to earth, sea and sky by the Indigenous people inhabiting the Great Land have run deep. Alaska has nearly 34,000 miles of shoreline, 12,000 rivers and three million lakes. Alaskans are proud of their home, and have come to appreciate the ancient history of the land far removed from the rest of the United States.

The state's wildlife jockeys for position as most popular attraction, regardless of species. Whether spying a humpback whale in a magnificent breach, watching a brown bear catch salmon with one swipe of a paw, or flying above a craggy peak where mountain goats inhabit the tiniest slivers of rock ledges, the combination of landscapes and living creatures inspire awe.

For those who thrive on heart-pounding adventure, Alaska delivers the best of the best.

From soaring above North America's highest peak to rafting a raging river, the list of activities knows no bounds, and each region features its own particular brand of excitement, from mountain biking to paddling or backcountry skiing.

A plethora of parks, trails, pathways and untracked areas open to hikers of any ability or age offer miles of wandering.

Pure, raw, unforgiving and humongous in scale, Alaska is a place that arouses basic instincts and ignites what Jack London termed the 'call of the wild.'

IULIA SHELIEPOVA/SHUTTERSTOCK

PRINCE WILLIAM SOUND
Imposing glaciers; isolated fishing ports. **p1050**

KENAI PENINSULA
Stunning views meet world-class fishing. **p1052**

KODIAK & KATMAI
Brown bears, historic architecture, Indigenous heritage. **p1053**

1038

ALASKA

THE GUIDE

Find Your Way

A vehicle greatly enhances travel in most populated parts of Alaska, but far-flung communities unreachable by road are numerous – ferries and charter flights are your new best friends. The train travel is epic, too.

Denali National Park & Preserve, p1054
Signature national park for spying Alaska's famed 'Big Five' animals: moose, bears, wolves, caribou and Dall sheep.

Juneau & the Alexander Archipelago, p1040
Watch for humpback whales, sea otters and brown bears, and take time to explore the hilly streets of Alaska's capital city.

Anchorage, p1046
Bike, hike, or paddle with locals and dine at some of the state's most famous restaurants in Alaska's urban hub.

CAR
Car rental in Alaska requires you to be at least 21 years old and have a valid driver's license and a major credit card (or pay a large cash deposit). An International Driving Permit (IDP) isn't required but is certainly recommended.

AIR, TRAIN & FERRY
Alaska Airlines (alaskaair.com) services 19 destinations in Alaska. **Alaska Railroad** (alaskarailroad.com) operates year-round between Fairbanks and Anchorage, as well as summer services (Anchorage/Whittier/Seward). **Alaska Marine Highway** (dot.alaska.gov/amhs) ferries call at 30 ports across the coastline.

Denali National Park (p1054)

Plan Your Time

Clocking in at roughly 586,400 sq miles, not only is Alaska the largest US state, but 80% of its land is generally inaccessible by car. It's a beautiful, pristine monster.

A Week of Wildlife & Wilderness

- Acclimatize to Alaska in **Anchorage** (p1046), enjoying seafood, craft beers and the mountain scenery, then travel south along the Seward Hwy – keep an eye out for whales in Turnagain Arm. The Seward Hwy is the only road connecting to the **Kenai Peninsula** (p1052) and offers year-round recreation, wildlife and scenery.

Slow Down & Stay Awhile

- Fly into **Juneau** (p1040), traversing the island-studded wilderness. Ferry to Whittier – eyes open for **Prince William Sound** (p1050) glaciers – and on to **Anchorage** (p1046). Then take a road trip, exploring out-of-this-world views of water, sky, mountain and forest in **Seward** (p1052). Drive north to ogle Alaska's 'Big Five' animals in **Denali National Park** (p1054) before returning to Anchorage.

SEASONAL HIGHLIGHTS

SPRING
As Alaska awakens, festivities abound, including dog-sled racing, while wildflowers bloom and bird migrate.

SUMMER
Summer brings solstice festivals, 20-hour days and peak salmon runs. Trails and passes are snow-free in August.

AUTUMN
The aurora borealis is visible from late September to early April, but the southeast can be rainy.

WINTER
Most activity companies close for winter. Longer and warmer days make late February best time for winter sports.

Juneau & the Alexander Archipelago

SCENIC TOWNS | GLACIERS | HISTORIC RAILS

☑ TOP TIP
On the 2nd floor of Glacier Bay Lodge, the **Glacier Bay National Park Visitor Center** is a good first stop for perusing exhibitions on the park, chatting with a ranger, and plotting talks and guided activities. For info on the park and Gustavus, check out *gustavusak.com*.

If you imagine Alaska as a treeless expanse of barren land and permafrost, the Alexander Archipelago will quickly destroy this notion. Stretching for some 300 miles along the state's southeastern panhandle, these 1100 islands are home to ice-blue glaciers, rugged snowcapped mountains and some of the most verdant wilderness on the planet. In fact, the entire region lies within the vast Tongass National Forest, the largest remaining temperate rainforest on Earth.

Long before the first European sailors arrived on the scene in the 18th century, Indigenous people flourished in small interwoven communities scattered across the archipelago. Before WWII, the Southeast was Alaska's heart and soul, and Juneau was not only the capital but the state's largest city. Today, the region is characterized by old-growth forests and small towns. Every town in this region is unique and none of them are connected to another by road.

Cultural Wanders in Downtown Juneau
Museums, mansions and churches

You could spend a full day exploring the sites of Juneau, which are all within walking distance of the lively waterfront. Start off with a visit to **Sealaska Heritage Institute** *(sealaskaheritage.org),* easily spotted by the totem poles in front and the beautifully carved panels framing the entrance. The whole place is a work of art, with much of the detail completed by Tsimshian artist David Boxley.

A few blocks west of Sealaska, the **Alaska State Museum** *(museums.alaska.gov/asm; adult/child $14/free)* displays one of the country's best collections devoted to Alaska Native culture and the state's history. There's a wealth of extraordinary pieces on display here: the Shaman's Vision Mask by Tlingit artist Jim Schoppert, bead- and quill-decorated jackets by Athabascan artisans, and diaphanous Yupik parkas made from animal innards. One of the museum's oldest pieces is a spruce basket made more than 5400 years ago. It's a short

JUNEAU & THE ALEXANDER ARCHIPELAGO

★ HIGHLIGHTS
1. Alaska State Museum

● SIGHTS
2. Alaska State Capitol
3. Governor's Mansion of Alaska
4. Juneau-Douglas City Museum
5. Sealaska Heritage Institute
6. St Nicholas Russian Orthodox Church
7. Wickersham State Historic Site

● ACTIVITIES
8. White Pass & Yukon Route Railway

● SLEEPING
9. Alaskan Hotel & Bar
10. Alaska's Capital Inn
11. Juneau Hotel
12. Silverbow Inn

● EATING
13. Bernadette's
14. Deckhand Dave's
15. Olivia's Bistro
16. Salt
17. Salty Siren
18. Skagway Fish Company
19. Tracy's King Crab Shack
20. Woadie's South East Seafood

THE GUIDE

ALASKA JUNEAU & THE ALEXANDER ARCHIPELAGO

GETTING AROUND

The **Alaska Marine Highway** (dot.alaska.gov/amhs), North America's longest public ferry system, connects the cities, towns and fishing ports around the archipelago. Juneau has a decent public bus system, though it doesn't go near the ferry terminal at Auke Bay (13 miles from town), nor does it quite reach the Mendenhall Glacier. For Glacier Bay National Park, some lodges provide free transportation to/from the airport or the ferry terminal. If not, **TLC taxi** (907-697-2239) can carry up to 10 people, gear and kayaks. Most of Skagway is fairly walkable.

walk from the museum up to Calhoun Ave for a look at the **Governor's Mansion of Alaska**, one of Juneau's most attractive homes. Built and furnished in 1912 at a cost of $44,000, this mansion has 26 rooms across some 14,400 sq ft. It's not open to the public.

The nearby **Alaska State Capitol** (alaskacapitol.gov) is easy to stroll right past. The boxy building went up between 1929 and 1931, and it looks more like an overgrown high school than a historic bastion of democracy. Inquire about free tours. One block away from the capitol building, the **Juneau-Douglas City Museum** (juneau.org/library/museum; adult/child $7/free) provides guests with an overview of key events from the past, with a focus on Tlingit culture, mining and politics.

It's a steep climb up to the **Wickersham State Historic Site** (dnr.alaska.gov/parks; adult/child $5/free), but worth the effort for the views alone. The garden-fringed house-museum was once the residence of pioneer judge and statesman James Wickersham. Heading back into downtown Juneau, stop for a peek at the **St Nicholas Russian Orthodox Church**. Dating from 1893 and etched against the backdrop of Mt Juneau, this diminutive onion-domed church is the oldest Russian Orthodox church in Alaska.

EATING IN JUNEAU: OUR PICKS

Bernadette's: Food stall doling out Filipino barbecue, sandwiches and *dinuguan* (pork stew). Wash it down with craft suds from Alaskan Brewing Company. *11am-7pm* $$

Deckhand Dave's: Outdoor spot with counters for fish tacos (wild salmon, rockfish, halibut), craft beer, and oysters and champagne. *11am-8pm Sun-Thu, to 9pm Fri & Sat* $$

Tracy's King Crab Shack: King crab with ample butter, plus outstanding crab bisque and mini crab cakes. *10am-9pm Mon-Tue & Thu-Fri, 12:30-6pm Wed, 11am-4pm Sat* $$$

Salt: This high-end spot serves up coconut salmon, weathervane scallops, halibut Dijonnaise and other mouthwatering fare alongside a commendable whisky list. *5-10pm* $$$

Margerie Glacier (p1044)

Boating into the World of Ice
Day trip in Glacier Bay

One of the best ways to experience **Glacier Bay National Park** *(nps.gov/glba)* is on a classic all-day boat trip with **Glacier Bay Lodge & Tours** *(visitglacierbay.com; day trip adult/child $266/139)*. The seven-hour excursion departs in the morning from Bartlett Cove and makes a 130-mile journey through Glacier Bay before its return in the late afternoon.

The first good viewing spot is the birding paradise of **South Marble Island**, where tufted and horned puffins, pigeon guillemots, surf scoters and pelagic cormorants are often seen. Near the shoreline, Steller sea lions bask on rocky ledges and watch idly as boats glide past.

Further along, the captain will slow the boat when sailing alongside **Gloomy Knob**, a barren rock face with steep cliffs where mountain goats are frequently spotted. Brown bears are also occasionally seen simply walking along the shoreline. It's well worth spending ample time out on the boat deck and studying the seas, coastline and sky. Binoculars come in handy.

The excursion offers dramatic views of the high peaks of the **Fairweather Range**, home to some of the world's highest

HOW BIG, HOW BLUE, HOW BEAUTIFUL

One of Juneau's biggest attractions is the **Mendenhall Glacier**, an impressive remnant from the last Ice Age and part of the 1500-sq-mile Juneau Icefield. Nestled amid a mountain valley, the glacier flows some 13 miles from its source, and it has a half-mile-wide face where it ends at Mendenhall Lake, with a shimmering waterfall nearby. On a sunny day Mendenhall Glacier is beautiful, with blue skies and snowcapped mountains in the background. On a cloudy and drizzly afternoon it can be even more photogenic, as the ice turns shades of deep blue. **Photo Point Trail** is a quick stroll (0.3 miles round trip) to a viewpoint, where there's a panoramic glacier view off in the distance.

EATING IN SKAGWAY: OUR PICKS

Olivia's Bistro: The bistro at Skagway Inn serves wild game, baked seafood and whatever is growing in their lovely garden. *10:30am-8pm* **$$**

Salty Siren: Ale-battered fish-and-chips, sockeye salmon sandwiches with a ginger shoyu glaze and burgers go perfectly with the local craft beers. *11am-7pm Mon-Fri* **$$**

Woadie's South East Seafood: Crab, halibut sandwiches and ceviche plus craft beer from nearby Klondike Brewing Company. *10am-7pm Mon-Fri, 11am-4pm Sat* **$$$**

Skagway Fish Company: The bar at this famous seafood eatery on the waterfront has the best view in town. *11am-8pm Mon-Sat, to 4pm Sun* **$$$**

GETTING TO GLACIER BAY

It's a short but scenic flight between Juneau and Gustavus (the gateway to Glacier Bay National Park), with both **Alaska Airlines** *(alaskaair. com; from $119)* and **Alaska Seaplanes** *(flyalaskaseaplanes. com; from $184)* making the 25-minute journey; the former runs one flight daily while the latter offers four to five daily services. If you're not in a hurry, the **Alaska Marine Highway** *(dot.alaska. gov/amhs; $55)* ferry is a great way to travel as whales and other marine life are frequently spotted along the way. The boat travels three times a week during the summer (twice weekly in winter), typically departing Juneau at 7am and arriving in Gustavus at 12:45pm. From Gustavus, boats sail at 1:30pm, arriving in Juneau at 7:15pm.

coastal mountains including Mt Fairweather, which tops out at 15,266ft. The landscape changes as you draw nearer to the ice field, with steeper mountains and sparser vegetation.

Boats will typically take the narrow passage of **Tarr Inlet**, which dead-ends near one of the national park's most spectacular glaciers. Well before you get there, however, you'll see the obvious presence of these frozen rivers with growlers and bergy bits (small and medium-sized icebergs) floating in the water.

At the northwest end of the inlet lies **Margerie Glacier**, a stunning and iconic tidewater glacier that stretches nearly a mile wide and towers some 250ft above the waterline (and another 100ft extending below the surface). Its terminus is just a small piece of this 21-mile-long river of ice that originates in the Fairweather Range. The snowy white surface appears blue in places, and its colors are more vivid on cloudy days. The boat will linger for the chance to possibly see calving, when huge icebergs sheer off the glacier and plunge into the water.

Apart from the striking backdrop – icebergs in the foreground, the wide glacier and chiseled mountains off in the distance –Tarr Inlet is also a good place to spot wildlife. Look for harbor seals stretched out on the ice, sea otters in the water, and black-legged kittiwake gulls flying past.

You'll pass other glaciers as you make the return journey, including the photogenic **Lamplugh Glacier** and slow-moving **Reid Glacier**, which was once the backdrop to a cabin built by the Ibachs, a pioneering family who, in the 1920s, searched for gold in the nearby mountains.

Riding the Rails in Skagway
Mining lore and grand views

The epic gold-rush era **White Pass & Yukon Route Railway** *(wpyr.com)* gives visitors a taste of a bygone era. The classic experience is the **White Pass Summit Excursion** *(adult/ child from $150/75)*, a 2½-hour journey departing several times daily between mid-April and late October. Take the first train (8am) to avoid the crowds.

The journey in old-fashioned carriages is magnificent. As the train chugs out of the station, skirting alongside the rushing **Yukon River**, you're quickly surrounded by nature's grandeur. The scenery just keeps getting better as you wind your way up forest-lined slopes and up to grand overlooks, like the aptly named **Inspiration Point** high above Skagway. You'll get fine views over **Lynn Canal**, a 90-mile-long fjord that reaches depths of 2000ft in some places. Further along, you'll pass over the headwaters of the Yukon River, dramatic trestle bridges and horseshoe curves (yielding photogenic views of the train itself), as well as the shimmering **Bridal Veil Falls**.

Haines

JIRI KULISEK/SHUTTERSTOCK

ARTIST HAVEN

Snowcapped peaks tower above Alaska's longest fjord, Lynn Canal, its blue-green waters lapping at the edge of one of Southeast Alaska's most captivating small towns. **Haines** has tranquil streets dotted with all the essentials of good living in Alaska: friendly restaurants, curio-filled museums, a cafe with house-roasted coffee beans, and separate drinking spots for microbrews, craft spirits and mead. The shop windows are full of arty handmade products, thanks to the surprising number of creative types who've relocated here over the years; in fact, Haines has more artists per capita than any other similarly sized town in the United States. Though just an hour ferry ride from Skagway, Haines sees only a fraction of Skagway's cruise traffic.

Anchorage

MUSEUMS | FOOD & DRINK | OUTDOOR ADVENTURES

GETTING AROUND

Downtown Anchorage is walkable but otherwise the city spreads far and wide (it's actually the fourth largest city in the US by area). The People Mover city bus system covers it decently, but you really need a car (or at least a bike) for efficient mobility. Over 120 miles of paved bike and multiuse trails canvas the municipality, connecting many parks and neighborhoods and allowing for two-wheel movement around parts of the city. In winter, add 130 miles of plowed winter walkways and 105 miles of maintained ski trails to the mix.

British explorer Captain James Cook sailed past what is current-day Anchorage as far back as 1779 in his pursuit for the elusive Northwest Passage. A century later, optimistic gold prospectors descended on Ship Creek, which today runs just off the city's compact downtown, in hopes of striking it rich. But it wasn't until 1915, when the Alaska Railroad settled in, that a tent city of 2000 leapt to life faster than a salmon runs. Today, Alaska's biggest city shares few traits with elsewhere. Enveloped by the extraordinary peaks of the Alaska Range on the northern horizon, the Chugach Mountains on its eastern doorstep and the Gulf of Alaska's Cook Inlet and its outstretched Arms to the west and south, its incredible surroundings are undeniable. The city itself isn't easy on the eyes but a cavalcade of locally owned, independent businesses running on the state's free-spirited nature ensure its charms.

Anchorage Away
An Alaska big city best-of

Anchorage's bricks-and-mortar aesthetic harbors restaurants serving the world's best salmon and halibut, breweries churning out fantastic craft beer, a wealth of both frontier and Alaska Native culture, and a fiercely local-driven ethos. Start at **Snow City Cafe** (*snowcitycafe.com*), an artsy, award-winning destination-breakfast joint for purveyors of finer morning things. Go for a 'crabby' omelet or a salmon cake Benedict.

Downtown Anchorage is a walkable delight of scenic overlooks and locally run businesses inhabiting a compact grid rubbing up against the shores of Cook Inlet. Anchorage's cultural crown jewel 10 blocks to the east, the wildly out-of-place **Anchorage Museum** (*anchoragemuseum.org; adult/child $25/12*) is a world-class facility that counts as Alaska's largest museum. The museum's flagship exhibit (2nd floor), 'Living Our Cultures, Sharing Our Heritage: The First Peoples of Alaska' beautifully displays more than 600 Alaska Native objects. Need a pick-me-up? The **Fire Island Rustic Bakeshop** (*fireislandbread.*

ANCHORAGE

HIGHLIGHTS
1. Alaska Railroad
2. Anchorage Museum

ACTIVITIES
3. Ghost Tours of Anchorage
4. Regal Air
5. Rust's Flying Service

SLEEPING
6. Aloft
7. Base Camp Anchorage Hostel
8. Copper Whale Inn
9. Historic Anchorage Hotel
10. Oscar Gill House
11. Susitna Place
12. Wildbirch Hotel

EATING
13. Fire Island Rustic Bakeshop
14. Humpy's Great Alaskan Alehouse
15. Moose's Tooth Brewpub
16. Snow City Cafe

DRINKING & NIGHTLIFE
17. Bernie's Bungalow Lounge
18. Chilkoot Charlie's
19. Crow's Nest
20. Forty-Ninth State Brewing
21. Glacier BrewHouse

TRANSPORT
22. Downtown Bicycle Rental
23. Flattop Mountain Shuttle

com), inside the trendy **K Street Market**, is a local staple doing scrumptious things with artisan baked goods, including incredible scones. For something more substantial, indulge in fine seafood at downtown favorites **Humpy's Great Alaskan Alehouse** (humpysalaska.com) or **Glacier BrewHouse** (glacierbrewhouse.com) – both do wonderful things with salmon, king crab or halibut, chased with a bounty of local brews. In the evenings, it's all about excellent craft beer, great pub food and outstanding patio views at **Forty-Ninth State Brewing** (49thstatebrewing.com).

Work off the eating and drinking on the two-hour, 11-mile **Tony Knowles Coastal Trail**, which hugs Knik Arm as it unravels

☑ TOP TIP

The **Flattop Mountain Shuttle** *($25)* travels to/from the Glen Alps trailhead for Anchorage's most climbed peak from May to early September, departing Downtown Bicycle Rental at 12:15pm, returning at 4:30pm. There are plenty of scenic views along the way.

PICTURESQUE PALMER

Born of a 1935 New Deal social experiment spearheaded by President Franklin D Roosevelt, **Palmer**, 43 miles northeast of Anchorage, saw the transplant of 203 farming refugees from the Depression-era Dust Bowl (the worst agricultural disaster in US history) to Alaska, where they would cultivate a new agriculturally driven society known as the Matanuska Colony. The so-called Valley Colonists, these transplants farmed the land and built the city, turning it into Alaska's only settlement founded on agriculture. Today, historic farming-related buildings pepper the town, juxtaposing 1930s ambience with antique furniture and wood floors plus modern restaurants and flowing craft-beer taps. It's all ringed by some of the region's most dramatic mountains.

PHOTO SPIRIT/SHUTTERSTOCK

through moose-heavy birch forest on its way to Kincaid Park. Fantastic views abound of Cook Inlet and the Alaska Range. Choose your adventure: cycle out and back for a 22-mile ride in a rental from **Downtown Bicycle Rental** *(per 3hr from $25)*; or go with **Alaska Trail Guides** *(alaskatrailguides.com; $119)*, who begin at **Kincaid Park** and leisurely soak up the scenery in the mostly descending route back to Anchorage.

Falling Up Flattop
Urban hiking, mountain views

If there's a quick way to bag your first Alaska peak, the 3-mile round-trip **Flattop Mountain Trail** to the 3510ft summit of Flattop Mountain is it. After all, this is the first peak every Anchorage kid summits, but be forewarned: this is not an easy hike (and these are kids from Alaska we're talking about!). Its namesake summit is as big as a football field, with panoramic views of Anchorage, Cook Inlet, Knik and Turnagain Arms and, on a clear day, the Alaska Range, including Denali.

The hike begins at **Glen Alps Trailhead**, 15.5 miles southeast of downtown, and begins to climb almost as soon as you leave the parking lot *($5 parking fee)*. The first section is through a wind-twisted grove of hemlock, but you soon emerge to talus

DRINKING IN ANCHORAGE: OUR PICKS

Bernie's Bungalow Lounge: See-and-be-seen venue; patio is the city's best for live music. *11am-10pm Tue-Thu, to 1:30am Fri, 3pm-1:30am Sat, 3-11pm Sun*

Crow's Nest: Cook Inlet views pair fantastically with award-winning cocktails at the top of Hotel Captain Cook. Also Anchorage's fanciest restaurant. *5-9pm Tue-Sat*

Anchorage Brewing Company: Excels at craft beer styles among giant foeders as scenic drinking backdrops. *2-9pm Mon-Thu, to 11pm Fri, noon-11pm Sat, noon-9pm Sun*

Chilkoot Charlie's: Rambling drinking den with live-music and nooks and crannies across 10 different environments. *11am-2:30am Sun-Thu, to 3am Fri & Sat*

Flattop Mountain Trail

slopes. There's a brief respite at a saddle before your final push to the summit. You'll need to scramble the last few hundred feet; the trail here is marked by spray-painted rocks.

Give yourself 90 minutes to climb the short but steep trail (you'll gain 1350ft in 1.7 miles) and an hour to get back down. Bring sturdy shoes, plenty of water and a hat and jacket. Always be wary of wildlife (moose in winter, moose and bears in summer).

The trail is closed in winter, and snow and mud can be rampant even in June, so novice and/or casual hikers should reconsider in these conditions (the easy 1.5-mile **Blueberry Loop** circles Flattop at a lower elevation and bags much of the same astonishing views).

After conquering Flattop, join everyone else at **Moose's Tooth Brewpub** *(moosestooth.net)* in Midtown for gourmet pizza and 22 taps of well-earned local beers.

All Aboard the Alaska Railway!
Historic railway, mountain scenery

Anchorage's roots as Alaska's biggest city were planted in 1914, when a hurriedly erected railway construction camp at Ship Creek roared to life to extend an existing 50-mile rail line from Seward to Fairbanks. Today, the famed all-weather **Alaska Railroad** *(alaskarailroad.com)*, inaugurated by President Warren G Harding shortly before his death in 1923, shuffles more than 400,000 passengers and 5.11 million tons of freight along 656 miles of track. From its downtown Anchorage depot, departing journeys include the **Denali Star**, heading north daily between May and September to Talkeetna *(adult/child from $123/62)*, Denali National Park *(from $199/100)* and Fairbanks *(from $285/143)*; the **Coastal Classic**, calling at Girdwood *(from $100/50)* and Seward *(from $129/65)*; and the **Glacier Discovery**, connecting Anchorage with Whittier *(from $111/56)*.

BEST ANCHORAGE TOURS

Alaska Photo Treks: Year-round, day/multiday professional photographer-led safaris frame Alaska's stunning natural beauty for budding wildlife paparazzi.

Ghost Tours of Anchorage: Ninety-minute downtown ghost tours led by local character, Rick Goodfellow, leave Tuesday to Sunday at 7:30pm from Snow City Cafe.

Mica Guides: A popular choice for a day of snow and ice on Matanuska Glacier, the largest roadside glacier in Alaska.

Rust's Flying Service: Three-hour Denali flights, including magnificent 40-mile-long Ruth Glacier *($525)*, and tours around Prince William Sound.

Regal Air: Flying from Lake Hood, Regal Air specializes in scenic flights (Denali, Knik Glacier) and backcountry bear-viewing excursions.

Beyond Anchorage

Places
Prince William Sound p1050
Kenai Peninsula p1052
Kodiak p1053

World-class fishing, unmatched glacier viewing, brown-bear ogling, historic architecture and rich Indigenous heritage characterize outposts southeast and southwest of Anchorage.

It's patently evident from any vantage point in Anchorage that the great outdoors beckons mere steps from the city. Prince William Sound clocks in at enormous 3800 miles of coastline in total, most of which is untarnished save three unique 'villages' that guard the gates to endless adventure possibilities. Kenai Peninsula is an angler's bucket-list destination for salmon and halibut and a top spot for road-accessible, stunning coastal mountain views, hikes to alpine lakes, world-class ocean kayaking and wildlife galore. Kodiak Island and Katmai National Park are home to rugged mountain peaks, old-growth forests and seemingly endless miles of untrammeled shoreline. More than anything else, however, it's the wildlife that has long captivated visitors.

Prince William Sound

TIME FROM ANCHORAGE: 1½HR TO 5HR

Glacier getaway

Both the quirky outpost of **Whittier** and Prince William Sound's most lively city, **Valdez** (both reachable by car) count glacier gawking as their main events. But don't fret about repeating experiences if you've already been chasing glaciers in one place or another – due to its mammoth size, Prince William Sound offers completely different sets of glaciers depending on your departure point.

From Whittier, founded in 1941 as an intake military base for United States soldiers deployed to Alaska, **Lazy Otter Charters** *(lazyottercharters.com)* operates out of a very pleasant cafe on the harbor and offers all the adventurous water activities you could hope for, including a grand eight-hour 'Best of Prince William Sound Cruise' *(per person $330)* that's limited to just six passengers. Depending on the weather and sea conditions, you'll take in innumerable sea lions and sea otters en route to/from a variety of astonishing tidewater glaciers such as the massive **Harvard** and **Yale Glaciers** (45 or so nautical miles from Whittier) or the smaller but no less spectacular glaciers of **Blackstone Bay**. Here, amid glacier

Blackstone Bay

slush and a smattering of vibrant-blue icebergs, the **Beloit** and **Blackstone Glaciers**, both flanked by numerous waterfalls, are absolutely staggering. And they are just the sideshow.

Valdez, a quaint and cool harbor, with excellent museums, good restaurants and outdoor adventures aplenty, offers direct access to the enormous but catastrophically retreating **Columbia Glacier**, the big daddy of Prince William Sound's glaciers and one of the world's fastest moving. The rub? Columbia is calving an unprecedented amount of ice by Alaska standards – over 8 million tons of ice daily falls from its face. While boats aim to get as close as a half-mile from Columbia's terminus, the sheer amount of ice and icebergs can sometimes prevent boats from giving passengers the up-close-and-personal look they came to Alaska to get.

Enter the second largest tidewater glacier in Alaska, the spectacular **Meares Glacier**. Due to its distance from Valdez, it's less visited than Columbia, but no less awe-inducing. In fact, the moment the boat rounds the northeastern corner of Unakwik Inlet for the grand unveiling of Meares is arguably Prince William Sound's most breath-snatching moment.

GETTING AROUND

Much of Prince William Sound and the Kenai Peninsula is a road-trip paradise, so exploring with your own wheels is highly recommended. Cordova can only be reached by **Alaska Airlines** (alaskaair.com) once daily or the **Alaska Marine Highway** (dot.alaska.gov/amhs). For Katmai, Alaska Airlines flies to King Salmon, from where a number of air-taxi companies offer the 20-minute floatplane flight to Brooks Camp. Alaska Airlines also flies to Kodiak three times daily.

EATING IN SEWARD: OUR PICKS

Chinooks: Seward's best waterfront eatery serves creative plates with local seafood and style. Try the fresh clam chowder. *4-8pm Sun-Thu, to 9pm Fri & Sat* **$$**

Ray's Waterfront: Great harbor views and delicious Alaska fare with a wide variety of seafood and non-seafood options. Retains its Alaskan vibe. *11am-9pm* **$$**

Alaska Seafood Grill: Delicious halibut fish and chips, wide variety of burgers, and pizza. Plenty of patio seating – perfect on a sunny day. *11am-8pm* **$$**

Cookery: Seward's top fine-dining destination. Reserve ahead and don't miss the local oysters and bubbly followed by whatever fresh seafood is on. *5-9pm Tue-Sat* **$$$**

CORDOVA CALLING

Isolated **Cordova** is unadulterated Alaska at its finest. With no road access, this small, eccentric fishing village has managed to starve off mass tourism – in fact, its newly adopted regenerative tourism model is best described as a 'conscious untouristing,' at least from the high-dollar, quick-fix cruise tourism that Whittier and Valdez have embraced (only five expedition-style cruise ships call here per year). Buzzwords like authenticity come to mind as a result, but without the usual ironic accompaniment. Think of the village as a choose-your-own-adventure port of call that wants its eco-altruistic tourism goals to not only benefit the local community without leaving a footprint but improve the destination as a whole.

Stan Stephens Glacier & Wildlife Cruises (*stephenscruises.com*), the biggest tour operator in town, runs wonderful and comfortable aluminum catamarans for up to 149 people to Columbia Glacier *(adult/child $170/85.50)* and 7½-hour trips *(adult/child $190/95.50)* to Meares Glacier.

Kenai Peninsula

TIME FROM ANCHORAGE: 2½HR

Dip into Seward's ocean bounty

Like much of the Kenai Peninsula, Seward is a top destination for sport and subsistence fishing for both Alaskans and visitors. Summer days here bring throngs of anglers looking for a fresh ocean catch via private or charter boat.

Start your own Seward fishing experience bright and early with the **Fish House** *(thefishhouse.net; per person $350-400)* on their salmon and halibut full-day trip. Setting out from the small boat harbor, travel up to four hours out of Resurrection Bay to the deep ocean where halibut is found. Pass by the towering fjords and keep an eye out for wildlife as you head out for this deep-sea fishing – harbor seals, whales, sea birds including adorable puffins, and Dall's porpoise are common sights out here.

Dropping lines from heavy poles into the sea, wait for a bite and then fight these monster fish onto the boat, some

EATING AROUND PRINCE WILLIAN SOUND: OUR PICKS

Nat Shack: Lines don't lie: Valdez' favorite food truck has worth-the-wait Cal-Mex street food (banh-mi crunch wrap, trust us!) and local craft beer. *noon-8pm* $

Roadside Potatohead Too: Valdez' must-stop for elevated street-food fare (black-bean corn salad breakfast wrap, pulled pork po'boys, rosemary and garlic fries). *7am-9pm* $

Wild Catch Cafe: Whittier mainstay: fantastic salmon burgers, halibut and chips, reindeer chili, decent beer, Kaladi Brothers coffee. *6am-9pm Sun-Thu, to 10pm Fri, 7am-10pm Sat* $$

Reluctant Fisherman: *The spot* in Cordova. Good burgers, fish and chips, pot roast, Copper River salmon, fusion. Fantastic views and a lively crowd. *4-9pm Fri-Wed* $$

Fish catch, Seward

weighing more than 90lb. Feel the excitement of reeling in other fish species that you're not specifically targeting, including rockfish and lingcod, before starting your return journey for salmon fishing in the bay.

Swapping equipment for lighter rods which are good for the comparatively small salmon, get ready for the fun of battle and the cry of 'fish on' around the boat as you pull in your limit of silvers before heading back to the harbor.

Kodiak

TIME FROM ANCHORAGE: 1HR

Nature and culture in downtown Kodiak

Kodiak's main sights make for pleasant downtown exploration. A great first stop is the small **Kodiak National Wildlife Refuge Visitor Center** *(fws.gov/refuge/kodiak)*, with intriguing, kid-friendly displays on the island's diverse ecosystems. The Kodiak brown bear, the most famous resident of the refuge, plays a starring role – with insight into their diet and their prevalence (the island is home to seven bears for every 10 sq miles, vs Denali with its one bear for every 12 sq miles), as well as the ongoing threats they face. See them for yourself with **Kodiak Treks** *(kodiaktreks.com; from $450)*; book way in advance!

Continued on p1056

FIVE SPECIES OF SALMON

Alaska's infamous salmon runs bring in five distinct species of salmon over the course of the summer. What type you target will depend on when the fish are running, current state restrictions and your personal preferences. **Chinook** or **king salmon** are large, fatty fish valued for their taste. They require immense patience to catch all season long. **Coho** or **silver salmon** have firm, bright orange-red meat. **Red** or **sockeye salmon** are prized for their flavor and deep red color. **Pink salmon** have a tender texture and are only open for fishing in even-numbered years. Finally, **chum** or **dog salmon** are generally not targeted for sportfishing, largely thanks to their unappealing appearance.

EATING & DRINKING IN KODIAK: OUR PICKS

Kodiak Hana: Tuck into Kodiak's best seafood at this elegant Japanese restaurant with waterfront deck seating. *11:30am-2pm & 5-9pm Tue-Thu, to 10pm Fri-Sat, 5-9pm Sun* **$$**

Nuniaq: Native and woman-owned; Kodiak-sourced seafood features in comfort dishes like rockfish tacos, salmon in bowls, melts and wraps and more. *11am-3pm* **$$**

Henry's Great Alaskan: Lively family-friendly pub with a big menu of fried seafood, sandwiches and salads. *11:30am-9pm Mon-Thu, to 9:30pm Fri-Sat, noon-8:30pm Sun* **$$**

Kodiak Island Brewing Co: Much-loved microbrewery; sample its latest ales including Liquid Sunshine, and bring your own food. *noon-8pm Sun-Wed, to 9pm Thu-Sat*

TOP EXPERIENCE

Denali National Park & Preserve

While the dominating profile of **Denali** the mountain is hard to ignore with its 20,310ft elevation, its shadow encompasses popular Denali National Park & Preserve, Alaska's most visited national park. Situated on the traditional lands of the Athabascan people, Denali's name means 'the tall one' or 'mountain-big,' reaching beyond the surrounding forests, tundra and braided rivers weaving through this pristine wilderness.

- Savage River Loop Trail
- Savage Alpine Trail
- Tundra Wilderness Tour
- Denali Natural History Tour
- Mountain Vista Loop Trail
- Murie Science & Learning Center

Get to Know the Park

Pay park admission fees, get maps, learn of ranger-led programs and wander the many exhibits about park history, wildlife and mountaineering at the **main visitor center**. Nearby, **Murie Science & Learning Center** focuses on the natural science side of Denali National Park. Ringing the entire entrance is a network of fully accessible trails winding through lush birch, aspen and spruce forests, including the **McKinley Station interpretive trail** toward Riley Creek Campground

PRACTICALITIES
- nps.gov/dena
- adult/child $15/free
- mid-May–mid-Sep (though open for winter recreation)

(note original sites for the railroad station, a hotel and other buildings from the park's early days); and **Rock Creek Trail**, which winds through a forest of birch and spruce.

Go Deeper into Denali

For those wanting to travel further and learn more about the history, flora and fauna of the park, a naturalist-led tour bus – offered between late May and early September – is a good option (fees include park entrance fees).

The five-hour **Denali Natural History Tour** *(adult/child $116.75/51)* travels from the entrance area to Primrose Ridge at Mile 15. The tour begins at the **Denali Bus Depot** with the film *Across Time and Tundra* explaining the natural history of this unique environment. Then, buses stop at the historic **Savage Cabin** to learn how the cabin was once used for housing, and how it continues to be used today by Denali's sled-dog teams and mushers. Finally, the bus will stop at **Primrose Ridge** where you will experience a memorable Alaska Native presentation that provides a background into how the First People have used this land for nearly 10,000 years.

The **Tundra Wilderness Tour** *(adult/child $144.50/64.75)* is the longest-running tour (in various forms since 1923) in the park. This is a 5½-hour trip traveling along the open sections of the Park Rd corridor, looking for wildlife and seasonal shifts in landscapes. A highlight is a stop at the **Murie Cabin** near the East Fork River (Mile 43) to experience where Adolph Murie lived while conducting his famous research inside what was then known as Mt McKinley National Park.

Hikes in the Park

For those looking to hike on maintained trails, the best bet is to drive or catch a shuttle bus to either **Mountain Vista Day Use Area** at Mile 13, or Savage River at Mile 15. **Mountain Vista Loop Trail** is a level, short (0.6-mile) trail perfect for catching a view of Denali on a clear day. The **Savage River parking area** is a trailhead for two popular hikes: the **Savage River Loop Trail** and **Savage Alpine Trail**. For the loop portion, hike along either side of Savage River through a scenic canyon, **Healy Ridge** and **Mt Margaret**. The trail winds along meadows and scrub brush for about a mile before crossing the river at a bridge (an excellent spot for photos) and continuing on the other side. The Savage Alpine Trail is tougher, traveling between **Savage River Campground** (next to Mountain Vista) at Mile 13 and the **Savage River Canyon**, traversing a high section of what's called the Outer Range. It's worth the climb, though, for the sweeping views of the valley.

DENALI STATE PARK

Most Alaska visitors pass right on by **Denali State Park** *(dnr.alaska.gov)* en route to Denali National Park further along George Parks Hwy. Don't be those people. This quiet park encompasses more than 500 sq miles (about half the size of Rhode Island). With excellent campgrounds, fabulous hiking trails and views of Denali from several locations, it's worth exploring without the crowds of the national park.

KATMAI NATIONAL PARK & PRESERVE

Katmai is famous for its salmon-trapping brown bears, epic sportfishing potential and unusual volcanic landscapes. Unconnected to the main Alaska road network and covering an area the size of Wales, a visit here, for most people, is a once-in-a-lifetime experience involving meticulous preplanning and quite a lot of cash. Nearly all park visitors fly in via floatplane to the main tourist area of Brooks Camp, 35 miles east of King Salmon. Here, they will stand spine-tinglingly close to formidable 1000lb brown bears pawing giant salmon out of the river. Beyond the bears, Katmai has an astonishing archaeological record, with evidence of humans in the Brooks River area more than 5000 years ago.

Holy Resurrection Cathedral

Continued from p1053

You can also step into the oldest Russian structure in Alaska. The **Kodiak History Museum** *(kodiakhistorymuseum.org; adult/child $10/free)* occupies Erskine House, which the Russians built in 1808 as a storehouse for precious sea-otter pelts. A short walk up Mission Rd, you'll spot the bright-blue onion domes of **Holy Resurrection Cathedral** *(oca.org/parishes/oca-ak-kodhrc)*. Established in 1794, the church serves the oldest Russian Orthodox parish in America.

Half a block further along Mission Rd, the thoughtfully designed **Alutiiq Museum** *(alutiiqmuseum.org; adult/child $10/free)* should not be missed. The Alutiiqs (not to be confused with the Aleuts) were the original inhabitants of the Kodiak archipelago and many of them remain members of the Russian Orthodox Church. Like many Native groups, their population was decimated during the 19th century, and the museum protects some precious Native heritage.

Places We Love to Stay

$ Budget $$ Midrange $$$ Top End

Juneau & the Alexander Archipelago MAP p1041

Alaskan Hotel & Bar $ With old wallpaper, creaky stairs and a rowdy downstairs bar, this 1913 penny-pincher exudes character.

Silverbow Inn $$$ This boutique inn has 16 rooms in a contemporary minimalist style, and there's a rooftop Jacuzzi.

Alaska's Capital Inn $$$ Period details mingle with modern comfort inside the gorgeously restored 1906 home of a prospector.

Juneau Hotel $$$ This handsome all-suites hotel is well equipped, each with full kitchens, washers and dryers.

Anchorage MAP p1047

Base Camp Anchorage Hostel $ Amid Midtown's action, this community-driven hostel has uncrowded dorm rooms and a wood-fired sauna.

Oscar Gill House $$ Three-room B&B occupying a historic 1913 clapboard home relocated from Knik by a former Anchorage mayor.

Susitna Place $$ View Alaska Range from this 4000-sq-ft, five-room home perched on a downtown bluff.

Copper Whale Inn $$ Ideal downtown location, elegant interiors and two relaxing waterfall courtyards at this top-choice inn.

Historic Anchorage Hotel $$$ Established one year after Anchorage itself, this distinguished, 26-room icon abounds in historic elegance.

Wildbirch Hotel $$$ In a downtown building that used to be a homeless shelter, this stylish boutique hotel has a cool bar and mid-century-modern vibes.

Aloft $$$ The brand is a bit predictable, but this 146-suite boutique hotel in Midtown is quite welcoming.

Denali National Park & Preserve p1054

K'esugi Ken $ Cabins, tent and RV sites. One of few state-park campgrounds that takes reservations and provides RV power hookups.

Byers Lake Campground $ Longtime favorite of Alaskans, with a dock for paddling access and three public-use cabins.

Carlo Creek Lodge $$ The 32-acre grounds here, nestled amidst the mountains, feature hand-hewn log cabins filled with genuine old-Alaska charm.

Denali Dome Home B&B $$ Huge, intriguing geodesic house on a 5-acre lot, offering a fantastic B&B experience with seven modern rooms (with partial antique furnishings).

Camp Denali $$$ Verging on legendary, Camp Denali has been the gold standard among Kantishna lodges for the last half-century.

Prince William Sound p1050

Keystone Hotel $ Utilitarian Valdez container hotel distinctly evocative of pipeline boom years. Clean rooms, if old-fashioned; friendly staff.

Reluctant Fisherman Inn $$$ Cordova harbor views and good bar/restaurant make up for the motel-basic rooms at this town focal point.

Best Western Valdez Harbor Inn $$$ Independently run waterfront comfort. Business-savvy rooms to Best Western standards.

Kenai Peninsula p1052

Best Western Edgewater Hotel $$$ Fabulous bay views and comfortable rooms in a chain-hotel setting.

Safari Lodge $$$ Adjacent to Seward's small-boat harbor with waterfront-facing patios for each room.

Harbor 360 Hotel $$$ Clean and comfortable with free breakfast plus a pool and hot tub – a Seward rarity.

Orca Island Cabins $$$ Private yurts in a stunning, immersive glamping setting accessed by water taxi.

Kodiak & Katmai p1053

Brooks Camp Campground $ Summer reservations open 8am, January 5 for this coveted national-park campground and fill within hours.

Channel View B&B $$ The friendly hosts have a wealth of Kodiak knowledge and both apartments have lovely water views.

Best Western Kodiak Inn $$$ The large centrally located Kodiak motel has modern rooms, a good restaurant and airport-shuttle service.

A Downtown BnB $$$ These well-equipped studio apartments in Kodiak include the use of a car (Fiat 500).

Brooks Lodge $$$ Reservations for these Katmai cabins are awarded by lottery; apply in December for the year after next.

Researched by
Sarah Etinas

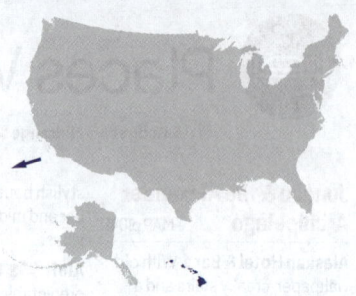

Hawai'i

ISLANDS OF ALOHA

Naturally beautiful and culturally rich, the Hawaiian Islands offer a travel experience unlike anywhere else in the US.

Most visitors to Hawai'i think of the islands as simply a tropical oasis – one with year-round warm weather, golden-sand beaches and swaying palm trees. While that may be true to some extent, there's more to the Hawaiian Islands than what fits on a postcard.

For one, there's the Native Hawaiian people and culture. Its core concept of aloha spirit – the belief that all of the kindness you give to others, the land, the world as a whole, will come back to you – is a significant reason that Hawai'i is the wonderful place that it is. It's why locals treat each other with warmth, why communities build up small businesses and why nature has continued to flourish. Let's not forget to mention the revival of Native Hawaiian cultural traditions – from hula dancing to lei making to 'Ōlelo Hawai'i (Hawaiian language) revitalization.

The many immigrant communities have done their part to make Hawai'i wonderful as well, with influences from Japan to the Philippines to Portugal. The result: a sort of multicultural haven, where potluck spreads and event calendars are about as diverse as it gets.

All of that said, Hawai'i is more than just a fantasy, of course. Native Hawaiians struggle to afford the rising costs of living, and to preserve their culture. The islands' endemic creatures are under threat from invasive species, development and climate change. There's no time like the present to behold these wonderful islands, but also to do your part in keeping it that way.

ELESSEUS/SHUTTERSTOCK

THE MAIN AREAS

O'AHU
Honolulu city life and Waikīkī beaches.
p1064

THE BIG ISLAND OF HAWAI'I
Coffee farms and active volcanoes.
p1070

MAUI
Romantic island of beaches and scenic drives. **p1075**

KAUA'I
Greenery-filled hikers' paradise. **p1079**

For places to stay in Hawai'i, see p1083

THE GUIDE

HAWAI'I

Left: Surfing, Waikīkī (1067); Above: Honolulu (p1064)

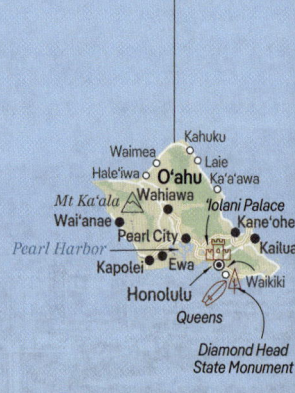

O'ahu, p1064
Home to Honolulu, Waikīkī and the North Shore, O'ahu is the most popular of Hawaiian Islands to visit.

Kaua'i, p1079
A nature lover's paradise, Kaua'i is filled with hikes, lookout points and botanical gardens that live up to the island's Garden Isle nickname.

Find Your Way

Hawai'i is composed of eight islands, six of which are visitable by the general public. O'ahu, the Big Island of Hawai'i, Maui and Kaua'i are the four main islands, while the smaller islands Lāna'i and Moloka'i round out the list.

AIRPLANE
To travel between most Hawaiian Islands, your only option (other than a cruise) is to take a plane. The only exception to this rule is the ferry between Maui and Lāna'i.

BUS
While almost all of the islands have some sort of public bus system, O'ahu's is the only one that can be reliably used to get around most of the island. It will take time, but you'll still get where you need to go.

CAR
Once you're at your island destination, a car is your best mode of transportation. It's quick, and it can get you to many spots that public transportation doesn't reach. You'll likely have to pay for overnight hotel parking, and be prepared for some traffic.

THE GUIDE

HAWAI'I

Maui, p1075
Escape to Maui for a getaway filled with scenic drives, mountaintop sunrise views and beach days.

The Big Island of Hawai'i, p1070
With active volcanoes, cascading waterfalls and sunny beaches, the Big Island's landscapes are as diverse as it gets.

Plan Your Time

While it may be tempting to hit as many islands as possible, it's best to explore fewer islands for a longer period of time.

Five Days to Travel Around

● With five days, you'll want to stick to one island, so why not opt for the most popular: O'ahu (p1064). Spend your days lounging on **Waikīkī's beaches** (p1067), watching surf competitions on the **North Shore** (p1069), and kayaking to the **Mokulua Islands** (p1069) on the Windward Side. Don't forget to make time to learn about Hawaiian history as well, with stops at **'Iolani Palace** (p1064) and **Kawaiaha'o Church** (p1066).

● Amid all the outdoor adventures and historic sites, be sure also to experience the local food scene, trying *poke* from **Off the Hook Poke Market** (p1066), *malasadas* (Portuguese-style doughnuts) from **Pipeline Bakeshop & Creamery** (p1067), and traditional Hawaiian fare from the James Beard Award–winning **Helena's Hawaiian Food** (p1066).

'Akaka Falls State Park (p1073)

Seasonal Highlights

No matter when you visit, there's always something happening – from Native Hawaiian cultural celebrations to surf competitions.

JANUARY

Cooler weather brings larger waves, making for fantastic **surfing** conditions. While certain shorelines stay calm enough for beginner surfers, others have 30ft-plus waves that are ideal for prestigious surf competitions.

FEBRUARY

Though the waves are still large in February, the whales don't mind. As a matter of fact, February is peak **whale season**, with humpbacks migrating down from the North Pacific Ocean.

APRIL

April brings lovely warm weather, relatively calm waters, and the renowned **Merrie Monarch Festival** (p1072) in Hilo, Hawai'i. This competitive hula event is a fantastic display of Native Hawaiian culture.

A Weeklong Stay

● With a weeklong stay, you have the option of adding a second island to your itinerary, and the **Big Island of Hawai'i** (p1070) is a fantastic option. Devote part of your visit to the Kona side of the island, taking tours of **Kona coffee farms** (p1071) and spending days at the golden **South Kohala beaches** (p1070).

● Then, drive across Saddle Rd over to the Hilo side, where the active volcanoes of **Hawai'i Volcanoes National Park** (p1074) are the stars. Walk through a lava tube, warm up by the steam vents and take a hike through a volcanic crater. If you have time, add an excursion to the stunning **'Akaka Falls** (p1073) or summit **Maunakea** (p1073) – the tallest mountain on earth – for unparalleled stargazing opportunities.

A Two-Week Escape

● With a two-week escape, three islands would be your best bet. **Maui** (p1075) is a fantastic option for couples and first-time visitors, with the scenic **Road to Hāna** (p1075) drive, mountaintop **Haleakalā** (p1077) sunrise views and sunny **Kā'anapali Beach** (p1077) visits.

● Alternatively, **Kaua'i** (p1079) – aptly named the Garden Isle – is ideal for nature lovers. Spend your days sailing past the gorgeous **Nā Pali Coast** (p1079) cliffs and hiking through the rust-orange **Waimea Canyon** (p1081). If you need a break from all of the blood-pumping activity, go for a lovely stroll through **Allerton Garden** (p1081) or settle in for a classic, heart-warming bowl of noodles from **Hamura Saimin** (p1082).

MAY
May 1 is May Day – or in Hawai'i, **Lei Day**. Across all of the islands, there are traditional flower-filled festivals and parades, rooted in Native Hawaiian culture. May is also an ideal time to visit, with smaller crowds before the summer rush.

JUNE
June 11 is **King Kamehameha Day**, a state holiday held in remembrance of the first ruler of the Kingdom of Hawai'i. While the largest celebration is on O'ahu, all of the major islands have events for the holiday.

JULY
The height of summer is prime time to enjoy most of the islands' ocean activities. Lather on reef-safe sunscreen, don your swimwear, and get ready for epic **swimming**, **snorkeling** and **scuba diving** opportunities.

SEPTEMBER
September is one of the few times of year when the tourist crowds abate a bit. This means that prices are more affordable, but be aware that it's one of the hottest months as well.

O'ahu

NATIVE HAWAIIAN HISTORY | SUNNY BEACHES | SURF COMPETITIONS

☑ TOP TIP

Time and again, O'ahu ranks as having some of the worst traffic in the US. Try to time your activities to avoid rush hour – essentially, don't head into Honolulu before 9am and don't try to leave between 4pm and 7pm.

Home to the famous cities of Honolulu and Waikīkī, O'ahu is the most frequently visited of all Hawaiian Islands – and it's as diverse as it is stunning. Start in Honolulu, the capital steeped in history and culture, where Chinatown eateries and Victorian-era royal buildings sit just steps away from beautiful beaches. Technically part of Honolulu, Waikīkī is by far the most world-renowned of its neighborhoods. Its name alone will have you thinking of boundless horizons, Pacific sunsets and hula dancers swaying to the beat of island rhythms. Find surfers catching beginner-friendly waves, locally owned fashion-forward boutiques, and island-inspired cocktail lounges.

But O'ahu has so much more to offer beyond its main city. The North Shore is known for its epic swells fit for the most challenging of surf competitions, while the Windward Coast – also known as the East Side – has golden-sand beaches and can't-miss kayaking adventures.

GETTING AROUND

Nothing beats having your own car on O'ahu. Hotels may have hefty parking fees, but most attractions allow you to park for free. O'ahu's public bus system, **TheBus** *(thebus.org)*, is a close second and a much more sustainable choice.

Evocative Home of Lost Royalty
Explore elegant 'Iolani Palace

No other place evokes a more poignant sense of Hawai'i's history. **'Iolani Palace** *(iolanipalace.org; adult/child from $33/15)* was built under King David Kalākaua of the Kingdom of Hawai'i in 1882. Only one year later, powerful US-influenced businessmen overthrew the kingdom. In 1895, Queen Lili'uokalani, who had succeeded her brother David to the throne, was convicted of treason and spent nine months imprisoned in her former home. Later, the palace served as the capitol of the republic, then the territory and finally the state of Hawai'i.

Today, visitors take a docent-led or self-guided tour (reserve ahead online during peak times) to see 'Iolani's restored interior, including grand re-creations of the throne room and residential quarters uph.

O'AHU

★ HIGHLIGHTS
1. Diamond Head State Monument
2. 'Iolani Palace

● SIGHTS
3. Kahuku Farms
4. Kawaiaha'o Church
5. Mokulua Islands
6. Pearl Harbor National Memorial

● ACTIVITIES
7. Kailua Beach

● SLEEPING
8. Aulani, A Disney Resort & Spa
9. Four Seasons Resort O'ahu at Ko Olina
10. Turtle Bay Resort

● EATING
11. Beach House by Roy Yamaguchi
12. Fête
13. Giovanni's Shrimp Truck
14. Helena's Hawaiian Food
15. Ken's Fresh Fish
16. Off the Hook Poke Market
17. Pig & the Lady
18. Pipeline Bakeshop & Creamery

● DRINKING & NIGHTLIFE
19. Bar Leather Apron

● ENTERTAINMENT
20. Da Hui Backdoor Shootout
21. Eddie Aikau Big Wave Invitational
22. Vans Pipe Masters

● SHOPPING
23. Cindy's Lei Shoppe
24. Fighting Eel
25. Open Sea Leather
26. Pegge Hopper Gallery
27. Roberta Oaks
28. Sig on Smith

WAIKĪKĪ'S ROYAL HISTORY

Less than 150 years ago, Waikīkī was almost entirely wetlands filled with fishponds and *lo'i kalo* (taro fields). Fed by mountain streams from the Mānoa Valley, Waikīkī (Spouting Water) was once one of O'ahu's most fertile farming areas. In 1795, Kamehameha I became the first *ali'i* (chief) to successfully unite the Hawaiian Islands under one sovereign's rule, bringing his royal court to Waikīkī. Later in the 19th century, Queen Kapi'olani had two homes here. One grander palatial estate was at the southeast end of today's Ala Wai Canal, near where her namesake park is now located. Another, more modest home was on the waterfront. She spent her days here writing poetry and working to preserve ancient forms of hula.

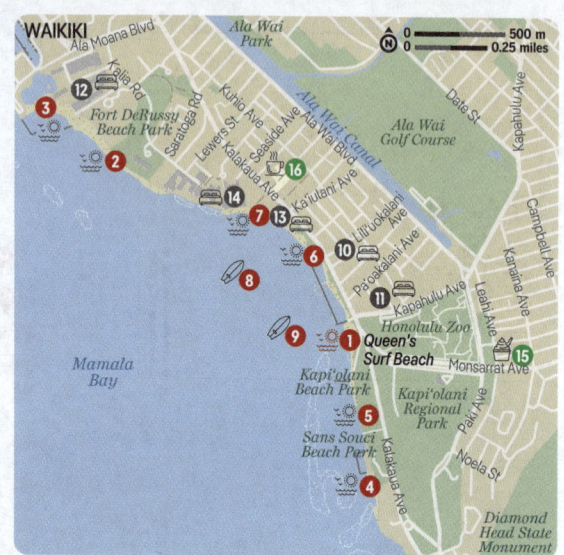

HIGHLIGHTS
1 Queen's Surf Beach

SIGHTS
2 Fort DeRussy Beach
3 Kahanamoku Beach
4 Kaimana Beach
5 Kapi'olani Beach Park
6 Kūhiō Beach Park
7 Waikīkī Beach

ACTIVITIES
8 Canoes
9 Queens

SLEEPING
10 'Alohilani Resort
11 Beach Waikiki Hostel by ALOH
12 Hilton Hawaiian Village
13 Moana Surfrider
14 Royal Hawaiian

EATING
15 Monsarrat Shave Ice

DRINKING & NIGHTLIFE
16 Kona Coffee Purveyors

Meet the 'Westminster Abbey of Hawai'i'

Admire the coral Kawaiaha'o Church

Built in 1842, this New England Gothic–style **church** (*kawaiahaochurch.com*) was made of 14,000 coral slabs and nicknamed the 'Westminster Abbey of Hawai'i.' Inspect those walls and pay your respects at the **Tomb of King Lunalilo**, the first monarch of the Kingdom of Hawai'i to be elected rather than succeed by birthright.

EATING IN HONOLULU & WAIKĪKĪ: OUR PICKS

Pig & the Lady: Modern Vietnamese restaurant, long known as one of the best eateries on O'ahu. *11:30am-2:30pm & 5:30-9:30pm Tue-Sat* **$$**

Helena's Hawaiian Food: Winner of the James Beard Award for 'America's Classics' for its traditional Hawaiian eats. *10am-7:30pm Tue-Fri* **$$**

Off the Hook Poke Market: Lines form early for superb *poke* (salad with cubed raw fish); spicy (yellowfin tuna) is sublime. *10am-6pm Mon-Sat* **$$**

Fête: The menus here are ever-changing; the seasonal island cuisine reflects the local farm-to-table scene. *11am-9pm Mon-Sat, from 4pm Sun* **$$**

The Ultimate Hawaiian Accessory
Get a lei
The tradition of lei dates back to the Polynesians, who wore garlands of everyday objects such as flowers and feathers for status, honor and beauty. While there are lei makers dotted all over the island, the most beloved vendors are found in Chinatown, including the landmark **Cindy's Lei Shoppe** *(cindysleishoppe.com)*. Here, you can watch aunties craft flower lei made of orchids, plumeria, twining maile, lantern *'ilima* (flowering ground-cover) and ginger for all occasions *(from $10)*.

Soak Up the Sun
Beach time in Waikīkī
The golden sand, sunshine and palm trees of Waikīkī's beaches have visitors dreaming of trips to the islands. While famed Waikīkī Beach steals the spotlight, there are other noteworthy shorelines in the area. At the westernmost edge lies **Kahanamoku Beach**, a large patch of sand that exists thanks to the curving breakwaters, and its neighboring (and less crowded) **Fort DeRussy Beach**. Swimmers, windsurfers, bodyboarders and board surfers all play here.

Heading east, find **Waikīkī Beach** in all its salty, sandy glory – with the expected crowds to go along with it. Nearby, **Kūhiō Beach Park** offers everything from protected swimming to outrigger canoe rides.

Queen's Surf Beach is a great place for families, with gentle waves, while next-door **Kapi'olani Beach Park**, backed by a green space of banyan trees and grassy lawns, offers a relaxing niche with none of the frenzy found on the beaches fronting the Waikīkī hotel strip. At the Diamond Head edge of Waikīkī, **Kaimana Beach** is a prime sandy triangle of oceanfront and a resident favorite.

Surf's Up!
Ride waves at Canoes and Queens
Waikīkī, where surfing began, is good for riding the waves year-round, with the largest waves rolling in during winter. Gentler summer surf breaks are best for beginners. Surfing lessons and surfboard, stand-up paddleboarding (SUP) and bodyboard rentals can be arranged at the beach concession stands.

QUEEN LILI'UOKALANI'S READING LIST

Queen Lili'uokalani of the Kingdom of Hawai'i was overthrown on January 17, 1893, in a colonial coup that still sparks outrage today. Chinatown's Native Books at Arts & Letters in conjunction with Ala Moana's Nā Mea Hawai'i has created a reading list of books they sell about this remarkable woman.

Lili'uokalani
Authored by playwright Aldyth Morris, who researched the queen's life in 1929.

Diaries of Queen Lili'uokalani of Hawai'i, 1885–1900
The queen's life in her own words, including her time in prison after the coup leaders jailed her for treason.

The Queen's Songbook
Lili'uokalani wrote music, including the iconic 'Aloha 'Oe.'

 DRINKING & DESSERTS IN HONOLULU & WAIKĪKĪ: OUR PICKS

Bar Leather Apron:	Kona Coffee Purveyors:	Monsarrat Shave Ice:	Pipeline Bakeshop & Creamery:
Old-school, casual yet elegant dark bar for Honolulu's best cocktails, crafted by wizards. *5pm-midnight Wed-Sat*	Get yourself a cup of Kona coffee and a flaky *kouign-amann* pastry from this Waikīkī coffee shop. *7am-4pm*	This hole-in-the-wall shave-ice spot stands out from the crowd with its almost jam-like natural fruit syrups. *11am-4pm* $	Kaimukī dessert shop with *malasadas* (Portuguese-style doughnuts) and ice cream. *8am-6pm Wed & Thu, 9am-7pm Fri-Sun* $

CHINATOWN'S BEST DESIGN & ART

Roberta Oaks: Namesake shop for a top Hawai'i designer known for women's wear and men's tailored shirts – aloha-print or *palaka* (plantation-style checkered).

Fighting Eel: One-stop made-in-Hawai'i shop for blowsy, draped dresses in modern solids, resort flowers and geometric prints.

Sig on Smith: Chinatown outlet for famed Hawaiian shirt designer Sig Zane of Hilo, Hawai'i. Not your polyester knock-offs – it's where you'll find the aloha wear that locals don.

Open Sea Leather: Get a new custom wallet or belt made while you wait at this stylish store and workshop.

Pegge Hopper Gallery: Distinctive prints and paintings depicting island women; good special exhibitions.

Kailua Beach

Right offshore, **Canoes** is famous and often busy with surfing classes. It's an easygoing mix of left and right breaks with a crowd from around the world enjoying long, consistent rides. **Queens** is the perfect break for beginners who've mastered Canoes. It's an all-round great wave that's a longboard dream and is usually crowded.

The Top of a Landmark

Climb Diamond Head

A dramatic backdrop for Waikīkī Beach, **Diamond Head State Monument** (dlnr.hawaii.gov/dsp/parks/oahu; adult/child $5/free) is one of the best-known landmarks in Hawai'i. Ancient Hawaiians called it Lē'ahi, and at its summit they built a *luakini*, a temple dedicated to the war god Kū and used for human sacrifices. Ever since 1825, when British sailors found calcite crystals sparkling in the sun and mistakenly thought they'd struck it rich, the sacred peak has been called Diamond Head.

Today, Diamond Head is one of O'ahu's top hikes. The 0.8-mile one-way climb to its windy summit affords fantastic 360-degree views of the southeast coast to Koko Head and the leeward coast to the Wai'anae Range. It's a fairly steep trail (you climb 560ft) but people of all ages make the hike,

EATING & DRINKING ON THE NORTH SHORE: OUR PICKS

Kahuku Farms: Working farm with a to-go food stand for goodies like locally grown acai bowls and veggie-laden paninis. *11am-4pm Thu-Mon* $

Beach House by Roy Yamaguchi: Chef-owned Turtle Bay Resort restaurant serving fancy pan-Asian food in a casual setting. *11:30am-2:30pm & 4:30-9pm* $$$

Ken's Fresh Fish: Small to-go eatery with some of the North Shore's freshest seafood; try the katsu-style ahi sandwich. *11am-4pm Tue, Wed & Fri, to 5pm Sat* $$

Giovanni's Shrimp Truck: Popular shrimp truck started in Kahuku. Its extra garlicky shrimp scampi plate is delicious, if messy. *10:30am-6:30pm* $

which takes about 90 minutes.

Watch Surf Pros at Work
North Shore surf competitions

O'ahu's North Shore has made a name for itself as one of the premier surfing destinations in the world. While you can find swells year-round, October to March typically bring the biggest waves – along with the surf competitions. Some of the most beloved North Shore surf competitions include **Vans Pipe Masters** (December), the **Da Hui Backdoor Shootout** (January) and the **Eddie Aikau Big Wave Invitational** (December to March).

Surf competitions need consistently large waves in order to take place, meaning organizers don't know if the event will actually run until that morning. The event dates you see are 'holding periods' for when the competition may occur. Check online to stay up to date.

Memories of a Nation Changed
Pay your respects at Pearl Harbor

The WWII-era rallying cry 'Remember Pearl Harbor!' once mobilized an entire nation. It was here that the surprise Japanese attack on December 7, 1941, hurtled the US into war in the Pacific. The iconic offshore shrine at the sunken USS *Arizona* is the focus of the **Pearl Harbor National Memorial** *(nps.gov/perl)* site, while the other unmissable museums and memorials – including the Battleship Missouri Memorial, the USS Oklahoma Memorial and the Pearl Harbor Aviation Museum – tell the story of the attack and the larger war.

A Kayaking Adventure
Kailua Beach to the Mokulua Islands

The **Mokulua Islands**, traditionally called Nā Mokulua and colloquially called 'the Mokes,' are a pair of islands that you can see throughout the Windward Coast – and the only way to get to them is by kayak (or paddleboard). Departing from the beautiful Kailua Beach, it's a four-hour expedition with about three hours of kayaking. Once you reach your destination, enjoy the peace while keeping an eye out for *honu* (sea turtles) and monk seals, and soaking up the views of the lush Ko'olau Mountains across the way. **Kailua Beach Adventures** *(kailuabeachadventures.com; adult/child from $179/159)* runs kayaking tours, so you can enjoy the fun without the planning.

REEF-SAFE SUNSCREEN

To help Hawai'i's marine animals live long, healthy lives, the state implemented a ban on the sale of chemical sunscreen. Studies have shown that chemical sunscreen bleaches coral reefs, disrupts fish endocrine systems and stops algae growth, among other things. Instead, use reef-safe sunscreen, particularly options from local brands like Little Hands Hawai'i, Project Reef and Mama Kuleana. This simple switch will not only continue to protect your skin, but it will also help O'ahu's marine environments survive and thrive for years to come. For a more active way to help O'ahu's marine environment, it's possible to volunteer with the nonprofit organization Mālama Maunalua to remove invasive seaweed species from the waters of Hawai'i Kai's Maunalua Bay.

The Big Island of Hawai'i

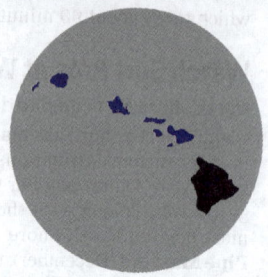

ACTIVE VOLCANOES | SUNNY BEACHES | COFFEE FARMS

☑ TOP TIP

The Big Island of Hawai'i is much larger than the rest of the Hawaiian Islands. Be prepared to do quite a bit of driving. To make the most of your time, consider splitting your trip between stays in Kona (the west side of the island) and Hilo (the east side).

GETTING AROUND

While there are taxis and rideshares, you'll want to rent your own vehicle to truly explore the best of the island. Be prepared to drive on island time (at a slower pace) to match the local flow of traffic. If a car isn't possible, the public **Hele-On Bus** *(heleonbus. hawaiicounty.gov)* system has over 20 different routes, though it's still rather limited. At the time of writing, Hele-On buses are free to ride – part of an experiment that may or may not wrap up at the end of 2025.

With 10 different climate zones, the Big Island (the island of Hawai'i) is one of the most ecologically diverse places on Earth. Roads wind through otherworldly lava fields and rolling green hills, hikes traverse dramatic valleys and tropical rainforests, and the island's rugged coastline and aquamarine waters teem with marine life. The largest and youngest in the archipelago, the Big Island is still growing. Four lava-spewing volcanoes, including the highly active Kīlauea – home of the fire goddess Pele – and Mauna Loa, the largest volcano in the world, regularly create and destroy in equal measure.

The Big Island of Hawai'i is five times the size of O'ahu but has just a fifth of the population, meaning there's room to breathe and life is notably more laid-back. Lava flows have warded off the modern development seen on nearby islands, and much of Big Island remains a beloved version of Hawai'i from the past.

A Hawai'i Beach Day

The Big Island's best sandy shores

Despite the Big Island's hundreds of miles of coastline, many of its sugary shores are concentrated in South Kohala. **Kauna'oa Beach**, more commonly known as **Maunakea Beach**, is perhaps the region's most coveted white-sand spot for lounging seaside. This curved, uncrowded shoreline is ideal for swimming, snorkeling and SUP.

The island's longest strip of white sand is found at **Hāpuna Beach State Recreation Area** *(adult/child $5/free)*. Its relaxed vibe (despite its popularity for family barbecues and birthdays) and soft stretch of shoreline makes it one of the island's best beaches.

THE BIG ISLAND OF HAWAI'I

- ⭐ **HIGHLIGHTS**
  1. Hawai'i Volcanoes National Park
  2. Kona Coffee Living History Farm
  3. Maunakea Summit Area
- 🔴 **SIGHTS**
  4. 'Akaka Falls State Park
  5. Greenwell Farms
  6. Hāpuna Beach State Recreation Area
  7. Kīlauea
  8. Kīlauea Overlook
  9. Mauna Loa
  10. Maunakea Beach
  11. Steam Vents & Steaming Bluff
- 🔴 **ACTIVITIES**
  12. Kīlauea Iki Trail
  13. Mauna Loa Observatory Trail
  14. Thurston Lava Tube
- ⚫ **SLEEPING**
  15. Dolphin Bay Hotel
  16. Fairmont Orchid
  17. Hilton Waikōloa Village
  18. My Hawaii Hostel
  19. Volcano House
- 🟢 **EATING**
  20. Hayashi's/You Make the Roll
  21. Ka'aloa's Super J's
  22. Merriman's
  23. Moon & Turtle
  24. Pine Tree Cafe
  25. Two Ladies Kitchen
- 🟢 **DRINKING & NIGHTLIFE**
  26. Big Island Coffee Roasters
  27. Ola Brew
- 🔴 **ENTERTAINMENT**
  28. Merrie Monarch Festival
- 🔵 **INFORMATION**
  29. Maunakea Visitor Information Station

Get Caffeinated

Coffee tours and tastings

With its strong, smooth flavor, Kona coffee is some of the world's best, and a trip to the Big Island would be incomplete without sampling its premier product (don't mess with the blends, though – the 100% pure Kona coffee is where it's at).

Why not dive even deeper with a Kona coffee farm visit? The **Kona Coffee Living History Farm** *(konahistorical. org; adult/child $20/free)* offers more than just an insight into

RAPID 'ŌHI'A DEATH

While hiking, you may encounter signage regarding Rapid 'Ōhi'a Death (ROD). This fungal disease grows inside *'ōhi'a lehua* trees, which are the backbone of most of the island's native forests. They protect watersheds, provide habitat and food for native birds and plants, and prevent erosion. When the fungus enters the tree, it cuts off the flow of water, and infected trees begin to die within a few days or weeks. Thousands of ROD-infected trees have been found across the Big Island, and there's no remedy or cure. To avoid spreading the fungus, don't cut branches or scrub up roots, which can allow for the fungus to enter the tree. At the trailheads' shoe-cleaning stations, brush the soil off your shoes and spray them with rubbing alcohol when provided.

Telescopes, Maunakea

coffee growing and harvesting; it's a self-guided experience of a 5.5-acre working coffee farm, complete with encounters with costumed interpreters who take visitors back in time to the farm's 1920s-era roots. Alternatively, **Greenwell Farms** *(greenwellfarms.com)*, a 150-acre, fourth-generation family farm, is one of Kona's oldest and best-known coffee plantations. On the free, hour-long guided tour, learn how coffee goes from seed to cup, with samples before and after.

Hula Masters at Work

Watch the Merrie Monarch Festival

During Easter week, the annual **Merrie Monarch Festival** *(merriemonarch.com; from $10)*, named for King David Kalākaua, is a huge hula celebration taking place in Hilo. Book tickets and accommodations months in advance.

 EATING & DRINKING ON THE BIG ISLAND'S KONA SIDE: OUR PICKS

Hayashi's/You Make the Roll: Prepare for hours-long waits at this takeout sushi spot in Kona Marketplace. *11am-4:30pm Mon-Sat* $

Ka'aloa's Super J's: Traditional Hawaiian dishes, such as *laulau* (steamed pork, chicken or fish wrapped in taro leaves). *10am-3pm Mon & Wed-Sat* $

Pine Tree Cafe: Short ribs, garlic fried chicken and *loco moco* (rice, fried egg and meat patty topped with gravy) in awe-inspiring portions. *6am-7pm* $

Merriman's: Original location of chef Peter Merriman's statewide chain of locavore eateries. Excellent Sunday brunch. Reserve for dinner. *hours vary* $$$

Maunakea above the Clouds
Atop the world's tallest mountain

Mighty **Maunakea** is the tallest point in the Hawaiian Islands, standing at 13,803ft. It's also the highest mountain on Earth – bigger than Mt Everest – when measured from base (underwater) to summit (33,476ft). This high-altitude spot offers an unforgettable, steep 4WD drive in a deeply sacred Hawaiian place.Thanks to its altitude and dry atmosphere, there's unparalleled clarity on the summit, which has become home to 13 telescopes (some controversial); working here is the pinnacle for astrophysicists. Take a tour up to the top of Maunakea to watch a celestial sunset, followed by an unparalleled stargazing experience.

Up an Active Volcano
Ascend Mauna Loa

Mauna Loa is the largest active volcano on Earth, last erupting in 2022. Its name means 'long mountain,' and it makes up half the Big Island of Hawai'i, stretching over 2035 sq miles. Even when the shield volcano isn't obscured by clouds, it's impossible to pick out the summit (13,678ft), as the gradual slope has built slowly over time from lava oozing down its flanks.

There are a few different paths to the summit, with the 6.4-mile **Mauna Loa Observatory Trail** being the easiest of the bunch – though 'easy' is relative, because it still requires climbing 2500ft in altitude. Prepare for snow at any time, and take a flashlight; it'll take longer than you think.

A Waterfall Wonder
Gape in awe at 'Akaka Falls

'Akaka Falls State Park *(dlnr.hawaii.gov/dsp/parks/hawaii; adult/child $5/free)* is home to two waterfalls – the 100ft **Kahuna Falls**, clasped by rainforest, and the epic 442ft **'Akaka Falls**, plunging into a moss-lined, emerald pool. Both cascades are accessed by an easy 0.5-mile loop through tropical flora.

ACCLIMATIZING ON MAUNAKEA

Altitude sickness is a very real risk on the summit (13,803ft) of Maunakea, especially during hard physical exertion when hiking on the volcano. It's advisable to stop at the **Visitor Information Station** *(hilo.hawaii.edu/maunakea/visitor-information/station)* to acclimatize for an hour before continuing to the summit.

Altitude sickness can be fatal and should be taken seriously. If you are short of breath, have a headache, stomachache or feel tired, clumsy or confused, head back down the mountain straight away. Don't go to the top of the mountain if you are unwell, if you have been scuba diving within the previous 24 hours, if you're pregnant or if you suffer from a medical condition.

 EATING & DRINKING ON THE BIG ISLAND'S HILO SIDE: OUR PICKS

Moon & Turtle: High-end restaurant in downtown Hilo serving up locally sourced seafood. Reservations recommended. *5:30-9pm Tue-Sat* $$$

Two Ladies Kitchen: Handmade rainbow-colored mochi with island-inspired flavors. Expect a queue out the door. *10am-4pm Tue-Sat* $

Big Island Coffee Roasters: Get your coffee fix at this farm-owned cafe. Its 'espresso bites' are made with coffee (instead of cacao) beans. *6:30am-5pm*

Ola Brew: Creative local crafts like *liliko'i* (passion fruit) lime milkshake IPA, plus hard juice, cider, tea and seltzer in a modern taproom. *hours vary*

TOP EXPERIENCE

Hawai'i Volcanoes National Park

From the otherworldly summit of the Mauna Loa to the windswept coastline where lava poured into the sea, **Hawai'i Volcanoes National Park** is a micro-continent of dripping rainforests, bizarre desertscapes, high-mountain meadows and coastal plains, with plenty of geological marvels in between. At the heart of it all is **Kīlauea** – the planet's youngest and most active shield volcano – which frequently erupted in 2025.

View of an eruption from Kīlauea Overlook

TOP TIPS

- Get an early start, especially when the volcanoes are active. The tour buses and crowds start arriving around 10am.

- Take advantage of the park's education programs, interpretive signs, ranger-led hikes and weekly lectures.

PRACTICALITIES

- nps.gov/havo
- $30 per vehicle
- open 24/7

Trails of Lava

If you can only do one day hike in the park, make it the **Kīlauea Iki Trail**, and do it counter-clockwise. The 4.5-mile loop traverses an astounding microcosm of the park, descending through ohia forests to a mile-wide, still-steaming crater that was filled by a fiery fountain that turned it into a lava lake. The 0.3-mile loop through the **Thurston Lava Tube** (aka Nāhuku Trail) starts in an ohia forest filled with birdsong, then heads underground through a gigantic (but short) lava tube.

Steamy Photo Ops

Head to the evocative **Steaming Bluff**, where curtains of steam frame the cliffs above a post-apocalyptic landscape.

An Active Volcano at Work

The **Kīlauea Overlook** is a front-row seat for one of the planet's most active volcanoes. Kīlauea and its steaming crater-within-a-crater, Halema'uma'u, have actively spewed lava for much of 2025 (and a good chunk of the last 25 years). How active the volcano will be when you visit is subject to the whims of Pele, the Hawaiian goddess of fire.

Maui

GOLDEN BEACHES | STUNNING WATERFALLS | MOUNTAIN SUNRISES

While Maui draws in all types of travelers, it's often thought of as a couples' escape. With picturesque sunrises above the clouds on Haleakalā, waterfall-filled drives along the Road to Hāna, and sunny beaches on nearly every coastline, the island certainly lives up to its romantic reputation. Amid the natural beauty, Maui also has its fair share of locally owned boutiques, multicultural restaurants and charming dessert shops.

Maui County also includes the small neighboring islands of Molokaʻi and Lānaʻi. The former could be called a taste of Hawaiʻi without the impact of tourism – the pace of life is slowed way down, development has been brought to a halt by locals, and more than 50% of residents are at least partially of Native Hawaiian descent. The latter is a luxurious escape (with two Four Seasons resorts and a billionaire owner) set within a beautiful natural setting of sunny beaches and lush pine forests.

It's about the Journey

The Road to Hāna

Drive the **Road to Hāna** *(roadtohana.com)*, a serpentine road lined with tumbling waterfalls, lush slopes, rugged coastline and serious hairpin turns. It's typically tackled in a day, with stops at waterfalls and sites along the way, and drivers then backtrack to their accommodations in the late afternoon. We recommend spending a night in Hāna so you don't have to rush: the experience is more fun if taken at a relaxed pace.

There are a dozen or so must-see stops on the Road to Hāna, from easy-access **Twin Falls** to the **Hāna Lava Tube** to Honokalani Black Sand Beach at **Waiʻānapanapa State Park**. Stagger them, so you'll have some stops to enjoy on the way there, and others on the return.

☑ TOP TIP

In Maui County – which includes the islands of Maui, Molokaʻi and Lānaʻi – you'll want to be a smidge more conscious of and courteous to the locals. Maui is still recovering from the devastating 2023 Lāhainā wildfire, while Molokaʻi and Lānaʻi are small islands that are impacted by each individual visitor's choices. When possible, buy local, drive slowly, and be kind to those you cross paths with.

GETTING AROUND

While there's a public bus system on Maui, you'll realistically need a car to get around the island. Rideshares can be an option within tourist hubs like Wailea and Kāʻanapali, but they're not ideal for long-distance journeys. If you'd like to travel to the other islands within Maui County, you'll need to take a flight (available for both Molokaʻi and Lānaʻi) or a ferry (only available for Lānaʻi).

MAUI HAWAI'I

★ HIGHLIGHTS
1. Haleakalā Summit Area
2. Kā'anapali Beach
3. 'Ohe'o Gulch

● SIGHTS
see 2 Kā'anapali Beach Walk
4. Twin Falls
5. Wai'ānapanapa State Park

● ACTIVITIES
6. Hāna Lava Tube
7. Keonehe'ehe'e Trail
see 3 Kūloa Point Trail
8. Pīpīwai Trail
9. Waihe'e Ridge Trailhead

● EATING
10. Four Seasons Maui at Wailea
11. Grand Wailea Resort Hotel & Spa
12. Hana-Maui Resort
13. Hotel Wailea
14. Hyatt Regency Maui Resort & Spa
15. Outrigger Napili Shores

● EATING
16. Kaohu Store
17. Leoda's Kitchen & Pie Shop
18. Lineage
19. Mama's Fish House
20. Sam Sato's
21. Tasaka Guri Guri
22. Tin Roof
23. Ululani's

● SLEEPING

Wander off the Beaten Path
Hike the glorious Waiheʻe Ridge Trail

For jaw-dropping views over the lush Waiheʻe Gorge, cascading waterfalls and Maui's northern tropical forests, it doesn't get much better than the moderate, 5-mile **Waiheʻe Ridge Trail**. You might even get a glimpse of Makamakaʻole Falls along the way!

Maui's Golden Sands
A day on Kāʻanapali Beach

Golden-sand beaches are a huge part of Maui's draw, and **Kāʻanapali Beach** is one of the best on the island. Scope out a prime spot for sunbathing during a dawn stroll on the hotel-lined **Kāʻanapali Beach Walk**. Surfers, bodyboarders and parasailers rip across the water, snorkelers admire the sea life, and sailboats pull up on the shore.

Watch the Heavens Awaken
Sunrise on Haleakalā

Haleakalā means 'House of the Sun,' so it's no surprise that people have been making pilgrimages up the **crater** *(nps.gov/hale; $30 per vehicle)* to watch the sunrise for hundreds of years. It's an experience that borders on the mystical. Mark Twain called it the 'sublimest spectacle' that he had ever seen. Plan to arrive at the summit an hour before the actual sunrise, guaranteeing that you'll have enough time to see the night stars fade away and pastel pinks, oranges and yellows come to light. Reservations are required for arrivals between 3am and 7am. Bring warm clothes, as temperatures hover around freezing at dawn.

A DAY TRIP TO LĀNAʻI

The tiny island of Lānaʻi has a population of just 3000 people and is a short ferry ride from Maui, making it perfect for a day trip. Start in Lānaʻi City, where you can grab a late breakfast from **Blue Ginger Cafe**, while overlooking **Dole Park**. Then, learn about the island's pineapple-filled past at the nearby **Lānaʻi Culture & Heritage Center** *(lanaichc.org)*. Consider a 4WD rental so you can do the island's top drive to the end of the sandy Keomuku Rd at **Naha**. With extra time in the afternoon, laze around and snorkel at **Hulopoʻe Beach**, where turtles and dolphins often make appearances.

 EATING & DRINKING ON MAUI: OUR PICKS

Tin Roof: Pick up a tin with *mochiko* chicken or garlic shrimp in Kahului. Owned by *Top Chef* alum Sheldon Simeon. *10am-8pm Tue-Sat* $	**Lineage:** At Wailea mall, old-school Hawaiian hospitality complements creative Asian-American dishes. *5-9pm Tue-Sat* $$	**Tasaka Guri Guri:** Century-old Kahului storefront serving flavored sherbets. *10am-4pm Mon-Sat* $	**Sam Sato's:** Get the dry *mein* (noodles) and a *teri* (teriyaki) stick, plus some *manjū* (Japanese cakes) in Wailuku. *7am-2pm Tue-Sat* $
Leoda's Kitchen & Pie Shop: Olowalu roadside bakery known for its pies. Start with a pot pie and save room for dessert options. *10am-6pm* $	**Mama's Fish House:** Celebrate a special occasion with exquisite fish, impeccable service and a beach view in Paʻia. *11am-8:45pm* $$$	**Kaohu Store:** Wailuku grocery store with excellent *poke* made in small batches with fresh fish. *6:30am-5:30pm Mon-Thu, to 6pm Fri* $	**Ululani's:** This Maui-started shave-ice shop in Kihei has mastered the perfect ice texture and fruit-based syrups. *10:30am-6:30pm* $

A DAY TRIP TO MOLOKA'I

Like Lāna'i, the island of Moloka'i is a small island that's part of greater Maui County. You'll have to fly over for a day trip to this less accessible island. Start by checking out timeless **Kaunakakai**, the largest (but still very small) town on Moloka'i, for food finds and local artist creations. Then, drive east toward the Hālawa Valley. Stop at **Mana'e Goods & Grindz** for lunch, then continue to the valley and its sensational waterfall hike, and **Hālawa Beach**. If time allows, snorkel at **Kūmimi Beach** on the way back. Last but not least, pause at **St Joseph's Church** *(damienchurchmolokai.org)* to learn about Father Damien, the first American saint.

'Ohe'o Gulch

High-Altitude Trails

Hiking Haleakalā

Stick around the Haleakalā summit for a bit longer after sunrise. There are over 30 miles of trails to explore, with the strenuous **Keonehe'ehe'e Trail** being a favorite, descending into Haleakalā crater itself, crossing through a cinder desert, and wandering through a cloud forest. The full 10.2-mile hike is recommended as a two-day excursion, but you can opt to do a fraction of the hike, turning around partway through. Keep an eye out for the rare *'āhinahina* (silversword) plant, as well as the handful of native honeycreeper bird species that make their home here.

Waterfall Vistas

Explore the Kīpahulu District

When people think of Haleakalā National Park, they usually think of the summit area. But what many fail to realize is that the park extends down the southeast slopes to the eastern shore of Maui, past the famed little town of Hāna. This area of the park is the **Kīpahulu District** *(nps.gov/hale; $30 per vehicle)*, and its crowning glory is the **'Ohe'o Gulch**, a magnificent cascade of 24 freshwater pools and interconnected waterfalls, tumbling into the ocean.

To get there, take the **Kūloa Point Trail**, a relaxing 0.5-mile loop with 80ft of elevation, to find the 'Ohe'o Gulch clearing, where you'll get an amazing view of both a waterfall and the ocean. Note that while the pools may look calm, flash floods have taken several lives here, so the Park Service does not recommend swimming in them.

If you have a little more energy, tackle the stunning 4-mile **Pīpīwai Trail** (with 800ft of elevation gain) for bamboo groves and waterfall views.

Kaua'i

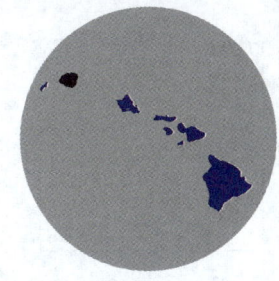

STUNNING CLIFFSIDES | IRON-RICH CANYONS | UNDERWATER ADVENTURES

One law in particular sums up the mindset of the island of Kaua'i: no building can be taller than a coconut tree. Nature is at its core, and development, while limited, still has its opportunities here. Aptly nicknamed the Garden Isle, Kaua'i feels a bit like a storybook oasis – the sea cliffs seem more precipitous, the waterfalls more thunderous and the trees a more luminous shade of green than reality would allow.

Amid the natural beauty, it's the locals that make Kaua'i such a special place. By embracing the aloha spirit, a core tenet of Native Hawaiian culture, residents extend kindness and respect to each other and to the land itself. Find them leaving trails better than they found them, frequenting local businesses and volunteering for conservation efforts, just to start. Visitors can do the same to keep the Garden Isle the stunning gem that it is.

A Jaw-Dropping Set of Cliffs
Experience the Nā Pali Coast's beauty

Pristine and hauntingly beautiful, the **Nā Pali Coast Wilderness State Park** *(dlnr.hawaii.gov/dsp/parks/kauai)* is a 16-mile stretch of soaring green-clad cliffs, white-sand beaches, turquoise coves and gushing waterfalls. While no road winds through this stark wilderness, there is the legendary **Kalalau Trail** for the first 11 miles or so, which the fittest of trekkers hike to get as far as Kalalau Valley. If a strenuous hike isn't a fit, hop on a boat or helicopter instead. The Native Hawaiian-owned **Makana Charters** and **Ali'i Kauai Air Tours & Charters** are both great options.

Wondrous Natural Trails
Hike through Kōke'e State Park

Kōke'e State Park *(dlnr.hawaii.gov/dsp/parks/kauai; adult/child $5/free)* is defined by vast canyons and thundering waterfalls, primeval forest and unique swampland. Some of the

☑ TOP TIP

Of all of the Hawaiian Islands, Kaua'i has an affinity for local businesses. You'll find vendors harvesting their own honey to sell at farmers markets, others sourcing island-inspired outfits for their charming boutiques, and quite a few opening food trucks to share their multicultural takes on food with the island.

GETTING AROUND

Like Maui, Kaua'i has a public bus system, but a rental car is the realistic way to go. While you can likely navigate tourist hot spots by rideshare, you'll still want a car of your own for the far-off landmarks like Waimea Canyon and Kōke'e State Park. Conversely, one of the island's main attractions, the Nā Pali Coast, is inaccessible by car; you'll need to go on foot, by boat or by helicopter to get a glimpse of these stunning cliffs.

KAUA'I

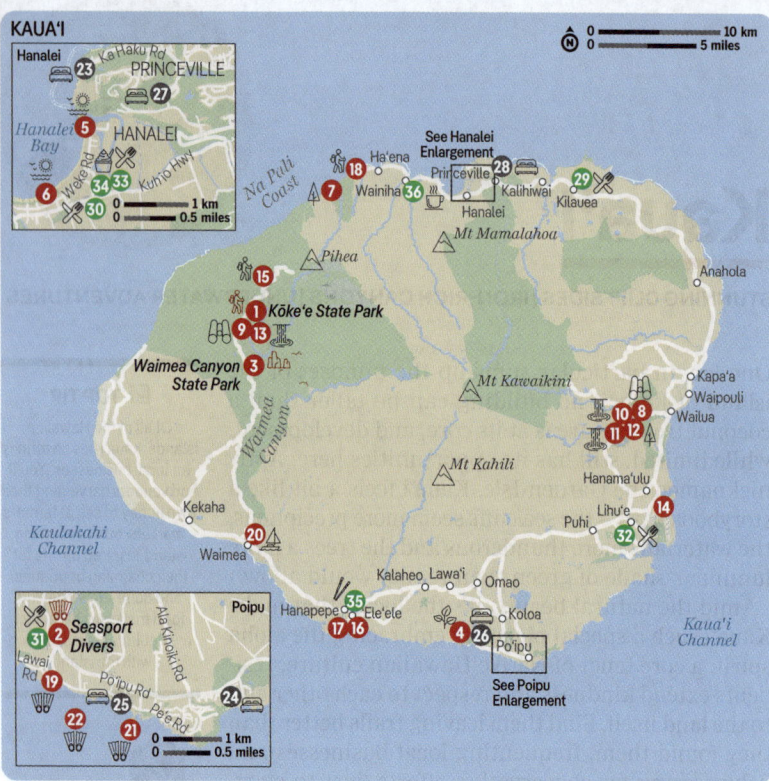

★ HIGHLIGHTS
1. Kōke'e State Park
2. Seasport Divers
3. Waimea Canyon State Park

● SIGHTS
4. Allerton Garden
5. Black Pot Beach Park (Hanalei Pier)
6. Hanalei Bay
7. Nā Pali Coast Wilderness State Park
8. 'Ōpaeka'a Falls Lookout
9. Pu'u Hinahina Lookout
10. Uluwehi Falls
11. Wailua Falls
12. Wailua River State Park
13. Waipo'o Falls

● ACTIVITIES
14. Ali'i Kauai Air Tours & Charters
15. Awa'awapuhi Trail
16. Blue Dolphin Charters
17. Holo Holo Charters
18. Kalalau Trail
19. Kōloa Landing
20. Makana Charters
21. Nukumoi Point
22. Sheraton Caverns

● SLEEPING
23. 1 Hotel Hanalei Bay
24. Grand Hyatt Kauai Resort & Spa
25. Ko'a Kea Hotel & Resort
26. Lodge at Kukui'ula
27. Makai Club Resort
28. Westin Princeville Ocean Resort Villas

● EATING
29. Avalon Gastropub
30. Bar Acuda
31. Eating House 1849
32. Hamura Saimin
33. Hanalei Dolphin
34. Holey Grail Donuts
35. Japanese Grandma

● DRINKING & NIGHTLIFE
36. Haven

island's most precious ecosystems and unusual creatures are protected here, and even a brief visit is hugely rewarding, thanks to the end-of-the-road lookouts perched atop the highest cliffs of the Nā Pali Coast.

Kōke'e is arguably the single best hiking destination in Hawai'i. If you only have time for one hike, make it the **Awa'awapuhi Trail**. Measuring 3.1 miles one-way, the hike culminates in unsurpassable vistas from the Awa'awapuhi Lookout, 2500ft above the Nā Pali Coast.

Welcome to the 'Grand Canyon of the Pacific'

Explore the Waimea Canyon

One of Kaua'i's most astounding natural features, **Waimea Canyon State Park** *(dlnr.hawaii.gov/dsp/parks/kauai; adult/child $5/free)* is a gaping abyss of lava rock stretching over 10 miles in length and plunging over 3500ft deep, all bisected by the Waimea River. While you can simply drive from one lookout point to the next, consider hitting the trails for a closer look. The 2.6-mile path to **Waipo'o Falls** via the Canyon Trail and **Pu'u Hinahina Lookout** is moderately challenging, but a crowd-pleaser, with its stunning views of the eponymous waterfall and the surrounding rust-orange canyon.

A Sun-Drenched Shoreline

Snorkel, surf and sunbathe

Venture to **Hanalei Bay** on the North Shore of Kaua'i for an unforgettable beach day. Stroll the white sandy contours of its shore surrounded by emerald mountain views, where novice surfers find their footing and kids (and kids-at-heart) leap off the **Hanalei Pier** near **Black Pot Beach**. The original, wooden pier was built in the 1890s, and was used to transport rice from Hanalei to Honolulu.

Kayak to a Waterfall

A paddle on the Wailua River

With its calm, rippling emerald waters – a color not unlike the foliage that flanks it – the regal **Wailua River State Park** *(dlnr.hawaii.gov/dsp/parks/kauai)* is not to be missed. Stretching 20 miles long from the top of Mt Wai'ale'ale, it feeds the cascades for **'Ōpaeka'a**, **Wailua** and **Uluwehi Falls** (Secret Falls) – the latter of which is only accessible via kayak. Most kayaking operators (rentals and tours) for Uluwehi Falls are found at the mouth of the Wailua River.

Stop & Smell the Flowers

The tropical oasis of Allerton Garden

You'll need to take a guided tour to visit **Allerton Garden** *(ntbg.org/gardens/allerton; adult/child from $65/32.50)*, but you'll be more than grateful for all of the flora facts your knowledgeable guide will provide. On a standard two-hour tour, explore the meticulously landscaped grounds, including the otherworldly Moreton Bay fig trees, golden bamboo groves, a pristine lagoon and bougainvillea-covered valley walls.

HIKING SAFETY

People have died hiking in Waimea Canyon and Kōke'e State Park, and it's important to prioritize safety on these trails.

Beware of rain, which creates hazardous conditions: red-dirt trails quickly become slick, and river fords rise to impassable levels.

Check the forecast before setting out, wear appropriate shoes and bring a waterproof jacket.

Don't stand near steep ledges, particularly in slippery areas.

Pack light, but carry enough water for your entire trip, especially the uphill return hike. Do not drink water from rivers or streams without treating it.

Cell phones won't work, so hike with a companion if possible, or at least tell someone your expected return time.

GETTING TO NI'IHAU

Off the West Side of Kaua'i lies the little island of Ni'ihau. Privately owned by one Native Hawaiian family since 1864, this island is closed off to visitors – for the most part. Some tours get close enough to Ni'ihau to technically snorkel in its waters, including **Holo Holo Charters** *(holoholokauaiboattours.com; adult/child $315/295)* and **Blue Dolphin Charters** *(bluedolphinkauai.com; adult/child $299/269)*, but there's only one way to step foot on Ni'ihau (that is, without a direct invitation from the owners). That's through **Niihau Helicopters** *(niihau.us; from $630)* – you'll land right on one of Ni'ihau's untouched beaches and spend the day swimming in the clear waters and maybe even seeing an endangered monk seal.

Manta ray off Kaua'i'

Diving Deeper
Scuba and SNUBA

Make the most of Hawai'i's prime ocean conditions by diving deep on Kaua'i's South Shore. Book a tour with a local company, like the Po'ipū-based **Seasport Divers** *(seasportdivers.com; from $179)*, who may take you to the best dive sites around (depending on your certification). **Sheraton Caverns** is a signature Kaua'i dive, with lava tubes and swim-thrus, sea turtles and moray eels. **Nukumoi Point** is ideal for beginners, and everything from sea turtles to Hawaiian lobsters call this area home. Finally, there's **Kōloa Landing**, the most protected shore dive on the South Coast and home to rays, octopuses, sea turtles and more.

EATING & DRINKING ON KAUA'I: OUR PICKS

Eating House 1849: In Po'ipu, renowned local restaurateur Roy Yamaguchi offers island-inspired 'plantation cuisine'. 5-9pm $$$	**Hanalei Dolphin:** At the back of the restaurant, the same company's fish market makes the best sushi and *poke* in town. 10am-6pm $$	**Japanese Grandma:** Hanapepe restaurant popular for its take on Japanese cuisine. Impeccable sushi. 3-8pm Thu-Mon $$$	**Holey Grail Donuts: Whipping** up fresh-to-order doughnuts made with Hanalei *kalo* (taro), this food truck is the talk of the town. 7am-1pm $
Hamura Saimin: Known for its brothy saimin (pan-Asian noodle dish) and *liliko'i* (passion fruit) chiffon pie. 10am-9:30pm $	**Haven:** This Wainiha hole-in-the-wall coffee shop is the place to get your morning latte, pour-over or cold brew. 6:30am-2pm	**Avalon Gastropub:** A Kilauea favorite thanks to its flavorful small plates, smoky drinks and fantastic atmosphere. 5-9pm Wed-Sat $$	**Bar Acuda:** Tapas tend to be the star of the show, but this restaurant's specialty cocktails are delicious. 5:30-9:30pm Tue-Sat $$$

Places We Love to Stay

$ Budget $$ Midrange $$$ Top End

Oʻahu
MAP p1065

Beach Waikiki Hostel by ALOH $ Guest rooms at this sociable hostel include four-, six- and eight-bed dorms plus various flavors of private rooms.

Moana Surfrider $$ Historic hotel and Westin Resort, with grand style and Hawaiian artwork hanging on the walls. The ocean-facing courtyard has a huge banyan tree.

Hilton Hawaiian Village $$ Waikīkī's largest resort hotel is practically a self-sufficient tourist fortress with 22 acres of towers, restaurants, bars, five pools and myriad franchise shops. It's geared to families.

Royal Hawaiian $$$ The original Waikīkī luxury hotel is a pink Spanish-Moorish–style landmark loaded with vintage opulence. A modern high-rise tower has sweeping ocean views.

ʻAlohilani Resort $$$ The lobby features a two-story aquarium that the hotel modestly calls the 'Oceanarium.' The pool deck is a destination itself, with a saltwater infinity pool and a kid-friendly pool.

Aulani, A Disney Resort & Spa $$$ Kid-friendly resort filled with iconic Disney characters, water slides and Polynesian-inspired rooms.

Four Seasons Resort Oʻahu at Ko Olina $$$ Luxurious resort that's popular with couples, thanks to its charming two-person rooms and adults-only amenities.

Turtle Bay Resort $$$ A locally beloved accommodations option that's known for its beachfront golfing opportunities.

The Big Island of Hawaiʻi
MAP p1071

My Hawaii Hostel $ Two miles from downtown Kailua-Kona, this simple, clean budget option offers dorms, private rooms and a friendly vibe.

Volcano House $$ Perched on the rim of Kīlauea caldera, this is the park's only hotel, with 33 spacious (if plain) rooms. Ask for a volcano view.

Hilton Waikōloa Village $$ This mega-hotel has a bit of a theme-park feel to it, with its artificial saltwater lagoons and trams.

Dolphin Bay Hotel $$ Mid-size Hilo hotel with a big aloha welcome and spotless apartment-like accommodations with kitchens.

Fairmont Orchid $$$ Elegant and almost formal (for Hawaiʻi), the Orchid never lets you forget that you're at an exclusive, luxury hotel.

Maui
MAP p1076

Outrigger Napili Shores $$ Condo units have full kitchens and beachy furnishings. Staff are accommodating, and the gazebo is on-site.

Four Seasons Maui at Wailea $$$ Rooms shine with understated elegance at this impressive getaway, the backdrop for *The White Lotus*.

Grand Wailea Resort Hotel & Spa $$$ Upscale joie de vivre alongside impressive fine art and water slides.

Hana-Maui Resort $$$ This historic resort has big cottages, gorgeous grounds and island-inspired activities. Great overnight stopping point on the Road to Hāna.

Hotel Wailea $$$ Roomy suites at this adults-only Relais & Châteaux hotel gleam with elegant but inviting beach-modern style.

Hyatt Regency Maui Resort & Spa $$$ Fresh from multimillion-dollar renovations, rooms give a nod to the islands with sleek modern style.

Kauaʻi
MAP p1080

Makai Club Resort $$ Casual resort with homey condos and cottages known for its ocean-view golf course.

Lodge at Kukuiʻula $$$ Guests stay in opulent villas and enjoy exclusive access to the over-the-top amenities, including farm-to-table restaurants and a dreamy pool complex.

Koʻa Kea Hotel & Resort $$$ A boutique oceanfront resort and spa with 121 rooms in a U-shaped design open to the beach and a central pool.

1 Hotel Hanalei Bay $$$ On the banks of Hanalei Bay, this luxury resort touts itself as a sustainable innovator in the Kauaʻi accommodations scene.

Westin Princeville Ocean Resort Villas $$$ Upscale clifftop resort with high-end villas, relaxing pools and a peaceful spa.

Grand Hyatt Kauai Resort & Spa $$$ This oceanfront resort features glamorous lounges and restaurants, and a magnificent pool complex.

TOOLKIT

The chapters in this section cover the most important topics you'll need to know about in the USA. They're full of nuts-and-bolts information and valuable insights to help you understand and navigate the USA and get the most out of your trip.

Arriving
p1086

Getting Around
p1087

Money
p1088

Accommodations
p1089

Family Travel
p1090

Health & Safe Travel
p1091

Food, Drink & Nightlife
p1092

Responsible Travel
p1094

LGBTQ+ Travelers
p1096

Accessible Travel
p1097

Nuts & Bolts
p1099

L train, Chicago (p504)
WONDERLUSTPICSTRAVEL/SHUTTERSTOCK

Arriving

The US has dozens of major airports that serve as both international and domestic gateways. You'll find the largest number of connections (and generally the most competitive prices) at the following major hubs: Atlanta (ATL), Chicago (ORD), Dallas (DFW), Houston (IAH), Los Angeles (LAX), Miami (MIA), New York (JFK), Newark (EWR), San Francisco (SFO) and Washington, DC (IAD).

Visas
Citizens of many countries are eligible for the Visa Waiver Program, which requires prior approval via Electronic System for Travel Authorization (ESTA). Fill out the online form at least 72 hours prior to departure.

ATMs
Choose wisely when selecting an ATM at the airport. It's better to go with machines linked to a bank rather than currency-exchange ATMs, which tend to charge higher fees.

Border Crossings
There are numerous border crossings with Canada and Mexico. Make sure your documents are in order, and plan your arrival carefully – avoid peak times like weekends and holidays if possible.

Wi-fi
All major airports offer free wi-fi. Elsewhere, you'll find free wi-fi at hotels and many restaurants and cafes, as well as in public libraries; some cities and towns also have free public wi-fi hot spots.

Travel to the City Center

	New York (JFK)	Los Angeles (LAX)	Miami (MIA)
TRAIN/ SUBWAY	45–90min; $12–20	45–90min; $2	30min; $2.25
BUS/ SHUTTLE	45–60min; $40	40–75min; $13	45–65min; $2.25
TAXI/ RIDESHARE	45–90min; $70–85	30–60min; $30–60	15–25min; $45–55

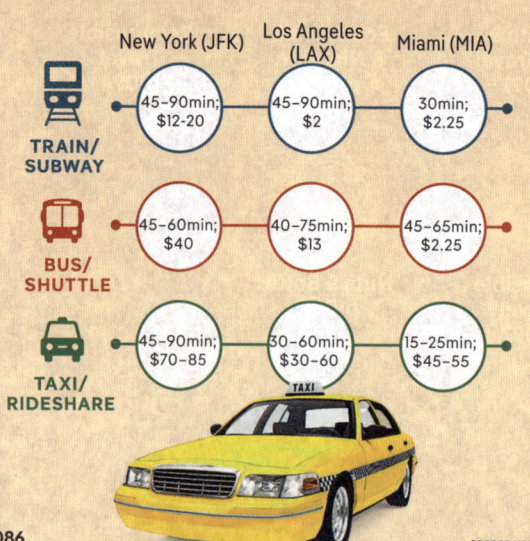

BRINGING ITEMS INTO THE US

The US has fairly strict rules regarding what you can bring into the country, so plan carefully before getting underway. In general, you're not allowed to bring any agricultural products (food, vegetables, plants etc) into the country. Bakery items and prepared foods (coffee, tea, honey) are permitted. You can bring in 1L of alcohol for personal use (but not if you're under 21). Although recreational or medical marijuana is legal in some states, it's illegal to bring marijuana and cannabis-infused products into the US. The exception is for CBD oil with less than 0.3% THC on a dry-weight basis.

CLOCKWISE FROM TOP LEFT: FUSE/GETTY IMAGES, GEORGE MDIVANIAN/EYEEM/GETTY IMAGES, NERTHUZ/SHUTTERSTOCK

Getting Around

Flights can get you to every state in the US, though the excellent highway system makes for memorable road trips. There are also trains and buses.

TRAVEL COSTS

Car rental
$40–60 per day

Gasoline
$3–5 per gallon

Bus/subway ride
$2.50–3.50

Bike rental
from $20 per half-day

Public Transportation

In large cities, you'll find good public transit networks. Most city networks now have transit apps, allowing you to purchase tickets. Key apps include MTA (New York City), Ventra (Chicago), TAP LA (Los Angeles), MBTA mTicket (Boston), SmarTrip (Washington, DC) and MuniMobile (San Francisco).

Ferry

Ferry services provide efficient, scenic links to islands off both coasts. In New England, boats are the best way to access Provincetown, Nantucket, Martha's Vineyard and Block Island. The **North Carolina Ferry System** *(ferry.ncdot.gov)* operates routes connecting the mainland with the Outer Banks. Ferries also link islands along the coast of Alaska.

TIP

Save money on parking by putting in a little extra legwork. Prices at parking lots fall significantly if you're willing to walk 10 minutes or more to the town center.

GETTING BEHIND THE WHEEL

Renting a car (or bringing your own) is the most convenient option for seeing rural areas, exploring small towns and partaking in outdoor adventures. But be prepared: traffic jams are common in built-up areas during peak hours – 7am to 9:30am and 3pm to 7pm – and all along the coast in the summer (especially on weekends).

Bus

Greyhound *(greyhound.com)* is the major long-distance company. Routes generally trace major highways and stop at larger population centers. Patience and/or a good sense of humor helps as problems sometimes arise (late buses, breakdowns, troubled fellow passengers). Other bus companies are Trailways, Megabus and FlixBus.

Train

Amtrak *(amtrak.com)* has an extensive rail system. Compared with other modes of travel in the US, trains are rarely the quickest, cheapest, timeliest or most convenient, but they turn the journey into a relaxing, social and scenic experience, especially on western routes, where double-decker trains boast spacious lounges with panoramic windows.

Air

When time is tight, book a flight. The domestic air system is extensive and reliable, with dozens of competing airlines, hundreds of airports and thousands of flights. Flying is usually (but not always) more expensive than traveling by bus, train or car, but it's the way to go when you're in a hurry. If you're after a bargain, check rates with Spirit, Frontier or Breeze Airways.

DRIVING ESSENTIALS

Drive on the right.

Speed limit is 25mph to 30mph on city roads, and 55mph to 70mph on highways and interstates.

.08

Blood alcohol limit is 0.08%.

Money

CURRENCY: US DOLLAR ($)

Credit Cards

Credit cards are widely accepted throughout the US, and required to make reservations for hotels and car rentals. Only a handful of places (mostly mom-and-pop restaurants) accept cash only. Visa and Mastercard are the most common credit cards. American Express and Discover are less widely accepted.

Tipping

Tipping is not optional. Many service workers make minimum wage and rely on tips. Tip at least $1 per drink ($2 or more for fancier cocktails). Add about 15% to fares for cabs and rideshares. At hotels and inns, $2 to $5 per day is typical for housekeeping.

ATMs

ATMs are ubiquitous in towns and cities throughout the US. Most banks charge at least $2 per withdrawal. The Cirrus and Plus systems both have extensive ATM networks.

Taxes

Taxes vary by state, but up to 10% is added to the sticker price of retail goods, prepared food and beverages. Additional taxes at hotels tack on 2% to 10.5%.

HOW MUCH FOR...

national park entry
free to $35

museum admission
$15–35

a movie ticket
$12–24

entry to a live-music club
$10–30

HOW TO... Save Money

In many parts of the US, the high prices can quickly burn through your budget. There are plenty of ways to save cash, however. Inexpensive state parks can be a great way to immerse yourself in nature, and beaches are free everywhere (though parking not so much). Many towns host free events on the first Friday or Saturday of the month, with gallery openings, music and sometimes wine.

FREE-ADMISSION DAYS

Many major cities have designated days when entrance to museums is free or reduced for visitors, potentially saving hundreds of dollars for families or keen cultural tourists. In NYC, for example, you'll find free or pay-what-you-wish admission days at top museums like the Guggenheim, Whitney and MoMA. Elsewhere, you'll find free days at major institutions like Los Angeles' LACMA, the Chicago Art Institute and Boston's Museum of Fine Arts. The national parks also offer free admission on six days of the year.

MOBILE PAYMENTS

Many shops, cafes and restaurants – and some transit systems – accept mobile payments such as Apple Pay and Google Pay, allowing you to pay with a tap of your phone.

Accommodations

Save Money in a Motel

Motels, located along main roads, at interstate highway exits or on the outskirts of towns and cities, range from dowdy 10-room places to more stylish abodes. Motels offer standard accommodations: a room with a private entrance, bathroom, TV, heating and air-con. Some have small refrigerators, and many provide a simple breakfast at no extra charge.

Stay in a B&B

Intimate, family-run guesthouses are often contained in historic or architecturally interesting homes. Accommodations and amenities can vary widely, from the very simple and rustic to the luxurious (and prices vary accordingly). Many B&Bs require a minimum stay of two or three nights during high season, and some places do not welcome children under a certain age.

Camp under the Stars

Available at private, state and national park campsites. The most basic have bathing facilities and electricity/water hookups, while some have pools, beaches and family activities. Most campsites open from mid-May to mid-October (with longer seasons in the south). If you prefer not to rough it, you'll find lots of glamping options, with safari-style tents, comfy beds and wilderness views.

Hotels & Resorts

Hotels, mostly found in cities, are generally large and full of amenities. Boutique hotels tend to have smaller footprints and lean toward the understatedly lavish. Resorts usually offer a wide variety of guest activities, such as skiing and water sports. Prices range from $200 upwards per night, though low-season discounts can bring substantial savings.

HOW MUCH FOR A NIGHT IN…

- a B&B **$150–300**
- a campsite **$20–60**
- a motel **$85–200**

Hostels

Budget-friendly hostels are disappearing from the US, but you'll still find several hundred of them scattered across the country, including in NYC, Chicago, Miami, New Orleans and San Francisco. As elsewhere in the world, the big draw (apart from saving money in shared dormitories) is meeting other travelers, and many places organize inexpensive activities – dinners, bar-hopping and walking tours.

RENTALS & AIRBNB

Across the US, you'll find thousands of vacation rentals for short- and long-term stays. Companies like Airbnb and Vrbo make it easy to find unique places to stay across the 50 states. Not everyone is thrilled with the ever-growing expansion of homestays, which has only exacerbated the housing crisis. Locals cite the rise in housing prices and lack of affordable rentals as more properties are taken off the market to become Airbnbs. There's also the negative effect on communities as long-term residents are displaced by transients.

Family Travel

Oceanside action, woodland walks, horseback riding and deliriously fun theme parks are all part of the allure of travel in the USA. You can get a nature fix in the mountains, within the rolling forests and on the seashore, or opt for a more urban itinerary. There are countless kid-friendly attractions in big and small cities all across the country.

Fun by the Water

Pencil in some water activities to keep everyone cool. The US has spectacular beaches on three coastlines, and there's never a bad season to visit (hit Florida in the winter and northern beaches in the summer). If you're not near the coast, don't despair: you can cool off at creeks, streams, lakes and waterfalls, which you'll find sprinkled across the nation.

Essentials for Babies

Urban areas are great for strollers, but if you plan on enjoying the great outdoors, child carriers are definitely a better option. Some attractions offer rental strollers. Diapers and other essentials are available in supermarkets and drugstores (some open 24 hours), while organics and specialty items can be found at higher-end supermarkets. Bathrooms with changing facilities are common, as are family bathrooms.

Car-Seat Laws

Laws vary between states, but in general children up to three years require federally approved car seats (rear-facing until one year or 20lb). Kids aged four to five need booster seats; those under 13 must travel in the back seat.

Discounts

Children's discounts are available for everything from museum admission to movie tickets. The definition of a 'child' varies but usually means kids under 12 years old (kids under two often go for free). Many restaurants offer less expensive children's menus.

BEST ATTRACTIONS FOR FAMILIES

Orlando theme parks, Florida (p472)

Disney, Universal, SeaWorld, LEGOLAND... all fail-safe hits with the kids.

Omaha's Henry Doorly Zoo & Aquarium (p626)

Explore rainforest and desert wildlife in one of America's best zoos.

Yosemite National Park, California (p928)

Epic Sierra Nevada scenery: gushing waterfalls, alpine lakes, glacier-carved peaks.

Field Museum, Chicago (p514)

Check out SUE, the largest and most complete fossilized T-Rex ever found.

Yellowstone National Park, Wyoming (p758)

See erupting geysers, bubbling mud pools and massive bison.

BE A JUNIOR RANGER

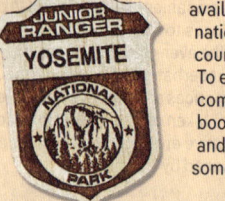

Kids can earn a cool badge through the Junior Ranger Program, available at numerous national park sites and countless state parks. To earn the badge, kids complete an activity book with questions and games, and for some parks complete an activity (such as a hike, while making observations along the way). The program is aimed at five- to 12-year-olds. Some parks have a range of activities for younger vs older kids, as well as specialties like nighttime stargazing, paleontology or sound exploration. Adults can enjoy it, too, and everyone is likely to gain a deeper understanding of the environment.

Health & Safe Travel

INSURANCE

Travel insurance to cover theft, loss and medical issues is essential, especially for international visitors. Domestic visitors should confirm they have proper coverage. Some policies don't cover 'risky' activities such as scuba diving, riding a motorcycle and skiing, so read the fine print.

Heat Dangers

During the summer (and even earlier in the south), when midday temperatures can soar, you'll need to prepare for the heat. Carry plenty of water to avoid dehydration, wear a wide-brimmed hat and use sunscreen. If you're out hiking or biking, know your limits: strenuous activity can lead to heat exhaustion.

Lyme Disease

Ticks can be present in many woodlands, so you'll want to check yourself carefully after visiting the park. Since some ticks can carry Lyme disease – an increasing concern in the Northeast and Upper Midwest – try to avoid them if possible. Using DEET repellent and wearing appropriate clothing (such as long pants and a hat) will minimize the risks.

POISON IVY

If you come into contact with poison ivy, wash the area within 30 minutes with soap and water.

OCEAN SAFETY

Green Flag Calm conditions – exercise caution

Yellow Flag Waters might be rough – use extreme caution

Red Flag Hazardous conditions – high surf or strong current

Double Red Flag Danger: do not enter the water

Purple and Blue Flags Dangerous marine life (sharks, jellyfish) spotted

Hurricanes & Wildfires

Hurricanes can strike the Gulf and Atlantic coasts from June until November. The most active period tends to be in August and September, when powerful winds and heavy rains can cause devastation. If you're in the path of a storm, be sure to follow all official directives. June to November are also peak months for wildfires out west (especially California). Stay weather-aware.

THOUSANDS WITHOUT HOMES

Despite billions spent annually to combat the country's homelessness crisis, the number of people living on the streets keeps inexorably growing. You'll see unhoused people – the current descriptor of choice – in large cities and small towns, living in tents, under tarps, in battered RVs etc. Solving the causes, which include housing costs, mental health and substance-abuse problems, is an elusive goal.

Food, Drink & Nightlife

When to Eat

Breakfast (7am to 10am, later on weekends) Order pancakes and eggs at a diner or head to a cafe for pastries, sandwiches and coffees.

Lunch (noon to 2pm) Anything from pork tacos off a food truck to veggie bowls or barbecue at a food hall.

Dinner (5pm to 9pm) Prime time for tucking into oysters, fresh-off-the-boat seafood and farm-to-table cooking.

Where to Eat

Cafes and bakeries Open during daytime, cafes are good for casual meals, sweet treats or coffee.

Food halls Typically six or more vendors offer a variety of diverse cuisines.

Food trucks Kitchen on wheels, parked where hungry pedestrians are found and often at breweries.

Crab, clam or lobster shacks Informal eateries along the East Coast serving simply prepared seafood.

Bars and pubs Many drinking establishments also serve food, from basic bar food to more innovative dishes (at gastropubs).

MENU DECODER

Entrée Always confusing to non-Americans – the word for the main course.

Oysters Normally served raw on the half-shell. You might also spot them chargrilled (drizzled with butter, garlic, herbs and cheese).

Lobster roll Lobster meat, usually with a touch of mayo, is served on a lightly toasted roll.

À la carte Choose anything from the menu; a side often must be ordered in addition to the main dishes.

Blue plate Special of the day in a diner.

Po'boy Large sandwich made on French bread and stuffed with a variety of fillings.

Brisket Beef that's been slow-cooked for hours over a low-heat fire.

Grits Popular in the south, this dish of ground corn cooked to a cereal-like consistency is often served with butter or melted cheese.

HOW TO... Order Barbecue

Ordering at a barbecue counter is fairly straightforward, but first-time visitors might feel lost with the variety of choices. Popular restaurants typically have a posted menu with some kind of notes on what is already sold out.

Take your pick among the variety of meats on display, sometimes priced by weight, which are immediately cut and weighed in front of you. Most adults will want from a third to half of a pound of meat. Ideally, get a group together to order family-style and try a little of everything.

Next come the side dishes, often displayed buffet-style, making it easy to point and choose whatever looks most promising. They're normally served in a range of sizes: individual, pint and quart.

Pay up, then pick a seat. Many restaurants use shared tables, so don't be afraid to plop down next to a stranger if you need to. They won't bite.

FROM LEFT: NATALIA LISOVSKAYA/SHUTTERSTOCK, NEW AFRICA/SHUTTERSTOCK

HOW MUCH FOR A...

breakfast in a diner
from $12

pizza slice
$3-6

taco
$2.50-4.50

small cappuccino
$5

pint of craft beer
$6-10

lobster roll
from $28

craft cocktail
$12-20

barbecue meal
$15-35

HOW TO... Eat Lobster

Whether sitting in an award-winning restaurant in Boston or ponying up to a seafood shack in Downeast Maine, lobster plays a starring role on many top menus, especially in New England. If you've never partaken, navigating a meal with a whole crustacean might seem daunting, but it's actually fairly straightforward once you know the basics. The most traditional method of preparation is simply boiling the crustacean and serving it up whole, with clarified butter for dipping the piping-hot meat into.

First off, make sure they gave you all the equipment you need: a claw cracker and a tiny fork for extracting difficult-to-reach meat. If you've received a bib, now's the time to put it on. You're about to get messy. Now, pick up the lobster, and break off the tail. Use a knife to cut lengthwise down the tail's underside. Remove the whole piece of tail meat (discarding the dark, vein-like thread, which is the digestive tract). The tail is one of the most delectable parts of the lobster. Dunk it in butter and indulge.

Next, move on to the claws. Use your cracker to break the shell, then pull out the meat with the fork. Dunk, enjoy. You can also crack open the legs, but there's not much meat in them.

Apart from whole lobster, there's also lobster bisque, a creamy soup featuring lobster meat and a rich stock that's made from the lobster shells.

Lobsters 101

Fisherfolk in the US harvest some 140 million pounds of lobster each year, with an at-the-docks value of over $900 million. It takes around five 1lb lobsters to make 1lb of lobster meat.

WHAT MAKES A NEW YORK BAGEL SPECIAL

The bagel may be the most iconic New York food of them all. Crispy on the outside and chewy on the inside, New York bagels are unlike any other in the world. Before they're baked, New York bagels are submerged in boiling tap water that's been mixed with barley malt. This process is what gives them their crisp exteriors and chewy interiors. They can be topped with sesame seeds, poppy seeds or everything seasoning; eating just half a bagel can make you feel like you've eaten an entire meal. Bagels became a New York staple in the 1930s. Local Jewish communities would cut them in half, smear them with cream cheese and layer on lox to create a kosher substitute for eggs Benedict. This is where the term 'schmear,' which you'll see on most bagel-shop menus, comes from. Back then, a schmear was a thin layer of cream cheese. Plus, you'll now it's not uncommon to unwrap a bagel that's been stuffed with 3oz or 4oz of cream cheese. And even bagels themselves have gotten larger over the years, now coming in at an average of 6oz or 7oz.

Nowadays, you'll find bagel shops well beyond the boundaries of New York. There are well-loved New York-style bagels in every major city and even in some rural areas (places like Native Bagel Company in Berea, Kentucky, have an avid following). The best plan is to go early. Bagels are considered a breakfast food and some shops close by 2pm.

Responsible Travel

Climate Change & Travel

It's impossible to ignore the impact we have when traveling; Lonely Planet urges all travelers to engage with their travel carbon footprint, which will mainly come from air travel. While there often isn't an alternative, travelers can look to minimize the number of flights they take, opt for newer aircrafts and use cleaner ground transportation, such as trains. One proposed solution – purchasing carbon offsets – unfortunately does not cancel out the impact of individual flights. While most destinations will depend on air travel for the foreseeable future, for now, pursuing ground-based travel where possible is the best course of action.

The **UN Carbon Offset Calculator** shows how flying impacts a household's emissions:

The **ICAO's carbon emissions calculator** allows visitors to analyse the CO^2 generated by point-to-point journeys:

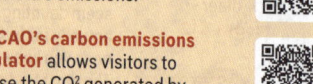

Cycle the Sights

Skip the noisy double-decker buses and rent a bicycle instead. Most cities have a good network of bike lanes and some towns are well connected to nature trails on former rail lines (*railstotrails.org*).

Travel by Train

Instead of flying, take Amtrak. Travel on the California Zephyr from San Francisco to Chicago over the Rocky Mountains, or traverse the northeast from Washington, DC to Burlington, Vermont aboard the Vermonter.

RESPECT THE WILDLIFE

Stay at least 50yd away from all wildlife in national parks. Never approach an animal, and if your presence changes the animal's behavior in any way, you're too close. Feeding wildlife is prohibited.

Nearly all the big cities in the US have extensive public transit networks. But even smaller places like Aspen (Colorado), Madison (Wisconsin) and Burlington (Vermont) have reliable transit, and it can be a pleasant way to see the city.

Going strong since 1995, the nonprofit **Seafood Watch** (*seafoodwatch.org*) publishes guides that list sustainably harvested seafood. Download the guide to the Northeast and bring it with you.

TIP STREET PERFORMERS

Whether performing on the street or playing in a bar or restaurant, musicians are the lifeblood of many cities. Show your appreciation with a tip in cash or through an app.

Go Electric
If you're renting a car during your stay, consider going electric. You'll find EV charging stations at a growing number of places, including hotels, grocery stores and campgrounds. Find the nearest one at *chargehub.com*.

Get Thrifty
Go secondhand shopping at flea markets, thrift stores and vintage shops. Every city, and even small towns, has secondhand stores packed with treasures waiting to be discovered.

Sleep under the Stars
Camping is a great way to go green while also immersing yourself in nature. You'll find many enchanting settings for pitching a tent, plus glamping spots for a dose of the outdoors without roughing it.

Green Adventures
Consider taking a low-impact tour in the wetlands rather than a mortorboat or an airboat excursion. Kayaking and canoeing are more immersive, with fewer crowds and more opportunities to experience the plant and animal life.

Buy Picnic Fare at a Farmers Market
You'll find farmers markets all across the US, with locally made cheeses, breads and other goodies along with seasonal temptations including berries and foraged mushrooms. Most markets are held on Saturday morning.

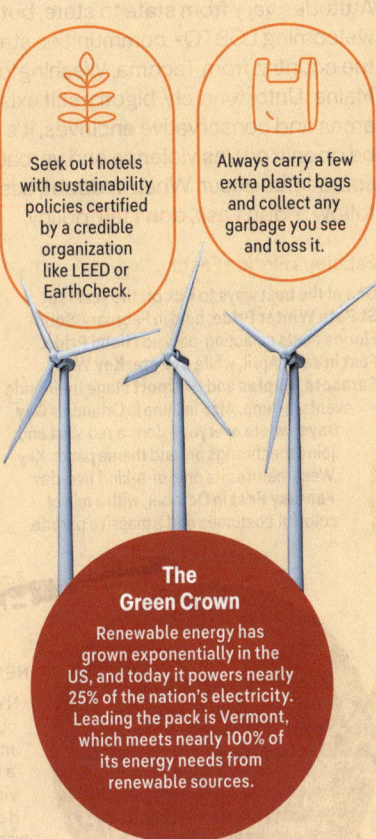

Seek out hotels with sustainability policies certified by a credible organization like LEED or EarthCheck.

Always carry a few extra plastic bags and collect any garbage you see and toss it.

The Green Crown
Renewable energy has grown exponentially in the US, and today it powers nearly 25% of the nation's electricity. Leading the pack is Vermont, which meets nearly 100% of its energy needs from renewable sources.

TOOLKIT RESPONSIBLE TRAVEL

RESOURCES

happycow.net
Vegetarian and vegan restaurants across the country.

environmentamerica.org
A citizen-based environmental advocacy organization.

thedyrt.com
Top campsites across the country.

CLOCKWISE FROM TOP LEFT: PHILIP PILOSIAN/SHUTTERSTOCK, AKRII_SS/SHUTTERSTOCK, DARIA RYBAKOVA/SHUTTERSTOCK, KRASOWIT/SHUTTERSTOCK, NEW AFRICA/SHUTTERSTOCK, YZ VECTOR/SHUTTERSTOCK

LGBTQ+ Travelers

Attitudes vary from state to state, but prominent, welcoming LGBTQ+ communities stretch all across the country, from Tacoma, Washington to Ogunquit, Maine. Unfortunately, bigotry still exists. In rural areas and conservative enclaves, it's unwise to be openly out, as violence and verbal abuse can sometimes occur. When in doubt, assume locals follow a 'don't ask, don't tell' policy.

Fabulous Florida Fests

One of the best ways to kick off the year is at **St Pete Winter Pride**, held in February. South Florida hosts an action-packed **Miami Pride Fest** in early April, while **St Pete**, **Key West**, **Sarasota**, **Naples** and **Gulfport** stage their Pride events in June. Also in June is Orlando's **Gay Days**, where everyone dons a red shirt and joins the throngs around theme parks. Key West features its one-of-a-kind five-day **Fantasy Fest** in October, with a mix of colorful costumes and a massive parade.

CALIFORNIA QUEER HAVENS

Many places in California are queer-friendly but the following are at another level. San Francisco's **Castro District**, the center of everything; **West Hollywood** and its extraordinary nightlife; **Guerneville** for summer escapes amid the redwoods; **Santa Cruz**, where lesbians could be open in the 1970s; and **Palm Springs**, with languid days spent by the pool. In March, head to the Sierra, for **Mammoth Gay Ski Week**.

New Orleans Nights

Bourbon St near St Anne marks the beginning of the so-called **Lavender Line**, with a dense concentration of LGBTQ bars, lounges and nightclubs. If you're up for a wild party, visit during **Southern Decadence** (early September) with its mix of street parties and club nights.

NEW YORK NEIGHBORHOODS

NYC is home to several gay neighborhoods. Hang out in **Greenwich Village**, where the gay liberation movement began (the still open Stonewall Inn is a National Historic Landmark). Dine at **Chelsea**'s vibrant restaurants. Eat and drink your way across **Hell's Kitchen**. Have a nightcap in **Astoria**, or wander through **Brooklyn Heights**, a historic hub of the New York gay community since the 1920s.

RESOURCES

Advocate *(advocate.com/travel)* News, LGBTQ travel features and destination guides.
Damron *(damron.com)* Long-running, advertiser-driven gay travel guides and app.
LGBT National Help Center *(lgbthotline.org)* Counseling, information and referrals for people of all ages; special resources for youths.
Out Traveler *(outtraveler.com)* Free online magazine articles with travel tips, guides and resort reviews.

Gay Stays

The lodging website and app **Misterb&b** *(misterbandb.com)* lists gay-friendly hotels, apartments, private rooms and vacation homes for rent. There are numerous options all across the country, and hosts are well vetted to ensure all visitors are welcome.

Accessible Travel

If you have a physical disability, the USA can be an accommodating place, though you'll need to plan your travels carefully. Bigger cities are generally more accessible, though you'll also find accessible beaches, state and national parks and other attractions sprinkled across the country.

Beach Accessibility

Among other states, Florida and California each have over 100 beaches with free or rentable wheelchairs designed for use on the sand. Find these beaches at *coastal.ca.gov/access/beach-wheelchairs.html* and *visitflorida.com/travel-ideas/articles/wheelchair-accessible-beaches*.

Airport

Most US airports provide barrier-free paths and accessible services throughout their terminals, including guided mobility assistance at designated locations. If a wheelchair is required upon arrival, be sure to request it in advance through your airline.

Accommodations

Hotels built since 1993 must meet modern accessibility requirements. Major chains usually have rooms adapted for accessibility needs, but book in advance and double-check they have what you require. Holiday rentals and older properties may not be accessible.

Disability Pride

Keep an eye out for special events in July, during Disability Pride Month. Events in LA, NYC, Washington (DC), Chicago and many other places host parades and other events.

Accessible Public Transit

In cities, many public buses are accessible thanks to 'kneeling' buses and automated ramps. Trains, including Amtrak, are generally accessible. Metro/underground systems are a mixed bag, ranging from excellent (Washington, DC) to poor (NYC).

BROADWAY & BEYOND

Dozens of Broadway theaters offer accessibility options including wheelchair seating, assistive listening devices, sign language and closed captioning. Many theaters elsewhere, including Chicago, Boston, Los Angeles, Philadelphia and DC are similarly accessible.

RESOURCES

AccessibleGO *(accessiblego.com)* Provides accessibility details and community reviews for hotels, flights and more.

Society for Accessible Tourism & Hospitality *(sath.org)* Brings together organizations serving travelers with disabilities; tons of helpful travel tips and access info.

Handiscover *(handiscover.com)* Useful for booking accessible accommodations.

Be My Eyes *(bemyeyes.com)* Excellent app that helps blind and vision-impaired travelers navigate their environment through AI and live video.

Hidden Disabilities Sunflower Program

Those who want to share that they have a non-visible disability should check out the **Hidden Disabilities Sunflower Program** *(hdsunflower.com/us)*. Users wear a sunflower-emblazoned lanyard, which alerts airports and other places that they need extra help.

New Year's celebrations, Washington DC (p242)

Nuts & Bolts

OPENING HOURS

The following is a general guideline for opening hours. Shorter hours may apply during low seasons, when some venues close completely.

Banks and offices 9am to 5pm Monday to Friday; sometimes 9am to noon Saturday

Bars and pubs 4pm to midnight, some until 2am (4am in places like NYC)

Restaurants Breakfast 7am to 10am, lunch 11am to 2:30pm, dinner 5pm to 10pm

Shops 9am to 7pm Monday to Saturday; some open noon to 5pm Sunday, or until evening in tourist areas

Weights & Measures

The US uses the imperial system, with mountain heights measured in feet (0.3m) and road distances in miles (1.6km). Weights are measured in pounds (0.45kg) and gasoline is sold by the gallon (3.8L).

Toilets

Look for free public restrooms inside shopping malls, public buildings, libraries, gas stations and some transportation hubs, as well as some parks and beaches.

Internet

Many hotels, restaurants and cafes offer free wi-fi. Some cities and towns have free public wi-fi hot spots.

GOOD TO KNOW

Time zones
Continental USA has four: California (GMT/UTC -7hr) is three hours behind NYC (GMT/UTC -4hr).

Country calling code
+1

Emergency number
911

Population
342 million

Electricity
Type A and B; 120V/60Hz

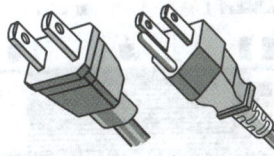

PUBLIC HOLIDAYS

On the following holidays, banks, schools and government offices (including post offices) are closed, and transportation, museums and other services may operate on a Sunday schedule. Holidays falling on a weekend are usually observed the following Monday.

New Year's Day January 1

Martin Luther King Jr Day Third Monday of January

Presidents' Day Third Monday of February

Memorial Day Last Monday of May

Independence Day July 4

Labor Day First Monday of September

Indigenous Peoples' Day (Columbus Day) Second Monday of October

Veterans' Day November 11

Thanksgiving Fourth Thursday of November

Christmas Day December 25

STORYBOOK

THE USA
STORYBOOK

Our writers delve deep into different aspects of The USA life

A History of the USA in 15 places

The story of the US features cliff dwellers, immigrants, warring states and a people in bondage.
Regis St Louis
p1102

Meet the Americans

A collection of diverse communities, peoples and views, the USA feels like many countries woven into one.
Regis St Louis
p1106

The Birth of America's Vacation

How stories about the Adirondacks became a prototype for the modern guidebook.
John Garry
p1108

Riding the Rails Through the USA

Think train travel is a thing of the past in the United States? Think again.
Lauren Keith
p1110

The Games That Bind Us

From football and baseball, nothing fires up Americans like their favorite sports team.
Karla Zimmerman
p1112

Statue of Liberty, Liberty Island (p72)
DIMASID/SHUTTERSTOCK

A HISTORY OF THE USA IN 15 PLACES

The story of the US spans centuries, and features mysterious cliff dwellers, hopeful immigrants, warring states and a people in bondage who helped build a nation. It's a history that's still being written, as communities grapple with the intractable problems of today, including the high cost of living and the grave threats of climate change.

MORE THAN 570 Native tribes called this land home before 15th-century explorers set foot on a continent later called America. The legacy of those with ancestral ties to the forests, plains and mountains lives on across the country, from the hidden canyon rims of Mesa Verde to the towering earthworks in the Mississippi Valley. They were followed by waves of new arrivals who left their own mark on the landscape, beginning with the primitive village of Plimoth and culminating in the planting of great cities on the edge of rivers, lakes and oceans.

As every American student (and *Hamilton* fan) can tell you, July 4, 1776, brought independence to the upstart colony. But it wasn't until much later that Thomas Jefferson's famous words 'All men are created equal' were actually realized, thanks to the courageous efforts of Civil Rights leaders like Martin Luther King Jr and Rosa Parks. They are a reminder that while conflict is woven into this nation, the US is also a place of extraordinary possibility. It's where millions of immigrants have sought a better life, and its diverse cultures have given the world everything from blues ballads to Cinderella castles, along with egalitarian ideas like creating national parks for all to enjoy.

1. Mesa Verde National Park
ANCIENT CLIFF DWELLERS

Ancestral Puebloans first arrived to the Mesa Verde area around 550 CE. Initially, they inhabited pit houses dug into the ground on the tops of mesas, but around 1000 CE, they began building multistory houses of carved stone. Elaborate in scope, these ranged in size from one-room dwellings to expansive villages of more than 150 rooms, and up to 5000 people lived in the community during its peak. Around the year 1300, after living for more than 700 years here, the cliff dwellers mysteriously abandoned their mesa homes and migrated elsewhere for reasons still unknown to archaeologists.

For more on Mesa Verde National Park, see p741.

2. Plimoth Patuxet Museums
PILGRIMS AND THE WAMPANOAG

In 1620, the *Mayflower* made landfall. It was the first of four ships bearing a group of religious dissidents from England who would create a new life in this unknown land. A painstakingly recreated village sheds light on the struggles of this fledgling colony – over half of the original 102 would die from cold and disease that first winter. The Native Wampanoag are also a big part of the story – indeed, without them, probably none of the pilgrims would have survived. Traditional huts, dugout canoes and historically accurate crops illustrate what life was like for Indigenous people in the early 17th century.

For more on the Plimoth Patuxet Museums, see p183.

3. Freedom Trail
THE ROAD TO INDEPENDENCE

In 1770, British soldiers opened fire on a group of protesting colonists outside Boston's Custom House. In 1773, colonial patriots hatched a plan inside the Old South Meeting House to sneak onto English merchant ships and dump its cargo in what would later be called the Boston Tea Party. Under a midnight sky in 1776, Paul Revere spurred his horse up the cobblestones to warn that the British were coming. These major events all unfolded along a 2.5-mile stretch known today as the Freedom Trail – 16 sites in all shed light on one the most important periods in America's early history.

For more on the Freedom Trail, see p172.

Cliff Palace (p741), Mesa Verde National Park

4. The National Mall
AMERICA'S FRONT YARD

In 1790, just three years after the US Constitution was written, the fledgling nation founded its capital on a marshy site along the Potomac and Anacostia Rivers. President George Washington – for whom the city was named – hired French architect Pierre Charles L'Enfant to design it. A key part of L'Enfant's vision was a grand avenue that would be open to all and embody the egalitarian nature of the new country. Today, this 2-mile strip is lined with grand museums, memorials and monuments, and it has hosted some of the nation's most important demonstrations and speeches, including Martin Luther King's 'I have a dream' in 1963.

For more on the National Mall, see p256.

5. First Americans Museum
NATIVE AMERICA

Present-day Oklahoma was designated 'Indian Territory' by Congress in 1830. In the decades that followed, numerous tribes were forcibly relocated there, including the 100,000 people who were marched across the country on a brutal journey later called the Trail of Tears. Today, Oklahoma is home to 39 tribes, and their rich ancestral heritage – with roots stretching across the continent – is celebrated in the stunning First Americans Museum (FAM). Nearly three decades in the making, the FAM delves into origin stories, collective histories and personal narrations by generations of Native Americans. The building is designed along the cardinal directions, which comes into focus during each solstice and equinox.

For more on the First Americans Museum, see p620.

6. Marshall Gold Discovery State Historic Park
THE GOLD RUSH

In 1848, while building a sawmill on the South Fork of the American River, James Marshall saw shiny flecks in the water. Examining the pieces, he realized he'd found gold. Word spread rapidly and thousands of fortune seekers flooded the area. Gold caused rapid growth and created boomtowns like San Francisco, whose population went from 800 to 25,000 between 1848 and 1851. The influx drew some 300,000 prospectors, hailing from the US, Europe, Latin America, Asia and even Australia. The gold rush accelerated California's statehood (which happened in 1850) while leading to the precipitous decline of the Native population.

For more on the Marshall Gold Discovery State Historic Park, see p935.

7. Gettysburg National Military Park
TURNING POINT OF THE CIVIL WAR

The American Civil War had been raging for two years when General Lee pushed his Confederate forces into Pennsylvania in 1863. By directly attacking the north, he aimed to crush Union morale and force a negotiated peace. Things didn't go according to plan, however, and the Confederacy suffered a staggering defeat. Today, Gettysburg is hallowed ground for many visitors who come to remember the battle's terrible costs (50,000 casualties) and pay homage to those who gave their lives so that '...government of the people, by the people, for the people, shall not perish from the earth,' as Abraham Lincoln stated four months later in his famous 'Gettysburg Address.'

For more on the Gettysburg National Military Park, see p152.

8. Yellowstone National Park
THE FIRST NATIONAL PARK

Native American tribes have inhabited the Yellowstone region for over 11,000 years, though it remained largely unknown to outsiders until the 19th century. When fur trapper John Colter crossed through an area of geysers and mud pools in 1807, few believed his tales of fire and brimstone. It would take another 60 years for a properly mounted expedition to visit the site. Among the surveyors and scientists was landscape artist Thomas Moran, whose striking paintings of a vast canyon, towering falls and steaming geothermal features left a deep impression on the public – and led Congress to permanently safeguard this wilderness. In 1872, Yellowstone became the world's first national park.

For more on Yellowstone National Park, see p758.

9. Ellis Island
GATEWAY TO A NEW LIFE

On January 1, 1892, a 17-year-old girl from Ireland named Annie Moore made history as the first immigrant to pass through Ellis Island. She was accompanied by her two younger brothers and would be followed over the next six decades by 12 million other immigrants from far-flung corners of Europe and beyond seeking a better life in the USA. As immigration policies changed and embassies opened, fewer people made the journey through Ellis Island. During WWII, it became a detention center for merchant seamen. The last of those detainees, a Norwegian named Arne Peterssen, left Ellis Island in 1954.

For more on Ellis Island, see p72.

10. Delta Blues Museum
BIRTHPLACE OF AMERICAN MUSIC

Created by freed African Americans in the late 1860s, the music known as the blues emerged from a place of farming and sharecropping in the sunbaked fields of the Mississippi Delta. This hardscrabble region is where greats like Robert Johnson, Muddy Waters and BB King got their start playing in dance halls and juke joints. Still packed with blues clubs, Clarksdale is home to the Delta Blues Museum, which charts the importance of this uniquely American sound – one that would become the foundation for virtually all popular music of today, including rock, soul, R&B, hip-hop and even country.

For more on the Delta Blues Museum, see p399.

11. Great Smoky Mountains National Park
PRESERVING WILDERNESS IN THE GREAT DEPRESSION

In 1929 the New York stock market crashed, and the economy collapsed. By 1932, one in four working-age Americans were unemployed. To help put people back to work, President Roosevelt launched a variety of New Deal programs, including the Civilian Conservation Corps (CCC), which provided work for more than three million young men from 1933 to 1942. Active across the country, the CCC played a pivotal role in conservation, particularly in state and national parks. The legacy of these laborers lives on in the Great Smoky Mountains, where CCC workers built fire towers, stone bridges, campgrounds and even hiking trails.

For more on Great Smoky Mountains National Park, see p337.

12. National WWII Museum
FROM THE BAYOU TO THE BATTLEFIELD

Before the outbreak of WWII, the US Army had just 174,000 troops, ranking it 17th in the world. The US was also woefully equipped when it came to war materials. After Japan's attack on Pearl Harbor in 1941, the US transformed its economy and millions of men enlisted. Crucial to the war's success was the Higgins boat, allowing soldiers to land directly on Normandy's beaches during D-Day. The vessels were developed and built in Louisiana – and modeled after the flat-bottom boats used in the bayous – which is why the nation's most important WWII museum resides in New Orleans.

For more on the National WWII Museum, see p425.

13. Dexter Avenue King Memorial Baptist Church
CHAMPION OF CIVIL RIGHTS

Martin Luther King Jr grew up in Atlanta, but Montgomery, Alabama, was where he first made his mark as a courageous defender of civil rights. Serving as pastor at Dexter Avenue Baptist Church, King met Rosa Parks, a Black woman who refused to give up her seat for a white passenger. The year was 1955, and as King organized the Montgomery bus boycott, he insisted on nonviolent protest – no matter the abuse and beatings protestors endured. In the years that followed, he inspired countless people to join his movement, won a Nobel Peace Prize and ultimately convinced a president to sign the Civil Rights Act.

For more on Dexter Avenue King Memorial Baptist Church, see p395

14. Walt Disney World®
A NEW TYPE OF RESORT

Walt Disney had already achieved monumental success as an animator, producer and entrepreneur when he began working on his next venture in the early 1960s. Rather than creating another theme park, he aimed to build a whole world of entertainment through multiple resorts and even a prototype city for the future across some 25,000 acres. Though Walt's more utopian plans were shelved after his death in 1966, Walt Disney World was a groundbreaking success when it opened in 1971. Today, the Florida park employs around 80,000 people and generates $40 billion in economic impact, thanks to 58 million annual visitors.

For more on Walt Disney World®, see p475.

15. International African American Museum
THE PEOPLE WHO BUILT A NATION

Gadsden's Wharf was the site of untold suffering. For nearly a century, tens of thousands of men, women and children who had been taken from Africa were sold into slavery from this dock in Charleston. In 2023, after 20 years of planning, the International African American Museum opened on this hallowed ground with thought-provoking galleries that take visitors on a journey from ancient Africa to the present day. There are exhibitions on the Black Atlantic world linking Africa, Europe and the Americas, as well as insight into the Gullah-Geechee – the Lowcountry descendants of enslaved people from West and Central Africa.

For more on the International African American Museum, see p344.

MEET THE AMERICANS

A collection of diverse communities, peoples and views, the USA feels like many countries woven into one grand landscape. Regis St Louis

IT'S EASY TO see why only 50% of Americans have passports. I often feel like I'm crossing continents when traveling in the US. How is it possible that fast-talking New Yorkers whizzing beneath rivers in steel subway cars live in the same country as cowboys on horseback, riding among the chiseled peaks and roaming grizzlies of Wyoming? Oftentimes 50 states feel more like 50 countries, with their own accents and distinct world views, not to mention the panoply of colors and creeds – after all, Spanish is the lingua franca in Miami, and Queens is more akin to a citified version of the UN, with its dizzying array of ethnic enclaves.

Like many Americans, I don't think about my nationality all that often. During the World Cup and the Olympics, country pride runs deep (especially when the powerhouse women's gymnastics team steps onto the mat). At other times, our focus narrows to the regions we live in and our communities. Though Texas and Louisiana are neighbors, their residents are nothing alike. And even within those states the regional variation is vast: New Orleanians follow different traditions and rhythms to those from Lafayette in Cajun Country, while Austinites and Houstonians might as well hail from different countries despite the mere 160-odd miles separating the two cities.

This far-reaching diversity makes it impossible to describe a typical American, though it does underly the very essence of this nation's character. Never mind what the politicians say – our diversity is our greatest strength, and it's evident in everything from music and films to fashion and urban design.

There's often talk of two Americas. It's mostly made in reference to the nation's dueling political parties, though sometimes employed to describe the rural–urban divide, or the chasm between the well-off and the working poor. But those divisions tend to disappear when it comes to food. The beloved dish, of course, changes from place to place: quahogs (hard-shell clams) in Rhode Island, smoked ribs in western Tennessee, green-chile enchiladas in New Mexico or Chinook salmon in Alaska. Locals may argue endlessly over who does it best, though they'll agree on the heart of the matter: that it's simply the finest thing you'll ever eat.

Festivals likewise collapse the walls of division and bring Americans of wide-ranging backgrounds together. As with other things, the biggest celebrations are rooted at the local level: Patriots' Day in Boston, which commemorates the start of the American Revolution, the flower-filled processions of Fiesta in San Antonio or weeks of pre-Lenten revelry in Mobile, home to the nation's oldest Mardi Gras parades.

Food and celebration – albeit of a more subdued nature – join hands in November during the country's best-loved gathering: Thanksgiving. It's a time when families and friends come together to cook, set the table and then give thanks before sitting down to the biggest feast of the year.

> **Who & How Many**
>
> The USA is home to 342 million people, though nine western states have more cows than humans residing there. The Hispanic/Latinx population makes up around 20%, while 14% identify as Black, and around 3% as Native American or Native Alaskan.

Pictured clockwise from top left: New York City Subway (p66); Surfer, Malibu (p959); Native American tribe, North Dakota (p645); Jazz musician, New Orleans (p415)

WE ARE ALL A MIX

Like most Americans, I have mixed background. My family line stretches across Europe (France, Canada, Scotland, Ireland and Slovenia), and my ancestors did everything from digging coal mines to building bridges. I was born in a small town in the Midwest, but my parents grew up in Colorado. Early visits to the Rockies perhaps fueled my wanderlust: since finishing university, I've lived in San Francisco, Los Angeles, Brooklyn and New Orleans. As I set out, I was in good company – each year around eight million Americans move to a different state. In the Northeast, I felt like a New Yorker the day I arrived. In fact, less than half of the city's residents were born in the state, with nearly 37% born outside the US. Not so in Louisiana, where I've met many people with multigenerational roots in the area. I wasn't surprised to later learn that out of the entire US, Louisiana has the highest percentage of residents born in the state where they reside.

THE BIRTH OF AMERICA'S VACATION

A series of 19th-century stories about New York's wild Adirondacks became a prototype for the modern guidebook and a passport to freedom. By John Garry

FOR MANY WATERFRONT destinations throughout the Mid-Atlantic, summer is more than a season – it's the most exciting time of year. Populations boom with vacationers who leave behind their cities and look forward to letting loose. The tradition may seem old hat, but it's relatively new. These are its origins.

Summer Arrives

Memorial Day sets off an East Coast alarm bell. Tiny waterfront towns that hibernated from October through April spring back to life by the last Monday of May. Summer has arrived. Vacationers are coming.

The wake-up call is particularly pronounced in Lake George – an Adirondack Mountains village where the population can swell from roughly 1000 to 50,000 throughout summer. When it comes to preparing for the incoming deluge, Lake George is a well-oiled machine. Mini-golf courses polish their fiberglass sculptures and fudge shops set out chunks of sweet treats. Marinas fill up their rental boats with gas. Campgrounds clean up winter's debris. The entire region simmers with the splendor of summer vacation until Labor Day, when the season's enchantment disappears. But for those few precious months, the Adirondacks ace the art of escapism. This is, after all, where the American vacation was born.

Rise of the Vacation Class

In the early 19th century, traveling for leisure was a privilege reserved for the rich. In New York, the well-heeled went to spa towns like Saratoga Springs, where 'taking the waters' supposedly cured various ailments, while newlyweds traveled to Niagara Falls to sojourn with the sublime. But the average American had no concept of 'vacation.' The word wasn't even used in common parlance.

All that changed after the Civil War. Rapid industrialization transformed America's demographics: urban factories gave rise to an affluent middle class, and Puritan prejudice against 'idle hands' was countered with arguments about relaxation's benefits. With time to kill and money to burn, the number of Americans traveling for rest and recreation began growing, aided by railroads. The nation was becoming an open book. The only thing nascent travelers needed was a guide.

America's Proto-Travel Guide

In the mid-1860s, a young clergyman named William HH Murray took his first trip to the Adirondacks – a vast wilderness known mostly by indigenous inhabitants and rugged outdoorsmen. Murray fell in love with the landscape and began writing about his off-the-radar adventures. By 1869, he published a book – Adventures in the Wilderness; or, Camp-Life in the Adirondacks.

Much like the poetic ponderings of his academic contemporaries Henry David Thoreau and Ralph Waldo Emerson, Murray persuasively preached the physical and spiritual benefits of connecting with nature. He argued that the pine-scented mountains could be the antidote to urban ailments, writing, 'no portion of our country surpasses, if indeed any equals, in health-giving qualities, the Adirondack Wilderness.'

His writing was simple and straightforward, and laid out plenty of practical information. This easy-to-follow advice – what to pack, where to stay, who to hire as a guide, how much money to spend – gave novice nature lovers confidence to rough it in the woods.

Murray also attempted to democratize the Adirondack experience by appealing to a group often left out of outdoor exploration – women. A section of the guide focused solely on what they should wear. He noted that 'none enjoy the experiences more than ladies, and certain it is that none are more benefited by it.'

While critical reviews of Murray's work were mixed, the public ate it up. Within months, New York's mountains erupted with stampedes of urbanites, who streamed in from NYC, Boston and beyond, clutching Murray's words like their wilderness Bible.

But the summer of '69 wasn't exactly the Edenic destination Murray described. Locusts of black flies left visitors bug-bitten and bloody. Rain came down in torrents. Lodges became overwhelmed. Untrained wilderness guides led groups astray. Even with Murray's instructions, travelers were ill-prepared. Critics of Murray's disgruntled disciples derided them as 'Murray's Fools.'

Still, many readers remained undeterred. Some even waxed poetic about their experiences. Journalist and lecturer Kate Field, who spent that summer camping with three pioneering female companions among the mountains, summed up the region's unflagging magnetism best: 'The moral of the Adirondacks is freedom.'

Signs of Overtourism

The promise of freedom continued luring masses to the Adirondacks in 1870, and as crowds multiplied, businesses sprang up to meet their demands. By the end of the century, hotels, railroads, steamboats and wagon roads dotted the wilds, ready to make a buck off the bucket-list destination.

NYC blue bloods like the Vanderbilts and Rockefellers joined their ranks, purchasing private lakeside properties where they could 'vacate' the city's heat for cool mountain air. Their sprawling estates became the sites of 'Great Camps' – Gilded Age fortresses constructed with logs, covered in tree bark and decorated with taxidermy.

At the same time, local farming and logging reached its feverish peak. In 1885, maps commissioned by New York State's legislature showed that an estimated 27.8% of what's now Adirondack Park had been cleared.

Murray's work presented a paradox, a dilemma plaguing sites from Machu Picchu to Venice today: extolling the virtues of the pristine Adirondacks inadvertently played a role in their decay.George says Tempest Tours helped consult on Twisters and that a lot of the technical stuff is correct, but at the end of the day, it's Hollywood. 'We don't drive through people's fields, and we don't see a tornado every 10 minutes,' she says. 'Storm chasing is all about driving the long distances to get to your target.' Tornadoes are seasonal, generally occurring between April and July. 'We know there are going to be storms during this season,' George says. On 'down days' on tour, travelers visit local attractions, but some tours in 2025 were out chasing daily.

Paradise Found

Thanks to state legislation and environmental activism, fortunately the story of the Adirondacks doesn't end in destruction. By 1885 New York's Governor established a law ensuring the Adirondacks would be 'forever kept as wild forest lands.'

As America marched into the 20th century and the nation's final frontiers vanished, no destination would quite match what Murray described in 1869. Still, plenty of other East Coast utopias emerged as getaway hot spots. New Jersey's Atlantic City and Brooklyn's Coney Island became blue-collar escapes for work-weary travelers. Jewish summer resorts took root in New York's Catskills. African Americans found relaxation at Maryland's Highland Beach. The country's first gay and lesbian summer community spread its wings in Cherry Grove.

More travel guides soon filled the shelves of bookstores while Murray's musings faded into obscurity, but an idea he planted permanently lodged itself in the American psyche: now and then, everyone deserves a vacation.

RIDING THE RAILS THROUGH THE USA

Think train travel is a thing of the past in the United States? Think again. By Lauren Keith

IF YOU'RE PLANNING a trip around the USA, you already know that you have a lot of ground to cover: more than 3.8 million sq miles of mountains, deserts, forests and prairie sprinkled with cities of all sizes. The most immersive way to see it all? By taking the train.

What to Expect on a US Train Trip

While the USA hasn't had the renaissance of train travel that Europe has seen, the country is getting back on track. Amtrak, the only national passenger rail service, posted record ridership numbers in 2024. Improvements and all-new trains are coming soon, but for now, train travel in the USA means slow travel. Trains are notoriously delayed, and some of the train cars are pretty old-fashioned. For example, the long-distance routes that can take days to get from end to end don't have wi-fi, and these trains depart only once a day (or even just a few times a week), sometimes at odd hours, depending on where you board.

Is taking a train in the USA the most efficient way to travel? Rarely. But it's sure to leave you with better stories than you'd have sitting at an airport. Disconnect from your devices and instead connect with your fellow passengers in the observation car, or simply sit back, relax and enjoy the ride.

Best for Cross-Country Scenery
California Zephyr: Chicago–Emeryville (San Francisco)

No train journey in the USA – or perhaps the world – is as epic as the California Zephyr. Clocking in at 2438 miles, it's the furthest you can go within the US by train, and it packag-

Union Station, Chicago (p504)

es up the best of the country. Between Reno and Sacramento, docents from the California State Railroad Museum often narrate the journey.

Southwest Chief: Chicago–Los Angeles

This route runs more southerly than the California Zephyr, opening up the grand landscapes of the Southwest through New Mexico and Arizona.

Empire Builder: Chicago–Seattle or Portland

Nature is the star of the show on the Empire Builder, which connects three epicenters of urban culture via Glacier National Park and the Columbia River Gorge (on the Portland branch).

Sunset Limited: Los Angeles–New Orleans

Amtrak's southernmost line might not have the same level of wow factor, but it's a quiet classic. This journey once extended to Miami, but after Hurricane Katrina walloped the Gulf Coast in 2005, the service was partially shut down. In August 2025, a new extension between New Orleans and Mobile, Alabama, called Amtrak Mardi Gras Service, opened two decades later.

Best for City Hopping

Acela & Northeast Regional: Washington, DC–Boston

The most European train travel experience on this side of the pond, these two services link up major East Coast cities, including Baltimore, Philadelphia and New York City, in just a few hours. The two lines cover much of the same ground, but Acela is the only high-speed service in the Americas, though in reality it doesn't shave a huge amount of time off the journey.

Borealis: Chicago–St Paul

Opened in 2024, Borealis joins up three major Great Lakes cities, traveling via Milwaukee. This route isn't new – the Empire Builder and Hiawatha take the same tracks – but this addition means more frequent services for day-trippers and weekenders.

Missouri River Runner: Kansas City–St Louis

It's difficult to get around the Great Plains without a car, but twice-daily trains run between two of the region's biggest cities, whose stations are conveniently located near their downtowns.

Best for Coastline

The best oceanside train routes are along the Pacific Coast, and you can combine all three for an epic international adventure stretching from Vancouver, Canada, to Tijuana, Mexico.

Coast Starlight: Seattle–Los Angeles

Tracing nearly all of the USA's western shore, the Coast Starlight curves atop high cliffs with surfer-dotted waves crashing below. An hour or so after sunset is a particularly good time to nab a seat in the observation car as the Golden State enters golden hour.

Amtrak Cascades: Eugene–Vancouver, Canada

Amtrak Cascades winds through a fairy-tale scene of rushing rivers, waterfalls and forests of moss-covered trees. The tracks get so close to the water of Puget Sound that it feels like you could reach out the train window and dip your hand in.

Pacific Surfliner: San Luis Obispo–San Diego

If you don't have the days to dedicate to the Coast Starlight, the Pacific Surfliner is the perfect option for a shorter train trip, covering many of the same stops. The Blue Line of the San Diego Trolley connects the train station with the San Ysidro border crossing into Mexico.

Best Private Routes

Amtrak is the only countrywide passenger train service in the United States, but private companies run scenic routes in some places.

Canyon Spirit: Salt Lake City–Denver

Formerly called 'Rocky Mountaineer,' Canyon Spirit offers a luxe three-day ride through Colorado's winding Glenwood Canyon and Utah's Martian deserts, which are best viewed through its glass-domed train cars.

Durango & Silverton Narrow Gauge Railroad

Opened in 1881, the Durango and Silverton Railroad once hauled silver and gold out of the San Juan Mountains but now has snap-happy travelers filling up its cars. This heritage line still runs old-school steam trains through the mountains and along rocky cliffs above the Animas River.

Grand Canyon Railway

Arrive in one of the country's most popular national parks like a traveler of yore aboard the historic Grand Canyon Railway, which has been bringing visitors to the Grand Canyon for longer than it's been a national park.

THE GAMES THAT BIND US

From football and baseball to women's basketball, nothing fires up Americans like their favorite sports team. By Karla Zimmerman

MAYBE IT'S THE Yankees, the Cowboys, the Buckeyes or the Bananas. Most Americans have a team: a loyalty they can't quite explain, one that makes them shout at the TV, rearrange their schedules or even wear team-colored body paint. Sports unite us – and spotlight the social issues we can't ignore.

More Than a Pastime

An obsession with sports isn't uniquely American. Many countries are die-hard.

The Washington Commanders versus the New York Giants in football

But the sheer scale of money poured into sports in the US is beyond compare. In 2024 alone, spectator-sports tourism generated $114 billion, according to the Sports Events and Tourism Association. Sports-betting revenue reached nearly $14 billion the same year – a number that keeps rising. Add in billions more for fantasy leagues, team merchandise, youth sports and media rights, and it's clear: this is more than just a pastime.

No wonder, because in America, sports aren't just games. They're social glue. They bond generations, with parents, grandparents and kids all cheering for the same team. They connect people across geography, like Ohio State fans gathering in a Dallas bar to watch a big game. And they bridge everyday life: listen in on any Monday morning, when coworkers from all walks of life rehash the weekend's heroes, villains and underdog triumphs from their favorite teams.

Football

Football is big, physical and flush with cash. With the shortest season and fewest games of any major American sport, each match carries the weight of an epic showdown. Weather adds to the drama, as football is played through rain, sleet and snow. The coldest game in National Football League (NFL) history? Green Bay, 1967, when temperatures dropped to -13°F (-48°F with the wind chill). Still, 50,000 fans stayed to cheer.

Passion runs deep. At pro games, body paint, profane chants and beer-fueled tailgate parties in stadium parking lots are customary. For those not on-site, the action shifts to bars, where locals don jerseys, yell at umpires through the TV screen and high-five after overtime wins. This ritual plays out every Sunday from September through January.

Meanwhile, fall Saturdays are for college football. The first thing to know about the scene is that many college stadiums are bigger than their NFL counterparts. Capacity of 100,000 or more is common, while NFL venues max out around 80,000. Some college arenas hold more people than the surrounding town holds.

So size matters. And so does pageantry. Each team has its time-honored traditions that are as crucial to the game as the players snapping the ball. Auburn's war eagle soars over the stadium before kickoff, and Ohio State's marching band forms a script 'Ohio' on the field at half-time. At Oklahoma, a pony-led covered wagon – the Sooner Schooner – charges onto the field after every home-team score.

Baseball

Baseball may not command the same TV viewership as football, but with 162 games over a spring-through-summer season (versus 17 games for football), its ubiquity helps maintain its popularity.

Besides, baseball isn't about seeing it on TV. It's all about the live version: being at the ballpark on a sunny day, sitting in the bleachers with a beer and hot dog, and indulging in the seventh-inning stretch, when the entire park erupts in a communal singalong of 'Take Me Out to the Ballgame.' Going to a game is an American rite of passage.

Minor-league baseball games are also a blast. They cost less and provide a more intimate setting, with lots of audience participation, stray chickens and dogs running across the field, and wild throws from the pitcher's mound. While there are 30 major league stadiums, more than 120 minor league ballparks offer action across the country.

Basketball

The fast-paced sport ignites the fervor of many true-blue fans. Teams in the National Basketball Association (NBA) play 82 games from late October through mid-April, offering plenty of chances to go to a game and experience the kiss cam (jumbotron images of smooching couples), T-shirt cannon (a bazooka-like device the team mascot uses to shoot shirts into the crowd) and high-energy dance squads.

College-level basketball also draws millions of fans, especially every spring when March Madness rolls around.

The single-elimination tournament features 68 teams competing over a three-week span and is packed with upsets, unexpected champions and other high drama. The games are widely televised and bet on, particularly in workplaces around the country.

Basketball is the sport leading the pack toward gender equality. Teams in the Women's National Basketball Association (WNBA) play 44 games between May and October – roughly half of the NBA's season.

Attendance figures are also smaller, but the league has gained major momentum in recent years. Crowds have surged thanks to rising stars like Caitlin Clark, and several new teams are slated to join the league.

Off the court, the WNBA has pioneered groundbreaking policies around child care, maternity rights and revenue sharing. It has also brought national attention to the ongoing issue of pay disparity, as player salaries remain a fraction of those in the men's league.

Beyond the Big Three

Ice hockey, once favored only in northern climes, is popular nationwide – even in warm-weather cities, whose teams have claimed the championship in recent years. Soccer continues to attract an ever-increasing number of fans with both the men's and women's pro leagues.

But beyond providing entertainment and community, sporting events have become public arenas where deeper issues take the field.

From Jackie Robinson becoming the first Black player in pro sports when he joined baseball's Dodgers in 1947, to NFL players kneeling during the national anthem some 70 years later, sports have sparked national conversations about racial injustice, gender equity, LGBTQ rights and mental health.

INDEX

A

Abilene 610
Abiquiú 869
Acadia National Park 236-8
accessible travel 1097
accommodations 1089, *see also individual locations*
activities 43, 48-9, 54-7
Adirondacks, the 117, 119-21
air travel 1078, 1079, 1087
Alabama 388-96, 432-3, **389**
Alaska 1037-57, **1038**
 accomodations 1057
 festivals & events 1039
 itineraries 1039
 navigation 1038
 travel seasons 1039
 travel within 1038
Albuquerque 865-7, 879, **866**
Alexandria 304
Ali, Muhammad 368
alligators 452, 455
Alpine 706-7
Amana Colonies 638-40, 662
Amarillo 710
Americana 27
Amherst 190
Amish people 151-2
amusement parks
 Adventure Landing Jacksonville Beach 484
 Aquatica 478
 Buffalo Heritage Carousel 125
 Carousel Gardens 426
 Cedar Point 540
 Centennial Wheel 509
 Deno's Wonder Wheel Park 105
 Disneyland 968-9
 Glen Echo Park 291
 Greenway Carousel 166
 Jane's Carousel 103
 LEGOLAND 476, 478
 Luna Park 105
 Orlando Eye 474
 Roger at the Pier 286
 SkyView Ferris wheel 378
 SkyWheel 349
 Slide Hill 67
 Trimper Rides 286
 Universal Orlando Resort™ 477
 Walt Disney World® 475, 496-7, 1105
 Water Works Park 492
 Wisconsin Dells 566
Anacortes 1001
Anchorage 1046-9, **1047**
 accomodations 1057
 beyond Anchorage 1050-6
Ann Arbor 551
Annapolis 282, 283
Antietam National Battlefield 291
Anza-Borrego 965-6
Apostle Islands 570-1
aquariums
 Echo Leahy Center for Lake Champlain 212
 Florida Aquarium 492
 Georgia Aquarium 376-7
 Greater Cleveland Aquarium 535, 537
 Mystic Aquarium 207
 National Aquarium 287
 New England Aquarium 167
 Save the Bay's Hamilton Family Aquarium 198
 SeaWorld 478
 Shedd Aquarium 515
 Tennessee Aquarium 363
 Witt Stephens Jr Nature Center 409
 Woods Hole Science Aquarium 186
Aransas National Wildlife Refuge 705
Arches National Park 854-5
architecture
 Buffalo 124
 Cape May 130
 Chicago 507, 509
 Columbus 531
 Lewes 278-9
 Michigan 548
 Newport 200
 Racine 564
Area 51 806
Arizona 808-42, **822, 836**
Arkansas 405-14, 433, **406**
Arlington 303-4
arriving 1086
art 1045, 1068, *see also galleries & art museums*
Asbury Park 132-3
Asheville 333-4
Aspen 734-6
Assateague Island 286-7
Astoria 1030-1
astronomy 1073
Atchison 607, 609
Athens 382
Atlanta 375-82, **376, 378, 379**
ATMs 1086, 1088
Auburn 528, 935
Aurora 123
Austin 670-9, **671, 672, 674**
 accommodations 712
 cinemas 677
 drinking 674, 679
 festivals 675
 food 672, 673, 675, 677, 678
 nightlife 678-9
 transportation 670

B

Bainbridge Island 1005
Balboa Park 976
Baltimore 287-91, **288, 290**
Bandera 687-8
barbecue 52, 53, 1092
 Kansas City 601-2
Bar Harbor 236-8
Bardstown 369
baseball 1113
 BASE jumping 787
 Comerica Park 548
 Fenway Park 179
 Frawley Stadium 273
 Nationals Park 262
 Oriole Park at Camden Yards 289
 Vermont Lake Monsters 212
 Wrigley Field 511
basics 44
basketball 1113
 Little Caesars Arena 548
Bay Area 977
beaches 22-3, 1109
 Amsterdam Beach 111
 Atlantic Beach 486
 Bethany Beach 278
 Big Island of Hawai'i, the 1070
 Boneyard Beach 486
 Bradford Beach 564
 Cape Hatteras National Seashore 326-7
 Castle Island 180
 Chicago 516
 Clearwater Beach 495
 Cocoa Beach 482
 Ditch Plains Beach 107
 Edgewater Park Beach 537
 Edisto Beach State Park 348
 Florida Keys 462
 Folly Beach 348
 Fort Lauderdale Beach 464
 Gansevoort Peninsula 86-7
 Gunnison Beach 134
 Hammonasset Beach State Park 205
 Harbor Heights Beach 481
 Jacksonville Beach 484, 486
 Jacobs Beach 205
 Kaua'i 1081
 Kiawah Beachwater Park 348
 Kirk Park Beach 111
 La Jolla 973
 Long Beach 1005-6
 Long Point Beach 189
 Maui 1077, 1078
 Meyers Beach 571
 Mid-Beach, Miami 440, 443
 Million Dollar Beach 119
 Montauk Beach 111
 Moonstone Beach 940-1
 Myrtle Beach 349

Map Pages **000**

Neptune Beach 486
Newport 970-1
North Beach 384
North Beach, Miami 443
O'ahu 1067
Point Reyes 907-8
Rehoboth Beach 276-7
San Francisco 904
Santa Barbara 939
Santa Cruz 946
Santa Monica to Malibu 959
South Beach, Miami 440
South Edison Beach 111
Springer's Point Preserve 327
St Pete Beach 495
Venice 959
Beacon 113
Bear Lake 730
bears 773, 933
Beartooth Scenic Highway 768
Beaufort (North Carolina) 324-5
Beaufort (South Carolina) 348
Bellingham 1001
Bend 1028-9
Bennington 221
Bentonville 413
Berkeley 905-7, **906**
Berkeley Springs 313
Berkshires, the 192-3
Beverly Hills 958
Big Island of Hawai'i, the 1070-4, **1071**
 accommodations 1083
 drinking 1072-3
 festivals & events 1072
 food 1072-3
Big Sur 944-5
Billings 768
birdwatching
 Alaska 1043
 Aransas National Wildlife Refuge 705
 Audubon Bird Sanctuary 396
 Biscayne National Park 457
 Boise River Greenbelt 779
 Cape May Bird Observatory 130
 Cape May Point State Park 131
 Delaware River 151
 Grand Island 630
 Montrose Point Bird Sanctuary 507
 Point Reyes 908
 Orlando Wetlands Park 476

Outer Banks 327
Shark Valley 452
Wekiwa Springs State Park 474
Birmingham 392-3, **393**
Bisbee 839, 841, 878
Biscayne Bay 445
Bismarck 648
Black Broadway 264-5
Black Hills 655-61, 663, **656-7**
Blackbeard 325
Blackfoot 787
Blowing Rock 335
Blue Ridge Parkway 35, 300
Blues, the (music) 37, 1104
boat tours
 Acadia National Park 237
 Alaska 1043
 Annapolis 282
 Apostle Islands 570-1
 Biscayne National Park 456-7
 Boothbay Harbor 233
 Boston 176
 Buffalo 125
 Burlington 212
 Charleston 347
 Chicago 507
 Fort Lauderdale 467
 Kaua'i 1082
 Lafayette 431
 Lake George 119-20
 Miami 445
 New Jersey 132
 New Orleans 419
 New York City 94-5
 Pennsylvania 144
 Portland 231
bodegas 99
Boerne 687-8
Boise 779-83, 789, **780**
Bonneville Dam 1027
books 45, 85, 335, 1067
Boothbay Harbor 233
border crossings 1086
Boston 33, 166-83, **168-9**, **170**, **178**
 accommodations 240
 children, travel with 180
 entertainment 176, 179
 food 167, 176
 history 175
 travel within Boston 166, 177
Boulder 728-9, 732, 788, **729**
Boundary Waters 583, 585
Boyne City 552
Bozeman 765-7, 789, **766**
Brandywine Valley 147
Branson 606
Brazos Bend 703

Brevard 335-6
breweries
 18th Ward Brewing 104
 Alaska 1047
 Anheuser-Busch Brewery 598
 Aslin Brewery 156
 Avondale Brewing Company 393
 Bold Monk Brewing Co 381
 Bookhouse Brewing 535
 Brooklyn Brewery 103-4
 Burial 334
 Cincinnati's Brewing Heritage Trail 537
 Fire Maker Brewing Company 381
 Founders Brewing Co 552
 Grand Rapids 551-2
 Great Lakes Brewing Company 535
 Grimm Artisanal Ales 104
 Hansa Brewery 535
 Harmony Brewing Company 552
 Highland Brewing Co 333
 Hop Lot Brewing Company 556
 Lakefront Brewery 561-2, 563
 Miller Brewing Company 561
 Mitten Brewing Company 552
 Monday Night Brewing 381
 New Holland Brewing Pub on 8th 555
 Scratch Brewing 523
 Sierra Nevada Brewing Company 334, 948
 South Slope Brewing District 334
 Talea 104
 Vine Street Brewing Co 603
 Vivant Brewery 552
 Warped Wing Brewing Company 543
 Wicked Weed 334
bridges
 Aerial Lift Bridge 580
 Bartonsville 221
 Brooklyn Bridge 67-9
 Cornish-Windsor Bridge 221
 Endless Bridge 577
 Fisher Railroad Bridge 221
 Golden Gate Bridge 890, 907
 John A Roebling Suspension Bridge 538
 Montgomery 221

New River Gorge Bridge 308
Nichols Bridgeway 506
Old Steel Railroad Bridge 492
Purple People Bridge 538
Three-in-a-Row Bridges 221
Brookings 1032-3
Brown County 531
Browning 774
Brunswick 387
Bryson City 336
budget 1087, 1088, 1089, 1093
Buffalo 124
Bunyan, Paul 580, 581
Burlington 212-13
Burning Man festivals 805-6
bus travel 14, 1087
business hours 24, 1099

cable cars 121
Cahokia Mounds 523
California 880-979, **882-3**, **912**, **938**, **970**
 accommodations 977-9
 festivals 884-5
 itineraries 884-5
 navigation 882-3
 travel seasons 884-5
 travel within 883
Cambria 940-1
camping 48, 228, 454
Cannon Beach 1031-2
canoeing, see kayaking & canoeing
Canyon de Chelly 830-1, 878
Cape Lookout National Seashore 325
Cape May 130-1
Capital Region, the 242-315, **244-5**
 accommodations 314-15
 climate 246-7
 itineraries 246-7
 navigation 244-5
Capitol Hill 254-5
Carmel-by-the-Sea 943-4
Carrboro 333
car travel 1087
Cascade Lakes Scenic Byway 1030
casinos
 California 972
 Las Vegas 797
 Montana 775
 Nevada 797, 803
cathedrals, see churches & cathedrals

Catskills, the 116-20
caves
  Ash Cave 542
  Blanchard Springs Caverns 414
  Cave Point 568
  Crystal Cave 930
  Eben Ice Caves 555
  Jewel Cave 660
  Lake Shasta Caverns 923
  Mammoth Cave National Park 371
  Marengo Cave 532
  Mitchell Caverns 966
  Old Man's Cave 542
  Wind Cave 652
cemeteries
  Arlington National Cemetery 303-4
  British Cemetery 327
  Gateway Walk 344
  Mount Hope Cemetery 551
  Oak Ridge Cemetery 521
  St Louis Cemetery No 1 420
Central Park 100-1
Champ 212
Chanhassen 578
Chapel Hill 331
Charleston 307, 342-8, **343, 346**
Charlevoix 552
Charlotte 329-30
Chattanooga 362-4
Chautauqua Park 732
Cherokee 336
Cherry Grove 111
Cheyenne 751-2, **752**
Chicago 38, 504-15, **505, 508, 510, 512, 513, 515, 516**
  accommodations 586
  children, travel with 511
  entertainment 507, 510-11, 512, 514
  food 504
  shopping 514
  travel within 504
Chico 947-8, 979
children, see family travel
Chimayó 868
Chinatown 71, 75
Chuckanut Drive 1001
churches & cathedrals

Map Pages **000**

16th Street Baptist Church 392
Basilica of St Patrick's Old Cathedral 80
Boston Avenue United Methodist Church 616
Cathedral Basilica of St Augustine 487
Cathedral Basilica of the Immaculate Conception 395-6
Chapel of the Holy Cross 823
Dexter Avenue King Memorial Church 393, 395
El Santuario de Chimayó 869
First Christian Church 531
Holy Resurrection Cathedral 1056
Kawaiaha'o Church 1066
Loretto Chapel 867
San Felipe de Neri Church 865
San Geronimo Church 873
Santuario Nacional de Nuestra Señora de la Caridad 451
St John Coltrane Church 894
St Nicholas Russian Orthodox Church 1042
Washington National Cathedral 268, 270
cideries 123
Cincinnati 537-8
cinemas, 80, 392
cities 14-15
Clarksdale 37
Cleveland 534-5, 537
climate 42-3
Clinton, Bill 405-7
clothing 44
coasts 22-3, see also beaches
Cocoa Village 482-3
Cody 756-7
Colorado 720-48, **721, 723**
  accommodations 788
  food 726, 728, 733, 735, 738, 742, 743, 747
Colorado River Scenic Byway 862
Colorado Springs 747
Columbia 350
Columbus 538-9
Compton 956
Coney Island 104-5
Connecticut 201-9, 240, **202**
coral 460
Coral Gables 450

Cordova 1052
Corolla 328-9
costs 1087, 1088, 1089, 1093
country music 36
Coupeville 1001
credit cards 1088
Crested Butte 737-8
crocodiles 455
Crow Fair 768
CSKT Bison Range 774
culture 1106
  Adena 543
  Amish 541-2
  Cajun 430, 431
  Caribbean 417
  Cherokee 336
  Creole 431
  Gullah 348, 350
  Gullah-Geechee 344, 346, 386
  Hopewell 543
  Mohican 192
  Shakers 193
  Tibetan 530
  Wampanoag 186
Cumberland 291-2
customs 1086
cycling & cycling tours 14, 55, 1048, see also mountain biking
  Assateague Island 287
  Austin 675, 676
  Bentonville 409, 413
  Boston 176, 182
  Burlington 212
  Chicago 515-16
  C&O Canal 292, 312
  Crested Butte 738
  Des Moines 641-2
  Falmouth 186
  Georgetown-Lewes Trail 278
  Greenville 351
  Indianapolis 527-8
  Iowa 643, 644
  Little Rock 409
  Moab 848-9
  Monarch Crest Trail 736-7
  Morgantown 312
  Mt Nebo 409
  New Jersey 132, 137
  Pennsylvania 153
  Portland 231
  Provincetown 189
  San Diego 975
  Taos 873
  Wilmington 273
  Wisconsin 565

Dallas 690-4, 712
Davenport 635
Davis 947, 979

Dayton 542-3
Deadwood 661
Dean, James 530
Dearborn 549-50
Death Valley 964, **965**
Delaware 271-9, 314, **272**
Denver 724-8, 788, **725**
Des Moines 640-1, 662-3, **641**
Desolation Wilderness 931
Detroit 545-9, **546**
Dimes Sq 84
diners 136
dinosaurs
  Dinosaur National Monument 745
  Moab 851
  Morrison Formation 753
  Museum of the Rockies 765
disabilities, travelers with 1097
distilleries
  Bardstown 369
  Frankfort 371
  Louisville 368
  Vikre Distillery 580
diving & snorkeling
  Biscayne National Park 457
  Cherokee National Forest 364
  John Pennekamp Coral Reef State Park 460
  Kaua'i 1082
Dodge City 613
dogsledding 757
dolphin-watching
  Charleston 348
  New Jersey 131, 132
  St Augustine 489
Door County 568-9
Douglass, Frederick 288
Dover 276
Doylestown 148-9
Driggs 787, 789
drinking 1092-3, see also individual locations
driving & driving tours 18-19, 1087
  Big Sur 944-5
  Blue Hill Peninsula 234-5, **235**
  Brandywine Valley 275, **275**
  Cape Cod 191, **191**
  Cherohala Skyway 364
  Eastern Shore, Maryland 285, **285**
  Florida Keys 461, **461**
  Great River Road 567, **567**
  Hwy 61, Minnesota 581
  Kancamagus Highway 228

Lassen Volcanic National Park 924, **924**
M-22, the 555-6
Maui 1075
Mt Washington 227-8
Natchez Trace Parkway 404
New River Gorge 308
Ohio River Scenic Byway 531-2
Route 66, Illinois 522, **522**
Stagecoach Trail 523
Vermont 215, 218-19, **219**
Western Catskills 118, **118**
Dubuque 635-8, 662, **637**
Duluth 580
dunes 22
 Arcadia Dunes 552
 Nordhouse Dunes 552
 Rosy Mound Natural Area 552
 Saugatuck Dunes State Park 552
 Silver Lake Dunes 552
 Sleeping Bear Dunes National Lakeshore 553
 Warren Dunes 552
 Whitefish Dunes State Park 568
Durham 331, 332
Dylan, Bob 583

E

eagle, bald 151
Earhart, Amelia 607, 609
East Burke 220
Eisenhower, Dwight 610
electricity 1099
El Paso 711, **711**
Ellington, Duke 265
Ellis Island 72-3
emergencies 1099
Empire State Building 88, 90
Enchanted Circle 872
entertainment 20, 36-7, see also individual locations, music, nightlife
environmental issues 460
Essex 205-6
etiquette 44
Eugene 1025
Eureka 920-1
Eureka Springs 412
events, see festivals & events
Everglades 452-7, 496, **453**

F

Fairhope 396
Fairmount 530
Falmouth 186-7
family travel 55, 1090
 Boston 180
 Chicago 511
 Houston 702
 Indianapolis 526-7
 Kansas City 603
 Maryland 284
 Myrtle Beach 349
 New Orleans 426
 Omaha 626
 Orlando 478
 Springfield, Massachusetts 190
 Tampa 492
 Washington, DC 260
Fargo 645, 647
farming 24
Fayetteville 309, 410-11, 413
ferry travel 1087
 Alaska 1042
 Isle Royale Ferries 582
 Madeline Island Ferry 571
 Maui 1077
 New York City 99
 Portland 231
 Rock Island Ferry 569
 Washington Island Ferry 569
festivals & events 21, 43, 51, see also food & wine festivals, film festivals, music festivals, individual locations
 Alabama 390
 Alaska 1039
 Arkansas 409
 Baltimore 287
 Fort Lauderdale 467
 Georgia 386
 Gettysburg 153
 Hawai'i 1062-3
 Indiana 526
 Kansas 609
 Kentucky 368, 369
 Maryland 287
 Michigan 554
 Milwaukee 563
 Mississippi 401
 Missouri 605
 Nebraska 633
 New Jersey 133
 New Orleans 415, 417
 New York City 77, 105
 Newport 200
 Ohio 538
 Oklahoma 619
 Providence 196
 St Paul 577
 Washington, DC 257-8, 259, 263
Fidalgo 1001
films 45
film festivals 409
Fire Island Pines 111
fishing
 Alaska 1053
 Boothbay Harbor 233
 Catskills, the 120
 Gallatin River 766-7
 Jacksonville 486
 Montana 766
 New Jersey 132
 Outer Banks 328
 Port Aransas 705
Fishtown 556
Fitzgerald, F Scott 578-9
fjords, see glaciers
Flagstaff 827-9, 878
Flint Hills 610-11
Florence 190
Florida 434-97, **436-7**, **461**
 accommodations 496-7
 driving tours 461
 itineraries 438-9
 navigation 436-7
Florida Keys 458-63, 496, **459**
Florida, Northeast 484-9
Florida, Southeast 464-71
food 24-5, 50-3, 1071, 1092-3, see also individual destinations
 barbecue 52, 53, 601-2, 1092
 bagels 1093
 cheese 570
 crabs 282
 coffee 1071
 gumbo 427
 ice-cream 215-16
 lobster 1093
 pizza 203
 supper clubs 571
 Tabasco 431
food & wine festivals
 Bowen's Wharf Seafood Festival 200
 Johnny Appleseed Festival 526
 Maine Lobster Festival 233
 Maryland Crab Cake Festival 287
 National Apple Harvest Festival 153
 National Cherry Festival 554
 Newport Oyster Festival 200
 Red, White & Blueberry Festival 133
 Shadfest 133
 South 9th Street Italian Market Festival 145-6
football 1112
 Bryant-Denny Stadium 393
 Dooley Field at Sanford Stadium 382
 Ford Field 548
 Lambeau Field 569-70
 Pro Football Hall of Fame 540
Forks 1005
Fort Davis 707-8
Fort Laramie 755
Fort Lauderdale 464-9, **465**
forts
 Fort Baker 905
 Fort Davis 707-8
 Fort Kearny 631
 Fort Laramie 755
 Fort Mason 893
 Fort Missoula 771
 Fort Robinson 632
 Fort Selden 875
 Fort Sill 622-3
 Fort Washakie 753-4, 789
 Fort Worth 694-6, 712-13
Franconia 228
Frankfort 370-1
Fredericksburg 304, 688, 689, **689**
Frost, Robert 213-14, 228

G

Galena 521, 523
Gallatin Valley 765-7, 789
galleries & art museums
 Addison/Ripley Fine Art 268
 Amazing World of Dr Seuss 190
 American Art Museum 260
 American Folk Art Museum 98
 American Visionary Art Museum 289
 Andy Warhol Museum 156
 Art Institute of Chicago 505-6
 Art Omi 114
 Asheville Art Museum 333
 Aspen Art Museum 735
 Attic Gallery 402
 Baltimore Museum of Art 289
 Barnes Foundation 146
 Bass, the 443
 Bechtler Museum of Modern Art 330
 Bennington Museum 221
 Biltmore 334

Broad 955
Broad Art Museum 551
Buffalo AKG Art Museum 125
Burchfield Penney Art Center 125
Cantor Arts Center 909
Carrie Haddad's 113
Chazen Museum of Art 565
Chicago Cultural Center 515
Chihuly Collection 495
Chinati Foundation 708
Cincinnati Art Museum 538
Cleveland Museum of Art 535
C.M. Russell Museum 775
Columbus Museum of Art 539
Contemporary Arts Museum Houston 700
Crystal Bridges Museum 413
Denver Art Museum 726
Des Moines Art Center 640
Detroit Institute of Arts 545
Dia Beacon 112
Dia Bridgehampton 112
Dia Chelsea 88
Down Creek Gallery 326
Drawing Center 71
Eastern Shore Art Center 396
Eric Carle Museum of Picture Book Art 190
Frick Art Museum 156
Frick Collection 98
Gagosian 88
Gallery Article 15 268
Georgia Museum of Art 382
Getty Center 960
Harvey B Gantt Center 330
Heidelberg Project 547
High Line Nine 88
High Museum of Art 379
Hill Center 262
Hirshhorn Museum 257
Hunter Museum of American Art 363

Huntsville Museum of Art 390
Imagine Museum 495
Indianapolis Museum of Art 527
Institute of Contemporary Art 180
International Center of Photography 81
James Museum of Western & Wildlife Art 495
Jay Etkin Gallery 357
Jepson Center 384
Joslyn Art Museum 628
Knoxville Museum of Art 365
KuBe Art Center 114
LACMA 956
Leslie-Lohman Museum of Art 71
LongHouse Reserve 112
Lucy Clark Gallery 335
Mackinac Art Museum 559
MacNider Art Museum 644
Magazzino Italian Art 114
Mattress Factory 156
Memphis Brooks Museum of Art 358
Menil Collection 702
Metropolitan Museum of Art 96-7
Miami Museum of Art & Design 446
Milwaukee Art Museum 563
Minneapolis Institute of Art 575
Mint Museum Uptown 329-30
Missoula Art Museum 770
Monongalia Arts Center 311
Museum of Contemporary Art (Chicago) 506
Museum of Contemporary Art Detroit 545
Museum of Contemporary Photography 515
Museum of Fine Arts (Boston) 177
Museum of Fine Arts (Houston) 697
Museum of Modern Art 91
Museum of Nebraska Art 631
Museum of the American Arts & Crafts Movement 495

National Gallery of Art 257
National Museum of African Art 256
National Museum of Asian Art 256
National Museum of Mexican Art 515
National Museum of Wildlife Art 757
National Museum of Women in the Arts 260
National Portrait Gallery 260
Nelson-Atkins Museum of Art 601
Neue Galerie 95
Nevada Museum of Art 804
New Museum 81
New Orleans Museum of Art 427
New York Earth Room 71
Nicholas Roerich Museum 98
Northwest Museum of Arts & Culture 1010
Opus 40 117
Otherworld 539
Pace Gallery 88
Paula Cooper Gallery 88
Pennsylvania Academy of the Fine Arts 146
Pérez Art Museum Miami 445
Philadelphia Museum of Art 140
Philbrook Museum of Art 618
Phillips Collection 267
Phoenix Art Museum 812
Plains Art Museum 647
Pollock-Krasner House 112
Portland Museum of Art 231, 233
Princeton University Art Museum 134
Rehoboth Art League 277
Renwick Gallery 248-9
RISD Museum of Art 196
River Gallery 362-3
Rodin Museum 146
Romero Britto Fine Art Gallery 443
Rubell Museum 260
San Antonio Museum of Art 684
San Francisco Museum of Modern Art (SFMOMA) 903
Sandwich Glass Museum 186
Seattle Art Museum 991

Skyspace 413
St Louis Art Museum 598
Stanley Museum of Art 638
Storm King Art Center 112-13
Studio Museum in Harlem 99
Tampa Museum of Art 492
Telfair Academy 384
Torpedo Factory Art Center 304
Transformer Station 535
Tucson Museum of Art 837
University of Michigan Museum of Art 551
Village Craftsmen 326
Virginia Museum of Fine Arts 295
Wadsworth Atheneum 208
Walters Art Museum 289
Washington Printmakers Gallery 268
Weisman Art Museum 575
Wexner Center for the Arts 539
Whitney Museum of American Art 81, 84
Wichita Art Museum 612
Wolfsonian-FIU 443
Galveston 704-5
gardens, *see* parks & gardens
Georgia 374-87, 432, **375**
Georgian Coast 384, 386
Geronimo 842
Geronimo (Goyahkla) 622
Getty Center 960
Gettysburg 152
ghost towns 830
  Garnet Ghost Town 769-70
  Vulture City & Mine 830
glaciers 1043, 1044, 1050
Glacier Trail 807
Going-to-the-Sun Rd 772-3
gorges
  Dismals Canyon 390
  Little River Canyon 390
  Columbia River Gorge 1026-7, 1035
Grand Canyon 41, 816-17
Grand Coulee Dam 1010
Grand Marais 582-3
Grand Rapids 551-2
Great Falls 774-5, 789
Great Lakes 499-587, **500-1, 520**
  accommodations 586-7
  festivals & events 502-3

itineraries 502-3
navigation 500-1
walking tours 520, **520**
Great Plains 588-663, **590**
 accommodations 662-3
 festivals 592-3
 itineraries 592-3
 navigation 590-1
 travel seasons 592-3
 travel within 590
Great River Road 640
Green Bay 569-70
Greensboro 330, 331
Greenville 350-1
Griffith Park 951
Gruene 686, 687
Guilford 205
Gulf Coast 704-5, 713

Haines 1045
Half Moon Bay 909-10
Harpers Ferry 34, 312
Hartford 207-8
Harvard University 171
Hatfield-McCoy Trails 309
Havre de Grace 282
Hawai'i 1058-83, **1060-1**
 accommodations 1083
 festivals & events 1062
 itineraries 1062-3
 navigation 1060
 travel around 1061
 travel seasons 1062-3
Healdsburg 916
health 1091
Helena 768-9, 789
Hemingway, Ernest 519, 552, 785
Hibbing 583
High Line 85-6
highlights 14-27
hiking 54, see also trails, walking & walking tours
 Acadia National Park 236
 Adirondacks, the 117, 119
 Alabama 390
 Alaska 1048, 1055
 Big Island of Hawai'i, the 1072, 1073
 Birmingham 392
 Boise 782-3
 Bryce Canyon National Park 858-9
 Cascadilla Gorge 122
 Catskills, the 116
 Cherokee National Forest 364
 Colorado National Monument 746
 Crater Lake National Park 1022
 Craters of the Moon National Monument & Reserve 786
 Everglades National Park 455
 Falmouth 186
 Fiery Furnace 855
 Flagstaff 827
 Gallatin Valley 765-6
 Georgia 382
 Glacier National Park 773
 Graham Creek Nature Preserve 396
 Grand Canyon 817
 Grand Teton National Park 762
 Great Basin National Park 807
 Gunflint Trail 583
 Hocking Hills 542
 Hudson Valley 115
 John Pennekamp Coral Reef State Park 458, 460
 Kaua'i 1079
 Lansing 550
 Letchworth State Park 123
 Mammoth Cave National Park 371
 Maroon Bells 736
 Marquette 559
 Maryland Heights Trail 312
 Maui 1077, 1078
 Monument Mountain 192-3
 Morgantown 312
 Mt Baker 1003
 Mt Elbert 734
 Mt Hood 1028
 Mt Katahdin 238-9
 Mt Konocti 918-19
 Mt Nebo 409-10
 Mt Sentinel 771
 Mt Shasta 922
 Mt Tom State Reservation 190
 Mt Washington 226
 Nashville 362
 Nevada City 936
 New River Gorge 308
 North Carolina 335
 North Cascades 1007
 Oak Creek Canyon 825
 Ohiopyle State Park 157
 Outer Banks 328
 Ozark Mountains 414
 Ozarks 605-6
 Palo Alto 908
 Pennsylvania Wilds 153
 Phoenix 810, 811
 Pikes Peak 747
 Pisgah National Forest 336
 Provincetown 189
 Quoddy Head State Park 238
 Rainbow Lake Wilderness Area 364-5
 Redwood National Park 921
 Rocky Mountain National Park 730-1
 Saguaro National Park 840
 San Luis Obispo 940
 Sedona 823
 Shawnee National Forest 523
 Shenandoah National Park 301
 Skinner State Park 190
 South Mountain Park 812
 Superior Hiking Trail 582
 Telluride 743
 Vermont 216
 White Mountains 228
 Wisconsin 565
 Zion National Park 860-1
Hill Country 686-9, 712
historic buildings & sites, see also notable buildings
 AG Gaston Motel 392
 Aiken-Rhett House 344
 Bachman-Wilson House 413
 Beaufort Historic Site 324
 Biltmore 334
 Biltmore Hotel 448
 Bolivar Heights Battlefield 312
 Boscobel House & Gardens 114
 Brown v Board of Education National Historical Park 609
 Cahokia Mounds State Historic Site 523
 Capitol Hill 254-5
 Castillo de San Marcos 489
 Chatham Manor 304
 Clayton House 156
 Clinton Presidential Center 405-7
 College of William & Mary 297
 Colonial Williamsburg 297
 Dealey Plaza 691-2
 Dexter Avenue King Memorial Baptist Church 393, 395, 1105
 Dover Green 276
 Eastern State Penitentiary 146
 Ellis Island 1104
 Embassy Row 267
 Emlen Physick Estate 130
 Empire State Building 88, 90
 Fisher Building 548
 Flannery O'Connor Childhood Home 384
 Fort Condé 396
 Fort Mackinac 556, 559
 Fort Matanzas 489
 Fort Morgan State Historic Site 396
 Fort Moultrie 347
 Fort Raleigh National Historic Site 327
 Fort Sumter 347
 Freedmen's Colony 327
 Freedom Trail 172-3, 1103
 George Floyd Square 575
 Gettysburg National Military Park 152, 1104
 Grand Central Terminal 91-2
 Guardian Building 548
 Heurich House 267
 Highland 298
 Historic Corolla Park 328-9
 Historic St Mary's City 282
 Hopewell Culture National Historical Park 543
 'Iolani Palace 1064
 Independence National Historical Park 142-3
 John Brown's Fort 312
 Judd Foundation 80
 Kane Manor Inn 153
 Kelly Ingram Park 392
 Kenmore 304
 Kentuck Knob 157
 Kykuit 114
 Larz Anderson House 267
 Laura Plantation 429
 Little Rock Central High School National Historic Site 410
 Mansion on O Street 267
 Marshall Gold Discovery State Historic Park 935
 Martin Luther King Jr National Historical Park 377
 Mary Washington House 304
 Mayflower Hotel 267
 Medicine Wheel National Historic Landmark 755-6
 Melrose Estate 404
 Mercer-Williams House 384

1119

Minidoka National Historic Site 785-6
Minute Man National Historical Park 182
Minuteman Missile National Historic Site 654
Mission Nombre de Dios 489
Monticello 298
Monument Valley Navajo Tribal Park 829-30
Moundville Archaeological Park 395
Mount Vernon 305
National Mall, the 1103
Ocmulgee Mounds 382-3
Olana 115
Old Salem 331
Old State Capitol 370
Old Swedes Historic Site 273-4
Old Town Alexandria 304
Owens-Thomas House & Slave Quarters 384
Pabst Mansion 564
Park Avenue Armory 95
Pearl Harbor 1069, 1105
Plant Riverside District 384
Point Park 364
Poverty Point 431
Reconstruction Era National Historical Park 348
Rookery 509
Rowan Oak 401
SC Johnson Administration Building & Research Tower 564
Sloss 392
Star-Spangled Banner Flag House 291
Stonewall Inn 84
Taliesin 566
Tennessee State Capitol 359
Thomas Cole National Historic Site 114-15
Tomb of King Lunalilo 1066
Tribune Tower 509
United Nations 92
Unity Temple 519

Map Pages **000**

Valley Forge National Historic Park 148
Vicksburg 402
Vicksburg National Military Park 403
Volta Laboratory and Bureau 268
Whalehead Club 329
Whitman Mission National Historic Site 1009-10
Whitney Plantation 429
Wickersham State Historic Site 1042
William Johnson House 404
Wingspread 564
Wormsloe State Historic Site 386
Wrigley Building 509
history 26, 1102-5
 Black Heritage Trail 224, 226
 Brooklyn 104
 Civil War, the 1104
 Hawai'i 1067
 National Archives 259-60
 Portsmouth 224
 Prohibition 131
 WWII 1069, 1105
Hollywood 949-51
Homolovi State Park 833-4
Hood River 1026
Hoover Dam 803-4
horse racing
 Lexington 370
 Louisville 368
horse riding
 Daniel Boone National Forest 373
 Mammoth Cave National Park 371
horses, wild 329, 387
hot springs 27, 660
 Black Hills 660-1
 Cascade Mountains 1026
 Ouray 742
 Strawberry Park Hot Springs 733
 Truth or Consequences 876
Houston 697-703, **698-9, 700**
 accommodations 713
 drinking 702
 festivals 701
 food 701, 703
 transportation 697
Hudson Valley 112-15
Hudson Yards 86
Humboldt 610
Huntsville 388, 390
hurricanes 42, 1091

Hutchinson 612-13
Hwy 61 399

ice hockey 1113
ice skating 125
Idaho 777-87, **778**
Idaho Panhandle 783-4
Illinois 517-23, 586, **518**
immigration 1104
Independence 604
Indiana 524-32, 586, **525**
Indian Key 460
Indianapolis 526-8
insurance 1091
internet 1086, 1099
Iowa 634-44, **635**
Iowa City 638
Iowa State Fair 640
islands
 Assateague Island 286-7
 Big Island of Hawai'i, the 1070
 Cape Lookout National Seashore 325-6
 Coney Island 104-5
 Cumberland Island 387
 Fenwick Island 278
 Fire Island 111
 Governors Island 66-7
 Grand Island 630
 Isle of Palms 348
 Jekyll Island 387
 Kaua'i 1079
 Kelleys Island 540-1
 Kiawah 348
 Lāna'i 1077
 Little Island 87
 Long Beach Island 133
 Madeline Island 571
 Maui 1075
 Nantucket Island 189
 Northerly Island 507
 O'ahu 1064
 Peaks Island 231
 Roanoke Island 327-8
 San Juan Island 1004
 San Juan Islands 1034
 South Marble Island 1043
 St Helena Island 348
 Sullivan's Island 348
 Tybee Island 384, 386
itineraries 32-41, see also individual regions

Jackson 401-2, 757, 760-1, **760**
Jacksonville 484-6, **485**
Jaega people 470
jazz music 36, 37

Jefferson, Thomas 258, 298, 300
Jerome 826, 878
John's Pass Village 495
Juneau & the Alexander Archipelago 1040-5, **1041**
 accomodations 1057
 food 1042

Kalamazoo 550
Kansas 607-13, **608**
Kansas City 36, 601-4, 662, **602**
Katmai 1053, 1057
Kaua'i 1079-82, **1080**
 accommodations 1083
 drinking 1082
 food 1082
kayaking & canoeing 55, see also rafting
 Acadia National Park 237
 Apostle Islands National Lakeshore 570
 Assateague Island 287
 Assawoman Bay 278
 Baxter State Park 239
 Beaufort 325
 Boundary Waters Canoe Area Wilderness 583, 585
 Buffalo 125
 Buffalo National River 414
 Burlington 213
 Cave Point 568
 Charleston 347-8
 Cypress Creek National Wildlife Refuge 523
 Daniel Boone National Forest 373
 Jones Lagoon 457
 Kaua'i 1081
 Lafayette 431
 Lake George 119
 Mammoth Cave National Park 371
 Minneapolis 577
 New York City 94
 O'ahu 1069
 Philadelphia 144
 Pocano Mountains 150
 Portland 231
 Providence 196
 Red River Gorge 372
 Traverse City 556
 Valentine 633
 Washington, DC 270
 Wekiwa Springs Adventures 474
Kearney 630-1
Keller, Helen 391
Kenai Peninsula 1052, 1057
Kennedy Space Center 479

Kentucky 366-73, **367**
Ketchum 783-4, 789
Key West 458-63, 496, **459**
King, Martin Luther Jr 257, 393, 395
Kingman 833-4
Knoxville 365
Kodiak 1053, 1057

La Jolla 972-3
Lafayette 430-1
lakes
　Bde Maka Ska 577
　Bear Lake 455
　Cedar Lake 577
　Finger Lakes 121-3
　Lake Champlain 212-13
　Lake George 119-20, 121
　Lake Harriet 577
　Lake of the Isles 577
　Lake Placid 120-1
　Lake Pontchartrain 430
　Lake Tahoe 931-4, 978, **932**
　Lake Willoughby 214
　Rainbow Lake 364-5
Lambertville 137
Lancaster 151-2
language 45
Lansing 550-1
Laramie 752-3
Las Cruces 875-6, 879
Las Vegas 796-801, 878, **798-9**
Last Green Valley 209
Laurel Highlands 156-7
Lawrence 609
Lawrence, DH 874
Leadville 734
leaf peeping 214
Leland 556
Lenox 192
Lexington 369-70
LGBTQ+ travelers, 753, 1096
　Austin 679
　Chicago 513-14
　Denver 726
　Fort Lauderdale 467
　Los Angeles 958
　Missouri 606
　New York City 84
　Portland 1014-15, 1018
　San Francisco 902
libraries
　Boston Athenaeum 175
　Nashville Public Library 359, 361
　New York Public Library 92

lighthouses
　Au Sable Point Light Station 558
　Cape Henry Lighthouse 302
　Cape May Lighthouse 130
　Currituck Beach Lighthouse 329
　Grand Marais Lighthouse 583
　Hereford Lighthouse 132
　Montauk Point Lighthouse 106
　Ocracoke Lighthouse 327
　Sandy Hook Lighthouse 133
　Tybee Island Light Station 384, 386
　West Quoddy Head Lighthouse 238
Lincoln 628-9, 662
Lincoln, Abraham 519, 521, 532
Lindsborg 610
Litchfield County 209
Little Rock 405-10, **407**
live music
　Boston 176, 179
　Chicago 510-11, 512
　Clarksdale 399-400
　Memphis 357
Lloyd Wright, Frank 643
Lockhart 686-7
Logan 542
Long Beach 1005-6
Long Island 106-7, 111-12, **110**
Los Alamos 870
Los Angeles 949-62, **952-3**, **954**
　accommodations 979
　drinking 950, 951
　food 954, 955, 956
　shopping 955
　travel within 949
Louisiana 428-31, 433, **429**
Louisville 368
Lowcountry 346
Lubbock 710
Lucas 613
Luckenbach 688
Luther King Jr, Martin 1105
lyme disease 1091

M

Mackinac Island 556, 559
Macon 382-3
Madison 205
Madison, Indiana 532
Madison, James 301
Madison, Wisconsin 564-6
Maine 229-39, 241, **230**
Marfa 708, **709**
Mariposa 925, 927

markets
　Alaska 1047
　Atlanta 381
　Carrboro 333
　Charleston 344
　Cincinnati 537
　Cleveland 535
　Lambertville 137
　Lancaster 151
　Litchfield 209
　Little Rock 409
　Madison, Wisconsin 565
　Michigan 547
　Milwaukee 564
　Nashville 359
　New Orleans 423
　New York City 81, 84-5, 92, 99, 103
　Orlando 476
　Philadelphia 144-5
　Pittsburgh 154
　Richmond 295
　Washington, DC 262, 267
　Wilmington 273
Marley, Bob 273
Maroon Bells 736
Marquette 559
Maryland 280-92, 314-15, **281**
Mason City 642-4, 663
Massachusetts 184-94, 240, **185**
Maui 1075-8, **1076**
　accommodations 1083
　drinking 1077
　food 1077
McMinnville 1024-5
Medora 648
Memphis 37, 355-9, **356**
Mendocino 916, 918
Mercer, Henry 148
Merck Forest 220
Mexico 976
Miami 440-51, **441**, **442**, **444**, **446**, **448**, **449**
　accommodations 496
　festivals & events 448
　shopping 447
　travel within Miami 440
　walking tour 442, **442**
Michigan 544-59, 586-7, **545**
Middlebury 213-14
Milford 276
Mill Mountain Star 300
Million Dollar Hwy 739
Milwaukee 560-4, **562**
Minneapolis 572-6, **574**, **576**
Minnesota 572-85, 587, **573**
Mississippi 397-404, 433, **398**
Mississippi Delta 399-400
Missoula 769-71, 789, **770**

Missouri 594-606, **595**
Mitchell Caverns 966
Moab 848-51, **850**
Mobile 395-6
Mojave Desert 802-3
money 1088
Monowi 633
Montana 763-76, **764**
Monterey 942-3
Montgomery 393-5
Montpelier 217, 220
monuments & memorials
　Bandelier National Monument 870
　Bears Ears National Monument 851-2
　Canyon of the Ancients National Monument 738-9
　Chiricahua National Monument 841-2
　Colorado National Monument 746
　Craters of the Moon National Monument 786
　Crazy Horse Memorial 658
　Devil's Tower National Monument 755
　Diamond Head State Monument 1068
　Dinosaur National Monument 745
　Freedom Monument Sculpture Park 394
　Indiana War Memorial 527
　Korean War Veterans Memorial 258
　Lincoln Memorial 258
　Little Bighorn Battlefield National Monument 776
　Navajo National Monument 832
　Make Way for Ducklings 174
　Martin Luther King Jr Memorial 257
　Mary Tyler Moore Statue 580
　Mt St Helens National Volcanic Monument 1007
　National Memorial for Peace & Justice 394
　National WWII Memorial 258
　Navajo National Monument 832
　Newberry National Volcanic Monument 1029-30
　Paul Bunyan Statue 580

1121

Pearl Harbor National Memorial 1069
Pilgrim Monument 187
Say Their Names Cemetery 575
Scotts Bluff National Monument 632
Stonewall National Monument 84
Vietnam Veterans Memorial 259
Vulcan 392
Washington Monument 252, 256
moonshine 365
Morgan, Zackquill 311
Morgantown 311-12
mosquitoes 582
mountain biking 55, see also cycling & cycling tours
Bentonville 411
Kingdom Trails 220
Wisconsin 565
mountains
Appalachians 34-5
Blood Mountain 382
Cadillac Mountain 236
Coler Mountain 413
Grandfather Mountain 335
Lookout Mountain 363-4
Maunakea 1073
Monument Mountain 192
Mt Baker 1002-3
Mt Greylock 193
Mt Hood 1027-8
Mt Katahdin 238-9
Mt Lemmon 837-8
Mt Magazine 410
Mt Mansfield 216
Mt Margaret 1055
Mt Nebo 409-10
Mt Rainier 39
Mt Rushmore 658
Mt Shasta 922, 978
Mt Washington 226-8
North Carolina Mountains 35
Old Rag Mountain 301
Ozark Mountains 414
White Mountains 228
Wichita Mountains 623
murals
Cumberland 292

Map Pages **000**

Detroit 545, 547
Miami 445, 447
Vicksburg 403
museums 27, see also galleries & art museums
Abbe Museum 236
Adams Museum 661
Agua Caliente Cultural Museum 963
AKC Museum of the Dog 92
Alabama Music Hall of Fame 391
Alaska State Museum 1040
Allegany Museum 291-2
Alutiiq Museum 1056
American Civil War Museum 295
American Museum of Natural History 98
American Writers Museum 506
America's Black Holocaust Museum 564
Anchorage Museum 1046
Arab American National Museum 551
Art Deco Museum 443
Asia Society & Museum 95
Atlanta History Center 381-2
Auburn Cord Duesenberg Automobile Museum 528
Automotive Hall of Fame 550
B&O Railroad Museum 289
Backstreet Cultural Museum 420
Baltimore Museum of Industry 289
Basque Museum & Cultural Center 781
BB King Museum 399
Bethel Woods Center for the Arts 117
Birmingham Civil Rights Institute 392
Bobblehead Hall of Fame and Museum 564
Boot Hill Museum 613
Boston Children's Museum 180
Boston Fire Museum 180
Boston Tea Party Ships & Museum 180
Bradbury Science Museum 870

Branch Museum of Architecture & Design 295
Bryan Museum 704
Buffalo Bill Center of the West 756-7
Buffalo History Museum 125
Buffalo Transportation Pierce-Arrow Museum 125
Cabildo 417
Capital City Museum 370
Carnegie Museums of Pittsburgh 156
Catfish Row Museum 403
Charleston Museum 342
Charlestown Navy Yard 181
Cincinnati Museum Center 537
City Museum (St Louis) 594-5
City Reliquary 103
Clay Center for the Arts and Sciences 307
Cooper-Hewitt Smithsonian Design Museum 95
Corning Museum of Glass 123
Country Music Hall of Fame & Museum 359
Cumberland Visitor Center & Museum 292
de Young Museum 891
Delaware Children's Museum 273
Delaware History Museum 274
Delta Blues Museum 399-400, 1104
Dexter Parsonage Museum 395
Discovery World at Pier Wisconsin 564
Durham 627
Dwight D Eisenhower Presidential Library & Museum 610
Eastern State Penitentiary 146-7
Edgar Allan Poe National Historic Site 146
Eiteljorg Museum 527-8
Electromagnetic Pinball Museum & Restoration 198
Evergreen Museum 289
Fairhope Museum of History 396
Field Museum 514-15
First Americans Museum 620

Flatwoods Monster Museum 310
Ford Piquette Avenue Plant 549
Fountain of Youth Archaeological Park 489
Frank Lloyd Wright Home & Studio 519
Frazier History Museum 368
Gallier House Museum 419
Gateway to the Blues Museum 399
German Village 538
Gettysburg National Military Park 152
Gilmore Car Museum 550
Grand Portage National Monument 581-2
Grand Rapids African American Museum & Archives 551
Grand Rapids Public Museum 551
Graveyard of the Atlantic Museum 326-7
Great Lakes Shipwreck Museum 551
Greyhound Bus Museum 580
Griffin Museum of Science & Industry 506
Harley-Davidson Museum 563
Hancock Shaker Village 193
Harry S Truman Presidential Library & Museum 604
Hatteras Island Ocean Center 327
Havre de Grace Decoy Museum 282
Heard Museum 809-10
Heinz History Center 154
Helen Keller Birthplace 391
Henry Ford Museum of American Innovation 549-50
Henry Whitfield State Museum 205
Highway 61 Blues Museum 399
Historic Jamestown Archaearium 298
Historic New Orleans Collection 417
History Jackson Hole 760
History Museum of Mobile 396

Historic Patuxet Homesit 183
Idaho Black History Museum 779
Idaho Potato Museum 787
Idaho State Museum 779
Insect Asylum 506
International African American Museum 344, 1105
International Civil Rights Center & Museum 331
International Spy Museum 262
International UFO Museum & Research Center 874-5
International Tennis Hall of Fame 198
Intrepid Sea, Air & Space Museum 94
Jewish Museum 95
Jewish Museum of Florida-FIU 443
Jewish Museum of Maryland 289
Jimmy Carter Presidential Library & Museum 382
John Brown Wax Museum 312
Johnny Cash Museum 359
Juliette Gordon Low Birthplace Museum 384
Juneau-Douglas City Museum 1042
Kalmar Nyckel Shipyard 273
Kentucky Historical Society 370
Kentucky Horse Park 369
Kentucky Military History Museum 370
Kodiak History Museum 1056
Kurt Vonnegut Museum & Library 528
Kykuit 114
Lake Placid Olympic Museum 120
Legacy Museum 394
Life-Saving Station Museum 286
Little Traverse History Museum 552
Living Sharks Museum 198
Louisiana Children's Museum 426
Louisville Slugger Museum & Factory 368

Lower Mississippi River Museum 402
Mark Twain House & Museum 207
Mayflower II 183
Memphis Rock 'n' Soul Museum 355
Mercer Museum 149
Merchant's House Museum 80
Merry-Go-Round Museum 540
Mid-America All-Indian Museum 612
Milford Museum 276
Mississippi Civil Rights Museum 401
Missouri History Museum 598-9
Mitchell Center for African American Heritage 274
Mob Museum 801
Mosaic Jekyll Island Museum 387
Motown Museum 547
Musée Mécanique 895
Museum at Bethel Woods 117
Museum at Eldridge Street 79
Museum of African American History 175-6
Museum of Broadway 90
Museum of Discovery 409
Museum of East Tennessee History 365
Museum of Illusions 260, 506
Museum of Mississippi History 401-2
Museum of Native American History 413
Museum of Northern Arizona 827
Museum of Pop Culture 987
Museum of the Cherokee People 336
Museum of the City of New York 95
Museum of the Mountain Man 754-5
Museum of the Plains Indians 774
Museum of the Rockies 765
Mütter Museum 146
Mystic Seaport Museum 206
Natchez Museum of African American Culture & History 404

National Air and Space Museum 257
National Archives 259-60
National Automobile Museum 805
National Auto & Truck Museum 528
National Building Museum 260
National Center for Civil & Human Right 375
National Children's Museum 260
National Civil Rights Museum 355
National Constitution Center 138, 140
National Cowboy & Western Heritage Museum 620
National Frontier Trails Museum 604
National Great Blacks in Wax Museum 289
National Jazz Museum 98
National Maritime Museum of the Gulf 396
National Mississippi River Museum 636
National Museum of African American History & Culture 249
National Museum of Natural History 249
National Museum of the American Indian 256-7
National Museum of the US Air Force 543
National Mustard Museum 566
National September 11 Memorial Museum 69
National Underground Railroad Freedom Center 538
National WWII Museum 425, 601, 1105
Natural History Museum of Utah 847
Negro Leagues Baseball Museum 603
Neon Museum 801
Nevada Historical Society Museum 805
Newport Art Museum 198
Newport Car Museum 198
New Mexico Museum of Space History 876
New Orleans Pharmacy Museum 417
New York Historical Society 98
Nichols House Museum 174

Oakland Museum of California 905
Ocracoke Preservation Museum 327
Oklahoma City National Memorial & Museum 620
Old Cowtown Museum 611-12
Old Slave Mart Museum 343
Old State House Museum 409
Old West Museum 751
Oldest Wooden School House Museum & Gardens 487
Orange County Regional History Center 478
Oregon Museum of Science & Industry 1015
Osage Nation Museum 619
Oscar Getz Museum of Bourbon History 369
Penn Center 348
Pin Point Heritage Museum 386
Planet Word 260
Plimoth Grist Mill 183
Plimoth Patuxet Museums 183, 1102
Poe Museum 297
Pony Express National Museum 604
Presbytère 417
Provincetown Museum 188
RE Olds Transportation Museum 551
Reginald F Lewis Museum 289
Roanoke Island Festival Park 327-8
Rock & Roll Hall of Fame & Museum 534
Rosa Parks Museum 395
Route 66 Museum 833
Sag Harbor Whaling & Historical Museum 111
Sailing Museum & National Sailing Hall of Fame 198
Science Museum of Virginia 295
Sealaska Heritage Institute 1040
Sixth Floor Museum 690-1
Smith Robertson Museum 402
Solomon R Guggenheim Museum 95
Sorrel Weed House 384
Spam Museum 580

Stax Museum of American Soul Music 355, 357
Strategic Air Command & Aerospace Museum 629
Strawbery Banke Museum 224
Studebaker National Museum 528
Stuhr Museum 630
Tampa Bay History Center 492
Temecula Valley Museum 971
Tenderloin Museum 900
Tenement Museum 77
Tennessee State Museum 359
University of Michigan Museum of Natural History 551
University of Mississippi Museum 401
University of Nebraska State Museum 629
US Olympic & Paralympic Museum 747
US Space & Rocket Center 390
USS *Alabama* 396
USS *Cairo* Museum 403
USS *Constitution* Museum 181
Ute Indian Museum 744
Vermont Historical Society Museum 220
Vicksburg Civil War Museum 402
Virginia Musical Museum 297
Vizcaya Museum & Gardens 451
Walmart Museum 413
Wadsworth-Longfellow House 231
Wells'Built Museum 472
West Virginia Bigfoot Museum 310
Western Antique Aeroplane & Automobile Museum 1026
Whaling Museum 189
Whaley House Museum 975
Wood River Museum of History & Culture 784
World Kite Museum 1006
World of Coca-Cola 376
World's Only Mothman Museum 310
Wright Brothers National Memorial 328
Wyoming State Museum 751
Yavapai Geology Museum 813
Ybor City Museum State Park 492
Zwaanendael Museum 278
mushrooms 148
music 20, 36-7, 45, 548, 1104, *see also* live music, *individual genres*
music festivals 133, 153, 192, 200, 273, 400, 401, 417, 526, 530, 554, 563
Myrtle Beach 349
Mystic 206-7

N

Nantucket Island 189
Napa 978
Napa Valley 913
NASA 703
Nashville 36, 359-62, **360, 361**
Natchez 403-4
National Mall 256
national parks & reserves 16, 27, 46-9, *see also* parks & gardens, state parks & reserves
Acadia National Park 236-8
Arches National Park 854-5
Badlands National Park 38, 650-1
Big Bend National Park 40, 708-9
Biscayne National Park 452-7, 496, 453
Black Canyon of the Gunnison National Park 744
Bryce Canyon National Park 858-9
Canyonlands National Park 856-7
Capitol Reef National Park 853
Cherokee National Forest 364
Crater Lake National Park 1022
Craters of the Moon National Park 789
Congaree National Park 352
Cuyahoga Valley National Park 536
Daniel Boone National Forest 373
Death Valley National Park 964, **965**
Denali National Park & Preserve 1054, 1057
Everglades National Park 454, 456
Gateway Arch National Park 600
Glacier Bay National Park 1043
Glacier National Park 39, 772-3
Grand Canyon National Park 813-20, **814-15**
Grand Teton National Park 762
Great Basin National Park 807
Great Sand Dunes National Park 748
Great Smoky Mountains National Park 35, 337-40, 363, 1104
Guadalupe Mountains National Park 709
Hawai'i Volcanoes National Park 1074
Homestead National Historical Park 630
Hot Springs National Park 408
Indiana Dunes National Park 529
Isle Royale National Park 557
Joshua Tree National Park 963-4
Junior Rangers 731
Katmai National Park & Preserve 1056
Kings Canyon National Park 930
Lassen Volcanic National Park 924
Mammoth Cave National Park 371
Mesa Verde National Park 740-1
Mojave National Preserve 966
Mt Rainier National Park 998
New River Gorge National Park & Preserve 34, 308-9
North Cascades National Park 1000
Ocmulgee Mounds 382-3
Olympic National Park 999
Oregon Dunes National Recreation Area 1032-3
Ozark National Scenic Riverways 605
Petrified Forest National Park 832-3
Pictured Rocks National Lakeshore 558
Redwood National Park 921
Ocmulgee Mounds 382-3
Saguaro National Park 840
Sawtooth National Recreation Area 784-5
Sequoia National Park 930
Shenandoah National Park 34, 300-1
Sinks Canyon State Park 753
Tallgrass Prairie National Preserve 610
Theodore Roosevelt National Park 646
Voyageurs National Park 584
White Sands National Park 877
Wind Cave National Park 652
Yellowstone National Park 38, 758-9, 1104
Yosemite National Park 41, 928-9, **929**
Zion National Park 41, 860-1
Native Americans 622, 1046, 1102, 1103
Oglala Lakota Sioux 654-5
Osage people 619-20
Native American sites
Agua Caliente Cultural Museum 963
Akta Lakota Museum & Cultural Center 659
Eastern Shoshone Indian Days 753-4
Havasupai Reservation 820
Heard Museum 808-9
Indian Pueblo Cultural Center 866
Little Bighorn Battlefield National Monument 776
Medicine Wheel National Historic Landmark 755-6

Map Pages **000**

Monument Valley Navajo Tribal Park 829-30
Museum of the Plains Indians 774
Navajo National Monument 832
Sand Creek Massacre National Historic Site 748
Shoshone Tribal Cultural Center 754
Ute Indian Museum 744
Wounded Knee 655
Nebraska 624-33, **625**
Nebraska Panhandle 632
Nevada 802-7, **803**
Nevada City 935-6
New Braunfels 686, 687
New England 161-241, **162-3**
 accommodations 240-1
 climate 164-5
 itineraries 164-5
 navigation 162-3
New Hampshire 222-8, 241, **223**
New Haven 203-5, **204**
New Hope 149-50
New Jersey 60-5, 128-37, **62-3**, **129**
 accommodations 159
 activities 64-5
 itineraries 64-5
 navigation 62-3
New Mexico 863-77, **864**
New Orleans 37, 415-27, **416**, **421**, **424**, **425**
 accommodations 433
 children, travel with 426
 drinking & nightlife 422, 423
 entertainment 419, 422, 423
 festivals & events 415, 417
 shopping 426
 travel within 415
New River Gorge 308-9
New York City 32, 60-1, 66-105, **68**, **70**, **72**, **74**, **78**, **82**, **89**, **93**, **102**
 accommodations 158
 drinking & nightlife 103-4
 entertainment 75, 81, 88, 90-1
 festivals & events 105
 food 71, 75, 77, 81, 84-5
 itineraries 64
 shopping 69, 75-6, 86
 travel within New York City 66
 walking tour 70, **70**
New York State 60-5, 106-27, **62-3**, **108-9**
 accommodations 158
 activities 64-5
 itineraries 64-5
 navigation 62-3
Newport 198-200
Newport Beach 970-1
Newport **199**
Niagara Falls 126-7
Nicodemus 610
nightlife 1092-3
Norfolk 302
North Carolina 322-40, 432, **323**
North Dakota 645-8, 663, **647**
North Shore 581-3
Northeast Florida 484-9, 497
Northport 556
notable buildings, see also historic buildings & sites
 520 W 28th St 86
 Alaska State Capitol 1042
 Empire State Building 88, 90
 Freedom Tower 443, 446
 Governor's Mansion of Alaska 1042
 Hearst Castle 941-2
 John F Kennedy Center for the Performing Arts 248
 Kennedy Center 248
 Marina City 509
 One World Trade Center 69
 Pritzker Pavilion 507
 St Regis Chicago 509
 Willis Tower 509

Oak Park 517, 519, 520
O'ahu 1064-9, **1065**, **1066**
 accommodations 1083
 drinking 1067, 1069
 food 1066-7, 1069
 surfing 1069
Oakland 905
Ocean City 286
Ocracoke 327
Ohio 533-43, 586, **534**
Ohio Amish Country 541-2
Ohio City 535
O'Keeffe, Georgia 869
Oklahoma 614-23, **615**
Oklahoma City 620-2, 662, **621**
Olympia 1005
Omaha 626-8, 662, **627**
opening hours 24, 1099
Oppenheimer, J Robert 870
Orcas Island 1004
Oregon 1021-33, **1023**, see also Portland
Oregon Trail 632
Orlando 472-8, 496-7, **473**
Osage people 619-20
Ouray 739, 742
Outer Banks 326-9
Oxford 400-1
oysters 75
Ozarks 605-6

Pacific Northwest 980-1035, **982-3**
 festivals 984-5
 itineraries 984-5
 navigation 982-3
 travel seasons 984-5
 travel within 982
Palm Springs 962, 979
Palmer 1048
Palo Alto 908, 909
Palouse Falls 1009
Park City 847-8
parks & gardens, see also national parks & reserves, state parks & reserves
 Airlie Gardens 324
 Alfred Caldwell Lily Pool 507
 Atlanta Botanical Garden 380
 Audubon Park 427
 Battle Green 181-2
 Bayfront Park 443, 445
 Beacon Park 549
 Belle Isle Park 549
 Bluff View Art District 362
 Bonnet House Museum & Gardens 467
 Boston Common 170
 Botanica 612
 Brickell Key Park 445
 Brookgreen Gardens 349
 Brooklyn Bridge Park 99, 103
 Bryant Park 92, 94
 Buffalo Bayou Park 701
 Burlington Greenway 212
 Campus Martius Park 549
 Centennial Olympic Park 378
 Centennial Park 362, 492
 Central Park 14, 100-1
 Charles River Esplanade 176
 Cheekwood 362
 City Park 427, 726-7
 Columbus Park 71, 75
 Concrete Park 566
 Confluence Park 724
 Curry Hammock 462
 Curtis Hixon Waterfront Park 492
 Delaware Botanic Gardens 279
 Delaware Park 124
 Dequindre Cut Greenway 549
 Desert Botanical Garden 810
 Domino Park 447
 Dr Evermor's Sculpture Park 566
 East Rock Park 203
 Elizabeth Street Garden 76
 Formal Gardens 358
 Fort Lauderdale Beach Park 464
 Fort Worth Botanic Garden 696
 Fort Zachary Taylor Park 462
 Garden of the Gods 747
 Gathering Place 618
 Golden Gate Park 891
 Governor Tom McCall Waterfront Park 1017
 Grant Park 507
 Harry P Leu Gardens 476
 Hermann Park 701
 Historic Fourth Ward Park 381
 Hudson River Park 86-7
 Huntsville Botanical Garden 390
 Institute Woods 135
 Jetty Park 481
 Labyrinth 166
 Lady Bird Johnson Wildflower Center 677
 Lincoln Park 507
 Longwood Gardens 147
 Lurie Garden 507
 Margaret Pace Park 445
 Martin's Park 180
 Maurice A Ferré Park 445
 Máximo Gómez Park 447
 Mill Ruins Park 577
 Millennium Park 506-7
 Minneapolis Sculpture Garden 575
 Minute Man National Historical Park 182
 Missouri Botanical Garden 599
 Morey's Piers 131
 Myriad Botanical Gardens 623
 New Orleans Botanical Garden 427
 Nichols Arboretum 551
 Overton Park 358
 Philadelphia's Magic Gardens 147

Piedmont Park 380
Pilgrims' First Landing Park 187-8
Point Park 364
Polk Bros Park 509
Public Garden 170, 174
Railroad Park 392
Red Butte Garden 847
RiverFront 626
Rose Kennedy Greenway 166-7
San Antonio Botanical Garden 684
Sarah P Duke Gardens 331
Saxapahaw Island Park 333
Schuylkill Banks 140, 144
Spohr Gardens 186
State Botanical Garden of Georgia 382
Storm King Art Center 112-13
Sunken Forest 111
Sydney & Walda Besthoff Sculpture Garden 427
Tubman Garrett Riverfront Park 273
Umpachenee Falls Park 192
Underline 445
United States National Arboretum 263, 267
Valley Forge National Historic Park 148
Veldheer Tulip Gardens 554
Virginia B Fairbanks Art & Nature Park 527
Vizcaya Museum & Gardens 451
Warner Parks 362
Washington Park 1017
Washington Square Park 87-8
Water Works Park 490, 492
Watson Island Park 445
Wild Gardens of Acadia 237
Windmill Island Garden 554
Women's Rights National Historical Park 123
Parks, Rosa 393, 395

Map Pages **000**

Paso Robles 941-2
Pawhuska 619-20
Peacham 221
Peñasco 869
Pendleton 1033-4
Pennsylvania 60-5, 138-57, **62-3, 139**
  accommodations 159
  activities 64-5
  itineraries 64-5
  navigation 62-3
Pennsylvania Wilds 152-3
people 1106
Petoskey 552
petroglyphs 541
Philadelphia 32, 138, 140-6, **141**
  accommodations 159
  drinking 144, 145
  food 144, 146, 147, 148, 149
Phoenix 808-12, **809**
pickles 154
Pine Ridge Reservation 654-5
Pinesdale 754-5
Pittsburgh 154-6, **155**
Pittsfield 193
planetariums 515
Plantation Country 429
Plymouth 182-3
Poconos, the 150-1
Point Pleasant 309-10
Point Reyes 907-8
poison ivy 1091
population 1099, 1106
Porcupine Mountains 559
Port Aransas 704-5
Port Canaveral 481-2
Portland 33, 231-3, 1011-20, **1012-13**
  accommodations 1034
  drinking 1014, 1018
  food 1015, 1016, 1017, 1019
  parks 1015
  travel within 1011
Portsmouth 224-6
Portuguese man o' war 466
powwows 768
Prescott 826-7, 878
Presley, Elvis 357
Prince 572-3, 578
Prince William Sound 1050, 1057
Princeton 134-7, Princeton **135**
Providence 196-7, **197**
Provincetown 33, 187-9
public holidays 1099

Racine 564
rafting 55, *see also* kayaking & canoeing

Arkansas River 736
Boise 779-80
Bryson City 336
Charlotte 330
Cherokee National Forest 364
Colorado River 849-50
Dinosaur National Monument 745
Grand Canyon 817
Merced River 927
Penobscot River 239
Rio Grande 874
Salmon River 785
Truckee River 806
Yakima River 1008
Rapid City 655
Red River Gorge 371, 372
Red Rock Canyon National Conservation Area 802-3
Red Rock Scenic Byway 825
Red Rocks Amphitheater 727-8
Redwood National Park 921
Rehoboth Beach 276-7
Reno 804-6, **805**
responsible travel 1072, 1094-5
Revere, Paul 1103
Rhode Island 194-200, 240, **195**
Richmond 295-7, **296**
rivers
  Blue River 532
  Buffalo National River 414
  Cuyahoga River 535
  Grand River 550
  Penobscot River 239
  Potomac River 270
  Red Cedar River 550
  Wabash River 532
  Yukon River 1044
road trips, *see* driving & driving tours
Roche Harbor 1004
rock climbing
  Acadia National Park 237
  Chattanooga 363
  Giant City 519
  Mississippi Palisades 519
  White Mountains 227
Rockland 233
Rocky Mountains 714-89, **716-17**
  accommodations 788
  festivals 718-19
  itineraries 718-19
  navigation 716-17
  travel seasons 718-19
  travel within 716
Rogue-Umpqua Scenic Byway 1033-4
roller-skating 550

Roosevelt, Franklin D 1048
Roosevelt, Theodore 648
Roswell 874-5, 879
Route 66
  Arizona 833-4
  Flagstaff 828
  Kansas 611
  Oklahoma 618
  Tulsa 616, 618
Russell, CM 775

Sacramento 946-7, 978-9
safety 49, 1081, 1091
Saguaro National Park 840
Salida 736-7
salmon 1053
Salt Lake City 845-7, **846**
salt marshes 206, 327
San Antonio 40, 680-6, 712, **681, 682**
San Diego 973-6, 979, **974**
San Francisco 886-904, **887, 888-9, 892, 900**
  accommodations 977
  cable cars 899
  drinking 901
  food 887, 894, 895, 896, 899, 902
  travel within 886
San Luis Obispo 939-40
Santa Barbara 937, 939
Santa Cruz 943-4, 946
sandboarding 328
Sandusky 539-40
Sandwich 186-7
Sandy Hook 133-4
Santa Fe 40, 867-9, 879, **867**
Santa Fe Trail 613, 748
Santa Monica 958-9
Sausalito 907-8
Savannah 384, 385
Saxapahaw 333
seals 132, 198
Seattle 39, 986-95, **988-9**
  accommodations 1034
  drinking 991, 995
  food 987, 990, 992-3
  shopping 993
  travel within 986
Seaview 1005-6
Sebastopol 915
Sedona 821-5, 878, **824**
Sequim 1005
Sequoia 978
Sequoyah 336
Seward 1051
sharks 22
Shasta Lake 922-3
Shawnee Hills 523
Shelter Cove 919-20
Shepard, Matthew 753

Shoals, the 390-1
Sioux City 644
Sioux Falls 649, 653-4, 663
Sisters 1030
Skagit Valley 1003
skiing
 Aspen 734-5
 Big Sky 767
 Bridger Bowl 767
 Canaan Valley 313
 Catamount Trail 216
 Colorado 722-3
 Cranmore 227
 Crested Butte Mountain Resort 737-8
 Jackson Hole Mountain Resort 761
 Jackson XC 227
 Lake Placid 120-1
 Michigan 555
 Mt Baker 1002
 Mt Hood 1027-8
 Park City 847-8
 Santa Fe 868
 Snowshoe Mountain Resort 313
 Steamboat Mountain Resort 732-3
 Stowe 214-15
 Sun Valley Resort 783
 Tahoe 931, 934
 Telluride Ski Resort 743
 Timberline Mountain 313
 Vail Mountain 733-4
 Whitefish Mountain Resort 774
 Winterplace Ski Resort 313
Slater, Kelly 483
slavery 1105
small towns 17
snorkeling, see diving & snorkeling
snowmobiling 555
soccer 1112, 1113, 262
Sonoma 914-15, 978
Sonora 936
South Bend 528, 530
South by Southwest 677
South Carolina 341-52, 432, **342**
South Dakota 649-61
South Padre Island 705
South, the 317-433, **318**
 accommodations 432-3
 festivals & events 320-1
 itineraries 320-1
 navigation 318-19
Southeast Florida 464-71, 496
Southwest Florida 490-5, 497
Southwest USA 790-879, **792-3**

festivals 794-5
itineraries 794-5
navigation 792-3
travel seasons 794-5
travel within 793
Space Center Houston 703
Space Coast 479-83, 497, **480**
spas
 Atlanta 379
 Berkeley Springs 313
 New York City 67, 80
 Williamstown 192
 Spokane 1010
sports 1112-13, 260, 724, 991-2, see also individual sports
Spring Green 566
Springfield 190, 519, 521, 1025
Stanford 908-9
Stanley 784-5
St Augustine 486-9, **488**
St Elmo 737
St Joseph 604-5
St Louis 36, 594-9, 662, **596-7**
St Mary's City 282, 284
St Paul 578-9
St Thomas Ghost Town 804
stargazing
 Big Bend 707
 Black Canyon of the Gunnison 744
 Bryce Canyon National Park 859
 Chiricahua National Monument 842
 Grand Canyon National Park 813
 John Glenn Astronomy Park 542
 Mesa Verde National Park 741
 Sisters 1030
state parks & reserves 46-9, see also national parks & reserves, parks & gardens
 'Akaka Falls State Park 1073
 Assateague State Park 286-7
 Balmorhea State Park 707-8
 Bash Bish Falls State Park 192
 Baxter State Park 238-9
 Berkeley Springs State Park 313
 Bicentennial Capitol Mall State Park 359
 Big Bay State Park 571

 Big Talbot Island State Park 486
 Blue Spring State Park 474
 Brown County State Park 531
 Buttermilk Falls State Park 122
 Camp Hero State Park 106-7
 Cape Disappointment State Park 1006
 Cape May Point State Park 131
 Cheesequake State Park 137
 Clark State Forest 528
 Clear Lake State Park 918
 Clifty Falls State Park 528
 Crater of Diamonds State Park 410
 Cumberland Falls State Resort Park 373
 Custer State Park 659-60
 Deception Pass State Park 1001
 Delaware Seashore State Park 278
 Devil's Den State Park 414
 DuPont State Fores 335-6
 Edisto Beach State Park 348
 Falls of the Ohio State Park 528
 First State Heritage Park 276
 Gooseberry Falls State Park 581
 Grand Haven State Park 559
 Grandfather Mountain State Park 335
 Gulf State Park 396
 Hammonasset Beach State Park 205
 High Point State Park 137
 Hither Hills State Park 111
 Holland State Park 559
 Hueston Woods State Park 542
 Hugh Taylor Birch State Park 466
 Hunting Island State Park 348-9
 Indian River Lagoon State Park 482
 Jekyll Island State Park 387
 Jockey's Ridge State Park 328
 John Bryan State Park 542

 John Pennekamp Coral Reef State Park 458, 460
 Judge CR Magney State Park 581
 Kelleys Island State Park 541
 Kittatinny Valley State Park 137
 Kōke'e State Park 1079
 Lake Guntersville State Park 390
 Leonard Harrison State Park 152
 Letchworth State Park 123
 Lignumvitae Key Botanical State Park 460, 462
 Lime Kiln Point State Park 1004
 Ludington State Park 559
 Malabar Farm State Park 542
 Marshall Gold Discovery State Historic Park 1103
 Matthiessen State Park 519
 Mendocino Headlands State Park 918
 Mohican-Memorial State Forest 542
 Montauk Point State Park 106
 Monte Sano State Park 390
 Mounds State Park 528
 Mt Tom State Reservation 190
 Myrtle Beach State Park 349
 Nā Pali Coast Wilderness State Park 1079
 Natural Bridge State Resort Park 372
 Newport State Park 568
 Norvin Green State Forest 137
 Oak Mountain State Park 392
 Ohiopyle State Park 157
 Old Forest State Natural Area 358
 Palo Duro Canyon State Park 710
 Palouse Falls State Park 1009
 Peninsula State Park 568
 Petit Jean 409
 Petoskey State Park 559
 Point Lookout State Park 284
 Porcupine Mountains 559

Princeton Battlefield State Park 135
Quoddy Head State Park 238
Rainbow Lake Wilderness Area 364-5
Robert H Treman State Park 122
Sebastian Inlet State Park 482
Shadmoor State Park 112
Silver Falls State Park 1025
Sinks Canyon State Park 753
Skinner State Park 190
Sleeping Bear Dunes National Lakeshore 553
South Bass Island State Park 542
Starved Rock 519
Tahquamenon Falls State Park 559
Tallulah Gorge State Park 382
Temperance River State Park 581
Turkey Run State Park 528
Underhill State Park 216-17
Unicoi State Park & Lodge 382
Vogel State Park 382
Waimea Canyon State Park 1081
Washington Crossing State Park 137
Watkins Glen State Park 122
Wekiwa Springs State Park 474
Wharton State Forest 137
White Pines Forest 519
White River State Park 527, 528
Statue of Liberty 72-3
Steamboat Springs 732-3
Stiltsville 457
Sturbridge 189-90
sun safety 1069, 1091
Sun Valley 783-4
surfing
  Jacksonville 486
  Long Island 107

New Jersey 134
O'ahu 1067
Port Canaveral 481
Santa Cruz 943
Virginia Beach 302
Sussex County 277-9
Sutton 310
Suttons Bay 556
swimming 1091
SXSW 677

Tahlequah 620
Tampa 490-3, **491**
Tampa Bay 490-5, 497
Taos 870-1, 873-4, 879, **871**
taxes 1088
telephones 1099
Telluride 743-4, 788
Temecula 971-2
temples 136
Tennessee 353-65, 432, **354**
Texas 40, 664-713, **666-7**
  accommodations 712-13
  festivals 668-9
  itineraries 668-9
  navigation 666-7
  travel seasons 668-9
  travel within 666
Texas Panhandle 710
theaters
  54 Below 91
  Alabama Theatre 392
  American Players Theatre 566
  Apollo Theater 99
  Atlantic Theater Company 88
  Broadway 90-1
  Bucks County Playhouse 149-50
  Chicago Theatre 514
  Chopin Theatre 514
  Clayton Theatre 277
  Clear Space Theatre Company 277
  Comedy Cellar 88
  Den Theatre 511
  GableStage 450
  Goodman Theatre 514
  Guthrie Theater 577
  Historic Ritz Theatre 387
  Howard Theatre 264
  iO Theater 511
  Jungle Theater 577
  Lincoln Center 98
  Lincoln Theatre 265
  Lucille Lortel Theatre 88
  Lyric 392
  Metropolitan Theatre 311
  Milton Theatre 277
  Miracle Theatre 262

National Theatre 260
Neo-Futurist Theater 514
Paramount Theater 298
Playhouse Square 535
Playwrights Horizons 90-1
Public Theater 75
Second City 511
Shakespeare Theatre Company 260
Slipper Room 81
Steppenwolf Theatre 514
Studio Theatre 263
TheaterSquared 411
University Theater 410-11
Village Vanguard 88
Walton Arts Center 411
Warner Theatre 260
Woolly Mammoth Theatre Company 260
theme parks, see amusement parks
Theodore Roosevelt National Park 646
Tillamook 1032-3
Times Square 92, 94
time zones 1099
tipping 1088
toilets 1099
Tombstone 841
Topeka 609-10
Torrey 879
tours 1049, 1055, see also boat tours, cycling & cycling tours, driving tours, train travel & tours, walking tours
Trail of Tears 620
trails
  Continental Divide Trail 869
  Katy Trail 692
  Mission Trail 685
  Monarch Crest Trail 736-7
  Perimeter Trail 742
  Royal Arch Trail 732
  Santa Fe Trail 748
  Tahoe Rim Trail 934
train tavel & tours 14, 32-3, 1110-11, 1087
  Alaska 1044
  Great Smoky Mountains Railroad 336
  Incline Railway 363-4
travel insurance 1091
travel seasons 42-3, 47, 1108, see also individual locations
travel to/from the USA 1086
travel within the USA 1087
Traverse City 556
Tremont 537
Triangle, the 331

Tri-Peaks Region 409-10
Truman, Harry S 604
Truth or Consequences 876
tubing 350
Tubman, Harriet 276
Tucson 835-9, 878, **838**
Tulsa 614-19, **617**
TV shows 45

universities
  Duke University 331
  Howard University 264
  Michigan State University 551
  University of Arkansas 410-11
  University of Georgia 382
  University of Michigan 551
  University of North Carolina 331
  University of Notre Dame 530
  University of Virginia 298
Utah 843-62, **844**

vacations 1108-9
Vail 733-4
Valentine 633
Vermont 210-21, 241, **211**
viewpoints
  Chicago 509
  New York City 90
  Washington, DC 252
Virginia 293-306, 315, **294**
visas 1086
volcanoes 1073, 1074, 1077
voodoo 417

Waikīkī 1066
walking & walking tours 54, 172, 180, 213, see also hiking
  Annapolis 283, **283**
  Boston 175
  Charleston 345, **345**
  Durham 332, **332**
  Echo Park 957
  El Paso 711, **711**
  Eureka Springs 412, **412**
  Flagstaff 828, **828**
  Fort Worth Stockyards 695, **695**
  Miami 442, **442**
  New Orleans 418, **418**
  New York City 70, 156, **70**

Oak Park 520, **520**
Portland 231, 232, **232**
Portsmouth 225, **225**
San Francisco 898, **898**
Savannah 385, **385**
Washington, DC 253, **253**
Williamsburg 297
Wall 654
Walla Walla 1008-9
Washington 996-1010, **997**
see also Seattle
Washington Cascades 1006-7
Washington, DC 32, 242-7, 248-70, **249**, **253**, **259**, **261**, **266**, **269**
accommodations 314
children, travel with 260
drinking & nightlife 268
entertainment 248, 260, 263, 264-5
food 262
shopping 268
travel within Washington, DC 248
walking tours 253, **253**
Washington, George 1103
waterfalls
Bastion Falls 116
Benton Falls Trail 364
Big Island of Hawai'i, the 1073
Cathedral Falls 308
Cedar Falls 542
Cumberland Falls 372, 373
Dingmans Falls 151
Eagles Falls 373
Glen Burney Falls Trail 335
Glory Hole Falls 414
Hemmed-in Hollow Falls 414
Ithaca Falls 122
Kaaterskill Falls 116
Kaua'i 1081

Maui 1075, 1078
Minnehaha Falls 577-8
Niagara Falls 126-7
Rainbow Lake Wilderness Area 364-5
Ruby Falls 364
Sabbaday Falls 228
Taughannock Falls 121
weather 42-3
West Palm Beach 469-71, **470**
West Texas 706-11, 713, **707**
West Virginia 306-13, 315, **307**
whale watching
Alaska 1044, 1052
Boothbay Harbor 233
New Jersey 131
Provincetown 188-9
whiskey 369, *see also* distilleries
White House, the 250-1
Whitefish 774
Wichita 611-12
wi-fi 1086, 1099
wildfires 1031, 1091
wildlife 18, 55, 1049, *see also individual species*
Glacier National Park 773
Grand Teton National Park 762
Minnesota 585
National Elk Refuge & Greater Yellowstone Visitor Center 757
Rocky Mountain National Park 731
wildlife sanctuaries & reserves, *see also* zoos
Archie Carr National Wildlife Refuge 482
Audubon Bird Sanctuary 396
Blackwater National Wildlife Refuge 285
Bon Secour National

Wildlife Refuge 396
Chincoteague National Wildlife Refuge 302-3
Cypress Creek National Wildlife Refuge 523
Du Pont Environmental Education Center 273
Duke Lemur Center 331
Manatee Lagoon 471
Merritt Island National Wildlife Refuge 482
Montrose Point Bird Sanctuary 507
Northern Chumash Heritage National Marine Sanctuary 941
Okefenokee National Wildlife Refuge 383
Pelican Island National Wildlife Refuge 471
Prime Hook National Wildlife Refuge 278
Rachel Carson National Wildlife Refuge 324-5
Seaside Seabird Sanctuary 495
Stellwagen Bank National Marine Sanctuary 189
Wildwood 131-2
Willamette Valley 1025-6, 1035
Williamsburg 297-8
Wilmington 273-5, 324, **274**
Wimberley 688
wine 52
wine regions
Finger Lakes 122
Hill Country 687
Michigan 555
Napa Valley 913
New Jersey 130
Pennsylvania 149
Shawnee Hills 523
Sonoma 914-15
Temecula 972

Verde Valley 825
Virginia 298, 300
Willamette Valley 1025-6
Yakima Valley 1008
Winslow 831
Winston-Salem 331
Wisconsin 560-71, 587, **561**
Wood, Grant 636, 638
Woods Hole 186
Woodstock 117
Wright Brothers 328, 542-3
Wright, Frank Lloyd 517, 519
Wyoming 749-62, **750**

Yakima Valley 1008
Ybor City 492-3
Yurok tribe 921

ziplining
Bryson City 336
Chattanooga 364
Harpers Ferry 312
Lake Placid 120
Wildcat Mountain 227
zoos, *see also* wildlife sanctuaries & reserves
Audubon Zoo 427
Central Florida Zoo & Botanic Gardens 478
Kansas City Zoo & Aquarium 603
Lincoln Park Zoo 511
Memphis Zoo 358
Potter Park Zoo 551
Smithsonian's National Zoo 263
St Louis Zoo 599
Woodland Park Zoo 993
Zoo Tampa at Lowry Park 492

NOTES

NOTES

NOTES

NOTES

"The Grand Canyon lives up to the hype: its immensity, its grandeur, its beauty and its very age all scream for superlatives."
– Anthony Ham

"Skyscraper canyons. Honking cabs. Rattling trains. Massive museums. Michelin-starred restaurants. The bright lights of Broadway. The list doesn't stop; New York doesn't either."
– John Garry

All rights reserved. No part of this publication may be copied, stored in a retrieval system, or transmitted in any form by any means, electronic, mechanical, recording or otherwise, except brief extracts for the purpose of review, and no part of this publication may be sold or hired, without the written permission of the publisher. Lonely Planet and the Lonely Planet logo are trademarks of Lonely Planet and are registered in the US Patent and Trademark Office and in other countries. Lonely Planet does not allow its name or logo to be appropriated by commercial establishments, such as retailers, restaurants or hotels. Please let us know of any misuses: lonelyplanet.com/legal/intellectual-property.

Mapping data sources:
© Lonely Planet
© OpenStreetMap http://openstreetmap.org/copyright

THIS BOOK

Destination Editor
Caroline Trefler

Coordinating Editor
Brana Vladisavljevic

Production Editor
Graham O'Neill

Image Editor
Megan Cassidy

Cartographer
Anthony Phelan

Assisting Editors
Melanie Dankel, Kate Mathews, Anne Mulvaney,

Cover Researcher
Giada de Agostinis

Thanks James Appleton, Janet Austin, Catalina Aragón, Andrew Bain, Imogen Bannister, Michelle Bennett, Nigel Chin, Peterjon Creswell, Shauna Daly, Andrea Dobbin, Natalie Howard, Rachel Imeson, Kate James, Valentina Kremenchutskaya, Helen Koehne, Kellie Langdon, Michael MacKenzie, Ailbhe MacMahon, Virginia Moreno, Karyn Noble, Katelyn Perry, Darren O'Connell, Saralinda Turner, Clifton Wilkinson, Robin Yule

Paper in this book is certified against the Forest Stewardship Council™ standards. FSC™ promotes environmentally responsible, socially beneficial and economically viable management of the world's forests.

Published by Lonely Planet Global Limited
CRN 554153
13th edition – Feb 2026
ISBN 978 1 83758 723 0
© Lonely Planet 2026
10 9 8 7 6 5 4 3 2 1
Printed in Malaysia